60th Annual Meeting of the Association for Computational Linguistics (ACL 2022)

Student Research Workshop

Dublin, Ireland
22-27 May 2022

ISBN: 978-1-7138-6723-4

Printed from e-media with permission by:

Curran Associates, Inc.
57 Morehouse Lane
Red Hook, NY 12571

Some format issues inherent in the e-media version may also appear in this print version.

Printed with permission by Curran Associates, Inc. (2023)

Association for Computational Linguistics
209 N. Eighth Street
Stroudsburg, Pennsylvania 18360

Phone: 1-570-476-8006
Fax: 1-570-476-0860

acl@aclweb.org

Additional copies of this publication are available from:

Curran Associates, Inc.
57 Morehouse Lane
Red Hook, NY 12571 USA
Phone: 845-758-0400
Fax: 845-758-2633
Email: curran@proceedings.com
Web: www.proceedings.com

ACL 2022

The 60th Annual Meeting of the Association for Computational Linguistics

Proceedings of the Student Research Workshop

May 22-27, 2022

Introduction

Welcome to the ACL 2022 Student Research Workshop!

The ACL 2022 Student Research Workshop (SRW) is a forum for student researchers in computational linguistics and natural language processing. The workshop provides a great opportunity for student participants to take part in a mentorship program, present their work and receive valuable feedback from the international research community.

Following the tradition of the previous student research workshops, we have two tracks: research papers and thesis proposals. The research paper track is a venue for students to describe completed work or work-in-progress along with preliminary results. The thesis proposal track is offered for Ph.D. students who have decided on a thesis topic and are interested in getting feedback on their proposal and ideas about future directions for their work.

Mentoring is at the heart of the SRW. In keeping with previous years, we had a pre-submission mentoring program before the submission deadline. Excluding 4 withdrawals and duplicates, a total of 29 papers participated in the pre-submission mentoring program. This program offered students the opportunity to receive feedback from a mentor to improve the writing style and presentation of their submissions.

This year, the student research workshop has again received wide attention. Excluding 7 withdrawals and duplicates, we received 100 submissions including 91 research papers (56 long papers and 35 short papers) and 9 thesis proposals. 3 submissions were desk rejected. 43 submissions (4 thesis proposals, 28 long papers and 11 short papers)were accepted. 1 long paper was withdrawn after acceptance. Excluding non-archival papers, 39 papers appear in these proceedings. All the accepted papers will be presented in person and/or virtually in the poster sessions of the main conference. Some will also have oral presentations.

We are deeply grateful to ACL for providing funds that covered registrations for part of the authors as volunteer students. We thank our program committee members for their careful reviews of each paper and all of our mentors for donating their time to provide feedback to our student authors. Thank you to our faculty advisors, Cecile Paris, Siva Reddy and German Rigau, for their advice and to the ACL 2022 organizing committee for their support. Finally, thank you to our student participants!

Program Committee

Organizers

Samuel Louvan, Fondazione Bruno Kessler
Andrea Madotto, Meta, Reality Lab
Brielen Madureira, University of Potsdam

Faculty Advisors

Cecile Paris, CSIRO, Australia
Siva Reddy, McGill University, Canada
German Rigau, Basque Country University, Spain

Program Committee

Talha olakolu, AI Enablement Department, Huawei Turkey Research and Development Center
Sree Harsha Ramesh, UMass Amherst
Barry Haddow, University of Edinburgh
Mariana Neves, German Federal Institute for Risk Assessment
Omri Abend, The Hebrew University of Jerusalem
Chris Develder, Ghent University
Alina Karakanta, Fondazione Bruno Kessler (FBK), University of Trento
Antoine Venant, Universite Toulouse 3/ IRIT
Glorianna Jagfeld, Spectrum Centre for Mental Health Research, University of Lancaster
Chia-Hui Chang, National Central University
Olga Zamaraeva, University of A Corua
Arkaitz Zubiaga, Queen Mary University of London
Masaaki Nagata, NTT Corporation
Ahsaas Bajaj, University of Massachusetts Amherst
Tatiana Anikina, DFKI / Saarland Informatics Campus
Nina Hosseini-Kivanani, University of Luxembourg
Sarthak Mittal, Mila
Silviu Oprea, University of Edinburgh
Ian Stewart, University of Michigan
Zhengbao Jiang, Carnegie Mellon University
Steven Wilson, Oakland University
Denis Emelin, The University of Edinburgh
Jana Gtze, University of Potsdam
Melissa Roemmele, SDL
Katira Soleymanzadeh, Ege University
Naoki Otani, Carnegie Mellon University
Tomoyuki Kajiwara, Ehime University
Dan Goldwasser, Purdue University
Denis Newman-Griffis, University of Pittsburgh
Arlene Casey, University of Edinburgh
Christopher Homan, Rochester Institute of Technology
Vikas Raunak, Microsoft
Anne Beyer, University of Potsdam

Mamoru Komachi, Tokyo Metropolitan University
Laurie Burchell, University of Edinburgh
Surangika Ranathunga, university of moratuwa
Chuan-Jie Lin, National Taiwan Ocean University
Kemal Kurniawan, University of Melbourne
Kornraphop Kawintiranon, Georgetown University
Diana Galvan-Sosa, Tohoku University
Nihal V. Nayak, Brown University
Xiang Dai, University of Copenhagen
Ronald Cardenas, University of Edinburgh
Gosse Minnema, University of Groningen
Jingzhou Liu, Carnegie Mellon University
Jad Kabbara, McGill University - MILA
Xinyi Zheng, University of Michigan, Ann Arbor
Carolina Scarton, University of Sheffield
Kirk Roberts, University of Texas Health Science Center at Houston
Junxian He, Carnegie Mellon University
Yasumasa Onoe, The University of Texas at Austin
Parisa Kordjamshidi, Michigan State University
Vasu Sharma, Carnegie Mellon University
Jannis Vamvas, Department of Computational Linguistics, University of Zurich
Kiet Nguyen, University of Information Technology, VNU-HCM
Alok Debnath, Trinity College, Dublin
Vivek Gupta, School of Computing, University of Utah
Vincent Ng, University of Texas at Dallas
Lucy Lin, University of Washington
Farig Sadeque, Educational Testing Service
Bharat Ram Ambati, Apple Inc.
Jeff Jacobs, Columbia University
Durgesh Nandini, University of Bamberg
Sudipta Kar, Amazon Alexa AI
Shruti Rijhwani, Carnegie Mellon University
Miguel A. Alonso, Universidade da Corua
Merel Scholman, Saarland University
Valentina Pyatkin, Bar-Ilan University
Bonnie Webber, University of Edinburgh
Marco Antonio Sobrevilla Cabezudo, University of So Paulo
Amita Misra, IBM
Deeksha Varshney, Indian Institute of Technology, Patna, India
Abhilasha Ravichander, Carnegie Mellon University
Adithya Pratapa, Carnegie Mellon University
Micha Elsner, The Ohio State University
Haoran Zhang, University of Pittsburgh
Guy Rotman, Faculty of Industrial Engineering and Management, Technion, IIT
Jakob Prange, Georgetown University
Maria Antoniak, Cornell University
Yusu Qian, New York University
Labiba Jahan, Florida International University
Cesare Spinoso-Di Piano, McGill University
Valentin Malykh, Huawei Noah's Ark Lab / Kazan Federal University
Oscar Sainz, University of the Basque Country (UPV/EHU)

ABULIKEMU ABUDUWEILI, Carnegie Mellon University
Bonaventure F. P. Dossou, Jacobs University Bremen
Jifan Chen, UT Austin
Vincent Nguyen, Australian National University & CSIRO Data61
Zihan Liu, Hong Kong University of Science and Technology
Koji Mineshima, Keio University
Rajaswa Patil, TCS Research
Ian Porada, Mila, McGill University
Valeria de Paiva, Topos Institute
Elizabeth Salesky, Johns Hopkins University
Iker Garca-Ferrero, HiTZ Center - Ixa, University of the Basque Country UPV/EHU
Devang Kulshreshtha, MILA Lab, McGill University
Ivan Vuli, University of Cambridge
Zhong Zhou, Carnegie Mellon University
eljko Agi, Unity Technologies
Najoung Kim, New York University
Meaghan Fowlie, Utrecht University
Gabriel Doyle, San Diego State University
Dimosthenis Kontogiorgos, PhD Student
Aitor Ormazabal, University of the Basque Country
Taiwo Kolajo, Federal University Lokoja
Kevin Small, Amazon
Tejas Srinivasan, University of Southern California
Badr Abdullah, Saarland University
Hai Pham, Carnegie Mellon University
Mandy Korpusik, Loyola Marymount University
Dayne Freitag, SRI International
Fangyu Liu, University of Cambridge
Ruken Cakici, METU
Marija Stanojevic, Center for Data Analytics and Biomedical Informatics, Temple University
Di Lu, Dataminr
Sina Sheikholeslami, KTH Royal Institute of Technology
Jorge Balazs, Amazon
Sowmya Vajjala, National Research Council
Da Yin, University of California, Los Angeles (UCLA)
Zeerak Talat, University of Sheffield
Eduardo Blanco, Arizona State University
David Demeter, Northwestern University
David Adelani, Saarland University
Ivaylo Radev, IICT, Bulgarian Academy of Sciences
Zi-Yi Dou, UCLA
Tom Hosking, University of Edinburgh
Abeer Aldayel, King Saud University
Piush Aggarwal, FernUniversitt in Hagen, Computational Linguistics
Endang Pamungkas, Universitas Muhammadiyah Surakarta
David Trye, University of Waikato
Bruno Martins, IST and INESC-ID
Alexandra Lavrentovich, Amazon Alexa
Gunhee Kim, Seoul National University
Aditi Chaudhary, Carnegie Mellon University
Amir Zeldes, Georgetown University

Jasy Suet Yan Liew, School of Computer Sciences, Universiti Sains Malaysia
Marius Mosbach, Saarland University
Carlos Escolano, Universitat Politcnica de Catalunya
Dat Quoc Nguyen, VinAI Research
Evelin Amorim, UFMG
Zara Kancheva, IICT-BAS
Maike Paetzel-Prsmann, University of Potsdam
Shane Steinert-Threlkeld, University of Washington
Marcos Garcia, Universidade de Santiago de Compostela
Manex Agirrezabal, University of Copenhagen
Tina Fang, University of Waterloo
Richard Sproat, Google, Japan
Rachel Bawden, Inria
Philipp Sadler, University of Potsdam
Yumo Xu, University of Edinburgh
Tatjana Scheffler, Ruhr-Universitt Bochum
Jonathan K. Kummerfeld, University of Michigan
Neat Dereli, Adjust GmbH
Meishan Zhang, Harbin Institute of Technology (Shenzhen), China
Valerio Basile, University of Turin
Shabnam Tafreshi, UMD:ARLIS
Anjali Bhavan, University of Washington
Samuel Pecar, PwC
Omid Moradiannasab, Saarland University
Tatiana Bladier, Heinrich Heine University Dsseldorf
Jonas Groschwitz, Saarland University
Christoph Teichmann, Bloomberg LP

Mentor

Mihai Surdeanu, University of Arizona
Yansong Feng, Peking University
Tatjana Scheffler, Ruhr-Universität Bochum
Hanna Suominen, Australian National University
Vincent Ng, utdallas
Rajaswa Patil Patil, TCS Research
Raffaella Bernardi, University of Trento
Jindřich Libovický, LMU Munich
Marco Basaldella, Amazon Alexa AI
Arkaitz Zubiaga Zubiaga, Queen Mary University of London
Clara Vania Vania, Amazon Alexa AI
Yi-Ling Chung Chung, University of Trento/Fondazione Bruno Kessler
Duygu Ataman, New York University
Fajri Koto, University of Melbourne
Miryam de Lhoneux, Uppsala University
Genta Indra Winata Indra Winata, Bloomberg
Alan Ramponi, Fondazione Bruno Kessler
Jinwook Choi, Seoul National University
Derry Tanti Wijaya, Boston University
Valerio Basile, U of Turin
Niranjan Balasubramanian, Stonybrook University

Marco Gaido, University of Trento/Fondazione Bruno Kessler
Greg Durrett, University of Texas, Austin
Sara Tonelli, Fondazione Bruno Kessler
Bonnie Webber, University of Edinburgh
Shujian Huang, Nanjing University
Malihe Alikhani, University of Pittsburgh
Peng Xu, Hong Kong University of Technology
Zhaojiang Lin, Facebook
Xiang Dai, University of Sydney

Table of Contents

Evaluating zero-shot transfers and multilingual models for dependency parsing and POS tagging within the low-resource language family Tupían

Frederic Blum
Institut für deutsche Sprache und Linguistik
Humboldt-Universität zu Berlin
frederic.blum@hu-berlin.de

Abstract

This work presents two experiments with the goal of replicating the transferability of dependency parsers and POS taggers trained on closely related languages within the low-resource language family Tupían. The experiments include both zero-shot settings as well as multilingual models. Previous studies have found that even a comparably small treebank from a closely related language will improve sequence labelling considerably in such cases. Results from both POS tagging and dependency parsing confirm previous evidence that the closer the phylogenetic relation between two languages, the better the predictions for sequence labelling tasks get. In many cases, the results are improved if multiple languages from the same family are combined. This suggests that in addition to leveraging similarity between two related languages, the incorporation of multiple languages of the same family might lead to better results in transfer learning for NLP applications.

1 Introduction

For most of the 7000 languages of the world, no NLP resources exist (Joshi et al., 2020; Mager et al., 2018). As a response to this situation, more and more initiatives emerged in recent years that work on NLP applications for underrepresented and low-resource languages (Orife et al., 2020; Nekoto et al., 2020; Mager et al., 2021). Despite those advances, access to tools like machine translation still is hindered by a large language barrier. Most of those languages do not have large text corpora, which have been used for the recent advantages in NLP like the building of large transformer models (Vaswani et al., 2017). Annotated data and parallel corpora thus remain an important but scarce tool for many of them. Yet, annotating this data is a challenge itself, and might be aided through the transfer of models from languages with more available resources.

The idea to leverage existing databases and models for cross-lingual transfer is not new (Aufrant et al., 2016; Duong et al., 2015; Lacroix et al., 2016; Vania et al., 2019; Wang et al., 2019). However, many studies even in this area remain within the environment of high-resource languages, and benchmarks with a typological sample as representative as possible - common nowadays in linguistic typology - are rarely found (Bender, 2009; de Lhoneux, 2019; Ponti et al., 2019). The main goal of this contribution is to replicate previous findings on cross-lingual transfer in low-resource settings (Meechan-Maddon and Nivre, 2019) within an underpresented language family, Tupían.

2 Data and Hypotheses

The data used for this study is taken from the Tupían Dependency Treebanks project (TuDeT, Gerardi et al., 2021)[1], which is openly available under a CC-BY-SA-4.0 License and is already partially present in the Universal Dependencies database. The author is not part of the team that developed these treebanks. There are currently seven languages in the dataset, which belong to different branches of the Tupían family (Hammarström et al., 2021). Except Tupinambá, which is extinct, the languages are spoken in Brazilian territory. All languages but Guajajára have SOV word order, while the former has VSO. The datasets are summarized in Table 1. There are some important differences with respect to the distribution of annotations data. For example, adjectives are absent for nearly all languages but Karo, either because they do not have adjectives and use stative verbs instead like Guajajára (Harrison, 2010), or because of low sample size. There are some tags, like NUM and INTJ, which are quite unevenly distributed between the available treebanks for the respective languages. As a consequence, this will result in low macro-f1

[1] https://github.com/tupian-language-resources/tudet

Proceedings of the 60th Annual Meeting of the Association for Computational Linguistics
Student Research Workshop, pages 1 - 9
May 22-27, 2022 ©2022 Association for Computational Linguistics

Language	Code	Branch	Word order	Tokens	Utterances	Tokens per utterance
Akuntsu	aqz	Tuparic	SOV	408	101	4.04
Guajajára	gub	Tupi-Guarani	VSO	3571	497	7.18
Kaapor	urb	Tupi-Guarani	SOV	366	83	4.41
Karo	arr	Ramarama	SOV	2318	674	3.44
Makuráp	mpu	Tuparic	SOV	146	31	4.71
Mundurukú	myu	Mundurukuic	SOV	828	124	6.68
Tupinambá	tpn	Tupi-Guarani	SOV	2576	353	7.30

Table 1: Treebanks used in the dataset

scores, making accuracy the more relevant measure for this research question. A detailed description of the distribution of UPOS-tags in the dataset is given in Appendix A, the distribution of dependency relations is given in Appendix B.

In this study, I primarily test the utility of cross-lingual transfer for POS-taggers and dependency parsers with special attention given to language phylogeny. Language phylogeny can be seen as a proxy to typological features, given that closely related languages usually show many structural similarities. Previous studies have shown that even a comparably small treebank from a closely related language will improve the results of annotation considerably (Meechan-Maddon and Nivre, 2019).

Recent studies suggest to leverage phylogenetic proximity in a more efficient way than simply comparing languages based on the language family they belong to (Dehouck and Denis, 2019). Which model generalizes best over the different treebanks used in this sample, and what role does language phylogeny play in this? In this study, 'closeness' of two languages is defined based on the proximity of their phylogenetic clades. This is used as a proxy to their typological similarity. Especially for languages which do not have extensive descriptive material available, such similarities cannot easily be computed from typological databases. Based on phylolinguistic inferences about Tupían (Galucio et al., 2015; Gerardi and Reichert, 2021), the following explicit hypotheses are postulated:

1. Guajajára and Tupinambá should provide the best results for the evaluation of Kaapor, given that all three are part of the Tupi-Guarani branch of the Tupían language family.

2. Despite belonging to three different branches, the remaining four languages are quite close to each other in networks of lexical similarity. Here, Mundurukú is closer to Akuntsú than to Makuráp, and Karo is closer to Makuráp than to Akuntsú. The results should mirror this relation.

3 Experiments

One of the challenges for NLP applications with low-resource languages is the lack of language-specific resources on which embeddings can be trained on (Mager et al., 2018). Even though there are useful pipelines which can sometimes be used to crawl monolingual data from published sources (Bustamante et al., 2020), those are not always available or accessible. The embeddings used for the experiments in this contributions are based on the jw300-corpus (Agić and Vulić, 2019). This corpus is derived specifically from 343 low-resource languages and shows greater typological diversity than most dominating multilingual models. The embeddings are implemented in flair (Akbik et al., 2018). They have been fine-tuned for the pooled set of source languages. Transformer word embeddings mBERT (Devlin et al., 2019) and ROBERTA (Conneau et al., 2020) were also evaluated for the model, but rarely surpassed 40% accuracy for the source languages and have thus been discarded from further experiments for now. This results further call into question the utility of such large models for typologically diverse languages, and strengthens previous findings that even the largest multilingual transformer models do not show good results when transferring to typologically different languages (Ahmad et al., 2019; Lauscher et al., 2020; Pires et al., 2019). However, the exact reasons for their failure in this experiment are not entirely clear and need further research with more typologically diverse low-resource languages.

The experiments will be done for both POS tagging and dependency parsing and include a zero-shot setting. Also, models trained on individual source languages will be compared against models trained on multiple datasets, with the evaluation set being the remaining treebanks of the dataset. Given the small amoung of training data and the models chosen, all model runs combined did not need more than three hours on CPU. The evaluation was done within the provided utilities by flair and SuPaR, respectively. All code is available on OSF.[2]

3.1 POS-tagging

For all experiments, the datasets have been separated into source (Guajajára, Karo, Tupinambá) and target languages (Akuntsu, Kaapor, Makuráp, Mundurukú). The split has been made according to the availability of data, and all treebanks with over 2000 annotated tokens have been used as source language. The main reason for this is to assure that the training sets have sufficient data for training and evaluating the models. Every treebank in the source set was further split into training, test and dev data (80/10/10). Given the scarcity of the data, all models were trained including the dev-set. The model itself a BiLSTM-CRF sequence tagger implemented using the *flair*-framework (Akbik et al., 2019, Version 0.10),[3] trained with a hidden size of 512. The following models were run:

1. training on the combined source set (tupi3)
2. training on the individual source languages Guajajára (gub), Karo (arr) and Tupinambá (tpn)
3. fine-tuning the tupi3 model for each Akuntsu (tupi3-aqz) and Mundurukú (tupi3+myu) on 50% of of the respective data, with the remaining part of the data used as evaluation
4. using a model pre-trained for 12 European UD languages, implemented in *flair* (Akbik et al., 2018).[4] This model was trained on treebanks from Czech, Danish, Dutch, English, Finnish, French, German, Italian, Norwegian, Polish, Spanish, and Swedish

The pre-trained model for European languages was used in order to provide a baseline of transferability of models based on unrelated, high-resource languages. All models were evaluated on each target language. Each model was run five times, and the average results are presented in Table 2. In case of the fine-tuning experiment, training accuracy describes the result on the test set, while the language-specific column gives the result for the overall treebank. The evaluation column is a summary over the evaluation set, without considering the source language. The best result for each of the languages in the evaluation set is boldfaced.

Unsurprisingly, the experiment conditions with fine-tuning for a specific language show the best results for the respective language. In both cases, the results for the other language were also improved, confirming the hypothesis that the results of Akuntsu and Mundurukú should be closely related. This could motivate training a model on Akuntsu and Mundurukú combined. The close relationship between Akuntsu and Makuráp, on the other hand, does not seem to lead to better results. The best predictions for Makuráp are instead based on the model trained for Karo, a relationship that was predicted by the second hypothesis, even though only as the second strongest effect. Despite those results, it should be considered that Makuráp has by far the smallest treebank available with only 146 annotated tokens, so no final evaluations should be made. This also reflects in the low overall accuracy in all settings for Makuráp, never surpassing 40%.

3.2 Dependency parsing

The experiment settings were mostly identical for the dependency parsing experiment. The main difference is that no pre-trained model for European languages is available for the dependency parser that was used for the experiments. For the same reason, no fine-tuning for the tupi3 setting is implemented so far. Instead, a single model for Mundurukú was added for further evaluation of Hypothesis 2. As model architecture, an implementation of the deep biaffine dependency parser (Dozat and Manning, 2017) from SuPar (Version 1.01) was used (Zhang et al., 2020).[5] The results are shown in Table 3. In case the language was the source language, the evaluation score only reflects the evaluation of the test split. This is the case for the tupi3 setting as well as the individual languages. All other languages in each row were evaluated against the entire dataset. As the main evaluation criteria, Labelled Attachment Scores (LAS) were chosen.

[2] https://doi.org/10.17605/OSF.IO/ZHDMP

[3] https://github.com/flairNLP/flair, MIT License

[4] https://huggingface.co/flair/upos-multi

[5] https://github.com/yzhangcs/parser, MIT License

Model	TrainAcc	TrainF1	EvalAcc	EvalF1	aqz	mpu	myu	urb
arr	0.84	0.68	0.30	0.10	0.35	**0.36**	0.30	0.24
gub	0.91	0.76	0.44	0.19	0.45	0.29	0.48	0.41
tpn	0.87	0.81	0.42	0.17	0.43	0.25	0.49	0.34
tupi3	0.86	0.64	0.46	0.20	0.49	0.35	0.47	**0.42**
tupi3+aqz	0.56	0.31	0.48	0.19	**0.52**	0.32	0.51	0.40
tupi3+myu	0.55	0.22	0.48	0.19	0.51	0.34	**0.53**	0.39
multi			0.33	0.13	0.38	0.23	0.36	0.23

Table 2: Average training and evaluation accuracy and F1-scores over five runs of the POS tagging experiment

Model	aqz	arr	gub	mpu	myu	tpn	urb
arr	0.00	**64.10**	0.00	**25.00**	0.00	0.00	0.00
gub	12.90	14.50	**73.30**	9.00	8.90	10.30	14.20
myu	**19.09**	14.98	10.65	7.64	**65.28**	7.85	13.89
tpn	13.30	0.00	20.90	14.30	0.00	**46.40**	15.80
tupi3	9.50	62.60	72.70	11.80	8.90	42.90	**21.80**

Table 3: Labelled Attachment Scores (LAS) of the dependency parsing experiment

4 Discussion

4.1 Discussing the POS tagging experiment

Against Hypothesis 1, the best result for Kaapor is not achieved by Guajajára or Tupinambá, but by the combined model trained on the pooled treebanks. However, the model of Guajajára is only 0.01% behind the pooled model and should be considerd equal, as it is well within the standard deviation of the average result (upos 0.02, gub 0.01). It should also not be forgotten that two of the three languages in the pooled set, including Guajajára itself, are part of the Tupí-Guarani branch, which can be reasonably postulated as part of the reason that tupi3 scores so high. Instead of a single language of that branch, it might just be the combination of two languages from the same branch that shows such strong results.

This leads to another result that should be highlighted, namely the overall usefulness of the multilingual Tupían model. While the European multilingual model had, perhaps expectedly without any fine-tuning, low results for most evaluations, the Tupían model was competitive in most settings. For both Makuráp and Kaapor it was basically equal with the best individual model, for Akuntsu it was second best behind the fine-tuned models, and even for Mundurukú it showed good results, even though it showed weaker predictions in this case. While previous studies suggested that at least 200 annotated utterances are sufficient to improve the results of a multilingual model considerably (Meechan-Maddon and Nivre, 2019), the results in this contribution suggest that as few as 50 or 60 training utterances could already provide a considerable improvement of the evaluation scores. These are only approximate numbers, and definitely need more experiments with other datasets in order to be confirmed.

All in all, the POS tagging experiment shows that language phylogeny is a strong, but not a deterministic predictor for the transferability of models. Given the low amount of training data for the models even in the combined tupi3 setting, the zero-shot transfer results are better than perhaps expected.

4.2 Discussing the Dependency Parsing experiment

Overall, the transfer LAS are much lower than the accuracy in the previous experiment. Given the complexity of dependency parsing compared to POS tagging, this is hardly surprising. This is also true for the training scores, never surpassing 75%. With regard to Hypothesis 1, we see again that both Guajajára and Tupinambá show better results for Kaapor than Karo and Mundurukú. The model hugely improves in the tupi3 setting, indicating again that both larger training treebanks and combining different closely related languages might show considerable effects to the evaluation of a new language. This has already been the case for the POS tagging, and will result in an additional experiment in the next phase of this study.

Hypothesis 2 is also largely confirmed. Karo

was hypothesized to achieve the best results for the evaluation of Makuráp, and this predictions is met strongly, with a LAS difference over 10%. As Mundurukú outperforms the other languages in the evaluation of Akuntsu, the second part of the hypothesis is also confirmed. The results for Mundurukú itself further show that even with a small treebank of only $\sim$ 100 utterances, good predictions can be achieved.

At the current state of this paper, an important gap is the missing detailed error analysis. One important source of errors for the models is the uneven distribution of dependency relations between the treebanks, as shown in Table 5. Partially due to the low amount of data and due to language-specific differences, some tags are distributed unevenly among languages, or are not present at all in some of them. However, even when accounting for this differences, the exact factors that determine failure and success of the transfer remain not fully explained. For example, whether the overall success of the combined model of various languages (tupi3) is due to the higher amount of training data, or whether there are other factors involved when combining data from multiple languages that could be leveraged for the development of NLP applications for low-resource languages, cannot be answered by this contribution.

5 Conclusion

This study further confirms previous findings that cross-lingual transfer of dependency parsers and POS taggers is a viable option in low-resource settings if a closely related language is available (Vania et al., 2019; Meechan-Maddon and Nivre, 2019). This extends previous evidence for phylogenetically informed transfer from Indo-European and Uralic (Dehouck and Denis, 2019) to Tupían. Further experiments on other language families should be conducted in order to confirm the exact features that make successful transfer possible.

Further, this study provided further evidence for extending the phylolinguistically informed combination of source languages. In all experiment settings of this study, the pooled source language set had very good results, and a targeted combination will likely further improve the results. Further follow-up experiments will consist of targeted combinations of annotated data from different languages, including an incorporation of typological features and delexicalized transfer. In preliminary experiments, CRF2o dependency parsing (Zhang et al., 2020) showed promising results for transfer results as well. Especially in the dependency parsing experiment the transfer scores were quite low, and further improving the training data as well as comparing different models should be a viable solution for this challenge.

References

Željko Agić and Ivan Vulić. 2019. JW300: A wide-coverage parallel corpus for low-resource languages. In *Proceedings of the 57th Annual Meeting of the Association for Computational Linguistics*, pages 3204–3210, Florence, Italy. Association for Computational Linguistics.

Wasi Ahmad, Zhisong Zhang, Xuezhe Ma, Eduard Hovy, Kai-Wei Chang, and Nanyun Peng. 2019. On difficulties of cross-lingual transfer with order differences: A case study on dependency parsing. In *Proceedings of the 2019 Conference of the North American Chapter of the Association for Computational Linguistics: Human Language Technologies, Volume 1 (Long and Short Papers)*, pages 2440–2452, Minneapolis, Minnesota. Association for Computational Linguistics.

Alan Akbik, Tanja Bergmann, Duncan Blythe, Kashif Rasul, Stefan Schweter, and Roland Vollgraf. 2019. FLAIR: An easy-to-use framework for state-of-the-art NLP. In *Proceedings of the 2019 Conference of the North American Chapter of the Association for Computational Linguistics (Demonstrations)*, pages 54–59, Minneapolis, Minnesota. Association for Computational Linguistics.

Alan Akbik, Duncan Blythe, and Roland Vollgraf. 2018. Contextual string embeddings for sequence labeling. In *COLING 2018, 27th International Conference on Computational Linguistics*, pages 1638–1649.

Lauriane Aufrant, Guillaume Wisniewski, and François Yvon. 2016. Zero-resource dependency parsing: Boosting delexicalized cross-lingual transfer with linguistic knowledge. In *Proceedings of COLING 2016, the 26th International Conference on Computational Linguistics: Technical Papers*, pages 119–130, Osaka, Japan. The COLING 2016 Organizing Committee.

Emily M. Bender. 2009. Linguistically naïve != language independent: Why NLP needs linguistic typology. In *Proceedings of the EACL 2009 Workshop on the Interaction between Linguistics and Computational Linguistics: Virtuous, Vicious or Vacuous?*, pages 26–32, Athens, Greece. Association for Computational Linguistics.

Gina Bustamante, Arturo Oncevay, and Roberto Zariquiey. 2020. No data to crawl? monolingual corpus creation from PDF files of truly low-resource languages in Peru. In *Proceedings of the 12th Language Resources and Evaluation Conference*, pages 2914–2923, Marseille, France. European Language Resources Association.

Alexis Conneau, Kartikay Khandelwal, Naman Goyal, Vishrav Chaudhary, Guillaume Wenzek, Francisco Guzmán, Edouard Grave, Myle Ott, Luke Zettlemoyer, and Veselin Stoyanov. 2020. Unsupervised cross-lingual representation learning at scale. In *Proceedings of the 58th Annual Meeting of the Association for Computational Linguistics*, pages 8440–8451, Online. Association for Computational Linguistics.

Miryam de Lhoneux. 2019. *Linguistically informed neural dependency parsing for typologically diverse languages*. Ph.D. thesis, Acta Universitatis Upsaliensis.

Mathieu Dehouck and Pascal Denis. 2019. Phylogenic multi-lingual dependency parsing. In *Proceedings of the 2019 Conference of the North American Chapter of the Association for Computational Linguistics: Human Language Technologies, Volume 1 (Long and Short Papers)*, pages 192–203, Minneapolis, Minnesota. Association for Computational Linguistics.

Jacob Devlin, Ming-Wei Chang, Kenton Lee, and Kristina Toutanova. 2019. BERT: Pre-training of deep bidirectional transformers for language understanding. In *Proceedings of the 2019 Conference of the North American Chapter of the Association for Computational Linguistics: Human Language Technologies, Volume 1 (Long and Short Papers)*, pages 4171–4186, Minneapolis, Minnesota. Association for Computational Linguistics.

Timothy Dozat and Christopher D. Manning. 2017. Deep biaffine attention for neural dependency parsing. In *ICLR 2017*.

Long Duong, Trevor Cohn, Steven Bird, and Paul Cook. 2015. A neural network model for low-resource Universal Dependency parsing. In *Proceedings of the 2015 Conference on Empirical Methods in Natural Language Processing*, pages 339–348, Lisbon, Portugal. Association for Computational Linguistics.

Ana Vilacy Galucio, Sérgio Meira, Joshua Birchall, Denny Moore, Nilson Gabas, Sebastian Drude, Luciana Storto, Gessiane Picanço, and Carmen Reis Rodrigues. 2015. Genealogical relations and lexical distances within the tupian linguistic family. *Boletim do Museu Paraense Emílio Goeldi. Ciências Humanas*, 10:229–274.

Fabrício Ferraz Gerardi and Stanislav Reichert. 2021. The tupí-guaraní language family. *Diachronica*, 38(2):151–188.

Fabrício Ferraz Gerardi, Stanislav Reichert, Carolina Aragon, Lorena Martín-Rodríguez, Gustavo Godoy, and Tatiana Merzhevich. 2021. Tudet: Tupían dependency treebank.

Harald Hammarström, Robert Forkel, Martin Haspelmath, and Sebastian Bank. 2021. glottolog/glottolog: Glottolog database 4.5.

Carl H. Harrison. 2010. Verb prominence, verb initialness, ergativity and typological disharmony in guajajara. In Desmond C. Derbyshire and Geoffrey K. Pullum, editors, *Volume 1 Handbook of Amazonian languages: Volume 1*, pages 407–439. De Gruyter Mouton.

Pratik Joshi, Sebastin Santy, Amar Budhiraja, Kalika Bali, and Monojit Choudhury. 2020. The state and fate of linguistic diversity and inclusion in the NLP world. In *Proceedings of the 58th Annual Meeting of the Association for Computational Linguistics*, pages 6282–6293, Online. Association for Computational Linguistics.

Ophélie Lacroix, Lauriane Aufrant, Guillaume Wisniewski, and François Yvon. 2016. Frustratingly easy cross-lingual transfer for transition-based dependency parsing. In *Proceedings of the 2016 Conference of the North American Chapter of the Association for Computational Linguistics: Human Language Technologies*, pages 1058–1063, San Diego, California. Association for Computational Linguistics.

Anne Lauscher, Vinit Ravishankar, Ivan Vulić, and Goran Glavaš. 2020. From zero to hero: On the limitations of zero-shot language transfer with multilingual Transformers. In *Proceedings of the 2020 Conference on Empirical Methods in Natural Language Processing (EMNLP)*, pages 4483–4499, Online. Association for Computational Linguistics.

Manuel Mager, Ximena Gutierrez-Vasques, Gerardo Sierra, and Ivan Meza-Ruiz. 2018. Challenges of language technologies for the indigenous languages of the Americas. In *Proceedings of the 27th International Conference on Computational Linguistics*, pages 55–69, Santa Fe, New Mexico, USA. Association for Computational Linguistics.

Manuel Mager, Arturo Oncevay, Annette Rios, Ivan Vladimir Meza Ruiz, Alexis Palmer, Graham Neubig, and Katharina Kann, editors. 2021. *Proceedings of the First Workshop on Natural Language Processing for Indigenous Languages of the Americas*. Association for Computational Linguistics, Online.

Ailsa Meechan-Maddon and Joakim Nivre. 2019. How to parse low-resource languages: Cross-lingual parsing, target language annotation, or both? In *Proceedings of the Fifth International Conference on Dependency Linguistics (Depling, SyntaxFest 2019)*, pages 112–120, Paris, France. Association for Computational Linguistics.

Wilhelmina Nekoto, Vukosi Marivate, Tshinondiwa Matsila, Timi Fasubaa, Taiwo Fagbohungbe, Solomon Oluwole Akinola, Shamsuddeen Muhammad, Salomon Kabongo Kabenamualu, Salomey Osei, Freshia Sackey, Rubungo Andre Niyongabo,

Ricky Macharm, Perez Ogayo, Orevaoghene Ahia, Musie Meressa Berhe, Mofetoluwa Adeyemi, Masabata Mokgesi-Selinga, Lawrence Okegbemi, Laura Martinus, Kolawole Tajudeen, Kevin Degila, Kelechi Ogueji, Kathleen Siminyu, Julia Kreutzer, Jason Webster, Jamiil Toure Ali, Jade Abbott, Iroro Orife, Ignatius Ezeani, Idris Abdulkadir Dangana, Herman Kamper, Hady Elsahar, Goodness Duru, Ghollah Kioko, Murhabazi Espoir, Elan van Biljon, Daniel Whitenack, Christopher Onyefuluchi, Chris Chinenye Emezue, Bonaventure F. P. Dossou, Blessing Sibanda, Blessing Bassey, Ayodele Olabiyi, Arshath Ramkilowan, Alp Öktem, Adewale Akinfaderin, and Abdallah Bashir. 2020. Participatory research for low-resourced machine translation: A case study in African languages. In *Findings of the Association for Computational Linguistics: EMNLP 2020*, pages 2144–2160, Online. Association for Computational Linguistics.

Iroro Orife, Julia Kreutzer, Blessing Sibanda, Daniel Whitenack, Kathleen Siminyu, Laura Martinus, Jamiil Toure Ali, Jade Z. Abbott, Vukosi Marivate, Salomon Kabongo, Musie Meressa, Espoir Murhabazi, Orevaoghene Ahia, Elan Van Biljon, Arshath Ramkilowan, Adewale Akinfaderin, Alp Öktem, Wole Akin, Ghollah Kioko, Kevin Degila, Herman Kamper, Bonaventure Dossou, Chris Emezue, Kelechi Ogueji, and Abdallah Bashir. 2020. Masakhane - machine translation for africa. *CoRR*, abs/2003.11529.

Telmo Pires, Eva Schlinger, and Dan Garrette. 2019. How multilingual is multilingual BERT? In *Proceedings of the 57th Annual Meeting of the Association for Computational Linguistics*, pages 4996–5001, Florence, Italy. Association for Computational Linguistics.

Edoardo Maria Ponti, Helen O'Horan, Yevgeni Berzak, Ivan Vulić, Roi Reichart, Thierry Poibeau, Ekaterina Shutova, and Anna Korhonen. 2019. Modeling language variation and universals: A survey on typological linguistics for natural language processing. *Computational Linguistics*, 45(3):559–601.

Clara Vania, Yova Kementchedjhieva, Anders Søgaard, and Adam Lopez. 2019. A systematic comparison of methods for low-resource dependency parsing on genuinely low-resource languages. In *Proceedings of the 2019 Conference on Empirical Methods in Natural Language Processing and the 9th International Joint Conference on Natural Language Processing (EMNLP-IJCNLP)*, pages 1105–1116, Hong Kong, China. Association for Computational Linguistics.

Ashish Vaswani, Noam Shazeer, Niki Parmar, Jakob Uszkoreit, Llion Jones, Aidan N Gomez, Łukasz Kaiser, and Illia Polosukhin. 2017. Attention is all you need. In *Advances in neural information processing systems*, pages 5998–6008.

Yuxuan Wang, Wanxiang Che, Jiang Guo, Yijia Liu, and Ting Liu. 2019. Cross-lingual BERT transformation for zero-shot dependency parsing. In *Proceedings of the 2019 Conference on Empirical Methods in Natural Language Processing and the 9th International Joint Conference on Natural Language Processing (EMNLP-IJCNLP)*, pages 5721–5727, Hong Kong, China. Association for Computational Linguistics.

Yu Zhang, Zhenghua Li, and Min Zhang. 2020. Efficient second-order TreeCRF for neural dependency parsing. In *Proceedings of the 58th Annual Meeting of the Association for Computational Linguistics*, pages 3295–3305, Online. Association for Computational Linguistics.

A POS-tags used in the dataset

	UPOS	Akuntsu	Guajajára	Kaapor	Karo	Makuráp	Mundurukú	Tupinambá
1	ADJ	2		3	103		5	
2	ADP	29	79	25	36	27	126	73
3	ADV	32	68	101	42	137	29	76
4	AUX	7	9	16	75	14	12	4
5	DET	49	24	8		41	5	20
6	INTJ	5	3			14	2	8
7	NOUN	429	250	240	244	219	408	338
8	NUM	15	1		2		2	4
9	PART	39	132	101	129	103	25	42
10	PRON	78	32	172	129	75	59	48
11	PROPN	42	41	55	5		4	34
12	PUNCT	88	176	16	1	14	115	209
13	VERB	184	181	246	222	329	179	140
14	CCONJ		2	11		27	2	1
15	SCONJ		2	5	10		23	1
16	X				2		4	1

Table 4: POS tags per 1.000 Tokens used in TuDeT

B Dependency relations used in the dataset

	deprel	Akuntsu	Guajajára	Kaapor	Karo	Makuráp	Mundurukú	Tupinambá
1	advmod	39	65	101	80	137	25	62
2	amod	5		25	29		6	1
3	appos	15	6		2		10	24
4	aux	2	9	16	57	14	8	4
5	case	34	56	19	36	27	121	62
6	ccomp	2	16	5	3		4	5
7	conj	15	8	5	3	21	12	30
8	dep	17	11		29	116	25	24
9	discourse	39	139	87	26	89	14	42
10	dislocated	2						1
11	iobj	2	14	14				1
12	nmod	135	52	63	60	48	63	94
13	nsubj	150	91	202	127	62	95	45
14	nummod	12	0		2		1	4
15	obj	91	55	156	65	82	54	42
16	obl	59	113	22	31	27	175	99
17	parataxis	44	5		3	96	34	32
18	punct	88	176	16	1	14	115	209
19	root	248	139	227	291	212	150	137
20	advcl		16	8	1	14	41	54
21	compound		1	5	19			1
22	det		18	3	3		4	3
23	flat		1				1	
24	list		2					
25	mark		7	5	47		28	0
26	orphan		1					
27	cc			11		21	1	2
28	csubj			5				
29	xcomp			3	8	21	1	7
30	acl				2			4
31	clf				66		10	
32	cop				9		1	
33	goeswith							1
34	obl:obj							3
35	obl:subj							5
36	vocative							1

Table 5: Dependency relations per 1.000 tokens used in TuDeT

RFBFN: A Relation-First Blank Filling Network for Joint Relational Triple Extraction

Zhe Li[1], **Luoyi Fu**[1], **Haisong Zhang**[3], **Chenghu Zhou**[2], **Xinbing Wang**[1]
[1]School of Electronic Information and Electrical Engineering,
Shanghai Jiao Tong University, Shanghai, China
[2]Chinese Academy of Sciences, Beijing, China
[3]Tencent AI Lab, Shenzhen, China
{lizhe2016,yiluofu,xwang8}@sjtu.edu.cn
zhouch@lreis.ac.cn, hansonzhang@tencent.com

Abstract

Joint relational triple extraction from unstructured text is an important task in information extraction. However, most existing works either ignore the semantic information of relations or predict subjects and objects sequentially. To address the issues, we introduce a new blank filling paradigm for the task, and propose a relation-first blank filling network (RFBFN). Specifically, we first detect potential relations maintained in the text to aid the following entity pair extraction. Then, we transform relations into relation templates with blanks which contain the fine-grained semantic representation of the relations. Finally, corresponding subjects and objects are extracted simultaneously by filling the blanks. We evaluate the proposed model on public benchmark datasets. Experimental results show our model outperforms current state-of-the-art methods. The source code of our work is available at: `https://github.com/lizhe2016/RFBFN`.

1 Introduction

Extracting pairs of entities with semantic relations from unstructured texts is essential in knowledge graph construction. Given a text, the aim of this task is to detect triples, i.e., in the form of *(subject, relation, object)* or *(s, r, o)*. Traditional pipeline methods (Chan and Roth, 2011; Lin et al., 2016) first extract entity mentions and then perform relation classification for each entity pair. However, they suffer from error propagation and ignore the interaction between the two tasks.

Different from the pipeline methods, joint learning methods (Yu et al., 2020; Zeng et al., 2020; Zheng et al., 2021) aim to extract entities and relations simultaneously in an end-to-end way, which achieve promising performance. They tend to decompose the task into several subtasks and solve the problem through a multi-task learning framework (Miwa and Bansal, 2016; Wei et al., 2020; Zheng et al., 2021).

Model	Relation Semantics	Relation-First Prediction	Simultaneous Subject-Object Extraction
Multi-Turn QA (Li et al., 2019)	Yes	No	No
PRGC (Zheng et al., 2021)	No	Yes	No
RFBFN (Ours)	Yes	Yes	Yes

Table 1: Comparison of our RFBFN and previous methods.

Although previous works have achieved great success, the semantic information of relations is still underutilized. Most models (Miwa and Bansal, 2016; Zeng et al., 2018; Zhong and Chen, 2021) treat the relation extraction as a classification task which only replace the relation with a meaningless class ID. To better capture the semantic information, machine reading comprehension (MRC) models (Li et al., 2019; Zhao et al., 2020; Goswami et al., 2020) are proposed to address the extraction task. Li et al. (2019) and Zhao et al. (2020) transform the task into a multi-turn question answering problem. The subjects are detected first by answering entity-specific questions. Then, relation-specific questions are generated to extract objects. However, they predict subjects and objects sequentially and separately, and thus question answering is required to perform for multiple turns.

More recently, the relation-first methods have shown promising performance in relational triple extraction (Zheng et al., 2021; Ma et al., 2021), which benefit from the fact that relations are usually triggered by the context rather than entities. For example, the *"creator"* relation will be directly detected from descriptions such as *"was created by"*. By predicting relations first, irrelevant relations are filtered out, which mitigates negative effects caused by useless relations and avoids the data imbalance issue. However, the subject-object

Proceedings of the 60th Annual Meeting of the Association for Computational Linguistics
Student Research Workshop, pages 10 - 20

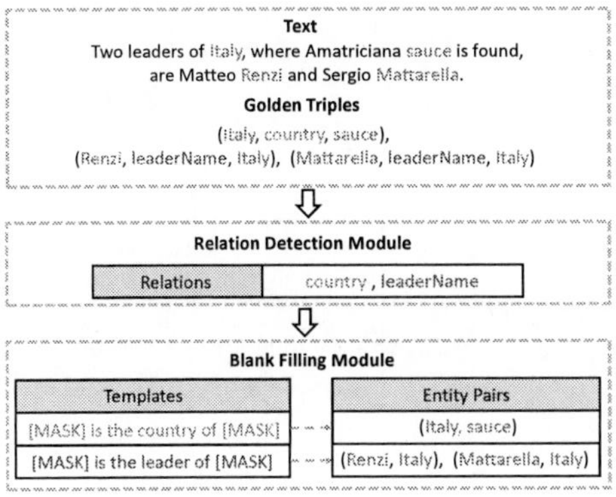

Figure 1: An illustration of the relational triple extraction in the proposed RFBFN. The relation templates contain blanks for entity extraction.

alignment mechanism is needed to align subjects and objects to form valid triples in these works. We review and compare previous methods in Table 1.

We propose an end-to-end relation-first framework for joint relational triple extraction, which can not only capture the semantics of relations, but also extract subjects and objects simultaneously. We formalize the task as a relation-first blank filling problem, inspired by the cloze task (Taylor, 1953). Our RFBFN includes a relation detection module and a blank filling module. For the relation detection module, we first obtain a subset of most relevant relations and filter out irrelevant ones. For the blank filling module, we transform relations to relation templates which contain significant semantics of relations. As shown in Figure 1, the model needs to fill the blanks in the templates like "`[MASK] is the country of [MASK]`" and "`[MASK] is the leader of [MASK]`" with the corresponding subjects and objects. Thus, entity pairs in the text which have the corresponding relations will be extracted by filling the blanks. Notably, our model detects subjects and objects simultaneously in a non-autoregressive decoder without aligning them. Besides, entities are allowed to be assigned with different relations, which naturally tackles the overlapping cases. Experiments on public datasets demonstrate that our proposed method outperforms the state-of-the-art methods. The main contributions of this paper are as follows:

- We propose a novel end-to-end relation-first blank filling network for relational triple extraction, which first detects relations, and then extracts subjects and objects simultaneously in a non-autoregressive transformer decoder.
- We tackle the entity pair extraction from a novel perspective which transforms the task to a blank filling problem. This paradigm allows the model to encode the prior knowledge of the relations in the templates and make use of semantic information of the relations.
- Extensive experiments on two public datasets show that the proposed framework achieves state-of-the-art results, especially for complex scenarios of overlapping triples. Further ablation studies and analyses confirm the effectiveness of our model.

2 Related Work

Early works (Zelenko et al., 2003; Chan and Roth, 2011; Lin et al., 2016) treat the extraction as a pipeline of two separate tasks: an entity model first identifies entities and then a relation model extracts the relations between the entity mentions. However, these methods ignore the correlation between the two steps and suffer from the error propagation issue. To overcome these shortcomings, joint models (Lin et al., 2020; Wang and Lu, 2020) are proposed, which can extract entities and relations simultaneously.

Traditional joint methods (Yu and Lam, 2010; Li and Ji, 2014; Miwa and Sasaki, 2014; Ren et al., 2017) are feature-based and heavily rely on feature engineering, which require intensive manual efforts. To reduce manual work, recent studies have investigated neural network models, which include sequence tagging methods (Zheng et al., 2017; Dai et al., 2019; Yu et al., 2020), sequence-to-sequence methods (Zeng et al., 2018, 2020) and table-filling methods (Gupta et al., 2016; Wang et al., 2021).

Although above models make great progress, they still only treat the relation type as a meaningless class ID or a trainable embedding (Yuan et al., 2020; Zheng et al., 2021) which is not enough to capture the fine-grained semantic information of a relation. Current works cast the task into a question answering problem with machine reading models. Goswami et al. (2020) perform unsupervised relation extraction without a fine-tuned extractive head. However, they only extract objects from the given contexts and subjects. To joint extract entities and relations, Li et al. (2019); Zhao et al. (2020) first predict subjects from the context by answering entity questions. Then, the extracted subjects are inserted to the slots to generate the relation ques-

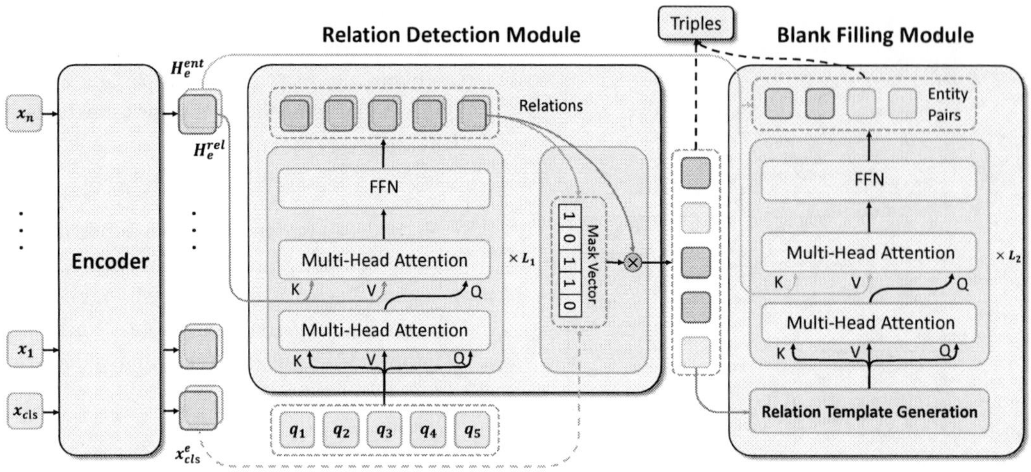

Figure 2: The overall architecture of RFBFN. Given a sentence X, RFBFN first predicts a subset of candidate relations in the relation detection module. Then for each candidate relation, corresponding entity pairs are extracted by filling the blanks of the transformed relation templates in the blank filling module. $q_1, q_2, ..., q_5$ are learnable embeddings to predict relations. L_1 and L_2 are the numbers of the decoder blocks.

tions and then objects can be extracted. Although the well developed machine reading comprehension models can be exploited, they extract subjects and objects sequentially and need multiple turns.

In this paper, we propose a joint relation-first blank filling network to extract triples. Different from previous works, we transform relations to specific relation templates to make use of semantic information of the relations. Moreover, we extract subjects and objects at the same time in a non-autoregressive decoder without aligning them.

3 Method

3.1 Overview

For relational triple extraction task, the input is a sentence $X = (x_1, x_2, ..., x_n)$, which comprises n tokens of the sentence with another special `[CLS]` token x_{cls}. Let $\mathcal{R}$ be the set of predefined relation types. The task is to predict all possible triples as $T(X) = (e_i, r_{ij}, e_j)$, where e_i, e_j are sequences of tokens denoting the subject and object respectively, and $r_{ij} \in \mathcal{R}$ is the relation that holds between e_i and e_j.

Figure 2 shows an overview architecture of the proposed RFBFN. It consists of three main parts: *Span-Level Encoder*, *Relation Detection Module* and *Blank Filling Module*. First, the encoder preprocesses the source text and extracts the span representations. Then the relation detection module predicts potential relations and filters out irrelevant ones. Finally, the blank filling module takes a set of relation templates as input and predicts the corresponding entity pairs. We model relation extraction as a blank filling task, which can not only capture the semantics of a relation, but also extract subjects and objects simultaneously.

3.2 Span-Level Encoder

The goal of this component is to obtain the contextualized representation of each span in a sentence. We utilize BERT (Devlin et al., 2019) as the feature encoder due to its effectiveness in representation learning. Let $S = (s_1, s_2, ..., s_{n_s})$ be all possible spans in X. Given a span $s_i \in S$, the span representation $\mathbf{h}_\mathrm{i}^\mathrm{e}$ is defined as:

$$\mathbf{h}_\mathrm{i}^\mathrm{e} = [\mathbf{x}^\mathrm{e}_{\mathrm{START(i)}}; \mathbf{x}^\mathrm{e}_{\mathrm{END(i)}}; \phi(\mathbf{x}_\mathrm{i})], \qquad (1)$$

where $\mathbf{x}^\mathrm{e}_{\mathrm{START(i)}}$ and $\mathbf{x}^\mathrm{e}_{\mathrm{START(i)}}$ are the context-aware representations of the boundary tokens. $\phi(\mathbf{x}_i)$ represents the feature vector denoting the span length (Wadden et al., 2019; Zhong and Chen, 2021). Unlike the token-level models, overlapping spans can be detected because each span is independent of others. The output of the encoder is the representation of spans, and is denoted as $\mathbf{H}^\mathrm{e} \in \mathbb{R}^{\mathrm{n_s} \times \mathrm{d}}$, where n_s is the number of spans and d is embedding dimension.

Then $\mathbf{H}^\mathrm{e}$ is fed into two separate *Feed-Forward Networks (FFN)* to generate the features for the *Relation Detection Module* and the *Blank Filling*

Module respectively:

$$\mathbf{H}_{\mathrm{e}}^{\mathrm{rel}} = \mathbf{W}_{rel}\mathbf{H}^{e} + \mathbf{b}_{rel},$$
$$\mathbf{H}_{\mathrm{e}}^{\mathrm{ent}} = \mathbf{W}_{ent}\mathbf{H}^{e} + \mathbf{b}_{ent}, \tag{2}$$

where $\mathbf{W}_{rel}, \mathbf{W}_{ent} \in \mathbb{R}^{d\times d}$ are trainable weights and $\mathbf{b}_{rel}, \mathbf{b}_{ent} \in \mathbb{R}^{d}$ are trainable biases.

3.3 Relation Detection Module

Different from previous works (Yuan et al., 2020; Wei et al., 2020) which redundantly perform entity extraction to every relation, we first predict a subset of candidate relations in a sentence, then entities only need to be extracted based on these target ones. This module first predicts potential relations with a non-autoregressive decoder, then irrelevant ones are excluded with a binary classifier.

Potential Relation Extractor We predict the relations with the transformer-based non-autoregressive decoder (Vaswani et al., 2017), as shown in Figure 2. The input of the decoder is initialized by n_q learnable embeddings $\mathbf{Q} \in \mathbb{R}^{\mathrm{n_q}\times \mathrm{d}}$, where n_q is set to be the maximum number of relations in a sentence. Different from the prior token-level cross-attention, we exploit the span representation $\mathbf{H}_{\mathrm{e}}^{\mathrm{rel}}$ as part of the input here. Given the output embedding $\mathbf{H}^{\mathrm{r}} \in \mathbb{R}^{\mathrm{n_q}\times \mathrm{d}}$, the predicted relation type is obtained by:

$$\mathbf{p}_{\mathrm{i}}^{\mathrm{r}} = \mathrm{Softmax}(\mathbf{W}_{\mathrm{r}}\mathbf{h}_{\mathrm{i}}^{\mathrm{r}} + \mathbf{b}_{\mathrm{r}}), \tag{3}$$

where $\mathbf{W}_{\mathrm{r}} \in \mathbb{R}^{|\mathcal{R}|\times \mathrm{d}}$, $\mathbf{b}_{\mathrm{r}} \in \mathbb{R}^{|\mathcal{R}|}$ are learnable parameters and $|\mathcal{R}|$ is the total number of relation types. We adopt the bipartite matching loss (Sui et al., 2020) in the training process, which is invariant to any permutation of predictions.

Candidate Relation Judgement After predicting a subset of potential relations, we filter out irrelevant ones to generate relation templates effectively. Given the output representation matrix $\mathbf{H}^{\mathrm{r}}$ of the non-autoregressive decoder and the embedding of `[CLS]`, this component predicts a boolean mask vector $\mathbf{M}$ from a binary classifier to guide the candidate relation set:

$$\mathbf{M} = \sigma(\mathbf{W}_{\mathrm{s}}[\mathbf{H}^{\mathrm{r}}; \mathbf{x}_{\mathrm{cls}}^{\mathrm{e}}] + \mathbf{b}_{\mathrm{s}}), \tag{4}$$

where $\mathbf{W}_s$ is the trainable weight, $\mathbf{b}_s$ is the bias and σ is the sigmoid activation function. The higher the value, the higher the confidence level that the relation contains in a sentence, and vice versa. In this step, for each sentence, we filter out useless relations and predict a subset $\mathcal{R}_i \in \mathcal{R}$ to discard most of the negative samples. If the text contains the j-th relation type, it will be fed into blank filling module to aid entity pair recognition.

3.4 Blank Filling Module

We propose a new blank filling paradigm for entity pair extraction, i.e., the extraction of entity pairs is transformed to the task of identifying answer spans from the context to fill the blanks. We transform each candidate relation type to a template with blanks (denoted as `[MASK]` here), which are then filled with the participating subjects and objects. In other words, if the context contains the corresponding entity pairs of the relation, entity spans will be extracted by filling the blanks.

Relation Template Generation Each relation type is associated with a type-specific template. A relation template is generated manually by combing the semantic information and two blanks as shown in Figure 1. For example, the relation "`leaderName`" corresponds to the template like "`[MASK] is the leader of [MASK]`". The relation template encodes the semantic information for the relation which is important for relational triple extraction. Formally, the input relation template can be denoted as:

$$T_r = (m_1^r, t_1^r, t_2^r, ..., t_{n_t}^r, m_2^r), \tag{5}$$

where m_1^r denotes the blank for the subject, m_2^r for the object and $t_1^r, t_2^r, ..., t_{n_t}^r$ are the relation tokens of the relation r. Each relation template is copied k times and then concatenated with the special `[SEP]` token, where k is larger than the typical triple number of the relation. Therefore, multiple entity pairs with the same relation can be extracted in one pass.

Entity Pair Extractor Given the relation template and the span representation $\bar{\mathbf{H}} = [\mathbf{H}_{\mathrm{e}}^{\mathrm{ent}}; \mathbf{x}_{\mathrm{cls}}^{\mathrm{e}}]$, the goal of this component is to extract corresponding entity pairs. We use a non-autoregressive span-level transformer decoder as our entity pair extractor, which is similar to the relation extractor. In each transformer layer, the multi-head self-attention is to model the association between blanks and relation semantics, and the multi-head cross-attention is to fuse the information of the spans. After the decoder, blanks are embedded into $\mathbf{H}_{\mathrm{r}}^{\mathrm{blk}} \in \mathbb{R}^{2\mathrm{k}\times \mathrm{d}}$.

Next, the decoder copies subjects and objects from possible spans in the source sentence as the

Dataset	#Relations	#Sentences			Details of Test Set				
		Train	Valid	Test	Normal	EPO	SEO	$N=1$	$N>1$
NYT*	24	56195	4999	5000	3266	978	1297	3244	1756
WebNLG*	171	5019	500	703	246	26	457	266	437
NYT	24	56196	5000	5000	3071	1168	1273	3089	1911
WebNLG	216	5019	500	703	239	6	448	256	447

Table 2: Statistics of the datasets in experiments, where N is the number of triples in a sentence. EPO and SEO refer to entity pair overlapping and single entity overlapping respectively (Zeng et al., 2018). Note that a sentence can belong to both EPO and SEO patterns.

predictions of the blanks in parallel. To handle the instances without corresponding entities, we set the answer as the `[CLS]` token. We calculate the span representations for each blank as:

$$\mathbf{h}^{\mathrm{b}}_{\mathrm{i,r}} = \tanh(\mathbf{W}^1_{\mathrm{b}}\bar{\mathbf{H}} + \mathbf{W}^2_{\mathrm{b}}\mathbf{h}^{\mathrm{blk}}_{\mathrm{i,r}} + \mathbf{b}_{\mathrm{b}}), \quad (6)$$

where $\mathbf{W}^1_{\mathrm{b}}, \mathbf{W}^2_{\mathrm{b}} \in \mathbb{R}^{\mathrm{d}\times\mathrm{d}}$ are the trainable weights and $\mathbf{b}_{\mathrm{b}} \in \mathbb{R}^{\mathrm{d}}$ is the trainable bias.

Finally, we apply softmax to obtain the probability distribution and select the span with the highest probability as the predicted entity:

$$\mathbf{p}^{\mathrm{b}}_{\mathrm{i,r}} = \mathrm{Softmax}(\mathbf{u}^{\mathrm{T}}_{\mathrm{b}} \cdot \mathbf{h}^{\mathrm{b}}_{\mathrm{i,r}}), \quad (7)$$

where $\mathbf{u}_b \in \mathbb{R}^d$ is the learnable parameter. We use the span-based method to predict entity pairs, so entities with multiple tokens can be extracted simultaneously without the pointer network or the sequence labeling scheme.

3.5 Joint Training

There are totally two tasks in our model: relation detection and entity pair extraction. During optimization, we train the model jointly in a multi-task manner and share the parameters of the encoder. To predict entity pairs, we sort them according to their order in the text, and adopt cross-entropy loss as the loss function for entity pair extraction:

$$\mathcal{L}_{ent} = -\sum_{r=1}^{n_d}\sum_{i=1}^{2k} \log \mathbf{p}^{\mathrm{b}}_{\mathrm{i,r}}(\mathrm{y}^{\mathrm{b}}_{\mathrm{i,r}}), \quad (8)$$

where $\mathrm{y}^{\mathrm{b}}_{\mathrm{i,r}}$ is the ground truth entity span for relation r and n_d is the detected relation number. However, for relation detection, there exists no suitable way to sort the relations, thus we adopt bipartite matching loss (Sui et al., 2020) which does not penalize small order shift. To find an optimal matching between the ground truth relations and predicted relations, we search for a permutation strategy π^* with the lowest cost:

$$\pi^* = \underset{\pi\in\Pi(\mathrm{n_q})}{\mathrm{argmin}}(-\sum_{\mathrm{i=1}}^{\mathrm{n_q}} \mathrm{I}(\mathrm{y}^{\mathrm{r}}_{\mathrm{i}}) \cdot \mathbf{p}^{\mathrm{r}}_{\pi(\mathrm{i})}(\mathrm{y}^{\mathrm{r}}_{\mathrm{i}})), \quad (9)$$

where $\Pi(n_q)$ is the space of all permutation strategies, $\mathrm{y}^{\mathrm{r}}_{\mathrm{i}}$ is the ground truth relation. $I(y^r_i)$ is a switching function: if $\mathrm{y}^{\mathrm{r}}_{\mathrm{i}} \neq \varnothing$, $\mathrm{I}(\mathrm{y}^{\mathrm{r}}_{\mathrm{i}}) = 1$, otherwise 0. We define the loss for relation detection as:

$$\mathcal{L}_{rel} = -\sum_{\mathrm{i=1}}^{\mathrm{n_q}} \log \mathbf{p}^{\mathrm{r}}_{\pi^*(\mathrm{i})}(\mathrm{y}^{\mathrm{r}}_{\mathrm{i}}) \quad (10)$$

The total loss is the sum of two parts:

$$\mathcal{L} = \lambda\mathcal{L}_{ent} + (1-\lambda)\mathcal{L}_{rel}, \quad (11)$$

where $\lambda \in \mathbb{R}$ is the parameter controlling the trade-off between the two objectives. During the training phase, the model learns to minimize $\mathcal{L}$ and optimizes the parameters jointly.

4 Experiments

4.1 Experimental Settings

Datasets We evaluate our approach on two benchmark datasets: NYT24 (Riedel et al., 2010) and WebNLG (Gardent et al., 2017). Both of them have two different versions. NYT* and WebNLG* annotate the last word of entities, while NYT and WebNLG annotate the whole entity span. We use the datasets released by (Zheng et al., 2021), in which the statistics of the datasets are shown in Table 2. To further study the capability of RFBFN in extracting overlapping and multiple relations, we also split the test set by overlapping patterns (Zeng et al., 2018) and triple numbers.

Baselines and Evaluation Metrics We compare our model with eleven strong baseline models including the state-of-the-art model GRTE$_{BERT}$ (Ren et al., 2021). The experimental results of the baseline models are from the original papers.

Model	NYT*			WebNLG*			NYT			WebNLG		
	Prec.	Rec.	F1	Prec.	Rec.	F1	Prec.	Rec.	F1	Prec.	Rec.	F1
NovalTagging (Zheng et al., 2017)	-	-	-	-	-	-	32.8	30.6	31.7	52.5	19.3	28.3
CopyRE (Zeng et al., 2018)	61.0	56.6	58.7	37.7	36.4	37.1	-	-	-	-	-	-
MutiHead (Bekoulis et al., 2018)	-	-	-	-	-	-	60.7	58.6	59.6	57.5	54.1	55.7
GraphRel (Fu et al., 2019)	63.9	60.0	61.9	44.7	41.1	42.9	-	-	-	-	-	-
ETL-span (Yu et al., 2020)	84.9	72.3	78.1	84.0	91.5	87.6	85.5	71.7	78.0	84.3	82.0	83.1
CasRel$_{BERT}$ (Wei et al., 2020)	89.7	89.5	89.6	93.4	90.1	91.8	-	-	-	-	-	-
TPLinker$_{BERT}$ (Wang et al., 2020)	91.3	92.5	91.9	91.8	92.0	91.9	91.4	92.6	92.0	88.9	84.5	86.7
SPN$_{BERT}$ (Sui et al., 2020)	93.3	91.7	92.5	93.1	93.6	93.4	92.5	92.2	92.3	-	-	-
PRGC$_{Random}$ (Zheng et al., 2021)	89.6	82.3	85.8	90.6	88.5	89.5	87.8	83.8	85.8	82.5	79.2	80.8
PRGC$_{BERT}$ (Zheng et al., 2021)	93.3	91.9	92.6	**94.0**	92.1	93.0	93.5	91.9	92.7	89.9	87.2	88.5
GRTE$_{BERT}$ (Ren et al., 2021)	92.9	93.1	93.0	93.7	**94.2**	93.9	93.4	93.5	93.4	**92.3**	87.9	90.0
RFBFN$_{Random}$	88.6	86.8	87.7	90.4	90.8	90.6	87.9	86.1	87.0	83.1	82.1	82.6
RFBFN$_{BERT}$	**93.4**	**93.2**	**93.3**	93.9	94.1	**94.0**	**93.7**	**93.6**	**93.6**	91.5	**89.4**	**90.4**

Table 3: Comparison of the proposed RFBFN method with the prior works. **Bold** marks the highest score. The subscript *Random* refers to a model with randomly initialized parameters.

In our experiments, to keep in line with previous works (Sui et al., 2020; Zheng et al., 2021; Ren et al., 2021), an extracted triple is regarded as correct only if it is an extract match with ground truth, which means the last word of entities in NYT* and WebNLG* or the whole entity span in NYT and WebNLG of both subject and object and the relation are all correct. The standard micro precision, recall, and F1 score are used to evaluate the results.

Implementation Details For fair comparison, we use the BERT-Base-Cased English model[1] as our embedding layer. We train our model with AdamW optimizer with batch size of 8 for 100 epochs. We set the learning rate $1e-5$ for the pre-trained parameters, $5e-5$ for cross-attention and $7e-5$ for others. The spans are up to 8 words and $\lambda = 0.5$ for loss. The duplicate number k of relation templates on NYT*, NYT, WebNLG* and WebNLG is set to 6, 8, 3 and 3 respectively. The learnable embedding number n_q is set to 15/12 in NYT(NYT*)/WebNLG(WebNLG*).

4.2 Main Results

The results of our model against other baseline methods are shown in Table 3. Our RFBFN model outperforms them in respect of almost all evaluation metrics even if compared with the recent strongest baseline (Ren et al., 2021). We also implement RFBFN$_{Random}$ where all parameters are randomly initialized. Especially, RFBFN$_{Random}$ improves 1.9% F1 on NYT*, 1.1% F1 on WebNLG*, 1.2% F1 on NYT and 1.8% F1 on WebNLG over PRGC$_{Random}$. The performance of RFBFN$_{Random}$ demonstrates that our framework still achieves better results than others which do not take BERT as the pre-trained language model.

Our RFBFN outperforms the most competitive GRTE$_{BERT}$ model in four F1 scores. There are two main reasons behind this. First, the relation detection module greatly reduces irrelevant relations compared to GRTE$_{BERT}$ which generates a table feature for each relation. In other words, filtering negative relations provides additional benefits compared to the models which perform entity extraction under every relation. Second, introduction of semantic information of the relations is significant for relational triple extraction. However, GRTE$_{BERT}$ only assigns trainable weights for the relations, which can not fully explore the semantic information of the relations. Moreover, our model detects subjects and objects simultaneously in the non-autoregressive decoder. By contrast, PRGC$_{BERT}$ is a relation-first model, which extracts subjects and objects in two separate sequence tagging operations and needs to check the corresponding score in a global matrix for subject-object alignment. We find that detects subjects and objects simultaneously can achieve better results.

4.3 Detailed Results on Complex Scenarios

Following previous works (Sui et al., 2020; Zheng et al., 2021; Ren et al., 2021), we conduct further experiments on NYT* and WebNLG* to verify

[1]Available at `https://huggingface.co/bert-base-cased`.

Model	NYT*								WebNLG*							
	Normal	SEO	EPO	$N=1$	$N=2$	$N=3$	$N=4$	$N\geq 5$	Normal	SEO	EPO	$N=1$	$N=2$	$N=3$	$N=4$	$N\geq 5$
CasRel	87.3	91.4	92.0	88.2	90.3	91.9	94.2	83.7	89.4	92.2	94.7	89.3	90.8	94.2	92.4	90.9
TPLinker	90.1	93.4	94.0	90.0	92.8	93.1	96.1	90.0	87.9	92.5	95.3	88.0	90.1	94.6	93.3	91.6
SPN	90.8	94.0	94.1	90.9	93.4	94.2	95.5	90.6	89.5	94.1	90.8	89.5	91.3	96.4	94.7	93.8
PRGC	91.0	94.0	94.5	91.1	93.0	93.5	95.5	93.0	90.4	93.6	95.9	89.9	91.6	95.0	94.8	92.8
GRTE	91.1	94.4	95.0	90.8	93.7	94.4	96.2	93.4	90.6	94.5	96.0	90.6	92.5	96.5	**95.5**	94.4
RFBFN	**91.2**	**95.2**	**95.6**	**91.4**	**93.8**	**94.8**	**96.4**	**93.9**	**91.0**	**94.6**	**96.5**	**90.8**	**92.6**	**96.6**	94.7	**94.5**

Table 4: F1 score on sentences with different overlapping patterns and different triple numbers. N is the number of triples in a sentence.

	Subtask	Prec.	Rec.	F1
NYT*	Potential Relation Extractor	96.8	96.0	96.4
	Candidate Relation Judgement	97.7	95.4	96.5
	Entity Pair Extractor	95.0	94.8	94.9
	Combination of Above All	93.4	93.2	93.3
WebNLG*	Potential Relation Extractor	95.8	95.9	95.9
	Candidate Relation Judgement	96.9	94.9	95.9
	Entity Pair Extractor	96.5	96.7	96.6
	Combination of Above All	93.9	94.1	94.0

Table 5: Results of different subtasks on NYT* and WebNLG* datasets. Relation performance after *Potential Relation Extractor* and *Candidate Relation Judgement*. Entity performance after *Entity Pair Extractor*.

Model	Prec.	Rec.	F1
RFBFN	**93.9**	94.1	**94.0**
– Relation Detection Module	81.7	89.0	85.2
– Candidate Relation Judgement	92.9	**94.3**	93.6
– Relation Template Generation	93.0	93.2	93.1
– Non-Autoregressive Entity Pair Extractor	88.8	88.2	88.5
– Joint Training	92.4	92.6	92.5

Table 6: Ablation study on WebNLG* dataset.

the capability of our model in handling different overlapping patterns and sentences with different numbers of triples. As shown in Table 4, we can see that RFBFN achieves the best results on all three overlapping patterns of both datasets. Besides, the performance of our model is better than others almost for all numbers of triples. In general, these two further experiments adequately show the advantages of our model in complex scenarios.

4.4 Results on Different Subtasks

To further verify the results of the subtasks, we present more detailed evaluations on NYT* and WebNLG* datasets which show the performance after each component of our model in Table 5. After the *Candidate Relation Judgement* component, we get higher precision in relation detection to reduce negative relations and ensure most detected relations are correct. In the *Entity Pair Extractor* component, golden relation templates are taken as input, which showcases the upper bound result that our model can achieve for relational triple extraction. The result shows the proposed blank filling module outperforms existing models by a large margin (up to 2.7%). This indicates that our method is able to capture the sufficient semantic information of relations which helps to extract entities.

For NYT*, we find that identifying relations is somehow easier than identifying entities. In contrast to NYT*, for WebNLG*, it is more challenging to identify the relations than entities, as the performance of the entity pair extractor is much higher than the overall performance. We attribute the difference to the different numbers of relations in two datasets (24 in NYT* and 171 in WebNLG*), which make identification of relations much harder in WebNLG*.

5 Analysis

5.1 Ablation Study

We conduct ablation experiments to evaluate the contributions of some main components in RFBFN. We remove one component at a time to obtain its impact on the experimental results, which is summarized in Table 6.

(1) – *Relation Detection Module* denotes that the model removes the *Relation Detection Module* from RFBFN, and uses all relations to extract entity pairs. It is not possible to enumerate all relations in WebNLG* (171 in all), and thus we randomly add 30% negative ones. As shown in Table 6, the performance significantly decreases without relation detection. It is because that redundant relations cause negative influence on entity pair extractor. Meanwhile, with the increase of relation number,

Texts	Ground Truth	Embeddings	Relation Templates
Acta Mathematica **Hungarica** is the publisher of Springer Science + Business **Media**, founded by Julius **Springer**.	(Hungarica, publisher, Media) (Springer, founder, Media)	(Springer, publisher, Media) ✖ (Springer, founder, Media)	(Hungarica, publisher, Media) (Springer, founder, Media)
Buzz **Aldrin** is a national of the United **States** whose leader is Joe **Biden**. He was born in Glen Ridge, Essex County, New **Jersey**.	(Jersey, birthPlace, Aldrin) (States, nationality, Aldrin) (Biden, leaderName, States) (Jersey, isPartOf, Jersey)	(Jersey, birthPlace, Aldrin) (States, nationality, Aldrin) (Biden, leaderName, Jersey) ✖ (Jersey, isPartOf, Jersey)	(Jersey, birthPlace, Aldrin) (States, nationality, Aldrin) (Biden, leaderName, States) (Jersey, isPartOf, Jersey)

Figure 3: Case study for ablation study of *–Relation Template Generation*. Examples are from WebNLG* dataset. The correct entities are in **bold**, the correct relations are colored and the red cross marks bad cases.

it results in a heavy computational burden.

(2) – *Candidate Relation Judgement* denotes that the model ablates the *Candidate Relation Judgement* component from RFBFN, which ignores the impact of negative relations. We note the performance decreases in the result, which indicates that this component contributes to reducing the noise brought by unrelated relations. In other words, filtering out irrelevant relations is helpful for relational triple extraction.

(3) – *Relation Template Generation* denotes that the model replaces relation templates with trainable embeddings. As shown in the results, the performance drops significantly. Through the case study in Figure 3, we observe that if the relation is only represented by a trainable embedding, the model cannot understand the underlying semantics of a relation and predicts wrong entity pairs. Although it has the ability to detect right entities, it ignores their relation. However, our relation template can capture fine-grained semantic information of the relation, which is helpful for extracting entities. We argue that the explicit semantic representation of a relation plays an important role for relational triple extraction which is ignored in most previous works.

(4) – *Non-Autoregressive Entity Pair Extractor* denotes that the decoder replaces the unmasked self-attention with the casual mask and the entity pair extractor starts with a detected relation. In this way, subjects and objects are generated sequentially. The results in Table 6 reveal that predicting subjects and objects simultaneously in our non-autoregressive decoder is reasonable.

(5) – *Joint Training* denotes that the relation detection module and the blank filling module are trained separately without parameter sharing. As shown in Table 6, joint learning framework brings a remarkable improvement (1.5%) in F1 score, which demonstrates that our potential relation extractor

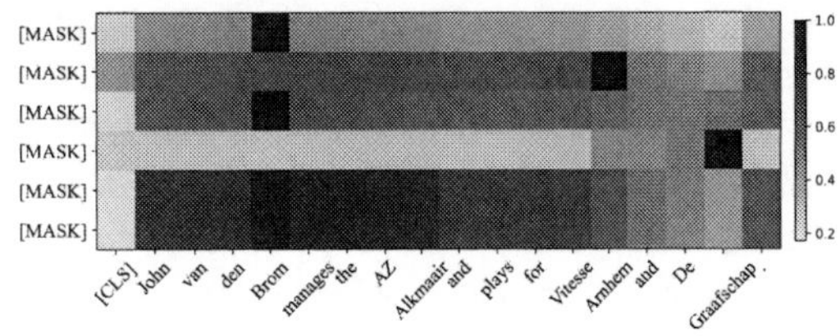

Figure 4: An illustration on how different blanks attend to the words in the text. The attention score is averaged over all attention heads in the last layer. The darker color denotes the higher score.

and entity pair extractor actually work in a mutually beneficial way.

5.2 Visualization

In order to validate that our model is able to fill the blanks with related entities in the sentence, we visualize the cross-attention score of the blank filling module in Figure 4. The source sentence contains two triples, i.e. *(Brom, club, Arnhem), (Brom, club, Graafschap)* and the input relation of the entity pair extractor is `club`. As shown in Figure 4, through span-level cross-attention, different blanks can attend to corresponding entities with the specific relation. In the entity pair extractor, subjects and objects with the same relation can be extracted simultaneously rather than sequentially. Besides, the extracting order is determined with the sorting scheme, thus we do not extract repetitive entity pairs. The visualization demonstrates the validity of our model.

6 Conclusion

In this paper, we design a novel blank filling paradigm for relational triple extraction, and present a relation-first blank filling network. We transform relations into relation templates with blanks to fill which can capture important semantic information of the relations. Meanwhile, subjects and objects are extracted simultaneously by filling the blanks in the non-autoregressive decoder. To the best of our knowledge, we are the first to cast relational triple extraction as a blank filling problem, which may motivate new ideas and inspire future research directions. The experiment results on public datasets show that our model achieves state-of-the-art performance.

Acknowledgements

This work is supported by National Key R&D Program of China (No.2018YFB2100302), NSF China (No. 42050105, 62020106005, 62061146002, 61960206002, 61822206, 61832013, 61829201), 2021 Tencent AI Lab RhinoBird Focused Research Program (No: JR202132), and the Program of Shanghai Academic/Technology Research Leader under Grant No. 18XD1401800.

References

Giannis Bekoulis, Johannes Deleu, Thomas Demeester, and Chris Develder. 2018. Joint entity recognition and relation extraction as a multi-head selection problem. *Expert Systems with Applications*, 114:34–45.

Yee Seng Chan and Dan Roth. 2011. Exploiting syntactico-semantic structures for relation extraction. In *Proceedings of the 49th Annual Meeting of the Association for Computational Linguistics: Human Language Technologies*, pages 551–560, Portland, Oregon, USA. Association for Computational Linguistics.

Dai Dai, Xinyan Xiao, Yajuan Lyu, Shan Dou, Qiaoqiao She, and Haifeng Wang. 2019. Joint extraction of entities and overlapping relations using position-attentive sequence labeling. *Proceedings of the AAAI Conference on Artificial Intelligence*, 33(01):6300–6308.

Jacob Devlin, Ming-Wei Chang, Kenton Lee, and Kristina Toutanova. 2019. BERT: Pre-training of deep bidirectional transformers for language understanding. In *Proceedings of the 2019 Conference of the North American Chapter of the Association for Computational Linguistics: Human Language Technologies, Volume 1 (Long and Short Papers)*, pages 4171–4186, Minneapolis, Minnesota. Association for Computational Linguistics.

Tsu-Jui Fu, Peng-Hsuan Li, and Wei-Yun Ma. 2019. GraphRel: Modeling text as relational graphs for joint entity and relation extraction. In *Proceedings of the 57th Annual Meeting of the Association for Computational Linguistics*, pages 1409–1418, Florence, Italy. Association for Computational Linguistics.

Claire Gardent, Anastasia Shimorina, Shashi Narayan, and Laura Perez-Beltrachini. 2017. Creating training corpora for NLG micro-planners. In *Proceedings of the 55th Annual Meeting of the Association for Computational Linguistics (Volume 1: Long Papers)*, pages 179–188, Vancouver, Canada. Association for Computational Linguistics.

Ankur Goswami, Akshata Bhat, Hadar Ohana, and Theodoros Rekatsinas. 2020. Unsupervised relation extraction from language models using constrained cloze completion. In *Findings of the Association for Computational Linguistics: EMNLP 2020*, pages 1263–1276, Online. Association for Computational Linguistics.

Pankaj Gupta, Hinrich Schütze, and Bernt Andrassy. 2016. Table filling multi-task recurrent neural network for joint entity and relation extraction. In *Proceedings of COLING 2016, the 26th International Conference on Computational Linguistics: Technical Papers*, pages 2537–2547, Osaka, Japan. The COLING 2016 Organizing Committee.

Qi Li and Heng Ji. 2014. Incremental joint extraction of entity mentions and relations. In *Proceedings of the 52nd Annual Meeting of the Association for Computational Linguistics (Volume 1: Long Papers)*, pages 402–412, Baltimore, Maryland. Association for Computational Linguistics.

Xiaoya Li, Fan Yin, Zijun Sun, Xiayu Li, Arianna Yuan, Duo Chai, Mingxin Zhou, and Jiwei Li. 2019. Entity-relation extraction as multi-turn question answering. In *Proceedings of the 57th Annual Meeting of the Association for Computational Linguistics*, pages 1340–1350, Florence, Italy. Association for Computational Linguistics.

Yankai Lin, Shiqi Shen, Zhiyuan Liu, Huanbo Luan, and Maosong Sun. 2016. Neural relation extraction with selective attention over instances. In *Proceedings of the 54th Annual Meeting of the Association for Computational Linguistics (Volume 1: Long Papers)*, pages 2124–2133, Berlin, Germany. Association for Computational Linguistics.

Ying Lin, Heng Ji, Fei Huang, and Lingfei Wu. 2020. A joint neural model for information extraction with global features. In *Proceedings of the 58th Annual Meeting of the Association for Computational Linguistics*, pages 7999–8009, Online. Association for Computational Linguistics.

Lianbo Ma, Huimin Ren, and Xiliang Zhang. 2021. Effective cascade dual-decoder model for joint entity and relation extraction. *arXiv preprint arXiv:2106.14163*.

Makoto Miwa and Mohit Bansal. 2016. End-to-end relation extraction using LSTMs on sequences and tree structures. In *Proceedings of the 54th Annual Meeting of the Association for Computational Linguistics (Volume 1: Long Papers)*, pages 1105–1116, Berlin, Germany. Association for Computational Linguistics.

Makoto Miwa and Yutaka Sasaki. 2014. Modeling joint entity and relation extraction with table representation. In *Proceedings of the 2014 Conference on Empirical Methods in Natural Language Processing (EMNLP)*, pages 1858–1869, Doha, Qatar. Association for Computational Linguistics.

Feiliang Ren, Longhui Zhang, Shujuan Yin, Xiaofeng Zhao, Shilei Liu, Bochao Li, and Yaduo Liu. 2021. A novel global feature-oriented relational triple extraction model based on table filling. In *Proceedings of the 2021 Conference on Empirical Methods in Natural Language Processing*, pages 2646–2656, Online and Punta Cana, Dominican Republic. Association for Computational Linguistics.

Xiang Ren, Zeqiu Wu, Wenqi He, Meng Qu, Clare R. Voss, Heng Ji, Tarek F. Abdelzaher, and Jiawei Han. 2017. Cotype: Joint extraction of typed entities and relations with knowledge bases. WWW '17, page 1015–1024, Republic and Canton of Geneva, CHE. International World Wide Web Conferences Steering Committee.

Sebastian Riedel, Limin Yao, and Andrew McCallum. 2010. Modeling relations and their mentions without labeled text. In *Machine Learning and Knowledge Discovery in Databases*, pages 148–163, Berlin, Heidelberg. Springer Berlin Heidelberg.

Dianbo Sui, Yubo Chen, Kang Liu, Jun Zhao, Xiangrong Zeng, and Shengping Liu. 2020. Joint entity and relation extraction with set prediction networks. *arXiv preprint arXiv:2011.01675*.

Wilson L Taylor. 1953. "cloze procedure": A new tool for measuring readability. *Journalism quarterly*, 30(4):415–433.

Ashish Vaswani, Noam Shazeer, Niki Parmar, Jakob Uszkoreit, Llion Jones, Aidan N. Gomez, Łukasz Kaiser, and Illia Polosukhin. 2017. Attention is all you need. In *Proceedings of the 31st International Conference on Neural Information Processing Systems*, NIPS'17, page 6000–6010, Red Hook, NY, USA. Curran Associates Inc.

David Wadden, Ulme Wennberg, Yi Luan, and Hannaneh Hajishirzi. 2019. Entity, relation, and event extraction with contextualized span representations. In *Proceedings of the 2019 Conference on Empirical Methods in Natural Language Processing and the 9th International Joint Conference on Natural Language Processing (EMNLP-IJCNLP)*, pages 5784–5789, Hong Kong, China. Association for Computational Linguistics.

Jue Wang and Wei Lu. 2020. Two are better than one: Joint entity and relation extraction with table-sequence encoders. In *Proceedings of the 2020 Conference on Empirical Methods in Natural Language Processing (EMNLP)*, pages 1706–1721, Online. Association for Computational Linguistics.

Yijun Wang, Changzhi Sun, Yuanbin Wu, Hao Zhou, Lei Li, and Junchi Yan. 2021. UniRE: A unified label space for entity relation extraction. In *Proceedings of the 59th Annual Meeting of the Association for Computational Linguistics and the 11th International Joint Conference on Natural Language Processing (Volume 1: Long Papers)*, pages 220–231, Online. Association for Computational Linguistics.

Yucheng Wang, Bowen Yu, Yueyang Zhang, Tingwen Liu, Hongsong Zhu, and Limin Sun. 2020. TPLinker: Single-stage joint extraction of entities and relations through token pair linking. In *Proceedings of the 28th International Conference on Computational Linguistics*, pages 1572–1582, Barcelona, Spain (Online). International Committee on Computational Linguistics.

Zhepei Wei, Jianlin Su, Yue Wang, Yuan Tian, and Yi Chang. 2020. A novel cascade binary tagging framework for relational triple extraction. In *Proceedings of the 58th Annual Meeting of the Association for Computational Linguistics*, pages 1476–1488, Online. Association for Computational Linguistics.

Bowen Yu, Zhenyu Zhang, Xiaobo Shu, Tingwen Liu, Yubin Wang, Bin Wang, and Sujian Li. 2020. Joint extraction of entities and relations based on a novel decomposition strategy. In *ECAI*, pages 2282–2289. IOS Press.

Xiaofeng Yu and Wai Lam. 2010. Jointly identifying entities and extracting relations in encyclopedia text via a graphical model approach. In *Coling 2010: Posters*, pages 1399–1407, Beijing, China. Coling 2010 Organizing Committee.

Yue Yuan, Xiaofei Zhou, Shirui Pan, Qiannan Zhu, Zeliang Song, and Li Guo. 2020. A relation-specific attention network for joint entity and relation extraction. In *Proceedings of the Twenty-Ninth International Joint Conference on Artificial Intelligence, IJCAI-20*, pages 4054–4060. International Joint Conferences on Artificial Intelligence Organization. Main track.

Dmitry Zelenko, Chinatsu Aone, and Anthony Richardella. 2003. Kernel methods for relation extraction. *Journal of machine learning research*, 3(Feb):1083–1106.

Daojian Zeng, Haoran Zhang, and Qianying Liu. 2020. Copymtl: Copy mechanism for joint extraction of entities and relations with multi-task learning. *Proceedings of the AAAI Conference on Artificial Intelligence*, 34(05):9507–9514.

Xiangrong Zeng, Daojian Zeng, Shizhu He, Kang Liu, and Jun Zhao. 2018. Extracting relational facts by an end-to-end neural model with copy mechanism. In *Proceedings of the 56th Annual Meeting of the Association for Computational Linguistics (Volume 1: Long Papers)*, pages 506–514, Melbourne, Australia. Association for Computational Linguistics.

Tianyang Zhao, Zhao Yan, Yunbo Cao, and Zhoujun Li. 2020. Asking effective and diverse questions: A machine reading comprehension based framework for joint entity-relation extraction. In *Proceedings of the Twenty-Ninth International Joint Conference on Artificial Intelligence, IJCAI-20*, pages 3948–3954. International Joint Conferences on Artificial Intelligence Organization. Main track.

Hengyi Zheng, Rui Wen, Xi Chen, Yifan Yang, Yunyan Zhang, Ziheng Zhang, Ningyu Zhang, Bin Qin, Xu Ming, and Yefeng Zheng. 2021. PRGC: Potential relation and global correspondence based joint relational triple extraction. In *Proceedings of the 59th Annual Meeting of the Association for Computational Linguistics and the 11th International Joint Conference on Natural Language Processing (Volume 1: Long Papers)*, pages 6225–6235, Online. Association for Computational Linguistics.

Suncong Zheng, Feng Wang, Hongyun Bao, Yuexing Hao, Peng Zhou, and Bo Xu. 2017. Joint extraction of entities and relations based on a novel tagging scheme. In *Proceedings of the 55th Annual Meeting of the Association for Computational Linguistics (Volume 1: Long Papers)*, pages 1227–1236, Vancouver, Canada. Association for Computational Linguistics.

Zexuan Zhong and Danqi Chen. 2021. A frustratingly easy approach for entity and relation extraction. In *Proceedings of the 2021 Conference of the North American Chapter of the Association for Computational Linguistics: Human Language Technologies*, pages 50–61, Online. Association for Computational Linguistics.

Building a Dialogue Corpus Annotated with Expressed and Experienced Emotions

Tatsuya Ide and **Daisuke Kawahara**
Department of Computer Science and Communications Engineering, Waseda University
{t-ide@toki., dkw@}waseda.jp

Abstract

In communication, a human would recognize the emotion of an interlocutor and respond with an appropriate emotion, such as empathy and comfort. Toward developing a dialogue system with such a human-like ability, we propose a method to build a dialogue corpus annotated with two kinds of emotions. We collect dialogues from Twitter and annotate each utterance with the emotion that a speaker put into the utterance (expressed emotion) and the emotion that a listener felt after listening to the utterance (experienced emotion). We built a dialogue corpus in Japanese using this method, and its statistical analysis revealed the differences between expressed and experienced emotions. We conducted experiments on recognition of the two kinds of emotions. The experimental results indicated the difficulty in recognizing experienced emotions and the effectiveness of multi-task learning of the two kinds of emotions. We hope that the constructed corpus will facilitate the study on emotion recognition in a dialogue and emotion-aware dialogue response generation.

1 Introduction

Text-based communication has become indispensable as society accelerates online. In natural language processing, communication between humans and machines has attracted attention, and the development of dialogue systems has been a hot topic. Through the invention of Transformer (Vaswani et al., 2017) and the success of transfer learning (e.g., Radford et al. (2018); Devlin et al. (2019)), the performance of natural language understanding models and dialogue systems continues to improve. In recent years, there have been studies toward building open-domain neural chatbots that can generate a human-like response (Zhou et al., 2020; Adiwardana et al., 2020; Roller et al., 2021).

One of the keys to building more human-like chatbots is to generate a response that takes into account the emotion of the interlocutor. A human would recognize the emotion of the interlocutor and respond with an appropriate emotion, such as empathy and comfort, or give a response that promotes positive emotion of the interlocutor. Accordingly, developing a chatbot with such a human-like ability (Rashkin et al., 2019; Lubis et al., 2018, 2019) is essential. Although several dialogue corpora with emotion annotation have been proposed, an utterance is annotated only with a speaker's emotion (Li et al., 2017; Hsu et al., 2018) or a dialogue as a whole is annotated (Rashkin et al., 2019), all of which are not appropriate for enabling the above ability.

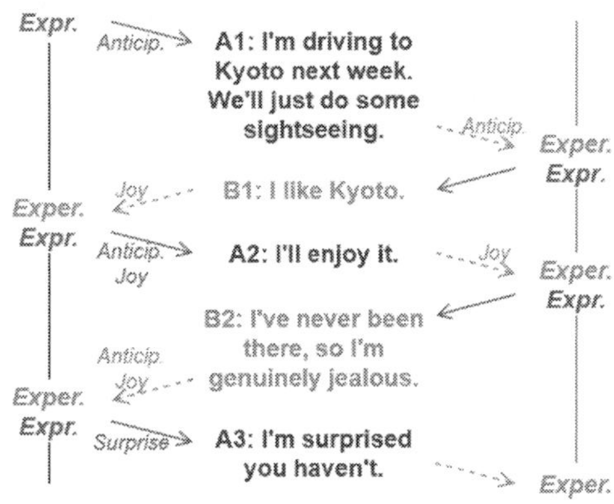

Figure 1: An example dialogue with expressed and experienced emotions.

In this paper, we propose a method to build an emotion-annotated multi-turn dialogue corpus, which is necessary for developing a dialogue system that can recognize the emotion of an interlocutor and generate a response with an appropriate emotion. We annotate each utterance in a dialogue with an **expressed emotion**, which a speaker put into the utterance, and an **experienced emotion**, which a listener felt when listening to the utterance.

To construct a multi-turn dialogue corpus annotated with these emotions, we collect dialogues

Proceedings of the 60th Annual Meeting of the Association for Computational Linguistics
Student Research Workshop, pages 21 - 30
May 22-27, 2022 ©2022 Association for Computational Linguistics

from Twitter and crowdsource their emotion annotation. As a dialogue corpus, we extract tweet sequences where two people speak alternately. For the emotion annotation, we adopt Plutchik's wheel of emotions (Plutchik, 1980) as emotion labels and ask crowdworkers whether an utterance indicates each emotion label for expressed and experienced emotion categories. Each utterance is allowed to have multiple emotion labels and has an intensity, strong and weak, according to the number of crowdworkers' votes. We build a Japanese dialogue corpus as a testbed in this paper, but our proposed method can be applied to any language.

Using the above method, we constructed a Japanese emotion-tagged dialogue corpus consisting of 3,828 dialogues and 13,806 utterances.[1] Statistical analysis of the constructed corpus revealed the characteristics of words for each emotion and the relationship between expressed and experienced emotions. We further conducted experiments to recognize expressed and experienced emotions using BERT (Devlin et al., 2019). We defined the task of emotion recognition as regression and evaluated BERT's performance using correlation coefficients. The experimental results showed that it was more difficult to infer experienced emotions than expressed emotions, and that multi-task learning of both emotion categories improved the overall performance of emotion recognition. From these results, we can see that expressed and experienced emotions are different, and that it is meaningful to annotate both. We expect that the constructed corpus will facilitate the study on emotion recognition in dialogue and emotion-aware response generation.

2 Related Work

2.1 Emotion-Tagged Corpora

Many non-dialogue corpora annotated with emotions have been constructed. EmoBank (Buechel and Hahn, 2017) is a corpus of social media or reviews with emotion annotation. They annotate sentences with the emotions of a person who read them and a person who wrote them. WRIME (Kajiwara et al., 2021) is an emotion-annotated corpus in Japanese, where SNS posts are tagged with both *subjective* and *objective* emotions. The concept of this corpus is similar to EmoBank. However, they emphasize the subjectivity of annotation and ask writers to annotate their own sentences with emotions. Furthermore, EmoInt (Mohammad and Bravo-Marquez, 2017) aims at the task of detecting emotion intensity. They annotate Twitter posts with anger, fear, joy, and sadness and give each emotion a real value between 0 and 1 as the intensity level.

Some corpora are tagged with non-emotional factors, along with emotions. EmotionStimulus (Ghazi et al., 2015) and GroundedEmotions (Liu et al., 2017) are corpora that focus on the reason for an expressed emotion. The former uses FrameNet to detect a cause, while the latter treats weather and news as external emotion factors. In terms of emotion labels, the two corpora adopt seven emotions (Ekman's six emotions (Ekman, 1992) and shame) and two emotions (only happiness and sadness), respectively. In StoryCommonsense (Rashkin et al., 2018), a series of sentences comprising of a short story is tagged with *motivation* and *emotional reaction* for each character. For emotion labels, they use some theories of psychology, including Plutchik's wheel of emotions (Plutchik, 1980).

None of the above corpora, however, are relevant to dialogue. StoryCommonsense is similar to ours but differs in that characters in a story are annotated instead of speakers' utterances.

2.2 Dialogue Corpora

Several dialogue corpora annotated with emotions are available. DailyDialog (Li et al., 2017) is one collected from educational websites and tagged with emotions and intentions. EmotionLines (Hsu et al., 2018) is a multi-turn dialogue corpus with annotation of emotions. Both of them use seven labels for tagging: Ekman's six emotions (Ekman, 1992) and an other/neutral emotion. MELD (Poria et al., 2019) is an extension of EmotionLines, tagged with not only emotions but also visual and audio modalities. EmpatheticDialogues (Rashkin et al., 2019) is a dialogue-level emotion-tagged corpus, considering two participants as a *speaker* and a *listener*, and tagged with the speaker's emotion and its context.

In EmpatheticDialogues, not each utterance but each dialogue is annotated, which is not suitable for recognizing emotional transition throughout a dialogue. For Japanese, there is a Japanese version of EmpatheticDialogues called JEmpatheticDialogues (Sugiyama et al., 2021), which suffers from the same problem. In this work, we conduct utterance-level annotation like DailyDialog

[1] We will release our corpus and code at `https://github.com/nlp-waseda/expr-exper-emo`.

Length	# Dialogues	# Utterances
2	1,330	2,660
3	1,071	3,213
4	509	2,036
5	310	1,550
6	225	1,350
7	158	1,106
8	134	1,072
9	91	819
2-9	3,828	13,806

Table 1: The statistics of dialogues and utterances.

Label	Expressed		Experienced	
	Strong	Weak	Strong	Weak
Anger	430	1,349	124	870
Anticipation	1,906	4,229	1,215	4,068
Joy	1,629	3,672	1.553	4,549
Trust	247	1,732	520	3,455
Fear	252	942	123	846
Surprise	602	2,018	434	2,798
Sadness	1,227	2,936	889	3,037
Disgust	476	1,979	186	1,535
Any	6,371	12,215	4,705	12,515

Table 2: The statistics of utterances for each emotion label.

and EmotionLines. Although these corpora contain only the speaker's emotion (expressed emotion), we also annotate an utterance with the emotion of a person who hears it (experienced emotion). Furthermore, while an utterance has only one emotion label in these corpora, we allow multiple emotion labels to be tagged per utterance and also consider their strength.

There are also some studies toward developing emotion-aware dialogue systems. Smith et al. (2020) propose three skills for a human-like dialogue system: recognizing emotions, using knowledge (Dinan et al., 2019), and considering personality (Zhang et al., 2018). Furthermore, Roller et al. (2021) build a dialogue system capable of blending these three skills.

3 Corpus Building

3.1 Dialogue Collection

We collect dialogue texts from Twitter by considering the interaction between tweets and their replies by two users as a dialogue. To improve the text quality, we exclude tweets that contain images or

Figure 2: An example of the crowdsourced task. Checkboxes allow crowdworkers to select multiple emotions for an utterance.

hashtags and set the maximum number of utterances included in a dialogue to nine. We also apply several filters: excluding dialogues that contain special symbols, emojis, repeated characters, and utterances that are too short. Note that the reason why we exclude emojis is that they are relatively explicit emotional factors, and we intend to analyze emotions implied from usual textual expressions.

We collected Japanese dialogues using this method. The numbers of dialogues and utterances are shown in Table 1. We obtained 3,828 dialogues that correspond to 13,806 utterances in total. Regarding the length of dialogues, the number of dialogues tends to decrease as that of utterances per dialogue increases.

3.2 Emotion Annotation

We adopt Plutchik's wheel of emotions (Plutchik, 1980) as annotation labels.[2] Specifically, our annotation labels consist of eight emotions: anger, anticipation, joy, trust, fear, surprise, sadness, and disgust. We annotate each utterance with two emotion categories: an expressed emotion, which is expressed by a speaker of the utterance, and an experienced emotion, which is experienced by a listener of the utterance. In other words, an utter-

[2]Ekman's six emotions (Ekman, 1992) and Plutchik's wheel of emotions (Plutchik, 1980) are commonly used in emotion-tagged corpora. Preliminary experiments by crowdsourcing showed that the latter is more appropriate for our crawled dialogues. In this work, therefore, we use eight emotions by Plutchik (1980).

Utterance	Expressed	Experienced
A1: 来週、車で京都行く 普通に観光してきます (I'm driving to Kyoto next week. We'll just do some sightseeing.)	{**Anticipation**, Joy}	{**Anticipation**}
B1: いいなぁ、京都 (I like Kyoto.)	{Anticipation}	{Anticipation, **Joy**}
A2: 楽しんできます (I'll enjoy it.)	{**Anticipation**, **Joy**}	{Anticipation, **Joy**}
B2: 行ったことないから純粋に羨ましい (I've never been there, so I'm genuinely jealous.)	{Anticipation}	{**Anticipation**, **Joy**}
A3: ないんや意外 (I'm surprised you haven't.)	{**Surprise**}	{Joy, Surprise}

Table 3: An example dialogue annotated with expressed and experienced emotions by crowdsourcing. The labels in bold indicate strong emotions.

Label	Expressed	Experienced
Anger	糞, せる, マジだ (shit, force, serious)	糞, うるさい, 居る (shit, noisy, exist)
Anticipation	教える, 願う, 待つ (teach, hope, wait)	待つ, 楽しみだ, 強い (wait, looking forward to, strong)
Joy	楽しい, 嬉しい, おもろい (joyful, glad, funny)	楽しい, 嬉しい, おもろい (joyful, glad, funny)
Trust	全然, 大丈夫だ, ちゃんと (at all, all right, properly)	やすみ, 教える, 大事だ (rest, teach, important)
Fear	怖い, やばい, どう (afraid, serious, how)	怖い, やばい, 危険だ (afraid, serious, dangerous)
Surprise	やばい, なんで, ? (serious, why, ?)	居る, ビックリ, 年 (exist, surprise, year)
Sadness	泣く, 痛い, 悲しい (cry, hurt, sad)	泣く, 辛い, 痛い (cry, hard, hurt)
Disgust	悪い, 嫌いだ, 嫌だ (bad, hate, dislike)	悪い, 気持ち, 嫌だ (bad, surprise, dislike)

Table 4: Top-3 frequent words for each emotion label. An IDF filtering is applied to exclude common words.

ance is annotated with both subjective and objective emotions, which is similar to EmoBank (Buechel and Hahn, 2017) for non-dialogue texts. By annotating expressed and experienced emotions, we can trace the changes in the emotion surrounding both an utterance and a participant in a dialogue.

As a crowdsourcing platform, we use Yahoo! Crowdsourcing.[3] By showing the target utterance and its context, we ask seven workers whether the target utterance has a specified emotion or not about each emotion label for expressed and experienced emotion categories. For the expressed emotions, we ask which emotion a speaker expressed when saying the utterance. For the experienced emotions, we ask which emotion a listener experienced when hearing the utterance. Workers are allowed to select multiple emotion labels or none of them. An interface of the crowdsourcing task for expressed emotions is shown in Figure 2.

Because a view of expressed and experienced emotions can vary among annotators, we employ many workers per an utterance and aggregate their votes to obtain highly reliable annotations.[4] We consider strength for each emotion according to the number of workers' votes; emotions selected by more than half of the workers are regarded as strong, and ones selected by more than a quarter are regarded as weak. Note that the set of strong emotions is a subset of the set of weak ones. We expect that providing the emotions with intensity enables us to handle their granularity.

We applied the above emotion annotation method to our dialogue corpus. The number of utterances for each emotion is shown in Table 2. For the expressed emotion, 46.15% and 88.48% of the utterances are tagged with at least one strong and weak emotion, respectively. For the experienced emotion, the percentages are 34.08% and 90.65%, respectively. Approximately 90% of the utterances are accompanied by one or more emotion labels, and thus our corpus is consequently suitable for recognizing emotions in dialogues and analyzing their changes. In contrast to ours, for example, less than 20% of utterances are tagged with a specific emotion in DailyDialog (Li et al., 2017). Hence it is difficult to analyze emotion changes using such corpora with a small amount of emotion annotation. In addition, we can see a bias among the emotion labels for both expressed and experienced emotions, with more instances of anticipation and joy and fewer instances of trust and fear. An example of a dialogue with the annotation is shown in Table 3.

[3] https://crowdsourcing.yahoo.co.jp/

[4] For the expressed emotion, we ask workers to annotate the emotion of the speaker of an utterance. This annotation, however, is not strictly what a speaker had in mind but what the workers think a speaker would want to express, which can be considered *objective* in some sense. Having truly subjective annotation as the expressed emotion, like Kajiwara et al. (2021), is our future work.

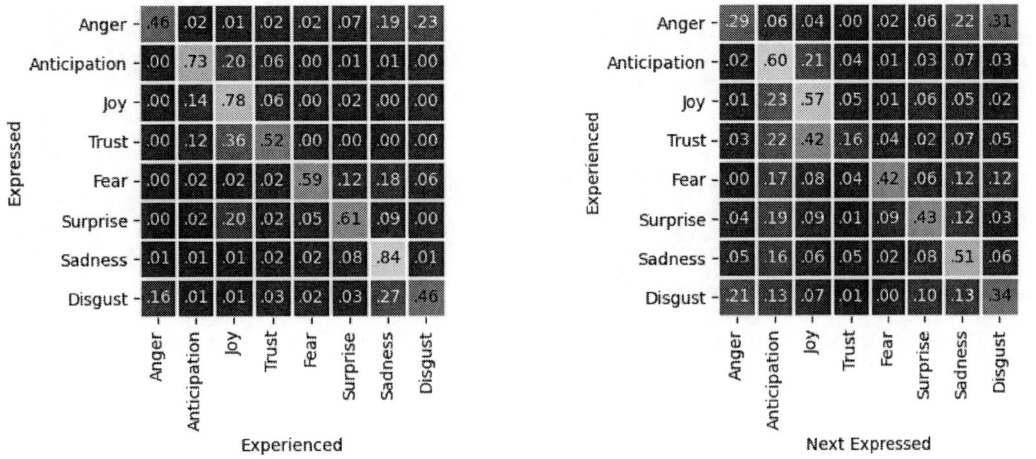

(a) Expressed and experienced emotions (for a certain utterance).

(b) Experienced and next expressed emotions (for a certain person).

Figure 3: The confusion matrices of the relationship between expressed and experienced emotions. In this analysis, we focus on only the strong labels. Note that the matrices' elements are normalized in the row direction.

4 Corpus Analysis

4.1 Frequent Words for Emotion Categories and Labels

To investigate the characteristics of utterances with different emotions, we count words for each strong emotion label in our corpus. In this analysis, we identify words by the Japanese morphological analyzer Juman++ (Tolmachev et al., 2018). To exclude common words likely to appear for all emotions, we apply an IDF filtering. Specifically, words with IDF less than half of the maximum are ignored.

Top-3 words appearing for strong emotion labels are shown in Table 4. The same words tend to appear in the two emotion categories for joy and sadness. In contrast, the frequent words in the two categories are different for anticipation, trust, and surprise.

4.2 Relationship Between Expressed and Experienced Emotions

We annotated utterances with the expressed and experienced emotions. Here, we focus on the relationship between these two emotion categories. Specifically, we investigate the following two relationships:

a. The expressed emotion and the experienced emotion for the same utterance (different persons).

b. The experienced emotion for an utterance and the expressed emotion for the next utterance (the same person).

The confusion matrices for the strong emotion labels are shown in Figure 3, where the elements are normalized in the row direction. First, diagonal components of the two confusion matrices have large values, indicating that the same emotions are likely to occur both for the same utterance and for the same person. Figure 3a shows that people are likely to experience joy for an utterance of anticipation, trust, and surprise in addition to the same emotion. People also tend to experience disgust and sadness for anger and disgust, respectively. Figure 3b shows that after experiencing trust, people are more likely to express joy than trust. For an anger experience, people are more likely to express disgust than anger. Figures 3a and 3b reveal that the relationship of sadness is particularly different. For a certain utterance, sadness makes the other person feel sad in most cases, but for a certain person, anticipation in addition to sadness can be expressed after experiencing sadness. We speculate that when a person experiences sadness from the interlocutor, the person brings an utterance with anticipation to comfort them.

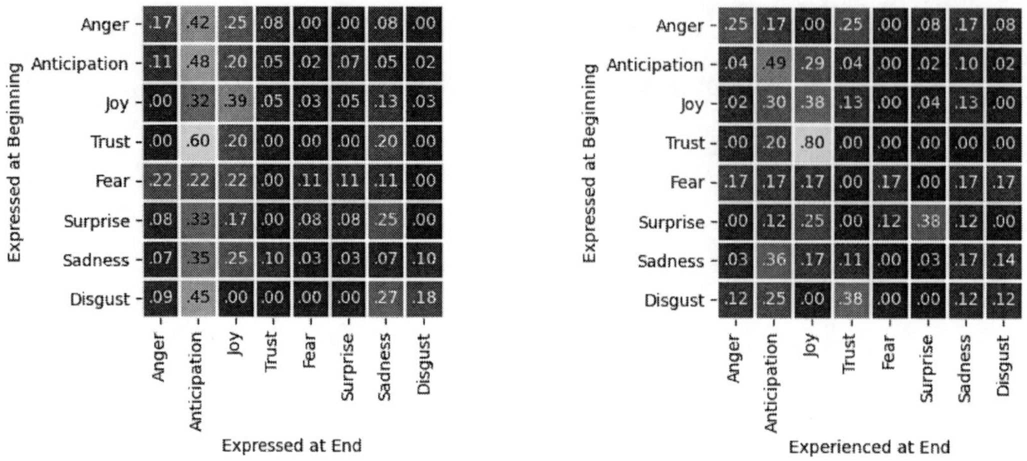

(a) Expressed emotions at the beginning and end of dialogue.

(b) Expressed emotions at the beginning and experienced emotions at the end of dialogue.

Figure 4: The confusion matrices for the emotion labels at the beginning and end of dialogue. In this analysis, we consider only the emotions of a person who begins a dialogue. Note that the targets are limited to the dialogues containing six to nine utterances, and the elements are normalized in the row direction.

4.3 Emotions at the Beginning and End of a Dialogue

To analyze the emotion changes through a dialogue, we compare emotions at the beginning and end of a dialogue. In other words, we see how the emotions of a person who starts the dialogue change through the dialogue. In this analysis, we focus on the following two relationships:

a. The emotion expressed first and the emotion *expressed* last by the same person.

b. The emotion expressed first and the emotion *experienced* last by the same person.

The confusion matrices for the strong emotion labels are shown in Figure 4. The targets are limited to dialogues containing six to nine utterances to analyze the emotion changes in long dialogues. Figure 4a shows that a speaker of the first utterance is likely to finally express anticipation and joy regardless of the first emotion. A speaker who first expresses surprise can express sadness through the dialogue. Figure 4b also shows that the first speaker can experience anticipation at the end of a dialogue. A person who first expresses anger and disgust tends to finally experience trust. From these two figures, we can see that a dialogue causes a person who first expresses fear to finally feel either a positive or negative emotion.

5 Experiments

5.1 Model Setup

We conduct experiments on expressed and experienced emotion recognition using our corpus. We solve a regression task of each emotion intensity for an utterance with its context for the emotion recognition task. We assign 0, 1, and 2 for none, weak, and strong emotion labels, respectively, and let a model regress these values for each emotion. As such, we train two separate models for expressed and experienced emotions with the mean squared error loss:

$$\mathcal{L} = \frac{1}{NK}\sum_{i=1}^{N}\sum_{j=1}^{K}(y_{ij} - t_{ij})^2, \quad (1)$$

where N is the number of samples and K is the number of emotion labels. y_{ij} is the output from the model for the jth label of the ith sample, and t_{ij} is its gold label.

We adopt a Japanese pre-trained BERT model and fine-tune it. We compare two pre-trained models from Kyoto University[5] and one from NICT[6]. We use the WWM and BPE versions for Kyoto University's and NICT's BERT models, respectively.

[5]https://nlp.ist.i.kyoto-u.ac.jp/?ku_bert_japanese

[6]https://alaginrc.nict.go.jp/nict-bert/index.html

Model	Expressed	Experienced
Kyoto (base)	58.84/44.33	53.60/41.84
Kyoto (large)	60.85/45.16	55.09/42.94
NICT	**61.50/46.05**	**56.23/43.88**

Table 5: The results of regression for expressed and experienced emotions. The metrics are Pearson's and Spearman's correlation coefficients.

Label	Expressed	Experienced
Anger	50.21/33.80	38.11/23.80
Anticipation	62.76/**55.55**	57.46/51.22
Joy	**67.25**/55.22	**61.92/54.47**
Trust	41.15/36.69	43.91/40.48
Fear	59.09/31.47	49.60/24.90
Surprise	49.86/39.58	40.58/33.86
Sadness	63.70/51.50	55.48/43.88
Disgust	47.76/38.18	37.32/28.13

Table 6: The correlation coefficients for each emotion label. The metrics are Pearson's and Spearman's correlation coefficients. The scores are from the NICT model that achieved the highest performance in Table 5.

Input utterances are segmented into words with Juman++ (Tolmachev et al., 2018) and tokenized into subwords by applying BPE. We join utterances with `[SEP]` and append `[CLS]` and `[SEP]` to the beginning and end, respectively. As there are two participants in a dialogue, we give each utterance a segment ID of 0 or 1. It provides the models with the information about the speaker of an utterance. Based on a series of utterances joined with `[SEP]`, we predict an emotion label for the last utterance. The vector corresponding to `[CLS]` is passed to a fully-connected layer, and an eight-dimensional vector representing the eight emotions is obtained. Each of the elements is supposed to regress the intensity of each emotion.

Since we are dealing with a regression task, Pearson's and Spearman's correlation coefficients are used as evaluation metrics. The dialogues in our corpus are split into 8:1:1, corresponding to training, validation, and test sets. We fine-tune our models for three epochs and evaluate them on the test set. The implementation of the models is based on HuggingFace Transformers[7]. The models are trained using NVIDIA Tesla V100 SXM2 GPU.

5.2 Results

For the regression task defined in Section 5.1, the correlation coefficients for each model are shown in Table 5. In terms of performance, the NICT model achieved the best score across all values. For the values regarding expressed and experienced emotions, the performance of the experienced emotion is inferior to that of expressed emotion in all models. This result indicated that it is more difficult to recognize the experienced emotion than the expressed emotion.

The correlation coefficients for each emotion inferred by the NICT model are shown in Table 6. For both the expressed and experienced emotions, the highest scores were achieved for *anticipation* and *joy*. In contrast, the emotions with lower values were *trust* and *fear* for the expressed emotion and *anger* and *disgust* for the experienced emotion. From Tables 6 and 2, we can see that the larger the number of the samples for an emotion is, the higher the correlation coefficient becomes. As a case study, we show example dialogues and their emotions predicted by the NICT model in Table 7.

5.3 Multi-Task Learning

Our analysis in Section 4.2 indicated that there is a correlation between expressed and experienced emotions. Therefore, we consider training a single model for recognizing both the emotion categories. The information for solving the two similar tasks is expected to allow a model to improve the performance of each other (Liu et al., 2019). We provide a model with two separate fully-connected layers for the tasks and train them simultaneously, where the inputs are the same as those in Section 5.1. Here, the mean of the losses for expressed and experienced emotions is optimized:

$$\mathcal{L}_{\text{multi-task}} = \frac{\mathcal{L}_{\text{expressed}} + \mathcal{L}_{\text{experienced}}}{2}. \quad (2)$$

Based on Figures 3a and 3b, we consider multi-task learning of expressed and experienced emotions for a certain utterance and a certain person. For the relationship in a certain person, we use the experienced emotion of an utterance and the expressed emotion of the following utterance. We also conduct experiments on the cases where the training and test sets are different from each other. In such a case, for example, expressed emotions are used

[7]`https://huggingface.co/transformers/`

Dialogue	Predicted	Gold
A1: ゲームの検証してる人が検証してほしいことあれば言ってください的なこと言ってたから依頼したら無視されて悲しくなったのはいい思い出 (I have a good memory of a guy who was verifying a game and said if there was anything he wanted verified, please let him know, so I made a request and he ignored it, which made me sad.) B1: それは悲しいね (That's sad.)	**Strong sadness**	**Strong sadness**
A1: youtubeでバーのマスターが氷砕いてる動画見てボーッとしてる (I've been watching videos of bar masters crushing ice on youtube and I'm in a daze.) B1: なんかしてよ (Do something.) A2: そのうちこういうときにツイキャスをしようかなと思っておる (One of these days I'm going to do a tweak for this.) B2: 天才の発想 スマホでも見やすいから助かる (It's a genius idea, and it's easy to watch on my phone.)	Weak anticipation and **joy**	Strong **joy** and weak trust
A1: 今、部活終わって帰るとこやけど 雨やばいしかっぱ持ってきてないし 最悪 (I'm on my way home after club activities, but it's raining and I didn't bring my hat, so that sucks.) B1: わたしも学校出た瞬間大雨降ってきた (I'm going back to school now, but it's raining really hard and I didn't bring my jacket.)	Strong surprise	Strong sadness

Table 7: Example dialogues with predicted and gold expressed emotions. The predicted emotion labels are taken from the predictions of the NICT model, which predicted an emotion label for the last utterance of each dialogue.

Train\Test	Expressed	Experienced
Expressed	61.50/46.05	52.89/40.91
Experienced	55.49/43.34	56.23/43.88
Multi-Task	**62.20/46.63**	**57.35/45.01**

Table 8: The results of multi-task learning with expressed and experienced emotions. The metrics are Pearson's and Spearman's correlation coefficients.

Train\Test	Experienced	Next Expressed
Experienced	54.62/43.47	29.53/25.46
Next Expressed	43.32/35.27	33.91/28.31
Multi-Task	**55.75/49.50**	**35.17/30.49**

Table 9: The results of multi-task learning with experienced and next expressed emotions. The metrics are Pearson's and Spearman's correlation coefficients.

for training, but experienced emotions are used for testing.

The correlation coefficients for an utterance and a speaker by multi-task learning are shown in Tables 8 and 9, respectively. First, the scores when the training and test sets are different from each other are lower than those when they are the same. This gap indicates the significance of annotating utterances with expressed and experienced emotions separately. In all columns, the multi-task models achieved higher performance than the single-task models. Especially, in Table 9, the multi-task scores for both the two tasks are higher than the single-task baselines by one point. In other words, expressed, experienced, and next expressed emotions have the information for helping the recognition of each other.

6 Conclusion

We proposed a method to build an emotion-tagged multi-turn dialogue corpus to help machines recognize emotional transition in a dialogue. Dialogues between two speakers are collected from Twitter, and each utterance is annotated with emotions by crowdsourcing. In the annotation process, we consider the emotions expressed by a speaker who said the utterance and the emotion experienced by a listener who heard the utterance. In addition, the labels are provided with their intensity, representing the granularity of emotions.

We built a Japanese emotion-tagged dialogue corpus and analyzed it. The results showed the characteristics of words for each emotion, the correlation between the emotions about a certain utterance and speaker, and the tendency for speakers to become positive through a dialogue. We also developed emotion recognition models for expressed and experienced emotions based on the Japanese pretrained BERT models. The experimental results indicated that it is more difficult to recognize a listener's emotion than a speaker's emotion. Multi-task learning of expressed and experienced emotions improved the performance of the two emotion recognition tasks about an utterance and a speaker.

For our future work, we will tackle response generation based on predicted emotions. With our corpus, a dialogue system is expected to predict which emotion it experiences from a given utterance and which emotion it should express for the next utterance. Once such emotions are recognized, the dialogue system should be able to generate an appropriate response depending on the predicted expressed emotion.

The corpus in this work is annotated only with expressed and experienced emotions about an utterance. In addition to the emotion annotation, we should also consider dialogue situations (Rashkin et al., 2019). The cause of a dialogue or an utterance helps recognize a speaker's emotion and how it changes. We can also consider non-emotional annotation, such as a dialogue's topic and an utterance's intention (Li et al., 2017). The relationship between emotions and non-emotional factors is also important for machines to better recognize a speaker's emotion.

Acknowledgements

This work was supported by a joint research grant from LINE Corporation.

Ethical Considerations

We built the dataset by collecting texts from Twitter and annotating them by crowdsourcing. For crowdsourcing, we employed 3,847 workers. It took approximately five minutes for a task of annotating 10 utterances. Every worker was paid 4 JPY per 10 utterances, and in total, the built dataset costs 195,700 JPY. Since the dataset was collected from Twitter, it may include contents that are harmful for some of the dataset or its application users. For building the dataset through the Twitter API and crowdsourcing, we did not include any sensitive information that allows personal identification.

The dataset or models trained on it enable downstream applications to infer the emotions of their users, resulting in facilitating communication between the users and the applications. In terms of dialogue systems, this ability is considered valuable for both task-oriented and non-task-oriented dialogue systems. For example, it assists the user in decision-making and solves the user's worry and trouble. In contrast to such benefit, it is difficult for the model to infer the emotion accurately, with the relatively small dataset. Therefore, prediction errors by the model, especially for sensitive utterances or negative emotions, may bring harmful experiences on the users.

References

Daniel Adiwardana, Minh-Thang Luong, David R. So, Jamie Hall, Noah Fiedel, Romal Thoppilan, Zi Yang, Apoorv Kulshreshtha, Gaurav Nemade, Yifeng Lu, and Quoc V. Le. 2020. Towards a human-like open-domain chatbot.

Sven Buechel and Udo Hahn. 2017. EmoBank: Studying the impact of annotation perspective and representation format on dimensional emotion analysis. In *Proceedings of the 15th Conference of the European Chapter of the Association for Computational Linguistics: Volume 2, Short Papers*, pages 578–585, Valencia, Spain. Association for Computational Linguistics.

Jacob Devlin, Ming-Wei Chang, Kenton Lee, and Kristina Toutanova. 2019. BERT: Pre-training of deep bidirectional transformers for language understanding. In *Proceedings of the 2019 Conference of the North American Chapter of the Association for Computational Linguistics: Human Language Technologies, Volume 1 (Long and Short Papers)*, pages 4171–4186, Minneapolis, Minnesota. Association for Computational Linguistics.

Emily Dinan, Stephen Roller, Kurt Shuster, Angela Fan, Michael Auli, and Jason Weston. 2019. Wizard of wikipedia: Knowledge-powered conversational agents. In *International Conference on Learning Representations*.

Paul Ekman. 1992. An argument for basic emotions. *Cognition and Emotion*, 6(3-4):169–200.

Diman Ghazi, Diana Inkpen, and Stan Szpakowicz. 2015. Detecting emotion stimuli in emotion-bearing sentences. In *Computational Linguistics and Intelligent Text Processing*, pages 152–165, Cham. Springer International Publishing.

Chao-Chun Hsu, Sheng-Yeh Chen, Chuan-Chun Kuo, Ting-Hao Huang, and Lun-Wei Ku. 2018. EmotionLines: An emotion corpus of multi-party conversations. In *Proceedings of the Eleventh International Conference on Language Resources and Evaluation (LREC 2018)*, Miyazaki, Japan. European Language Resources Association (ELRA).

Tomoyuki Kajiwara, Chenhui Chu, Noriko Takemura, Yuta Nakashima, and Hajime Nagahara. 2021. WRIME: A new dataset for emotional intensity estimation with subjective and objective annotations. In *Proceedings of the 2021 Conference of the North American Chapter of the Association for Computational Linguistics: Human Language Technologies*, pages 2095–2104, Online. Association for Computational Linguistics.

Yanran Li, Hui Su, Xiaoyu Shen, Wenjie Li, Ziqiang Cao, and Shuzi Niu. 2017. DailyDialog: A manually labelled multi-turn dialogue dataset. In *Proceedings of the Eighth International Joint Conference on Natural Language Processing (Volume 1: Long Papers)*, pages 986–995, Taipei, Taiwan. Asian Federation of Natural Language Processing.

Vicki Liu, Carmen Banea, and Rada Mihalcea. 2017. Grounded emotions. In *2017 Seventh International Conference on Affective Computing and Intelligent Interaction (ACII)*, pages 477–483.

Xiaodong Liu, Pengcheng He, Weizhu Chen, and Jianfeng Gao. 2019. Multi-task deep neural networks for natural language understanding. In *Proceedings of the 57th Annual Meeting of the Association for Computational Linguistics*, pages 4487–4496, Florence, Italy. Association for Computational Linguistics.

Nurul Lubis, Sakriani Sakti, Koichiro Yoshino, and Satoshi Nakamura. 2018. Eliciting positive emotion through affect-sensitive dialogue response generation: A neural network approach. *Proceedings of the AAAI Conference on Artificial Intelligence*, 32(1).

Nurul Lubis, Sakriani Sakti, Koichiro Yoshino, and Satoshi Nakamura. 2019. Positive emotion elicitation in chat-based dialogue systems. *IEEE/ACM Transactions on Audio, Speech, and Language Processing*, 27(4):866–877.

Saif Mohammad and Felipe Bravo-Marquez. 2017. Emotion intensities in tweets. In *Proceedings of the 6th Joint Conference on Lexical and Computational Semantics (*SEM 2017)*, pages 65–77, Vancouver, Canada. Association for Computational Linguistics.

Robert Plutchik. 1980. A general psychoevolutionary theory of emotion. In *Theories of emotion*, pages 3–33. Elsevier.

Soujanya Poria, Devamanyu Hazarika, Navonil Majumder, Gautam Naik, Erik Cambria, and Rada Mihalcea. 2019. MELD: A multimodal multi-party dataset for emotion recognition in conversations. In *Proceedings of the 57th Annual Meeting of the Association for Computational Linguistics*, pages 527–536, Florence, Italy. Association for Computational Linguistics.

Alec Radford, Karthik Narasimhan, Tim Salimans, and Ilya Sutskever. 2018. Improving language understanding by generative pre-training.

Hannah Rashkin, Antoine Bosselut, Maarten Sap, Kevin Knight, and Yejin Choi. 2018. Modeling naive psychology of characters in simple commonsense stories. In *Proceedings of the 56th Annual Meeting of the Association for Computational Linguistics (Volume 1: Long Papers)*, pages 2289–2299, Melbourne, Australia. Association for Computational Linguistics.

Hannah Rashkin, Eric Michael Smith, Margaret Li, and Y-Lan Boureau. 2019. Towards empathetic open-domain conversation models: A new benchmark and dataset. In *Proceedings of the 57th Annual Meeting of the Association for Computational Linguistics*, pages 5370–5381, Florence, Italy. Association for Computational Linguistics.

Stephen Roller, Emily Dinan, Naman Goyal, Da Ju, Mary Williamson, Yinhan Liu, Jing Xu, Myle Ott, Eric Michael Smith, Y-Lan Boureau, and Jason Weston. 2021. Recipes for building an open-domain chatbot. In *Proceedings of the 16th Conference of the European Chapter of the Association for Computational Linguistics: Main Volume*, pages 300–325, Online. Association for Computational Linguistics.

Eric Michael Smith, Mary Williamson, Kurt Shuster, Jason Weston, and Y-Lan Boureau. 2020. Can you put it all together: Evaluating conversational agents' ability to blend skills. In *Proceedings of the 58th Annual Meeting of the Association for Computational Linguistics*, pages 2021–2030, Online. Association for Computational Linguistics.

Hiroaki Sugiyama, Masahiro Mizukami, Tsunehiro Arimoto, Hiromi Narimatsu, Yuya Chiba, Hideharu Nakajima, and Toyomi Meguro. 2021. Empirical analysis of training strategies of transformer-based japanese chit-chat systems.

Arseny Tolmachev, Daisuke Kawahara, and Sadao Kurohashi. 2018. Juman++: A morphological analysis toolkit for scriptio continua. In *Proceedings of the 2018 Conference on Empirical Methods in Natural Language Processing: System Demonstrations*, pages 54–59, Brussels, Belgium. Association for Computational Linguistics.

Ashish Vaswani, Noam Shazeer, Niki Parmar, Jakob Uszkoreit, Llion Jones, Aidan N Gomez, Ł ukasz Kaiser, and Illia Polosukhin. 2017. Attention is all you need. In *Advances in Neural Information Processing Systems*, volume 30. Curran Associates, Inc.

Saizheng Zhang, Emily Dinan, Jack Urbanek, Arthur Szlam, Douwe Kiela, and Jason Weston. 2018. Personalizing dialogue agents: I have a dog, do you have pets too? In *Proceedings of the 56th Annual Meeting of the Association for Computational Linguistics (Volume 1: Long Papers)*, pages 2204–2213, Melbourne, Australia. Association for Computational Linguistics.

Li Zhou, Jianfeng Gao, Di Li, and Heung-Yeung Shum. 2020. The design and implementation of XiaoIce, an empathetic social chatbot. *Computational Linguistics*, 46(1):53–93.

Darkness can not drive out darkness: Investigating Bias in Hate Speech Detection Models

Fatma Elsafoury
School of Physics, Engineering, and Computing
The University of The West of Scotland
fatma.elsafoury@uws.ac.uk

Abstract

It has become crucial to develop tools for automated hate speech and abuse detection. These tools would help to stop the bullies and the haters and provide a safer environment for individuals especially from marginalized groups to freely express themselves. However, recent research shows that machine learning models are biased and they might make the right decisions for the wrong reasons. In this thesis, I set out to understand the performance of hate speech and abuse detection models and the different biases that could influence them. I show that hate speech and abuse detection models are not only subject to social bias but also to other types of bias that have not been explored before. Finally, I investigate the causal effect of the social and intersectional bias on the performance and unfairness of hate speech detection models.

1 Introduction

Over the last decade, there have been attempts to use machine learning models (Dinakar et al., 2011; Dadvar et al., 2014; Rafiq et al., 2015; Waseem and Hovy, 2016a; Raisi and Huang, 2017; Agrawal and Awekar, 2018a; Kumar et al., 2019; Pavlopoulos et al., 2019; Mozafari et al., 2019; Yadav et al., 2020; Paul and Saha, 2020) for the task of hate speech and abuse detection. However, those studies focused mainly on enhancing models' performance, without providing any insight into the models' inner workings.

In recent years, the research community started to pay more attention to machine learning models' explainability and the biases in these models and the datasets. Wagner et al. (2021) describe the term *algorithmically infused societies* as the societies that are shaped by algorithmic and human behavior. The data collected from these societies carry the same bias in algorithms and humans, like population bias and behavioral bias (Olteanu et al., 2019). These biases are important in the field of Natural Language Processing (NLP) because unsupervised models like word embeddings encode them during training. (Brunet et al., 2019; Joseph and Morgan, 2020). This includes racial biases (Garg et al., 2018; Manzini et al., 2019; Sweeney and Najafian, 2019), gender biases (Garg et al., 2018; Bolukbasi et al., 2016; Chaloner and Maldonado, 2019), and personality stereotypes (Agarwal et al., 2019).

Recent research in social science explains that using racial slurs and third person profanity goes beyond offending individuals or groups of people and that it actually aims at stressing on inferiority of the identity of marginalized groups (Kukla, 2018). However, the research on bias in NLP have not payed attention to how this type of offensive stereotyping being encoded in machine learning models that are trained on data from social media. So I introduce systematic offensive stereotyping (SOS) bias which includes associating offensive terms to different groups of people, especially marginalized people, based on their ethnicity, gender, or sexual orientation. On the other hand, studies that focused on the same type of bias in hate speech detection models studied it within hate speech datasets (Dixon et al., 2018; Waseem and Hovy, 2016b; Zhou et al., 2021), but not in the widely-used word embeddings which are, in contrast, not trained on data specifically curated to contain offensive content.

Moreover, the proposed methods to study social biases like gender bias in word embeddings focused on studying the statistical association between words that describe women e.g., wife, mother, sister, girl, woman, and words related to femininity e.g. nurturing, sensitive, and emotional (Caliskan et al., 2017; Garg et al., 2018; Sweeney and Najafian, 2019; Dev and Phillips, 2019). However, social science literature has shown that femininity differs in conceptualization among White and black people (Giddings, 2006; Rosenfield, 2012). Additionally, the claim that the bias found in the word

Proceedings of the 60th Annual Meeting of the Association for Computational Linguistics Student Research Workshop, pages 31 - 43
May 22-27, 2022

embeddings influence the NLP downstream tasks has not been proven (Blodgett et al., 2020). A few studies have used statistical correlation to show that influence (De-Arteaga et al., 2019). However, correlation is not causation and causal inferences have not been used to understand the influence of bias that exists in word embeddings, on the downstream task of hate speech detection.

The limitations enlisted here could have negative implications as hate speech detection models might learn to associate marginalized groups with extremism and abuse. As a result, these models that were supposed to provide a protective environment for the marginalized people to express themselves are the ones that could lead to silencing them or flagging their content as inappropriate. In this thesis, I aim to understand and investigate the performance and the biases of hate speech and abuse detection models through achieving the following research goals: 1) Understand the performance of state-of-the-art hate speech and abuse detection models. 2) Inspect other biases than social stereotypical bias in commonly used static word embeddings. 3) Investigate intersectional bias in contextual word embeddings and the causal effect of social and intersectional bias on the task of hate speech detection.

2 Literature review

2.1 Hate speech detection

In the literature on hate speech and abuse detection, there is a lack of clear distinction between hate speech and related concepts like online abuse (Elsafoury et al., 2021). There are different definitions of online abuse but most of them can be summarized as "*one form or another of insulting, spread using mobile or internet technology*" (Elsafoury et al., 2021). On the other hand, Fortuna et al. studied hate speech in the literature in relation to four dimensions: physical violence encouragement, targets, attack language, and humorous hate speech and introduced the following definition "*a language that attacks or diminishes, that incites violence or hate against groups, based on specific characteristics such as physical appearance, religion, descent, national or ethnic origin, sexual orientation, gender identity or other, and it can occur with different linguistic styles, even in subtle forms or when humor is used*" (Fortuna and Nunes, 2018). I could distinguish between online abuse and online hate speech through the target of the attack. If the target is an individual then it is online abuse but if the target is a group of people then it is online hate speech. Since I'm investigating bias which is related to groups of people, so in this thesis, I focus on hate speech detection rather than abuse detection except for the first research goal where online abuse datasets are used.

Different approaches have been developed to detect hate speech and abuse detection from social media including rule-based, conventional, deep learning, and attention-based machine learning models (BERT) (Elsafoury et al., 2021). These studies have shown that BERT outperformed all the other models on the task of hate speech and abuse detection (Paul and Saha, 2020; Mozafari et al., 2019). However, none of them explain why. In the last few years, there have been published studies on the analysis of BERT's attention weights on the GLUE tasks (Kovaleva et al., 2019; Rogers et al., 2021; Sun and Lu, 2020; Vashishth et al., 2019; Serrano and Smith, 2019) but none of them were employed for the task of hate speech and abuse detection. Inspired by this research, one of my research goals in this thesis is to gain a better understanding of BERT's strong performance on the task of hate speech and abuse detection.

2.2 Bias in word embeddings

The term *bias* is defined and used in many different ways (Olteanu et al., 2019). Most of the studies that measure bias in NLP use the statistical definition of bias as "systematic distortion in the sampled data that compromises its representatives" (Olteanu et al., 2019). In the case of bias in distributional word representations (static word embeddings), the most commonly used methods for quantifying bias are WEAT , RND, RNSB, and ECT (Badilla et al., 2020). For WEAT, the authors were inspired by the Implicit Association Test (IAT) to develop a statistical test to demonstrate human-like biases in word embeddings (Caliskan et al., 2017). They used the cosine similarity and statistical significance tests to measure the unfair correlations for two different demographics, as represented by manually curated word lists. For RND, the authors used the Euclidean distance between neutral words, like professions, and a representative group vector created by averaging the word vectors for words that describe a stereotyped group (gender/ethnicity) (Garg et al., 2018). In RNSB, a logistic regression model has first trained on the word vectors of unbiased labeled sentiment words (positive and negative) extracted from biased word embeddings. Then, that model was used to predict the sentiment of words that describe certain demographics (Sweeney and Najafian, 2019). In ECT, the authors proposed a method to measure how much bias has been removed from the word embeddings after debiasing them (Dev and Phillips, 2019). These metrics, except RNSB, are based on the polarity between two opposing points, like male and female, allowing for binary comparisons. This forces practitioners to model gender as a spectrum between more "male" and "female" words, requiring an overly simplified view of the construct, leading to similar problems for other stereotypical types of bias, like racial and sexual orientation, where there are more than two categories that need to be represented (Sweeney and Najafian, 2019). These metrics also use lists of seed words that are unreliable as explained by (Antoniak and Mimno, 2021). Since I am interested in measuring the systematic offensive stereotypes of different marginalized groups based on race and sexual orientation, these metrics would fall short of my needs. As for the RNSB metric, even though it is possible to include more than two identities, the sentiment dimension is represented as positive or negative (binary). But in my case, I am interested in a variety of offensive language targeted at different marginalized groups. Additionally, the literature on bias in word embeddings claims that it influences downstream tasks, like translation, classification, and text generation. Still, these claims have not yet been tested (Blodgett et al., 2020). In this thesis, I aim to address these limitations by introducing the systematic offensive stereotyping (SOS) bias, proposing a method to measure it, and investigating the statistical association between the SOS bias and the task of hate speech detection.

2.3 Intersectionality of bias

Intersectionality as a term is coined by Kimberle Crenshaw (Crenshaw, 1989) to describe that Black women experience a different type of bias other than the ones experienced by White women and Black men. She states that "*This intersectional experience is greater than the sum of racism and sexism, any analysis that does not take intersectionality into account can not sufficiently address the particular manner in which Black women are subordinated*" (Crenshaw, 1989). Ever since there has been increasing research on intersectionality in social sciences. For example, European American people associate femininity with characteristics like submissiveness, nurturing, sensitivity, and emotional expressiveness. On the contrary, for African American people, femininity incorporate paid work and achievement. African American people conceptualize gender as flexible with greater gender role equality and less traditional attitudes towards women's roles than European American people (Giddings, 2006; Rosenfield, 2012). Similarly, O'Brien et al., show that African American women are more likely to major in STEM fields in comparison to European American women. They also found that African Americans had a weaker implicit gender-STEM stereotype than European Americans (O'Brien et al., 2015). These Examples show that the methods used in the literature to measure the gender bias in word embeddings (WEAT, RND, and ECT) measure the gender bias that European American women suffer from "White gender bias" which does not reflect the experience of women of color especially African American women.

A few studies focus on the intersectionality of bias in pre-trained contextual word embeddings (Guo and Caliskan, 2021; Tan and Celis, 2019; Lepori, 2020). These studies have used seed words from the literature for their tests without mitigating for their limitations as specified by (Antoniak and Mimno, 2021). The limitations include the lack of motivation behind choosing and the lack of coherence among the words that describe the same group of people like using people's names to infer their ethnicity or race. Additionally, the inspected intersectional biases have not been tested for their influence on downstream tasks. For example, (Kim et al., 2020) investigated the intersectional bias in hate speech datasets again without analyzing their influence on the model's outcome.

In this thesis, I aim to mitigate this limitation by creating a new bias dataset and propose a method to measure interseactional bias in contextual word embeddings. Additionally, I am going to investigate the causal influence of the studied intersectional bias on the task of hate speech detection.

2.4 Causality in NLP

As mentioned earlier the research community has mainly focused on measuring bias in word embeddings without understanding how this bias influences the downstream NLP tasks. Even the few studies that investigated that influence, have re-

Dataset	Samples	Positive samples	
Kaggle-insults	7425	35%	(Kaggle, 2012)
Twitter-sex	14742	23%	(Waseem and Hovy, 2016a)
Twitter-rac	13349	15%	(Waseem and Hovy, 2016a)
HateEval	12722	42%	(Basile et al., 2019)
Twitter-hate	5569	25%	(Davidson et al., 2017)
WTP-agg	114649	13%	(Wulczyn et al., 2017)
WTP-tox	157671	10%	(Wulczyn et al., 2017)

Table 1: Dataset statistics

Dataset	LSTM	Bi-LSTM	BERT(FT)
Kaggle-insults	0.6420	0.653	0.768
Twitter-sex	0.6569	0.649	0.760
Twitter-rac	0.6400	0.678	0.757
WTP-agg	0.7110	0.679	0.753
WTP-tox	0.7230	0.737	0.786

Table 2: F1-scores achieved for each dataset

lied on statistical correlations. For example, De-Arteaga et al., measure the correlation between the true positive rates gap between genders in the task of occupation classification and the existing gender imbalances in those occupations (De-Arteaga et al., 2019).

Given that correlation is not causation, there has been a recent trend in NLP that uses causal inference to understand the influence of different concepts on different NLP tasks (Feder et al., 2021a). Some of these studies have focused on understanding the causal inference of concepts (e.g. social bias in the datasets) on the task of text classification using counterfactual causal inference (Feder et al., 2021b; Qian et al., 2021; Elazar et al., 2021). Others have focused on using causal inferences to understand the influence of some concepts (e.g. syntax representation, and social biases in pre-trained word embeddings) on tasks like consistency with English grammar (Ravfogel et al., 2021; Tucker et al., 2021). However, causal inference methods have not been used to investigate the influence of bias in pre-trained word embeddings on hate speech. In this thesis, I aim to fill that research gap by using counterfactual causal inference to measure that influence and to measure how harmful that influence is on the task of hate speech detection.

3 Proposed Methods

In this section, I describe the proposed methods to achieve my research goals and the outcomes of the research goals that have been achieved. The datasets used in the experiments discussed in sections 3.1 and section 3.2 are described in Table 1.

3.1 Research objective 1

To achieve my first research goal, I started with reviewing the literature on hate speech and abuse detection models including the most used ML models, and datasets. Then, weused BERT in comparison to RNN models on the task of hate speech and abuse detection using some. or fine-tuning, BERT was trained for 10 epochs with a batch size of 32 and a learning rate of $2e^{-5}$, as suggested in (Devlin et al., 2019). The sequence length parameter changed across datasets depending on their maximum token length. For the Twitter-sexism and Twitter-racism datasets, a sequence length of 64 was used because it is the closest to the maximum observed sequence length in the dataset, while 128 was used for the rest because it is the maximum I could use due to available computational resources limitations. A single linear layer was added on top of the pooled output of BERT for sentence classification. I also used LSTM (Hochreiter and Schmidhuber, 1997) and Bi-directional LSTM (Schuster and Paliwal, 1997), with the same architecture as in (Agrawal and Awekar, 2018a), who used RNN models to detect cyberbullying. To this end, I first used the Keras tokeniser (Tensorflow.org, 2020) to convert the text into numerical vectors (each integer being the index of a token in a dictionary) with a maximum length of 600 (the maximum I could use due to computational resources limitations) for the Kaggle and WTP datasets and 41 (maximum observed sequence length in the dataset) for the Twitter datasets. A trainable embedding layer was used as the first hidden layer of the LSTM and Bi-LSTM-based networks, with an input size equal to the number of unique tokens of the dataset after pre-processing and an output size of 128. The two models were then trained for 100 epochs with a batch size of 32, using the Adam optimiser and a learning rate of 0.01 which is the default of the Keras Optimiser. The results show that BERT outperforms other commonly used deep learning models on multiple hate speech and abuse-related datasets achieving the highest F1 (Table 2).

I built on these results by analyzing the performance of BERT to understand the reason behind BERT's good performance (Elsafoury). To achieve that I first examined how fine-tuning affects BERT's attention weights, the results show that there is a difference in attention weights' patterns between BERT with and without fine-tuning. Then, to investigate the role of attention weights

Dataset	No. tokens	PCC (attention vs importance)	PCC (attention vs no. occurrences)	PCC (importance vs no. occurrences)
Twitter-Sexism	3878	0.108	-0.047	-0.002
Twitter-Racism	3991	0.056	-0.015	-0.002
Kaggle-Insults	4452	0.171	-0.023	-0.004
WTP-Aggression	4457	0.125	-0.101	-0.009
WTP-Toxicity	4524	0.163	-0.076	-0.011

Table 3: PCC between mean attention weights of fine-tuned BERT, mean absolute feature importance and number of occurrences per token

of a fine-tuned BERT in the model's performance, I compared the mean feature importance score of individual tokens, obtained using the Integrated Gradients algorithm (Sundararajan et al., 2017), to their mean attention weights. I computed the Pearson's correlation coefficient (PCC) between the mean attention weights of fine-tuned BERT of all heads across the last layers (9-12) and the tokens' absolute importance score, as it has been shown that fine-tuning effects mostly BERT's last layers (9-12) (Rogers et al., 2021).

The results show that even though the patterns of the attention weights of fine-tuned BERT are different from those of BERT without fine-tuning, results show that attention weights are not meaningful when it comes to the model's prediction. As I found no linear correlation between the absolute importance score and the mean attention weights of BERT, Table 3, for the examined datasets ($0.056 \leq$ PCC ≤ 0.171), as well as between the number of occurrences of a token and the mean attention weights ($-0.101 \leq$ PCC ≤ -0.015) or the mean importance scores ($-0.011 \leq$ PCC ≤ -0.002). These results suggest that attention weights don't play a direct role in explaining BERT's performance, which is in line with previous studies (Sun and Lu, 2020; Serrano and Smith, 2019; Vashishth et al., 2019).

Finally, I analyzed the importance scores of POS tags of fine-tuned BERT to find out the features that BERT relies on to make its prediction. The results show that BERT captures syntactical biases in the datasets. As the results in Figure 1 show that the POS tags with the highest importance scores are auxiliaries, punctuation, determiners, adpositions, and pronouns which are not informative for the task of hate speech and abuse detection. Among these, the most informative tag for hate speech and abuse detection is the pronoun. These results suggest that BERT relies on syntactical biases and shortcuts in the datasets for its good performance. I speculate that this syntactical bias is resulted from the upstream datasets that BERT was pre-trained on. To mitigate the effect of that bias, I fine-tuned BERT on an intermediate task which is English POS tags classification dataset following the work suggested in (Zhou et al., 2020). However the results show almost the same distribution of the feature importance scores. This results suggest that Post-processing bias mitigation in BERT is not effective and mitigating the bias during the pre-training might be more effective. The results in this section motivate the second and the third research objectives.

Group	Word
LGBTQ*	lesbian, gay, queer, homosexual, lgbt, bisexual, transgender, trans, non-binary
Women*	woman, female, girl, wife, sister, mother, daughter
Other ethnicities*	african, african american, black, asian, hispanic, latin, mexican, indian, arab
Straight	hetrosexual, cisgender
Men	man, male, boy, son, father, husband, brother
White ethnicities	white, caucasian, european american, european, norwegian, canadian, german, australian, english, french, american, swedish, dutch

*Marginalised group

Table 4: NOI words and the group they describe.

3.2 Research objective 2

To achieve my second research goal and to find out if there are other biases in the commonly used word embeddings that are used in the task of hate speech and abuse detection models, I aim to reveal whether word embeddings associate offensive language with words describing marginalized groups. I define systematic offensive stereotypes (SOS) from a statistical perspective as "*A systematic association in the word embeddings between profanity and marginalized groups of people*". In other words, SOS refers to associating offensive terms to different groups of people, especially marginalized people, based on their ethnicity, gender, or sexual orientation. Based on my definition of SOS, I want a method to measure the association that each word embedding model has between profanity and marginalized groups of people. I propose to measure that association using the cosine similarity between swear words and words that describe marginalized social groups.

For the swear words, I used a list of 427 swear words from (Agrawal and Awekar, 2018b). For

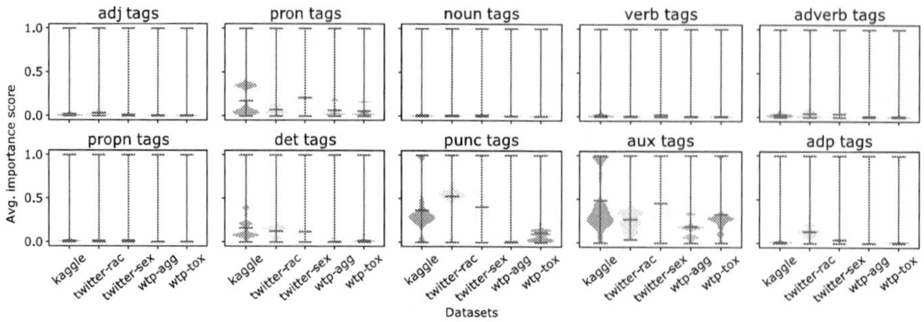

Figure 1: Mean normalised importance scores assigned by fine-tuned BERT to POS tags in the datasets.

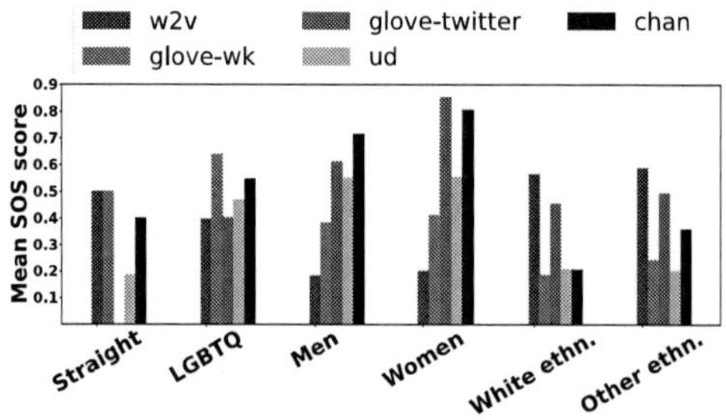

Figure 2: Mean SOS scores for the examined word embeddings and groups.

describing marginalized social groups, I used a word list that contains non-offensive identity (NOI) names to describe marginalized groups of people (Zhou et al., 2021; Dixon et al., 2018) and non-marginalized ones (Sweeney and Najafian, 2019), as summarised in Table 4. Similar to RNSB, I use NOI words to describe the different groups, unlike WEAT, ECT, and RND which used seed words like people's names to infer their nationality or pronouns. The motivation behind using NOI words is clearer than using seed words used in the literature (Antoniak and Mimno, 2021). Moreover, According to the reported coherence scores in (Antoniak and Mimno, 2021), The used NOI words for women, men, white and non-white ethnicity groups, score the highest coherence which are 0.090 and 0.910 respectively which shows that the NOI that describe two different groups, e.g. Women vs Men, are far apart which is ideal. However, they don't provide analysis for seed words related to sexual orientation. Since we used the same method to collect these seed words like gender and ethnicity related seed words, I assume that sexual oriented seed words would also have accepted coherence scores.

To measure the SOS bias, let $W_{NOI} = \{w_1, w_2, w_3, ...w_n\}$ be the list of NOI words w_i, $i = 1, 2, ..., n$, and $W_{sw} = \{o_1, o_2, o_3, ...o_m\}$ be the list of swear words o_j, $j = 1, 2, ..., m$. To measure the SOS bias for a specific word embedding we, I first compute the average vector $\overrightarrow{\mathbf{W}_{\mathbf{sw}}^{\mathbf{we}}}$ of the swear words for we, e.g. for Word2Vec, Glove, etc. $SOS_{i,we}$ for a NOI word w_i and a word embedding we is then defined (Equation 1) as the cosine similarity between $\overrightarrow{\mathbf{W}_{\mathbf{sw}}^{\mathbf{we}}}$ and the word vector $\overrightarrow{w_{i,we}}$, for the word embedding we, normalised to the range $[0, 1]$ using min-max normalisation across all NOI words (W_{NOI}).

$$SOS_{i,we} = \frac{\overrightarrow{\mathbf{W}_{\mathbf{sw}}^{\mathbf{we}}} \cdot \overrightarrow{w_{i,we}}}{||\overrightarrow{\mathbf{W}_{\mathbf{sw}}^{\mathbf{we}}}|| \cdot ||\overrightarrow{w_{i,we}}||} \quad (1)$$

The normalized SOS score takes values within the range $[0, 1]$ and indicates the similarity of an NOI word to the average representation of swear words. Consequently, a higher $SOS_{i,we}$ value for word w_i indicates that the word embedding $\overrightarrow{w_{i,we}}$ for the word w_i, is more associated with profanity. The metric is intended to be used comparatively among word embeddings, e.g. w2v vs Glove-WK, or among different groups of people, e.g. Women vs Men, rather than to determine an objective threshold below which no bias exists.

I computed the mean SOS score over the examined word embeddings(Word2Vec, Glove-WK, Glove-Twitter, UD, and Chan) for each examined group individually. Figure 2 shows that some word embeddings are more biased than others and that the biased word embeddings are more biased towards the marginalized group than the non-marginalized groups.

To validate my SOS bias metric, I compared the SOS bias, measured by my proposed method and state-of-the-art metrics (WEAT, RNSB, RND, ECT), to the published statistics on online abuse

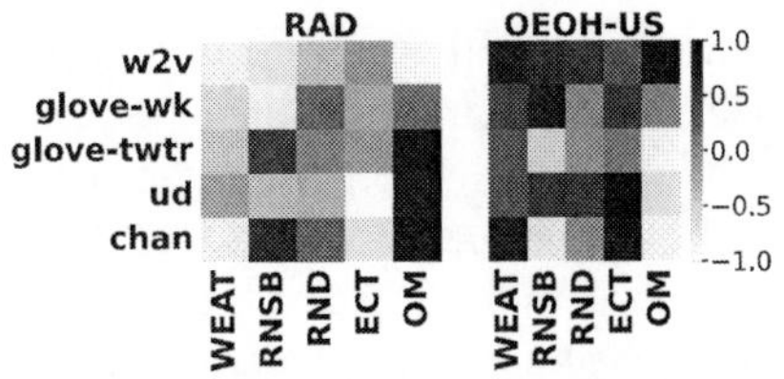

Figure 3: ThePearson's correlation between the different metrics and the percentages of people belonging to the examined marginalized groups who experienced abuse and extremism online for each published surveys for the examined word embedding. For RAD heatmap, correlation is computed between the SOS scores and the differences in RAD between the percentage of (women and men), (LGTBQ and straight), and (Non-white ethnicities and White ethnicities).

and extremism that is targeted at marginalized groups (Women, LGBTQ, Non-white ethnicities). The WEFE framework (Badilla et al., 2020) was used to measure the SOS bias of the examined word embeddings using the state-of-the-art metrics. The metrics in the WEFE platform take 4 inputs: Target list 1: a word list describing a group of people, e.g. women; Target list 2: a word list that describes a different group of people, e.g. men; Attribute list 1: a word list that contains attributes that are believed to be associated with target group 1, e.g. housewife; and Attribute list 2: a word list that contains attributes that are believed to be associated with target group 2, e.g. engineer. Each metric then measures these associations.

To measure the SOS_{women} using the state-of-the-art metrics, target list W1 contained the NOI words that describe women in Table 4, target list W2 contained the NOI words that describe men, attribute list 1 contained the same swear words used earlier to measure the SOS bias, and attribute list 2 a list of positive words provided by the WEFE framework. To measure the $SOS_{ethnicity}$, I used the same process, with the same attribute lists, but with target list E1 that contained NOI words that describe non-white ethnicities and target list E2 that contained NOI words that describe white ethnicities. Similarly, to measure SOS_{lgbtq}, I used the same attribute lists and target list L1, which contained NOI words that describe LGBTQ, and target list L2 which contained NOI words that describe straight and cisgender people. To measure SOS_{women}, SOS_{lgbtq}, and $SOS_{ethnicity}$ with my proposed metric, I computed the mean SOS scores of the NOI words that describe Women, LGBTQ, and Non-white ethnicities. The percentages of people belonging to the examined marginalized groups who experienced abuse and extremism online were then acquired fromthe following surveys: the Rad Campaign Online Harassment Survey 2014 (Rad Campaign, 2014) where 1,000 adult Americans (aged 18+) were surveyed about being harassed online and the online extremism and online hate survey (OEOH), collected by (Hawdon et al., 2015) from Finland (FI) (n=555), Germany (GR) (n=999), the US (n=1,033), and the UK (n=999) in 2013 and 2014, for individuals aged 15 - 30.

Then, I computed the Pearson's correlation coefficient between the SOS* scores, measured by the different metrics for Women, LGTBQ, and Non-white ethnicities for the examined word embeddings and the percentages of people belonging to the examined marginalized groups who experienced abuse and extremism online. The results in Figure 3† show that my proposed SOS bias metric, for Chan, UD, and Glove-Twitter, has a high positive correlation with the published statistics on online abuse (RAD), whereas the correlation is very small or negative for word2vec and Glove-WK. On the contrary, for the online hate and extremism surveys OEOH (US, UK, GR, and FI), my SOS bias metric for Word2Vec and Glove-WK shows a positive correlation, whereas the correlation for Glove-Twitter, UD, and Chan is negative or very small. A similar pattern is exhibited by the RNSB metric to a lesser extend. On the other hand, WEAT, RND, and ECT exhibit almost the opposite pattern, as they show a negative or very small correlation to the statistics of the surveys on online abuse (RAD) for all the word embeddings, but show a high positive correlation with the statistics of the surveys of online hate and extremism OEOH (US, UK, GR, and FI).

These results suggest that my metric highlights the difference in the SOS bias between the different word embeddings, as the word embeddings that were trained on the social media datasets (Glove-Twitter, UD, and Chan) encode the online abuse towards marginalized people, while word embeddings that were trained on Google news and Wikipedia articles encode the hate and extremism against the marginalized groups shared in those sources. On the contrary, the other metrics fail to

*Contrary to all other metrics, ECT scores have an inverse relationship with the level of bias, so I subtract all ECT scores from 1 to enforce that higher scores for all metrics indicate greater levels of bias.

†The correlation results for OEOH-US are similar to OEOH-UK, OEOH-GR, and OEOH-FI, so the latter were omitted from the figure.

capture that difference between the word embeddings. Consequently, the results suggest that my bias metric is more reflective of the SOS bias in the different word embeddings than the-state-of-the-art bias metrics.

Dataset	Model	F1-score				
		Word2Vec	Glove-WK	Glove-Twitter	UD	Chan
HateEval	MLP	0.593	0.583	0.623	0.597	**0.627**
	BiLSTM	0.663	0.651	**0.671**	0.661	0.661
Twitter-sexism	MLP	0.587	0.587	**0.589**	0.578	0.563
	BiLSTM	0.659	0.661	**0.661**	0.625	0.631
Twitter-racism	MLP	**0.683**	0.681	0.680	0.679	0.650
	BiLSTM	0.717	**0.727**	0.6999	0.698	0.712
Twitter-hate	MLP	0.681	0.713	0.775	**0.780**	0.692
	BiLSTM	0.772	0.821	**0.851**	0.837	0.84

Note: Numbers in bold indicate best performance per model and dataset

Table 5: F1 scores for the used models using the examined word embeddings on my datasets.

Dataset	Model	Spearman's correlation				
		WEAT	RNSB	RND	ECT	Our_metric
HateEval	MLP	**0.900**	-0.300	0.400	-0.100	0.500
	BiLSTM	0.102	-0.974	-0.461	-0.205	**0.974**
Twitter-sexism	MLP	-0.359	-0.564	-0.359	-0.615	**0.461**
	BiLSTM	-0.205	-0.102	0.153	-0.872	**0.205**
Twitter-racism	MLP	-0.900	-0.200	-0.600	-0.100	**0.100**
	BiLSTM	-0.500	**0.500**	0.200	-0.300	-0.300
Twitter-hate	MLP	**0.300**	-0.100	0	0	-0.200
	BiLSTM	**0.900**	-0.300	0.500	-0.500	0.400

Table 6: Spearman's rank correlation coefficient of the SOS bias scores of the different word embeddings and the F1 scores of the used models for each bias metric and dataset.

I also investigate the influence that my SOS bias metric and state-of-the-art metrics have on the downstream task of hate speech detection. By correlating the F1 scores of machine learning models on different hate speech datasets (Table 5) and the SOS bias scores as measured by my proposed methods and the state-of-the-art metrics. The results in Table 6 show that my metric exhibits a positive correlation with the F1 scores of the Bi-LSTM and MLP models on the HateEval and Twitter-sexism datasets. For Twitter-racism, RNSB shows the highest positive correlation with the F1-score of the Bi-LSTM model, while for the Twitter-hate dataset, WEAT shows the highest positive correlation with the F1-scores of the MLP and Bi-LSTM models. These results suggest that my SOS bias metric correlates consistently positively with the F1 scores of the deep learning models on the different datasets compared to the other metrics. My findings in this section suggest that there is an influence of the SOS bias in the word embeddings on the downstream task of hate speech detection. However, the results are not conclusive and more experiments are required.

The results in this section suggest that the SOS bias provides important information to be used in addition to the social bias to get a fuller picture of the bias in the word embeddings. They also suggest that impact of the SOS and the social bias in the word embeddings on the performance of hate speech detection models. Which means it is important for the future studies on hate speech detection to pay attention to the influence of bias on the models' performance to develop fairer models.

My findings in this section motivate my next research objective to use counterfactual causal inference to understand the influence of the bias in word embedding on the downstream tasks of hate speech and abuse detection.

3.3 Research objective 3

This research goal can be achieved by answering the following research question: 1) How to measure the intersectional bias in pre-trained contextual word embeddings? 2) What is the causal influence of bias, social and intersectional, in the pre-trained contextual word embeddings on the task of hate speech detection? and how harmful that bias is it on the models' fairness?

To answer the first research question and to measure the intersectional bias (gender and race) in contextual word embeddings, I plan to first create an intersectional bias dataset similar to SteroSet (Nadeem et al., 2021) and CrowS-Pairs (Nangia et al., 2020) bias datasets but with focus on intersectionality of gender and race. Then, I plan to use the same method proposed to measure the bias in contextual word embeddings using the same method proposed in (Nangia et al., 2020).

To answer the first part of the second questions and to measure the influence of social and intersectional bias on the task of hate speech detection, I plan to compute the Average Treatment Effect (ATE) on the model's prediction probability distribution (Feder et al., 2021b). I plan to compute the ATE of the prediction probability distribution of a biased contextual word embeddings on a hate speech dataset (factual) and the prediction probability distribution of a debiased contextual word embeddings (counterfactual) on hate speech datasets. I plan to use contextual word embeddings without fine-tuning to avoid unobserved con-founders like the bias in the hate speech datasets.

To answer the second half of the second research question and measure the potential harm of the bias on the task of hate speech detection, I plan to measure the unfairness model for the marginalized and the non-marginalized groups. To measure the unfairness of hate speech detection models, I plan to use similar fairness metric to the one suggested in (De-Arteaga et al., 2019) where the authors measure the difference of the true positive rates (TPR) scores between the different groups of people (marginalised vs. non-marginalized). But instead of the TPRs scores, I plan to use the false positive rate (FPR) scores since FPR is a better estimate of unfairness in hate speech detection models as suggested by (Dixon et al., 2018). Our metric to measure unfairness in hate speech models is described in Equation 2 where g is the marginalized group of people (women, non-white ethnicities, and LGBTQ) and $\hat{g}$ is hte non-marginalized groups of peaple (men, white-ethnciities, and straight).

$$Unfairness_{g,y} = TPR_g - TPR_{\hat{g}} \quad (2)$$

Similarly I plan to use contextual word embeddings without fine-tuning to avoid the unfairness that might result from the imbalances in the datasets. For the experiments I plan to use distilled versions of different pre-trained contextual word embedding, e.g. Distill-BERT, Distill-Roberta, and Distill-GPT2. due to limited access to computational resources. I also plan to use the hate speech datasets described in Table 7, as they contain detailed information on the target of the hate based on attributes like race, gender, and sexual orientation.

This work is expected to reveal the intersectional bias in the contextual word embeddings and how, in addition to the social bias, it causally influence the performance and the unfairness of the hate speech detection models. Understanding this causal influence on performance and fairness would be helpful in developing more effective and targeted debias techniques that address the unfairness of the hate speech detection models instead of generic superficial debias techniques (Gonen and Goldberg, 2019).

Dataset	Size	
ETHOS	433	(Mollas et al., 2022)
MLMa	5647	(Ousidhoum et al., 2019)
Jigsaw	1,902,194	(Jigsaw, 2019)
MIT	59,179	(Huang et al., 2020)
SBIC	112,900	(Sap et al., 2020)

Table 7: Targeted Hate speech datasets

3.4 Limitations

Even though this work has a positive implications , it also has its limitations. One of the limitations is studying bias only from the western society perspective as the way bias is measured might differ in different societies. As for intersectional bias, this work focus only on the intersectionality of gender and race. This work focuses only on models and datasets that are in English which is another limitation. Finally, this work studies the influence of bias only on hate speech detection models using only supervised machine learning models.

3.5 Ethical consideration

This work has a positive impact on the society since it is targeted at revealing the different biases in the commonly used NLP models. It gives insight into the potential risks and unfairness of these NLP models.

4 Conclusion

Hate speech and abuse detection is a very important task to provide a safe inclusive environment for people from different backgrounds to express themselves. However, the different types of biases that have been shown in different NLP tasks could have a counter effect on these hate speech and abuse detection models as they could associate minorities with hate and abuse which could lead to flagging their content as inappropriate and silencing which is the exact opposite of the aim of hate speech and abuse detection models. In this thesis, I look at the different biases in hate speech and abuse detection models and what is the influence of that bias on the performance of hate speech detection models and how this bias could harm the model's fairness. This work reveal types of biases other than social bias in some of the most common NLP models. And it gives insight into developing targeted and effective techniques to mitigate the effect of the different biases and to develop fairer hate speech detection models.

References

Oshin Agarwal, Funda Durupınar, Norman I. Badler, and Ani Nenkova. 2019. Word embeddings (also) encode human personality stereotypes. In *Proceedings of the Eighth Joint Conference on Lexical and Computational Semantics (*SEM 2019)*, pages 205–211, Minneapolis, Minnesota. Association for Computational Linguistics.

Sweta Agrawal and Amit Awekar. 2018a. Deep learning for detecting cyberbullying across multiple social media platforms. In *Advances in Information Retrieval*, pages 141–153, Cham. Springer International Publishing.

Sweta Agrawal and Amit Awekar. 2018b. Deep learning for detecting cyberbullying across multiple social media platforms. In *Advances in Information Retrieval - 40th European Conference on IR Research, ECIR 2018, Grenoble, France, March 26-29, 2018, Proceedings*, volume 10772 of *Lecture Notes in Computer Science*, pages 141–153. Springer.

Maria Antoniak and David Mimno. 2021. Bad seeds: Evaluating lexical methods for bias measurement. In *Proceedings of the 59th Annual Meeting of the Association for Computational Linguistics and the 11th International Joint Conference on Natural Language Processing (Volume 1: Long Papers)*, pages 1889–1904, Online. Association for Computational Linguistics.

Pablo Badilla, Felipe Bravo-Marquez, and Jorge Pérez. 2020. WEFE: the word embeddings fairness evaluation framework. In *Proceedings of the Twenty-Ninth International Joint Conference on Artificial Intelligence, IJCAI 2020*, pages 430–436. ijcai.org.

Valerio Basile, Cristina Bosco, Elisabetta Fersini, Debora Nozza, Viviana Patti, Francisco Manuel Rangel Pardo, Paolo Rosso, and Manuela Sanguinetti. 2019. SemEval-2019 task 5: Multilingual detection of hate speech against immigrants and women in Twitter. In *Proceedings of the 13th International Workshop on Semantic Evaluation*, pages 54–63, Minneapolis, Minnesota, USA. Association for Computational Linguistics.

Su Lin Blodgett, Solon Barocas, Hal Daumé III, and Hanna Wallach. 2020. Language (technology) is power: A critical survey of "bias" in NLP. In *Proceedings of the 58th Annual Meeting of the Association for Computational Linguistics*, pages 5454–5476, Online. Association for Computational Linguistics.

Tolga Bolukbasi, Kai-Wei Chang, James Zou, Venkatesh Saligrama, and Adam Kalai. 2016. Man is to computer programmer as woman is to homemaker? debiasing word embeddings. In *Proceedings of the 30th International Conference on Neural Information Processing Systems*, NIPS'16, page 4356–4364, Red Hook, NY, USA. Curran Associates Inc.

Marc-Etienne Brunet, Colleen Alkalay-Houlihan, Ashton Anderson, and Richard S. Zemel. 2019. Understanding the origins of bias in word embeddings. In *Proceedings of the 36th International Conference on Machine Learning, ICML 2019, 9-15 June 2019, Long Beach, California, USA*, volume 97 of *Proceedings of Machine Learning Research*, pages 803–811. PMLR.

Aylin Caliskan, Joanna J. Bryson, and Arvind Narayanan. 2017. Semantics derived automatically from language corpora contain human-like biases. *Science*, 356(6334):183–186.

Kaytlin Chaloner and Alfredo Maldonado. 2019. Measuring gender bias in word embeddings across domains and discovering new gender bias word categories. In *Proceedings of the First Workshop on Gender Bias in Natural Language Processing*, pages 25–32, Florence, Italy. Association for Computational Linguistics.

Kimberlé Crenshaw. 1989. Demarginalizing the intersection of race and sex: A black feminist critique of antidiscrimination doctrine, feminist theory and antiracist politics. *u. Chi. Legal f.*, page 139.

Maral Dadvar, Dolf Trieschnigg, and Franciska de Jong. 2014. Experts and machines against bullies: A hybrid approach to detect cyberbullies. In *Advances in Artificial Intelligence*, pages 275–281, Cham. Springer International Publishing.

Thomas Davidson, Dana Warmsley, Michael W. Macy, and Ingmar Weber. 2017. Automated hate speech detection and the problem of offensive language. In *Proceedings of the Eleventh International Conference on Web and Social Media, ICWSM 2017, Montréal, Québec, Canada, May 15-18, 2017*, pages 512–515. AAAI Press.

Maria De-Arteaga, Alexey Romanov, Hanna Wallach, Jennifer Chayes, Christian Borgs, Alexandra Chouldechova, Sahin Geyik, Krishnaram Kenthapadi, and Adam Tauman Kalai. 2019. Bias in bios: A case study of semantic representation bias in a high-stakes setting. In *proceedings of the Conference on Fairness, Accountability, and Transparency*, pages 120–128.

Maria De-Arteaga, Alexey Romanov, Hanna M. Wallach, Jennifer T. Chayes, Christian Borgs, Alexandra Chouldechova, Sahin Cem Geyik, Krishnaram Kenthapadi, and Adam Tauman Kalai. 2019. Bias in bios: A case study of semantic representation bias in a high-stakes setting. In *Proceedings of the Conference on Fairness, Accountability, and Transparency, FAT* 2019, Atlanta, GA, USA, January 29-31, 2019*, pages 120–128. ACM.

Sunipa Dev and Jeff M. Phillips. 2019. Attenuating bias in word vectors. In *The 22nd International Conference on Artificial Intelligence and Statistics, AISTATS 2019, 16-18 April 2019, Naha, Okinawa, Japan*, volume 89 of *Proceedings of Machine Learning Research*, pages 879–887. PMLR.

Jacob Devlin, Ming-Wei Chang, Kenton Lee, and Kristina Toutanova. 2019. BERT: pre-training of deep bidirectional transformers for language understanding. In *NAACL-HLT (1)*, pages 4171–4186. Association for Computational Linguistics.

Karthik Dinakar, Roi Reichart, and Henry Lieberman. 2011. Modeling the detection of textual cyberbullying. In *5th International AAAI Conference on Weblogs and Social Media.*

Lucas Dixon, John Li, Jeffrey Sorensen, Nithum Thain, and Lucy Vasserman. 2018. Measuring and mitigating unintended bias in text classification. In *Proceedings of the 2018 AAAI/ACM Conference on AI, Ethics, and Society*, AIES '18, page 67–73, New York, NY, USA. Association for Computing Machinery.

Yanai Elazar, Shauli Ravfogel, Alon Jacovi, and Yoav Goldberg. 2021. Amnesic probing: Behavioral explanation with amnesic counterfactuals. *Trans. Assoc. Comput. Linguistics*, 9:160–175.

Fatma Elsafoury. BERT attention explanation. `https://github.com/efatmae/BERT_Attention_Explanation`.

Fatma Elsafoury, Stamos Katsigiannis, Zeeshan Pervez, and Naeem Ramzan. 2021. When the timeline meets the pipeline: A survey on automated cyberbullying detection. *IEEE Access*, 9:103541–103563.

Amir Feder, Katherine A Keith, Emaad Manzoor, Reid Pryzant, Dhanya Sridhar, Zach Wood-Doughty, Jacob Eisenstein, Justin Grimmer, Roi Reichart, Margaret E Roberts, et al. 2021a. Causal inference in natural language processing: Estimation, prediction, interpretation and beyond. *arXiv preprint arXiv:2109.00725.*

Amir Feder, Nadav Oved, Uri Shalit, and Roi Reichart. 2021b. Causalm: Causal model explanation through counterfactual language models. *Comput. Linguistics*, 47(2):333–386.

Paula Fortuna and Sérgio Nunes. 2018. A survey on automatic detection of hate speech in text. *ACM Computing Surveys (CSUR)*, 51(4):1–30.

Nikhil Garg, Londa Schiebinger, Dan Jurafsky, and James Zou. 2018. Word embeddings quantify 100 years of gender and ethnic stereotypes. *Proceedings of the National Academy of Sciences*, 115(16):E3635–E3644.

Paula Giddings. 2006. *When and where I enter*. Bantam Doubleday Dell Publishing Group Incorporated.

Hila Gonen and Yoav Goldberg. 2019. Lipstick on a pig: Debiasing methods cover up systematic gender biases in word embeddings but do not remove them. In *NAACL-HLT.*

Wei Guo and Aylin Caliskan. 2021. Detecting emergent intersectional biases: Contextualized word embeddings contain a distribution of human-like biases. In *Proceedings of the 2021 AAAI/ACM Conference on AI, Ethics, and Society*, AIES '21, page 122–133, New York, NY, USA. Association for Computing Machinery.

James Hawdon, Atte Oksanen, and Pekka Räsänen. 2015. Online extremism and online hate. *NORDICOM*, page 29.

Sepp Hochreiter and Jürgen Schmidhuber. 1997. Long short-term memory. *Neural computation*, 9(8):1735–1780.

Xiaolei Huang, Linzi Xing, Franck Dernoncourt, and Michael J. Paul. 2020. Multilingual twitter corpus and baselines for evaluating demographic bias in hate speech recognition. In *Proceedings of The 12th Language Resources and Evaluation Conference, LREC 2020, Marseille, France, May 11-16, 2020*, pages 1440–1448. European Language Resources Association.

Jigsaw. 2019. Jigsaw unintended bias in toxicity classification. Accessed: 2022-02-15.

Kenneth Joseph and Jonathan Morgan. 2020. When do word embeddings accurately reflect surveys on our beliefs about people? In *Proceedings of the 58th Annual Meeting of the Association for Computational Linguistics*, pages 4392–4415, Online. Association for Computational Linguistics.

Kaggle. 2012. Detecting insults in social commentary. `https://www.kaggle.com/c/detecting-insults-in-social-commentary/data`. Accessed: 2020-09-28.

Jae Yeon Kim, Carlos Ortiz, Sarah Nam, Sarah Santiago, and Vivek Datta. 2020. Intersectional bias in hate speech and abusive language datasets. *arXiv preprint arXiv:2005.05921.*

Olga Kovaleva, Alexey Romanov, Anna Rogers, and Anna Rumshisky. 2019. Revealing the dark secrets of BERT. In *EMNLP/IJCNLP (1)*, pages 4364–4373. Association for Computational Linguistics.

Rebecca Kukla. 2018. Slurs, interpellation, and ideology. *The Southern Journal of Philosophy*, 56:7–32.

Akshi Kumar, Shashwat Nayak, and Navya Chandra. 2019. Empirical analysis of supervised machine learning techniques for cyberbullying detection. In *International Conference on Innovative Computing and Communications*, pages 223–230, Singapore. Springer Singapore.

Michael A. Lepori. 2020. Unequal representations: Analyzing intersectional biases in word embeddings using representational similarity analysis. In *Proceedings of the 28th International Conference on Computational Linguistics, COLING 2020, Barcelona, Spain (Online), December 8-13, 2020*, pages 1720–1728. International Committee on Computational Linguistics.

Thomas Manzini, Lim Yao Chong, Alan W Black, and Yulia Tsvetkov. 2019. Black is to criminal as caucasian is to police: Detecting and removing multiclass bias in word embeddings. In *Proceedings of the 2019 Conference of the North American*

Chapter of the Association for Computational Linguistics: Human Language Technologies, Volume 1 (Long and Short Papers), pages 615–621, Minneapolis, Minnesota. Association for Computational Linguistics.

Ioannis Mollas, Zoe Chrysopoulou, Stamatis Karlos, and Grigorios Tsoumakas. 2022. ETHOS: a multi-label hate speech detection dataset. *Complex & Intelligent Systems*.

Marzieh Mozafari, Reza Farahbakhsh, and Noel Crespi. 2019. A bert-based transfer learning approach for hate speech detection in online social media. In *International Conference on Complex Networks and Their Applications*, pages 928–940. Springer.

Moin Nadeem, Anna Bethke, and Siva Reddy. 2021. Stereoset: Measuring stereotypical bias in pre-trained language models. In *Proceedings of the 59th Annual Meeting of the Association for Computational Linguistics and the 11th International Joint Conference on Natural Language Processing, ACL/IJCNLP 2021, (Volume 1: Long Papers), Virtual Event, August 1-6, 2021*, pages 5356–5371. Association for Computational Linguistics.

Nikita Nangia, Clara Vania, Rasika Bhalerao, and Samuel R. Bowman. 2020. CrowS-Pairs: A Challenge Dataset for Measuring Social Biases in Masked Language Models. In *Proceedings of the 2020 Conference on Empirical Methods in Natural Language Processing*, Online. Association for Computational Linguistics.

Laurie T O'Brien, Alison Blodorn, Glenn Adams, Donna M Garcia, and Elliott Hammer. 2015. Ethnic variation in gender-stem stereotypes and stem participation: An intersectional approach. *Cultural Diversity and Ethnic Minority Psychology*, 21(2):169.

Alexandra Olteanu, Carlos Castillo, Fernando Diaz, and Emre Kıcıman. 2019. Social data: Biases, methodological pitfalls, and ethical boundaries. *Frontiers in Big Data*, 2:13.

Nedjma Ousidhoum, Zizheng Lin, Hongming Zhang, Yangqiu Song, and Dit-Yan Yeung. 2019. Multilingual and multi-aspect hate speech analysis. In *Proceedings of EMNLP*. Association for Computational Linguistics.

Sayanta Paul and Sriparna Saha. 2020. Cyberbert: Bert for cyberbullying identification. *Multimedia Systems*.

John Pavlopoulos, Nithum Thain, Lucas Dixon, and Ion Androutsopoulos. 2019. Convai at semeval-2019 task 6: Offensive language identification and categorization with perspective and bert. In *Proceedings of the 13th international Workshop on Semantic Evaluation*, pages 571–576.

Chen Qian, Fuli Feng, Lijie Wen, Chunping Ma, and Pengjun Xie. 2021. Counterfactual inference for text classification debiasing. In *Proceedings of the 59th Annual Meeting of the Association for Computational Linguistics and the 11th International Joint Conference on Natural Language Processing, ACL/IJCNLP 2021, (Volume 1: Long Papers), Virtual Event, August 1-6, 2021*, pages 5434–5445. Association for Computational Linguistics.

Rad Campaign. 2014. The rise of online harassment. [Online] Accessed 13/9/2021.

Rahat Ibn Rafiq, Homa Hosseinmardi, Richard Han, Qin Lv, Shivakant Mishra, and Sabrina Arredondo Mattson. 2015. Careful what you share in six seconds: Detecting cyberbullying instances in vine. In *Proceedings of the 2015 IEEE/ACM International Conference on Advances in Social Networks Analysis and Mining 2015*, ASONAM '15, page 617–622. ACM.

E. Raisi and B. Huang. 2017. Cyberbullying detection with weakly supervised machine learning. In *2017 IEEE/ACM International Conference on Advances in Social Networks Analysis and Mining (ASONAM)*, pages 409–416.

Shauli Ravfogel, Grusha Prasad, Tal Linzen, and Yoav Goldberg. 2021. Counterfactual interventions reveal the causal effect of relative clause representations on agreement prediction. In *Proceedings of the 25th Conference on Computational Natural Language Learning, CoNLL 2021, Online, November 10-11, 2021*, pages 194–209. Association for Computational Linguistics.

Anna Rogers, Olga Kovaleva, and Anna Rumshisky. 2021. A primer in bertology: What we know about how BERT works. *Transactions of the Association for Computational Linguistics*, 8:842–866.

Sarah Rosenfield. 2012. Triple jeopardy? mental health at the intersection of gender, race, and class. *Social Science & Medicine*, 74(11):1791–1801.

Maarten Sap, Saadia Gabriel, Lianhui Qin, Dan Jurafsky, Noah A. Smith, and Yejin Choi. 2020. Social bias frames: Reasoning about social and power implications of language. In *Proceedings of the 58th Annual Meeting of the Association for Computational Linguistics, ACL 2020, Online, July 5-10, 2020*, pages 5477–5490. Association for Computational Linguistics.

Mike Schuster and Kuldip K Paliwal. 1997. Bidirectional recurrent neural networks. *IEEE Transactions on Signal Processing*, 45(11):2673–2681.

Sofia Serrano and Noah A. Smith. 2019. Is attention interpretable? In *Proceedings of the 57th Annual Meeting of the Association for Computational Linguistics*, pages 2931–2951, Florence, Italy. Association for Computational Linguistics.

Xiaobing Sun and Wei Lu. 2020. Understanding attention for text classification. In *Proceedings of the 58th Annual Meeting of the Association for Computational Linguistics*, pages 3418–3428. Association for Computational Linguistics.

Mukund Sundararajan, Ankur Taly, and Qiqi Yan. 2017. Axiomatic attribution for deep networks. In *Proceedings of the 34th International Conference on Machine Learning - Volume 70*, ICML'17, page 3319–3328.

Chris Sweeney and Maryam Najafian. 2019. A transparent framework for evaluating unintended demographic bias in word embeddings. In *Proceedings of the 57th Annual Meeting of the Association for Computational Linguistics*, pages 1662–1667, Florence, Italy. Association for Computational Linguistics.

Yi Chern Tan and L. Elisa Celis. 2019. Assessing social and intersectional biases in contextualized word representations. In *Advances in Neural Information Processing Systems 32: Annual Conference on Neural Information Processing Systems 2019, NeurIPS 2019, December 8-14, 2019, Vancouver, BC, Canada*, pages 13209–13220.

Tensorflow.org. 2020. Text tokenization utility class. `https://www.tensorflow.org/api_docs/python/tf/keras/preprocessing/text/Tokenizer`. Accessed: 2020-09-28.

Mycal Tucker, Peng Qian, and Roger Levy. 2021. What if this modified that? syntactic interventions with counterfactual embeddings. In *Findings of the Association for Computational Linguistics: ACL-IJCNLP 2021*, pages 862–875, Online. Association for Computational Linguistics.

Shikhar Vashishth, Shyam Upadhyay, Gaurav Singh Tomar, and Manaal Faruqui. 2019. Attention interpretability across NLP tasks. *arXiv.org*, arXiv:1909.11218.

Claudia Wagner, Markus Strohmaier, Alexandra Olteanu, Emre Kıcıman, Noshir Contractor, and Tina Eliassi-Rad. 2021. Measuring algorithmically infused societies. *Nature*, 595(7866):197–204.

Zeerak Waseem and Dirk Hovy. 2016a. Hateful symbols or hateful people? predictive features for hate speech detection on Twitter. In *Proceedings of the NAACL Student Research Workshop*, pages 88–93, San Diego, California. Association for Computational Linguistics.

Zeerak Waseem and Dirk Hovy. 2016b. Hateful symbols or hateful people? predictive features for hate speech detection on twitter. In *Proceedings of the Student Research Workshop, SRW@HLT-NAACL 2016, The 2016 Conference of the North American Chapter of the Association for Computational Linguistics: Human Language Technologies, San Diego California, USA, June 12-17, 2016*, pages 88–93. The Association for Computational Linguistics.

Ellery Wulczyn, Nithum Thain, and Lucas Dixon. 2017. Ex machina: Personal attacks seen at scale. In *Proceedings of the 26th International Conference on World Wide Web*, WWW '17, page 1391–1399. International World Wide Web Conferences Steering Committee.

Jaideep Yadav, Devesh Kumar, and Dheeraj Chauhan. 2020. Cyberbullying detection using pre-trained bert model. In *2020 International Conference on Electronics and Sustainable Communication Systems (ICESC)*, pages 1096–1100. IEEE.

Junru Zhou, Zhuosheng Zhang, Hai Zhao, and Shuailiang Zhang. 2020. LIMIT-BERT : Linguistics informed multi-task BERT. In *Findings of the Association for Computational Linguistics: EMNLP 2020*, pages 4450–4461, Online. Association for Computational Linguistics.

Xuhui Zhou, Maarten Sap, Swabha Swayamdipta, Yejin Choi, and Noah A. Smith. 2021. Challenges in automated debiasing for toxic language detection. In *Proceedings of the 16th Conference of the European Chapter of the Association for Computational Linguistics: Main Volume, EACL 2021, Online, April 19 - 23, 2021*, pages 3143–3155. Association for Computational Linguistics.

Ethical Considerations for Low-resourced Machine Translation

Levon Haroutunian
Department of Linguistics
University of Washington
levonh@uw.edu

Abstract

This paper considers some ethical implications of machine translation for low-resourced languages. I use Armenian as a case study and investigate specific needs for and concerns arising from the creation and deployment of improved machine translation between English and Armenian. To do this, I conduct stakeholder interviews and construct Value Scenarios (Nathan et al., 2007) from the themes that emerge. These scenarios illustrate some of the potential harms that low-resourced language communities may face due to the deployment of improved machine translation systems. Based on these scenarios, I recommend 1) collaborating with stakeholders in order to create more useful and reliable machine translation tools, and 2) determining which other forms of language technology should be developed alongside efforts to improve machine translation in order to mitigate harms rendered to vulnerable language communities. Both of these goals require treating low-resourced machine translation as a language-specific, rather than language-agnostic, task.

1 Introduction

The challenge of building machine translation systems for low-resourced languages is often seen merely a problem of data scarcity, but such a framing obscures the systemic differences between low-resourced languages and high-resourced languages, as well as between their corresponding speaker communities. Before building machine translation systems for low-resourced languages, it is important to consider the real impact that these systems can have on their intended users. This paper investigates the ethical implications for improvements to machine translation for low-resourced languages using a Value Scenarios (Nathan et al., 2007) framework to identify potential harms and construct recommendations to mitigate them.

The remainder of this paper uses the Armenian language as a case study and considers the specific circumstances of speakers in the Armenian Diaspora. I conducted interviews with four stakeholders (Armenian speakers who use machine translation systems) and analyzed their responses to identify common desires and concerns for machine translation. I then used these analyses to construct Value Scenarios, which illustrate potential unintended consequences of improving the quality of machine translation between English and Armenian to the level of current machine translation between English and other high-resourced languages.

In examining machine translation for Armenian, I hope to provide examples of the kinds of harms that may be caused to speakers of low-resourced languages in the development of machine translation tools. This paper is not meant as an exhaustive exploration of all possible harms; instead, it provides a starting point for considering how the specific circumstances of a language community can inform the creation of ethically-produced machine translation tools.

My findings show that machine translation for low-resourced languages should not be undertaken as an aggregated language-agnostic task, but should instead be approached in a language-specific way that contextualizes speakers' needs and other facets of existing language technology. Such an approach would allow NLP researchers to move away from a data-first paradigm that privileges high-resourced languages and varieties towards one that can take into account the particular circumstances of vulnerable groups in order to ensure that we build machine translation tools that are genuinely useful and reliable.

The rest of this paper is organized as follows. Section 2 provides background information on machine translation for low-resourced languages and describes Value Scenarios. Following that, Section 3 gives an overview of considerations for Armenian. Section 4 describes the methodology I followed to conduct stakeholder interviews, the results of

Proceedings of the 60th Annual Meeting of the Association for Computational Linguistics
Student Research Workshop, pages 44 - 54
May 22-27, 2022

which are analyzed in Section 5. Based on interviewees' responses, two Value Scenarios are presented and analyzed in Section 6, and recommendations based on these scenarios are given in Section 7. Section 8 describes ethical considerations for this project, and Section 9 provides a conclusion.

2 Background

2.1 (Neural) Machine Translation for Low-Resourced Languages

In the past few years, neural machine translation (NMT) (Bahdanau et al., 2016) has become the dominant model for machine translation applications. NMT systems generally show a wide gap in translation quality for low-resourced languages and high-resourced languages (Caswell and Liang, 2020). This difference in performance has significant consequences for speakers of low-resourced languages. As Joshi et al. (2020) argue, the divergence in the quality of NLP applications for high-resourced languages and low-resourced languages can exacerbate conditions that lead to language decline.

There have been many efforts to improve machine translation for low-resourced languages (e.g. Gu et al., 2018; Lample et al., 2018; Ko et al., 2021; Zoph et al., 2016; Fadaee et al., 2017), many of which take a transfer learning approach that applies models trained on multilingual data to languages for which there is less data available. Many current NMT models are trained on large, uncurated datasets, such as Wikipedia dumps (Gu et al., 2018). As a result, NMT systems generally work better for standard language varieties than non-standard ones (Kumar et al., 2021).

When approaching the task of machine translation for low-resourced languages, it is important to consider the relationship between the NLP community and communities that speak low-resourced languages. As Nekoto et al. (2020) detail, understanding low-resourcedness as merely a lack of data is reductive, as this framing fails to capture the corresponding lack of linguistic and geographic diversity of NLP scholars. Nekoto et al. (2020) also describe how much of the work in machine translation is Anglo-centric, as it prioritizes the quality of translations to and from English.

Both of these observations point to a disconnect between the NLP community and speakers of low-resourced languages. As a result, language technologists building applications for low-resourced languages may not have a clear picture of the wants and needs of these languages' speaker communities, and may not understand the benefits and harms rendered to these communities by the language technology they build. The number of languages considered to be low-resourced is vast, and communities that speak low-resourced languages have diverse needs; often, these needs are very different from the needs of speakers of high-resourced languages (e.g. Joshi et al., 2019).

2.2 Value Scenarios

Incorporating stakeholders' perspectives is crucial for creating useful improvements in language technology for low-resourced languages (e.g. Nekoto et al., 2020; Joshi et al., 2019).

To do that, this work will draw on the principles of Value-Sensitive Design (Friedman, 1996), particularly Value Scenarios (Nathan et al., 2007), to identify ethical challenges in the improvements of machine translation for low-resourced languages. A Value Scenario imagines the systemic impacts of a proposed technology in order to anticipate and mitigate negative consequences before that technology is deployed. Considering how many efforts are underway to improve the quality of machine translation for low-resourced languages, it is pertinent to examine a range of impacts that these improvements may have for speakers of low-resourced languages. The utility of Value Scenarios in this use case is to illustrate the needs and concerns of a particular group of stakeholders in a way that generates specific avenues for harm mitigation.

The Value Scenarios framework (Nathan et al., 2007) identifies five key elements to explore: stakeholders (people who are impacted by the technology either directly or indirectly), pervasiveness (the effects of the technology when it has widespread use), time (the effect of the technology in short- and long-term scales), systemic effects (how the technology interacts with various areas of life), and value implications (potential positive and negative influences that impact use of the technology). My analysis in this paper will draw on each of these five components.

It should be noted that the purpose of Value Scenarios is not to generate predictions for the future, nor is it possible to use Value Scenarios to imagine every possible consequence of a proposed technology (Nathan et al., 2007). The task of preventing harms to marginalized groups is complex and ever-changing, and requires the integration of many types of expertise and a variety of tools. This paper considers the use of Value Scenarios as one such tool.

3 Considerations for Armenian

In this section, I present two important challenges specific to the improvement of machine translation for Armenian: language variation and orthography. While the details of these challenges pertain to the particular situation of the Armenian language and of Armenian speakers, it is likely that improvements to other low-resourced languages would require similar considerations.

3.1 Variation

Modern Armenian has two main varieties: Modern Eastern Armenian and Modern Western Armenian. While these two varieties are mostly mutually intelligible, there are large distinctions between them in phonology, morphology, syntax, and lexical items.

The following characterization of Armenian-speaking populations is consistent with Eberhard et al. (2021). Eastern Armenian speakers are predominantly those in Armenia, Artsakh, Russia, and Iran. Western Armenian speakers are predominantly those in the United States, Lebanon, Georgia, and Argentina. There are about 3.8 million Eastern Armenian speakers and about 1.4 million Western Armenian speakers worldwide.

There is a large imbalance in the amount of data available in each of the two main varieties; for example, the Eastern Armenian Wikipedia (called simply Armenian Wikipedia) has about 291 thousand articles in early 2022, while the Western Armenian Wikipedia has only about 10 thousand.[1]

3.2 Orthography

The following description is based on Hagopian (2007). While all varieties of Armenian are written with the same alphabet, there are two sets of spelling conventions: Classical Orthography and Reformed Orthography. There are substantial differences between the two systems, though it is generally possible for someone who typically uses one orthography to read text written in the other. Speakers of all varieties of Western Armenian and of the *Barskahye* variety of Eastern Armenian use Classical Orthography, while all other speakers of Eastern Armenian use Reformed Orthography. The vast majority of text in Armenian on the Internet is in Reformed Orthography. See Table 1 for an example of differences between varieties and orthographies.

Eastern, Reformed	իմ քույրը խոսում է
Eastern, Classical	իմ քոյրը խօսում է
Eastern, IPA	im ˈkʰui.ɾə ˈχo.sum e
Western, Classical	իմ քոյրս կը խօսի
Western, IPA	im ˈkʰui.ɾəs gə χo.ˈsi

Table 1: The phrase "my sister speaks" in both Eastern and Western Armenian. The transcriptions in IPA show roughly standard pronunciations for both main varieties.

Additionally, many Armenian speakers often write using ad-hoc Romanization rather than Armenian script, which is an additional challenge for machine translation.

4 Methodology

This section describes the process by which I conducted stakeholder interviews. This study was approved by the Institutional Review Board (IRB) at the University of Washington.

4.1 Participants

Four volunteer participants were recruited on the basis of their status as Armenian and English speakers who have previously used machine translation technology. To avoid the unwanted identification of these participants, the following description and the discussion in Section 5 include only details that are necessary for contextualizing the perspectives described in this paper.

Each participant speaks a different variety of Armenian: Standard Eastern Armenian, the *Karabaghtsi* (Artsakhi) variety of Eastern Armenian, the *Barskahye* (Iranian) variety of Eastern Armenian, and Standard Western Armenian. These varieties cover a large swath of Armenian speakers, although of course they do not constitute the totality of variation in Armenian.

While the stakeholders I interviewed are diverse in the varieties they speak, they are otherwise a somewhat homogeneous group. All of the interviewees are below the age of 35, and all have resided in the United States for the majority of their lives. Additionally, while all four interviewees speak Armenian at home and in some social settings, they also all speak English as their primary language in other settings. Therefore, the perspectives described in this paper reflect a partic-

[1] meta.wikimedia.org/wiki/List_of_Wikipedias

ularly diasporic and English-dominant experience of Armenian identity, which has a clear influence on the desires and concerns described in Section 5. It should also be noted that all of the interviewees were people in my own network, and do not form a representative sample of Armenian speakers as a whole or even of Armenian speakers in the United States.

4.2 Interviews

Before the interviews were conducted, participants were provided with a description of this study's purpose and the topics that would be discussed during the interview, along with a description of how their data would be stored and used. Each participant was interviewed separately over a video call that lasted between one and two hours in length. With the participants' consent, the interviews were recorded to aid later analysis. To protect the interviewees' privacy, all recording files are secured in accordance with the guidelines established by the Human Subjects Division at the University of Washington.

These interviews were conducted in a semi-structured format: some questions were predetermined, and others were based on participants' responses in the moment. I constructed a set of basic questions for each topic I planned to discuss with interviewees, and these questions served as starting points to informal conversations. This format was chosen in order to illuminate comparisons between different interviewees' experiences with machine translation while allowing the course of each interview to be shaped by particulars of the interviewee's perspective. The length of the interviews was determined by the length of interviewees' responses.

Each interview covered the same set of topics, including the participant's 1) use of Armenian, 2) experience of being an Armenian person in online spaces, 3) use of machine translation technology, 4) desired improvements for Armenian-English machine translation, and 5) expected benefits and harms for Armenian-English machine translation. Below is a sample of the questions that I determined prior to the interviews; a complete list can be found in Appendix A.

- What is your experience using machine translation tools? How usable are they for you?

- What is your experience as an Armenian speaker online?

- When you translate from English to Armenian, do machine translation tools give you something that sounds like the way you would speak?

- When you translate from Armenian to English, do you run into any problems that relate to the way you speak Armenian?

- If machine translation for Armenian (to and from English) improved, how do you think it would affect you? How do you imagine other people (both Armenians and non-Armenians) would use it?

4.3 Limitations

To contextualize the results in Section 5 and the Value Scenarios in Section 6, it is important to acknowledge the limitations of this project.

First, as stated previously, the participant group forms a non-representative sample of Armenian speakers. There are only four interviewees, and they have similar backgrounds: they all live in the United States, they all speak English as a primary language, and they are all relatively young. Likewise, all of the speakers I interviewed indicated the same types of uses for machine translation and largely similar concerns. It is very likely that different results would have emerged if I had been able to interview a more diverse group of Armenian speakers, particularly if I was able to incorporate the perspectives of older speakers and those who speak a language other than English as a primary language. This is not to say that the needs and concerns identified below are any less relevant – merely that there are likely many other needs and concerns that I was not able to identify. The perspectives in this paper should not be taken as representative of all Armenian speakers.

Second, as stated in Section 2, the Value Scenarios approach cannot uncover every possible consequence of a proposed technology, since many harms are emergent. The harms described in this paper do not constitute the totality of potential negative impacts for low-resourced machine translation.

5 Results

Below is an overview of significant themes that emerged from my stakeholder interviews.

5.1 State of Current Machine Translation Tools for Armenian

In general, respondents said that they mostly used translation tools to look up words or short phrases. The most common usages respondents reported was to help them remember words that they already knew or to find words specific to Standard Eastern Armenian. One respondent said that she occasionally used machine translation to look up specific terms she knew in English but not Armenian in order to facilitate communication with family members who do not speak English well.

All interviewees were familiar with Google Translate[2], which has several features that they found useful. One such feature is transliterated output, which makes interpretation easier for interviewees who are unable to read Armenian or less practiced. Audio output was similarly useful. Respondents reported that they were usually able to find the English translation of an Armenian word they were not able to spell correctly, which was helpful.

On the other hand, every respondent reported a lack of trust in Google Translate's accuracy, with multiple respondents reporting that they usually verified the output with another Armenian speaker before incorporating it into their own speech. Additionally, all respondents noted that the output from Google Translate had a markedly Standard Eastern Armenian style, including the exclusive use of Reformed Orthography. As a result, only the respondent who speaks Standard Eastern Armenian reported that she was able to consistently get output from Google Translate that matches the way she speaks.

Most of the participants were also familiar with Nayiri Armenian Dictionary[3], which is an online resource that supports Western Armenian (in Classical Orthography) and Eastern Armenian (in Reformed Orthography). Nayiri, which is maintained by a small team of Armenian software engineers and linguists, incorporates a database of digitized Armenian dictionaries into its search. Respondents who used Nayiri reported that they trusted its output far more than they trusted that of Google Translate, but that Nayiri was more challenging to use: the site is less user-friendly, there is less forgiveness for misspellings, and Nayiri only supports single-word look-ups rather than phrase or sentence translations.

The respondent who reported the least amount of resources for her variety was the *Barskahye* speaker, who reported that she was unable to find any translation tool that outputs results in Eastern Armenian using Classical Orthography.

Respondents reported that neither tool was useful for translating full sentences or paragraphs in either direction. When respondents have tried to translate longer utterances on Google Translate, output was generally jumbled or nonsensical.

5.2 Desires for and Anticipated Benefits of Improved Machine Translation

The speakers I interviewed were enthusiastic about the prospect of improved machine translation tools, and each of them was able to identify both personal and communal benefits. Beyond a general improvement in translation quality, interviewees most strongly desired 1) expanded support for varieties other than Standard Eastern Armenian, and 2) output in Reformed Orthography, Classical Orthography, and in Roman characters.

There was a wide variety of potential uses that the interviewees identified for improved machine translation tools:

- *Language learning.* All of the stakeholders I interviewed said that they would hope to utilize improved machine translation tools to expand their own knowledge of the Armenian language, specifically to improve their vocabulary (in their own and other varieties) and to strengthen their literacy.

- *Transmitting urgent information.* Two stakeholders identified machine translation as a tool to help Armenians in the diaspora more rapidly understand urgent news coming out of Armenia and Artsakh. This is a particularly pressing need in the wake of the 2020 war between Artsakh and Azerbaijan.

- *Connecting to other Armenians.* Related to the above points, interviewees stated that they would use improved machine translation tools to better communicate with other Armenians, both those that speak their variety and those that speak other varieties. In particular, one interviewee spoke of the potential to use such tools to build bridges between diaspora communities and Armenia and Artsakh.

[2]translate.google.com

[3]nayiri.com

- *Connecting outsiders to Armenia.* One interviewee suggested that improved machine translation would bolster tourism prospects for Armenia, while another suggested that it would allow outsiders easier access to information and history that has thus far only been available in Armenian.

5.3 Concerns about harassment and disinformation

All respondents described seeing frequent online harassment against Armenians, generally from Turkish and Azerbaijani ultra-nationalists. According to respondents, there has been a substantial increase in harassment since the beginning of the 2020 war between Artsakh and Azerbaijan.

Two respondents reported receiving harassment on social media themselves, and all respondents reported seeing other Armenians be harassed. This harassment generally comes in the form of spam, specifically the use of particular emojis (e.g. Azerbaijani and Turkish flags, skulls, coffins, pigs, wolves, and knives) and inflammatory or disturbing hashtags. Other forms of harassment include 1) comments advocating violence against Armenians, denying the Armenian Genocide, celebrating the Armenian Genocide, and claiming Azerbaijani ownership of Armenian cultural monuments; 2) hateful or disturbing memes; and 3) videos of Azerbaijani soldiers desecrating Armenian churches and cemeteries, flying Azerbaijani flags over Armenian buildings and monuments, destroying Armenian homes and property, and in the worst cases, torturing and murdering Armenian soldiers and civilians.

All respondents stated that their relationship with social media changed in the wake of the war, with anti-Armenian harassment being one factor that influenced this change. When I asked respondents what negative impacts they could imagine from the deployment of an effective machine translation tool for Armenian, three of the four respondents independently brought up the potential for production of hateful content. These respondents expressed concerns that malicious actors could use improved machine translation to further their harassment of Armenians, either by using it to better understand posts written in Armenian and attacking creators of those posts, or to translate hateful messages into Armenian (which would potentially be more disturbing than hateful messages written in English).

Additionally, interviewees were concerned about the possibility of machine translation tools being used for disinformation campaigns and propaganda from Azerbaijani military forces.

5.4 Concerns about standardization

When presented with the possibility of machine translation tools being improved only for Standard Eastern Armenian and not for other varieties, three of the four interviewees expressed concern that this move would negatively impact speakers of Western Armenian and non-standard varieties of Eastern Armenian. Specifically, interviewees were concerned that the hegemony of Standard Eastern Armenian online, amplified by machine translation tools that exclusively produce output in Standard Eastern Armenian, would contribute to the common belief that Eastern Armenian written in Reformed Orthography is the most "correct" or "pure" form of Armenian.

6 Value Scenarios

In this section, I present two value scenarios that I have constructed based on the above findings. These value scenarios are intended to illustrate *potential* unwanted consequences of improving machine translation for low-resourced languages. They are not meant to be predictions of real events; rather, they are deliberately dark imaginings of the impacts that new technology could have (Nathan et al., 2007). The purpose of creating these value scenarios is to uncover considerations that may need to be made before developing improvements to machine translation for low-resourced languages.

While the two scenarios below are presented as separate outcomes, it should be noted they could occur simultaneously. The distinction between them is merely for the purpose of more easily illustrating different possible consequences.

6.1 Value Scenario 1

Thanks to advances in unsupervised neural machine translation, there have been large improvements in translation between English and languages with relatively large monolingual corpora; Standard Eastern Armenian is one such language. Due to these developments, machine translation in Standard Eastern Armenian on platforms like Google Translate is much more reliable than it used to be.

For people looking to learn Standard Eastern Armenian either to connect with their family or to visit Armenia on vacation, these applications are very useful. However, speakers of minoritized varieties of Armenian receive none of these benefits. On top of that, machine translation for Armenian is now regarded as a solved task, so there is little motivation for expanding machine translation capabilities for other varieties.

Many more websites and platforms are able to support Armenian text and Armenian users, but it assumed that all of these users are willing and able to communicate in Standard Eastern Armenian written in Reformed Orthography. This contributes to the perception that Standard Eastern Armenian is the only legitimate form of Armenian, leading other speakers to feel alienated from their communities. Speakers of Western Armenian and non-standard varieties of Eastern Armenian alter their speech to fit in, or they avoid speaking Armenian at all when other languages are available. Artsakhi refugees of the 2020 war are ridiculed for their speech in their new homes in Armenia; many of them face additional burdens at school or work because their speech is seen as unintelligent.

Over time, other varieties' speaker populations decline, and the linguistic diversity of Armenian speakers around the world is replaced with homogeneity. Along with these varieties, numerous artifacts of minoritized Armenian cultures become less accessible and, in some cases, are lost. This is particularly painful for Western Armenian communities, for whom language was one of the most significant cultural resources that persisted in the wake of the Armenian Genocide.

Analysis In this scenario, improvements to machine translation only for the most high-resourced variety of Armenian exacerbate existing biases against speakers of lower-resourced varieties. The implicit standardization of one variety leads to further marginalization of the others, which has social and cultural consequences, including the erasure of distinct minoritized cultures.

6.2 Value Scenario 2

After substantial time and effort, improvements to machine translation tools are rolled out for a number of low-resourced languages, including Armenian. These improvements increase the accuracy of translation between English and Armenian to a level that is currently only seen among the most high-resourced language pairs. These improvements give Armenians in the diaspora better tools for developing their language skills, which allows some users to communicate more freely with their families and friends and connect with communities in Armenia and Artsakh.

On the other hand, Armenians are facing an extreme increase in online harassment. Turkish and Azerbaijani ultra-nationalists, seizing upon capabilities of newly released machine translation systems, gleefully descend into Armenians' DMs, retweets, and comments with translated messages expressing their hatred of Armenian people. Unlike the harassment that Armenians had been receiving previously, this time the comments are lengthier, more descriptive, and more disturbing – and they're in Armenian. While these comments are not translated perfectly, their meaning and intent is clear enough; the fact that they appear in the users' own language only adds more pain to the experience.

Because major social media platforms have yet to implement content moderation policies for content written in Armenian, the platforms are unable or unwilling to address this influx of harassment. Armenian users are able to delete messages containing harassment and block the senders' accounts, but this does not prevent trolls from making new accounts and sending more messages. For many Armenians on social media, this becomes an exhausting part of their daily routine. With all this effort expended, they still have to see the disturbing messages.

To escape harassment, many Armenian users, particularly those with large followings, leave social media for good. They are unable to use platforms like Twitter, Instagram, or Facebook to connect with friends and family or to engage with their communities. It becomes more challenging for Armenians to find job opportunities that are advertised on social media or to establish professional online profiles. Armenian artists and small business owners have to weigh the prospect of harassment if they maintain public profiles against losses in income if they don't.

The number of Armenian voices online gradually diminishes; in their absence, disinformation, anti-Armenian propaganda, and genocide denial flourishes.

Analysis It is crucial to account for the ways that machine translation interacts with existing technology, particularly on social media. Many Armenians already have to contend with harassment on social media, which affects their ability to engage with these platforms (as detailed in Section 5.3). If a new machine translation tool is deployed without taking these circumstances into account, there could be dire consequences.

Improved machine translation can allow for a sudden proliferation of text in a low-resourced language like Armenian online, potentially from bad actors. To prevent unwanted harms, it is necessary for social media platforms to take proactive steps to support these language communities. In the above scenario, that means creating more robust content moderation policies and the infrastructure needed to enforce these policies. Depending on community-specific vulnerabilities, there are likely other possible harms that would need to be mitigated using other strategies.

7 Recommendations

The potential benefits of improved machine translation for low-resourced languages are enormous. The stakeholders I interviewed all named specific uses they would have for better translation tools, ranging from improving their literacy skills to strengthening their connections to their families and communities. The potential harms are enormous as well, as the above scenarios illustrate. Different speaker communities will have other uses for and concerns about machine translation (Paullada, 2020). Ensuring that improved machine translation tools maximize the benefits and mitigate the harms requires the NLP community to take explicit steps to collaborate with and support low-resourced language communities.

First, it is necessary to examine the particular wants and needs that language communities have during the planning stage of a project. This paper demonstrates the efficacy of a Value-Sensitive Design approach in surfacing a particular community's needs and anticipating potential harms before technology is built. The interviews described in Section 5 and the resulting Value Scenarios illuminate concerns that otherwise might only be apparent to Armenian speakers. Similar efforts can be undertaken with speakers of low-resourced languages to uncover other community-specific considerations. Value-Sensitive Design provides a number of other practical techniques for collaborating with stakeholders (Friedman et al., 2017), which may be useful in future efforts.

Second, we must consider what other facets of language technology should be developed alongside improvements to machine translation. The deployment of robust machine translation allows for the generation of large volumes of text in a low-resourced language, which can have negative impacts for language communities. These impacts are likely impossible to prevent without actions taken by entities outside of NLP; for instance, preventing the outcome described in Value Scenario 2 requires social media platforms to implement stronger content moderation policies in low-resourced languages. NLP researchers can, however, work to expand the capabilities of other facets of language technology (in this case, hate speech detection for Armenian) that can mitigate potential harms caused by improved machine translation.

Fulfilling these goals requires disaggregating the task of machine translation; rather than creating translation tools for many languages at once, each language should be considered separately. Doing this would undoubtedly be more resource-intensive than a language-agnostic approach, but it is a necessary step towards prioritizing the needs of low-resourced language speakers. The scenarios in Section 6 illustrate just a couple of the ways that speakers of low-resourced languages may have very different circumstances than speakers of high-resourced languages, both linguistically and geopolitically, that need to be taken into account when machine translation applications are deployed. In both scenarios, harms fall unduly on groups that are already marginalized: in the first scenario, minoritized Armenian speakers bear the brunt of these harms, while in the second, Armenians in general are impacted negatively. Treating machine translation as an abstract language-agnostic task, divorced from the specific needs of distinct groups of users, obscures harms like these. Worse, it risks exacerbating inequitable conditions.

Taking a language-specific, stakeholder-focused approach does more than prevent potential harms; it also builds better, more reliable technology. When researchers assemble datasets for languages they are not familiar with, they are often unable to verify the validity of a data source and may not be able to find an existing high-quality data source (Nekoto et al., 2020). This is illustrated by the difference in reliability that interviewees reported for Google Translate and Nayiri: while Google Translate has more useful features, Nayiri is more trustworthy because it is built by a team with deep knowledge of the language and communities it serves, using carefully curated resources that may be inaccessible to outsiders.

The current paradigm of building NMT systems that rely on vast quantities of unlabelled data, whose size prevents careful curation (Bender et al., 2021; Paullada et al., 2021), makes it difficult to build systems that can account for language variation and serve users that speak minoritized varieties. As a result, machine translation systems cannot produce reliable and useful output for speakers whose varieties do not have substantial bodies of data. Building better and more equitable systems requires moving away from data-first approaches and investing in holistic methods that take into consideration the state of existing language technology and external circumstances of the communities in question, as well as developing higher-quality data sources (Hanna and Park, 2020; Paullada et al., 2021). This process does not need to begin from scratch; as with the example of Nayiri, low-resourced language communities may already have ongoing intra-community projects that would be fruitful sites for investment from and collaboration with NLP practitioners.

8 Ethical Considerations

As described in Section 4.3, the methodology used in this paper has a number of limitations that affect how these results may be generalized. Most prominently, the stakeholder group that I interviewed was small and represented only a small subsection of the perspectives of Armenian speakers.

Additionally, the group of participants described in this paper comprises speakers of only one low-resourced language; speakers of other low-resourced languages would likely have very different needs and concerns. This case study is meant only to provide examples of the concerns of speakers of a particular low-resourced language. It is important to avoid generalizing low-resourced languages and their speakers.

This paper does not cover all of the potential harms of machine translation; further efforts are needed to uncover other concerns for individual language communities. If only the harms I described in this paper were taken into consideration in the development of a machine translation system, it is certain that other important concerns would be missed, which could cause substantial harms to speaker populations.

9 Conclusion

Using Value Scenarios, this paper illustrates some potential harms that a general-purpose machine translation system could have for speakers of a low-resourced language. Avoiding these harms requires direct collaboration with stakeholders before the creation of a machine translation system intended for low-resourced languages. To do so, machine translation for low-resourced languages should be undertaken as a language-specific task.

Acknowledgments

I express my deep appreciation to my interviewees for sharing their time and insights with me, as well as to Emily Bender and my classmates at the University of Washington for their helpful feedback. Additionally, I am grateful to the anonymous reviewers of this work for their constructive comments.

References

Dzmitry Bahdanau, Kyunghyun Cho, and Yoshua Bengio. 2016. Neural Machine Translation by Jointly Learning to Align and Translate. In *Proceedings of the 3rd International Conference on Learning Representations*, San Diego, California. ArXiv: 1409.0473.

Emily M. Bender, Timnit Gebru, Angelina McMillan-Major, and Shmargaret Shmitchell. 2021. On the Dangers of Stochastic Parrots: Can Language Models Be Too Big? 🦜. In *Proceedings of the 2021 ACM Conference on Fairness, Accountability, and Transparency*, pages 610–623, Virtual Event Canada. ACM.

Isaac Caswell and Bowen Liang. 2020. Recent Advances in Google Translate.

David M. Eberhard, Gary F. Simons, and Charles D. Fennig, editors. 2021. *Ethnologue: Languages of the World*, 24th edition. SIL International, Dallas, Texas.

Marzieh Fadaee, Arianna Bisazza, and Christof Monz. 2017. Data augmentation for low-resource neural machine translation. In *Proceedings of the 55th Annual Meeting of the Association for Computational Linguistics (Volume 2: Short Papers)*, pages 567–573, Vancouver, Canada. Association for Computational Linguistics.

Batya Friedman. 1996. Value-sensitive design. *Interactions*, 3(6):16–23.

Batya Friedman, David G. Hendry, and Alan Borning. 2017. A Survey of Value Sensitive Design Methods. *Foundations and Trends® in Human–Computer Interaction*, 11(2):63–125.

Jiatao Gu, Hany Hassan, Jacob Devlin, and Victor O.K. Li. 2018. Universal neural machine translation for extremely low resource languages. In *Proceedings of the 2018 Conference of the North American Chapter of the Association for Computational Linguistics: Human Language Technologies, Volume 1 (Long Papers)*, pages 344–354, New Orleans, Louisiana. Association for Computational Linguistics.

Gayané Hagopian. 2007. *Armenian for Everyone: Western And Eastern Armenian in Parallel Lessons.*, 2nd edition. Yerevan Printing, Glendale, California, USA. OCLC: 150335569.

Alex Hanna and Tina M. Park. 2020. Against Scale: Provocations and Resistances to Scale Thinking. *Proceedings of the CSCW 2020 Workshop: Reconsidering Scale and Scaling in CSCW Research.* ArXiv: 2010.08850.

Pratik Joshi, Christain Barnes, Sebastin Santy, Simran Khanuja, Sanket Shah, Anirudh Srinivasan, Satwik Bhattamishra, Sunayana Sitaram, Monojit Choudhury, and Kalika Bali. 2019. Unsung challenges of building and deploying language technologies for low resource language communities. In *Proceedings of the 16th International Conference on Natural Language Processing*, pages 211–219, International Institute of Information Technology, Hyderabad, India. NLP Association of India.

Pratik Joshi, Sebastin Santy, Amar Budhiraja, Kalika Bali, and Monojit Choudhury. 2020. The state and fate of linguistic diversity and inclusion in the NLP world. In *Proceedings of the 58th Annual Meeting of the Association for Computational Linguistics*, pages 6282–6293, Online. Association for Computational Linguistics.

Wei-Jen Ko, Ahmed El-Kishky, Adithya Renduchintala, Vishrav Chaudhary, Naman Goyal, Francisco Guzmán, Pascale Fung, Philipp Koehn, and Mona Diab. 2021. Adapting high-resource NMT models to translate low-resource related languages without parallel data. In *Proceedings of the 59th Annual Meeting of the Association for Computational Linguistics and the 11th International Joint Conference on Natural Language Processing (Volume 1: Long Papers)*, pages 802–812, Online. Association for Computational Linguistics.

Sachin Kumar, Antonios Anastasopoulos, Shuly Wintner, and Yulia Tsvetkov. 2021. Machine translation into low-resource language varieties. In *Proceedings of the 59th Annual Meeting of the Association for Computational Linguistics and the 11th International Joint Conference on Natural Language Processing (Volume 2: Short Papers)*, pages 110–121, Online. Association for Computational Linguistics.

Guillaume Lample, Alexis Conneau, Ludovic Denoyer, and Marc'Aurelio Ranzato. 2018. Unsupervised Machine Translation Using Monolingual Corpora Only. In *Proceedings of the 6th International Conference on Learning Representations*, page 14.

Lisa P. Nathan, Predrag V. Klasnja, and Batya Friedman. 2007. Value scenarios: a technique for envisioning systemic effects of new technologies. In *CHI '07 Extended Abstracts on Human Factors in Computing Systems*, pages 2585–2590, San Jose CA USA. ACM.

Wilhelmina Nekoto, Vukosi Marivate, Tshinondiwa Matsila, Timi Fasubaa, Taiwo Fagbohungbe, Solomon Oluwole Akinola, Shamsuddeen Muhammad, Salomon Kabongo Kabenamualu, Salomey Osei, Freshia Sackey, Rubungo Andre Niyongabo, Ricky Macharm, Perez Ogayo, Orevaoghene Ahia, Musie Meressa Berhe, Mofetoluwa Adeyemi, Masabata Mokgesi-Selinga, Lawrence Okegbemi, Laura Martinus, Kolawole Tajudeen, Kevin Degila, Kelechi Ogueji, Kathleen Siminyu, Julia Kreutzer, Jason Webster, Jamiil Toure Ali, Jade Abbott, Iroro Orife, Ignatius Ezeani, Idris Abdulkadir Dangana, Herman Kamper, Hady Elsahar, Goodness Duru, Ghollah Kioko, Murhabazi Espoir, Elan van Biljon, Daniel Whitenack, Christopher Onyefuluchi, Chris Chinenye Emezue, Bonaventure F. P. Dossou, Blessing Sibanda, Blessing Bassey, Ayodele Olabiyi, Arshath Ramkilowan, Alp Öktem, Adewale Akinfaderin, and Abdallah Bashir. 2020. Participatory research for low-resourced machine translation: A case study in African languages. In *Findings of the Association for Computational Linguistics: EMNLP 2020*, pages 2144–2160, Online. Association for Computational Linguistics.

Amandalynne Paullada. 2020. How does Machine Translation Shift Power? *Resistance AI Workshop at 34th Conference on Neural Information Processing Systems (NeurIPS 2020).*

Amandalynne Paullada, Inioluwa Deborah Raji, Emily M. Bender, Emily Denton, and Alex Hanna. 2021. Data and its (dis)contents: A survey of dataset development and use in machine learning research. *Patterns*, 2(11):100336.

Barret Zoph, Deniz Yuret, Jonathan May, and Kevin Knight. 2016. Transfer learning for low-resource neural machine translation. In *Proceedings of the 2016 Conference on Empirical Methods in Natural Language Processing*, pages 1568–1575, Austin, Texas. Association for Computational Linguistics.

A Appendix: Interview Topics and questions

Below are the questions that I used to guide each interview, separated by topics. Because the interviews were conducted in a semi-structured format, this list does not include every question I asked participants.

Topic 1: Use of Armenian Language

- Can you describe how you speak Armenian?
- What variety do you speak?
- How often do you speak it?
- With whom do you speak Armenian?
- How do you use Armenian online?

Topic 2: Experience of Being Armenian Online

- What is your experience as an Armenian speaker online?
- How do you engage with other Armenians or Armenian communities online?
- How do you engage with non-Armenians online?
- How difficult is it for you to communicate in Armenian online?
- Have you ever been the subject of harassment? If so, can you tell me more about that?

Topic 3: Use of Machine Translation Tools

- What is your experience using machine translation tools?
- What tools do you use?
- How well does it work for your variety?
- How usable is it for you?
- When you translate from English to Armenian, does it give you something that sounds like the way you would speak?
- When you translate from Armenian to English, do you run into any problems that relate to the way you speak Armenian?
- What is your understanding of how it works?

Topic 4: Desired Improvements and Potential Uses

- What concerns do you have about how machine translation currently works for Armenian?
- What would have to change about machine translation for Armenian to make it more useful for you?
- If machine translation for Armenian (to and from English) improved, how do you think it would affect you?
- How would it affect people you know?

Topic 5: Anticipating Improvements to Machine Translation

- How do you imagine other people (both Armenians and non-Armenians) would use an improved machine translation system?
- What benefits do you anticipate?
- What harms do you anticipate?
- How would it affect you if your data (speech or text) was used to improve it?
- What if machine translation was substantially improved for Standard Eastern Armenian, but not for other varieties? What impact would this have on you? What are the potential benefits you would expect in this scenario? What are the potential harms?
- How would it affect you if non-Armenians were able to understand you when you speak Armenian? Specifically, how would it affect you if you were understood by a) your friends, b) strangers on the internet, or c) trolls?
- Let's imagine a best-case scenario for improved machine translation. What would that look like? How do you think people would use it? How would you use it?
- Let's imagine a worst-case scenario. What would that look like? How would that affect you and people you know?

Topic 6: Miscellaneous

- What other concerns do you have about improvements to machine translation for Armenian?
- Is there anything else you'd like to add?

Integrating Question Rewriting in Conversational Question Answering: A Reinforcement Learning Approach

Etsuko Ishii*, **Bryan Wilie***, **Yan Xu***, **Samuel Cahyawijaya***, **Pascale Fung**
The Hong Kong University of Science and Technology
{eishii, bwilie, yxucb, scahyawijaya}@connect.ust.hk

Abstract

Resolving dependencies among dialogue history is one of the main obstacles in the research on conversational question answering (CQA). The conversational question rewrites (QR) task has been shown to be effective to solve this problem by reformulating questions in a self-contained form. However, QR datasets are limited and existing methods tend to depend on the assumption of the existence of corresponding QR datasets for every CQA dataset. This paper proposes a reinforcement learning approach that integrates QR and CQA tasks without corresponding labeled QR datasets. We train a QR model based on the reward signal obtained from the CQA, and the experimental results show that our approach can bring improvement over the pipeline approaches. The code is available at `https://github.com/HLTCHKUST/cqr4cqa`.

1 Introduction

Conversational Question Rewrites (QR) systems paraphrase a question into a self-contained format using its dialogue history so as to make it easier to understand by the Conversational Question Answering (CQA) system. Prior works (Elgohary et al., 2019a; Anantha et al., 2021a; Kim et al., 2021) have shown that explicit guidance of QR benefits the performance of the CQA models in multiple questions answering datasets.

However, the existing works on QR in the context of CQA are often ignorant of two critical issues. Firstly, they are dependent on the assumption that QR datasets exist on target CQA datasets, although existing QR datasets only cover a small amount of CQA. It is also notable that building a novel QR dataset is expensive. Current works mainly focus on QuAC (Choi et al., 2018) datasets thanks to QR datasets constructed from it (Elgohary et al., 2019a; Anantha et al., 2021a), however, the other popular CQA datasets such as CoQA (Reddy et al., 2019) remain less explored. Secondly, although QR task evaluation is mainly done by automatic metrics that compute n-gram overlaps with BLEU (Papineni et al., 2002) or ROUGE (Lin, 2004), and by human evaluation, there is no correlation guaranteed between those metrics and the performance in CQA. In fact, Petrén Bach Hansen and Søgaard (2020) and Buck et al. (2018) suggest "better" rewrites in the human eye are not necessarily better for machines.

To this end, we propose to alleviate the limitation of the QR system by introducing a reinforcement learning framework that utilizes QR to overcome the aforementioned two obstacles. In this framework, a QR model plays the role of "the agent" which receives rewards from a CQA model which acts as "the environment." During training, a QR model aims to maximize the performance on the CQA task by generating better rewrites of the questions. Exploiting the reinforcement learning nature, we can benefit CQA regardless of the existence of QR annotation, and we can ensure that QR contributes to the final objective of improving CQA. Experimental results show that our framework successfully improves the CQA performance by 4.1 to 8.6 F1 score on CoQA and 4.7 to 9.2 F1 on QuAC compared to the pipeline baselines that combine a QR model and a QA model.

Our contributions in this paper can be summarized three-fold as follow:

- We propose a reinforcement learning framework for CQA which can be applied regardless of the existence of corresponding QR datasets.
- Our experimental results on two popular CQA datasets show that our approach improves the performance over the simple combination baselines of a QA and QR model.

* Equal Contribution

Proceedings of the 60th Annual Meeting of the Association for Computational Linguistics Student Research Workshop, pages 55 - 66
May 22-27, 2022

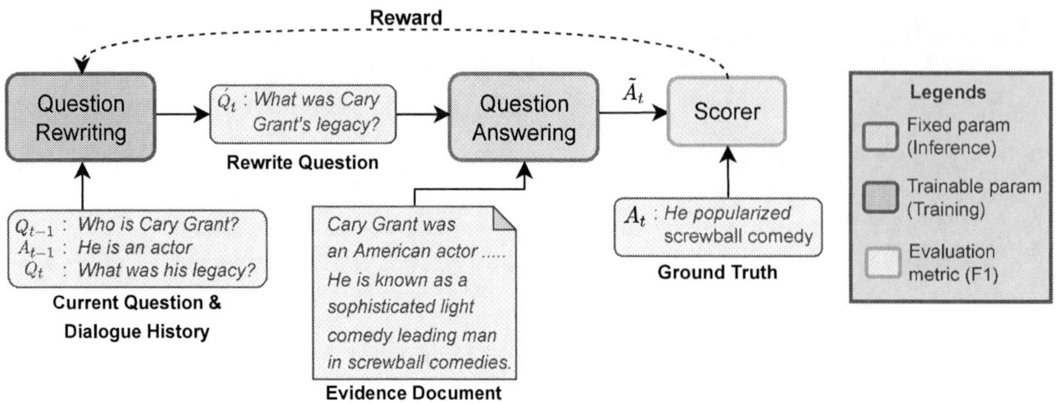

Figure 1: Overview of our reinforcement learning approach for CQA task that involves a QR model and a QA model. The current question Q_t and its dialogue history are reformulated into a self-contained question $\acute{Q}_t$ by the QR model. Then, $\acute{Q}_t$ and optionally, its dialogue history is passed to the QA model to extract an answer span $\tilde{A}_t$ from the provided evidence document. We train the QR model by maximizing the reward signal (F1 score) obtained by the comparison between the predicted answer span $\tilde{A}_t$ and the gold span A_t.

- We provide extensive analysis on suitable settings for our approach, such as training algorithms for the QR model and existing QR datasets for the QR model initialization.

2 Related Work

2.1 Conversational Question Answering

Recently, along with the raised popularity of works on dialogue systems (Madotto et al., 2020b,a; Ishii et al., 2021; Lin et al., 2021; Xu et al., 2021a; Liu et al., 2019b) and question answering(Su et al., 2020, 2019, 2022), conversational question answering (CQA) has gained more attention. CQA task aims to assist users for information-seeking purpose. It has been widely studied in the recent years and many CQA datasets have been made publicly available, such as CoQA (Reddy et al., 2019), QuAC (Choi et al., 2018), ShARC(Saeidi et al., 2018), Doc2Dial (Feng et al., 2020), and DoQA (Campos et al., 2020). Existing works focus on improving the model structure (Zhu et al., 2018; Huang et al., 2018; Yeh and Chen, 2019; Ohsugi et al., 2019; Zhang et al., 2021; Zhao et al., 2021) to deal with the dialogue history, leveraging different training techniques, such as adversarial training (Ju et al., 2019), or utilizing data augmentation via multi-task learning (Xu et al., 2021b) to improve the model performance in an end-to-end fashion. Unlike the aforementioned works, we propose to increase performance on CQA tasks by improving the readability of the questions via reinforcement learning. It may not align with the question readability for human beings. Furthermore, Our proposed approach does not contradict with the above methods, but can co-exist with them in the CQA system instead.

2.2 Question Rewrites

As the key challenge in CQA is to understand a highly-contextualized question, several QR datasets are proposed to offer a subtask in CQA which is to paraphrase a question in a self-contained style (Elgohary et al., 2019a; Petrén Bach Hansen and Søgaard, 2020; Anantha et al., 2021a). While many of the existing works put more effort on generating high-quality rewrites (Lin et al., 2020; Vakulenko et al., 2021), Kim et al. (2021) recently introduced a framework to leverage QR to improve the performance of CQA models by additional a consistency-based regularization. Their EXCORD feeds the original questions together with the rewritten questions, whereas we only use the rewritten questions. Similar to our work, Buck et al. (2018) train a question rewriting model in reinforcement learning framework interacting with the question answering environment to transform a given query from a declarative sentence into an interrogative one. It is noteworthy that QR in CQA requires more effort than in their setting, since we seek a QR model to elaborate dialogue history so as to resolve anaphora or ellipsis in a question to rewrite, rather than simple grammatical transformation of the given query.

2.3 Reinforcement Learning in Natural Language Generation

One of the most common reasons to adopt reinforcement learning (RL) methods in natural language generation (NLG) is due to inconsistency between train/test measurement (Keneshloo et al., 2019). If we apply deep neural network, we often train with differentiable loss function such as token-wise cross-entropy; but in test time, we use BLEU or ROUGE which we cannot directly use as a loss function. Motivated as such, RL approaches have been investigated in various NLG tasks, for example, in machine translation (Ranzato et al., 2016; Wu et al., 2016; He et al., 2017; Bahdanau et al., 2017), abstractive summarization (Ranzato et al., 2016; Paulus et al., 2018; Böhm et al., 2019), or dialogue generation (Li et al., 2016). If we train an NLG model from scratch with reinforcement learning, however, a model frequently suffers from too large exploration space (Ranzato et al., 2016). Thanks to the recent advance in large pretrained language models, RL approaches are investigated as an alternative fine-tuning approach which can reflect human preferences (Ziegler et al., 2019; Stiennon et al., 2020; Jaques et al., 2020) or reduce non-normative text (Peng et al., 2020). Our work also utilize large pretrained language models and use RL approach for fine-tuning.

3 Methodology

In this section, we present our reinforcement learning framework and the training algorithm. Firstly, we offer several preliminary definitions used throughout the paper, and secondly, we describe the strategy to train the whole framework.

3.1 Preliminary Definition

We denote a CQA dataset as $\{\mathcal{D}^n\}_{n=1}^N$ and the dialogue history at turn t as $\mathcal{D}_t = \{(Q_i, A_i)\}_{i=1}^t$, where Q_t is the question and A_t is the answer. Along with the QA pairs, the corresponding evidence document Y_t is also given.

In our proposed framework, a QA model and a QR model are involved. In CQA tasks, the answers to the questions are composed as pairs of start indexes and end indexes in the given paragraphs, where we denote as $A_t = \{{a_t}^s, {a_t}^e\}$. Let's denote a generated rewrite question sequence of Q_t as $\acute{Q}_t = \{\acute{q}_l\}_{l=1}^L$. The objective of the QR model is to rewrite the question Q_t at turn t into a self-contained version, based on the current question

Algorithm 1 RL training process of our QR agent

Require: $\{\mathcal{D}^n\}$: CQA dataset
Require: π_{θ_0}: Pretrained language model
Train an environment f_ϕ on $\{\mathcal{D}^n\}$
Initialize an agent π_θ with π_{θ_0}
while not done **do**
  Sample an input state from the CQA dataset $X_t \sim \{\mathcal{D}^n\}$
  Construct a rewrite sequence $\acute{Q}_t$ which maximize $\pi_\theta(\acute{Q}_t|X_t)$
  Calculate F1-score r via $r(f_\phi(\acute{X}_t))$
  Update π_θ using an RL algorithm with state X_t, action Q_t, and reward R_t
end while

and the dialogue history $\mathcal{D}_{t-1}$.

As shown in Figure 1, we consider in a reinforcement learning framework. An agent takes an input state $X_t = (\mathcal{D}_{t-1}, Q_t)$ and generates a paraphrase $\acute{Q}_t$. Then, $\acute{X}_t = (\mathcal{D}_{t-1}, \acute{Q}_t)$ and an evidence document Y_t are provided to an environment, namely, a QA model f_ϕ, which extracts an answer span $\tilde{A}_t = f_\phi(\acute{X}_t, Y_t)$. We aim the agent, a QR model π_θ, to learn to generate a high-quality paraphrase of given question based on the reward received from the environment.

The policy, in our case the QR model, assigns the probability

$$\pi_\theta(\acute{Q}_t|X_t) = \prod_{l=1}^{L} p(\acute{q}_l|\acute{q}_1, \ldots, \acute{q}_{l-1}, X_t). \quad (1)$$

Our goal is to maximize the expected reward of the answer returned under the policy, namely,

$$\mathrm{E}_{\acute{q}_t \sim \pi_\theta(\cdot|q_t)}[r(f_\phi(\acute{X}_t))], \quad (2)$$

where r is a reward function. We apply the token-level F1-score between the predicted answer span $\tilde{A}_t$ and the gold span A_t as the reward r. We can directly optimize the expected reward in Eq. 2 using reinforcement learning algorithms.

3.2 Training Algorithm

Prior to the training process, the QA model f_ϕ is fine-tuned on $\{\mathcal{D}^n\}$ and the QR model is initialized with $\pi_\theta = \pi_{\theta_0}$, where π_{θ_0} is a pretrained language model. We apply Proximal Policy Optimization (PPO) (Schulman et al., 2017; Ziegler et al., 2019) to train π_θ. PPO is a policy gradient method which alternate between sampling data through interaction with the environment and optimizing a surrogate objective function via stochastic gradient ascent. PPO makes use of learned state-value function to compute the variance-reduced advantage-function. The overview of our training process is shown in Algorithm 1.

Following Ziegler et al. (2019), we penalize the reward r with a KL-penalty so as to prevent the policy π_θ from drifting too far away from π_{θ_0}:

$$R_t = R(\acute{X}_t) = r(f_\phi(\acute{X}_t)) - \beta \mathrm{KL}(\pi_\theta, \pi_{\theta_0}),$$

where β represents a weight factor. We perform reinforce learning on the modified reward of R_t instead of r.

Inspired by MIXER (Ranzato et al., 2016), we apply a cross-entropy loss on the first m tokens of the generated sequence $\acute{Q}_t$ by using the tokens from the original question Q_t as the label to enhance training stability in addition to the KL-penalty. We decrease the number of tokens where we apply the cross-entropy loss over time steps, allowing the policy π_θ to explore more. By applying the cross-entropy constraint, the PPO objective function $\mathcal{L}(\theta)$ is modified into:

$$\mathcal{L}_l = \begin{cases} -\sum_{i=1}^{|\mathcal{V}|} q_{i,l} \log(\acute{q}_{i,l}) & (l \leq m) \\ \mathcal{L}^{\mathrm{CLIP}}(\acute{q}_l) + c\mathcal{L}^{\mathrm{VF}}(\acute{q}_l) & (l > m) \end{cases} \tag{3}$$

$$\mathcal{L}(\theta) = \frac{1}{m}\sum_{l=1}^{m} \mathcal{L}_l + \sum_{l=m+1}^{L} \mathcal{L}_l, \tag{4}$$

where $|\mathcal{V}|$ is the vocabulary size, $\mathcal{L}^{\mathrm{CLIP}}$ is the clipped surrogate loss (see Eq. 7 in Schulman et al. (2017)), c is a value loss coefficient, and $\mathcal{L}^{\mathrm{VF}}$ is the value function loss (see Eq. 9 in Schulman et al. (2017)).

In addition to MIXER, we introduce another strategy to improve exploration (denoted as EXPLORE) that comes along with beam-search decoding. The strategy of using beam-search is to search for top-k sequences with the highest likelihood during the generation process and take the one with the highest likelihood over k sequences. Our approach is utilizing the top-k' $(1 \leq k' \leq k)$ sequences collected during beam search for PPO training. With this approach, we can improve the exploration capability of the QR model without requiring additional exploration steps.

4 Experiments

4.1 Datasets

We conduct our experiments on two CQA datasets, CoQA (Reddy et al., 2019) and QuAC (Choi et al., 2018). Since the test set is not publicly available for both CoQA and QuAC, we follow the splitting introduced by (Kim et al., 2021). We leverage the train/dev/test split provided by Kim et al. (2021) for the QuAC experiments. We randomly sample 5% of data samples in the training set in units of dialogues and adopt them as our validation set for CoQA since there is no public split available.

CoQA CoQA dataset contains 127K questions with answers in the conversation form (8K conversations in total). The questions are highly contextualized with the dialogues, and the answers are free-form text with their corresponding evidence in the passage for reference. In this paper, following the settings of the other existing works (Huang et al., 2018; Yeh and Chen, 2019; Ju et al., 2019), we still construct the answers as spans extracted from the passages, where the gold labels used in training are the snippets with the highest F1 score compared to the annotated answers.

QuAC QuAC is also a crowd-sourced CQA dataset that contains 14K information-seeking QA conversations. In contrast to CoQA, QuAC is designed as a span-extraction dataset with dialogue acts. Moreover, 20% of the questions in QuAC are unanswerable questions, whereas those in CoQA take up $\sim$1.3%.

We initialize the QR model with a pre-trained language model that is fine-tuned on QR datasets. We apply two QR datasets, i.e., QReCC and CANARD, for the fine-tuning to obtain more insights on the influence of the QR model initialization with different data sources.

CANARD CANARD dataset (Elgohary et al., 2019b) is a question-rewriting (QR) dataset which aims at conducting question-in-context rewriting to convert the questions with long conversation histories into short and self-contained questions. The questions are generated by rewriting a subset of the original questions in QuAC dataset. The dataset is split in to training, development, and test sets in size of 31K, 3.4K, and 5.6K.

QReCC QReCC dataset (Anantha et al., 2021b) is another QR dataset. In contrast to CANARD,

Models		CoQA						QuAC		
		Overall F1	Child.	Liter.	M&H	News	Wiki.	F1	HEQ-Q	HEQ-D
	end-to-end	84.5	**84.4**	82.4	**82.9**	86.0	86.9	**67.8**	63.5	7.9
QReCC	pipeline-eval	80.6	80.8	78.6	78.3	81.7	83.7	62.9	58.5	5.2
	pipeline-train	82.9	82.9	80.9	81.5	84.4	84.8	66.3	62.0	6.6
	ours	**84.7**	84.3	**83.1**	82.7	**86.3**	86.8	67.6	63.2	7.8
CANARD	pipeline-eval	75.9	75.5	74.8	73.1	76.3	79.8	58.2	54.5	5.2
	pipeline-train	82.8	83.4	80.1	80.8	84.4	85.6	66.5	62.5	7.4
	EXCORD†	83.4	**84.4**	81.2	79.8	84.6	**87.0**	67.7	**64.0**	**9.3**
	ours	84.4	84.1	82.7	82.6	86.0	86.7	67.4	62.7	8.1

Table 1: Evaluation results of our approach and baselines on the test set. EXCORD† follows the results reported in Kim et al. (2021). **Bold** are the best results amongst all. Underlined represents the best score on each combination of the CQA and QR datasets.

QReCC dataset is built upon three publicly available datasets: QuAC, TREC Conversational Assistant Track (CAsT) (Dalton et al., 2020) and Natural Questions (NQ) (Kwiatkowski et al., 2019), where QreCC contains 14K dialogues with 80K questions in total, and 9.3K dialogues are from QuAC. The sampled data are further extended to the open-domain CQA setting. It also supports the passage retrieval and reading comprehension tasks. The dataset is split into training, development, and test sets. However, in the released version, the training and development set are merged. In the experiments, we directly train the model with the merged training set and use the test set for evaluation.

4.2 Evaluation Metrics

To automatically evaluate the performance of the QA models, following Reddy (2020), we leverage the unigram F1 score. In CoQA evaluation, the models are also evaluated per domain on all six domains as listed in the official validation set (our test set instead), i.e., Children Stories (Child.), Literature (Liter.), Mid-High School (M&H), News, and Wikipedia (Wiki.). Following the leaderboard, for the QuAC dataset, we incorporate the human equivalence score HEQ-Q and HEQ-D for QuAC evaluation. HEQ-Q indicates the percentage of questions on which the model outperforms human beings and HEQ-D represents the percentage of dialogues on which the model outperforms human beings for every question in the dialogue.

4.3 Models

QA model In all the experiments, we leverage pre-trained RoBERTa (Liu et al., 2019a) model as the initial model and adapt it to different CQA tasks (see Table A1 in Appendix for more details). The RoBERTa model is the leading pre-trained model according to different leaderboards and it has shown its effectiveness on QA tasks (Ju et al., 2019; Zhao et al., 2021; Yasunaga et al., 2021; Zhu et al., 2021). The model is trained to predict the start positions and the end positions of the given contexts with respect to the questions. Since our proposed method is model-agnostic, the QA component in the framework can be replaced with any existing QA models.

QR model We use GPT-2 (Radford et al., 2019) as the base model to train the QR models (see Table A2 in Appendix for more details). In the QR training process, we provide the dialogue history and the current question as the inputs and train the model to rewrite the current question into a self-contained version that is able to be answered without considering the dialogue history.

Model selection and initialization in RL Before applying our methods, the QA and QR models are initialized with the best QA and QR baseline models. For both QA models that are trained on CoQA and QuAC datasets, the models with the highest F1 score on the validation set are selected. We use different metrics for the QR model selection on two datasets, following the original metrics that are used for model evaluation. We select the best QR model checkpoint on the CANARD dataset and

... Far on in the hot days of June the Excommunication, for some weeks arrived from Rome, was solemnly published in the Duomo. Romola went to witness the scene, that the resistance it inspired might invigorate that sympathy with Savonarola ...			... Jenny loves singing. But her baby sister is crying so loud that Jenny can't hear herself, so she was angry! Her Mom said she could try to play with her sister, but that only made ...		
	Utterance	F1 Score		Utterance	F1 Score
Q_{t-1}	**Where was the Excommunication published?**		Q_{t-1}	**How is she feeling?**	
A_{t-1}	in the Duomo		A_{t-1}	Angry.	
Q_t	When?	0.61	Q_t	Why?	0.82
$\acute{Q}_t$	When was **the Excommunication published?**	1.0	$\acute{Q}_t$	Why **is she feeling?**	0.98

Table 2: Examples of rewritten questions by the trained QR model initialized with QReCC. We can see that the model learns how to recover the abbreviated contents from the dialogue history to get a better score on CoQA.

QReCC dataset based on the BLEU [1] score and the unigram recall (ROUGE-1 R) score respectively.

4.4 Baselines

We compare our proposed approach with three different settings: (i) directly finetuning the QA model on the CQA tasks without the QR model (**end-to-end**), (ii) inferencing the QA model with questions rewritten by the QR model (**pipeline-eval**), and (iii) finetuning the QA model with questions rewritten by the QR model (**pipeline-train**).

4.5 Experimental Setup

Our implementation is based on Wolf et al. (2020). We conduct all of the experiments with GeForce RTX 2080 Ti. To obtain the models for initialization, GPT-2 is trained on QReCC and CANARD dataset as the QR model, and RoBERTa is trained on CoQA and QuAC datasets as the QA model with Adam optimizer (Kingma and Ba, 2015) with a learning rate of $3e-5$. We report other hyperparameters used in the model initialization in Table A1 and Table A2 in Appendix.

For PPO training, we train the QR model with Adam optimizer with a learning rate of $1e-7$. Further, we use beam search with beam size of 5, preventing generation repetition (Keskar et al., 2019) with using repetition penalty of 1.1, and set the maximum input sequence length to 512. On the MIXER settings, we initialize cross entropy length as 3 and limits its minimum to 1. We then run the PPO with value function coefficient of 1.0, while ensuring the sequence length of question rewriting model input to be 150 tokens maximum and the generations length to be 50 tokens at maximum. To ensure that the learned policy does not deviate too much, we apply an additional reward signal, adaptive KL factor β according to the magnitude of the KL-penalty with a KL-coefficient $K_\beta = 0.1$. Other hyperparameters are listed in Table A3 in Appendix.

4.6 Results

We report our experimental results in Table 1. Our approach achieves 84.7 and 67.6 F1 scores on the CoQA and QuAC datasets, respectively, and constantly outperforms the pipeline baselines. As shown in the examples listed in Table 2, our approach successfully teaches the QR model to refer to the dialogue history and recover the abbreviated contents if necessary. Comparing to the pipeline-eval, our approach scores at least 4.1 F1 score better, which indicates that our reinforcement learning approach successfully trains the QR model to paraphrase the questions into more preferred format of the QA model from the QR model initialization. Our approach performs better at least by 1.0 overall F1 score than EXCORD (Kim et al., 2021) on CoQA, and comparably on QuAC. However, our approach could not contribute to the considerable improvement over the end-to-end baseline, which poses the need for further investigation.

5 Discussion

In this section, we provide our findings regarding the most suitable settings of our approach, including the comparison of the QR datasets for initialization, the QR model architectures, the training algorithms, and the effect of the decoding strategy. For automatic evaluation, we report Exact Match (EM) in addition to the unigram F1 score. EM in-

[1]`https://github.com/moses-smt/mosesdecoder/blob/master/scripts/generic/multi-bleu-detok.perl`

Models	# Params	Evaluation	
		F1	EM
GPT-2	243M	**84.7**	**76.6**
BART-base	210M	83.6	75.7

Table 3: Comparison of the QR model architectures initialized with QReCC and further trained on CQA. GPT-2 achieves a higher F1 score and EM than BART-base. Note that we have twice as many parameters as GPT-2 and 1.5 times as BART-base since we copy the decoders and train them for estimating the value function.

dicates that the percentage of the predictions is the same as the gold answers, while the F1 score evaluates the performance with uni-gram overlapping.

5.1 Comparison of QR datasets for Initialization

We compare the effect of QR dataset initialization, i.e., QReCC and CANARD, to the evaluation performance of the CQA task. As shown in Table 1, QR models trained with QReCC dataset almost always performs better than the ones trained with CANARD dataset, with one exception on the pipeline-train approach on the QuAC dataset. We assume this is because QReCC gives more generalization ability to the QR models since QReCC is composed of several QA datasets, whereas CANARD is more devoted to QuAC as it is a subset of QuAC.

5.2 Comparison of QR Model Architectures

In the search for suitable architecture, we compare the architectures of the QR models in the RL training both using GPT-2 and BART-base (Lewis et al., 2020). First, we train BART with QReCC in the same way as GPT-2 and then fine-tune it with CoQA using our reinforcement learning approach. It is noteworthy that utilizing the BART-base serves the system worse fits compared with using GPT-2 as reported in Table 3. However, this performance gap could be due to our implementation. For BART, we only copy the decoder to estimate the value function, resulting in 70M parameters for estimating the value function, but GPT-2 uses all 117M parameters for it. In future, we plan to attempt to use the whole parameters of BART for estimating the value function.

Algorithm	CoQA		QuAC	
	F1	EM	F1	EM
PPO	**84.7**	**76.6**	**67.6**	**51.3**
REINFORCE	84.2	76.1	64.8	49.3

Table 4: Comparison between training algorithms of the QR model. PPO scores constantly better than the REINFORCE algorithm.

5.3 Comparison of RL algorithms

In addition to the PPO approach, we explore the REINFORCE algorithm (Williams, 1992) to train π_θ. We use self-critical sequence training (Rennie et al., 2017) instead of MIXER in REINFORCE experiments. In self-critical sequence training, we normalize the reward r derived from the sampled rewrites $\acute{X}_t$ with the reward derived from another rewrite which is generated by greedy decoding. We use Adam optimizer with a learning rate of $1\mathrm{e}-7$ and keep the other hyperparameters the same as the PPO training.

We report the evaluation results of CoQA and QuAC with the initialization of QReCC in Table 4. REINFORCE could not outperform PPO, although bringing some improvement over the majority of the pipeline baselines. This observation that PPO is better than the REINFORCE supports the experimental results reported in Andrychowicz et al. (2021).

5.4 Ablation Study

We examine the effects of different exploration strategies, namely, EXPLORE and MIXER, on our approach and report it in Table 5. The QR models in the experiments are initialized with QReCC. Both EXPLORE and MIXER improve performance, although the combination does not outperform MIXER-only settings. We assume this is because the benefit of MIXER offsets the contribution of EXPLORE.

EXPLORE helps to explore more by sampling multiple candidates of question rewrites, and improves F1 scores by 2.5 for CoQA and 1.2 for QuAC. On the other hand, MIXER teaches the QR model to copy the first m tokens from the original question to limit the exploration space and stabilize the training process, resulting in a 3.6 F1 score gain in CoQA and 2.9 F1 score gain in QuAC. Combined, MIXER and EXPLORE offset the benefits of each other. To further improve the

Algorithm	CoQA		QuAC	
	F1	EM	F1	EM
PPO	81.1	73.3	64.7	49.4
+ EXPLORE	83.8	75.9	65.9	50.3
+ MIXER	**84.7**	**76.6**	**67.6**	**51.3**
+ MIXER + EXPLORE	84.2	76.2	67.5	51.2

Table 5: Effects of EXPLORE and MIXER in our framework. Both EXPLORE and MIXER benefit performance, while the combination does not outperform MIXER-only.

Repetition penalty	Evaluation	
	F1	EM
1.0	67.37	51.46
1.1	**67.47**	**51.40**
1.3	67.12	51.12

Table 6: Using smaller or no repetition penalty tends to yield better results.

performance, we plan to seek an adequate balance of exploration and exploitation since we believe more exploration can boost the performance but stabilizing the training is challenging according to our observation.

5.5 Effects of Decoding Strategies

We explore the effect of decoding strategies for generating question rewrites for inference. We find the greedy search significantly worsens the performance by around 3 to 6 F1 score loss. While the performance steadily improves along with the increase of the beam size, we can not see non-trivial improvement when the beam size is equal or larger than three. We also examine the different sets of hyperparameters, for example, repetition penalty, sampling (combination of temperature, top-k, and top-p) approaches. As reported in Table 6, using smaller or no repetition penalty yields better results. We observe that sampling methods only alter the results marginally. We assume that beam search works satisfactorily because the optimal rewritten questions are more or less predictable similar to machine translation (Yang et al., 2018; Murray and Chiang, 2018).

6 Conclusion and Future Work

In this paper, we propose a reinforcement learning framework for CQA that a QR model that acts as an agent and a QA model as an environment. Our experiments show that the QR model learned to paraphrase questions into a more suitable format for the QA model by reward signal obtained from the CQA performance. Since our exploration is conducted with limited combinations of QA/QR model structures and datasets, we plan to explore the other combinations to justify our approach. Moreover, it would be beneficial to train the QR model without the dialogue history to enforce the QR model and make the question more self-contained. If we can minimize the contribution of the dialogue history in CQA, we can treat the CQA task as a single-turn QA task, and it enormously expands possible solutions for the CQA.

Ethical Considerations

This work is not related to any specific real-world application. All the datasets used in our experiments are collected by crowdsourcing (Anantha et al., 2021a), especially through Amazon Mechanical Turk (Reddy et al., 2019; Choi et al., 2018; Elgohary et al., 2019a), and they are publicly available. As the nature of the task, the data collection of CQA and QR is done anonymously and does not involve any privacy or intellectual property concern.

Acknowledgement

We thank the anonymous reviewers for their valuable comments. This work has been partially supported by the China NSFC Project (No. NSFC21EG14), Hong Kong PhD Fellowship Scheme, Research Grant Council, Hong Kong (PF18-25016, PF20-43679), and School of Engineering PhD Fellowship Award, the Hong Kong University of Science and Technology.

References

Raviteja Anantha, Svitlana Vakulenko, Zhucheng Tu, Shayne Longpre, Stephen Pulman, and Srinivas Chappidi. 2021a. Open-domain question answering goes conversational via question rewriting. In *Proceedings of the 2021 Conference of the North American Chapter of the Association for Computational Linguistics: Human Language Technologies*, pages 520–534, Online. Association for Computational Linguistics.

Raviteja Anantha, Svitlana Vakulenko, Zhucheng Tu, Shayne Longpre, Stephen Pulman, and Srinivas Chappidi. 2021b. Open-domain question answering goes conversational via question rewriting. In

Proceedings of the 2021 Conference of the North American Chapter of the Association for Computational Linguistics: Human Language Technologies, pages 520–534.

Marcin Andrychowicz, Anton Raichuk, Piotr Stańczyk, Manu Orsini, Sertan Girgin, Raphaël Marinier, Leonard Hussenot, Matthieu Geist, Olivier Pietquin, Marcin Michalski, Sylvain Gelly, and Olivier Bachem. 2021. What matters for on-policy deep actor-critic methods? a large-scale study. In *International Conference on Learning Representations*.

Dzmitry Bahdanau, Philemon Brakel, Kelvin Xu, Anirudh Goyal, Ryan Lowe, Joelle Pineau, Aaron C. Courville, and Yoshua Bengio. 2017. An actor-critic algorithm for sequence prediction. In *5th International Conference on Learning Representations, ICLR 2017, Toulon, France, April 24-26, 2017, Conference Track Proceedings*. OpenReview.net.

Florian Böhm, Yang Gao, Christian M. Meyer, Ori Shapira, Ido Dagan, and Iryna Gurevych. 2019. Better rewards yield better summaries: Learning to summarise without references. In *Proceedings of the 2019 Conference on Empirical Methods in Natural Language Processing and the 9th International Joint Conference on Natural Language Processing (EMNLP-IJCNLP)*, pages 3110–3120, Hong Kong, China. Association for Computational Linguistics.

Christian Buck, Jannis Bulian, Massimiliano Ciaramita, Wojciech Gajewski, Andrea Gesmundo, Neil Houlsby, and Wei Wang. 2018. Ask the right questions: Active question reformulation with reinforcement learning. In *International Conference on Learning Representations*.

Jon Ander Campos, Arantxa Otegi, Aitor Soroa, Jan Deriu, Mark Cieliebak, and Eneko Agirre. 2020. DoQA - accessing domain-specific FAQs via conversational QA. In *Proceedings of the 58th Annual Meeting of the Association for Computational Linguistics*, pages 7302–7314, Online. Association for Computational Linguistics.

Eunsol Choi, He He, Mohit Iyyer, Mark Yatskar, Wen-tau Yih, Yejin Choi, Percy Liang, and Luke Zettlemoyer. 2018. QuAC: Question answering in context. In *Proceedings of the 2018 Conference on Empirical Methods in Natural Language Processing*, pages 2174–2184, Brussels, Belgium. Association for Computational Linguistics.

Jeffrey Dalton, Chenyan Xiong, and Jamie Callan. 2020. Trec cast 2019: The conversational assistance track overview. *arXiv preprint arXiv:2003.13624*.

Ahmed Elgohary, Denis Peskov, and Jordan Boyd-Graber. 2019a. Can you unpack that? learning to rewrite questions-in-context. In *Proceedings of the 2019 Conference on Empirical Methods in Natural Language Processing and the 9th International Joint Conference on Natural Language Processing (EMNLP-IJCNLP)*, pages 5918–5924, Hong Kong, China. Association for Computational Linguistics.

Ahmed Elgohary, Denis Peskov, and Jordan Boyd-Graber. 2019b. Can you unpack that? learning to rewrite questions-in-context. In *Proceedings of the 2019 Conference on Empirical Methods in Natural Language Processing and the 9th International Joint Conference on Natural Language Processing (EMNLP-IJCNLP)*, pages 5918–5924.

Song Feng, Hui Wan, Chulaka Gunasekara, Siva Patel, Sachindra Joshi, and Luis Lastras. 2020. doc2dial: A goal-oriented document-grounded dialogue dataset. In *Proceedings of the 2020 Conference on Empirical Methods in Natural Language Processing (EMNLP)*, pages 8118–8128, Online. Association for Computational Linguistics.

Di He, Hanqing Lu, Yingce Xia, Tao Qin, Liwei Wang, and Tie-Yan Liu. 2017. Decoding with value networks for neural machine translation. In *Advances in Neural Information Processing Systems*, volume 30. Curran Associates, Inc.

Hsin-Yuan Huang, Eunsol Choi, and Wen-tau Yih. 2018. Flowqa: Grasping flow in history for conversational machine comprehension. In *International Conference on Learning Representations*.

Etsuko Ishii, Genta Indra Winata, Samuel Cahyawijaya, Divesh Lala, Tatsuya Kawahara, and Pascale Fung. 2021. ERICA: An empathetic android companion for covid-19 quarantine. In *Proceedings of the 22nd Annual Meeting of the Special Interest Group on Discourse and Dialogue*, pages 257–260, Singapore and Online. Association for Computational Linguistics.

Natasha Jaques, Judy Hanwen Shen, Asma Ghandeharioun, Craig Ferguson, Agata Lapedriza, Noah Jones, Shixiang Gu, and Rosalind Picard. 2020. Human-centric dialog training via offline reinforcement learning. In *Proceedings of the 2020 Conference on Empirical Methods in Natural Language Processing (EMNLP)*, pages 3985–4003, Online. Association for Computational Linguistics.

Ying Ju, Fubang Zhao, Shijie Chen, Bowen Zheng, Xuefeng Yang, and Yunfeng Liu. 2019. Technical report on conversational question answering. *arXiv preprint arXiv:1909.10772*.

Y Keneshloo, T Shi, N Ramakrishnan, and CK Reddy. 2019. Deep reinforcement learning for sequence-to-sequence models. *IEEE Transactions on Neural Networks and Learning Systems*, 31(7):2469–2489.

Nitish Shirish Keskar, Bryan McCann, Lav R. Varshney, Caiming Xiong, and Richard Socher. 2019. CTRL: A conditional transformer language model for controllable generation. *CoRR*, abs/1909.05858.

Gangwoo Kim, Hyunjae Kim, Jungsoo Park, and Jaewoo Kang. 2021. Learn to resolve conversational dependency: A consistency training framework for conversational question answering. In *Proceedings of the 59th Annual Meeting of the Association for Computational Linguistics and the 11th International*

Joint Conference on Natural Language Processing (Volume 1: Long Papers), pages 6130–6141, Online. Association for Computational Linguistics.

Diederik P. Kingma and Jimmy Ba. 2015. Adam: A method for stochastic optimization. In *3rd International Conference on Learning Representations, ICLR 2015, San Diego, CA, USA, May 7-9, 2015, Conference Track Proceedings*.

Tom Kwiatkowski, Jennimaria Palomaki, Olivia Redfield, Michael Collins, Ankur Parikh, Chris Alberti, Danielle Epstein, Illia Polosukhin, Jacob Devlin, Kenton Lee, et al. 2019. Natural questions: A benchmark for question answering research. *Transactions of the Association for Computational Linguistics*, 7:452–466.

Mike Lewis, Yinhan Liu, Naman Goyal, Marjan Ghazvininejad, Abdelrahman Mohamed, Omer Levy, Veselin Stoyanov, and Luke Zettlemoyer. 2020. BART: Denoising sequence-to-sequence pre-training for natural language generation, translation, and comprehension. In *Proceedings of the 58th Annual Meeting of the Association for Computational Linguistics*, pages 7871–7880, Online. Association for Computational Linguistics.

Jiwei Li, Will Monroe, Alan Ritter, Dan Jurafsky, Michel Galley, and Jianfeng Gao. 2016. Deep reinforcement learning for dialogue generation. In *Proceedings of the 2016 Conference on Empirical Methods in Natural Language Processing*, pages 1192–1202, Austin, Texas. Association for Computational Linguistics.

Chin-Yew Lin. 2004. ROUGE: A package for automatic evaluation of summaries. In *Text Summarization Branches Out*, pages 74–81, Barcelona, Spain. Association for Computational Linguistics.

Sheng-Chieh Lin, Jheng-Hong Yang, Rodrigo Nogueira, Ming-Feng Tsai, Chuan-Ju Wang, and Jimmy Lin. 2020. Conversational question reformulation via sequence-to-sequence architectures and pretrained language models. *arXiv preprint arXiv:2004.01909*.

Zhaojiang Lin, Zihan Liu, Genta Indra Winata, Samuel Cahyawijaya, Andrea Madotto, Yejin Bang, Etsuko Ishii, and Pascale Fung. 2021. XPersona: Evaluating multilingual personalized chatbot. In *Proceedings of the 3rd Workshop on Natural Language Processing for Conversational AI*, pages 102–112, Online. Association for Computational Linguistics.

Yinhan Liu, Myle Ott, Naman Goyal, Jingfei Du, Mandar Joshi, Danqi Chen, Omer Levy, Mike Lewis, Luke Zettlemoyer, and Veselin Stoyanov. 2019a. Roberta: A robustly optimized bert pretraining approach. *arXiv preprint arXiv:1907.11692*.

Zihan Liu, Jamin Shin, Yan Xu, Genta Indra Winata, Peng Xu, Andrea Madotto, and Pascale Fung. 2019b. Zero-shot cross-lingual dialogue systems with transferable latent variables. In *Proceedings of the 2019 Conference on Empirical Methods in Natural Language Processing and the 9th International Joint Conference on Natural Language Processing (EMNLP-IJCNLP)*, pages 1297–1303, Hong Kong, China. Association for Computational Linguistics.

Andrea Madotto, Samuel Cahyawijaya, Genta Indra Winata, Yan Xu, Zihan Liu, Zhaojiang Lin, and Pascale Fung. 2020a. Learning knowledge bases with parameters for task-oriented dialogue systems. In *Findings of the Association for Computational Linguistics: EMNLP 2020*, pages 2372–2394, Online. Association for Computational Linguistics.

Andrea Madotto, Etsuko Ishii, Zhaojiang Lin, Sumanth Dathathri, and Pascale Fung. 2020b. Plug-and-play conversational models. In *Findings of the Association for Computational Linguistics: EMNLP 2020*, pages 2422–2433, Online. Association for Computational Linguistics.

Kenton Murray and David Chiang. 2018. Correcting length bias in neural machine translation. In *Proceedings of the Third Conference on Machine Translation: Research Papers*, pages 212–223, Brussels, Belgium. Association for Computational Linguistics.

Yasuhito Ohsugi, Itsumi Saito, Kyosuke Nishida, Hisako Asano, and Junji Tomita. 2019. A simple but effective method to incorporate multi-turn context with bert for conversational machine comprehension. In *Proceedings of the First Workshop on NLP for Conversational AI*, pages 11–17.

Kishore Papineni, Salim Roukos, Todd Ward, and Wei-Jing Zhu. 2002. Bleu: a method for automatic evaluation of machine translation. In *Proceedings of the 40th Annual Meeting of the Association for Computational Linguistics*, pages 311–318, Philadelphia, Pennsylvania, USA. Association for Computational Linguistics.

Romain Paulus, Caiming Xiong, and Richard Socher. 2018. A deep reinforced model for abstractive summarization. In *International Conference on Learning Representations*.

Xiangyu Peng, Siyan Li, Spencer Frazier, and Mark Riedl. 2020. Reducing non-normative text generation from language models. In *Proceedings of the 13th International Conference on Natural Language Generation*, pages 374–383, Dublin, Ireland. Association for Computational Linguistics.

Victor Petrén Bach Hansen and Anders Søgaard. 2020. What do you mean 'why?': Resolving sluices in conversations. *Proceedings of the AAAI Conference on Artificial Intelligence*, 34(05):7887–7894.

Alec Radford, Jeffrey Wu, Rewon Child, David Luan, Dario Amodei, Ilya Sutskever, et al. 2019. Language models are unsupervised multitask learners. *OpenAI blog*, 1(8):9.

Marc'Aurelio Ranzato, Sumit Chopra, Michael Auli, and Wojciech Zaremba. 2016. Sequence level training with recurrent neural networks. In *4th International Conference on Learning Representations, ICLR 2016, San Juan, Puerto Rico, May 2-4, 2016, Conference Track Proceedings*.

Saichethan Reddy. 2020. Detecting tweets reporting birth defect pregnancy outcome using two-view CNN RNN based architecture. In *Proceedings of the Fifth Social Media Mining for Health Applications Workshop & Shared Task*, pages 125–127, Barcelona, Spain (Online). Association for Computational Linguistics.

Siva Reddy, Danqi Chen, and Christopher D. Manning. 2019. CoQA: A conversational question answering challenge. *Transactions of the Association for Computational Linguistics*, 7:249–266.

S. J. Rennie, E. Marcheret, Y. Mroueh, J. Ross, and V. Goel. 2017. Self-critical sequence training for image captioning. In *2017 IEEE Conference on Computer Vision and Pattern Recognition (CVPR)*, pages 1179–1195, Los Alamitos, CA, USA. IEEE Computer Society.

Marzieh Saeidi, Max Bartolo, Patrick Lewis, Sameer Singh, Tim Rocktäschel, Mike Sheldon, Guillaume Bouchard, and Sebastian Riedel. 2018. Interpretation of natural language rules in conversational machine reading. In *Proceedings of the 2018 Conference on Empirical Methods in Natural Language Processing*, pages 2087–2097, Brussels, Belgium. Association for Computational Linguistics.

John Schulman, Filip Wolski, Prafulla Dhariwal, Alec Radford, and Oleg Klimov. 2017. Proximal policy optimization algorithms. *CoRR*, abs/1707.06347.

Nisan Stiennon, Long Ouyang, Jeffrey Wu, Daniel Ziegler, Ryan Lowe, Chelsea Voss, Alec Radford, Dario Amodei, and Paul F Christiano. 2020. Learning to summarize with human feedback. In *Advances in Neural Information Processing Systems*, volume 33, pages 3008–3021. Curran Associates, Inc.

Dan Su, Xiaoguang Li, Jindi Zhang, Lifeng Shang, Xin Jiang, Qun Liu, and Pascale Fung. 2022. Read before generate! faithful long form question answering with machine reading. *arXiv preprint arXiv:2203.00343*.

Dan Su, Yan Xu, Genta Indra Winata, Peng Xu, Hyeondey Kim, Zihan Liu, and Pascale Fung. 2019. Generalizing question answering system with pre-trained language model fine-tuning. In *Proceedings of the 2nd Workshop on Machine Reading for Question Answering*, pages 203–211, Hong Kong, China. Association for Computational Linguistics.

Dan Su, Yan Xu, Tiezheng Yu, Farhad Bin Siddique, Elham Barezi, and Pascale Fung. 2020. CAiRE-COVID: A question answering and query-focused multi-document summarization system for COVID-19 scholarly information management. In *Proceedings of the 1st Workshop on NLP for COVID-19 (Part 2) at EMNLP 2020*, Online. Association for Computational Linguistics.

Svitlana Vakulenko, Shayne Longpre, Zhucheng Tu, and Raviteja Anantha. 2021. Question rewriting for conversational question answering. In *Proceedings of the 14th ACM International Conference on Web Search and Data Mining*, pages 355–363.

Ronald J. Williams. 1992. Simple statistical gradient-following algorithms for connectionist reinforcement learning. *Mach. Learn.*, 8(3–4):229–256.

Thomas Wolf, Lysandre Debut, Victor Sanh, Julien Chaumond, Clement Delangue, Anthony Moi, Pierric Cistac, Tim Rault, Remi Louf, Morgan Funtowicz, Joe Davison, Sam Shleifer, Patrick von Platen, Clara Ma, Yacine Jernite, Julien Plu, Canwen Xu, Teven Le Scao, Sylvain Gugger, Mariama Drame, Quentin Lhoest, and Alexander Rush. 2020. Transformers: State-of-the-art natural language processing. In *Proceedings of the 2020 Conference on Empirical Methods in Natural Language Processing: System Demonstrations*, pages 38–45, Online. Association for Computational Linguistics.

Yonghui Wu, Mike Schuster, Zhifeng Chen, Quoc V Le, Mohammad Norouzi, Wolfgang Macherey, Maxim Krikun, Yuan Cao, Qin Gao, Klaus Macherey, et al. 2016. Google's neural machine translation system: Bridging the gap between human and machine translation. *arXiv preprint arXiv:1609.08144*.

Yan Xu, Etsuko Ishii, Samuel Cahyawijaya, Zihan Liu, Genta Indra Winata, Andrea Madotto, Dan Su, and Pascale Fung. 2021a. [link].

Yan Xu, Etsuko Ishii, Genta Indra Winata, Zhaojiang Lin, Andrea Madotto, Zihan Liu, Peng Xu, and Pascale Fung. 2021b. Caire in dialdoc21: Data augmentation for information seeking dialogue system. In *Proceedings of the 1st Workshop on Document-grounded Dialogue and Conversational Question Answering (DialDoc 2021)*, pages 46–51.

Yilin Yang, Liang Huang, and Mingbo Ma. 2018. Breaking the beam search curse: A study of (re-)scoring methods and stopping criteria for neural machine translation. In *Proceedings of the 2018 Conference on Empirical Methods in Natural Language Processing*, pages 3054–3059, Brussels, Belgium. Association for Computational Linguistics.

Michihiro Yasunaga, Hongyu Ren, Antoine Bosselut, Percy Liang, and Jure Leskovec. 2021. Qa-gnn: Reasoning with language models and knowledge graphs for question answering. In *Proceedings of the 2021 Conference of the North American Chapter of the Association for Computational Linguistics: Human Language Technologies*, pages 535–546.

Yi-Ting Yeh and Yun-Nung Chen. 2019. Flowdelta: Modeling flow information gain in reasoning for conversational machine comprehension. In *Proceedings of the 2nd Workshop on Machine Reading for Question Answering*, pages 86–90.

Zhuosheng Zhang, Junjie Yang, and Hai Zhao. 2021. Retrospective reader for machine reading comprehension. *Proceedings of the AAAI Conference on Artificial Intelligence*, 35(16):14506–14514.

Jing Zhao, Junwei Bao, Yifan Wang, Yongwei Zhou, Youzheng Wu, Xiaodong He, and Bowen Zhou. 2021. RoR: Read-over-read for long document machine reading comprehension. In *Findings of the Association for Computational Linguistics: EMNLP 2021*, pages 1862–1872, Punta Cana, Dominican Republic. Association for Computational Linguistics.

Chenguang Zhu, Michael Zeng, and Xuedong Huang. 2018. Sdnet: Contextualized attention-based deep network for conversational question answering. *arXiv preprint arXiv:1812.03593*.

Hongyin Zhu, Prayag Tiwari, Ahmed Ghoneim, and M Shamim Hossain. 2021. A collaborative ai-enabled pretrained language model for aiot domain question answering. *IEEE Transactions on Industrial Informatics*.

Daniel M Ziegler, Nisan Stiennon, Jeffrey Wu, Tom B Brown, Alec Radford, Dario Amodei, Paul Christiano, and Geoffrey Irving. 2019. Fine-tuning language models from human preferences. *arXiv preprint arXiv:1909.08593*.

What Do You Mean by Relation Extraction? A Survey on Datasets and Study on Scientific Relation Classification

Elisa Bassignana[♣] and **Barbara Plank**[♣◇]
[♣]Department of Computer Science, IT University of Copenhagen, Denmark
[◇]Center for Information and Language Processing (CIS), LMU Munich, Germany
`{elba, bapl}@itu.dk`

Abstract

Over the last five years, research on Relation Extraction (RE) witnessed extensive progress with many new dataset releases. At the same time, setup clarity has decreased, contributing to increased difficulty of reliable empirical evaluation (Taillé et al., 2020). In this paper, we provide a comprehensive survey of RE datasets, and revisit the task definition and its adoption by the community. We find that cross-dataset and cross-domain setups are particularly lacking. We present an empirical study on scientific Relation Classification across two datasets. Despite large data overlap, our analysis reveals substantial discrepancies in annotation. Annotation discrepancies strongly impact Relation Classification performance, explaining large drops in cross-dataset evaluations. Variation within further sub-domains exists but impacts Relation Classification only to limited degrees. Overall, our study calls for more rigour in reporting setups in RE and evaluation across multiple test sets.

1 Introduction

Information Extraction (IE) is a key step in Natural Language Processing (NLP) to extract information, which is useful for question answering and knowledge base population, for example. Relation Extraction (RE) is a specific case of IE (Grishman, 2012) with the focus on the identification of semantic relations between entities (see Figure 1). The aim of the most typical RE setup is the extraction of informative triples from texts. Given a sequence of tokens $[t_0, t_1 ..., t_n]$ and two entities (spans), $s_A = [t_i, \ldots, t_j]$ and $s_B = [t_u, \ldots, t_v]$, RE triples are in the form (s_A, s_B, r), where $r \in R$ and R is a pre-defined set of relation labels. Because of the directionality of the relations, (s_B, s_A, r) represents a different triple.

We survey existing RE datasets—outside the biomedical domain—with an additional focus on the task definition.[1] Existing RE surveys mainly focus on modeling techniques (Bach and Badaskar, 2007; Pawar et al., 2017; Aydar et al., 2021; Liu, 2020). To the best of our knowledge, we are the first to give a comprehensive overview of available RE datasets. We also revisit RE papers from the ACL community over the last five years, to identify what part(s) of the task definition recent work focuses on. As it turns out, this is often not easy to determine, which makes fair evaluation difficult. We aim to shed light on such assumptions.[2]

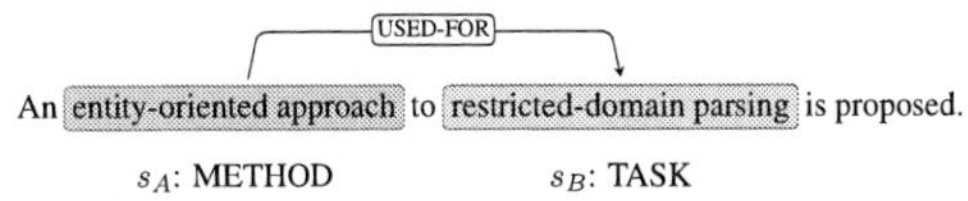

Figure 1: RE annotation sample. The sentence contains two annotated spans denoting two entities, with respective types `METHOD` and `TASK`, and a semantic relation between them labeled as `USED-FOR`.

Moreover, recent work in NLP has shown that single test splits and in-distribution evaluation overestimate generalization performance, arguing for the use of multiple test sets or split evaluation (Gorman and Bedrick, 2019; Søgaard et al., 2021). While this direction has started to be followed by other NLP tasks (Petrov and McDonald, 2012; Pradhan et al., 2013; Williams et al., 2018; Yu et al., 2019; Zhu et al., 2020a; Liu et al., 2021), for RE *cross-dataset* and *cross-domain* evaluation have received little attention. We explore this direction in the scientific domain and propose to study the possible presence of distinctive *sub-domains* (Lippincott et al., 2010). Sub-domains are differences between subsets of a domain that may be expected to behave homogeneously. Using two scientific datasets, we study to what degree: (*a*) they contain overlapping data; (*b*) their annotations differ;

[1]We refer the reader to Luo et al. (2016) for a survey on biomedical RE and event extraction.

[2]Pyysalo et al. (2008) discuss similar difficulties in the biomedical domain.

Proceedings of the 60th Annual Meeting of the Association for Computational Linguistics
Student Research Workshop, pages 67 - 83

and (*c*) sub-domains impact Relation Classification (RC)—the task of classifying the relation type held between a pair of entities (details in Section 3).

The contributions of this paper are:

- To the best of our knowledge, we are the first to provide a comprehensive survey on currently available RE datasets.
- We define RE considering its modularity. We analyze previous works and find unclarity in setups; we call for more rigour in specifying which RE sub-part(s) are tackled.
- We provide a case study on Relation Classification in the scientific domain, to fill a gap on cross-domain and cross-dataset evaluation.

2 Relation Extraction Datasets Survey

RE has been broadly studied in the last decades and many datasets were published. We survey widely used RE datasets in chronological order, and broadly classify them into three domains based on the data source: (1) news and web, (2) scientific publications and (3) Wikipedia. An overview of the datasets is given in Table 1. Our empirical target here focuses on the scientific domain as so far it has received no attention in the cross-domain direction; a similar investigation on overlaps in data, annotation, and model transferability between datasets in other domains is interesting future work.

The CoNLL 2004 dataset (Roth and Yih, 2004) is one of the first works. It contains annotations for named entities and relations in news articles. In the same year, the widely studied ACE dataset was published by Doddington et al. (2004). It contains annotated entities, relations and events in broadcast transcripts, newswire and newspaper data in English, Chinese and Arabic. The corpus is divided into six domains.

Another widely used dataset is The New York Times (NYT) Annotated Corpus,[3] first presented by Riedel et al. (2010). It contains over 1.8 million articles by the NYT between 1987 and 2007. NYT has been created with a distant supervision approach (Mintz et al., 2009), using Freebase (Bollacker et al., 2008) as knowledge base. Two further versions of it followed recently: Zhu et al. (2020b) (NYT-H) and Jia et al. (2019) published manually annotated versions of the test set in order to perform a more accurate evaluation.

RE has also been part of the SemEval shared tasks for four times so far. The two early SemEval shared tasks focused on the identification of semantic relations between nominals (Nastase et al., 2021). For SemEval-2007 Task 4, Girju et al. (2007) released a dataset for RC into seven generic semantic relations between nominals. Three years later, for SemEval-2010 Task 8, Hendrickx et al. (2010) revised the annotation guidelines and published a corpus for RC, by providing a much larger dataset (10k instances, in comparison to 1.5k of the 2007 shared task).

Since 2017, three RE datasets in the scientific domain emerged, two of the three as SemEval shared tasks. In SemEval-2017 Task 10 Augenstein et al. (2017) proposed a dataset for the identification of keyphrases and considered two generic relations (`HYPONYM-OF` and `SYNONYM-OF`). The dataset is called ScienceIE and consists of 500 journal articles from the Computer Science, Material Sciences and Physics fields. The year after, Gábor et al. (2018) proposed a corpus for RC and RE made of abstracts of scientific papers from the ACL Anthology for SemEval-2018 Task 7. The data will be described in further detail in Section 4.1. Following the same line, Luan et al. (2018) published SciERC, which is a scientific RE dataset further annotated for coreference resolution. It contains abstracts from scientific AI-related conferences. From the existing three scientific RE datasets summarized in Table 1, in our empirical investigation we focus on two (SemEval-2018 and SciERC). We leave out ScienceIE as it focuses on keyphrase extraction and it contains two generic relations only.

The Wikipedia domain has been first introduced in 2013. Google released GoogleRE,[4] a RE corpus consisting of snippets from Wikipedia. More recently, Kassner et al. (2021) proposed mLAMA, a multilingual version (53 languages) of GoogleRE with the purpose of investigating knowledge in pretrained language models. The multi-lingual dimension is gaining more interest for RE. Following this trend, Seganti et al. (2021) presented SMiLER, a multilingual dataset (14 languages) from Wikipedia with relations belonging to nine domains.

Previous datasets were restricted to the same label collection in the training set and in the test set. To address this gap and make RE experimental scenarios more realistic, Han et al. (2018) published Few-Rel, a Wikipedia-based few-shot learning

[3] `http://iesl.cs.umass.edu/riedel/ecml/`

[4] `https://code.google.com/archive/p/relation-extraction-corpus/downloads`

Dataset	Paper	Data Source	# Relation Types
News and Web			
CoNLL04	Roth and Yih (2004)	News articles	5
ACE*	Doddington et al. (2004)	News and conversations	24
NYT	Riedel et al. (2010)	New York Times articles	24-57◇
SemEval-2007	Girju et al. (2007)	Sentences from the web	7
SemEval-2010	Hendrickx et al. (2010)	Sentences from the web	10
TACRED	Zhang et al. (2017b)	Newswire and web text	42
FSL TACRED	Sabo et al. (2021)	TACRED data	42
DWIE	Zaporojets et al. (2021)	Deutsche Welle articles	65
Scientific publications			
ScienceIE	Augenstein et al. (2017)	Scientific articles	2
SemEval-2018	Gábor et al. (2018)	NLP abstracts	6
SciERC	Luan et al. (2018)	Abstracts of AI proceedings	7
Wikipedia			
GoogleRE	-	Wikipedia	5
mLAMA*	Kassner et al. (2021)	GoogleRE data	5
FewRel	Han et al. (2018)	Wikipedia	100
FewRel 2.0	Gao et al. (2019)	FewRel data + Biomedical literature	100 + 25
DocRED	Yao et al. (2019)	Wikipedia and Wikidata	96
SMiLER	Seganti et al. (2021)	Wikipedia	36

Table 1: Overview of the RE datasets for the English language grouped by macro domains. (⋆): Multilingual datasets. (◇): The original paper does not state the number of considered relations and different work describe different dataset setups.

(FSL) RC dataset annotated by crowdworkers. One year later, Gao et al. (2019) published a new version (Few-Rel 2.0), adding a new test set in the biomedical domain and the `None-Of-The-Above` relation (cf. Section 3).

Back to the news domain, Zhang et al. (2017b) published a large-scale RE dataset built over newswire and web text, by crowdsourcing relation annotations for sentences with named entity pairs. This resulted in the TACRED dataset with over 100k instances, which is particularly well-suited for neural models. Sabo et al. (2021) used TACRED to make a FSL RC dataset and compared it to FewRel 1.0 and FewRel 2.0, aiming at a more realistic scenario (i.e., non-uniform label distribution, inclusion of pronouns and common nouns).

All datasets so far present a sentence level annotation. To address this, Yao et al. (2019) published DocRED, a document-level RE dataset from Wikipedia and Wikidata. The difference with a traditional sentence-level corpus is that both the intra- and inter-sentence relations are annotated, increasing the challenge level. In addition to RE, DocRED annotates coreference chains. DWIE by Zaporojets et al. (2021) is another document-level dataset, specifically designed for multi-task IE (Named Entity Recognition, Coreference Resolution, Relation Extraction, and Entity Linking).

Lastly, there are works focusing on creating datasets for specific RE aspects. Cheng et al. (2021), for example, proposed a Chinese document-level RE dataset for *hard cases* in order to move towards even more challenging evaluation setups.

Domains in RE Given our analysis, we observe a shift in target domains: from news text in seminal works, over web texts, to emerging corpora in the scientific domain and the most recent focus on Wikipedia. Similarly, we observe the emerging trend for FSL.

Different datasets lend themselves to study different aspects of the task. Concerning cross-domain RE, we propose to distinguish three setups:

1. Data from different domains, but same relation types, which are general enough to be present in each domain (limited and often confined to the ACE dataset) (e.g., Plank and Moschitti, 2013).

2. Stable data domain, but different relation sets (e.g., FewRel by Han et al., 2018). Note that when labels change, approaches such as FSL must be adopted.

3. A combination of both: The data changes and so do the relation types (e.g., FewRel 2.0 by Gao et al., 2019).

In the case study of this paper, given the scientific datasets available, we focus on the first setup.

3 The Relation Extraction Task

Conceptually, RE involves a pipeline of steps (see Figure 2). Starting from the raw text, the first step consists in identifying the entities and eventually assigning them a type. Entities involve either nominals or named entities, and hence it is either Named Entity Recognition (NER) or, more broadly, Mention Detection (MD).[5] After entities are identified, approaches start to be more blurry as studies have approached RE via different angles.

One way is to take two steps, Relation Identification (RI) and subsequent Relation Classification (RC) (Ye et al., 2019), as illustrated in Figure 2. This means to first identify from all the possible entity pairs the ones which are in some kind of relation via a binary classification task (RI). As the proportion of positive samples over the negative is usually extremely unbalanced towards the latter (Gormley et al., 2015), a priori heuristics are generally applied to reduce the possible combinations (e.g., entity pairs involving distant entities, or entity type pairs not licensed by the relations are not even considered). The last step (RC) is usually a multi-class classification to assign a relation type r to the positive samples from the previous step. Some studies merge RI and RC (Seganti et al., 2021) into one step, by adding a `no-relation` (`no-rel`) label. Other studies instead reduce the task to RC, and assume there exists a relation between two entities and the task is to determine the type (without a `no-rel` label). Regardless, RI is influenced by the RC setup: Relations which are not in the RC label set are considered as negative samples in the RI phase. Some studies address this approximation by distinguishing between the `no-rel` and the `None-Of-The-Above` (`NOTA`) relation (Gao et al., 2019). Note that, in our definition, the `NOTA` label differs from `no-rel` in the sense that a relation holds between the two entities, but its type is not in the considered RC label set.[6]

What Do You Mean by Relation Extraction? RE studies rarely address the whole pipeline. We

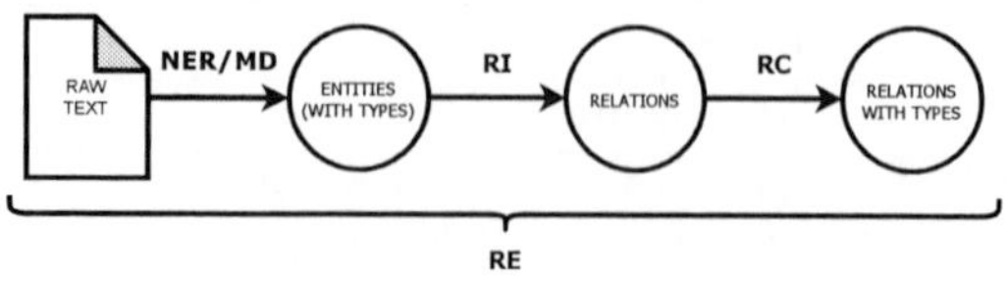

Figure 2: Relation Extraction pipeline. NER: Named Entity Recognition; MD: Mention Detection; RI: Relation Identification; RC: Relation Classification.

analyze all the ACL papers published in the last five years which contain the *Relation Extraction* keyword in the title and determine which sub-task is performed (NER/MD, RI, RC). Table 2 shows such investigation. We leave out from this analysis (*a*) papers which make use of distant supervision or which somehow involve knowledge bases, (*b*) shared task papers, (*c*) the bioNLP field, (*d*) temporal RE, and (*e*) Open RE.

The result shows that gold entities are usually assumed for RE, presumably given the complexity of the NER/MD task on its own. Most importantly, for end-to-end models, recent work has shown that ablations for steps like NER are lacking (Taillé et al., 2020). Our analysis further shows that it is difficult to determine the RI setup. While RC is always performed, the situation is different for RI (or `no-rel`). Sometimes RI is clearly not done (i.e., the paper assumes a scenario in which every instance contains at least one relation), but most of the times it is either not clear from the paper, or done in a simplified scenario (e.g., datasets which already clear out most of the `no-rel` entity pair instances). As this blurriness hampers fair evaluation, we propose that *studies clearly state which step they include*, i.e., whether the work focus is on RC, RI+RC or the full RE pipeline and how special cases (`no-rel` and `NOTA`) are handled. These details are utterly important as they impact both model estimation and evaluation.

Pipeline or Joint Model? The traditional RE pipeline is, by definition of pipeline, prone to error propagation by sub-tasks. Joint entity and relation extraction approaches have been proposed in order to alleviate this problem (Miwa and Bansal, 2016; Zhang et al., 2017a; Bekoulis et al., 2018a,b; Wang and Lu, 2020; Wang et al., 2021). However, Taillé et al. (2020) recently discussed the challenge of properly evaluating such complex models. They surveyed the evaluation metrics of recently published works on end-to-end RE referring to the *Strict*, *Boundaries*, *Relaxed* evaluation setting pro-

[5]Some studies divide the entity extraction into two substeps: identification (often called MD), and subsequent classification into entity types.

[6]Some studies name such relation `Other` (Hendrickx et al., 2010).

Relation Extraction Paper	Task Performed NER/MD	RI	RC
2021			
Wang et al. (2021)	✓	✓	✓
Cui et al. (2021)			✓
Tang et al. (2021)		(?)	✓
Xie et al. (2021)	✓	(?)	✓
Tian et al. (2021)			✓
Ma et al. (2021)		✓	✓
Mathur et al. (2021)			✓
Yang et al. (2021)			✓
Huang et al. (2021b)		(?)	✓
Huang et al. (2021a)		(?)	✓
2020			
Kruiper et al. (2020)	✓		✓
Nan et al. (2020)			✓
Alt et al. (2020)		✓	✓
Yu et al. (2020)		✓	✓
Shahbazi et al. (2020)		(?)	✓
Pouran Ben Veyseh et al. (2020)			✓
2019			
Trisedya et al. (2019)	✓	(?)	✓
Guo et al. (2019)		✓	✓
Yao et al. (2019)			✓
Zhu et al. (2019)		✓	✓
Li et al. (2019)	✓	(?)	✓
Ye et al. (2019)		✓	✓
Fu et al. (2019)	✓	✓	✓
Dixit and Al-Onaizan (2019)	✓	✓	✓
Obamuyide and Vlachos (2019)		(?)	✓
2018			
Christopoulou et al. (2018)		✓	✓
Phi et al. (2018)			✓
2017			
Lin et al. (2017)		(?)	✓

Table 2: ACL paper analysis: over the last 5 years, which RE sub-task is performed. *(?)* indicates that either the paper does not state if the step is considered, either it is performed, but in a simplified scenario.

posed by Bekoulis et al. (2018a). They observe unfair comparisons and overestimations of end-to-end models, and claim the need for more rigorous reports of evaluation settings, including detailed datasets statistics.

While some recent work shifts to joint models, it is still an open question which approach (joint or pipeline) is the most robust. Zhong and Chen (2021) found that when incorporating modern pretrained language models (e.g., BERT) using separate encoders can surpass existing joint models. Since the output label space is different, separate encoders could better capture distinct contextual information. At the moment it is not clear if one approach is more suitable than the other for RE. For this reason and because of our final goal, which is a closer look to sub-domains in the scientific field, we follow the pipeline approach and, following most work from Table 2, we here restrict the setup by focusing on the RC task.

Open Issues To summarize, open issues are: *1)* The unclarity of RE setups, as illustrated in Table 2 —specially regarding RI—leads to problematic evaluation comparisons; *2)* A lack of cross-domain studies, for all three setups outlined in Section 2.

4 Scientific Domain Data Analysis

In this section, we present the two English corpora involved in the experimental study (Section 4.1), explain the label mapping adopted for the cross-dataset experiments (Section 4.2), discuss the overlap between the datasets and the annotation divergence between them (Section 4.3), and introduce the sub-domains considered (Section 4.4).

4.1 Datasets

SemEval-2018 Task 7 (Gábor et al., 2018) The corpus contains 500 abstracts of published research papers in computational linguistics from the ACL Anthology. Relations are classified into six classes. The task was split into three sub-tasks: (1.1) RC on clean data (manually annotated), (1.2) RC on noisy data (automatically annotated entities) and (2) RI+RC (identifying instances + assigning class labels). For each sub-task, the training data contains 350 abstracts and the test data 150. The train set for sub-task (1.1) and (2) is identical.

SciERC (Luan et al., 2018) The dataset consists of 500 abstracts from scientific publications annotated for entities, their relations and coreference clusters. The authors define six scientific entity types and seven relation types. The original paper presents a unified multi-task model for entity extraction, RI+RC and coreference resolution. SciERC is assembled from different conference proceedings. As the data is released with original abstract IDs, this allows us to identify four major sub-domains: AI and ML, Computer Vision (CV), Speech Processing, and NLP, sampled over a time frame from 1980 to 2016. Details of the sub-domains are provided in Table 9 in Appendix A. To the best of our knowledge, we are the first to analyze the corpus at this sub-domain level.

4.2 Cross-dataset Label Mapping

We homogenize the relation label sets via a manual analysis performed after an exploratory data analy-

	SemEval-2018	SciERC
Considered in this study	COMPARE	COMPARE
	USAGE	USED-FOR
	PART_WHOLE	PART-OF
	MODEL-FEATURE	FEATURE-OF
	RESULT	EVALUATE-FOR*
Not-considered	TOPIC	-
	-	HYPONYM-OF
	-	CONJUNCTION

Table 3: Label mapping. (*): Same semantic relation, but inverse direction: We homogenized the two versions by flipping the head with the tail.

Whole corpus		
	SemEval-2018	SciERC
# abstracts	500	500
# relations	1,583	4,648
Datasets Overlap (307 abstracts)		
# relations	1,087	2,476
# common relations	1,071	1,922
Same entity pair		394
Same entity pair + same relation type		327

Table 4: SemEval-2018 and SciERC annotation comparison. The common relations are the ones with a direct correspondent in both datasets (see Table 3).

sis, as we find that most of the labels in SemEval-2018 and SciERC have a direct correspondent, and hence we mapped them as shown in Table 3. The gold label distribution of the relations on the two datasets is shown in Figure 4 in Appendix B. We decided to leave out the two generic labels from SciERC and one relation from SemEval-2018 which does not have any correspondent and is rare.

4.3 Overlap of the Datasets and Annotation Divergences

Our analysis further reveals a high overlap in articles between SemEval-2018 and SciERC corresponding to 307 ACL abstracts.[7] Interestingly, the overlap contains a huge annotation divergence. In more detail, we identify three main annotation disagreement scenarios between the two datasets (represented by the 3 samples in Table 5):

- **Sample 1**: *The annotated entities differ and so the annotated relations do as well.* SemEval-2018 annotates just one entity and thus there can not even exist a relation; as the corresponding sentence in SciERC is annotated with two entities, it contains a relation.

- **Sample 2**: *The amount of annotated entities and the amount of annotated relations are the same, but the annotations do not match.* The relations involve non-mutual entities and so do not correspond.

- **Sample 3**: *The annotated entities are the same, but the relation annotations differ.* This involves conflicting annotations, e.g., the bold arrow shows the same entity pair annotated with a different relation label.

Table 4 shows the annotation statistics from the two corpora and their overlap. Overall both datasets contain the same amount of abstracts, but the amount of annotated relations differs substantially. The overlap between the two corpora reports a similar trend. Even the fairer count of the common labels (see Table 3) reveals that the annotation gap still holds (ratio of 1:1.8). In more detail, the entity pairs annotated in both dataset by using a strict criterion (i.e., entity spans with the same boundaries) are only 394 (considering relations from the whole relation sets). Out of them, only 327 are labeled with the same relation type, meaning that there are 67 conflicting instances as the bold arrow in Table 5 (Sample 3).

4.4 Experimental Sub-domains

We use the metadata described in Section 4.1 to divide SciERC into four sub-domains. Figure 5 in Appendix B shows the label distribution over the new SciERC split. As we are particularly interested in the annotation divergence impact, we leave out of this study 193 abstracts from SemEval-2018 which are not in overlap with SciERC.

We assume a setup which takes the NLP domain as source training domain in all experiments, as it is the largest sub-domain in both datasets. The considered sub-domains and their relative amount of data are reported in Table 6.

5 Experiments

5.1 Model Setup

Since the seminal work by Nguyen and Grishman (2015), Convolutional Neural Networks (CNNs) are widely used for IE tasks (Zeng et al., 2014; Nguyen and Grishman, 2015; Fu et al., 2017; Augenstein et al., 2017; Gábor et al., 2018; Yao et al.,

[7]Note that in our study, regarding SemEval-2018, for fair comparison with SciERC, which is manually annotated, we consider the dataset related to sub-task (1.1).

Sample 1: Different number of entity (and relation) annotations	
SemEval-2018	We evaluate the utility of this constraint in two different algorithms.
SCIERC	EVALUATE-FOR We evaluate the utility of this constraint in two different algorithms .
Sample 2: Different entity annotations	
SemEval-2018	PART_WHOLE We propose a detection method for orthographic variants caused by transliteration in a large corpus .
SCIERC	USED-FOR We propose a detection method for orthographic variants caused by transliteration in a large corpus.
Sample 3: Different relation annotations	
SemEval-2018	MODEL-FEATURE The speech-search algorithm is implemented on a board with a single Intel i860 chip , which provides a factor of 5 speed-up over a SUN 4 for straight C code .
SCIERC	USED-FOR PART-OF USED-FOR COMPARE USED-FOR The speech-search algorithm is implemented on a board with a single Intel i860 chip , which provides a factor of 5 speed-up over a SUN 4 for straight C code .

Table 5: Annotated sentence pairs from SemEval-2018 and SCIERC. The underlined spans are the entities.

Dataset	Sub-domain	train	dev	test
SemEval-2018	NLP	257	50	50
SCIERC	NLP	257	50	50
	AI-ML	-	-	52
	CV	-	-	105
	SPEECH	-	-	35

Table 6: Sub-domains and relative amount of abstracts.

2019). Similarly, since the advent of contextualized representations (Peters et al., 2018; Devlin et al., 2019), BERT-like representations are commonly used (Seganti et al., 2021), but non-contextualized embeddings (i.e., GloVe, fastText) are still widely adopted (Yao et al., 2019; Huang et al., 2021b). We compare the best CNN setup to fine-tuning a full transformer model. For the latter we use the MaChAmp toolkit (van der Goot et al., 2021)

Our CNN follows Nguyen and Grishman (2015). We tests both non-contextualized word embeddings—fastText (Bojanowski et al., 2017)—and contextualized ones—BERT (Devlin et al., 2019) and the domain-specific SciBERT (Beltagy et al., 2019). Further details about the model implementation and hyperparameter settings can be found in Appendix C. We use macro F1-score as evaluation metric. All experiments were run over three different seeds and the results reported are the mean.[8]

5.2 Cross-dataset Evaluation

We test the following training configurations:[9] (1) *cross-dataset*: Training on SemEval-2018 and testing on SCIERC, and vice versa; (2) *cross-annotation*: Training on a mix of SemEval-2018 and SCIERC overlap: (2.1) *exclusive*: Considering either abstracts from the two corpora, (2.2) *repeated labeling*: Including every abstract twice, once from each dataset; this approach repeats instances with different annotations and is a simple method to handle divergences in annotation (Sheng et al., 2008; Uma et al., 2021), (2.3) *filter*: Double annotation of the abstracts as in (2.2), but filtering out conflicting annotations.

Results Table 7 reports the results of the experiments. The *cross-dataset* experiments (1) confirm the expected drop across datasets, in both directions (Sem: 40.28 → 34.81 and SCI: 34.29 → 31.37). Considering the *cross-annotation* setups, results are mixed in the *exclusive* version (2.1). The overall amount of training data is the same as the cross-dataset experiments, but there is less dataset-specific data, which hurts SemEval-2018. In contrast, regarding (2.2) and (2.3), in both setups improvements are evident on both test sets. Compared to (2.1), the training data amount is effectively doubled and the model benefits from it. Removing the conflicting instances results in a slightly smaller train set, but an overall higher average performance (43.81 → 44.16). The improvement of (2.3) over (2.2) is significant, which we test by the *almost stochastic dominance* test (Dror et al., 2019). Details about significance are in Appendix D.

5.3 Contextualized Word Embeddings

We pick the best performing training scenario (*cross-annotation filter*, 2.3) and compare fastText with contextualized embeddings: BERT and the domain-specific SciBERT. The central columns of Table 7 report the results. While BERT does not bring relevant improvements over the best fastText setup, SciBERT confirms the strength of domain-

[8] https://github.com/elisabassignana/scientific-re

[9] The development set follows the train set distributions.

Model	CNN							Transformer [tuned]	
Word embedding	FastText					BERT	SciBERT	SciBERT	SciBERT
↓Test | Train (NLP) →	Sem	SCI	[½ + ½]	2A	2A w/o CR	2A w/o CR	2A w/o CR	2A	2A w/o CR
SemEval NLP	40.28	34.81	39.91	50.17	48.95	42.54	49.27	79.16	77.79
SCIERC NLP	31.37	34.29	36.29	39.36	41.48	38.63	51.99	67.36	69.90
SCIERC AI-ML	37.00	50.44	46.78	49.52	49.66	40.81	51.14	72.48	76.80
SCIERC CV	33.32	41.30	37.24	44.59	45.60	38.51	48.18	73.55	76.11
SCIERC SPEECH	29.60	35.00	33.71	35.39	35.11	31.62	42.72	64.17	65.21
avg.	34.31	39.17	38.79	43.81	**44.16**	38.34	**48.66**	71.34	**73.56**

Table 7: Macro F1-scores of the cross-dataset and cross-domain experiments. (2.1) [½ + ½] refers to the case in which the train is made half by SemEval-2018 and half by SCIERC; (2.2) 2A means double annotation from the two datasets; (2.3) CR are the conflicting relations (bold sample in Table 5).

specific trained language models (improvement of 4.5 F1 points and *almost stochastic dominance*). Compared to the CNN, full transformer fine-tuning results in the best model (rightmost columns). We tested different setups to feed the input to the transformer (see appendix E), finding two entity spans and the full sentence as best setup. The full fine-tuned transformer model confirms the *dominance* of training setup (2.3) over (2.2).

5.4 Cross-domain Evaluation

Next, we look at *cross-domain* variation: Training on NLP, and testing on all sub-domains. The lower rows in Table 7 show the results. If we focus on the SciBERT models, we observe that there is some drop in performance from NLP, but mostly to CV and SPEECH. Interestingly, in some cases, AI-ML even outperforms the in-domain performance. Over all models, the SPEECH domain shows the clearest drop in transfer from NLP.[10] From an analysis of the predictions of the RC trained on SciBERT, we notice that the classifier struggles with identifying the most frequent USAGE relation (see Appendix B) across sub-domains (confusion from lowest to highest: AI-ML, CV and SPEECH), and it is most confused with MODEL-FEATURE. Figure 7 in Appendix F contains the detailed confusion matrices. The overall evaluation suggests that in this setup sub-domain variation impacts RC performance to a limiting degree only.

In order to confirm this qualitatively, we (1) inspect whether model-internal representations are able to capture sub-domain variation, and we (2) test whether sub-domain variation is identifiable. To answer (1), we visualise the PCA representation of the CNN trained on setup (2.3) with SciBERT. The result is shown in Figure 3. The plot confirms

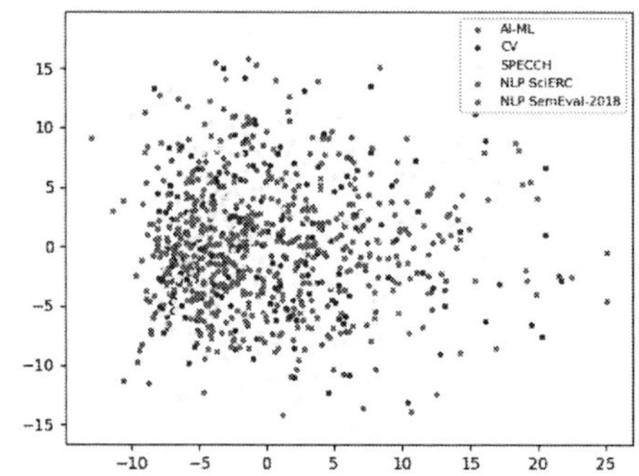

Figure 3: PCA representation of the CNN hidden state (just before the linear layer) using SciBERT.

that the representations do not contain visible clusters: The relation instances from each sub-domain are equally spread over it, and thus the performance of the relation classifier is similar for each of them. Our intuition is that the unified label set contains relations general enough to be equally covered by every sub-domain.

We explore the sub-domains more deeply apart from the RC task. To answer (2), we built a domain classifier to investigate how hard it is to tear apart the sub-domains. We hypothesize that, if sub-domains are distinguishable, a classifier should be able to easily distinguish them by looking at the coarsest level (the abstract). The classifier consists of a linear layer on top of the SciBERT encoder and achieves a F1-score of 62.01, over a random baseline of 25.58. This shows that the sub-domains are identifiable at the abstract level but with modest performance. As we would expect, SPEECH and NLP are highly confused (Figure 6 in Appendix G reports the confusion matrix) and the large vocabulary overlap shown in Table 8 between these sub-

[10]We note that the data amount for speech is the smallest in respect to the other sub-corpora, which might have an impact.

Domain	# word types	# overlap	% overlap
NLP	5,646	-	-
AI-ML	1,895	917	48.39%
CV	3,387	1,205	35.58%
SPEECH	1,398	715	51.14%

Table 8: Vocabulary overlap between NLP and the other sub-domains. *# word types*, *# overlap* in word types, and *% overlap* as relative percentages. Note that the amount of abstracts varies, cf. Table 6.

domains confirms this observation. Overall, sub-domains are identifiable but have limited impact on the RC task in the setup considered.

6 Conclusions

We present a survey on datasets for RE, revisit the task definition, and provide an empirical study on scientific RC. We observe a domain shift in RE datasets, and a trend towards multilingual and FSL for RE. Our analysis shows that our surveyed ACL RE papers focus mostly on RC and assume gold entities. Other steps are more blurry, concluding with a call for reporting RE setups more clearly.

As testing on only one dataset or domain bears risks of overestimation, we carry out a cross-dataset evaluation. Despite large data overlaps, we find annotations to substantially differ, which impacts classification results. Sub-domains extracted from meta-data instead only slightly impact performance. This finding on sub-domain variation is specific to the explored RC task on the scientific setup considered. Our study contributes to the first of three cross-domain RE setups we propose (Section 2) to aid further work on generalization for RE.

Limitations and Ethical Considerations

This work focuses on a limited view of the whole RE research field. Our dataset survey excludes specific angles of RE such as temporal RE or bioNLP, as they are large sub-fields which warrant a dedicated analysis in itself. From a methodological point of view, in our analysis we did not further cover weakly-supervised (e.g., distant supervision) and un-supervised approaches. Finally, given that our study points out gaps in RE, specifically cross-dataset, our experiments are still limited to RC only and next steps are to extend to the whole pipeline and to additional datasets and domains.

The data analyzed in this work is based on existing publicly-available datasets (based on published research papers).

Acknowledgements

We thank the NLPnorth group for insightful discussions on this work—in particular Mike Zhang and Max Müller-Eberstein. We would also like to thank the anonymous reviewers for their comments to improve this paper. Last, we also thank the ITU's High-performance Computing cluster for computing resources. This research is supported by the Independent Research Fund Denmark (Danmarks Frie Forskningsfond; DFF) grant number 9063-00077B.

References

Christoph Alt, Aleksandra Gabryszak, and Leonhard Hennig. 2020. TACRED revisited: A thorough evaluation of the TACRED relation extraction task. In *Proceedings of the 58th Annual Meeting of the Association for Computational Linguistics*, pages 1558–1569, Online. Association for Computational Linguistics.

Isabelle Augenstein, Mrinal Das, Sebastian Riedel, Lakshmi Vikraman, and Andrew McCallum. 2017. SemEval 2017 task 10: ScienceIE - extracting keyphrases and relations from scientific publications. In *Proceedings of the 11th International Workshop on Semantic Evaluation (SemEval-2017)*, pages 546–555, Vancouver, Canada. Association for Computational Linguistics.

Mehmet Aydar, Özge Bozal, and Furkan Özbay. 2021. Neural relation extraction: a review. *Turkish Journal of Electrical Engineering & Computer Sciences*, 29(2):1029–1043.

Nguyen Bach and Sameer Badaskar. 2007. A review of relation extraction. *Literature review for Language and Statistics II*, 2:1–15.

Livio Baldini Soares, Nicholas FitzGerald, Jeffrey Ling, and Tom Kwiatkowski. 2019. Matching the blanks: Distributional similarity for relation learning. In *Proceedings of the 57th Annual Meeting of the Association for Computational Linguistics*, pages 2895–2905, Florence, Italy. Association for Computational Linguistics.

Giannis Bekoulis, Johannes Deleu, Thomas Demeester, and Chris Develder. 2018a. Adversarial training for multi-context joint entity and relation extraction. In *Proceedings of the 2018 Conference on Empirical Methods in Natural Language Processing*, pages 2830–2836, Brussels, Belgium. Association for Computational Linguistics.

Giannis Bekoulis, Johannes Deleu, Thomas Demeester, and Chris Develder. 2018b. Joint entity recognition and relation extraction as a multi-head selection problem. *Expert Systems with Applications*, 114:34–45.

Iz Beltagy, Kyle Lo, and Arman Cohan. 2019. SciBERT: A pretrained language model for scientific text. In *Proceedings of the 2019 Conference on Empirical Methods in Natural Language Processing and the 9th International Joint Conference on Natural Language Processing (EMNLP-IJCNLP)*, pages 3615–3620, Hong Kong, China. Association for Computational Linguistics.

Piotr Bojanowski, Edouard Grave, Armand Joulin, and Tomas Mikolov. 2017. Enriching word vectors with subword information. *Transactions of the Association for Computational Linguistics*, 5:135–146.

Kurt Bollacker, Colin Evans, Praveen Paritosh, Tim Sturge, and Jamie Taylor. 2008. Freebase: a collaboratively created graph database for structuring human knowledge. In *Proceedings of the 2008 ACM SIGMOD international conference on Management of data*, pages 1247–1250.

C.E. Bonferroni. 1936. *Teoria statistica delle classi e calcolo delle probabilità*. Pubblicazioni del R. Istituto superiore di scienze economiche e commerciali di Firenze. Seeber.

Qiao Cheng, Juntao Liu, Xiaoye Qu, Jin Zhao, Jiaqing Liang, Zhefeng Wang, Baoxing Huai, Nicholas Jing Yuan, and Yanghua Xiao. 2021. HacRED: A large-scale relation extraction dataset toward hard cases in practical applications. In *Findings of the Association for Computational Linguistics: ACL-IJCNLP 2021*, pages 2819–2831, Online. Association for Computational Linguistics.

Fenia Christopoulou, Makoto Miwa, and Sophia Ananiadou. 2018. A walk-based model on entity graphs for relation extraction. In *Proceedings of the 56th Annual Meeting of the Association for Computational Linguistics (Volume 2: Short Papers)*, pages 81–88, Melbourne, Australia. Association for Computational Linguistics.

Li Cui, Deqing Yang, Jiaxin Yu, Chengwei Hu, Jiayang Cheng, Jingjie Yi, and Yanghua Xiao. 2021. Refining sample embeddings with relation prototypes to enhance continual relation extraction. In *Proceedings of the 59th Annual Meeting of the Association for Computational Linguistics and the 11th International Joint Conference on Natural Language Processing (Volume 1: Long Papers)*, pages 232–243, Online. Association for Computational Linguistics.

Jacob Devlin, Ming-Wei Chang, Kenton Lee, and Kristina Toutanova. 2019. BERT: Pre-training of deep bidirectional transformers for language understanding. In *Proceedings of the 2019 Conference of the North American Chapter of the Association for Computational Linguistics: Human Language Technologies, Volume 1 (Long and Short Papers)*, pages 4171–4186, Minneapolis, Minnesota. Association for Computational Linguistics.

Kalpit Dixit and Yaser Al-Onaizan. 2019. Span-level model for relation extraction. In *Proceedings of the 57th Annual Meeting of the Association for Computational Linguistics*, pages 5308–5314, Florence, Italy. Association for Computational Linguistics.

George Doddington, Alexis Mitchell, Mark Przybocki, Lance Ramshaw, Stephanie Strassel, and Ralph Weischedel. 2004. The automatic content extraction (ACE) program – tasks, data, and evaluation. In *Proceedings of the Fourth International Conference on Language Resources and Evaluation (LREC'04)*, Lisbon, Portugal. European Language Resources Association (ELRA).

Rotem Dror, Segev Shlomov, and Roi Reichart. 2019. Deep dominance - how to properly compare deep neural models. In *Proceedings of the 57th Annual Meeting of the Association for Computational Linguistics*, pages 2773–2785, Florence, Italy. Association for Computational Linguistics.

Lisheng Fu, Thien Huu Nguyen, Bonan Min, and Ralph Grishman. 2017. Domain adaptation for relation extraction with domain adversarial neural network. In *Proceedings of the Eighth International Joint Conference on Natural Language Processing (Volume 2: Short Papers)*, pages 425–429, Taipei, Taiwan. Asian Federation of Natural Language Processing.

Tsu-Jui Fu, Peng-Hsuan Li, and Wei-Yun Ma. 2019. GraphRel: Modeling text as relational graphs for joint entity and relation extraction. In *Proceedings of the 57th Annual Meeting of the Association for Computational Linguistics*, pages 1409–1418, Florence, Italy. Association for Computational Linguistics.

Kata Gábor, Davide Buscaldi, Anne-Kathrin Schumann, Behrang QasemiZadeh, Haïfa Zargayouna, and Thierry Charnois. 2018. SemEval-2018 task 7: Semantic relation extraction and classification in scientific papers. In *Proceedings of The 12th International Workshop on Semantic Evaluation*, pages 679–688, New Orleans, Louisiana. Association for Computational Linguistics.

Tianyu Gao, Xu Han, Hao Zhu, Zhiyuan Liu, Peng Li, Maosong Sun, and Jie Zhou. 2019. FewRel 2.0: Towards more challenging few-shot relation classification. In *Proceedings of the 2019 Conference on Empirical Methods in Natural Language Processing and the 9th International Joint Conference on Natural Language Processing (EMNLP-IJCNLP)*, pages 6250–6255, Hong Kong, China. Association for Computational Linguistics.

Roxana Girju, Preslav Nakov, Vivi Nastase, Stan Szpakowicz, Peter Turney, and Deniz Yuret. 2007. SemEval-2007 task 04: Classification of semantic relations between nominals. In *Proceedings of the Fourth International Workshop on Semantic Evaluations (SemEval-2007)*, pages 13–18, Prague, Czech Republic. Association for Computational Linguistics.

Kyle Gorman and Steven Bedrick. 2019. We need to talk about standard splits. In *Proceedings of the 57th Annual Meeting of the Association for Computational Linguistics*, pages 2786–2791, Florence, Italy. Association for Computational Linguistics.

Matthew R. Gormley, Mo Yu, and Mark Dredze. 2015. Improved relation extraction with feature-rich compositional embedding models. In *Proceedings of the 2015 Conference on Empirical Methods in Natural Language Processing*, pages 1774–1784, Lisbon, Portugal. Association for Computational Linguistics.

Ralph Grishman. 2012. Information extraction: Capabilities and challenges.

Zhijiang Guo, Yan Zhang, and Wei Lu. 2019. Attention guided graph convolutional networks for relation extraction. In *Proceedings of the 57th Annual Meeting of the Association for Computational Linguistics*, pages 241–251, Florence, Italy. Association for Computational Linguistics.

Xu Han, Hao Zhu, Pengfei Yu, Ziyun Wang, Yuan Yao, Zhiyuan Liu, and Maosong Sun. 2018. FewRel: A large-scale supervised few-shot relation classification dataset with state-of-the-art evaluation. In *Proceedings of the 2018 Conference on Empirical Methods in Natural Language Processing*, pages 4803–4809, Brussels, Belgium. Association for Computational Linguistics.

Iris Hendrickx, Su Nam Kim, Zornitsa Kozareva, Preslav Nakov, Diarmuid Ó Séaghdha, Sebastian Padó, Marco Pennacchiotti, Lorenza Romano, and Stan Szpakowicz. 2010. SemEval-2010 task 8: Multi-way classification of semantic relations between pairs of nominals. In *Proceedings of the 5th International Workshop on Semantic Evaluation*, pages 33–38, Uppsala, Sweden. Association for Computational Linguistics.

Kevin Huang, Peng Qi, Guangtao Wang, Tengyu Ma, and Jing Huang. 2021a. Entity and evidence guided document-level relation extraction. In *Proceedings of the 6th Workshop on Representation Learning for NLP (RepL4NLP-2021)*, pages 307–315, Online. Association for Computational Linguistics.

Quzhe Huang, Shengqi Zhu, Yansong Feng, Yuan Ye, Yuxuan Lai, and Dongyan Zhao. 2021b. Three sentences are all you need: Local path enhanced document relation extraction. In *Proceedings of the 59th Annual Meeting of the Association for Computational Linguistics and the 11th International Joint Conference on Natural Language Processing (Volume 2: Short Papers)*, pages 998–1004, Online. Association for Computational Linguistics.

Wei Jia, Dai Dai, Xinyan Xiao, and Hua Wu. 2019. ARNOR: Attention regularization based noise reduction for distant supervision relation classification. In *Proceedings of the 57th Annual Meeting of the Association for Computational Linguistics*, pages 1399–1408, Florence, Italy. Association for Computational Linguistics.

Nora Kassner, Philipp Dufter, and Hinrich Schütze. 2021. Multilingual LAMA: Investigating knowledge in multilingual pretrained language models. In *Proceedings of the 16th Conference of the European Chapter of the Association for Computational Linguistics: Main Volume*, pages 3250–3258, Online. Association for Computational Linguistics.

Ruben Kruiper, Julian Vincent, Jessica Chen-Burger, Marc Desmulliez, and Ioannis Konstas. 2020. In layman's terms: Semi-open relation extraction from scientific texts. In *Proceedings of the 58th Annual Meeting of the Association for Computational Linguistics*, pages 1489–1500, Online. Association for Computational Linguistics.

Xiaoya Li, Fan Yin, Zijun Sun, Xiayu Li, Arianna Yuan, Duo Chai, Mingxin Zhou, and Jiwei Li. 2019. Entity-relation extraction as multi-turn question answering. In *Proceedings of the 57th Annual Meeting of the Association for Computational Linguistics*, pages 1340–1350, Florence, Italy. Association for Computational Linguistics.

Yankai Lin, Zhiyuan Liu, and Maosong Sun. 2017. Neural relation extraction with multi-lingual attention. In *Proceedings of the 55th Annual Meeting of the Association for Computational Linguistics (Volume 1: Long Papers)*, pages 34–43, Vancouver, Canada. Association for Computational Linguistics.

Tom Lippincott, Diarmuid Ó Séaghdha, Lin Sun, and Anna Korhonen. 2010. Exploring variation across biomedical subdomains. In *Proceedings of the 23rd International Conference on Computational Linguistics (Coling 2010)*, pages 689–697, Beijing, China. Coling 2010 Organizing Committee.

Kang Liu. 2020. A survey on neural relation extraction. *Science China Technological Sciences*, 63(10):1971–1989.

Zihan Liu, Yan Xu, Tiezheng Yu, Wenliang Dai, Ziwei Ji, Samuel Cahyawijaya, Andrea Madotto, and Pascale Fung. 2021. Crossner: Evaluating cross-domain named entity recognition. *Proceedings of the AAAI Conference on Artificial Intelligence*, 35(15):13452–13460.

Yi Luan, Luheng He, Mari Ostendorf, and Hannaneh Hajishirzi. 2018. Multi-task identification of entities, relations, and coreference for scientific knowledge graph construction. In *Proceedings of the 2018 Conference on Empirical Methods in Natural Language Processing*, pages 3219–3232, Brussels, Belgium. Association for Computational Linguistics.

Yuan Luo, Özlem Uzuner, and Peter Szolovits. 2016. Bridging semantics and syntax with graph algorithms—state-of-the-art of extracting biomedical relations. *Briefings in Bioinformatics*, 18(1):160–178.

Ruotian Ma, Tao Gui, Linyang Li, Qi Zhang, Xuanjing Huang, and Yaqian Zhou. 2021. SENT: Sentence-level distant relation extraction via negative training. In *Proceedings of the 59th Annual Meeting of the Association for Computational Linguistics and the 11th International Joint Conference on Natural Language Processing (Volume 1: Long Papers)*, pages 6201–6213, Online. Association for Computational Linguistics.

Puneet Mathur, Rajiv Jain, Franck Dernoncourt, Vlad Morariu, Quan Hung Tran, and Dinesh Manocha. 2021. TIMERS: Document-level temporal relation extraction. In *Proceedings of the 59th Annual Meeting of the Association for Computational Linguistics and the 11th International Joint Conference on Natural Language Processing (Volume 2: Short Papers)*, pages 524–533, Online. Association for Computational Linguistics.

Mike Mintz, Steven Bills, Rion Snow, and Daniel Jurafsky. 2009. Distant supervision for relation extraction without labeled data. In *Proceedings of the Joint Conference of the 47th Annual Meeting of the ACL and the 4th International Joint Conference on Natural Language Processing of the AFNLP*, pages 1003–1011, Suntec, Singapore. Association for Computational Linguistics.

Makoto Miwa and Mohit Bansal. 2016. End-to-end relation extraction using LSTMs on sequences and tree structures. In *Proceedings of the 54th Annual Meeting of the Association for Computational Linguistics (Volume 1: Long Papers)*, pages 1105–1116, Berlin, Germany. Association for Computational Linguistics.

Guoshun Nan, Zhijiang Guo, Ivan Sekulic, and Wei Lu. 2020. Reasoning with latent structure refinement for document-level relation extraction. In *Proceedings of the 58th Annual Meeting of the Association for Computational Linguistics*, pages 1546–1557, Online. Association for Computational Linguistics.

Vivi Nastase, Stan Szpakowicz, Preslav Nakov, and Diarmuid Ó Séagdha. 2021. Semantic relations between nominals. *Synthesis Lectures on Human Language Technologies*, 14(1):1–234.

Thien Huu Nguyen and Ralph Grishman. 2015. Relation extraction: Perspective from convolutional neural networks. In *Proceedings of the 1st Workshop on Vector Space Modeling for Natural Language Processing*, pages 39–48, Denver, Colorado. Association for Computational Linguistics.

Abiola Obamuyide and Andreas Vlachos. 2019. Meta-learning improves lifelong relation extraction. In *Proceedings of the 4th Workshop on Representation Learning for NLP (RepL4NLP-2019)*, pages 224–229, Florence, Italy. Association for Computational Linguistics.

Sachin Pawar, Girish K Palshikar, and Pushpak Bhattacharyya. 2017. Relation extraction: A survey. *arXiv preprint arXiv:1712.05191*.

Matthew E. Peters, Mark Neumann, Mohit Iyyer, Matt Gardner, Christopher Clark, Kenton Lee, and Luke Zettlemoyer. 2018. Deep contextualized word representations. In *Proceedings of the 2018 Conference of the North American Chapter of the Association for Computational Linguistics: Human Language Technologies, Volume 1 (Long Papers)*, pages 2227–2237, New Orleans, Louisiana. Association for Computational Linguistics.

Slav Petrov and Ryan McDonald. 2012. Overview of the 2012 shared task on parsing the web. In *First Workshop on Syntactic Analysis of Non-Canonical Language (SANCL), NAACL-HLT*.

Van-Thuy Phi, Joan Santoso, Masashi Shimbo, and Yuji Matsumoto. 2018. Ranking-based automatic seed selection and noise reduction for weakly supervised relation extraction. In *Proceedings of the 56th Annual Meeting of the Association for Computational Linguistics (Volume 2: Short Papers)*, pages 89–95, Melbourne, Australia. Association for Computational Linguistics.

Barbara Plank and Alessandro Moschitti. 2013. Embedding semantic similarity in tree kernels for domain adaptation of relation extraction. In *Proceedings of the 51st Annual Meeting of the Association for Computational Linguistics (Volume 1: Long Papers)*, pages 1498–1507, Sofia, Bulgaria. Association for Computational Linguistics.

Amir Pouran Ben Veyseh, Franck Dernoncourt, Dejing Dou, and Thien Huu Nguyen. 2020. Exploiting the syntax-model consistency for neural relation extraction. In *Proceedings of the 58th Annual Meeting of the Association for Computational Linguistics*, pages 8021–8032, Online. Association for Computational Linguistics.

Sameer Pradhan, Alessandro Moschitti, Nianwen Xue, Hwee Tou Ng, Anders Björkelund, Olga Uryupina, Yuchen Zhang, and Zhi Zhong. 2013. Towards robust linguistic analysis using OntoNotes. In *Proceedings of the Seventeenth Conference on Computational Natural Language Learning*, pages 143–152, Sofia, Bulgaria. Association for Computational Linguistics.

S. Pyysalo, R. SÃ¦tre, J. Tsujii, and T. Salakoski. 2008. Why biomedical relation extraction results are incomparable and what to do about it. In *Proceedings of the Third International Symposium on Semantic Mining in Biomedicine (SMBM 2008)*, pages 149–152.

Sebastian Riedel, Limin Yao, and Andrew McCallum. 2010. Modeling relations and their mentions without labeled text. In *Joint European Conference on Machine Learning and Knowledge Discovery in Databases*, pages 148–163, Berlin, Heidelberg. Springer Berlin Heidelberg.

Dan Roth and Wen-tau Yih. 2004. A linear programming formulation for global inference in natural language tasks. In *Proceedings of the Eighth Conference on Computational Natural Language Learning (CoNLL-2004) at HLT-NAACL 2004*, pages 1–8, Boston, Massachusetts, USA. Association for Computational Linguistics.

Ofer Sabo, Yanai Elazar, Yoav Goldberg, and Ido Dagan. 2021. Revisiting Few-shot Relation Classification: Evaluation Data and Classification Schemes. *Transactions of the Association for Computational Linguistics*, 9:691–706.

Alessandro Seganti, Klaudia Firląg, Helena Skowronska, Michał Satława, and Piotr Andruszkiewicz. 2021. Multilingual entity and relation extraction dataset and model. In *Proceedings of the 16th Conference of the European Chapter of the Association for Computational Linguistics: Main Volume*, pages 1946–1955, Online. Association for Computational Linguistics.

Hamed Shahbazi, Xiaoli Fern, Reza Ghaeini, and Prasad Tadepalli. 2020. Relation extraction with explanation. In *Proceedings of the 58th Annual Meeting of the Association for Computational Linguistics*, pages 6488–6494, Online. Association for Computational Linguistics.

Victor S. Sheng, Foster Provost, and Panagiotis G. Ipeirotis. 2008. Get another label? improving data quality and data mining using multiple, noisy labelers. In *Proceedings of the 14th ACM SIGKDD International Conference on Knowledge Discovery and Data Mining*, KDD '08, page 614–622, New York, NY, USA. Association for Computing Machinery.

Anders Søgaard, Sebastian Ebert, Jasmijn Bastings, and Katja Filippova. 2021. We need to talk about random splits. In *Proceedings of the 16th Conference of the European Chapter of the Association for Computational Linguistics: Main Volume*, pages 1823–1832, Online. Association for Computational Linguistics.

Bruno Taillé, Vincent Guigue, Geoffrey Scoutheeten, and Patrick Gallinari. 2020. Let's Stop Incorrect Comparisons in End-to-end Relation Extraction! In *Proceedings of the 2020 Conference on Empirical Methods in Natural Language Processing (EMNLP)*, pages 3689–3701, Online. Association for Computational Linguistics.

Jialong Tang, Hongyu Lin, Meng Liao, Yaojie Lu, Xianpei Han, Le Sun, Weijian Xie, and Jin Xu. 2021. From discourse to narrative: Knowledge projection for event relation extraction. In *Proceedings of the 59th Annual Meeting of the Association for Computational Linguistics and the 11th International Joint Conference on Natural Language Processing (Volume 1: Long Papers)*, pages 732–742, Online. Association for Computational Linguistics.

Yuanhe Tian, Guimin Chen, Yan Song, and Xiang Wan. 2021. Dependency-driven relation extraction with attentive graph convolutional networks. In *Proceedings of the 59th Annual Meeting of the Association for Computational Linguistics and the 11th International Joint Conference on Natural Language Processing (Volume 1: Long Papers)*, pages 4458–4471, Online. Association for Computational Linguistics.

Bayu Distiawan Trisedya, Gerhard Weikum, Jianzhong Qi, and Rui Zhang. 2019. Neural relation extraction for knowledge base enrichment. In *Proceedings of the 57th Annual Meeting of the Association for Computational Linguistics*, pages 229–240, Florence, Italy. Association for Computational Linguistics.

Dennis Ulmer. 2021. deep-significance: Easy and Better Significance Testing for Deep Neural Networks. Https://github.com/Kaleidophon/deep-significance.

Alexandra N. Uma, Tommaso Fornaciari, Dirk Hovy, Silviu Paun, Barbara Plank, and Massimo Poesio. 2021. Learning from disagreement: A survey. *The Journal of Artificial Intelligence Research*, Forthcoming.

Rob van der Goot, Ahmet Üstün, Alan Ramponi, Ibrahim Sharaf, and Barbara Plank. 2021. Massive choice, ample tasks (MaChAmp): A toolkit for multi-task learning in NLP. In *Proceedings of the 16th Conference of the European Chapter of the Association for Computational Linguistics: System Demonstrations*, pages 176–197, Online. Association for Computational Linguistics.

Jue Wang and Wei Lu. 2020. Two are better than one: Joint entity and relation extraction with table-sequence encoders. In *Proceedings of the 2020 Conference on Empirical Methods in Natural Language Processing (EMNLP)*, pages 1706–1721, Online. Association for Computational Linguistics.

Yijun Wang, Changzhi Sun, Yuanbin Wu, Hao Zhou, Lei Li, and Junchi Yan. 2021. UniRE: A unified label space for entity relation extraction. In *Proceedings of the 59th Annual Meeting of the Association for Computational Linguistics and the 11th International Joint Conference on Natural Language Processing (Volume 1: Long Papers)*, pages 220–231, Online. Association for Computational Linguistics.

Adina Williams, Nikita Nangia, and Samuel Bowman. 2018. A broad-coverage challenge corpus for sentence understanding through inference. In *Proceedings of the 2018 Conference of the North American Chapter of the Association for Computational Linguistics: Human Language Technologies, Volume 1 (Long Papers)*, pages 1112–1122, New Orleans, Louisiana. Association for Computational Linguistics.

Chenhao Xie, Jiaqing Liang, Jingping Liu, Chengsong Huang, Wenhao Huang, and Yanghua Xiao. 2021. Revisiting the negative data of distantly supervised relation extraction. In *Proceedings of the 59th Annual Meeting of the Association for Computational*

Linguistics and the 11th International Joint Conference on Natural Language Processing (Volume 1: Long Papers), pages 3572–3581, Online. Association for Computational Linguistics.

Shan Yang, Yongfei Zhang, Guanglin Niu, Qinghua Zhao, and Shiliang Pu. 2021. Entity concept-enhanced few-shot relation extraction. In *Proceedings of the 59th Annual Meeting of the Association for Computational Linguistics and the 11th International Joint Conference on Natural Language Processing (Volume 2: Short Papers)*, pages 987–991, Online. Association for Computational Linguistics.

Yuan Yao, Deming Ye, Peng Li, Xu Han, Yankai Lin, Zhenghao Liu, Zhiyuan Liu, Lixin Huang, Jie Zhou, and Maosong Sun. 2019. DocRED: A large-scale document-level relation extraction dataset. In *Proceedings of the 57th Annual Meeting of the Association for Computational Linguistics*, pages 764–777, Florence, Italy. Association for Computational Linguistics.

Wei Ye, Bo Li, Rui Xie, Zhonghao Sheng, Long Chen, and Shikun Zhang. 2019. Exploiting entity BIO tag embeddings and multi-task learning for relation extraction with imbalanced data. In *Proceedings of the 57th Annual Meeting of the Association for Computational Linguistics*, pages 1351–1360, Florence, Italy. Association for Computational Linguistics.

Dian Yu, Kai Sun, Claire Cardie, and Dong Yu. 2020. Dialogue-based relation extraction. In *Proceedings of the 58th Annual Meeting of the Association for Computational Linguistics*, pages 4927–4940, Online. Association for Computational Linguistics.

Tao Yu, Rui Zhang, Michihiro Yasunaga, Yi Chern Tan, Xi Victoria Lin, Suyi Li, Heyang Er, Irene Li, Bo Pang, Tao Chen, Emily Ji, Shreya Dixit, David Proctor, Sungrok Shim, Jonathan Kraft, Vincent Zhang, Caiming Xiong, Richard Socher, and Dragomir Radev. 2019. SParC: Cross-domain semantic parsing in context. In *Proceedings of the 57th Annual Meeting of the Association for Computational Linguistics*, pages 4511–4523, Florence, Italy. Association for Computational Linguistics.

Klim Zaporojets, Johannes Deleu, Chris Develder, and Thomas Demeester. 2021. Dwie: An entity-centric dataset for multi-task document-level information extraction. *Information Processing Management*, 58(4):102563.

Daojian Zeng, Kang Liu, Siwei Lai, Guangyou Zhou, and Jun Zhao. 2014. Relation classification via convolutional deep neural network. In *Proceedings of COLING 2014, the 25th International Conference on Computational Linguistics: Technical Papers*, pages 2335–2344, Dublin, Ireland. Dublin City University and Association for Computational Linguistics.

Meishan Zhang, Yue Zhang, and Guohong Fu. 2017a. End-to-end neural relation extraction with global optimization. In *Proceedings of the 2017 Conference on Empirical Methods in Natural Language Processing*, pages 1730–1740, Copenhagen, Denmark. Association for Computational Linguistics.

Yuhao Zhang, Victor Zhong, Danqi Chen, Gabor Angeli, and Christopher D. Manning. 2017b. Position-aware attention and supervised data improve slot filling. In *Proceedings of the 2017 Conference on Empirical Methods in Natural Language Processing*, pages 35–45, Copenhagen, Denmark. Association for Computational Linguistics.

Zexuan Zhong and Danqi Chen. 2021. A frustratingly easy approach for entity and relation extraction. In *Proceedings of the 2021 Conference of the North American Chapter of the Association for Computational Linguistics: Human Language Technologies*, pages 50–61, Online. Association for Computational Linguistics.

Hao Zhu, Yankai Lin, Zhiyuan Liu, Jie Fu, Tat-Seng Chua, and Maosong Sun. 2019. Graph neural networks with generated parameters for relation extraction. In *Proceedings of the 57th Annual Meeting of the Association for Computational Linguistics*, pages 1331–1339, Florence, Italy. Association for Computational Linguistics.

Qi Zhu, Kaili Huang, Zheng Zhang, Xiaoyan Zhu, and Minlie Huang. 2020a. CrossWOZ: A large-scale Chinese cross-domain task-oriented dialogue dataset. *Transactions of the Association for Computational Linguistics*, 8:281–295.

Wanrong Zhu, Xin Wang, Pradyumna Narayana, Kazoo Sone, Sugato Basu, and William Yang Wang. 2020b. Towards understanding sample variance in visually grounded language generation: Evaluations and observations. In *Proceedings of the 2020 Conference on Empirical Methods in Natural Language Processing (EMNLP)*, pages 8806–8811, Online. Association for Computational Linguistics.

Appendix

A SciERC Conference Division

The metadata relative to the IDs of the SciERC abstracts contains information about the proceedings in which the papers have been published. We use this information to divide SciERC into four sub-domains as shown in Table 9.

Conference	# abs
Artificial Intelligence - Machine Learning (AI-ML)	52
NeurIPS Neural Information Processing Systems	20
IJCAI International Joint Conference on Artificial Intelligence	14
ICML International Conference on Machine Learning	10
AAAI Association for the Advancement of Artificial Intelligence	8
Computer Vision (CV)	105
CVPR Conference on Computer Vision and Pattern Recognition	66
ICCV International Conference on Computer Vision	23
ECCV European Conference on Computer Vision	16
Speech	35
INTERSPEECH Annual Conference of the International Speech Communication Association	25
ICASSP International Conference on Acoustics, Speech, and Signal Processing	10
Natural Language Processing (NLP)	308
ACL Association for Computational Linguistics	307
IJCNLP International Joint Conference on Natural Language Processing	1

Table 9: SciERC division into conferences and relative amount of abstracts for each of them.

B Data Analysis

Figure 4 reports the gold label distribution over SemEval-2018 and SciERC respectively.

Figure 5, instead, contains the gold label distributions of SciERC sub-domains over the five matching labels between the two datasets (see Table 3).

C Model Details

Our RC model is a CNN with four layers (Nguyen and Grishman, 2015). The layers consist of lookup embedding layers for word embeddings and entity position information (detailed below), convolutional layers with n-gram kernel sizes (2, 3 and

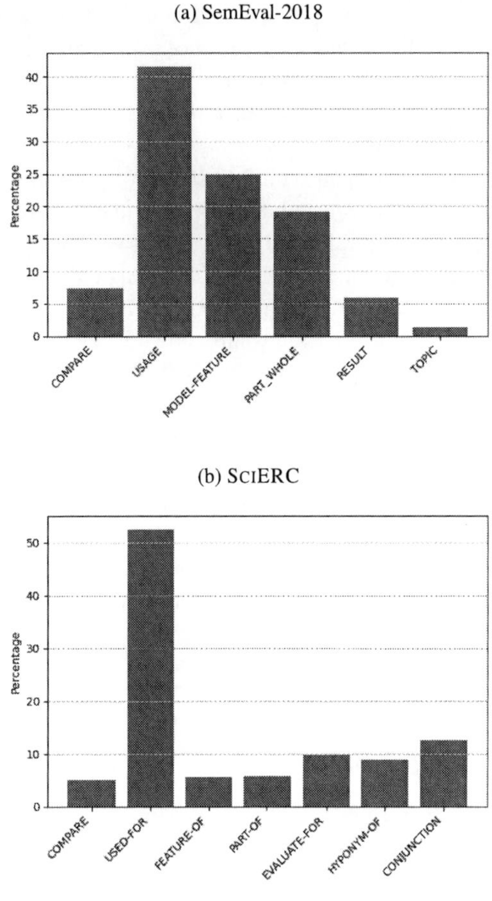

Figure 4: Gold label distribution in the SemEval-2018 sub-task (1.1) and SciERC datasets.

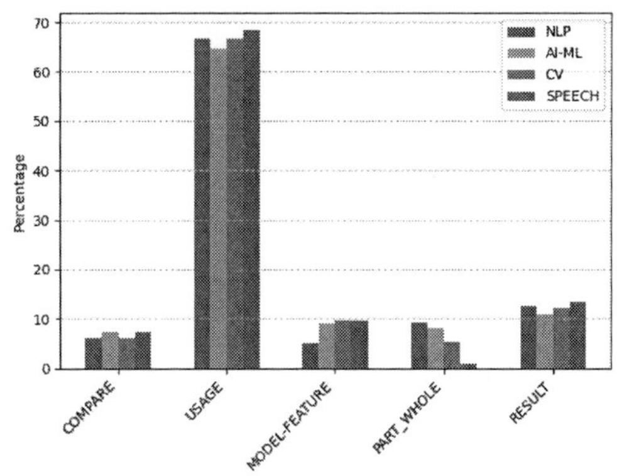

Figure 5: Gold label distribution of the five considered relations over SciERC sub-domains.

4), a max-pooling layer and a linear softmax relation classification layer with dropout of 0.5. Each input to the network is a sentence containing a pair of entities—which positions in the sentence are given—and a label within R, the set of five considered relations.

We experiment with three types of pre-trained *word embeddings*: one non-contextualized, fastText (Bojanowski et al., 2017), and two contextualized representations, BERT (Devlin et al., 2019) and the domain-specific SciBERT (Beltagy et al., 2019). For word split into subword-tokens, we adopt the strategy of keeping only the first embedding for each token. For every token we also consider two *position embeddings* following Nguyen and Grishman (2015). Each of them encodes the relative distance of the token from each of the two entities involved in the relation.

Hyperparameters were determined by tuning the model on a held-out development set.

All experiments were ran on an NVIDIA® A100 SXM4 40 GB GPU and an AMD EPYC™ 7662 64-Core CPU.

D Significance Testing

We compare our setups using Almost Stochastic Order (ASO; Dror et al., 2019).[11] Given the results over multiple seeds, the ASO test determines whether there is a stochastic order. The method computes a score (ϵ_{min}) which represents how far the first is from being significantly better in respect to the second. The possible scenarios are therefore *(a)* $\epsilon_{min} = 0.0$ (*truly stochastic dominance*) and *(b)* $\epsilon_{min} < 0.5$ (*almost stochastic dominance*). Table 10 reports the ASO scores with a confidence level of $\alpha = 0.05$ adjusted by using the Bonferroni correction (Bonferroni, 1936). See Section 5 for the setup details.

E Transformer setups

The MaChAmp toolkit (van der Goot et al., 2021) allows for a flexible amount of textual inputs (separated by the `[SEP]` token) to train the transformer and test the fine-tuned model on. We used SciBERT (Beltagy et al., 2019) and tested the following input configurations:

1. The two entities:
   [*ent-1* `[SEP]` *ent-2*]

[11] Implementation by Ulmer (2021).

	2A [fastText]*	2A w/o CR [fastText]*	2A w/o CR [BERT]*	2A w/o CR [SciBERT]*	2A [SciBERT]†	2A w/o CR [SciBERT]†
2A [fastText]*	-	1.0	**0.0**	1.0	1.0	1.0
2A w/o CR [fastText]*	**0.0**	-	**0.0**	1.0	1.0	1.0
2A w/o CR [BERT]*	1.0	1.0	-	1.0	1.0	1.0
2A w/o CR [SciBERT]*	**0.0**	**0.0**	**0.0**	-	1.0	1.0
2A [SciBERT]†	**0.0**	**0.0**	**0.0**	**0.0**	-	1.0
2A w/o CR [SciBERT]†	**0.0**	**0.0**	**0.0**	**0.0**	**0.0**	-

Table 10: ASO scores of the main experimental setups described in Section 5. (*) CNN model. (†) full fine-tuned transformer model. Read as row → column.

↓Test | Input Setup →	①	②	③	④	⑤
SemEval NLP	58.15	42.08	77.79	74.85	75.12
SciERC NLP	51.42	42.16	69.90	69.09	71.32
SciERC AI-ML	54.63	40.35	76.80	75.08	74.93
SciERC CV	53.16	41.09	76.11	74.73	74.21
SciERC SPEECH	49.59	40.42	67.21	66.78	67.56
avg.	53.39	41.22	**73.56**	72.11	72.63

Table 11: Macro F1-scores of the RC using SciBERT (Beltagy et al., 2019) within the MaChAmp toolkit (van der Goot et al., 2021). Setups 1-5 described in Appendix E.

2. The sentence containing the two entities:
   [*sentence*]

3. The two entities and the sentence containing them:
   [*ent-1* `[SEP]` *ent-2* `[SEP]` *sentence*]

4. For the third setup, we introduce a marker between the two entities, resulting in a 2-inputs configuration:
   [*ent-1* `[MARK]` *ent-2* `[SEP]` *sentence*]

5. Finally—following Baldini Soares et al. (2019)—we augment the input sentence with four word pieces to mark the beginning and the end of each entity mention (`[E1-START]`, `[E1-END]`, `[E2-START]`, `[E2-END]`):
   [*sentence-with-entity-markers*]

Table 11 reports the results of the experiments using MaChAmp on the setups described above.

F Scientific Sub-domain Analysis

Figure 7 contains the confusion matrices of the CNN trained with SciBERT for the AI-ML, CV and SPEECH sub-domains. For fair comparison between the different data amounts the numbers reported are percentages.

G Conference Classifier

Figure 6 represents the confusion matrix relative to the conference classifier described in Section 5.4.

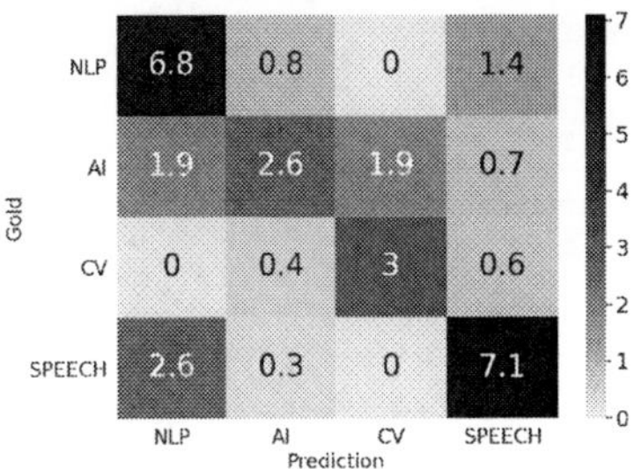

Figure 6: Confusion matrix of the conference classification experiment. The numbers reported are the average over three runs on different seeds.

(a) AI-ML (52 abstracts)

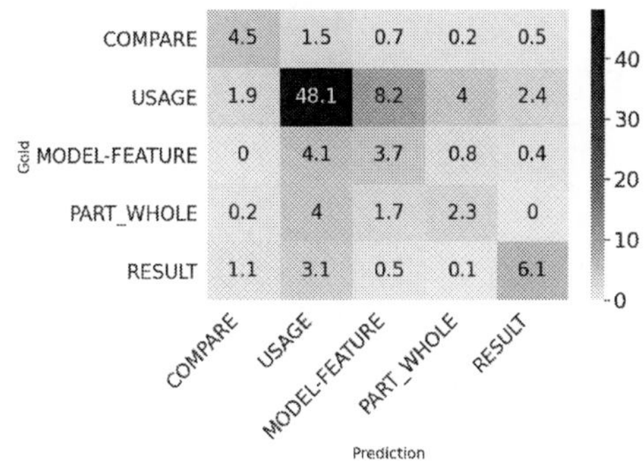

(b) CV (105 abstracts)

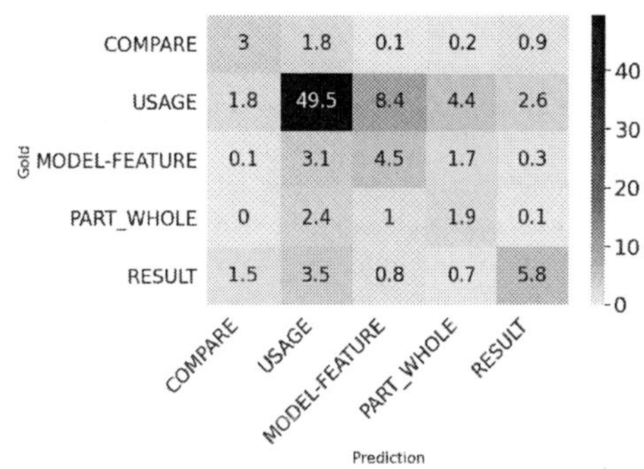

(c) SPEECH (35 abstracts)

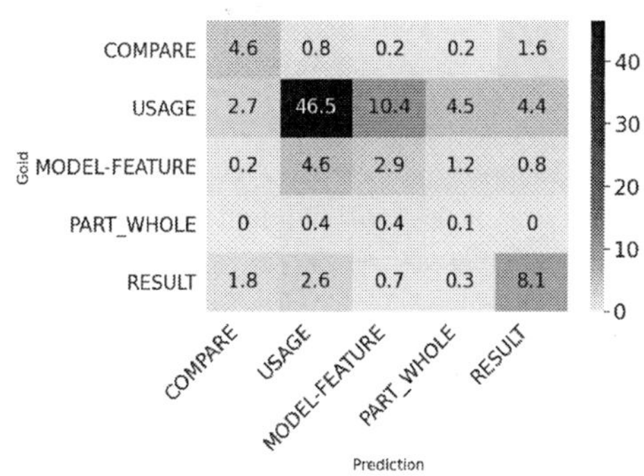

Figure 7: Percentage confusion matrices of the CNN on SciERC sub-domains.

Logical Inference for Counting on Semi-structured Tables

Tomoya Kurosawa and **Hitomi Yanaka**
The University of Tokyo
{kurosawa-tomoya, hyanaka}@is.s.u-tokyo.ac.jp

Abstract

Recently, the Natural Language Inference (NLI) task has been studied for semi-structured tables that do not have a strict format. Although neural approaches have achieved high performance in various types of NLI, including NLI between semi-structured tables and texts, they still have difficulty in performing a numerical type of inference, such as counting. To handle a numerical type of inference, we propose a logical inference system for reasoning between semi-structured tables and texts. We use logical representations as meaning representations for tables and texts and use model checking to handle a numerical type of inference between texts and tables. To evaluate the extent to which our system can perform inference with numerical comparatives, we make an evaluation protocol that focuses on numerical understanding between semi-structured tables and texts in English. We show that our system can more robustly perform inference between tables and texts that requires numerical understanding compared with current neural approaches.

1 Introduction

Natural Language Inference (NLI) (Dagan et al., 2006) is one of the most fundamental tasks to determine whether a premise entails a hypothesis. Recently, researchers have developed benchmarks not only for texts but for other kinds of resources as well, a table being one example. Previous studies have targeted database-style structured tables (Pasupat and Liang, 2015; Wiseman et al., 2017; Krishnamurthy et al., 2017) and semi-structured tables, such as the infoboxes in Wikipedia (Lebret et al., 2016; Gupta et al., 2020). Our focus here is on the NLI task on semi-structured tables, where we handle a semi-structured table as a premise and a sentence as a hypothesis.

In Figure 1, for example, we consider the semi-structured table as a given premise and take *Joe Biden was born in November* as Hypothesis 1. We can conclude that Hypothesis 1 is entailed by the table. A semi-structured table has only two columns and describes a single object, which is indicated in the title. We call elements of the first column, such as **Political Party**, *keys*, each of which has an associated *value* in the second column such as *Democratic* (*1969–present*). Pairs of keys and values are called *rows*. It is relatively difficult to understand the information contained in infobox tables because (i) values are not limited to words or phrases, and sometimes whole sentences, and (ii) a row can contain more than one type of information, such as the birthday and birthplace in the **Born** row.

Joe Biden	
Born	Joseph Robinette Biden Jr. November 20, 1942 (age 79) Scranton, Pennsylvania, U.S.
Political party	Democratic (1969–present)
Spouse(s)	Neilia Hunter (m. 1966; died 1972) Jill Jacobs (m. 1977)

Hypothesis 1: Joe Biden was born in November.
Hypothesis 2: Joe Biden has had more than two wives.

Figure 1: A semi-structured table describing Joe Biden[1] and two hypothesis sentences. This table entails Hypothesis 1 and contradicts Hypothesis 2.

In recent years, modern neural network (NN) approaches have achieved high performance in many Natural Language Understanding benchmarks, such as BERT (Devlin et al., 2019). NN-based approaches (Neeraja et al., 2021) have also achieved high accuracy on the NLI task between semi-structured tables and texts, but previous studies have questioned whether NN-based models truly understand the various linguistic phenomena

[1]The table was retrieved from https://en.wikipedia.org/wiki/Joe_Biden on February 25, 2022. Some rows have been removed to save space.

Proceedings of the 60th Annual Meeting of the Association for Computational Linguistics
Student Research Workshop, pages 84 - 96
May 22-27, 2022 ©2022 Association for Computational Linguistics

(Jia and Liang, 2017; Naik et al., 2018; Rozen et al., 2019; Ravichander et al., 2019; Richardson et al., 2020). These studies have shown that NN-based approaches have failed to achieve a high performance in numerical reasoning.

In this paper, we focus on a numerical type of inference on semi-structured tables, which requires understanding the number of items in a table as well as numerical comparisons. Numerical comparatives are among the more challenging linguistic phenomena that involve generalized quantifiers. For example, the phrase *more than* in Hypothesis 2 in Figure 1 is a numerical comparative and compares two and the number of wives. For dealing with numerical comparatives, Haruta et al. (2020a,b) achieved high performance by developing a logical inference system based on formal semantics. However, Haruta et al. (2020a,b) concentrated on the inference between texts only, and inference systems that reliably perform inference between tables and texts involving numerical comparatives have not yet been developed.

Thus, we aim to develop a logical inference system between semi-structured tables and texts, especially for numerical reasoning. While previous work (Pasupat and Liang, 2015; Wiseman et al., 2017; Krishnamurthy et al., 2017) has provided semantic parsers of constructing query languages such as SQLs for question answering on database-style tables, we present logical representations for semi-structured tables to enable a numerical type of inference on semi-structured tables. Furthermore, the existing NLI dataset for semi-structured tables (Gupta et al., 2020) does not contain sufficient test cases for understanding numerical comparatives. Thus, there is a need for an evaluation protocol that investigates the numerical reasoning skills of NLI systems for semi-structured tables.

Given this background, our main contributions in this paper are the following:

1. We propose a logical inference system for handling numerical comparatives that is based on formal semantics for NLI between semi-structured tables and texts.

2. We provide an evaluation protocol and dataset that focus on numerical comparatives between semi-structured tables and texts.

3. We demonstrate the increased performance of our inference system compared with previous NN models on the NLI dataset, focusing on numerical comparatives between semi-structured tables and texts.

Our system and dataset will be publicly available at `https://github.com/ynklab/sst_count`.

2 Related Work and Background

This section explains the related work of logic-based NLI approaches and the background of model checking, which is used for inference between semi-structured tables and sentences in our proposed system.

2.1 Logic-based Approach

Based on the analysis of formal semantics, logic-based NLI approaches can handle a greater variety of linguistic phenomena than NN-based approaches can. Some logic-based NLI approaches using syntactic and semantic parsers based on formal semantics have been proposed (Bos, 2008; Abzianidze, 2015; Mineshima et al., 2015; Hu et al., 2020; Haruta et al., 2020a,b). These logic-based approaches can derive semantic representations of sentences involving linguistically challenging phenomena, such as generalized quantifiers and comparatives, based on Combinatory Categorial Grammar (CCG) (Steedman, 2000) syntactic analysis. CCG is often used in these approaches because it has a tiny number of combinatory rules, which is suitable for semantic composition from syntactic structures. In addition, robust CCG parsers are readily available (Clark and Curran, 2007; Yoshikawa et al., 2017).

Regarding logic-based approaches for inference other than inference between texts, Suzuki et al. (2019) proposed a logical inference system for inference between images and texts. Their system converts images to first-order logic (FOL) structures by using image datasets where structured representations of the images are annotated. They then get FOL formulas P for images from these structures along with the associated image captions. Hypothesis sentences are translated into FOL formulas H through the use of a semantic parser (Martínez-Gómez et al., 2016). For inference, they used automated theorem proving and sought to prove $P \vdash H$. Our proposed inference system between semi-structured tables and texts is inspired by Suzuki et al. (2019). While the previous system uses automated theorem proving for in-

$$
\begin{aligned}
D &= \{B_1, G_1, G_2\} \\
V &= \{(\textsc{alice}, \{G_1\}), (\textsc{bob}, \{B_1\}), (\textsc{cathy}, \{G_2\}), \\
&\quad (\textsc{boy}, \{B_1\}), (\textsc{girl}, \{G_1, G_2\}), \\
&\quad (\textsc{like}, \{(B_1, G_1), (B_1, G_2), (G_1, B_1)\})\}
\end{aligned}
$$

Logical formula	Output
$\exists x.\exists y.(\textsc{boy}(x) \wedge \textsc{like}(x, y))$	True
$\exists x.\exists y.(\textsc{girl}(x) \wedge \textsc{girl}(y) \wedge \textsc{like}(x, y))$	False
$\exists x.\exists y.(\textsc{cat}(y) \wedge \textsc{like}(x, y))$	Undefined

Figure 2: Outputs of model checking based on an example model and three formulas.

ference between images and texts, our system uses model checking to judge whether a given text is true under a given table, and it is expected to be a faster method.

2.2 Model Checking

We use model checking in the Natural Language Toolkit (NLTK) (Bird and Loper, 2004; Garrette and Klein, 2009) for making inference between tables and texts. This system judges a truth-value of an FOL formula based on FOL structures. An FOL structure (called *model*) is defined by a pair of the domain $\boldsymbol{D}$ and the valuation $\boldsymbol{V}$, where $\boldsymbol{D}$ is a finite set of variables and $\boldsymbol{V}$ is a finite set of functions. Each element of $\boldsymbol{V}$ is a pair of symbols, the name of the function and its domain.

Based on the model used, the system will return

- *true* if the FOL formula is satisfiable,
- *false* if the formula is unsatisfiable, and
- *undefined* if there is an undefined function in the formula.

Figure 2 shows outputs from model checking based on an example model and three formulas.

3 Method

3.1 System Overview

Figure 3 shows the overview of our proposed system. The system takes a table and a sentence as inputs and determines whether the table entails, contradicts, or is neutral toward the sentence. We represent the meaning of tables as FOL structures (see Section 3.2) and the meaning of sentences as FOL formulas (see Section 3.3). In the process of translating a table, we first make a filtered table, and then translate that table to an FOL structure.

In the process of translating a sentence, we convert the sentence to a CCG derivation tree using a CCG parser (Yoshikawa et al., 2017). Before parsing, we use a Named Entity Recognition (NER) system in spaCy[2] to identify a proper noun in sentences and add extra underscores to spaces and at the end of phrases so that such phrases can be categorized as one proper noun. This derivation tree is modified by a tree transformation so that it handles numerical expressions correctly. For the tree transformation, we use tsurgeon (Levy and Andrew, 2006) (see Appendix A for more details). We then construct semantic representations (FOL formulas) of the hypothesis sentences according to the CCG derivation tree. For semantic parsing based on CCG, we use ccg2lambda (Martínez-Gómez et al., 2016). As a result, we obtain an FOL formula representing the whole sentence.

We apply model checking between the FOL structure and the FOL formula for inference using NLTK with optimization (see Section 3.4). Under the FOL formula and the FOL structure, we assume

- *entailment* if our system returns *true*,
- *contradiction* if our system returns *false*, and
- *neutral* otherwise.

3.2 Meaning Representations for Tables

The top of the Figure 3 shows the processes of translating from premise tables to FOL models. We select the **Children** and **Parents** rows from the table (a) using rows filtering (see Section 3.2.1). Then, the filtered table (b) is translated into an FOL structure (c). In (c), have is a meta-predicate (see Section 3.2.2), a predicate connecting a title and other values.

3.2.1 Rows Filtering

To isolate rows from a premise table that are related to the hypothesis sentence, we apply Distracting Rows Removal (DRR), which was proposed by the previous approach (Neeraja et al., 2021). Since that approach was NN-based, a sentence vector representation was generated for each row in the table, and the original DRR was applied to the sentence representation. Then, the similarity score between each generated sentence and the hypothesis sentence was calculated. In this process, the previous approach used fastText (Joulin et al., 2016) to obtain the embedding vectors of words. They represented a hypothesis vector sequence of length p as $(\boldsymbol{h}_0, \boldsymbol{h}_1, \ldots, \boldsymbol{h}_{p-1})$ and an i-th row

[2] https://github.com/explosion/spaCy

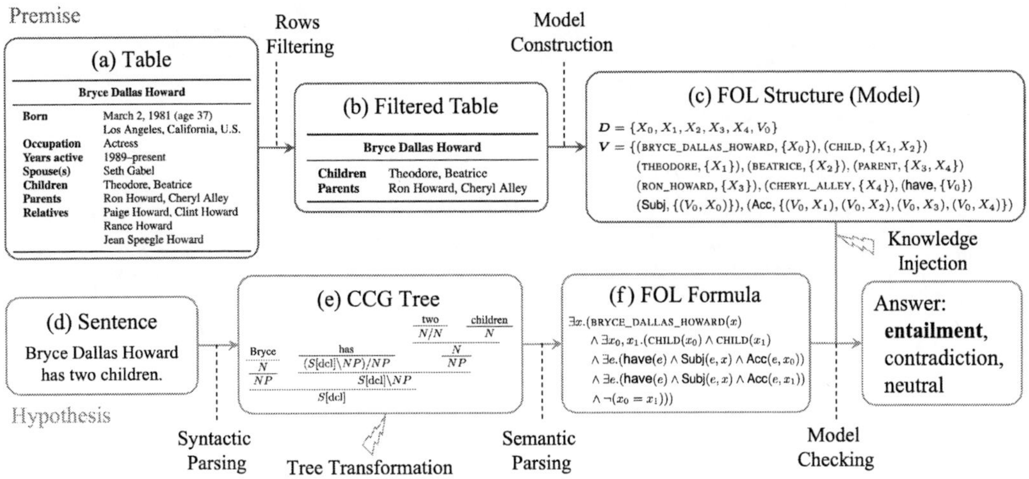

Figure 3: Overview of our proposed system with the example set for premise-hypothesis pair describing Bryce Dallas Howard. Our system returns *true* (*entailment*) for this pair.

vector sequence of length q as $(\boldsymbol{t}_0^i, \boldsymbol{t}_1^i, \ldots, \boldsymbol{t}_{q-1}^i)$. The similarity score was then calculating using

$$\text{SCORE}_i = \sum_{0 \leq j < p} \max_{0 \leq k < q} (\boldsymbol{h}_j \cdot \boldsymbol{t}_k^i)$$

Finally, the four rows which were the most similar were selected as the premise.

We follow most of the original DRR, but with a slight modification. First, since we directly represent a set of rows as FOL structures, we do not need to generate a sentence for each row. Thus, our system makes a simple concatenation (not using any words) of keys and values rather than a proper sentence. Also, to improve the similarity score calculation, we include numbers in a list of stopwords. In rows filtering, we select the top two most similar rows as the premise.

3.2.2 Model Construction

We construct a model based on the title and rows selected in Section 3.2.1. First, we define an entity variable X_0 that indicates a title. For keys and values in rows,

- when the key is a noun, we define entity variables X_i $(i \geq 1)$ indicating the value of each, and
- when the key is a verb, we define event variables V_j $(j \geq 1)$, whose subject is the title entity and whose accusative is the value of each.

To classify the parts of speech of the keys as nouns or verbs of the keys, we use spaCy for part-of-speech (POS) tagging. Keys are usually composed of nouns, verbs, adjectives, and prepositions, as shown in Figure 1. Since morphosyntactic ambiguity rarely appears in keys, we can classify keys into nouns and verbs by simply using a POS tagger.

We also introduce a meta-predicate have, with an event variable V_0. The subject of have is the variable X_0 indicating the title entity, and the accusatives are any of the entities in values.

3.2.3 Knowledge Injection

In some inference problems, an inference system needs to capture paraphrases (restatements of phrases that have the same meaning but are worded differently) in a premise table and a hypothesis sentence. For example, the function WIFE is injected in a model because *spouse* can be paraphrased as *wife*.

Using knowledge graphs to paraphrase some words in keys, we calculate the relatedness score between each word in keys (*key_term*) and each word in the hypothesis sentence (*hypo_term*). When the score exceeds the threshold (0.5), the *hypo_term* is introduced as a function, and the domain of which is the same as that of the *key_term*. In this process, we use the standard knowledge graph ConceptNet (Liu and Singh, 2004) to get the relatedness score between *key_term* and *hypo_term*. ConceptNet is a knowledge base that

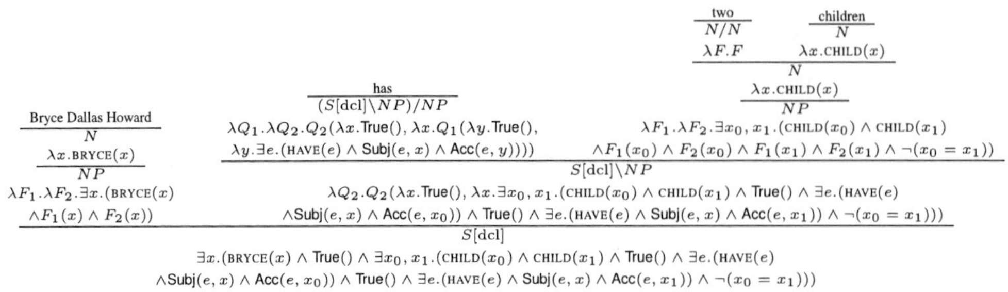

Figure 4: A derivation tree of *Bryce Dallas Howard has two children.* True is a predicate which always returns true regardless of arity and argument. The function BRYCE is an abbreviation for BRYCE_DALLAS_HOWARD_.

	Phrase	Logical formula
(a)	less than two books	$\lambda F_1 F_2.\forall x_0 x_1.((\textsc{book}(x_0) \wedge \textsc{book}(x_1) \wedge F_1(x_0) \wedge F_2(x_0) \wedge F_1(x_1) \wedge F_2(x_1)) \rightarrow (x_0 = x_1))$
(b)	at least two books	$\lambda F_1 F_2.\exists x_0 x_1.(\textsc{book}(x_0) \wedge \textsc{book}(x_1) \wedge F_1(x_0) \wedge F_2(x_0) \wedge F_1(x_1) \wedge F_2(x_1) \wedge \neg(x_0 = x_1))$
(c)	twice	$\lambda VQK.\exists e_1 e_2.(V(Q, \lambda e.(K(e) \wedge (e = e_1))) \wedge V(Q, \lambda e.(K(e) \wedge (e = e_2))) \wedge \neg(e_1 = e_2))$

Table 1: Examples of FOL formulas. F_1 and F_2 in (a) and (b) are unary predicates representing additional attributes of *books* on the bottom of the syntactic tree. In (c), V is a unary predicate for verb phrases, Q is a binary predicate for noun phrases, and K is a unary predicate for additional attributes of the event.

includes WordNet (Miller, 1995). We select ConceptNet because InfoTabS requires paraphrases based on not only hypernymy and hyponymy relations considered in WordNet, but also common knowledge. For example, to understand whether the hypothesis *Joe Biden has married twice* is entailed or not by Figure 1, we need to capture paraphrases between **Spouse** in the premise table and *marry* or *marriage* in the hypothesis.

3.3 Meaning Representations for Sentences

We construct meaning representations of hypothesis sentences based on the CCG derivation tree and Neo-Davidsonian Event Semantics (Parsons, 1990). ccg2lambda (Mineshima et al., 2015; Martínez-Gómez et al., 2016) is used to obtain meaning representations (FOL formulas) of hypothesis sentences based on CCG and λ-calculus. We extend the semantic template that defines lexical entries and schematic entries assigned to CCG categories in Mineshima et al. (2015) so that it can handle the numerical expressions for this task. In total, we add 251 extra lexical entries for the numerical expressions. Figure 4 shows an example of CCG derivation trees with meaning representations involving numerical expressions.

We focus on expressions related to numerical comparatives: *less than*, *no more than*, *exactly*, *at least*, *no less than*, and *more than*. We need to consider how to represent the meaning of a noun phrase (NP as its CCG category) that involves a numerical comparative and the number of entities, such as *less than two books*. The meaning of this phrase is analyzed in Table 1a. We also analyze the meaning of the phrase *at least two books* in Table 1b. The meaning representation of *exactly two books* is given as the composition of the representation of *at least two books* and the representation of *no more than two books* (van Benthem, 1986).

Adverbs of frequency such as *twice* describe the number of events, and their CCG category is $(S\backslash NP)\backslash(S\backslash NP)$. The semantic representation of *twice* is given in Table 1c.

In previous work, Haruta et al. (2020a,b) handled generalized quantifiers including numerical comparatives as binary predicates many. For example, the noun phrase *two cats* is represented as $\textsc{cat}(x) \wedge \mathsf{many}(x, 2)$, which indicates that x has the property of CAT and is composed of at least 2 entities. Since one of the aims of our system is to count the elements in the values of premise tables, our system assigns different entities for every word or phrase in the values.

3.4 Optimization of Model Checking

To optimize the process of model checking between tables and texts, we extend the implementation of model checking in NLTK. Figure 5 shows the program that evaluates the truth-value of $\exists x.A$. NLTK is implemented in Python and uses a set,

```
1: for y in D do
2:     if the truth-value of A[y/x] is true then
3:         return true
4:     end if
5: end for
6: return false
```

Figure 5: A program for evaluating the truth-value of $\exists x.A$.

Karachi	
Country	Pakistan
Province	Sindh
Metropolitan corporation	2011
City council	City Complex, Gulshan-e-Iqbal Town
Districts	Central Karachi, East Karachi, South Karachi, West Karachi, Korangi, Malir

Table 2: The premise table for the hypothesis *Karachi has a half dozen districts.*

which is an unordered collection, to represent the domain D of an FOL structure. When evaluating a for loop with a set (line 1 of Figure 5), an order of values in the set is not fixed for each run. To fix the order, we changed the implementation of the domain from a set to a list.

We also modify the original program for model checking in NLTK to make judgments faster. First, we sort the domain D to facilitate faster evaluation, giving $(X_0, X_1, \ldots, X_{n-1}, V_0, V_1, \ldots, V_{m-1})$, where n and m are the number of entities and events, respectively. It is sorted this way because the title variable X_0 is often the subject of the hypothesis sentence, which can be found at the top of the meaning representations.

Second, we use constraints for both the existential and universal quantifiers ($\exists$ and $\forall$). We do not substitute one variable for the other type of bounded variable in the evaluation scheme during quantification. Third, we use constraints for existential quantifiers ($\exists$) so as not to use the same variables for two or more bounded variables during substitution. We apply this restriction for only to entity variables because the same variable may be applied to different bounded variables for each event. In the process of model checking, we set a timeout of 10 seconds for judging whether the formula is satisfiable.

4 Experiments

We evaluate the extent to which our system can perform inference with numerical comparatives. We make an evaluation protocol that focuses on the numerical understanding between semi-structured tables and texts in English.

4.1 Dataset

We created a new dataset for the numerical understanding of semi-structured tables. There are two motivations for doing so. One is that the number of test cases for numerical understanding is limited to the previous NLI dataset for semi-structured tables, InfoTabS (Gupta et al., 2020). In addition, to evaluate whether NLI systems consistently perform inference with numerical comparatives, we need to analyze whether the prediction labels change correctly when the numbers in the hypothesis sentence are slightly changed from those in the original hypothesis sentence.

To create the dataset for numerical understanding of semi-structured tables, we first manually extracted 105 examples involving numerical expressions from the α_1, α_2, and α_3 test sets in InfoTabS. The inference for these examples requires an understanding of the number of entities and events. We then made a *problem set* from each example and defined the *base hypothesis* of the test cases by rewriting to the actual value n with *exactly* entailed from a premise table.

Table 2 shows a premise table for the hypothesis *Karachi has a half dozen districts*, which was extracted from InfoTabS. This premise-hypothesis pair is an example, and it makes a problem set for the statement *how many districts Karachi has*. Because we can precisely see six districts in Karachi from the premise table, the base hypothesis of this problem set is *Karachi has exactly six districts*, where *a half dozen* is defined as the number *six*. When the gold label of an example extracted from InfoTabS is *neutral*, a base hypothesis of the example is made by simply replacing the numerical comparatives with *exactly*. The gold label of the base hypothesis is the same as that of the original example. For instance, if the original hypothesis is *Bob has more than two dogs*, and its gold label is *neutral*, then the base hypothesis becomes *Bob has exactly two dogs*. Finally, we make test cases from each base hypothesis using the following process:

(i) We make a new hypothesis sentence S by removing *exactly* from the base hypothesis.

Hypothesis	Gold	Note
Karachi has less than five districts.	C	[2]
Karachi has less than six districts.	C	[1]
Karachi has less than seven districts.	E	
Karachi has five districts.	E	[1]
Karachi has six districts.	E	
Karachi has seven districts.	C	
Karachi has more than five districts.	E	[1]
Karachi has more than six districts.	C	
Karachi has more than seven districts.	C	

Table 3: A part of the test cases made from the problem set for the base hypothesis *Karachi has exactly six districts.* $[i]$ $(i = 1, 2)$ as noted means that the test case is not defined when $n \leq i$, n being the actual value. E and C are *entailment* and *contradiction*, respectively.

(ii) We make two new hypothesis sentences, S_+ and S_- by replacing the number n in S with $n + 1$ and $n - 1$ in S, respectively.

(iii) We make six additional hypothesis sentences each from S, S_+, and S_- by adding the expressions related to numerical comparatives, *less than*, *no more than*, *exactly*, *at least*, *no less than*, and *more than*, thus making a problem set consisting of 21 hypothesis sentences with correct gold labels. Table 3 shows a part of the hypothesis sentences.

(iv) We remove unnatural hypothesis sentences from the problem set, including such as *at least zero* and *less than one*.

Note that here *two* has the same meaning as *at least two*. Our dataset consists of 105 problem sets with 1,979 test cases. The distribution of gold labels is (*entailment*, *neutral*, *contradiction*) = (965, 176, 838). This dataset includes ten problem sets that are filled with *neutral* labels. We confirmed all words are commonly used in a training set in InfoTabS and our dataset.

4.2 Experimental Setup for Previous Research

Neeraja et al. (2021) proposed an NN-based model for inference between semi-structured tables and texts and tested it by InfoTabS. We compare our system to +KG explicit, which was the setting for which the previous model (Neeraja et al., 2021) achieved the highest performance. +KG explicit consists of the following four methods for making sentence representations of tables.

	+KG	Ours
All problem sets	0.03	**0.31**
All problem sets excluding *neutral*-filled	0.00	**0.27**

Table 4: The accuracy of problem sets whose test cases were all predicted correctly. +KG is an abbreviation for +KG explicit.

Implicit Knowledge Addition The model adds information that is not in the tables and texts to models by pre-training with a large-scale NLI corpus, MultiNLI (Williams et al., 2018).

Better Paragraph Representation The model generates more grammatical sentences for specific entity types, such as money, date, and cardinal, with carefully crafted templates when making sentence representations of tables.

Distracting Rows Removal (DRR) The model removes several rows from the premise table that are unrelated to the hypothesis sentence. For a detailed explanation of DRR, see Section 3.2.1.

Explicit Knowledge Addition The model adds a suitable meaning to the keys for each premise from WordNet (Miller, 1995) or Wikipedia articles by calculating similarity based on the BERT embedding.

+KG explicit makes sentence representations of tables and uses RoBERTa-large (Liu et al., 2019) for encoding premise-hypothesis pairs. Almost all of the setups are identical to what was used in previous research except (i) the batch size is set to 4 and (ii) we adopt the result of one seed rather than the average of three seeds.

4.3 Results

Accuracy per Problem Set Table 4 shows the accuracy of the previous model (+KG) and our system (Ours) for a number of problem sets. Our proposed system could correctly predict 31% of all problem sets, while the previous model only predicted 3%. Premise-hypothesis pairs whose gold labels are *neutral* can be predicted correctly without a precise numerical understanding. Table 4 also shows that +KG could not perform inference on any problem set whose gold labels were *entailment* or *contradiction* at all. On the other hand, the accuracy of our logic-based system was 27%. These results indicate that our system better handles inference involving numerical comparatives

	+KG	Ours
less than k	0.10	**0.36**
no more than k	0.10	**0.35**
exactly k	0.19	**0.32**
k	0.24	**0.33**
at least k	0.08	**0.32**
no less than k	0.19	**0.33**
more than k	0.17	**0.35**

Table 5: The accuracy for each numerical comparative construction. +KG is an abbreviation for +KG explicit. k indicates a number.

than the previous model, being able to more robustly predict *entailment* and *contradiction* labels. This shows that our proposed dataset for numerical understanding is challenging for current systems. We describe the error analysis of our system in the fourth paragraph of this section.

Understanding for Each Numerical Comparative Table 5 shows the accuracy of both methods for each numerical comparative construction. We observe that our proposed method can predict correct labels more often than the existing method for all numerical comparatives.

Run Time for Model Checking with Optimization We compare the run times for model checking with and without our optimization for model checking (see Section 3.4). We chose six problem sets involving different numbers of values, which consist of two problem sets each whose numbers of values are 2, 4, and 6. All of the problems require understanding the number of entities. The number of test cases is 124. Table 6 shows the average and maximum run times for ten trials. We observe that our optimization made model checking much faster.

Error Analysis Error analysis shows that main errors are caused by the failure of knowledge injection. Figure 6 shows two premise-hypothesis pairs, one for which our system was able to perform inference and one for which it was not. In Figure 6a, the function HUSBAND was added to the model in the knowledge injection process because the relatedness score between *spouse* and *husband* was high (0.747). On the other hand, in Figure 6b, the function WIN was not added to the model because the relatedness score between *award* and *win* was low (0.336). In addition, even though we improved the speed of the original model checking program, several test cases still ran out of time.

Optimization	Average	Maximum
disabled	3.20	185.17
enabled	**0.04**	**1.26**

Table 6: Average and maximum run time (seconds) for model checking with and without optimization.

For example, the problem with the hypothesis sentence *Jimmy Eat World has been on 13 labels* (this gold label is *contradiction*) exceeded the maximum time limit (10 seconds).

Discussion We discuss how to handle various types of inference other than the numerical one in InfoTabS with our inference system. First, we have to correctly parse values in various tables and extract information from them. For example, to determine whether Hypothesis 1 in Figure 1 is entailed by the premise table, we need to parse the noun phrase *November 20, 1942* into one date format. In addition to this, various formats are needed to be provided, such as age, duration, and year of marriage. Also, some test cases require arithmetic operations other than counting, such as *Joe Biden and Neilia Hunter divorced six years after their marriage*, based on the premise table in Figure 1. Although such issues are tricky, we believe that our logic-based approach is applicable with adding premises related to arithmetic operations.

5 Conclusion

In this study, we proposed a logic-based system for an NLI task that requires numerical understanding in semi-structured tables. We built an NLI dataset that focuses on numerical comparatives between semi-structured tables and texts. Using this dataset, we showed that our system performed more robustly than the previous NN-based model.

In future work, we will improve knowledge injection process to cover various problems. We also seek to handle other generalized quantifiers such as *many*. We believe that our system and dataset for performing numerical inference between semi-structured tables and texts could pave the way for applications of inference between resources other than texts.

Acknowledgements

We thank the three anonymous reviewers for their helpful comments and feedback. This work was

Jodie Whittaker	
Spouse	Christian Contreras

i. Part of the filtered table describing Jodie Whittaker.

$$\boldsymbol{D} = \{X_0, X_1, V_0\}$$
$$\boldsymbol{V} = \{(\text{JODIE\_WHITTAKER\_}, \{X_0\}), (\text{SPOUSE}, \{X_1\}), (\text{CHRISTIAN\_CONTRERASM}, \{X_1\}), \underline{(\text{HUSBAND}, \{X_1\})}, (\text{HAVE}, \{V_0\}), (\mathsf{Subj}, \{(V_0, X_0)\}), (\mathsf{Acc}, \{(V_0, X_1)\})\}$$

ii. Part of the model constructed by our system for (a-i).

$$\exists x.(\text{JODIE\_WHITTAKER\_}(x) \wedge \exists x_0.(\underline{\text{HUSBAND}(x_0)} \wedge \exists e.(\mathsf{have}(e) \wedge \mathsf{Subj}(e, x) \wedge \mathsf{Acc}(e, x_0))))$$

iii. An FOL formula constructed from the hypothesis *Jodie Whittaker has had one husband.*

(a) Outputs of our system to the premise-hypothesis pair describing Jodie Whittaker. Our system was able to perform inference correctly.

Karl Ferdinand Braun	
Awards	Nobel Prize in Physics (1909)

i. Part of the filtered table describing Karl Ferdinand Braun.

$$\boldsymbol{D} = \{X_0, X_1, V_0\}$$
$$\boldsymbol{V} = \{(\text{KARL}, \{X_0\}), (\text{AWARD}, \{X_1\}), (\text{NOBEL\_PRIZE\_PHYSIC}, \{X_1\}), (\text{HAVE}, \{V_0\}), (\mathsf{Subj}, \{(V_0, X_0)\}), (\mathsf{Acc}, \{(V_0, X_1)\})\}$$

ii. Part of the model constructed by our system for (b-i).

$$\exists x.(\text{KARL}(x) \wedge \exists x_0.(\text{AWARD}(x_0) \wedge \exists e.(\underline{\text{WIN}(e)} \wedge \mathsf{Subj}(e, x) \wedge \mathsf{Acc}(e, x_0))))$$

iii. An FOL formula constructed from the hypothesis *Karl Ferdinand Braun won one award.*

(b) Outputs of our system to the premise-hypothesis pair describing Karl Ferdinand Braun. Our system was not able to perform inference correctly.

Figure 6: Two premise-hypothesis pairs, one for which our system was able to perform inference (a) and one for which it was not (b). The function KARL in (b-ii, b-iii) is an abbreviation for KARL_FERDINAND_BRAUN_. The underlined functions are added in the knowledge injection process to perform inference.

supported by PRESTO, JST Grant Number JPMJPR21C8, Japan.

References

Lasha Abzianidze. 2015. A tableau prover for natural logic and language. In *Proceedings of the 2015 Conference on Empirical Methods in Natural Language Processing*, pages 2492–2502, Lisbon, Portugal. Association for Computational Linguistics.

Steven Bird and Edward Loper. 2004. NLTK: The natural language toolkit. In *Proceedings of the ACL Interactive Poster and Demonstration Sessions*, pages 214–217, Barcelona, Spain. Association for Computational Linguistics.

Johan Bos. 2008. Wide-coverage semantic analysis with Boxer. In *Semantics in Text Processing. STEP 2008 Conference Proceedings*, pages 277–286. College Publications.

Stephen Clark and James R. Curran. 2007. Wide-coverage efficient statistical parsing with CCG and log-linear models. *Computational Linguistics*, 33(4):493–552.

Ido Dagan, Oren Glickman, and Bernardo Magnini. 2006. The pascal recognising textual entailment challenge. In *Machine Learning Challenges. Evaluating Predictive Uncertainty, Visual Object Classification, and Recognising Tectual Entailment*, pages 177–190, Berlin, Heidelberg. Springer Berlin Heidelberg.

Jacob Devlin, Ming-Wei Chang, Kenton Lee, and Kristina Toutanova. 2019. BERT: Pre-training of deep bidirectional transformers for language understanding. In *Proceedings of the 2019 Conference of the North American Chapter of the Association for Computational Linguistics: Human Language Technologies, Volume 1 (Long and Short Papers)*, pages 4171–4186, Minneapolis, Minnesota. Association for Computational Linguistics.

Dan Garrette and Ewan Klein. 2009. An extensible toolkit for computational semantics. In *Proceedings of the Eight International Conference on Computational Semantics*, pages 116–127, Tilburg, The Netherlands. Association for Computational Linguistics.

Vivek Gupta, Maitrey Mehta, Pegah Nokhiz, and Vivek Srikumar. 2020. INFOTABS: Inference on tables as semi-structured data. In *Proceedings of the 58th Annual Meeting of the Association for Computational Linguistics*, pages 2309–2324, Online. Association for Computational Linguistics.

Izumi Haruta, Koji Mineshima, and Daisuke Bekki. 2020a. Combining event semantics and degree semantics for natural language inference. In *Proceedings of the 28th International Conference on Computational Linguistics*, pages 1758–1764, Barcelona, Spain (Online). International Committee on Computational Linguistics.

Izumi Haruta, Koji Mineshima, and Daisuke Bekki. 2020b. Logical inferences with comparatives and generalized quantifiers. In *Proceedings of the*

58th Annual Meeting of the Association for Computational Linguistics: Student Research Workshop, pages 263–270, Online. Association for Computational Linguistics.

Hai Hu, Qi Chen, Kyle Richardson, Atreyee Mukherjee, Lawrence S. Moss, and Sandra Kuebler. 2020. MonaLog: a lightweight system for natural language inference based on monotonicity. In *Proceedings of the Society for Computation in Linguistics 2020*, pages 334–344, New York, New York. Association for Computational Linguistics.

Robin Jia and Percy Liang. 2017. Adversarial examples for evaluating reading comprehension systems. In *Proceedings of the 2017 Conference on Empirical Methods in Natural Language Processing*, pages 2021–2031, Copenhagen, Denmark. Association for Computational Linguistics.

Armand Joulin, Edouard Grave, Piotr Bojanowski, Matthijs Douze, Hérve Jégou, and Tomas Mikolov. 2016. FastText.zip: Compressing text classification models. *Computing Research Repository*, arXiv:1612.03651.

Jayant Krishnamurthy, Pradeep Dasigi, and Matt Gardner. 2017. Neural semantic parsing with type constraints for semi-structured tables. In *Proceedings of the 2017 Conference on Empirical Methods in Natural Language Processing*, pages 1516–1526, Copenhagen, Denmark. Association for Computational Linguistics.

Rémi Lebret, David Grangier, and Michael Auli. 2016. Neural text generation from structured data with application to the biography domain. In *Proceedings of the 2016 Conference on Empirical Methods in Natural Language Processing*, pages 1203–1213, Austin, Texas. Association for Computational Linguistics.

Roger Levy and Galen Andrew. 2006. Tregex and tsurgeon: tools for querying and manipulating tree data structures. In *Proceedings of the Fifth International Conference on Language Resources and Evaluation (LREC'06)*, Genoa, Italy. European Language Resources Association (ELRA).

Hugo Liu and Push Singh. 2004. Conceptnet - a practical commonsense reasoning tool-kit. *BT Technology Journal*, 22:211–226.

Yinhan Liu, Myle Ott, Naman Goyal, Jingfei Du, Mandar Joshi, Danqi Chen, Omer Levy, Mike Lewis, Luke Zettlemoyer, and Veselin Stoyanov. 2019. RoBERTa: A robustly optimized bert pretraining approach. *Computing Research Repository*, arXiv:1907.11692.

Pascual Martínez-Gómez, Koji Mineshima, Yusuke Miyao, and Daisuke Bekki. 2016. ccg2lambda: A compositional semantics system. In *Proceedings of ACL-2016 System Demonstrations*, pages 85–90, Berlin, Germany. Association for Computational Linguistics.

George A. Miller. 1995. Wordnet: A lexical database for english. *Commun. ACM*, 38(11):39–41.

Koji Mineshima, Pascual Martínez-Gómez, Yusuke Miyao, and Daisuke Bekki. 2015. Higher-order logical inference with compositional semantics. In *Proceedings of the 2015 Conference on Empirical Methods in Natural Language Processing*, pages 2055–2061, Lisbon, Portugal. Association for Computational Linguistics.

Aakanksha Naik, Abhilasha Ravichander, Norman Sadeh, Carolyn Rose, and Graham Neubig. 2018. Stress test evaluation for natural language inference. In *Proceedings of the 27th International Conference on Computational Linguistics*, pages 2340–2353, Santa Fe, New Mexico, USA. Association for Computational Linguistics.

J. Neeraja, Vivek Gupta, and Vivek Srikumar. 2021. Incorporating external knowledge to enhance tabular reasoning. In *Proceedings of the 2021 Conference of the North American Chapter of the Association for Computational Linguistics: Human Language Technologies*, pages 2799–2809, Online. Association for Computational Linguistics.

Terence Parsons. 1990. *Events in the Semantics of English: A Study in Subatomic Semantics*. The MIT Press, Cambridge, MA.

Panupong Pasupat and Percy Liang. 2015. Compositional semantic parsing on semi-structured tables. In *Proceedings of the 53rd Annual Meeting of the Association for Computational Linguistics and the 7th International Joint Conference on Natural Language Processing (Volume 1: Long Papers)*, pages 1470–1480, Beijing, China. Association for Computational Linguistics.

Abhilasha Ravichander, Aakanksha Naik, Carolyn Rose, and Eduard Hovy. 2019. EQUATE: A benchmark evaluation framework for quantitative reasoning in natural language inference. In *Proceedings of the 23rd Conference on Computational Natural Language Learning (CoNLL)*, pages 349–361, Hong Kong, China. Association for Computational Linguistics.

Kyle Richardson, Hai Hu, Lawrence Moss, and Ashish Sabharwal. 2020. Probing natural language inference models through semantic fragments. *Proceedings of the AAAI Conference on Artificial Intelligence*, 34(05):8713–8721.

Ohad Rozen, Vered Shwartz, Roee Aharoni, and Ido Dagan. 2019. Diversify your datasets: Analyzing generalization via controlled variance in adversarial datasets. In *Proceedings of the 23rd Conference on Computational Natural Language Learning (CoNLL)*, pages 196–205, Hong Kong, China. Association for Computational Linguistics.

Mark Steedman. 2000. *The Syntactic Process*. The MIT Press, Cambridge, MA.

Riko Suzuki, Hitomi Yanaka, Masashi Yoshikawa, Koji Mineshima, and Daisuke Bekki. 2019. Multimodal logical inference system for visual-textual entailment. In *Proceedings of the 57th Annual Meeting of the Association for Computational Linguistics: Student Research Workshop*, pages 386–392, Florence, Italy. Association for Computational Linguistics.

Johan van Benthem. 1986. *Essays in Logical Semantics*. Springer, Dordrecht.

Adina Williams, Nikita Nangia, and Samuel Bowman. 2018. A broad-coverage challenge corpus for sentence understanding through inference. In *Proceedings of the 2018 Conference of the North American Chapter of the Association for Computational Linguistics: Human Language Technologies, Volume 1 (Long Papers)*, pages 1112–1122, New Orleans, Louisiana. Association for Computational Linguistics.

Sam Wiseman, Stuart Shieber, and Alexander Rush. 2017. Challenges in data-to-document generation. In *Proceedings of the 2017 Conference on Empirical Methods in Natural Language Processing*, pages 2253–2263, Copenhagen, Denmark. Association for Computational Linguistics.

Masashi Yoshikawa, Hiroshi Noji, and Yuji Matsumoto. 2017. A* CCG parsing with a supertag and dependency factored model. In *Proceedings of the 55th Annual Meeting of the Association for Computational Linguistics (Volume 1: Long Papers)*, pages 277–287, Vancouver, Canada. Association for Computational Linguistics.

Knowledge injection	Accuracy
disabled	0.23
enabled	**0.34**

Table 7: The accuracy of our proposed system with and without knowledge injection.

A Examples of Tree Transformation

We detect where to transform by tregex (Levy and Andrew, 2006), the regular expression for trees. We have three tsurgeon scripts, all of which are for handling numerical expressions involving the number of events. For example, as Figure 7 shows, we transform the CCG subtree (a) for *exactly* n *times*, where n is a number, into the CCG subtree (b).

B Ablation Study for Knowledge Injection

We conducted an ablation study for knowledge injection (see Section 3.2.3). We picked all of the base hypotheses in our dataset (105 cases in total) and experimented to see how effective our knowledge injection method is. As seen in Table 7, our knowledge injection method provided increased accuracy by 11% (12 cases).

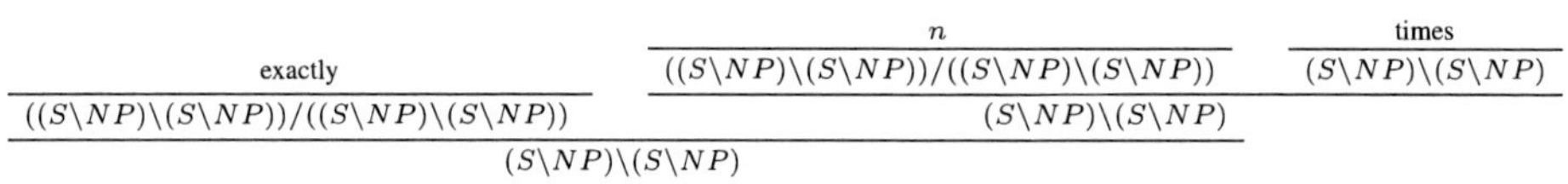

(a)

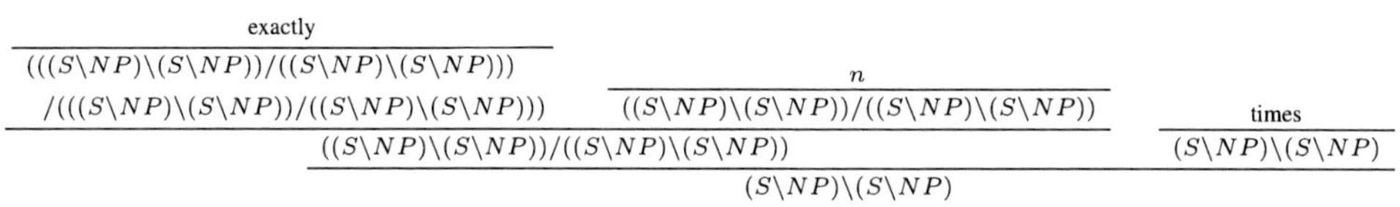

(b)

Figure 7: An example tree transformation process for *exactly n times*, where n is a number. (a) is transformed into (b).

GNNer: Reducing Overlapping in Span-based NER Using Graph Neural Networks

Urchade Zaratiana[*†], **Nadi Tomeh**[†], **Pierre Holat**[*†], **Thierry Charnois**[†]
[*] FI Group, Puteaux, France
[†] LIPN, Université Sorbonne Paris Nord - CNRS UMR 7030, Villetaneuse, France
{urchade.zaratiana,pierre.holah}@fi-group.com
{charnois,tomeh}@lipn.fr

Abstract

There are two main paradigms for Named Entity Recognition (NER): sequence labelling and span classification. Sequence labelling aims to assign a label to each word in an input text using, for example, BIO (Begin, Inside and Outside) tagging, while span classification involves enumerating all possible spans in a text and classifying them into their labels. In contrast to sequence labelling, unconstrained span-based methods tend to assign entity labels to overlapping spans, which is generally undesirable, especially for NER tasks without nested entities. Accordingly, we propose GNNer, a framework that uses Graph Neural Networks to enrich the span representation to reduce the number of overlapping spans during prediction. Our approach reduces the number of overlapping spans compared to strong baseline while maintaining competitive metric performance. Code is available at `https://github.com/urchade/GNNer`.

1 Introduction

Named Entity Recognition (NER) is an information extraction task that aims to identify named entities such as locations, organizations and person names from textual data. Frequently, NER is designed as a sequence labelling task where each word is classified into its respective label using an annotation scheme such as BIO (Huang et al., 2015; Lample et al., 2016). Such schemes are used to encode segment information on the token level. Recently, span-based NER has gained a lot of popularity by handling segments, instead of individual words, as the basic units for labelling (Luan et al., 2018; Wadden et al., 2019). Specifically, span-based NER enumerates every segment in a text and classifies them by their entity label, whereby non-entity segments are classified into an allocated `null` label. While this method has shown good empirical results, it often assigns entity labels to overlapping spans, which is not desirable, especially for flat NER tasks.

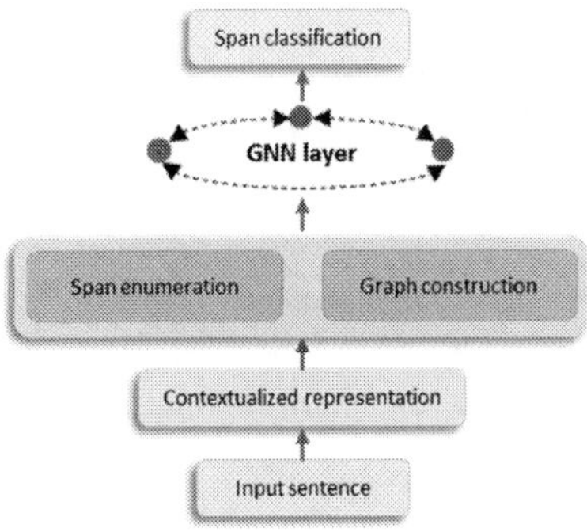

Figure 1: **The overall architecture of our framework**: GNNer

Therefore, to ensure that entities do not overlap, a constraint must be explicitly applied during decoding through, for example, Semi-Markov CRFs (Sarawagi and Cohen, 2005; Sato et al., 2017). Recent work by Fu et al. (2021) and Li et al. (2021) address overlapping entities using heuristic decoding: conflict between overlapping spans is resolved by retaining the span with the highest prediction probability, dropping the others. This approach has proven effective, however, the no-overlap constraint is not imposed during learning, which is sub-optimal. In this work, we consider that the no-overlap constraint could be optimized directly by injecting inductive biases into the model.

In this regard, we propose a new approach to reduce overlapping in span-based NERs without affecting the efficiency of heuristic-based decoding. The idea is to make the representation of each span directly influenced by other spans overlapping with it. Specifically, we encode overlapping information as a graph and feed it into the span representation using an equivariant graph neural network layer. In this way, we bias the model towards predictions that implicitly respect the constraints without explicitly modelling them. Our results

Proceedings of the 60th Annual Meeting of the Association for Computational Linguistics Student Research Workshop, pages 97 - 103
May 22-27, 2022

demonstrate that injecting this graph during model training significantly reduces the number of overlaps compared to our baseline model while achieving better performance. We propose, in this paper, two variants of our model, `GNNer-Conv` based on the graph convolution network (Kipf and Welling, 2017) and `GNNer-AT` based on the graph attention network (Velickovic et al., 2018). We observe that `GNNer-AT` is best at preventing span overlaps at the cost of a low recall, while `GNNer-Conv` provides a better trade-off between the number of violated constraints and metric performance (precision, recall and F-score).

2 Model

Given an input sequence, our task involves enumerating and classifying every span. The architecture of our model, summarized in Figure 1, includes the following components: token representation layer, span representation layer, GNN layer and span classification layer. Our model is similar to the vanilla span-based NER models (Lee et al., 2017; Luan et al., 2019), to which we add the GNN layer.

2.1 Word Representation

The primary component of our architecture is the word representation layer. The purpose of this layer is to return a set of embedding vectors $\{\boldsymbol{h}^0, \boldsymbol{h}^1, \ldots, \boldsymbol{h}^L\}$ from a sequence of tokens $\{w^0, w^1, \ldots, w^L\}$. For this part, we employ pre-trained Transformer models such as BERT (Devlin et al., 2019). However, since pre-trained Transformer models produce sub-word instead of word representations, we retain for each word its first sub-word representation. This choice works well in practice for token classification tasks (Devlin et al., 2019; Beltagy et al., 2019).

2.2 Span Representation

After representing words with their contextualized embeddings, we enumerate all the spans of the sentence up to a maximum span width, which we set to 6 in all our experiments, following prior works (Sarawagi and Cohen, 2005; Xia et al., 2019). Next, we compute the representation of a span as the concatenation of word embeddings of its left and right extremities, along with a learned embedding of the span width. Specifically, a span (i, j) of width k is represented by the vector $s_{ij} = \boldsymbol{h}^i \otimes \boldsymbol{h}^j \otimes \boldsymbol{z}_k$ where $\boldsymbol{h}^i$ and $\boldsymbol{h}^j$ are respectively the representation of the words at indexes i and j, and $\boldsymbol{z}_k$ corresponds to the embedding vector for spans of width k; the $\otimes$ symbol denotes the concatenation operation.

2.3 Graph construction

Given two spans s_1 and s_2, our graph as represented by the adjacency matrix $\boldsymbol{A}$ is defined as follows:

$$\boldsymbol{A}[s_1, s_2] = \begin{cases} 1, & \text{if } s_1 = s_2 \\ 0, & \text{if } |s_1 \cap s_2| = 0 \\ -1, & \text{otherwise} \end{cases} \quad (1)$$

In the adjacency matrix, the edge weight 1 corresponds to self-connection, 0 to non-overlapping nodes, and -1 to overlapping spans. The choice of -1 for the overlap case is supposed to bias the model to learn dissimilar representations for overlapping spans. However, we believe that there may be a better choice to achieve this objective, which would require more in-depth investigation. The addition of the span graph information to the model before the classification layer gives each span information about the spans connected to it and thus allows them to make predictions in a collaborative way, i.e. to make their predictions according to the predictions of their neighbours in the graph.

2.4 Span refinement with GNN

After the initial BERT-based representations of all spans are obtained, we refine them using a GNN layer exploiting the previously constructed graph. We propose two versions of the GNN layer: `GNNer-CONV`, based on graph convolution; and `GNNer-AT` based on attention mechanisms. By exploiting the graph information, we expect the model to implicitly learn that two overlapping spans should not be predicted as a named entity at the same time by learning dissimilar representations for them.

2.4.1 GNNer-CONV

The first variant of our model uses a GCN (Kipf and Welling, 2017) layer, but since GCN is not well suited in the presence of negative edges (Derr et al., 2018), we run two independent 1-layer GCNs over the span representations S: a first GCN, GCN_+ using only positive edges E^+ and another GCN GCN_- using only negative edges E^- for which we concatenate the two representations to get the final

	Architecture	Precision	Recall	F1	Num. Ov.
Conll 2003	Baseline	89.83±0.48	90.31±0.26	90.06±0.15	83±27
	GNNer-CONV	90.12±0.32	89.88±0.36	**90.16±0.52**	52±1
	GNNer-AT	89.54±0.84	79.32±0.04	84.12±0.37	24±11
SciERC	Baseline	66.69±0.49	69.89±0.45	68.25±0.33	87±4
	GNNer-CONV	66.89±1.59	70.34±0.50	**68.57±0.96**	35±3
	GNNer-AT	63.21±0.51	58.06±0.86	60.53±0.69	13±2
NCBI	Baseline	85.30±0.45	89.59±0.74	87.39±0.13	43±12
	GNNer-CONV	85.98±0.45	88.93±0.45	**87.43±0.45**	16±5
	GNNer-AT	84.78±0.18	79.41±0.61	81.98±0.38	10±4

Table 1: **The results of the experiments on the test datasets**. We report the micro-averaged precision, recall and F1-score as well as Num. OV., the total number of overlapping spans on all the test set (without normalization). The numbers are the result of averaging across 3 different/independent runs using different random seeds.

span representation:

$$\begin{aligned} S^+ &= GCN_+(S, E^+) \\ S^- &= GCN_-(S, E^-) \\ S^{final} &= S^+ \otimes S^- \end{aligned} \quad (2)$$

Note that running a 1-layer GCN on the positive edges is equivalent to a linear layer since the positive edges are self-connections.

2.4.2 GNNer-AT

The second variant of our method uses a graph attention network (Velickovic et al., 2018) but instead of using additive attention, we employ a dot product attention which is much faster and more space-efficient in practice, according to Vaswani et al. (2017). More specifically, we project the span representation into keys $\boldsymbol{K}$, queries $\boldsymbol{Q}$, and values $\boldsymbol{V}$ using a two-layer feed-forward network, and compute the attention score as the dot product of the queries and all keys. We further include the scaling factor $\frac{1}{\sqrt{d_{model}}}$ following (Vaswani et al., 2017) to prevent saturation. We then multiply this attention score by the weighted adjacency matrix. We compute the final span representation as follows:

$$S^{final} = \left(\frac{\boldsymbol{Q}\boldsymbol{K}^T}{\sqrt{d_{model}}} \odot \boldsymbol{A}\right)\boldsymbol{V} \quad (3)$$

In the above equation, $\odot$ denotes element-wise multiplication or Hadamard product which is used to mask the attention for null edges. One downside to this approach is that the self-attention mechanism has a quadratic complexity in the number of spans.

2.5 Span classification

Lastly, the final representation of the spans is passed to a linear layer with softmax activation to predict the span labels. Remember that for non-entity spans, we allocate a `null` label.

$$Y = \text{softmax}(S^{final}\boldsymbol{W}^{(f)}) \quad (4)$$

Here, $\boldsymbol{W}^{(f)}$ is a weight matrix that project the span representations into the label space and the softmax activation function is applied to the label dimension.

3 Experiments

3.1 Experimental Setup

Datasets We evaluate our approach on three benchmark datasets: Conll-2003 (Tjong Kim Sang and De Meulder, 2003), SciERC NER (Luan et al., 2018) and NCBI (Doğan et al., 2014). Conll-2003 is a general domain NER dataset that extracts person, organization and location entity mentions from text. SciERC is a dataset for scientific information extraction that consists of article abstracts extracted from Artificial Intelligence related articles. NCBI is a NER dataset that is designed to identify disease mentions in biomedical texts. For all the datasets, we employed the standard train, test and validation splits.

	Domain	Train	Dev	Test
Conll 2003	News	14,987	3,466	3,684
NCBI	Bio	5432	923	940
SciERC	CS	350	50	50

Table 2: **The statistics of the datasets**

Evaluation We evaluate our models on the test splits of the corresponding datasets. Our evaluation is based on the exact match between true and gold entities by discarding non-entity spans. We report the micro-averaged precision, recall and F1. In addition, we also measure the ability of each model to avoid entity overlaps during classification by reporting the number of entity overlaps (Num. Ov.) across all the test set, where a lower number is better.

Implementation details For all our experiments, we used either pre-trained BERT (Devlin et al., 2019) or SciBERT (Beltagy et al., 2019) as the word encoder depending on the dataset used i.e. BERT for conll-2003, and SciBERT for SciERC and NCBI. We employed a span width embedding of 128 dimensions, and down-projected the span representation (768 * 2 + 128) into 128 units before the GNN layer, using a linear layer. We used only one layer for all GNN variants, which resulted in the best performance on the dev set. In fact, we noticed in our preliminary experiments that adding more layers resulted in decreased performance and slower convergence during training. For all experiments, we set our learning rate to 1e-5 and used Adam (Kingma and Ba, 2017) as our optimizer. We ran all our models for up to 50 epochs and kept the checkpoint with the best validation performance for testing. All our models are implemented in the PyTorch (Paszke et al., 2019) and we used the heavily tested GCN layer provided by PyTorch Geometric library (Fey and Lenssen, 2019).

Baseline We used the same architecture without the GNN layer as our baseline. For fair comparisons, we increased the size of the baseline layers to obtain a comparable number of parameters to our proposed models.

3.2 Results

Table 1 summarizes the results of our experiments by reporting the performance measures (micro-averaged Precision, Recall and F1-score) and the Num. Ov. on the test set. The numbers are the result of averaging across 3 independent runs using different random seeds.

Main results From the table 1 we can draw several conclusions. First, `GNNer-AT` outperforms every approach at reducing Num. Ov. On average. It produces 4 times fewer overlaps than the baseline model and 2 times fewer than the `GNNer-CONV` model. However, it has low recall (-11 absolute points compared to the baseline on conll-2003) but can maintain a comparable precision score. The problem of low recall could be caused by overly restricting the span representation through the use of negative edges in our span graph, which could prevent the model from predicting many entities. Second, `GNNer-CONV` gets competitive results while maintaining a low Num. Ov. compared to the baseline model, making it the best balance between Num. Ov. and metric performance.

Learning curves Figure 2 shows the evolution of precision, recall, and Num. Ov. during model training. The plot is shown for training on the SciERC dataset, we obtained similar curves on Conll-2003 and NCBI datasets. We observe that the baseline model trains faster than the GNN-based method, which can be explained by the non-overlap constraint induced by the GNN that favours low recall. On the other hand, the Num. Ov. of the graph-based approach remains low during training, especially for the GNNer-AT approach, while the baseline model increases at the first stage of training before gradually decreasing.

4 Limitations

There are several limitations to our approach. First, the addition of GNN does not completely remove the overlapping spans in contrast to heuristic approches. Moreover, the inclusion of GNN layer bring more comptation to the model which result into a slower model than the baseline span-based NER. In fact since, the overlaping span graph is dense (contains many egde), the model does not really benefit of efficient sparse operations of GNN layers.

5 Related works

Approaches for NER NER is an important tasks in Natural Language Processing and is used in many downstream information extraction applications. Usually, NER tasks are designed as sequence labelling (Chiu and Nichols, 2016; Huang et al., 2015; Ma and Hovy, 2016; Lample et al., 2016; Akbik et al., 2018; Zaratiana et al., 2022). The goal is to predict BIO tags in which a word is labelled as B-tag if it is the beginning of an entity, I-tag if it is within but not the first in the entity and O for non-entity words. Recently, different approaches have been proposed to perform NER tasks that go beyond traditional sequence labelling. One approach that has been widely adopted is the span-based approach (Luan et al., 2018, 2019; Wadden et al., 2019; Xue et al., 2020) where the representation of

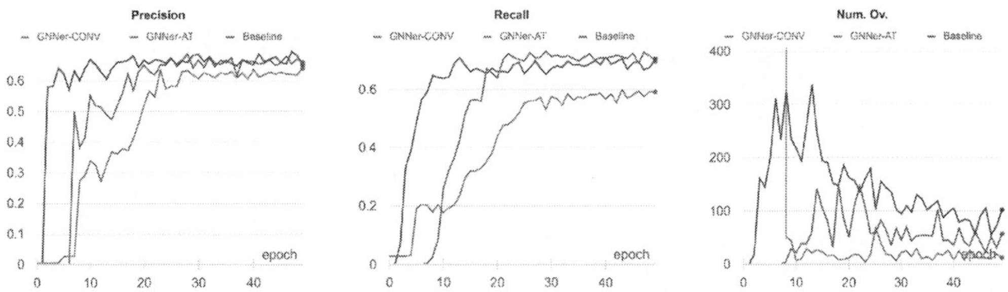

Figure 2: **Evolution of precision, recall and number of overlaps (Num. Ov.) on the SciERC validation set.**

each segment is computed using a neural network, then fed to a classifier. To prevent overlapping span, priors works either used heuristic decoding (Fu et al., 2021; Li et al., 2021; Xia et al., 2019) or structured decoding using semi-CRFs (Sato et al., 2017; Ye and Ling, 2018). However, to the best of our knowledge, no work have used GNN for the purpose of reducing span overlap for NER. Some work (Li et al., 2020) has also approached NER as a question answering task in which named entities are extracted by retrieving answer spans. In addition, with the growing popularity of prompt-based learning, recent work such as (Cui et al., 2021) considers NER as template filling by fine-tuning a BART (Lewis et al., 2019) encoder-decoder model. In contrast we focus on learning appropriate span representations.

GNN for NLP GNNs have gained a lot of popularity recently due to their powerful ability to represent arbitrary shapes of data (Hamilton et al., 2018; Wu et al., 2019; Hamilton, 2020). Specifically, GNNs provide a way to inject prior knowledge into NLP systems through, for example, dependency graphs (Liu et al., 2018; Zhang et al., 2019), constituency graphs (Marcheggiani and Titov, 2020) or knowledge graphs (Sun et al., 2018; Lin et al., 2021). As a result, GNNs have been widely applied to different NLP tasks such as Neural Machine Translation (Bastings et al., 2017; Beck et al., 2018), Semantic Parsing (Xu et al., 2018; Shao et al., 2020), Information Extraction (Fu et al., 2019; Sun et al., 2019) and text classification (Yao et al., 2018; Liu et al., 2020). More relevant to our work, DyGiE (Luan et al., 2019; Wadden et al., 2019) used GNNs to refine the span representation for joint NER and RE extraction, but in contrast, they learn their graph dynamically during training while we used a static span graph. For a detailed review of GNNs for NLP, please refer to Wu et al. (2021).

6 Conclusion

In this work, we investigated new span-based NER method using Graph Neural Networks. Our best approach, built on a Graph Convolution Network, significantly reduces the number of overlapping spans compared to a strong baseline (up to 2 times less) while maintaining competitive metric performance. In future work, we will explore ways to integrate GNN-enhanced representations into architectures for joint named entity recognition and relation extraction tasks.

Ethical considerations

There are ethical considerations to take into account when using NER technology. For example, the technology may disproportionately work worse for some populations with uncommon name structure. This could have a negative impact on these groups, as their names may not be accurately recognized and classified by the software. It is important that we are aware of potential biases in our data and algorithms, so that we can avoid unfairly discriminating against certain groups of people.

Acknowledgments

This work was performed using HPC resources from GENCI-IDRIS (Grant 20XX-AD011013096).

References

Alan Akbik, Duncan Blythe, and Roland Vollgraf. 2018. Contextual string embeddings for sequence labeling. In *Proceedings of the 27th International Conference on Computational Linguistics*, pages 1638–1649, Santa Fe, New Mexico, USA. Association for Computational Linguistics.

Jasmijn Bastings, Ivan Titov, Wilker Aziz, Diego Marcheggiani, and Khalil Sima'an. 2017. Graph convolutional encoders for syntax-aware neural machine translation. In *Proceedings of the 2017 Conference on Empirical Methods in Natural Language Processing*, pages 1957–1967, Copenhagen, Denmark. Association for Computational Linguistics.

Daniel Beck, Gholamreza Haffari, and Trevor Cohn. 2018. Graph-to-sequence learning using gated graph neural networks.

Iz Beltagy, Kyle Lo, and Arman Cohan. 2019. SciBERT: A pretrained language model for scientific text. In *Proceedings of the 2019 Conference on Empirical Methods in Natural Language Processing and the 9th International Joint Conference on Natural Language Processing (EMNLP-IJCNLP)*, pages 3615–3620, Hong Kong, China. Association for Computational Linguistics.

Jason P. C. Chiu and Eric Nichols. 2016. Named entity recognition with bidirectional lstm-cnns.

Leyang Cui, Yu Wu, Jian Liu, Sen Yang, and Yue Zhang. 2021. Template-based named entity recognition using bart.

Tyler Derr, Yao Ma, and Jiliang Tang. 2018. Signed graph convolutional network.

Jacob Devlin, Ming-Wei Chang, Kenton Lee, and Kristina Toutanova. 2019. BERT: Pre-training of deep bidirectional transformers for language understanding. In *Proceedings of the 2019 Conference of the North American Chapter of the Association for Computational Linguistics: Human Language Technologies, Volume 1 (Long and Short Papers)*, pages 4171–4186, Minneapolis, Minnesota. Association for Computational Linguistics.

Rezarta Islamaj Doğan, Robert Leaman, and Zhiyong Lu. 2014. Ncbi disease corpus: A resource for disease name recognition and concept normalization. *Journal of Biomedical Informatics*, 47:1–10.

Matthias Fey and Jan Eric Lenssen. 2019. Fast graph representation learning with pytorch geometric.

Jinlan Fu, Xuanjing Huang, and Pengfei Liu. 2021. Spanner: Named entity re-/recognition as span prediction.

Tsu-Jui Fu, Peng-Hsuan Li, and Wei-Yun Ma. 2019. GraphRel: Modeling text as relational graphs for joint entity and relation extraction. In *Proceedings of the 57th Annual Meeting of the Association for Computational Linguistics*, pages 1409–1418, Florence, Italy. Association for Computational Linguistics.

William L. Hamilton. 2020. Graph representation learning. *Synthesis Lectures on Artificial Intelligence and Machine Learning*, 14(3):1–159.

William L. Hamilton, Rex Ying, and Jure Leskovec. 2018. Representation learning on graphs: Methods and applications.

Zhiheng Huang, Wei Xu, and Kai Yu. 2015. Bidirectional lstm-crf models for sequence tagging.

Diederik P. Kingma and Jimmy Ba. 2017. Adam: A method for stochastic optimization.

Thomas Kipf and Max Welling. 2017. Semi-supervised classification with graph convolutional networks. *ArXiv*, abs/1609.02907.

Guillaume Lample, Miguel Ballesteros, Sandeep Subramanian, Kazuya Kawakami, and Chris Dyer. 2016. Neural architectures for named entity recognition. In *Proceedings of the 2016 Conference of the North American Chapter of the Association for Computational Linguistics: Human Language Technologies*, pages 260–270, San Diego, California. Association for Computational Linguistics.

Kenton Lee, Luheng He, Mike Lewis, and Luke Zettlemoyer. 2017. End-to-end neural coreference resolution. In *Proceedings of the 2017 Conference on Empirical Methods in Natural Language Processing*, pages 188–197, Copenhagen, Denmark. Association for Computational Linguistics.

Mike Lewis, Yinhan Liu, Naman Goyal, Marjan Ghazvininejad, Abdelrahman Mohamed, Omer Levy, Ves Stoyanov, and Luke Zettlemoyer. 2019. Bart: Denoising sequence-to-sequence pre-training for natural language generation, translation, and comprehension.

Xiaoya Li, Jingrong Feng, Yuxian Meng, Qinghong Han, Fei Wu, and Jiwei Li. 2020. A unified mrc framework for named entity recognition.

Yangming Li, lemao liu, and Shuming Shi. 2021. Empirical analysis of unlabeled entity problem in named entity recognition. In *International Conference on Learning Representations*.

Yuxiao Lin, Yuxian Meng, Xiaofei Sun, Qinghong Han, Kun Kuang, Jiwei Li, and Fei Wu. 2021. Bertgcn: Transductive text classification by combining gcn and bert.

Xiao Liu, Zhunchen Luo, and Heyan Huang. 2018. Jointly multiple events extraction via attention-based graph information aggregation. In *Proceedings of the 2018 Conference on Empirical Methods in Natural Language Processing*, pages 1247–1256, Brussels, Belgium. Association for Computational Linguistics.

Xien Liu, Xinxin You, Xiao Zhang, Ji Wu, and Ping Lv. 2020. Tensor graph convolutional networks for text classification.

Yi Luan, Luheng He, Mari Ostendorf, and Hannaneh Hajishirzi. 2018. Multi-task identification of entities, relations, and coreference for scientific knowledge graph construction. In *Proceedings of the 2018 Conference on Empirical Methods in Natural Language Processing*, pages 3219–3232, Brussels, Belgium. Association for Computational Linguistics.

Yi Luan, Dave Wadden, Luheng He, Amy Shah, Mari Ostendorf, and Hannaneh Hajishirzi. 2019. A general framework for information extraction using dynamic span graphs.

Xuezhe Ma and Eduard Hovy. 2016. End-to-end sequence labeling via bi-directional lstm-cnns-crf.

Diego Marcheggiani and Ivan Titov. 2020. Graph convolutions over constituent trees for syntax-aware semantic role labeling. In *Proceedings of the 2020 Conference on Empirical Methods in Natural Language Processing (EMNLP)*, pages 3915–3928, Online. Association for Computational Linguistics.

Adam Paszke, Sam Gross, Francisco Massa, Adam Lerer, James Bradbury, Gregory Chanan, Trevor Killeen, Zeming Lin, Natalia Gimelshein, Luca Antiga, Alban Desmaison, Andreas Köpf, Edward Yang, Zach DeVito, Martin Raison, Alykhan Tejani, Sasank Chilamkurthy, Benoit Steiner, Lu Fang, Junjie Bai, and Soumith Chintala. 2019. Pytorch: An imperative style, high-performance deep learning library.

Sunita Sarawagi and William W Cohen. 2005. Semi-markov conditional random fields for information extraction. In *Advances in Neural Information Processing Systems*, volume 17. MIT Press.

Motoki Sato, Hiroyuki Shindo, Ikuya Yamada, and Yuji Matsumoto. 2017. Segment-level neural conditional random fields for named entity recognition. In *Proceedings of the Eighth International Joint Conference on Natural Language Processing (Volume 2: Short Papers)*, pages 97–102, Taipei, Taiwan. Asian Federation of Natural Language Processing.

Bo Shao, Yeyun Gong, Weizhen Qi, Guihong Cao, Jianshu Ji, and Xiaola Lin. 2020. Graph-based transformer with cross-candidate verification for semantic parsing. *Proceedings of the AAAI Conference on Artificial Intelligence*, 34(05):8807–8814.

Changzhi Sun, Yeyun Gong, Yuanbin Wu, Ming Gong, Daxin Jiang, Man Lan, Shiliang Sun, and Nan Duan. 2019. Joint type inference on entities and relations via graph convolutional networks. In *Proceedings of the 57th Annual Meeting of the Association for Computational Linguistics*, pages 1361–1370, Florence, Italy. Association for Computational Linguistics.

Haitian Sun, Bhuwan Dhingra, Manzil Zaheer, Kathryn Mazaitis, Ruslan Salakhutdinov, and William Cohen. 2018. Open domain question answering using early fusion of knowledge bases and text. In *Proceedings of the 2018 Conference on Empirical Methods in Natural Language Processing*, pages 4231–4242, Brussels, Belgium. Association for Computational Linguistics.

Erik F. Tjong Kim Sang and Fien De Meulder. 2003. Introduction to the CoNLL-2003 shared task: Language-independent named entity recognition. In *Proceedings of the Seventh Conference on Natural Language Learning at HLT-NAACL 2003*, pages 142–147.

Ashish Vaswani, Noam Shazeer, Niki Parmar, Jakob Uszkoreit, Llion Jones, Aidan N. Gomez, Lukasz Kaiser, and Illia Polosukhin. 2017. Attention is all you need.

Petar Velickovic, Guillem Cucurull, Arantxa Casanova, Adriana Romero, Pietro Lio', and Yoshua Bengio. 2018. Graph attention networks. *ArXiv*, abs/1710.10903.

David Wadden, Ulme Wennberg, Yi Luan, and Hannaneh Hajishirzi. 2019. Entity, relation, and event extraction with contextualized span representations. *ArXiv*, abs/1909.03546.

Lingfei Wu, Yu Chen, Kai Shen, Xiaojie Guo, Hanning Gao, Shucheng Li, Jian Pei, and Bo Long. 2021. Graph neural networks for natural language processing: A survey.

Zonghan Wu, Shirui Pan, Fengwen Chen, Guodong Long, Chengqi Zhang, and Philip S. Yu. 2019. A comprehensive survey on graph neural networks.

Congying Xia, Chenwei Zhang, Tao Yang, Yaliang Li, Nan Du, Xian Wu, Wei Fan, Fenglong Ma, and Philip Yu. 2019. Multi-grained named entity recognition. In *Proceedings of the 57th Annual Meeting of the Association for Computational Linguistics*, pages 1430–1440, Florence, Italy. Association for Computational Linguistics.

Kun Xu, Lingfei Wu, Zhiguo Wang, Mo Yu, Liwei Chen, and Vadim Sheinin. 2018. Exploiting rich syntactic information for semantic parsing with graph-to-sequence model.

Mengge Xue, Bowen Yu, Zhenyu Zhang, Tingwen Liu, Yue Zhang, and Bin Wang. 2020. Coarse-to-fine pre-training for named entity recognition.

Liang Yao, Chengsheng Mao, and Yuan Luo. 2018. Graph convolutional networks for text classification.

Zhixiu Ye and Zhen-Hua Ling. 2018. Hybrid semi-Markov CRF for neural sequence labeling. In *Proceedings of the 56th Annual Meeting of the Association for Computational Linguistics (Volume 2: Short Papers)*, pages 235–240, Melbourne, Australia. Association for Computational Linguistics.

Urchade Zaratiana, Pierre Holat, Nadi Tomeh, and Thierry Charnois. 2022. Hierarchical transformer model for scientific named entity recognition. *ArXiv*, abs/2203.14710.

Chen Zhang, Qiuchi Li, and Dawei Song. 2019. Aspect-based sentiment classification with aspect-specific graph convolutional networks. In *Proceedings of the 2019 Conference on Empirical Methods in Natural Language Processing and the 9th International Joint Conference on Natural Language Processing (EMNLP-IJCNLP)*, pages 4568–4578, Hong Kong, China. Association for Computational Linguistics.

Compositional Semantics and Inference System for Temporal Order based on Japanese CCG

Tomoki Sugimoto and **Hitomi Yanaka**
The University of Tokyo
{sugimoto.tomoki, hyanaka}@is.s.u-tokyo.ac.jp

Abstract

Natural Language Inference (NLI) is the task of determining whether a premise entails a hypothesis. NLI with temporal order is a challenging task because tense and aspect are complex linguistic phenomena involving interactions with temporal adverbs and temporal connectives. To tackle this, temporal and aspectual inference has been analyzed in various ways in the field of formal semantics. However, a Japanese NLI system for temporal order based on the analysis of formal semantics has not been sufficiently developed. We present a logic-based NLI system that considers temporal order in Japanese based on compositional semantics via Combinatory Categorial Grammar (CCG) syntactic analysis. Our system performs inference involving temporal order by using axioms for temporal relations and automated theorem provers. We evaluate our system by experimenting with Japanese NLI datasets that involve temporal order. We show that our system outperforms previous logic-based systems as well as current deep learning-based models.

1 Introduction

Natural Language Inference (NLI) is the task of determining whether a premise entails a hypothesis. In particular, NLI involving temporal expressions is crucial. (1) is an example of English NLI involving temporal expressions.

(1) *P*: I arrived in April 2021.
H: I arrived before May 2021. (entailment)

The inference example with temporal expressions is challenging. This is because we need to represent the meaning of sentences that contain temporal adverbs like *before* and *in*, temporal expressions like *April* 2021, and verb tenses like *arrived*, and to compute temporal order of events written in the sentences.

Thukral et al. (2021) showed that deep learning-based models (Liu et al., 2019; He et al., 2020) trained on a standard NLI dataset such as Multi-Genre Natural Language Inference (MultiNLI; Williams et al. (2018)) failed to perform simple temporal inference as in (1). Furthermore, deep learning-based models have performed poorly on challenging NLI datasets that involve various temporal inferences such as FraCaS (Cooper et al., 1996) for English and JSeM (Kawazoe et al., 2015) for Japanese.

Recently, logical inference systems based on compositional semantics (Bos and Markert, 2005; Abzianidze, 2015; Mineshima et al., 2015, 2016; Bernardy and Chatzikyriakidis, 2017, 2020; Onishi et al., 2020) (i.e., semantics in which the meaning of a phrase is determined compositionally from the syntax and the meaning of the lexicon contained in the phrase) achieved high accuracy in FraCaS and JSeM. However, most previous systems did not cover temporal inference.

In addition, because most previous research on NLI has focused on English, research on other languages is desirable. In particular, research on NLI in Japanese is still in its infancy and is limited to deep learning-based systems using pre-trained language models and a few logical inference systems (Mineshima et al., 2016; Onishi et al., 2020). Onishi et al. (2020) attempted to implement a Japanese logical inference system for temporal inference. However, the focus of this previous research was limited to a few temporal clauses in Japanese, and temporal adverbs are out of scope. Thus, there is still room for improvement in the accuracy of temporal inference in Japanese.

In this study, our aim is to realize the compositional semantics and a logical inference system for temporal inference in Japanese based on Combinatory Categorial Grammar (CCG) (Steedman, 2000; Bekki, 2010) to derive a transparent syntax-semantics interface and the analysis of tense and aspect studied in formal semantics (Kamp and Reyle, 1993; Yoshimoto, 2000; Kaufmann and Miyachi,

Proceedings of the 60th Annual Meeting of the Association for Computational Linguistics
Student Research Workshop, pages 104 - 114
May 22-27, 2022

2011; Utsugi and Bekki, 2015; Ogihara, 2017; Jacobsen, 2018). We focus on temporal order and develop a Japanese logical inference system for temporal order.

In our system, a CCG parser first parses the premise and hypothesis sentences and converts them into CCG trees. Based on the analysis of the compositional semantics, we then modify the obtained CCG trees. Next, using ccg2lambda (Martínez-Gómez et al., 2016), the meaning of the whole sentence is derived as a logical form. Finally, we attempt to prove the entailment relations between the obtained logical forms by an automated theorem prover Vampire (Kovács and Voronkov, 2013).

We experiment with two NLI datasets involving temporal order in Japanese: JSeM and a Japanese translation of the NLI dataset focusing on temporal inference (Thukral et al., 2021). We compare our system with the previous Japanese logical inference system (Onishi et al., 2020) and the Japanese BERT model (Devlin et al., 2019). Our experiments show that our system outperforms previous logical inference systems as well as current deep learning-based models. Our system will be available for research use at `https://github.com/ynklab/ccgtemp`.

2 Background

Tense and aspect are important linguistic phenomena related to temporal expressions. This section provides standard background on the semantics of temporal expressions in Japanese, which have been analyzed in previous studies (Yoshimoto, 2000; Kaufmann and Miyachi, 2011; Utsugi and Bekki, 2015; Ogihara, 2017; Jacobsen, 2018).

In Japanese, verb tense is classified into past (-*ta*) and non-past (-*ru*), and aspect is classified into stative (like *iru*) and non-stative (like *kuru*). The temporal interpretation of a matrix clause (i.e., a clause that contains a subordinate clause) is determined by the combination of tense and aspect, and is expressed by the constraints imposed on the relation between speech time and reference time. Speech time represents the time that a sentence is uttered, and reference time is a concept proposed by Reichenbach (1947) and refers to the time used with location time (i.e., time when an event occurs) and speech time to represent the meaning of tense. Table 1 shows the temporal interpretation of a matrix clause determined by the combination of tense and aspect and example sentences corresponding to each combination.

Past	Stative	Relation	Example
$+$	$+$	$r < s$	*Taro-ga ita* 'Taro was here'
	$-$	$r < s$	*Taro-ga kita* 'Taro came'
$-$	$+$	$r \geq s$	*Taro-ga iru* 'Taro is here'
	$-$	$r > s$	*Taro-ga kuru* 'Taro is coming'

Table 1: Constraints imposed on the relation between speech time s and reference time r by tense and aspect and example sentences

To analyze the temporal interpretation of embedded clauses, the concepts of absolute tense and relative tense are necessary. Absolute tense means that the temporal interpretation is determined by the relation between the speech time and the reference time, as in the matrix clause. However, relative tense means an interpretation in which the temporal interpretation does not depend on the relation between the speech time and the reference time. We explain the details with examples in Section 3.2.

This paper uses CCG to formalize the syntactic analysis of our method and analyzes the compositional semantics of temporal expressions based on the analysis by Kaufmann and Miyachi (2011).

3 Compositional Semantics and Inference for Tense

3.1 Semantic Representations for Verb Tense

This section explains the semantic representations for verb tense. Consider the following sentences.

(2) a. Taro-ga kuru
   Taro-NOM come-NP
   'Taro is coming'

b. Taro-ga kita
   Taro-NOM come-P
   'Taro came'

(2a) is non-past tense (NP), and (2b) is past tense (P). (2a) means that the event of Taro's coming occurs after the speech time, whereas (2b) means that the event occurred before the speech time. Thus, for the speech time s and the reference time r, $r > s$ in (2a) and $r < s$ in (2b). Here, r and s both

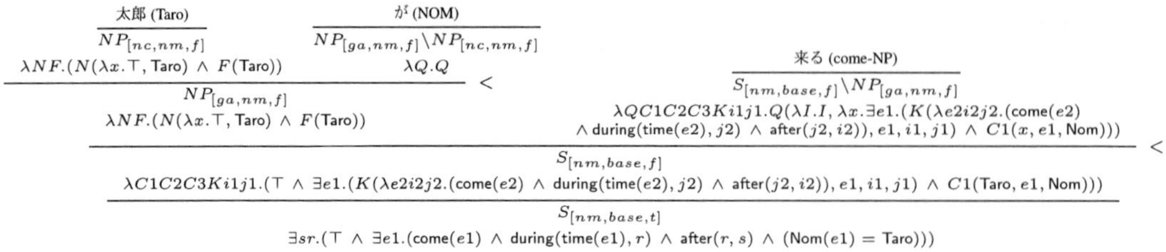

Figure 1: CCG derivation tree for *Taro-ga kuru* (*Taro is coming*). $\top$ denotes the tautology.

represent intervals and $r < s$ means the end of the interval r is before the beginning of the interval s. Another interpretation of time is instance semantics, which treats time as an instance, but in this study, we follow the standard treatment of time as an interval (Kamp and Reyle, 1993; Bernardy and Chatzikyriakidis, 2020).

Following Kamp and Reyle (1993), in this study, the time of an event is represented by its relationship with the reference time. Then, the meaning of (2a) and (2b) can be expressed by the following logical expressions, where tgk is the predicate that represents the event Taro's coming, time is the function that returns the time when the event occurred and e is a variable representing the event.

(3) a. $\exists e.(\text{tgk}(e) \wedge \text{time}(e) \subseteq r \wedge r > s)$

b. $\exists e.(\text{tgk}(e) \wedge \text{time}(e) \subseteq r \wedge r < s)$

The meanings of (3a) and (3b) are as shown in the Figure 2 and Figure 3. Figure 1 shows the CCG derivation tree for (2a).

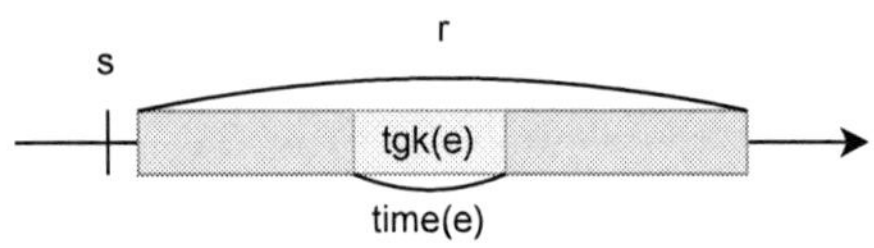

Figure 2: Temporal interpretation of (2a)

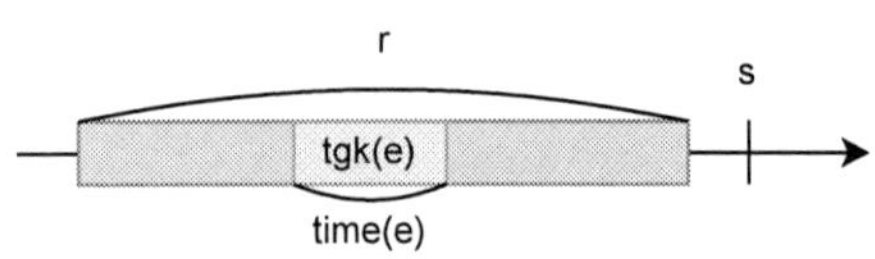

Figure 3: Temporal interpretation of (2b)

3.2 Semantic Representations for Temporal Clause

Next, consider the following sentences with an embedded clause.

(4) a. Taro-ga kuru mae-ni oyoida
Taro-NOM come-NP before-LOC swim-P
'I swam before Taro came'

b. Taro-ga kita ato-ni oyoida
Taro-NOM come-NP after-LOC swim-P
'I swam after Taro came'

In (4a), the embedded clause is the non-past tense, and in (4b), the embedded clause is the past tense. As mentioned in Section 2, the temporal meaning of embedded clauses is interpreted using "relative tense." Thus, the temporal meaning of embedded clauses is determined not by the relation between the speech time and the reference time of the embedded clause but by the relation between the reference time of the matrix clause and the reference time of the embedded clause. For the reference time of the embedded clause t and the reference time of the matrix clause r, we then have $t > r$ in (4a), and $t < r$ in (4b).

Therefore, using the same predicates and functions as Section 3.1, the meaning of the embedded clauses can be expressed by the following logical formulas.

(5) a. $\exists e.(\text{tgk}(e) \wedge \text{time}(e) \subseteq t \wedge t > r)$

b. $\exists e.(\text{tgk}(e) \wedge \text{time}(e) \subseteq t \wedge t < r)$

By combining these logical formulas with the meanings of the matrix clauses interpreted in the same way as Section 3.1, the meanings of sentences with the embedded clauses can be expressed by the following logical formulas, where o is the predicate that represents the event of my swimming.

(6) a. $\exists t.(\exists e_1.(\text{tgk}(e_1) \wedge \text{time}(e_1) \subseteq t \wedge t > r) \wedge \exists e_2.(\text{o}(e_2) \wedge \text{time}(e_2) \subseteq r \wedge r < s))$

b. $\exists t.(\exists e_1.(\text{tgk}(e_1) \wedge \text{time}(e_1) \subseteq t \wedge t < r) \wedge \exists e_2.(\text{o}(e_2) \wedge \text{time}(e_2) \subseteq r \wedge r < s))$

The meanings of (6a) and (6b) are as shown in the Figure 4 and Figure 5.
This study interprets the temporal meaning of sentences with embedded clauses in this way.

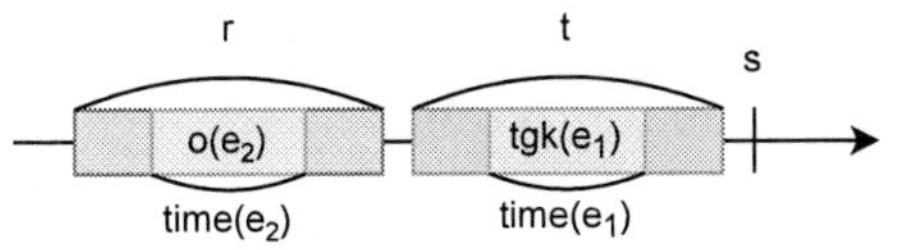

Figure 4: Temporal interpretation of (4a)

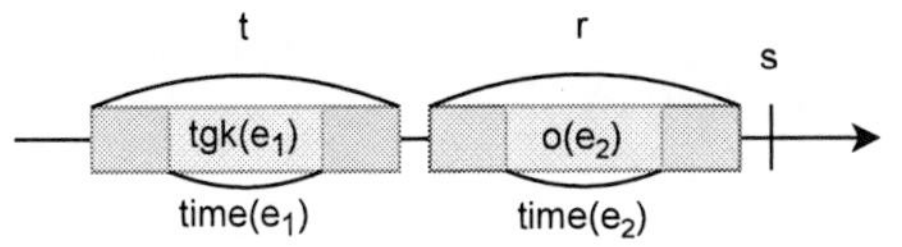

Figure 5: Temporal interpretation of (4b)

3.3 Semantic Representations for Temporal Adverb

3.3.1 Syntactic analysis

An example of the temporal adverbs targeted in this paper is shown in bold in the following.

(7) Taro-ga **4 gatsu 3 nichi izen-ni** kita
  Taro-NOM **4 month 3 day before** come-P
  'Taro came **before April 3**'

More generally, we analyze temporal adverbs comprising various types of absolute temporal expressions (e.g., date, day of the week, and time) and temporal connectives *izen* (*before*) and *ikou* (*after*). Absolute temporal expressions are temporal expressions that do not depend on the speech time, in contrast to relative temporal expressions such as *today* that depend on the speech time. In this study, temporal adverbs containing relative temporal expressions are out of scope and left for future work.

In temporal adverbs containing absolute temporal expressions, the particle *-ni* is unnecessary. For example, the following three sentences are all acceptable and have the same meaning.

(8) a. 4 gatsu 3 nichi ni Taro-ga kita
  4 month 3 day on Taro-NOM come-P
  'Taro came on April 3'

b. 4 gatsu 3 nichi, Taro-ga kita
  4 month 3 day Taro-NOM come-P
  'Taro came on April 3'

c. 4 gatsu 3 nichi Taro-ga kita
  4 month 3 day Taro-NOM come-P
  'Taro came on April 3'

Thus, *-ni* can be analyzed as a separation of clauses like a comma and does not have any meaning. Before considering the syntactic category of *-ni*, let us consider absolute temporal expressions. As shown in (8c), absolute temporal expressions are combined with sentences such as *Taro-ga kita*. Therefore, S/S is assigned as the syntactic category of the absolute temporal expression 4 *gatsu* 3 *nichi*. As mentioned above, because *-ni* plays the role of connecting the preceding and following clauses, $(S/S)\backslash(S/S)$ is appropriate as its syntactic category.

In addition, absolute temporal expressions like 4 *gatsu* 3 *nichi* can be a noun phrase NP, as in Figure 6. In this example, the syntactic category of 4 *gatsu* 3 *nichi* is NP, and the syntactic category of *izen* is $(S/S)\backslash NP$. We explain the reason why absolute temporal expressions are used as both NP and S/S from a semantic perspective in the next paragraph.

4月3日 (April 3) 以前 (before) に
NP $(S/S)\backslash NP$
S/S $(S/S)\backslash(S/S)$
S/S

Figure 6: CCG derivation tree for 4 *gatsu* 3 *nichi izen ni* (*before April* 3).

3.3.2 Semantic analysis

We treat absolute temporal expressions (e.g., 4 *gatsu* 3 *nichi* (*April* 3)) as multi-word expressions. Consider the expression 4 *gatsu* 3 *nichi*. We can decompose the expression into four constituents as follows.

$$
\begin{aligned}
[4\ gatu\ 3\ nichi] &= [4\ gatu][3\ nichi] \\
&= [[4][gatu]][[3][nichi]]
\end{aligned}
$$

A current Japanese CCG parser (Yoshikawa et al., 2017) analyzes each constituent as the syntactic category $4 = NP, gatsu = (NP/NP)\backslash NP, 3 = NP$, and $nichi = NP/NP$, respectively. The semantic template for NP is $\lambda E\ N\ F.^{\exists}x.(N(E,x) \wedge F(x))$, which means "some bound variable x is associated with the word E." Now 4 and 3 are both NP, so 4 and 3 have different bound variables associated with them. This bound variable refers to the interval. Essentially, because 4 *gatsu* 3 *nichi* refers to only one interval, 4 and 3 need to be associated with the same interval. The correct meaning cannot be derived when 4 and 3 are associated with different bound variables.

Thus, we treat temporal expressions such as 4 *gatsu* 3 *nichi* as multi-word expressions and set

Category	Expression	Semantic Template
$S\backslash NP$	来る (is coming)	$\lambda Q\ C1\ C2\ C3\ K\ i1\ j1.Q(\lambda I.I, \lambda x.^{\exists}e1.(K(\lambda e2\ i2\ j2.(\mathsf{come}(e2) \wedge \mathsf{during}(\mathsf{time}(e2), j2) \wedge \mathsf{after}(j2, i2)), e1, i1, j1) \wedge C1(x, e1, \mathsf{Nom})))$
$S\backslash NP$	来た (came)	$\lambda Q\ C1\ C2\ C3\ K\ i1\ j1.Q(\lambda I.I, \lambda x.^{\exists}e1.(K(\lambda e2\ i2\ j2.(\mathsf{come}(e2) \wedge \mathsf{during}(\mathsf{time}(e2), j2) \wedge \mathsf{before}(j2, i2)), e1, i1, j1) \wedge C1(x, e1, \mathsf{Nom})))$
NP	4月3日 (April 3rd)	$\lambda N\ F.^{\exists}x.(N(\lambda y.(\mathsf{normalized\_time}(y) = 40300), x) \wedge F(x))$
S/S	4月3日 (April 3rd)	$\lambda S\ C1\ C2\ C3\ K\ i1\ j1.S(C1, C2, C3, \lambda J\ e1\ i2\ j2.K(\lambda e2\ i3\ j3.(J(e2, i3, j3) \wedge {}^{\exists}x.((\mathsf{normalized\_time}(x) = 40300) \wedge (x = j3))), e1, i2, j2), i1, j1)$
$(S/S)\backslash NP$	以前 (before)	$\lambda Q\ S\ C1\ C2\ C3\ K\ i1\ j1.S(C1, C2, C3, \lambda J\ e1\ i2\ j2.K(\lambda e2\ i3\ j3.(J(e2, i3, j3) \wedge Q(\lambda I.I, \lambda x.\mathsf{before}(j3, x))), e1, i2, j2), i1, j1)$
$(S/S)\backslash(S/S)$	に (on)	$\lambda V3.V3$

Table 2: Examples of semantic templates.

up a semantic template as shown in Table 2. This semantic template allows us to derive the meaning of a temporal expression associated with only one bound variable. In this template, the function normalized_time takes interval as an argument and returns its actual time, which can be set in the format YYYYMMDDHH from absolute temporal expressions. For example, for interval x, which represents *April* 3, the value is $\mathsf{normalized\_time}(x) = 0000040300$. In this example, year and hour are not explicitly written, so zero-padding is applied to them.

As shown in Figure 6, 4 *gatsu* 3 *nichi* functions as NP when connected to *izen* and as S/S when used by itself. This phenomenon can be analyzed as follows. Temporal expressions such as 4 *gatsu* 3 *nichi* and 4 *gatsu* 3 *nichi izen* play the role of representing the time of the sentence. Consider the following sentences.

(9) 4 gatsu 3 nichi ni Taro-ga kita
4 month 3 day on Taro-NOM come-P
'Taro came on April 3'

(10) 4 gatsu 3 nichi izen-ni Taro-ga kita
4 month 3 day before Taro-NOM come-P
'Taro came before April 3'

In (9), the location time of the event *Taro-ga kita* (*Taro came*) is 4 *gatsu* 3 *nichi* (*April* 3), and in (10), the location time of the event *Taro-ga kita* (*Taro came*) is 4 *gatsu* 3 *nichi izen* (*before April* 3). The expressions that represent temporal adverbs such as 4 *gatsu* 3 *nichi* (*April* 3) and 4 *gatsu* 3 *nichi izen* (*before April* 3) must have the syntactic category of S/S, so 4 *gatsu* 3 *nichi* changes from NP to S/S.

Next, the semantic template for *izen* was determined as shown in Table 2. The temporal meaning of *izen* is represented as the lambda expression $\lambda x.\mathsf{before}(j3, x)$, which indicates that the expression "doing before x" means "doing in $j3$ before x." Finally, the meaning of temporal expressions can be derived by setting up a template with *-ni* and a comma as meaningless words, as described in Section 3.3.1.

3.4 Inference with Tense

We introduce a set of axioms for temporal relations and temporal expressions to perform inference for temporal order. Allen (1983) defined 13 relations between time intervals. The previous logic-based inference system (Onishi et al., 2020) introduced 169 axioms for these 13 temporal relations. Six of the 13 temporal relations, meets, met_by, starts, started_by, finishes, and finished_by are special cases of other relations in implementing axioms. For example, meets is a special case of before where the end of the preceding interval coincides with the beginning of the following interval. meets is necessary for inferences involving temporal clauses such as *soon after*. Thus, we consider that those six relations are redundant in performing the temporal inference involving temporal order in this study. We therefore merged them into the most similar relations: merged meets into before, met_by into after, starts into during, started_by into contains, finishes into during, and finished_by into contains, respectively. In summary, we introduce 49 axioms corresponding to seven temporal relations: before, after, overlaps, overlapped_by, during, contains, and equal.

In addition, we speculate 30 additional axioms for temporal expressions in Japanese such as *izen* (*before*) and *ikou* (*after*), and those for identity conditions of speech times between premises and hypotheses. Table 3 shows examples of the axioms.

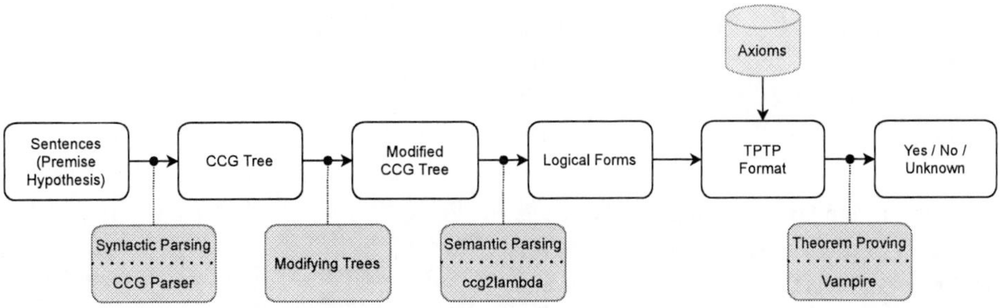

Figure 7: Overview of our system

Pattern	Axiom
transitivity of before relations	$^\forall A, B, C.(\mathsf{before}(A, B) \wedge \mathsf{before}(B, C) \rightarrow \mathsf{before}(A, C))$
insertion of *izen*	$^\forall I, X, R.((\mathsf{nort}(X) = I \wedge (X = R)) \rightarrow (^\forall J.((I \leq J)$ $\rightarrow (^\exists Y.(\mathsf{nort}(Y) = J \wedge ^\exists Z.(\mathsf{before}(Z, Y) \wedge (Z = R))))))).$
replacement of *izen*	$^\forall I, X, R.((\mathsf{nort}(X) = I \wedge \mathsf{before}(R, X)) \rightarrow (^\forall J.((I \leq J)$ $\rightarrow (^\exists Z.(\mathsf{nort}(Z) = J \wedge \mathsf{before}(R, Z))))))$
identity condition of speech times	$^\forall S_1, S_2.(\mathsf{speech\_time}(S_1) \wedge \mathsf{speech\_time}(S_2) \rightarrow S_1 = S_2)$

Table 3: Examples of axioms. nort indicates a normalized_time function.

4 System Overview

Figure 7 shows the pipeline of our system. Our system consists of three main steps. First, natural language sentences of premises and hypotheses are converted into modified CCG trees by CCG parsing and modifying trees. Next, a meaning from the semantic templates is assigned to each lexical item. The semantics in lexical items are then composed by ccg2lambda to derive a logical formula that represents the meaning of the whole sentence. Finally, an automated theorem prover determines whether the logical formula of the hypothesis is provable from the logical formula of the premises. In this section, we describe each of these steps.

4.1 Syntactic Analysis

The syntactic analysis, which obtains CCG parsing trees of input sentences, consists of two steps. First, we use the tokenizer to tokenize sentences and a CCG parser to obtain a CCG tree. We use depccg (Yoshikawa et al., 2017), a standard Japanese CCG parser, trained on the Japanese CCG-Bank (Uematsu et al., 2013) for the first step.

Second, if the sentence contains temporal expressions, we extract the subtrees in which the leaves are temporal expressions from the CCG tree of the whole sentence. The extracted CCG subtree is then transformed into an appropriate form. Figure 8 and Figure 9 show the temporal expression subtrees 4 *gatsu* 3 *nichi ni* (*on April* 3) before and after the conversion. As another possible way of implementation for obtaining correct CCG trees for temporal expressions, we can improve the CCG parser itself. However, to do that, we need to re-train the morphological analyzer and the CCG parser to correctly handle a variety of temporal expressions. We do not take this approach because it is too costly.

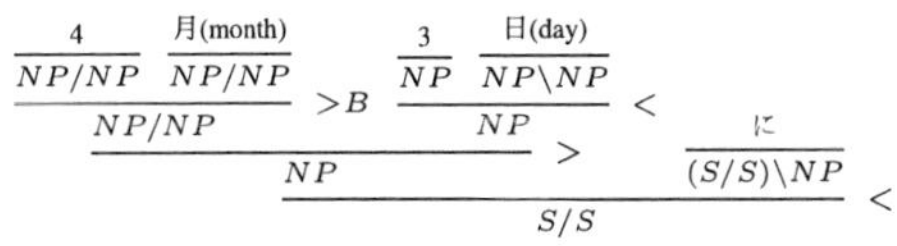

Figure 8: CCG derivation tree before conversion.

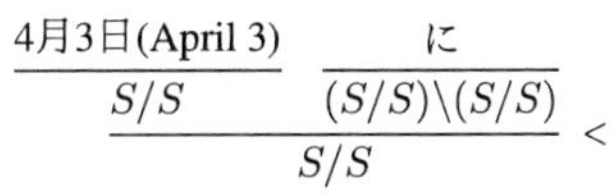

Figure 9: CCG derivation tree after conversion.

4.2 Semantic Analysis

In semantic analysis, each leaf (lexical item) of the CCG tree obtained in the syntactic analysis is assigned a meaning from the semantic templates. The lexical items are then combined according to the CCG derivation tree to derive a logical formula that expresses the meaning of the entire sentence. The composition is performed using ccg2lambda in Japanese (Mineshima et al., 2016).

In order to assign meaning to the temporal expressions, we set up semantic templates for lexical items such as absolute temporal expressions and *izen*. We provide a set of semantic templates, which contains 150 lexical entries. The number of lexical entries assigned to CCG categories is 92, and the number of entries directly assigned to specific words is 58. Table 2 shows the examples of semantic templates.

As a representation language, we use the typed first-order form of the Thousands of Problems for Theorem Provers (TPTP; Sutcliffe (2017)) format. We use standard interval semantics (Dowty, 1979; Bennett and Partee, 1978) and introduce an interval type to express time instances as intervals and their relations in logical expressions. We use four basic types: E (Entity), Ev (Event), Prop (Proposition) and I (Interval). The types of expressions we adopt are defined by

$$\mathsf{T} ::= \mathsf{E} \mid \mathsf{Ev} \mid \mathsf{Prop} \mid \mathsf{I} \mid \mathsf{T1} \Rightarrow \mathsf{T2}$$

where $\mathsf{T1} \Rightarrow \mathsf{T2}$ is a function type. Because the logical expressions derived by ccg2lambda are not typed, we implement automatic completion of variable types, predicate types, and definitions of predicates.

4.3 Theorem Proving

In theorem proving, we use the state-of-the-art first-order logic automated theorem prover Vampire (Kovács and Voronkov, 2013) which accepts TPTP formats to determine whether or not a hypothesis is provable from premises using the logical formula derived in Section 4.2. The system outputs "yes" (entailment) when the hypothesis can be proved from the premises, "no" (contradiction) when the negation of the hypothesis can be proved from the premises, and "unknown" (neutral) when neither can be proved. We use the fastest mode, CASC mode, and set the timeout of Vampire to a maximum of 300 sec for our experiments.

Even though Vampire is a fast theorem prover, it takes too long to prove the problems, whose premises and hypothesis are too complex. When proving the negation of a hypothesis, it turns out that simply negating the logical formula increases the complexity. Therefore, this study uses the symmetrical relationship between *ikou* and *izen* to replace *izen* and *ikou* in the hypothesis with *ikou* and *izen*, respectively, to negate the logical formula without increasing the complexity.

5 Experiments

5.1 Experimental Setup

We evaluate our system on two datasets. First, JSeM (Kawazoe et al., 2015) is a Japanese version of the FraCaS (Cooper et al., 1996) test suite, which consists of nine sections, each containing representative problems of semantically challenging inferences involving various linguistic phenomena. In this study, we use 23 problems involving temporal order in temporal reference section. The distribution of gold answer labels for the problems is (yes/no/unknown) = (12/4/7).

PLMUTE Section: time_multi, No. 11, Gold answer: yes	
P	午後7時以降ロビンは両親を訪ねた。 (After 7 p.m. Robin visited her parents.)
H	16時以降ロビンは両親を訪ねた。 (After 16:00 Robin went to visit her parents.)
PLMUTE Section: day, No. 239, Gold answer: no	
P	月曜日以前、食料品店が閉店した。 (Before Monday, the grocery store was closed.)
H	火曜日以降、食料品店が閉店した。 (After Tuesday, the grocery store was closed.)
JSeM No. 645, Gold answer: yes	
P	1992年以来、ITELはバーミンガムにある。 (Since 1992 ITEL has been in Birmingham.) 現在、1996年である。 (It is now 1996.)
H	ITELは1993年にはバーミンガムにあった。 (ITEL was in Birmingham in 1993.)

Table 4: Examples of problems from JSeM and PLMUTE_ja.

Second, we created an NLI dataset focusing on temporal order in Japanese from the existing NLI dataset (which we refer to as PLMUTE) for temporal inference in English proposed by Thukral et al. (2021) because Japanese NLI datasets involving diverse temporal adverbs were not well developed. We used the ordering section of PLMUTE, which collects problems related to ordering various temporal adverbs for a date, day of the week, and time. The original PLMUTE is automatically generated from 71 templates by a program. Thus, we manually translated the templates into Japanese and modified the program to generate the dataset to make the generated dataset natural in Japanese. We automatically generated a Japanese translation of the original PLMUTE by using the translated templates and modified program. We call the dataset PLMUTE_ja. PLMUTE_ja consists of nine sections: year (340 problems), month (480 problems), date (560 problems), date_DMY (340 problems), date_MY (340 problems), day

System		year	month	date	date _dmy	date _my	day	time _12	time _24	time _multi
Majority		.382	.421	.425	.403	.379	.396	.368	.415	.418
BERT	JSNLI	.394	.413	.382	.400	.400	.380	.378	.415	.368
	few	.509	.517	.509	.491	.476	.518	.440	.453	.515
	all	.997	1.000	.998	.985	.982	1.000	1.000	.998	.960
Onishi et al. (2020)		.238	.265	.239	.206	.244	.291	.290	.225	.253
Our system		1.000	1.000	.980	.971	.974	.984	.943	.970	.953

Table 5: Accuracy on the PLMUTE_ja test suite.

(560 problems), time_12 (400 problems), time_24 (400 problems), and time_multi (400 problems). The distribution of gold answer labels for the problems is (yes/no/unknown) = (1353/1502/965). Table 4 shows examples of problems in JSeM and PLMUTE_ja.

We compared our system with the following previous logic-based inference system and deep learning-based models in Japanese.

Logic-based inference system We used the logic-based inference system for temporal inference in Japanese proposed by Onishi et al. (2020). Onishi et al. (2020)'s system used Coq, a higher-order theorem prover based on natural deduction.

Deep learning-based model We used the Japanese BERT (Devlin et al., 2019) model (cl-tohoku/bert-base-japanese-whole-word-masking) of Huggingface transformers[1] as a deep learning-based model. This Japanese BERT model is the most commonly used pre-trained language model for Japanese in huggingface/transformers. In this study, we experimented with the following three models: **BERT_JSNLI** is Japanese BERT fine-tuned on a large Japanese NLI dataset JSNLI (Yoshikoshi et al., 2020) (533,005 examples), a Japanese translation of the SNLI dataset (Bowman et al., 2015), which is one of the most widely used NLI datasets. **BERT_few** is Japanese BERT fine-tuned on the PLMUTE_ja minimal training set with two examples each of different combinations of tenses and sections (360 examples). **BERT_all** is Japanese BERT fine-tuned on the entire PLMUTE_ja training set (11,220 examples).

[1]https://huggingface.co/transformers/

System		Accuracy
BERT	JSNLI	.522
	few	.217
	all	.435
Onishi et al. (2020)		.478
Our system		.783

Table 6: Accuracy on the problems involving temporal order in the JSeM test suite.

6 Results and Discussion

6.1 Results

The results on the problems involving temporal order in JSeM are shown in Table 6. As the table shows, our system outperforms all models.

The results on the PLMUTE_ja test set are shown in Table 5. As the table shows, our system outperforms all models except BERT_all. Although the performance is slightly inferior to BERT_all, the performance is comparable to BERT_all with 11,220 training data. The experiment with Japanese BERT + PLMUTE_ja reproduced the results of the experiment with English RoBERTa + PLMUTE conducted by Thukral et al. (2021). That is, although the model trained on all of the PLMUTE training sets could achieve high accuracy, the model trained on either the large standard NLI dataset or the minimal training set could only achieve low accuracy.

We also compared the average proof time for all four problems for which both our system and Onishi et al. (2020)'s system output "yes". Our system was faster than the previous logic-based system: the average proof time for our system was 1.98 seconds, while Onishi et al. (2020)'s system was 3.11 seconds.

P_1	ジョーンズが契約書を修正した。 (Jones revised the contract.)
P_2	スミスが契約書を修正した。 (Smith revised the contract.)
P_3	ジョーンズがスミスより先に契約書を修正した。 (Jones revised the contract after Smith did.)
H	スミスはジョーンズより後に契約書を修正した。 (Smith revised the contract before Jones did.)
	Gold answer: yes (JSeM No. 659)

Table 7: An example of problem our system did not solve.

6.2 Error Analysis

In this section, we discuss the error analysis in the experiments. Our system did not solve the problems involving comparative deletion and temporal connectives such as *yori mae* (*before*) and *yori ato* (*after*), as shown in Table 7.

Although *yori mae* and *yori ato* have similar meanings to *izen* and *ikou*, they have different meanings. For example, 4 *gatsu* 3 *nichi izen* includes April 3rd, while 4 *gatsu* 3 *nichi yori-mae* does not include April 3rd. In addition, *yori mae* is more difficult to analyze than *izen* because it consists of two words, *yori* and *mae* that require the analysis of comparative deletion, which we leaves for future work.

7 Conclusion

In this paper, we compositionally derived semantic representations of sentences with tense and aspect in Japanese based on CCG. We developed a logic-based NLI system that considers temporal order in Japanese. We evaluated our system by experimenting with two Japanese NLI datasets involving temporal order. Our system performed more robustly than previous logic-based systems as well as current deep learning-based models. The experimental results of our system suggest that a logical NLI system based on an analysis of tense in formal semantics is effective for temporal inference. Other previous studies of logic-based methods have shown the effectiveness of NLI systems based on the analysis of various semantics such as degree semantics (Haruta et al., 2020). By combining them, we will be able to construct one NLI system capable of performing a variety of inferences. In the future, we plan to cover various temporal inferences involving comparative deletion and temporal anaphora. Furthermore, we plan to construct inference test sets for these challenging inferences.

Acknowledgements

We thank the three anonymous reviewers for their helpful comments and feedback. This work was supported by PRESTO, JST Grant Number JP-MJPR21C8, Japan.

References

Lasha Abzianidze. 2015. A tableau prover for natural logic and language. In *Proceedings of the 2015 Conference on Empirical Methods in Natural Language Processing*, pages 2492–2502, Lisbon, Portugal. Association for Computational Linguistics.

James F. Allen. 1983. Maintaining knowledge about temporal intervals. *Commun. ACM*, 26(11):832–843.

Daisuke Bekki. 2010. *A Formal Theory of Japanese Grammar: The Conjugation System, Syntactic Structures, and Semantic Composition (in Japanese)*. Kuroshio.

Michael Bennett and Barbara Hall Partee. 1978. *Toward the logic of tense and aspect in English*, volume 84. Indiana University Linguistics Club Bloomington.

Jean-Philippe Bernardy and Stergios Chatzikyriakidis. 2017. A type-theoretical system for the FraCaS test suite: Grammatical framework meets coq. In *IWCS 2017 - 12th International Conference on Computational Semantics - Long papers*.

Jean-Philippe Bernardy and Stergios Chatzikyriakidis. 2020. Fracas: Temporal analysis. *arXiv preprint arXiv:2012.10668*.

Johan Bos and Katja Markert. 2005. Recognising textual entailment with logical inference. In *Proceedings of Human Language Technology Conference and Conference on Empirical Methods in Natural Language Processing*, pages 628–635, Vancouver, British Columbia, Canada. Association for Computational Linguistics.

Samuel R. Bowman, Gabor Angeli, Christopher Potts, and Christopher D. Manning. 2015. A large annotated corpus for learning natural language inference. In *Proceedings of the 2015 Conference on Empirical Methods in Natural Language Processing*, pages 632–642, Lisbon, Portugal. Association for Computational Linguistics.

Robin Cooper, Richard Crouch, Jan van Eijck, Chris Fox, Josef van Genabith, Jan Jaspars, Hans Kamp, Manfred Pinkal, David Milward, Massimo Poesio, Stephen Pulman, Ted Briscoe, Holger Maier, and Karsten Konrad. 1996. Using the framework. Technical report, Technical Report LRE 62-051 D-16, The FraCaS Consortium.

Jacob Devlin, Ming-Wei Chang, Kenton Lee, and Kristina Toutanova. 2019. BERT: Pre-training of deep bidirectional transformers for language understanding. In *Proceedings of the 2019 Conference of the North American Chapter of the Association for Computational Linguistics: Human Language Technologies, Volume 1 (Long and Short Papers)*, pages 4171–4186, Minneapolis, Minnesota. Association for Computational Linguistics.

David R Dowty. 1979. *Word meaning and Montague grammar: The semantics of verbs and times in generative semantics and in Montague's PTQ*. Reidel, Dordrecht.

Izumi Haruta, Koji Mineshima, and Daisuke Bekki. 2020. Logical inferences with comparatives and generalized quantifiers. In *Proceedings of the 58th Annual Meeting of the Association for Computational Linguistics: Student Research Workshop*, pages 263–270, Online. Association for Computational Linguistics.

Pengcheng He, Xiaodong Liu, Jianfeng Gao, and Weizhu Chen. 2020. DeBERTa: Decoding-enhanced BERT with disentangled attention. *arXiv preprint arXiv:2006.03654*.

Wesley M. Jacobsen. 2018. *Tense and Aspect*, page 332–356. Cambridge University Press.

Hans Kamp and Uwe Reyle. 1993. *From Discourse to Logic: Introduction to Modeltheoretic Semantics of Natural Language, Formal Logic and Discourse Representation Theory*. Dordrecht: Kluwer Academic Publishers.

Stefan Kaufmann and Misa Miyachi. 2011. On the temporal interpretation of japanese temporal clause. *Journal of East Asian Linguistics*, 20(1):33–76.

Ai Kawazoe, Ribeka Tanaka, Koji Mineshima, and Daisuke Bekki. 2015. An inference problem set for evaluating semantic theories and semantic processing systems for japanese. In *JSAI International Symposium on Artificial Intelligence*, pages 58–65. Springer.

Laura Kovács and Andrei Voronkov. 2013. First-order theorem proving and Vampire. In *International Conference on Computer Aided Verification*, pages 1–35. Springer.

Yinhan Liu, Myle Ott, Naman Goyal, Jingfei Du, Mandar Joshi, Danqi Chen, Omer Levy, Mike Lewis, Luke Zettlemoyer, and Veselin Stoyanov. 2019. RoBERTa: A robustly optimized BERT pretraining approach. *arXiv preprint arXiv:1907.11692*.

Pascual Martínez-Gómez, Koji Mineshima, Yusuke Miyao, and Daisuke Bekki. 2016. ccg2lambda: A compositional semantics system. In *Proceedings of ACL-2016 System Demonstrations*, pages 85–90, Berlin, Germany. Association for Computational Linguistics.

Koji Mineshima, Pascual Martínez-Gómez, Yusuke Miyao, and Daisuke Bekki. 2015. Higher-order logical inference with compositional semantics. In *Proceedings of the 2015 Conference on Empirical Methods in Natural Language Processing*, pages 2055–2061, Lisbon, Portugal. Association for Computational Linguistics.

Koji Mineshima, Ribeka Tanaka, Pascual Martínez-Gómez, Yusuke Miyao, and Daisuke Bekki. 2016. Building compositional semantics and higher-order inference system for a wide-coverage Japanese CCG parser. In *Proceedings of the 2016 Conference on Empirical Methods in Natural Language Processing*, pages 2236–2242, Austin, Texas. Association for Computational Linguistics.

Toshiyuki Ogihara. 2017. Tense and aspect. *The handbook of Japanese linguistics*, pages 326–348.

Maiko Onishi, Hitomi Yanaka, Koji Mineshima, and Daisuke Bekki. 2020. Recognizing temporal relations in natural language based on ccg and theorem proving (in japanese). In *Proceedings of the Annual Conference of JSAI*, volume JSAI2020, pages 1E3GS904–1E3GS904.

Hans Reichenbach. 1947. *Elements of Symbolic Logic*. London: Dover Publications.

Mark Steedman. 2000. *The syntactic process*, volume 24. MIT press Cambridge, MA.

Geoff Sutcliffe. 2017. The TPTP problem library and associated infrastructure. *Journal of Automated Reasoning*, 59(4):483–502.

Shivin Thukral, Kunal Kukreja, and Christian Kavouras. 2021. Probing language models for understanding of temporal expressions. In *Proceedings of the Fourth BlackboxNLP Workshop on Analyzing and Interpreting Neural Networks for NLP*, pages 396–406, Punta Cana, Dominican Republic. Association for Computational Linguistics.

Sumire Uematsu, Takuya Matsuzaki, Hiroki Hanaoka, Yusuke Miyao, and Hideki Mima. 2013. Integrating multiple dependency corpora for inducing wide-coverage Japanese CCG resources. In *Proceedings of the 51st Annual Meeting of the Association for Computational Linguistics (Volume 1: Long Papers)*, pages 1042–1051, Sofia, Bulgaria. Association for Computational Linguistics.

Maika Utsugi and Daisuke Bekki. 2015. Towards an analysis of tense and aspect in japanese by dependent type semantics (in japanese). In *Proceedings of the Annual Conference of JSAI*, volume JSAI2015, pages 2F4OS01a3–2F4OS01a3.

Adina Williams, Nikita Nangia, and Samuel Bowman. 2018. A broad-coverage challenge corpus for sentence understanding through inference. In *Proceedings of the 2018 Conference of the North American Chapter of the Association for Computational Linguistics: Human Language Technologies, Volume*

1 (Long Papers), pages 1112–1122, New Orleans, Louisiana. Association for Computational Linguistics.

Masashi Yoshikawa, Hiroshi Noji, and Yuji Matsumoto. 2017. A* CCG parsing with a supertag and dependency factored model. In *Proceedings of the 55th Annual Meeting of the Association for Computational Linguistics (Volume 1: Long Papers)*, pages 277–287, Vancouver, Canada. Association for Computational Linguistics.

Takumi Yoshikoshi, Daisuke Kawahara, and Sadao Kurohashi. 2020. Multilingualization of a natural language inference dataset using machine translation (in japanese). In *The 244th Meeting of Natural Language Processing*, pages 1–8.

Kei Yoshimoto. 2000. *Tense and Aspect in Japanese and English*. Peter Lang Publisher Inc.

Combine to Describe: Evaluating Compositional Generalization in Image Captioning

Georgios Pantazopoulos
Heriot-Watt University
Edinburgh, Scotland
gmp2000@hw.ac.uk

Alessandro Suglia
Heriot-Watt University
Edinburgh, Scotland
a.suglia@hw.ac.uk

Arash Eshghi
Heriot-Watt University
Edinburgh, Scotland
a.eshghi@hw.ac.uk

Abstract

Compositionality – the ability to combine simpler concepts to understand & generate arbitrarily more complex conceptual structures – has long been thought to be the cornerstone of human language capacity. With the recent, notable success of neural models in various NLP tasks, attention has now naturally turned to the compositional capacity of these models. In this paper, we study the compositional generalization properties of image captioning models. We perform a set of experiments under controlled conditions using model and data ablations, each designed to benchmark a particular facet of compositional generalization: *systematicity* is the ability of a model to create novel combinations of concepts out of those observed during training, *productivity* is here operationalised as the capacity of a model to extend its predictions beyond the length distribution it has observed during training, and *substitutivity* is concerned with the robustness of the model against synonym substitutions. While previous work has focused primarily on systematicity, here we provide a more in-depth analysis of the strengths and weaknesses of state of the art captioning models. Our findings demonstrate that the models we study here do not compositionally generalize in terms of systematicity and productivity, however, they are robust to some degree to synonym substitutions[1].

1 Introduction

Deep neural networks have undoubtedly become the standard option for many Natural Language Processing (NLP) tasks with tangible results across a variety of tasks (Vaswani et al., 2017; Devlin et al., 2019; Raffel et al., 2020; Brown et al., 2020; Liu et al., 2019). Despite their success, neural networks are regularly criticized from a growing body of research for their limited capacity to generalize beyond the distribution of the data on which they were trained. A frequent topic of discussion is *compositionality* of meaning. Humans can understand or generate novel and more complex conceptual structures or sentences out of simpler constituent representations, without needing to encounter any instances of these more complex structures. On the other hand, to what extent different neural models exhibit compositional behavior remains an open problem (Fodor and Pylyshyn, 1988; Smolensky, 1990; Hupkes et al., 2020; Baroni, 2020).

Previous work studying compositionality has primarily focused on artificially created datasets, where compositional rules can be isolated from other natural language phenomena (Baroni, 2020). In this setting, the majority of prior work has largely focused on systematicity under the prism of a downstream task. While these approaches have provided valuable insights, compositionality is multifaceted and a single test can yield misleading findings regarding compositional generalization.

In this paper, we explore compositionality from the perspective of image captioning as a grounded natural language task and propose an evaluation framework with multiple dimensions of compositionality for captioning models. In particular, we adapt the independent and task-agnostic compositionality tests from Hupkes et al. (2020) to the task of image captioning using data and model ablations. Each test is designed to quantify the behavior of a model along a specific dimension of compositionality. In particular, we evaluate three facets of compositionality: (1) *systematicity* (Fodor and Pylyshyn, 1988; Fodor and Lepore, 2002): the ability to generalize to unseen combinations of concepts learned in isolation during training; (2) *productivity*: the capacity to extend predictions beyond the observations; and (3) *substitutivity*: the robustness of predictions under synonym substitution. Previous approaches investigating compositionality in image captioning have focused primarily on systematicity (Atzmon et al., 2016; Nikolaus et al.,

[1]Code & data are available here.

Proceedings of the 60th Annual Meeting of the Association for Computational Linguistics Student Research Workshop, pages 115 - 131
May 22-27, 2022 ©2022 Association for Computational Linguistics

2019; Bugliarello and Elliott, 2021). Our work thus constitutes a more in-depth analysis on the compositional capabilities of captioning models.

Our findings regarding systematicity indicate that the standard fine-tuning approach using reinforcement learning provides gains in word-overlap metrics but hinders systematic generalization. In productivity, we demonstrate that models struggle to extend the length of their prediction beyond the training distribution. Finally, with substitutivity, we demonstrate that state of the art captioning models we study here are robust against substitutions of fine-grained with more high-level synonyms.

2 Related Work

In mathematical logic, the *principle of compositionality* declares that the meaning of an expression can be derived from the meanings of its constituent expressions (Frege, 1950). From the perspective of natural language, if all lexical/word meaning is abstracted out from a sentence, then what remains are the rules of composition. Implications of the principle influence research to this day with longstanding debates regarding compositional properties of vector space and neural models.

Compositionality in Neural Language Processing Initial approaches on distributional, vector-space semantics use tensors as word and phrase meaning representations, and has studied various tensor operations for composition (Mitchell and Lapata, 2008; Baroni and Zamparelli, 2010; Coecke et al., 2010; Sadrzadeh and Grefenstette, 2011; Purver et al., 2021). In all this work, the compositional operations are fixed in advance based on some linguistic theory. In contrast, neural models learn to encode meaning: compositional operations are neither fixed during processing, nor given in advance. To encourage compositionality of neural models, prior work clusters around data augmentation (Akyürek et al., 2020; Qiu et al., 2021), loss functions that encode different inductive biases (Yin et al., 2021; Jiang and Bansal, 2021), as well as meta-learning (Conklin et al., 2021).

Benchmarking compositionality Compositionality is often measured as systematic generalization in different tasks including: in navigation environments (Lake and Baroni, 2018), where the objective is to translate commands into sequences of actions; or in question-answering, (Sinha et al., 2019; Keysers et al., 2019; Kim and Linzen, 2020), where to answer a question the model needs to infer underlying relationships between entities. Additional benchmarks include evaluating arithmetic expressions (Veldhoen et al., 2016; Saxton et al., 2019), and logical entailment (Bowman et al., 2015; Mul and Zuidema, 2019).

Compositionality in Visually Grounded Natural Language Compositionality has also been studied from the perspective of visually grounded natural language. Previous work on visual question answering (VQA) measures generalization to novel question-answer pairs on natural (Agrawal et al., 2017; Whitehead et al., 2021), and synthetic datasets (Bahdanau et al., 2018; Johnson et al., 2017). Similarly, Suglia et al. (2020), proposes an evaluation framework that accounts for a model's systematic generalization capacity coupled with task performance in the context of visual guessing games. More closely related to this paper, prior work has examined compositionality for image captioning (Atzmon et al., 2016; Nikolaus et al., 2019; Bugliarello and Elliott, 2021). However, the aforementioned works mainly focus on systematicity alone and thus provide valuable, but limited insights on compositional properties.

Some prior work has studied compositionality along different prisms. Ruis et al. (2020) examines compositionality under multiple dimensions extending the work of Lake and Baroni (2018) by grounding language to grid world environments. Hupkes et al. (2020) provides a multifaceted view on compositional properties of neural models under a set of task-agnostic tests instantiated with an artificial translation task. The distilled conclusion of this work is that the performance on a single downstream task is not a representative indicator of compositional awareness, even if this task is designed to be highly compositional. This paper can be viewed as an extension of the latter line of work, where we adapt the more fine-grained compositionality tests to the visually grounded image captioning task.

3 Testing Compositionality in Image Captioning

In this section, we describe the proposed tests for evaluating compositionality in image captioning. Figure 1 illustrates examples from each test. We adopt a subset of task-agnostic tests proposed by Hupkes et al. (2020). Our suite consists of three tests: systematicity, productivity, and substitutivity.

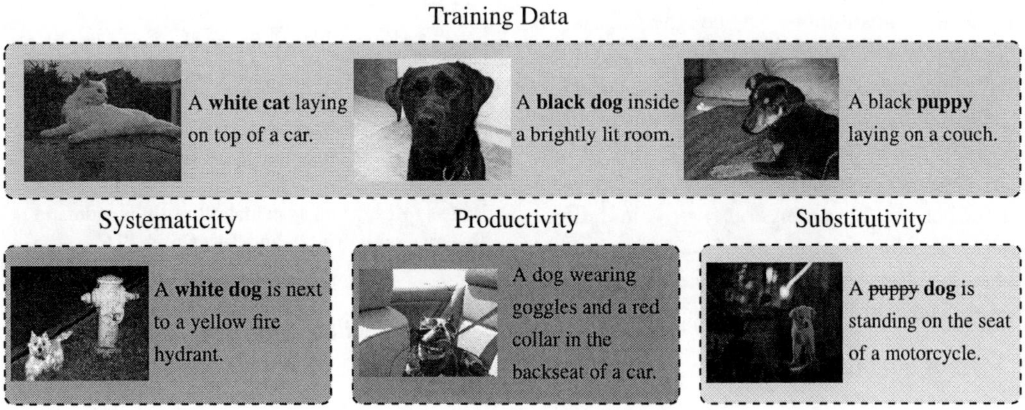

Figure 1: Illustration of different compositionality tests. In the systematicity test, we evaluate the ability to combine concepts (white cat, black dog) to form novel output (white dog). With productivity we focus on the conditions where a model can produce output extending beyond the observable samples. In the substitutivity test, we investigate if models are robust to synonym substitutions. Note that the training data is different across each compositional test.

For each test we define custom training and evaluation splits of the MSCOCO dataset (Lin et al., 2014). Appendix A contains additional details concerning dataset splits, and we will release this data in the public domain.

Systematicity The first test asserts the model's ability to combine known concepts into new expressions. If somebody can understand the meaning of a 'black dog' and a 'white cat', then they can understand the meaning of a 'white dog' (Szabó, 2012). Consequently, a model should be able to describe a white dog even though it has only observed pairs of black dogs and white cats during training.

To probe for systematic behavior, we consider pairs of concepts where their combination is observed during testing and independently during training. In the above example, the pairs 'black dog' and 'white cat' belong to the training while the pair 'white dog' is assigned to the evaluation split. Following Nikolaus et al. (2019), we adopt systematicity splits with pairs of adjectives and nouns, as well as verbs and nouns. For comparative analysis we use a second evaluation set where the constituents of the pairs are observed separately.

Productivity Natural languages are said to be productive in the sense that the speakers of a language are able to understand & generate a theoretically infinite set of expressions or sentences. While there is broad agreement that much of this productivity is buttressed by systematicity, there are also exceptional cases of non-systematic, or partial productivity (Baroni, 2020).

In this paper, we operationalise the broad concept of productivity in two very specific ways. First, we take the productivity of a model to be its ability to generate captions beyond the length it has observed during training (Graves et al., 2014). We tokenize each caption and compute the average caption length for each image. We assign the images at the tail of the histogram of the average caption length to the evaluation set. From the remaining pool of images we sample a second equally-sized evaluation set for comparative analysis. The remaining images are used for training. Second, we assume a model exhibits productive behavior if it can describe significantly denser, more complex images than it has observed during training. We use the number of ground truth bounding boxes from MSCOCO as an indicator of the number of objects present in a scene, and as a measure of their density; and use this measure to create controlled training and evaluation splits.

Substitutivity Substitutivity states that the meaning of a complex expression is not altered after replacement of one of its constituents with another constituent that has the same meaning (Pagin, 2003). Therefore, if a model is compositional then replacing an expression with its synonym should not affect the structure nor the meaning of the whole expression. In the above example a model should be able to infer that the word 'puppy' and 'dog' are synonyms, thus the substitution should preserve the meaning and structure of the caption.

We use a subset of the synonyms of the 80 MSCOCO categories defined by Lu et al. (2018).

We consider substitutions between the original object category and the corresponding retrieved synonym. For each object category and its synonyms, we select pairs that make valid substitutions given the visual context by manually inspecting ground truth captions containing each constituent word. We further exclude ambiguous words and divide object categories to ensure that the substitutions we make are always valid. For instance, we divide the 'person' category into 'man', 'woman' and 'child'.

4 Experiments and results

Model We use $\mathcal{M}^2$-transformer (Cornia et al., 2020), and adopt the configuration with the best reported results. Following standard protocol (Anderson et al., 2018; Lu et al., 2018; Cornia et al., 2020), the training scheme in all experiments consists of two phases: cross-entropy (XE) and CIDEr optimization. For XE, we apply teacher forcing where the model is trained to predict the next token given the previous ground truth tokens. We adopt Self Critical Sequence Training (SCST) (Rennie et al., 2017), as the reinforcement learning paradigm for CIDEr optimization. The reward function is the CIDEr score obtained with sampled sentences using beam search. For both phases, we applied the same training hyperparameters as in Cornia et al. (2020). The training phases are performed sequentially. We start by optimizing XE and then fine-tune the model using SCST. We used early stopping to terminate a training phase, whenever the CIDEr score on the validation set did not improve for 5 consecutive epochs.

Evaluation We evaluate compositional generalization using standard metrics in image captioning: BLEU (B1, B4, Papineni et al., 2002), METEOR (M, Denkowski and Lavie, 2014), ROUGE (R, Lin, 2004), and CIDEr (C, Vedantam et al., 2015. We also quantify semantic similarity using the multi-reference BERTSCORE (Yi et al., 2020). For the case of systematicity, we follow previous approaches (Nikolaus et al., 2019; Bugliarello and Elliott, 2021), and additionally report Recall@K of the pair of interest over the K generated captions using beam search ($K = 1 \ldots 5$).

4.1 Systematicity

In the first set of experiments, we investigate whether or not the model can combine known concepts disjointly observed during training. We adopt a subset of the pairs of adjectives and nouns, verbs and nouns defined by Nikolaus et al. (2019), and modify the proposed train, validation, and test sets. The examined pairs are presented in Table 7.

		B1	B4	M	R	C	BS
V	$\mathcal{M}^2$	75.71	37.01	27.81	58.22	106.25	45.07
	$\mathcal{M}^2_{SCST}$	78.68	39.37	28.93	59.51	116.81	46.15
TNC	$\mathcal{M}^2$	75.22	35.94	27.35	56.42	115.95	43.78
	$\mathcal{M}^2_{SCST}$	80.36	39.14	28.59	58.41	130.16	45.20
TC	$\mathcal{M}^2$	75.83	36.08	27.56	57.79	105.90	44.83
	$\mathcal{M}^2_{SCST}$	79.02	38.66	28.56	59.36	116.11	45.80

Table 1: Results on systematicity split in validation (V), Test no Comb (TNC), and Test Comb (TC).

With these pairs we test the model under two different conditions: Test no Comb (TNC) consists of images where the constituents of the pairs are not observed in the same image; and Test Comb (TC) is the test set defined in Nikolaus et al. (2019). For TNC, we sampled random images from the proposed train set ensuring that both test sets have the same number of images. Finally, we used the same validation set as the proposed split. Notably, the validation set consists of images where at least one of the captions contains the concept of interest. This means that while the model is not directly exposed to the combination of the concepts, it is tuned by optimizing the evaluation metrics on a set that contains these combinations.

Table 1 shows the performance of both models in terms of standard captioning metrics. In particular, SCST improves the performance of the model in terms of word similarity metrics, but also in terms of semantic equivalence as shown by BERTSCORE. Furthermore, there are no significant performance drops between the validation and TC set. However, TNC appears to be much easier for both models presumably because it lacks the combined pair. Importantly, out of all the evaluation metrics used here, BLEU has the weakest (Elliott and Keller, 2014), and METEOR and CIDEr have the strongest correlations with human judgements (Yi et al., 2020). In terms of capturing semantics, SCST yields a more robust model than XE optimization as indicated by the 0.6 and 1 decline in BERTSCORE units respectively.

Considering that we kept all the conditions the same, differences must be due to the poor ability of the model to combine concepts without having observed the combinations during training, i.e. lack of systematicity. To confirm this, we inspect the Recall@K of the pairs after testing on TC. Because the combination of the pairs occur approximately

	$\mathcal{M}^2$					$\mathcal{M}^2_{SCST}$				
	R@1	R@2	R@3	R@4	R@5	R@1	R@2	R@3	R@4	R@5
black cat	1.12	2.01	3.13	3.58	4.03	1.79	1.79	2.46	3.13	4.03
big bird	0	0.81	0.81	0.81	0.81	0	0	0	0	0
red bus	10.39	14.29	19.48	22.94	27.71	12.12	13.42	15.15	16.88	17.32
small plane	0	0	0	0	0	0	0	0	0	0
eat man	11.67	13.75	17.5	21.25	22.08	8.33	8.75	10.42	12.08	12.08
lie woman	4.23	10.56	12.68	14.79	16.2	5.63	6.34	9.15	10.56	11.27
Average	4.57	6.9	8.93	10.56	11.8	4.65	5.05	6.2	7.11	7.45

Table 2: Recall scores for each pair of interest in the systematicity test.

in 1.57 of the 5 ground truth captions, it is not expected by the model to generate the combination in a single caption (Nikolaus et al., 2019). We therefore use the top 5 most likely captions generated using beam search. Table 2 illustrates recall scores for all pairs. Both models rarely perform any systematic generalizations. On average, only 4.57% (4.65%) of the time the model under XE (SCST) includes the pair in the description.

Surprisingly, SCST fine-tuning actually hinders the systematic performance of the model. While both models perform similarly when taking into account the single most likely caption, XE optimization yields significant gains by taking into account additional generations. Intuitively, SCST should facilitate exploration of the caption space. Because the reward value is a function of word overlap, for images where the majority of the reference captions do not contain the examined pair, the model will be penalized when making any systematic generalizations. This is further exacerbated by the lack of diversity in each active hypothesis during beam search decoding (Li et al., 2016; Vijayakumar et al., 2016). If most of the active hypotheses have significant overlaps with minor variations, then there is little hope for the model to make systematic generalizations in any of the K most likely generations. An alternative approach would be to modify the reward function to not penalize plausible descriptions that deviate from the ground truth. For instance, a model should not be penalized if it describes properties of objects in an image even if these properties are not mentioned in the ground truth. We leave this direction for future work.

4.2 Productivity

With productivity, we explore to what degree a captioning model can extend its predictions beyond the length distribution it has observed during training. We expose the models in two different test conditions. First, we tokenize each caption using spaCy (Honnibal et al., 2020) and compute the histogram of the average caption length for each image. The distribution of the average caption length is shown in Figure 2. For each condition, we use the same number (5000) of images for validation and testing as in Karpathy and Fei-Fei (2015). From the histogram, we assign the 5000 images with the highest caption length to the first condition, denoted Test Rich (TR). From the remaining examples, we randomly select 5000 images and assign them to the second condition - Test Base (TB), and 5000 images for validation. Lastly, the remaining $82,783$ images are used for training.

		B1	B4	M	R	C	BS
V	$\mathcal{M}^2$	76.22	36.17	28.35	57.11	115.90	44.33
	$\mathcal{M}^2_{SCST}$	81.31	39.39	29.26	59.26	130.03	45.56
TB	$\mathcal{M}^2$	76.22	35.91	28.17	56.92	116.11	44.30
	$\mathcal{M}^2_{SCST}$	80.98	39.38	29.22	59.49	130.42	45.54
TR	$\mathcal{M}^2$	75.72	35.97	24.99	53.31	85.01	40.28
	$\mathcal{M}^2_{SCST}$	80.79	39.53	26.31	55.58	95.73	41.47

Table 3: Results on productivity split in validation (V), Test Base (TB), and Test Rich (TR).

This procedure yields two independent tests, where the base test follows the same distribution of caption lengths as the train set. The rich test contains images with significantly greater length. Table 9 illustrates the average POS tags and the length of each caption per image. On average captions of images from TR have approximately 14.47% more adjectives, 31.75% more nouns, and 29.70% verbs than the train, validation, and TB.

We report the performance on the productivity test in Table 3. Overall, it appears that images containing longer captions are difficult for both models as showcased by standard captioning and semantic metrics. The performance on the TB is comparable with the validation set, however, both models perform considerably worse on the TR set. The model after XE optimization reports a drop of 31.1

CIDEr units when evaluated on longer captions. The same trend can be observed for SCST where the performance gap between TB and TR is even greater than solely training using XE. In terms of semantics, we observe a drop of approximately 4 BERTSCORE units across both methods.

	$\mathcal{M}^2$		$\mathcal{M}^2_{SCST}$	
	TB	TR	TB	TR
ADJ	0.56	0.48	0.43	0.37
ADP	1.73	1.77	1.68	1.82
ADV	0.09	0.11	0.05	0.07
CCONJ	0.15	0.19	0.20	0.24
DET	2.3	2.40	2.41	2.56
NOUN	3.42	3.49	3.45	3.62
PRON	0.03	0.03	0.04	0.04
VERB	1	1.01	0.92	0.91
LENGTH	9.36	9.58	9.34	9.74

Table 4: Average POS tags and length of generated captions in Test Base (TB) and Test Rich (TR).

Further insights can also be obtained from the average POS tags and caption length illustrated in Table 4. We observe that the model from XE optimization generates more adjectives and verbs as opposed to the model using SCST. However, the latter is generating substantially more nouns especially to describe images from the TR set. This observation also supports the findings on systematicity. If a model is generating more adjectives and verbs then it is capable of making more (adjective, noun) and (noun, verb) compositions. It is likely that the model receives greater reward by describing additional objects in the image rather than their attributes or their relations (eg 'a blue bird sitting on a bench' vs 'a bird next to two people'). As a result, the generated captions contain additional DET and ADP tags present in the caption which is also supported by the presented findings.

4.2.1 Visual Density

		B1	B4	M	R	C	BS
V	$\mathcal{M}^2$	75.89	36.38	27.83	56.65	115.0	44.06
	$\mathcal{M}^2_{SCST}$	80.74	39.43	29.08	59.01	129.11	45.38
TLD	$\mathcal{M}^2$	75.98	36.12	27.81	56.57	114.86	43.97
	$\mathcal{M}^2_{SCST}$	80.97	39.88	29.02	59.24	130.21	45.31
THD	$\mathcal{M}^2$	77.23	37.96	27.07	56.56	90.76	41.60
	$\mathcal{M}^2_{SCST}$	81.57	40.36	28.52	58.8	103.52	43.26

Table 5: Results on productivity (visual density) split in validation (V), Test Low Density (TLD), and Test High Density (THD).

The caption length may correlate with the visual information from the image and thus it may contain lots of words because the image has rich content. While this would be a nice property of captioning models, it would mean that the models do not necessarily exhibit productive behavior but simply are capable of describing additional concepts in the image. However, there is no linear dependency between the number of concepts in an image and with the length of its description (Figure 4). Consequently, a model may actually behave differently in terms of productivity if it is exposed to images with less number of objects during training.

Motivated by this observation, we repeat the productivity experiments but this time we are interested in exposing the model to images with low visual density and evaluating on images with high density. We split the dataset in a way that the test images contain significantly more numbers of concepts. Similarly, we have two test conditions: Test Low Density (TLD) and High Density (THD).

Table 5 illustrates the results in the productivity split based on image density. The word overlap evaluation metrics showcase that the models exhibit the same behavior with the previous experiments. We also observe performance drop in terms of semantic equivalence using BERTSCORE. However, it is worth mentioning that the degradation in capturing semantics is less significant than the productivity experiments using caption length. Previously, XE and CIDEr optimization recorded a difference of 4 BERTSCORE units between TLD and THD, whereas BERTSCORE declined by 2.37 and 2.05 units respectively.

4.3 Substitutivity

		B1	B4	M	R	C	BS
$\mathcal{O}$ vs $\mathcal{GT}$	$\mathcal{M}^2$	77.12	37.5	30.12	58.64	110.54	45.18
	$\mathcal{M}^2_{SCST}$	81.74	40.63	31.00	60.42	122.14	46.24
$\mathcal{S}$ vs $\mathcal{GT}$	$\mathcal{M}^2$	72.78	29.35	26.6	52.76	95.42	43.87
	$\mathcal{M}^2_{SCST}$	76.13	33.19	28.26	54.74	109.62	45.54
$\mathcal{O}$ vs $\mathcal{S}$	$\mathcal{M}^2$	62.57	35.18	32.98	60.8	304.27	65.79
	$\mathcal{M}^2_{SCST}$	77.0	55.88	44.89	75.16	466.76	77.71
$\mathcal{O}_t$ vs $\mathcal{S}_t$	$\mathcal{M}^2$	66.27	46.16	34.9	64.55	446.13	69.30
	$\mathcal{M}^2_{SCST}$	85.21	74.37	50.93	82.76	707.9	83.51

Table 6: Results on substitutivity test. ($\mathcal{GT}$) ground truth captions, ($\mathcal{O}$) original caption without substitution, ($\mathcal{S}$) caption after substitution, ($\mathcal{O}_t$) sub-caption after the synonym word, ($\mathcal{S}_t$) sub-caption after substituting the synonym word.

The objective of the final test is to evaluate the robustness of a model against synonym substitutions. In order to create a substitutivity test, we manually create two sets of words S_1, S_2. For every word

$w \in S_1$, there is another word $s \in S_2$ such that w can always be replaced by s without altering the meaning of the caption. We initially considered the 80 COCO object categories and used the mapping between objects and fine-grained classes defined by Lu et al. (2018). We excluded object categories with no synonyms ('cup') and categories containing more than one word ('baseball glove'). Next, we manually inspected ground truth captions to ensure that pairs of object categories and their synonyms are interchangeable. With this process we further divided the 'person' category into 'man', 'woman', 'boy', and 'girl' with 'person' and 'child' as synonyms. Finally, we discarded words with multiple meanings.

The pairs of object categories and synonyms used to test substitutivity are illustrated in Table 10. In order to ensure that the model is exposed to both object categories and fine-grained classes, we selected those that appeared adequate times during training. We trained a model on the train set of the Karpathy split and selected pairs of categories and fine-grained classes, where each word appears at least 200 times in the ground truth training examples. Note that in substitutivity we are not exclusively interested in images where the pair of words is jointly observed in its captions. Finally, we selected images from the test set in the Karpathy split where the generated captions of the trained model contained the fine-grained class. To verify that a substitution is performed adequate times during inference, we used pairs where the fine-grained class appeared at least 10 times in the generated captions. The distribution of the number of images with captions containing either a selected object category or fine-grained class for the train and test set are illustrated in Figure 5.

We inspect how the model behaves under replacement of a word with its synonym. During inference we apply beam search. For each active hypothesis, if the current most likely word belongs in S_1, we substitute the word with its synonym from S_2. To ensure that the substitution is preserved after each decoding stage, we set the probability of the synonym word to 1. We compute standard metrics using the original caption ($\mathcal{O}$), the caption after substitution ($\mathcal{S}$), the sub-caption after the synonym word ($\mathcal{O}_t$), and the sub-caption after replacing the synonym word ($\mathcal{S}_t$). In this setting, high values regarding overlap metrics such as BLEU and ROUGE indicate robustness of a model while semantic equivalence BERTSCORE also provides valuable insights.

The substitutivity results are illustrated in Table 6. In the first two rows we compare the ground truth caption with the originally generated caption and the caption after substitution. For both model variations we observe considerable performance drops after replacing a word with its synonym. This is expected as we intervened during decoding and replaced the original word with its synonym that had lower probability. In this case, the main concern is not whether the model generates plausible captions but whether its prediction matches the prediction before the substitution. The last two rows of the table compare the generated caption and the caption after substitution. Overall, both models performed exceptionally well with SCST providing consistent gains across all metrics. The sub-caption after substituting the synonym word appears to match with the sub-caption after the synonym word both in terms of n-gram metrics as well as semantics. This claim also holds for the captions as a whole; the high scores indicate that the models may be meaning-invariant with regards substitutions from fine-grained classes to more generic ones.

Our findings suggest that the model is robust against these substitutions. However, it may be straightforward for the model to substitute a fine-grained object description with another that has a broader concept. A more challenging scenario would involve the same experiment but replacing generic descriptions with more fine-grained categories. For instance, replacing 'person' in 'A person driving truck' with 'firefighter'.

5 Qualitative Analysis

For each proposed test we randomly sampled 100 examples from the derived splits and inspected the generated captions. In this section, we report the main findings based on that pool. Additional material is provided in the Appendix C.

Systematicity We observed that the models from both training procedures are reluctant to make systematic generalizations. In the case of adjective and noun pairs the models consistently avoided using adjectives or used adjectives that describe a different property of the object. In these cases the models do not actually learn to combine pairs but instead learn co-occurrence statistics in the data (e.g., 'a double decker bus' and 'a red bus'). With regards to pairs of nouns and verbs the models tended to replace the verb with a generic phrase. We also found an adequate number of examples where the generated caption did not contain any verb at all.

Productivity Overall, both models favored short captions. We observed cases where the ground truth captions provided fine-grained explanations, yet the generated caption contained only a handful of these descriptions. However, this does not entail that the generated caption is incorrect or of poor quality. Both models generally performed reasonably well, without hallucinating objects in the scenes or assigning incorrect properties to described objects. We also frequently observed cases where at least one of the reference captions constitutes an outlier in terms of caption length. In these cases the annotator provided a thorough description of the image. To maximize its performance, the model prioritizes matching the generated with the remaining reference captions whose lengths cluster around similar values.

Substitutivity In the cases of mismatch between the originally generated caption and its modification, the majority of the examples differed exclusively in the part of the caption after the substitution. The modified caption either contained the same objects and their attributes with a simple reordering or the objects were described with more detail including additional properties or relations. We observed a few examples where the caption was completely restructured and identified two cases of such behavior. On the one hand, the original caption contained multiple occurrences of fine-grained objects (e.g., 'a man and a woman riding on a motorcycle' & 'a person riding a motorcycle with a person on the back'). On the other hand, the caption was altered to include additional properties of the substituted word (e.g., 'a living room with a television and a fireplace' & 'a flat screen tv in a living room with a fireplace'). These cases could be due to the decoding policy as substituting the original word with its synonym in an active hypothesis results in a sequence with lower marginal probability. The active hypothesis is then discarded as it does not fit in the beam width. This is a common problem in decoding, where high probability words are concealed behind low probability words.

6 Conclusion

We presented a series of tests for compositionality in image captioning. This work contributes towards what it means for a captioning model to be 'compositional', and what properties we would like them to have. We performed data and model ablations to identify limitations of state of the art models across three dimensions of compositionality.

Our findings in the systematicity align with the findings from previous works. We find that transformer-based captioning models rarely make systematic generalizations. However, as shown by the experiments in productivity, this is also partially due to the model not producing adjectives and nouns. We demonstrated that the well-established CIDEr fine-tuning coupled with beam search decoding actually exacerbates the already poor performance on systematicity.

In productivity, we found out that models struggle to extend their predictions to match the length of the ground truth captions. Both models trained using XE and SCST generated less number of adjectives, nouns, and verbs compared to the ground truth captions. On average we observed that models after XE optimization provide captions with more adjectives and verbs, while models incorporating SCST generate descriptions with more nouns. We further included a set of experiments concerning the visual density of the image with similar results.

The substitutivity experiment showcased that it is easy for the models to substitute a fine-grained with abstract descriptions of concepts. In most cases, the part of the caption following the synonym word was identical to the part of the caption after the substitution with its synonym. A natural extension to the substitutivity experiment would include the performance after substituting more abstract with fine-grained descriptions.

With our framework we provided insights regarding the evaluation and training of image captioning models. Word overlap metrics favor models that generate sequences closer to the target rather than more 'grounded' models that focus on actual properties of the objects in the image. This calls for a training regime that mitigates this issue by introducing multimodal metrics that take both text and vision into account (e.g., *CLIPScore* (Hessel et al., 2021)). Additionally, different training strategies should be adopted to allow the model to explore the search space, and learn to generate sequences that go beyond the average sequence length.

7 Ethical statement

The presented paper introduces a framework to evaluate compositionality of image captioning models from multiple perspectives. The dataset and the model under evaluation are publicly available for academic purposes and not intended for downstream deployment.

Despite recent advances, our findings challenge the systematicity and productivity of current models. This suggests that the generalization capacity and robustness remain a barrier to overcome, before exposing the outputs of these models to end users. As a result, we believe that comprehensive evaluations can help expose biases in the model and minimize the impact in real-world deployment of language technologies.

Acknowledgements

This research was supported by Alana AI. The views, and/or opinions presented are those of the authors and not of the funding agency.

References

Aishwarya Agrawal, Aniruddha Kembhavi, Dhruv Batra, and Devi Parikh. 2017. C-vqa: A compositional split of the visual question answering (vqa) v1. 0 dataset. *arXiv preprint arXiv:1704.08243*.

Ekin Akyürek, Afra Feyza Akyürek, and Jacob Andreas. 2020. Learning to recombine and resample data for compositional generalization. In *International Conference on Learning Representations*.

Peter Anderson, Xiaodong He, Chris Buehler, Damien Teney, Mark Johnson, Stephen Gould, and Lei Zhang. 2018. Bottom-up and top-down attention for image captioning and visual question answering. In *Proceedings of the IEEE conference on computer vision and pattern recognition*, pages 6077–6086.

Yuval Atzmon, Jonathan Berant, Vahid Kezami, Amir Globerson, and Gal Chechik. 2016. Learning to generalize to new compositions in image understanding. *arXiv preprint arXiv:1608.07639*.

Dzmitry Bahdanau, Shikhar Murty, Michael Noukhovitch, Thien Huu Nguyen, Harm de Vries, and Aaron Courville. 2018. Systematic generalization: What is required and can it be learned? In *International Conference on Learning Representations*.

Marco Baroni. 2020. Linguistic generalization and compositionality in modern artificial neural networks. *Philosophical Transactions of the Royal Society B*, 375(1791):20190307.

Marco Baroni and Roberto Zamparelli. 2010. Nouns are vectors, adjectives are matrices: Representing adjective-noun constructions in semantic space. In *Proceedings of the 2010 Conference on Empirical Methods in Natural Language Processing*, pages 1183–1193, Cambridge, MA. Association for Computational Linguistics.

Samuel R. Bowman, Christopher Potts, and Christopher D. Manning. 2015. Recursive neural networks can learn logical semantics. In *Proceedings of the 3rd Workshop on Continuous Vector Space Models and their Compositionality*, pages 12–21, Beijing, China. Association for Computational Linguistics.

Tom Brown, Benjamin Mann, Nick Ryder, Melanie Subbiah, Jared D Kaplan, Prafulla Dhariwal, Arvind Neelakantan, Pranav Shyam, Girish Sastry, Amanda Askell, Sandhini Agarwal, Ariel Herbert-Voss, Gretchen Krueger, Tom Henighan, Rewon Child, Aditya Ramesh, Daniel Ziegler, Jeffrey Wu, Clemens Winter, Chris Hesse, Mark Chen, Eric Sigler, Mateusz Litwin, Scott Gray, Benjamin Chess, Jack Clark, Christopher Berner, Sam McCandlish, Alec Radford, Ilya Sutskever, and Dario Amodei. 2020. Language models are few-shot learners. In *Advances in Neural Information Processing Systems*, volume 33, pages 1877–1901. Curran Associates, Inc.

Emanuele Bugliarello and Desmond Elliott. 2021. The role of syntactic planning in compositional image captioning. In *Proceedings of the 16th Conference of the European Chapter of the Association for Computational Linguistics: Main Volume*, pages 593–607.

Bob Coecke, Mehrnoosh Sadrzadeh, and Stephen Clark. 2010. Mathematical foundations for a compositional distributional model of meaning. *arXiv preprint arXiv:1003.4394*.

Henry Conklin, Bailin Wang, Kenny Smith, and Ivan Titov. 2021. Meta-learning to compositionally generalize. In *Proceedings of the 59th Annual Meeting of the Association for Computational Linguistics and the 11th International Joint Conference on Natural Language Processing (Volume 1: Long Papers)*, pages 3322–3335, Online. Association for Computational Linguistics.

Marcella Cornia, Matteo Stefanini, Lorenzo Baraldi, and Rita Cucchiara. 2020. Meshed-memory transformer for image captioning. In *Proceedings of the IEEE/CVF Conference on Computer Vision and Pattern Recognition*, pages 10578–10587.

Michael Denkowski and Alon Lavie. 2014. Meteor universal: Language specific translation evaluation for any target language. In *Proceedings of the Ninth Workshop on Statistical Machine Translation*, pages 376–380. Association for Computational Linguistics.

Jacob Devlin, Ming-Wei Chang, Kenton Lee, and Kristina Toutanova. 2019. BERT: Pre-training of deep bidirectional transformers for language understanding. In *Proceedings of the 2019 Conference of the North American Chapter of the Association for Computational Linguistics: Human Language Technologies, Volume 1 (Long and Short Papers)*, pages 4171–4186, Minneapolis, Minnesota. Association for Computational Linguistics.

Desmond Elliott and Frank Keller. 2014. Comparing automatic evaluation measures for image description. In *Proceedings of the 52nd Annual Meeting of the Association for Computational Linguistics (Volume 2: Short Papers)*, pages 452–457, Baltimore, Maryland. Association for Computational Linguistics.

Jerry A Fodor and Ernest Lepore. 2002. *The compositionality papers*. Oxford University Press.

Jerry A Fodor and Zenon W Pylyshyn. 1988. Connectionism and cognitive architecture: A critical analysis. *Cognition*, 28(1-2):3–71.

Gottlob Frege. 1950. *The foundations of arithmetic: A logico-mathematical enquiry into the concept of number*. Northwestern University Press.

Alex Graves, Greg Wayne, and Ivo Danihelka. 2014. Neural turing machines. *arXiv preprint arXiv:1410.5401*.

Jack Hessel, Ari Holtzman, Maxwell Forbes, Ronan Le Bras, and Yejin Choi. 2021. Clipscore: A reference-free evaluation metric for image captioning. In *Proceedings of the 2021 Conference on Empirical Methods in Natural Language Processing*, pages 7514–7528.

Matthew Honnibal, Ines Montani, Sofie Van Landeghem, and Adriane Boyd. 2020. spaCy: Industrial-strength Natural Language Processing in Python.

Dieuwke Hupkes, Verna Dankers, Mathijs Mul, and Elia Bruni. 2020. Compositionality decomposed: how do neural networks generalise? *Journal of Artificial Intelligence Research*, 67:757–795.

Yichen Jiang and Mohit Bansal. 2021. Inducing transformer's compositional generalization ability via auxiliary sequence prediction tasks. In *Proceedings of the 2021 Conference on Empirical Methods in Natural Language Processing*, pages 6253–6265.

Justin Johnson, Bharath Hariharan, Laurens Van Der Maaten, Li Fei-Fei, C Lawrence Zitnick, and Ross Girshick. 2017. Clevr: A diagnostic dataset for compositional language and elementary visual reasoning. In *Proceedings of the IEEE Conference on Computer Vision and Pattern Recognition*, pages 2901–2910.

Andrej Karpathy and Li Fei-Fei. 2015. Deep visual-semantic alignments for generating image descriptions. In *Proceedings of the IEEE conference on computer vision and pattern recognition*, pages 3128–3137.

Daniel Keysers, Nathanael Schärli, Nathan Scales, Hylke Buisman, Daniel Furrer, Sergii Kashubin, Nikola Momchev, Danila Sinopalnikov, Lukasz Stafiniak, Tibor Tihon, et al. 2019. Measuring compositional generalization: A comprehensive method on realistic data. In *International Conference on Learning Representations*.

Najoung Kim and Tal Linzen. 2020. COGS: A compositional generalization challenge based on semantic interpretation. In *Proceedings of the 2020 Conference on Empirical Methods in Natural Language Processing (EMNLP)*, pages 9087–9105, Online. Association for Computational Linguistics.

Brenden Lake and Marco Baroni. 2018. Generalization without systematicity: On the compositional skills of sequence-to-sequence recurrent networks. In *International Conference on Machine Learning*, pages 2873–2882. PMLR.

Jiwei Li, Michel Galley, Chris Brockett, Jianfeng Gao, and Bill Dolan. 2016. A diversity-promoting objective function for neural conversation models. In *Proceedings of the 2016 Conference of the North American Chapter of the Association for Computational Linguistics: Human Language Technologies*, pages 110–119, San Diego, California. Association for Computational Linguistics.

Chin-Yew Lin. 2004. ROUGE: A package for automatic evaluation of summaries. In *Text Summarization Branches Out*, pages 74–81, Barcelona, Spain. Association for Computational Linguistics.

Tsung-Yi Lin, Michael Maire, Serge Belongie, James Hays, Pietro Perona, Deva Ramanan, Piotr Dollár, and C Lawrence Zitnick. 2014. Microsoft coco: Common objects in context. In *European conference on computer vision*, pages 740–755. Springer.

Yinhan Liu, Myle Ott, Naman Goyal, Jingfei Du, Mandar Joshi, Danqi Chen, Omer Levy, Mike Lewis, Luke Zettlemoyer, and Veselin Stoyanov. 2019. Roberta: A robustly optimized bert pretraining approach. *arXiv preprint arXiv:1907.11692*.

Jiasen Lu, Jianwei Yang, Dhruv Batra, and Devi Parikh. 2018. Neural baby talk. In *Proceedings of the IEEE conference on computer vision and pattern recognition*, pages 7219–7228.

Jeff Mitchell and Mirella Lapata. 2008. Vector-based models of semantic composition. In *Association for Computational Linguistics Human Language Technology Conference*, pages 236–244.

Mathijs Mul and Willem Zuidema. 2019. Siamese recurrent networks learn first-order logic reasoning and exhibit zero-shot compositional generalization. *arXiv preprint arXiv:1906.00180*.

Mitja Nikolaus, Mostafa Abdou, Matthew Lamm, Rahul Aralikatte, and Desmond Elliott. 2019. Compositional generalization in image captioning. In *Proceedings of the 23rd Conference on Computational*

Natural Language Learning (CoNLL), pages 87–98. Association for Computational Linguistics.

Peter Pagin. 2003. Communication and strong compositionality. *Journal of Philosophical Logic*, 32(3):287–322.

Kishore Papineni, Salim Roukos, Todd Ward, and Wei-Jing Zhu. 2002. Bleu: a method for automatic evaluation of machine translation. In *Proceedings of the 40th annual meeting of the Association for Computational Linguistics*, pages 311–318.

Matthew Purver, Mehrnoosh Sadrzadeh, Ruth Kempson, Gijs Wijnholds, and Julian Hough. 2021. Incremental composition in distributional semantics. *Journal of Logic, Language and Information*, 30(2):379–406.

Linlu Qiu, Peter Shaw, Panupong Pasupat, Paweł Krzysztof Nowak, Tal Linzen, Fei Sha, and Kristina Toutanova. 2021. Improving compositional generalization with latent structure and data augmentation. *arXiv preprint arXiv:2112.07610*.

Colin Raffel, Noam Shazeer, Adam Roberts, Katherine Lee, Sharan Narang, Michael Matena, Yanqi Zhou, Wei Li, and Peter J. Liu. 2020. Exploring the limits of transfer learning with a unified text-to-text transformer. *Journal of Machine Learning Research*, 21(140):1–67.

Steven J Rennie, Etienne Marcheret, Youssef Mroueh, Jerret Ross, and Vaibhava Goel. 2017. Self-critical sequence training for image captioning. In *Proceedings of the IEEE conference on computer vision and pattern recognition*, pages 7008–7024.

Laura Ruis, Jacob Andreas, Marco Baroni, Diane Bouchacourt, and Brenden M Lake. 2020. A benchmark for systematic generalization in grounded language understanding. *Advances in neural information processing systems*, 33:19861–19872.

Mehrnoosh Sadrzadeh and Edward Grefenstette. 2011. A compositional distributional semantics, two concrete constructions, and some experimental evaluations. In *International Symposium on Quantum Interaction*, pages 35–47. Springer.

David Saxton, Edward Grefenstette, Felix Hill, and Pushmeet Kohli. 2019. Analysing mathematical reasoning abilities of neural models. In *International Conference on Learning Representations*.

Koustuv Sinha, Shagun Sodhani, Jin Dong, Joelle Pineau, and William L. Hamilton. 2019. CLUTRR: A diagnostic benchmark for inductive reasoning from text. In *Proceedings of the 2019 Conference on Empirical Methods in Natural Language Processing and the 9th International Joint Conference on Natural Language Processing (EMNLP-IJCNLP)*, pages 4506–4515, Hong Kong, China. Association for Computational Linguistics.

Paul Smolensky. 1990. Tensor product variable binding and the representation of symbolic structures in connectionist systems. *Artificial intelligence*, 46(1-2):159–216.

Alessandro Suglia, Ioannis Konstas, Andrea Vanzo, Emanuele Bastianelli, Desmond Elliott, Stella Frank, and Oliver Lemon. 2020. CompGuessWhat?!: A multi-task evaluation framework for grounded language learning. In *Proceedings of the 58th Annual Meeting of the Association for Computational Linguistics*, pages 7625–7641, Online. Association for Computational Linguistics.

Zoltan Szabó. 2012. The case for compositionality. *The Oxford handbook of compositionality*, 64:80.

Ashish Vaswani, Noam Shazeer, Niki Parmar, Jakob Uszkoreit, Llion Jones, Aidan N Gomez, Lukasz Kaiser, and Illia Polosukhin. 2017. Attention is all you need. In *NIPS*.

Ramakrishna Vedantam, C Lawrence Zitnick, and Devi Parikh. 2015. Cider: Consensus-based image description evaluation. In *Proceedings of the IEEE conference on computer vision and pattern recognition*, pages 4566–4575.

Sara Veldhoen, Dieuwke Hupkes, and Willem H Zuidema. 2016. Diagnostic classifiers revealing how neural networks process hierarchical structure. In *CoCo@ NIPS*.

Ashwin K Vijayakumar, Michael Cogswell, Ramprasath R Selvaraju, Qing Sun, Stefan Lee, David Crandall, and Dhruv Batra. 2016. Diverse beam search: Decoding diverse solutions from neural sequence models. *arXiv preprint arXiv:1610.02424*.

Spencer Whitehead, Hui Wu, Heng Ji, Rogerio Feris, and Kate Saenko. 2021. Separating skills and concepts for novel visual question answering. In *Proceedings of the IEEE/CVF Conference on Computer Vision and Pattern Recognition*, pages 5632–5641.

Yanzhi Yi, Hangyu Deng, and Jinglu Hu. 2020. Improving image captioning evaluation by considering inter references variance. In *Proceedings of the 58th Annual Meeting of the Association for Computational Linguistics*, pages 985–994, Online. Association for Computational Linguistics.

Pengcheng Yin, Hao Fang, Graham Neubig, Adam Pauls, Emmanouil Antonios Platanios, Yu Su, Sam Thomson, and Jacob Andreas. 2021. Compositional generalization for neural semantic parsing via span-level supervised attention. In *Proceedings of the 2021 Conference of the North American Chapter of the Association for Computational Linguistics: Human Language Technologies*, pages 2810–2823, Online. Association for Computational Linguistics.

A Dataset splits

We created custom splits of the MSCOCO dataset (Lin et al., 2014), a collection of images described in English.

A.1 Systematicity

black cat
big bird
red bus
small plane
eat man
lie woman

Table 7: Pairs of concepts used to test systematicity.

Recall scores

	Color	Size	Verb
BUTD Nikolaus et al.	15.95	0.32	10.55
$\mathcal{M}^2$	15.78	0.41	19.14
$\mathcal{M}^2_{SCST}$	8.66	0	11.7

Table 8: Recall@5 for each grouped category of concepts of interest.

Additional insights can be obtained by observing the individual recall scores for each concept of interest. Both models cannot make systematic generalizations in terms of adjectives describing size. This aligns with the view of (Nikolaus et al., 2019) who also showcased that the actual bounding box of the referred noun does not correlate with its size modifiers in the description of an image. For additional comparison with the work of Nikolaus et al. (2019), we group the pairs in terms of color, size, and verb as shown in Table 8. Interestingly, our findings suggest that transformer-based architectures are more capable of systematic composition when they describe verbs. On the other hand, BUTD recorded the best generalization performance when they describe color and noun pairs. There is no reported performance of BUTD for the systematicity split using SCST.

A.2 Productivity

The distribution of the average caption length is shown Figure 2. An overview of the average POS tags and the length of each caption per image is illustrated in Table 9, where the left and right part of the table account for the Karpathy and the proposed productivity split. On average captions of images

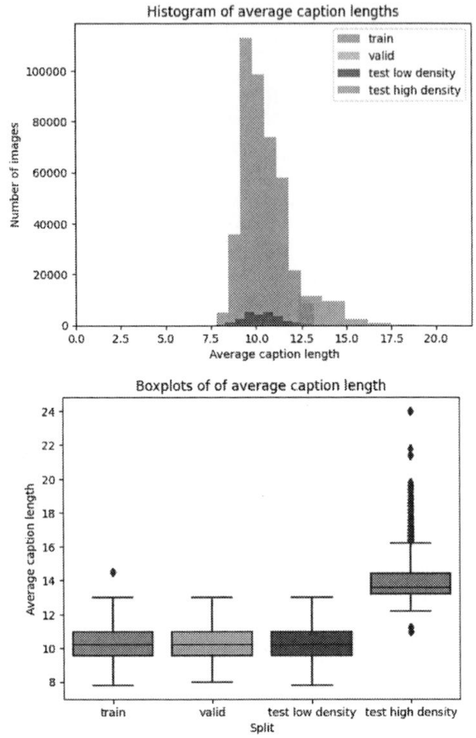

Figure 2: Histogram and boxplots of average caption length for each image in the train, validation, and test sets of the productivity split.

from Test Rich have approximately 14.47% more adjectives, 31.75% more nouns, and 29.70% verbs than the train, validation, and test base sets. We apply the same procedure for the visual density experiment. Figure 3 shows the distribution of the number of instances on each split.

A.3 Substitutivity

We initially considered the 80 COCO categories and used the mapping between objects and fine-grained classes defined by Lu et al. (2018). We excluded object categories with no synonyms ('cup') and categories containing more than one word ('baseball glove'). Next, we manually inspected ground truth captions to ensure that pairs of object categories and their synonyms are interchangeable. With this process we further divided the 'person' category into 'man', 'woman', 'boy', and 'girl' with 'person' and 'child' as synonyms. Finally, we discarded the 'dog' category completely as we found that it often referred to the actual animal or 'hot dog'.

	Train	Valid	Test	Train	Valid	Test Base	Test Rich
ADJ	0.76	0.76	0.77	0.76	0.77	0.76	0.87
ADP	1.74	1.75	1.75	1.71	1.71	1.71	2.46
ADV	0.15	0.15	0.16	0.15	0.15	0.14	0.21
CCONJ	0.24	0.24	0.24	0.23	0.23	0.23	0.45
DET	2.2	2.21	2.2	2.17	2.17	2.18	2.9
NOUN	3.64	3.64	3.62	3.59	3.58	3.58	4.73
PRON	0.18	0.18	0.18	0.17	0.18	0.17	0.32
VERB	1.02	1.02	1.01	1.01	1	1.01	1.31
LENGTH	11.34	11.35	11.32	11.19	11.17	11.2	15.03

Table 9: Comparison of average POS tags and caption lengths in each image between train, validation, and test sets in the Karpathy (Karpathy and Fei-Fei, 2015) and the productivity split.

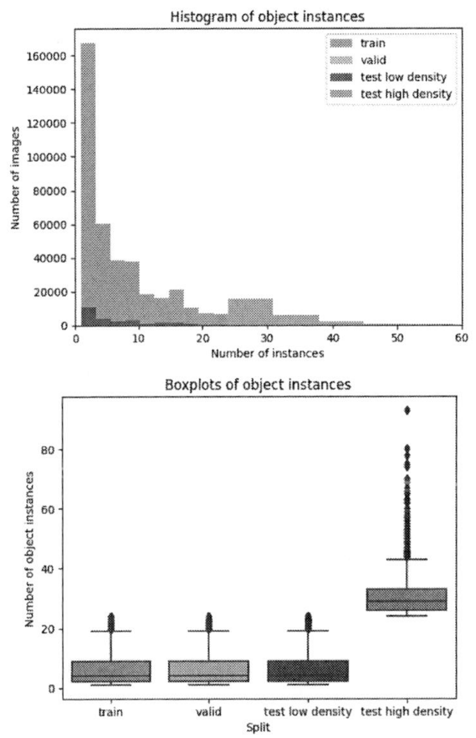

Figure 3: Histogram and boxplots of number of instances for each image in the train, validation, and test sets of the productivity split concerning visual density.

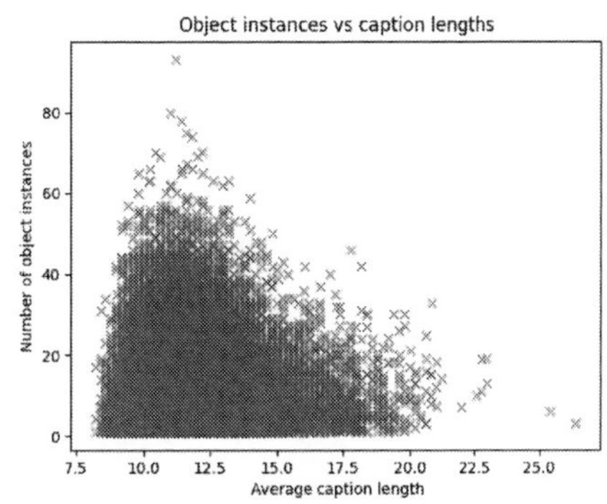

Figure 4: Illustration of the number of instances and the caption length of images in MSCOCO (Lin et al., 2014).

Object category	Fine-grained class
`person`	`man`, `woman`
`child`	`boy`, `girl`
`bicycle`	`bike`
`airplane`	`plane`, `jet`, `jetliner`
`cow`	`cattle`
`tv`	`television`
`refrigerator`	`freezer`
`laptop`	`computer`

Table 10: Selected pairs of object categories and fine-grained classes used in substitutivity split. During inference, we replace the generated fine-grained word with its synonym.

B Model details

Our implementation is based on the publicly available PyTorch codebase of $\mathcal{M}^2$-transformer (`https://github.com/aimagelab/meshed-memory-transformer`). Following Cornia et al. (2020) we use 3 encoding and decoding layers, 8 attention heads, and 40 memory vectors.

We also noticed during SCST, that the model occasionally produced incomplete captions (e.g., 'a man is riding a horse in a'). Our interpretation here is that the model is reluctant to produce that noun and the learnt policy indicates that it is better to generate an incomplete caption and receive the adjusted reward rather than make a 'risky' prediction. The paper introducing SCST (Rennie et al., 2017) states in the supplementary materials (sec-

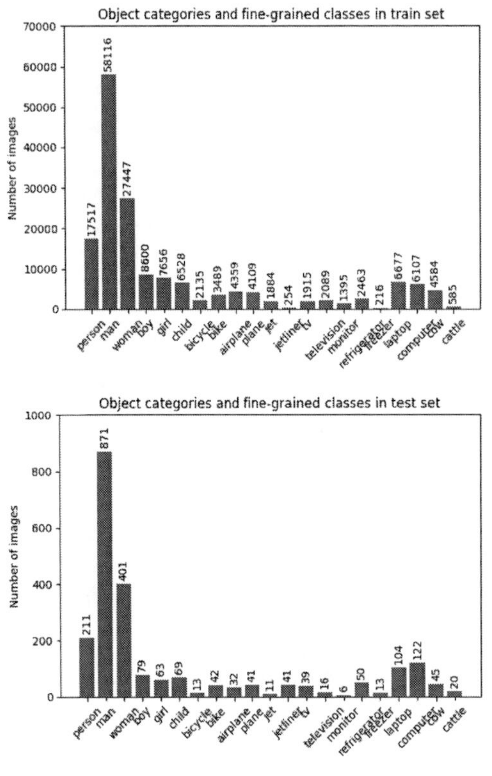

Figure 5: Distribution of object categories and fine-grained classes in train (left) and test (right) substitutivity split.

tion E): "*One detail that was crucial to optimizing CIDEr to produce better models was to include the EOS tag as a word.*" If the EOS word is omitted, trivial sentence fragments such as 'with a' and 'and a' receive significant reward values, as opposed to their full sentence counterparts. However, including the EOS tag lowers the reward allocated to the incomplete captions. We apply the same procedure by appending EOS token to both candidate and reference captions.

C Qualitative analysis

We examined qualitatively the behavior of the models under each compositional test by randomly sampling 100 examples. For systematicity (Figure 6), we compared the occurrences of systematic generalization in Test Comb. Similarly, for productivity (Figure 7) we studied the captions over images belonging to Test Rich with a focus on the part-of-speech tags produced during generation as opposed to the reference captions. Finally, for substitutivity (Figure 8) we examined the originally generated and the modified caption and emphasized on their similarity.

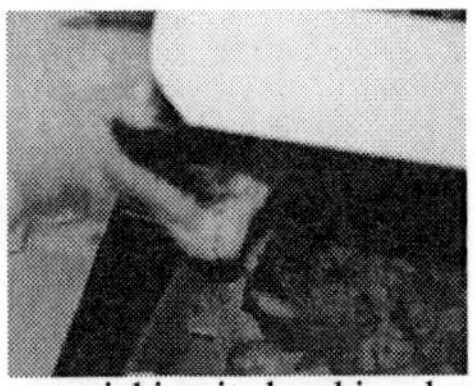

$\mathcal{GT}$: a cute cat sticking its head in a box of pizza,
a white and black cat with its head inside a box smelling the food,
a cat pokes its head into a box and smells the food inside it,
a cat with its head in a box of pizza,
a cat trying to sneak a bite of pizza
$\mathcal{M}^2$: a white and **black cat** eating a piece of pizza
$\mathcal{M}^2_{SCST}$: a cat is eating a pizza in a box

$\mathcal{GT}$: a couple of black cats laying on top of a bed,
two black cats cuddle together on a blanket,
two black cats sleeping together on a bed,
two black cats cuddled together on a bed,
a couple of cats relaxing with each other on the bed
a woman sitting in the drivers seat of a car with a cat in her lap
$\mathcal{M}^2$: a cat laying on a blanket on a bed
$\mathcal{M}^2_{SCST}$: a **black cat** laying on a bed

$\mathcal{GT}$: two red buses headed to the same place are right next to each other on the road,
buses lined up on the street in traffic,
there are many red busses coming down the street together,
the buses are lined up waiting for passengers,
a couple of buses drive next to each other
$\mathcal{M}^2$: a couple of **red buses** driving down a street
$\mathcal{M}^2_{SCST}$: two **red buses** driving down a city street

$\mathcal{GT}$: a red bus on street next to buildings,
a public transit bus on a city street,
a large red bus on a city street,
a red bus crossing a street next to tall buildings,
a red bus is parked along the side of a street
$\mathcal{M}^2$: a double decker bus driving down a city street
$\mathcal{M}^2_{SCST}$: a double decker bus driving down a city street

$\mathcal{GT}$: a bright blue and white amx jet is in the clear sky,
a blue airplane is flying during a clear day,
an airplane flying in a blue sky,
a small two toned blue airplane flying,
a small plane is seen flying on a clear day
$\mathcal{M}^2$: a blue and white airplane flying in the sky
$\mathcal{M}^2_{SCST}$: an airplane is flying in the blue sky

$\mathcal{GT}$: an airplane with wheels wheels barely off ground tilted slightly upward from the pavement to the blue sky,
a small plane is taking off from a sandy beach,
a white airplane is driving down the runway,
small plane inches above flat surface near water,
a small plane on the sand near a beach
$\mathcal{M}^2$: an airplane is on the runway on a sunny day
$\mathcal{M}^2_{SCST}$: an airplane is taking off from an airport runway

$\mathcal{GT}$: a man holding a slice of pizza while wearing glasses,
there is a man eating a sandwich with lots of cheese on it,
a man in red is eating some food,
a full view of an individual in the image,
a man looks at the camera while holding a hot dog
$\mathcal{M}^2$: a man in a red shirt holding two hot dogs
$\mathcal{M}^2_{SCST}$: a man in a red shirt holding a hot dog

$\mathcal{GT}$: three guys sitting down eating sandwiches and smiling,
three men eating sandwiches at a corner table,
two young men one old enjoying a meal at a restaurant,
three men all eating sub sandwiches at a restaurant,
three men are sitting in a restaurant eating sandwiches
$\mathcal{M}^2$: three **men** sitting at a table **eating** food
$\mathcal{M}^2_{SCST}$: three **men** sitting at a table **eating** a sandwich

Figure 6: Examples of generated captions for different concept pairs from the Test Comb. Bold phrases indicate successful systematic generalization.

$\mathcal{GT}$: a woman driving a car while holding a cat on her lap
a woman driving her car with a cat riding in her lap,
a lady driving her car with a black and white cat in her lap,
a woman sitting in a car with a black and white cat,
a woman sitting in the drivers seat of a car with a cat in her lap
$\mathcal{M}^2$: a person in a car with a cat
$\mathcal{M}^2_{SCST}$: a woman in a car with a black and white cat

$\mathcal{GT}$: a bunch of people sitting on and standing around a bench with bikes,
some people sit on a bench near bicycles,
a group of people sit on and near a park bench,
several people sit on a blue bench with their bikes around them,
a bench seats a few people as bikes are parked nearby and one man sits on a brick walkway as another boy in blue stands near them
$\mathcal{M}^2$: a couple of people sitting on top of a bench
$\mathcal{M}^2_{SCST}$: a bike with a bench and people in it

$\mathcal{GT}$: a man holding an orange frisbee in his mouth with a dog,
a dog and its owner battling over a frisbee,
a person with a frisbee in his mouth bending over to his dog who has the other end of the frisbee in its mouth,
a man in the snow holding a disc in his mouth as a dog bites it also,
a man and dog use their teeth to fight for the same frisbee
$\mathcal{M}^2$: a man holding an orange dog in the snow
$\mathcal{M}^2_{SCST}$: a man holding an orange frisbee with a dog

$\mathcal{GT}$: a wooden kitchen table topped with baked goods and pie,
a tray with some food a pot and some bottles,
there is a pan with lettuce in it near a tray of meat,
a tray of food and a boiler with a vegetable sit on a kitchen counter,
a counter with a pot with a vegetable in it as well as chicken breasts on the side
$\mathcal{M}^2$: a wooden cutting board topped with lots of food
$\mathcal{M}^2_{SCST}$: a wooden table with a pan of food and a knife

$\mathcal{GT}$: father and daughter leaning over small cake with large candle on it,
a man and a woman blowing out a candle in a cake,
a guy and girl celebrating an occasion with a cake with chocolate frosting and 1 candle,
a man and woman stand before a small cake with a single candle in it,
a couple blowing out an enormous candle on a small chocolate
$\mathcal{M}^2$: a man blowing out candles on a birthday cake
$\mathcal{M}^2_{SCST}$: a man and a woman blowing out candles on a birthday cake

$\mathcal{GT}$: a kitchen counter top with a tray of sliced tomatoes and a plate of whole tomatoes,
there is a large plate of tomatoes and a pan of sliced tomatoes,
a cookie sheet with red sliced tomatoes and a platter of whole tomatoes on a crowded kitchen counter, there 's plenty of red tomatoes on the kitchen counter,
a sloe up of sliced tomatoes on a baking pan
$\mathcal{M}^2$: a close up of a plate of food with tomatoes
$\mathcal{M}^2_{SCST}$: a kitchen counter with a bunch of tomatoes and other vegetables

Figure 7: Productivity: examples of generated captions from images in the Test Rich.

$\mathcal{GT}$: an airport with large jetliners and a bus traveling on a tarmac,
an airplane and busses are lined up at the airport,
a group of buses driving around at the airport,
airplanes sit at the gate as transportation vehicles move about,
a busy runway with buses and luggage carts driving around
$\mathcal{M}^2$: a large jetliner sitting on top of an airport tarmac
$\mathcal{M}^2$ (S): a large airplane that is on a runway
$\mathcal{M}^2_{SCST}$: a plane is parked at an airport terminal
$\mathcal{M}^2_{SCST}$ (S): a airplane parked at an airport with cars and planes

$\mathcal{GT}$: a person sits on top of a motorcycle with a stuffed toy,
a person riding a motorcycle with a stuffed animal on the back,
a person on a motorcycle with a stuffed animal on back,
a motorcyclist riding with a stuffed animal attached to the back,
a person in full leather riding a motorcycle with a stuff animal on the back
$\mathcal{M}^2$: a man riding on the back of a motorcycle
$\mathcal{M}^2$ (S): a person riding a motorcycle on a street
$\mathcal{M}^2_{SCST}$: a man riding a motorcycle on a road
$\mathcal{M}^2_{SCST}$ (S): a person riding a motorcycle on a road

$\mathcal{GT}$: an older woman sits in a sweater at the beach,
a person wearing sun glasses and blue jeans sitting on a rock by the ocean,
a woman is sitting on the beach,
a lady near some rocks during the daytime looking at the camera,
an older woman sitting on a drift log at a beach
$\mathcal{M}^2$: a woman sitting on a log near the water
$\mathcal{M}^2$ (S): an older person sitting on a log in front of a mountain
$\mathcal{M}^2_{SCST}$: a woman sitting on a log by the water
$\mathcal{M}^2_{SCST}$ (S): an older person sitting on a log near the water

$\mathcal{GT}$: two girls in a library seated at a table cutting large brown paper,
girls sitting in a library cutting brown paper,
two girls working on a project in the library,
a couple of girls cutting paper with some scissors,
two teenaged girls sitting in armchairs at a public library and cutting sheets of craft paper with scissors $\mathcal{M}^2$: two girls sitting on chairs in a library
$\mathcal{M}^2$ (S): two young children sitting together in a library
$\mathcal{M}^2_{SCST}$: two girls sitting in chairs in a library
$\mathcal{M}^2_{SCST}$ (S): two children sitting in chairs in a library

$\mathcal{GT}$: a young man standing next to a race car with the red sox logo on it 's hood,
a young boy standing in front of a sponsored car,
a man standing near a red sox nascar,
a young boy standing by a red sox car wearing red sox shirt and visor,
a young man standing next to a racecar on a display lot
$\mathcal{M}^2$: a young boy wearing a red hat standing in front of a car
$\mathcal{M}^2$ (S): a young child standing in front of a car
$\mathcal{M}^2_{SCST}$: a young boy is standing next to a car
$\mathcal{M}^2_{SCST}$ (S): a young child standing next to a police car

$\mathcal{GT}$: a low flying commercial plane passing tall buildings,
an airplane is flying in the sky beyond some skyscrapers,
a jetliner flying low as viewed between two skyscrapers,
an airplane is seen in the air between two buildings,
an airplane flying pass building and a bank building
$\mathcal{M}^2$: a large jetliner flying over a tall building
$\mathcal{M}^2$ (S): a large airplane flying over a city skyline
$\mathcal{M}^2_{SCST}$: a large jetliner flying over a tall building
$\mathcal{M}^2_{SCST}$ (S): a large airplane flying over a city skyline

Figure 8: Substitutivity: examples of generated captions from images in the substitutivity test.

Towards Unification of Discourse Annotation Frameworks

Yingxue Fu
School of Computer Science
University of St Andrews
KY16 9SX, UK
yf30@st-andrews.ac.uk

Abstract

Discourse information is difficult to represent and annotate. Among the major frameworks for annotating discourse information, RST, PDTB and SDRT are widely discussed and used, each having its own theoretical foundation and focus. Corpora annotated under different frameworks vary considerably. To make better use of the existing discourse corpora and achieve the possible synergy of different frameworks, it is worthwhile to investigate the systematic relations between different frameworks and devise methods of unifying the frameworks. Although the issue of framework unification has been a topic of discussion for a long time, there is currently no comprehensive approach which considers unifying both discourse structure and discourse relations and evaluates the unified framework intrinsically and extrinsically. We plan to use automatic means for the unification task and evaluate the result with structural complexity and downstream tasks. We will also explore the application of the unified framework in multi-task learning and graphical models.

1 Introduction

A text is not a simple collection of isolated sentences. These sentences generally appear in a certain order and are connected with each other through logical or semantic means to form a coherent whole. In recent years, modelling beyond the sentence level is attracting more attention, and different natural language processing (NLP) tasks use discourse-aware models to obtain better performance, such as sentiment analysis (Bhatia et al., 2015), automatic essay scoring (Nadeem et al., 2019), machine translation (Sim Smith, 2017), text summarization (Xu et al., 2020) and so on.

As discourse information typically involves the interaction of different levels of linguistic phenomena, including syntax, semantics, pragmatics and information structure, it is difficult to represent and annotate. Different discourse theories and discourse annotation frameworks have been proposed. Accordingly, discourse corpora annotated under different frameworks show considerable variation, and a corpus can be hardly used together with another corpus for natural language processing (NLP) tasks or discourse analysis in linguistics. Discourse parsing is a task of uncovering the underlying structure of text organization, and deep-learning based approaches are used in recent years. However, discourse annotation takes the whole document as the basic unit and is a laborious task. To boost the performance of neural models, we typically need a large amount of data.

Due to the above issues, the unification of discourse annotation frameworks has been a topic of discussion for a long time. Researchers have proposed varied methods to unify discourse relations and debated over whether trees are a good representation of discourse (Egg and Redeker, 2010; Lee et al., 2008; Wolf and Gibson, 2005). However, existing research either focuses on mapping or unifying discourse relations of different frameworks (Bunt and Prasad, 2016; Benamara and Taboada, 2015; Sanders et al., 2018; Demberg et al., 2019), or on finding a common discourse structure (Yi et al., 2021), without giving sufficient attention to the issue of relation mapping. There is still no comprehensive approach that considers unifying both discourse structure and discourse relations.

Another approach to tackling the task is to use multi-task learning so that information from a discourse corpus annotated under one framework can be used to solve a task in another framework, thus achieving synergy between different frameworks. However, existing studies adopting this method (Liu et al., 2016; Braud et al., 2016) do not show significant performance gain by incorporating a part of discourse information from a corpus annotated under a different framework. How to leverage discourse information from different frameworks

Proceedings of the 60th Annual Meeting of the Association for Computational Linguistics
Student Research Workshop, pages 132 - 142
May 22-27, 2022 ©2022 Association for Computational Linguistics

remains a challenge.

Discourse information may be used in downstream tasks. Huang and Kurohashi (2021) and Xu et al. (2020) use both coreference relations and discourse relations for text summarization with graph neural networks (GNNs). The ablation study by Huang and Kurohashi (2021) shows that using coreference relations only brings little performance improvement but incorporating discourse relations achieves the highest performance gain. While different kinds of discourse information can be used, how to encode different types of discourse information to improve discourse-awareness of neural models is a topic that merits further investigation.

The above challenges motivate our research on unifying different discourse annotation frameworks. We will focus on the following research questions:

RQ1: Which structure can be used to represent discourse in the unified framework?

RQ2: What properties of different frameworks should be kept and what properties should be ignored in the unification?

RQ3: How can entity-based models and lexical-based models be incorporated into the unified framework?

RQ4: How can the unified framework be evaluated?

The first three questions are closely related to each other. Automatic means will be used, although we do not preclude semi-automatic means, as exemplified by Yi et al. (2021). We will start with the methods suggested by existing research and focus on the challenges of incorporating different kinds of discourse information in multi-task learning and graphical models.

The unified framework can be used for the following purposes:

1. A corpus annotated under one framework can be used jointly with another corpus annotated under a different framework to augment data, for developing discourse parsing models or for discourse analysis. We can train a discourse parser on a corpus annotated under one framework and compare its performance with the case when it is trained on augmented data, similar to Yi et al. (2021).

2. Each framework has its own theoretical foundation and focus. A unified framework may have the potential of combining the strengths of different frameworks. Experiments can be done with multi-task learning so that discourse parsing tasks of different frameworks can be solved jointly. We can also investigate how to enable GNNs to better capture different kinds of discourse information.

3. A unified framework may provide a common ground for exploring the relations of different frameworks and validating annotation consistency of a corpus. We can perform comparative corpus analysis and obtain new understanding of how information expressed in one framework is conveyed in another framework, thus validating corpus annotation consistency and finding some clues for solving problems in a framework with signals from another framework, similar to Poláková et al. (2017) and Bourgonje and Zolotarenko (2019).

2 Related Work

2.1 An Overview of Discourse Theories

A number of discourse theories have been proposed. The theory by Grosz and Sidner (1986) is one of those earlier few whose linguistic claims about discourse are also computationally significant (Mann and Thompson, 1987). With this theory, it is believed that discourse structure is composed of three separated but interrelated components: linguistic structure, intentional structure and attentional structure. The linguistic structure focuses on cue phrases and discourse segmentation. The intentional structure mainly deals with why a discourse is performed (discourse purpose) and how a segment contributes to the overall discourse purpose (discourse segment purpose). The attentional structure is not related to the discourse participants, and it records the objects, properties and relations that are salient at each point in discourse. These three aspects capture discourse phenomena in a systematic way, and other discourse theories may be related to this theory in some way. For instance, the Centering Theory (Grosz et al., 1995) and the entity-grid model (Barzilay and Lapata, 2008) focus on the attentional structure, and the Rhetorical Structure Theory (RST) (Mann and Thompson, 1988) focuses on the intentional structure.

The theory proposed by Halliday and Hasan (1976) studies how various lexical means are used to achieve cohesion, these lexical means including reference, substitution, ellipsis, lexical cohesion and conjunction. Cohesion realized through the first four lexical means is in essence anaphoric dependency and conjunction is the only source of discourse relation under this theory (Webber, 2006).

The other discourse theories can be divided into two broad types: relation-based discourse theories and entity-based discourse theories (Jurafsky and Martin, 2018). The former studies how coherence is achieved with discourse relations and the latter focuses on local coherence achieved through shift of focus, which abstracts a text into a set of entity transition sequences (Barzilay and Lapata, 2008).

RST is one of the most influential relation-based discourse theories. The RST Discourse Treebank (RST-DT) (Carlson et al., 2001) is annotated based on this theory. In the RST framework, discourse can be represented by a tree structure whose leaves are Elementary Discourse Units (EDUs), typically clauses, and whose non-terminals are adjacent spans linked by discourse relations. The discourse relations can be symmetric or asymmetric, the former being characterized by equally important spans connected in parallel, and the latter typically having a nucleus and a satellite, which are assigned based on their importance in conveying the intended effects. An RST tree is built recursively by connecting the adjacent discourse units, forming a hierarchical structure covering the whole text. An example of RST discourse trees can be seen in Figure 1.

Another influential framework is the Penn Discourse Treebank (PDTB) framework, which is represented by the Penn Discourse Treebank (Prasad et al., 2008, 2018). Unlike the RST framework, the PDTB framework does not aim at achieving complete annotation of the text but focuses on local discourse relations anchored by structural connectives or discourse adverbials. When there are no explicit connectives, the annotators will read adjacent sentences and decide if a connective can be inserted to express the relation. The annotation is not committed to a specific structure at the higher level. PDTB 3.0 adopts a three-layer sense hierarchy, including four general categories called classes at the highest level, the middle layer being more specific divisions, which are called types, and the lowest layer containing directionality of the arguments, called subtypes. An example of the PDTB-style annotation is shown as follows (Prasad et al., 2019):

The Soviet insisted that aircraft be brought into the talks,(implicit=but){arg2-as-denier} **then argued for exempting some 4,000 Russian planes because they are solely defensive.**

The first argument is shown in italics and the second argument is shown in bold font for distinction. As the discourse relation is implicit, the annotator adds a connective that is considered to be suitable for the context.

The Segmented Discourse Representation Theory (SDRT) (Asher and Lascarides, 2003) is based on the Discourse Representation Theory (Kamp and Reyle, 1993), with discourse relations added, and discourse structure is represented with directed acyclic graphs (DAGs). Elementary discourse units may be combined recursively to form a complex discourse unit (CDU), which can be linked with another EDU or CDU (Asher et al., 2017). The set of discourse relations developed in this framework overlap partly with those in the RST framework but some are motivated from pragmatic and semantic considerations. In Asher and Lascarides (2003), a precise dynamic semantic interpretation of the rhetorical relations is defined. An example of discourse representation in the SDRT framework is shown in Figure 2, which illustrates that the SDRT framework provides full annotation, similar to the RST framework, and it assumes a hierarchical structure of text organization. The vertical arrow-headed lines represent subordinate relations, and the horizontal lines represent coordinate relations. The textual units in solid-line boxes are EDUs and π' and π" represent CDUs. The relations are shown in bold.

2.2 Research on Relations between Different Frameworks

The correlation between different frameworks has been a topic of interest for a long time. Some studies explore how different frameworks are related, either in discourse structures or in relation sets. Some studies take a step further and try to map the relation sets of different frameworks.

2.2.1 Comparison/unification of discourse structures of different frameworks

Stede et al. (2016) investigate the relations between RST, SDRT and argumentation structure. For the purpose of comparing the three layers of annotation, the EDU segmentation in RST and SDRT is harmonized, and an "argumentatively empty" JOIN relation is introduced to address the issue that the basic unit of the argumentation structure is coarser than the other two layers. The annotations are con-

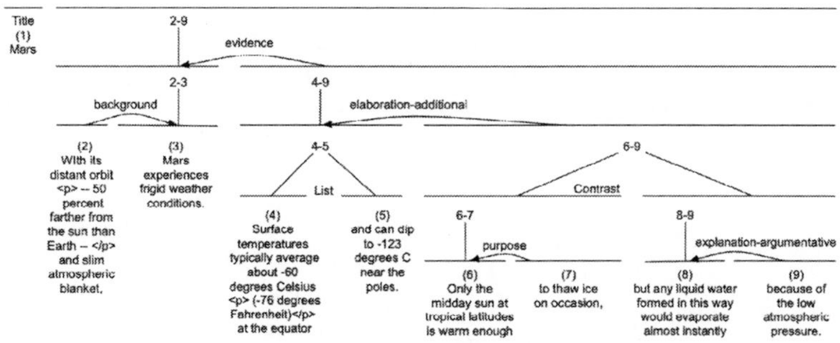

Figure 1: An RST discourse tree, originally from Marcu (2000a).

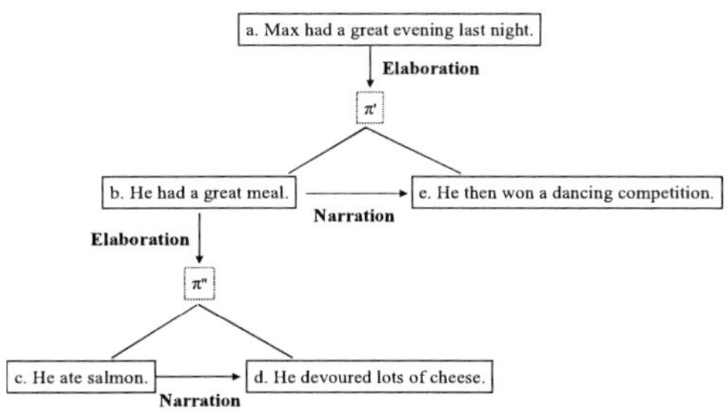

Figure 2: SDRT representation of the text *a. Max had a great evening last night. b. He had a great meal. c. He ate salmon. d. He devoured lots of cheese. e. He then won a dancing competition.* The example is taken from Asher and Lascarides (2003).

verted to a common dependency graph format for calculating correlations. To transform RST trees to the dependency structure, the method introduced by Li et al. (2014) is used. The RST trees are binarized and the left-most EDU is treated as the head. In the transformation of the SDRT graphs to the dependency structure, the CDUs are simplified by a *head replacement strategy*. The authors compare the dependency graphs in terms of common edges and common connected components. The relations of the argumentation structure are compared with those of RST and SDRT, respectively, through a co-occurrence matrix. Their research shows the systematic relations between the argumentation structure and the two discourse annotation frameworks. The purpose is to investigate if discourse parsing can contribute to automatic argumentation analysis. The authors exclude the PDTB framework because it does not provide full discourse annotation.

Yi et al. (2021) try to unify two Chinese discourse corpora annotated under the PDTB framework and the RST framework, respectively, with a corpus annotated under the dependency framework. They use semi-automatic means to transform the corpora to the discourse dependency structure which is presented in Li et al. (2014). Their work shows that the major difficulty is the transformation from the PDTB framework to the discourse dependency structure, which requires re-segmenting texts and complementing some relations to construct complete dependency trees. They use the same method as Stede et al. (2016) to transform the RST trees to the dependency structure. Details about relation mapping across the frameworks are not given.

2.2.2 Comparison/unification of discourse relations of different frameworks

The methods of mapping discourse relations of different frameworks presented by Scheffler and Stede (2016), Demberg et al. (2019) and Bourgonje and Zolotarenko (2019) are empirically grounded. The main approach is to make use of the same texts annotated under different frameworks.

Scheffler and Stede (2016) focus on mapping between explicit PDTB discourse connectives and RST rhetorical relations. The Potsdam Commentary Corpus (Stede and Neumann, 2014), which contains annotations under both frameworks, is used. It is found that the majority of the PDTB connectives in the corpus match exactly one RST relation and mismatches are caused by different segment definitions and focuses, i.e., PDTB focuses on local/lexicalized relations and RST focuses on global structural relations.

As the Potsdam Commentary Corpus only contains explicit relations under the PDTB framework, Bourgonje and Zolotarenko (2019) try to induce implicit relations from the corresponding RST annotation. Since RST trees are hierarchical and the PDTB annotation is shallow, RST relations that connect complex spans are discarded.

Moreover, because the arguments of explicit and implicit relations under the PDTB framework are determined based on different criteria, only RST relations that are signalled explicitly are considered in the experiment. It is shown that differences in segmentation and partially overlapping relations pose challenges for the task.

Demberg et al. (2019) propose a method of mapping RST and PDTB relations. Since the number of PDTB relations is much smaller than that of RST relations for the same text, the PDTB relations are used as the starting point for the mapping. They aim for mapping as many relations as possible while making sure that the relations connect the same segments. Six cases are identified: direct mapping, which is the easiest case; when PDTB arguments are non-adjacent, the Strong Compositionality hypothesis (Marcu, 2000b) (i.e., if a relation holds between two textual spans, that relation also holds between the most important units of the constituent spans) is used to check if there is a match when the complex span of an RST relation is traced along the nucleus path to its nucleus EDU; in the case of multi-nuclear relations, it is checked if a PDTB argument can be traced to the nucleus of the RST relation along the nucleus path; the mismatch caused by different segmentation granularity is considered innately unalignable and discarded; centrally embedded EDUs in RST-DT are treated as a whole and compared with an argument of the PDTB relation; and the PDTB EntRel relation is included to test its correlation with some RST relations that tend to be associated with cohesion.

Other studies are more theoretical. Hovy (1990) is the first to attempt to unify discourse relations proposed by researchers from different areas and suggests adopting a hierarchy of relations, with the top level being more general (from the functional perspective: ideational, interpersonal and textual) and putting no restrictions on adding fine-grained relations, as long as they can be subsumed under existing taxonomy. The number of researchers who propose a specific relation is taken as a vote of confidence of the relation in the taxonomy. The study serves as a starting point for research in this direction. There are a few other proposals for unifying discourse relations of different frameworks to facilitate cross-framework discourse analysis, including: introducing a hierarchy of discourse relations, similar to Hovy (1990), where the top level is general and fixed, and the lowest level is more specific and allows variations based on genre and language (Benamara and Taboada, 2015), finding some dimensions based on cognitive evidence where the relations can be compared with each other and re-grouped (Sanders et al., 2018), and formulating a set of core relations that are shared by existing frameworks but are open and extensible in use, with the outcome being ISO-DR-Core (Bunt and Prasad, 2016). When the PDTB sense hierarchy is mapped to the ISO-DR-Core, it is found that the directionality of relations cannot be captured by the existing ISO-DR-Core relations and it remains a question whether to extend the ISO-DR-Core relations or to redefine the PDTB relations so that the directionality of arguments can be captured (Prasad et al., 2018).

3 Research Plan

RST-DT is annotated on texts from the Penn Treebank (Marcus et al., 1993) that have also been annotated in PDTB. The texts are formally written Wall Street Journal articles. The English corpora annotated under the SDRT framework, i.e., the STAC corpus (Asher et al., 2016) and the Molweni corpus (Li et al., 2020), are created for analyzing multi-party dialogues, making it difficult to be used together with the other two corpora. Therefore, in addition to RST-DT and PDTB 3.0, we will use the ANNODIS corpus (Péry-Woodley et al., 2009), which consists of formally written French texts. We will first translate the texts into English with an MT system and then manually check the translated texts to reduce errors.

In the following, the research questions and the approach in our plan will be discussed. These questions are closely related to each other and the research on one question is likely to influence how the other questions should be addressed. They are presented separately just for easier description.

RQ1: Which structure can be used to represent discourse in the unified framework?

Although there is a lack of consensus on how to represent discourse structure, in a number of studies, the dependency structure is taken as a common structure that the other structures can be converted to (Muller et al., 2012; Hirao et al., 2013; Venant et al., 2013; Li et al., 2014; Yoshida et al., 2014; Stede et al., 2016; Morey et al., 2018; Yi et al., 2021). This choice is mainly inspired by research in the field of syntax, where the dependency grammar is better studied and its computational and representational properties are well-understood[1]. The research by Venant et al. (2013) provides a common language for comparing discourse structures of different formalisms, which is used in the transformation procedure presented by Stede et al. (2016). Another possibility is the constrained directed acyclic graph introduced by Danlos (2004). While Venant et al. (2013) focus on the expressivity of different structures, the constrained DAG is motivated from the perspective of strong generative capacity (Danlos, 2008). Although neither of the studies deals with the PDTB framework, since they are both semantically driven, we believe it is possible to deal with the PDTB framework using either of the two structures. We will start with the investigation of the two structures.

Another issue is how to maintain one-to-one correspondence during the transformation of the original structure and the unified structure back and forth. As indicated by Stede et al. (2016), the transformation from the RST or SDRT structures into dependency structures always produces the same structure, but going back to the initial RST or SDRT structures is ambiguous. Morey et al. (2018) introduces head-ordered dependency trees in syntactic parsing (Fernández-González and Martins, 2015) to reduce the ambiguity. We may start with a similar method.

As is clear from Section 2, using the dependency structure as a common ground for studying the relations between different frameworks is not new in existing literature, but comparing the RST, PDTB and SDRT frameworks with this method has not yet been done. This approach will be our starting point, and the suitability of the dependency structure in representing discourse will be investigated empirically. The SciDTB corpus (Yang and Li, 2018), which is annotated under the dependency framework, will be used for this purpose.

RQ2:[2] What properties of different frameworks should be kept and what properties should be ignored in the unification?

We present a non-exhaustive list of properties, which we consider to have considerable influence on the unified discourse structure.

1. Nuclearity: Marcu (1996) uses the nuclearity principle as the foundation for a formal treatment of compositionality in RST, which means that two adjacent spans can be joined into a larger span by a rhetorical relation if and only if the relation holds between the most salient units of those spans. This assumption is criticized by Stede (2008). The remedy provided by Stede (2008) is to separate different levels of discourse information, which is in line with the suggestions in Knott et al. (2000) and Moore and Pollack (1992). Our strategy is to keep this property in the initial stage of experimentation. The existing methods for transforming RST trees to dependency structure (Hirao et al., 2013; Li et al., 2014) rely heavily on the nuclearity principle and we will use these methods in the transformation and see what kinds of problems this procedure will cause, particularly with respect to the PDTB framework, which does not enforce a hierarchical structure for complete coverage of the text.

2. Sentence-boundedness: The RST framework does not enforce well-formed discourse sub-trees for each sentence. However, it is found that 95% of the discourse parse trees in RST-DT have well-formed sub-trees at the sentence level (Soricut and Marcu, 2003). For the PDTB framework, there is no restriction on how far an argument can be from its corresponding connective: it can be in the same sentence as the connective, in the sentence immediately preceding that of the connective, or in some non-adjacent sentence (Prasad et al., 2006). Moreover, the arguments are determined based on the *Minimality Principle*, which means that clauses and/or sentences that are minimally required for the interpretation of the relation should be included in the argument, and other spans that are relevant but not necessary can be annotated as supplementary information, which is labeled depending on which argument it is supplementary to (Prasad et al., 2008). The SDRT framework developed in Asher and Lascarides (2003) does not specify the basic discourse unit, but in the annotation of the ANNODIS corpus, EDU segmentation follows similar principles as RST-DT. The formation of CDU and the attachment of relations are where SDRT differs significantly from RST. A segment can be attached to another segment from the same sentence, the same paragraph or a larger context,

[1] In communication with Bonnie Webber, January, 2022.

[2] In communication with Bonnie Webber, January, 2022. We thank her for pointing out this aspect.

and by one or possibly more relations. A CDU can be of any size and can have segments that are far apart in the text, and relations may be annotated within the CDU[3].

The differences in the criteria on location and extent for basic discourse unit identification and relation labeling of the RST framework and the PDTB framework may be partly attributed to different annotation procedures. In RST, EDU segmentation is performed first and EDU linking and relation labelling are performed later. The balance between consistency and granularity is the major concern behind the strategy for EDU segmentation (Carlson et al., 2001). In contrast, in PDTB, the connectives are identified first, and their arguments are determined afterwards. Semantic relatedness is given greater weight and the location and extent of the arguments can be determined more flexibly. On the whole, neither SDRT nor PDTB shows any tendency of sentence-boundedness. We will investigate to what extent the tendency of sentence-boundedness complicates the unification and what the consequences are if entity-based models and lexical-based models are incorporated.

3. Multi-sense annotation: As shown above, SDRT and PDTB allow multi-sense annotation while RST only allows one relation to be labeled. The single-sense constraint actually gives rise to ambiguity because of the multi-faceted nature of local coherence (Stede, 2008). For the unification task, we assume that multi-sense annotation is useful. However, we agree with the view mentioned in Stede (2008) that incrementally adding more relations as phenomena are being recognized is not a promising direction. There are two possible approaches: one is to separate different dimensions of discourse information (Stede, 2008) and the other is to represent different kinds of discourse information simultaneously, similar to the approach adopted in Knott et al. (2000). While multi-level annotation may reveal the interaction between discourse and other linguistic phenomena, it is less helpful for developing a discourse parser and requires more efforts in annotation. The second approach may be conducive to computationally cheaper discourse processing when proper constraints are introduced.

RQ3: How can entity-based models and lexical-based models be incorporated into the unified framework?

The PDTB framework believes that lexical-based discourse relations are associated with anaphoric dependency, which is anchored by discourse adverbials (Webber et al., 2003) and annotated as a type of explicit relations. As for entity-based relations, PDTB uses the ENTREL label to annotate this type of relations when neither explicit nor implicit relations can be identified and only entity-based coherence relations are present. In the RST framework, the ELABORATION relation is actually a relation between entities. However, it is encoded in the same way as the other relations between propositions, which bedevils the framework (Knott et al., 2000). Further empirical studies may be needed to identify how different frameworks represent these different kinds of discourse information. The main challenge is to use a relatively simple structure to represent different types of discourse information while keeping the complexity relatively low.

RQ4: How can the unified framework be evaluated?

We will use intrinsic evaluation to assess the complexity of the discourse structure.

Extrinsic evaluation will be used to assess the effectiveness of the unified framework. The downstream tasks in the extrinsic evaluation include text summarization and document discrimination, which are two typical tasks for evaluating discourse models. The document discrimination task asks a score of coherence to be assigned to a document. The originally written document is considered to be the most coherent, and with more permutations, the document becomes less coherent. For comparison with previous studies, we will use the CNN and Dailymail dataset (Hermann et al., 2015) for the text summarization task, and use the method and dataset[4] in Shen et al. (2021) to control the degree of coherence for the document discrimination task.

[3]See section 3 of the ANNODIS annotation manual, available through http://w3.erss.univ-tlse2.fr/textes/publications/CarnetsGrammaire/carnGram21.pdf

[4]https://github.com/AiliAili/Coherence_Modelling

Previous studies that use multi-task learning and GNNs to encode different types of discourse information will be re-investigated to test the effectiveness of the unified framework.

As we may have to ignore some properties, we will examine what might be lost with the unified framework.

4 Conclusion

We propose to unify the RST, PDTB and SDRT frameworks, which may enable discourse corpora annotated under different frameworks to be used jointly and achieve the potential synergy of different frameworks. The major challenges include determining which structure to use in the unified framework, choosing what properties to keep and what to ignore, and incorporating entity-based models and lexical-based models into the unified framework. We will start with existing research and try to find a computationally less expensive way for the task. Extensive experiments will be conducted to investigate how effective the unified framework is and how it can be used. An empirical evaluation of what might be lost through the unification will be performed.

5 Acknowledgements

We thank Bonnie Webber for valuable feedback that greatly shaped the work. We are grateful to the anonymous reviewers for detailed and insightful comments that improved the work considerably, and Mark-Jan Nederhof for proof-reading the manuscript. The author is funded by University of St Andrews-China Scholarship Council joint scholarship (NO.202008300012).

6 Ethical Considerations and Limitations

The corpora are used in compliance with the licence requirements:

The ANNODIS corpus is available under Creative Commons By-NC-SA 3.0.

RST-DT is distributed on Linguistic Data Consortium:

Carlson, Lynn, Daniel Marcu, and Mary Ellen Okurowski. RST Discourse Treebank LDC2002T07. Web Download. Philadelphia: Linguistic Data Consortium, 2002.

PDTB 3.0 is also distributed on Linguistic Data Consortium:

Prasad, Rashmi, et al. Penn Discourse Treebank Version 3.0 LDC2019T05. Web Download. Philadelphia: Linguistic Data Consortium, 2019.

Bender Rule English is the language studied in this work.

References

Nicholas Asher, Julie Hunter, Mathieu Morey, Benamara Farah, and Stergos Afantenos. 2016. Discourse structure and dialogue acts in multiparty dialogue: the STAC corpus. In *Proceedings of the Tenth International Conference on Language Resources and Evaluation (LREC'16)*, pages 2721–2727, Portorož, Slovenia. European Language Resources Association (ELRA).

Nicholas Asher and Alex Lascarides. 2003. *Logics of conversation*. Cambridge University Press.

Nicholas Asher, Philippe Muller, Myriam Bras, Lydia Mai Ho-Dac, Farah Benamara, Stergos Afantenos, and Laure Vieu. 2017. ANNODIS and related projects: case studies on the annotation of discourse structure. In *Handbook of Linguistic Annotation*, pages 1241–1264. Springer.

Regina Barzilay and Mirella Lapata. 2008. Modeling local coherence: An entity-based approach. *Computational Linguistics*, 34(1):1–34.

Farah Benamara and Maite Taboada. 2015. Mapping different rhetorical relation annotations: A proposal. In *Proceedings of the Fourth Joint Conference on Lexical and Computational Semantics*, pages 147–152, Denver, Colorado. Association for Computational Linguistics.

Parminder Bhatia, Yangfeng Ji, and Jacob Eisenstein. 2015. Better document-level sentiment analysis from RST discourse parsing. In *Proceedings of the 2015 Conference on Empirical Methods in Natural Language Processing*, pages 2212–2218, Lisbon, Portugal. Association for Computational Linguistics.

Peter Bourgonje and Olha Zolotarenko. 2019. Toward cross-theory discourse relation annotation. In *Proceedings of the Workshop on Discourse Relation Parsing and Treebanking 2019*, pages 7–11, Minneapolis, MN. Association for Computational Linguistics.

Chloé Braud, Barbara Plank, and Anders Søgaard. 2016. Multi-view and multi-task training of RST discourse parsers. In *Proceedings of COLING 2016, the 26th International Conference on Computational Linguistics: Technical Papers*, pages 1903–1913, Osaka, Japan. The COLING 2016 Organizing Committee.

Harry Bunt and Rashmi Prasad. 2016. ISO DR-Core (ISO 24617-8): Core concepts for the annotation of discourse relations. In *Proceedings 12th Joint ACL-ISO Workshop on Interoperable Semantic Annotation (ISA-12)*, pages 45–54.

Lynn Carlson, Daniel Marcu, and Mary Ellen Okurovsky. 2001. Building a discourse-tagged corpus in the framework of Rhetorical Structure Theory. In *Proceedings of the Second SIGdial Workshop on Discourse and Dialogue*.

Laurence Danlos. 2004. Discourse dependency structures as constrained DAGs. In *Proceedings of the 5th SIGdial Workshop on Discourse and Dialogue at HLT-NAACL 2004*, pages 127–135, Cambridge, Massachusetts, USA. Association for Computational Linguistics.

Laurence Danlos. 2008. Strong generative capacity of rst, sdrt and discourse dependency dagss. In *Constraints in discourse*. Citeseer.

Vera Demberg, Merel CJ Scholman, and Fatemeh Torabi Asr. 2019. How compatible are our discourse annotation frameworks? insights from mapping rst-dt and pdtb annotations. *Dialogue & Discourse*, 10(1):87–135.

Markus Egg and Gisela Redeker. 2010. How complex is discourse structure? In *Proceedings of the Seventh International Conference on Language Resources and Evaluation (LREC'10)*, Valletta, Malta. European Language Resources Association (ELRA).

Daniel Fernández-González and André F. T. Martins. 2015. Parsing as reduction. In *Proceedings of the 53rd Annual Meeting of the Association for Computational Linguistics and the 7th International Joint Conference on Natural Language Processing (Volume 1: Long Papers)*, pages 1523–1533, Beijing, China. Association for Computational Linguistics.

Barbara J. Grosz, Aravind K. Joshi, and Scott Weinstein. 1995. Centering: A framework for modeling the local coherence of discourse. *Computational Linguistics*, 21(2):203–225.

Barbara J. Grosz and Candace L. Sidner. 1986. Attention, intentions, and the structure of discourse. *Computational Linguistics*, 12(3):175–204.

Michael Alexander Kirkwood Halliday and Ruqaiya Hasan. 1976. *Cohesion in English (1st ed.)*. Routledge.

Karl Moritz Hermann, Tomáš Kočiský, Edward Grefenstette, Lasse Espeholt, Will Kay, Mustafa Suleyman, and Phil Blunsom. 2015. Teaching machines to read and comprehend. In *Proceedings of the 28th International Conference on Neural Information Processing Systems - Volume 1*, NIPS'15, page 1693–1701, Cambridge, MA, USA. MIT Press.

Tsutomu Hirao, Yasuhisa Yoshida, Masaaki Nishino, Norihito Yasuda, and Masaaki Nagata. 2013. Single-document summarization as a tree knapsack problem. In *Proceedings of the 2013 Conference on Empirical Methods in Natural Language Processing*, pages 1515–1520, Seattle, Washington, USA. Association for Computational Linguistics.

Eduard H. Hovy. 1990. Parsimonious and profligate approaches to the question of discourse structure relations. In *Proceedings of the Fifth International Workshop on Natural Language Generation*, Linden Hall Conference Center, Dawson, Pennsylvania. Association for Computational Linguistics.

Yin Jou Huang and Sadao Kurohashi. 2021. Extractive summarization considering discourse and coreference relations based on heterogeneous graph. In *Proceedings of the 16th Conference of the European Chapter of the Association for Computational Linguistics: Main Volume*, pages 3046–3052, Online. Association for Computational Linguistics.

Daniel Jurafsky and James H Martin. 2018. Speech and language processing (draft). *preparation [cited 2022 Jan 3], Available from: https://web. stanford. edu/~ jurafsky/slp3*.

Hans Kamp and Uwe Reyle. 1993. *From Discourse to Logic: Introduction to Model theoretic Semantics of Natural Language, Formal Logic and Discourse Representation Theory*. Dordrecht: Kluwer Academic Publishers.

Alistair Knott, Jon Oberlander, Michael O'Donnell, and Chris Mellish. 2000. Beyond elaboration: The interaction of relations and focus in coherent text. In *Text Representation: Linguistic and Psycholinguistic Aspects, chapter 7*, pages 181–196. John Benjamins.

Alan Lee, Rashmi Prasad, Aravind Joshi, and Bonnie Webber. 2008. Departures from tree structures in discourse: Shared arguments in the penn discourse treebank. In *Proceedings of the constraints in discourse iii workshop*, pages 61–68.

Jiaqi Li, Ming Liu, Min-Yen Kan, Zihao Zheng, Zekun Wang, Wenqiang Lei, Ting Liu, and Bing Qin. 2020. Molweni: A challenge multiparty dialogues-based machine reading comprehension dataset with discourse structure. In *Proceedings of the 28th International Conference on Computational Linguistics*, pages 2642–2652, Barcelona, Spain (Online). International Committee on Computational Linguistics.

Sujian Li, Liang Wang, Ziqiang Cao, and Wenjie Li. 2014. Text-level discourse dependency parsing. In *Proceedings of the 52nd Annual Meeting of the Association for Computational Linguistics (Volume 1: Long Papers)*, pages 25–35, Baltimore, Maryland. Association for Computational Linguistics.

Yang Liu, Sujian Li, Xiaodong Zhang, and Zhifang Sui. 2016. Implicit discourse relation classification via multi-task neural networks. In *Proceedings of the AAAI Conference on Artificial Intelligence*, volume 30.

William C Mann and Sandra A Thompson. 1987. *Rhetorical structure theory: A theory of text organization*. University of Southern California, Information Sciences Institute Los Angeles.

William C Mann and Sandra A Thompson. 1988. Rhetorical structure theory: Toward a functional theory of text organization. *Text*, 8(3):243–281.

Daniel Marcu. 1996. Building up rhetorical structure trees. In *Proceedings of the National Conference on Artificial Intelligence*, pages 1069–1074.

Daniel Marcu. 2000a. The rhetorical parsing of unrestricted texts: a surface-based approach. *Computational Linguistics*, 26(3):395–448.

Daniel Marcu. 2000b. *The theory and practice of discourse parsing and summarization*. MIT press.

Mitchell P. Marcus, Beatrice Santorini, and Mary Ann Marcinkiewicz. 1993. Building a large annotated corpus of English: The Penn Treebank. *Computational Linguistics*, 19(2):313–330.

Johanna D. Moore and Martha E. Pollack. 1992. A problem for RST: The need for multi-level discourse analysis. *Computational Linguistics*, 18(4):537–544.

Mathieu Morey, Philippe Muller, and Nicholas Asher. 2018. A dependency perspective on RST discourse parsing and evaluation. *Computational Linguistics*, 44(2):197–235.

Philippe Muller, Stergos Afantenos, Pascal Denis, and Nicholas Asher. 2012. Constrained decoding for text-level discourse parsing. In *Proceedings of COLING 2012*, pages 1883–1900, Mumbai, India. The COLING 2012 Organizing Committee.

Farah Nadeem, Huy Nguyen, Yang Liu, and Mari Ostendorf. 2019. Automated essay scoring with discourse-aware neural models. In *Proceedings of the Fourteenth Workshop on Innovative Use of NLP for Building Educational Applications*, pages 484–493, Florence, Italy. Association for Computational Linguistics.

Marie-Paule Péry-Woodley, Nicholas Asher, Patrice Enjalbert, Farah Benamara, Myriam Bras, Cécile Fabre, Stéphane Ferrari, Lydia-Mai Ho-Dac, Anne Le Draoulec, Yann Mathet, Philippe Muller, Laurent Prévot, Josette Rebeyrolle, Ludovic Tanguy, Marianne Vergez-Couret, Laure Vieu, and Antoine Widlöcher. 2009. ANNODIS: une approche outillée de l'annotation de structures discursives. In *Actes de la 16ème conférence sur le Traitement Automatique des Langues Naturelles. Articles courts*, pages 41–46, Senlis, France. ATALA.

Lucie Poláková, Jirí Mírovský, and Pavlína Synková. 2017. Signalling implicit relations: A PDTB-RST comparison. *Dialogue & Discourse*, 8(2):225–248.

R. Prasad, Eleni Miltsakaki, Nikhil Dinesh, Alan Lee, Aravind K. Joshi, Livio Robaldo, and Bonnie Lynn Webber. 2006. The Penn Discourse Treebank 2.0 annotation manual.

Rashmi Prasad, Nikhil Dinesh, Alan Lee, Eleni Miltsakaki, Livio Robaldo, Aravind Joshi, and Bonnie Webber. 2008. The Penn Discourse TreeBank 2.0. In *Proceedings of the Sixth International Conference on Language Resources and Evaluation (LREC'08)*, Marrakech, Morocco. European Language Resources Association (ELRA).

Rashmi Prasad, Bonnie Webber, and Alan Lee. 2018. Discourse annotation in the PDTB: The next generation. In *Proceedings 14th Joint ACL - ISO Workshop on Interoperable Semantic Annotation*, pages 87–97, Santa Fe, New Mexico, USA. Association for Computational Linguistics.

Rashmi Prasad, Bonnie Webber, Alan Lee, and Aravind Joshi. 2019. Penn Discourse Treebank Version 3.0 LDC2019T05.

Ted JM Sanders, Vera Demberg, Jet Hoek, Merel CJ Scholman, Fatemeh Torabi Asr, Sandrine Zufferey, and Jacqueline Evers-Vermeul. 2018. Unifying dimensions in coherence relations: How various annotation frameworks are related. *Corpus Linguistics and Linguistic Theory*.

Tatjana Scheffler and Manfred Stede. 2016. Mapping PDTB-style connective annotation to RST-style discourse annotation. In *Proceedings of the 13th Conference on Natural Language Processing*, pages 242–247.

Aili Shen, Meladel Mistica, Bahar Salehi, Hang Li, Timothy Baldwin, and Jianzhong Qi. 2021. Evaluating document coherence modeling. *Transactions of the Association for Computational Linguistics*, 9:621–640.

Karin Sim Smith. 2017. On integrating discourse in machine translation. In *Proceedings of the Third Workshop on Discourse in Machine Translation*, pages 110–121, Copenhagen, Denmark. Association for Computational Linguistics.

Radu Soricut and Daniel Marcu. 2003. Sentence level discourse parsing using syntactic and lexical information. In *Proceedings of the 2003 Human Language Technology Conference of the North American Chapter of the Association for Computational Linguistics*, pages 228–235.

Manfred Stede. 2008. Disentangling nuclearity. *'Subordination' versus 'Coordination' in Sentence and Text: A cross-linguistic perspective*, 98:33.

Manfred Stede, Stergos Afantenos, Andreas Peldszus, Nicholas Asher, and Jérémy Perret. 2016. Parallel discourse annotations on a corpus of short texts. In *Proceedings of the Tenth International Conference on Language Resources and Evaluation (LREC'16)*, pages 1051–1058, Portorož, Slovenia. European Language Resources Association (ELRA).

Manfred Stede and Arne Neumann. 2014. Potsdam commentary corpus 2.0: Annotation for discourse research. In *Proceedings of the Ninth International*

Conference on Language Resources and Evaluation (LREC'14), pages 925–929, Reykjavik, Iceland. European Language Resources Association (ELRA).

Antoine Venant, Nicholas Asher, Philippe Muller, Pascal Denis, and Stergos Afantenos. 2013. Expressivity and comparison of models of discourse structure. In *Proceedings of the SIGDIAL 2013 Conference*, pages 2–11, Metz, France. Association for Computational Linguistics.

Bonnie Webber. 2006. Accounting for discourse relations: constituency and dependency. *Intelligent linguistic architectures*, pages 339–360.

Bonnie Webber, Matthew Stone, Aravind Joshi, and Alistair Knott. 2003. Anaphora and discourse structure. *Computational Linguistics*, 29(4):545–587.

Florian Wolf and Edward Gibson. 2005. Representing discourse coherence: A corpus-based study. *Computational Linguistics*, 31(2):249–287.

Jiacheng Xu, Zhe Gan, Yu Cheng, and Jingjing Liu. 2020. Discourse-aware neural extractive text summarization. In *Proceedings of the 58th Annual Meeting of the Association for Computational Linguistics*, pages 5021–5031, Online. Association for Computational Linguistics.

An Yang and Sujian Li. 2018. SciDTB: Discourse dependency TreeBank for scientific abstracts. In *Proceedings of the 56th Annual Meeting of the Association for Computational Linguistics (Volume 2: Short Papers)*, pages 444–449, Melbourne, Australia. Association for Computational Linguistics.

Cheng Yi, Li Sujian, and Li Yueyuan. 2021. Unifying discourse resources with dependency framework. In *Proceedings of the 20th Chinese National Conference on Computational Linguistics*, pages 1058–1065, Huhhot, China. Chinese Information Processing Society of China.

Yasuhisa Yoshida, Jun Suzuki, Tsutomu Hirao, and Masaaki Nagata. 2014. Dependency-based discourse parser for single-document summarization. In *Proceedings of the 2014 Conference on Empirical Methods in Natural Language Processing (EMNLP)*, pages 1834–1839, Doha, Qatar. Association for Computational Linguistics.

AMR Alignment for Morphologically-rich and Pro-drop Languages

Elif Oral
NLP Research Group,
Faculty of Computer&Informatics,
Istanbul Technical University,
Istanbul, Turkey
oralk19@itu.edu.tr

Gülşen Eryiğit
Department of Artificial Intelligence &
Data Engineering,
Istanbul Technical University,
Istanbul, Turkey
gulsen.cebiroglu@itu.edu.tr

Abstract

Alignment between concepts in an abstract meaning representation (AMR) graph and the words within a sentence is one of the important stages of AMR parsing. Although there exist high performing AMR aligners for English, unfortunately, these are not well suited for many languages where many concepts appear from morpho-semantic elements. For the first time in the literature, this paper presents an AMR aligner tailored for morphologically-rich and pro-drop languages by experimenting on the Turkish language being a prominent example of this language group. Our aligner focuses on the meaning considering the rich Turkish morphology and aligns AMR concepts that emerge from morphemes using a tree traversal approach without additional resources or rules. We evaluate our aligner over a manually annotated gold data set. Our aligner outperforms the Turkish adaptations of the previously proposed aligners for English and Portuguese by an F1 score of 0.87 and provides a relative error reduction of up to 76%.

1 Introduction

AMR (Banarescu et al., 2013) is a semantic formalism that represents sentence meaning as directed graphs. The nodes in the graphs represent the *concepts* in the sentence, and the edges show the *relations* between the concepts. The purpose of AMR is to abstract sentence meaning from syntactic features. It gathers the semantic aspects of the sentence (semantic roles, time concepts, entity names, etc.) under a formalism and focuses on the sentence's meaning. Words that do not contribute to meaning and some syntactic features (tenses, passive voice, etc.) are not shown in AMR graphs.

With its increasing popularity in recent years, AMR has attracted the attention of many researchers (Žabokrtský et al., 2020; Bos, 2016) and has been used in several applications such as text generation (Wang et al., 2020; Mager et al., 2020; Zhao et al., 2020; Fan and Gardent, 2020), text summarization (Dohare et al., 2017; Liu et al., 2018a; Liao et al., 2018), event extraction (Huang et al., 2016; Li et al., 2020). An important branch of this research is AMR parsing. Most parsing studies require an alignment between graph nodes and sentence concepts to create the training set for converting sentences to AMR graphs (Flanigan et al., 2014; Wang et al., 2015; Zhou et al., 2016). Many studies in the literature have reported that the alignment process greatly affects the parsing performance and has offered different solutions for the alignment process (Flanigan et al., 2014; Liu et al., 2018b; Pourdamghani et al., 2014; Anchiêta and Pardo, 2020). Lyu and Titov (2018) use alignments as latent variables during parsing, while Konstas et al. (2017); Zhang et al. (2019) could be given as an example study which does not require an alignment stage before parsing. However, since in these studies the learning process requires large amounts of sentence-AMR graph pairs, it is hard to apply them directly to a resource-poor languages.

The popular approaches in the literature for automatic AMR alignment aim to match concepts (either with fuzzy or semantic match) with the word lemmas with the help of a rule list. Although these approaches seem to be suitable for English, they do not perform well on languages with different characteristics (Anchiêta and Pardo, 2020). Morphologically-rich and pro-drop languages pose interesting challenges for AMR alignment as well as other NLP tasks. In these languages, many concepts appear from morpho-semantic elements rather than the entire word surface-form, yielding multiple concepts from a single word. In this paper, we introduce an AMR aligner for Turkish, a morphologically-rich and pro-drop language. Our alignment strategy handles concepts that emerge from the morphemes without the need for any extension of external resources or rules. Differing from the literature, with this approach, instead of

Proceedings of the 60th Annual Meeting of the Association for Computational Linguistics Student Research Workshop, pages 143 - 152

looking for a match over the rule list, we use a two-stage strategy: we first map words to lexical concepts by using a similarity measure, and then navigate through the nodes over these matches, aligning the remaining concepts (i.e., abstract and morphology-based concepts) that do not have a word correspondence in the sentence. We evaluate our approach on manually annotated sentences randomly selected from IMST (Sulubacak et al., 2016) using the same evaluation methods from Flanigan et al. (2014). The results show that the proposed alignment strategy performs better for Turkish than the existing approaches originally proposed for English and Portuguese. The aligner will be available for researchers in GitHub [1].

The paper is organized as follows: Section 2 provides alignment fundamentals and briefly represents the related studies from the literature. Section 3 introduces the aligner and Section 4 gives the evaluation. Finally, 5 provides the conclusion.

2 Background and Related Work

In AMR parsing, although the parser takes sentences as input and produces AMR graphs, it is challenging to learn complete semantic representation from the sentences directly by using sentence-AMR graph pairs. Therefore, several parsing approaches need a word-concept alignment stage to know the semantic representation of words separately. One should note that concepts' names may differ substantially (e.g., due to inflections, derivations, or semantic closeness) from the related lexical words, and it is probable that they could not be mapped directly: for example, the word 'desirous' or 'desires' could be related to the concept name 'desire.01' in an AMR graph. This situation may be even harder in morphologically rich languages, where the character length of the inflectional affixes could be longer then the length of the lemma. Another example could be the word 'afraid' related to the concept 'fear-01'. An aligner is a tool that maps AMR concepts to the related words within the sentence. The outputs of the aligner are used as input data to train the AMR parsers.

JAMR (Flanigan et al., 2014) aligner, the first AMR aligner in the literature, is built on heuristic rules and greedy search. In this method, fuzzy matching between words and concepts is searched using heuristic rules. The aligner moves down from the first rule and looks for a fuzzy match based on the rule currently being processed. While some rules are applied to all nodes by traversing the entire graph for each rule, some are only applied to some specific nodes (e.g., entity names). The TAMR (Liu et al., 2018b) aligner is an extension of the method presented in JAMR with emphasis on meaning. The list of JAMR rules has been expanded with syntactic and semantic matching, where semantic and morpho-semantic matching are used together with fuzzy matching. The connection between verb-invoking nouns and their verb frames (e.g., example - exemplify) is provided by the morphological meaning database (Fellbaum et al., 2007). Pourdamghani et al. (2014) used syntax-based statistical machine translation with an unsupervised word alignment method in the alignment approach. During the alignment, they linearize AMR graphs with the IBM word alignment model (Brown et al., 1993) and map the nodes to English sentences. Anchiêta and Pardo (2020) presents an AMR aligner for Portuguese which is a morphologically rich language. The authors solve the word-concept alignment using the Word Mover's Distance (Kusner et al., 2015) and lexical lists for the alignment of the abstract concepts and entity names.

```
::snt The boy wants to be believed by the girl.
::alignments 1-2|0.0 2-3|0 5-6|0.1 8-9|0.1.0

(w / want-01                        0
   :ARG0 (b / boy)                  0.0
   :ARG1 (b2 / believe-01           0.1
             :ARG0 (g / girl)       0.1.0
             :ARG1 b))
```

Figure 1: Alignment format of JAMR

The alignment format adopted in the literature is presented by JAMR, where alignment blocks are separated with white space (Figure 1). Each alignment block includes a word span and its graph fragment where a pipe sign ('|') separates them. Graph fragments consist of nodes represented with their position in the AMR graphs. A root node is located at position 0 ('want-01'); its children take 0.x where x represents the order of the children. For example, the first child of the root node takes 0.0 as a position indicator ('boy'); the second takes 0.1 ('believe-01').

[1] https://github.com/amr-turkish/turkish-amr-aligner

3 The Aligner

For Turkish, an alignment approach depending only on word-concept matching (Flanigan et al., 2014; Liu et al., 2018b) does not fully cover all concepts. On the other hand, unsupervised machine translation approaches (Pourdamghani et al., 2014) are not easily applicable due to representation issues (Oflazer and Durgar El-Kahlout, 2007) and the need for high-volume of parallel data. In Turkish, some of the correspondences are not present explicitly as a word, and are hidden inside the words as morphemes (e.g., personal markers, modality markers) due to its complex morphology and pro-drop nature. Consider the sentences in Figure 2 "Sana geleceğimi bilebilmene şaşırdım" (*I am surprised that you could know that I would be coming to you.*). The lemma of the words are 'sen' (*you*), 'gel'(*come*), 'bil' (*know*) and 'şaşır' (*be shocked*). The lexical concepts related to these may be aligned using fuzzy matching, however, the other concepts 'ben' (*I*) and mümkün.01 (*possible-01*)) deriving from their suffixes could not be matched. 'ben' is a dropped pronoun represented with a the first personal suffix (*-m*) that attach to verb lemma 'gel', 'mümkün.01' is originated from the modality marker (*-ebil*).

Figure 2 shows the aligned version of the sentence "Sana geleceğimi bilebilmene şaşırdım" (*I am surprised that you could know that I would be coming to you.*).

::snt Sana / gelece**ğimi** / bil**ebil**mene / şaşırdım
::eng to you / that I would be coming / that you could know / I am surprised
::alignments 0-1|0.1.1 1-2|0.1.1.0 2-3|0.1.0+0.1 3-4|0+0.0

```
(ş / şaşır.01                0
  :ARG0 (b / ben)            0.0
  :ARG1 (m / mümkün.01.      0.1
      :ARG1 (b2 / bil.01.    0.1.0
          :ARG0 (s / sen).   0.1.1
          :ARG1 (g / gel.01  0.1.1.0
              :ARG0 b
              :ARG4 s))))
```

Figure 2: AMR representation of the sentence "Sana geleceğimi bilebilmene şaşırdım" (*I am surprised that you could know that I would be coming to you*) and its alignment in JAMR format

To align such concepts, one alternative is to follow the literature and expand the rule list of JAMR (Flanigan et al., 2014) with the new rules to handle morphology based concepts. We believe this is not an option due to the following reasons: (i) There may be morphemes whose meaning can be changed according to the context. In order to align them, their meaning should be determined first and this needs semantic interpretation. Modality marker (*-meli*) is such an example and could carry out different meanings (i.e., 'should' or 'have to') depending on the context. (ii) There may be morphemes that invoke predicates, and the predicates invoked by the same morphemes can be different based on the nouns being attached. For example, when the very productive suffix *-CI* (with surface forms *ci, cı, çi, çı* under different vowel harmonies) attaches to nouns, it may mean 1) 'a person who sells' the item given in the noun lemma (e.g., 'simit**çi**' is the person who sells bagels where 'simit' is bagel), 2) 'a person who runs' the item given in the noun lemma (e.g., 'lokanta**cı**' is a person who runs a restaurant where 'lokanta' is restaurant) 3) 'a person who plays' (e.g., 'bas**cı**' is a person who plays bass guitar where 'bas' is bass guitar), and so forth. Covering all possible meanings with defining rules requires numerous rules. (iii) Construction of a solution on top of the morphemes (i.e., aligning morphemes using a predefined list) requires a preliminary morphological analysis stage. The aligner would become very dependent on the performance of the morphological analysis, and its errors propagate throughout the alignment. Considering these, we believe that a better approach should be proposed for the alignment of handling morphology-based concepts.

We propose an alignment strategy which relies on the word-concept similarity and tree traversal. Our aligner has two steps. In the first step, it builds a map where concepts are mapped to their word correspondence. This mapping is done by using similarity between pre-trained word embeddings for the words of the sentence and the node labels of the graph. The mapping does not necessarily include all concepts in this step: morphology derived and abstract concepts are left unmapped. The second step focuses on aligning all concepts. First, it starts aligning with concept-words pairs in the mapping obtained in the first step. Then it aligns the remaining concepts (i.e., morphology derived and abstract concepts) by traversing the AMR graph through the mapping. For each concept-word pair, the aligner visits neighbors of the concept by following the heuristically determined paths, and any unaligned neighbors are simply added to the alignments for the word. Our aligner is detailed in the following subsections: Section 3.1 and 3.2.

3.1 Similarity Mapping

The similarity mapping aims to create lemma-concept pairs to be aligned in the next step. Our approach is similar to TAMR in which both syntactic and semantic similarities are used. However, we do not use morpho-semantic matching from TAMR despite Turkish being an morphologically rich language. Since Turkish is an agglutinative language, there is a direct link between the nouns invoking verbs and the verb frames. Therefore, semantic similarity can easily be used to match such nouns and the use of extra databases is not necessary.

The mapping is started with the semantic similarity calculation. A similarity score is calculated for each lemma-concept pair in the cross of lemma and concept set. We use Fasttext[2] (Grave et al., 2018) vectors, and empirically define threshold of 0.5 for the similarity score. Lemma-concept pairs with similarity scores above this limit are considered 'close'. The closest ones are matched with each other when they satisfy the condition that the closeness should be bi-directional. In other words, a mapping occurs when the closest concept of a lemma 'A' is B when B's closest pair is A (Function $mapping$ in Algorithm 2). It should be noted the aligner allows the lemma A to map more than one concept since there may be cases where A should have more than one concept as pair.

In some cases, word vectors fail to converge words having the same stem semantically; to handle them, we use syntactic similarity ($mFuzzy$) since their lemmas are the same[3]. After these two similarity matching processes, it is considered that remaining words that can not be mapped to any concept do not contribute to sentence meaning.

Similarity mapping seems straightforward; however, ellipsis makes the mapping difficult. An elliptical construction is the omission of one or more words that we call omitted words and their existence may be understood from the remaining words within the context. The AMR representation of such constructions varies across languages (Migueles-Abraira et al., 2018; Liu et al., 2019). Similar to (Liu et al., 2019), the omitted words are also restored and represented with concepts in Turkish AMR. This results in a situation that there may appear concepts whose correspondence words do not exist within the sentence. We call these concepts 'elliptic concepts' since they should align with the elided words. The elliptic concepts should be aligned with the words, but the aligned words may change according to the ellipsis type. Generally, we align elliptic concepts with the words that can help to understand the omitted words by semantic inference: these can be either the re-occurrences or the antecedents of the elided words. For the sake of simplicity, we name these words infer-words.

We gather the alignment of elliptic concepts under two categories: alignment with re-occurrences and alignment with antecedents. Similarity mapping of the first category is straightforward since re-occurrences can easily be matched with the elliptic concepts such as gapping ellipses. In the sentence "Herkes şeker (*verirdi*), o çikolata verirdi." (*Everybody would give chocolate*, s/he would give a candy.), 'verirdi' in parenthesis is omitted, but we can understand its existence by the last predicate (i.e., the infer-word). Its AMR graph has to have two 'ver.01' (give) frames since two different people perform different actions. We map both 'ver.01' concepts to 'verirdi'.

The latter category deserves more attention since the infer-words may cause ambiguity. Nominal ellipsis is such an example where there could exist syntactically similar words within the same sentence to the elliptic concrete concept, while the elliptic concept should actually be aligned to some other words (e.g., nominal adjectives) that derive the ellipsis instead of the syntactically similar one. This means that we need to match the concepts with the words that are not similar neither semantically nor syntactically, even if there exist completely identical words within the sentence.

Figure 3a provides such an example of the alignment of an English sentence ("S/he preferred the red dress over the white."). The elliptic concept (i.e., the second dress) is also derived from 'dress'. However, the morphologically-rich nature of Turkish poses extra challenges in such situations since the meaning carried by the 'dress' (first dress) will be provided by the suffix 'a' attached to the adjective (Figure 3b). This situation yields the need of mapping the elliptic concept to the nominal adjective.

To deal with this, we add a disambiguation (Funtion $disambiguation$ in Algorithm 2) step. Simi-

[2]https://fasttext.cc/docs/en/crawl-vectors.html

[3]We set threshold of 0.95 for the similarity score

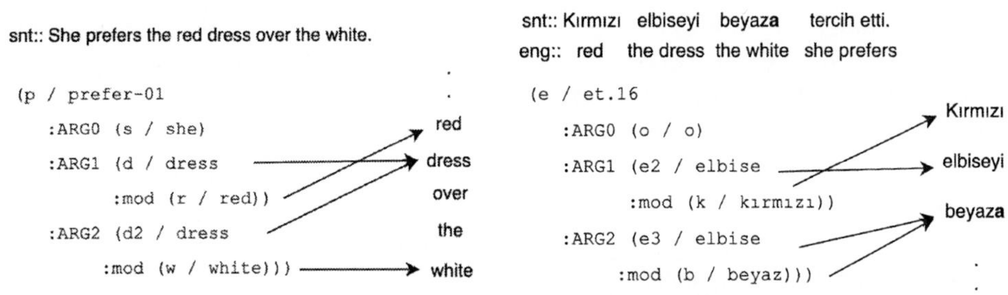

(a) The alignment of nominal ellipsis in English. AMR graph on the left, the words of the actual sentence on the right. The elliptic concept 'd2' should be aligned with the word 'dress'.

(b) The alignment of nominal ellipsis in Turkish. AMR graph on the left, the words of the actual sentence on the right. The elliptic concept 'e3' should be aligned with "beyaza" (the lemma 'beyaz' (*white*) in dative form carrying the meaning of the dress).

Figure 3: The alignment of nominal ellipsis

larity mapping and disambiguation operate simultaneously. When there is more than one concept candidate paired with a single word within the sentence, a disambiguator is invoked to decide if a removal of a concept-word match is necessary: At this stage multiple mapping is allowed for the first category describe above (i.e., gapping ellipsis). For the second category (i.e., nominal ellipsis), the disambiguator reduces the possible multiple mappings into a selected one; i.e., selects one of the candidates.

The disambiguator searches for common syntactic structures (i.e., modifiers of the concept-lemma pair in focus) between the candidate concept and lemma. However, since we do not use any extra resources at this stage such as a dependency parser, we make a general assumption that the modifiers (e.g., adjectives describing a noun) would appear on the left side of a noun in the actual sentence word order. Although, most of the time, this assumption holds for English and several other languages, where modifiers frequently precede nouns, the direction may be changed if necessary for the language in focus.

First, the aligner calculates an overlap score between the 1-degree neighbors of each candidate concepts and the neighboring words in the 1-word window of the word in focus (i.e., the focus word to be mapped). Then, the candidate having a higher overlap score is matched with the word in focus. For example, possible mappings of the word in focus 'dress' in the actual sentence provided in Figure 3a are the two concepts d and d2. The overlap between the word in focus' neighbors is the word 'red', which eliminates the second possible mapping: the white dress. As one would notice, the introduced assumption does not have any effect in this example since the single overlapped word is enough for the elimination. However, when we look to the second example (Figure 3b) in the same figure, the 1-word window neighbor set of the word 'elbise' (*dress*) contain both the words 'red' and 'white' where our assumption helps to select the most possible candidate concept.

3.2 Alignment Algorithm

The alignment procedure (Algorithm 1) starts with similarity mapping ($simMap$) where word-concept pairs are determined as described in the previous section. Consider a set of words $W = \{w_1, w_2, ..., w_n\}$ in sentence S, where n is the number of words, the AMR graph is shown as $G = \{C, V\}$, where $C = \{c_1, c_2, ..., c_m\}$ is the set of concepts, and V is the relation set between these concepts. It should be noted that concept indexes and word indexes are not directly related to each other. As the output of similarity mapping, we get a list, each element of which is also a list (*pl*). This list *pl* contains $< w_j, c_i >$ pairs where j depicts the word-order index of the current word within the sentence. Our aligner processes each $< w_j, c_i >$ pair and first aligns c_i with w_j. Then it searches for c_i's one-edge away neighbors to find unmatched concepts during previous stage that need to be aligned with w_j. c_i is accepted as a central node and the aligner visits its neighbors. If a neighbor has a word pair, the aligner turns back to c_i. Otherwise the neighbor node is added to a list of visited concepts and the aligner moves to that node to search unmapped concepts in its neighborhood. This recursive process stops when there are no more mapped concepts in the neighborhood and the aligner returns to c_i. Concepts added into the visited list during neighbor search are aligned with w_j. Then, the aligner moves to another concept-word pair and repeats the same steps. The alignment algorithm terminates when all pairs are processed.

Algorithm 1: Alignment Algorithm

Input: $S = List(w_1 \dots w_n), G = (C, V)$
Output: $Alignments$
$M \leftarrow simMap(S, G)$
$M \leftarrow sort(M)$
$T \leftarrow removeReent(G)$
$Alignments \leftarrow \emptyset$
for $j = 0$ ***to*** n **do**
  $pl_j \leftarrow M[j]$
  for $< w_j, c_i > \in pl_j$ **do**
    $Alignments[j] \cup \{c_i\}$
    $Alignments[j] \cup getVisited(c_i, T, M)$
  end
end
$Alignments \leftarrow postprocess(Alignments)$
Function *getVisited* (c, T, M)**:**
  $visited \leftarrow \emptyset$
  $n \leftarrow NeighInAllowedPath(c, T, M)$
  for $n_i, \in n$ **do**
    if $< \forall w, n_i > \notin M$ **then**
      $visited \cup getVisited(n_i, T, M)$
  end
  return $visited$

Morphologicallly rich languages lead to frequent reification (i.e., conversion of a role into a concept (Banarescu et al., 2013)) situations in AMR. This results in nested concepts. Remember the example 'simitçi' (the person who sells bagels) from Section 3, which produces 3 concepts: 'person', 'sell.01', and 'bagel'. We use the above-explained recursive search for finding unmapped concepts within the nested relation chains.

At the beginning of the alignment procedure, we remove reentrancy[4] relations (function $removeReent$ in the Algorithm 1) and the graphs are transformed into trees. The reasons for this are that (i) we aim to align words whose alignments are graph fragments, and reentrancy connections appear on the linguistic phenomena such as co-reference, coordination, repetition, etc. (Blodgett and Schneider, 2021) rather than morphology-based ones where such graph fragments emerge. Therefore, we assume that the graph fragments do not include reentrancy connections. (ii) the majority of the reentrancy relations come from the personal suffixes whose concepts are mostly morphology originated. In figure 2, the concept 'ben' comes from the personal suffix *-Im* and can be aligned with 'geleceğ**imi**' or 'şaşırd**ım**', both alignments are correct. Since one of them is enough for the aligner to be used in concept generation as the first stage of parsing, we ignore the reentrancy connections during the alignment to be handled later during parsing.

Our aligner greedily searches neighbor nodes and the ordering of the concepts in the mapping list (M) is crucial for our aligner. The unmapped morphology-based concepts should be reached from their children nodes first since they tend to appear on top of the lexical concepts in the AMR graph. In order to ensure this, we add a sorting ($sort$) operation which moves the predicate concepts to the end of the mapping list to ensure that they are handled later than the leaf nodes. Moreover, we put constraints to force the aligner to visit neighbor nodes only in allowed path ($NeighInAllowedPath$) so that some nodes are reachable only via specified relations. These constraints guarantee the alignment of the abstract concepts of AMR. For instance, '*-quantity*' concepts are only reachable over the relations *:unit* and *:value*. The constraints are taken from JAMR rules responsible for alignments of abstract concepts.

Up to this stage, the aligner produces alignments for words. However, in order to produce alignments for word spans (e.g., named entities, reduplications, multi-word expressions), we need an additional stage to combine some words and their alignments. Therefore, we use a two stage post-processing step: The first stage focuses on the alignment of named entities: it unifies the alignment of consecutive words which were initially aligned to some concepts connected to the same 'name'[5] concept. In other words, consecutive words are merged into word spans, and their related concepts are also merged similarly for named entities.

[4]A single word in a sentence might be argument of more than one predicate. This is called reentrancy (Banarescu et al., 2013) in AMR.

[5]In AMR, the abstract 'name' concept is used for representing the named entities.

Algorithm 2: Similarity Mapping Algorithm ($simMap$)

Input: $S = List(w_1 \dots w_n)$, $G = (C, V)$, wv, t
Output: M
sim $\leftarrow n \times m$, M $\leftarrow \emptyset$
for $j = 0$ ***to*** n **do**
    $w_j \leftarrow S[j]$
    $v_{wj} \leftarrow wv(wj)$
    for $c_i \in C$ **do**
        $v_{c_i} \leftarrow wv(c_i)$
        if $CosSim(v_{wj}, v_{c_i}) \geq t$ **then**
            sim$[w_j][c_i] \leftarrow CosSim(v_{wj}, v_{c_i})$
        else if $mFuzzy(v_{wj}, v_{c_i} \geq 0.95$ **then**
            sim$[w_j][c_i] \leftarrow mFuzzy(v_{wj}, v_{c_i})$
    end
end
for $j = 0$ *to* n **do**
    $concepts \leftarrow mapping(sim, S, j, G)$
    for each c_i *in* $concepts$ **do**
        M[j] $\cup \{< S[j], c_i >\}$
    end
end
Function *mapping (sim,S,j,G)*
    $w_j \leftarrow S$[j]
    $s \leftarrow max$(sim$[w_j]$)
    for $c_l \in C$ **do**
        $w_k \leftarrow argmax$(sim$[:, c_l]$)
        if $w_k = w_j$ **then**
            $cands \cup \{c_l\}$ if $s =$ sim$[w_k, c_l]$
    end
    if $length(cands) \geq 2$ **then**
        $cands \leftarrow$
          $disambugate(cands, S, j, G)$
    end
    return $cands$
Function *disambugate (candidates,S,i,G)*
    $max \leftarrow 0$, $v \leftarrow \emptyset$
    for each c *in* $candidates$ **do**
        if *c is verb frame* **then**
            return $candidates$
        else
            $children \leftarrow getChildren(c, G)$
            $prev \leftarrow \{S[i-1]\}$
            $next \leftarrow \{S[i+1]\}$
            $parents \leftarrow getParent(c, G)$
            $overlap \leftarrow \{ prev \cap children \} \cup$
                    $\{ next \cap parents \}$
            if $length(overlap) \geq$ max **then**
                $v \leftarrow$ candidate
                $max \leftarrow length(overlap)$
            end
        end
    end
    return $\{ v \}$

The second stage focuses on multi-word expressions (i.e., idioms) and reduplications [6]. The previous stages can only align one word of such constructions, and the other words in the expression or reduplication remain unaligned. The post-processor checks each unaligned word within a sentence and creates word spans by combining them with their consecutive neighbours whose related concept name includes the unaligned word's lemma. For the languages which do not have these phenomena, this latter post processing steps could be omitted.

4 Experiments and Results

In order to evaluate the performance of our aligner, we randomly choose 100 sentences from a Turkish AMR corpus (Oral et al., 2022). and manually align the concepts of the AMR graphs with the words within sentences.[7]

Following the same evaluation method used in JAMR[8], we compare our aligner with TAMR (Liu et al., 2018b), JAMR (Flanigan et al., 2014) , and Portuguese-Aligner (shortly, PrAMR) (Anchiêta and Pardo, 2020). We adapt these aligners to Turkish. The predefined dictionaries such as months, conjunctions, etc., are replaced with their Turkish counterparts, and Fasttext is used in TAMR and PrAMR. We set similarity thresholds as 0.5 and 1.5 respectively. Since PrAMR uses lexical lists for named entities, we localized these as far as possible via a Portuguese to Turkish translator and adding additional Turkish gazetteers. Table 1 shows the results. Our aligner achieves an F1-score of 87% and outperforms the other aligners developed for English and Portuguese. Although TAMR and JAMR have a precision score relatively close to our aligner, they fall far behind the F1 score due to their low recalls. The recalls obviously show that the proposed methods for alignment fail to align around half of the concepts; these are the concepts derived from morphology. Furthermore, the alignment approach with Word Mover's Distance (PrAMR) has poorer performance than the fuzzy matching.

We design another experiment to evaluate our ap-

[6]Reduplication is the repetition of a word or part of a word (Göksel and Kerslake, 2004).

[7]The alignment gold set was annotated by one of the authors in two iterations. In the first iteration, the alignments were built from scratch. In the second iteration, the same annotator checked the correctness of the alignments, and the ones having alignment mistakes were corrected.

[8]https://github.com/jflanigan/jamr/blob/Semeval-2016/src/EvalSpans.scala

Output	P	R	F1
JAMR	0.73	0.48	0.58
TAMR	0.70	0.43	0.53
PrAMR	0.55	0.39	0.45
Ours	**0.89**	**0.84**	**0.87**

Table 1: The evaluation of our aligner

proach's effectiveness and investigate our aligner's alignment performance on different concept types. We evaluate our aligner on the sentence constituents concerning only the concept types in focus.

	P	R	F1
Elliptic Concepts	0.60	0.42	0.50
NEs	0.86	0.89	0.88
Abstract Concepts	0.90	0.82	0.86
Morphological Concepts	0.87	0.86	0.86

Table 2: Alignment performance of our aligner on different concept types

As shown in Table 2, our aligner's performance is in parallel to its overall score except elliptic concepts. Ellipsis is one of the most challenging parts of AMR alignment in Turkish. As a future work, we aim to improve the approach for this phenomenon.

We make a further error analysis to see the weaknesses of our aligner. One of our aligner's mistakes is the mismatch/unmatch of specific concepts. Since our alignment algorithm greedily searches unmapped concepts, any mistakes in the mapping phase result in the wrong alignments. Although our aligner uses the power of the pre-trained word embeddings, it fails to match the punctuation marks when they create concepts, especially the cases when they have a coordination role in the sentence: for example the comma mark is related to the concept 'and', and the colon mark is related to the concept 'de.01'(*say.01*), however these punctuation marks are not similar to the concept names neither semantically nor syntactically. The alignment of the light verbs is another unmatched case where our aligner fails. The Turkish Propbank (Şahin, 2016) represents them as frames of auxiliary verbs, which is how the AMR uses them too. Therefore, our aligner maps only the verb part due to semantic similarity; the first part of the verb is left unmatched. For example 'tercih et-' (*to prefer*) is represented with 'et.16' our aligner aligns only 'et' (*do*). Our aligner also shows poor performance on the alignment of the auxiliary verb 'ol'. This verb has 26 frames, including the widespread meanings 'have' (ol.04) and 'become' (ol.03). When there are multiple occurrences within the same sentence, the aligner does not have enough information to distinguish these frames. As a result, it may produce wrong mappings. An option to solve this ambiguity problem could be to integrate Propbank verb frames as an external resource in future works. One should note that this kind of additions would increase the alignment cost.

5 Conclusions and Feature Work

In this paper, we proposed an alignment approach for morphologically-rich and pro-drop languages and presented the first AMR aligner designed for Turkish which is prominent language of morphologically rich languages. Our aligner uses pre-trained word vectors and fuzzy matching for aligning concrete concepts. Furthermore, we present an algorithm for the alignment problem of concepts that emerged from the morphemes; this simple approach may be adopted to other morphologically rich and pro-drop languages with little effort. Our study reveals the challenging points in the Turkish alignment study, and we believe that our findings will accelerate the development of multilingual AMR parsing studies. As a future work, we plan to expand our study on the other morphologically rich and pro-drop languages (e.g., Portuguese).

References

Rafael Anchiêta and Thiago Pardo. 2020. Semantically inspired AMR alignment for the Portuguese language. In *Proceedings of the 2020 Conference on Empirical Methods in Natural Language Processing (EMNLP)*, pages 1595–1600, Online. Association for Computational Linguistics.

Laura Banarescu, Claire Bonial, Shu Cai, Madalina Georgescu, Kira Griffitt, Ulf Hermjakob, Kevin Knight, Philipp Koehn, Martha Palmer, and Nathan Schneider. 2013. Abstract meaning representation for sembanking. In *Proceedings of the 7th linguistic annotation workshop and interoperability with discourse*, pages 178–186.

Austin Blodgett and Nathan Schneider. 2021. Probabilistic, structure-aware algorithms for improved variety, accuracy, and coverage of amr alignments. *arXiv preprint arXiv:2106.06002*.

Johan Bos. 2016. Expressive power of abstract meaning representations. *Computational Linguistics*, 42(3):527–535.

Peter F Brown, Stephen A Della Pietra, Vincent J Della Pietra, and Robert L Mercer. 1993. The mathematics of statistical machine translation: Parameter estimation. *Computational linguistics*, 19(2):263–311.

Gözde Gül Şahin. 2016. Framing of verbs for Turkish propbank. *Turkish Computational Linguistics*, pages 3–9.

Shibhansh Dohare, Harish Karnick, and Vivek Gupta. 2017. Text summarization using Abstract Meaning Representation. *arXiv preprint arXiv:1706.01678*.

Angela Fan and Claire Gardent. 2020. Multilingual AMR-to-text generation. In *Proceedings of the 2020 Conference on Empirical Methods in Natural Language Processing (EMNLP)*, pages 2889–2901, Online. Association for Computational Linguistics.

Christiane Fellbaum, Anne Osherson, and Peter E Clark. 2007. Putting semantics into wordnet's" morphosemantic" links. In *Language and technology conference*, pages 350–358. Springer.

Jeffrey Flanigan, Sam Thomson, Jaime Carbonell, Chris Dyer, and Noah A. Smith. 2014. A discriminative graph-based parser for the Abstract Meaning Representation. In *Proceedings of the 52nd Annual Meeting of the Association for Computational Linguistics (Volume 1: Long Papers)*, pages 1426–1436, Baltimore, Maryland. Association for Computational Linguistics.

Aslı Göksel and Celia Kerslake. 2004. *Turkish: A comprehensive grammar*. Routledge.

Edouard Grave, Piotr Bojanowski, Prakhar Gupta, Armand Joulin, and Tomas Mikolov. 2018. Learning word vectors for 157 languages. In *Proceedings of the International Conference on Language Resources and Evaluation (LREC 2018)*.

Lifu Huang, Taylor Cassidy, Xiaocheng Feng, Heng Ji, Clare R. Voss, Jiawei Han, and Avirup Sil. 2016. Liberal event extraction and event schema induction. In *Proceedings of the 54th Annual Meeting of the Association for Computational Linguistics (Volume 1: Long Papers)*, pages 258–268, Berlin, Germany. Association for Computational Linguistics.

Ioannis Konstas, Srinivasan Iyer, Mark Yatskar, Yejin Choi, and Luke Zettlemoyer. 2017. Neural AMR: Sequence-to-sequence models for parsing and generation. *arXiv preprint arXiv:1704.08381*.

Matt Kusner, Yu Sun, Nicholas Kolkin, and Kilian Weinberger. 2015. From word embeddings to document distances. In *International conference on machine learning*, pages 957–966. PMLR.

Manling Li, Alireza Zareian, Qi Zeng, Spencer Whitehead, Di Lu, Heng Ji, and Shih-Fu Chang. 2020. Cross-media structured common space for multimedia event extraction. *arXiv preprint arXiv:2005.02472*.

Kexin Liao, Logan Lebanoff, and Fei Liu. 2018. Abstract meaning representation for multi-document summarization. *arXiv preprint arXiv:1806.05655*.

Fei Liu, Jeffrey Flanigan, Sam Thomson, Norman Sadeh, and Noah A Smith. 2018a. Toward abstractive summarization using semantic representations. *arXiv preprint arXiv:1805.10399*.

Yihuan Liu, Bin Li, Peiyi Yan, Li Song, and Weiguang Qu. 2019. Ellipsis in chinese amr corpus. In *Proceedings of the First International Workshop on Designing Meaning Representations*, pages 92–99.

Yijia Liu, Wanxiang Che, Bo Zheng, Bing Qin, and Ting Liu. 2018b. An AMR aligner tuned by transition-based parser. *arXiv preprint arXiv:1810.03541*.

Chunchuan Lyu and Ivan Titov. 2018. AMR parsing as graph prediction with latent alignment. *arXiv preprint arXiv:1805.05286*.

Manuel Mager, Ramón Fernandez Astudillo, Tahira Naseem, Md Arafat Sultan, Young-Suk Lee, Radu Florian, and Salim Roukos. 2020. Gpt-too: A language-model-first approach for AMR-to-text generation. *arXiv preprint arXiv:2005.09123*.

Noelia Migueles-Abraira, Rodrigo Agerri, and Arantza Diaz de Ilarraza. 2018. Annotating abstract meaning representations for spanish. In *Proceedings of the Eleventh International Conference on Language Resources and Evaluation (LREC 2018)*.

Kemal Oflazer and İlknur Durgar El-Kahlout. 2007. Exploring different representational units in English-to-Turkish statistical machine translation. In *Proceedings of the Second Workshop on Statistical Machine Translation*, pages 25–32, Prague, Czech Republic. Association for Computational Linguistics.

Elif Oral, Ali Acar, and Gülşen Eryiğit. 2022. Abstract meaning representation of Turkish. *Natural Language Engineering*.

Nima Pourdamghani, Yang Gao, Ulf Hermjakob, and Kevin Knight. 2014. Aligning english strings with abstract meaning representation graphs. In *Proceedings of the 2014 Conference on Empirical Methods in Natural Language Processing (EMNLP)*, pages 425–429.

Umut Sulubacak, Gülşen Eryiğit, and Tuğba Pamay. 2016. IMST: A revisited Turkish Dependency Treebank. In *Proceedings of TurCLing 2016, the 1st International Conference on Turkic Computational Linguistics*, pages 1–6, Turkey. EGE UNIVERSITY PRESS.

Chuan Wang, Nianwen Xue, and Sameer Pradhan. 2015. A transition-based algorithm for amr parsing. In *Proceedings of the 2015 Conference of the North American Chapter of the Association for Computational Linguistics: Human Language Technologies*, pages 366–375.

Tianming Wang, Xiaojun Wan, and Hanqi Jin. 2020. AMR-To-Text Generation with Graph Transformer. *Transactions of the Association for Computational Linguistics*, 8:19–33.

Zdeněk Žabokrtský, Daniel Zeman, and Magda Ševčíková. 2020. Sentence meaning representations across languages: what can we learn from existing frameworks? *Computational Linguistics*, 46(3):605–665.

Sheng Zhang, Xutai Ma, Kevin Duh, and Benjamin Van Durme. 2019. Broad-coverage semantic parsing as transduction. pages 3786–3798, Hong Kong, China. Association for Computational Linguistics.

Yanbin Zhao, Lu Chen, Zhi Chen, Ruisheng Cao, Su Zhu, and Kai Yu. 2020. Line graph enhanced AMR-to-text generation with mix-order graph attention networks. In *Proceedings of the 58th Annual Meeting of the Association for Computational Linguistics*, pages 732–741, Online. Association for Computational Linguistics.

Junsheng Zhou, Feiyu Xu, Hans Uszkoreit, Weiguang Qu, Ran Li, and Yanhui Gu. 2016. Amr parsing with an incremental joint model. In *Proceedings of the 2016 conference on empirical methods in natural language processing*, pages 680–689.

Sketching a Linguistically-Driven Reasoning Dialog Model for Social Talk

Alex Lưu
Brandeis University
alexluu@brandeis.edu

Abstract

The capability of holding social talk (or casual conversation) and making sense of conversational content requires context-sensitive natural language understanding and reasoning, which cannot be handled efficiently by the current popular open-domain dialog systems and chatbots. Heavily relying on corpus-based machine learning techniques to encode and decode context-sensitive meanings, these systems focus on fitting a particular training dataset, but not tracking what is actually happening in a conversation, and therefore easily derail in a new context. This work sketches out a more linguistically-informed architecture to handle social talk in English, in which corpus-based methods form the backbone of the relatively context-insensitive components (e.g. part-of-speech tagging, approximation of lexical meaning and constituent chunking), while symbolic modeling is used for reasoning out the context-sensitive components, which do not have any consistent mapping to linguistic forms. All components are fitted into a Bayesian game-theoretic model to address the interactive and rational aspects of conversation.[1]

1 Introduction and Background

Developing dialog systems that can socially communicate with humans and make sense of conversational content would demonstrate that we are able to put together all linguistic knowledge and skills in action in a truly personalized manner, i.e. the dialog systems can use the same language competence to produce different coherent contents in different conversational situations. Such domain-independence would allow a dialog system to be robustly used across multiple content and task domains. While the benefit of using social interaction style in real-life dialog systems is a controversial topic (e.g. Chattaraman et al., 2019; Clark et al., 2019), the availability of social dialog agents can alleviate the critical shortage of human resources, e.g. in language education (Swanson and Mason, 2018), among other domains. Worldwide language learners often have little time to develop their communication skills with their teachers in the classroom setting; consequently teachers do not have enough clues to analyze their students' communication competence and their own teaching effectiveness. Having a dialog system that can socially converse with students at least about the learning materials outside the classroom and being able to access the content of these conversations for further analysis would be a plausible solution to the bottleneck of human resources in language education.

Research on social dialog systems has thrived in recent years thanks to optimism about the robustness of Natural Language Processing (NLP) techniques based on big data and deep learning. Within this period, emerging dialog systems either (1) seek to accommodate the open-domain information exchange by expanding the list of predefined interlocutors' intents and conversational topics for modular architectures, e.g. systems competing in Alexa Prize Socialbot Challenges (Khatri et al., 2018), or (2) focus on generating utterances to prolong the conversation based on neural network sequence-to-sequence approaches, such as Google's Meena (Adiwardana et al., 2020) and Meta's BlenderBot (Roller et al., 2021). Primarily motivated by the available data and statistical techniques but not the sociocultural characteristics of social talk, these dialog systems focus on fitting pre-existing training datasets, but not tracking what is actually happening in a conversation. As a consequence, they easily derail in a new context, as illustrated in Figure 1: the chatbot seems to interpret *bank* in the question *What do you do at a river bank?* as a financial institution, which is statistically preferred given the training data, instead of the land alongside a river, which is more felicitous in this particular context.

[1]The live version of this publication is located at https://osf.io/xz65k/.

Proceedings of the 60th Annual Meeting of the Association for Computational Linguistics
Student Research Workshop, pages 153 - 170

```
Enter Your Message: I just had a walk along the Connecticut river. The bank is gorgeous.
[TransformerGenerator]: i ' ll have to check it out , thanks !
Enter Your Message: What do you do at a river bank?
[TransformerGenerator]: i ' m a teller at a local bank .
```

Figure 1: A dialog between me and a state-of-the-art (SOTA) chatbot developed by Meta Research (Roller).

To address that shortcoming, this work takes a novel approach, relying on in-depth analysis of naturally occurring data to sketch out a more linguistically-informed[2] architecture to handle social talk in English, in which corpus-based methods form the backbone of the relatively context-insensitive components (e.g. part-of-speech (POS) tagging, approximation of lexical meaning, and constituent chunking), while symbolic modeling is used for reasoning out the context-sensitive components, which do not have any consistent mapping to linguistic forms. All components are fitted into a Bayesian game-theoretic model to address the interactive and rational aspects of conversation.

This paper is organized as follows. Section 2 provides a working definition of interlocutors' shared goal in social talk and its implications. Section 3 presents the key aspects of coherence with respect to the shared goal[3]. Section 4 outlines the conversational context that accounts for the coherence-based and goal-directed nature of social talk. Section 5 describes a simple worked example of the proposed model. Section 6 discusses the key differences between the proposed approach and current popular approaches to social dialog systems, analyzing its advantages and limitations, research priorities, and ethics and social impact considerations. Section 7 concludes and presents a plan for future work.

2 Interlocutors' Shared Social Goal

Lưu and Malamud (2020b) provides evidence of non-content based coherence in social talk that is not constrained by the purpose of information exchange. Specifically, the new-topic utterances in social talk, which begin a new topic not linguistically correlating with the content of prior discourse, signal certain sequential adjustment of the distances between the active conversational topic and each interlocutor, such as switching social focus from one interlocutor to another. This finding suggests that the definition of interlocutors' shared goal in social talk must be based on a social interaction formalism that goes beyond an information exchange framework (cf. Hovy and Yang, 2021 – a recent advocate for incorporating language's social factors into computational models of language use, given the SOTA NLP advancements).

Following the literature on intersubjectivity in communication (e.g. Rommetveit, 1976; Schiffrin, 1990; Wertsch, 2000; Tirassa and Bosco, 2008), I propose that the shared goal of interlocutors in social talk is **to create a coherent experience of together making sense of Self, the Other, and the relationship between them** (but not necessarily to share the same perspective on any aspect of the conversational content). This shared goal is not only primarily addressed by social talk but also forms a part of natural task-oriented conversation when the interlocutors attempt to build mutual rapport. Even the task-related conversational goals can be considered instantiations of this shared goal when Self and the Other are playing specific social roles in the task domains, e.g. seller – buyer or consultant – client. Within this shared goal, performing a conversational move implies taking a stance, i.e. a public social act of simultaneously **evaluating** objects (directly or indirectly) discussed in the conversational move, **positioning** subjects (Self or the Other or both), and **aligning** with the other subject, with respect to any salient dimension of the sociocultural field (Du Bois, 2007, p. 163). Regarding the sociocultural field, I adopt the proposal in Stevanovic and Peräkylä (2014) and Stevanovic and Koski (2018) for representing conversational interactions between Self and the Other as falling into one of three dimensions: **epistemic** (knowledge/information exchange - *how knowledgeable the interlocutors are*), **normative**[4] (power/social distance - *how powerful the interlocutors are*), and **affective** (affect/emotion - *how emotional the interlocutors are*). By explicitly paying attention to the normative and affective domains in the conversational context, we can expand current models of dialog that involve a representation of context but focus on the epistemic domain (such as those that build on Stalnaker, 1974, 1978; Roberts, 1996/2012, inter alia), and therefore can adequately

[2]As theory-neutral as possible.

[3]Detailed discussion on the concepts of "social talk" and "coherence" can be found in Lưu and Malamud (2020b).

[4]The original term, **deontic**, can be confusing since it expresses duty or obligation in the linguistics literature.

handle the multifaceted coherence in social talk and the corresponding social reasoning.

3 Multifaceted Coherence in Social Talk

Lưu and Malamud (2020b) shows that conversational coherence in social talk arises from at least two different sources, depending on whether the target utterance bears any content-based coherence relations to prior discourse.

Where there is at least one content-based coherence relation between the target utterance and prior discourse, this relation is shaped by certain **discourse hooks**[5] (located in the target utterance) that are pragmatically accessible to the hearer, and can be discourse-old, discourse-new bearing inferential relation to discourse-old, or discourse-new and related to discourse-old in a non-inferential manner (cf. Prince, 1992; Birner, 2012, inter alia). For example, in the social dialog in Table 1 the utterance 132-A is connected to the utterance 131-A by a coherence relation that is explicitly triggered by the conjunction *and* and shaped by several discourse hooks: the pronoun *it* is evoked as discourse-old information, referring to *a lovely red dress* which first appeared in 131-A, and *everything* is arguably inferrable from that *dress* via the entity/attribute inferential relation. Another coherence relation can be established between 133-A and 136-B since the clause *she totally ditched it* in the former utterance presupposes that there is a reason behind that action, which becomes the focus of the latter.

When there is no content-based coherence relation between the target utterance and prior discourse, conversational coherence is demonstrated by the **shift of social focus** created by certain explicit positioning or alignment signals in the target utterance. For example, the utterance 147-A of the excerpt shown in Table 1 switches the social focus from the speaker A to the hearer B by raising a question related to B, given that the preceding topic of discussion is A's difficulty in searching for a dress. By extending the conversation with new content relevant to the social subject who has received less focus in the preceding discourse, this utterance does contribute to the process of 'together making sense of Self, the Other, and the relationship between them' in a coherent way and seems to get its motivation from the non-epistemic domains:

Utt.	Simplified transcript
131-A	*Well Rosemary and I went in for a look and uhm I found a lovely red dress*
132-A	*And I was like delighted with it and everything*
133-A	*And I brought mum up to see it and she totally ditched it*
134-B	*Yeah*
135-B	*Yeah*
136-B	*Why*
137-A	*She said it looked like she was she was saying it didn't do anything for my hips*
138-A	*It made my hips look big and like you know my bum and hips and everything*
139-A	*I was really excited cos I had the dress and then I just*
140-B	*But did you like it*
141-A	*Yeah*
142-B	*But she turned you off it*
143-A	*Yeah well I mean I'm hardly going to wear it now seeing everyone thinking I've big hip*
144-A	*Hip girl*
145-A	*I'll be called hippy*
146-A	*Hippo*
147-A	***Ah so how are you anyway***

Table 1: An excerpt, with indexed utterances, from telephone dialog *P1A-099* in the SPICE-Ireland corpus[6] (Kallen and Kirk, 2012) between two students A and B.

speaker A probably wants to show her attentiveness to speaker B (affective dimension), and her social closeness to B makes her think that this move is appropriate (normative dimension).

Coherence and Relevance It is worth noting that to be coherent, an utterance must not only be connected to the prior discourse via certain inferences, but also be **relevant** to the conversational goals, which coordinate the sequences of action performed by interlocutors' utterances (cf. Clift, 2016, pp. 89-94 for the discussion on coherence in interaction). Within the shared goal of interlocutors in social talk defined in Section 2, the expression of this relevance varies according to sociocultural dimensions. To be epistemically relevant, an utterance must, at least, introduce a new focus of discussion instead of simply repeating the old information. To be affectively relevant, an utterance can mimic the emotional intensity or support the sentiment of the immediately preceding discourse. For example, the interlocutors clearly show their matching emotional intensity in the excerpt of a face-to-face social dialog in Table 2 whose second

[5] I follow Birner to step away from the term 'topic' which "has not succeeded in becoming a unified concept within linguistic theory" (Birner, 2012, p. 214).

[6] This corpus can be obtained upon request to its directors.

half is full of laughter (see Ginzburg et al., 2020 for the discussion on emotive aspects of laughter). Finally, to be normatively relevant, the utterance should not, for example, provoke any controversial discussion that may hurt the social relationship between interlocutors, which is usually handled by profanity filters in current dialog systems (e.g. Khatri et al., 2018).

Coherence and Consistency Another aspect of conversational coherence is the consistency of the interlocutors' conversational contents and psychological behaviors, which are subsumed in the term '**speaker type**' in this paper. An utterance is incoherent if it commits an object evaluation, e.g. *I like cats*, that conflicts with another evaluation of the same object by the same speaker in prior discourse, e.g. *I hate cats*. One of the popular attempts to address this problem is the creation of the PERSONA-CHAT dataset for training and testing the aspects of persona consistency in chatbot models (Zhang et al., 2018). An utterance is also less coherent if it demonstrates some dramatic change in its speaker's behaviors, e.g. a rude statement from a speaker who is very polite in prior discourse. From the production perspective, a speaker would like to maintain their behavioral consistency; while from the interpretation perspective, a hearer would assume this consistency from the speaker to effectively decode the meaning of the speaker's utterance. Previous work such as Fang et al. (2018) shows that understanding the speaker's personality in the dialog helps the hearer in having better interaction strategies. It's worth noting that interlocutors' psychological behaviors vary according to different factors of the speech situation such as the cultural conditions, the interlocutors' personalities, and the relationship between interlocutors. For example, the social distance between interlocutors can affect the course and topics of discussion. Comparing the dialog in Table 2 between two friends and the dialog in Table 3 between a couple, we see that even though both of them are casual, the higher intimacy in the latter can be observed in all sociocultural dimensions:

- epistemic: the discussion topics are more personal (e.g. *two things I got out of my marriage, the marriage itself I mean as hellish*) and involve more creative association (e.g. *it pulled me under like a giant octopus or a giant giant shark, it's not the way with food*)
- affective: more instances of highly expressive language such as *really interesting*, *really got me grounded*, *as hellish as it was*, *like a giant octopus or a giant giant shark*, *the silent scream*, *so much better*, *very hellish*
- normative: the fact that the interlocutors are

Utt.	Simplified transcript
1442-M	*You know I wish I was uh the person whose voice they used in the telephone when it tells you the number has been changed*
...	...
1458-M	*They certainly use her a lot*
1459-M	*But I mean they only use what as uh five seconds total or something*
1460-M	*You know it's a*
1461-J	*Probably took her a long time to to say every possible combination*
1462-M	*Oh but they the computer does that*
1463-M	*All she has to do is say each digit*
1464-M	*And the computer*
1465-J	*Oh that's all it is*
1466-M	*Yeah*
1467-M	*It's like a series of samples*
1468-J	*And it automatically sorts em*
...	...
1474-M	*It would be much more pleasant if they had done all the combinations though*
1475-M	*You know call it up and there's something that actually says your number*
1476-M	*In toto*
1477-M	*You know **[laughter]***
1478-J	*Yeah*
1479-J	*Or because it recognizes your phone number it automatically goes into the computer finds that*
1480-M	*Yeah that sample*
1481-J	*And and names the name*
1482-J	*Thank you Mister Smith for calling Pacific Bell*
1483-J	***[laughter]***
1484-M	*Yeah right*
1485-M	*You know **[laughter]***
1486-J	*I am your personal computer representative*
1487-J	*[inhalation]*
1488-M	*That'd be great*
1489-J	***[laughter]***
1490-M	***[laughter]***

Table 2: An excerpt, with indexed utterances, from face-to-face dialog *SBC017Notions*[7] in the NEWT-SBCSAE corpus (Lưu and Malamud, 2020a; Riou, 2015; Du Bois et al., 2000) between two friends Michael and Jim.

[7]The original audio recording and transcript of the dialog can be conveniently browsed here.

comfortable with more personal topics and more expressive language; and the emphasis on positioning by explicitly involving Self in the story (e.g. *I used to have ..., two things I got out of my marriage, ... got me grounded, ... pulled me..., there I was, then I found that I was on my own two feet again, a way out of me*) but not on alignment as in the other dialog in which the interlocutors use the phrase *you know* as an alignment signal more frequently.

The difference in the normative dimension confirms that explicit positioning and alignment play an important role in the dynamics of social relationship between the interlocutors.

Utt.	Simplified transcript
2494-P	*I used to have this sort of standard line that there were two things I got out of my marriage*
2495-P	*One was a name that was easy to spell and one was a a child*
2496-P	*That really got me grounded*
2497-P	*But the fact of the matter is*
2498-P	*That the marriage itself I mean as hellish as it was it's like it pulled me under like a giant octopus*
2499-P	*Or a giant giant shark*
2500-P	*And it pulled me all the way under*
2501-P	*And then*
2502-P	*And there I was*
2503-P	*It was like the silent scream*
2504-P	*And then then I found that I was on my own two feet again*
2505-P	*And it really was what was hell in that that marriage became became a way out of me*
2506-P	*It was the flip side*
2507-P	*It's like sometimes you go through things and you come out the other side of them*
2508-P	*You come out so much better*
2509-P	*And if I hadn't had that if I hadn't had*
2510-P	*[inhalation]*
2511-D	*It's not the way with food*
2512-P	*What do you mean*
2513-D	*What goes in one way doesn't come out* ***[laughter]***
2514-P	***[laughter]***
2515-P	***[laughter]***
2516-P	*[inhalation]*
2517-P	*Comes out very hellish*

Table 3: An excerpt, with indexed utterances, from face-to-face dialog *SBC005Book*[8] in the NEWT-SBCSAE corpus (Lưu and Malamud, 2020a; Riou, 2015; Du Bois et al., 2000) between a couple, Pamela and Darryl.

4 Context Representation and Update

To be capable of reasoning about multifaceted coherence in social talk presented in Section 3, a linguistically-driven dialog model needs an adequate representation of the conversational context that consists of essential linguistic information obtained from either neural or symbolic knowledge. To optimally exploit both sources of knowledge, the relatively context-insensitive components of the conversational context are deduced by machine learning techniques; while the more context-sensitive components, which do not have any consistent mapping to linguistic forms, are reasoned out by symbolic methods. This division of labor takes advantage of the knowledge of pretrained statistical models as prior experiences to approximate linguistic meanings, at the same time separate them from the real-time meanings co-constructed by interlocutors in a specific conversational context via symbolic reasoning. To facilitate the reasoning, the conversational context has direct access to knowledge sources including linguistic dictionaries and thesauri, and world knowledge bases. An all-in-one option for knowledge sources is Wolfram Engine.

Specifically, using statistical models of off-the-shelf NLP libraries such as spaCy, we can automatically obtain basic linguistic annotations of an utterance including word tokens, their POS tags and contextual embeddings, syntactic relations between word tokens (as the result of dependency parsing), and linguistic constituents (including named entities). Based on these pieces of linguistic information, the discourse hooks in an utterance are identified by various heuristics such as:

Relying on linguistic definitions and relations:

- use dictionaries to obtain the senses of a word token and the corresponding definitions and examples of their usage in context
- select the most probable senses of that token in the target utterance based on the similarity scores between the contextual embeddings of the token and each of its senses
- use linguistic thesauri, such as WordNet (Fellbaum, 2010), to obtain the set of related lexical items of each selected sense, e.g. its synonyms, hypernyms and hyponyms
- identify and weigh potential discourse hook relations between each selected sense or related lexical item of the examined token and

[8]The original audio recording and transcript of the dialog can be conveniently browsed here.

other tokens in prior context based on the similarity scores between their embeddings

Relying on world knowledge bases:

- map a linguistic constituent to a concept in knowledge bases based on the similarity scores between their embeddings
- obtain a set of neighbor concepts of that linguistic constituent in knowledge bases
- identify and weigh potential discourse hook relations between each neighbor concept and other concepts in prior context based on the similarity scores between their embeddings

Relying on discourse knowledge:

- use the conversational context itself as a knowledge source to infer those potential discourse hook relations such as co-references between a pronoun in the target utterance and entities in immediately preceding discourse, and the temporal and spatial relations between an event or object in the target utterance and other events or objects in preceding discourse

These heuristics mainly address the first two types of discourse hook discussed in Section 3, discourse-old and discourse-new bearing inferential relation to discourse-old; the final type, discourse-new and related to discourse-old in a non-inferential manner, requires more sophisticated linguistic reasoning about presupposed content of an utterance. It is worth noting that by establishing potential discourse hook relations we not only connect two utterances but also lengthen various conversational threads which reflect different sequences of actions performed by the interlocutors, and therefore provide a deeper contextual structure in comparison with the contextual representation in which prior discourse is treated as a single conversational thread, usually called the dialog history.

Further, to represent non-epistemic dimensions, it is necessary to annotate at least the following:

Affective: intances of highly expressive language in the target utterance such as adjectives and idioms (which can be identified by analyzing their definition and properties recorded in the linguistic dictionaries) and their sentiments (which can retrieved from off-the-shelf sentiment analysis models)

Normative: default and emphasized positioning and alignment in the target utterance which can be identified based on the clause type of the utterance and the absence or presence of Self and the Other in its linguistic content; for example:

- If the target utterance is a declarative:
  - if Self is present in the utterance: emphasized Self positioning
  - else: default Self positioning
- If the target utterance is an interrogative:
  - if the Other is present in the utterance: emphasized alignment
  - else: default alignment
- If the target utterance is an imperative:
  - emphasized alignment
  - if Self is present in the utterance: emphasized Self positioning
  - else: default Self positioning

As discussed in Section 3, instances of highly expressive language help the dialog model estimate the emotional intensity or sentiment conveyed by its partner and flavor its own utterances with appropriate affective connotations; while emphasized positioning and alignment assist the model in recognizing a potential shift of social focus or of social distance expressed by its partner. Using clause types to reason out emphasized positioning is a basic pragmatic calculation of social acts encoded in an utterance in the proposed architecture. System designers can enrich the pragmatic calculation with additional normative rules for a more fine-grained representation of social acts[9]. Although clause type classification is not a current component of a typical automatic linguistic annotation pipeline, this task should not be as challenging as speech act/intent classification and should be robustly handled by statistical models because clause types are distinguished by specific form-based features, at least in English (Siemund, 2018).

A Minimally Viable Dialog Model A minimally viable linguistically-driven reasoning dialog model for social talk is an honest conversational companion in that it behaves as a conversing computer without wearing any superficial persona. It is equipped with all components listed in this section. From the interpretation perspective, whenever it receives the transcript of an utterance from the human interlocutor, it will obtain the automatic linguistic annotations of the utterance and apply predefined heuristics (1) to establish potential discourse hook relations between the words/constituents of

[9]Which can be informed by additional sociolinguistic knowledge, e.g. variant linguistic forms of the English suffix (ING) signal different levels of formality (an embodiment of social distance): the standard form *-ing* is more formal than the marked form *-in'* (Labov, 2012).

the utterance and other words/constituents in prior discourse, (2) to mark the instances of highly expressive language in the utterance with their sentiments, and (3) to capture the default/emphasized positioning and alignment in the utterance.

The model is aware that there may exist different alternatives in its interpretation; for example, each word in the utterance can have different discourse hook relations for different senses and therefore the number of alternatives for the whole utterance is the product of the numbers of senses. To select the best interpretation alternative, the model assigns a discourse salience score to each alternative.

This salience score is compositionally calculated based on how strongly an alternative is grounded in the context, including, for example, the weights of the discourse hook relations characterizing that alternative, and the recentness of discourse threads they participate in. Each alternative is also indexed with the sociocultural dimension that is most relevant to it: epistemic if it is full of discourse hooks, affective if it stands out with plenty of highly expressive language, or normative if it is highlighted by emphasized positioning/alignment. The interpretation alternative that has the highest discourse salience score will be added to the conversational context. Its salience factors and relevant sociocultural dimension provide human-readable evidence of what makes it a coherent move within the shared social goal, as discussed in Section 3.

From the production perspective, the model can heuristically generate a set of utterances as production alternatives which are salient with respect to the current conversational context and relevant to the conversational goal in at least one sociocultural dimension. For example, if the model knows that the human interlocutor just evaluated some aspect of an object and manages to find other information about the object in its knowledge bases, it can generate an utterance evaluating the object in the newly found aspect. In another scenario when the model has nothing else to comment on the object under discussion, it can switch social focus to the human interlocutor using the emphasized alignment technique, e.g. *What else are you interested in?* Similarly to the case of interpretation, the model can index each production alternative with the sociocultural dimension that is most relevant to it, and heuristically assign discourse salience scores to the alternatives in order to select the best one and update the context with its content.

Game-Theoretic Reasoning The selection of the best alternative from either interpretation or production perspectives can be formalized in a game-theoretic style, which pairs Lewis (1969/2002)'s signaling games (between two communicators) with the Bayesian approach to speaker/listener reasoning (see Tenenbaum et al., 2011 for an overview). Specifically, the probability $P(m|u, C)$ that the model assigns the hidden meaning m to the observable utterance u in the conversational context C depends on the prior probability $P(m)$ of the human interlocutor having m in mind and the utility value $U(u, m, C)$, corresponding to the salience of m with respect to u in C[10].

$P(m|u, C) \propto P(m) \times exp(\alpha \times U(u, m, C))$
(where α is a normalizing constant)

The prior probability $P(m)$ is used to account for the consistency of the speaker type discussed in Section 3. Specifically it captures the personal inclination of the human interlocutor towards a particular sociocultural dimension (cf. Yoon et al., 2020 for a different way to integrate these dimensions into a game-theoretic model and Asher and Lascarides, 2013 for a similar way to integrate a different aspect of speaker types into a game-theoretic model). There are three values of $P(m)$ for the three sociocutural dimension indexes:

- $P_{epi}(m) + P_{aff}(m) + P_{nor}(m) = 1$

These values are paired with the utility values of alternatives which share the same sociocultural dimension index. They can be learned offline based on a sample of human interlocutors or assigned by the interlocutor at the beginning of a conversation. These values can also be updated in a real time manner, e.g. if the human interlocutor produces a series of conversational moves that are highly relevant to the conversational goal in the affective dimension, $P_{aff}(m)$ will be increased accordingly.

5 A Worked Example

To demonstrate how the proposed dialog model works, a proof-of-concept text-based dialog system was developed based on the Free Wolfram

[10]This formalism simplifies the Bayesian inference in that it doesn't require the separation between speaker and listener behaviors as in recent popular game-theoretic frameworks for pragmatic reasoning, e.g. Iterated Best Response (Franke, 2009), Rational Speech Act (Frank and Goodman, 2012), and Social Meaning Game (Burnett, 2019). That simplification results from the fact that the model reasons based on a predefined shared goal and a rich representation of conversational context which accounts for all relevant aspects of real-time meanings co-constructed by interlocutors.

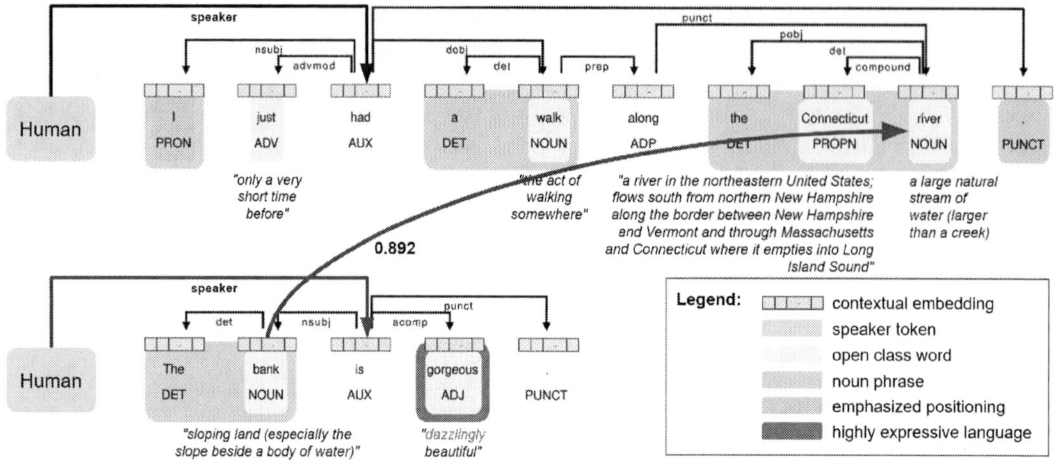

Figure 2: Contextual representation of a dialog turn.

Engine for Developers and spaCy v2.3.5[11], including its small core model for English and the DistilBERT model (Sanh et al., 2019), accessed via spacy-transformers v0.6.x[11]. Figure 2 shows the conversational context created by the system after the human interlocutor enters the text string *I just had a walk along the Connecticut river. The bank is gorgeous.* (please refer to Appendix A for the snapshots of step-by-step context update).

The system uses spaCy's core model to tokenize the text string into word tokens (including punctuation marks), provide their POS tags, and then segment the sequence of tokens into sentences with their dependency structures. The system relies on DistilBERT to obtain the contextual embeddings of tokens and sequences of tokens so that it can calculate similarity scores between these embeddings to reason out the most appropriate senses of semantically ambiguous words as well as the potential discourse hook relations between linguistic constituents. For each open class word, i.e. an adjective, adverb, interjection, noun or verb, the system first retrieves all of WordNet senses from Wolfram knowledge base (via Wolfram Engine), and then identifies the real-time context-sensitive sense, as shown under each of these words in Figure 2. Each real-time sense is the one whose contextual embedding (calculated based on its textual definition) is the most similar to the contextual embedding of the corresponding word. They not only represent the human-readable meanings, but also participate in the creation of future discourse hook relations. Next, the system adds a meta-data token storing speaker information to each sentence before performing more context-sensitive reasoning.

Based on the pronoun *I*, the punctuation "." and the dependency links, the system recognizes that the first sentence is a declarative which has Self as the subject. Consequently, this sentence features the emphasized Self positioning. Moving to the second sentence, the system first examines alternative discourse hook relations between its sole noun phrase and other noun phrases in prior discourse, which results in the selection of the most salient relation between *the bank* and *the Connecticut river*, corresponding to the highest similarity score (0.892) between the embeddings of the real-time senses of the head nouns *bank* and *river*. The system then marks the adjective *gorgeous* as an instance of highly expressive language because its definition contains a degree adverb (*dazzlingly*).

To produce the most relevant response, the system puts more weight on the candidates addressing the second sentence as it is more recent. The highest salience score is achieved when the response includes both *the bank* and the emotional resonance of *gorgeous*, an instance of positive sentiment. Consequently, the system adds positive elements such as the predicate *like* to its planned response. A possible template for this planned response is "It seems that you like ... a lot, right?", which results in the ultimate response as *It seems that you like the bank a lot, right?*[12]

6 Discussion

Departing from current popular approaches to social dialog systems, which rely on available mod-

[11] Under the MIT License.

[12] Using templates is the simplest technique for the proof-of-concept system, but not a categorical implementation choice.

els for similar tasks[13] and conversational data created in artificial or asynchronous settings (Huang et al., 2020), this work starts with empirical analysis of naturally occurring data, i.e. human–human casual conversation in real life, to systematically define key linguistic characteristics of social dialog which can be modeled based on SOTA NLP techniques. This approach is in line with the preregistration practice promoted by van Miltenburg et al. (2021), entailing both advantages and limitations. By specifying what I want to capture in my model before the actual implementation, I can avoid the post-hoc problems faced by heavily data-driven architectures (e.g. Henderson et al., 2018). However, not relying on benchmark data and their corresponding techniques, I can not prove the practicality and reproducibility of my model in an actionable way before a full-blown dialog system is implemented. In addition, while this work starts with human–human conversation, its ultimate outcome is human–computer conversation which definitely diverges from the input guiding data and can potentially direct the research agenda into unplanned territories. It is also worth noting that while the modularity of the proposed architecture allows independent and simultaneous improvements of its components, its effectiveness can suffer from cumulative parsing errors caused by its pipeline design. Moreover, the statistical models of off-the-shelf NLP libraries used in the proposed architecture, mostly trained on planned text (e.g. Weischedel et al., 2013), may not work well on spontaneous conversation.

Research Priorities As the ultimate goal of the proposed dialog model is to truly facilitate mutual understanding in human–computer social communication, the model must aim at effectively co-constructing the real-time conversational context with its interlocutors and reasoning about their conversational moves (Kopp and Krämer, 2021). Thus, within the proposed framework I will focus on coherence-based context modeling and discourse salience calculation, taking into account the shared social goal. In other words, the research question that captivates me most is how to dynamically construct meaning in the context of social conversation (cf. Trott et al., 2020 for a broader research agenda). This priority implies the necessity of novel evaluation protocols to validly and reliably assess human–computer mutual understanding, which is ignored in current evaluation practices for in social dialog systems (Finch and Choi, 2020).

Another direction for exploration, which is more application-oriented, is how to optimally incorporate additional knowledge sources into the dialog model or spotlight a portion of the existing ones to seamlessly change salience calculation results, which conform to the system owner's desire. For example, imagine the scenario in which a language learner want to chat with the dialog system to enhance their vocabulary on a specific topic, they would definitely want the system to pay more attention to the area of knowledge sources which covers that topic. Ultimately, the dialog model could be systematically adapted for task-oriented dialog by integrating domain-specific knowledge bases.

Ethics and Social Impact Considerations The proposed dialog model is explainable in both its development approach and its interactions with different stakeholders (Kaur et al., 2022). First, its design is explicitly informed by empirical analysis of relevant data and its operational decisions are interpretable, using human-readable symbolic representation of conversational context. Second, the transparency of the proposed architecture with well-defined functional components can provide adequate and personalized explanations to the involved developers, domain experts, and end users.

Relying on publicly accessible NLP resources and featuring a widely integrable structure, the proposed dialog model can be freely implemented and used by independent end users, and continuously developed and enhanced by domain experts.

7 Conclusion and Future Work

This paper sketches out a novel dialog model for social conversation in English, motivated by a thorough investigation of the nature and linguistic characteristics of the phenomenon, including the shared goal between interlocutors and multifaceted coherence across different sociocultural dimensions. Next, I will implement a full-blown dialog system based on this model and develop adequate evaluation protocols, before iteratively evaluating and improving the system until it can consistently hold casual conversations with humans. Subsequently, I will use these conversations and their contextual representation as a new window into the social interaction between humans and reasoning machines.

[13]Either in the application aspect, e.g. task-oriented dialog models, or technical aspect, e.g. sequence-to-sequence machine translation models.

Acknowledgments

My deepest gratitude goes to Sophia A. Malamud, who exhaustively discussed every aspect of this paper with me. I am extremely grateful to Nianwen Xue, Anton Benz, Ralf Klabunde, and Malihe Alikhani for sharing their valuable perspectives on my work. Finally, I would like to thank the anonymous reviewers of EMNLP 2021, SCiL 2022, ARR (Dec 2021 deadline) and ACL-SRW 2022 for their detailed, constructive and actionable feedback.

References

Daniel Adiwardana, Minh-Thang Luong, David R So, Jamie Hall, Noah Fiedel, Romal Thoppilan, Zi Yang, Apoorv Kulshreshtha, Gaurav Nemade, Yifeng Lu, et al. 2020. Towards a human-like open-domain chatbot. *arXiv preprint arXiv:2001.09977*.

Nicholas Asher and Alex Lascarides. 2013. Strategic conversation. *Semantics and Pragmatics*, 6:1–62.

Betty J Birner. 2012. *Introduction to Pragmatics*. John Wiley & Sons.

Heather Burnett. 2019. Signalling games, sociolinguistic variation and the construction of style. *Linguistics and Philosophy*.

Veena Chattaraman, Wi-Suk Kwon, Juan E. Gilbert, and Kassandra Ross. 2019. Should AI-Based, conversational digital assistants employ social- or task-oriented interaction style? A task-competency and reciprocity perspective for older adults. *Computers in Human Behavior*, 90:315–330.

Leigh Clark, Nadia Pantidi, Orla Cooney, Philip Doyle, Diego Garaialde, Justin Edwards, Brendan Spillane, Emer Gilmartin, Christine Murad, Cosmin Munteanu, Vincent Wade, and Benjamin R. Cowan. 2019. What Makes a Good Conversation? Challenges in Designing Truly Conversational Agents. In *Proceedings of the 2019 CHI Conference on Human Factors in Computing Systems*, CHI '19, pages 1–12, New York, NY, USA. Association for Computing Machinery.

Rebecca Clift. 2016. *Conversation Analysis*. Cambridge University Press.

John W Du Bois. 2007. The stance triangle. *Stancetaking in discourse: Subjectivity, evaluation, interaction*, 164(3):139–182.

John W Du Bois, Wallace L Chafe, Charles Meyer, Sandra A Thompson, and Nii Martey. 2000. Santa Barbara corpus of spoken American English. *CD-ROM. Philadelphia: Linguistic Data Consortium*.

Hao Fang, Hao Cheng, Maarten Sap, Elizabeth Clark, Ari Holtzman, Yejin Choi, Noah A. Smith, and Mari Ostendorf. 2018. Sounding board: A user-centric and content-driven social chatbot. In *Proceedings of the 2018 Conference of the North American Chapter of the Association for Computational Linguistics: Demonstrations*, pages 96–100, New Orleans, Louisiana. Association for Computational Linguistics.

Christiane Fellbaum. 2010. WordNet. In Roberto Poli, Michael Healy, and Achilles Kameas, editors, *Theory and Applications of Ontology: Computer Applications*, pages 231–243. Springer Netherlands, Dordrecht.

Sarah E. Finch and Jinho D. Choi. 2020. Towards unified dialogue system evaluation: A comprehensive analysis of current evaluation protocols. In *Proceedings of the 21th Annual Meeting of the Special Interest Group on Discourse and Dialogue*, pages 236–245, 1st virtual meeting. Association for Computational Linguistics.

Michael C. Frank and Noah D. Goodman. 2012. Predicting pragmatic reasoning in language games. *Science*, 336(6084):998–998.

Michael Franke. 2009. *Signal to Act: Game Theory in Pragmatics*. Ph.D. thesis, Universiteit van Amsterdam.

Jonathan Ginzburg, Chiara Mazzocconi, and Ye Tian. 2020. Laughter as language. *Glossa: a journal of general linguistics*, 5(1):104. Number: 1 Publisher: Ubiquity Press.

Peter Henderson, Koustuv Sinha, Nicolas Angelard-Gontier, Nan Rosemary Ke, Genevieve Fried, Ryan Lowe, and Joelle Pineau. 2018. Ethical Challenges in Data-Driven Dialogue Systems. In *Proceedings of the 2018 AAAI/ACM Conference on AI, Ethics, and Society*, AIES '18, pages 123–129, New York, NY, USA. Association for Computing Machinery.

Dirk Hovy and Diyi Yang. 2021. The importance of modeling social factors of language: Theory and practice. In *Proceedings of the 2021 Conference of the North American Chapter of the Association for Computational Linguistics: Human Language Technologies*, pages 588–602, Online. Association for Computational Linguistics.

Minlie Huang, Xiaoyan Zhu, and Jianfeng Gao. 2020. Challenges in Building Intelligent Open-domain Dialog Systems. *ACM Transactions on Information Systems*, 38(3):21:1–21:32.

Jeffrey L Kallen and John Monfries Kirk. 2012. *SPICE-Ireland: A User's Guide; Documentation to Accompany the SPICE-Ireland Corpus: Systems of Pragmatic Annotation in ICE-Ireland*. Cló Ollscoil na Banríona.

Davinder Kaur, Suleyman Uslu, Kaley J. Rittichier, and Arjan Durresi. 2022. Trustworthy Artificial Intelligence: A Review. *ACM Computing Surveys*, 55(2):39:1–39:38.

Chandra Khatri, Anu Venkatesh, Behnam Hedayatnia, Raefer Gabriel, Ashwin Ram, and Rohit Prasad. 2018. Alexa Prize — state of the art in conversational AI. *AI Magazine*, 39(3):40–55.

Stefan Kopp and Nicole Krämer. 2021. Revisiting Human-Agent Communication: The Importance of Joint Co-construction and Understanding Mental States. *Frontiers in Psychology*, 12.

William Labov. 2012. *Dialect Diversity in America: The Politics of Language Change*. University of Virginia Press, Charlottesville, VA.

David Lewis. 1969/2002. *Convention: A Philosophical Study*. John Wiley & Sons.

Alex Lưu and Sophia A. Malamud. 2020a. Annotating coherence relations for studying topic transitions in social talk. In *Proceedings of the 14th Linguistic Annotation Workshop*, pages 174–179, Barcelona, Spain. Association for Computational Linguistics.

Alex Lưu and Sophia A. Malamud. 2020b. Non-topical coherence in social talk: A call for dialogue model enrichment. In *Proceedings of the 58th Annual Meeting of the Association for Computational Linguistics: Student Research Workshop*, pages 118–133, Online. Association for Computational Linguistics.

Ellen Prince. 1992. The ZPG letter: Subjects, definiteness, and information status. In William C. Mann and Sandra A. Thompson, editors, *Discourse Description: Discourse Analyses of a Fundraising Text*, pages 295–325. Amsterdam: John Benjamins.

Marine Riou. 2015. *The Grammar of Topic Transition in American English Conversation. Topic Transition Design and Management in Typical and Atypical Conversations (Schizophrenia)*. Ph.D. thesis, Université Sorbonne Paris Cité.

Craige Roberts. 1996/2012. Information structure: Towards an integrated formal theory of pragmatics. *Semantics and Pragmatics*, 5:6–1.

Stephen Roller. ParlAI tutorial (accessed on 10/10/2021).

Stephen Roller, Emily Dinan, Naman Goyal, Da Ju, Mary Williamson, Yinhan Liu, Jing Xu, Myle Ott, Eric Michael Smith, Y-Lan Boureau, and Jason Weston. 2021. Recipes for building an open-domain chatbot. In *Proceedings of the 16th Conference of the European Chapter of the Association for Computational Linguistics: Main Volume*, pages 300–325, Online. Association for Computational Linguistics.

Ragnar Rommetveit. 1976. On the architecture of intersubjectivity. In Lloyd H. Strickland, Frances E. Aboud, and Kenneth J. Gergen, editors, *Social Psychology in Transition*, pages 201–214. Springer US, Boston, MA.

Victor Sanh, Lysandre Debut, Julien Chaumond, and Thomas Wolf. 2019. DistilBERT, a distilled version of BERT: smaller, faster, cheaper and lighter. In *The 5th Workshop on Energy Efficient Machine Learning and Cognitive Computing*, Vancouver, Canada.

Deborah Schiffrin. 1990. The principle of intersubjectivity in communication and conversation. *Semiotica*, 80(1-2):121–185.

Peter Siemund. 2018. *Speech Acts and Clause Types: English in a Cross-Linguistic Context*. Oxford Textbooks in Linguistics. Oxford University Press, Oxford, New York.

Robert Stalnaker. 1974. Pragmatic presuppositions. In Milton K. Munitz and Peter K. Unger, editors, *Semantics and Philosophy*, pages 197–213. New York University Press.

Robert Stalnaker. 1978. Assertion. In P. Cole, editor, *Syntax and Semantics 9: Pragmatics*, volume 9, pages 315–332. Academic Press, New York.

Melisa Stevanovic and Sonja E Koski. 2018. Intersubjectivity and the domains of social interaction: Proposal of a cross-sectional approach. *Psychology of Language and Communication*, 22(1):39–70.

Melisa Stevanovic and Anssi Peräkylä. 2014. Three orders in the organization of human action: On the interface between knowledge, power, and emotion in interaction and social relations. *Language in Society*, 43(2):185–207.

Pete Swanson and Shannon Mason. 2018. The world language teacher shortage: Taking a new direction. *Foreign Language Annals*, 51(1):251–262.

Joshua B. Tenenbaum, Charles Kemp, Thomas L. Griffiths, and Noah D. Goodman. 2011. How to Grow a Mind: Statistics, Structure, and Abstraction. *Science*, 331(6022):1279–1285. Publisher: American Association for the Advancement of Science.

Maurizio Tirassa and Francesca M Bosco. 2008. On the nature and role of intersubjectivity in communication. In *Enacting intersubjectivity: A cognitive and social perspective to the study of interactions*, pages 81–95. Amsterdam: IOS Press.

Sean Trott, Tiago Timponi Torrent, Nancy Chang, and Nathan Schneider. 2020. (Re)construing meaning in NLP. In *Proceedings of the 58th Annual Meeting of the Association for Computational Linguistics*, pages 5170–5184, Online. Association for Computational Linguistics.

Emiel van Miltenburg, Chris van der Lee, and Emiel Krahmer. 2021. Preregistering NLP research. In *Proceedings of the 2021 Conference of the North American Chapter of the Association for Computational Linguistics: Human Language Technologies*, pages 613–623, Online. Association for Computational Linguistics.

Ralph Weischedel, Martha Palmer, Mitchell Marcus, Eduard Hovy, Pradhan, Lance Ramshaw, Nianwen Xue, Ann Taylor, Jeff Kaufman, Michelle Franchini, Mohammed El-Bachouti, Robert Belvin, and Ann Houston. 2013. OntoNotes Release 5.0. Artwork Size: 2806280 KB Pages: 2806280 KB Type: dataset.

James V Wertsch. 2000. Intersubjectivity and alterity in human communication. *Communication: An arena of development*, pages 17–31.

Erica J. Yoon, Michael Henry Tessler, Noah D. Goodman, and Michael C. Frank. 2020. Polite Speech Emerges From Competing Social Goals. *Open Mind*, 4:71–87. Publisher: MIT Press.

Saizheng Zhang, Emily Dinan, Jack Urbanek, Arthur Szlam, Douwe Kiela, and Jason Weston. 2018. Personalizing dialogue agents: I have a dog, do you have pets too? In *Proceedings of the 56th Annual Meeting of the Association for Computational Linguistics (Volume 1: Long Papers)*, pages 2204–2213, Melbourne, Australia. Association for Computational Linguistics.

A Step-by-Step Context Update

Figures 3–20 capture the sequence of context changes discussed in Section 5.

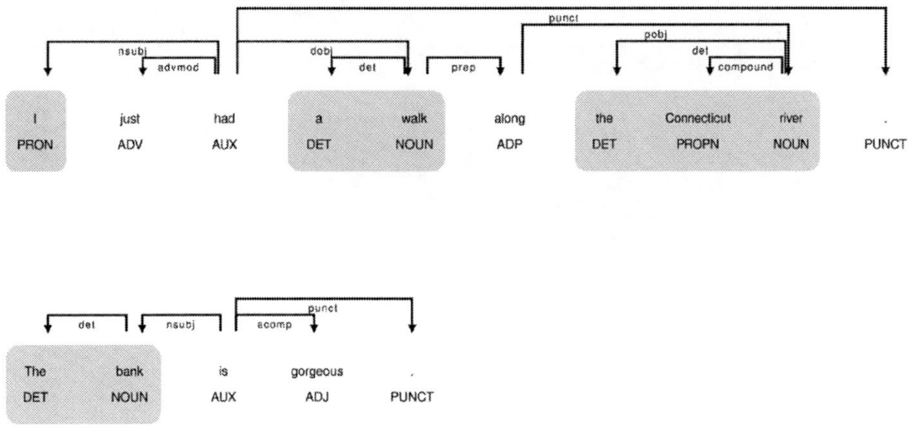

Figure 3: Add spaCy's linguistic annotations.

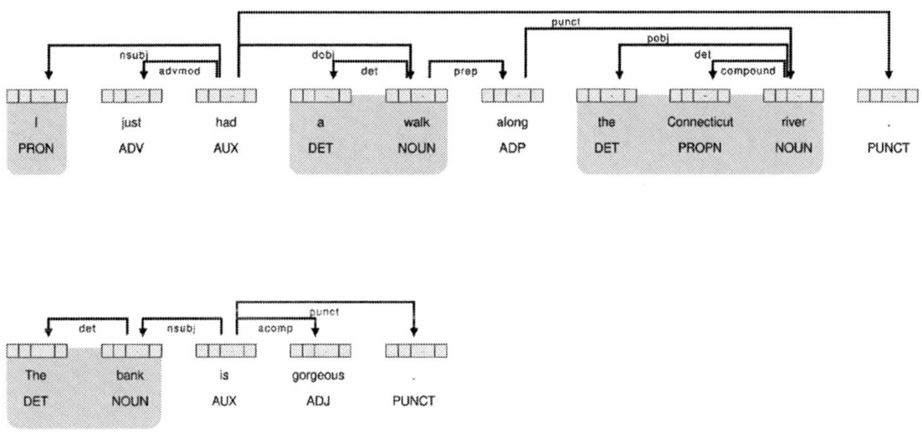

Figure 4: Add DistilBERT embeddings.

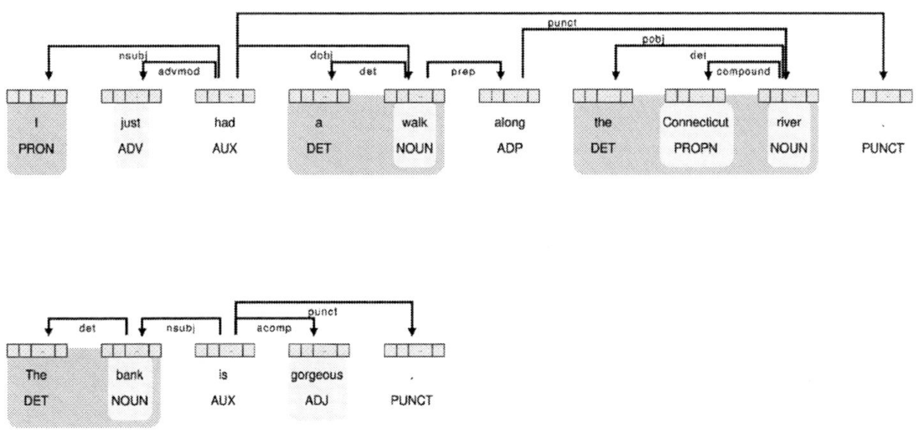

Figure 5: Navigate open class words, which are *just*, *walk*, *Connecticut*, *river*, *bank* and *gorgeous*.

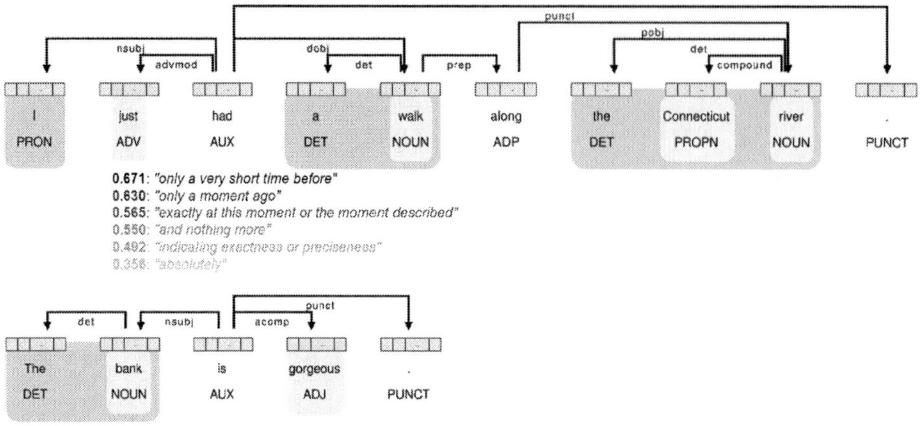

Figure 6: Calculate and rank similarity scores between *just* and each of its dictionary sense definitions.

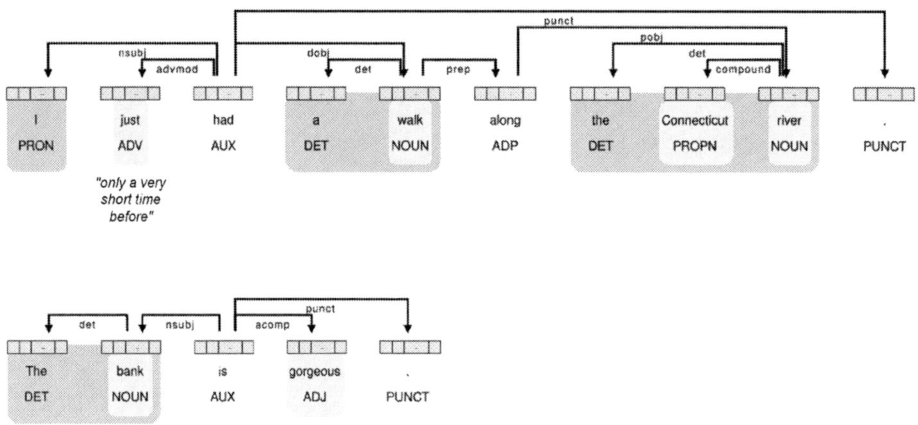

Figure 7: Add the contextually identified sense of *just*.

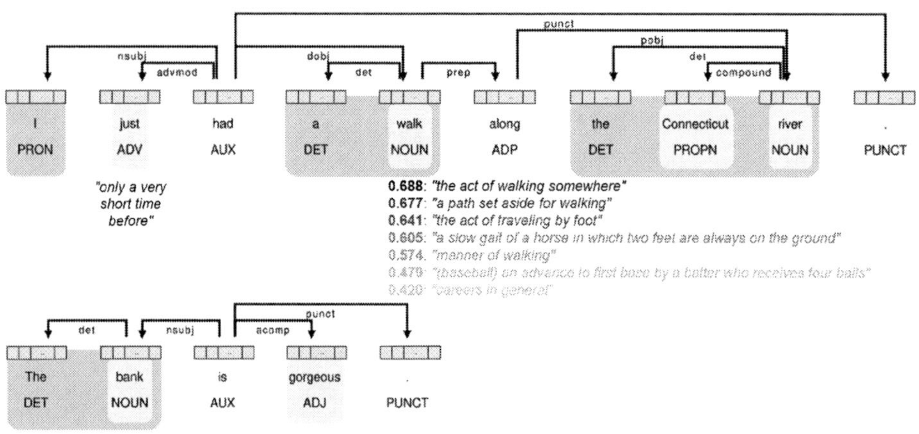

Figure 8: Calculate and rank similarity scores between *walk* and each of its dictionary sense definitions.

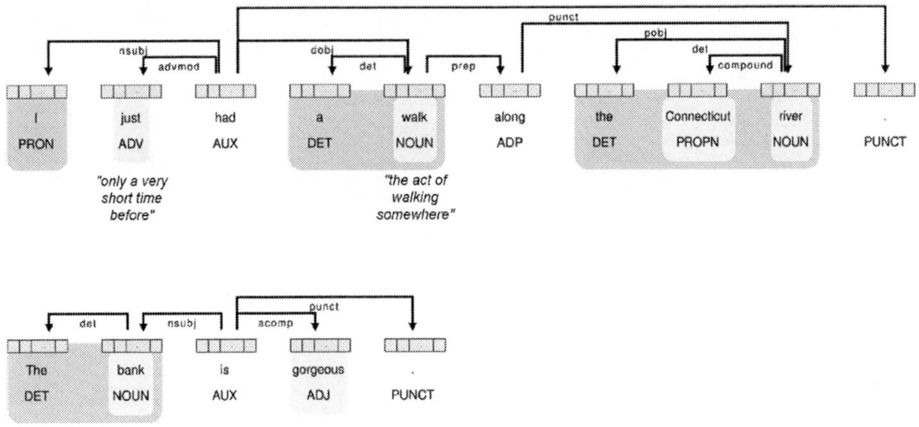

Figure 9: Add the contextually identified sense of *walk*.

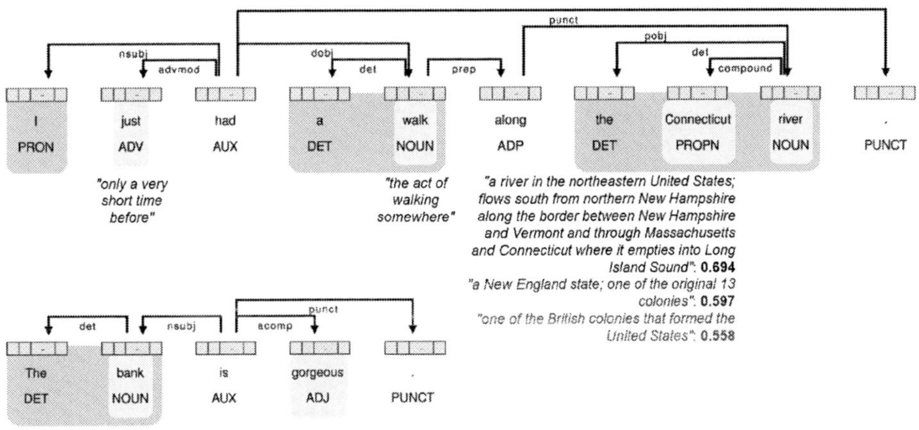

Figure 10: Calculate and rank similarity scores between *Connecticut* and each of its dictionary sense definitions.

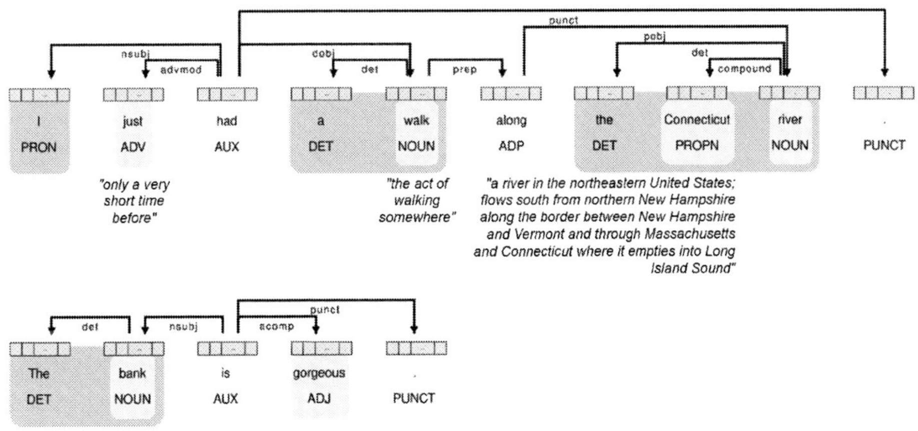

Figure 11: Add the contextually identified sense of *Connecticut*.

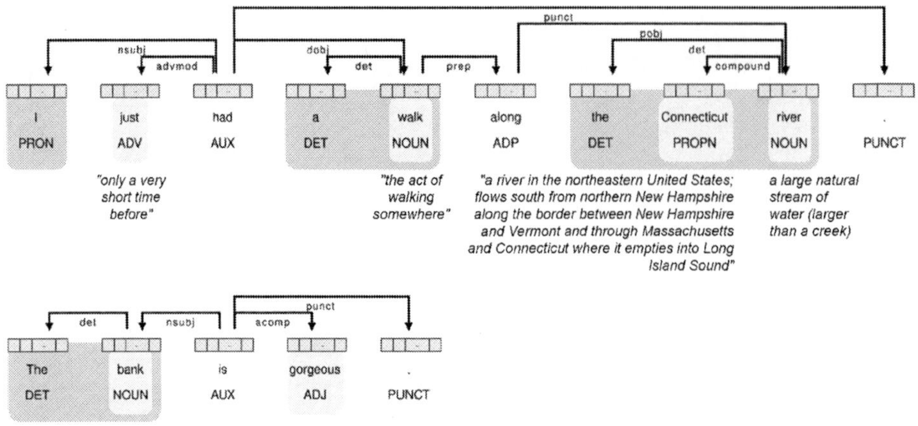

Figure 12: Add the sole sense of *river*.

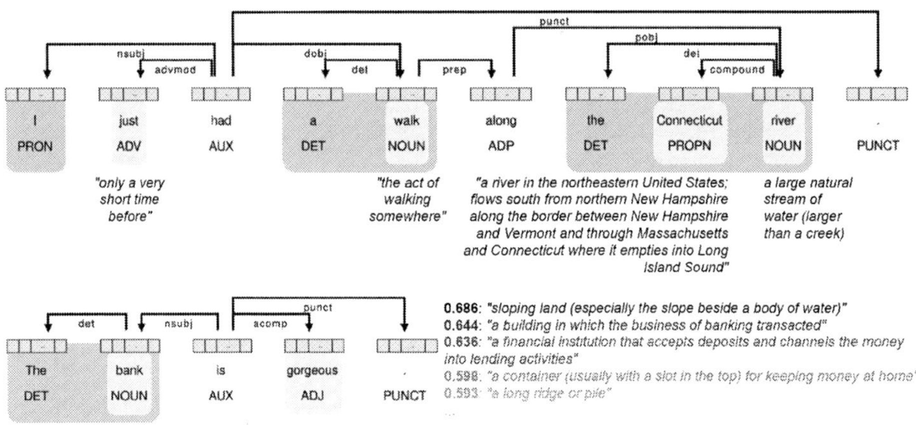

Figure 13: Calculate and rank similarity scores between *bank* and each of its dictionary sense definitions. Before that, the contextual embedding of *bank* was recalculated based on a modified version of the second sentence, which is *The Connecticut river, the bank is gorgeous.* This enhancement of the real-time context-sensitive meaning of *bank* is informed by the fact that *the Connecticut river* is the noun phrase in the first sentence whose head noun, i.e. *river*, is the closest to *bank* in terms of similarity scores between their contextual embeddings.

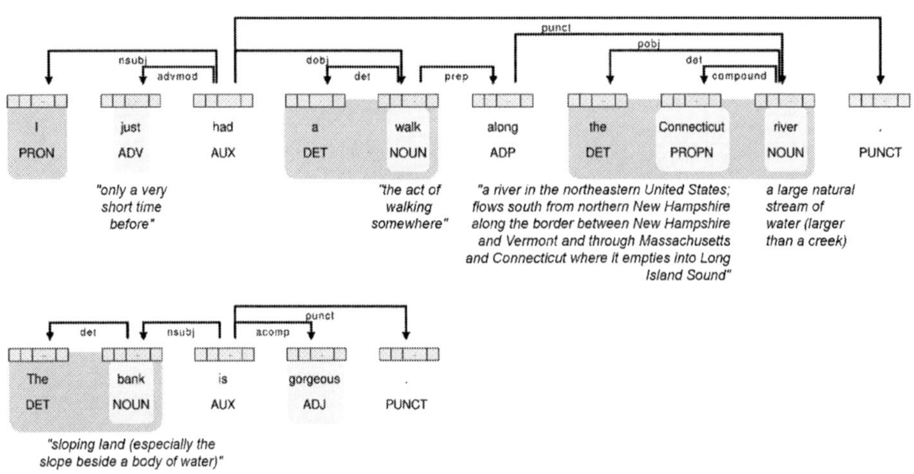

Figure 14: Add the contextually identified sense of *bank*.

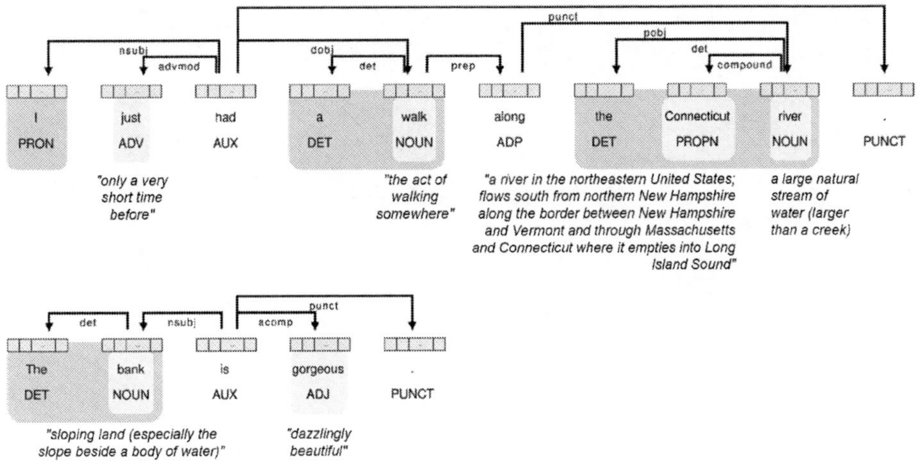

Figure 15: Add the sole sense of *gorgeous*.

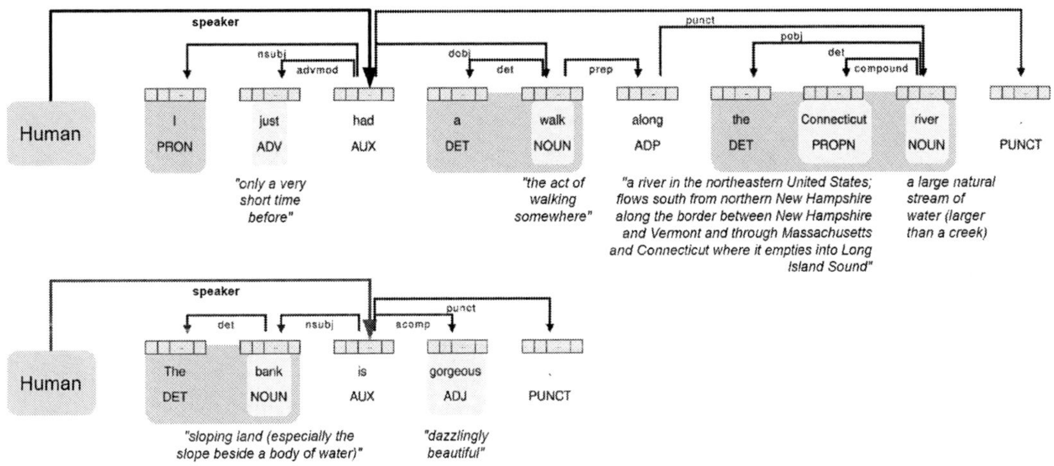

Figure 16: Add speaker tokens **Human** to each sentence.

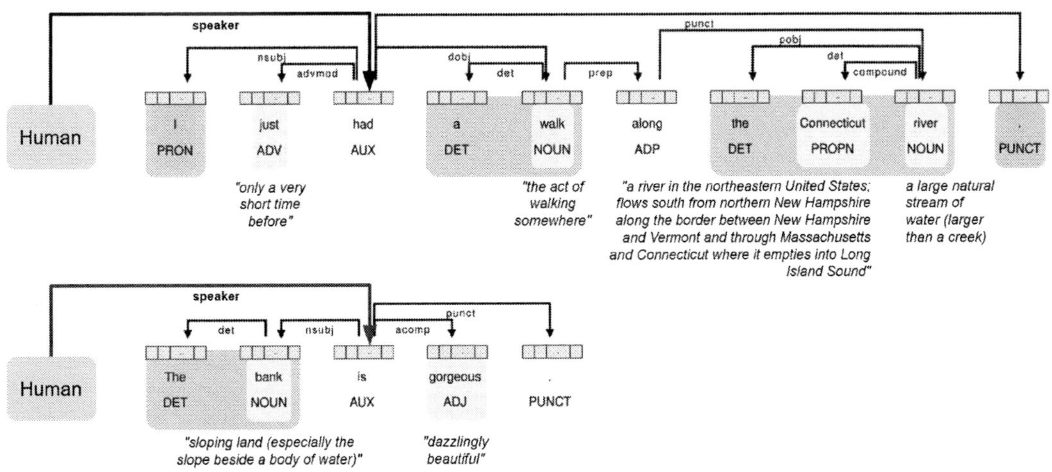

Figure 17: Identify emphasized positioning present in the first sentence. This is an instance of emphasized Self positioning, embodied by the first person pronoun *I* in a declarative sentence.

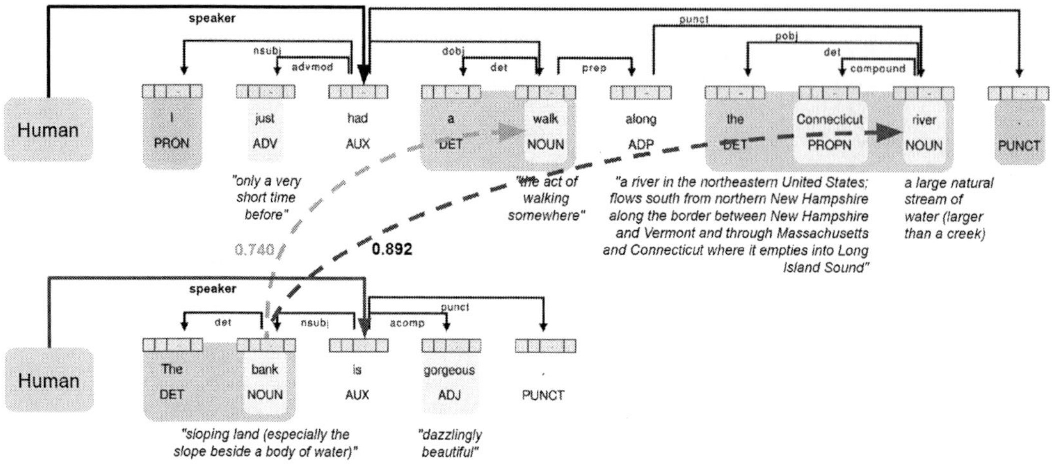

Figure 18: Identify potential discourse hook relations which connect the second sentence to the first sentence by calculating relevant similarity scores between the definitions of identified senses of head nouns of noun phrases.

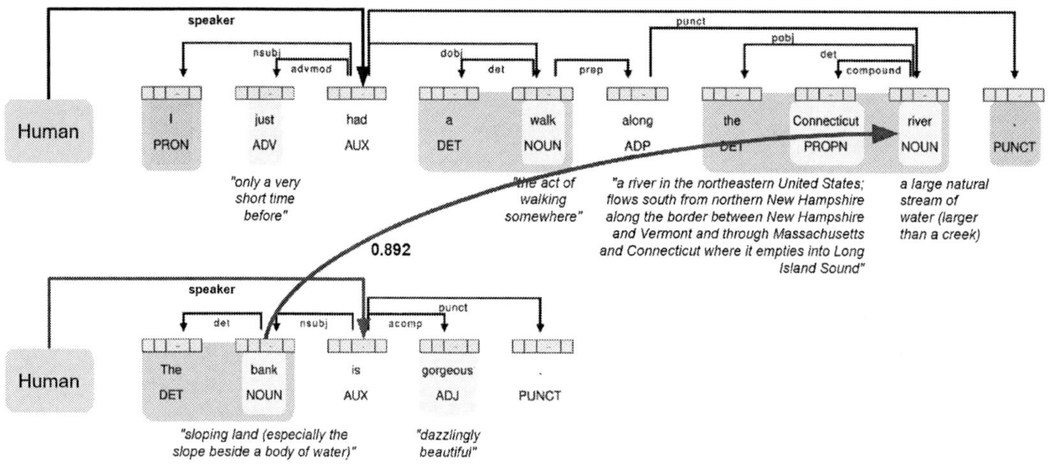

Figure 19: Select the most salient discourse hook relation, shaped by the similarity score between *bank* and *river*.

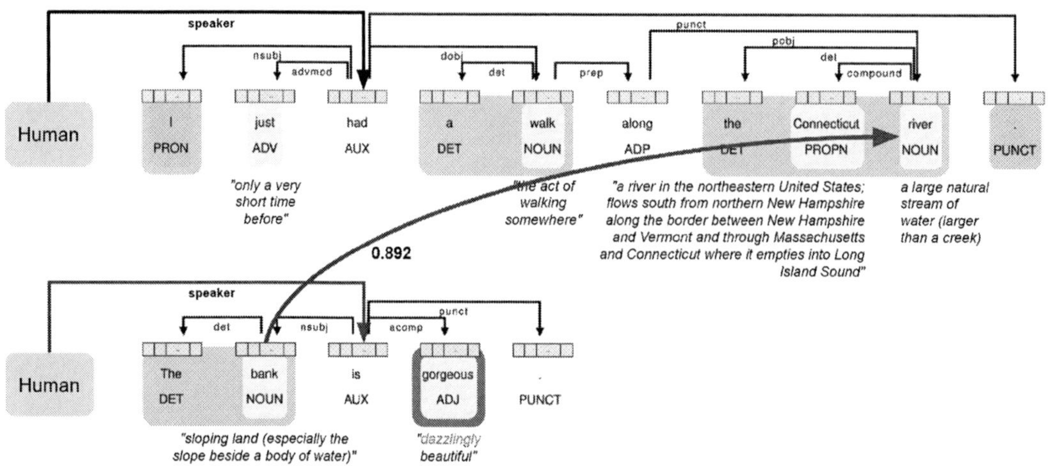

Figure 20: Identify highly expressive language present in the second sentence. This is an instance of positive sentiment expressed by the adjective *gorgeous*.

Scoping natural language processing in Indonesian and Malay for education applications

Zara Maxwell-Smith[1] **Michelle Kohler**[2] **Hanna Suominen**[1,3]
1. The Australian National University / Canberra, ACT, Australia
2. University of South Australia / Adelaide, SA, Australia
3. University of Turku / Turku, Finland
Zara.Maxwell-Smith@anu.edu.au, Michelle.Kohler@unisa.edu.au,
Hanna.Suominen@anu.edu.au

Abstract

Indonesian and Malay are underrepresented in the development of natural language processing (NLP) technologies and available resources are difficult to find. A clear picture of existing work can invigorate and inform how researchers conceptualise worthwhile projects. Using an education sector project to motivate the study, we conducted a wide-ranging overview of Indonesian and Malay human language technologies and corpus work. We charted 657 included studies according to Hirschberg and Manning's 2015 description of NLP, concluding that the field was dominated by exploratory corpus work, machine reading of text gathered from the Internet, and sentiment analysis. In this paper, we identify most published authors and research hubs, and make a number of recommendations to encourage future collaboration and efficiency within NLP in Indonesian and Malay.

1 Introduction

Limited natural language processing (NLP) resources currently available for Indonesian and Malay varieties do not reflect large speaker populations of these languages in Indonesia, Malaysia, and other South-East Asian nations[1]. Difficulties locating resources and existing work hinders progress in the field; it can result in duplicated or unnecessary work, clouding the ability of researchers to formulate useful research questions and study designs. Since Indonesian and Malay varieties are closely related (Sneddon, 2003; Basuki and Antaputra, 2020b), connecting research and technologies developed for either language could provide useful insights and shortcuts for work in the other language.[2]

These challenges restrict the impact that advances in NLP might have in the education sector in Indonesia and Malaysia, and in the teaching of these languages. Ideally, teachers of Indonesian or Malay as a second or foreign language would draw on a wide range of human language technologies, machine learning methods, and corpus linguistics tools to enhance teaching and learning outcomes [3].

As part of a broader project investigating teacher-speech and materials for Indonesian language teaching (Maxwell-Smith et al., 2020; Maxwell-Smith, 2021), the aims of this study were to scope the state of play of existing work in Indonesian and Malay NLP to assist in the formulation of realistic research goals, and to identify useful networks and resources. As such, our study draws on the notion of scoping work as "reconnaisance" (Peters et al., 2015), where the goal is to first determine what range of quantitative and/or qualitative evidence is available on a topic and then to chart, map, or otherwise represent this located evidence visually.

Our research questions were as follows:

1. What language technologies and NLP resources exist for Indonesian/Malay (and therefore for education sector applications)?

2. How do they align with the trends seen more widely in NLP?

We begin by describing our search strategy and methods for charting 657 included studies by their

[1]In 2011, the Indonesian Census recorded 197 million Indonesians as literate in Indonesian (Zein, 2020). In Malaysia, nearly the whole population speak Malay as a first or additional language (Coluzzi, 2017); in 2021, according to the Department of Statistics Malaysia, this was about 32 million people.

[2]As indicated in Lin et al. (2019c) and Nomoto et al. (2018a), some significant differences should caution NLP researchers from regarding the Indonesian and Malay languages as one.

[3]See for example Lee et al. (2020) in journals such as CALL and LLT.

Proceedings of the 60th Annual Meeting of the Association for Computational Linguistics Student Research Workshop, pages 171 - 228

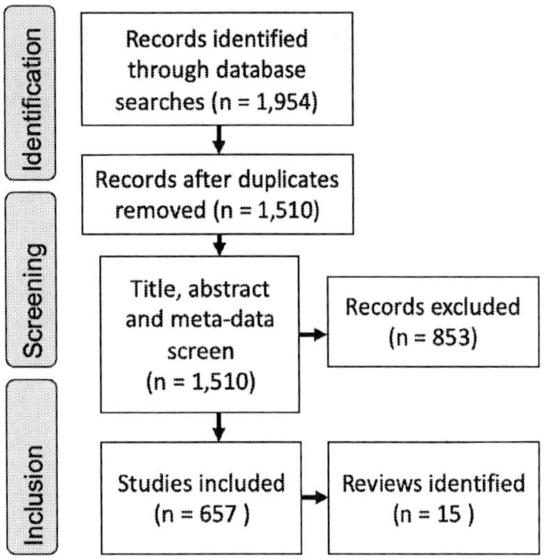

Figure 1: Screening Process and Study Selection

topic and year of publication. We summarize existing literature reviews and notable work, graph most published authors and their affiliated research hubs, and describe recent educational applications of NLP. Finally, we make 7 recommendations to build collaboration and efficiency in Indonesian and Malay NLP, highlighting our contribution to these goals.

2 Methods

In order to capture a broad and rich picture of the recent literature, we applied a simplification of the Systematic Reviews and Meta-Analyses (PRISMA) for scoping reviews (Tricco et al., 2018; Page et al., 2021). Generally, we aimed to provide a descriptive overview and visualization of the reviewed material without detailed critical appraisal of individual studies or synthesis of evidence from different studies (Pham et al., 2014; Peters et al., 2015).

The review engaged with literature from many disciplines, including, but not limited to, Computational Linguistics, Computer Science, Indonesian Language Teaching, and NLP. Extensive consultations with research librarians resulted in a broad search strategy of the databases and terms (Figure 2). Both Indonesian/Malay and English search terms were used to maximize coverage. Additional search terms focused on our interest in Indonesian language teaching were used to mitigate the risk of missing relevant literature.

We experienced significant problems identifying studies with the Association for Computational Linguistics (ACL) as their publisher. In searches via Google Scholar, Scopus, and Proquest; many ACL publications (e.g., Koto et al. (2020a) and Wilie et al. (2020)) were not returned[4]. We then added a direct ACL Anthology search to our database search list. Unexplained behaviour in the ACL Anthology sort by 'Year of Publication' functionality cut results by over 400%, missing, for example, the aforementioned two relevant papers. To identify a reasonable portion of the work presented at ACL events, we extended the set of identified records semi-automatically by manually opening and exporting studies from ACL Anthology searches.

Our inclusion criteria specified that studies be recent (published in 2016 or later), peer-reviewed, written in English, Indonesian or Malay, and relevant to our topic (work about other languages or unrelated to NLP was excluded). Topical relevance was determined by a single reviewer (the first author of this paper) screening the title, abstract, and metadata of each identified study ($n = 1,954$) that was unique ($n = 1,510$) (Figure 1).

Included studies were then classified according to Hirschberg and Manning's 2015 characterization of advances in NLP. We refer to these classifications in brief as: *Broad NLP*; *Machine Reading*; *Machine Translation*; *Spoken Dialogue Systems*; *Speaker State*; and *Social Media*. We added a class — *Statistical Work* — to group work which primarily contributes corpus data or statistical and preprocessing work which stands at the foundation of most NLP.

Two reviewers (the first and last author of this paper) worked as a classification team, thereby assuring the quality of this 'light-touch' manual content analysis (Saldaña, 2016). In total, 80 of the 657 included studies (12.2%) were classified independently by both reviewers, including studies whose classification was perceived as uncertain by the first reviewer, as well as a random selection of further studies to increase confidence in reviewer agreement. Reviewers' classification disagreements were resolved through reference to full-text articles and discussion reaching consensus[5].

While many studies were classified as belonging to more than one 'grouping', the primary class was

[4]Not in the top 100 search results on Google Scholar.

[5]Both reviewers are academic researchers in NLP and teachers. Reviewer agreement of classification was very high. Most often the selection of a primary class was discussed and resolved by looking beyond brief, and at times misleading, information in article abstracts.

Database/Search Engine and search date/details	NLP and Indonesian/Malay keywords	Additional education keywords added to search string
Scopus **ProQuest** **EBSCO** **Limited to peer-review** **21 October 2021**	("natural language processing" OR nlp OR corpus OR corpora OR "computational linguistics" OR "pemrosesan bahasa alami" OR "pengolahan bahasa alami" OR korpus OR korpora OR "linguistik komputasional") AND ("indonesian language" OR "bahasa indonesia" OR malay)	AND ("language teaching" OR "language learning" OR "foreign language" OR bipa OR tifl OR tisol OR "belajar bahasa")
Google **Reduced length due to character limit** **8 July 2021**	("natural language processing" OR corpus OR corpora OR "computational linguistics" OR "pemrosesan bahasa alami" OR "pengolahan bahasa alami" OR korpus OR korpora OR "linguistik komputasional") AND ("indonesian language" OR "bahasa indonesia" OR malay)	("natural language processing" OR corpus OR "computational linguistics" OR "pemrosesan bahasa alami" OR korpus OR "linguistik komputasional") AND (indonesia OR malay) AND ("language teaching" OR "language learning" OR bipa OR "belajar bahasa")
ACL Anthology **25 October 2021**	(indonesian OR malay OR bahasa) AND ("language teaching" OR "language learning" OR "foreign language")	indonesian OR malay OR bahasa

Figure 2: Search Strategy

used in our analysis below. Appendix B is sorted by the second and third classification levels to improve search-ability and provide further information.

A search of titles and abstracts uncovered pre-existing reviews. These reviews were screened in full text and their findings are outlined in our results section to complement the scoping or quantitative map of the field. Literature outside our inclusion criteria which appeared highly relevant was retained separately for full-text review.

Unique names in the raw list of the top 50 most-published authors were manually normalized to prepare a publication-by-author count. Manual identification of name variants for authors with many publications were identified by matching author initials, affiliations, and profiles where possible to create Figure 5. Author affiliations for Figure 6 were taken from the most recent study of a given author included in this overview.

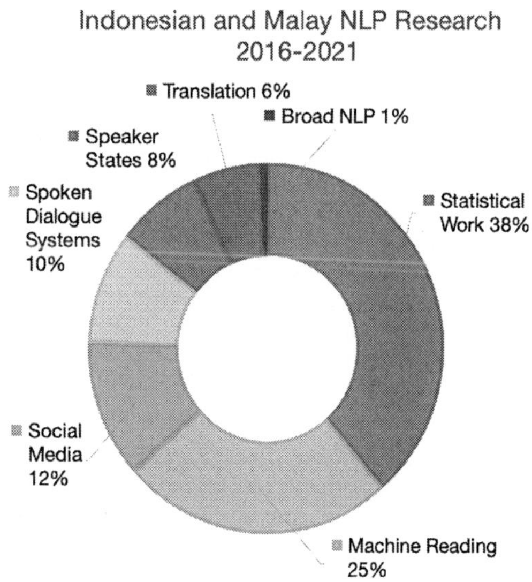

Figure 3: Indonesian and Malay NLP Research in 2016–2021

3 Results

A total of 657 from 1,954 studies met our inclusion criteria. Statistical and corpus work dominated throughout the last 5 years (from 2016 — Figure 3). Studies related to machine reading and sentiment analysis of online text such as news websites (included in 'Speaker States') and social media (sentiment analysis comprises much of our 'Social Media' classification) were popular and showed growth (Figure 4). The largest growth area was in 'Speaker Dialogue Systems' with a relative boom in publishing in 2019 (26 studies).

While our search terms were bilingual, the majority of studies that met our inclusion criteria were written in English or had an English title and abstract. The apparent stagnation of publications in 2020 (Figure 4) with a rebound in the first half of 2021 (which our search covered) could be related to the context of the COVID19 pandemic.

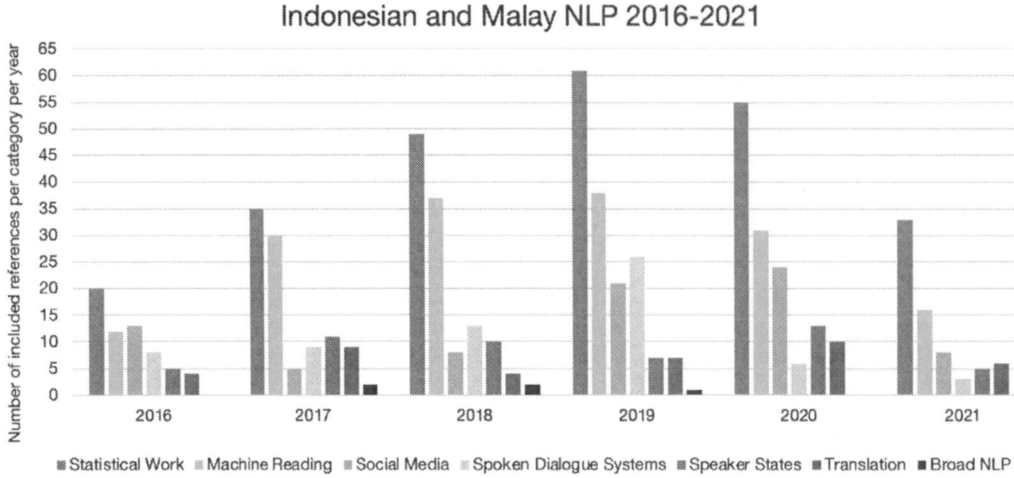

Figure 4: Categorisation of Indonesian and Malay NLP Research in 2016–2021 by Year

However, as "country-specific variables play a significant role" (Abramo et al., 2022) in pandemic publication trends, this is very difficult to determine.

As noted by Hirschberg and Manning in 2015, machine reading research makes use of the vast quantities of text available in the modern world while the mining of text from social media has "revolutionized the amount and types of information available today to NLP researchers". The presence of work in all classifications indicates Indonesian and Malay NLP has advanced from its 2015 state, when Hirschberg and Manning said it had "no such resources or systems available" (2015). To complement the quantitative picture in Figures 3 and 4, we identified existing reviews and provide a summary below. A detailed full-text review of all articles identified in a given classification is needed to fully investigate progress in each respective field.

3.1 Existing Reviews

Of the included studies, 15 were identified as reviews and read in full-text. Lan and Logeswaran (2020) discussed NLP in Indonesian/Malay in general. They did not identify their search methods nor their inclusion criteria, and their reference list had a strong focus on Malaysian research. Their description of statistical work on morphological and lexical analysis, the development of stop word lists, text normalization and named entity recognition concluded that "most researchers have no choice but to resort to compile their own corpus specific to their domain" (Lan and Logeswaran, 2020). According to their discussion, applications of NLP, such as those for machine translation, sentiment analysis, sarcasm and spam detection, as well as text summarization, were hampered by an absence of language-specific tools and resources. For example, they stated that the Jawi Malay script (which is based on Arabic) appeared to be missing characters, lemmatizers for translation seemed to struggle with affixes as they were loaned from English NLP, and sentiment analysis tended to rely on translated sentiment lexicons.

A 16th review article — "An Overview of Natural Language Processing for Indonesian and Malay" by Jiang et al. (2020), written in Mandarin — was identified at the screening stage. It fell outside the scope of this study but we did note that it provided a detailed overview of Indonesian/Malay NLP. The authors characterized the field as "widely distributed, covering stemming, part-of-speech tagging, syntactic analysis, semantic analysis, and other underlying technologies, as well as upper-level applications such as machine translation, spell checking, sentiment analysis, named entity recognition" (Jiang et al., 2020). However, similarly to Lan and Logeswaran (2020), they noted that "the basic resources, open data platforms and open-source language processing tools for these two languages are also lacking, and there are few mature and available text analysis systems" (Jiang et al., 2020).

Statistical or corpus based NLP is important to further the field; however, only 2 reviews had a special focus on corpora and these were specific to Malay (Awang Abu Bakar et al. (2018) and Nasharuddin et al. (2018)). These reviews provided some insight into Malay resources, and Nasharuddin et al. (2018) suggested document alignment as an avenue to overcome parallel corpus scarcity in cross and bilingual information retrieval, however, a thorough picture of existing corpora was lacking.

A further review by Kassim et al. (2016b) discussed morphology related challenges in stemming tools for Malay as perceived by the authors. However, this review did not fully address the complex steps necessary to uncover lemmas. As later described by Nomoto (2020), what has been "thought of as stemming and lemmatization [· · ·] is in fact 'root'-ing, that is, undoing all morphological processes to get a root". Future work needs to make use of the sort of stem and lemma information in MALINDO Morph to create Indonesian/Malay stemmers.

Machine translation was discussed in a single review of Indonesian translation by Rahutomo et al. (2019)[6], who identified that many researchers had created their own web-crawled parallel corpora. They described a range of techniques used in Indonesian translation, noting that Moses was commonly used and that attention-based approaches were improving neural machine translation. Their list of studies spanned languages: Sundanese, Javanese, Lampung, as well as English, Japanese, and Korean — a very limited list given there are between 652–701 languages in use in Indonesia (Zein, 2020). Thereby translation needs are yet to be met.

Machine reading was the focus of 5 reviews. Gunawan and Amalia (2018) reviewed single document text summarization and identified evaluation methods as a significant concern among 10 papers reporting research into extractive text summarization. They concluded that a text-summary dataset created by experts is needed to advance the field and to calibrate the diverse results reported in the literature.

Looking only at Malay, Mohemad et al. (2020b) suggested relatively poor results across the field. They found summaries were often longer than the original text and Malay anaphora proved difficult to condense, resulting in poor comprehensibility.[7]

In 2021, Widodo et al. remained concerned with evaluation measures in text summarization. Their review of 6 studies found all text summarization work was in extractive summarization — as opposed to abstractive — and that it was dominated by single document summarization of online news. To expand the usability and scope of these tools for Indonesian, they suggested that journal articles should be used as data to support multi-document summarization, as existing summaries of these documents could be used to enhance results.

Malay named entity recognition and classification (NERC) was carefully reviewed by Mohemad et al. (2020a), finding that differences in Malay morphology and textual ambiguities, as well as limitations on corpora and annotated data, are difficult challenges affecting both rule-based and machine learning methods. In addition, they found that the "majority of the systems developed [were] based on manually predefined dictionaries by a human" (Mohemad et al., 2020a) and that deep learning methods were yet to be studied with Malay NERC.

All 4 reviews of sentiment analysis were primarily concerned with social media in the Malaysian context (see both 'Speaker States' and 'Social Media' in Appendix B). Abdullah et al. (2017) found hybrid approaches of lexicon based and supervised machine learning were most common, while Handayani et al. (2018) added a more detailed discussion of techniques and datasets found in 10 carefully selected studies. Abu Bakar et al. (2020) foregrounded the 'noise' of social media data to confront the more complex language often found on the Internet. Abdullah and Rusli (2021) pushed this further, examining literature on multilingual sentiment analysis to inform the development of sentiment analysis for the Malaysian social media context, which they described as characterized by the multilingual use of English, Malay, and Chinese.

No reviews of spoken dialogue systems, such as automated speech recognition (ASR) or Text To Speech (TTS) toolkits (which are typically considered later-generation NLP), were found. This is not surprising given text-based NLP (e.g., machine reading) dominated the research agenda (Figure 4).

3.2 Notable Work Responding to the Lack of Data and Evaluation Methods, and Other Recent Contributions

Common to all reviews was a scarcity of freely available NLP resources, and subsequently the creation of custom datasets, loaned preprocessing tools from NLP in English, and difficulties in benchmarking performance without reliable eval-

[6]see also Septarina et al. (2019)

[7]Providing a brief reference to Malay language corpora, Omar et al. (2021) outlined advances in text summarization techniques.

uation techniques and reference datasets. In this context, we note the growing use of zero and few shot methods which are supported by pipelines such as HuggingFace[8]. We also note four projects and respective papers that develop benchmarking and open access corpora for:

- language modelling; Indonesian Language Evaluation Montage (IndoLEM) and Indonesian Bidirectional Encoder Representations from Transformers (IndoBERT);
- Indonesian Natural Language Understanding (IndoNLU); as well as
- Indonesian Natural Language Generation (IndoNLG) and Indonesian Natural Language Inference (IndoNLI).

Recently available, but not included in our study as it was published after our analysis was complete, Aji et al. (2022) provide a detailed discussion of NLP for the 700+ languages spoken in Indonesia. They outline challenges for NLP in Indonesia, describing limited resources, language diversity, orthography variation, and societal challenges such as the poor distribution of technology and education across Indonesia.

3.3 Highly Active Researchers and Research Hubs

Highly active researchers in the field are identified in Figure 5. While we made substantial efforts to ensure author publications were grouped accurately, name variations appeared to be prevalent in this field. We concentrated our efforts on normalizing the raw list of the top 50 authors. In contrast to broader trends (Mohammad, 2020), we note that 7 of the 11 authors in Figure 5 are female, though some are not first authors on many papers.

Research hubs in Indonesia and Malaysia are illustrated in Figure 6. The affiliations of the 25 authors with the most publications were used to identify these hubs. All affiliated universities listed by these 25 authors (as indicated in their most recent publication which met our inclusion criteria) were in either Malaysia or Indonesia. While there was an even spread between the two countries, overall Malaysia dominated with a ratio of 14:11 affiliations in Malaysia and Indonesia, respectively.

3.4 Education Specific Studies

The number of education specific studies was 41 (see Appendix A), based on the title and abstract. Of these 41 studies, 15 focused on assessment, with an emphasis on expediting and improving the efficiency of grading and providing feedback. Earlier studies (2016–2018) tended to focus on word-level error correction and short-answer grading while later studies (2019–2021) seemed to address whole of text evaluation, assessment task design (particularly questioning techniques), and providing feedback. Within the limited time frame of our study, we tentatively noted a shift from micro language level applications and their intrinsic evaluations to more macro, holistic language use applications that proceed to extrinsic or broader NLP evaluations.

A portion of education studies considered teaching practices and teacher training. Generally the studies reflected the design of our search-terms to target Indonesian language teaching; 10 papers were geared towards using NLP to improve the teaching and learning of Indonesian/Malay for non-background language learners. Bahasa Indonesia bagi Penutur Asing (BIPA — *Indonesian language for Foreign Learners*) and the Malay equivalent were discussed separately. Two studies were related to using NLP to improve the training of teachers of Indonesian as a foreign language. Another 2 studies focused on NLP for improving the teaching of translation for local students (i.e., Indonesian background speakers). Beyond studies from a language teaching setting, a further 6 studies related to instruction in general or other areas of the curriculum such as Mathematics, study skills, and values education.

Overall the body of work indicates a need for greater resourcing generally, and greater resourcing in education, with a shift towards more sophisticated language concerns and potential uses for these methods. Pleasingly, researchers identified for a high number of publications in Figure 5, such as Amalia, A[9] were also identified among those developing NLP for education (Amalia et al., 2019a), indicating high profile NLP researchers are invested in education sector applications.

4 Discussion

This study sheds significant light on the state of play and progress of Indonesian and Malay NLP.

[8] See, for example, Cahya Wirawan's pre-trained Wikipedia model.

[9] (see also name variant: *Amalia, Amalia* and Google Scholar profile *Amalia, Mahdi*)

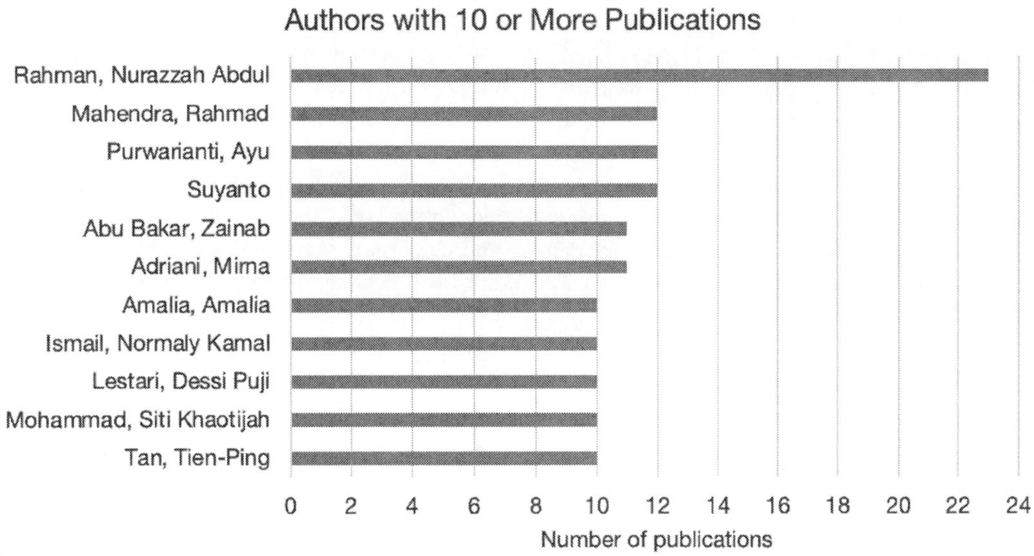

Figure 5: Authors with 10 or More Publications

Figure 6: Author Affiliation of the Top 25 Authors with Most Publications

We make the following 7 recommendations and outline our related contributions to encourage collaboration and support appropriate investment in the development of Indonesian and Malay NLP, and its application in education.

4.1 Recommendations

1. Broader adoption of best-practices for findable, open, sustainable, and future-proof data. All 15 reviews raised the difficulty of locating data, tools, and existing work as a significant problem. Our study responds to this problem and is unique in that Appendix B offers a catalogue of recent work, identifies a variety of openly shared datasets and tools, and locates research hubs. Our results complement reviews such as Lan and Logeswaran (2020) and Jiang et al. (2020) by providing an empirical picture of published research on Indonesian and Malay NLP. While our study was not specifically focused on corpora like Awang Abu Bakar et al. (2018), over 50 of the papers listed at the top of 'Statistical Work' in Appendix B point to datasets which may be useful to future projects.

Useful advice to implement the FAIR Principles (Findable, Accessible, Interoperable, Reusable) and further advice for individual researchers/teams to develop metadata, choose file formats, and think beyond their immediate plans for linguistic data is set out by Janda (2022) and Mattern (2022), respectively. Funding requirements that encourage data reuse (given ethics restraints) and which provide financial support for adequate digital stewardship are recommended.

2. Expanded evaluation methods and datasets, and negative result publication

As identified by Gunawan and Amalia (2018) and Widodo et al. (2021), evaluation of Indonesian and Malay NLP is poorly supported due to a lack of clear methods and few reference datasets. Open, accessible data from studies can assist with this, but to encourage further efficiency in the field, we also recommend authors consider the publication of 'unsuccessful' experiments in venues such as Workshop on Insights from Negative Results in NLP and organize or participate in evaluation challenges (a.k.a. shared tasks) and their workshops, for example, as part of ACL conferences.

3. Collaboration and connection between Indonesian and Malay NLP research and projects to speed development and allow cross-fertilisation

Many of the reviews discussed in our results focused on Malaysian research specifically looking at Malay NLP. By using both Indonesian and Malay in our search terms we connect these reviews to the work of Indonesian authors. To illustrate, Handayani et al. (2018), Abu Bakar et al. (2020), and Abdullah et al. (2021) examine one study which included Malay in the application of multilingual sentiment analysis. Our findings connect this work in Malay to more recent work by Tho et al. (2021), who looked at Indonesian and Javanese code-mixed sentiment analysis.

Indonesian and Malay are closely related (Sneddon, 2003). With a caveat that corpus metadata must clearly describe which languages are present, and that projects must clearly state how Indonesian and Malay are used in training data, we recommend future work seek out synergies that could be leveraged by using both languages.

4. Flexible author name formats and consistent author name use

Many authors of studies we included had only one name, but appeared to double this name in some publications but not others, perhaps to suit forms built with an (eurocentric) expectation of family names. Similarly, many authors with lengthy names used various forms.

We recommend publishers adapt their submission forms to accommodate diverse name traditions and support existing unique author identifiers (e.g., the ORCID system). We also recommend authors choose a publication name and use it as consistently as possible to increase the findability of their work.

5. Investment in spoken language data and transcription protocols

Our findings indicate only modest developments of 'later-generation' NLP in Indonesian and Malay. Significant investment is needed to give users of these languages access to a broader gamut of NLP applications, including applications in the education sector.

In this space it is also essential to recognise differences in the actual usage of these languages in real-life, spoken situations. Transcription which records code-mixed and often diglossic use of spoken varieties of Indonesian and Malay in a machine readable format needs to be investigated and scrutinised (Maxwell-Smith et al., 2020).

6. Investment in other languages of Indonesia and Malaysia

As a necessary endeavour for equitable access to advances in NLP for speakers, and to limit the further endangerment of many languages as a consequence of the expansion of Indonesian (Zein, 2020), we recommend simultaneous investment in other languages of Indonesia and Malaysia. Linked to Recommendation 5, to reflect actual usage and to allow NLP to be useful in real-world contexts where code-mixing is the norm, investment in other languages is also likely crucial.

7. Education and NLP researchers should consider the use of datasets by researchers outside their field

A research project such as ours, investigating teacher-speech and teaching materials for Indonesian language teaching (Maxwell-Smith et al., 2020) should take advantage of human language technologies. This article contributes a language-specific characterization of the field which will help scope future projects.

Education researchers should be aware that computational methods such as data normalization scripts and stemming tools are yet to be fully developed for their use with the Indonesian language. If working with spoken language, ASR toolkits for working on low resource languages are suitable for consideration but may require significant investment of time and training before they are capable of managing complex code-switching behaviours common in education settings.

For education researchers and teachers to use NLP resources they need clear information about the profile of language/s in corpora and also about what data has been used when training models/tools. This allows proper assessment of the cultural and political suitability of NLP resources.

Education researchers also need to consider the possible use of datasets by researchers outside their field. Ensuring data they collect is recorded in 'future-proof' formats and prepared with consideration of the FAIR principles (see Recommendation 1 — Janda (2022) and Mattern (2022)) is an investment which encourages NLP applications specifically built for or amenable to education settings.

4.2 Limitations and Future Work

With regard to the limitations of this study, we employed a 'light-touch', subjective coding method with a discrete set of class labels to scope relevant literature; we did not undertake the act of synthesis (Peters et al., 2015). We screened only the title and abstract for the vast majority of references. Unintentional misinterpretation could have taken place. Our analysis provides an approximate area within NLP for each reference to assist researchers studying an NLP application or use-case. Researchers interested in a particular algorithm (e.g., Random Forest Decision Trees or Transformers), or the use of a particular performance indicator (e.g., F1 or Word Error Rate), might not find our work as useful, but we encourage them to scan related categories in Appendix A for work relevant to their interest. Most references were labelled as belonging to multiple categories, with the identification of the first category an educated but ultimately subjective decision. Reading every study carefully beyond title and abstract was beyond the scope of this study.

Future studies to target Indonesian and Malay language publications may identify further literature on Indonesian and Malay NLP. Unfortunately, our initial searches through databases such as the University of Indonesia's Research Portal, produced varied results, with a large proportion of returned studies not necessarily having been as rigorously peer-reviewed (encompassing for example many 'skripsi' or honours dissertations). Indonesia's national library service OneSearch has grown dramatically, and with over 3748 libraries affiliated in February 2022, it should also be included in future reviews of Indonesian and Malay NLP.

Since we conducted our review, Aji et al. (2022) have proposed potential research directions in the Indonesian context such as data-efficient and compute-efficient NLP. Given the low number of studies in our *Speaker Dialogue Systems* class, we support their call for "NLP Beyond Text". The 'superglossic' translanguaging practices of Indonesia (Zein, 2020), and language classrooms (Maxwell-Smith et al., 2020), correspond with their call for "Robustness to Code-mixing and Non-Standard Orthography". Applications of Indonesian NLP necessitate involvement with other languages of Indonesia and inevitably impact many at-risk languages. There is an ethical obligation for "careful assessment of individual usage scenarios of language technology, so they are implemented for the good of the local population" (Aji et al., 2022).

5 Conclusion

Overall, this scoping study provides a baseline picture of Indonesian and Malay NLP. It shows an emerging research community engaged with the wide range of NLP advances identified in 2015 by Hirschberg and Manning. Researchers in the field continue to experience difficulties in benchmarking performance without reliable evaluation techniques and reference datasets, re-engineering of loaned preprocessing tools from English NLP, and thankless tasks such as the creation of custom datasets and resources. NLP applications in education are limited, as are tools for language which is not in text format. Our results highlight the importance of creating and releasing well-described and maintained resources openly and fostering collaboration. IndoLEM-IndoBERT, IndoNLU, IndoNLG, and IndoNLI are notable releases that are already helping to orientate researchers and future projects using Indonesian and Malay NLP.

Acknowledgements

We are grateful to Murray Hall, Chenchen Xu, and Rebecca Barber for their technical, translation, and search strategy assistance, respectively. We also thank the anonymous reviewers for their helpful feedback.

References

Muhammad Aasim Asyafi'Ie bin Ahmad, Mokhtar bin Harun, Puspa Inayat binti Khalid, Mohd Ibrahim Shapiai, Md. Najib bin Ibrahi, and Siti Zaleha Abdul Hamid. 2017. Comparison of the themes of Malaysian Friday sermons between the year 2010 and 2015. *Indonesian Journal of Electrical Engineering and Computer Science*, 6(1):212–218.

Nurazzah Abd Rahman, Nursyahidah Alias, Nomaly Kamal Ismail, Zulhilmi Bin Mohamed Nor, and Muhammad Nazir bin Alias. 2016. An identification of authentic narrator's name features in Malay hadith texts. *IEEE Conference on Open Systems, ICOS 2015*, pages 79–84.

Imran Ho Abdullah, Anis Nadiah Che Abdul Rahman, and Azhar Jaludin. 2021. The development of the Malaysian Hansard Corpus: A corpus of parliamentary debates 1959-2020. *Jurnal Linguistik*, 25(1).

Nur Atiqah Sia Abdullah and Nur Ida Aniza Rusli. 2021. Multilingual sentiment analysis: A systematic literature review. *Pertanika Journal of Science and Technology*, 29(1):445–470.

Nur Atiqah Sia Abdullah, Nurul Iman Shaari, and Abd Rasul Abd Rahman. 2017. Review on sentiment analysis approaches for social media data. *Journal of Engineering and Applied Sciences*, 12(3):462–467.

Enid Zureen Zainal Abidin, Nik Farhan Mustapha, Normaliza Abd Rahim, and Syed Nurulakla Syed Abdullah. 2020. Translation of idioms from Arabic into Malay via Google Translate: What needs to be done? *GEMA Online Journal of Language Studies*, 20(3):156–180.

Zaenal Abidin and Permata Permata. 2021. Pengaruh penambahan korpus paralel pada mesin penerjemah statistik Bahasa Indonesian ke Bahasa Lampung Dialek Nyo. *Jurnal Teknoinfo*, 15(1):13–19.

Zaenal Abidin, Permata Permata, I. Ahmad, and Rusliyawati. 2021. Effect of mono corpus quantity on statistical machine translation Indonesian-Lampung dialect of Nyo. *3rd International Conference on Applied Sciences Mathematics and Informatics, ICASMI 2020*, 1751.

Achmad Fatchuttamam Abka. 2017. Evaluating the use of word embeddings for part-of-speech tagging in Bahasa Indonesia. *2016 International Conference on Computer, Control, Informatics and its Applications, IC3INA 2016*, pages 209–214.

Giovanni Abramo, Ciriaco Andrea D'Angelo, and Ida Mele. 2022. Impact of Covid-19 on research output by gender across countries. *Scientometrics*.

M. Abu, A. Amir, N. A. H. Zahri, and R. Ngadiran. 2020. Voice-based Malay commands recognition by using audio fingerprint method for smart house applications. *IOP Conference Series. Materials Science and Engineering*, 767(1).

Muhammad Fakhrur Razi Abu Bakar, Norisma Idris, Liyana Shuib, and Norazlina Khamis. 2020. Sentiment analysis of noisy Malay text: State of art, challenges and future work. *IEEE Access*, 8:24687–24696.

Muhammad Yuslan Abu Bakar, Adiwijaya, and Said Al Faraby. 2019a. Multi-label topic classification of hadith of Bukhari (Indonesian language translation) using information gain and backpropagation neural network. *22nd International Conference on Asian Language Processing, IALP 2018*, pages 344–350.

Normi Sham Awang Abu Bakar, Ros Aziehan Rahmat, and Umar Faruq Othman. 2019b. Polarity classification tool for sentiment analysis in Malay language. *IAES International Journal of Artificial Intelligence*, 8(3):258–263.

Rike Adelia, Suyanto Suyanto, and Untari Novia Wisesty. 2019. Indonesian abstractive text summarization using bidirectional gated recurrent unit. *4th International Conference on Computer Science and Computational Intelligence, ICCSCI 2019*, 157:581–588.

Rifki Adhitama, Retno Kusumaningrum, and Rahmat Gernowo. 2017. Topic labeling towards news document collection based on Latent Dirichlet Allocation and ontology. *1st International Conference on Informatics and Computational Sciences, ICICoS 2017*, 2018-January:247–251.

Ryan Adipradana, Bagas Pradipabista Nayoga, Ryan Suryadi, and Derwin Suhartono. 2021. Hoax analyzer for Indonesian news using RNNs with fasttext and glove embeddings. *Bulletin of Electrical Engineering and Informatics*, 10(4):2130–2136.

Dwi Intan Af'idah, Retno Kusumaningrum, and Bayu Surarso. 2020. Long short term memory convolutional neural network for Indonesian sentiment analysis towards touristic destination reviews. *2020 International Seminar on Application for Technology of Information and Communication, iSemantic 2020*, pages 630–637.

Afiyati, Edi Winarko, and Anis Cherid. 2018. Recognizing the sarcastic statement on WhatsApp Group with Indonesian language text. *2017 International Conference on Broadband Communication, Wireless Sensors and Powering, BCWSP 2017*, 2018-January:1–6.

Zaaba Ahmad, Syaheerah Lebai Lutfi, Albin Lemuel Kushan, Mohamad Hafiz Khairuddin, Anwar Farhan Zolkeplay, Mohammad Hafidz Rahmat, and Mohd Taufik Mishan. 2017. Construction of the Malay language psychometric properties using LIWC from Facebook statuses. *Advanced Science Letters*, 23(8):7911–7914.

Mohd Zakree Ahmad Nazri, Tri Basuki Kurniawan, Abdul Razak Hamdan, Salwani Abdullah, and Mohammed Azlan Mis. 2018. Taxonomy development from Malay text using firefly bisection algorithm. *GEMA Online Journal of Language Studies*, 18(2):182–201.

Noor Bazilah Ahmat Baseri, Juhaida Abu Bakar, Azizah Ahmad, Hawa Jafferi, and Muhammad Faiz Zamri. 2020. SMVS: A web-based application for graphical visualization of Malay text corpus. *10th IEEE Symposium on Computer Applications and Industrial Electronics, ISCAIE 2020*, pages 30–35.

Alham Fikri Aji, Genta Indra Winata, Fajri Koto, Samuel Cahyawijaya, Ade Romadhony, Rahmad Mahendra, Kemal Kurniawan, David Moeljadi, Radityo Eko Prasojo, Timothy Baldwin, Jey Han Lau, and Sebastian Ruder. 2022. One country, 700+ languages: Nlp challenges for underrepresented languages and dialects in indonesia.

Try Ajitiono and Yani Widyani. 2017. Indonesian essay grading module using natural language processing. *3rd International Conference on Data and Software Engineering, ICoDSE 2016*.

Herley Shaori Al-Ash and Wahyu Catur Wibowo. 2018. Fake news identification characteristics using named entity recognition and phrase detection. *10th International Conference on Information Technology and Electrical Engineering, ICITEE 2018*, pages 12–17.

Tareq Al-Moslmi, Nazlia Omar, Mohammed Albared, and Ade Alshabi. 2017. Enhanced Malay sentiment analysis with an ensemble classification machine learning approach. *Journal of Engineering and Applied Sciences*, 12(20):5226–5232.

Ahmed Al-Saffar, Suryanti Awang, Hai Tao, Nazlia Omar, Wafaa Al-Saiagh, and Mohammed Al-bared. 2018. Malay sentiment analysis based on combined classification approaches and Senti-lexicon algorithm. *PLoS ONE*, 13(4):e0194852.

Andry Alamsyah, Muhammad Fadhli Rachman, Cindy Septiani Hudaya, Rimba Pratama Putra, Aulia Ichsan Rifkyano, and Fivi Nurwianti. 2019. A progress on the personality measurement model using ontology based on social media text. *4th International Conference on Information Management and Technology, ICIMTech 2019*, pages 581–586.

Andry Alamsyah, Sri Widiyanesti, Rizqy Dwi Putra, and Puspita Kencana Sari. 2020. Personality measurement design for ontology based platform using social media text. *Advances in Science, Technology and Engineering Systems*, 5(3):100–107.

Ika Alfina, Ruli Manurung, and Mohamad Ivan Fanany. 2017. DBpedia entities expansion in automatically building dataset for Indonesian NER. *8th International Conference on Advanced Computer Science and Information Systems, ICACSIS 2016*, pages 335–340.

Ika Alfina, Rio Mulia, Mohamad Ivan Fanany, and Yudo Ekanata. 2018. Hate speech detection in the Indonesian language: A dataset and preliminary study. *9th International Conference on Advanced Computer Science and Information Systems, ICACSIS 2017*, 2018-January:233–237.

Rayner Alfred, Leow Ching Leong, and Joe Henry Obit. 2017. An evolutionary-based term reduction approach to bilingual clustering of Malay-English corpora. *Proceedings of the International Conference on Advances in Information and Communication Technology, ICTA 2016*, 538 AISC:132–141.

Rayner Alfred, Leow Jia Ren, and Joe Henry Obit. 2016. Assessing factors that influence the performances of automated topic selection for Malay articles. *2nd International Conference on Soft Computing in Data Science, SCDS 2016*, 652:300–309.

Nursyahidah Alias, Nurazzah Abd Rahman, Normaly Kamal Ismail, Zulhilmi Mohamed Nor, and Muhammad Nazir Alias. 2017a. Graph-based text representation for Malay translated hadith text. *3rd International Conference on Information Retrieval and Knowledge Management, CAMP 2016*, pages 60–66.

Suraya Alias, Siti Khaotijah Mohammad, Keng Hoon Gan, and Tan Tien Ping. 2018a. MYTextSum: A Malay text summarizer model using a constrained pattern-growth sentence compression technique. *4th International Conference on Computational Science and Technology, ICCST17*, 488:141–150.

Suraya Alias, Siti Khaotijah Mohammad, Gan Keng Hoon, and Tan Tien Ping. 2016. A Malay text corpus analysis for sentence compression using pattern-growth method. *Jurnal Teknologi*, 78(8):197–206.

Suraya Alias, Siti Khaotijah Mohammad, Gan Keng Hoon, and Tan Tien Ping. 2017b. A Malay text summarizer using pattern-growth method with sentence compression rules. *3rd International Conference on Information Retrieval and Knowledge Management, CAMP 2016*, pages 7–12.

Suraya Alias, Siti Khaotijah Mohammad, Gan Keng Hoon, and Tan Tien Ping. 2017c. Extract, compress and summarize – An experiment using Malay news article. *Advanced Science Letters*, 23(5):4336–4340.

Suraya Alias, Siti Khaotijah Mohammad, Gan Keng Hoon, and Tan Tien Ping. 2018b. A text representation model using Sequential Pattern-Growth method. *Pattern Analysis and Applications*, 21(1):233–247.

Suraya Alias, Siti Khaotijah Mohammad, Gan Keng Hoon, and Mohd Shamrie Sainin. 2018c. Understanding human sentence compression pattern for Malay text summarizer. *4th International Conference on Information Retrieval and Knowledge Management: Diving into Data Sciences, CAMP 2018*, pages 42–47.

Suraya Alias, Mohd Shamrie Sainin, and Siti Khaotijah Mohammad. 2020. Bilingual extractive text summarization model using textual pattern constraints. *GEMA Online Journal of Language Studies*, 20(3):70–95.

Suraya Alias, Mohd Shamrie Sainin, and Siti Khaotijah Mohammad. 2021. A syntactic-based sentence validation technique for Malay text summarizer. *Journal of Information and Communication Technology*, 20(3):329–352.

A. Amalia, D. Gunawan, Y. Fithri, and I. Aulia. 2019a. Automated Bahasa Indonesia essay evaluation with latent semantic analysis. *Journal of Physics: Conference Series*, 1235(1).

Amalia Amalia, Opim Salim Sitompul, Erna Budhiarti Nababan, Maya Silvi Lydia, and Nadia Rahmatunnisa. 2019b. Bahasa Indonesia text corpus generation using web corpora approaches. *Journal of Theoretical and Applied Information Technology*, 97(24):3810–3821.

Amalia Amalia, Opim Salim Sitompul, Erna Budhiarti Nababan, and Teddy Mantoro. 2020a. A comparison study of document clustering using DOC2VEC versus TFIDF combined with LSA for small corpora. *Journal of Theoretical and Applied Information Technology*, 98(17):3644–3657.

Amalia Amalia, Opim Salim Sitompul, Erna Budhiarti Nababan, and Teddy Mantoro. 2020b. An efficient text classification using fasttext for Bahasa Indonesia documents classification. *2020 International Conference on Data Science, Artificial Intelligence, and Business Analytics, DATABIA 2020*, pages 69–75.

Rizkiana Amalia, Moch Arif Bijaksana, and Dhinta Darmantoro. 2018. Negation handling in sentiment classification using rule-based adapted from Indonesian language syntactic for Indonesian text in Twitter. *International Conference on Data and Information Science 2017, ICoDIS 2017*, 971.

Andi Tenri Ampa, Muhammad D Basri, and Sri Ramdayani. 2019. A morphophonemic analysis on the affixation in the Indonesian Language. *International Journal of Scientific and Technology Research*, 8(7):267–273.

Ahmad Zuli Amrullah, Rudy Hartanto, and I Wayan Mustika. 2017. A comparison of different part-of-speech tagging technique for text in Bahasa Indonesia. *7th International Annual Engineering Seminar, InAES 2017*.

Ratna Anak Agung Putri, Purnamasari Prima Dewi, Boma Anantasatya Adhi, F. Astha Ekadiyanto, Muhammad Salman, Mardiyah Mardiyah, and Winata Darien Jonathan. 2017. Cross-language plagiarism detection system using latent semantic analysis and learning vector quantization. *Algorithms*, 10(2):69.

Muhammad Bagus Andra and Tsuyoshi Usagawa. 2020. Automatic transcription and captioning system for Bahasa Indonesia in multi-speaker environment. *5th International Conference on Intelligent Informatics and Biomedical Sciences, ICIIBMS 2020*, pages 51–56.

Muhammad Bagus Andra and Tsuyoshi Usagawa. 2021. Improved transcription and speaker identification system for concurrent speech in Bahasa Indonesia using recurrent neural network. *IEEE Access*, 9:70758–70774.

Vincent Andreas, Alexander Agung Santoso Gunawan, and Widodo Budiharto. 2019. Anita: Intelligent humanoid robot with self-learning capability using Indonesian language. *4th Asia-Pacific Conference on Intelligent Robot Systems, ACIRS 2019*, pages 144–147.

Miftah Andriansyah, Antonius Irianto Sukowati, Marshal Samos, Imam Purwanto, Ali Akbar, and Muhammad Subali. 2018. Developing Indonesian corpus of pornography using simple nlp-text mining (NTM) approach to support government anti-pornography program. *2nd International Conference on Informatics and Computing, ICIC 2017*, 2018-January:1–4.

Sandhya Aneja, Siti Nur Afikah Bte Abdul Mazid, and Nagender Aneja. 2020. Neural machine translation model for university email application. *2nd Symposium on Signal Processing Systems, SSPS 2020*, pages 74–79.

Dina Anggraini, Achmad Benny Mutiara, Tb. Maulana Kusuma, and Lily Wulandari. 2018. Algorithm for simple sentence identification in Bahasa Indonesia. *3rd International Conference on Informatics and Computing, ICIC 2018*.

Sarudin Anida, Redzwan Husna Faredza Mohamed, Zulkifli Osman, Shah Raja Noor Farah Azura Raja Ma'amor, and Albakri Intan Safinas Mohd Ariff. 2019. Menangani kekaburan kemahiran prosedur dan terminologi awal matematik: Pendekatan leksis berdasarkan teori prosodi semantik. *Malaysian Journal of Learning and Instruction*, 16(2):255–294.

Laksmi Anindyati, Ayu Purwarianti, and Ade Nursanti. 2019. Optimizing deep learning for detection cyberbullying text in Indonesian language. *2019 International Conference on Advanced Informatics: Concepts, Theory, and Applications, ICAICTA 2019*.

Ani Anisyah, Tricya Esterina Widagdo, and Fazat Nur Nur Azizah. 2019. Natural language interface to database (NLIDB) for decision support queries. *2019 International Conference on Data and Software Engineering, ICoDSE 2019*.

Lalitia Ansari and Totok Suhardijanto. 2019. Where is the head positioned in Indonesian language?: A corpus study of head directionality from a dependency perspective. *22nd International Conference on Asian Language Processing, IALP 2018*, pages 171–177.

Nurfarihah Apandi and Nursuriati Jamil. 2017. An analysis of Malay language emotional speech corpus for emotion recognition system. *2016 IEEE Industrial Electronics and Applications Conference, IEACon 2016*, pages 225–231.

William Aprilius, Seng Hansun, and Dennis Gunawan. 2017. Entity annotation WordPress plugin using TAGME technology. *Telkomnika (Telecommunication Computing Electronics and Control)*, 15(1):486–493.

Winda Widya Ariestya, Ida Astuti, and I Made Wiryana. 2018. Preprocessing for crawler of short message social media. *3rd International Conference on Informatics and Computing, ICIC 2018*.

Siti Noor Allia Noor Ariffin and Sabrina Tiun. 2018. Part-of-speech tagger for Malay social media texts. *GEMA Online Journal of Language Studies*, 18(4):124–142.

Siti Noor Allia Noor Ariffin and Sabrina Tiun. 2020. Rule-based text normalization for Malay social media texts. *International Journal of Advanced Computer Science and Applications*, 11(10):156–162.

Y. Arifin, S. M. Isa, L. A. Wulandhari, and E. Abdurachman. 2018. Plagiarism detection for Indonesian language using winnowing with parallel processing. *Journal of Physics: Conference Series*, 978(1).

Bayu Aryoyudanta, Teguh Bharata Adji, and Indriana Hidayah. 2017. Semi-supervised learning approach for Indonesian Named Entity Recognition (NER) using co-training algorithm. *2016 International Seminar on Intelligent Technology and Its Application, ISITIA 2016*, pages 7–12.

Siti Azirah Asmai, Muhammad Sharilazlan Salleh, Halizah Basiron, and Sabrina Ahmad. 2018. An enhanced Malay named entity recognition using combination approach for crime textual data analysis. *International Journal of Advanced Computer Science and Applications*, 9(9):474–483.

Asniar and B. R. Aditya. 2017. A framework for sentiment analysis implementation of Indonesian language tweet on Twitter. *Journal of Physics: Conference Series*, 801(1).

Atqia Aulia, Dewi Khairani, Rizal Broer Bahaweres, and Nashrul Hakiem. 2017a. WatsaQ: Repository of al hadith in Bahasa (case study: Hadith Bukhari). *4th International Conference on Electrical Engineering, Computer Science and Informatics, EECSI 2017*, 2017-December.

Atqia Aulia, Dewi Khairani, and Nashrul Hakiem. 2017b. Development of a retrieval system for al hadith in Bahasa (case study: Hadith Bukhari). *5th International Conference on Cyber and IT Service Management, CITSM 2017*.

Indra Aulia and Ari Moesriami Barmawi. 2016. An automatic health surveillance chart interpretation system based on Indonesian language. *International Conference on Advanced Computer Science and Information Systems, ICACSIS 2015*, pages 163–170.

Indra Aulia, Ainul Hizriadi, Seniman, and Muhibuddin. 2020. Preliminary research design on sensor data gathering for air quality text generation. *4th International Conference on Computing and Applied Informatics 2019, ICCAI 2019*, 1566.

Normi Sham Awang Abu Bakar, Hamwira Yaacob, Dini Handayani, and Mustafa Ali Abuzaraida. 2018. Malay Online Virtual Integrated Corpus (MOVIC): A systematic review. *2018 International Conference on Information and Communication Technology for the Muslim World, ICT4M 2018*, pages 243–248.

Media Anugerah Ayu, Teddy Mantoro, and Jelita Asian. 2018. Quality translation enhancement using sequence knowledge and pruning in statistical machine translation. *Telkomnika (Telecommunication Computing Electronics and Control)*, 16(2):718–727.

Media Anugerah Ayu, Sony Surya Wijaya, and Teddy Mantoro. 2019. An automatic lexicon generation for Indonesian news sentiment analysis: A case on governor elections in Indonesia. *Indonesian Journal of Electrical Engineering and Computer Science*, 16(3):1555–1561.

Indira Suri Azarine, Moch Arif Bijaksana, and Ibnu Asror. 2019. Named entity recognition on Indonesian tweets using hidden markov model. *7th International Conference on Information and Communication Technology, ICoICT 2019*.

Shaari Azianura Hani, Kamaluddin Mohammad Rahim, Fauzi Wan Fariza Paizi, and Mohd Masnizah. 2019. Online-dating romance scam in Malaysia: An analysis of online conversations between scammers and victims. *GEMA Online Journal of Language Studies*, 19(1):97–115.

Jamaluddin Aziz. 2019. Exploring gender issues associated with wanita/woman and perempuan/woman in Malaysian parliamentary debates: A culturomic approach. *GEMA Online Journal of Language Studies*, 19(4):278–303.

Nadhia Salsabila Azzahra, Muhammad Okky Ibrohim, Junaedi Fahmi, Bagus Fajar Apriyanto, and Oskar Riandi. 2020. Developing name entity recognition for structured and unstructured text formatting dataset. *5th International Conference on Informatics and Computing, ICIC 2020*.

Juhaida Abu Bakar, Khairuddin Omar, Mohammad Faidzul Nasrudin, and Mohd Zamri Murah. 2016. NUWT: Jawi-specific buckwalter corpus for Malay word tokenization. *Journal of Information and Communication Technology*, 15(1):107–131.

Muhammad Fakhrur Razi Abu Bakar, Norisma Idris, and Liyana Shuib. 2019. An enhancement of Malay social media text normalization for lexicon-based sentiment analysis. *23rd International Conference on Asian Language Processing, IALP 2019*, pages 211–215.

Normi Sham Abu Bakar. 2020. The development of an integrated corpus for Malay language. *6th International Conference on Computational Science and Technology, ICCST 2019*, 603:425–433.

Zamri Abu Bakar, Nomaly Kamal Ismail, and Mohd Izani Mohamed Rawi. 2017. Detection of compound word with combination noun and adjective using rule based technique in Malay standard document. *Journal of Telecommunication, Electronic and Computer Engineering*, 9(3-5 Special Issue):129–134.

Zamri Abu Bakar, Normaly Kamal Ismail, and Mohd Izani Mohamed Rawi. 2018a. Identification of noun + verb compound nouns in Malay standard document based on rule based. *3rd IEEE International Conference on Engineering Technologies and Social Sciences, ICETSS 2017*, 2018-January:1–6.

Zamri Abu Bakar, Normaly Kamal Ismail, Mohd Izani Mohamed Rawi, and Nurazzah Abdul Rahman. 2018b. Automatic detection of compound word in Malay standard document using rule based technique. *2017 IEEE Conference on Open Systems, ICOS 2017*, 2018-January:59–64.

Vimala Balakrishnan, Mohammed Kaity, Hajar Abdul Rahim, and Nazari Ismail. 2021. Social media analytics using sentiment and content analyses on the 2018 Malaysia's general election. *Malaysian Journal of Computer Science*, 34(2):171–183.

Anab Maulana Barik, Rahmad Mahendra, and Mirna Adriani. 2019. Normalization of Indonesian-English code-mixed Twitter data. In *Proceedings of the 5th Workshop on Noisy User-generated Text (W-NUT 2019)*, pages 417–424. Association for Computational Linguistics.

Thomas Agung Basuki and Benediktus Giovanito Antaputra. 2020a. How similar is similar: A comparison of Bahasa Indonesia and Bahasa Malaysia. *3rd International Conference on Electronics, Communications and Control Engineering, ICECC 2020*, pages 8–12.

Thomas Anung Basuki and Benediktus Giovanito Antaputra. 2020b. How similar is similar: A comparison of Bahasa Indonesia and Bahasa Malaysia. In *Proceedings of the 3rd International Conference on Electronics, Communications and Control Engineering*, ICECC 2020, page 8–12, New York, NY, USA. Association for Computing Machinery.

Shaiful Bakhtiar Bin Rodzman, Mohammad Hanif Rashid, Normaly Kamal Ismail, Nurazzah Abd Rahman, Syed Ahmad Aljunid, and Hayati Abd Rahman. 2019a. Experiment with lexicon based techniques on domain-specific Malay document sentiment analysis. *9th IEEE Symposium on Computer Applications and Industrial Electronics, ISCAIE 2019*, pages 330–334.

Shaiful Bakhtiar Bin Rodzman, Nomaly Kamal Ismail, and Nurazzah Abd Rahman. 2018a. A survey on context-aware information retrieval research. *4th International Conference on Computational Science and Technology, ICCST17*, 488:399–409.

Shaiful Bakhtiar Bin Rodzman, Normaly Kamal Ismail, Nurazzah Abd Rahman, and Zulhilmi Mohamed Nor. 2018b. The implementation of fuzzy logic controller for defining the ranking function on Malay text corpus. *2017 IEEE Conference on Big Data and Analytics, ICBDA 2017*, 2018-January:93–98.

Shaiful Bakhtiar Bin Rodzman, Normaly Kamal Ismail, Nurazzah Abd Rahman, Syed Ahmad Aljunid, Hayati Abd Rahman, Zulhilmi Mohamed Nor, Ku Muhammad Naim Ku Khalif, and Ahmad Yunus Mohd Noor. 2019b. Experiment with text summarization as a positive hierarchical fuzzy logic ranking indicator for domain specific retrieval of Malay translated hadith. *9th IEEE Symposium on Computer Applications and Industrial Electronics, ISCAIE 2019*, pages 299–304.

Maslida Binti Yusof and Nurul Jamilah Binti Rosly. 2018. Conceptual structure representation of causative verb in Malay language and relation with syntax. *GEMA Online Journal of Language Studies*, 18(4):143–167.

Francis Bond, Hiroki Nomoto, Luis Morgado da Costa, and Arthur Bond. 2020. Linking the TUFS Basic Vocabulary to the Open Multilingual Wordnet. In *Proceedings of the 12th Language Resources and Evaluation Conference*, pages 3181–3188. European Language Resources Association.

Prachya Boonkwan, Thepchai Supnithi, Wandee Tosuwan, and Chai Wutiwiwatchai. 2016. The development of an audible Pattani Malay-Thai electronic phrasebook for military purposes. *5th Workshop on Spoken Language Technologies for Under-resourced languages, SLTU 2016*, 81:237–242.

Annisa Briliani, Budhi Irawan, and Casi Setianingsih. 2019. Hate speech detection in Indonesian language on Instagram comment section using K-nearest neighbor classification method. *2019 IEEE International Conference on Internet of Things and Intelligence System, IoTaIS 2019*, pages 98–104.

Widodo Budiharto, Vincent Andreas, and Alexander Agung Santoso Gunawan. 2021. A novel model and implementation of humanoid robot with facial expression and natural language processing (NIP). *ICIC Express Letters, Part B: Applications*, 12(3):275–281.

Marvin Jerremy Budiman and Dessi Puji Lestari. 2020. Multi speaker speech synthesis system for Indonesian language. *7th International Conference on Advanced Informatics: Concepts, Theory and Applications, ICAICTA 2020.*

Sari Dewi Budiwati and Masayoshi Aritsugi. 2019. Multiple pivots in statistical machine translation for low resource languages. *33rd Pacific Asia Conference on Language, Information and Computation, PACLIC 2019*, pages 345–355.

Sakti Putra Perdana Bunga Batara, Budhi Irawan, and Casi Setianingsih. 2019. Hate speech detection in Indonesian language on Instagram comment section using deep neural network classification method. *5th IEEE Asia Pacific Conference on Wireless and Mobile, APWiMob 2019*, pages 143–149.

Ghulam Asrofi Buntoro, Rizal Arifin, Gus Nanang Syaifuddiin, Ali Selamat, O. Krejcar, and H. Fujita. 2021. Implementation of a machine learning algorithm for sentiment analysis of Indonesia's 2019 presidential election. *IIUM Engineering Journal*, 22(1):78–92.

Francesco Burroni, Sireemas Maspong, Pittayawat Pittayaporn, and Pimthip Kochaiyaphum. 2020. A new look at Pattani Malay initial geminates: a statistical and machine learning approach. In *Proceedings of the 34th Pacific Asia Conference on Language, Information and Computation*, pages 21–29.

Bianka Buschbeck and Miriam Exel. 2020. A parallel evaluation data set of software documentation with document structure annotation. In *Proceedings of the 7th Workshop on Asian Translation*, pages 160–169. Association for Computational Linguistics.

Alson Cahyadi and Masayu Leylia Khodra. 2018. Aspect-based sentiment analysis using convolutional neural network and bidirectional long short-term memory. *5th International Conference on Advanced Informatics: Concepts Theory and Applications, ICAICTA 2018*, pages 124–129.

Denis Eka Cahyani, Langlang Gumilar, and Ajie Pangestu. 2020. Indonesian parsing using Probabilistic Context-Free Grammar (PCFG) and Viterbi-Cocke Younger Kasami (Viterbi-CYK). *3rd International Seminar on Research of Information Technology and Intelligent Systems, ISRITI 2020*, pages 56–61.

Denis Eka Cahyani, Ruli Manurung, and Rahmad Mahendra. 2016. Knowledge representation system for copula sentence in Bahasa Indonesia based on Web Ontology Language (OWL). *International Conference on Advanced Computer Science and Information Systems, ICACSIS 2015*, pages 137–142.

Denis Eka Cahyani and Mtchael Juan Vindiyanto. 2019. Indonesian part of speech tagging using hidden markov model - ngram viterbi. *4th International Conference on Information Technology, Information Systems and Electrical Engineering, ICITISEE 2019*, pages 353–358.

Elok Cahyaningtyas and Dhany Arifianto. 2018. Development of under-resourced Bahasa Indonesia speech corpus. *9th Asia-Pacific Signal and Information Processing Association Annual Summit and Conference, APSIPA ASC 2017*, 2018-February:1097–1101.

Risma Mustika Cahyaningtyas, Retno Kusumaningrum, Sutikno, Suhartono, and Djalal Er Riyanto. 2017. Emotion detection of tweets in Indonesian language using LDA and expression symbol conversion. *1st International Conference on Informatics and Computational Sciences, ICICoS 2017*, 2018-January:253–257.

Zefeng Cai, Nankai Lin, Chuyu Ma, and Shengyi Jiang. 2019. Indonesian automatic text summarization based on a new clustering method in sentence level. *2019 International Conference on Big Data Engineering, BDE 2019*, pages 30–35.

A. Candra, Wella, and A. Wicaksana. 2021. Bidirectional encoder representations from transformers for cyberbullying text detection in Indonesian social media. *International Journal of Innovative Computing, Information and Control*, 17(5):1599–1615.

Henri Chambert-Loir. 2019. The particle pun in modern Indonesian and Malaysian (La particule pun en Indonésien et Malaisien modernes.). *Archipel. Études interdisciplinaires sur le monde insulindien*, (98):177–237.

Reza Chandra, M. Agung Sucipta Iskandar, Lintang Yuniar Banowosari, Adang Suhendra, and Prihandoko Prihandoko. 2019. Building corpus in Bahasa Indonesia for pornographic indicated website content. *5th International Conference on Computing Engineering and Design, ICCED 2019*.

Khalifa Chekima and Rayner Alfred. 2016. An automatic construction of Malay stop words based on aggregation method. *2nd International Conference on Soft Computing in Data Science, SCDS 2016*, 652:180–189.

Khalifa Chekima and Rayner Alfred. 2018. Sentiment analysis of Malay social media text. *4th International Conference on Computational Science and Technology, ICCST17*, 488:205–219.

Khalifa Chekima, Rayner Alfred, and Kim On Chin. 2018. Rule-based model for Malay text sentiment analysis. *4th International Conference on Computational Science and Technology, ICCST17*, 488:172–185.

Feng Chen, Jian Yang, and Lixuan Zhao. 2020. A bilingual speech synthesis system of standard Malay and Indonesian based on HMM-DNN. *2020 International Conference on Asian Language Processing, IALP 2020*, pages 181–186.

Andry Chowanda and Alan Darmasaputra Chowanda. 2017. Recurrent neural network to deep learn conversation in Indonesian. *2nd International Conference on Computer Science and Computational Intelligence, ICCSCI 2017*, 116:579–586.

Andry Chowanda and Alan Darmasaputra Chowanda. 2018. Generative Indonesian conversation model using recurrent neural network with attention mechanism. *3rd International Conference on Computer Science and Computational Intelligence, ICCSCI 2018*, 135:433–440.

Christianto, Julio Christian Young, and Andre Rusli. 2020. Evaluating RNN architectures for handling imbalanced dataset in multi-class text classification in Bahasa Indonesia. *International Journal of Advanced Trends in Computer Science and Engineering*, 9(5):8418–8423.

Chong Chai Chua, Tek Yong Lim, Lay-Ki Soon, Enya Kong Tang, and Bali Ranaivo-Malançon. 2017. Meaning preservation in Example-based Machine Translation with structural semantics. *Expert Systems with Applications*, 78:242–258.

S. Chua and P. N. E. Nohuddin. 2017. Relationship analysis of keyword and chapter in Malay-translated tafseer of Al-Quran. *Journal of Telecommunication, Electronic and Computer Engineering*, 9(2-10):185–189.

Siaw-Fong Chung. 2019. Lagi in standard Malaysian Malay: Its meaning conceptualization. *Concentric: Studies in Linguistics*, 45(1):82–111.

Siaw-Fong Chung and Meng-Hsien Shih. 2019. An annotated news corpus of Malaysian Malay. *Nusa*, pages 7–34.

Paolo Coluzzi. 2017. Language planning for Malay in Malaysia: A case of failure or success? *International Journal of the Sociology of Language*, 2017(244):17–38.

Mohammad Darwich, Shahrul Azman Mohd Noah, and Nazlia Omar. 2017. Minimally-supervised sentiment lexicon induction model: A case study of Malay sentiment analysis. *11th Multi-disciplinary International Workshop on Artificial Intelligence, MIWAI 2017*, 10607 LNAI:225–237.

Robby Darwis, Herry Sujaini, and Rudy Dwi Nyoto. 2019. Peningkatan mesin penerjemah statistik dengan menambah kuantitas korpus monolingual (studi kasus: Bahasa Indonesia-Sunda). *JUSTIN (Jurnal Sistem dan Teknologi Informasi)*, 7(1):27–32.

Karlina Denistia and R. Harald Baayen. 2019. The Indonesian prefixes PE- and PEN-: A study in productivity and allomorphy. *Morphology*, 29(3):385.

Destiani, Andayani, and Muhammad Rohmadi. 2018a. Vocabulary load on two mainstream Indonesian textbooks for foreign learners: A comparative study. *International Journal of Social Sciences & Educational Studies*, 5(2):137–151.

Andayani Destiani, Andayani Andayani, and Muhammad Rohmadi. 2018b. Perbandingan deiksis pada dua buku ajar: Analisis kontrastif BIPA dan Bahasa Inggris. *Jurnal Pendidikan Bahasa dan Sastra*, 18(2):151–162.

Dyah Ayu Cyntya Dewi, Shaufiah, and Ibnu Asror. 2018. Analysis and implementation of cross lingual short message service spam filtering using graph-based k-nearest neighbor. *International Conference on Data and Information Science 2017, ICoDIS 2017*, 971.

Haru Deliana Dewi, Andika Wijaya, and Rahayu S. Hidayat. 2021. English legalese translation into Indonesian. *Wacana*, 21(3):446–474.

Intan Novita Dewi, Rahmat Nurcahyo, and Farizal. 2020. Word cloud result of mobile payment user review in Indonesia. *7th IEEE International Conference on Industrial Engineering and Applications, ICIEA 2020*, pages 989–992.

Dhammajoti, Julio Christian Young, and Andre Rusli. 2020. A comparison of supervised text classification and resampling techniques for user feedback in Bahasa Indonesia. *5th International Conference on Informatics and Computing, ICIC 2020*.

Fudholi Dhomas Hatta and Juwairi Kiki Purnama. 2021. Classifying medical document in Bahasa Indonesia using semi-supervised learning. *IOP Conference Series. Materials Science and Engineering*, 1077(1).

M. M. Din, N. H. H. Hashim, and M. M. Siraj. 2017. Comparative study on corpus development for Malay investment fraud detection in website. *Journal of Fundamental and Applied Sciences*, 9(6S):828–838.

Arawinda Dinakaramani and Totok Suhardijanto. 2019. Building a web-based application for language resources in Indonesia. *2nd International Conference on Data and Information Science, ICoDIS 2018*, 1192.

Chenchen Ding, Masao Utiyama, and Eiichiro Sumita. 2016. Similar southeast Asian languages: Corpus-based case study on Thai-Laotian and Malay-Indonesian. In *Proceedings of the 3rd Workshop on Asian Translation (WAT2016)*, pages 149–156. The COLING 2016 Organizing Committee.

Zuraidah Mohd Don and Gerry Knowles. 2020. New tools for old tasks: A new approach to the investigation of Malay. *Journal on Asian Linguistic Anthropology*, 2(3):21–38.

Mohamad Draman, Din Chai Tee, Zainuddin Lambak, Mohd Razman Yahya, Mohd Izwardi Bin Mohd Yusoff, S. H. Ibrahim, Shahril Saidon, N. Abu Haris, and Tien-Ping Tan. 2017. Malay speech corpus of telecommunication call center preparation for ASR. *5th International Conference on Information and Communication Technology, ICoIC7 2017*.

Meisyarah Dwiastuti. 2019. English-Indonesian neural machine translation for spoken language domains. In *Proceedings of the 57th Annual Meeting of the Association for Computational Linguistics: Student Research Workshop*, pages 309–314. Association for Computational Linguistics.

Suci Dwijayanti, Muhammad Abid Tami, and Bhakti Yudho Suprapto. 2021. Speech-to-text conversion in Indonesian language using a deep bidirectional long short-term memory algorithm. *International Journal of Advanced Computer Science and Applications*, 12(3):225–230.

Diyan Ermawan Effendi and Muchammadun. 2018. “happiness” in Bahasa Indonesia and its implication to health and community well-being. *Asian EFL Journal*, 20(8):279–291.

Sukmawati Nur Endah, Satriyo Adhy, and Sutikno. 2017. Comparison of feature extraction MFCC and LPC in automatic speech recognition for Indonesian. *Telkomnika (Telecommunication Computing Electronics and Control)*, 15(1):292–298.

Elvira Erizal, Budhi Irawan, and Casi Setianingsih. 2019. Hate speech detection in Indonesian language on Instagram comment section using maximum entropy classification method. *2nd International Conference on Information and Communications Technology, ICOIACT 2019*, pages 533–538.

Muhammad Izzuddin Eshak, Rohiza Ahmad, and Aliza Sarlan. 2018. A preliminary study on hybrid sentiment model for customer purchase intention analysis in social commerce. *2017 IEEE Conference on Big Data and Analytics, ICBDA 2017*, 2018-January:61–66.

Ditari Salsabila Esperanti and Ayu Purwarianti. 2016. Relation extraction using dependency tree kernel for Bahasa Indonesia. *4th IGNITE Conference and 2016 International Conference on Advanced Informatics: Concepts, Theory and Application, ICAICTA 2016*.

Alaba Ayotunde Fadele, Amirrudin Kamsin, Khadher Ahmad, and Rasheed Abubakar Rasheed. 2020. A novel hadith authentication mobile system in Arabic to Malay language translation for android and iOS phones. *International Journal of Information Technology (Singapore)*, 13(4):1683–1692.

Ahmad Fadly. 2018. Pengembangan kamus pemelajar Bahasa Indonesia bagi penutur asing tingkat dasar di Universitas Muhammadiyah Jakarta. *Pena Literasi*, 1(2):74–80.

Fahmi Fahmi, Meganingrum Arista Jiwanggi, and Mirna Adriani. 2020. Speech-emotion detection in an Indonesian movie. In *Proceedings of the 1st Joint Workshop on Spoken Language Technologies for Under-resourced languages (SLTU) and Collaboration and Computing for Under-Resourced Languages (CCURL)*, volume Language Resources and Evaluation Conference (LREC 2020), pages 185–193. European Language Resources Association (ELRA).

Muhammad Fairuzz Fairuzz Hiloh, Mohd Juzaiddin Ab Aziz, and Lailatul Qadri Zakaria. 2018. The effectiveness of bottom up technique with probabilistic approach for a Malay parser. *GEMA Online Journal of Language Studies*, 18(2):124–133.

Edi Faisal, Farza Nurifan, and Riyanarto Sarno. 2018. Word sense disambiguation in Bahasa Indonesia using svm. *3rd International Seminar on Application for Technology of Information and Communication, iSemantic 2018*, pages 239–243.

Ahmad Muammar Fanani and Suyanto Suyanto. 2021. Syllabification model of Indonesian language named-entity using syntactic n-gram. *5th International Conference on Computer Science and Computational Intelligence, ICCSCI 2020*, 179:721–727.

Laina Farsiah, Yi-Shin Chen, and Alim Misbullah. 2020. Multi-classes emotion detection for unbalanced indonesian tweets. *2020 International Conference on Electrical Engineering and Informatics, ICELTICs 2020*, 2020-October.

M. Ali Fauzi. 2018. Random forest approach fo sentiment analysis in Indonesian language. *Indonesian Journal of Electrical Engineering and Computer Science*, 12(1):46–50.

M. Ali Fauzi and Anny Yuniarti. 2018. Ensemble method for Indonesian Twitter hate speech detection. *Indonesian Journal of Electrical Engineering and Computer Science*, 11(1):294–299.

Ridi Ferdiana, William Fajar, Desi Dwi Purwanti, Artmita Sekar Tri Ayu, and Fahim Jatmiko. 2019. Twitter sentiment analysis in under-resourced languages using byte-level recurrent neural model. *International Journal of Advanced Computer Science and Applications*, 10(8):108–112.

Ivan Ferdino and Andre Rusli. 2019. Using naïve bayes classifier for application feedback classification and management in Bahasa Indonesia. *5th International Conference on New Media Studies, CONMEDIA 2019*, pages 217–222.

Mohammad Fikri and Riyanarto Sarno. 2019. A comparative study of sentiment analysis using svm and senti word net. *Indonesian Journal of Electrical Engineering and Computer Science*, 13(3):902–909.

Devi Fitrianah, Dwiki Jatikusumo, and Ida Nurhaida. 2020. D-loc apps: A location detection application based on social media platform in the event of a flood disaster. *2nd Asia Pacific Information Technology Conference, APIT 2020*, pages 41–45.

Novi Sofia Fitriasari, Khalifa Esha Iftitah, and Rizky Rachman Judhie Putra. 2017. Indonesian document retrieval using vector space method. *3rd International Conference on Science in Information Technology, ICSITech 2017*, 2018-January:664–668.

Yingwen Fu, Nankai Lin, Xiaotian Lin, and Shengyi Jiang. 2021. Towards corpus and model: Hierarchical structured-attention-based features for Indonesian named entity recognition. *Journal of Intelligent & Fuzzy Systems*, 41(1):1–12.

Shamsan Gaber, Mohd Zakree Ahmad Nazri, Nazlia Omar, and Salwani Abdullah. 2020. Part-of-speech (pos) tagger for Malay language using naÏve bayes and k-nearest neighbor model. *Journal of Critical Reviews*, 7(16):248–257.

Garmastewira Garmastewira and Masayu Leylia Khodra. 2019. Summarizing Indonesian news articles using graph convolutional network. *Journal of Information and Communication Technology*, 18(3):345–365.

Beat Gfeller, Vlad Schogol, and Keith Hall. 2016. Cross-lingual projection for class-based language models. In *Proceedings of the 54th Annual Meeting of the Association for Computational Linguistics (Volume 2: Short Papers)*, pages 83–88.

Hishshah Ghassani and Tricya Esterina Widagdo. 2018. Access to relational databases using interrogative sentences in Indonesian language. *5th International Conference on Data and Software Engineering, ICoDSE 2018*.

Yohanes Gultom and Wahyu Catur Wibowo. 2018. Automatic open domain information extraction from Indonesian text. *2017 International Workshop on Big Data and Information Security, WBIS 2017*, 2018-January:23–30.

Gunarso Gunarso, Hammam Riza, Elvira Nurfadhilah, M. Teduh Uliniansyah, Agung Santosa, and Lyla R. Aini. 2016. An overview of BPPT's Indonesian language resources. In *Proceedings of the 12th Workshop on Asian Language Resources (ALR12)*, pages 73–77.

D. Gunawan and A. Amalia. 2017. The design of lexical database for Indonesian language. *IOP Conference Series. Materials Science and Engineering*, 180(1).

D. Gunawan, A. Amalia, M. S. Lydia, and M. I. Muthaqin. 2018a. The observation of Bahasa Indonesia official computer terms implementation in scientific publication. *Journal of Physics: Conference Series*, 979(1).

D. Gunawan, A. Amalia, and O. N. Maringga. 2019a. Building the application to identify incorrect capital letters writing in Bahasa Indonesia. *Journal of Physics: Conference Series*, 1235(1).

D. Gunawan, A. Pasaribu, R. F. Rahmat, and R. Budiarto. 2017a. Automatic text summarization for Indonesian language using textteaser. *IOP Conference Series. Materials Science and Engineering*, 190(1).

Dani Gunawan and Amalia Amalia. 2018. Review of the recent research on automatic text summarization in Bahasa Indonesia. *3rd International Conference on Informatics and Computing, ICIC 2018*.

Dani Gunawan, Amalia Amalia, and Indra Charisma. 2017b. Automatic extraction of multiword expression candidates for Indonesian language. *6th IEEE International Conference on Control System, Computing and Engineering, ICCSCE 2016*, pages 304–309.

Dani Gunawan, Siti Hazizah Harahap, and Romi Fadillah Fadillah Rahmat. 2019b. Multi-document summarization by using textrank and maximal marginal relevance for text in Bahasa Indonesia. *10th International Conference on ICT for Smart Society, ICISS 2019*.

Dani Gunawan, Syaiful Anwar Husen Lubis, Romi Fadillah Rahmat, and Ainul Hizriadi. 2019c. Building the pornography corpus for Bahasa Indonesia based on TRUST+™ positif database. *10th International Conference on ICT for Smart Society, ICISS 2019*.

Dani Gunawan, Fanindia Purnamasari, Ranti Ramadhiana, and Romi Fadillah Rahmat. 2020. Keyword extraction from scientific articles in Bahasa Indonesia using textrank algorithm. *4th International Conference on Electrical, Telecommunication and Computer Engineering, ELTICOM 2020*, pages 260–264.

Dani Gunawan, Hardiani Putri Siregar, and Opim Salim Sitompul. 2019d. Identifying sentence structure in Bahasa Indonesia by using pos tag and lalr parser. *5th International Conference on Computing Engineering and Design, ICCED 2019*.

Deri Gunawan, Rendra Mahardika, Feri Ranja, Sarah Purnamawati, and Ivan Jaya. 2019e. The identification of pornographic sentences in Bahasa Indonesia. *5th Information Systems International Conference, ISICO 2019*, 161:601–606.

Reza Gunawan, Ichan Taufik, Edi Mulyana, Opik Taupik Kurahman, Muhammad Ali Ramdhani, and Mahmud Mahmud. 2019f. Chatbot application on internet of things (iot) to support smart urban agriculture. *5th International Conference on Wireless and Telematics, ICWT 2019*.

Teddy Surya Gunawan, Rashida Husain, and Mira Kartiwi. 2018b. Development of language identification system using mfcc and vector quantization. *4th IEEE International Conference on Smart Instrumentation, Measurement and Applications, ICSIMA 2017*, 2017-November:1–4.

William Gunawan, Derwin Suhartono, Fredy Purnomo, and Andrew Ongko. 2018c. Named-entity recognition for Indonesian language using bidirectional lstm-cnns. *3rd International Conference on Computer Science and Computational Intelligence, ICCSCI 2018*, 135:425–432.

Tri Wahyu Guntara, Alham Fikri Aji, and Radityo Eko Prasojo. 2020. Benchmarking multidomain English-Indonesian machine translation. In *Proceedings of the 13th Workshop on Building and Using Comparable Corpora*, pages 35–43.

Abid Nurul Hakim, Rahmad Mahendra, Mima Adriani, and Adrianus Saga Ekakristi. 2018. Corpus development for Indonesian consumer-health question answering system. *9th International Conference on Advanced Computer Science and Information Systems, ICACSIS 2017*, 2018-January:222–227.

Harnisa Azrin Hakimi and Nurazzah Abd Rahman. 2021. Developing the covid-19 Malay corpus using wordpress content management system (cms). In *5th International Conference on Information Retrieval and Knowledge Management, CAMP 2021*, pages 75–83. Institute of Electrical and Electronics Engineers Inc.

Christian Halim, Alfan Farizki. Wicaksono, and Mirna Adriani. 2018. Extracting disease-symptom relationships from health question and answer forum. *21st International Conference on Asian Language Processing, IALP 2017*, 2018-January:87–90.

Mohd Pouzi Hamzah and Syarifah Fatem Na'imah Binti Syed Kamaruddin. 2021. Open text ontology mining to improve retrievals of information. *International Journal of Advanced Computer Science and Applications*, 12(7):504–511.

Raseeda Hamzah, Nursuriati Jamil, Khyrina Airin Fariza Abu Samah, Nur Nabilah Abu Mangshor, Nurbaity Sabri, and Rosniza Roslan. 2017. Comparing statistical classifiers for emotion classification. *7th IEEE International Conference on System Engineering and Technology, ICSET 2017*, pages 183–188.

Novita Hanafiah, Alexander Kevin, Charles Sutanto, Fiona, Yulyani Arifin, and Jaka Hartanto. 2017. Text normalization algorithm on Twitter in complaint category. *2nd International Conference on Computer Science and Computational Intelligence, ICCSCI 2017*, 116:20–26.

Dini Handayani, Normi Sham Awang Abu Bakar, Hamwira Yaacob, and Mustafa Ali Abuzaraida. 2018. Sentiment analysis for Malay language: systematic literature review. *2018 International Conference on Information and Communication Technology for the Muslim World (ICT4M)*, pages 305–310.

Dellon Handrata, Christian Nathaniel Purwanto, Fransisca Haryanti Chandra, Joan Santoso, and Gunawan. 2019. Part of speech tagging for Indonesian language using bidirectional long short-term memory. *1st International Conference on Cybernetics and Intelligent System, ICORIS 2019*, pages 85–88.

Rafizah Mohd Hanifa, Khalid Isa, Shamsul Mohamad, Shaharil Moh Shah, Shelena Soosay Nathan, Rosni Ramle, and Mazniha Berahim. 2019. Voiced and unvoiced separation in Malay speech using zero crossing rate and energy. *Indonesian Journal of Electrical Engineering and Computer Science*, 16(2):775–780.

Haslizatul Mohamed Hanum and Zainab Abu Bakar. 2016a. Evaluation of energy and duration on Malay phrase breaks. *9th Asia International Conference on Mathematical Modelling and Computer Simulation - Asia Modelling Symposium, AMS 2015*, pages 101–104.

Haslizatul Mohamed Hanum and Zainab Abu Bakar. 2016b. Sentence segmentation and phrase strength estimation in Malay continuous speech. *8th Speech Prosody 2016*, 2016-January:1163–1166.

Haslizatul Mohamed Hanum, Syazwani Nasaruddin, and Zainab Abu Bakar. 2017. Prosodic breaks on Malay speech corpus: Evaluation of pitch, intensity and duration. *3rd International Conference on Information Retrieval and Knowledge Management, CAMP 2016*, pages 43–47.

Haslizatul Mohamed Hanum, Nur Farhana Rasip, and Zainab Abu Bakar. 2019. Multi-word similarity and retrieval model for a refined retrieval of quranic sentences. *6th International Conference on Advances in Visual Informatics, IVIC 2019*, 11870 LNCS:380–389.

Mukhtar Haris, Moch Arif Bijaksana, and Totok Suhardijanto. 2019. Warning and suggestion system on syntax tree maker application. *22nd International Conference on Asian Language Processing, IALP 2018*, pages 113–117.

Hanny Haryanto and Aripin. 2019. A finite state machine model to determine syllables of Indonesian text. *1st International Conference on Cybernetics and Intelligent System, ICORIS 2019*, pages 238–241.

Uswatun Hasanah, Tri Astuti, Rizki Wahyudi, Zanuar Rifai, and Rilas Agung Pambudi. 2018. An experimental study of text preprocessing techniques for automatic short answer grading in Indonesian. *3rd International Conference on Information Technology, Information Systems and Electrical Engineering, ICITISEE 2018*, pages 230–234.

Siti Zubaidah Mohd Hashim and Hajar Abdul Rahim. 2016. Defying the global: The cultural connotations of "Islam" in Malaysia. *Kemanusiaan*, 23(Supp. 2):81–98.

Ramos Janoah Hasudungan and Ayu Purwarianti. 2019. Relation detection for Indonesian language using deep neural network - support vector machine. *22nd International Conference on Asian Language Processing, IALP 2018*, pages 290–296.

Mohamad Hazim, Nor Badrul Anuar, Mohd Faizal Ab Razak, and Nor Aniza Abdullah. 2018. Detecting opinion spams through supervised boosting approach. *PLoS ONE*, 13(6):e0198884.

Alex Henry and Debbie G. E. Ho. 2016. Code-switching in bruneian online retail transactions. *World Englishes*, 35(4):554–570.

Herlawati, Rahmadya Trias Handayanto, Didik Setiyadi, and Endang Retnoningsih. 2019. Corpus usage for sentiment analysis of a hashtag Twitter. *4th International Conference on Informatics and Computing, ICIC 2019*.

John Hewitt, Daphne Ippolito, Brendan Callahan, Reno Kriz, Derry Tanti Wijaya, and Chris Callison-Burch. 2018. Learning translations via images with a massively multilingual image dataset. In *Proceedings of the 56th Annual Meeting of the Association for Computational Linguistics (Volume 1: Long Papers)*, pages 2566–2576.

Risanuri Hidayat, Priyatmadi, and Welly Ikawijaya. 2016. Wavelet based feature extraction for the vowel sound. *2nd International Conference on Information Technology Systems and Innovation, ICITSI 2015.*

A. F. Hidayatullah and M. R. Ma'arif. 2017. Preprocessing tasks in Indonesian Twitter messages. *Journal of Physics: Conference Series*, 801(1).

Ahmad Fathan Hidayatullah, Wisnu Kurniawan, and Chanifah Indah Ratnasari. 2019. Topic modeling on Indonesian online shop chat. *3rd International Conference on Natural Language Processing and Information Retrieval, NLPIR 2019*, pages 121–126.

Ahmad Fathan Hidayatullah, Elang Cergas Pembrani, Wisnu Kurniawan, Gilang Akbar, and Ridwan Pranata. 2018. Twitter topic modeling on football news. *3rd International Conference on Computer and Communication Systems, ICCCS 2018*, pages 94–98.

Ahmad Fathan Hidayatullah, Chanifah Indah Ratnasari, and Satrio Wisnugroho. 2016. Analysis of stemming influence on Indonesian tweet classification. *Telkomnika (Telecommunication Computing Electronics and Control)*, 14(2):665–673.

Satria Nur Hidayatullah and Suyanto. 2019. Developing an adaptive language model for Bahasa Indonesia. *International Journal of Advanced Computer Science and Applications*, 10(1):488–492.

Mohd Hanafi Ahmad Hijazi, Lyndia Libin, Rayner Alfred, and Frans Coenen. 2017. Bias aware lexicon-based sentiment analysis of Malay dialect on social media data: A study on the Sabah language. *2nd International Conference on Science in Information Technology, ICSITech 2016*, pages 356–361.

Awaliyatul Hikmah, Sumarni Adi, and Mulia Sulistiyono. 2020. The best parameter tuning on rnn layers for Indonesian text classification. *3rd International Seminar on Research of Information Technology and Intelligent Systems, ISRITI 2020*, pages 94–99.

Xavier Hinaut and Johannes Twiefel. 2020. Teach your robot your language! Trainable neural parser for modeling human sentence processing: Examples for 15 languages. *IEEE Transactions on Cognitive and Developmental Systems*, 12(2):179–188.

Julia Hirschberg and Christopher D. Manning. 2015. Advances in natural language processing. *Science*, 349(6245):261–266.

Devin Hoesen, Dessi Puji Lestari, and Dwi Hendratmo Widyantoro. 2018. Shared-hidden-layer deep neural network for under-resourced language the content. *Telkomnika (Telecommunication Computing Electronics and Control)*, 16(3):1226–1238.

Devin Hoesen, Fanda Yuliana Putri, and Dessi Puji Lestari. 2019. Automatic pronunciation generator for Indonesian speech recognition system based on sequence-to-sequence model. *22nd Conference of the Oriental COCOSDA International Committee for the Co-ordination and Standardisation of Speech Databases and Assessment Techniques, O-COCOSDA 2019.*

Tom G. Hoogervorst. 2018. Utterance-final particles in Klang Valley Malay. *Wacana*, 19(2):291–326.

Ahmad Hany Hossny and Lewis Mitchell. 2019. Event detection in Twitter: A keyword volume approach. *18th IEEE International Conference on Data Mining Workshops, ICDMW 2018*, 2018-November:1200–1208.

Tan Kim Hua, Hamdi Khalis, Nur Ehsan Mohd-Said, and Ong Song Howe. 2021. The polarity of war metaphors in sports news: A corpus-informed analysis. *GEMA Online Journal of Language Studies*, 21(2):238–252.

Tan Kim Hua, Shahidatul Maslina Mat So'od, and Bahiyah Abdul Hamid. 2019. Communicating insults in cyberbullying. *SEARCH (Malaysia)*, 11(3):91–109.

Khodijah Hulliyah, Husni Teja Sukmana, Normi Sham Abu Bakar, and Amelia Ritahani Ismail. 2019. Indonesian affective word resources construction in valence and arousal dimension for sentiment analysis. *6th International Conference on Cyber and IT Service Management, CITSM 2018.*

Khodijah Hulliyah, Abdul Wahab, Norhaslinda Kamaruddin, Sevki Erdogan, and Yusuf Durachman. 2017. Analysis of Indonesian sentiment text based on affective space model (ASM) using electroencephalogram (EEG) signals. *1st International Conference on Informatics and Computing, ICIC 2016*, pages 325–328.

Mohd Zabidin Husin, Saidah Saad, and Shahrul Azman Mohd Noah. 2018. Syntactic rule-based approach for extracting concepts from quranic translation text. *6th International Conference on Electrical Engineering and Informatics, ICEEI 2017*, 2017-November:1–6.

Husni, Ika Oktavia Suzanti, Yoga Dwitya Pramudita, Putro Sigit Susanto, and Lukman Heryawan. 2020. Web service for search engine Bahasa Indonesia (sebi). *Journal of Physics: Conference Series*, 1569(2).

Amalia Asti Hutami, Moch Arif Bijaksana, and Arie Ardiyanti Suryani. 2019. Paraphrase construction of Al Quran in Indonesian language translation. *7th International Conference on Information and Communication Technology, ICoICT 2019.*

Jacqueline Ibrahim and Dessi Puji Lestari. 2018. Classification and clustering to identify spoken dialects in Indonesian. *4th International Conference on Data and Software Engineering, ICoDSE 2017*, 2018-January:1–6.

Noor Jamaliah Ibrahim, Mohd Yamani Idna Idris, Mohd Yakub Zulkifli Mohd Yusoff, Noor Naemah Abdul Rahman, and Mawil Izzi Dien. 2019. Robust feature extraction based on spectral and prosodic features for classical Arabic accents recognition. *Malaysian Journal of Computer Science*, 2019(Special Issue 3):46–72.

Muhammad Okky Ibrohim and Indra Budi. 2019a. Multi-label hate speech and abusive language detection in Indonesian Twitter. Proceedings of the Third Workshop on Abusive Language Online, pages 46–57. Association for Computational Linguistics.

Muhammad Okky Ibrohim and Indra Budi. 2019b. Translated vs non-translated method for multilingual hate speech identification in Twitter. *International Journal on Advanced Science, Engineering and Information Technology*, 9(4):1116–1123.

Muhammad Okky Ibrohim, Muhammad Akbar Setiadi, and Indra Budi. 2019. Identification of hate speech and abusive language on Indonesian Twitter using the word2vec, part of speech and emoji features. *2019 International Conference on Advanced Information Science and System, AISS 2019*.

Nur Oktavin Idris, Widyawan, and Teguh Bharata Adji. 2019. Classification of radicalism content from Twitter written in Indonesian language using long short term memory. *3rd International Conference on Informatics and Computational Sciences, ICICOS 2019*.

M. Ikhwan Syafiq, M. Shukor Talib, Naomie Salim, Habibollah Haron, and Razana Alwee. 2019. A concise review of named entity recognition system: Methods and features. *International Conference on Green Engineering Technology and Applied Computing 2019, IConGETech2 019 and International Conference on Applied Computing 2019, ICAC 2019*, 551.

Helmi Imaduddin, Widyawan, and Silmi Fauziati. 2019. Word embedding comparison for Indonesian language sentiment analysis. *1st International Conference of Artificial Intelligence and Information Technology, ICAIIT 2019*, pages 426–430.

Imamah, Husni, Eka Malasari Rachman, Ika Oktavia Suzanti, and Fifin Ayu Mufarroha. 2020. Text mining and support vector machine for sentiment analysis of tourist reviews in bangkalan regency. *Journal of Physics: Conference Series*, 1477(2).

Zul Indra, Jafreezal Jaafar, Norshuhani Zamin, and Zainab Abu Bakar. 2016. A language identifier for Indonesian and Malay text document. *2015 International Symposium on Mathematical Sciences and Computing Research, iSMSC 2015*, pages 127–131.

Budi Irmawati, Hiroyuki Shindo, and Yuji Matsumoto. 2016. Exploiting syntactic similarities for preposition error corrections on Indonesian sentences written by second language learner. *5th Workshop on Spoken Language Technologies for Under-resourced languages, SLTU 2016*, 81:214–220.

Budi Irmawati, Hiroyuki Shindo, and Yuji Matsumoto. 2017a. A dependency annotation scheme to extract syntactic features in Indonesian sentences. *International Journal of Technology*, 8(5):957–967.

Budi Irmawati, Hiroyuki Shindo, and Yuji Matsumoto. 2017b. Generating artificial error data for Indonesian preposition error corrections. *International Journal of Technology*, 8(3):549–558.

Ann Irvine and Chris Callison-Burch. 2017. A comprehensive analysis of bilingual lexicon induction. *Computational Linguistics*, 43(2):273.

Asiah Ismail, Anida Sarudin, Zulkifli Osman, and Husna Faredza Mohamed Redzwan. 2021. The process of forming a more complex idiomatic meaning using a principle of integration metaphors. *GEMA Online Journal of Language Studies*, 21(2):86–110.

B. H. Iswanto and V. Poerwoto. 2018. Sentiment analysis on Bahasa Indonesia tweets using unibigram models and machine learning techniques. *IOP Conference Series. Materials Science and Engineering*, 434(1).

Jafreezal Jaafar, Zul Indra, and Nurshuhaini Zamin. 2016. A category classification algorithm for Indonesian and Malay news documents. *Jurnal Teknologi*, 78(8-2):121–132.

Aris Tri Jaka Harjanta and Bambang Agus Herlambang. 2020. Extraction sentiment analysis using naive bayes algorithm and reducing noise word applied in Indonesian language. *7th International Conference on DV-Xa Method: The Advances-Related Experiments and Theories on Material Science, ICDM 2019*, 835.

Norezmi Jamal, N Fuad, and M. N. A. H. Sha'abani. 2020. A hybrid approach for single channel speech enhancement using deep neural network and harmonic regeneration noise reduction. *International Journal of Advanced Computer Science and Applications*, 11(10):243–248.

Muhammad Nabil Fikri Jamaluddin, Siti Zaleha Zainal Abidin, and Nasiroh Omar. 2017. Classification and quantification of user's emotion on Malay language in social network sites using latent semantic analysis. *2016 IEEE Conference on Open Systems, ICOS 2016*, pages 65–70.

Muhammad Ihsan Jambak, Fathey Mohammed, Novita Hidayati, Rusdi Efendi, and Rifkie Primartha. 2019. The impacts of singular value decomposition algorithm toward Indonesian language text documents clustering. *3rd International Conference of Reliable Information and Communication Technology, IRICT 2018*, 843:173–183.

Muhammad Ihsan Jambak and Putri Sanggabuana Setiawan. 2018. The development of Bahasa Indonesia corpora for machine learning model in combating cyber bullying: A case study of the Indonesian 2017 capital city governor election. *Journal of Theoretical and Applied Information Technology*, 96(7):1971–1988.

Nursuriati Jamil, Farihah Apandi, and Raseeda Hamzah. 2017. Influences of age in emotion recognition of spontaneous speech: A case of an under-resourced language. *9th International Conference on Speech Technology and Human-Computer Dialogue, SpeD 2017*.

Nurul Syafidah Jamil, Siti Sakira Kamaruddin, and Farzana Kabir Ahmad. 2019. Social tension and crime related events detection method on Twitter. *International Journal of Advanced Trends in Computer Science and Engineering*, 8(6):2821–2824.

Laura A. Janda. 2022. Managing Data and Statistical Code According to the FAIR Principles. In *The Open Handbook of Linguistic Data Management*. The MIT Press.

S. Jiang, S. Li, S. Fu, and N. Lin. 2020. An overview of natural language processing for Indonesian and Malay. *Moshi Shibie yu Rengong Zhineng/Pattern Recognition and Artificial Intelligence*, 33(6):530–541.

Meganingrum Arista Jiwanggi and Mirna Adriani. 2016. Topic summarization of microblog document in Bahasa Indonesia using the phrase reinforcement algorithm. *5th Workshop on Spoken Language Technologies for Under-resourced languages, SLTU 2016*, 81:229–236.

Andreas Jodhinata and Lusia Hartanti. 2016. Naïve bayes implementation into Bahasa Indonesia stemmer for content based webpage classification. *International Journal of Applied Business and Economic Research*, 14(11):8211–8223.

Mohammed Kaity and Vimala Balakrishnan. 2020. An integrated semi-automated framework for domain-based polarity words extraction from an unannotated non-English corpus. *Journal of Supercomputing*, 76(12):9772–9799.

Constantijn Kaland and Stefan Baumann. 2020. Demarcating and highlighting in Papuan Malay phrase prosody. *Journal of the Acoustical Society of America*, 147(4):2974–2988.

Constantijn Kaland and Nikolaus P. Himmelmann. 2020. Repetition reduction revisited: The prosody of repeated words in Papuan Malay. *Language and Speech*, 63(1):31–55.

Constantijn Kaland, Nikolaus P. Himmelmann, and Angela Kluge. 2019. Stress predictors in a Papuan Malay random forest. In *Proceedings of the 19th International Congress of Phonetic Sciences*, pages 2871–2875.

Constantijn Kaland, Angela Kluge, and Vincent J. Van Heuven. 2021. Lexical analyses of the function and phonology of Papuan Malay word stress. *Phonetica*, 78(2):141–168.

Syarifah Fatem Na'imah Binti Syed Kamaruddin, Fatihah Mohd, Mohd Pouzi Hamzah, Fadilah Harun, Noor Raihani Zainol, and Nurul Izyan Mat Daud. 2021. Information retrieval for Malay text: A decade review of research (2008-2019). In *5th International Conference on Information Retrieval and Knowledge Management, CAMP 2021*, pages 2–7. Institute of Electrical and Electronics Engineers Inc.

Rathimala Kannan, Ki Soon Lay, and Menagaeswary Govindasamy. 2019. Review on the role of social media for dengue prevention and monitoring. *Applied Mechanics and Materials*, 892:228–233.

Yeni Karlina, Amin Rahman, and Raqib Chowdhury. 2020. Designing phonetic alphabet for Bahasa Indonesia (PABI) for the teaching of intelligible English pronunciation in indonesia. *Indonesian Journal of Applied Linguistics*, 9(3):724–732.

Junaini Kasdan, Rusmadi Baharuddin, and Anis Shahira Shamsuri. 2020. Covid-19 dalam korpus peristilahan Bahasa Melayu: Analisis sosioterminologi (Covid-19 in the corpus of Malay terminology: A socio-terminological analysis). *GEMA Online Journal of Language Studies*, 20(3):221–241.

Junaini Kasdan, Harshita Aini Haroon, Nor Suhaila Che Pa, and Zuhairah Idrus. 2017. Gandaan separa dalam terminologi Bahasa Melayu: Analisis sosioterminologi (Partial reduplication in Malay terminology: A socio-terminological analysis). *GEMA Online Journal of Language Studies*, 17(1):183–202.

Emaliana Kasmuri and Halizah Basiron. 2019. Building a Malay-English code-switching subjectivity corpus for sentiment analysis. *International Journal of Advances in Soft Computing and its Applications*, 11(1):112–130.

Emaliana Kasmuri and Halizah Basiron. 2020. Segregation of code-switching sentences using rule-based technique. *International Journal of Advances in Soft Computing and its Applications*, 12(1):49–64.

Mohamad Nizam Kassim, Shaifal Hisham Mat Jali, Mohd Aizaini Maarof, and Anazida Zainal. 2019. Towards stemming error reduction for Malay texts. *5th International Conference on Computational Science and Technology, ICCST 2018*, 481:13–23.

Mohamad Nizam Kassim, Shaifal Hisham Mat Jali, Mohd Aizaini Maarof, Anazida Zainal, and Amirudin Abdul Wahab. 2020a. Design consideration of Malay text stemmer using structured approach. In *3rd International Conference on Smart Trends for Information Technology and Computer Communications, SmartCom 2019*, volume 165, pages 421–432. Springer.

Mohamad Nizam Kassim, Shaifal Hisham Mat Jali, Mohd Aizaini Maarof, Anazida Zainal, and Amirudin Abdul Wahab. 2020b. Enhanced text stemmer with noisy text normalization for Malay texts. In *3rd International Conference on Smart Trends for*

Information Technology and Computer Communications, SmartCom 2019, volume 165, pages 433–444. Springer.

Mohamad Nizam Kassim, Mohd Aizaini Maarof, Anazida Zainal, and Amirudin Abdul Wahab. 2016a. Enhanced rules application order to stem affixation, reduplication and compounding words in Malay texts. *14th International Workshop on Knowledge Management and Acquisition for Intelligent Systems, PKAW2016*, 9806 LNCS:71–85.

Mohamad Nizam Kassim, Mohd Aizaini Maarof, Anazida Zainal, and Amirudin Abdul Wahab. 2016b. Malay word stemmer to stem standard and slang word patterns on social media. *Lecture Notes in Computer Science (including subseries Lecture Notes in Artificial Intelligence and Lecture Notes in Bioinformatics)*, 9714 LNCS:391–400.

Mohamad Nizam Kassim, Mohd Aizaini Maarof, Anazida Zainal, and Amirudin Abdul Wahab. 2016c. Word stemming challenges in Malay texts: A literature review. *4th International Conference on Information and Communication Technology, ICoICT 2016*.

Wandeep Kaur and Vimala Balakrishnan. 2016. Bilingual sentiment detection - investigating impact of tweet translation. *7th International Conference on Applications of Digital Information and Web Technologies, ICADIWT 2016*, 282:105–111.

Siti Oryza Khairunnisa, Aizhan Imankulova, and Mamoru Komachi. 2020. Towards a standardized dataset on Indonesian named entity recognition. In *Proceedings of the 1st Conference of the Asia-Pacific Chapter of the Association for Computational Linguistics and the 10th International Joint Conference on Natural Language Processing: Student Research Workshop*, pages 64–71. Association for Computational Linguistics.

Nur Firza Shafiqa Khalid and Normaliza Abd Rahim. 2021. Pola penggunaan Bahasa Melayu dalam Twitter mantan Perdana Menteri ke-enam, Dato' Seri Najib Razak (Patterns of Malay language usage on Twitter of former sixth Prime Minister, Dato' Seri Najib Razak). *Jurnal Komunikasi: Malaysian Journal of Communication*, 37(2):195–209.

Yen-Min Jasmina Khaw, Tien-Ping Tan, and Bali Ranaivo-Malançon. 2017. Automatic phoneme identification for Malay dialects. *Journal of Telecommunication, Electronic and Computer Engineering*, 9(2-9):85–94.

Lau Su Kia and Awab Su'Ad. 2019. A study of education-related Chinese words used in Malaysia-based computer corpus. *Kajian Malaysia*, 37(1):83–107.

Xuan Kong and Jian Yang. 2018. Indonesian corpus constructing and text processing for speech synthesis. In *2018 International Conference on Asian Language Processing (IALP)*, pages 193–196. IEEE.

Fajri Koto. 2016. A publicly available Indonesian corpora for automatic abstractive and extractive chat summarization. In *Proceedings of the Tenth International Conference on Language Resources and Evaluation (LREC'16)*, pages 801–805.

Fajri Koto and Ikhwan Koto. 2020. Towards computational linguistics in Minangkabau language: Studies on sentiment analysis and machine translation. In *Proceedings of the 34th Pacific Asia Conference on Language, Information and Computation*, pages 138–148.

Fajri Koto, Jey Han Lau, and Timothy Baldwin. 2020a. Liputan6: A large-scale Indonesian dataset for text summarization. In *Proceedings of the 1st Conference of the Asia-Pacific Chapter of the Association for Computational Linguistics and the 10th International Joint Conference on Natural Language Processing*, pages 598–608.

Fajri Koto, Afshin Rahimi, Jey Han Lau, and Timothy Baldwin. 2020b. IndoLEM and IndoBERT: A benchmark dataset and pre-trained language model for Indonesian nlp. Proceedings of the 28th International Conference on Computational Linguistics, page 7. International Committee on Computational Linguistics.

Dinar Ajeng Kristiyanti, Akhmad Hairul Umam, Mochamad Wahyudi, Ruhul Amin, and Linda Marlinda. 2019. Comparison of svm naïve bayes algorithm for sentiment analysis toward West Java governor candidate period 2018-2023 based on public opinion on Twitter. *6th International Conference on Cyber and IT Service Management, CITSM 2018*.

Deffri Kun Indarta and Ade Romadhony. 2021. Aspect and opinion extraction of Indonesian lipsticks product reviews using conditional random field (crf). *13th International Conference Knowledge and Smart Technology, KST 2021*, pages 113–117.

Rafly Indra Kurnia and Abba Suganda Girsang. 2021. Classification of user comment using word2vec and deep learning. *International Journal of Emerging Technology and Advanced Engineering*, 11(5):1–8.

Lilis Kurniasari and Arief Setyanto. 2020a. Sentiment analysis using recurrent neural network-lstm in Bahasa Indonesia. *Journal of Engineering Science and Technology*, 15(5):3242–3256.

Lilis Kurniasari and Arif Setyanto. 2020b. Sentiment analysis using recurrent neural network. *Journal of Physics: Conference Series*, 1471(1).

Farhan Wahyu Kurniawan and Warih Maharani. 2020. Indonesian Twitter sentiment analysis using word2vec. *2020 International Conference on Data Science and Its Applications, ICoDSA 2020*.

Kemal Kurniawan and Samuel Louvan. 2018. Empirical evaluation of character-based model on neural named-entity recognition in Indonesian conversational texts.

In *Proceedings of the 2018 EMNLP Workshop W-NUT: The 4th Workshop on Noisy User-generated Text*, pages 85–92. Association for Computational Linguistics.

Rahmad Kurniawan, Fitra Lestari, Abdul Somad Batubara, Mohd Zakree Ahmad Nazri, Khairunnas Rajab, and Rinaldi Munir. 2021. Indonesian lexicon-based sentiment analysis of online religious lectures review. In *2021 International Congress of Advanced Technology and Engineering, ICOTEN 2021*. Institute of Electrical and Electronics Engineers Inc.

Selvia Ferdiana Kusuma, Daniel Siahaan, and Umi Laili Yuhana. 2016. Automatic Indonesia's questions classification based on bloom's taxonomy using natural language processing a preliminary study. *2nd International Conference on Information Technology Systems and Innovation, ICITSI 2015*.

Renny Pradina Kusumawardani and Siti Oryza Khairunnisa. 2019. Author-topic modelling for reviewer assignment of scientific papers in Bahasa Indonesia. *22nd International Conference on Asian Language Processing, IALP 2018*, pages 351–356.

Renny Pradina Kusumawardani and Muhammad Wildan Maulidani. 2020. Aspect-level sentiment analysis for social media data in the political domain using hierarchical attention and position embeddings. *2020 International Conference on Data Science and Its Applications, ICoDSA 2020*.

Renny Pradina Kusumawardani, Stezar Priansya, and Faizal Johan Atletiko. 2018. Context-sensitive normalization of social media text in Bahasa Indonesia based on neural word embeddings. *3rd International Neural Network Society Conference on Big Data and Deep Learning, INNS BDDL 2018*, 144:105–117.

Deny A. Kwary. 2019. A corpus platform of Indonesian academic language. *SoftwareX*, 9:102–106.

Teguh Puji Laksono, Ahmad Fathan Hidayatullah, and Chanifah Indah Ratnasari. 2019. Speech to text of patient complaints for Bahasa Indonesia. *22nd International Conference on Asian Language Processing, IALP 2018*, pages 79–84.

Tang Sui Lan and Rajasvaran Logeswaran. 2020. Challenges and development in Malay natural language processing. *Journal of Critical Reviews*, 7(3):61–65.

Anisa Larassati, Nina Setyaningsih, Raden Arief Nugroho, Valentina Widya Suryaningtyas, Setyo Prasiyanto Cahyono, and Stephani Diah Pamelasari. 2019. Google vs. Instagram machine translation: Multilingual application program interface errors in translating procedure text genre. *2019 International Seminar on Application for Technology of Information and Communication, iSemantic 2019*, pages 554–558.

Jeremia Jason Lasiman and Dessi Puji Lestari. 2019. Speech emotion recognition for Indonesian language using long short-term memory. *6th International Conference on Computer, Control, Informatics and its Applications, IC3INA 2018*, pages 40–43.

Tuan Anh Le, David Moeljadi, Yasuhide Miura, and Tomoko Ohkuma. 2016. Sentiment analysis for low resource languages: A study on informal Indonesian tweets. In *Proceedings of the 12th Workshop on Asian Language Resources (ALR12)*, pages 123–131.

Joanna Chiew Ling Lee, Phoey Lee Teh, Sian Lun Lau, and Irina Pak. 2019. Compilation of Malay criminological terms from online news. *Indonesian Journal of Electrical Engineering and Computer Science*, 15(1):355–364.

Sungyoon Lee, Li-Jen Kuo, Zhihong Xu, and Xueyan Hu. 2020. The effects of technology-integrated classroom instruction on k-12 english language learners' literacy development: a meta-analysis. *Computer Assisted Language Learning*, 0(0):1–32.

Rezka Aufar Leonandya, Bayu Distiawan, and Nursidik Heru Praptono. 2016. A semi-supervised algorithm for Indonesian named entity recognition. *3rd International Symposium on Computational and Business Intelligence, ISCBI 2015*, pages 45–50.

Boon Pang Lim, Faith Wong, Yuyao Li, and Jia Wei Bay. 2016. Transfer learning with bottleneck feature networks for whispered speech recognition. *17th Annual Conference of the International Speech Communication Association, INTERSPEECH 2016*, 08-12-September-2016:1578–1582.

Hui Ting Lim, Sharin Hazlin Huspi, and Roliana Ibrahim. 2021. A conceptual framework for Malay-English mixed-language question answering system. In *2021 International Congress of Advanced Technology and Engineering, ICOTEN 2021*. Institute of Electrical and Electronics Engineers Inc.

Shin Huei Lim and Terry Halpin. 2016. Automated verbalization of orm models in Malay and Mandarin. *International Journal of Information System Modeling and Design*, 7(4):1–16.

Nankai Lin, Sihui Fu, Jiawen Huang, and Shengyi Jiang. 2019a. Exploring letter's differences between partial Indonesian branch language and English. *23rd International Conference on Asian Language Processing, IALP 2019*, pages 84–89.

Nankai Lin, Sihui Fu, Shengyi Jiang, Chen Chen, Lixian Xiao, and Gangqin Zhu. 2019b. Learning Indonesian frequently used vocabulary from large-scale news. *22nd International Conference on Asian Language Processing, IALP 2018*, pages 234–239.

Nankai Lin, Sihui Fu, Shengyi Jiang, Gangqin Zhu, and Yanni Hou. 2019c. Exploring lexical differences between Indonesian and Malay. *22nd International Conference on Asian Language Processing, IALP 2018*, pages 178–183.

Chen Liu, Anderson De Andrade, and Muhammad Osama. 2019a. Exploring multilingual syntactic sentence representations. In *Proceedings of the 5th Workshop on Noisy User-generated Text (W-NUT 2019)*, pages 153–159.

Wuying Liu and Lin Wang. 2019. Malay-corpus-enhanced Indonesian-Chinese neural machine translation. *10th International Symposium on Intelligence Computation and Applications, ISICA 2018*, 986:239–248.

Wuying Liu and Lin Wang. 2020. Transfer building of multiword expression resource from Indonesian to Malay. *2020 International Conference on Asian Language Processing, IALP 2020*, pages 299–304.

Wuying Liu, Lin Xiao, Shengyi Jiang, and Lin Wang. 2019b. Language resource extension for Indonesian-Chinese machine translation. *22nd International Conference on Asian Language Processing, IALP 2018*, pages 221–225.

Chek Kim Loi and Jason Miin-Hwa Lim. 2019. Hedging in the discussion sections of English and Malay educational research articles. *GEMA Online Journal of Language Studies*, 19(1):36–61.

Yu-Zane Low, Lay-Ki Soon, and Shageenderan Sapai. 2020. A neural machine translation approach for translating Malay parliament hansard to English text. *2020 International Conference on Asian Language Processing, IALP 2020*, pages 316–320.

Manuel Mager, Özlem Çetinoğlu, and Katharina Kann. 2020. Tackling the low-resource challenge for canonical segmentation. In *Proceedings of the 2020 Conference on Empirical Methods in Natural Language Processing (EMNLP)*, pages 5237–5250. Association for Computational Linguistics.

Made Raharja Surya Mahadi, Anditya Arifianto, and Kurniawan Nur Ramadhani. 2020. Adaptive attention generation for Indonesian image captioning. *8th International Conference on Information and Communication Technology, ICoICT 2020*.

Nurul Husna Mahadzir, Mohd Faizal Omar, and Mohd Nasrun Mohd Nawi. 2018. Semantic similarity measures for Malay-English ambiguous words. *Journal of Telecommunication, Electronic and Computer Engineering*, 10(1-11):109–112.

Rahmad Mahendra, Abid Nurul Hakim, and Mirna Adriani. 2018a. Towards question identification from online healthcare consultation forum post in bahasa. *21st International Conference on Asian Language Processing, IALP 2017*, 2018-January:399–402.

Rahmad Mahendra, Heninggar Septiantri, Haryo Akbarianto Wibowo, Ruli Manurung, and Mirna Adriani. 2018b. Cross-lingual and supervised learning approach for Indonesian word sense disambiguation task. In *Proceedings of the 9th Global Wordnet Conference*, pages 245–250.

Syiti Liviani Mahfiz and Ade Romadhony. 2020. Aspect-based opinion mining on beauty product reviews. *3rd International Seminar on Research of Information Technology and Intelligent Systems, ISRITI 2020*, pages 488–493.

Nurul Hashimah Ahamed Hassain Malim, Saravanan Sagadevan, and Nurul Izzati Ridzuwan. 2019. Criminality recognition using machine learning on Malay language tweets. *Pertanika Journal of Science and Technology*, 27(4):1803–1820.

Gamaria Mandar and Gunawan Gunawan. 2017. Peringkasan dokumen berita Bahasa Indonesia menggunakan metode cross latent semantic analysis. *Register: Jurnal Ilmiah Teknologi Sistem Informasi*, 3(2):94–104.

Lindung Parningotan Manik, Hani Febri Mustika, Zaenal Akbar, Yulia Aris Kartika, Dadan Ridwan Saleh, Foni Agus Setiawan, and Ika Atman Satya. 2020. Aspect-based sentiment analysis on candidate character traits in Indonesian presidential election. *2020 International Conference on Radar, Antenna, Microwave, Electronics, and Telecommunications, ICRAMET 2020*, pages 224–228.

Lindung Parningotan Manik, Arida Ferti Syafiandini, Hani Febri Mustika, Achmad Fatchuttamam Abka, and Yan Rianto. 2019. Evaluating the morphological and capitalization features for word embedding-based pos tagger in Bahasa Indonesia. *6th International Conference on Computer, Control, Informatics and its Applications, IC3INA 2018*, pages 49–53.

N. A. W. Mansor and Nor Hashimah Jalaluddin. 2016. The implicit meaning in Malay figurative language: Synergising communication, cognition and semantics. *Jurnal Komunikasi: Malaysian Journal of Communication*, 32(1):189–206.

Teddy Mantoro, Media Anugerah Ayu, and Rahmadya Trias Handayanto. 2020. Machine learning approach for sentiment analysis in crime information retrieval. *3rd International Conference on Computer and Informatics Engineering, IC2IE 2020*, pages 96–100.

Ngalim Markhamah Abdul, Muhammad Muinudinillah Basri, and Atiqa Sabardila. 2017. Comparison of personal pronoun between Arabic and its Indonesian translation of Koran. *International Journal of Applied Linguistics & English Literature*, 6(5):238–254.

Marlyn Maseri and Mazlina Mamat. 2019. Malay language speech recognition for preschool children using Hidden Markov Model (HMM) system training. *Computational Science and Technology*, pages 205–214.

Ruhaila Maskat, Muhammad Faizzuddin Zainal, Nurrissammimayantie Ismail, Norizah Ardi, Amirah Ahmad, and Norizah Daud. 2020. Automatic labelling of Malay cyberbullying Twitter corpus using combinations of sentiment, emotion and toxicity polarities.

3rd International Conference on Algorithms, Computing and Artificial Intelligence, ACAI 2020.

Ruhaila Maskat and Yuda Munarko. 2019. A taxonomy of Malay social media text. *Indonesian Journal of Electrical Engineering and Computer Science*, 16(1):465–472.

Ruhaila Maskat and Nurazzah Abdul Rahman. 2020. Categorization of Malay social media text and normalization of spelling variations and vowel-less words. *International Journal on Advanced Science, Engineering and Information Technology*, 10(4):1380–1386.

Mohd Masnizah, Fauzi Wan Fariza Paizi, and Amri Jasin. 2018. Teknik pengukuhan perangkak tumpuan melalui modul pengesan bahasa bagi capaian web Bahasa Melayu (Focused crawler enhancement technique with language detection module for Malay web retrieval). *GEMA Online Journal of Language Studies*, 18(3):170–185.

Eleanor Mattern. 2022. The Linguistic Data Life Cycle, Sustainability of Data, and Principles of Solid Data Management. In *The Open Handbook of Linguistic Data Management*. The MIT Press.

Muhammad Rizki Aulia Rahman Maulana and Mohamad Ivan Fanany. 2018a. Indonesian audio-visual speech corpus for multimodal automatic speech recognition. *9th International Conference on Advanced Computer Science and Information Systems, ICACSIS 2017*, 2018-January:381–385.

Muhammad Rizki Aulia Rahman Maulana and Mohamad Ivan Fanany. 2018b. Sentence-level Indonesian lip reading with spatiotemporal cnn and gated rnn. *9th International Conference on Advanced Computer Science and Information Systems, ICACSIS 2017*, 2018-January:375–380.

Nur Maulidiah Elfajr and Riyanarto Sarno. 2018. Sentiment analysis using weighted emoticons and SentiWordNet for Indonesian language. *3rd International Seminar on Application for Technology of Information and Communication, iSemantic 2018*, pages 234–238.

Candy Olivia Mawalim, Dessi Puji Lestari, and Ayu Purwarianti. 2017. Rule-based reordering and post-processing for Indonesian-Korean statistical machine translation. Proceedings of the 31st Pacific Asia Conference on Language, Information and Computation, pages 287–295. The National University (Phillippines).

Zara Maxwell-Smith. 2021. Fossicking in dominant language teaching: Javanese and Indonesian 'low' varieties in language teaching resources. *Proceedings of the Workshop on Computational Methods for Endangered Languages*, 1:24–32.

Zara Maxwell-Smith and Ben Foley. 2021. Developing ASR for Indonesian-English bilingual language teaching. In *Proceedings of the Fifth Workshop on Computational Approaches to Linguistic Code-Switching*, pages 131–132.

Zara Maxwell-Smith, Simón González Ochoa, Ben Foley, and Hanna Suominen. 2020. Applications of natural language processing in bilingual language teaching: An Indonesian-English case study. In *Proceedings of the Fifteenth Workshop on Innovative Use of NLP for Building Educational Applications*, pages 124–134.

Dian Sa'adillah Maylawati, Cecep Nurul Alam, Muhammad Fakhri Muharram, Muhammad Ali Ramdhani, Abdusy Syakur Amin, and Hilmi Aulawi. 2020. The purpose of bellman-ford algorithm to summarize the multiple scientific Indonesian journal articles. *6th International Conference on Wireless and Telematics, ICWT 2020.*

Dian Sa'adillah Maylawati, Yogan Jaya Kumar, Fauziah Binti Kasmin, and Basit Raza. 2019. Sequential pattern mining and deep learning to enhance readability of Indonesian text summarization. *International Journal of Advanced Trends in Computer Science and Engineering*, 8(6):3147–3159.

Niknik Mediyawati, Julio Christian Young, and Samiaji Bintang Nusantara. 2021. U-tapis: Automatic spelling filter as an effort to improve Indonesian language competencies of journalistic students. *Cakrawala Pendidikan*, 40(2):402–412.

Mirwan, Aryo Nugroho, Ferial Hendarta, Rumaisah Hidayatillah, Firdaus Hassan, and Kristovel Printo Nana. 2018. Virtual assistant using lstm networks in Indonesian. *2018 International Seminar on Research of Information Technology and Intelligent Systems, ISRITI 2018*, pages 652–655.

Paramita Mirza. 2016. Recognizing and normalizing temporal expressions in Indonesian texts. *14th International Conference of the Pacific Association for Computaitonal Linguistics, PACLING 2015*, 593:135–147.

Vivensius Mitra, Herry Sujaini, and Arif Bijaksana Putra Negara. 2017. Rancang bangun aplikasi web scraping untuk korpus paralel indonesia-inggris dengan metode html dom. *JUSTIN (Jurnal Sistem dan Teknologi Informasi)*, 5(1):36–41.

David Moeljadi and Francis Bond. 2016. Identifying and exploiting definitions in wordnet bahasa. In *Proceedings of the 8th Global WordNet Conference (GWC)*, pages 227–233. Global Wordnet Association.

Abdul Karim Mohamad, Mailasan Jayakrishnan, and Nurnajwa Hazwani Nawi. 2020a. Classification of Twitter data by sentiment analysis in the Malay language. *International Journal of Emerging Trends in Engineering Research*, 8(6):2730–2738.

Abdul Karim Mohamad, Mailasan Jayakrishnan, and Nurnajwa Hazwani Nawi. 2020b. Employ Twitter data to perform sentiment analysis in the Malay language. *International Journal of Advanced Trends in Computer Science and Engineering*, 9(2):1404–1412.

Hasnah Mohamad, Noorul Khairien Abdul Malek, and Noor Husna Abd. Razak. 2020c. Formation of health science terminology by users in general Malay language texts. *GEMA Online Journal of Language Studies*, 20(3):96–112.

Noor Hasnoor Mohamad Nor, Eizah Mat Hussain, and Ahmad Ramizu Abdullah. 2019. Politeness in communication through local children's animated film. *Jurnal Komunikasi: Malaysian Journal of Communication*, 35(4):368–385.

Hassan Mohamed, Nazlia Omar, and Mohd Juzaiddin Ab Aziz. 2018. The effectiveness of using Malay affixes for handling unknown words in unsupervised hmm pos tagger. *International Journal of Engineering & Technology*, 7(4.29):9–12.

Haslizatul Mohamed Hanum and Zainab Abu Bakar. 2016. Detection of Malay phrase breaks using energy and duration. *International Journal of Simulation: Systems, Science and Technology*, 17(32).

Saif M. Mohammad. 2020. Gender gap in natural language processing research: Disparities in authorship and citations. In *Proceedings of the 58th Annual Meeting of the Association for Computational Linguistics*, pages 7860–7870, Online. Association for Computational Linguistics.

Syuhairah Rahifah Mohammad Najib, Nurazzah Abd Rahman, Normaly Kamal Ismail, Nursyahidah Alias, Zulhilmi Mohamed Nor, and Muhammad Nazir Alias. 2017. Comparative study of machine learning approach on Malay translated hadith text classification based on sanad. *8th International Conference on Mechanical and Manufacturing Engineering, ICME 2017*, 135.

Mohd Amin Mohd Yunus, Aida Mustapha, Rizwan Iqbal, and Noor Azah Samsudin. 2017. An ontological approach towards dialogue based information visualization system: Quran corpus for Juz' Amma. *8th International Conference on Mechanical and Manufacturing Engineering, ICME 2017*, 135.

Nazri Mohd Zakree Ahmad, Kurniawan Tri Basuki, Hamdan Abdul Razak, Salwani Abdullah, and Mohammed Azlan Mis. 2018. Pembangunan taksonomi dari teks Melayu menggunakan algoritma kunang-kunang pembahagi dua sama (Taxonomy development from Malay text using firefly bisection algorithm). *GEMA Online Journal of Language Studies*, 18(2):182–201.

Rosmayati Mohemad, Nazratul Naziah Mohd Muhait, Noor Maizura Mohamad Noor, and Zulaiha Ali Othman. 2020a. A review of named entity recognition and classification on unstructured Malay data. *Journal of Theoretical and Applied Information Technology*, 98(23):3741–3756.

Rosmayati Mohemad, Nazratul Naziah Mohd Muhait, Noor Maizura Mohamad Noor, and Zulaiha Ali Othman. 2020b. Technique on Malay text summarization: A review. *International Journal of Advanced Science and Technology*, 29(6 Special Issue):814–822.

Rosmayati Mohemad, Muhait Nazratul Naziah Mohd, Noor Noor Maizura Mohamad, and Othman Zulaiha Ali. 2020c. Unstructured Malay text analytics model in crime. *IOP Conference Series. Materials Science and Engineering*, 769(1).

Itaza Afiani Mohtar, Masurah Mohamad, Puteri Nursyawati Azzuri, Nurazzah Abd Rahman, and Saidi Adnan Md Nor. 2021. Development of a web-based Jahai-Malay language repository. In *5th International Conference on Information Retrieval and Knowledge Management, CAMP 2021*, pages 14–18. Institute of Electrical and Electronics Engineers Inc.

Putra Fissabil Muhammad, Retno Kusumaningrum, and Adi Wibowo. 2021. Sentiment analysis using word2vec and long short-term memory (lstm) for Indonesian hotel reviews. *5th International Conference on Computer Science and Computational Intelligence, ICCSCI 2020*, 179:728–735.

Muljono, Umriya Afini, and Catur Supriyanto. 2017a. Morphology analysis for hidden markov model based Indonesian part-of-speech tagger. *1st International Conference on Informatics and Computational Sciences, ICICoS 2017*, 2018-January:237–240.

Muljono, Agus Harjoko, Sri Winarsih Nurul Anisa, and Catur Supriyanto. 2020. An evaluation of sentence selection methods on the different phone-sized units for constructing Indonesian speech corpus. *International Journal of Speech Technology*, 23(1):141–147.

Muljono, Surya Sumpeno, Dhany Arifianto, Kiyoaki Aikawa, and Mauridhi Purnomo. 2016. Developing an online self-learning system of Indonesian pronunciation for foreign learners. *International Journal of Emerging Technologies in Learning*, 11(4):83–89.

Muljono, Askarya Qaulan Syadida, De Rosal Ignatius Moses Setiadi, and A. Setyono. 2017b. Sphinx4 for Indonesian continuous speech recognition system. *2017 International Seminar on Application for Technology of Information and Communication, iSemantic 2017*, 2018-January:264–267.

Muljono Muljono, Umriya Afini, Catur Supriyanto, and Raden Nugroho. 2017c. The development of Indonesian POS tagging system for computer-aided independent language learning. *International Journal of Emerging Technologies in Learning*, 12(11):138–150.

Devi Munandar, Endang Suryawati, Dianadewi Riswantini, Achmad Fatchuttamam Abka, Rini Wijayanti, and Andria Arisal. 2017. Pos-tagging for non-English tweets: An automatic approach: (study in Bahasa Indonesia). *1st International Conference on Informatics and Computational Sciences, ICICoS 2017*, 2018-January:219–224.

Yohei Murakami. 2019. Indonesia language sphere: An ecosystem for dictionary development for low-resource languages. *Journal of Physics: Conference Series*, 1192(1).

Nurul Amelina Nasharuddin, Muhamad Taufik Abdullah, Azreen Azman, and Rabiah Abdul Kadir. 2017. English and Malay cross-lingual sentiment lexicon acquisition and analysis. *8th International Conference on Information Science and Applications, ICISA 2017*, 424:467–475.

Nurul Amelina Nasharuddin, Muhamad Taufik Abdullah, Azreen Azman, and Rabiah Abdul Kadir. 2018. A review on building bilingual comparable corpora for resource-limited languages. *4th International Conference on Information Retrieval and Knowledge Management: Diving into Data Sciences, CAMP 2018*, pages 113–118.

Nurul Amelina Nasharuddin, Muhamad Taufik Abdullah, Azreen Azman, and Rabiah Abdul Kadir. 2019. A framework for English and Malay cross-lingual document alignment method. *International Journal of Advanced Trends in Computer Science and Engineering*, 8(1.3 S1):190–195.

Muhammad Zahier Nasrudin, Ruhaila Maskat, and Ramli Musa. 2019. Detecting candidates of depression, anxiety and stress through Malay-written tweets: A preliminary study. *Indonesian Journal of Electrical Engineering and Computer Science*, 16(2):787–793.

Arbi Haza Nasution, Yohei Murakami, and Toru Ishida. 2019. Designing a collaborative process to create bilingual dictionaries of Indonesian ethnic languages. *11th International Conference on Language Resources and Evaluation, LREC 2018*, pages 3397–3404.

Halim Nataprawira and Michael D. Carey. 2020. Towards developing colloquial Indonesian language pedagogy: A corpus analysis. *Indonesian Journal of Applied Linguistics*, 10(2):382–396.

Rizka Putri Nawangsari, Retno Kusumaningrum, and Adi Wibowo. 2019. Word2vec for Indonesian sentiment analysis towards hotel reviews: An evaluation study. *4th International Conference on Computer Science and Computational Intelligence, ICCSCI 2019*, 157:360–366.

Shekhar Nayak, C Shiva Kumar, G. Ramesh, Saurabhchand Bhati, and K. Sri Rama Murty. 2019. Virtual phone discovery for speech synthesis without text. *7th IEEE Global Conference on Signal and Information Processing, GlobalSIP 2019*.

Bagas Pradipabista Nayoga, Ryan Adipradana, Ryan Suryadi, and Derwin Suhartono. 2021. Hoax analyzer for Indonesian news using deep learning models. *5th International Conference on Computer Science and Computational Intelligence, ICCSCI 2020*, 179:704–712.

Wayan Suastini Ni, Ketut Artawa, Yadnya Ida Bagus Putra, and I. Ketut Darma Laksana. 2018. Translation and markedness. *International Journal of Comparative Literature & Translation Studies*, 6(4):28–32.

Annisa Maulida Ningtyas and Guntur Budi Herwanto. 2018. The influence of negation handling on sentiment analysis in Bahasa Indonesia. *5th International Conference on Data and Software Engineering, ICoDSE 2018*.

Made Nindyatama Nityasya, Rahmad Mahendra, and Mirna Adriani. 2019. Hypernym-hyponym relation extraction from Indonesian wikipedia text. *22nd International Conference on Asian Language Processing, IALP 2018*, pages 285–289.

Muhammad Nizami and Ayu Purwarianti. 2017. Modification of chu-liu/edmonds algorithm and mira learning algorithm for dependency parser on Indonesian language. *2017 International Conference on Advanced Informatics: Concepts, Theory and Applications, ICAICTA 2017*.

Shahrul Azman Mohd Noah, Nazlena Mohamad Ali, and Mohd Sabri Hasan. 2018. Generation of news headline for Malay language based on term features. *GEMA Online Journal of Language Studies*, 18(4):42–59.

Zakiah Noh, Siti Zaleha Zainal Abidin, and Nasiroh Omar. 2019. Poetry visualization in digital technology. *Knowledge Management and Organizational Learning*, 7:171–195.

Hiroki Nomoto. 2020. Towards genuine stemming and lemmatization in Malay/Indonesian. In *Proceedings of the 26th Annual Meeting of the Natural Language Processing Society (March 2020)*.

Hiroki Nomoto, Shiro Akasegawa, and Asako Shiohara. 2018a. Reclassification of the leipzig corpora collection for Malay and Indonesian. *Nusa*, 65:47–66.

Hiroki Nomoto and David Moeljadi. 2019. Linguistic studies using large annotated corpora: introduction. *Nusa*, pages 1–6.

Hiroki Nomoto, Kenji Okano, David Moeljadi, and Hideo Sawada. 2018b. Tufs Asian language parallel corpus (talpco). *Proceedings of the Twenty-Fourth Annual Meeting of the Association for Natural Language Processing*, pages 436–439.

Huzaimi Karimah Mohd Noor Noor, Shahrul Azman Mohd Noah, and Mohd Juzaiddin Ab Aziz. 2020. Classification of short possessive clitic pronoun nya in Malay text to support anaphor candidate determination. *Journal of Information and Communication Technology*, 19(4):513–532.

Noorhuzaimi Moh Noor, Junaida Sulaiman, and Shahrul Azman Noah. 2016. Malay name entity recognition using limited resources. *Advanced Science Letters*, 22(10):2968–2971.

Muhamad Nor Azlizawati Binti, Norisma Idris, and Saloot Mohammad Arshi. 2017. Proposal: A hybrid dictionary modelling approach for Malay tweet normalization. *Journal of Physics: Conference Series*, 806(1).

Nor Nor Fariza Mohd, Rahman Anis Nadiah Che Abdul, Azhar Jaluddin, Abdullah Imran Ho, and Sabrina Tiun. 2019. A corpus driven analysis of representations around the word 'ekonomi' in Malaysian hansard corpus. *GEMA Online Journal of Language Studies*, 19(4):66–95.

Awal Norsimah Mat, Azhar Jaludin, Rahman Anis Nadiah Che Abdul, and Imran Ho-Abdullah. 2019. "Is Selangor in Deep Water?": A corpus-driven account of air/water in the Malaysian hansard corpus (mhc). *GEMA Online Journal of Language Studies*, 19(2):99–120.

Sashi Novitasari, Dessi Puji Lestari, Sakriani Sakti, and Ayu Purwarianti. 2019. Rude-words detection for Indonesian speech using support vector machine. *22nd International Conference on Asian Language Processing, IALP 2018*, pages 19–24.

Sashi Novitasari, Andros Tjandra, Sakriani Sakti, and Satoshi Nakamura. 2020. Cross-lingual machine speech chain for Javanese, Sundanese, Balinese, and Bataks speech recognition and synthesis. In *Proceedings of the 1st Joint Workshop on Spoken Language Technologies for Under-resourced languages (SLTU) and Collaboration and Computing for Under-Resourced Languages (CCURL)*, pages 131–138.

Aditya Alif Nugraha, Anditya Arifianto, and Suyanto. 2019. Generating image description on Indonesian language using convolutional neural network and gated recurrent unit. *7th International Conference on Information and Communication Technology, ICoICT 2019*.

Yanuar Nurdiansyah, Saiful Bukhori, and Rahmad Hidayat. 2018. Sentiment analysis system for movie review in Bahasa Indonesia using naive bayes classifier method. *Journal of Physics: Conference Series*, 1008(1).

M. Nurilman Baehaqi, Med. Irzal, and Fariani Hermin Indiyah. 2019. Morphological analysis of speech translation into Indonesian sign language system (SIBI) on android platform. *11th International Conference on Advanced Computer Science and Information Systems, ICACSIS 2019*, pages 205–210.

Vessa Rizky Oktavia, Umi Laili Laili Yuhana, Chastine Fatichah, and Ayu Purwarianti. 2021. WPS: Application for generating answer of word problem in Bahasa Indonesia. In *8th International Conference on ICT for Smart Society, ICISS 2021*. Institute of Electrical and Electronics Engineers Inc.

Ikmi Nur Oktavianti. 2019. A corpus-based analysis of English core modal verbs and their counterparts in Indonesian. *International Journal of Scientific and Technology Research*, 8(12):2811–2819.

Ikmi Nur Oktavianti and Zanuar Anggun Pramesti. 2019. Frequency of verbs in lifestyle column in the Jakarta Post and the relation to text characteristics: A corpus-based analysis. *IDEAS: Journal on English Language Teaching and Learning, Linguistics and Literature*, 7(2):233–246.

Nasiroh Omar, Ahmad Farhan Hamsani, Nur Atiqah Sia Abdullah, and Siti Zaleha Zainal Abidin. 2017. Construction of Malay abbreviation corpus based on social media data. *Journal of Engineering and Applied Sciences*, 12(3):468–474.

Salehah Omar, Juhaida Abu Bakar, Maslinda Mohd Nadzir, Nor Hazlyna Harun, and Nooraini Yusoff. 2021. Text simplification for Malay corpus: A review. In *6th International Conference on Computer and Information Sciences, ICCOINS 2021*, pages 345–350. Institute of Electrical and Electronics Engineers Inc.

Veronica Ong, Anneke Dwi Sesarika Rahmanto, Williem, Derwin Suhartono, Aryo E. Nugroho, Esther W. Andangsari, and Muhamad N. Suprayogi. 2017. Personality prediction based on Twitter information in Bahasa Indonesia. *2017 Federated Conference on Computer Science and Information Systems, FedCSIS 2017*, pages 367–372.

Veronica Ong, Anneke Dwi Sesarika Rahmanto, Williem Williem, Nicholaus H. Jeremy, Derwin Suhartono, and Esther W. Andangsari. 2021. Personality modelling of Indonesian Twitter users with xgboost based on the five factor model. *International Journal of Intelligent Engineering and Systems*, 14(2):248–261.

Norzanita Othman, Nor Nor Fariza Mohd, and Noraini Ibrahim. 2019. Linguistic representation of violence in judicial opinions in Malaysia. *GEMA Online Journal of Language Studies*, 19(2):82–98.

Matthew J. Page, Joanne E. McKenzie, Patrick M. Bossuyt, Isabelle Boutron, Tammy C. Hoffmann, Cynthia D. Mulrow, Larissa Shamseer, Jennifer M. Tetzlaff, Elie A. Akl, Sue E. Brennan, Roger Chou, Julie Glanville, Jeremy M. Grimshaw, Asbjørn Hróbjartsson, Manoj M. Lalu, Tianjing Li, Elizabeth W. Loder, Evan Mayo-Wilson, Steve McDonald, Luke A. McGuinness, Lesley A. Stewart, James Thomas, Anea C. Tricco, Vivian A. Welch, Penny Whiting, and David Moher. 2021. The PRISMA 2020 statement: an updated guideline for reporting systematic reviews. *BMJ (Clinical research ed.)*, 10(1):89–89.

Endang Wahyu Pamungkas and Divi Galih Prasetyo Putri. 2017. An experimental study of lexicon-based sentiment analysis on Bahasa Indonesia. *6th International Annual Engineering Seminar, InAES 2016*, pages 28–31.

Ningrum Panggih Kusuma, Tatdow Pansombut, and Attachai Ueranantasun. 2020. Text mining of online job advertisements to identify direct discrimination during job hunting process: A case study in Indonesia. *PLoS ONE*, 15(6):e0233746.

Bagus Pragnya Paramarta. 2018. Analisis korpus terhadap idiom Bahasa Indonesia yang berbasis nama binatang. *Lingua*, 14(1):18–25.

Edwina Anky Parande and Suyanto Suyanto. 2019. Indonesian graphemic syllabification using a nearest neighbour classifier and recovery procedure. *International Journal of Speech Technology*, 22(1):13–20.

Jasman Pardede and Mira Musrini Barmawi. 2016. Implementation of lsi method on information retrieval for text document in Bahasa Indonesia. *Internetworking Indonesia Journal*, 8(1):83–87.

W. G. S. Parwita. 2020. A document recommendation system of stemming and stopword removal impact: A web-based application. *Journal of Physics: Conference Series*, 1469(1).

Fahmi Candra Permana, Yusep Rosmansyah, and Atje Setiawan Abdullah. 2017. Naive bayes as opinion classifier to evaluate students satisfaction based on student sentiment in Twitter social media. *Asian Mathematical Conference 2016, AMC 2016*, 893.

Micah D.J. Peters, Christina M. Godfrey, Hanan Khalil, Patricia McInerney, Deborah Parker, and Cassia Baldini Soares. 2015. Guidance for conducting systematic scoping reviews. *JBI Evidence Implementation*, 13(3):141–146.

Mai T. Pham, Andrijana Rajić, Judy D. Greig, Jan M. Sargeant, Andrew Papadopoulos, and Scott A. McEwen. 2014. A scoping review of scoping reviews: Advancing the approach and enhancing the consistency. *Research synthesis methods*, 5(4):371–385.

Yuen Chi Phang, Azleena Mohd Kassim, and Ernest Mangantig. 2021. Concerns of thalassemia patients, carriers, and their caregivers in Malaysia: Text mining information shared on social media. *Healthcare Informatics Research*, 27(3):200–213.

Yeong-Tsann Phua, Kwang-Hooi Yew, Oi-Mean Foong, and Matthew Yok-Wooi Teow. 2020. Assessing suitable word embedding model for Malay language through intrinsic evaluation. *2020 International Conference on Computational Intelligence, ICCI 2020*, pages 202–210.

Dion Ajie Poetra, Tricya Esterina Widagdo, and Fazat Nur Azizah. 2019. Natural language interface to database (NLIDB) for query with temporal aspect. *2019 International Conference on Data and Software Engineering, ICoDSE 2019*.

Faizal Adhitama Prabowo, Muhammad Okky Ibrohim, and Indra Budi. 2019. Hierarchical multi-label classification to identify hate speech and abusive language on Indonesian Twitter. *6th International Conference on Information Technology, Computer and Electrical Engineering, ICITACEE 2019*.

Bayu Trisna Pratama, Ema Utami, and Andi Sunyoto. 2019. A comparison of the use of several different resources on lexicon based Indonesian sentiment analysis on app review dataset. *1st International Conference of Artificial Intelligence and Information Technology, ICAIIT 2019*, pages 282–287.

Septya Egho Pratama, Wahyudin Darmalaksana, Dian Sa'adillah Maylawati, Hamdan Sugilar, Teddy Mantoro, and Muhammad Ali Ramdhani. 2020. Weighted inverse document frequency and vector space model for hadith search engine. *Indonesian Journal of Electrical Engineering and Computer Science*, 18(2):1004–1014.

Timothy Pratama and Ayu Purwarianti. 2017. Topic classification and clustering on Indonesian complaint tweets for Bandung government using supervised and unsupervised learning. *2017 International Conference on Advanced Informatics: Concepts, Theory and Applications, ICAICTA 2017*.

Inggrid Yanuar Risca Pratiwi, Rosa Andrie Asmara, and Faisal Rahutomo. 2018. Study of hoax news detection using naïve bayes classifier in Indonesian language. *11th International Conference on Information and Communication Technology and System, ICTS 2017*, 2018-January:73–78.

Nur Indah Pratiwi, Indra Budi, and Ika Alfina. 2019. Hate speech detection on Indonesian Instagram comments using fasttext approach. *10th International Conference on Advanced Computer Science and Information Systems, ICACSIS 2018*, pages 447–450.

Prihantoro. 2016. The influence of students' L1 and spoken English in English writing: A corpus-based research. *TEFLIN Journal*, 27(2):217–245.

Prihantoro. 2021. An evaluation of morphind's morphological annotation scheme for Indonesian. *Corpora*, 16(2):287.

D. Purnamasari, R. Arianty, D. T. Susetianingtias, and R. D. Kusumawati. 2016. Query rewriting and corpus of semantic similarity as encryption method for documents in Indonesian language. *2nd International Conference on Electrical Systems, Technology and Information, ICESTI 2015*, 365:565–571.

K. K. Purnamasari and I. S. Suwardi. 2018. Rule-based part of speech tagger for Indonesian language. *International Conference on Informatics, Engineering, Science and Technology, INCITEST 2018*, 407.

Yohanes Sigit Purnomo W.P, Yogan Jaya Kumar, and Nur Zareen Zulkarnain. 2020. Understanding quotation extraction and attribution: towards automatic extraction of public figure's statements for journalism in Indonesia. *Global Knowledge, Memory and Communication*.

Dewi Puspita and Kamal Yusuf. 2020. Sketching the semantic change of jahanam and hijrah: A corpus based approach to manuscripts of Arabic-Indonesian lexicon. *Arabi: Journal of Arabic Studies*, 5(1):1–10.

Nurnasran Puteh, Mohd Zabidin Husin, Hatim Mohamad Tahir, and Azham Hussain. 2019. Building a question classification model for a Malay question answering system. *International Journal of Innovative Technology and Exploring Engineering*, 8(5s):184–190.

I Gede Manggala Putra and Dade Nurjanah. 2020. Hate speech detection in Indonesian language Instagram. *12th International Conference on Advanced Computer Science and Information Systems, ICACSIS 2020*, pages 413–420.

M. Iqbal D. Putra, Budi Irmawati, Wirarama Wedashwara, Dita Pramesti, and Siti Oryza Khairunnisa. 2020. Age group based document classification in Bahasa Indonesia. *2020 International Conference on Advancement in Data Science, E-Learning and Information Systems, ICADEIS 2020*.

Rahardyan Bisma Setya Putra, Ema Utami, and Suwanto Raharjo. 2018a. Non-formal affixed word stemming in Indonesian language. *1st International Conference on Information and Communications Technology, ICOIACT 2018*, 2018-January:531–536.

Rahardyan Bisma Setya Putra, Ema Utami, and Suwanto Raharjo. 2019. Accuracy measurement on Indonesian non-formal affixed word stemming with levenhstein. *2nd International Conference on Information and Communications Technology, ICOIACT 2019*, pages 486–490.

Syopiansyah Jaya Putra, Muhamad Nur Gunawan, Ismail Khalil, and Teddy Mantoro. 2017. Sentence boundary disambiguation for Indonesian language. *19th International Conference on Information Integration and Web-Based Applications and Services, iiWAS2017*, pages 587–590.

Syopiansyah Jaya Putra, Ismail Khalil, Muhamad Nur Gunawan, Riva'l Amin, and Tata Sutabri. 2018b. A hybrid model for social media sentiment analysis for Indonesian text. *20th International Conference on Information Integration and Web-Based Applications and Services, iiWAS 2018*, pages 297–301.

Fanda Yuliana Putri, Devin Hoesen, and Dessi Puji Lestari. 2019a. Rule-based pronunciation models to handle oov words for Indonesian automatic speech recognition system. *5th International Conference on Science in Information Technology, ICSITech 2019*, pages 246–251.

S. K. Putri, A. Amalia, E. B. Nababan, and O. S. Sitompul. 2021. Bahasa Indonesia pre-trained word vector generation using word2vec for computer and information technology field. In *5th International Conference on Computing and Applied Informatics, ICCAI 2020*, volume 1898. IOP Publishing Ltd.

Wahyuningdiah Trisari Harsanti Putri, Muhammad Singgih Prastio, Retno Hendrowati, Yustiana Sari, and Harry Tursulistyono Yani Achsan. 2019b. Content-based filtering model for recommendation of Indonesian legal article study case of klinik hukumonline. *2019 International Workshop on Big Data and Information Security, IWBIS 2019*, pages 9–14.

Xin Ying Qiu and Gangqin Zhu. 2016. Learning Indonesian-Chinese lexicon with bilingual word embedding models and monolingual signals. In *Proceedings of the 6th Workshop on South and Southeast Asian Natural Language Processing (WSSANLP2016)*, pages 188–193.

Valdi Rachman, Rahmad Mahendra, Alfan Farizki Wicaksono, Ahmad Rizqi Meydiarso, and Fariz Ikhwantri. 2018a. Semantic role labeling in conversational chat using deep bi-directional long short-term memory networks with attention mechanism. In *Proceedings of the 32nd Pacific Asia Conference on Language, Information and Computation*. Association for Computational Linguistics.

Valdi Rachman, Septiviana Savitri, Fithriannisa Augustianti, and Rahmad Mahendra. 2018b. Named entity recognition on Indonesian Twitter posts using long short-term memory networks. *9th International Conference on Advanced Computer Science and Information Systems, ICACSIS 2017*, 2018-January:228–232.

Suwanto Raharjo, Retantyo Wardoyo, and Agfianto E. Putra. 2018. Rule based sentence segmentation of Indonesian language. *Journal of Engineering and Applied Sciences*, 13(21):8986–8992.

Suwanto Raharjo, Retantyo Wardoyo, and Agfianto E. Putra. 2020. Detecting proper nouns in Indonesian-language translation of the Quran using a guided method. *Journal of King Saud University - Computer and Information Sciences*, 32(5):583–591.

Anis Nadiah Che Abdul Rahman, Imran Ho Abdullah, Intan Safinaz Zainudin, Sabrina Tiun, and Azhar Jaludin. 2021a. Domain-specific stop words in Malaysian parliamentary debates 1959 - 2018. *GEMA Online Journal of Language Studies*, 21(2):1–27.

Arief Rahman. 2018. Medical named entity recognition for Indonesian language using word representations. *IOP Conference Series. Materials Science and Engineering*, 325(1).

Arief Rahman and Ayu Purwarianti. 2017. Ensemble technique utilization for Indonesian dependency parser. In *Proceedings of the 31st Pacific Asia Conference on Language, Information and Computation*, pages 64–71.

Nurazzah Abd Rahman, Faiz Ikhwan Mohd Rafhan Syamil, and Shaiful Bakhtiar Bin Rodzman. 2020. Development of mobile application for Malay translated hadith search engine. *Indonesian Journal of Electrical Engineering and Computer Science*, 20(2):932–938.

Nurazzah Abd Rahman, Siti Nur Afiqah Ramlam, Natasha Aleza Azhar, Haslizatul Mohamed Hanum,

Noor Ida Ramli, and Najahudin Lateh. 2021b. Automatic text summarization for Malay news documents using latent dirichlet allocation and sentence selection algorithm. In *5th International Conference on Information Retrieval and Knowledge Management, CAMP 2021*, pages 36–40. Institute of Electrical and Electronics Engineers Inc.

Nurazzah Abd Rahman, Afiqah Bazlla Md Soom, and Normaly Kamal Ismail. 2017. Enhancing latent semantic analysis by embedding tagging algorithm in retrieving Malay text documents. *Studies in Computational Intelligence*, 710:309–319.

Rinaldi Andrian Rahmanda, Mirna Adriani, and Dipta Tanaya. 2019. Cross language information retrieval using parallel corpus with bilingual mapping method. *23rd International Conference on Asian Language Processing, IALP 2019*, pages 222–227.

Muhammad Abdillah Rahmat, Indrabayu, and Intan Sari Areni. 2019. Hoax web detection for news in bahasa using support vector machine. *2nd International Conference on Information and Communications Technology, ICOIACT 2019*, pages 332–336.

Laili Etika Rahmawati, Anggi Niasih, Hari Kusmanto, and Harun Joko Prayitno. 2020. Environmental awareness content for character education in grade 10 in Indonesian language student textbooks. *International Journal of Innovation, Creativity and Change*, (4):161–174.

F. Rahutomo, A. A. Septarina, M. Sarosa, A. Setiawan, and M. M. Huda. 2019. A review on Indonesian machine translation. *4th Annual Applied Science and Engineering Conference, AASEC 2019*, 1402.

Faisal Rahutomo, Alfi Samudro Mulyo, and Pramana Yoga Saputra. 2018. Automatic grammar checking system for Indonesian. *1st International Conference on Applied Science and Technology, iCAST 2018*, pages 308–313.

Reza Rahutomo, Arif Budiarto, Kartika Purwandari, and Anzaludin Samsinga Perbangsa. 2020. Ten-year compilation of #savekpk Twitter dataset. *5th International Conference on Information Management and Technology, ICIMTech 2020*, pages 185–190.

Roza Athirah Raja, Soon Lay-Ki, and Haw Su-Cheng. 2019. Exploring edit distance for normalising out-of-vocabulary Malay words on social media. *MATEC Web of Conferences*, 255:03001.

Gede Primahadi Wijaya Rajeg. 2020. Linguistik korpus kuantitatif dan kajian semantik leksikal sinonim emosi Bahasa Indonesia. *Linguistik Indonesia*, 38(2):123–150.

Gede Primahadi Wijaya Rajeg, Karlina Denistia, and Simon Musgrave. 2019. Vector space models and the usage patterns of Indonesian denominal verbs: a case study of verbs with meN-, meN-/-kan, and meN-/-i affixes. *Nusa*, pages 35–76.

Rajesvary Rajoo and Ching Chee Aun. 2016. Influences of languages in speech emotion recognition: A comparative study using Malay, English and Mandarin languages. *2016 IEEE Symposium on Computer Applications and Industrial Electronics, ISCAIE 2016*, pages 35–39.

Nahda Rosa Ramadhanti and Siti Mariyah. 2019. Document similarity detection using Indonesian language word2vec model. *3rd International Conference on Informatics and Computational Sciences, ICICOS 2019*.

Muhammad Ali Ramdhani, Dian Sa'adillah Maylawati, and Teddy Mantoro. 2020. Indonesian news classification using convolutional neural network. *Indonesian Journal of Electrical Engineering and Computer Science*, 19(2):1000–1009.

Al-khulaidi Rami Ali and Akmeliawati Rini. 2017. Speech to text translation for Malay language. *IOP Conference Series. Materials Science and Engineering*, 260(1).

I. Ramli, N. Jamil, N. Seman, and N. Ardi. 2017. The first Malay language storytelling text-to-speech (TTS) corpus for humanoid robot storytellers. *Journal of Fundamental and Applied Sciences*, 9(4S):340–354.

Izzad Ramli, Jamil Nursuriati, and Noraini Seman. 2021. An iterated two-step sinusoidal pitch contour formulation for expressive speech synthesis. *Journal of Information and Communication Technology*, 20(4):489–510.

Izzad Ramli, Noraini Seman, Norizah Ardi, and Nursuriati Jamil. 2016. Prosody analysis of Malay language storytelling corpus. *18th International Conference on Speech and Computer, SPECOM 2016*, 9811 LNCS:563–570.

Bali Ranaivo-Malançon, Suhaila Saee, Rosita Mohamed Othman, and Jennifer Fiona Wilfred Busu. 2017. Transforming semi-structured indigenous dictionary into machine-readable dictionary. *Journal of Telecommunication, Electronic and Computer Engineering*, 9(3-11):7–11.

Francisco Rangel, Paolo Rosso, Julian Brooke, and Alexandra L Uitdenbogerd. 2018. Cross-corpus native language identification via statistical embedding. In *Proceedings of the Second Workshop on Stylistic Variation*, pages 39–43.

Ihda Rasyada, Yuliana Setiowati, Aliridho Barakbah, and M. Tafaquh Fiddin Al Islami. 2020. Sentiment analysis of bpjs kesehatan's services based on affective models. *2020 International Electronics Symposium, IES 2020*, pages 549–556.

Anak Agung Putri Ratna, Randy Sanjaya, Tomi Wirianata, and Prima Dewi Purnamasari. 2017. Word level auto-correction for latent semantic analysis based essay grading system. *15th International Conference on Quality in Research: International Symposium on Electrical and Computer Engineering, QiR 2017*, 2017-December:235–240.

Anak Agung Putri Ratna, Naiza Astri Wulandari, Aaliyah Kaltsum, Ihsan Ibrahim, and Prima Dewi Purnamasari. 2019. Answer categorization method using k-means for Indonesian language automatic short answer grading system based on latent semantic analysis. *16th International Conference on Quality in Research, QIR 2019*.

Sitti Munirah Abdul Razak, Muhamad Sadry Abu Seman, Wan Ali, Wan Yusoff Wan, Noor Hasrul Nizan, and Mohammad Noor. 2019. Malay manuscripts transliteration using statistical machine translation (SMT). *1st International Conference on Artificial Intelligence and Data Sciences, AiDAS 2019*, pages 137–141.

Sitti Munirah Abdul Razak, Muhamad Sadry Abu Seman, Wan Ali Wan Yusoff Wan Mamat, and Noor Hasrul Nizan Mohammad Noor. 2018. Transliteration engine for union catalogue of Malay manuscripts in Malaysia: E-JAWI version 3. *2018 International Conference on Information and Communication Technology for the Muslim World, ICT4M 2018*, pages 58–63.

Husna Faredza Mohamed Redzwan, Khairul Azam Bahari, Anida Sarudin, and Zulkifli Osman. 2020. Strategi pengukuran upaya berbahasa menerusi kesantunan berbahasa sebagai indikator profesionalisme guru pelatih berasaskan skala morfofonetik, sosiolinguistik dan sosiopragmatik (Linguistic politeness as an indicator of trainee teacher professionalism: A language abilty measurement strategy based on morphophonetic, sociolinguistic and sociopragmatic scales). *Malaysian Journal of Learning and Instruction*, 17(1):213–254.

Rianto, Achmad Benny Mutiara, Eri Prasetyo Wibowo, and Paulus Insap Santosa. 2021. Improving stemming techniques for non-formal Indonesian sentences using incorbiz. *ICIC Express Letters*, 15(1):67–74.

Mohd Arizal Shamsil Mat Rifin and Mohd Pouzi Hamzah. 2017. Incorporating knowledge base in unsupervised approach of word sense disambiguation of Malay documents. *Journal of Telecommunication, Electronic and Computer Engineering*, 9(3-4 Special Issue):119–122.

Muhammad Rif'at, Rahmad Mahendra, Indra Budi, and Haryo Akbarianto Wibowo. 2018. Towards product attributes extraction in Indonesian e-commerce platform. *Computacion y Sistemas*, 22(4):1367–1375.

Dewi Riyanti, M. Arif Bijaksana, and Adiwijaya. 2018. Automatic semantic orientation of adjectives for Indonesian language using pmi-ir and clustering. *International Conference on Data and Information Science 2017, ICoDIS 2017*, 971.

Faizal Riza, Saefulloh Rifai, Akmal Dirgantara, Sfenrianto, Rasenda, and Syarifudin Herdyansyah. 2020. Information retrieval technique for Indonesian pdf document with modified stemming porter method using php. *Journal of Physics: Conference Series*, 1477(3).

Hammam Riza, Michael Purwoadi, Gunarso, Teduh Uliniansyah, Aw Ai Ti, Sharifah Mahani Aljunied, Luong Chi Mai, Vu Tat Thang, Nguyen Phuong Thái, Vichet Chea, Vichet Sun, Sethserey Sam, Sopheap Seng, Khin Mar Soe, Khin Thandar Nwet, Masao Utiyama, and Chenchen Ding. 2017. Introduction of the asian language treebank. *19th Annual Conference of the Oriental Chapter of International Committee for Coordination and Standardization of Speech Databases and Assessment Techniques, O-COCOSDA 2016*, pages 1–6.

Arra'Di Nur Rizal and Sara Stymne. 2020. Evaluating word embeddings for Indonesian–English codemixed text based on synthetic data. In *Proceedings of the The 4th Workshop on Computational Approaches to Code Switching*, pages 26–35. European Language Resources Association.

Afian Syafaadi Rizki, Aris Tjahyanto, and Rahmat Trialih. 2019. Comparison of stemming algorithms on Indonesian text processing. *TELKOMNIKA*, 17(1):95–102.

Shaiful Bakhtia Rodzman, Sumayyah Hasbullah, Nomaly Kamal Ismail, Nurazzah Abd Rahman, Zulhilmi Mohamed Nor, and Ahmad Yunus Mohd Noor. 2020. Fabricated and Shia Malay translated hadith as negative fuzzy logic ranking indicator on Malay information retrieval. *ASM Science Journal*, 13(Special Issue 3):101–108.

Shaiful Bakhtia Rodzman, Nomaly Kamal Ismail, Nurazzah Abd Rahman, Syed Ahmad Aljunid, Zulhilmi Mohamed Nor, and Ahmad Yunus Mohd Noor. 2019. Domain specific concept ontologies and text summarization as hierarchical fuzzy logic ranking indicator on Malay text corpus. *Indonesian Journal of Electrical Engineering and Computer Science*, 15(3):1527–1534.

Shaiful Bakhtia Rodzman, Mohamad Fitri Izuan Abdul Ronie, Normaly Kamal Ismail, Nurazzah Abd Rahman, Fatimah Ahmad, and Zulhilmi Mohamed Nor. 2018. Analyzing Malay stemmer performance towards fuzzy logic ranking function on Malay text corpus. *4th International Conference on Information Retrieval and Knowledge Management: Diving into Data Sciences, CAMP 2018*, pages 36–41.

Ade Romadhony, Ayu Purwarianti, and Dwi Hendratmo Widyantoro. 2018. Rule-based Indonesian open information extraction. *5th International Conference on Advanced Informatics: Concepts Theory and Applications, ICAICTA 2018*, pages 107–112.

Fadhilah Rosdi, Mumtaz Begum Mustafa, and Siti Salwah Salim. 2017. Assessing automatic speech recognition in measuring speech intelligibility: A study of

Malay speakers with speech impairments. *2017 6th International Conference on Electrical Engineering and Informatics (ICEEI)*, pages 1–6.

Rosiyana Rosiyana. 2020. Pengajaran bahasa dan pemerolehan bahasa kedua dalam pembelajaran BIPA (Bahasa Indonesia Penutur Asing). *Jurnal Ilmiah KORPUS*, 4(3):374–382.

Suhanah Rosnan, Nurazzah Abd Rahman, Shahirah Mohamed Hatim, and Zahirah Hamid Ghul. 2019. Performance evaluation of inverted files, b-tree and b+ tree indexing algorithm on Malay text. *4th International Conference and Workshops on Recent Advances and Innovations in Engineering, ICRAIE 2019.*

Raphael Rubino, Benjamin Marie, Raj Dabre, Atushi Fujita, Masao Utiyama, and Eiichiro Sumita. 2020. Extremely low-resource neural machine translation for asian languages. *Machine Translation*, 34(4):347–382.

Fitrah Rumaisa, Halizah Basiron, Zurina Saaya, and Noorli Khamis. 2019. Development of multilingual social media data corpus: Development and evaluation. *International Journal of Innovation, Creativity and Change*, 6(5):1–14.

Fitrah Rumaisa, Halizah Basiron, Zurina Saaya, and Yoki Muchsam. 2020. BMBI: A development of a special corpus on homonyms for multi-lingual sentiment analysis. *International Journal of Advanced Trends in Computer Science and Engineering*, 9(4).

Andre Rusli, Julio Christian Young, and Ni Made Satvika Iswari. 2020. Identifying fake news in Indonesian via supervised binary text classification. *2020 IEEE International Conference on Industry 4.0, Artificial Intelligence, and Communications Technology, IAICT 2020*, pages 86–90.

Tatyana Ruzsics and Tanja Samardzic. 2017. Neural sequence-to-sequence learning of internal word structure. In *Proceedings of the 21st Conference on Computational Natural Language Learning (CoNLL 2017)*, pages 184–194. Association for Computational Linguistics.

Mastura Md Saad, Nursuriati Jamil, and Raseeda Hamzah. 2018a. Evaluation of support vector machine and decision tree for emotion recognition of Malay folklores. *Bulletin of Electrical Engineering and Informatics*, 7(3):479–486.

Nurui Huda Mohd Saad and Nor Hashimah Jalaluddin. 2020. Imbuhan meN- dengan kata nama konkrit unsur alam: Analisis teori relevans (Prefix meN- with concrete nouns of natural elements: A relevance theory analysis). *GEMA Online Journal of Language Studies*, 20(3):136–155.

Saidah Saad and Mansor Mohamed Kamil. 2018. Pendekatan teknik pengecaman entiti nama bagi capaian berita jenayah Bahasa Melayu (Named entity recognition approach for Malay crime news retrieval). *GEMA Online Journal of Language Studies*, 18(4):216–235.

Suziana Mat Saad, Nor Hashimah Jalaluddin, and Imran Ho-Abdullah. 2018b. Conceptual metaphor and linguistic manifestations in Malay and French: A cognitive analysis. *GEMA Online Journal of Language Studies*, 18(3):114–134.

Johnny Saldaña. 2016. *The Coding Manual for Qualitative Researchers*, third edition edition. SAGE, London; Los Angeles, CA.

Calvin Erico Rudy Salim and Derwin Suhartono. 2021. Long short-term memory for hate speech and abusive language detection on Indonesian YouTube comment section. In *2021 11th International Workshop on Computer Science and Engineering, WCSE 2021*, pages 193–200. International Workshop on Computer Science and Engineering (WCSE).

M. S. Salleh, S. A. Asmai, H. Basiron, and S. Ahmad. 2018. Named entity recognition using fuzzy c-means clustering method for Malay textual data analysis. *Journal of Telecommunication, Electronic and Computer Engineering*, 10(2-7):121–126.

Muhammad Sharilazlan Salleh, Siti Azirah Asmai, Halizah Basiron, and Sabrina Ahmad. 2017. A Malay named entity recognition using conditional random fields. *5th International Conference on Information and Communication Technology, ICoIC7 2017.*

Mohammad Arshi Saloot, Norisma Idris, AiTi Aw, and Dirk Thorleuchter. 2016. Twitter corpus creation: The case of a Malay chat-style-text corpus (MCC). *Digital Scholarship in the Humanities*, 31(2):227–243.

Nur-Hana Samsudin and Lukman Nurhaqi Rahim. 2019. Rapid heteronym disambiguation for text-to-speech system. *4th International Conference and Workshops on Recent Advances and Innovations in Engineering, ICRAIE 2019.*

Lidia Sandra and Ford Lumbangaol. 2021. When homecoming is not coming: 2021 homecoming ban sentiment analysis on Twitter data using support vector machine algorithm. In *8th International Conference on ICT for Smart Society, ICISS 2021*. Institute of Electrical and Electronics Engineers Inc.

Agung Santosa, Andi Djalal Latief, Hammam Riza, Asril Jarin, Lyla Ruslana Aini, Gunarso, Gita Citra Puspita, Muhammad Teduh Uliniansyah, Elvira Nurfadhilah, Harnum A. Prafitia, and Made Gunawan. 2019. The architecture of speech-to-speech translator for mobile conversation. *22nd Conference of the Oriental COCOSDA International Committee for the Coordination and Standardisation of Speech Databases and Assessment Techniques, O-COCOSDA 2019.*

Joan Santoso, Gunawan Gunawan, Hermes Vincentius Gani, Eko Mulyanto Yuniarno, Mochamad Hariadi, and Mauridhi Hery Purnomo. 2016. Noun phrases extraction using shallow parsing with c4.5 decision tree algorithm for Indonesian language ontology building. *15th International Symposium on Communications and Information Technologies, ISCIT 2015*, pages 149–152.

Joan Santoso, Esther Irawati Setiawan, Christian Nathaniel Purwanto, Eko Mulyanto Yuniarno, Mochamad Hariadi, and Mauridhi Hery Purnomo. 2021. Named entity recognition for extracting concept in ontology building on Indonesian language using end-to-end bidirectional long short term memory. *Expert Systems with Applications*, 176.

Erikson Saragih, Syahron Lubis, Amrin Saragih, Roswita Silalahi, and M. Hum. 2017. Ideational grammatical metaphors in doctrinal verses of The Bible in Indonesian version. *Theory and Practice in Language Studies*, 7(10):847–854.

Anida Sarudin, Mazura Mastura Muhammad, Muhamad Fadzllah Zaini, Zulkifli Osman, and Muhammad Anas Al Muhsin. 2020a. Collocation analysis of variants of intensifies in classical Malay texts. In *2020 Conference of the Global Council on Anthropological Linguistics in Asia, GLOCAL 2020*, volume 2020-January, pages 352–357. Global Council on Anthropological Linguistics.

Anida Sarudin, Mazura Mastura Muhammad, Muhamad Fadzllah Zaini, Husna Faredza Mohamed Redzwan, and Siti Saniah Abu Bakar. 2020b. The relationship between astronomy and architecture as an element of Malay intelligentsia. In *2020 Conference of the Global Council on Anthropological Linguistics in Asia, GLOCAL 2020*, volume 2020-January, pages 358–363. Global Council on Anthropological Linguistics.

Dhanang Hadhi Sasmita, Alfan Farizki Wicaksono, Samuel Louvan, and Mirna Adriani. 2018. Unsupervised aspect-based sentiment analysis on Indonesian restaurant reviews. *21st International Conference on Asian Language Processing, IALP 2017*, 2018-January:383–386.

Siti Syakirah Sazali, Zainab Abu Bakar, and Jafreezal Jaafar. 2016. Word prediction algorithm in resolving ambiguity in Malay text. *3rd International Conference on Computing for Sustainable Global Development, INDIACom 2016*, pages 1347–1352.

Siti Syakirah Sazali, Nurazzah Abdul Rahman, and Zainab Abu Bakar. 2017. Information extraction: Evaluating named entity recognition from classical Malay documents. *3rd International Conference on Information Retrieval and Knowledge Management, CAMP 2016*, pages 48–53.

Siti Syakirah Sazali, Nurazzah Abdul Rahman, and Zainab Abu Bakar. 2020. Characteristics of Malay translated hadith corpus. *Journal of King Saud University - Computer and Information Sciences*.

Noraini Seman and Ahmad Firdaus Norazam. 2019. Hybrid methods of Brandt's generalised likelihood ratio and short-term energy for Malay word speech segmentation. *Indonesian Journal of Electrical Engineering and Computer Science*, 16(1):283–291.

Amalia Agung Septarina, Faisal Rahutomo, and Moechammad Sarosa. 2019. Machine translation of Indonesian: A review. *Communications in Science and Technology*, 4(1):12–19.

Garin Septian, Ajib Susanto, and Guruh Fajar Shidik. 2017. Indonesian news classification based on nabana. *2017 International Seminar on Application for Technology of Information and Communication, iSemantic 2017*, 2018-January:175–180.

Ali Akbar Septiandri, Yosef Ardhito Winatmoko, and Ilham Firdausi Putra. 2020. Knowing right from wrong: Should we use more complex models for automatic short-answer scoring in Bahasa Indonesia? In *Proceedings of SustaiNLP: Workshop on Simple and Efficient Natural Language Processing*, pages 1–7.

Reza Setiabudi, Ni Made Satvika Iswari, and Andre Rusli. 2021. Enhancing text classification performance by preprocessing misspelled words in Indonesian language. *TELKOMNIKA*, 19(4):1234–1241.

Evelyn Setiani and Win Ce. 2018. Text classification services using naïve bayes for Bahasa Indonesia. *3rd International Conference on Information Management and Technology, ICIMTech 2018*, pages 361–366.

Esther Irawati Setiawan, Andy Januar Wicaksono, Joan Santoso, Yosi Kristian, Surya Sumpeno, and Mauridhi Hery Purnomo. 2018. N-gram keyword retrieval on association rule mining for predicting teenager deviant behavior from school regulation. *2018 International Conference on Computer Engineering, Network and Intelligent Multimedia, CENIM 2018*, pages 325–328.

Roziyani Setik, Raja Mohd Tariqi Raja Lope Ahmad, and Suziyanti Marjudi. 2021. Aspect-based sentiment analysis for posts on friday prayer during mco in Malaysia. In *2021 International Congress of Advanced Technology and Engineering, ICOTEN 2021*. Institute of Electrical and Electronics Engineers Inc.

Roziyani bt Setik, Raja Mohd Tariqi Bin Raja Ahmad, Suziyanti bt Marjudi, Azhar bin Hamid, Wan Hassan Basri bin Wan Ismail, Zuraidy bin Adnan, and Wan Azlan bin Wan Hassan. 2018. Exploiting Malay corpus on islamic issue using sketch engine. *2018 International Seminar on Research of Information Technology and Intelligent Systems, ISRITI 2018*, pages 281–286.

Yuliana Setiowati, Arif Djunaidy, and Daniel Oranova Siahaan. 2019. Pair extraction of aspect and implicit opinion word based on its co-occurrence in corpus of Bahasa Indonesia. *2nd International Seminar on*

Research of Information Technology and Intelligent Systems, ISRITI 2019, pages 73–78.

Verena Severina and Masayu Leylia Khodra. 2019. Multidocument abstractive summarization using abstract meaning representation for Indonesian language. *2019 International Conference on Advanced Informatics: Concepts, Theory, and Applications, ICAICTA 2019*.

Noah Shahrul Azman Mohd, Ali Nazlena Mohamad, and Hasan Mohd Sabri. 2018a. Penentuan fitur bagi pengekstrakan tajuk berita akhbar Bahasa Melayu (Determining features of news headline in Malay news document). *GEMA Online Journal of Language Studies*, 18(2):154–167.

Noah Shahrul Azman Mohd, Ali Nazlena Mohamad, and Hasan Mohd Sabri. 2018b. Penjanaan ringkasan isi utama berita Bahasa Melayu berdasarkan ciri kata (Generation of news headline for Malay language based on term features). *GEMA Online Journal of Language Studies*, 18(4):42–60.

Gayane Shalunts, Gerhard Backfried, and Helmy Syakh Alam. 2018. Sentiment analysis in Indonesian and French by sentisail. *9th Asia-Pacific Signal and Information Processing Association Annual Summit and Conference, APSIPA ASC 2017*, 2018-February:69–75.

Nurul Fathiyah Shamsudin, Halizah Basiron, and Zurina Sa'aya. 2016. Lexical based sentiment analysis - verb, adverb & negation. *Journal of Telecommunication, Electronic and Computer Engineering*, 8(2):161–166.

Asako Shiohara, Yuta Sakon, and Hiroki Nomoto. 2019. Discourse functions of the two non-active voices in Indonesian: based on the web corpus in MALINDO Conc. *Nusa*, pages 77–101.

Rizka Wakhidatus Sholikah, Agus Zainal Arifin, Diana Purwitasari, and Chastine Fatichah. 2017. Cooccurrence technique and dictionary based method for Indonesian thesaurus construction. *5th International Conference on Information and Communication Technology, ICoIC7 2017*.

Deardo Dibrianto Sinaga and Seng Hansun. 2018. Indonesian text document similarity detection system using rabin-karp and confix-stripping algorithms. *International Journal of Innovative Computing, Information and Control*, 14(5):1893–1903.

Sandhya Singh, Anoop Kunchukuttan, and Pushpak Bhattacharyya. 2016. IIT Bombay's English-Indonesian submission at wat: Integrating neural language models with SMT. In *Proceedings of the 3rd Workshop on Asian Translation (WAT2016)*, pages 68–74.

Ahmad Hasan Siregar and Dina Chahyati. 2020. Visual question answering for monas tourism object using deep learning. *12th International Conference on Advanced Computer Science and Information Systems, ICACSIS 2020*, pages 381–386.

Roswani Siregar. 2017. Teaching specific purpose translation: Utilization of bilingual contract document as parallel corpus. *English Language Teaching*, 10(7):175–182.

Samuel I. G. Situmeang, Ramosan K. Lubis, Fany J. N. Siregar, and Benyamin J. D. C. Panjaitan. 2019. Movie summarization based on Indonesian subtitles with restricted boltzmann machine. *4th International Conference on Sustainable Information Engineering and Technology, SIET 2019*, pages 338–342.

Verawaty Situmorang, Tia Elyani, Roberto Tambunan, and Yohana Gulto. 2019. Applying opinion mining technique on tourism study case: Lake Toba. *Journal of Physics: Conference Series*, 1175(1).

James Neil Sneddon. 2003. *The Indonesian Language: Its History and Role in Modern Society*. UNSW Press.

Rudy Sofyan and Bahagia Tarigan. 2018. Theme markedness in the translation of student translators. *Indonesian Journal of Applied Linguistics*, 8(1):235–243.

Shahidatul Maslina Mat Sood, Tan Kim Hua, and Bahiyah Abdul Hamid. 2020. Cyberbullying through intellect-related insults. *Jurnal Komunikasi: Malaysian Journal of Communication*, 36(1):278–297.

Dewi. Soyusiawaty and Eko. Aribowo. 2016. Designing and implementing parsing for ambiguous sentences in Indonesian language. *Journal of Theoretical and Applied Information Technology*, 84(3):339–347.

Ivan Stefanus, R.S. Joko Sarwono, and Miranti Indar Mandasari. 2017. Gmm based automatic speaker verification system development for forensics in Bahasa Indonesia. *5th International Conference on Instrumentation, Control, and Automation, ICA 2017*, pages 56–61.

Mary Fatimah Subet and Mohd Ridzuan Md Nasir. 2019. Inquisitive semantic analysis of Malay language proverbs. *Malaysian Journal of Learning and Instruction*, 16(2):227–253.

Syamsul Zahri Subir. 2019. Beyond the closet? The trends and visibility of homosexuality coverage in Malaysian newspapers, 1998 - 2012. *e-BANGI*, 16(9):13–30.

Mohd Suhairi Md Suhaimin, Mohd Hanafi Ahma Hijazi, Rayner Alfred, and Frans Coenen. 2019. Modified framework for sarcasm detection and classification in sentiment analysis. *Indonesian Journal of Electrical Engineering and Computer Science*, 13(3):1175–1183.

Mohd Suhairi Md Suhaimin, Mohd Hanafi Ahmad Hijazi, Rayner Alfred, and Frans Coenen. 2017. Natural language processing based features for sarcasm detection: An investigation using bilingual social media texts. *8th International Conference on Information Technology, ICIT 2017*, pages 703–709.

Totok Suhardijanto, Rahmad Mahendra, Zahroh Nuriah, and Adi Budiwiyanto. 2020. The framework of multiword expression in Indonesian language. Proceedings of the 34th Pacific Asia Conference on Language, Information and Computation, pages 582–588. Association for Computational Linguistics.

Totok Suhardijanto and Deodatus Perdana Putra. 2019. Acquiring extended units of meaning: The role of learner corpus in teaching Indonesian as a foreign language. In *KEBIPAAN 2019: Proceedings of the 2nd Konferensi BIPA Tahunan by Postgraduate Program of Javanese Literature and Language Education in Collaboration with Association of Indonesian Language and Literature Lecturers, KEBIPAAN, 9 November, 2019, Surakarta, C*, page 8.

Derwin Suhartono, Aryo Pradipta Gema, Suhendro Winton, Theodorus David, Mohamad Ivan Fanany, and Aniati Murni Arymurthy. 2020. Argument annotation and analysis using deep learning with attention mechanism in Bahasa Indonesia. *Journal of Big Data*, 7(1).

Adang Suhendra, Juwita Winadwiastuti, Astie Darmayantie, and Nuke Farida. 2018. Terrorism domain corpus building using latent dirichlet allocation (LDA) and its ontology relationship building using global similarity hierarchy learning(GSHL). *11th International Conference on Information and Communication Technology and System, ICTS 2017*, 2018-January:253–257.

Gilang Julian Suherik and Ayu Purwarianti. 2017. Experiments on coreference resolution for Indonesian language with lexical and shallow syntactic features. *5th International Conference on Information and Communication Technology, ICoIC7 2017*.

Herry Sujaini. 2018. Peningkatan akurasi penerjemah bahasa daerah dengan optimasi korpus paralel. *Jurnal Nasional Teknik Elektro dan Teknologi Informasi (JNTETI)*, 7(1):7–12.

Sahrul Sukardi, Meredita Susanty, Ade Irawan, and Randi Fermana Putra. 2020. Low complexity named-entity recognition for Indonesian language using bilstm-cnns. *3rd International Conference on Information and Communications Technology, ICOIACT 2020*, pages 137–142.

I Made Sukarsa, I Ketut Gede Darma Putra, Nyoman Putra Sastra, and Lie Jasa. 2018. A new framework for information system development on instant messaging for low cost solution. *Telkomnika (Telecommunication Computing Electronics and Control)*, 16(6):2799–2808.

O. R. Sulaeman, W. Gata, E. Wahyudi, M. J. Hakim, R. Subandi, R. Setiyawan, and B. Pratama. 2020. Information retrieval system to find articles and clauses in uud 1945 using vector space model method. *Journal of Physics: Conference Series*, 1471(1).

Mohamed Zain Sulaiman and Muhamad Jad Hamiza Bin Mohamad Yusoff. 2020. Bila dan mengapa 'you' menjadi 'kita': Satu analisis perbandingan Inggeris-Melayu (When and why 'you' becomes 'kita': A contrastive English-Malay analysis). *GEMA Online Journal of Language Studies*, 20(4):151–165.

S. Sulaiman, R. A. Wahid, and F. Morsidi. 2017. Feature extraction using regular expression in detecting proper noun for Malay news articles based on knn algorithm. *Journal of Fundamental and Applied Sciences*, 9(5S):210–231.

Fazal Mohamed Mohamed Sultan and Syafika Atika Binti Othman. 2021. Frasa topik dan fokus dalam Bahasa Melayu: Analisis program minimalis (Topic and focus phrase in Malay language: Minimalist program analysis). *GEMA Online Journal of Language Studies*, 21(2):195–214.

Meng Sun, Marie Stephen Leo, Eram Munawwar, Paul C Condylis, Sheng-yi Kong, Seong Per Lee, Albert Hidayat, and Muhamad Danang Kerianto. 2020. Semi-supervised category-specific review tagging on Indonesian e-commerce product reviews. In *Proceedings of The 3rd Workshop on e-Commerce and NLP*, pages 59–63. Association for Computational Linguistics.

Dedy Suryadi. 2021. Does it make you sad? a lexicon-based sentiment analysis on covid-19 news tweets. *IOP Conference Series. Materials Science and Engineering*, 1077(1).

Endang Suryawati, Munandar Devi, Dianadewi Riswantini, Achmad Fatchuttamam Abka, and Andria Arisal. 2018. Pos-tagging for informal language (study in Indonesian tweets). *International Conference on Data and Information Science 2017, ICoDIS 2017*, 971.

Tata Sutabri and Miftah Ardiansyah. 2017. Framework of sentiment annotation for document specification in Indonesian language base on topic modeling and machine learning. *5th International Conference on Cyber and IT Service Management, CITSM 2017*.

Taufic Leonardo Sutejo and Dessi Puji Lestari. 2019. Indonesia hate speech detection using deep learning. *22nd International Conference on Asian Language Processing, IALP 2018*, pages 39–43.

Wiwin Suwarningsih and Nuryani. 2019. Opinion qa-pairs generation from Indonesian Twitter. *6th International Conference on Computer, Control, Informatics and its Applications, IC3INA 2018*, pages 209–213.

Suyanto Suyanto. 2019a. Flipping onsets to enhance syllabification. *International Journal of Speech Technology*, 22(4):1031–1038.

Suyanto Suyanto. 2019b. Incorporating syllabification points into a model of grapheme-to-phoneme conversion. *International Journal of Speech Technology*, 22(2):459–470.

Suyanto Suyanto. 2020. Phonological similarity-based backoff smoothing to boost a bigram syllable boundary detection. *International Journal of Speech Technology*, 23(1):191–204.

Suyanto Suyanto, Anditya Arifianto, Anis Sirwan, and Angga P. Rizaendra. 2020. End-to-end speech recognition models for a low-resourced Indonesian language. *8th International Conference on Information and Communication Technology, ICoICT 2020.*

Suyanto Suyanto, Sri Hartati, Agus Harjoko, and Dirk Van Compernolle. 2016. Indonesian syllabification using a pseudo nearest neighbour rule and phonotactic knowledge. *Speech Communication*, 85:109–118.

Suyanto Suyanto, Andi Sunyoto, Rezza Nafi Ismail, Ema Rachmawati, and Warih Maharani. 2021. Stemmer and phonotactic rules to improve n-gram tagger-based Indonesian phonemicization. *Journal of King Saud University - Computer and Information Sciences.*

Arida Ferti Syafiandini, Hani Febri Mustika, Lindung Parningotan Manik, Yan Rianto, and Zaenal Akbar. 2019. Implementing graph based rank on online news media keyword extraction. *7th International Conference on Computer, Control, Informatics and its Applications, IC3INA 2019*, pages 108–113.

Indira Syawanodya and Arief Fatchul Huda. 2018. Improvement on stemmer algorithm for Indonesian language with spellchecker. *3rd International Conference on Informatics and Computing, ICIC 2018.*

Kathleen Swee Neo Tan, Tong Ming Lim, and Yee Mei Lim. 2020. Emotion analysis using self-training on Malaysian code-mixed Twitter data. In *13th IADIS International Conferences ICT, Society, and Human Beings 2020; Connected Smart Cities 2020; and Web Based Communities and Social Media 2020*, pages 181–188. IADIS.

Kim Hua Tan, Abdullah Imran Ho, Nur Azureen Zulkifli, and Shukor Shamirr Muhammad Mohd. 2017a. Trend penggunaan bahasa samar dalam persidangan parlimen Malaysia (Trend of adjunctive and disjunctive extenders usage in the Malaysian parliament). *GEMA Online Journal of Language Studies*, 17(4):84–100.

Tien-Ping Tan, Bali Ranaivo-Malançon, Laurent Besacier, Yin-Lai Yeong, Keng Hoon Gan, and Enya Kong Tang. 2017b. Evaluating lstm networks, hmm and wfst in Malay part-of-speech tagging. *Journal of Telecommunication, Electronic and Computer Engineering*, 9(2-9):79–83.

Yi-Fei Tan, Hai-Shuan Lam, Asyraf Azlan, and Wooi King Soo. 2016. Sentiment analysis for telco popularity on Twitter big data using a novel Malaysian dictionary. *7th International Conference on Applications of Digital Information and Web Technologies, ICADIWT 2016*, 282:112–125.

Theo Tanadi. 2018. Time series neural network model for part-of-speech tagging Indonesian language. In *International Conference on Information Technology and Digital Applications ICITDA 2017*, volume 325 of *IOP Conference Series. Materials Science and Engineering*. Institute of Physics Publishing.

Vincentius Gabriel Tandra, Yowen Yowen, Ravel Tanjaya, William Lucianto Santoso, and Nunung Nurul Qomariyah. 2021. Short message service filtering with natural language processing in Indonesian language. In *8th International Conference on ICT for Smart Society, ICISS 2021*. Institute of Electrical and Electronics Engineers Inc.

Dewa Ayu Nadia Taradhita and I Ketut Gede Darma Putra. 2021. Hate speech classification in Indonesian language tweets by using convolutional neural network. *Journal of ICT Research and Applications*, 14(3):225–239.

Natanael Taufik, Alfan Farizki Wicaksono, and Mirna Adriani. 2017. Named entity recognition on Indonesian microblog messages. *20th International Conference on Asian Language Processing, IALP 2016*, pages 358–361.

Syafi Muhammad Tauhid and Yova Ruldeviyani. 2020. Sentiment analysis of Indonesians response to influencer in social media. *7th International Conference on Information Technology, Computer, and Electrical Engineering, ICITACEE 2020*, pages 90–95.

B. Tawaqal and S. Suyanto. 2021. Recognizing five major dialects in Indonesia based on mfcc and drnn. *Journal of Physics: Conference Series*, 1844(1).

Mohammad Teduh Uliniansyah, Hammam Riza, Agung Santosa, Gunarso, Made Gunawan, and Elvira Nurfadhilah. 2018. Development of text and speech corpus for an Indonesian speech-to-speech translation system. *20th Conference of the Oriental Chapter of International Committee for Coordination and Standardization of Speech Databases and Assessment Techniques, O-COCOSDA 2017*, 2018-January:53–57.

H. Thamrin, G. Ariyanto, E. W. Pamungkas, and Y. Sulistyono. 2018. User participation in building language repository: The case of Google Translate. *IOP Conference Series. Materials Science and Engineering*, 403(1).

Husni Thamrin, Gunawan Ariyanto, Irma Yuliana, and Wawan Joko Pranoto. 2019a. Crowdsourcing in developing repository of phrase definition in Bahasa Indonesia. *Telkomnika (Telecommunication Computing Electronics and Control)*, 17(5):2321–2326.

Husni Thamrin, Gunawan Ariyanto, Irma Yuliana, and Dian Purworini. 2019b. An application that invites users to participate in developing repository of Bahasa Indonesia. *6th International Conference on Computer, Control, Informatics and its Applications, IC3INA 2018*, pages 72–76.

Agustinus Theodorus, Tio Kristian Prasetyo, Reynaldi Hartono, and Derwin Suhartono. 2021. Short message service (sms) spam filtering using machine learning in Bahasa Indonesia. *3rd East Indonesia Conference on Computer and Information Technology, EIConCIT 2021*, pages 199–202.

Moch. Fadli Shadiqin Thirafi and Faisal Rahutomo. 2018. Implementation of naïve bayes classifier algorithm to categorize Indonesian song lyrics based on age. *3rd International Conference on Sustainable Information Engineering and Technology, SIET 2018*, pages 106–109.

C. Tho, Y. Heryadi, L. Lukas, and A. Wibowo. 2021. Code-mixed sentiment analysis of Indonesian language and Javanese language using lexicon based approach. *Journal of Physics: Conference Series*, 1869(1).

Cuk Tho, Arden S. Setiawan, and Andry Chowanda. 2018. Forming of dyadic conversation dataset for Bahasa Indonesia. *3rd International Conference on Computer Science and Computational Intelligence, ICCSCI 2018*, 135:315–322.

Ye Kyaw Thu, Win Pa Pa, Masao. Utiyama, Andrew Finch, and Eiichiro Sumita. 2016. Introducing the Asian language treebank (ALT). *10th International Conference on Language Resources and Evaluation, LREC 2016*, pages 1574–1578.

Su-Hie Ting, Kee-Man Chuah, Collin Jerome, and Audea Johnson. 2021. Spotlight on LGBT in Malaysian online newspapers: Insights from textual analytics. *EDPACS*.

Su-Hie Ting, David Chen-On Then, and Oliver Guan-Bee Ong. 2020. Prestige of products and code-switching in retail encounters. *International Journal of Multilingualism*, 17(2):215–231.

Sabrina Tiun and Liew Siaw Hong. 2020. Identification of features in predicting prominent Malay words using decision tree. *Malaysian Journal of Computer Science*, 33(4):298–305.

Sabrina Tiun, Nor Fariza Mohd Nor, Azhar Jalaludin, and Anis Nadiah Che Abdul Rahman. 2020a. Word embedding for small and domain-specific Malay corpus. *6th International Conference on Computational Science and Technology, ICCST 2019*, 603:435–443.

Sabrina Tiun, Saidah Saad, Nor Fariza Mohd Nor, Azhar Jalaludin, and Anis Nadiah Che Abdul Rahman. 2020b. Quantifying semantic shift visually on a Malay domain-specific corpus using temporal word embedding approach. *Asia-Pacific Journal of Information Technology and Multimedia*, 9(2):1–10.

Parmonangan R. Togatorop, Roso Siagian, Yolanda Nainggolan, and Kaleb Simanungkalit. 2020. Implementation of ontology-based on word2vec and dbscan for part-of-speech. *5th International Conference on Sustainable Information Engineering and Technology, SIET 2020*, pages 51–56.

Andrea C. Tricco, Erin Lillie, Wasifa Zarin, Kelly K. O'Brien, Heather Colquhoun, Danielle Levac, David Moher, Micah D.J. Peters, Tanya Horsley, Laura Weeks, Susanne Hempel, Elie A. Akl, Christine Chang, Jessie McGowan, Lesley Stewart, Lisa Hartling, Adrian Aldcroft, Michael G. Wilson, Chantelle Garritty, Simon Lewin, Christina M. Godfrey, Marilyn T. Macdonald, Etienne V. Langlois, Karla Soares-Weiser, Jo Moriarty, Tammy Clifford, Özge Tunçalp, and Sharon E. Straus. 2018. PRISMA extension for scoping reviews (PRISMA-ScR): Checklist and explanation. *Annals of Internal Medicine*, 169(7):467–473. PMID: 30178033.

Hai-Long Trieu and Le-Minh Nguyen. 2018. Enhancing pivot translation using grammatical and morphological information. *15th International Conference of the Pacific Association for Computational Linguistics, PACLING 2017*, 781:137–151.

Hai-Long Trieu, Duc-Vu Tran, Ashwin Ittoo, and Le-Minh Nguyen. 2019. Leveraging additional resources for improving statistical machine translation on Asian low-resource languages. *ACM Transactions on Asian and Low-Resource Language Information Processing*, 18(3):1–22.

I Nyoman Prayana Trisna, Aina Musdholifah, and Yunita Sari. 2020. Utilizing morphological features for part-of-speech tagging of Bahasa Indonesia in bidirectional lstm. *6th International Conference on Science in Information Technology, ICSITech 2020*, pages 51–56.

I Nyoman Prayana Trisna and Arif Nurwidyantoro. 2020. Single document keywords extraction in Bahasa Indonesia using phrase chunking. *Telkomnika (Telecommunication Computing Electronics and Control)*, 18(4):1917–1925.

Sulis Triyono, Wening Sahayu, and Margana. 2020. Form and function of negation in German and Indonesian: Searching for equivalent construction of meaning. *Indonesian Journal of Applied Linguistics*, 9(3):675–684.

Tatiana Tsygankova, Francesca Marini, Stephen Mayhew, and Dan Roth. 2021. Building low-resource ner models using non-speaker annotations. In *Proceedings of the Second Workshop on Data Science with Human in the Loop: Language Advances*, pages 62–69.

Ajeng Aulia Turdjai and Kusprasapta Mutijarsa. 2017. Simulation of marketplace customer satisfaction analysis based on machine learning algorithms. *2016 International Seminar on Application of Technology for Information and Communication, ISEMANTIC 2016*, pages 157–162.

Mohammad Teduh Uliniansyah, Gunarso, Elvira Nurfadhilah, Lyla Ruslana Aini, Juliati Junde, Fara Ayuningtyas, and Agung Santosa. 2016. A tool to solve sentence segmentation problem on preparing speech database for Indonesian text-to-speech system. *5th*

Workshop on Spoken Language Technologies for Under-resourced languages, SLTU 2016, 81:188–193.

Mohammad Teduh Uliniansyah, Elvira Nurfadhilah, Harnum Annisa, Made Gunawan, Lyla Ruslana Aini, Agung Santosa, Asril Jarin, Gunarso, Fara Ayuningtyas, and Hammam Riza. 2019. Utilizing Indonesian allophones and intraword short pauses handling to improve performance of Indonesian text-to-speech. *22nd International Conference on Asian Language Processing, IALP 2018*, pages 143–146.

Priva Uriel Cohen. 2017. Informativity and the actuation of lenition. *Language*, 93(3):569–597.

Ema Utami, Anggit Dwi Hartanto, Sumarni Adi, Irwan Oyong, and Suwanto Raharjo. 2019a. Profiling analysis of disc personality traits based on Twitter posts in Bahasa Indonesia. *Journal of King Saud University - Computer and Information Sciences*.

Ema Utami, Anggit Dwi Hartanto, Sumarni Adi, Rahardyan Bisma. Setya Putra, and Suwanto Raharjo. 2019b. Formal and non-formal Indonesian word usage frequency in Twitter profile using non-formal affix rule. *1st International Conference on Cybernetics and Intelligent System, ICORIS 2019*, pages 173–176.

Ema Utami, Irwan Oyong, Suwanto Raharjo, Anggit Dwi Hartanto, and Sumarni Adi. 2021. Supervised learning and resampling techniques on disc personality classification using Twitter information in Bahasa Indonesia. *Applied Computing and Informatics*.

Dominique Vervoort and Jessica G. Luc. 2020. Hashtag global surgery: The role of social media in advancing the field of global surgery. *Cureus*, 12(6):e8468.

C. B. Vista, C. H. Satriawan, D. P. Lestari, and D. H. Widyantoro. 2018. Specific acoustic models for spontaneous and dictated style in Indonesian speech recognition. *2nd International Conference on Computing and Applied Informatics 2017, ICCAI 2017*, 978.

Agung Wahana, Diena Rauda Ramdania, Dhanis Al Ghifari, Ichsan Taufik, Faiz M. Kaffah, and Yana Aditia Gerhana. 2020. Breakdown film script using parsing algorithm. *Telkomnika (Telecommunication Computing Electronics and Control)*, 18(4):1976–1982.

Ummi Nadjwa Binti Wahiyudin and Taj Rijal Bin Muhamad Romli. 2021. Translating Malay compounds into Arabic based on dynamic theory and arabization method. *Journal of Islamic Thought and Civilization*, 11(1):43–58.

Eka Dyar Wahyuni, Amalia Anjani Arifiyanti, and Mohamad Irwan Afandi. 2020. School from home situation in Indonesia: An exploratory data analysis of Indonesian tweet data. *6th Information Technology International Seminar, ITIS 2020*, pages 103–108.

Lei Wang, Rong Tong, Cheung-Chi Leung, Sunil Sivadas, Chongjia Ni, and Bin Ma. 2018. Cloud-based automatic speech recognition systems for southeast Asian languages. *5th International Conference on Orange Technologies, ICOT 2017*, 2018-January:147–150.

Lianxi Wang, Xiaotian Lin, and Nankai Lin. 2021. Research on pseudo-label technology for multi-label news classification. In J. Llados, D. Lopresti, and S. Uchida, editors, *16th International Conference on Document Analysis and Recognition, ICDAR 2021*, volume 12822 LNCS, pages 683–698. Springer Science and Business Media Deutschland GmbH.

Pidong Wang, Preslav Nakov, and Hwee Tou Ng. 2016. Source language adaptation approaches for resource-poor machine translation. *Computational Linguistics*, 42(2):277–306.

Vivien Arief Wardhany, Muhammad Hendrick Kurnia, Sritrusta Sukaridhoto, Amang Sudarsono, and Dadet Pramadihanto. 2016. Smart presentation system using hand gestures and Indonesian speech command. *17th International Electronics Symposium, IES 2015*, pages 68–72.

Harco Leslie Hendric Spits Warnars, Jessica Aurellia, and Kendrick Saputra. 2021. Translation learning tool for local language to Bahasa Indonesia using knuth-morris-pratt algorithm. *TEM Journal*, 10(1):55–62.

Tifani Warnita and Dessi Puji Lestari. 2017. Identifying deception in Indonesian transcribed interviews through lexical-based approach. *31st Pacific Asia Conference on Language, Information and Computation, PACLIC 2017*, pages 148–154.

Kok Weiying, Duc Nghia Pham, Ngo Chuan Hai, and Hong Hoe Ong. 2018. Topic modelling for Malay news aggregator. *4th International Conference on Advances in Computing, Communication and Automation, ICACCA 2018*.

Annabelle Wenas, Smita Sjahputri, Takwin Bagus, Alfindra Primaldhi, and Muhamad Roby. 2016. Measuring happiness in large population. *IOP Conference Series. Earth and Environmental Science*, 31(1).

Haryo Akbarianto Wibowo, Tatag Aziz Prawiro, Muhammad Ihsan, Alham Fikri Aji, Radityo Eko Prasojo, Rahmad Mahendra, and Suci Fitriany. 2020. Semi-supervised low-resource style transfer of Indonesian informal to formal language with iterative forward-translation. *2020 International Conference on Asian Language Processing, IALP 2020*, pages 310–315.

Nelly Indriani Widiastuti and Maulvi Inayat Ali. 2021. Elman recurrent neural network for aspect based sentiment analysis. *Journal of Engineering Science and Technology*, 16(3):1991–2000.

W. Widodo, M. Nugraheni, and I. P. Sari. 2021. A comparative review of extractive text summarization in Indonesian language. *IOP Conference Series. Materials Science and Engineering*, 1098(3).

Bambang Dwi Wijanarko, Yaya Heryadi, Hapnes Toba, and Widodo Budiharto. 2020. Automated question generating method based on derived keyphrase structures from bloom's taxonomy. *ICIC Express Letters*, 14(11):1059–1067.

Bambang Dwi Wijanarko, Yaya Heryadi, Hapnes Toba, and Widodo Budiharto. 2021. Question generation model based on key-phrase, context-free grammar, and bloom's taxonomy. *Education and Information Technologies*, 26(2):2207–2223.

Wilbert Wijaya, I Made Murwantara, and Aditya Rama Mitra. 2020. A simplified method to identify the sarcastic elements of Bahasa Indonesia in YouTube comments. *8th International Conference on Information and Communication Technology, ICoICT 2020*.

Rini Wijayanti, Masayu Leylia Khodra, and Dwi Hendratmo Widyantoro. 2021. Indonesian abstractive summarization using pre-trained model. *3rd East Indonesia Conference on Computer and Information Technology, EIConCIT 2021*, pages 79–84.

Bryan Wilie, Karissa Vincentio, Genta Indra Winata, Samuel Cahyawijaya, Xiaohong Li, Zhi Yuan Lim, Sidik Soleman, Rahmad Mahendra, Pascale Fung, Syafri Bahar, and Ayu Purwarianti. 2020. IndoNLU: Benchmark and resources for evaluating Indonesian natural language understanding. Proceedings of the 1st Conference of the Asia-Pacific Chapter of the Association for Computational Linguistics and the 10th International Joint Conference on Natural Language Processing, pages 843–857. Association for Computational Linguistics.

Gabriella Putri Wiratama and Andre Rusli. 2019. Sentiment analysis of application user feedback in Bahasa Indonesia using multinomial naive bayes. *5th International Conference on New Media Studies, CONMEDIA 2019*, pages 223–227.

Tri Wiratno and Hisham Dzakiria. 2016. Examining the writing genre in journal articles of natural science and social science. *Advanced Science Letters*, 22(12):4431–4435.

Maulana Wisnu Prabowo, Indra Budi, and Harry Budi Santoso. 2021. Developing question generation system for Bahasa Indonesia using Indonesian standard language regulation. In *10th International Conference on Software and Computer Applications, ICSCA 2021*, pages 258–261. Association for Computing Machinery.

Sri Ratna Wulan and Suhono Harso Supangkat. 2018. Semi-supervised learning self-training for Indonesian motivational messages classification. *2017 International Conference on ICT for Smart Society, ICISS 2017*, 2018-January:1–7.

Benjamin Chu Min Xian, Mohammad Arshi Saloot, Amiera Syazreen Mohd Ghazali, Khalil Bouzekri, Rohana Mahmud, and Dickson Lukose. 2016. Benchmarking Mi-AR: Malay anaphora resolution. *2016 International Conference on Optoelectronics and Image Processing, ICOIP 2016*, pages 59–69.

Fuad Yahaya, Nurazzah Abdul Rahman, and Zainab Abu Bakar. 2017a. Resolving Malay word sense disambiguation utilizing cross-language learning sources approach. *Advanced Science Letters*, 23(11):11320–11324.

M. F. Yahaya, N. A. Rahman, Z. A. Bakar, and H. Hasmy. 2017b. Evaluation on knowledge extraction and machine learning in resolving Malay word ambiguity. *Journal of Fundamental and Applied Sciences*, 9(5S):115–130.

Mohd Fuad Yahaya, Nurazzah Abd Rahman, and Zainab Abu Bakar. 2018. Morphological analysis of Malay words for resolving ambiguity. *4th International Conference on Information Retrieval and Knowledge Management: Diving into Data Sciences, CAMP 2018*, pages 31–35.

Nurenzia Yannuar, Emalia Iragiliati, and Zen Evynurul Laily. 2017. Bòsò walikan malang's address practices. *GEMA Online Journal of Language Studies*, 17(1):107–123.

Muhamad Rizky Yanuar and Shun Shiramatsu. 2020. Aspect extraction for tourist spot review in Indonesian language using bert. *2nd International Conference on Artificial Intelligence in Information and Communication, ICAIIC 2020*, pages 298–302.

Yangfan Yao, Jian Cao, Tao Wang, Rui Liu, Zhenyuan Dai, and Haoqiang Yuan. 2020. Efficient implementation of dirty words detection in decision tree model. *5th IEEE International Conference on Signal and Image Processing, ICSIP 2020*, pages 60–64.

Yin-Lai Yeong, Tien-Ping Tan, Keng Hoon Gan, and Siti Khaotijah Mohammad. 2018. Hybrid machine translation with multi-source encoder-decoder long short-term memory in English-Malay translation. *International Journal on Advanced Science, Engineering and Information Technology*, 8(4-2):1446–1452.

Yin-Lai Yeong, Tien-Ping Tan, and Siti Khaotijah Mohammad. 2016. Using dictionary and lemmatizer to improve low resource English-Malay statistical machine translation system. *5th Workshop on Spoken Language Technologies for Under-resourced languages, SLTU 2016*, 81:243–249.

Ong Jun Ying, Muhammad Mun'im Ahmad Zabidi, Norhafizah Ramli, and Usman Ullah Sheikh. 2020. Sentiment analysis of informal Malay tweets with deep learning. *IAES International Journal of Artificial Intelligence*, 9(2):212–220.

Emny Harna Yossy, Syaeful Karim, and Dannys Dian Rachmantyo. 2020. Development of Indonesian language speech recognition algorithm model in knowledge database. *7th International Conference on Information Technology, Computer, and Electrical Engineering, ICITACEE 2020*, pages 126–129.

Julio Christian Young and Andre Rusli. 2019. Review and visualization of Facebook's fasttext pretrained word vector model. *2019 International Conference on Engineering, Science, and Industrial Applications, ICESI 2019*.

Grelly Lucia Yovellia Londo, Dwiky Hutomo Kartawijaya, Hesti Tri Ivariyani, Yohanes Sigit Purnomo W.P, Aryasuta P. Muhammad Rafi, and Dipo Ariyandi. 2019. A study of text classification for Indonesian news article. *1st International Conference of Artificial Intelligence and Information Technology, ICAIIT 2019*, pages 205–208.

Ranu Yulianto and Siti Mariyah. 2017. Building automatic mind map generator for natural disaster news in Bahasa Indonesia. *4th International Conference on Information Technology Systems and Innovation, ICITSI 2017*, 2018-January:177–182.

Rajif Agung Yunmar and I. Wayan Wiprayoga Wisesa. 2019. Design of ontology-based question answering system for incompleted sentence problem. *International Conference on Science, Infrastructure Technology and Regional Development 2018, ICoSITeR 2018*, 258.

Ahmad Rizal Mohd Yusof, Mohd Firdaus Hamdan, Shamsul Amri Baharuddin, and Mohd Syariefudin Abdullah. 2017. Bahasa Melayu sebagai bahasa ilmu (BMBI) di ruang siber: Suatu analisis sosiologi tehadap pembangunan pangkalan data BMBI. *e-BANGI*, 12(3):1–15.

Maslida Yusof and Karim Harun. 2021. Spesifikasi ruang dalam kata kerja deiktik datang dan pergi (Spatial specification in deictic verbs datang and pergi). *Geografia*, 17(2).

Maslida Yusof, Karim Harun, and Nasrun Alias. 2016. 'Sampai Di' vs 'Sampai Ke': Accomplishment or achievement verb? *Pertanika Journal of Social Sciences and Humanities*, 24(March):49–64.

Yusmeera Yusof, Siti Zamaratol-Mai Sarah Mukari Mukari, Kartini Ahmad, Mariam Adawiah Dzulkifli, Kalaivani Chellapan, Nashrah Maamor, and Wan Syafira Ishak. 2019. Development of Malay word materials for auditory-cognitive training for older adults. *International Journal on Disability and Human Development*, 18(2):153–160.

Yusra, Muhammad Fikry, Bambang Riyanto Trilaksono, Rado Yendra, and Ahmad Fudholi. 2017. Music interest classification of Twitter users using support vector machine. *Journal of Theoretical and Applied Information Technology*, 95(11):2352–2358.

Kamal Yusuf and Dewi Puspita. 2020. Diachronic corpora as a tool for tracing etymological information of Indonesian-Malay lexicon. *Register Journal*, 13(1):153–182.

Nuhu Yusuf, Mohd Amin Mohd Yunus, Norfaradilla Wahid, and Mohd Najib Mohd Salleh. 2021. A statistical linguistic terms interrelationship approach to query expansion based on terms selection value. *3rd International Conference on Information and Communication Technology and Applications, ICTA 2020*, 1350:234–244.

Raden Sandra Yuwana, Endang Suryawati, and Hilman F. Pardede. 2019. On empirical evaluation of deep architectures for Indonesian pos tagging problem. *6th International Conference on Computer, Control, Informatics and its Applications, IC3INA 2018*, pages 204–208.

Raden Sandra Yuwana, Asri Rizki. Yuliani, and Hilman F. Pardede. 2018. On part of speech tagger for Indonesian language. *2nd International Conferences on Information Technology, Information Systems and Electrical Engineering, ICITISEE 2017*, 2018-January:369–372.

Nur Imanina Zabha, Zakiah Ayop, Syarulnaziah Anawar, Erman Hamid, and Zaheera Zainal Abidin. 2019. Developing cross-lingual sentiment analysis of Malay Twitter data using lexicon-based approach. *International Journal of Advanced Computer Science and Applications*, 10(1):346–351.

Muhamad Fadzllah Zaini, Anida Saruddin, Mazura Mastura Muhammad, and Siti Saniah Abu Bakar. 2020a. Perception and metaphorical smell: A Malay manuscript study (petua membina rumah) as an Asian text. In *2020 Conference of the Global Council on Anthropological Linguistics in Asia, GLOCAL 2020*, volume 2020-January, pages 345–351. Global Council on Anthropological Linguistics.

Muhamad Fadzllah Zaini, Anida Sarudin, Mazura Mastura Muhammad, and Siti Saniah Abu Bakar. 2020b. Representatif leksikal ukuran sebagai metafora linguistik berdasarkan teks klasik Melayu (Representatives of lexical ukuran as linguistics metaphors based on Malay classic text). *GEMA Online Journal of Language Studies*, 20(2):168–187.

Muhamad Fadzllah Zaini, Anida Sarudin, Mazura Mastura Muhammad, Zulkifli Osman, Husna Faredza Mohamed Redzwan, and Muhammad Aanas Al-Muhsin. 2021. House building tips (HBT) corpus dataset as a resource to discover Malay architectural ingenuity and identity. *Data in Brief*, 36:107013.

Zamahsyari and Arif Nurwidyantoro. 2017. Sentiment analysis of economic news in Bahasa Indonesia using majority vote classifier. *3rd International Conference on Data and Software Engineering, ICoDSE 2016*.

Bakar Zamri Abu, Ismail Normaly Kamal, and Rawi Mohd Izani Mohamed. 2017. Rule-based approach on extraction of Malay compound nouns in standard Malay document. *IOP Conference Series. Materials Science and Engineering*, 226(1).

Subhan Zein. 2020. *Language Policy in Superdiverse Indonesia*. Taylor & Francis Group.

Zhiping Zeng, Van Tung Pham, Haihua Xu, Yerbolat Khassanov, Eng Siong Chng, Chongjia Ni, and Bin Ma. 2021. Leveraging text data using hybrid transformer-lstm based end-to-end ASR in transfer learning. *12th International Symposium on Chinese Spoken Language Processing, ISCSLP 2021.*

Lixuan Zhao, Jian Yang, and Qinglai Qin. 2020. Enhancing prosodic features by adopting pre-trained language model in Bahasa Indonesia speech synthesis. *3rd International Conference on Algorithms, Computing and Artificial Intelligence, ACAI 2020.*

Nurul Syeilla Syazhween Zulkefli, Nurazzah Abdul Rahman, and Mazidah Puteh. 2017. A survey: Framework of an information retrieval for Malay translated hadith document. *8th International Conference on Mechanical and Manufacturing Engineering, ICME 2017*, 135.

A Appendix

A more accessible table will be available here.

Table 1

Education Specific Studies		
Title	Author	Year
The Development of an Audible Pattani Malay- ...	Boonkwan et al.	2016
A corpus platform of Indonesian academic language	Kwary	2019
U-tapis: Automatic spelling filter as an effort to ...	Mediyawati et al.	2021
Word level auto-correction for latent semantic ...	Ratna et al.	2017
The development of Indonesian POS tagging sys ...	Muljono et al.	2017c
A morphophonemic analysis on the affixation in ...	Ampa et al.	2019
Learning Indonesian Frequently Used Vocabulary ...	Lin et al.	2019b
Towards developing colloquial Indonesian lan ...	Nataprawira and Carey	2020
Pengajaran bahasa dan pemerolehan bahasa ke ...	Rosiyana	2020
Cross-corpus native language identification via ...	Rangel et al.	2018
Acquiring Extended Units of Meaning: The Role ...	Suhardijanto and Putra	2019
Designing Phonetic Alphabet for Bahasa Indone ...	Karlina et al.	2020
Indonesian essay grading module using Natural ...	Ajitiono and Widyani	2017
Automated Bahasa Indonesia essay evaluation ...	Amalia et al.	2019a
Exploiting Syntactic Similarities for Preposition ...	Irmawati et al.	2016
Vocabulary Load on Two Mainstream Indonesian ...	Destiani et al.	2018a
Perbandingan Deiksis pada Dua Buku Ajar: Anal ...	Destiani et al.	2018b
Pengembangan kamus pemelajar Bahasa Indone ...	Fadly	2018
Teaching Specific Purpose Translation: Utiliza ...	Siregar	2017
Theme markedness in the translation of student ...	Sofyan and Tarigan	2018
Strategi Pengukuran Upaya Berbahasa Menerusi ...	Redzwan et al.	2020
Generating artificial error data for Indonesian ...	Irmawati et al.	2017b
Menangani Kekaburan Kemahiran Prosedur dan ...	Anida et al.	2019
Environmental awareness content for character ...	Rahmawati et al.	2020
Inquisitive semantic analysis of Malay language ...	Subet and Md Nasir	2019
An experimental study of text preprocessing tech ...	Hasanah et al.	2018
N-Gram Keyword Retrieval on Association Rule ...	Setiawan et al.	2018
Semi-supervised learning self-training for Indone ...	Wulan and Supangkat	2018
Evaluating rnn architectures for handling imbal ...	Christianto et al.	2020
A comparison of supervised text classification ...	Dhammajoti et al.	2020
Automatic Indonesia's questions classification ...	Kusuma et al.	2016
Answer categorization method using K-means for ...	Ratna et al.	2019
Knowing Right from Wrong: Should We Use ...	Septiandri et al.	2020
WPS: Application for Generating Answer of ...	Oktavia et al.	2021
Question generation model based on key-phrase, ...	Wijanarko et al.	2021
Developing Question Generation System for Ba ...	Wisnu Prabowo et al.	2021
Applications of natural language processing in ...	Maxwell-Smith et al.	2020
Developing an online self-learning system of In ...	Muljono et al.	2016
Automatic Pronunciation Generator for Indone ...	Hoesen et al.	2019
Anita: Intelligent Humanoid Robot with Self- ...	Andreas et al.	2019
A novel model and implementation of humanoid ...	Budiharto et al.	2021
End of Table		

B Appendix

A more accessible table will be available here.

Table 2

Broad NLP		
Title	Author	Year
IndoLEM and IndoBERT: A Benchmark Dataset...	Koto et al.	2020b
Unstructured Malay Text Analytics Model in Crime	Mohemad et al.	2020c
A new framework for information system devel...	Sukarsa et al.	2018
An overview of BPPT's Indonesian language re...	Gunarso et al.	2016
Challenges and development in Malay natural lan...	Lan and Logeswaran	2020

Statistical and Corpus Work		
Title	Author	Year
The Development of an Audible Pattani Malay-...	Boonkwan et al.	2016
Linking the TUFS Basic Vocabulary to the Open...	Bond et al.	2020
Hypernym-Hyponym Relation Extraction from...	Nityasya et al.	2019
Linguistik Korpus Kuantitatif dan Kajian Seman...	Rajeg	2020
Characteristics of Malay translated hadith corpus	Sazali et al.	2020
Syllabification Model of Indonesian Language...	Fanani and Suyanto	2021
A corpus platform of Indonesian academic language	Kwary	2019
Examining the writing genre in journal articles of...	Wiratno and Dzakiria	2016
An annotated news corpus of Malaysian Malay	Chung and Shih	2019
Introduction of the Asian Language Treebank	Riza et al.	2017
Information extraction: Evaluating named entity...	Sazali et al.	2017
Comparative study on corpus development for...	Din et al.	2017
Building the Pornography Corpus for Bahasa In...	Gunawan et al.	2019c
Building a Malay-English code-switching subjec...	Kasmuri and Basiron	2019
IndoNLU: Benchmark and Resources for Evaluat...	Wilie et al.	2020
Development of a retrieval system for Al Hadith...	Aulia et al.	2017b
An Ontological Approach towards Dialogue...	Mohd Yunus et al.	2017
Co-occurrence technique and dictionary based...	Sholikah et al.	2017
Penentuan Fitur bagi Pengekstrakan Tajuk Berita...	Shahrul Azman Mohd et al.	2018a
The Development of the Malaysian Hansard Cor...	Abdullah et al.	2021
Rancang bangun aplikasi web scraping untuk kor...	Mitra et al.	2017
NUWT: Jawi-specific buckwalter corpus for...	Bakar et al.	2016
Towards Computational Linguistics in Minangk...	Koto and Koto	2020
Indonesia Language Sphere: an ecosystem for...	Murakami	2019
Designing a collaborative process to create bilin...	Nasution et al.	2019
Tufs asian language parallel corpus (talpco)	Nomoto et al.	2018b
Sentence segmentation and phrase strength esti...	Hanum and Bakar	2016b
Evaluation of Energy and Duration on Malay...	Hanum and Bakar	2016a
Prosodic breaks on Malay speech corpus: Evalua...	Hanum et al.	2017
Demarcating and highlighting in Papuan Malay...	Kaland and Baumann	2020
Repetition Reduction Revisited: The Prosody of...	Kaland and Himmelmann	2020
Stress predictors in a Papuan Malay random forest	Kaland et al.	2019
Lexical analyses of the function and phonology...	Kaland et al.	2021
Development of under-resourced Bahasa Indone...	Cahyaningtyas and Arifianto	2018
Generative Indonesian Conversation Model using...	Chowanda and Chowanda	2018
An evaluation of sentence selection methods on...	Muljono et al.	2020
Indonesian Affective Word Resources Construc...	Hulliyah et al.	2019

Continuation of Table 2		
Title	Author	Year
Analysis of Indonesian sentiment text based on ...	Hulliyah et al.	2017
An integrated semi-automated framework for ...	Kaity and Balakrishnan	2020
BMBI: A Development of a Special Corpus on ...	Rumaisa et al.	2020
Sentiment analysis in Indonesian and French by ...	Shalunts et al.	2018
Preliminary Research Design on Sensor Data ...	Aulia et al.	2020
Review on the Role of Social Media for Dengue ...	Kannan et al.	2019
Twitter corpus creation: The case of a Malay ...	Saloot et al.	2016
An Application that Invites Users to Participate ...	Thamrin et al.	2019b
A publicly available Indonesian corpora for auto ...	Koto	2016
Development of multilingual social media data ...	Rumaisa et al.	2019
Bahasa Indonesia text corpus generation using ...	Amalia et al.	2019b
WatsaQ: Repository of Al Hadith in Bahasa (Case ...	Aulia et al.	2017a
Malay Online Virtual Integrated Corpus ...	Awang Abu Bakar et al.	2018
The Development of an Integrated Corpus for ...	Bakar	2020
Building Corpus in Bahasa Indonesia for Porno ...	Chandra et al.	2019
Building a web-based application for language ...	Dinakaramani and Suhardijanto	2019
Development of a Web-based Jahai-Malay Lan ...	Mohtar et al.	2021
A Review on Building Bilingual Comparable Cor ...	Nasharuddin et al.	2018
Linguistic studies using large annotated corpora: ...	Nomoto and Moeljadi	2019
Introducing the Asian language treebank (ALT)	Thu et al.	2016
Bahasa Melayu sebagai Bahasa Ilmu (BMBI) di ...	Yusof et al.	2017
A dependency annotation scheme to extract syn ...	Irmawati et al.	2017a
Domain-specific stop words in Malaysian parlia ...	Rahman et al.	2021a
Transforming semi-structured indigenous dictio ...	Ranaivo-Malançon et al.	2017
Rule-based text normalization for Malay social ...	Ariffin and Tiun	2020
Evaluating the use of word embeddings for part- ...	Abka	2017
Information Retrieval System to Find Articles and ...	Sulaeman et al.	2020
U-tapis: Automatic spelling filter as an effort to ...	Mediyawati et al.	2021
Building the Application to Identify Incorrect Cap ...	Gunawan et al.	2019a
Feature extraction using regular expression in de ...	Sulaiman et al.	2017
Incorporating Knowledge Base in Unsupervised ...	Rifin and Hamzah	2017
Movie Summarization based on Indonesian Subti ...	Situmeang et al.	2019
Semantic similarity measures for Malay-English ...	Mahadzir et al.	2018
Recognizing and normalizing temporal expres ...	Mirza	2016
Automatic Grammar Checking System for Indone ...	Rahutomo et al.	2018
Rapid Heteronym Disambiguation for Text-to- ...	Samsudin and Rahim	2019
Identification Of Features In Predicting Promi ...	Tiun and Hong	2020
An Enhancement of Malay Social Media Text ...	Bakar et al.	2019
Text Normalization Algorithm on Twitter in Com ...	Hanafiah et al.	2017
Pre-processing Tasks in Indonesian Twitter Messages	Hidayatullah and Ma'arif	2017
Proposal: A Hybrid Dictionary Modelling Ap ...	Nor Azlizawati Binti et al.	2017
Normalization of Indonesian-English code-mixed ...	Barik et al.	2019
Review and Visualization of Facebook's FastText ...	Young and Rusli	2019
Bidirectional encoder representations from trans ...	Candra et al.	2021
Categorization of Malay social media text and ...	Maskat and Rahman	2020
Exploring Edit Distance for Normalising Out-of- ...	Raja et al.	2019
An automatic construction of Malay stop words ...	Chekima and Alfred	2016
Word Sense Disambiguation in Bahasa Indonesia ...	Faisal et al.	2018
Cross-Lingual and Supervised Learning Ap ...	Mahendra et al.	2018b

Continuation of Table 2

Title	Author	Year
Enhancing Latent Semantic Analysis by Embed...	Rahman et al.	2017
Word level auto-correction for latent semantic...	Ratna et al.	2017
Evaluating Word Embeddings for Indone...	Rizal and Stymne	2020
Designing and implementing parsing for ambigu...	Soyusiawaty and Aribowo	2016
Word Embedding for Small and Domain-specific...	Tiun et al.	2020a
Resolving Malay word sense disambiguation uti...	Yahaya et al.	2017a
Morphological Analysis of Malay Words for Re...	Yahaya et al.	2018
Evaluation on knowledge extraction and machine...	Yahaya et al.	2017b
Naïve Bayes implementation into Bahasa Indone...	Jodhinata and Hartanti	2016
Analyzing Malay Stemmer Performance Towards...	Rodzman et al.	2018
Information Retrieval Technique for Indonesian...	Riza et al.	2020
Stemmer and phonotactic rules to improve n-gram...	Suyanto et al.	2021
Analysis of Stemming Influence on Indonesian...	Hidayatullah et al.	2016
Towards stemming error reduction for Malay texts	Kassim et al.	2019
Enhanced Text Stemmer with Noisy Text Normal...	Kassim et al.	2020b
Design Consideration of Malay Text Stemmer...	Kassim et al.	2020a
Malay word stemmer to stem standard and slang...	Kassim et al.	2016b
Enhanced rules application order to stem affixa...	Kassim et al.	2016a
Word stemming challenges in Malay texts: A lit...	Kassim et al.	2016c
Non-formal affixed word stemming in Indonesian...	Putra et al.	2018a
Accuracy measurement on Indonesian non-formal...	Putra et al.	2019
Improving stemming techniques for non-formal...	Rianto et al.	2021
Comparison of stemming algorithms on Indone...	Rizki et al.	2019
Improvement on stemmer algorithm for Indone...	Syawanodya and Huda	2018
The development of Indonesian POS tagging sys...	Muljono et al.	2017c
Semantic Role Labeling in Conversational Chat...	Rachman et al.	2018a
POS-Tagging for informal language (study in In...	Suryawati et al.	2018
Part-of-speech tagger for Malay social media texts	Ariffin and Tiun	2018
A comparison of different part-of-speech tagging...	Amrullah et al.	2017
Indonesian part of speech tagging using hidden...	Cahyani and Vindiyanto	2019
Part-of-speech (pos) tagger for Malay language...	Gaber et al.	2020
Part of Speech Tagging for Indonesian Language...	Handrata et al.	2019
Evaluating the Morphological and Capitalization...	Manik et al.	2019
Morphology analysis for Hidden Markov Model...	Muljono et al.	2017a
POS-tagging for non-English tweets: An auto...	Munandar et al.	2017
An evaluation of MorphInd's morphological an...	Prihantoro	2021
Rule-based Part of Speech Tagger for Indonesian...	Purnamasari and Suwardi	2018
Evaluating lstm networks, hmm and wfst in...	Tan et al.	2017b
Time Series Neural Network Model for Part-of-...	Tanadi	2018
Implementation of ontology-based on Word2Vec...	Togatorop et al.	2020
Utilizing Morphological Features for Part-of-...	Trisna et al.	2020
On Empirical Evaluation of Deep Architectures...	Yuwana et al.	2019
On part of speech tagger for Indonesian language	Yuwana et al.	2018
Identifying Sentence Structure in Bahasa Indone...	Gunawan et al.	2019d
Breakdown film script using parsing algorithm	Wahana et al.	2020
Algorithm for simple sentence identification in...	Anggraini et al.	2018
Indonesian Parsing using Probabilistic Context-...	Cahyani et al.	2020
The effectiveness of bottom up technique with...	Fairuzz Hiloh et al.	2018
Warning and Suggestion System on Syntax Tree...	Haris et al.	2019

Continuation of Table 2		
Title	Author	Year
A Finite State Machine Model to Determine Syl . . .	Haryanto and Aripin	2019
Tackling the Low-resource Challenge for Canoni . . .	Mager et al.	2020
Modification of Chu-Liu/Edmonds algorithm and . . .	Nizami and Purwarianti	2017
Sentence boundary disambiguation for Indone . . .	Putra et al.	2017
Rule based sentence segmentation of Indonesian . . .	Raharjo et al.	2018
Ensemble technique utilization for Indonesian de . . .	Rahman and Purwarianti	2017
How Similar is Similar: A Comparison of Bahasa . . .	Basuki and Antaputra	2020a
New tools for old tasks: A new approach to the . . .	Don and Knowles	2020
Identifying and Exploiting Definitions in Wordnet . . .	Moeljadi and Bond	2016
A morphophonemic analysis on the affixation in . . .	Ampa et al.	2019
A study of education-related Chinese words used . . .	Kia and Su'Ad	2019
Learning Indonesian Frequently Used Vocabulary . . .	Lin et al.	2019b
Towards developing colloquial Indonesian lan . . .	Nataprawira and Carey	2020
Pengajaran bahasa dan pemerolehan bahasa ke . . .	Rosiyana	2020
An identification of authentic narrator's name fea . . .	Abd Rahman et al.	2016
The process of forming a more complex idiomatic . . .	Ismail et al.	2021
Exploring Lexical Differences Between Indone . . .	Lin et al.	2019c
A Corpus Driven Analysis of Representations . . .	Nor Fariza Mohd et al.	2019
Exploiting Malay corpus on islamic issue using . . .	Setik et al.	2018
English legalese translation into Indonesian	Dewi et al.	2021
A corpus-based analysis of English core modal . . .	Oktavianti	2019
Comparison of Personal Pronoun between Arabic . . .	Markhamah Abdul et al.	2017
Prosody analysis of Malay language storytelling . . .	Ramli et al.	2016
Code-switching in Bruneian online retail transactions	Henry and Ho	2016
Comparison of the themes of Malaysian Friday . . .	Aasim Asyafi'Ie bin Ahmad et al.	2017
Where is the Head Positioned in Indonesian Lan . . .	Ansari and Suhardijanto	2019
Online-Dating Romance Scam in Malaysia: An . . .	Azianura Hani et al.	2019
Conceptual structure representation of causative . . .	Binti Yusof and Binti Rosly	2018
A new look at Pattani Malay Initial Geminates: a . . .	Burroni et al.	2020
The particle pun in modem Indonesian and . . .	Chambert-Loir	2019
Lagi in standard Malaysian Malay: Its meaning . . .	Chung	2019
The Indonesian prefixes PE- and PEN-: A study . . .	Denistia and Baayen	2019
Similar southeast asian languages: Corpus-based . . .	Ding et al.	2016
The Design of Lexical Database for Indonesian . . .	Gunawan and Amalia	2017
Automatic extraction of multiword expression can . . .	Gunawan et al.	2017b
The Observation of Bahasa Indonesia Official . . .	Gunawan et al.	2018a
Utterance-final particles in Klang Valley Malay	Hoogervorst	2018
Covid-19 dalam Korpus Peristilahan Bahasa . . .	Kasdan et al.	2020
Gandaan Separa dalam Terminologi Bahasa . . .	Kasdan et al.	2017
Compilation of Malay criminological terms from . . .	Lee et al.	2019
Exploring Letter's Differences between Partial . . .	Lin et al.	2019a
Hedging in the discussion sections of English and . . .	Loi and Lim	2019
Formation of health science terminology by users . . .	Mohamad et al.	2020c
Politeness in communication through local chil . . .	Mohamad Nor et al.	2019
Translation and Markedness	Ni et al.	2018
Frequency of Verbs in Lifestyle Column in the . . .	Oktavianti and Pramesti	2019
The influence of students' L1 and spoken English . . .	Prihantoro	2016
Sketching the Semantic Change of Jahanam and . . .	Puspita and Yusuf	2020
Vector Space Models and the usage patterns of . . .	Rajeg et al.	2019

Continuation of Table 2

Title	Author	Year
Cross-corpus native language identification via...	Rangel et al.	2018
Imbuhan meN- dengan Kata Nama Konkrit Unsur...	Saad and Jalaluddin	2020
Ideational Grammatical Metaphors in Doctrinal...	Saragih et al.	2017
Collocation analysis of variants of intensifies in...	Sarudin et al.	2020a
Discourse functions of the two non-active voices...	Shiohara et al.	2019
The Framework of Multiword Expression in In...	Suhardijanto et al.	2020
Acquiring Extended Units of Meaning: The Role...	Suhardijanto and Putra	2019
Bila dan Mengapa 'You' Menjadi 'Kita': Satu...	Sulaiman and Bin Mohamad Yusoff	2020
Frasa Topik Dan Fokus Dalam Bahasa Melayu:...	Sultan and Othman	2021
Prestige of products and code-switching in retail...	Ting et al.	2020
Quantifying semantic shift visually on a Malay...	Tiun et al.	2020b
Informativity and the actuation of lenition	Uriel Cohen	2017
Spesifikasi ruang dalam kata kerja deiktik datang...	Yusof and Harun	2021
'Sampai Di' Vs 'Sampai Ke': Accomplishment...	Yusof et al.	2016
Diachronic Corpora as a Tool for Tracing Etymo...	Yusuf and Puspita	2020
Representatif Leksikal Ukuran sebagai Metafora...	Zaini et al.	2020b
Designing Phonetic Alphabet for Bahasa Indone...	Karlina et al.	2020
Indonesian essay grading module using Natural...	Ajitiono and Widyani	2017
Automated Bahasa Indonesia essay evaluation...	Amalia et al.	2019a
Exploiting Syntactic Similarities for Preposition...	Irmawati et al.	2016
Vocabulary Load on Two Mainstream Indonesian...	Destiani et al.	2018a
Perbandingan Deiksis pada Dua Buku Ajar: Anal...	Destiani et al.	2018b
Pengembangan kamus pemelajar Bahasa Indone...	Fadly	2018
Fossicking in dominant language teaching: Ja...	Maxwell-Smith	2021
Teaching Specific Purpose Translation: Utiliza...	Siregar	2017
Theme markedness in the translation of student...	Sofyan and Tarigan	2018
Strategi Pengukuran Upaya Berbahasa Menerusi...	Redzwan et al.	2020
Generating artificial error data for Indonesian...	Irmawati et al.	2017b
Menangani Kekaburan Kemahiran Prosedur dan...	Anida et al.	2019
Environmental awareness content for character...	Rahmawati et al.	2020
Development of Malay word materials for...	Yusof et al.	2019
Exploring gender issues associated with...	Aziz	2019
"Happiness" in Bahasa Indonesia and its implica...	Effendi and Muchammadun	2018
Defying the global: The cultural connotations of...	Hashim and Rahim	2016
The implicit meaning in Malay figurative lan...	Mansor and Jalaluddin	2016
"Is Selangor in Deep Water?": A Corpus-driven...	Norsimah Mat et al.	2019
Linguistic Representation of Violence in Judicial...	Othman et al.	2019
Text mining of online job advertisements to iden...	Panggih Kusuma et al.	2020
Inquisitive semantic analysis of Malay language...	Subet and Md Nasir	2019
Spotlight on LGBT in Malaysian online newspa...	Ting et al.	2021
The polarity of war metaphors in sports news: A...	Hua et al.	2021
Communicating insults in cyberbullying	Hua et al.	2019
Analisis korpus terhadap idiom Bahasa Indonesia...	Paramarta	2018
Conceptual metaphor and linguistic manifesta...	Saad et al.	2018b
The relationship between astronomy and architec...	Sarudin et al.	2020b
Beyond the closet? The trends and visibility of...	Subir	2019
Trend Penggunaan Bahasa Samar dalam Persidan...	Tan et al.	2017a
Form and function of negation in German and...	Triyono et al.	2020
Bòsò Walikan Malang's Address Practices	Yannuar et al.	2017

Continuation of Table 2		
Title	Author	Year
Perception and metaphorical smell: A Malay ...	Zaini et al.	2020a
House building tips (HBT) corpus dataset as a ...	Zaini et al.	2021
Understanding quotation extraction and attribu ...	Purnomo W.P et al.	2020
An automatic health surveillance chart interpreta ...	Aulia and Barmawi	2016
A text representation model using Sequential ...	Alias et al.	2018b
Relationship analysis of keyword and chapter in ...	Chua and Nohuddin	2017
Relation extraction using dependency tree kernel ...	Esperanti and Purwarianti	2016
An experimental study of text preprocessing tech ...	Hasanah et al.	2018
Relation Detection for Indonesian Language Us ...	Hasudungan and Purwarianti	2019
Classification of short possessive clitic pronoun ...	Noor et al.	2020
Assessing Suitable Word Embedding Model for ...	Phua et al.	2020
Experiments on coreference resolution for Indone ...	Suherik and Purwarianti	2017
Malay manuscripts transliteration using statistical ...	Razak et al.	2019
Transliteration engine for union catalogue of ...	Razak et al.	2018
SMVS: A Web-based Application for Graphical ...	Ahmat Baseri et al.	2020
Exploring Multilingual Syntactic Sentence Repre ...	Liu et al.	2019a
Transfer Building of Multiword Expression Re ...	Liu and Wang	2020
Reclassification of the Leipzig Corpora Collec ...	Nomoto et al.	2018a
Learning Indonesian-Chinese Lexicon with Bilin ...	Qiu and Zhu	2016
Machine Reading		
Title	Author	Year
Towards corpus and model: Hierarchical ...	Fu et al.	2021
Towards a Standardized Dataset on Indonesian ...	Khairunnisa et al.	2020
Semi-supervised learning approach for Indone ...	Aryoyudanta et al.	2017
Named entity recognition for extracting concept ...	Santoso et al.	2021
Rule-based Approach on Extraction of Malay ...	Zamri Abu et al.	2017
A review of named entity recognition and classifi ...	Mohemad et al.	2020a
Detecting proper nouns in Indonesian-language ...	Raharjo et al.	2020
Named entity recognition on Indonesian tweets ...	Azarine et al.	2019
Named entity recognition on Indonesian Twitter ...	Rachman et al.	2018b
An enhanced Malay named entity recognition us ...	Asmai et al.	2018
Named entity recognition using fuzzy c-means ...	Salleh et al.	2018
Named entity recognition on Indonesian mi ...	Taufik et al.	2017
DBpedia entities expansion in automatically build ...	Alfina et al.	2017
Entity annotation WordPress plugin using ...	Aprilius et al.	2017
Developing name entity recognition for structured ...	Azzahra et al.	2020
Detection of compound word with combination ...	Bakar et al.	2017
Identification of Noun + Verb Compound Nouns ...	Bakar et al.	2018a
Automatic detection of compound word in Malay ...	Bakar et al.	2018b
Named-Entity Recognition for Indonesian Lan ...	Gunawan et al.	2018c
A Concise Review of Named Entity Recognition ...	Ikhwan Syafiq et al.	2019
Empirical Evaluation of Character-Based Model ...	Kurniawan and Louvan	2018
A Semi-supervised Algorithm for Indonesian ...	Leonandya et al.	2016
Malay name entity recognition using limited re ...	Noor et al.	2016
Medical Named Entity Recognition for Indone ...	Rahman	2018
Pendekatan Teknik Pengecaman Entiti Nama ...	Saad and Mohamed Kamil	2018
A Malay named entity recognition using condi ...	Salleh et al.	2017
Low Complexity Named-Entity Recognition for ...	Sukardi et al.	2020
Building Low-Resource NER Models Using Non- ...	Tsygankova et al.	2021

Continuation of Table 2

Title	Author	Year
Hate speech detection in the Indonesian language: ...	Alfina et al.	2018
Developing Indonesian corpus of pornography ...	Andriansyah et al.	2018
Bahasa Indonesia pre-trained word vector genera ...	Putri et al.	2021
Indonesian text document similarity detection sys ...	Sinaga and Hansun	2018
N-Gram Keyword Retrieval on Association Rule ...	Setiawan et al.	2018
The Effectiveness of Using Malay Affixes for Han ...	Mohamed et al.	2018
Author-Topic Modelling for Reviewer Assign ...	Kusumawardani and Khairunnisa	2019
Benchmarking Mi-AR: Malay anaphora resolution	Xian et al.	2016
Fake news identification characteristics using ...	Al-Ash and Wibowo	2018
Graph-based text representation for Malay trans ...	Alias et al.	2017a
Building automatic mind map generator for natu ...	Yulianto and Mariyah	2017
Neural sequence-to-sequence learning of internal ...	Ruzsics and Samardzic	2017
Classification of user comment using word2vec ...	Kurnia and Girsang	2021
Short Message Service (SMS) Spam Filtering us ...	Theodorus et al.	2021
Analysis and implementation of cross lingual ...	Dewi et al.	2018
Long short-term memory for hate speech and abu ...	Salim and Suhartono	2021
Semi-supervised learning self-training for Indone ...	Wulan and Supangkat	2018
Multi-Label Topic Classification of Hadith of ...	Abu Bakar et al.	2019a
Hoax analyzer for Indonesian news using rnns ...	Adipradana et al.	2021
An evolutionary-based term reduction approach ...	Alfred et al.	2017
Assessing factors that influence the performances ...	Alfred et al.	2016
A comparison study of document clustering using ...	Amalia et al.	2020a
An Efficient Text Classification Using fastText ...	Amalia et al.	2020b
Optimizing Deep Learning for Detection Cyber ...	Anindyati et al.	2019
Evaluating rnn architectures for handling imbal ...	Christianto et al.	2020
A comparison of supervised text classification ...	Dhammajoti et al.	2020
Classifying Medical Document in Bahasa Indone ...	Dhomas Hatta and Kiki Purnama	2021
Using naïve bayes classifier for application feed ...	Ferdino and Rusli	2019
The identification of pornographic sentences in ...	Gunawan et al.	2019e
The Best Parameter Tuning on RNN Layers for ...	Hikmah et al.	2020
A language identifier for Indonesian and Malay ...	Indra et al.	2016
A category classification algorithm for Indonesian ...	Jaafar et al.	2016
The impacts of singular value decomposition al ...	Jambak et al.	2019
Automatic Indonesia's questions classification ...	Kusuma et al.	2016
Comparative Study of Machine Learning Ap ...	Mohammad Najib et al.	2017
Hoax Analyzer for Indonesian News Using Deep ...	Nayoga et al.	2021
Study of hoax news detection using naïve bayes ...	Pratiwi et al.	2018
Building a question classification model for a ...	Puteh et al.	2019
Age Group Based Document Classification in Ba ...	Putra et al.	2020
Hoax web detection for news in bahasa using sup ...	Rahmat et al.	2019
Indonesian news classification using convolu ...	Ramdhani et al.	2020
Answer categorization method using K-means for ...	Ratna et al.	2019
Identifying fake news in Indonesian via super ...	Rusli et al.	2020
Indonesian news classification based on NaBaNA	Septian et al.	2017
Knowing Right from Wrong: Should We Use ...	Septiandri et al.	2020
Enhancing text classification performance by pre ...	Setiabudi et al.	2021
Text Classification Services Using Naïve Bayes ...	Setiani and Ce	2018
Argument annotation and analysis using deep ...	Suhartono et al.	2020
Semi-supervised Category-specific Review Tag ...	Sun et al.	2020

Continuation of Table 2		
Title	Author	Year
Short Message Service Filtering with Natural Lan ...	Tandra et al.	2021
Implementation of Naïve Bayes Classifier Algo ...	Thirafi and Rahutomo	2018
Research on Pseudo-label Technology for Multi- ...	Wang et al.	2021
Efficient Implementation of Dirty Words Detec ...	Yao et al.	2020
A Study of Text Classification for Indonesian ...	Yovellia Londo et al.	2019
Developing the COVID-19 Malay Corpus Using ...	Hakimi and Rahman	2021
Query rewriting and corpus of semantic similarity ...	Purnamasari et al.	2016
Performance Evaluation of Inverted Files, B-Tree ...	Rosnan et al.	2019
Word prediction algorithm in resolving ambiguity ...	Sazali et al.	2016
Implementation of LSI method on information ...	Pardede and Barmawi	2016
A document recommendation system of stem ...	Parwita	2020
Weighted inverse document frequency and vector ...	Pratama et al.	2020
Cross Language Information Retrieval Using Par ...	Rahmanda et al.	2019
Machine Learning Approach for Sentiment Anal ...	Mantoro et al.	2020
Natural Language Interface to Database (NLIDB) ...	Anisyah et al.	2019
A Survey on Context-Aware Information Re ...	Bin Rodzman et al.	2018a
The implementation of fuzzy logic controller for ...	Bin Rodzman et al.	2018b
Experiment with text summarization as a positive ...	Bin Rodzman et al.	2019b
Indonesian document retrieval using vector space ...	Fitriasari et al.	2017
Access to Relational Databases Using Interroga ...	Ghassani and Widagdo	2018
Automatic open domain information extraction ...	Gultom and Wibowo	2018
Open Text Ontology Mining to Improve Re ...	Hamzah and Kamaruddin	2021
Multi-word similarity and retrieval model for a ...	Hanum et al.	2019
Syntactic rule-based approach for extracting con ...	Husin et al.	2018
Web Service for Search Engine Bahasa Indonesia ...	Husni et al.	2020
Information Retrieval for Malay Text: A Decade ...	Kamaruddin et al.	2021
Teknik Pengukuhan Perangkak Tumpuan melalui ...	Masnizah et al.	2018
Natural Language Interface to Database (NLIDB) ...	Poetra et al.	2019
Content-based Filtering Model for Recommenda ...	Putri et al.	2019b
Fabricated and Shia Malay translated hadith as ...	Rodzman et al.	2020
Domain specific concept ontologies and text sum ...	Rodzman et al.	2019
Rule-based Indonesian Open Information Extraction	Romadhony et al.	2018
A Statistical Linguistic Terms Interrelationship ...	Yusuf et al.	2021
A Survey: Framework of an Information Retrieval ...	Zulkefli et al.	2017
Crowdsourcing in developing repository of phrase ...	Thamrin et al.	2019a
Single document keywords extraction in Bahasa ...	Trisna and Nurwidyantoro	2020
Topic modeling on Indonesian online shop chat	Hidayatullah et al.	2019
Indonesian abstractive text summarization using ...	Adelia et al.	2019
Topic labeling towards news document collection ...	Adhitama et al.	2017
MYTextSum: A Malay Text Summarizer Model ...	Alias et al.	2018a
A Malay text corpus analysis for sentence com ...	Alias et al.	2016
Extract, compress and summarize–An experiment ...	Alias et al.	2017c
A Malay text summarizer using pattern-growth ...	Alias et al.	2017b
Understanding Human Sentence Compression Pat ...	Alias et al.	2018c
Bilingual extractive text summarization model ...	Alias et al.	2020
A Syntactic-based Sentence Validation Technique ...	Alias et al.	2021
Indonesian Automatic Text Summarization Based ...	Cai et al.	2019
Summarizing Indonesian news articles using ...	Garmastewira and Khodra	2019
Review of the recent research on automatic text ...	Gunawan and Amalia	2018

Continuation of Table 2		
Title	Author	Year
Multi-document Summarization by using Tex...	Gunawan et al.	2019b
Automatic Text Summarization for Indonesian...	Gunawan et al.	2017a
Liputan6: A Large-scale Indonesian Dataset for...	Koto et al.	2020a
Peringkasan dokumen berita Bahasa Indonesia...	Mandar and Gunawan	2017
The purpose of bellman-ford algorithm to summa...	Maylawati et al.	2020
Sequential pattern mining and deep learning to...	Maylawati et al.	2019
Technique on Malay text summarization: A review	Mohemad et al.	2020b
Generation of news headline for Malay language...	Noah et al.	2018
Text simplification for Malay corpus: A Review	Omar et al.	2021
Automatic Text Summarization for Malay News...	Rahman et al.	2021b
Towards product attributes extraction in Indone...	Rif'at et al.	2018
Multidocument Abstractive Summarization using...	Severina and Khodra	2019
Penjanaan Ringkasan Isi Utama Berita Bahasa...	Shahrul Azman Mohd et al.	2018b
Terrorism domain corpus building using Latent...	Suhendra et al.	2018
Topic Modelling for Malay News Aggregator	Weiying et al.	2018
A comparative review of extractive text summa...	Widodo et al.	2021
Indonesian Abstractive Summarization using Pre-...	Wijayanti et al.	2021
A Conceptual Framework for Malay-English...	Lim et al.	2021
Design of Ontology-based Question Answering...	Yunmar and Wayan Wiprayoga Wisesa	2019
Corpus development for Indonesian consumer-...	Hakim et al.	2018
Towards question identification from online...	Mahendra et al.	2018a
WPS: Application for Generating Answer of...	Oktavia et al.	2021
Automated question generating method based on...	Wijanarko et al.	2020
Question generation model based on key-phrase,...	Wijanarko et al.	2021
Developing Question Generation System for Ba...	Wisnu Prabowo et al.	2021
Developing an adaptive language model for Ba...	Hidayatullah and Suyanto	2019
Pembangunan Taksonomi dari Teks Melayu...	Mohd Zakree Ahmad et al.	2018
Document Similarity Detection Using Indonesian...	Ramadhanti and Mariyah	2019
Paraphrase construction of Al Quran in Indone...	Hutami et al.	2019
Rude-Words Detection for Indonesian Speech Us...	Novitasari et al.	2019
Taxonomy development from Malay text using...	Ahmad Nazri et al.	2018
Cross-Language Plagiarism Detection System Us...	Anak Agung Putri et al.	2017
Plagiarism Detection for Indonesian Language...	Arifin et al.	2018
Knowledge representation system for copula sen...	Cahyani et al.	2016
Keyword extraction from scientific articles in Ba...	Gunawan et al.	2020
Extracting disease-symptom relationships from...	Halim et al.	2018
Segregation of Code-Switching Sentences using...	Kasmuri and Basiron	2020
Automated verbalization of ORM models in...	Lim and Halpin	2016
Noun phrases extraction using shallow parsing...	Santoso et al.	2016
Implementing Graph Based Rank on Online News...	Syafiandini et al.	2019
Translation		
Title	Author	Year
A framework for English and Malay cross-lingual...	Nasharuddin et al.	2019
User participation in building language reposi...	Thamrin et al.	2018
Google vs. Instagram Machine Translation: Mul...	Larassati et al.	2019
Neural Machine Translation model for University...	Aneja et al.	2020
Quality translation enhancement using sequence...	Ayu et al.	2018
Meaning preservation in Example-based Machine...	Chua et al.	2017
English-Indonesian Neural Machine Translation...	Dwiastuti	2019

Continuation of Table 2

Title	Author	Year
Benchmarking multidomain English-Indonesian ...	Guntara et al.	2020
A Neural Machine Translation Approach for ...	Low et al.	2020
IIT Bombay's English-Indonesian submission at ...	Singh et al.	2016
Source language adaptation approaches for ...	Wang et al.	2016
Hybrid machine translation with multi-source ...	Yeong et al.	2018
Using Dictionary and Lemmatizer to Improve ...	Yeong et al.	2016
Semi-Supervised Low-Resource Style Transfer ...	Wibowo et al.	2020
Morphological analysis of speech translation into ...	Nurilman Baehaqi et al.	2019
Pengaruh Pennambahan Korpus Paralel pada ...	Abidin and Permata	2021
Effect of mono corpus quantity on statistical ma ...	Abidin et al.	2021
Peningkatan Mesin Penerjemah Statistik dengan ...	Darwis et al.	2019
Peningkatan Akurasi Penerjemah Bahasa Daerah ...	Sujaini	2018
Translation Learning Tool for Local Language to ...	Warnars et al.	2021
Leveraging additional resources for improving ...	Trieu et al.	2019
Rule-based Reordering and Post-Processing for ...	Mawalim et al.	2017
A novel Hadith authentication mobile system in ...	Fadele et al.	2020
Translation of idioms from Arabic into Malay via ...	Abidin et al.	2020
Multiple pivots in statistical machine translation ...	Budiwati and Aritsugi	2019
A Parallel Evaluation Data Set of Software Docu ...	Buschbeck and Exel	2020
A Comprehensive Analysis of Bilingual Lexicon ...	Irvine and Callison-Burch	2017
Malay-corpus-enhanced Indonesian-Chinese neu ...	Liu and Wang	2019
Language Resource Extension for Indonesian- ...	Liu et al.	2019b
Development of mobile application for Malay ...	Rahman et al.	2020
Enhancing Pivot Translation Using Grammatical ...	Trieu and Nguyen	2018
Translating Malay Compounds into Arabic Based ...	Wahiyudin and Romli	2021
Generating image description on Indonesian lan ...	Nugraha et al.	2019
Visual question answering for monas tourism ob ...	Siregar and Chahyati	2020
Learning translations via images with a massively ...	Hewitt et al.	2018
Adaptive Attention Generation for Indonesian Im ...	Mahadi et al.	2020
Cross-lingual projection for class-based language ...	Gfeller et al.	2016
Extremely Low-Resource Neural Machine Trans ...	Rubino et al.	2020
Machine translation of Indonesian: A review	Septarina et al.	2019
See also - A review on Indonesian machine trans ...	Rahutomo et al.	2019
Spoken Dialogue Systems		
Title	Author	Year
Malay speech corpus of telecommunication call ...	Draman et al.	2017
Detection of Malay phrase breaks using energy ...	Mohamed Hanum and Abu Bakar	2016
A hybrid approach for single channel speech en ...	Jamal et al.	2020
Developing ASR for Indonesian-English Bilin ...	Maxwell-Smith and Foley	2021
Applications of natural language processing in ...	Maxwell-Smith et al.	2020
Robust Feature Extraction Based On Spectral And ...	Ibrahim et al.	2019
Transfer learning with bottleneck feature net ...	Lim et al.	2016
Cross-Lingual Machine Speech Chain for Ja ...	Novitasari et al.	2020
Comparing statistical classifiers for emotion clas ...	Hamzah et al.	2017
Influences of age in emotion recognition of spon ...	Jamil et al.	2017
Influences of languages in speech emotion recog ...	Rajoo and Aun	2016
Voice-Based Malay Commands Recognition by ...	Abu et al.	2020
Automatic Transcription and Captioning System ...	Andra and Usagawa	2020
Improved Transcription and Speaker Identifica ...	Andra and Usagawa	2021

Continuation of Table 2		
Title	Author	Year
Speech-to-Text Conversion in Indonesian Lan...	Dwijayanti et al.	2021
Comparison of feature extraction MFCC and LPC...	Endah et al.	2017
Development of language identification system...	Gunawan et al.	2018b
Voiced and unvoiced separation in Malay speech...	Hanifa et al.	2019
Wavelet based feature extraction for the vowel sound	Hidayat et al.	2016
Shared-hidden-layer deep neural network for...	Hoesen et al.	2018
Classification and clustering to identify spoken...	Ibrahim and Lestari	2018
Automatic phoneme identification for Malay dialects	Khaw et al.	2017
Speech to Text of Patient Complaints for Bahasa...	Laksono et al.	2019
Malay language speech recognition for preschool...	Maseri and Mamat	2019
Indonesian audio-visual speech corpus for multi...	Maulana and Fanany	2018a
Sentence-level Indonesian lip reading with spa...	Maulana and Fanany	2018b
Sphinx4 for Indonesian continuous speech recog...	Muljono et al.	2017b
Indonesian graphemic syllabification using a near...	Parande and Suyanto	2019
Rule-Based Pronunciation Models to Handle...	Putri et al.	2019a
Speech to Text Translation for Malay Language	Rami Ali and Rini	2017
Assessing automatic speech recognition in mea...	Rosdi et al.	2017
Hybrid methods of Brandt's generalised likeli...	Seman and Norazam	2019
Incorporating syllabification points into a model...	Suyanto	2019b
Flipping onsets to enhance syllabification	Suyanto	2019a
Phonological similarity-based backoff smoothing...	Suyanto	2020
End-to-End Speech Recognition Models for a...	Suyanto et al.	2020
Indonesian syllabification using a pseudo nearest...	Suyanto et al.	2016
Recognizing Five Major Dialects in Indonesia...	Tawaqal and Suyanto	2021
Specific acoustic models for spontaneous and dic...	Vista et al.	2018
Cloud-based automatic speech recognition sys...	Wang et al.	2018
Smart presentation system using hand gestures...	Wardhany et al.	2016
Leveraging Text Data Using Hybrid Transformer-...	Zeng et al.	2021
Indonesian Corpus Constructing and Text Process...	Kong and Yang	2018
Utilizing Indonesian Allophones and Intraword...	Uliniansyah et al.	2019
Developing an online self-learning system of In...	Muljono et al.	2016
Automatic Pronunciation Generator for Indone...	Hoesen et al.	2019
Multi Speaker Speech Synthesis System for In...	Budiman and Lestari	2020
A Bilingual Speech Synthesis System of Standard...	Chen et al.	2020
Poetry visualization in digital technology	Noh et al.	2019
The first Malay language storytelling text-to-...	Ramli et al.	2017
An Iterated Two-Step Sinusoidal Pitch Contour...	Ramli et al.	2021
A Tool to Solve Sentence Segmentation Problem...	Uliniansyah et al.	2016
Enhancing Prosodic Features by Adopting Pre-...	Zhao et al.	2020
Anita: Intelligent Humanoid Robot with Self-...	Andreas et al.	2019
A novel model and implementation of humanoid...	Budiharto et al.	2021
Teach your robot your language! trainable neural...	Hinaut and Twiefel	2020
The Architecture of Speech-to-Speech Translator...	Santosa et al.	2019
Development of text and speech corpus for an...	Teduh Uliniansyah et al.	2018
Chatbot Application on Internet of Things (IoT)...	Gunawan et al.	2019f
Virtual assistant using lstm networks in Indonesian	Mirwan et al.	2018
Forming of Dyadic Conversation Dataset for Ba...	Tho et al.	2018
Development of Indonesian Language Speech...	Yossy et al.	2020
GMM based automatic speaker verification sys...	Stefanus et al.	2017

Continuation of Table 2		
Title	Author	Year
Recurrent Neural Network to Deep Learn Conver...	Chowanda and Chowanda	2017
Virtual phone discovery for speech synthesis with...	Nayak et al.	2019

Speaker States		
Title	Author	Year
An automatic lexicon generation for Indonesian...	Ayu et al.	2019
Minimally-supervised sentiment lexicon induc...	Darwich et al.	2017
Extraction Sentiment Analysis Using naive Bayes...	Jaka Harjanta and Herlambang	2020
Automatic Semantic Orientation of Adjectives for...	Riyanti et al.	2018
Enhanced Malay sentiment analysis with an en...	Al-Moslmi et al.	2017
Aspect and Opinion Extraction of Indonesian Lip...	Kun Indarta and Romadhony	2021
Identifying deception in Indonesian transcribed...	Warnita and Lestari	2017
Aspect Extraction for Tourist Spot Review in In...	Yanuar and Shiramatsu	2020
Framework of sentiment annotation for document...	Sutabri and Ardiansyah	2017
Evaluation of support vector machine and deci...	Saad et al.	2018a
Sentiment analysis for low resource languages: A...	Le et al.	2016
Indonesian Lexicon-Based Sentiment Analysis of...	Kurniawan et al.	2021
A Simplified Method to Identify the Sarcastic Ele...	Wijaya et al.	2020
Experiment with lexicon based techniques on...	Bin Rodzman et al.	2019a
Implementation of a Machine Learning Algo...	Buntoro et al.	2021
Sentiment Analysis of Malay Social Media Text	Chekima and Alfred	2018
Random forest approach fo sentiment analysis in...	Fauzi	2018
Word embedding comparison for Indonesian lan...	Imaduddin et al.	2019
Text Mining and Support Vector Machine for Sen...	Imamah et al.	2020
Unsupervised aspect-based sentiment analysis on...	Sasmita et al.	2018
Elman recurrent neural network for aspect based...	Widiastuti and Ali	2021
Multilingual sentiment analysis: A systematic lit...	Abdullah and Rusli	2021
Polarity classification tool for sentiment analysis...	Abu Bakar et al.	2019b
Long short term memory convolutional neural...	Af'idah et al.	2020
Malay sentiment analysis based on combined clas...	Al-Saffar et al.	2018
An analysis of Malay language emotional speech...	Apandi and Jamil	2017
Aspect-Based Sentiment Analysis Using Convo...	Cahyadi and Khodra	2018
Rule-Based Model for Malay Text Sentiment...	Chekima et al.	2018
Speech-Emotion Detection in an Indonesian Movie	Fahmi et al.	2020
A comparative study of sentiment analysis using...	Fikri and Sarno	2019
Sentiment analysis for Malay language: system...	Handayani et al.	2018
Sentiment analysis using recurrent neural...	Kurniasari and Setyanto	2020a
Sentiment Analysis using Recurrent Neural Network	Kurniasari and Setyanto	2020b
Aspect-based Opinion Mining on Beauty Product...	Mahfiz and Romadhony	2020
Aspect-Based Sentiment Analysis on Candidate...	Manik et al.	2020
Sentiment Analysis Using Word2vec and Long...	Muhammad et al.	2021
English and Malay cross-lingual sentiment lexi...	Nasharuddin et al.	2017
Word2vec for Indonesian sentiment analysis to...	Nawangsari et al.	2019
The Influence of Negation Handling on Sentiment...	Ningtyas and Herwanto	2018
Sentiment analysis system for movie review in...	Nurdiansyah et al.	2018
An experimental study of lexicon-based sentiment...	Pamungkas and Putri	2017
A comparison of the use of several different re...	Pratama et al.	2019
Pair Extraction of Aspect and Implicit Opinion...	Setiowati et al.	2019
Sentiment analysis of application user feedback...	Wiratama and Rusli	2019
Sentiment analysis of economic news in Bahasa...	Zamahsyari and Nurwidyantoro	2017

Continuation of Table 2		
Title	Author	Year
Indonesia Hate Speech Detection Using Deep...	Sutejo and Lestari	2019
Criminality recognition using machine learning...	Malim et al.	2019
Personality Measurement Design for Ontology...	Alamsyah et al.	2020
A preliminary study on hybrid sentiment model...	Eshak et al.	2018
A Progress on the Personality Measurement...	Alamsyah et al.	2019
Speech Emotion Recognition for Indonesian Lan...	Lasiman and Lestari	2019
Social Media		
Title	Author	Year
Opinion QA-Pairs Generation from Indonesian...	Suwarningsih and Nuryani	2019
Preprocessing for crawler of short message social...	Ariestya et al.	2018
Pola Penggunaan Bahasa Melayu dalam Twitter...	Khalid and Rahim	2021
Cyberbullying through intellect-related insults	Sood et al.	2020
Formal and Non-Formal Indonesian Word Usage...	Utami et al.	2019b
Ten-year compilation of #savekpk Twitter dataset	Rahutomo et al.	2020
Word Cloud Result of Mobile Payment User Re...	Dewi et al.	2020
Ensemble method for Indonesian Twitter hate...	Fauzi and Yuniarti	2018
Event detection in Twitter: A keyword volume...	Hossny and Mitchell	2019
Multi-label Hate Speech and Abusive Language...	Ibrohim and Budi	2019a
Identification of hate speech and abusive language...	Ibrohim et al.	2019
Classification of Radicalism Content from Twitter...	Idris et al.	2019
Hierarchical multi-label classification to identify...	Prabowo et al.	2019
Topic classification and clustering on Indonesian...	Pratama and Purwarianti	2017
Twitter Topic Modeling on Football News	Hidayatullah et al.	2018
Topic Summarization of Microblog Document in...	Jiwanggi and Adriani	2016
Negation handling in sentiment classification us...	Amalia et al.	2018
A Framework for Sentiment Analysis Implemen...	Asniar and Aditya	2017
Social Media Analytics using Sentiment and Con...	Balakrishnan et al.	2021
Multi-Classes Emotion Detection for Unbalanced...	Farsiah et al.	2020
Twitter sentiment analysis in under-resourced lan...	Ferdiana et al.	2019
Corpus Usage for Sentiment Analysis of a Hash...	Herlawati et al.	2019
Sentiment analysis on Bahasa Indonesia tweets...	Iswanto and Poerwoto	2018
Social tension and crime related events detection...	Jamil et al.	2019
Bilingual sentiment detection - Investigating im...	Kaur and Balakrishnan	2016
Comparison of SVM Naïve Bayes Algorithm for...	Kristiyanti et al.	2019
Indonesian Twitter Sentiment Analysis Using...	Kurniawan and Maharani	2020
Aspect-level Sentiment Analysis for Social Media...	Kusumawardani and Maulidani	2020
Sentiment Analysis Using Weighted Emoticons...	Maulidiah Elfajr and Sarno	2018
Employ Twitter data to perform sentiment analy...	Mohamad et al.	2020b
Classification of Twitter data by sentiment analy...	Mohamad et al.	2020a
Detecting candidates of depression, anxiety and...	Nasrudin et al.	2019
Naive Bayes as opinion classifier to evaluate stu...	Permana et al.	2017
Sentiment Analysis of BPJS Kesehatan's Services...	Rasyada et al.	2020
When Homecoming is not Coming: 2021 Home...	Sandra and Lumbangaol	2021
Aspect-Based Sentiment Analysis for Posts on...	Setik et al.	2021
Applying Opinion Mining Technique on Tourism...	Situmorang et al.	2019
Does it make you sad? A lexicon-based sentiment...	Suryadi	2021
Emotion analysis using self-training on...	Tan et al.	2020
Sentiment analysis for telco popularity on Twitter...	Tan et al.	2016
Hate speech classification in Indonesian language...	Taradhita and Putra	2021

Continuation of Table 2

Title	Author	Year
Sentiment Analysis of Indonesians Response to ...	Tauhid and Ruldeviyani	2020
Code-mixed sentiment analysis of Indonesian lan ...	Tho et al.	2021
Simulation of marketplace customer satisfaction ...	Turdjai and Mutijarsa	2017
Hashtag Global Surgery: The Role of Social Me ...	Vervoort and Luc	2020
School from home situation in Indonesia: An ex ...	Wahyuni et al.	2020
Measuring happiness in large population	Wenas et al.	2016
Sentiment analysis of informal Malay tweets with ...	Ying et al.	2020
Developing cross-lingual sentiment analysis of ...	Zabha et al.	2019
Automatic Labelling of Malay Cyberbullying ...	Maskat et al.	2020
Personality prediction based on Twitter informa ...	Ong et al.	2017
Personality Modelling of Indonesian Twitter ...	Ong et al.	2021
Profiling analysis of DISC personality traits based ...	Utami et al.	2019a
Supervised learning and resampling techniques ...	Utami et al.	2021
D-Loc Apps: A Location Detection Application ...	Fitrianah et al.	2020
Music interest classification of Twitter users us ...	Yusra et al.	2017
Lexical based sentiment analysis - Verb, adverb ...	Shamsudin et al.	2016
Construction of the Malay language psychometric ...	Ahmad et al.	2017
Hate speech detection in Indonesian language on ...	Bunga Batara et al.	2019
Hate speech detection in Indonesian language on ...	Erizal et al.	2019
Hate speech detection on Indonesian Instagram ...	Pratiwi et al.	2019
Hate speech detection in Indonesian language In ...	Putra and Nurjanah	2020
Hate speech detection in Indonesian language on ...	Briliani et al.	2019
Recognizing the sarcastic statement on WhatsApp ...	Afiyati et al.	2018
Construction of Malay abbreviation corpus based ...	Omar et al.	2017
Context-sensitive normalization of social media ...	Kusumawardani et al.	2018
A taxonomy of Malay social media text	Maskat and Munarko	2019
Detecting opinion spams through supervised ...	Hazim et al.	2018
The development of Bahasa Indonesia corpora for ...	Jambak and Setiawan	2018
Review on sentiment analysis approaches for so ...	Abdullah et al.	2017
Sentiment Analysis of Noisy Malay Text: State ...	Abu Bakar et al.	2020
Emotion detection of tweets in Indonesian lan ...	Cahyaningtyas et al.	2017
Bias aware lexicon-based Sentiment Analysis of ...	Hijazi et al.	2017
Translated vs non-translated method for multilin ...	Ibrohim and Budi	2019b
Classification and quantification of user's emo ...	Jamaluddin et al.	2017
A hybrid model for social media sentiment analy ...	Putra et al.	2018b
Natural language processing based features for ...	Suhaimin et al.	2017
Modified framework for sarcasm detection and ...	Suhaimin et al.	2019
Concerns of thalassemia patients, carriers, and ...	Phang et al.	2021

End of Table

English-Malay Cross-Lingual Embedding Alignment using Bilingual Lexicon Augmentation

Lim Ying Hao, Jasy Liew Suet Yan
School of Computer Sciences, Universiti Sains Malaysia
11800 Penang, Malaysia
yinghaoly@student.usm.my, jasyliew@usm.my

Abstract

As high-quality Malay language resources are still a scarcity, cross lingual word embeddings make it possible for richer English resources to be leveraged for downstream Malay text classification tasks. This paper focuses on creating an English-Malay cross-lingual word embeddings using embedding alignment by exploiting existing language resources. We augmented the training bilingual lexicons using machine translation with the goal to improve the alignment precision of our cross-lingual word embeddings. We investigated the quality of the current state-of-the-art English-Malay bilingual lexicon and worked on improving its quality using Google Translate. We also examined the effect of Malay word coverage on the quality of cross-lingual word embeddings. Experimental results with a precision up till 28.17% show that the alignment precision of the cross-lingual word embeddings would inevitably degrade after 1-NN but a better seed lexicon and cleaner nearest neighbours can reduce the number of word pairs required to achieve satisfactory performance. As the English and Malay monolingual embeddings are pre-trained on informal language corpora, our proposed English-Malay embeddings alignment approach is also able to map non-standard Malay translations in the English nearest neighbours.

1 Introduction

Distributional semantic models produce word embeddings that allow us to compare the relationship between words. In (static) word embeddings, each word is associated to a continuous real-valued vector such that words that are semantically similar to each other will be in close proximity when we visualize them. Word embeddings that have been adopted extensively include but are not limited to CBOW (Mikolov, Chen, et al., 2013), Skip-gram (Mikolov, Chen, et al., 2013) and GloVe (Pennington et al., 2014).

Word embeddings that are pre-trained monolingually are limited to tasks solely in its own language. For this reason, we are unable to compare the meaning of words between languages or transfer models trained on one language to another language (Ruder et al., 2019). Cross-lingual word embeddings could overcome the language constraint and make it possible for the more abundant English resources to be leveraged for emotion or other text classification in Malay (i.e., the resource poor language of interest). In cross-lingual word embeddings, words that are semantically similar regardless of the languages, will appear to be close to each other in the vector space.

The current state-of-the-art multilingual language models like mBERT (Devlin et al., 2019) and XLM-RoBERTa (Conneau et al., 2020) for cross-lingual transfer are computationally expensive. Cross-lingual word embeddings offers an alternative that is cost-effective for cross-lingual transfer requiring a model to be trained only using the source language, which can then subsequently be applied to perform zero-shot or few-shot learning (Ghasemi et al., 2020) on the target language.

In this study, we attempt to align English and Malay monolingual static word embeddings pre-trained on informal text (i.e., tweets or Instagram posts) using the transformation method proposed by Smith et al. (2017). Corpora used to pre-train the embeddings are neither parallel nor aligned, and the only bilingual signal comes from the training bilingual lexicon. Instead of constructing the

Proceedings of the 60th Annual Meeting of the Association for Computational Linguistics
Student Research Workshop, pages 229 - 238
May 22-27, 2022 ©2022 Association for Computational Linguistics

training bilingual lexicon from parallel corpora (Dinu et al., 2015; Smith et al., 2017), we exploit and extend an existing English-Malay bilingual lexicon. The drawback of using the set of word pairs in this bilingual lexicon is that there are numerous invalid word pairs that need to be filtered out. However, using the bilingual lexicon, we are able to generalize the mapping to word embeddings trained on corpora of other domains. We also created a new bilingual lexicon that was shown to be better than the baseline seed lexicon in alignment precision.

To the best of our knowledge, there is no gold-standard bilingual lexicon available for our evaluation task. We select a portion of the bilingual lexicon available on Malaya Documentation (Husein, 2018) and manually extracted the Malay translations for the English-side seed words from *Dewan Bahasa dan Pustaka Malaysia* [1] (DBP). Malaya Documentation offers a current state-of-the-art Malay-English lexicon, which is currently not validated.

The contributions of this study are three-fold.:

a) We created a better English-Malay bilingual lexicon in terms of alignment precision than that the one from Malaya Documentation that has been widely used.
b) We created a gold-standard bilingual lexicon containing approximately 1,200 word pairs to be used as the seed dictionary to induce a better embedding mapping or as a test set to evaluate the quality of cross-lingual word embeddings for future research.
c) We aligned monolingual word embeddings trained independently on informal corpora to create the first English-Malay cross-lingual word embeddings in the social media domain and evaluated its quality using bilingual lexicon induction.

2 Related Work

Word embeddings alignment is one of the approaches used to bridge the language gap between the source (resource rich) and target (resource poor) languages. Prior studies can be categorized into those that require and do not require a set of bilingual seed lexicons.

Mikolov et al. (2013) were one of the earliest and influential studies using bilingual seed lexicons for word embeddings alignment. A transformation matrix was learnt from the seed word pairs to linearly map the source word embeddings to the target embeddings space. Dinu et al. (2015) enhanced this approach by introducing an L2-regularization least-squares error in the objective function.

Xing et al. (2015) improved the method proposed by Mikolov et al. (2013) by restricting the word vectors to a unit length and constraining the transformation matrix to be orthogonal. They also redefined the objective function by using cosine similarity between the transformed source and target embeddings. These additional steps solved the inconsistency uncovered in Mikolov et al. (2013) and achieved better performance. On top of these constraints, Artetxe et al. (2016) enforced dimension-wise mean centering on the word embeddings so that randomly chosen words would not be semantically similar. Their study also discovered that the improvement attained by Xing et al. (2015) was solely from the orthogonal constraint instead of solving the inconsistency problem. Smith et al. (2017) proved that an orthogonal transformation matrix must also be self-consistent.

Faruqui and Dyer (2014) used Canonical Correlation Analysis (CCA) to learn the transformation matrices from the seed lexicon. Unlike Mikolov et al. (2013), a transformation matric was learnt for both source language and target language, respectively. The source and target word embeddings were then mapped to a new shared vector space where the seed word pairs from a lexicon would be maximally correlated.

Lu et al. (2015) adopted a non-linear extension of CCA to train the transformation matrices. Two neural networks were trained to obtain the transformation matrices by maximizing the correlation of the transformed source and target word embeddings in the new vector space.

Barone (2016) aligned word embeddings by eliminating the need for seed lexicons. They adopted an adversarial autoencoder in mapping the source embeddings to target embeddings. The source embeddings were transformed using an encoder, and the discriminator then tried to match

[1] A government body that coordinates the use of the Malay language in Malaysia.

the latent representations to the distribution of the target embeddings.

Zhang et al. (2017) matched the distribution of the transformed source embeddings to target embeddings using adversarial training. They learnt an orthogonal transformation matrix using the generator, and the discriminator would then try to distinguish the transformed source embeddings from target embeddings. Additionally, they also attempted to relax the orthogonality constraint by using an adversarial autoencoder.

Artetxe et al. (2018) induced the initial seed word pairs by exploiting the similarity distribution between words using an unsupervised method. These initial seed word pairs were then refined through iterative self-learning. They also enforced the transformation matrices used to map the source and target embeddings to the new vector space to be orthogonal.

Feng and Wan (2019) proposed an approach to nonlinearly map the source word embeddings and target word embeddings to a new vector space. They induced the seed word pairs using nearest neighbour retrieval, and the seed word pairs were then refined iteratively using self-learning. Instead of orthogonality, they adopted the Euclidean Norm to guide the learning of the transformation matrices.

Recent studies proposed to align contextual embeddings. Schuster et al. (2019) generalized the approach by Mikolov et al. (2013) and Conneau et. al (2018) to align embeddings from mBERT. Since one word can have different embeddings based on the context, Schuster et al. represented each word using the embedding anchor that was obtained by averaging a subset of its contextual embeddings.

Aldarmaki and Diab (2019) adopted the approach by Mikolov et al. (2013) to map contextual embeddings from the ELMo (Peters et al., 2018). Instead of using the embedding anchor, they constructed a dynamic bilingual lexicon from a parallel corpus with word alignment. Additionally, they also proposed sentence-level mapping in which the transformation matrix was learnt on aligned sentences.

Wang et al. (2020) also extended the method by Mikolov et al. (2013) to contextual embeddings. Similar to Aldarmaki and Diab (2019), they formed the alignment matrix based on aligned word pairs extracted from parallel corpora. The representations extracted from mBERT were then aligned by multiplying with the alignment matrix.

Existing studies have not explored static or contextual word embeddings alignment between English and Malay languages. As word embeddings alignment has shown promising performance in cross-lingual transfer tasks in other language pairs, it provides strong motivation for us to explore how word embeddings alignment can also benefit the English-Malay language pair, and subsequently any future study that may require English-Malay cross-lingual word embeddings.

3 Data Sources

The method requires a monolingual English embedding, a monolingual Malay embedding and a bilingual English-Malay lexicon to map the two monolingual embeddings into a bilingual Malay-English embedding. The quality of the bilingual English-Malay lexicon plays an important role because it serves as the only bridge to map two separate English and Malay monolingual lexicons into a single shared space. Malay is written in the Latin alphabet and shares lexical similarities with Indonesian as they are from the same language family.

3.1 Word Embeddings

Our study used the word2vec **English monolingual word embedding (EWE)** pre-trained on tweets by Godin (2019) using the Skip-gram architecture and contained approximately 3 million words. The words were represented by 400-dimensional vectors.

Word2vec **Malay monolingual word embedding (MYWE)** were pre-trained on tweets and Instagram posts by Husein (2018) using the Skip-gram architecture and contained approximately 1.3 million words. Normalization and spell-check were performed to standardize non-standard Malay words in the embeddings.

We trimmed the vocabulary of the embeddings to the top 200,000 most frequent words from the subset of the training corpora used to train the word embeddings (**top200k-MYWE**). This naïve filter was an attempt to remove non-Malay words from the vocabulary. Additionally, we trimmed the original embeddings separately to the top 800,000 most frequent words from the same corpora and compared them against the words extracted from selected corpora by DBP written in standard Malay to remove non-standard Malay words from the vocabulary (**top800k-MYWE**).

3.2 Bilingual Lexicon

An **English-Malay bilingual lexicon** was obtained from Malaya Documentation (Husein, 2018). Invalid words, non-English words and non-Malay words were filtered out. We used English spell-check in Microsoft Excel to filter English words and *Dewan Eja Pro*[2] to filter Malay words. We randomly selected 90% of these lexicon word pairs for mapping in the training phase (**T-BL**) and regarded it as our baseline, while the remaining 10% were used to create a set of gold standard test English-Malay word pairs. For every word pair, we retained its English side, for which we manually extracted its corresponding Malay translations from the English-Malay dictionary by DBP[1] to create a gold standard bilingual lexicon (**G-BL**). G-BL contains 1273 entries of which one English word can have one or many Malay translations from G-BL. This bilingual lexicon consists of 3675 unique Malay words.

4 Methodology

4.1 Cross-lingual Word Embeddings

To create cross-lingual word embeddings, we mapped the English embeddings, $\boldsymbol{E}$ to the Malay embeddings space using the orthogonal transformations approach proposed by Smith et al. (2017). Malay embeddings were first made to have the same dimensions as English embeddings by post-padding with arrays of zeros. We also normalized both embeddings to a unit length.

From the bilingual lexicons (T-BL) containing n word pairs, two ordered matrices $S_D \in \mathbb{R}^{n\times 400}$ and $T_D \in \mathbb{R}^{n\times 400}$ were formed where i^{th} row of the matrices corresponded to the English and Malay word vectors of the i^{th}word pairs. We then performed Singular Value Decomposition (SVD) operation on the matrix product $P = {S_D}^T T_D \in \mathbb{R}^{400\times 400}$ and subsequently, P was represented by $U\Sigma V^T$. The English embeddings, $\boldsymbol{E}$, were then aligned to the Malay embeddings space by multiplying it with the transformation matrix $\boldsymbol{O} = UV^T$ that was subject to the orthogonal constraint:

$$\max_{O} \textstyle\sum_{i=1}^{n} {t_i}^T \boldsymbol{O} s_i \text{, subject to } \boldsymbol{O}^T\boldsymbol{O} = \boldsymbol{I} \quad (1)$$

4.2 Experiment Extensions

We explored three different directions to extend the initial embeddings mapping using T-BL. The first direction examined how the coverage of the Malay words in the training lexicon could affect the translation accuracy. The second direction investigated if the quality of T-BL is satisfactory, and the third direction aimed to improve the quality of the training bilingual lexicon used for mapping.

Direction 1: We hypothesized that a higher coverage of the Malay words in the training lexicon would improve the translation accuracy of English words. To investigate this hypothesis, we augmented T-BL by using the English-side words from the lexicon as the seed words. A different number (1, 5, 10) of nearest neighbours (NN) of the seed English words was selected using the dot product from their respective embeddings space. This is equivalent to using cosine similarity after normalizing the embeddings to a unit length as shown below:

$$cos(\theta) = \frac{\boldsymbol{V}_i \cdot \boldsymbol{V}_j}{\parallel \boldsymbol{V}_i \parallel \parallel \boldsymbol{V}_j \parallel} \; for \; i \neq j \quad (2)$$

where $\boldsymbol{V}_i$ is the vector representation of the ith seed word and $\boldsymbol{V}_j$ is the vector representation of other English words in the embeddings space.

Selected nearest neighbours were then translated into Malay language using either Google Cloud Translation API or Google Translate function in Google Sheets. This comparison is to help us determine which tool returns better translation as we notice they could return different translations for the same English word. Translated Malay words that are longer than one token were omitted as words in the vocabulary were restricted to be one-token long. Furthermore, the English nearest neighbours that happened to be in G-BL were also discarded to prevent possible data leakage.

Direction 2: We extracted the English-side words of T-BL and translated them into Malay language using Google Cloud Translation API to form a completely new set of seed lexicon (**N-BL**). This resulted in a completely new set of training word pairs having the same size as T-BL to allow direct comparison of the quality of the word pairs.

Direction 3: We observed that the English nearest neighbours could contain noise as the

[2] A Malay proofing tool produced by Dewan Bahasa dan Pustaka.

vocabulary of the English embeddings was not trimmed. Therefore, to remove this noise, we sent selected English nearest neighbours through a word filter to ensure that the nearest neighbours only comprised English words. Two different and independent filters were applied, resulting in two different sets of augmented training lexicons.

The **first filter** was built using words from WordNet. WordNet resembles a thesaurus in which words were grouped into synonymous sets (synsets) based on their concept and these words are known as lemmas. This filter gathered lemmas extracted from every synset into a list and omitted nearest neighbour words that did not match the words in the list.

The **second filter** was built using words from the Words Corpus. Words Corpus is a list of dictionary words attainable from /usr/share/dict/words file in Unix that some spell checkers use. It is a built-in corpus in the Natural Language Toolkit (NLTK) (Bird et al., 2009). Similarly, this filter gathered all words in this corpus into a list and omitted nearest neighbour words that did not have a match in the list.

4.3 Evaluation Metric

We used bilingual lexicon induction to evaluate the quality of our embeddings mapping by finding the top-*N* most semantically similar Malay words to the English words in the test set (G-BL) using cosine similarity from the shared vector space (P@N), where *N* is 1, 5 or 10. To avoid confusion from the translations obtained from Google Translate or bilingual English-Malay dictionary, we use "induced translation" to specifically indicate Malay words from the Malay embeddings that are mapped to the corresponding English words from the English embeddings. P@N measures the proportion of English words in G-BL which have at least one true Malay translation among the *N* Malay induced translations. Formally, P@N can be computed using the following equation:

$$P@N = \frac{\sum_{i=1}^{M} I_i}{M} \quad (3)$$

where M is the number of English words in G-BL. I_i is an indicator function that will take 1 if and only if i^{th} English word in G-BL has at least one correct Malay translation appearing in its corresponding *N* Malay induced translations, and take 0 otherwise. Therefore, the numerator indicates the number of English words that have at least one correct Malay induced translation. An induced translation will not be counted as correct if it does not appear in G-BL.

As our word embeddings were not trained on English-Malay parallel or aligned corpora, the investigation of a different number of Malay nearest neighbours is necessary to determine the extent of correct translations from the English words,. Furthermore, the word embeddings were pre-trained on tweets or Instagram posts known to mostly contain informal words.

5 Results and Discussion

5.1 Comparing Malay Embeddings Coverage

While we fixed the number of word pairs in G-BL, top200k-MYWE and top800k-MYWE have a smaller vocabulary size, and hence different number of effective word pairs for evaluation as reflected in the denominator in the P@10 column of Table 1. We only adopted P@10 in this experiment to justify the choice of the embeddings for subsequent experiments and not to compare the quality of the bilingual lexicon.

Embeddings	P@10
MYWE	22.2041 (274/1234)
top200k-MYWE	25.4036 (299/1177)
top800k-MYWE	24.9167 (299/1200)

Table 1: Performance comparison between embeddings using T-BL

The improvement when using top200k-MYWE and top800k-MYWE was attributed to the reduced noise in the cross-lingual space since the filters removed numerous non-Malay words from the Malay embeddings space. In other words, the English words were not obscured by irrelevant 'Malay' neighbours and could induce the correct Malay translations more easily.

The seemingly higher P@10 from top200k-MYWE was actually due to the lower number of effective word pairs (1177 in the denominator) for evaluation than top800k-MYWE when both embeddings, in fact, returned an exact number of correct translations (299). In this regard, we conclude that there is no difference in the mapping quality using these embeddings. However, given that our downstream task is cross-lingual emotion classification, we are inclined towards

		Google Translate function			Googletranslate API		
	0-NN	1-NN	5-NN	10-NN	1-NN	5-NN	10-NN
P@1	9.2500	9.4167	9.5000	8.9167	9.7500	9.3333	9.1667
P@5	19.0833	19.5833	18.7500	19.5000	19.5000	18.6667	18.0000
P@10	24.9167	25.2500	24.1667	23.6667	25.5000	25.0000	23.1667

Table 2: Performance comparison using T-BL as the seed lexicon and augmenting using different translation tools (0NN: T-BL without augmentation, 1-NN: T-BL augmented with one nearest neighbour, 5NN: T-BL augmented with 5 nearest neighbours, 10-NN: T-BL augmented with 10 nearest neighbours).

top800k-MYWE, which has a broader coverage of Malay words. This would ensure that fewer Malay words in our downstream task get encoded with zero vectors. Thus, for any subsequent extensions of the experiment, we would be using top800k-MYWE.

5.2 Augmentation of T-BL for Bilingual Lexicon Extension

As shown in Table 2, regardless of the translation tools, we managed to obtain a maximum P@1 of 9.8%, P@5 of 19.6% and P@10 of 25.5% on the test bilingual lexicon (G-BL) after augmentation using T-BL. However, the mapping quality seems to be generally better when we augmented T-BL with its 1-NN and 5-NN using Google Cloud Translation API. In other words, Google Cloud Translation API returned more accurate Malay translations independent of the context of English words. For this reason, we used it for subsequent translations.

The coverage of Malay words will always increase with the number of nearest neighbours. In other words, the more number of nearest neighbours included, the higher the coverage. Based on Table 2, our hypothesis positing that higher coverage of Malay words in T-BL does not hold beyond 1-NN using either translation tool. The precisions that initially increased with Malay words coverage using 1-NN augmentation are still aligned with our hypothesis.

However, the precision started to degrade afterwards even though our augmentation broadened the coverage significantly using either translation tool. We speculate that the drop in precision after 1-NN is due to the additional noise (English nearest neighbours that are not legitimate English words) introduced to our training bilingual lexicon, thus lowering the quality of T-BL. This noise will affect the transformation matrix induction adversely when the corresponding Malay translation returned by Google happened to be in the Malay word embeddings vocabulary, as we observed that the translation tool would attempt to correct the spelling of the noise before translation. For example, 'zeroo' was translated to *sifar* (zero), 'weeka' to *mingguan* (weekly), 'talkn' to *bercakap* (talking).

5.3 Quality of T-BL

As shown in Table 3, we managed to obtain better mapping quality in terms of alignment precision using just the naïve approach.

Lexicons	P@1	P@5	P@10
T-BL	9.2500	19.0833	24.9167
N-BL	10.9167	23.3333	27.3333

Table 3: Performance comparison between T-BL and N-BL

The new set of word pairs in the bilingual lexicon (N-BL) improves P@1 by 1.7%, P@5 by 4.2%, and P@10 by 2.4%, suggesting that there is still room for improvement in T-BL quality. It is possible that the words were paired up imprecisely or paired with less frequently used words. In fact, we removed a large number of word pairs from the original non-validated English-Malay bilingual lexicon to form T-BL. This removal gave us the signal that T-BL was below par. Hence, for the experiments in Section 5.4, N-BL is used as the seed lexicon.

5.4 Augmentation of N-BL for Bilingual Lexicon Extension

As shown in Table 4, we managed to achieve a maximum P@1 of 10.9%, P@5 of 23.3% and P@10 of 28.2% on the test bilingual lexicon (G-BL) after filtering the nearest neighbours using the WordNet filter. We also observed marginal improvement over N-BL in the P@10 when augmenting with 1-NN and 5-NN using the NLTK filter. However, the best P@10 using the NLTK filter (27.8% at 1-NN) is still slightly lower than

		NLTK filter			WordNet filter		
	0-NN	1-NN	5-NN	10-NN	1-NN	5-NN	10-NN
P@1	10.9167	10.5000	8.9167	9.5000	10.9167	9.9167	9.7500
P@5	22.333	22.5000	21.2500	19.0833	23.2500	21.5000	19.5000
P@10	27.3333	27.8333	27.4167	25.4167	28.1667	26.2500	24.5000

Table 4: Performance comparison using N-BL as the seed lexicon and filtering the nearest neighbours using different filters.

the best precision using the WordNet filter (28.2% at 1-NN). While the precisions generally degraded after 1-NN, they are still higher than most of the combinations in Section 5.2 without filters.

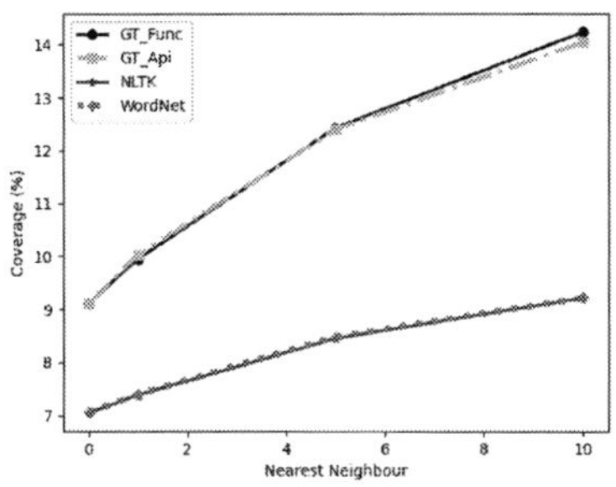

Figure 1: Comparison of the changes of coverage for experiments in Table 2 and Table 4.

Moreover, it is also worth noting from Figure 1 that the general coverage of the Malay words using N-BL is significantly lower than when using T-BL, but we managed to achieve better precisions most of the time with lower amount of computational time. This implies again that our N-BL along with the filter, is better in terms of word pairing quality than T-BL. We hit a P@10 of 28.2% at a lower coverage of about 7.4% when augmenting N-BL with 1-NN along with the WordNet filter. However, at a higher coverage of about 10%, augmenting T-BL with 1-NN using Google Translate API only resulted in a P@10 of 25.5%.

We acknowledged that having an enormous training set of English-Malay word pairs is not desirable. Using N-BL + 10NN still took us significantly longer than N-BL + 5NN and N-BL + 1NN to perform the embeddings mapping, yet the general performance degraded. From the results in Table 4, augmentation using 1-nearest neighbour is deemed ideal as it required the least translation time and training time but yielded the best mapping quality based on our experiments.

Additionally, we also compare our bilingual lexicon (N-BL + 1NN with WordNet filter) with the bilingual lexicons used for MUSE (Conneau et al., 2018) and by Anastasopoulos and Neubig (2020), which are also currently publicly available. We refer to the bilingual lexicons by Anastasopoulos and Neubig (2020) as AN-BL. Both MUSE and AN-BL have two sets of bilingual lexicons: full and train.

Lexicons	P@1	P@5	P@10
N-BL+1NN	10.9167	23.25	28.1667
MUSE-full	8.4167	18.3333	23.0000
MUSE-train	6.6667	16.0833	20.7500
AN-BL-full	8.0000	19.000	23.5833
AN-BL-train	7.4167	16.0833	21.0000

Table 5: Performance comparison between N-BL + 1NN, MUSE-full, MUSE-train, AN-BL-full and AN-BL-train.

As seen in Table 5, our bilingual lexicon also outperformed these bilingual lexicons by a minimum of 4.6%. We observe that there are bilingual lexicons contain word pairs of identical strings in English like *your-your*, *state-state* and *old-old* (i.e., the second word in the pair is identical to the first English word instead of being paired with its corresponding Malay word). While it is possible for English words to appear in Malay embeddings, these word pairs may disrupt the mapping to some extent if the English word also appears in the vocabulary of the Malay embeddings. In addition, our bilingual lexicon is smaller in size and requires 5 times less computational time than MUSE-full and AN-BL-full, but we show that the quality of our bilingual lexicon is better in terms of alignment precision.

5.5 Nearest Neighbours Analysis

Table 6 shows some interesting Malay translations of the English words from our G-BL test set. The term "rrc" in Table 6 is not a legitimate

Malay word as it could be the abbreviation of any words depending on the context, or possibly a result of typing errors that slipped through the cracks in spell-check. Thus, we consider this word as noise. Although none of the induced Malay translations returned matched the gold-standard translation for the word "criminal", some translations are related to this word in a way. For example, *korup* (corrupt), *pelacur* (prostitute), *siber* (cyber), *liwat* (sodomi) and *bersenjata* (armed). The word *kriminal* is not a legitimate Malay word but it is 'homophonically translated' to Malay and has been used to mean "criminal" instead of the correct Malay words *penjenayah* (the person) or *jenayah* (the noun). Such observation proves that Malay words that share similar semantic meaning to their English counterparts are mapped correctly in the bilingual word embedding space and is further strengthened by the mapping to informal Malay words even though our training bilingual lexicon contains only formal words. Since *kriminal* is non-standard and thus not included in our gold-standard bilingual lexicon (G-BL), we did not count this as a correct translation. Similarly, for the word "research", the gold standard only contains *penyelidikan* (the noun) or *menyelidik* (the verb) as its translations, completely leaving out other correct translations such as *kajian*. Moreover, the word *studi* is also an informal Malay word commonly used to represent "study" or "research".

criminal	research	vegetable	sad
korup	pemantauan	perasa	cemburu
kriminal	penyelidikan	makaroni	jijik
rrc	analisis	pete	kecewa
pelacur	penulisan	petai	menyampah
siber	pembelajaran	pindang	cuak
liwat	kajian	bayam	rimas
zalim	riset	tomat	berdosa
rasis	statistik	salmon	terharu
lgbt	studi	sayuran	sebak
bersenjata	penelitian	sardin	sedih

Table 6: Nearest neighbours of selected English words

For the Malay word "vegetable", we observed several semantically similar words to "vegetable" are returned such as *petai* (bitter bean), *bayam* (spinach) and *sayuran* (a variety of vegetables). Regardless of the plurality, *sayuran* is the closest Malay word to vegetable among the induced translations. *Tomat* is possibly a result of typing error for the word *tomato*. On the other hand, we observed Malay words of negative emotions are also returned in addition to the correct translation *sedih* for the word "sad" such as *cemburu* (jealous), *kecewa* (disappointed), *cuak* (scared) and *rimas* (uneasy or anxious). Although there are some Indonesian words in our Malay embeddings space which were not filtered out during the pre-training, such as *riset* and *pete*, these words will be eliminated as Indonesian tweets are removed in our downstream task.

6 Conclusion

In this study, we attempted to create English-Malay cross-lingual word embeddings using an English-Malay bilingual lexicon to map the English and Malay monolingual word embeddings into a single representation that was empirically and intrinsically evaluated based on word pair coverage and alignment precision. Despite the fact that the bilingual lexicon from Malaya Documentation being the current state-of-the-art, we demonstrated that its quality has room for improvement. Our bilingual lexicons (N-BL) obtained using a naïve approach easily outperformed Malaya Documentation in terms of the English-Malay alignment precision. We also investigated the effect of Malay word coverage on bilingual lexicon induction and discovered that a higher coverage would not necessarily improve the alignment precision. Also, we did not select our training or test lexicons based on word frequency in any corpora, thus our evaluation is more unbiased and generalizable.

We are aware that there are semi-supervised and unsupervised approaches in creating cross-lingual word embeddings that require limited or almost no bilingual signals. However, we did not adopt such an approach because both our embeddings were pre-trained on informal corpora, especially our Malay monolingual embeddings still containing significant noise even after applying the filter. Hence, legitimate words would easily be paired up with noise, or vice versa, without bilingual supervision. We adopted word2vec in this study as we were not aware of any existing Malay fastText embeddings pre-trained on the social media domain, and pre-training it ourselves is not within the scope of this study. In the future, we wish to pre-train Malay fastText embeddings that may work better on informal corpora and subsequently explore the feasibility of creating embeddings using semi-supervised and unsupervised methods.

We also plan to evaluate the performance of our English-Malay cross-lingual word embeddings on downstream tasks such as emotion classification.

Acknowledgement

This study was supported by the Ministry of Higher Education Malaysia for Fundamental Research Grant Scheme with Project Code: FRGS/1/2020/ICT02/USM/02/3.

References

Aldarmaki, Hanan, & Diab, Mona. (2019). Context-Aware Cross-Lingual Mapping. Proceedings of the 2019 Conference of the North American Chapter of the Association for Computational Linguistics: Human Language Technologies, Volume 1 (Long and Short Papers), 3906–3911.

Anastasopoulos, Antonios, & Neubig, Graham. (2020). Should All Cross-Lingual Embeddings Speak English? Proceedings of the 58th Annual Meeting of the Association for Computational Linguistics, 8658–8679.

Artetxe Mikel, Labaka Gorka and Agirre Eneko. (2016). Learning principled bilingual mappings of word embeddings while preserving monolingual invariance. Proceedings of the 2016 Conference on Empirical Methods in Natural Language Processing, 2289–2294.

Artetxe Mikel, Labaka Gorka and Agirre Eneko. (2018). A robust self-learning method for fully unsupervised cross-lingual mappings of word embeddings. Proceedings of the 56th Annual Meeting of the Association for Computational Linguistics (Volume 1: Long Papers), 789–798

Barone Antonio Valerio Miceli. (2016). Towards cross-lingual distributed representations without parallel text trained with adversarial autoencoders. Proceedings of the 1st Workshop on Representation Learning for NLP, 121–126.

Bird, Steven, Klein, Ewan, & Loper, Edward. (2009). Natural Language Processing With Python: Analyzing Text With The Natural Language Toolkit. O'Reilly Media, Inc.

Conneau, Alexis, Khandelwal, Kartikay, Goyal, Naman, Chaudhary, Vishrav, Wenzek, Guillaume, Guzmán, Franciso, Grave, Edouard, Ott, Myle, Zettlemoyer, Luke, & Stoyanov, Veselin. (2020). Unsupervised Cross-Lingual Representation Learning At Scale. Proceedings of the 58th Annual Meeting of the Association for Computational Linguistics, 8440–8451.

Conneau, Alexis, Lample, Guillaume, Ranzato, Marc' Aurelio, Denoyer, Ludovic, & Jégou, Hervé. (2018). Word Translation Without Parallel Data. ArXiv:1710.04087 [Cs].

Devlin, Jacob, Chang, Ming-Wei, Lee, Kenton, & Toutanova, Kristina. (2019). BERT: Pre-Training Of Deep Bidirectional Transformers For Language Understanding. Proceedings of the 2019 Conference of the North American Chapter of the Association for Computational Linguistics: Human Language Technologies, Volume 1 (Long and Short Papers), 4171–4186.

Dinu, Georgiana, Lazaridou, Angeliki, & Baroni, Marco. (2015). Improving zero-shot learning by mitigating the hubness problem. ArXiv:1412.6568 [Cs].

Faruqui Manaal and Dyer Chris. (2014). Improving Vector Space Word Representations Using Multilingual Correlation. Proceedings of the 14th Conference of the European Chapter of the Association for Computational Linguistics, 462–471.

Feng Yanlin and Wan Xiaojun. (2019). Learning Bilingual Sentiment-Specific Word Embeddings without Cross-lingual Supervision. Proceedings of the 2019 Conference of the North American Chapter of the Association for Computational Linguistics: Human Language Technologies, Volume 1 (Long and Short Papers), 420–429.

Ghasemi, Rouzbeh, Ashrafi Asli, Syed Arad, & Momtazi, Saeedeh. (2020). Deep Persian Sentiment Analysis: Cross-Lingual Training For Low-Resource Languages. Journal of Information Science, 016555152096278.

Godin Fréderic. 2019. "Improving and Interpreting Neural Networks for Word-Level Prediction Tasks in Natural Language Processing." Ghent University, Belgium.

Husein Zolkepli. (2018). Malaya, Natural-Language-Toolkit library for bahasa Malaysia, powered by Deep Learning Tensorflow [Github]. Malaya.

Lu Ang, Wang Weiran, Bansal Mohit, Gimpel Kevin, and Livescu Karen. (2015). Deep Multilingual Correlation for Improved Word Embeddings. Proceedings of the 2015 Conference of the North American Chapter of the Association for Computational Linguistics: Human Language Technologies, 250–256.

Mikolov Tomas, Chen Kai, Corrado Greg and Dean Jeffrey. (2013). Efficient Estimation of Word Representations in Vector Space. ArXiv:1301.3781 [Cs].

Mikolov Tomas, Le Quoc V., and Sutskever Ilya. (2013). Exploiting Similarities among Languages for Machine Translation. ArXiv:1309.4168 [Cs].

Pennington Jeffrey, Socher Richard and Manning Christoper. (2014). Glove: Global Vectors for Word Representation. Proceedings of the 2014 Conference on Empirical Methods in Natural Language Processing (EMNLP), 1532–1543.

Peters, Matthew. E., Neumann, Mark, Iyyer, Mohit, Gardner, Matt, Clark, Christopher, Lee, Kenton, & Zettlemoyer, Luke. (2018). Deep Contextualized Word Representations. Proceedings of the 2018 Conference of the North American Chapter of the Association for Computational Linguistics: Human Language Technologies, Volume 1 (Long Papers), 2227–2237.

Ruder Sebastian, Vulić Ivan and Søgaard Anders. (2019). A Survey of Cross-lingual Word Embedding Models. Journal of Artificial Intelligence Research, 65, 569–631.

Schuster, Tal, Ram, Ori, Barzilay, Regina, & Globerson, Amir. (2019). Cross-Lingual Alignment of Contextual Word Embeddings, with Applications to Zero-shot Dependency Parsing. Proceedings of the 2019 Conference of the North American Chapter of the Association for Computational Linguistics: Human Language Technologies, Volume 1 (Long and Short Papers), 1599–1613.

Smith Samuel L., Turban David H. P., Hamblin Steven and Hammerla Nils Y. (2017). Offline bilingual word vectors, orthogonal transformations and the inverted softmax. ArXiv:1702.03859 [Cs].

Wang, Zirui, Xie, Jiateng, Xu, Ruochen, Yang, Yiming, Neubig, Graham, & Carbonell, Jaime. (2020, May). Cross-lingual Alignment vs Joint Training: A Comparative Study And A Simple Unified Framework. Proceedings of the 8th International Conference on Learning Representations, ICLR 2020.

Xing Chao, Wang Dong, Liu Chao and Lin Yiye (2015). Normalized Word Embedding and Orthogonal Transform for Bilingual Word Translation. Proceedings of the 2015 Conference of the North American Chapter of the Association for Computational Linguistics: Human Language Technologies, 1006–1011.

Zhang Meng, Liu Yang, Luan Huanbo and Sun Maosong. (2017). Adversarial Training for Unsupervised Bilingual Lexicon Induction. Proceedings of the 55th Annual Meeting of the Association for Computational Linguistics (Volume 1: Long Papers), 1959–1970.

Towards Detecting Political Bias in Hindi News Articles

Samyak Agrawal **Kshitij Gupta*** **Devansh Gautam*** **Radhika Mamidi**
International Institute of Information Technology Hyderabad
samyak.agrawal@research.iiit.ac.in
{kshitij.gupta, devansh.gautam}@research.iiit.ac.in,
radhika.mamidi@iiit.ac.in

Abstract

Political propaganda in recent times has been amplified by media news portals through biased reporting, creating untruthful narratives on serious issues causing misinformed public opinions with interests of siding and helping a particular political party. This issue proposes a challenging NLP task of detecting political bias in news articles. We propose a transformer-based transfer learning method to fine-tune the pre-trained network on our data for this bias detection. As the required dataset for this particular task was not available, we created our dataset comprising 1388 Hindi news articles and their headlines from various Hindi news media outlets. We marked them on whether they are biased towards, against, or neutral to BJP, a political party, and the current ruling party at the centre in India.

1 Introduction

Biased news reporting is a widespread phenomenon present in most of the news circulating today .Bias is detected manually, but that is a tedious and time-consuming task; therefore, automation of bias detection in media articles can prove helpful in verifying these articles for their validity more efficiently.

Hindi is an Indo-Aryan language spoken mainly in North India. According to Ethnologue list[1] of most spoken languages worldwide, Hindi ranks third, and a total of 600.5 million Hindi speakers exist in the world[2]. It is also the most spoken language in India with a total of 528,3 million native speakers, which makes up around 43.6 per cent of India's population according to the 2011 census of India[3].

*The authors have contributed equally.

[1]https://www.ethnologue.com/guides/ethnologue200

[2]https://www.ethnologue.com/language/hin

[3]https://censusindia.gov.in/2011Census/Language-2011/Statement-4.pdf

We can observe political bias in news media articles by looking at different factors. We observe biases when the author of the article uses strong language trying to sensationalise an event, is partial to a particular political party, does not give a thorough review of held events etc. The headline in such an article is also essential as it is often filled with bias and is the first thing that catches a reader's attention before they start to read the article. As there is no such dataset annotated for political bias Hindi language, we created our dataset by collecting articles and their headlines from different Hindi news websites. We then annotated the dataset according to whether the article was biased towards or against Bhartiya Janta Party (BJP, the current ruling party at the centre in India) or was neutral.

We present several baseline Machine learning and Deep Learning approaches to detecting political bias on our dataset. We observe that XLM-RoBERTa (Conneau et al. (2020)), a transformer-based model, outperforms other baseline models and achieves a score of 83% accuracy, 76.4% F1-macro, and 72.1% MCC.

The main contributions of our work are as follows:

- We present an annotated dataset consisting of Hindi news articles for political bias detection.
- We propose several baselines using machine learning and deep learning approaches.
- We achieve an F1-macro score of 76.4% by fine-tuning XLM-RoBERTa, a multilingual transformer-based model, on the given dataset.

The rest of the paper is organized as follows. We discuss prior work related to bias detection. We describe the proposed dataset and analyse the annotations. We describe our baseline models and compare the performance of our approaches. We discuss the societal impacts of bias detection. We

Proceedings of the 60th Annual Meeting of the Association for Computational Linguistics Student Research Workshop, pages 239 - 244
May 22-27, 2022 ©2022 Association for Computational Linguistics

conclude with a direction for future work and highlight our main findings.

2 Related Work

Detection of bias has been studied before with attempts in detecting media bias and its effects on public perception of news and its impact on sociopolitical events like elections.

Misra and Basak (2016) developed an LSTM network model and used it to detect implicit political bias even in the absence of words that relates to either liberal or conservative ideology on two datasets - The Ideological Books Corpus (IBC) and ontheissues (OTI).

LIM et al. (2020) introduces a news bias dataset with sentence-level bias, which allows the development of approaches of bias detection on articles that have subtle bias.

Wei (2020) introduces a dataset of 200,00 sentences regarding Donald Trump and used GloVe vector embeddings to train CNN and RNN to predict the news source of the sentence. They analyze the top 5-grams with their model to gain meaningful insight into Trump's portrayal by different media sources.

Gangula et al. (2019) created a dataset of news articles and headlines collected from Telugu newspapers for bias detection and annotated them for bias towards a particular political party. They also propose a headline attention network model for the detection of bias on their dataset.

Pant et al. (2020) Worked on detecting subjective bias in Wiki Neutrality Corpus (WNC). They propose BERT-based ensemble models for bias detection, which utilizes predictions from multiple models to get better accuracy results.

Some independent organizations also work to fight misinformation. Alt News[4] is a fact-checking website that works to debunk misinformation and disinformation on mainstream social media platforms. Vishwas News[5] is another fact-checking website that is certified by International Fact-Checking Network (IFCN).

3 Dataset Description

We have looked at two major types of biases present in an article while annotating: Coverage / visibility bias and tonality / statement bias (D'Alessio and Allen, 2006). We have annotated our dataset using these biases into 3 categories, biased towards the BJP, biased against the BJP, and neutral if these biases are not visible in the article.

3.1 Target Classes

Coverage bias is concerned with the amount of coverage each side receives over an issue. Articles would at times present only one side of an argument and give undue amount of coverage to that side over the other in order to make viewers side with a particular party. Tonality bias measures the evaluation of a particular actor in the media coverage. In an article, a politician can either be framed positively or negatively changing perception of the general public about them.[6]

3.2 Data Collection

We collected hindi news articles along with their headlines from Indian news websites. We collected these articles from websites of four different news sources. The Wire, The Quint, OPIndia and The Frustrated Indian. The former two are known to be critical of the current government and more liberal media houses, while the latter are known for their pro BJP articles and being more right-wing. We did it to ensure a balance in the number of biased articles for and against the BJP. We collected the links to articles from TheWire using tweets from their Twitter handle @thewirehindi. We used the advanced search feature of Twitter and used hashtags based on the news that was relevant during data collection; for example, #modi, #yogi, #CAA, #BJP, #NRC, #covid etc. For the other three media houses, articles were selected directly from their websites using words relevant to the BJP like modi, bjp, yogi etc. Articles were then scraped from the websites using Selenium[7]. We collected over 8000 articles from all four media websites. Out of these articles, we manually removed irrelevant articles. In the end, a total of 1388 articles were left, which we then annotated for bias.

3.3 Data Annotation

Two annotators did the annotations. Both the annotators are native Hindi speakers and have a good grasp and proficiency in the language. One of the annotators is a self-reported liberal and the other one is a self-reported conservative. Both the annotators were politically up to date with the current

[4] https://www.altnews.in/

[5] https://www.vishvasnews.com/english/

[6] Examples of these biases in our dataset is given in the appendix

[7] https://www.selenium.dev/

	Neutral	For	Against
Articles	234	593	561
Avg #words in headline	15.5	17.8	14.9
Avg #words in article	844	750.9	1222.5
Avg #sentences in article	37.5	31.5	53.4

Table 1: Dataset statistics

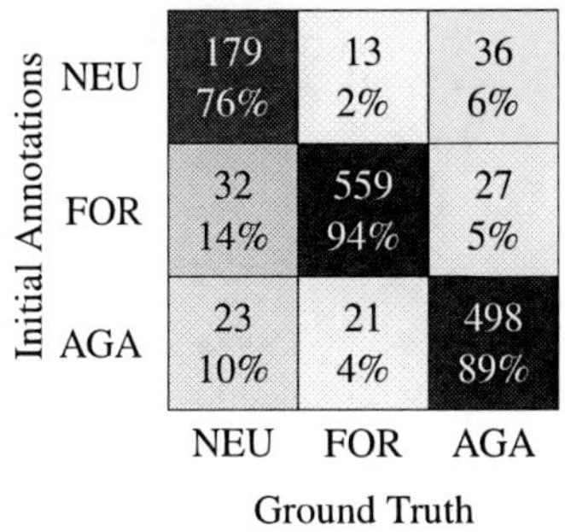

Figure 1: Confusion matrix of the classes annotated by both the annotators. The percentages show the ratio of the ground truth class, which was initially annotated as that class. NEU: Neutral, FOR: For BJP, AGA: Against BJP.

affairs of the country. In the annotation process, we provided both the headline and the article to the annotators. We asked them to read and annotate whether the article and the headline are biased towards the BJP, against it or neutral. We also asked the annotators to do the annotation keeping in mind whether the article exhibits coverage or tonality bias and not deciding on it based on whether the coverage or review is negative or positive. The observed kappa score of the annotations was 0.65. Cases where the two annotators disagreed, were then resolved by a third annotator.

Further, since articles from the same news outlet might have similar biases, we hide the information about the news source and shuffle all the articles before annotating.

3.4 Dataset Analysis

The Dataset contains of 1,388 articles along with their headlines. The general statistics of the dataset are demonstrated in Table 1.

To gauge the difficulty level of each class in the dataset, we analyse the confusion for each class between the two annotators. The results are demonstrated in Figure 1. The confusion matrix indicates that the neutral class is the hardest to detect compared to the other classes. A plausible explanation is the subjective nature of the class, and an article might seem biased to a person while unbiased to another.

4 System Description

In this section, we describe the data splits we use, the evaluation metrics we consider, and the baselines we propose.

4.1 Dataset Splits

The dataset consists of 1,388 articles. We divide the dataset into train and validation sets in the ratio of 10:1 by randomly choosing articles from the dataset. We use the same dataset split for all our models and report the performances on the validation set.

4.2 Evaluation Metrics

We use the following metrics, which are popularly known for classification tasks.

Accuracy is one of the most popular and easy-to-understand metrics. It is a good choice for classification tasks when the data does not suffer from class imbalance.

F1-Score represents a more balanced view, but it could still produce a biased result since it does not consider true negatives. Nonetheless, F1-macro can also handle class imbalance as it gives equal weight to all the classes.

MCC Matthews Correlation Coefficient (Matthews, 1975) takes all parameters of the confusion matrix into account and is less vulnerable to bias. It reports a number in the range -1 to 1, and a key advantage of it is its easy interpretability.

4.3 Baselines

In this section, we provide an overview of the baselines we propose. We experiment with pre-trained language models such as BERT (Devlin et al., 2019) and XLM-RoBERTa (Conneau et al., 2020) on our dataset. We also experiment with traditional machine learning approaches such as SVM, Random Forest to provide exhaustive baselines on the dataset.

4.3.1 mBERT

mBERT is the multilingual version of BERT, which has been trained on a multilingual corpus of 104 languages (including Hindi) using articles from Wikipedia as its training corpus. We leverage the

Model	Accuracy	F1-macro	MCC
mBERT	80.2 ± 1.4	72.4 ± 2.1	67.1 ± 2.2
XLM-RoBERTa	**83** $\pm \mathbf{1.1}$	**76.4** $\pm \mathbf{1.3}$	**72.1** $\pm \mathbf{1.8}$
XLM-RoBERTa (Hindi)	79.2 ± 1.5	72.5 ± 3.1	65.8 ± 2.6
IndicBERT	78.9 ± 1.2	69.2 ± 4.5	65.5 ± 2.1
SVM	78.7	59.6	64.6
Logistic Regression	77.1	55.1	61.5
Random Forest	78.7	59.6	64.6

Table 2: Mean and std dev are reported across five runs of all the models.

Hindi pre-training of the model and fine-tune the model on our dataset.

We use a [SEP] token between the headline and the contents of the article to prepare the input for the transformer network. For classification, we attach a feed-forward network on the [CLS] token embedding with two linear layers having the model's default dropout of 0.1 and *Tanh* activation layer in between. To train our model, we use Adam optimizer with a learning rate of $1e^{-5}$ and a batch size of 16 with a maximum sequence length of 256. We use the standard cross entropy loss to train our model.

4.3.2 XLM-RoBERTa

XLM-RoBERTa (Conneau et al., 2020) is the multilingual version of RoBERTa (Liu et al., 2019) which is an optimized version of BERT. XLM-RoBERTa has been pre-trained on 2.5TB of filtered CommonCrawl data containing 100 different languages. We leverage the Hindi pre-training of the model and fine-tune the model on our dataset for bias detection.

Since multilingual versions often perform slightly worse than their monolingual counterparts, we also experiment with a monolingual version of XLM-RoBERTa (Jain et al., 2020). The model has been pre-trained on 3GB of Hindi monolingual data majorly taken from OSCAR (Ortiz Suárez et al., 2020).

To train the models, we use the same classification network and training parameters as mentioned in Section 4.3.1.

4.3.3 IndicBERT

IndicBERT (Kakwani et al., 2020) is a multilingual model based on ALBERT (Lan et al., 2020) which has been pre-trained on 12 major Indian languages. The model has much fewer parameters than mBERT and XLM-RoBERTa, but it can still achieve similar performances or even better in most of the tasks.

To train the model, we use the same classification network and training parameters as mentioned in Section 4.3.1.

4.3.4 SVM

Support Vector Machines are models for classification and regression problems. First, the textual data is transformed to a set of features by using methods like Bag of words, Bag-of-n-grams, or Tf-Idf. Later, the classification model is applied on the transformed features. The kernel we used is the Radial Basis Function (RBF) kernel which is a non-linear kernel. The RBF kernel function computes the similarity between two points ($\mathbf{x}$, $\mathbf{x}'$) or how close they are to each other. This kernel can be explained as:

$$K(\mathbf{x}, \mathbf{x}') = \exp(-\gamma \|\mathbf{x} - \mathbf{x}'\|^2) \quad (1)$$

where γ is a free parameter.

We first generate the count matrix of all the tokens in the text. We use Term frequency (TF)-Inverse Document Frequency (IDF) to normalize the count matrix and use it to train our model.The regularization parameter is set to 1. The loss function used is hinge loss.

4.3.5 Logistic Regression

Logistic Regression is a another supervised learning approach like SVM which differs by using the weighted combination of the input features and passes them through a sigmoid function.

Similar to SVM, here we use TF-IDF to get features from the articles which are then given to our model. We use the standard cross entropy loss to train our model.

4.3.6 Random Forest

Random forests is a classification algorithm which creates an ensemble of decision trees. It uses bag-

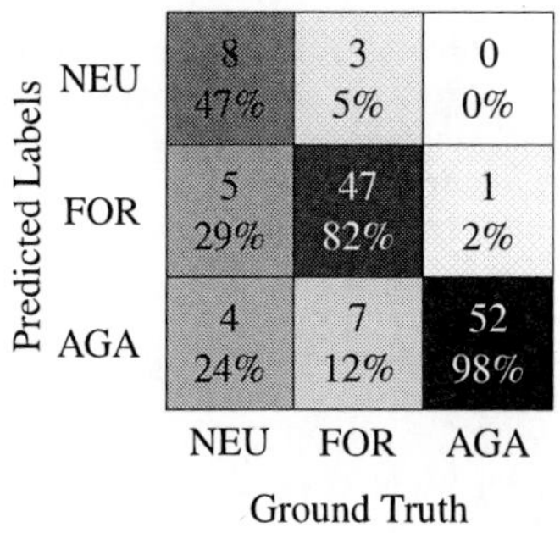

Figure 2: Confusion matrix of the classes predicted by the best performing model in the validation set. The percentages show the ratio of the target class, which was predicted as that class. NEU: Neutral, FOR: For BJP, AGA: Against BJP.

ging and feature randomness to build each individual tree and then use the predictions of the forest of trees which is more accurate than the prediction of any individual tree.

Similar to SVM, here we again use TF-IDF to get features from the articles which are then given to our model. We use the standard cross entropy loss to train our model. The quality of the split is measures using the gini criterion. The minimum sample split was kept at 2.

5 Results and Discussion

We report the results of our models in Table 2. We observe that the deep learning models perform better than the machine learning approaches. The results further indicate that even simpler models can give decent performances on the given problem.

To further analyse the results, we compare the class-wise results of the best models. We show the confusion matrix of the predictions compared to the ground truth values in Figure 2. The model is performing very well on the biased classes but suffers heavily on the neutral class. We observe the same pattern during the annotation process and believe that predicting whether an article is unbiased is comparatively more challenging than predicting the type of bias.

5.1 Societal Implications and Limitations

Online news in today's day and age strongly influences the general public's opinion. Ideally, news media should report the news objectively and from a neutral standpoint, but that is seldom the case. The news these days is highly subjective, biased and thus, these media companies put in a lot of opinionated information through sections of society. Biased news can have long-term and far-reaching implications for public opinion on societal issues and how they view government policies, laws and elections (Baum and Gussin, 2005; Bernhardt et al., 2008). People should have access to an unbiased and objective form of news reporting. In India, we can see news channels and news websites online pushing out one-sided and highly opinionated news. Chadha et al. (2019) discuss the discourse of several news portals with an inherent bias towards right-wing politics and how they talk about their "aims to provide a counter to the mainstream media narrative about India" which they consider to be "left-liberal" and "pseudo-secular". They also discuss how the members of political parties fund these websites to carry out propaganda on their behalf. This shows that instead of news sources providing unbiased news, we have news portals at two opposite sides of the political spectrum which will publish information and make opinion pieces keeping their political leaning in mind. Such biased news portals make the detection of political bias even more important and relevant in today's times.

Our system is trained on articles from a limited number of sources and thus might not be fitted well to make predictions on news articles from other sources. Also, predictions from our model which might be incorrect can be used to accuse certain media houses as biased. Thus, our system should rather be used as a method to filter out potentially biased articles from a larger set of articles rather than using it as a gold standard to mark articles as being biased.

6 Conclusion

In this paper, we proposed a dataset to detect biases in Hindi news articles. We analysed the difficulty level of each class, and our experiments indicate that detecting whether an article is unbiased is a more challenging problem than detecting the type of bias. Further, we provided several baseline models on the proposed dataset and found out that multilingual deep learning models outperform other approaches by a large margin and should be the choice for performance metrics. We perform error analysis on the best performing model to further understand the shortcomings of our proposed system. Lastly, we also discussed the ethical and societal implications of the proposed work.

As a part of future work, we aim to extend the

system by shifting our focus from a particular political party and propose a general approach for any set of political parties.

References

Matthew A Baum and Phil Gussin. 2005. Issue bias: How issue coverage and media bias affect voter perceptions of elections. In *Meeting of the American Political Science Association. Washington, DC: Apsa*. Citeseer.

Dan Bernhardt, Stefan Krasa, and Mattias Polborn. 2008. Political polarization and the electoral effects of media bias. *Journal of Public Economics*, 92(5-6):1092–1104.

K Chadha, P Bhat, and Shakuntala Rao. 2019. The media are biased: Exploring online right-wing responses to mainstream news in india. *Indian journalism in a New Era: Changes, challenges and perspectives*, pages 115–139.

Alexis Conneau, Kartikay Khandelwal, Naman Goyal, Vishrav Chaudhary, Guillaume Wenzek, Francisco Guzmán, Edouard Grave, Myle Ott, Luke Zettlemoyer, and Veselin Stoyanov. 2020. Unsupervised cross-lingual representation learning at scale. In *Proceedings of the 58th Annual Meeting of the Association for Computational Linguistics*, pages 8440–8451, Online. Association for Computational Linguistics.

Dave D'Alessio and Mike Allen. 2006. Media Bias in Presidential Elections: A Meta-Analysis. *Journal of Communication*, 50(4):133–156.

Jacob Devlin, Ming-Wei Chang, Kenton Lee, and Kristina Toutanova. 2019. BERT: Pre-training of deep bidirectional transformers for language understanding. In *Proceedings of the 2019 Conference of the North American Chapter of the Association for Computational Linguistics: Human Language Technologies, Volume 1 (Long and Short Papers)*, pages 4171–4186, Minneapolis, Minnesota. Association for Computational Linguistics.

Rama Rohit Reddy Gangula, Suma Reddy Duggenpudi, and Radhika Mamidi. 2019. Detecting political bias in news articles using headline attention. In *Proceedings of the 2019 ACL Workshop BlackboxNLP: Analyzing and Interpreting Neural Networks for NLP*, pages 77–84, Florence, Italy. Association for Computational Linguistics.

Kushal Jain, Adwait Deshpande, Kumar Shridhar, Felix Laumann, and Ayushman Dash. 2020. Indic-transformers: An analysis of transformer language models for indian languages. *CoRR*, abs/2011.02323.

Divyanshu Kakwani, Anoop Kunchukuttan, Satish Golla, Gokul N.C., Avik Bhattacharyya, Mitesh M. Khapra, and Pratyush Kumar. 2020. IndicNLPSuite: Monolingual corpora, evaluation benchmarks and pre-trained multilingual language models for Indian languages. In *Findings of the Association for Computational Linguistics: EMNLP 2020*, pages 4948–4961, Online. Association for Computational Linguistics.

Zhenzhong Lan, Mingda Chen, Sebastian Goodman, Kevin Gimpel, Piyush Sharma, and Radu Soricut. 2020. Albert: A lite bert for self-supervised learning of language representations. In *International Conference on Learning Representations*.

Sora LIM, Adam JATOWT, and Masatoshi YOSHIKAWA. 2020. Creating a dataset for fine-grained bias detection in news articles. In *Forum on Data Engineering and Information Management*, volume 12, pages 1–35.

Yinhan Liu, Myle Ott, Naman Goyal, Jingfei Du, Mandar Joshi, Danqi Chen, Omer Levy, Mike Lewis, Luke Zettlemoyer, and Veselin Stoyanov. 2019. Roberta: A robustly optimized bert pretraining approach.

B.W. Matthews. 1975. Comparison of the predicted and observed secondary structure of t4 phage lysozyme. *Biochimica et Biophysica Acta (BBA) - Protein Structure*, 405(2):442–451.

Arkajyoti Misra and Sanjib Basak. 2016. Political bias analysis.

Pedro Javier Ortiz Suárez, Laurent Romary, and Benoît Sagot. 2020. A monolingual approach to contextualized word embeddings for mid-resource languages. In *Proceedings of the 58th Annual Meeting of the Association for Computational Linguistics*, pages 1703–1714, Online. Association for Computational Linguistics.

Kartikey Pant, Tanvi Dadu, and Radhika Mamidi. 2020. Towards detection of subjective bias using contextualized word embeddings. In *Companion Proceedings of the Web Conference 2020*, WWW '20, page 75–76, New York, NY, USA. Association for Computing Machinery.

Jerry Wei. 2020. Newb: 200, 000+ sentences for political bias detection. *CoRR*, abs/2006.03051.

Restricted or Not: A General Training Framework for Neural Machine Translation

Zuchao Li[1,2], Masao Utiyama[3,*], Eiichiro Sumita[3], and Hai Zhao[1,2,*]
[1]Department of Computer Science and Engineering, Shanghai Jiao Tong University
[2]MoE Key Lab of Artificial Intelligence, AI Institute, Shanghai Jiao Tong University
[3]National Institute of Information and Communications Technology (NICT), Kyoto, Japan
charlee@sjtu.edu.cn, {mutiyama,eiichiro.sumita}@nict.go.jp, zhaohai@cs.sjtu.edu.cn

Abstract

Restricted machine translation incorporates human prior knowledge into translation. It restricts the flexibility of the translation to satisfy the demands of translation in specific scenarios. Existing work typically imposes constraints on beam search decoding. Although this can satisfy the requirements overall, it usually requires a larger beam size and far longer decoding time than unrestricted translation, which limits the concurrent processing ability of the translation model in deployment, and thus its practicality. In this paper, we propose a general training framework that allows a model to simultaneously support both unrestricted and restricted translation by adopting an additional auxiliary training process without constraining the decoding process. This maintains the benefits of restricted translation but greatly reduces the extra time overhead of constrained decoding, thus improving its practicality. The effectiveness of our proposed training framework is demonstrated by experiments on both original (WAT21 En$\leftrightarrow$Ja) and simulated (WMT14 En$\rightarrow$De and En$\rightarrow$Fr) restricted translation benchmarks.

1 Introduction

Neural machine translation (NMT) has recently entered use because of rapid improvements in its performance (Bahdanau et al., 2015; Gehring et al., 2017; Vaswani et al., 2017). The translation mechanism of an NMT model is a black box because it is a special deep neural network model, which means that translation generation is uncontrollable (Moryossef et al., 2019; Mehta et al., 2020; Miyata and Fujita, 2021). Although uncontrollable (or unguaranteed) translation can satisfy basic requirements, it is unacceptable in some formal scenarios, particularly for key numbers, time, and proper nouns. To address this concern, the restricted translation task has been proposed (Hokamp and Liu, 2017; Post and Vilar, 2018; Song et al., 2019; Chen et al., 2020; Chousa and Morishita, 2021; Li et al., 2021). This restricts translation by forcing the inclusion of prespecified words and phrases in the generation output, which enables explicit control over the system output.

Lexically constrained (or guided) decoding (CD) (Post and Vilar, 2018; Hu et al., 2019b,a), a modification of beam search, has commonly been used in recent restricted translation studies. Although CD is a reasonable option for restricted translation, its slow decoding limits the practicality of restricted translation. Therefore, we propose a novel training framework for restricted translation that requires only minor changes to the ordinary translation model, to address the inconvenience of the decoding time overhead caused by additional constraints. In this framework, restricted machine translation is achieved by the model structure instead of the CD.

Specifically, we perform translation in two modes in the training framework: end-to-end translation and restricted translation, and reuse the self-attention and cross-attention in the decoder of the translation model. To make the restricted translation training mode adapt to the training data situation with only parallel sentences available, we propose the Sampled Constraints as Concentration (SCC) training approach. In this approach, we sample the target sequence to simulate the constraint words and impose additional penalties on the loss of these sampled words.

Because the restricted translation is embedded with the model structure and training objective in the translation model trained with our framework, restricted translation is performed without CD. Consequently, the inference speed is substantially increased, which greatly improves the practicality of restricted translation. Experimental re-

[*]Corresponding author. This work was partially funded by the Key Projects of National Natural Science Foundation of China (U1836222 and 61733011).

Proceedings of the 60th Annual Meeting of the Association for Computational Linguistics
Student Research Workshop, pages 245 - 251

sults show that our end-to-end translation model can achieve approximately the same performance as the end-to-end translation baseline; moreover, although it only requires unconstrained decoding, it can achieve performance competitive or even superior with that of the baseline with CD.

2 Our Training Framework

Our training framework comprises two training subprocesses: end-to-end translation and restricted translation. Recent restricted translation studies have focused mainly on the decoding phase, but we set out to integrate restricted translation into the training phase, which makes the motivation of our work completely different from that of previous studies. Our implementation is based on the existing mainstream Transformer NMT baseline; however, because the training method is independent of the baseline, our training framework can easily be generalized to other NMT models and language generation tasks. Due to space limitations, please refer to Appendix A.2 for training details.

2.1 End-to-end Translation Training

The most widely adopted form of machine translation is end-to-end translation, which usually employs an encoder–decoder architecture. In the training of end-to-end machine translation, given a source language input $\mathbf{X} = \{x_1, x_2, ..., x_n\}$ and target language translation $\mathbf{Y} = \{y_1, y_2, ..., y_m\}$, the model with parameter θ is trained to generate the target output sequence $\mathbf{Y}$ according to the source input sequence $\mathbf{X}$.

Taking the Transformer model as an example, the encoder is composed of the multi-head self-attention module, whose purpose is to vectorize and contextualize the source input sequence. This module can be formalized as:

$$\mathbf{H}^X = \mathit{SelfAttn}_{enc}(\mathbf{X} + \mathit{Pos}(\mathbf{X})),$$

where $\mathit{Pos}(\cdot)$ represents the position encoding of a sequence, $\mathit{SelfAttn}_{enc}$ denotes the stacked multi-head self-attention encoder, and $\mathbf{H}^X$ is the contextualized source representation. A typical decoder comprises two main components: self-attention and cross-attention. In the self-attention component, the target representation is encoded with similar multi-head attention structures,

$$\hat{\mathbf{H}}^Y = \mathit{SelfAttn}_{dec}(\mathit{IncMask}(\hat{\mathbf{Y}} + \mathit{Pos}(\hat{\mathbf{Y}}))),$$

where $\hat{\mathbf{Y}} = \{BOS, y_1, y_2, ..., y_{m-1}\}$ is the shifted version of the target sequence $\mathbf{Y}$, $\mathit{SelfAttn}_{dec}$ denotes the stacked multi-head self-attention layers (similar to the encoder), and *IncMask* is the extra incremental mask adopted because the sequence on the decoder side is generated incrementally. The target representation is fed to the cross-attention component, as a query, and the source representation is used as the key and value to obtain the final representation, which is then mapped to the target vocabulary space through a linear and softmax layer. The final predicted probabilities can be written as follows:

$$P(\mathbf{Y}) = \mathit{Softmax}(\mathit{CrossAttn}(\hat{\mathbf{H}}^Y, \mathbf{H}^X)).$$

The model parameter θ is optimized by minimizing the negative log-likelihood of the gold tokens, according to their predicted probabilities:

$$\begin{aligned} \mathcal{L}_{\text{E2E}} &= -\sum_{i=1}^{m} logP(y_i) \\ &= -\sum_{i=1}^{m} logP(y_i|\mathbf{X}; \hat{\mathbf{Y}}_{<i}; \theta), \end{aligned} \tag{1}$$

where $\hat{\mathbf{Y}}_{<i}$ indicates the sequence before token y_i. In the inference stage, greedy (or beam) search is employed to generate the translation sequence according to predicted probabilities $P(y_i) = P(y_i|\mathbf{X}; \tilde{\mathbf{Y}}_{<i}; \theta)$, where $\tilde{\mathbf{Y}}$ is the generated token sequence.

2.2 Restricted Translation Training

In recent work on restricted translation, CD, a modification of beam search, has generally been adopted. In CD, $P(y_i)$ remains unchanged and external search processes are employed, which increases the decoding time overhead. In this paper, we focus on improving the efficiency of restricted translation by modifying $P(y_i)$ to eliminate the additional search processes. Given the constrained word sequence $\mathbf{C} = \{c_1, c_2, ..., c_k\}$, CD adds additional terms to the predicted probability of the model, and $\mathbf{C}$ is treated as an additional input prompt. The output probability $P(y_i)$ then becomes:

$$P(y_i) = P(y_i|\mathbf{X}; \mathbf{C}; \hat{\mathbf{Y}}_{<i}; \theta).$$

According to this change in the form of probability, we made a simple modification to the workflow of the model, keeping the model structure unchanged. First, we encoded the constrained word sequence with the self-attention component of the decoder. Because the input order of the constrained word sequence is usually inconsistent with the word order of the target sequence, we removed the positional encoding, taking advantage of the position invariance of the self-attention layer. In addition, these constrained words are visible during the entire translation generation process, so there is no need to use the incremental mask strategy. Finally, the constrained words representation is as follows:

$$\mathbf{H}^C = \mathit{SelfAttn}_{dec}(\mathbf{C}).$$

Regarding such a representation as an additional context, outside of the source representation, the predicted probability of the model can be written as:

$$P(\mathbf{Y}) = \mathit{Softmax}(\mathit{CrossAttn}(\hat{\mathbf{H}}^Y, \mathbf{H}^X) + \mathit{CrossAttn}(\hat{\mathbf{H}}^Y, \mathbf{H}^C)). \quad (2)$$

2.3 Sampled Constraints as Concentration

The training of end-to-end NMT models generally uses parallel sentences between source and target languages, whereas restricted machine translation requires an additional constraint sequence. To hide the difference between restricted translation training and testing, we propose the SCC training strategy.

Because restricted machine translation training requires additional given constraint sequences, we randomly sample the target sequence to obtain constrained words in this training strategy. However, this is insufficient. Because these additional target words are already exposed to the decoder, the generation of these tokens would become quite easy, and the goal of fully training the model would not be accomplished (i.e., there are shortcuts). This would have an undesirable impact on end-to-end translation (as when no constrained words are prespecified) and reduce the model's robustness, which is incompatible with our general training framework. Therefore, we propose additional concentration penalties for the losses of these exposed constrained tokens. Denoting the sampled sequence as $\mathbf{S}_\alpha^Y$, where α is the sampling ratio, and the penalty factor as γ, the final loss is:

$$\mathcal{L}_{\text{RT}} = -\sum_{i=1}^{m} \left((1 + \gamma \mathbb{1}(y_i \in \mathbf{S}_\alpha^Y)\right) \mathit{log} P(y_i | \mathbf{X}; \mathbf{S}_\alpha^Y; \hat{\mathbf{Y}}_{<i}; \theta)), \quad (3)$$

where $\mathbb{1}(\cdot)$ is the indicator function. Please refer to Appendix A.1 for an illustrated figure and more details.

3 Empirical Evaluation and Analysis

Our method was evaluated on the ASPEC (Nakazawa et al., 2016) En↔Ja benchmark and the WMT14 En→De and En→Fr benchmarks. The constrained words for the ASPEC En↔Ja test set were provided by the WAT21 restricted translation shared task and, for WMT14 En→De and En→Fr, we followed previous work by adopting random sampling to extract the constraints. We chose two typical Transformer model settings as our baseline: Transformer-base and Transformer-big, both of which are consistent with (Vaswani et al., 2017). During training, we set $\alpha = 0.15$ and $\gamma = 1.0$. For a fair comparison, the beam size was set to 10 and the batch size was fixed at 64.

We reported MultiBLEU scores in our experiments and calculated them using the Moses script. For En, De, and Fr, we use the default tokenizer provided by Moses (Hoang and Koehn, 2008), and for Ja, we adopted Mecab[1] for word segmentation. In the evaluation of WAT21 EN↔JA, we also reported a consistency metric – the Exact Match (EM) score - according to the WAT21 official instructions. This score is the ratio of sentences in the whole corpus that exactly match the given constraints. For the EM score evaluation, we use lowercase hypotheses and constraints, then use character-level sequence matching (including whitespaces) for each constraint in En, while for Ja, we use character-level sequence matching (including whitespaces) for each constraint without preprocessing. Please see Appendix A.3 for more preparation details.

3.1 Results and Analysis

We present the performance of the models on the WAT21 En↔Ja restricted translation tasks in Table 1. First, for both model architectures (Transformer-base (T-base) and Transformer-big (T-big)), the end-to-end translation performance (E2E) of our approach's models is almost the same as our baselines. This demonstrates that our training framework still maintains high end-to-end translation performance, even with restricted translation added, meaning it effectively supports both end-to-end translation and restricted translation simultaneously.

Second, on our end-to-end baselines, CD can also be used to accommodate restricted translation. Its very substantial gain in translation performance suggests that CD is a reasonable op-

[1] `https://taku910.github.io/mecab/`

Model	Alg.	En→Ja	Ja→En	Speed (sent./s)
T-base	E2E	41.82 [26.49]	28.18 [21.96]	53.98 / 63.39
	CD	47.11 [98.29]	31.55 [99.11]	0.74 / 0.78
Ours	E2E	41.87 [26.55]	28.20 [22.01]	53.95 / 63.40
	CAC	47.15 [60.26]	35.46 [56.68]	36.01 / 39.32
	CD+	**47.30 [98.56]**	**35.49 [99.30]**	0.73 / 0.81
T-big	E2E	43.33 [27.51]	29.45 [22.70]	29.68 / 32.53
	CD	47.89 [98.30]	32.04 [99.16]	0.68 / 0.71
Ours	E2E	43.40 [27.60]	29.41 [23.25]	29.55 / 32.21
	CAC	47.93 [60.77]	35.71 [57.42]	18.13 / 19.32
	CD+	**48.01 [98.60]**	**35.75 [99.44]**	0.65 / 0.70

Table 1: Performance on WAT21 En↔Ja test sets. In the form $a[b]$, a represents the BLEU score and b the EM score (see Appendix A.3).

Model	En→De	En→Fr	Speed (sent./s)
(Vaswani et al., 2017)	28.40	41.80	–
T-big (Ours)	28.15	43.12	39.23 / 34.95
+CAC (*rand1*)	29.95	44.27	31.27 / 29.38
+CAC (*rand2*)	31.62	45.53	30.63 / 28.37
+CAC (*rand3*)	33.13	47.21	29.43 / 27.46
+CAC (*rand4*)	34.51	48.16	28.19 / 26.40
+CAC (*phr4*)	36.07	48.95	28.26 / 26.38

Table 2: Performance on WMT14 En→De and En→Fr test sets.

tion for restricted translation. However, under the same conditions, its decoding speed is much lower than that of ordinary decoding, which prevents it from being deployed at a large scale. In our proposed framework, restricted translation is successfully supported with constraints as context (CAC), without using CD. Like CD methods, our method obtains a similar and substantial performance improvement, but it does so without sacrificing too much decoding speed, which demonstrates that our proposed method is efficient and effective.

Because CAC employs constrained word sequences as additional context, it only imposes soft constraints on the decoder, whereas CD imposes hard constraints. However, because CAC and CD do not conflict, we combined the two as CD+ to produce better results. Our experimental findings attest to the effectiveness of this practice. Furthermore, CAC significantly outperforms CD in Ja→En. This may be due to the beam size of 10, which is insufficient for longer constrained sequences and limits CD performance (a larger beam size will be better, see Figure 1(a)), but our proposed CAC alleviates this shortcoming obviously. Furthermore, for the EM score, CD adheres to hard constraints that the given constrained word must appear in the translation, whereas CAC leverages soft constraints and instead focuses on the overall translation, resulting in a higher BLEU for CAC and a higher EM for CD. CD+, however, provides higher scores for both these metrics.

As in previous studies on restricted translation, we also investigated the impact of constrained words on restricted translation. The constrained words were sampled from the translation references of popular translation datasets (WMT14 En→De and En→Fr). There are five common sampling strategies: *rand1*, *rand2*, *rand3*, *rand4*, and *phr4*. *randk* means that the translation is sampled without replacement k times, and *phrk* means that k consecutive words are sampled. For a translation length less than k, an empty string is output because no constrained words are given.

Table 2 compares the end-to-end translation performance of our T-big model with that of Vaswani et al. (2017)'s model. Although we used the same model size and number of training steps, our model's performance was inferior on En→De but superior on En→Fr. This is a consequence of the use of a larger beam size and the potential benefits of restricted translation training on end-to-end translation. The results also show that the translation performance improved dramatically even when only one constrained word was used. This shows that our method of using constraints as a soft restriction is very effective, and it also demonstrates that translation can be improved substantially with some prior knowledge of translation. The disparities between *rand1* and *rand4* show that accurate prior knowledge of translation can lead to more accurate translation, as the translation uncertainty has been gradually reduced. Additionally, comparing *rand4* and *phr4* demonstrates that the continuous sampling of four constrained words can result in a greater performance improvement than the discrete sampling of four constrained words. This is because *phr4* generally carries more useful information than *rand4*.

3.2 Ablation Study

To further demonstrate the advantages of our method, we plotted the performance in BLEU score and total decoding time with different beam sizes in Figure 1. The results of BLEU score vs. beam size show that, for CD methods or variants (CD+), the translation improves at first as the beam size increases. However, after the beam size increases

Model	En→Ja	Ja→En	Speed (sent./s)
T-base (E2E)	41.82	28.18	53.98 / 63.39
Ours (CAC)	47.15	35.46	36.01 / 39.32
- *SCC*	45.63	33.05	36.05 / 39.25
- *RTT*	19.42	10.56	36.07 / 39.30
+ *CPos*	43.36	29.55	35.91 / 39.04
+ *IncMask*	43.78	29.61	35.79 / 38.93

Table 3: Results of ablation study on WAT21 En↔Ja test sets.

beyond a certain threshold, the translation performance decreases. Moreover, we have also observed that CD methods require a larger beam size to outperform beam search methods, and they perform worse when beam size is small; because taking additional constraint words into consideration requires more searching. There is no such issue with our CAC method that employs beam search, however.

Figure 1(b) depicts the total decoding time for various beam sizes. The test set contains 1,812 sentences. We use two y-axes , a larger-scale one on the right to accommodate and denote CD and CD+'s longer decoding times, and a smaller-scale one on the left to denote E2E and CAC's decoding times. The decoding time results show that our CAC method can come close to beam search, a practical restricted translation solution, but CD and CD+ are extremely slow in comparison.

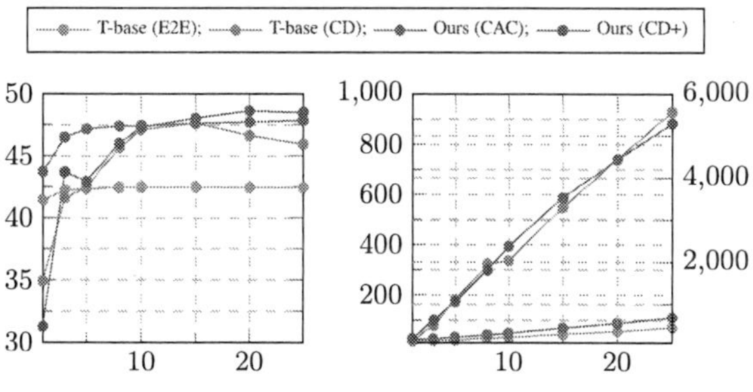

(a) BLEU vs. beam size (b) Time vs. beam size

Figure 1: BLEU score vs. beam size and Decoding time vs. beam size on WAT21 En→Ja test set.

We conducted ablation studies on the model structures and training options of our proposed framework, as shown in Table 3. Using a general MLE loss in restricted translation training; without using SCC loss (-SCC); outperforms the baseline, which shows that the use of restricted translation training can effectively support restricted translation; however, including SCC loss still leads to an improvement over this. This reveals that imposing additional penalties on the loss of constrained words exposed to the decoder is an important design decision. We also evaluated complete removal of the restricted translation training and directly using the end-to-end translation training model for CAC decoding (-RTT). Our results show that the performance greatly suffered, which illustrates the necessity of using restricted translation training for the restricted translation of CAC decoding.

4 Related Work

Lexically constrained (or guided) decoding (CD), a modification of beam search, has commonly been used in recent restricted translation studies. Specifically, some prespecified words or phrases are forced in translation choice. However, although these approaches can theoretically achieve the goal of restricted translation, existing methods are very expensive in terms of decoding time; this limits the practicality of CD. Starting from (Post and Vilar, 2018), in which CD was introduced and utilized in NMT, attempts have been made to reduce the time overhead of CD by the use of dynamic beam allocation. Although the time complexity is formally consistent with that of general beam search, it remains too inefficient to be used on a large scale (Hu et al., 2019b). Hu et al. (2019a) further extended CD and improved the throughput of restricted translation systems by using batching in vectorized dynamic beam allocation. Although these efforts have improved the practicality of restricted translation, the decoding speed is still far less than that of ordinary decoding.

5 Conclusion

In this paper, we proposed novel training and decoding methods for restricted translation that do not use CD. Furthermore, we established a general training framework. With our framework, end-to-end translation and restricted translation can be implemented in the same model. Compared to using CD in the end-to-end translation model, we achieved better translation results, as well as smaller beam size and consistently higher decoding speed. We evaluated the framework on multiple benchmarks, and demonstrated the performance advantages of restricted translation. Using our training framework and decoding method, restricted translation can overcome the limitation of its extremely slow decoding speed and become practical.

References

Dzmitry Bahdanau, Kyunghyun Cho, and Yoshua Bengio. 2015. Neural machine translation by jointly learning to align and translate. In *3rd International Conference on Learning Representations, ICLR 2015, San Diego, CA, USA, May 7-9, 2015, Conference Track Proceedings*.

Guanhua Chen, Yun Chen, Yong Wang, and Victor O. K. Li. 2020. Lexical-constraint-aware neural machine translation via data augmentation. In *Proceedings of the Twenty-Ninth International Joint Conference on Artificial Intelligence, IJCAI 2020*, pages 3587–3593. ijcai.org.

Katsuki Chousa and Makoto Morishita. 2021. Input augmentation improves constrained beam search for neural machine translation: NTT at WAT 2021. In *Proceedings of the 8th Workshop on Asian Translation (WAT2021)*, pages 53–61, Online. Association for Computational Linguistics.

Jonas Gehring, Michael Auli, David Grangier, Denis Yarats, and Yann N. Dauphin. 2017. Convolutional sequence to sequence learning. In *Proceedings of the 34th International Conference on Machine Learning, ICML 2017, Sydney, NSW, Australia, 6-11 August 2017*, volume 70 of *Proceedings of Machine Learning Research*, pages 1243–1252. PMLR.

Hieu Hoang and Philipp Koehn. 2008. Design of the Moses decoder for statistical machine translation. In *Software Engineering, Testing, and Quality Assurance for Natural Language Processing*, pages 58–65, Columbus, Ohio. Association for Computational Linguistics.

Chris Hokamp and Qun Liu. 2017. Lexically constrained decoding for sequence generation using grid beam search. In *Proceedings of the 55th Annual Meeting of the Association for Computational Linguistics (Volume 1: Long Papers)*, pages 1535–1546, Vancouver, Canada. Association for Computational Linguistics.

J. Edward Hu, Huda Khayrallah, Ryan Culkin, Patrick Xia, Tongfei Chen, Matt Post, and Benjamin Van Durme. 2019a. Improved lexically constrained decoding for translation and monolingual rewriting. In *Proceedings of the 2019 Conference of the North American Chapter of the Association for Computational Linguistics: Human Language Technologies, Volume 1 (Long and Short Papers)*, pages 839–850, Minneapolis, Minnesota. Association for Computational Linguistics.

J. Edward Hu, Rachel Rudinger, Matt Post, and Benjamin Van Durme. 2019b. PARABANK: monolingual bitext generation and sentential paraphrasing via lexically-constrained neural machine translation. In *The Thirty-Third AAAI Conference on Artificial Intelligence, AAAI 2019, The Thirty-First Innovative Applications of Artificial Intelligence Conference, IAAI 2019, The Ninth AAAI Symposium on Educational Advances in Artificial Intelligence, EAAI 2019, Honolulu, Hawaii, USA, January 27 - February 1, 2019*, pages 6521–6528. AAAI Press.

Zuchao Li, Masao Utiyama, Eiichiro Sumita, and Hai Zhao. 2021. NICT's neural machine translation systems for the WAT21 restricted translation task. In *Proceedings of the 8th Workshop on Asian Translation (WAT2021)*, pages 62–67, Online. Association for Computational Linguistics.

Sneha Mehta, Bahareh Azarnoush, Boris Chen, Avneesh Saluja, Vinith Misra, Ballav Bihani, and Ritwik Kumar. 2020. Simplify-then-translate: Automatic preprocessing for black-box translation. In *The Thirty-Fourth AAAI Conference on Artificial Intelligence, AAAI 2020, The Thirty-Second Innovative Applications of Artificial Intelligence Conference, IAAI 2020, The Tenth AAAI Symposium on Educational Advances in Artificial Intelligence, EAAI 2020, New York, NY, USA, February 7-12, 2020*, pages 8488–8495. AAAI Press.

Rei Miyata and Atsushi Fujita. 2021. Understanding pre-editing for black-box neural machine translation. In *Proceedings of the 16th Conference of the European Chapter of the Association for Computational Linguistics: Main Volume*, pages 1539–1550, Online. Association for Computational Linguistics.

Amit Moryossef, Roee Aharoni, and Yoav Goldberg. 2019. Filling gender & number gaps in neural machine translation with black-box context injection. In *Proceedings of the First Workshop on Gender Bias in Natural Language Processing*, pages 49–54, Florence, Italy. Association for Computational Linguistics.

Toshiaki Nakazawa, Manabu Yaguchi, Kiyotaka Uchimoto, Masao Utiyama, Eiichiro Sumita, Sadao Kurohashi, and Hitoshi Isahara. 2016. ASPEC: asian scientific paper excerpt corpus. In *Proceedings of the Tenth International Conference on Language Resources and Evaluation LREC 2016, Portorož, Slovenia, May 23-28, 2016*. European Language Resources Association (ELRA).

Myle Ott, Sergey Edunov, Alexei Baevski, Angela Fan, Sam Gross, Nathan Ng, David Grangier, and Michael Auli. 2019. fairseq: A fast, extensible toolkit for sequence modeling. In *Proceedings of the 2019 Conference of the North American Chapter of the Association for Computational Linguistics (Demonstrations)*, pages 48–53, Minneapolis, Minnesota. Association for Computational Linguistics.

Matt Post and David Vilar. 2018. Fast lexically constrained decoding with dynamic beam allocation for neural machine translation. In *Proceedings of the 2018 Conference of the North American Chapter of the Association for Computational Linguistics: Human Language Technologies, Volume 1 (Long Papers)*, pages 1314–1324, New Orleans, Louisiana. Association for Computational Linguistics.

Rico Sennrich, Barry Haddow, and Alexandra Birch. 2016. Neural machine translation of rare words with subword units. In *Proceedings of the 54th Annual Meeting of the Association for Computational Linguistics (Volume 1: Long Papers)*, pages 1715–1725, Berlin, Germany. Association for Computational Linguistics.

Kai Song, Yue Zhang, Heng Yu, Weihua Luo, Kun Wang, and Min Zhang. 2019. Code-switching for enhancing NMT with pre-specified translation. In *Proceedings of the 2019 Conference of the North American Chapter of the Association for Computational Linguistics: Human Language Technologies, Volume 1 (Long and Short Papers)*, pages 449–459, Minneapolis, Minnesota. Association for Computational Linguistics.

Ashish Vaswani, Noam Shazeer, Niki Parmar, Jakob Uszkoreit, Llion Jones, Aidan N. Gomez, Lukasz Kaiser, and Illia Polosukhin. 2017. Attention is all you need. In *Advances in Neural Information Processing Systems 30: Annual Conference on Neural Information Processing Systems 2017, December 4-9, 2017, Long Beach, CA, USA*, pages 5998–6008.

What do Models Learn From Training on More Than Text? Measuring Visual Commonsense Knowledge

Lovisa Hagström
Chalmers University of Technology
lovhag@chalmers.se

Richard Johansson
University of Gothenburg
richard.johansson@gu.se

Abstract

There are limitations in learning language from text alone. Therefore, recent focus has been on developing multimodal models. However, few benchmarks exist that can measure what language models learn about language from multimodal training. We hypothesize that training on a visual modality should improve on the visual commonsense knowledge in language models. Therefore, we introduce two evaluation tasks for measuring visual commonsense knowledge in language models[1] and use them to evaluate different multimodal models and unimodal baselines. Primarily, we find that the visual commonsense knowledge is not significantly different between the multimodal models and unimodal baseline models trained on visual text data.

1 Introduction

Language models (LMs) trained on large amounts of textual data have shown great performance on several textual tasks (Devlin et al., 2019; Brown et al., 2020). However, recent work has illuminated limitations with text-only training of LMs. These limitations arise from a lack of meaning (Bender and Koller, 2020) and experience (Bisk et al., 2020), together with the problem of reporting bias (Gordon and Van Durme, 2013). Multimodal training has been identified as one way to create models that do not suffer from the aforementioned limitations (Paik et al., 2021; Huang et al., 2021). While several multimodal models have been developed (Tan and Bansal, 2019; Li et al., 2019, 2020), few evaluation methods exist that can tell us whether multimodal training mitigates text-only training limits.

If we wish to successfully create multimodal LMs that learn from more than text, we need a way to evaluate them for what we expect them to have learned from their multimodal training.

[1]Code publicly available at: github.com/lovhag/measure-visual-commonsense-knowledge

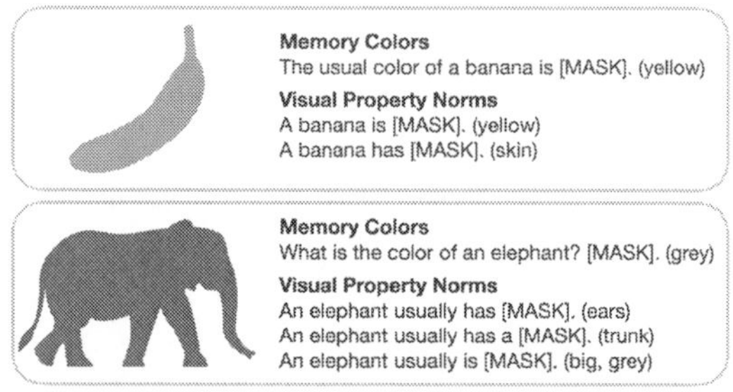

Figure 1: We introduce the two evaluation tasks Memory Colors and Visual Property Norms for measuring visual commonsense knowledge in a LM.

One hypothesis is that multimodal training should aid LMs in learning commonsense knowledge (Zhang et al., 2021). There are several text-only evaluation tasks that aim to measure the commonsense knowledge in LMs (Zellers et al., 2019b; Zhou et al., 2020), but none of them focus explicitly on the commonsense knowledge learned through training on more than text.

In this work, we focus on models trained on images and text, denoted *vision-and-language models*. We reason that if there is any additional information to be learnt from a visual modality it should firstly be basic visual commonsense knowledge. That is, visual conceptual knowledge that is viewed as commonsense by humans, and thus not attainable from text alone due to reporting bias.

We propose a simple method for measuring the visual commonsense knowledge of a model using two zero-shot masked language text-only tasks, depicted in Figure 1. The first task is the Memory Colors evaluation task (Norlund et al., 2021) and the second we create based on the visual features in the Centre for Speech, Language and the Brain (CSLB) concept property norms dataset (Devereux et al., 2014). We refer to the latter task as the Visual Property Norms evaluation task. We complement our work with the results of four vision-and-language models and four baselines on these two tasks.

Proceedings of the 60th Annual Meeting of the Association for Computational Linguistics Student Research Workshop, pages 252 - 261

2 Evaluation Tasks

Our aim is to evaluate models for visual commonsense knowledge. To do this we make use of the existing Memory Colors evaluation task described in section 2.1, and introduce a new evaluation task, Visual Property Norms in section 2.2. Memory Colors is smaller than Visual Property Norms and specifically focuses on visual information related to the color of different concepts, so it is potentially easier. We include both tasks to get a performance curve over increasing difficulty.

Common for both tasks is that they contain queries in English relating to visual properties of tangible concepts and that these queries are based on the knowledge of multiple human participants. Therefore, the tasks can be considered to evaluate a basic aspect of visual commonsense knowledge.

Also common for both tasks is that they use textual templates containing a `[MASK]` token to be predicted by a model in a cloze-style fashion, similarly to the method used by Kassner and Schütze (2020) and Petroni et al. (2019). The advantages with querying the models in this fashion is that most LMs[2] already have been exposed to this type of query format, including most multimodal models. We can then evaluate any model in a masked language modelling fashion on these tasks without additional training or having to make model-specific adaptations, enabling easy evaluation for researchers who wish to use these evaluation tasks.

This form of cloze-style evaluation is also referred to as *prompt-based retrieval*. The reliability of this method has recently been questioned by Jiang et al. (2020) and Cao et al. (2021) due to the query format sensitivity of LMs. To alleviate this issue, we evaluate the models using several different prompts for each of the two tasks.

2.1 Memory Colors

The Memory Colors evaluation task is a text-only zero-shot cloze test in English that evaluates a model for its knowledge of memory colors. It queries a model for the color of 109 typical objects using 13 different query templates. The task has been created with the help of 11 human participants, so to some extent it encodes human visual commonsense knowledge limited to colors. Some examples of queries can be seen in Figure 1.

We use the same evaluation metric as specified by Norlund et al. (2021), i.e. the accuracy score after masking the model output for the 11 possible colors black, blue, brown, green, grey, orange, pink, purple, red, white and yellow.

2.2 Visual Property Norms

We also introduce a new cloze task in English to evaluate for visual commonsense knowledge, denoted Visual Property Norms. It is the largest query-based pure-language evaluation task capable of evaluating LMs for visual commonsense knowledge, containing 6,541 visual conceptual features produced by human participants.

We base it on the CSLB concept property norms dataset (Devereux et al., 2014) that contains the conceptual knowledge of 30 human participants for each of 541 concrete objects, with 123 participants in total. This knowledge is represented as a set of features per object, for which each feature is specified with a production frequency (PF). The PF describes how many of 30 participants produced that feature, so a feature with a high PF can be considered to be more apparent to the participants, since more came to think of it. All features are also categorized as either *encyclopaedic*, *functional*, *other perceptual*, *taxonomic* or *visual perceptual*. Table 1 contains some examples of visual perceptual features in the dataset.

Concept	Relation	Feature	PF
Cherry	has a	stalk	17
Fern	is	green	29
Hair	is	thin	22
Plum	has	flesh	9

Table 1: Some concepts and their visual perceptual features in the concept property norms dataset.

We create our evaluation task from the concept property norms dataset in a set of steps. Firstly, since our goal is to measure visual commonsense knowledge, we only make use of the *visual perceptual* features. Since we wish to perform cloze tests through masked language modelling, only feature alternatives describable by one wordpiece from the BERT base uncased tokenizer are included.

Furthermore, we only include the four most common feature relations in the task. These are *has*, *has a*, *made of* and *is*. We then part the data into five different segments based on production frequency. This is done by thresholding the features for each concept such that only features with a PF above the set threshold for a certain data segment

[2]Excluding autoregressive LMs.

are included as gold labels in that segment. The segments and their PF thresholds are listed in the appendix.

Lastly, we create queries from the concepts in each data segment using 8 different query templates, seen in the appendix. Some examples of Visual Property Norms queries can be seen in Figure 1.

Similarly to Weir et al. (2020) we use the mean average precision (mAP) as our evaluation metric, since there may be multiple correct answers for each query in our evaluation data. We calculate this score for each concept and relation, per query template and production frequency segment. We then get a final score for each production frequency segment by taking the average score over all query templates and concepts per segment. This metric is measured over a vocabulary that has been masked to only contain the 614 possible answer alternatives in the Visual Property Norms evaluation data.

3 Models

We evaluate four multimodal pre-trained models for their visual commonsense knowledge. These are CLIP-BERT both with and without imagination[3] (Norlund et al., 2021), a LXMERT base uncased (Tan and Bansal, 2019) and VisualBERT (Li et al., 2019). We also evaluate four unimodal baseline models. These are a BERT base uncased pre-trained on English Wikipedia and BookCorpus, a BERT base uncased further trained on the pure-text part of the CLIP-BERT training data (BERT-CLIP-BERT-train) and two BERT base uncased models trained on the pure-text part of the LXMERT training data, one from scratch and one initialized from pre-trained BERT weights (BERT-LXMERT-train-scratch and BERT-LXMERT-train).

All models are to some extent based on the BERT base architecture and consequently share the same vocabulary and tokenizer. They are also of similar sizes with $\sim$ 110M trainable weights, the exception being LXMERT with $\sim$ 230M trainable weights. Additional information about the models can be found in the appendix.

Adapting the models for pure-text queries The majority of current multimodal models have not been developed to be queried only with text. In this case, both CLIP-BERT and VisualBERT should work well with only removing their visual features input, since they are single-stream models. However, LXMERT is a dual-stream model that requires a visual feature input. We handle the removal of visual information by simply removing the visual processing chain in LXMERT, making the language input the only input given to the Cross-Modality Encoder in the model. This would not work if we still wanted to use the model in a multimodal fashion, but we can make this adaption since we are only interested in querying the model for visual commonsense knowledge via language.

4 Results

The results of the models on our two evaluation tasks can be seen in Figure 2. We format the analysis of the results around a set of questions.

Do the multimodal models display more memory colors knowledge? The multimodal CLIP-BERT-explicit model has the best performance on this task. So to some extent, yes. But it is worth noting that the unimodal BERT model trained on LXMERT training data is second best on the task, outperforming both LXMERT and VisualBERT, indicating a small multimodal advantage.

Is performance on Memory Colors indicative of performance on Visual Property Norms? The ranking visible in Figure 2a does not entirely differ from that in Figure 2b. The main exception being CLIP-BERT-explicit, which has the best performance on Memory Colors, but is outperformed by most other models on Visual Property Norms. We perform a closer analysis of how these results compare by extracting Visual Property Norm results for colors in the appendix.

Do the models perform better when evaluated on more apparent concept features? We can observe how the model performance unanimously increases with increased production frequency threshold in Figure 2b. Thus, it appears as though the models agree more with concept features that can be regarded as more apparent.

Do the multimodal models contain more visual commonsense knowledge? The results in Figure 2b do not really indicate clear advantage of either unimodal or multimodal models. The multimodal model CLIP-BERT-implicit may generally have the best performance on the task, but the unimodal models trained on visual text data do not differ much in performance. For example, the unimodal BERT-LXMERT-train performs almost on par with CLIP-BERT-implicit.

[3] The explicit version has the ability to "imagine" visual features when queried with text.

(a) Memory Colors

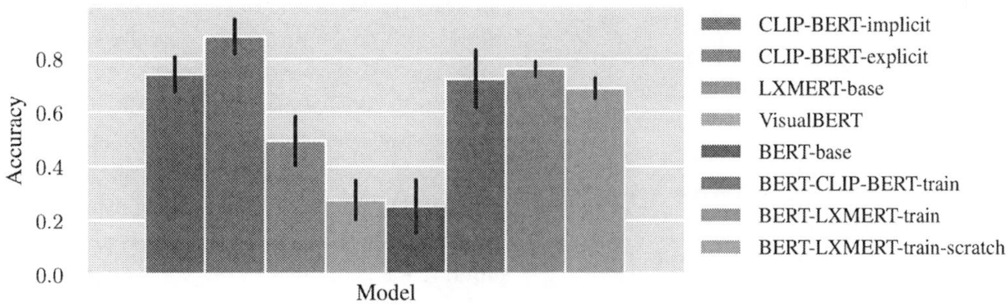

(b) Visual Property Norms

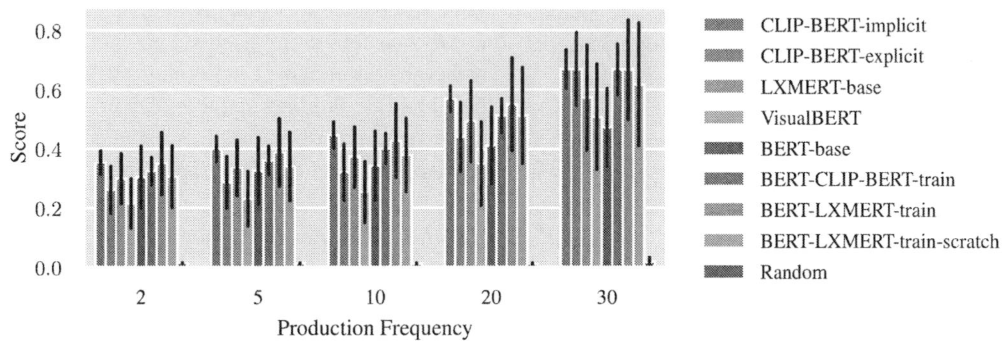

Figure 2: The model accuracy on Memory Colors and model scores on Visual Property Norms per production frequency segment. The multimodal model results are depicted with warmer colors, and the unimodal model results are depicted in cooler colors. The error bars indicate the standard deviation of the model performance over the different query templates. The score has been calculated by masking the vocabulary of the models to only contain the possible answers of the task.

This conclusion is similar to that of Yun et al. (2021), who also compared vision-and-language models to text-only models trained on captions. They found that the models have similar performance with respect to their internal linguistic representations for general tasks.

These results do not mean that the idea of having models learn language from more than text has failed. They do however indicate that there is more work to be done on developing models that use multimodal pretraining to improve on their natural language understanding.

However, we cannot exclude the possibility in our work that the multimodal models suffer in performance due to a lack of visual feature input. Future work investigating this would be valuable.

Are the models sensitive to how they are queried? Prevalent for all models is that their performance varies greatly with how they are queried. BERT-LXMERT-train may have the best performance on Visual Property Norms if queried differently. We evaluate the model performances depending on query template in the appendix. This highlights the importance of querying the models with different prompts, since the models may perform dissimilarily depending on prompt due to the degree of prompt-dataset fitness, as reported by Cao et al. (2021).

Does fine-tuning on visual language develop visual commonsense knowledge? In both Figures 2a and 2b it is visible that unimodal model performance greatly improves with fine-tuning on visual text corpora. Potential explanations for this are that the models become more attuned to the task with fine-tuning, or that corpora from VQA and image captioning do not suffer as much from reporting bias compared to more common corpora. Thus, text that has been curated to explicitly contain visual information may suffice as a replacement for images.

5 Related Work

Weir et al. (2020) also use the CSLB concept property norms to probe LMs for commonsense knowledge. Our work differs from theirs in that we focus on visual commonsense knowledge and evaluate several multimodal models for whether their multimodal training grants them additional visual commonsense knowledge.

Norlund et al. (2021) also query a multimodal model for visual commonsense knowledge but with a focus on memory colors. Paik et al. (2021) present similar work but with more focus on probing and reporting bias. In our work, we include general visual commonsense knowledge concepts and evaluate several multimodal models.

Additionally, Iki and Aizawa (2021) evaluate several vision-and-language models on GLUE, to investigate the effect of an additional visual modality on the general linguistic capabilities of a model. Our work differs in that we evaluate the models specifically for visual commonsense knowledge.

Other tasks that have been developed to evaluate the performance of vision-and-language models are Visual Question Answering (VQA) tasks and Visual Commonsense Reasning (VCR) tasks (Goyal et al., 2017; Hudson and Manning, 2019; Zellers et al., 2019a). Our work differs from these in that we evaluate for visual knowledge in models without conditioning on an image, to investigate whether the linguistic capabilities of a model improve from training on more than text. In the aforementioned tasks, the text prompts are always conditioned on an image provided with the prompt, obstructing equal comparisons with text-only models.

6 Limitations

Our work is limited to a subset of vision-and-language models, so the results found may not translate to all such model types. Also, since our evaluation utilizes prompt-based retrieval, its measurement accuracy depends on how well this method works for LMs. Additionally, as previously mentioned, we do not investigate how well the multimodal models adapt to a unimodal input. Thus, our results depend on whether the models were functioning adequately with our method of adapting them to a unimodal input.

7 Ethical Considerations

Our work should not have any direct ethical implications, since we mainly introduce evaluation tasks and evaluate different models on them. We do however investigate visual conceptual perceptions based on data from a potentially small group of people whose world-view may be culturally different from that of other individuals. This means that we may encourage knowledge that benefits some people more than others. Similar issues are discussed by Liu et al. (2021). Our investigation is limited to English-language models and datasets, limiting the generality of our conclusions.

8 Conclusions

We introduce new evaluation methods for measuring the visual commonsense knowledge in LMs and evaluate a number of multimodal LMs on these benchmarks. We find that there are no significant differences in performance between models trained on pure text and models trained on images and text. Most prominently, we find that a unimodal LM trained on image captions and VQA queries can attain a visual commonsense knowledge on par with that of a multimodal model.

We also confirm the results by Jiang et al. (2020) and Cao et al. (2021), that LMs are sensitive to query format even when querying for commonsense knowledge. This casts some doubts on what is really measured in a model for a cloze task and whether we can reason about LMs as having knowledge. An interesting future step would be to investigate this further and see if it would be more applicable to use e.g. probing or some other evaluation method.

Nonetheless, this is a first step towards measuring the visual commonsense knowledge in multimodal as well as unimodal LMs. We hope that the evaluation tasks introduced here may aid other researchers in their aim to create models that learn language from more than text.

Acknowledgements

We thank the anonymous reviewers for their valuable feedback and knowledge sharing.

This work was partially supported by the Wallenberg AI, Autonomous Systems and Software Program (WASP) funded by the Knut and Alice Wallenberg Foundation.

Additionally, the computations were enabled by resources provided by the Swedish National Infrastructure for Computing (SNIC), partially funded by the Swedish Research Council through grant agreement no. 2018-05973.

References

Emily M. Bender and Alexander Koller. 2020. Climbing towards NLU: On meaning, form, and understanding in the age of data. In *Proceedings of the 58th Annual Meeting of the Association for Computational Linguistics*, pages 5185–5198, Online. Association for Computational Linguistics.

Yonatan Bisk, Ari Holtzman, Jesse Thomason, Jacob Andreas, Yoshua Bengio, Joyce Chai, Mirella Lapata, Angeliki Lazaridou, Jonathan May, Aleksandr Nisnevich, Nicolas Pinto, and Joseph Turian. 2020. Experience grounds language. In *Proceedings of the 2020 Conference on Empirical Methods in Natural Language Processing (EMNLP)*, pages 8718–8735, Online. Association for Computational Linguistics.

Tom Brown, Benjamin Mann, Nick Ryder, Melanie Subbiah, Jared D Kaplan, Prafulla Dhariwal, Arvind Neelakantan, Pranav Shyam, Girish Sastry, Amanda Askell, Sandhini Agarwal, Ariel Herbert-Voss, Gretchen Krueger, Tom Henighan, Rewon Child, Aditya Ramesh, Daniel Ziegler, Jeffrey Wu, Clemens Winter, Chris Hesse, Mark Chen, Eric Sigler, Mateusz Litwin, Scott Gray, Benjamin Chess, Jack Clark, Christopher Berner, Sam McCandlish, Alec Radford, Ilya Sutskever, and Dario Amodei. 2020. Language models are few-shot learners. In *Advances in Neural Information Processing Systems*, volume 33, pages 1877–1901. Curran Associates, Inc.

Boxi Cao, Hongyu Lin, Xianpei Han, Le Sun, Lingyong Yan, Meng Liao, Tong Xue, and Jin Xu. 2021. Knowledgeable or educated guess? revisiting language models as knowledge bases. In *Proceedings of the 59th Annual Meeting of the Association for Computational Linguistics and the 11th International Joint Conference on Natural Language Processing (Volume 1: Long Papers)*, pages 1860–1874, Online. Association for Computational Linguistics.

Barry J Devereux, Lorraine K Tyler, Jeroen Geertzen, and Billi Randall. 2014. The centre for speech, language and the brain (cslb) concept property norms. *Behavior research methods*, 46(4):1119–1127.

Jacob Devlin, Ming-Wei Chang, Kenton Lee, and Kristina Toutanova. 2019. BERT: Pre-training of deep bidirectional transformers for language understanding. In *Proceedings of the 2019 Conference of the North American Chapter of the Association for Computational Linguistics: Human Language Technologies, Volume 1 (Long and Short Papers)*, pages 4171–4186, Minneapolis, Minnesota. Association for Computational Linguistics.

Jonathan Gordon and Benjamin Van Durme. 2013. Reporting bias and knowledge acquisition. In *Proceedings of the 2013 workshop on Automated knowledge base construction*, pages 25–30.

Yash Goyal, Tejas Khot, Douglas Summers-Stay, Dhruv Batra, and Devi Parikh. 2017. Making the V in VQA matter: Elevating the role of image understanding in Visual Question Answering. In *Conference on Computer Vision and Pattern Recognition (CVPR)*.

Yu Huang, Chenzhuang Du, Zihui Xue, Xuanyao Chen, Hang Zhao, and Longbo Huang. 2021. What makes multi-modal learning better than single (provably). *Advances in Neural Information Processing Systems*, 34.

Drew A Hudson and Christopher D Manning. 2019. Gqa: A new dataset for real-world visual reasoning and compositional question answering. *Conference on Computer Vision and Pattern Recognition (CVPR)*.

Taichi Iki and Akiko Aizawa. 2021. Effect of visual extensions on natural language understanding in vision-and-language models. In *Proceedings of the 2021 Conference on Empirical Methods in Natural Language Processing*, pages 2189–2196, Online and Punta Cana, Dominican Republic. Association for Computational Linguistics.

Zhengbao Jiang, Frank F. Xu, Jun Araki, and Graham Neubig. 2020. How Can We Know What Language Models Know? *Transactions of the Association for Computational Linguistics*, 8:423–438.

Nora Kassner and Hinrich Schütze. 2020. Negated and misprimed probes for pretrained language models: Birds can talk, but cannot fly. In *Proceedings of the 58th Annual Meeting of the Association for Computational Linguistics*, pages 7811–7818, Online. Association for Computational Linguistics.

Liunian Harold Li, Mark Yatskar, Da Yin, Cho-Jui Hsieh, and Kai-Wei Chang. 2019. Visualbert: A simple and performant baseline for vision and language. *arXiv preprint arXiv:1908.03557*.

Xiujun Li, Xi Yin, Chunyuan Li, Pengchuan Zhang, Xiaowei Hu, Lei Zhang, Lijuan Wang, Houdong Hu, Li Dong, Furu Wei, Yejin Choi, and Jianfeng Gao. 2020. Oscar: Object-semantics aligned pre-training for vision-language tasks. In *Computer Vision - ECCV 2020 - 16th European Conference, Glasgow, UK, August 23-28, 2020, Proceedings, Part XXX*, volume 12375 of *Lecture Notes in Computer Science*, pages 121–137. Springer.

Fangyu Liu, Emanuele Bugliarello, Edoardo Maria Ponti, Siva Reddy, Nigel Collier, and Desmond Elliott. 2021. Visually grounded reasoning across languages and cultures. In *Proceedings of the 2021 Conference on Empirical Methods in Natural Language Processing*, pages 10467–10485, Online and Punta Cana, Dominican Republic. Association for Computational Linguistics.

Tobias Norlund, Lovisa Hagström, and Richard Johansson. 2021. Transfering knowledge from vision to language: How to achieve it and how to measure it? In *Proceedings of the Fourth BlackboxNLP*

Workshop on Analyzing and Interpreting Neural Networks for NLP, pages 149–162, Punta Cana, Dominican Republic.

Cory Paik, Stéphane Aroca-Ouellette, Alessandro Roncone, and Katharina Kann. 2021. The World of an Octopus: How Reporting Bias Influences a Language Model's Perception of Color. In *Proceedings of the 2021 Conference on Empirical Methods in Natural Language Processing*, pages 823–835, Online and Punta Cana, Dominican Republic. Association for Computational Linguistics.

Fabio Petroni, Tim Rocktäschel, Sebastian Riedel, Patrick Lewis, Anton Bakhtin, Yuxiang Wu, and Alexander Miller. 2019. Language models as knowledge bases? In *Proceedings of the 2019 Conference on Empirical Methods in Natural Language Processing and the 9th International Joint Conference on Natural Language Processing (EMNLP-IJCNLP)*, pages 2463–2473, Hong Kong, China. Association for Computational Linguistics.

Hao Tan and Mohit Bansal. 2019. LXMERT: Learning cross-modality encoder representations from transformers. In *Proceedings of the 2019 Conference on Empirical Methods in Natural Language Processing and the 9th International Joint Conference on Natural Language Processing (EMNLP-IJCNLP)*, pages 5100–5111, Hong Kong, China. Association for Computational Linguistics.

Nathaniel Weir, Adam Poliak, and Benjamin Van Durme. 2020. Probing neural language models for human tacit assumptions. In *42nd Annual Virtual Meeting of the Cognitive Science Society (CogSci)*.

Tian Yun, Chen Sun, and Ellie Pavlick. 2021. Does vision-and-language pretraining improve lexical grounding? In *Findings of the Association for Computational Linguistics: EMNLP 2021*, pages 4357–4366, Punta Cana, Dominican Republic. Association for Computational Linguistics.

Rowan Zellers, Yonatan Bisk, Ali Farhadi, and Yejin Choi. 2019a. From recognition to cognition: Visual commonsense reasoning. In *The IEEE Conference on Computer Vision and Pattern Recognition (CVPR)*.

Rowan Zellers, Ari Holtzman, Yonatan Bisk, Ali Farhadi, and Yejin Choi. 2019b. HellaSwag: Can a machine really finish your sentence? In *Proceedings of the 57th Annual Meeting of the Association for Computational Linguistics*, pages 4791–4800, Florence, Italy. Association for Computational Linguistics.

Yian Zhang, Alex Warstadt, Xiaocheng Li, and Samuel R. Bowman. 2021. When do you need billions of words of pretraining data? In *Proceedings of the 59th Annual Meeting of the Association for Computational Linguistics and the 11th International Joint Conference on Natural Language Processing (Volume 1: Long Papers)*, pages 1112–1125, Online. Association for Computational Linguistics.

Xuhui Zhou, Yue Zhang, Leyang Cui, and Dandan Huang. 2020. Evaluating commonsense in pretrained language models. *Proceedings of the AAAI Conference on Artificial Intelligence*, 34(05):9733–9740.

A Additional model information

Additional information about the models used in our work and their training datasets can be found in Tables 2 and 3. We can observe that VisualBERT has been trained on a data amount that is quite small compared to those of CLIP-BERT and LXMERT.

It is also worth noting on the different backbones of the models. CLIP-BERT is a single-stream multimodal model with a CLIP backbone for visual processing. LXMERT is a dual-stream multimodal model with a Faster R-CNN detector backbone. While VisualBERT is a single-stream model that also utilizes Faster R-CNN detector backbone. Since CLIP has been trained on the immense WIT dataset, the backbone data sizes differ greatly between CLIP-BERT and the other multimodal models.

B Additional information on Visual Property Norms

Information about the different segments and number of entries per segment in the Visual Property Norms can be seen in Table 4.

C Additional results on Visual Property Norms

Additional model results on the Visual Property Norms can be found here.

Figure 3 indicates model performance per feature relation across the production frequency segments. We can observe how the models show the best performance for the *is made of* relation, which arguably can be associated more with visual perceptual properties.

Figure 4 shows model score per query template across all production frequency segments, indicating that CLIP-BERT-implicit benefits from being more robust to different query templates. Additionally, these results indicate that BERT-LXMERT-train would have the best overall score on Visual Property Norms if the queries containing "q: a" were to be removed.

Lastly, Figure 5 contains the results of the models on the color part of Visual Property Norms which has been filtered to only contain queries with

Model	Text	Visual text	Images+Text	Backbone	Training objectives
BERT	80M				MLM, NSP
CLIP-BERT-implicit	80M		4.7M	400M	MLM
CLIP-BERT-explicit	80M		4.7M	400M	MLM
BERT-CLIP-BERT-train	80M	4.7M			MLM
LXMERT			9.2M	0.1M	MLM, RFR, DLC, ITM, IQA
BERT-LXMERT-train	80M	9.0M			MLM
BERT-LXMERT-train-scratch		9.0M			MLM
VisualBERT	80M		1.7M	0.1M	MLM, ITM

Table 2: An overview of the pre-trained models, the sizes of their training datasets and their pre-training objectives. The sizes are measured in number of training samples. The backbone column indicates the training data sizes for the image processing backbones of the models. For the training objectives, ITM refers to Image-Text Matching, RFR to RoI-Feature Regression, DLC to Detected Label Classification, MVM to Masked Visual Modeling and IQA to image QA.

Dataset	Data sources	# of text	# of images
CLIP-BERT V+L	MS COCO, SBU Captions, VG-QA, CC	4.72M	2.91M
LXMERT V+L	MS COCO, VG, VQA, GQA, VG-QA	9.18M	0.18M
VisualBERT V+L	MS COCO, VQA	1.27M	0.12M

Table 3: The vision-language datasets on which the multimodal models originally were trained. More information about the datasets can be found in the articles that introduced the models.

PF	entries	*has*	*has a*	*made of*	*is*
2	6,541	1,675	1,190	1,176	2,500
5	3641	1,016	642	760	1,223
10	2001	583	347	509	562
20	613	169	88	209	147
30	27	5	2	10	10

Table 4: The data segments segmented based on production frequencies together with their number of entries. The entries are calculated as the number of feature-concept-label entries, where there can be several features belonging to the same feature and concept. The PF column indicates the production frequency threshold for each segment, all features with a production frequency higher or equal to this threshold are included in the segment. We also list the number of labels per feature relation type.

gold labels describing colors. Here, we see some indications of a better performance of CLIP-BERT-explicit for colors. Potentially, the imagination capacity of this model is more helpful for queries with answers relating to more basic visual properties, such as color.

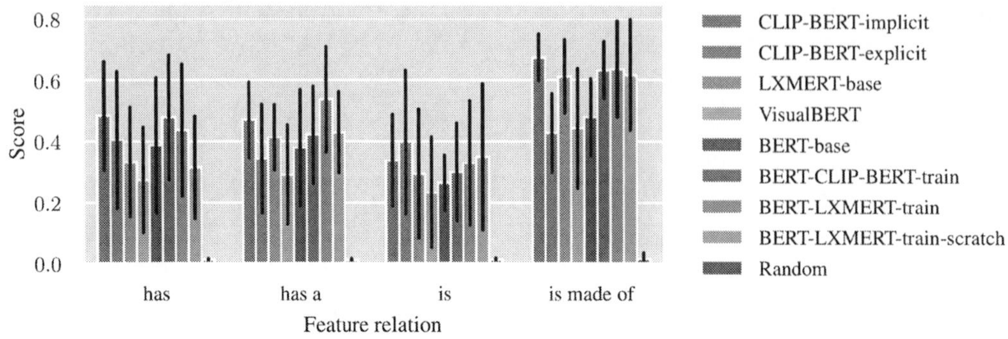

Figure 3: The model scores on Visual Property Norms per feature relation. The error bars indicate the standard deviation of the model performance over the different query templates. The score has been calculated by masking the vocabulary of the models to only contain the possible answers of the task.

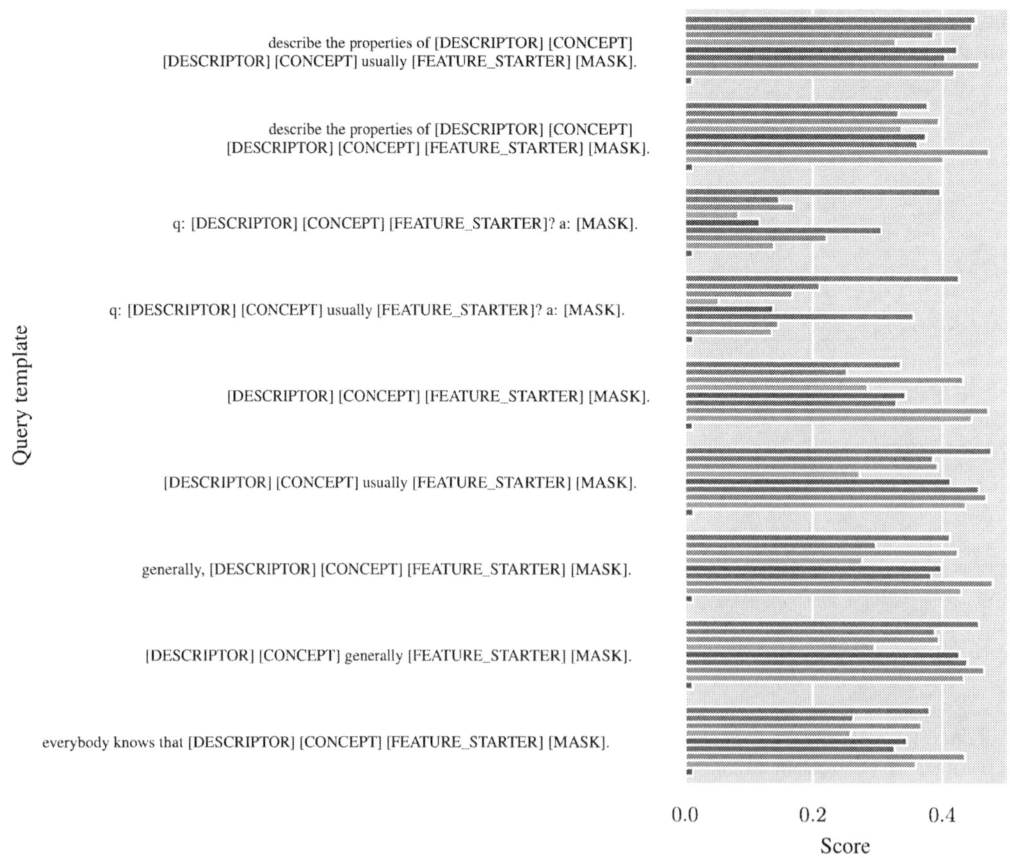

Figure 4: The score for each model on Visual Property Norms per query template. The score has been calculated by masking the vocabulary of the models to only contain the possible answers of the task.

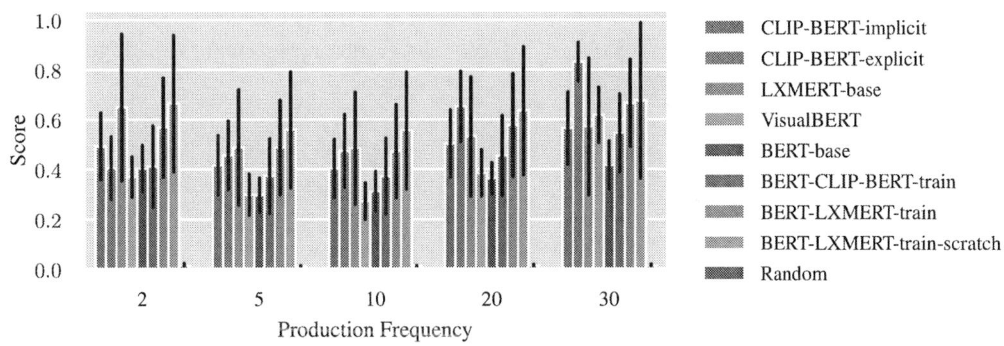

Figure 5: The score for each model per production frequency segment on Visual Property Norms that has been filtered to only contain samples for which the correct answer is one or more out of 11 possible colors. The score has been calculated by masking the vocabulary of the models to only contain the possible answers of the task.

TeluguNER: Leveraging Multi-Domain Named Entity Recognition with Deep Transformers

Suma Reddy Duggenpudi[1], **Subba Reddy Oota**[1,2], **Mounika Marreddy**[1] **Radhika Mamidi**[1]
[1]IIIT Hyderabad, India; [2]INRIA, Bordeaux, France
sumareddy.duggenpudi@research.iiit.ac.in, subba-reddy.oota@inria.fr
mounika.marreddy@research.iiit.ac.in, radhika.mamidi@iiit.ac.in

Abstract

Named Entity Recognition (NER) is a successful and well-researched problem in English due to the availability of resources. The transformer models, specifically the masked-language models (MLM), have shown remarkable performance in NER in recent times. With growing data in different online platforms, there is a need for NER in other languages too. NER remains underexplored in Indian languages due to the lack of resources and tools. Our contributions in this paper include (i) Two annotated NER datasets for the Telugu language in multiple domains: Newswire Dataset (ND) and Medical Dataset (MD), and we combined ND and MD to form a Combined Dataset (CD) (ii) Comparison of the finetuned Telugu pretrained transformer models (*BERT-Te*, *RoBERTa-Te*, and *ELECTRA-Te*) with other baseline models (CRF, LSTM-CRF, and BiLSTM-CRF) (iii) Further investigation of the performance of Telugu pretrained transformer models against the multilingual models mBERT (Devlin et al., 2018), XLM-R (Conneau et al., 2020), and IndicBERT (Kakwani et al., 2020). We find that pretrained Telugu language models (*BERT-Te* and *RoBERTa*) outperform the existing pretrained multilingual and baseline models in NER. On a large dataset (CD) of 38,363 sentences, the *BERT-Te* achieves a high F1-score of 0.80 (entity-level) and 0.75 (token-level). Further, these pretrained Telugu models have shown state-of-the-art performance on various Telugu NER datasets. We open-source our dataset, pretrained models, and code[1].

1 Introduction

Named Entity Recognition (NER) aims to identify various named entities from the raw text. Typically these named entities are broadly categorized into person names, locations, organizations, and other categories depending on the domain. Identifying these named entities is necessary and is proven to be very helpful in Natural Language Processing (NLP), Information Retrieval (IR), and Information Extraction (IE). Moreover, when so much data is generated daily today, NER becomes very important in processing and extracting meaningful information from the text. However, most NER work is limited to the resource-rich English language due to the availability of annotated datasets, efficient feature representations, and tools to process the data.

English has many huge annotated datasets like CoNLL-2003 (Sang and De Meulder, 2003), OntoNotes (Weischedel et al., 2013) and WNUT (Derczynski et al., 2017). Traditional models like Conditional Random Fields (CRF) (Lafferty et al., 2001) have been used for NER modeling by training them on these datasets. With the development in deep learning, solutions like Lample et al. (2016) and Ma and Hovy (2016) used Long Short-Term Memory (LSTMs) for sequence-labelling tasks like NER. Further, the combination of the LSTM-CRF model proposed by Huang et al. (2015) has achieved even better performance. Recently, transformer models (Devlin et al., 2019) have proven to be achieving similar results to the state-of-the-art models (Akbik et al., 2018; Peters et al., 2018). Hence, we can infer that there has been extensive and rapid research in NER for English with significant advancements. However, NER developed in English cannot be generalized and extended due to the rich morphological nature of Indian languages.

Unlike English, most of the resources created for Indian languages are for machine translation. However, in the NER task, the meaning of context, the roles of named entities, differentiations amongst categories, and syntactic and semantic structures will be lost if we translate English sentences to Telugu. Examples of Telugu language NER sentences, their WX notation (a standard notation used

[1]https://github.com/mors-ner/anonymous_telner

Proceedings of the 60th Annual Meeting of the Association for Computational Linguistics Student Research Workshop, pages 262 - 272

ఆంధ్ర[B-LOC] ప్రదేశ్[I-LOC] యొక్క ముఖ్యమంత్రి వైఎస్ఆర్[B-NORP] కాంగ్రెస్[I-NORP] పార్టీ[I-NORP] అధినేత వైఎస్[B-PER] జగన్[I-PER]. AMXra[B-LOC] praxeS[I-LOC] yoVkka muKyamaMwri vEeVsAr[B-NORP] kAMgreVs[I-NORP] pArtI[I-NORP] aXinewa vEeVs[B-PER] jagan[I-PER]. Chief Minister[TITLE] of Andhra Pradesh[PER] is YSR Congress Party[ORG] leader YS Jagan[PER].
జికా[B-DIS] వైరస్[I-DIS] దోమ[B-ORGANISM] కాటు వలన వ్యాప్తి చెందుతుంది. jikA[B-DIS] vEras[I-DIS] xoma[B-ORGANISM] kAtu valana vyApwi ceVMxuwuMxi. Zika[PER] virus spreads by mosquito bites.

Figure 1: Example sentences of NER tags in Telugu (top), WX notation (middle) and their English translations (bottom) with NER tagging using CoreNLP (Manning et al., 2014) respectively.

for Indian languages)[2], and their English translations are reported in Figure 1. From the examples, we can notice that Telugu's context and the actual NER tags are not captured by English-translated sentences when given to the Stanford CoreNLP NER tool [3]. Therefore, we understand the need for NER to address these challenges even in morphologically rich languages like Telugu. Hence, we created an annotated dataset for NER in Telugu, which will be a good resource for those working in Telugu NLP areas such as Dialog Systems, Text Summarization, Machine Translation, and Question Answering. Furthermore, we used pretrained Telugu transformer models (Marreddy et al., 2021) and finetuned on the Telugu NER dataset to achieve NER in multiple domains.

In this paper, we aim at creating resources for NER in Telugu. Overall, we make the following contributions to this paper: (1) We publicly release two diverse annotated NER datasets, which will be pioneering resources for building automated NER systems in Telugu, (2) We build NER models using Telugu pretrained transformer models to analyze the entity-level and token-level class performance across the multi-domain datasets and (3) We achieve the state-of-the-art results on existing NER datasets.

Our extensive experiments also lead us to these crucial insights: (i) Telugu pretrained transformer models fine-tuned for the NER task outperform the existing baseline methods. (ii) It is widely known that language-specific models (*BERT-Te* and *RoBERTa-Te*) outperform the existing pretrained multilingual models (mBERT, XLM-R, and IndicBERT), this holds to be true for Telugu as well. (iii) *ELECTRA-Te* performs on par with the existing pretrained multilingual models.

2 Related Work

Traditional Methods: The early NER experiments were studied to identify specific categories of named entities like Proper Names (Wakao et al., 1996), Organizations, and Locations (Grishman, 1995). They were based on rules, heuristics, and gazetteers. However, they could not handle out-of-gazetteer and ambiguous cases. Unlike earlier work, Lafferty et al. (2001) and Rabiner (1989) proposed CRF and HMM models to handle numerous sequence to sequence tasks such as NER and POS tagging. Nevertheless, the main limitation of these models is the computational complexity and that they cannot handle unknown words.

Later, it was found that deep learning (DL) based models like LSTM-CRF (Lample et al., 2016) and BiLSTM-CRF (Huang et al., 2015) focused on long-term dependencies and handled the feedback mechanism on sequence labeling tasks with high accuracy. However, these models compute token representation one by one (sequentially), which hinders the full exploitation of parallel computation and bidirectional context.

Transformers Based NER: In recent years, Transformers (Vaswani et al., 2017) have successfully performed various NLP tasks like Machine Translation, Language Modelling, and Semantic Role Labeling. Recently introduced Bidirectional Encoder Representations from Transformers (BERT), developed by Devlin et al. (2019), is a powerful language modeling technique to handle Masked-Language Modelling (MLM) and next-sentence prediction tasks. Furthermore, by fine-tuning the BERT model on the CoNLL dataset, a high F1 score of 92.8% was reported in Devlin et al. (2019) for NER. The success of BERT led to other variations like RoBERTa (Liu et al., 2019) and ELECTRA (Clark et al., 2019).

NER for Telugu: Though NER is a well-researched problem in English, very few works describe NER for Telugu. Existing NER sys-

[2] `https://en.wikipedia.org/wiki/WX_notation`

[3] `https://corenlp.run/`

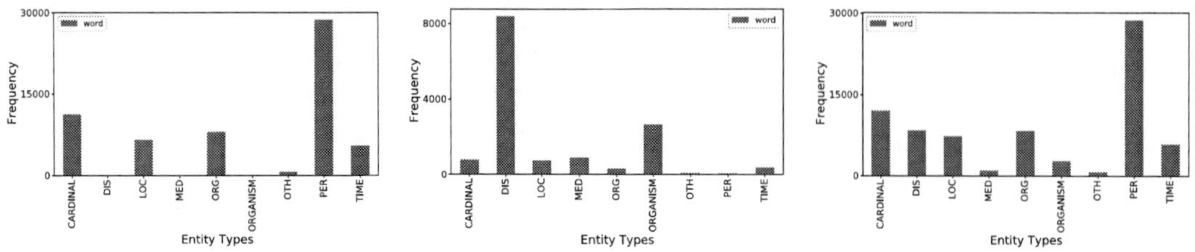

(a) Newswire (b) Medical (c) Combined

Figure 2: Frequency of named entities across three datasets: *(a)* Newswire *(b)* Medical, and *(c)* Combined Dataset

tems mainly use small datasets and limited categories like Person, Location, and Organisation. In addition, these systems are developed based on heuristics (Sasidhar et al., 2011), traditional ML (Shishtla et al., 2008; Srikanth and Murthy, 2008) or DL (Reddy et al., 2018) methods.

To the best of our knowledge, we are the first to create such a large and diverse annotated dataset of 38,363 sentences for the NER task in Telugu. Further, we create a multi-domain dataset that incorporates both Newswire and Medical domains. Finally, we take inspiration from the transformer models and use *BERT-Te* to model NER in Telugu.

3 Annotated Dataset for NER task

Existing NER datasets are small and mainly focus on limited categories like Person (PER), Location (LOC), and Organisation (ORG). There are two significant existing datasets for NER in Telugu: (i) WikiAnn (Pan et al., 2017) (ii) LREC-NER (Reddy et al., 2018). The WikiAnn dataset has PER, LOC, and ORG entity types, with a total of 6,495 annotated sentences. On the other hand, even though the LREC-NER dataset has 32,610 sentences, it consists only of PER, ORG, LOC, and Miscellaneous Named Entity category (MISC).

Hence, we came up with three datasets consisting of diverse named entity categories for NER in Telugu: (i) Newswire Dataset (ND), (ii) Medical Dataset (MD), and (iii) Combined Dataset [Newswire+Medical] (CD).

The ND focuses on the general named entity categories in the news domain, while the MD focuses on data related to the biomedical domain. Ultimately, by combining ND and MD, we form the CD. Detailed statistics of the three datasets are shown in Figures 2a, 2b, and 2c. Further, details regarding the dataset have been discussed below.

Data Collection and Preprocessing: For the ND, we crawled around 50,000 sentences from Telugu360[4], GreatAndhra[5], and Eenadu[6] websites that generally publish articles related to current affairs, sports, movies, gossips, and the latest news. However, while doing so, we noticed that in the prevailing COVID-19 situation, much information on the Telugu websites focuses on health and diseases. So then, we created a separate dataset by crawling 20,000 sentences for MD. We collected this data from Boldsky[7] and Telugu-Wikipedia[8] websites. After crawling, we cleaned and preprocessed the data by removing the unwanted URLs, hashtags, hyperlinks, English text, and duplicate sentences.

Entity Types in Datasets: After analyzing the preprocessed data, we identified the following named entity categories that would best suit to describe the data:

1. **Diseases and Symptoms** (DIS): Names of diseases and symptoms comprise this category (Patil, 2020). It is a part of MD and CD. Ex: *Tuberculosis* is an airborne disease.

2. **Cardinal** (CARDINAL): The number based entities that represent quantities fall into this category (Weischedel et al., 2013). It is a part of ND, MD and CD. Ex: Mahua tree reaches *20 meters* height.

3. **Medical and Pharmacological Terms** (MED): Names of medical procedures, treatments and medicines fall under MED (Patil, 2020). It is a part of MD and CD. Ex: *Laparoscopy* is a safe procedure.

4. **Organisms** (ORGANISM): Names of all living organisms, along with their biological equivalent terms constitute ORGAN-

[4]https://www.telugu360.com
[5]https://telugu.greatandhra.com
[6]https://www.eenadu.net
[7]https://telugu.boldsky.com/health/
[8]https://te.wikipedia.org/wiki/

ISM (Patil, 2020). It is a part of MD and CD. Ex: *Coronavirus* causes COVID-19.

5. **Location** (LOC): The names of places can be classified as LOC (Sang and De Meulder, 2003). It is a part of ND, MD and CD. Ex: *India* is a beautiful country.

6. **Organization** (ORG): The names of organizations belong to this category (Sang and De Meulder, 2003). It is a part of ND, MD and CD. Ex: *Vodafone* is a telecom company.

7. **Person** (PER): The names of people fall under PER (Sang and De Meulder, 2003). It is a part of ND and CD. Ex: *Priyanka* is an actress.

8. **Date and Time** (TIME): The words used to specify particular time and other precise temporal objects can be classified into this category (Loper and Bird, 2002). It is a part ND, MD and CD. Ex: I have a party on *June 20.*

9. **Other Miscellaneous Named Entities** (OTH): Other named entities that do not fit into the above categories form OTH (Sang and De Meulder, 2003). Ex:- *Names of currencies.* It is a part of ND and CD.

Data Annotation and Statistics: Usually, named entities can be of a single word or multiple words (chunks). Hence, we used the IOB2 tagging format for annotation to capture these types of named entities. IOB2 is similar to the BIO (Ramshaw and Marcus, 1999) format. The only difference is that in IOB2, the B- tag is used at the start of all chunks.

Dataset	Sentences	Words	Named Entities	Entity Types
Newswire Data	34,109	345,202	60,491	12
Medical Data	4,254	40,352	14,260	14
Combined Data	38,363	385,554	74,751	18

Table 1: Dataset Statistics for the NER task

We provided the data to an *Elancer IT Solutions Private Limited*[9] company for NER annotation. In order to perform the annotation process, *Elancer IT Solutions Private Limited* chose five native speakers of Telugu with excellent fluency, the company itself properly remunerates all the annotators. We provided the annotators with detailed annotation guidelines and example sentences. As a first step, we gave 100 sentences to all the annotators to verify their proficiency in the annotation. The Fleiss Kappa Score (Fleiss and Cohen, 1973) for this step was 0.92, and any minor issues found were conveyed as feedback to the annotator. After this step, five qualified native Telugu speakers provided annotations for $58,712$ sentences using provided annotation guidelines. As part of the annotation, we requested annotators to provide the named entities for every sentence. However, $20,349$ sentences are removed from the final dataset due to the following reasons: (i) redundant sentences, (ii) sentences that do not have one or no named entity, and (iii) sentences with bad quality tags. Finally, there were $38,363$ annotated sentences for the dataset, out of which $4,254$ sentences belong to the MD, and $34,109$ sentences belong to the ND. Table 1 includes the detailed statistics of all datasets. The Inter-Annotator agreement for this annotation was 0.91. Finally, we performed our experiments on the ND, MD, and CD datasets.

[9]http://elancerits.com/

4 Methodology

4.1 Approaches

This section presents the eight models we investigated for the NER study in more detail and their configuration.

CRF: The CRF (Lafferty et al., 2001) concept has been successfully adopted as a popular solution for sequence tagging tasks and is also a primary solution in NER. We use One-Hot Vector representations as input for the CRF model, and the output is a sequence of tags associated with each input word. The following hyperparameters were used for training the CRF model viz obtained from sklearn_crfsuite [10] library:- (i) Training Algorithm: *Gradient Descent with L-BFGS method (Liu and Nocedal, 1989)*, (ii) Coefficients of L1 and L2 regularization: *c1 = 0.1* and *c2 = 0.1*, and (iii) Maximum iterations: *1000*.

LSTM-CRF: In this model, we combined the LSTM with CRF to form an LSTM-CRF model (Huang et al., 2015). We used LSTM and other required layers from the Keras library [11], while the CRF layer from keras_contrib [12] library. For input, we compare the performance of both One-Hot vectors, which are trained from scratch, and Telugu FastText embeddings (Marreddy et al.,

[10]https://sklearn-crfsuite.readthedocs.io/en/latest/

[11]https://keras.io

[12]https://github.com/keras-team/keras-contrib

2021) (each word dimension is 200), while the output is a sequence of tags associated with each input word.

The following hyperparameters were used to train the model:- (i) Activation function: *Sigmoid*, (ii) Recurrent Dropout: *0.5*, (iii) Loss: *Negative log-likelihood*, (iv) Number of epochs: *50*, (v) Optimizer: *RMSProp*, (vi) Batch size: *64*, (vii) Hidden units in LSTM layer: *128*, and (viii) Hidden units in Dense Layer: *128*.

BiLSTM-CRF: We combine BiLSTM with CRF to form a BiLSTM-CRF model (Huang et al., 2015). Due to the additional context that BiLSTM receives, it generally performs better than the LSTM-CRF model. We used the same setup and hyperparameters as the LSTM-CRF model.

BERT-Telugu (*BERT-Te*): Like Pretrained BERT (Devlin et al., 2019) (a pretrained model trained on the BooksCorpus (Zhu et al., 2015) and English Wikipedia), we chose a model based on the Transformer structure of BERT-base-cased for Telugu (large corpora of 8 million sentences) (Marreddy et al., 2021). The BERT-base-cased model consists of 12 transformer blocks, 768 hidden layers, 12 self-attention blocks, and 110 million parameters in total. For this study, we finetune a *BERT-Te* model on each dataset separately. In order to finetune a *BERT-Te* model, we observe that the following hyper-parameters yields best performances: (i) Batch size: *32*, (ii) Learning rate: $3e^{-5}$, (iii) Number of training epochs: *10*, (iv) ϵ constant set to $1e^{-8}$ to avoid division by zero in the AdamW calculation when the gradient approaches zero, and (iv) *AdamW* as optimizer. We stopped training to overcome the over-fitting problem if the validation loss did not decrease for five consecutive epochs.

RoBERTa-Telugu (*RoBERTa-Te*): Similar to *BERT-Te*, we chose *RoBERTa-Te*, a pretrained RoBERTa-base model for Telugu (Marreddy et al., 2021). We then finetuned this Telugu RoBERTa model on NER datasets as well. Testing on the ND, MD, and CD, we found that parameters similar to *BERT-Te* reported the best macro-F1 score.

ELECTRA-Telugu (*ELECTRA-Te*): Here, we used a pretrained model created on Telugu Corpus (Marreddy et al., 2021) called *ELECTRA-Te*, and then we made it more relevant by finetuning it on NER datasets. We use the same hyper-parameters as *BERT-Te* when finetuning the *ELECTRA-Te* model.

It is to be noted that casing has no impact in Telugu script.

4.2 Dataset Splitting

To make sure our model is time sensitive, we used the data from the most recent articles of the dataset for testing (7,672 sentences), and the older data for training (30,691 sentences). We achieve this by dividing our data into 20% and 80% ratio based on the recency. We then use the latest data (20%) for testing and the remaining data (80%) for training and validation. We calculated the average of 5-folds on the 80% of train data and reported the results on the 20% of the latest data for each model.

4.3 Evaluation Metrics

Seqeval (Entity-Level): To assess the performance of the chunking task i.e. NER, we use the *seqeval* (Nakayama, 2018) tool to measure classification metrics for sequence labeling evaluation. For measuring these classification metrics, the first step is to predict all the sequences of NER tags on the test dataset using each trained model. To understand how each class performs, we choose macro averaging that gives each class equal weight for evaluating the system's performance across the 9-classes. Here, we report the macro-average precision, recall, and F1-score to measure the per entity classification performance.

Token-Level: We measure the NER system using the most typical evaluation method to calculate precision, recall, and F1-score at a token level. The final macro-average precision, recall, and F1-score values are reported at token level between empirical and predicted tokens on the test dataset.

5 Results

This section presents the entity and token-level macro-averaged classification metrics for models trained on ND, MD, and CD in Tables 2 and 3. To further examine each class's performance, we show the performance of eight models on each dataset in section 5.1 and answer several research questions.

Entity-Level Results: We make the following observations from Table 2: (i) The CRF model, LSTM-CRF and BiLSTM-CRF models are on par in performance, where the input representations of LSTM models are One-hot and FastText (FT). (ii)

Model Type→	CRF			LSTM-CRF			LSTM-CRF-FT			BiLSTM-CRF			BiLSTM-CRF-FT			**BERT-Te**			RoBERTa-Te			ELECTRA-Te		
Dataset↓	P	R	F1	P	R	F1	P	R	F1	P	R	F1	P	R	F1	P	R	F1	P	R	F1	P	R	F1
Newswire Dataset	0.72	0.54	0.61	0.57	0.69	0.62	0.61	0.62	0.61	0.59	0.69	0.63	0.63	0.61	0.62	**0.83**	**0.83**	**0.83**	0.80	0.79	0.79	0.78	0.78	0.78
Medical Dataset	0.71	0.46	0.54	0.64	0.52	0.56	0.51	0.52	0.51	0.60	0.54	0.56	0.55	0.47	0.51	0.71	0.74	0.72	**0.74**	**0.73**	**0.73**	0.72	0.73	0.72
Combined Dataset	0.83	0.60	0.68	0.72	0.67	0.69	0.69	0.58	0.63	0.69	0.68	0.68	0.69	0.64	0.66	**0.79**	**0.81**	**0.80**	0.78	0.78	0.77	0.76	0.77	0.76

P = Precision, R = Recall, F1 = F1-score

Table 2: Telugu NER Results Entity-Level classification.

Model Type→	CRF			LSTM-CRF			LSTM-CRF-FT			BiLSTM-CRF			BiLSTM-CRF-FT			**BERT-Te**			RoBERTa-Te			ELECTRA-Te		
Dataset↓	P	R	F1	P	R	F1	P	R	F1	P	R	F1	P	R	F1	P	R	F1	P	R	F1	P	R	F1
Newswire Dataset	0.69	0.52	0.58	0.53	0.55	0.54	0.59	0.51	0.53	0.60	0.58	0.58	0.60	0.52	0.56	**0.72**	**0.72**	**0.72**	0.69	0.72	0.70	0.71	0.70	0.70
Medical Dataset	0.67	0.53	0.52	0.49	0.45	0.44	0.59	0.40	0.48	0.44	0.40	0.42	0.63	0.35	0.49	**0.71**	**0.79**	**0.75**	0.68	0.75	0.71	0.69	0.73	0.71
Combined Dataset	0.78	0.53	0.60	0.62	0.57	0.59	0.62	0.54	0.57	0.59	0.62	0.60	0.60	0.56	0.58	**0.74**	**0.76**	**0.75**	0.72	0.72	0.72	0.73	0.72	0.72

P = Precision, R = Recall, F1 = F1-score

Table 3: Telugu NER Results: Token-Level classification.

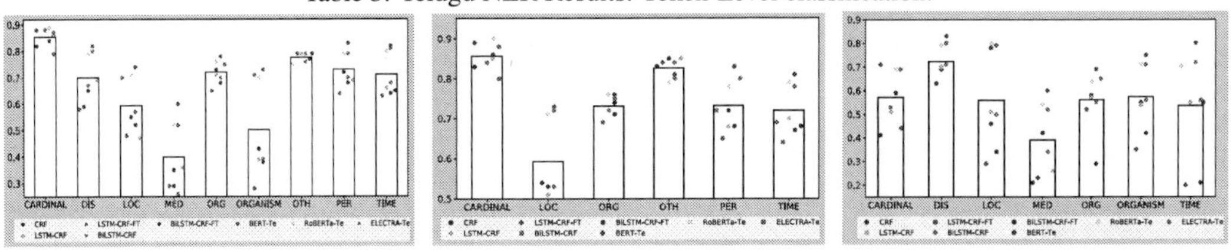

(a) Combined Dataset (b) Newswire Dataset (c) Medical Dataset

Figure 3: Distribution of F1 scores across three datasets: (a) Combined Dataset, (b) Newswire Dataset, and (c) Medical Dataset.

Wrt to precision, recall & f1-score, finetuned Telugu pretrained transformer models such as *BERT-Te*, *RoBERTa-Te*, and *ELECTRA-Te* show an improved performance than CRF, LSTM-CRF, and BiLSTM-CRF models. (iii) Specifically, the *BERT-Te*, *RoBERTa-Te*, and *ELECTRA-Te* models yield the highest, second-highest, and third-highest recall and F1 scores for all the classes except for OTH and CARDINAL categories, as shown in Figures 3(a) and 3(b). (iv) We observe that the *BERT-Te* model is better than all the models for ND (0.83) and CD (0.80) in terms of F1-score, whereas *RoBERTa-Te* model performs the best on MD (0.73). This demonstrates that the pre-training models capture the word context better. (v) The performance of all models on MD is comparatively low compared to ND and CD. This can be explained by analyzing entity class differences across the eight training models as discussed in 5.1.

Token-Level Results: Table 3 illustrates the token-level classification performance for three NER datasets using eight trained models. We observe from Table 3 that: (i) For all three datasets, the F1-scores (0.65, 0.73, 0.75) show that the *BERT-Te* model predicts the NER tags with high accuracy at token level. (ii) Similar to entity-level results, Telugu pretrained transformer models outperform the baseline CRF and LSTM-CRF based models. (iii) Since the number of classes in token-level is 2X than entity-level classes, we observe a comparatively low F1-score at token-level than entity-level.

5.1 Do Telugu pretrained transformer models outperform the baseline models for the NER task?

Class Distribution Performance: To understand the performance of models on each class, we show the individual class performance wrt entity-level macro-average classification metrics, including precision, recall, and F1-score.

Entity-Level Class Distribution: Figures 3(a), 3(b), and 3(c) display each class performance at entity-level wrt F1-score on three datasets. We also report the F1-score of three best performing models such as *BERT-Te*, *RoBERTa-Te*, and *ELECTRA-Te* for each class at entity-level on three datasets in Figures 4, 5, and 6. Further, we showcase the recall of each class at entity-level on three datasets (refer to Figures 10, 11, and 12 in Appendix). Overall, the results indicate that the transformer-based models outperform CRF and LSTM-CRF based models in terms of recall and F1 score across the three datasets. *BERT-Te* achieves the highest recall and F1-score in 7 out of the 9 classes. However, the CRF and LSTM-CRF based models have similar performance but display relatively lower class performance in terms of recall and F1-score when compared to the finetuned Telugu pretrained models. Specifically, LSTM-CRF and BiLSTM-CRF models with FT as

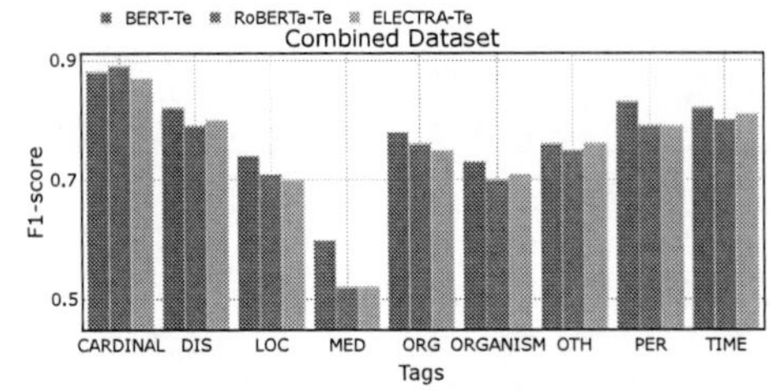

Figure 4: Distribution of F1 scores across three best-performing systems on Combined Dataset.

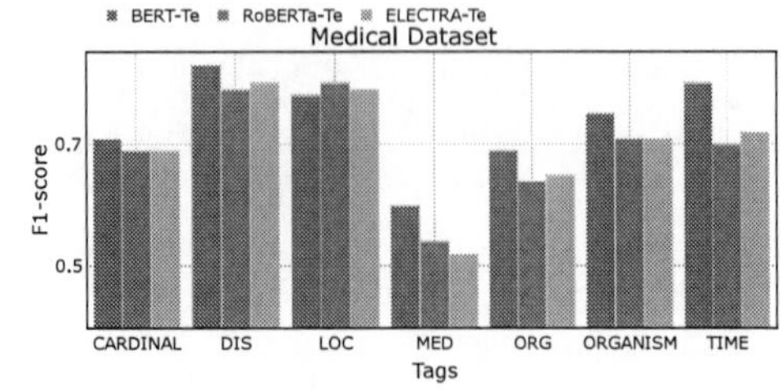

Figure 6: Distribution of F1 scores across three best-performing systems on Medical Dataset.

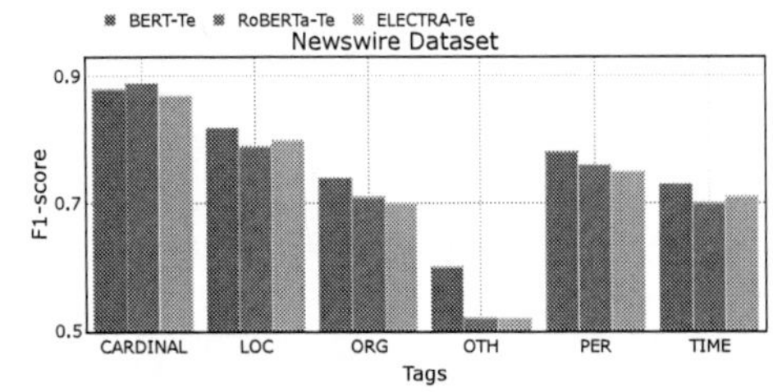

Figure 5: Distribution of F1 scores across three best-performing systems on Newswire Dataset.

input have shown a trend of lower performance in most classes.

Token-Level Class Distribution: Figure 7 shows the token-level class performance wrt F1-score across eight models on CD. Similar to entity-level, the transformer-based models *BERT-Te*, *RoBERTa-Te*, and *ELECTRA-Te* outperform the other models wrt F1-score in Figure 7. *BERT-Te* and *RoBERTa-Te* show an increasing F1-score performance for every class, while LSTM-CRF-FT and BiLSTM-CRF-FT report an overall lower F1-score across all the classes.

Model	#Sentences	#Parameters
mBERT	2.5TB	110M
XLM-R	2.5TB	125M
IndicBERT	452.8M	11M
BERT-Te	8.2M	108M
RoBERTa-Te	8.2M	125M
ELECTRA-Te	8.2M	14M

Table 4: Models and their Training Corpus size for the NER task

5.2 Do Telugu pretrained transformer models outperform the existing multilingual transformer models for the NER task?

Here, we compare the performance of three finetuned Telugu pretrained models (*BERT-Te*, *RoBERTa-Te*, and *ELECTRA-Te*) with existing multilingual transformer models (mBERT (Devlin et al., 2018), XLM-R (Conneau et al., 2020), and IndicBERT (Kakwani et al., 2020)) for the NER task. Figure 8 showcases the entity-level class performance across the three datasets. From Figure 8, we observe that *BERT-Te*, and *RoBERTa-Te* outperform mBERT, XLM-R, and IndicBERT across the three datasets. On the other hand, the *ELECTRA-Te* model has a similar performance as mBERT and XLM-R. Further, we report the pretrained model parameters of each model, as depicted in Table 4. Here, we noticed that *ELECTRA-Te* and IndicBERT models have comparatively fewer parameters than other models.

5.3 Do Telugu pretrained transformer models outperform the state-of-the-art Telugu NER systems?

In this section, we evaluate the performance of the Telugu Transformer models on the existing NER datasets: (i) WikiAnn (Pan et al., 2017) and (ii) LREC-NER (Reddy et al., 2018) and compare it with the previous state-of-the-art results. We report the various models and their performance against the datasets mentioned above in Table 5. From Table 5, we observe that *BERT-Te* and *RoBERTa-Te* deliver state-of-the-art performance on the WikiAnn dataset. Due to the simplicity of the LREC-NER dataset, all the Transformer models display 100% accurate predictions.

5.4 Quantitative Analysis

Figure 9 shows the macro F1-score of the BERT-Te model with varying training data set sizes across three datasets: CD, ND, and MD. We ran the model with three different settings - 25%, 50%, and 75% of the data for training and subsequently tested with the remaining data. As expected, the macro F1-score of the proposed model increases with the size of the training set. At 25% of the data, it is 0.74, at 50% of the data, it stands at 0.77, and finally, at 75% of the data, it stands at 0.80 for the CD. Similarly, we can observe an increasing level of performance for the ND and MD by varying the

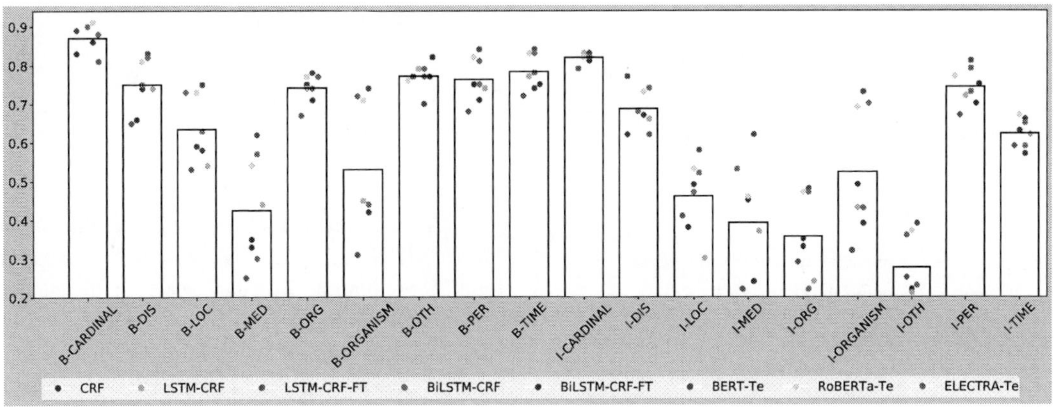

Figure 7: Combined-Dataset: Distribution of F1 scores at Token-Level.

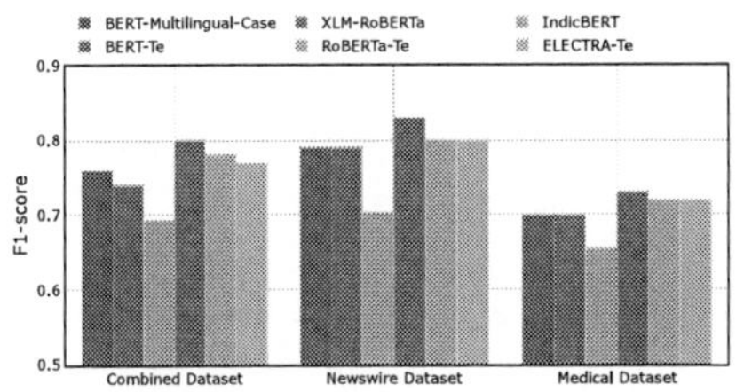

Figure 8: Entity-Level: Comparison of F1-score performance of (i) mBERT, (ii) XLM-R, (iii) IndicBERT, (iv) *BERT-Te*, (v) *RoBERTa-Te*, and (vi) *ELECTRA-Te* embeddings across three datasets: CD, ND, and MD. The *BERT-Te* fine-tuned on NER shows a higher F1-score compared to all the models.

Dataset	WikiAnn	LREC-NER
Model	F1-score	F1-score
LSTM-CRF (Reddy et al., 2018)	57.03	85.13
mBERT (Kakwani et al., 2020)	84.31	100
XLM-R (Kakwani et al., 2020)	81.71	100
IndicBERT base (Kakwani et al., 2020)	84.38	100
IndicBERT large (Kakwani et al., 2020)	80.12	100
BERT-Te	**87.03**	100
RoBERTa-Te	**87.16**	100

Table 5: Models comparison on existing Telugu NER datasets

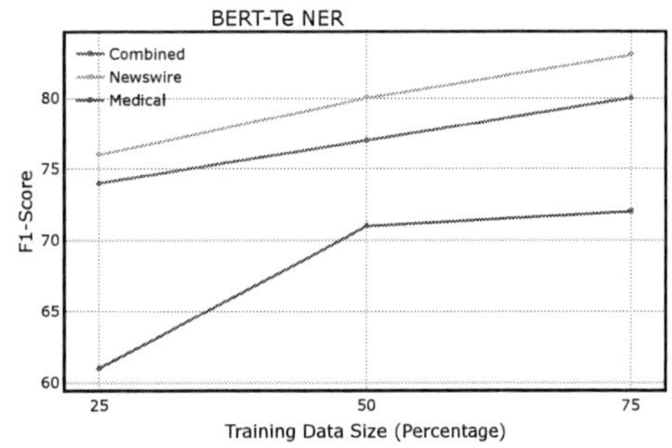

Figure 9: Entity-Level: Effect of changing the training set size on the *BERT-Te* model performance across three datasets: CD, ND, and MD.

		Predicted								
		CARDINAL	DIS	LOC	MED	ORG	ORGANISM	OTH	PER	TIME
Actual	CARDINAL	6386	14	1	0	0	0	14	20	108
	DISL	10	10153	1	110	23	121	17	5	2
	LOC	12	0	8809	8	268	44	4	138	20
	MED	0	24	6	692	14	7	19	2	6
	ORG	22	0	442	10	9077	0	0	106	3
	ORGANSIM	0	134	23	54	0	2763	12	14	0
	OTH	3	23	0	0	0	4	326	4	0
	PER	30	52	124	0	85	9	0	29895	5
	TIME	87	5	7	0	0	0	4	14	5162

Table 6: Combined: Confusion matrix for BERT-Te

size of the training set. However, the increase in performance is marginal as the BERT-Te model yields a similar level of performance with a smaller training dataset, possibly because the pretrained transformer captures the named entities mentioned in unstructured text into predefined categories.

5.5 Error Analysis

We analyzed the error cases in detail for three datasets using our best-performing model - *BERT-Te*. Tables 6, 7, and 8 reports the entity-level confusion matrices for the CD, ND, and MD. Table 6 shows that 2.8% of the LOC class were predicted as ORG and 1.45% as PER. Similarly, 4.5% were predicted as LOC for the ORG class, and 1.09% were predicted as PER. We can even observe a similar analysis from Table 7, where the model confused LOC, PER, and ORG tags. It is mainly because many last names derive from places in Telugu, and many Organisations are named after Person Names.

In the medical dataset, we observe from Table 8 that, for the DIS class, 1.1% were predicted as MED, and 1.7% were predicted as ORGANISM which indicates that the *BERT-Te* model gets confused with DIS, MED, and ORGANISM classes.

6 Conclusion

This paper presented annotated datasets and an empirical study of the performance of various fine-

		Predicted					
		CARDINAL	LOC	ORG	OTH	PER	TIME
Actual	CARDINAL	5729	1	25	2	22	104
	LOC	5	7308	194	5	106	12
	ORG	34	552	8417	0	79	3
	OTH	4	11	0	302	0	0
	PER	30	133	112	11	29293	21
	TIME	72	18	0	0	17	4608

Table 7: Newswire: Confusion matrix for BERT-Te

		Predicted						
		CARDINAL	DIS	LOC	MED	ORG	ORGANISM	TIME
Actual	CARDINAL	474	4	0	0	0	9	8
	DIS	3	10333	2	127	10	185	0
	LOC	5	7	1044	11	17	39	0
	MED	8	103	16	735	7	66	0
	ORG	0	16	3	0	250	0	0
	ORGANISM	0	179	32	43	0	2995	0
	TIME	6	0	8	0	0	0	404

Table 8: Medical: Confusion matrix for BERT-Te

tuned Telugu pretrained transformer models for the NER task. We compare these results with the commonly used architectures like CRF, LSTM-CRF, and BiLSTM-CRF models in all three datasets. We even compare these pretrained Telugu models to existing multilingual models like mBERT, XLM-R, and IndicBERT. We conclude that finetuned Telugu pretrained transformer models outperform all the other models across multiple domains and they give state-of-the-art performance on existing datasets. We also notice that *ELECTRA-Te* yields significantly equal performance when compared with multilingual models even after being trained on a much smaller corpus. In the future, we would like to perform Fine-Grained NER and also expand NER to more domains for the Telugu language.

7 Ethical Statement

We created two Telugu NER datasets corresponding to two different domains (Newswire and Medical), and we open source the two datasets. The code and datasets can be downloaded from `https://github.com/mors-ner/anonymous_telner`.

We reused publicly available datasets (WikiAnn and LREC-NER) to compare state-of-the-art methods.

WikiAnn dataset can be downloaded from `https://drive.google.com/drive/folders/1Q-xdT99SeaCghihGa7nRkcXGwRGUIsKN?usp=sharing`. WikiAnn dataset is licensed under `https://opendatacommons.org/licenses/by/`. Please read their terms of use[13] for more details.

[13]https://elisa-ie.github.io/wikiann/

LREC-NER dataset can be downloaded from `http://ltrc.iiit.ac.in/ner-ssea-08/index.cgi?topic=5`. LREC-NER dataset is licensed under a Creative Commons License. Please read their terms of use[14] for more details.

Fair Compensation: We provided the data to an *Elancer IT Solutions Private Limited*[15] company for NER annotation. In order to perform the annotation process, *Elancer IT Solutions Private Limited* chose five native speakers of Telugu with excellent fluency, the company itself properly remunerates all the annotators.

Privacy Concerns: We have gone through the privacy policy of various websites mentioned in the paper. For example, the website privacy policy of `www.greatandhra.com` is provided here [16]. We do not foresee any harmful uses of using the data from these websites.

8 Limitations & Social Impact

Multilingual pretrained models are usually evaluated by their capacity for knowledge transfer across languages. This can be done either by training the NER model on English data only or English+Telugu NER data using (for example) mBERT representations. It allows the model to benefit from high resource languages. During the testing phase, the NER model is evaluated in Telugu only. However, this paper evaluated the NER model where training and testing on Telugu data only. In the future, it would be interesting to evaluate how the knowledge transfer from the high resource languages model performs in Telugu to assess the usefulness of the proposed datasets better.

This paper studies NER with two large, strongly annotated datasets corresponding to two different domains. Further, we compared our model to existing small labeled Telugu NER datasets. Our investigation neither introduces any social/ethical bias to the model nor amplifies any bias in the data. We do not foresee any direct social consequences or ethical issues.

References

Alan Akbik, Duncan Blythe, and Roland Vollgraf. 2018. Contextual string embeddings for sequence labeling.

[14]http://ltrc.iiit.ac.in/ner-ssea-08/index.cgi?topic=5

[15]http://elancerits.com/

[16]https://www.greatandhra.com/privacy.php

In *Proceedings of the 27th International Conference on Computational Linguistics*, pages 1638–1649.

Kevin Clark, Minh-Thang Luong, Quoc V Le, and Christopher D Manning. 2019. Electra: Pre-training text encoders as discriminators rather than generators. In *International Conference on Learning Representations*.

Alexis Conneau, Kartikay Khandelwal, Naman Goyal, Vishrav Chaudhary, Guillaume Wenzek, Francisco Guzmán, Édouard Grave, Myle Ott, Luke Zettlemoyer, and Veselin Stoyanov. 2020. Unsupervised cross-lingual representation learning at scale. In *Proceedings of the 58th Annual Meeting of the Association for Computational Linguistics*, pages 8440–8451.

Leon Derczynski, Eric Nichols, Marieke van Erp, and Nut Limsopatham. 2017. Results of the wnut2017 shared task on novel and emerging entity recognition. In *Proceedings of the 3rd Workshop on Noisy User-generated Text*, pages 140–147.

Jacob Devlin, Ming-Wei Chang, Kenton Lee, and Kristina Toutanova. 2018. Multilingual bert -r. *https://github.com/google-research/bert/blob/master/multilingual.md*.

Jacob Devlin, Ming-Wei Chang, Kenton Lee, and Kristina Toutanova. 2019. Bert: Pre-training of deep bidirectional transformers for language understanding. In *Proceedings of the 2019 Conference of the North American Chapter of the Association for Computational Linguistics: Human Language Technologies, Volume 1 (Long and Short Papers)*, pages 4171–4186.

Joseph L Fleiss and Jacob Cohen. 1973. The equivalence of weighted kappa and the intraclass correlation coefficient as measures of reliability. *Educational and Psychological Measurement*, 33(3):613–619.

Ralph Grishman. 1995. The nyu system for muc-6 or where's the syntax? In *Sixth Message Understanding Conference (MUC-6): Proceedings of a Conference Held in Columbia, Maryland, November 6-8, 1995*.

Zhiheng Huang, Wei Xu, and Kai Yu. 2015. Bidirectional lstm-crf models for sequence tagging. *arXiv preprint arXiv:1508.01991*.

Divyanshu Kakwani, Anoop Kunchukuttan, Satish Golla, NC Gokul, Avik Bhattacharyya, Mitesh M Khapra, and Pratyush Kumar. 2020. inlpsuite: Monolingual corpora, evaluation benchmarks and pre-trained multilingual language models for indian languages. In *Proceedings of the 2020 Conference on Empirical Methods in Natural Language Processing: Findings*, pages 4948–4961.

John Lafferty, Andrew McCallum, and Fernando CN Pereira. 2001. Conditional random fields: probabilistic models for segmenting and labeling sequence data. In *Proceedings of the 18th International Conference on Machine Learning (ICML-2001)*.

Guillaume Lample, Miguel Ballesteros, Sandeep Subramanian, Kazuya Kawakami, and Chris Dyer. 2016. Neural architectures for named entity recognition. In *Proceedings of NAACL-HLT*, pages 260–270.

Dong C Liu and Jorge Nocedal. 1989. On the limited memory bfgs method for large scale optimization. *Mathematical Programming*, 45(1):503–528.

Yinhan Liu, Myle Ott, Naman Goyal, Jingfei Du, Mandar Joshi, Danqi Chen, Omer Levy, Mike Lewis, Luke Zettlemoyer, and Veselin Stoyanov. 2019. Roberta: A robustly optimized bert pretraining approach. *arXiv preprint arXiv:1907.11692*.

Edward Loper and Steven Bird. 2002. Nltk: the natural language toolkit. In *Proceedings of the ACL-02 Workshop on Effective Tools and Methodologies for Teaching Natural Language Processing and Computational Linguistics-Volume 1*, pages 63–70.

Xuezhe Ma and Eduard Hovy. 2016. End-to-end sequence labeling via bi-directional lstm-cnns-crf. In *Proceedings of the 54th Annual Meeting of the Association for Computational Linguistics (Volume 1: Long Papers)*, pages 1064–1074.

Christopher D Manning, Mihai Surdeanu, John Bauer, Jenny Rose Finkel, Steven Bethard, and David McClosky. 2014. The stanford corenlp natural language processing toolkit. In *Proceedings of 52nd Annual Meeting of the Association for Computational Linguistics: System Demonstrations*, pages 55–60.

Mounika Marreddy, Subba Reddy Oota, Lakshmi Sireesha Vakada, Venkata Charan Chinni, and Radhika Mamidi. 2021. Clickbait detection in telugu: Overcoming nlp challenges in resource-poor languages using benchmarked techniques. In *2021 International Joint Conference on Neural Networks (IJCNN)*.

Hiroki Nakayama. 2018. seqeval: A python framework for sequence labeling evaluation. Software available from https://github.com/chakki-works/seqeval.

Xiaoman Pan, Boliang Zhang, Jonathan May, Joel Nothman, Kevin Knight, and Heng Ji. 2017. Cross-lingual name tagging and linking for 282 languages. In *Proceedings of the 55th Annual Meeting of the Association for Computational Linguistics (Volume 1: Long Papers)*, pages 1946–1958, Vancouver, Canada. Association for Computational Linguistics.

Ashish Patil. 2020. Medical dataset for named entity recognition in cord 19 research challenge. `https://www.kaggle.com/finalepoch/medical-ner`.

Matthew Peters, Mark Neumann, Mohit Iyyer, Matt Gardner, Christopher Clark, Kenton Lee, and Luke Zettlemoyer. 2018. Deep contextualized word representations. In *Proceedings of the 2018 Conference of the North American Chapter of the Association for Computational Linguistics: Human Language Technologies, Volume 1 (Long Papers)*, pages 2227–2237.

Lawrence R Rabiner. 1989. A tutorial on hidden markov models and selected applications in speech recognition. *Proceedings of the IEEE*, 77(2):257–286.

Lance A Ramshaw and Mitchell P Marcus. 1999. Text chunking using transformation-based learning. In *Natural Language Processing using Very Large Corpora*, pages 157–176. Springer.

Aniketh Janardhan Reddy, Monica Adusumilli, Sai Kiranmai Gorla, Lalita Bhanu Murthy Neti, and Aruna Malapati. 2018. Named entity recognition for telugu using lstm-crf. In *WILDRE4–4th Workshop on Indian Language Data: Resources and Evaluation*, page 6.

Erik Tjong Kim Sang and Fien De Meulder. 2003. Introduction to the conll-2003 shared task: Language-independent named entity recognition. In *Proceedings of the Seventh Conference on Natural Language Learning at HLT-NAACL 2003*, pages 142–147.

B Sasidhar, PM Yohan, A Vinaya Babu, and A Govardhan. 2011. Named entity recognition in telugu language using language dependent features and rule based approach. *International Journal of Computer Applications*, 22(8):30–34.

Praneeth M Shishtla, Karthik Gali, Prasad Pingali, and Vasudeva Varma. 2008. Experiments in telugu ner: A conditional random field approach. In *Proceedings of the IJCNLP-08 Workshop on Named Entity Recognition for South and South East Asian Languages*.

P Srikanth and Kavi Narayana Murthy. 2008. Named entity recognition for telugu. In *Proceedings of the IJCNLP-08 Workshop on Named Entity Recognition for South and South East Asian Languages*.

Ashish Vaswani, Noam Shazeer, Niki Parmar, Jakob Uszkoreit, Llion Jones, Aidan N Gomez, Lukasz Kaiser, and Illia Polosukhin. 2017. Attention is all you need. In *NIPS*.

Takahiro Wakao, Robert Gaizauskas, and Yorick Wilks. 1996. Evaluation of an algorithm for the recognition and classification of proper names. In *COLING 1996 Volume 1: The 16th International Conference on Computational Linguistics*.

Ralph Weischedel, Martha Palmer, Mitchell Marcus, Eduard Hovy, Sameer Pradhan, Lance Ramshaw, Nianwen Xue, Ann Taylor, Jeff Kaufman, Michelle Franchini, et al. 2013. Ontonotes release 5.0 ldc2013t19. *Linguistic Data Consortium, Philadelphia, PA*, 23.

Yukun Zhu, Ryan Kiros, Rich Zemel, Ruslan Salakhutdinov, Raquel Urtasun, Antonio Torralba, and Sanja Fidler. 2015. Aligning books and movies: Towards story-like visual explanations by watching movies and reading books. In *The IEEE International Conference on Computer Vision (ICCV)*.

A Entity-Level Class Distribution Performance

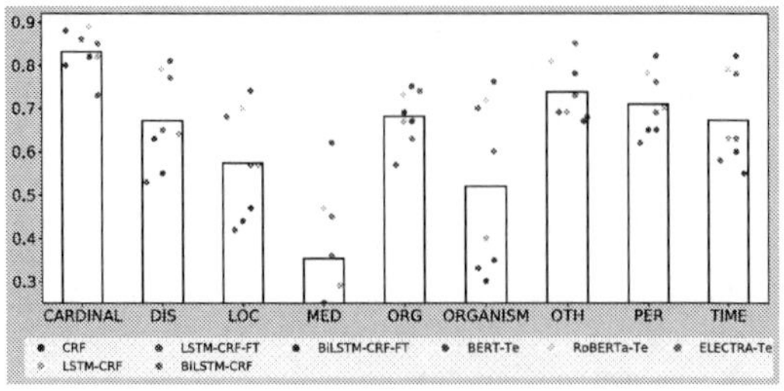

Figure 10: Combined Dataset: Distribution of Recall

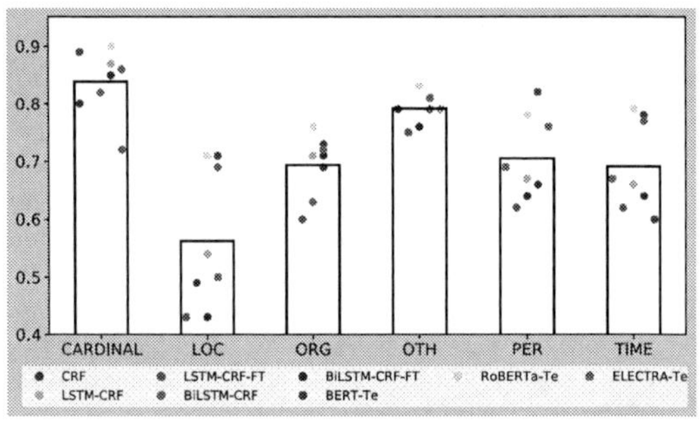

Figure 11: Newswire Dataset: Distribution of Recall

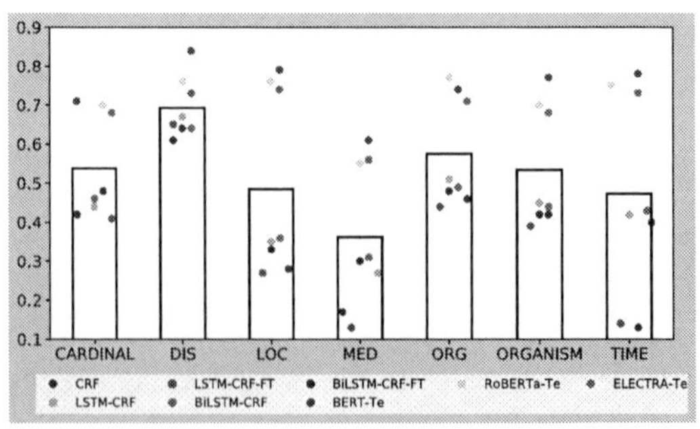

Figure 12: Medical Dataset: Distribution of Recall

Using Neural Machine Translation Methods for Sign Language Translation

Galina Angelova[1] and **Eleftherios Avramidis**[1] and **Sebastian Möller**[1,2]
[1] Technical University of Berlin, [2] German Research Center for Artificial Intelligence (DFKI)
g.angelova@campus.tu-berlin.de
{eleftherios.avramidis,sebastian.moeller}@dfki.de

Abstract

We examine methods and techniques, proven to be helpful for the text-to-text translation of spoken languages in the context of gloss-to-text translation systems, where the glosses are the written representation of the signs. We present one of the first works that include experiments on both parallel corpora of the German Sign Language (PHOENIX14T and the Public DGS Corpus). We experiment with two NMT architectures with optimization of their hyperparameters, several tokenization methods and two data augmentation techniques (back-translation and paraphrasing). Through our investigation we achieve a substantial improvement of 5.0 and 2.2 BLEU scores for the models trained on the two corpora respectively. Our RNN models outperform our Transformer models, and the segmentation method we achieve best results with is BPE, whereas back-translation and paraphrasing lead to minor but not significant improvements.

1 Introduction

Sign languages (SL), the main medium of exchanging information for the deaf and the hard of hearing, are visual-spatial natural languages with their own linguistic rules. In contrast to the spoken ones, they lack a written form, on one hand, and use face, hands and body to convey meaning, on the other. However, in our society, spoken languages are used by and large, leading to social exclusion in the everyday life of the deaf and hard of hearing. Therefore, recent research is making the most out of the technical advances in the fields of Natural Language Processing (NLP), Deep Neural Networks (DNN), and Machine Translation (MT), with the aim to develop systems that are able to translate between signed and spoken languages in order to fill the gap of communication between the SL speaking communities and the people using vocal language. Most latest approaches tackle the problem, dividing it into two sub-tasks: Sign Language Recognition (SLR), also called *video-to-gloss*, and Sign Language Translation (SLT), also known as *gloss-to-text* translation. The latter uses as an intermediate representation the glosses, described in Section 3.1 and Section 4.2.1. Isolating gloss-to-text translation serves as a building block of a bigger project, which considers SL as a whole and is done in direct co-operation with members of the SL community.

For the rest of this work, we focus on the gloss-to-text sub-task and treat it as a low-resource text-to-text machine translation problem. We explore different known techniques for MT of written languages on the glosses, and report our findings during our experiments with:

- two neural architectures (RNN and Transformer)
- several tokenization and sub-word segmentation methods (BPE, unigram and custom tokenization of the gloss annotations)
- two data augmentation techniques (back-translation and paraphrasing)

Preprocessing scripts and data are publicly available.[1]

The rest of our work is organized as follows: In Section 2, there is a review of previous related work in the field. In Section 3, we describe the essence of the gloss-to-text translation task, and briefly present the neural machine translation methods we have used throughout our experiments on the two corpora, both of them introduced in Section 4. Further, we present the experiments in Section 5 as well as all our results and findings, described in Section 6. In the last Section 7 we conclude our work and discuss possibilities for future research.

2 Related work

Sign language translation is a relatively new research field with recent findings made possible

[1] https://github.com/DFKI-SignLanguage/gloss-to-text-sign-language-translation

Proceedings of the 60th Annual Meeting of the Association for Computational Linguistics
Student Research Workshop, pages 273 - 284

thanks to the continuous advances in neural machine translation (NMT). Several experiments with SL gloss-to-text translation have taken place in the previous decade using statistical phrase-based machine translation (Stein et al., 2012; Morrissey et al., 2013). Camgoz et al. (2018) and Camgoz et al. (2020) use the Transformer architecture for SL translation, and are the first to realize an end-to-end system, combining SLR and SLT, jointly training based on both video embeddings, glosses and text, being currently the state-of-the-art work in the field. Yin and Read (2020) employ the Spatial-Temporal Multi-Cue (STMC) Network (Zhou et al., 2020) for the task. There have also been several experiments on the opposite direction: text-to-gloss (Othman and Jemni, 2011; Egea Gómez et al., 2021).

To the best of our knowledge, currently Moryossef et al. (2021) is the only published work experimenting with back-translation in the context of gloss-to-text translation. Their research has been conducted parallel and independent from our studies, and has concluded similar results concerning the use of back-translation in a low-resource SL setting. The main difference is that we further focus on other machine translation techniques, e.g. different models and tokenization schemes, whereas they explore in more detail the gloss-text pairs and their linguistic properties, proposing their own rule-based heuristics with the purpose to generate SL glosses, bearing in mind the specifics of the signed languages. The recent work of Yin et al. (2021), focusing on the problems related to the machine translation between signed and spoken language pairs, reports the first BLEU score on the Public DGS corpus, but contrary to our work, no details are given on how the models were trained and evaluated and therefore there can be no direct comparison of the results.

3 Methods

3.1 The gloss-to-text task

Glosses are the most commonly used written form for annotating SL, where each sign has a written gloss transcription. However, a limitation of using them is the fact that they do not sufficiently capture all the information, expressed through body posture, movement of the head and mimics, which also occur in parallel. As a result, there is a loss of information on a semantic level (Camgoz et al., 2020; Yin et al., 2021). Moreover, each SL corpus, offering gloss annotations, uses its own way of glossing, therefore the annotation is not standardized, and as a consequence different SL corpora cannot be concatenated.

Source: HUND3* AUCH1A SPRINGEN1
Target: Der Hund springt hinterher.

Table 1: Example of a parallel gloss sentence - German sentence pair.

In contrast to the classical text-to-text translation task, where the pairs consist of pre-aligned sentences - one in the source language and one in the target language, for our gloss-to-text translation models we work with matching pairs of gloss sentences on the source side, and German sentences on the target side (see Table 1). Hence the name *gloss-to-text*.

3.2 Architectures for neural machine translation

In our work we investigate two model architectures implementing different types of attention mechanisms - RNN and Transformer.

RNN is an encoder-decoder architecture with attention suggested by Sennrich et al. (2017b) (implemented in Nematus), similar to the one proposed in Bahdanau et al. (2014). A key difference is the initialization of the decoder hidden state with the averaged sum of the encoder concatenated hidden states, instead of with the last backward encoder state.

The Transformer is another encoder-decoder architecture (Vaswani et al., 2017), implementing the self-attention function. Without using RNNs the neural system computes representations of the input and output sequences. The encoder and decoder of the Transformer both consist of 6 identical layers, and each of these layers has two sub-layers. The decoder adds one additional sub-layer, which is using *multi-head decoder-encoder attention* on the encoder output helping the decoder to focus on the relevant parts of the input sequence.

3.3 Tokenization

Tokenizing text can be done at word, subword or character level. Investigation of possible tokenization variations for the glosses is particularly relevant in our work, because of the different gloss annotations in the two used corpora (Sections 4.2.1 and 5.2).

	Train	Dev	Test
PHOENIX14T	7,096	519	642
DGS	54,325	4,470	5,113

Table 2: Statistics of the two corpora.

Gloss	Meaning
ZU^3	to squeeze, squeezed
ZU7	closed
ZU9	towards

Table 3: Meaning of different variants of the German word "zu".

Byte Pair Encoding (BPE) is a simple data compression technique that has been succesfully applied to NMT (Sennrich et al., 2016b). The idea behind this algorithm is to replace the most common pairs of consecutive bytes with one single new byte. In order to rebuild the original data, a table of all the replacements is needed (Gage, 1994).

Unigram sub-word segmentation (Kudo, 2018) considers multiple segmentation variations of a word with their respective probabilities calculated based on a unigram language model.

3.4 Back-translation

Back-translation is a semi-supervised method for improving the quality of translation relying on monolingual data (Edunov et al., 2018). It allows using a big amount of monolingual target data, when available, in order to produce synthetic data for the source side. This technique may be beneficial in cases where the bilingual data is scarce, as is the case of the gloss-to-text task.

3.5 Paraphrasing

Paraphrasing is the task of using an alternative formulation to express the same semantic content (Madnani and Dorr, 2010). By using paraphrased sentences in the training set, we hope that the model may be lexically enriched by the provided variations. Here, we follow the paraphrasing method known as *bilingual pivoting* (Mallinson et al., 2017; Turkerud and Mengshoel, 2021).

4 Datasets

For our experiments we utilize the following corpora of the German SL, which due to the different gloss annotations are used only separately for our experiments. Statistics of the two corpora can be seen in Table 2.

4.1 RWTH-PHOENIX-Weather 2014T

Introduced by Camgoz et al. (2018), the corpus contains sign language videos with gloss annotations as well as their corresponding German sentences, and is a popular benchmark in SL translation. The project consists of a training set of 7,097 parallel sentences. For our experiments we used the already publicly available annotated data.[2] Contrary to the DGS corpus, this corpus doesn't contain any gloss suffix annotations.

4.2 The Public DGS Corpus

DGS is the result of a long-term project, conducted at the Institute for German Sign Language and Communication of the Deaf at the Hamburg University. The corpus, introduced by Hanke et al. (2020), is a subset of the full project. All resources are publicly accessible[3] via two formats. Our work will focus on the second one, MY DGS-annotated[4]. The data was extracted via the ELAN[5] format of the files (see Appendix, Figure 3). In the following sub-sections we describe the nature and the format of the DGS corpus as well as the required pre-processing steps. The final version of the corpus consists of 63,908 parallel sentence pairs.

4.2.1 DGS gloss annotation conventions

The gloss annotations of the DGS corpus are far more complex and comprehensive than the ones of the PHOENIX14T corpus. Konrad et al. (2020) give a detailed explanation of the glossing conventions. We use this information to construct the gloss sentences and to build our parallel data set. The glosses are written in capitalized letters - a common convention used for annotating SL. An essential part of the annotations are the gloss suffixes. For instance, they are used to represent lexical variants or to indicate different meanings of a word, as can be seen in the example with the German word "zu" (Konrad et al., 2020). It can be used as a preposition - locative, temporal or causal, as an adverb or as a conjunction. In order to differentiate between

[2] https://www-i6.informatik.rwth-aachen.de/~koller/RWTH-PHOENIX/

[3] https://www.sign-lang.uni-hamburg.de/dgs-korpus/index.php/welcome.html

[4] http://ling.meine-dgs.de

[5] https://archive.mpi.nl/tla/elan

these meanings, a combination of the word itself with a number and, in some cases, a sign, is used (see Table 3).

Focusing in depth on all of the linguistic rules used to create the different gloss annotations is out of scope for this work. Therefore, here we mention briefly some of the main sign categories. The *lexical signs* are approximately equivalent to the commonsense notion of the words, and also form the corpus dictionary. The *productive signs* in combination with other signs illustrate intended meaning, but they do not convey meaning of their own. The *pointing signs* indicate orientation or movement. There are also *fingerspelling signs* for annotating when the signers sketch the form of letters in the air. The *number type* forms a special system for easily representing different kind of numbers.

4.2.2 Creating the parallel corpus

The annotation of the sign language videos is structured in parallel channels, the *tiers*, supporting multi-level and multi-participant annotations (Appendix, Figure 3). The tiers we used to form the parallel sentence pairs are the ones containing the German sentences for each signer and those containing the glosses for the right and for the left hand of each signer. The first step was to access the textual data from all videos, using Beautiful Soup.[6] For this purpose we created a python script, which extracted the links to the files, read the content, and created an XML parse tree of each recording.

The ordering of glosses to a gloss sentence was achieved by considering the starting and the ending time of the corresponding German sentence and of the individual glosses. One particular obstacle we encountered during the formation of the parallel data set were the overlapping timestamps of some glosses done with both hands. Such is the case of the fingerspelling signs. Because signers have a "dominant" and a "non-dominant" hand, the dominant one is usually used for one-handed signs and for fingerspellings (Crasborn, 2011). For the purpose of constructing our gloss sentences we chose a uniform way to order the overlapping signs. We counted all the "left-handed" glosses and all the "right-handed" glosses for each file, and considered files with more "left-handed" ones to have signers with a dominant left hand, whereas files with more "right-handed" glosses to have signers with a dominant right hand. We refer to the glosses as "left" and "right" because of the annotations used in the corpus, although the distinction between "left" and "right" does not seem to have any linguistic role in any SL (Crasborn, 2011). Moreover, the native signers usually don't remember if a new signer is left-handed or right-handed. Thus, we decided to choose a convention for our work so that the gloss sentences formation is consistent, and therefore we always placed the glosses of the dominant hand in front of those of the non-dominant one.

5 Experiments

We separate our experiments in three main groups. In the first one, described in Section 5.1 we initially train two baseline models for both corpora and consecutively make changes to them with the goal to investigate how different model architectures and known configurations of neural MT systems influence them. Therefore, we use the best performing models from the first group to further continue our experiments in the second one, described in Section 5.2, where we apply three different tokenization schemes - BPE, unigram and custom tokenization, on the gloss and on the German sides of the corpora. Ultimately, we utilize the models, which produce the best translations up to this point, in the third group of experiments in Section 5.3, where we separately look into two data augmentation techniques - back-translation and paraphrasing. All models are trained using MarianNMT (Junczys-Dowmunt et al., 2018) and all configuration parameters are detailed in our repository.

5.1 Neural MT architecture

Our initial motivation to approach the gloss-to-text translation task as a classical low-resource MT problem were the findings by Koehn and Knowles (2017) and Sennrich and Zhang (2019). Therefore, we compare Transformer and RNN (Sennrich et al., 2017b) on which is the optimal model architecture for gloss-to-text translation. As baselines we train two off-the-shelf models on the PHOENIX14T and the Public DGS corpora separately, using the default parameters of MarianNMT.

We continue the first set of experiments using techniques for improving the MT quality in a low-resource setting (Sennrich and Zhang, 2019). We perform an extensive hyperparameter search, initiating from the configurations suggested by the above authors in order to reduce the chances that

[6] `https://www.crummy.com/software/BeautifulSoup/bs4/doc/`

other hyperparameters can lead to different conclusions. We achieve the best configuration when we reduce the size of the encoder to 1 layer, and the size of the decoder to 2 for both types of models. Furthermore, we implement an aggressive dropout of 0.5 and a word dropout of 0.4 on the source and the target sides. We reduce the beam size to 2, as suggested by Camgoz et al. (2018), and keep the learning rate 0.0005, the batch size 32, and the vocabulary size 1,010 and 2,600 for the PHOENIX14T and the DGS corpora, respectively. We use simple word tokenization. For the next group of experiments we continue only with the improved RNN configuration, following our conclusions regarding the best architecture (Section 6.2).

5.2 Tokenization experiments

During the tokenization experiments, using the best performing models up to this point, we investigate if and to what extend existing tokenization methods - BPE, unigram and custom tokenization - proven to be effective for NMT of written natural languages, could be beneficial in the gloss-to-text setting. The tokenization of BPE and unigram was done using SentencePiece (Kudo and Richardson, 2018) with the parameters that have been established as default, due to their good performance in WMT shared tasks (Sennrich et al., 2017a, e.g. 2 BPE iterations).

5.2.1 Tokenizing the PHOENIX14T corpus

On the PHOENIX14T corpus we train RNN systems using the same parameters as the ones from the previous group of experiments. The only difference is the way the input and output sentences are tokenized. We conduct additional experiments where we reduce the vocabulary size of the BPE models and compare the translation scores.

5.2.2 Tokenizing the DGS corpus

The DGS corpus has groups of glosses that are more complicated and rich in annotations, which we describe in Section 4. A comparison can be seen in Figure 1. Thus we make the assumption that there should be a difference in the translation quality of the models in favor of the subword tokenization. For our first experiment we use word tokenization and compare the results with the ones of the following models which use either BPE, unigram or custom tokenizations. The vocabulary size is 2,600.

Stripping the gloss parameters In a different, more naive, experiment on the DGS corpus we decide to strip the gloss parameters - such as signs or numbers, as shown in Figure 2, to see if they are making our model too complex, aware of the fact that they convey meaning to each annotation.

Custom tokenization for the glosses For our custom tokenization experimenent on the DGS corpus, we choose to add the token "@@" to separate prefix, suffix and compound glosses without losing this information in difference to the above case of leaving only the stem. The chosen custom token is not a part of the gloss parameters.

5.3 Data augmentation

For the last group of experiments we make the assumption that, according to Edunov et al. (2018), on one hand, back-translation has proven to be effective when using strong baselines with a big amount of data, but, on the other hand, it could also have a positive effect in low-resource NMT settings. Thus we decide to try this method for our corpora, together with one additional data augmentation technique - paraphrasing.

5.3.1 Back-translation on the PHOENIX14T corpus

We start with the PHOENIX14T corpus. As a first step, we train a model in the opposite direction, German sentences on the source side and gloss sentences on the target side. Based on the suggestions on back-translation in previous work (Sennrich et al., 2016a; Dou et al., 2019), we focus on in-domain data and we consider filtering sentences from an out-of-domain (ood) corpus separately, as too many out-of-domain sentences would result in adding a lot of noise, which may not be helpful for the translation quality. To confirm our hypothesis for the back-translation experiments, we mainly investigate the quality of the translation when adding in-domain data, different amounts of out-of-domain data or a mixture of in-domain and out-of-domain data.

In-domain back-translation A major challenge for the purpose of using back-translation is to find a big monolingual corpus of the target languages, given the very specific domain of the PHOENIX14T corpus, because it contains strictly weather-related sentences. Our first idea is to try and find weather-related corpus, but unfortunately,

DGS German: **Die Überflutung kam vom starken Regen.**

DGS Gloss: **REGEN**1C **STRÖMUNG**1^*

PHOENIX14T German: **am donnerstag im südosten ergiebiger dauerregen mit der gefahr von überflutungen**

PHOENIX14T Gloss: **DONNERSTAG SUED SUEDOST MOEGLICH DURCHGEHEND REGEN MOEGLICH GEFAHR UEBERFLUTUNG**

Figure 1: Comparison between gloss annotations for the two different corpora. The specific DGS gloss parameters are shown in orange.

stripping: **AUTOMATISCH**2B* ⇨ **AUTOMATISCH**

custom: **AUTOMATISCH**2B* ⇨ **AUTOMATISCH** @@2B*

Figure 2: Example of the two manual tokenizations of a gloss in the DGS corpus

popular crawled monolingual corpora do not contain such specific sentences. We collect data manually by selecting sentences from online German weather-related articles or German weather websites. We pay attention to not only choose recent articles, but also to search sentences from some available archive sources. Additionally, we manually process the sentences which includes splitting them in shorter ones, removing some words we know are out-of-vocabulary for our models, rewriting complex verb forms. Needless to say, this process is slow and not scalable. Hence, we stop at 1,202 sentences and add their back-translated variants to our training data.

In the first of the two following experiments we observe the effect of adding filtered out-of-domain back-translated sentences to our training data, and in the second one we combine in-domain and out-of-domain sets.

Filtered sentences from out-of-domain corpus We use crawled data from the German part of the News Crawl corpus (Barrault et al., 2019). We extract 5,000 sentences from the whole dataset using a custom python script. Further, we filter sentences, containing the most frequently used weather-related words in the PHOENIX data set. For example, words or phrases such as: "wetter", "wettervorhersage", "temperatur", "es regnet", "es scheint", "wolken", "böen", "gewitter". It is important to mention here, that even though our filtered sentences contain one of the following words or phrases, these sentences cannot be fully considered in-domain. One reason for this is the fact that the crawled sentences are still different in structure and style than our original training data. Another reason is the fact that many of the words we use for filtering could also have a different not weather-related meaning, depending on the context.

Mixing in and out-of-domain sentences Here we mix our 1,202 in-domain and a part of the out-of-domain back-translated sentences (3,418) from the previous two experiments.

Usage of back-translation tag Since Sennrich et al. (2016a) mix their synthetic data with their original data without distinguishing between them, we conduct a further experiment to investigate if the **bt** tag, indicating synthetic data, is actually helping the neural system or worsening the performance.

5.3.2 Back-translation experiments on the DGS corpus

Considering our low scores on the DGS corpus and the conclusions of Moryossef et al. (2021) regarding the limitations of the back-translation in low resource SL settings, we conduct only one experiment as a proof of our premise that back-translation is not beneficial in a very low-resource setting in combination with a poor model to back-translate. For this purpose we filter the first 10,000 sentences from the news-crawl without taking into account their domains, because the DGS Corpus also does not have a specific domain.

5.3.3 Data augmentation using paraphrasing

For the last experiment we add 3,612 translated sentences from our original training set, using DeepL Translate[7], from German to English and then back from English to German. The paraphrased sentences are firstly reviewed to guarantee their grammatical correctness. Here, our goal is to create more variety in the words (synonyms) on the target side or in their order.

[7] https://www.deepl.com/en/translator

6 Results

In this section we report the results from the three groups of experiments we have conducted.

6.1 Evaluation

We evaluate all our models using SacreBLEU (Post, 2018). We also use the original dev and test sets of the PHOENIX14T corpus. For the DGS corpus we separate our own dev and test sets using 15% of the collected data - 4,470 sentences for the dev set, and 5,113 sentences for the test set.

6.2 Model architecture results

The results from our first group of experiments, described in Section 5.1, where we compare two types of model architecture, combined with adjustment of hyperparameters for improving the translation quality in a low-resource setting, are shown in Table 4. Whereas the baseline models perform better with a Transformer architecture for both corpora, we observe substantial improvements in the BLEU scores for the RNN models, trained on the PHOENIX14T corpus, after optimizing the hyperparameters. These results confirm our hypothesis that the architecture is also a suitable choice for the task of NMT of sign languages.

6.3 Tokenization results

After conducting the first tokenization experiments, described in Section 5.2, we observe the results, shown in Table 5, and conclude that using BPE and unigram, compared to word tokenization, does not lead to a substantial difference in the translation quality of the PHOENIX14T models. We believe that this is a result of the low word inflection in the corpus, and because of that the low number of unique glosses in the training set. Therefore, we decrease the size of the vocabulary for the model with BPE tokenization from 2,600 to 2,000 and gain an increase of 0.5 on the test set. In contrast, in the DGS corpus we have more complicated and rich in annotations different groups of glosses. Our assumption that there should be a greater difference in the translation quality of the models in favor of the subword tokenization is verified by the score we achieve on the test set with BPE (3.7 BLEU) substantially higher score than the previous one (2.7 BLEU) for the model trained with word tokenization, and the highest score we manage to obtain on that corpus. This confirms our hypothesis that subword tokenization is a more suitable choice for machine translation of signed languages with more complex and diverse annotations.

Stripping The BLUE score we achieve on the DGS corpus after stripping the parameters from the glosses is only 2.8 which, we assume, is due to the fact that each gloss annotation consists of important parameters, both contributing to the meaning, and communicating nuances. Removing this information, makes it impossible for our model to learn meaningful and correct representations as the stems of many glosses may be the same, but with added parameters the annotations may have very different meanings.

Custom tokenization By adding a custom token to split the parameters from the stem of the glosses we achieve 3.3 BLEU score on the test set, which is the second best score we manage to obtain. Unfortunately, the translation performance remains low.

6.4 Data augmentation results

Before conducting the back-translation experiments based on previous work (Sennrich et al., 2016a), we consider that (a) when having a very narrow domain, it is useful that the sentences, used for back-translation, are similar in structure and domain to the original ones, and (b) adding a number of sentences less than half of the training set size could not lead to substantial improvements. We also add a tag to each back-translated sentence - **{bt}**, to indicate for the neural system that this data is synthetic. After we train a model with added in-domain synthetic data, we manage to obtain a BLEU score of 22.3 on the test set, which is very close to our current best model (22.5 BLEU), and 22.2 BLEU score on the dev set, where we have a small improvement of 0.3 BLEU, compared to 21.9 BLEU. Results are shown in Table 6. We believe that this is a sign that the performance of our model does not get worse, confirming (a), although with such a small number of data it cannot get substantially better, confirming (b). On the contrary, it is possible that the model is less prone to overfitting, compared to the one without noise from synthetic data.

The model trained with only out-of-domain back-translated data reaches 22.2 BLEU on the test set, and does not improve the BLEU score on the dev set. With these results and the small amount of sentences we have in our original training set, combined with the rather poor quality of translation of

Model	BLEU dev	BLEU test
phoenix-baseline-rnn	18.3	17.7
phoenix-baseline-transformer	18.6	18.2
phoenix-rnn-improved	21.6	22.2
phoenix-transformer-improved	18.8	18.5
dgs-baseline-rnn	1.8	1.6
dgs-baseline-transformer	2.5	2.0
dgs-rnn-improved	2.9	2.7
dgs-transformer-improved	1.9	1.9

Table 4: Model architecture comparison for the baseline and improved systems.

Model	Tokenization	BLEU dev	BLEU test	Vocab size
phoenix-word-tok	word	21.6	22.2	1,010
phoenix-unigram-tok	unigram	22.4	21.5	1,010
phoenix-bpe-tok	bpe	22.5	22	2,600
phoenix-bpe-tok*	bpe	21.9	**22.5**	2,000
dgs-word-tok	word	2.9	2.7	2,600
dgs-bpe-tok	bpe	**4.2**	**3.7**	2,600
dgs-unigram-tok	unigram	3.5	3.2	2,600
dgs-bpe-tok-stemmed	bpe	3.1	2.8	2,600
dgs-custom-tok	word	3.5	**3.3**	2,600

Table 5: Tokenization experiments on PHOENIX14T and The Public DGS Corpus. The last bpe model, marked with *, is indicating the one with reduced vocabulary size.

our back-translating model, our intuition is that adding more sentences, which are poorly back-translated, will not lead to any improvements. It will rather add more noise to the model, which is not beneficial anymore for the diversity of the data.

Our last model that combines in-domain and out-of-domain data, achieves 22.7 BLEU on the test set, which is our best score. It is +0.2 over phoenix-bpe-tok - the best performing model with no synthetic data, but unfortunately, it is not significantly better, based on a bootstrap resampling significance test. It improves the score on the dev set - from 21.9 BLEU to 23.4 BLEU confirming our assumption that this noise is creating some diversity in the data without worsening the performance.

Results from the comparison of models with synthetic sentences, using a tag and not, can also be seen in Table 6. Since they show no substantial difference, we decide that at least in our case the tag does not play an important role for the quality of the translation.

Using back-translation on the DGS corpus we achieve only a small improvement of +0.1 on the test set (results are also shown in Table 6), confirming our hypothesis and the findings of Moryossef et al. (2021) and Edunov et al. (2018) that in a very low-resource setting back-translation cannot be clearly beneficial for the translation quality of the neural systems.

Finally, our model with added grammatically correct paraphrased sentences reaches 22.5 BLEU score on the test set - the same as the PHOENIX14T model without added synthetic data. We believe that the technique does not lead to worse performance. On the contrary, we suppose that it makes a small improvement, which can be again noticed on the dev set in Table 6.

7 Conclusion and Future work

In this work we investigated the effect of several methods used in NMT on the gloss-to-text translation task for a sign language. We present one of the first works that does extensive experiments on both

Model	#added sentences	dev	test
phoenix-bpe-tok	0	21.9	22.5
phoenix-indomain	1,202	23.3	22.3
phoenix-ood	5,000	22.1	22.2
phoenix-mixed	1,202 + 3,418	**23.4**	**22.7**
phoenix-paraphrasing	3,612	23.1	22.5
phoenix-mixed-no-tag	1,202 + 3,418	23	22.3
dgs-bpe-tok	0	4.2	3.7
dgs-bt-10000	10,000	4.2	**3.8**

Table 6: Data augmentation experiments on the PHOENIX14T corpus and the DGS corpus. The "ood" in the names stands for "out-of-domain", the "bt" - for "back-translation".

existing corpora for the German Sign Language - PHOENIX14T and the DGS Corpus. Further, we ran three successive groups of experiments:

Neural MT architectures, contrasting RNN and Transformer, with extensive search of hyperparameters and techniques, proven to be effective in a low-resource setup. In contrary to previous research, we found that RNN performs better than the Transformer.

Tokenization schemes, where our findings were in favor of the BPE tokenization for both corpora. This improved our PHOENIX14T model by 0.3 BLEU on the test set (reaching 22.5 BLEU), and our DGS model by 1 BLEU on the test set (reaching 3.7 BLEU).

Data augmentation techniques, i.e. back-translation and paraphrasing via bilingual pivoting, with the intention to create variance in the data. Back-translation gave small improvements: +0.2 on the PHOENIX14T corpus and +0.1 on the DGS corpus. Further investigation on the reasons for the limited contribution of the above augmentation techniques may be directed to the extremely low-resource scenario, the amount and domain of the data, or the particular nature of the sign language glosses.

All above methods allowed an improvement of 5 BLEU points on the test set (22.7 BLEU) for the PHOENIX14T model, and 2.2 BLEU points on the test set (3.8 BLEU) for the DGS one.

In conclusion, in line with previous research (Yin et al., 2021; Moryossef et al., 2021), we believe that in order to achieve better translation performance, research and experiments should concentrate on two major problems - collecting and annotating more resources, and better understanding the nature of the sign languages with the intention to develop new SL-specific tools.

Acknowledgements

The work was accomplished as a Bachelor thesis, as part of the program Digital Media and Technology at the Technical University of Berlin. Supervision, computational resources and conference participation were supported by the project SocialWear (German Ministry of Research and Education; BMBF). We would also like to thank the anonymous reviewers for critically reading this work and suggesting improvements.

Ethical considerations

Our work concerns the German Sign Language (DGS) and is only a part of a bigger research line that intends to provide communication improvements for the the deaf and hard of hearing communities. In order to respect these communities and ensure proper representation of their interests, members of them have been included in our project as part of the research team, consultants or participants in user studies and ELSI workshops (e.g. Nguyen et al., 2021), as per the recommendations of the SLLS ethics statement. The isolation of glosses, known to be inferior to the full linguistic capacity of the sign language does not intend to simplify the language but is rather used as a tool for aiding further research.

References

Dzmitry Bahdanau, Kyunghyun Cho, and Yoshua Bengio. 2014. Neural machine translation by jointly learning to align and translate. *arXiv preprint arXiv:1409.0473*.

Loïc Barrault, Ondřej Bojar, Marta R. Costa-jussà, Christian Federmann, Mark Fishel, Yvette Graham, Barry Haddow, Matthias Huck, Philipp Koehn, Shervin Malmasi, Christof Monz, Mathias Müller, Santanu Pal, Matt Post, and Marcos Zampieri. 2019. Findings of the 2019 conference on machine translation (WMT19). In *Proceedings of the Fourth Conference on Machine Translation (Volume 2: Shared Task Papers, Day 1)*, pages 1–61, Florence, Italy. Association for Computational Linguistics.

Necati Cihan Camgoz, Simon Hadfield, Oscar Koller, Hermann Ney, and Richard Bowden. 2018. Neural sign language translation. In *2018 IEEE/CVF Conference on Computer Vision and Pattern Recognition*, pages 7784–7793.

Necati Cihan Camgoz, Oscar Koller, Simon Hadfield, and Richard Bowden. 2020. Sign language transformers: Joint end-to-end sign language recognition and translation. In *Proceedings of the IEEE/CVF conference on computer vision and pattern recognition*, pages 10023–10033.

Onno Crasborn. 2011. The other hand in sign language phonology. In Keren van Oostendorp, Marc ; Ewen, Colin J.; Hume, Elizabeth V.; Rice, editor, *The Blackwell companion to phonology*, chapter 5, pages 223–240. Wiley-Blackwell.

Zi-Yi Dou, Junjie Hu, Antonios Anastasopoulos, and Graham Neubig. 2019. Unsupervised domain adaptation for neural machine translation with domain-aware feature embeddings. In *Proceedings of the 2019 Conference on Empirical Methods in Natural Language Processing and the 9th International Joint Conference on Natural Language Processing (EMNLP-IJCNLP)*, pages 1417–1422, Hong Kong, China. Association for Computational Linguistics.

Sergey Edunov, Myle Ott, Michael Auli, and David Grangier. 2018. Understanding back-translation at scale. In *Proceedings of the 2018 Conference on Empirical Methods in Natural Language Processing*, pages 489–500, Brussels, Belgium. Association for Computational Linguistics.

Santiago Egea Gómez, Euan McGill, and Horacio Saggion. 2021. Syntax-aware Transformers for Neural Machine Translation: The Case of Text to Sign Gloss Translation. In *Proceedings of the 14th Workshop on Building and Using Comparable Corpora (BUCC 2021)*, pages 18–27, Online (Virtual Mode). INCOMA Ltd.

Philip Gage. 1994. A new algorithm for data compression. *C Users Journal*, 12(2):23–38.

Thomas Hanke, Marc Schulder, Reiner Konrad, and Elena Jahn. 2020. Extending the Public DGS Corpus in size and depth. In *Proceedings of the LREC2020 9th Workshop on the Representation and Processing of Sign Languages: Sign Language Resources in the Service of the Language Community, Technological Challenges and Application Perspectives*, pages 75–82, Marseille, France. European Language Resources Association (ELRA).

Marcin Junczys-Dowmunt, Roman Grundkiewicz, Tomasz Dwojak, Hieu Hoang, Kenneth Heafield, Tom Neckermann, Frank Seide, Ulrich Germann, Alham Aji, Nikolay Bogoychev, André Martins, and Alexandra Birch. 2018. Marian: Fast neural machine translation in c++. pages 116–121.

Philipp Koehn and Rebecca Knowles. 2017. Six challenges for neural machine translation. In *Proceedings of the First Workshop on Neural Machine Translation*, pages 28–39, Vancouver. Association for Computational Linguistics.

Reiner Konrad, Thomas Hanke, Gabriele Langer, Susanne König, Lutz König, Rie Nishio, and Anja Regen. 2020. Public DGS Corpus: Annotation Conventions / Öffentliches DGS-Korpus: Annotationskonventionen.

Taku Kudo. 2018. Subword regularization: Improving neural network translation models with multiple subword candidates. In *Proceedings of the 56th Annual Meeting of the Association for Computational Linguistics (Volume 1: Long Papers)*, pages 66–75, Melbourne, Australia. Association for Computational Linguistics.

Taku Kudo and John Richardson. 2018. SentencePiece: A simple and language independent subword tokenizer and detokenizer for neural text processing. In *Proceedings of the 2018 Conference on Empirical Methods in Natural Language Processing: System Demonstrations*, pages 66–71, Brussels, Belgium. Association for Computational Linguistics.

Nitin Madnani and Bonnie J. Dorr. 2010. Generating phrasal and sentential paraphrases: A survey of data-driven methods. *Computational Linguistics*, 36(3):341–387.

Jonathan Mallinson, Rico Sennrich, and Mirella Lapata. 2017. Paraphrasing revisited with neural machine translation. In *Proceedings of the 15th Conference of the European Chapter of the Association for Computational Linguistics: Volume 1, Long Papers*, pages 881–893, Valencia, Spain. Association for Computational Linguistics.

Sara Morrissey, Andy Way, S Morrissey, and A Way. 2013. Manual labour: tackling machine translation for sign languages. *Machine Translation 2013 27:1*, 27(1):25–64.

Amit Moryossef, Kayo Yin, Graham Neubig, and Yoav Goldberg. 2021. Data augmentation for sign language gloss translation. In *Proceedings of the 1st*

International Workshop on Automatic Translation for Signed and Spoken Languages (AT4SSL), pages 1–11, Virtual. Association for Machine Translation in the Americas.

Lan Thao Nguyen, Florian Schicktanz, Aeneas Stankowski, and Eleftherios Avramidis. 2021. Evaluating the translation of speech to virtually-performed sign language on ar glasses. In *2021 13th International Conference on Quality of Multimedia Experience (QoMEX)*, pages 141–144.

Achraf Othman and Mohamed Jemni. 2011. Statistical Sign Language Machine Translation: from English written text to American Sign Language Gloss. *International Journal of Computer Science Issues*, 8(5):65–73.

Matt Post. 2018. A call for clarity in reporting BLEU scores. In *Proceedings of the Third Conference on Machine Translation: Research Papers*, pages 186–191, Brussels, Belgium. Association for Computational Linguistics.

Rico Sennrich, Alexandra Birch, Anna Currey, Ulrich Germann, Barry Haddow, Kenneth Heafield, Antonio Valerio Miceli Barone, and Philip Williams. 2017a. The University of Edinburgh's neural MT systems for WMT17. In *Proceedings of the Second Conference on Machine Translation*, pages 389–399, Copenhagen, Denmark. Association for Computational Linguistics.

Rico Sennrich, Orhan Firat, Kyunghyun Cho, Alexandra Birch, Barry Haddow, Julian Hitschler, Marcin Junczys-Dowmunt, Samuel Läubli, Antonio Valerio Miceli Barone, Jozef Mokry, and Maria Nădejde. 2017b. Nematus: a toolkit for neural machine translation. In *Proceedings of the Software Demonstrations of the 15th Conference of the European Chapter of the Association for Computational Linguistics*, pages 65–68, Valencia, Spain. Association for Computational Linguistics.

Rico Sennrich, Barry Haddow, and Alexandra Birch. 2016a. Improving neural machine translation models with monolingual data. In *Proceedings of the 54th Annual Meeting of the Association for Computational Linguistics (Volume 1: Long Papers)*, pages 86–96, Berlin, Germany. Association for Computational Linguistics.

Rico Sennrich, Barry Haddow, and Alexandra Birch. 2016b. Neural machine translation of rare words with subword units. In *Proceedings of the 54th Annual Meeting of the Association for Computational Linguistics (Volume 1: Long Papers)*, pages 1715–1725, Berlin, Germany. Association for Computational Linguistics.

Rico Sennrich and Biao Zhang. 2019. Revisiting low-resource neural machine translation: A case study. In *Proceedings of the 57th Annual Meeting of the Association for Computational Linguistics*, pages 211–221, Florence, Italy. Association for Computational Linguistics.

Daniel Stein, Christoph Schmidt, and Hermann Ney. 2012. Analysis, preparation, and optimization of statistical sign language machine translation. *Machine Translation 2012 26:4*, 26(4):325–357.

Ingrid Ravn Turkerud and Ole Jakob Mengshoel. 2021. Image captioning using deep learning: Text augmentation by paraphrasing via backtranslation. In *2021 IEEE Symposium Series on Computational Intelligence (SSCI)*, pages 01–10.

Ashish Vaswani, Noam Shazeer, Niki Parmar, Jakob Uszkoreit, Llion Jones, Aidan N Gomez, Łukasz Kaiser, and Illia Polosukhin. 2017. Attention is all you need. In *Advances in neural information processing systems*, pages 5998–6008.

Kayo Yin, Amit Moryossef, Julie Hochgesang, Yoav Goldberg, and Malihe Alikhani. 2021. Including signed languages in natural language processing. In *Proceedings of the 59th Annual Meeting of the Association for Computational Linguistics and the 11th International Joint Conference on Natural Language Processing (Volume 1: Long Papers)*, pages 7347–7360, Online. Association for Computational Linguistics.

Kayo Yin and Jesse Read. 2020. Better sign language translation with STMC-transformer. In *Proceedings of the 28th International Conference on Computational Linguistics*, pages 5975–5989, Barcelona, Spain (Online). International Committee on Computational Linguistics.

Hao Zhou, Wengang Zhou, Yun Zhou, and Houqiang Li. 2020. Spatial-temporal multi-cue network for continuous sign language recognition. In *Proceedings of the Fourth AAAI Conference on Artificial Intelligence*, volume 34, pages 13009–13016.

Appendix

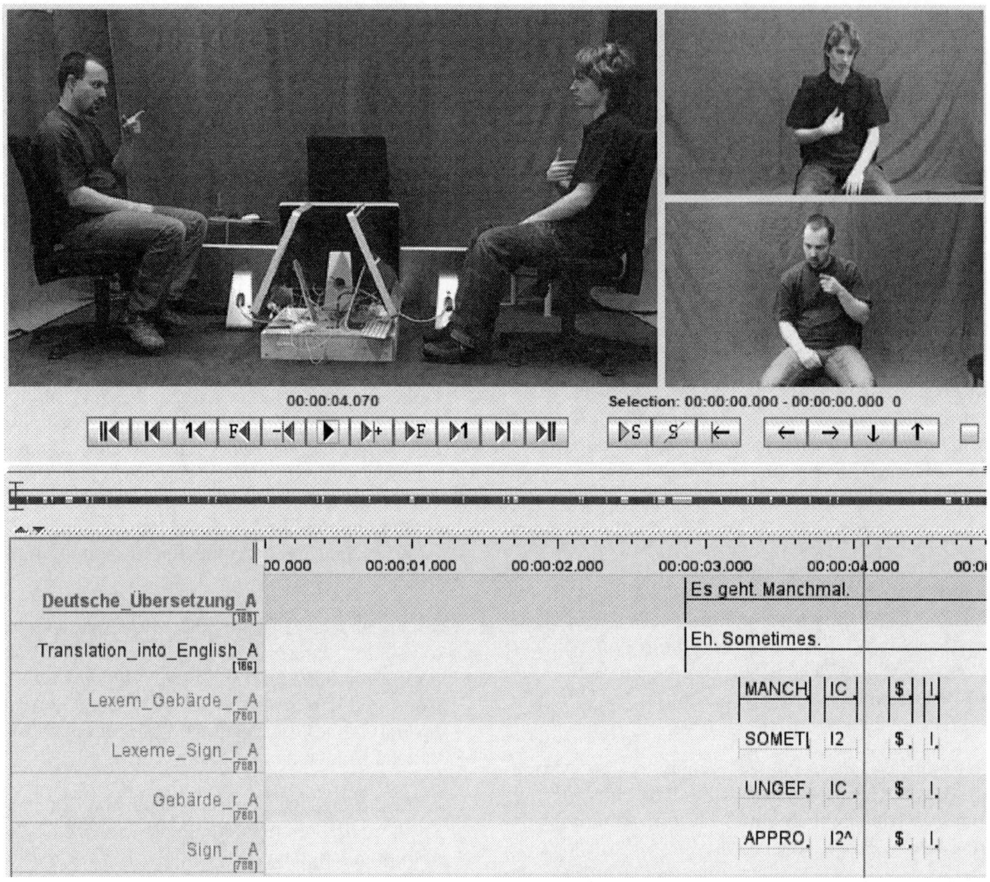

Figure 3: Sample of a short sentence form the DGS corpus in the ELAN software. Video with participants is shown above, and the different tiers can be seen underneath - e.g. "Deutsche_Übersetzung_A" for the German sentence, "Lexem_Gebärde_l_A" and "Lexem_Gebärde_r_A" for the gloss annotations for the left and right hands of signer A. Source: Hanke et al. (2020)

Flexible Visual Grounding

Yongmin Kim Chenhui Chu Sadao Kurohashi
Kyoto University, Kyoto, Japan
{yongmin, chu, kuro}@nlp.ist.i.kyoto-u.ac.jp

Abstract

Existing visual grounding datasets are artificially made, where every query regarding an entity must be able to be grounded to a corresponding image region, i.e., answerable. However, in real-world multimedia data such as news articles and social media, many entities in the text cannot be grounded to the image, i.e., unanswerable, due to the fact that the text is unnecessarily directly describing the accompanying image. A robust visual grounding model should be able to flexibly deal with both answerable and unanswerable visual grounding. To study this flexible visual grounding problem, we construct a pseudo dataset and a social media dataset including both answerable and unanswerable queries. In order to handle unanswerable visual grounding, we propose a novel method by adding a pseudo image region corresponding to a query that cannot be grounded. The model is then trained to ground to ground-truth regions for answerable queries and pseudo regions for unanswerable queries. In our experiments, we show that our model can flexibly process both answerable and unanswerable queries with high accuracy on our datasets.[1]

1 Introduction

Starting from conventional vision-and-language tasks such as image captioning (Vinyals et al., 2015) and visual question answering (Wu et al., 2017), many studies have been conducted to promote joint vision-and-language understanding. Visual grounding, which aims to find a specific region in an image given a query regarding an entity, is a fundamental task for enhancing the performance of various joint vision-and-language tasks (Plummer et al., 2015). For instance, in image captioning, it is important to ground to the corresponding image region while generating words for that region; in VQA, it is crucial to understand to which image region the question is referring. Because of the importance of visual grounding, many research efforts have been dedicated to improve its accuracy (Plummer et al., 2015; Wang et al., 2016a; Fukui et al., 2016; Rohrbach et al., 2016; Wang et al., 2016b; Yeh et al., 2017; Plummer et al., 2017; Chen et al., 2017; Yu et al., 2018b; Yang et al., 2020a,b; Dong et al., 2021).

Figure 1: A comparison between previous visual grounding work and our flexible visual grounding work. In previous work, a query must be able to be grounded (see the left sub-figure), while our work can deal with both answerable and unanswerable visual grounding flexibly (in the right sub-figure, "two wonderful horses" can be grounded, while "my favorite picture," "a beautiful sunrise," and "a frosty day" cannot be grounded). The green bounding boxes are the ground-truth for answerable queries.

Previous visual grounding work assume that a query must be able to be grounded to an image region and create many datasets such as the Flickr30k entities (Plummer et al., 2015), RefClef (Kazemzadeh et al., 2014), RefCOCO, RefCOCO+ (Yu et al., 2016), RefCOCOg (Mao et al., 2016), and Visual7W datasets (Zhu et al., 2016) for the task. However, this assumption is not true in real-world multimedia data such as news, TV dramas,

[1]The social media dataset is available at https://github.com/ku-nlp/SMD4FVG.

Proceedings of the 60th Annual Meeting of the Association for Computational Linguistics Student Research Workshop, pages 285 - 299
May 22-27, 2022 ©2022 Association for Computational Linguistics

and social media, where entities in the text are not always able to be grounded to the visual data due to the fact that text and visual data in these multimedia data are unnecessarily directly corresponding to each other.

We name the case that a query can be grounded to an image region as *answerable* visual grounding; otherwise, *unanswerable* visual grounding from here. The ignorance of unanswerable visual grounding in previous work can lead to problems for downstream tasks. For instance, in VQA, if the VQA model cannot understand the case that entities in the question cannot be grounded to the image, it cannot deal with the case that a question cannot be answered given the image either. Therefore, a robust visual grounding model should be able to flexibly deal with both answerable and unanswerable visual grounding. In this work, we study this flexible visual grounding problem. Figure 1 compares our work with previous work.

To study flexible visual grounding, we construct two types of datasets. The first one is a pseudo dataset, which is constructed by randomly selecting queries from other images and combining it with a target image in the RefCOCO+ dataset (Yu et al., 2016). The second one is a social media dataset (SMD4FVG), which contains unanswerable real-world queries. We construct the SMD4FVG dataset by crawling tweets consisting of both images and text and annotating answerable and unanswerable queries via crowdsourcing.

Previous visual grounding models cannot handle unanswerable visual grounding. To give a model the ability to flexibly identify whether the input query can be grounded or not, we propose a novel method for unanswerable visual grounding by adding a pseudo region corresponding to a query that cannot be grounded. The model is then trained to ground to ground-truth regions for answerable queries and pseudo regions for unanswerable queries. Experiments conducted on both the pseudo and SMD4FVG datasets indicate that our model can flexibly process both answerable and unanswerable queries with high accuracy. In addition, we study the possibility of the usage of using the pseudo dataset to improve the accuracy on the SMD4FVG dataset.

The contributions of this paper are in three-folds:

- We propose a flexible visual grounding task that includes unanswerable visual grounding, where the unanswerable visual grounding problem has not been studied before.
- We construct a pseudo dataset based on the RefCOCO+ dataset and a social media dataset based on tweets consisting of both images and text via crowdsourcing for studying the flexible visual grounding task.
- We propose a flexible visual grounding model, which can deal with both answerable and unanswerable queries and achieves high accuracy on our datasets.

2 Related Work

Previous visual grounding studies have been conducted on different datasets. In the Flickr30k entities dataset (Plummer et al., 2015), a query corresponds to a noun phrase (i.e., entity) containing in a caption of an image. In the RefClef (Kazemzadeh et al., 2014), RefCOCO, RefCOCO+ (Yu et al., 2016), and RefCOCOg (Mao et al., 2016) datasets, a query is an phrase referring to an object in an image. In the Visual7W dataset (Zhu et al., 2016), a query corresponds to a question regarding an image region. However, all these datasets do not consider unanswerable visual grounding. In contrast, we propose flexible visual grounding and construct a pseudo dataset and a social media dataset.

Regarding visual grounding models, Plummer et al. (2015) proposed a method based on canonical correlation analysis (Hardoon et al., 2004) that learns joint embeddings of phrases and image regions. Wang et al. (2016a) proposed a two-branch neural network for joint phrasal and visual embeddings. Fukui et al. (2016) used multimodal compact bilinear pooling to fuse phrasal and visual embeddings. Rohrbach et al. (2016) proposed a method to first detect a candidate region for a given phrase and then reconstruct the phrase using the detected region. Wang et al. (2016b) proposed an agreement-based method, which encourages semantic relations among phrases to agree with visual relations among regions. Yeh et al. (2017) proposed a framework that can search over all possible regions instead of a fixed number of region proposals. Plummer et al. (2017) used spatial relationships between pairs of phrases connected by verbs or prepositions. Chen et al. (2017) proposed a reinforcement learning-based model that rewards the grounding results with image-level context. Yu et al. (2018b) improved the region proposal network by training it on the Visual Genome dataset

(Krishna et al., 2016) to increase the diversity of object classes and attribute labels. Sadhu et al. (2019) proposed to combine object detection and grounding models to deal with unseen nouns during training. Yang et al. (2020a) propagated relations among noun phrases in a query based on the linguistic structure of it. Yang et al. (2020b) addressed the long and complex queries by recursive sub-query construction. Dong et al. (2021) proposed a cross-lingual visual grounding task, which transfers the knowledge from an English model to improve the performance of a French model.

Inspired by the success of pre-training language models such as BERT (Devlin et al., 2019), vision-and-language pre-training on large image caption datasets such as the conceptual captions dataset (Sharma et al., 2018) has been proposed such as ViLBERT (Lu et al., 2019) VL-BERT (Su et al., 2020; Lu et al., 2020), and UNITER (Chen et al., 2020). Those vision-and-language pre-training models differ from the model architecture. Vision-and-language pre-training is evaluated on tasks including visual grounding. However, same to previous studies, the visual grounding task does not consider unanswerable cases (Lu et al., 2019; Su et al., 2020; Chen et al., 2020). Our flexible visual grounding model is based on the multi-task ViLBERT model (Lu et al., 2020), which achieves state-of-the-art performance on visual grounding.

3 Dataset Construction

Because there are no existing visual grounding datasets where unanswerable queries are contained, we present two ways to construct two types of datasets to study the flexible visual grounding problem.

3.1 RefCOCO+ Pseudo Dataset

As the construction of a new large-scale dataset is costive and time-consuming, firstly, we constructed a pseudo dataset based on the RefCOCO+ dataset (Yu et al., 2016) using the negative pair sampling method presented in (Yu et al., 2018a). To generate unanswerable data, we randomly select an image and a query of another image from the RefCOCO+ dataset and combine them as a pair of visual grounding data. Because the query is from a different image, we can assume that the query cannot be grounded to the selected image. However, there is still a possibility that the randomly selected query can be grounded to the image, which may lead to noise. We will discuss this problem in Section 6.1. Next, we combined the generated unanswerable data to the original RefCOCO+ dataset to make a pseudo dataset containing both answerable and pseudo unanswerable queries.

3.2 Social Media Dataset (SMD4FVG)

Unanswerable visual grounding exists in real-world multimedia data consisting of both text and visual information such as news, TV dramas, and social media. Among these, social media is one typical case where there are many unanswerable visual grounding data because the text and visual information posted by users are not necessarily closely related to each other. Due to this characteristic, in social media, there could be more unanswerable visual grounding data than answerable ones. This might result in an unbalanced dataset, making training and evaluation difficult. In order to construct a balanced dataset, we propose a pipeline shown in Figure 2. We describe each step in detail in this section.

Data Crawling

To construct the SMD4FVG dataset, we first crawled image and text pairs from Twitter. We will follow the fair use policy of Twitter regarding copyright of the crawled data.[2] We used Twitter's official library tweepy[3] for this process. In order to inherit previous visual grounding studies, we decided to crawl data from the same domain as the RefCOCO+ dataset. To this end, we searched the hashtags in Twitter that match the object classes in the RefCOCO+ dataset and only crawled the data that hit. As a result, $20,941$ tweets of images and text pairs were crawled.

Image Filtering

In order to construct a visual grounding dataset balanced on both answerable and unanswerable queries, we further conducted image filtering from the crawled tweets. For the image filtering process, we used EfficientnNet (Tan and Le, 2019) to classify images, Yolov4 (Bochkovskiy et al., 2020) to detect objects and CRAFT (Baek et al., 2019) to detect text in images.

The EfficientNet model was pre-trained on the ImageNet dataset (Deng et al., 2009). With the

[2] `https://help.twitter.com/en/rules-and-policies/fair-use-policy`

[3] `https://www.tweepy.org/`

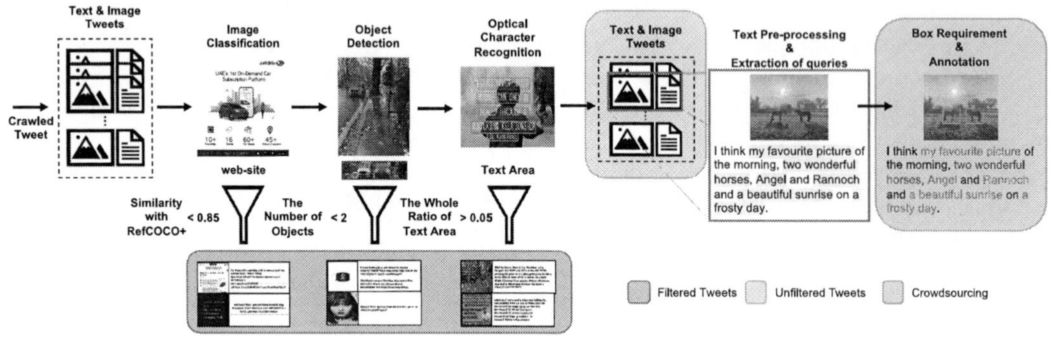

Figure 2: The pipeline for constructing the social media dataset. After crawling tweets containing both images and text, we first filter images that do not belong to the RefCOCO+ classes, contain less than two objects, or are dominated with text in the image step by step. After that, we extract noun phrases as queries in the tweet text. Finally, we annotate answerable and unanswerable queries via crowdsourcing in two steps where in the first step, unanswerable queries are identified, and in the second step, bounding boxes are annotated for answerable queries.

same purpose of inheriting previous visual grounding studies, from the ImageNet classes output by EfficientNet, we only chose the classes similar to RefCOCO+ classes and removed the others. When determining the similarities between the RefCOCO+ classes, we calculated the Wu & Palmer similarity (Wu and Palmer, 1994) and chose classes that surpassed a similarity score of 0.85. It calculates similarity by considering the depths of the two synsets $(s1, s2)$ within the WordNet (Feinerer and Hornik, 2020) hierarchy, along with the depth of the least common subsumer (LCS) as:

$$\mathrm{Wu-Palmer} = 2 * \frac{depth(LCS(s1, s2))}{depth(s1) + depth(s2)} \tag{1}$$

As a result of the image classification-based filtering, the crawled $20,941$ tweets decreased to $6,813$ tweets.

For the next step, we filtered more tweets using the Yolov4 object detection model. The object detection model was pre-trained with the Microsoft COCO dataset (Lin et al., 2014). We chose images that had two or more objects because images with only one single object or background are considered to be too easy for our task. As a result, $4,028$ tweets were chosen from the $6,813$ tweets.

In the crawled tweets, we found that many images consisted of mostly text and website information. As visual grounding is almost impossible for text/website-dominated images, we further filtered those images. To this end, we used the optical character recognition model of CRAFT. Based on the results of the optical character recognition model, we calculated a text proportion ratio in an image. We only kept images that had a proportion ratio lower than 0.05 with respective to the entire image. As a result, $3,425$ images were left.

Due to the limitations of the above image processing models, advertisement, inappropriate, and duplicate images were still left in the dataset after the above filtering process. Therefore, we further manually checked the data and discarded them. As a result, 988 tweets were finally left.

Query Extraction

Tweets contain emoji, links, and mentions, which make query extraction difficult. Therefore, we pre-processed the data and eliminated those expressions. From the pre-processed text, we extracted sentences and used the chunking model (Akbik et al., 2018) to chunk the noun phrases within the sentences. We did not use the pronoun (such as he, her, she) and relative pronoun (such as which, who, that) as queries. As for complex noun phrases that contain other noun phrases within them, we split them and only used single noun phrases as queries. As a result, we obtained $8,827$ queries for the 988 images.

Crowdsourcing Annotation

From the $8,827$ pairs of image and query obtained, we annotated image regions that can be grounded by queries and finally constructed the SMD4FVG dataset. For the annotation, we used Amazon Mechanical Turk. The compensation was 8-9 dollars per hour.

The annotation process consists of two steps.[4] The first step is the "bounding box requirement" task. In this step, we asked workers if a query can be grounded, and if not, which of the following cases it belongs to: 1) What the query refers to cannot be seen in the image. 2) The query does not refer to something specific in the image but rather to the background. 3) The query is an abstract noun that might be confusing based on the contents of the image.

In case 1, the query refers to an entity, but the image does not contain that entity. For instance, in the right part of Figure 1, the query "my favorite picture" entity does not appear in the image. In case 2, if the query is the background of an image, it might make the annotation regions different by different workers, or as there are many objects in the background, it might make the definition of background vague. For instance, in the right part of Figure 1, it is hard to clearly determine the region for the query "a beautiful sunrise." Also, there might be many objects in the annotation. Therefore, we asked workers to annotate this case as unanswerable. In case 3, if the query is an abstract noun, the judgment of annotation might differ from workers. For instance, if the query is "sport," and some workers might define "sport" as a person doing a sport and determine the query as answerable based on the contents of an image, and some workers might define "sport" as something invisible and determine the query as unanswerable. Thus, we set this case as unanswerable. As a result of the crowdsourcing annotation for this step, we obtained $6,941$ unanswerable queries in total.

The second step is the "drawing the bounding box" task. In this step, the annotation was done for data that were not annotated as unanswerable in the first step. Workers were asked to draw a bounding box for an image region corresponding to a query. The difficult part of this process was when there were multiple instances that corresponded to one query in an image. In this case, we instructed the workers to annotate multiple instances to one bounding box if the instances are not clearly separated; otherwise, we annotate them with individual bounding boxes. Besides that, queries in social media data can contain proper nouns, which are special compared to previous datasets and could be interesting to study; thus, we asked workers to indicate if an answerable query belongs to these. In total, $1,886$ answerable queries were annotated, among which 576 queries belong to proper nouns.

Finally, we manually checked the results of the two steps. We checked 100 unanswerable pairs and found that 7 of them were wrongly labeled. Most of them were simple misses where the entity that the query refers to does exist in an image, which we plan to improve as our future work. In addition, we checked and corrected the bounding boxes that were miss-labeled by workers of all answerable pairs. As a result, we obtained $8,827$ annotated query and image pairs for our SMD4FVG dataset.

4 Flexible Visual Grounding Model

We propose to add a pseudo region to a visual grounding model to achieve flexible visual grounding for both answerable and unanswerable queries. An overview of our proposed model is shown in Figure 3. In this section, we first present our visual grounding model, followed by the way to add pseudo regions for unanswerable queries.

4.1 Visual Grounding Model

Our visual grounding model follows (Lu et al., 2020), which consists of 2 stages. In the first stage, we extract region proposals and feature vectors of all regions with an object detection model. We employ the Faster RCNN (Ren et al., 2015) model in the first stage. In the second stage, a similarity score between a region proposal and an input query is calculated. We utilize the multi-task ViLBERT (Lu et al., 2020) for the calculation of the similarity between a region proposal and the input query. Our model is trained to minimize a binary cross-entropy (BCE) loss between a label vector and a similarity score vector similar to (Sadhu et al., 2019). In inference, the input query will be grounded to the region with the highest similarity score.

In detail, after extracting a feature vector $\mathbf{f}_v \in \mathbb{R}^{d_v}$ for a region proposal by Faster RCNN, a spatial vector $\mathbf{f}_s \in \mathbb{R}^5$ is incorporated to it. The spatial vector is encoded to a 5-d vector from normalized top-left and bottom-right coordinates as:

$$\mathbf{f_s} = \left[\frac{x_{tl}}{W}, \frac{y_{tl}}{H}, \frac{x_{br}}{W}, \frac{y_{br}}{W}, \frac{wh}{WH}\right], \quad (2)$$

where (x_{tl}, y_{tl}) is the top-left coordinate, (w_{br}, y_{br}) is the bottom-right coordinate, w and h are the the width and the height of the region, and W and H are the width and the height of the image, respectively. The spatial vector is then projected to match

[4]The screenshot of the interfaces for these two steps can be found in Appendix A.

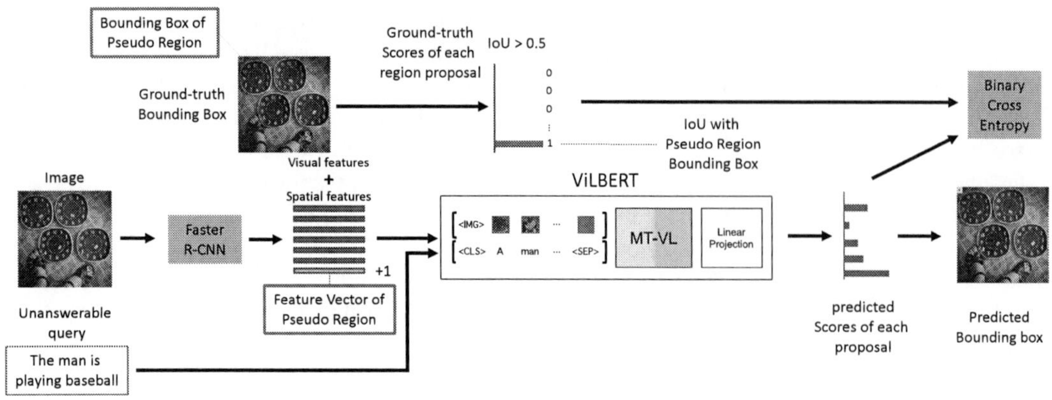

Figure 3: The proposed flexible visual grounding model. For an unanswerable query, we add a pseudo region and train the model to ground the query to the pseudo region.

the dimension of the visual feature by a learnable weight matrix $W_s \in \mathbb{R}^{5 \times d_v}$ and then added to $\mathbf{f}_v$ to generate the final region feature vector $\mathbf{v}_r$ as:

$$\mathbf{v}_r = \mathbf{f}_v + W_s \mathbf{f}_s. \tag{3}$$

The query is given in both training and inference. It is denoted as $\mathbf{q}$. Next, $\mathbf{v}_r$ and $\mathbf{q}$ are input to the multi-task ViLBERT model, which generates a representation $\mathbf{h}_i \in \mathbb{R}^{d_i}$ for the ith region and the query as:

$$\mathbf{h}_i = \texttt{ViLBERT}(\mathbf{v}_r, \mathbf{q}). \tag{4}$$

$\mathbf{h}_i$ is then used to calculate a similarity score for the ith region by:

$$s_i = W_i \mathbf{h}_i, \tag{5}$$

where $W_i \in \mathbb{R}^{d_i \times 1}$ is a learnable weight matrix.

The ground-truth label score is set to 1 if the IoU between a region proposal and the ground-truth region is larger than 0.5; otherwise, it is set to 0. The similarity score vector s_{ji} and the ground-truth label vector l_{ji} for the ith region in the jth image are then used to minimize a BCE loss as:

$$\text{BCE} = -\frac{1}{N}\sum_{j=1}^{N}\sum_{i=1}^{M} l_{ji} log(s_{ji}) + (1 - l_{ji}) log(1 - s_{ji}), \tag{6}$$

where N is the number of image and query pairs in a dataset, and M is the number of region proposals for an image.

4.2 Pseudo Region

To make our visual grounding model deal with unanswerable queries, we propose to incorporate a pseudo region corresponding to an unanswerable query into the region proposals. An example is shown in Figure 3. In Figure 3, the input query "man is playing baseball" is not related to the input image, where the image is about feet and clocks; thus, the query cannot be grounded to the image. For this query, we add a pseudo region to the regions proposed by Faster RCNN (Ren et al., 2015). The position of the pseudo region is set to the top-left of the input image, and all the x and y coordinate values of its spatial vector are set to 0 in Eq. (2). All components of the feature vector $\mathbf{f}_v \in \mathbb{R}^{d_v}$ for the pseudo region are set to $+1$.

Our visual grounding model calculates the similarity score between the pseudo region incorporated region vectors and the query same as Section 4.1. The model is then trained to give the highest similarity score for the pseudo region when the query cannot be grounded. During inference, the model will output the region with the highest score as the prediction. For instance, in the example of Figure 3, the pseudo region will be chosen for the input query because the input query is not corresponding to the input image.

5 Experimental Settings

In our experiments, we verify the effectiveness of the proposed model on both the RefCOCO+ pseudo and SMD4FVG datasets. Here, we first describe the statistics of each dataset and settings, followed by training details.

5.1 Settings on the RefCOCO+ Pseudo Dataset

For the pseudo dataset, based on the RefCOCO+ dataset, we generated unanswerable data and com-

Dataset	Split	Answerable	Unanswerable
	Train	42,278	21,139
Pseudo	Validation	3,805	1,905
	Test	3,773	1,886
	Train	1,270	4,775
SMD4FVG	Validation	330	1,097
	Test	286	1,069

Table 1: Statistics of our datasets (i.e., number of query and image pairs).

bined them with the original dataset with the ratio of 1:2. The upper part of Table 1 shows the statistics of the pseudo dataset.

For the pseudo dataset, we investigated the performance of our model with the following settings:

- **RefCOCO+**: A baseline that trained our visual grounding model in Section 4 on the original RefCOCO+ dataset to evaluate answerable visual grounding only, and compared the performance with (Lu et al., 2020).

- **RefCOCO+Thres**: A baseline based on the RefCOCO+ setting but sets a threshold according to the similarity score (Eq. (4)) distribution for all queries during inference. Queries with the highest similarity scores below the threshold were treated as unanswerable otherwise answerable. The threshold was tuned on the validation split of the pseudo dataset to achieve the highest accuracy for all queries.

- **Pseudo**: We directly trained and evaluated our model on the pseudo dataset.

- **SM→Pseudo**: We first trained our model on the training data of the SMD4FVG dataset and then further fine-tuned it on the pseudo dataset. We hope that the annotated SMD4FVG dataset could boost the performance on the pseudo dataset.

5.2 Settings on the SMD4FVG Dataset

The lower part of Table 1 shows the statistics of the SMD4FVG dataset, where we split the annotated $8,827$ query and image pairs into train/validation/test with a 69%:16%:15% distribution. We evaluated the performance on the SMD4FVG dataset with the following settings:

- **RefCOCO+Thres**: A baseline similar to the RefCOCO+Thres setting on the pseudo dataset, but the threshold was tuned on the validation split of the SMD4FVG dataset.

- **Pseudo**: Aiming to investigate the difference between the pseudo and SMD4FVG datasets, we trained our model on the training data of the pseudo dataset and evaluated it on the SMD4FVG dataset.

- **SM**: This is a straightforward setting that directly trained and evaluated our visual grounding model on the SMD4FVG dataset.

- **Pseudo→SM**: We first trained our model on the training data of the pseudo dataset and then further fine-tuned it on the SMD4FVG dataset. We hope that the large scale of the pseudo dataset could boost the performance on the SMD4FVG dataset.

5.3 Training Details

Visual features and region proposals were extracted from the ResNeXT-152 Faster-RCNN model (Ren et al., 2015) trained on the Visual Genome dataset (Krishna et al., 2016) with an attribute loss. It was not fine-tuned during training. We used the multi-task ViLBERT model (Lu et al., 2020) for calculating the similarity score between region proposals and the query, which contains a 6 / 12 layer of transformer blocks for visual/linguistic streams individually. The multi-task ViLBERT was trained simultaneously with 4 vision-and-language tasks on 12 datasets. We set the region feature dimension d_v to $2,048$, the joint ViLBERT representation dimension d_i to $1,024$, and the number of region proposals N to 100. We trained our model on 8 TitanX GPUs with a batch size of 256, 20 epochs, and the AdamW optimizer with a linear warmup and linear decay learning rate scheduler following (Lu et al., 2020) for all settings.

6 Results

6.1 Results on the Pseudo Dataset

The upper part of Table 2 shows the accuracy of our model on the pseudo dataset. For the RefCOCO+ setting, our model achieves an accuracy of 73.3%, which is almost the same as the result 73.2% when we evaluated the original model of (Lu et al., 2020) using their codes. This indicates that adding a pseudo region has little effect on the performance for answerable visual grounding. However, it cannot deal with unanswerable queries due to the absence of such data in the RefCOCO+ dataset. The

Dataset	Setting	Ans.	Unans.	All
Pseudo	RefCOCO+	73.3	N/A	73.3
	RefCOCO+Thres	**90.3**	46.9	75.9
	Pseudo	69.7	**91.2**	76.8
	SM→Pseudo	70.3	89.9	**76.9**
SMD4FVG	RefCOCO+Thres	0	**100.0**	78.9
	Pseudo	**49.7**	65.6	62.2
	SM	31.8	95.0	**81.7**
	Pseudo→SM	41.3	91.3	80.7

Table 2: Visual grounding results on the pseudo and SMD4FVG datasets. Ans., Unans., and All denote the accuracy for answerable, unanswerable, and all queries, respectively.

RefCOCO+Thres setting works well for answerable queries but fails for answerable ones. The similarity score distribution is in Appendix B.

For the pseudo setting, our model achieves an accuracy of 69.7% and 91.2% for answerable and unanswerable queries, respectively. Our model can ground unanswerable queries with high accuracy. However, it drops 2.6% point for answerable queries compared to the RefCOCO+ setting. We think the reason for this is due to the mixture of unanswerable queries to the original RefCOCO+ dataset, leading the judgment to answerable visual grounding be more complex. SM→Pseudo only slightly boots the All accuracy due to the small-scale of the SMD4FVG dataset. Some incorrect predictions for unanswerable queries are due to the randomness of the dataset, and qualitative examples can be found in Appendix C.

6.2 Results on the SMD4FVG Dataset

The lower part of Table 2 shows the accuracy of our model on the SMD4FVG dataset. We can see that the RefCOCO+Thres setting forces all queries to be unanswerable ones. The similarity score distribution can be found in Appendix B.

Among the other three settings, the pseudo setting achieves the highest accuracy of 49.7% for answerable queries. We think the reason for this is that there are only a few answerable queries in the SMD4FVG dataset, while both the amount and ratio for that are higher in the pseudo dataset, making the model learn answerable grounding well. However, the accuracy for unanswerable queries is only 65.6%, which is significantly worse than the other two settings that use the SMD4FVG dataset for training. We think this is due to the different characteristics of unanswerable queries in the pseudo and SMD4FVG datasets, wherein the pseudo dataset the unanswerable queries are unrelated to the images, but in the SMD4FVG dataset they are more complex. The SM setting achieves high accuracy of 95.0% for unanswerable queries and the best accuracy of 81.7% for all queries. The reason for this can be that our model is optimized in the SMD4FVG dataset directly with the SM setting. However, the accuracy for answerable queries with the SM setting is the lowest due to the small ratio of answerable queries and complex answerable queries in the SMD4FVG dataset. The Pseudo→SM setting achieves a trade-off between the pseudo and SM settings, where there is an improvement for answerable queries compared to the SM setting and a big improvement for unanswerable queries compared to the pseudo setting. We think the reason for this is that Pseudo→SM can take the balance between the pseudo and SM settings via fine-tuning the model pre-trained on the pseudo dataset to the SMD4FVG dataset. We also observe a 1% accuracy drop of all queries from SM to Pseudo→SM. We think it is caused by the big ratio of unanswerable queries in the SMD4FVG dataset. The SM model was more biased to unanswerable queries and thus performed better in accuracy for all queries because of the big ratio of unanswerable queries. Qualitative examples can be found in Appendix C.

For both the pseudo and SMD4FVG datasets, we observe better performance on unanswerable queries than answerable queries besides RefCOCO+Thres on the pseudo dataset. We think the reason could be that it is much easier to learn that a query is unrelated to an image (i.e., unanswerable) instead of finding the exact region that a query refers to (i.e., answerable) by our models.

7 Conclusion

Previous studies on visual grounding ignored the case of unanswerable queries, which is common in real-world such as social media data. In this paper, we proposed flexible visual grounding to address both answerable and unanswerable visual grounding. To this end, we constructed a pseudo dataset based on the RefCOCO+ dataset and a social media dataset based on tweets consisting of both images and text via crowdsourcing. In addition, we proposed a flexible visual grounding model, which can deal with both answerable and unanswerable queries. Experiments on our datasets indicated that our model could achieve high accuracy, especially for unanswerable queries, but there is still room for further improvement.

To make our social media dataset balanced, we constrained it to the RefCOCO+ classes, which may also limit the ability of our model on real-world data. In the future, we plan to construct a dataset without such constraints.

Acknowledgement

This work was supported by ACT-I, JST.

References

Alan Akbik, Duncan Blythe, and Roland Vollgraf. 2018. Contextual string embeddings for sequence labeling. In *COLING 2018, 27th International Conference on Computational Linguistics*, pages 1638–1649.

Youngmin Baek, Bado Lee, Dongyoon Han, Sangdoo Yun, and Hwalsuk Lee. 2019. Character region awareness for text detection. *CoRR*, abs/1904.01941.

Alexey Bochkovskiy, Chien-Yao Wang, and Hong-Yuan Mark Liao. 2020. YOLOv4: Optimal Speed and Accuracy of Object Detection. *arXiv e-prints*, page arXiv:2004.10934.

Kan Chen, Rama Kovvuri, and Ram Nevatia. 2017. Query-guided regression network with context policy for phrase grounding. In *ICCV*, pages 824–832.

Yen-Chun Chen, Linjie Li, Licheng Yu, Ahmed El Kholy, Faisal Ahmed, Zhe Gan, Yu Cheng, and Jingjing Liu. 2020. Uniter: Universal image-text representation learning. In *ECCV*.

J. Deng, W. Dong, R. Socher, L. Li, Kai Li, and Li Fei-Fei. 2009. Imagenet: A large-scale hierarchical image database. In *2009 IEEE Conference on Computer Vision and Pattern Recognition*, pages 248–255.

Jacob Devlin, Ming-Wei Chang, Kenton Lee, and Kristina Toutanova. 2019. BERT: Pre-training of deep bidirectional transformers for language understanding. In *NAACL: HLT*, pages 4171–4186.

Wenjian Dong, Mayu Otani, Noa Garcia, Yuta Nakashima, and Chenhui Chu. 2021. Cross-lingual visual grounding. *IEEE Access*, 9:349–358.

Ingo Feinerer and Kurt Hornik. 2020. *wordnet: WordNet Interface*. R package version 0.1-15.

Akira Fukui, Dong Huk Park, Daylen Yang, Anna Rohrbach, Trevor Darrell, and Marcus Rohrbach. 2016. Multimodal compact bilinear pooling for visual question answering and visual grounding. In *EMNLP*, pages 457–468.

David R. Hardoon, Sandor R. Szedmak, and John R. Shawe-taylor. 2004. Canonical correlation analysis: An overview with application to learning methods. *Neural Computation*, 16(12):2639–2664.

Sahar Kazemzadeh, Vicente Ordonez, Mark Matten, and Tamara Berg. 2014. ReferItGame: Referring to objects in photographs of natural scenes. In *Proceedings of the 2014 Conference on Empirical Methods in Natural Language Processing (EMNLP)*, pages 787–798, Doha, Qatar. Association for Computational Linguistics.

Ranjay Krishna, Yuke Zhu, Oliver Groth, Justin Johnson, Kenji Hata, Joshua Kravitz, Stephanie Chen, Yannis Kalantidis, Li-Jia Li, David A Shamma, Michael Bernstein, and Li Fei-Fei. 2016. Visual genome: Connecting language and vision using crowdsourced dense image annotations.

Tsung-Yi Lin, Michael Maire, Serge Belongie, James Hays, Pietro Perona, Deva Ramanan, Piotr Dollár, and C Lawrence Zitnick. 2014. Microsoft coco: Common objects in context. In *ECCV*, pages 740–755.

Jiasen Lu, Dhruv Batra, Devi Parikh, and Stefan Lee. 2019. Vilbert: Pretraining task-agnostic visiolinguistic representations for vision-and-language tasks. In *NeurIPS*, pages 13–23.

Jiasen Lu, Vedanuj Goswami, Marcus Rohrbach, Devi Parikh, and Stefan Lee. 2020. 12-in-1: Multi-task vision and language representation learning. In *The IEEE/CVF Conference on Computer Vision and Pattern Recognition (CVPR)*.

Junhua Mao, Jonathan Huang, Alexander Toshev, Oana Camburu, Alan L. Yuille, and Kevin Murphy. 2016. Generation and comprehension of unambiguous object descriptions. In *Proceedings of the IEEE Conference on Computer Vision and Pattern Recognition (CVPR)*.

Bryan A. Plummer, Arun Mallya, Christopher M. Cervantes, Julia Hockenmaier, and Svetlana Lazebnik. 2017. Phrase localization and visual relationship detection with comprehensive image-language cues. In *ICCV*, pages 1928–1937.

Bryan A. Plummer, Liwei Wang, Chris M. Cervantes, Juan C. Caicedo, Julia Hockenmaier, and Svetlana Lazebnik. 2015. Flickr30k entities: Collecting region-to-phrase correspondences for richer image-to-sentence models. In *ICCV*, pages 2641–2649.

Shaoqing Ren, Kaiming He, Ross Girshick, and Jian Sun. 2015. Faster r-cnn: Towards real-time object detection with region proposal networks. In *NIPS*, pages 91–99.

Anna Rohrbach, Marcus Rohrbach, Ronghang Hu, Trevor Darrell, and Bernt Schiele. 2016. Grounding of textual phrases in images by reconstruction. In *ECCV*, pages 817–834.

Arka Sadhu, Kan Chen, and Ram Nevatia. 2019. Zero-shot grounding of objects from natural language queries. In *The IEEE International Conference on Computer Vision (ICCV)*.

Piyush Sharma, Nan Ding, Sebastian Goodman, and Radu Soricut. 2018. Conceptual captions: A cleaned, hypernymed, image alt-text dataset for automatic image captioning. In *ACL*, pages 2556–2565.

Weijie Su, Xizhou Zhu, Yue Cao, Bin Li, Lewei Lu, Furu Wei, and Jifeng Dai. 2020. Vl-bert: Pre-training of generic visual-linguistic representations. In *ICLR*.

Mingxing Tan and Quoc V. Le. 2019. Efficientnet: Rethinking model scaling for convolutional neural networks. *CoRR*, abs/1905.11946.

Oriol Vinyals, Alexander Toshev, Samy Bengio, and Dumitru Erhan. 2015. Show and tell: A neural image caption generator. In *CVPR*, pages 3156–3164.

Liwei Wang, Yin Li, and Svetlana Lazebnik. 2016a. Learning deep structure-preserving image-text embeddings. In *CVPR*, pages 5005–5013.

Mingzhe Wang, Mahmoud Azab, Noriyuki Kojima, Rada Mihalcea, and Jia Deng. 2016b. Structured matching for phrase localization. In *ECCV*, pages 696–711.

Qi Wu, Damien Teney, Peng Wang, Chunhua Shen, Anthony Dick, and Anton van den Hengel. 2017. Visual question answering: A survey of methods and datasets. *CVIU*, pages 1–20.

Zhibiao Wu and Martha Palmer. 1994. Verb semantics and lexical selection. *CoRR*, abs/cmp-lg/9406033.

Sibei Yang, Guanbin Li, and Yizhou Yu. 2020a. Propagating over phrase relations for one-stage visual grounding. In *ECCV*.

Zhengyuan Yang, Tianlang Chen, Liwei Wang, and Jiebo Luo. 2020b. Improving one-stage visual grounding by recursive sub-query construction. In *ECCV*.

Raymond Yeh, Jinjun Xiong, Wen-Mei W. Hwu, Minh Do, and Alexander G. Schwing. 2017. Interpretable and globally optimal prediction for textual grounding using image concepts. In *NIPS*, pages 1909–1919.

Licheng Yu, Zhe Lin, Xiaohui Shen, Jimei Yang, Xin Lu, Mohit Bansal, and Tamara L Berg. 2018a. Mattnet: Modular attention network for referring expression comprehension. In *CVPR*.

Licheng Yu, Patrick Poirson, Shan Yang, Alexander C. Berg, and Tamara L. Berg. 2016. Modeling context in referring expressions. In *ECCV*.

Zhou Yu, Jun Yu, Chenchao Xiang, Zhou Zhao, Qi Tian, and Dacheng Tao. 2018b. Rethinking diversified and discriminative proposal generation for visual grounding. In *IJCAI*, pages 1114–1120.

Yuke Zhu, Oliver Groth, Michael Bernstein, and Li Fei-Fei. 2016. Visual7w: Grounded question answering in images. In *Proceedings of the IEEE Conference on Computer Vision and Pattern Recognition (CVPR)*.

A Annotation Interfaces

Figure 4 shows the screenshot of the first step of crowdsourcing. This step is the "bounding box requirement" task. We instruct workers to check if the given query is answerable or not. For unanswerable queries, we further ask workers to check which unanswerable type the query is.

Figure 5 shows the screenshot of the second step of crowdsourcing. This step is the "drawing bounding box" task. For an answerable query, we instruct workers to draw bounding boxes to which the query refers.

B Similarity Score Distribution

Figure 6 shows the similarity score distribution of the RefCOCO+Thres setting on the testsets of the pseudo dataset and SMD4FVG dataset, respectively. We can see that the similarity score and the grounding possibility have a very low correlation.

C Qualitative Examples

Figure 7 shows examples of our model with the RefCOCO+ setting on unanswerable queries in the pseudo dataset. We can see that the RefCOCO+ setting cannot identify unanswerable queries, which gives wrong predictions for them. However, there are also some ambiguous queries, such as the ones in examples 1, 6, and 7, for which we cannot confidently claim that the predictions are wrong due to the random combination characteristics of unanswerable queries in the pseudo dataset.

Figure 8 shows example outputs of our model with the pseudo setting. Examples 1 and 2 in Figure 8 are two successful examples for answerable visual grounding; we can see that our model can ground queries with and without modifiers. Examples 3 and 4 in Figure 8 are two successful examples for unanswerable visual grounding; we can see that for the queries that are unrelated to the images, our model can correctly identify that they cannot be grounded. Examples 5 and 6 in Figure 8 are two unsuccessful examples for answerable visual grounding; our model fails on example 5 in Figure 8 where the ground-truth is the other person with the number 160 on the vest; for example 6 in Figure 8, the query "taller one" itself is actually ambiguous, and our model makes the judgment that it cannot be grounded, while the ground-truth is annotated for the "taller refrigerator" in the RefCOCO+ dataset. Although our model achieves 91.2% accuracy for unanswerable queries, it still makes some mistakes. Examples 7 and 8 in Figure 8 show two unsuccessful examples for unanswerable visual grounding; we can see that for example 7 in Figure 8, the query "lady" actually can be grounded, but it is annotated as unanswerable in our pseudo dataset due to the fact that the query is taken from another image randomly and it could be grounded in coincidence; the query for example 8 in Figure 8 is again ambiguous, and thus it is actually difficult to claim that our model is wrong here.

Figure 9 shows example outputs of our model with the SNS setting, which achieves the best overall accuracy among the three settings. Examples 1 and 2 in Figure 9 are two successful examples for answerable visual grounding; we can see that our model can do grounding for both a single object (example 1) and multiple objects (example 2). Examples 3 and 4 in Figure 9 are two successful examples for unanswerable visual grounding; we can see that our model correctly identifies that the abstract noun query "sport" and the query "the east coast" that cannot be inferred from the image directly, cannot be grounded. Examples 5 and 6 in Figure 9 are two unsuccessful examples for answerable visual grounding; for example 5, the query "airbus320ceo" is a proper noun, which is difficult for grounding; while for example 6, "coach" is difficult to infer from the image though "bus" is clear. Examples 7 and 8 in Figure 9 show two unsuccessful examples for unanswerable visual grounding; for example 7, due to the failure of our query extraction model, an adjective query "automotive" is generated, which should not be grounded; for example 8, it is a human dressed up as a bear but not a real bear, and thus should not be grounded.

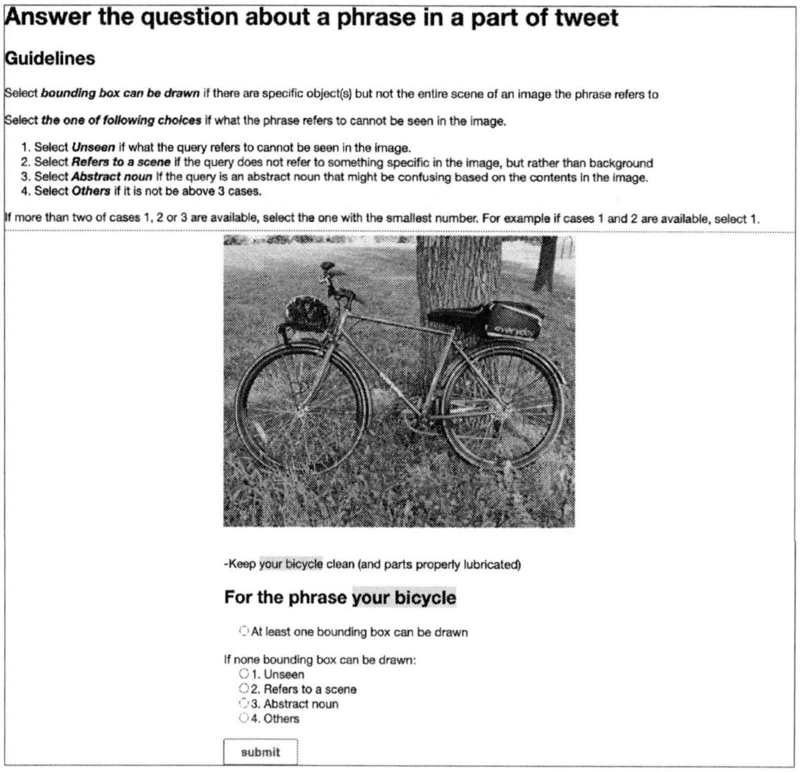

Figure 4: The bounding box requirement interface. This is the first step of crowdsourcing. In this step, we instruct workers to check whether the given query is answerable or not. If the query is unanswerable, we ask workers to further check which unanswerable type the query is.

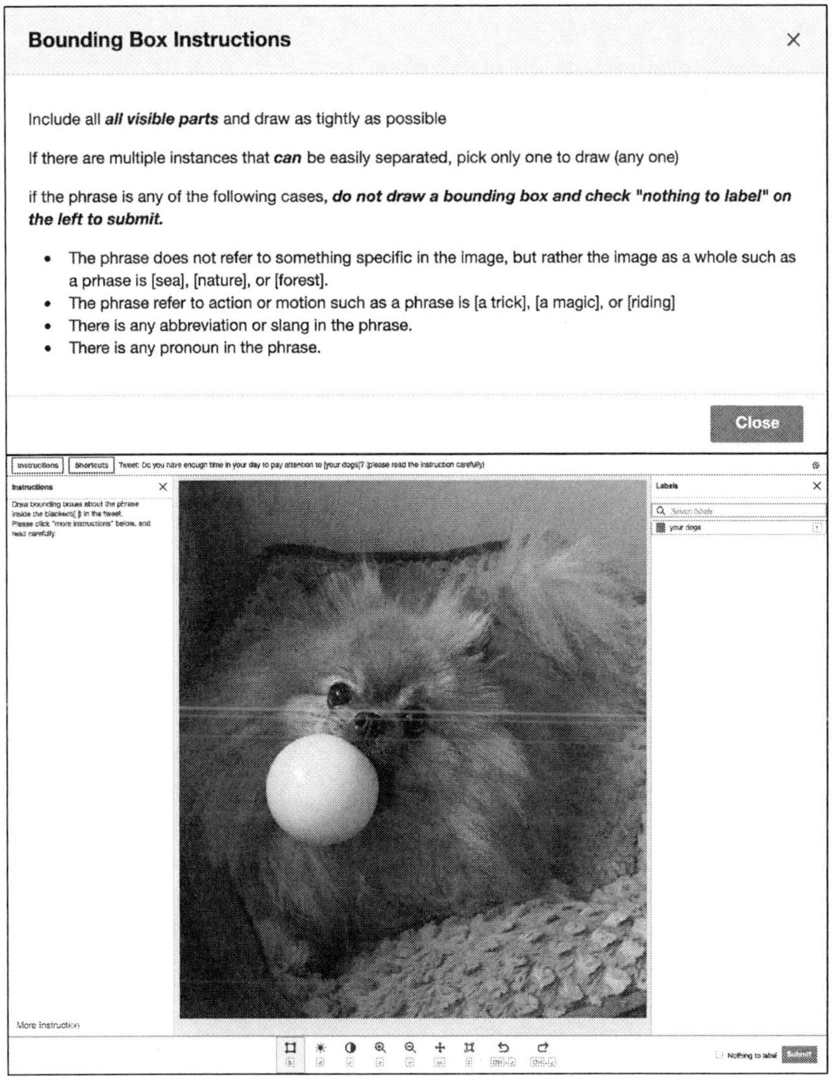

Figure 5: The drawing bounding box interface. This is the second step of crowdsourcing. In this step, we instruct workers to draw bounding boxes to which the query refers. The annotation is done for query and image pairs that are classified as answerable in the first step.

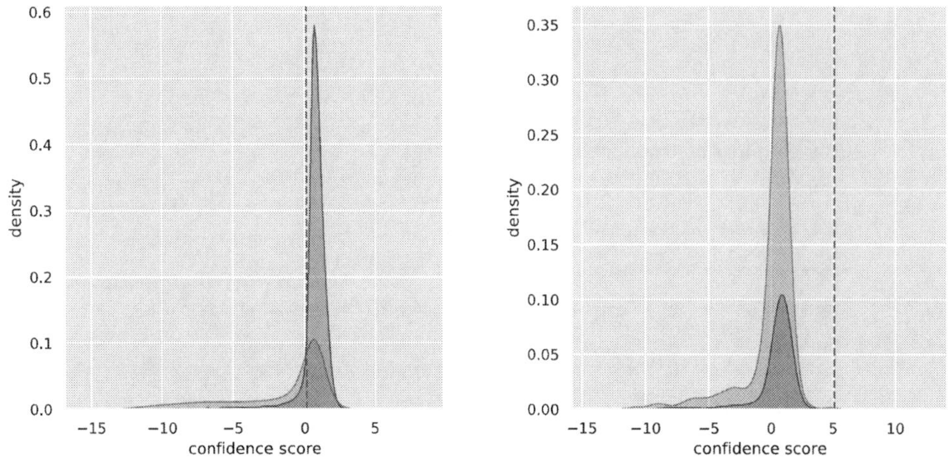

Pseudo dataset | SMD4FVG dataset

Figure 6: The similarity score distribution of the RefCOCO+Thres setting on the testsets of the pseudo dataset and SMD4FVG dataset, respectively. X-axis and Y-axis denote the similarity/confidence score and density, respectively. The solid blue and orange curves represent answerable and unanswerable queries, respectively. The vertical dotted red lines denote the thresholds.

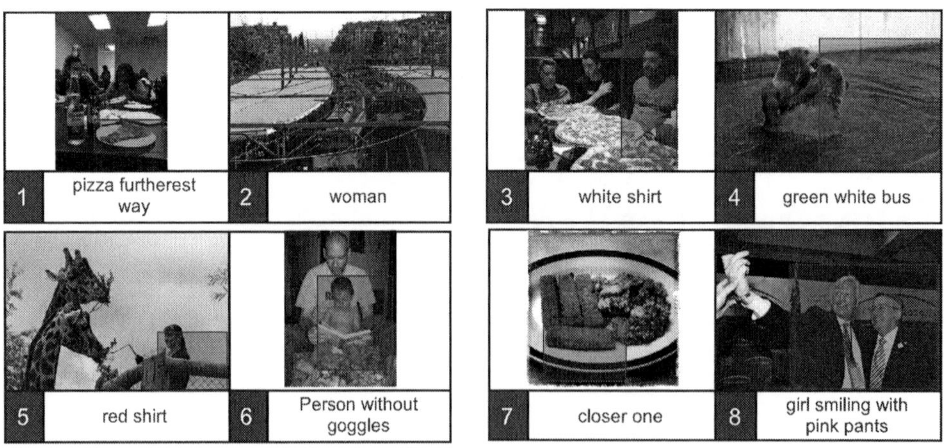

Figure 7: Examples of visual grounding for unanswerable queries in the pseudo dataset. The blue bounding boxes are the prediction of our model with the RefCOCO+ setting.

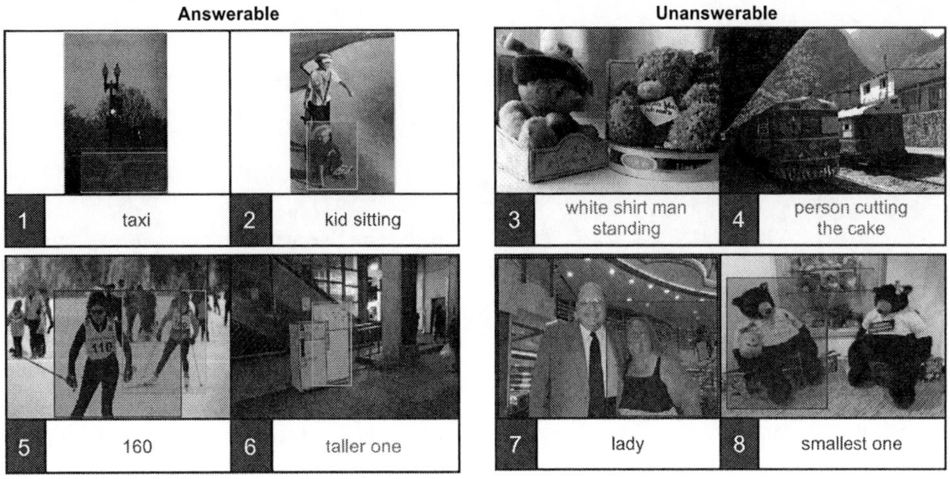

Figure 8: Examples of successful (top) and unsuccessful (bottom) visual grounding for answerable and unanswerable queries in the pseudo dataset. The green and blue bounding boxes are ground-truth and the prediction of our model with the pseudo setting, respectively.

Figure 9: Examples of successful (top) and unsuccessful (bottom) visual grounding for answerable and unanswerable queries in the SMD4FVG dataset. The green and blue bounding boxes are ground-truth and the prediction of our model with the SNS setting, respectively.

A large-scale computational study of content preservation measures for text style transfer and paraphrase generation

Nikolay Babakov, David Dale, Varvara Logacheva, and Alexander Panchenko
Skolkovo Institute of Science and Technology (Skoltech)
{n.babakov, d.dale, v.logacheva, a.panchenko}@skoltech.ru

Abstract

Text style transfer and paraphrasing of texts are actively growing areas of NLP, dozens of methods for solving these tasks have been recently introduced. In both tasks, the system is supposed to generate a text which should be semantically similar to the input text. Therefore, these tasks are dependent on methods of measuring textual semantic similarity. However, it is still unclear which measures are the best to automatically evaluate content preservation between original and generated text. According to our observations, many researchers still use BLEU-like measures, while there exist more advanced measures including neural-based that significantly outperform classic approaches. The current problem is the lack of a thorough evaluation of the available measures. We close this gap by conducting a large-scale computational study by comparing 57 measures based on different principles on 19 annotated datasets. We show that measures based on cross-encoder models outperform alternative approaches in almost all cases. We also introduce the Mutual Implication Score (MIS), a measure that uses the idea of paraphrasing as a bidirectional entailment and outperforms all other measures on the paraphrase detection task and performs on par with the best measures in the text style transfer task.

1 Introduction

Text style transfer (TST) and paraphrases generation (PG) are active areas of research in NLP, with dozens of papers proposing new methods. These methods could be applied for practical purposes, such as supporting human writers, personalizing digital assistants, or even creating artificial personalities.

Research and development of TST models require fast feedback loops, and they require fast and reliable automatic quality measures. TST is hard to evaluate for several reasons. First, golden answers, even if available, are not the only valid way to rewrite the text. Second, parallel corpora with different styles do not emerge naturally and are hard to find. This means that reference-based evaluation is often prohibitive and creates a need for manual evaluation of TST or for clever automatic measures.

The basic desired properties of TST are style accuracy, content preservation, and fluency (Mir et al., 2019). For many methods of unsupervised TST, keeping the content of the original text and automatically measuring its preservation is one of the most difficult tasks (see e.g. Dale et al. (2021)).

During development, the only way to control content preservation is to use automatic measures. Such measure takes two sentences and return the value which indicates the similarity of their content. More formally, the measure sim quantifies semantic relatedness of two utterances, an original text x and a style-transferred or paraphrased text y : $sim(x, y) \rightarrow [0; 1]$. The measure sim yields high score for the pairs with similar content and low score for ones with different content.

As Krishna et al. (2020) and Yamshchikov et al. (2021) show, most TST works evaluate the content preservation with BLEU (Papineni et al., 2002) or similar measures based on word overlap between two texts. The situation in PG is almost identical. Most works including the most recent ones (Sun et al., 2021; Fu et al., 2020) also still rely on BLEU.

Even though measures like BLEU, based on a word or character-level n-grams are pretty intuitive and straightforward, they don't take into account synonyms and distributively related words. Moreover, there already exist several pieces of evidence that correlation of standard BLEU-like automatic measures is relatively low (Briakou et al., 2021). The recent development of vector representations of textual information (Mikolov et al., 2013; Zhang et al., 2019) and various ways to handle these vectors provides room for improvement of the approaches to scoring the content preservation. It

Proceedings of the 60th Annual Meeting of the Association for Computational Linguistics
Student Research Workshop, pages 300 - 321
May 22-27, 2022

is, therefore, crucial to perform a thorough analysis of all existing content preservation measures and to gather best practices from the top-performing approaches to create a new approach that could demonstrate stable performance in terms of both PG and TST tasks.

In this work, we further extend a comprehensive study of Yamshchikov et al. (2021) by analyzing a much more diverse set of measures including recently developed transformers-based ones, and also by proposing a new measure specially developed for TST and PG content preservation scoring. The contributions of our paper are as follows:

- We perform a large-scale evaluation of automatic content preservation measures for text style transfer and paraphrase generation tasks, which includes 57 measures applied to 9 paraphrasing datasets and 10 text style transfer datasets. To the best of our knowledge, this is the largest and the most comprehensive evaluation of this kind;
- We introduce Mutual Implication Score (MIS): a measure of content preservation based on predictions of NLI models in two directions. We show that it outperforms all known measures in paraphrase detection and shows consistently high results for TST. We opensource the model on Huggingface Model Hub.[1]

The code for measures and experiments is released publicly.[2]

2 Related work

2.1 Measures of content preservation

There exists a large number of content preservation measures that can be classified into several groups. In this section, we describe all of these approaches. Refer to Figure 1 for a schematic description of all approaches.

Words or characters n-grams (ngram) The most simple and intuitive way to compare two texts is based on the overlap of word or character n-grams. The standard method used to evaluate the quality of a generated text is to compare it with a human-written reference text via BLEU score (Papineni et al., 2002), which is the precision of word n-grams. In TST and PG papers, BLEU is often used to evaluate content preservation relative to the original text or a reference. Other popular measures based on words or n-grams are ROUGE (Lin, 2004), METEOR (Banerjee and Lavie, 2005), chrF (Popović, 2015). Such approaches as Levenshtein distance (Levenshtein et al., 1966), Jaro-Winkler distance (Jaro, 1989) also work at the subword level by calculating the edit distance between two sequences, so we also refer them to the ngram group. Panchenko and Morozova (2012) provided a comparative study of classic word similarity measures and their combinations. The ngram measures are simple and intuitive but do not handle well such linguistic phenomena as synonyms, negation, and issues with word order.

Similarity between static embeddings (emb-static) Another family of measures partially overcomes these difficulties by representing texts with their embeddings and calculating the distance (e.g. cosine similarity) between the embeddings of two texts. This group of measures can be further divided by the way the embeddings are generated. The basic way of obtaining the embedding of a text is by averaging across static word embeddings: Word2vec (Mikolov et al., 2013), GloVe (Pennington et al., 2014), FastText (Bojanowski et al., 2017).

Similarity between contextualized embeddings (emb-context) Special distance function (e.g. WMD (Kusner et al., 2015), POS-distance (Tian et al., 2018a)) can be also applied to context-dependent vectors: BERTScore (Zhang et al., 2019), MoverScore (Zhao et al., 2019).

Similarity between embeddings from bi-encoders (emb-bi-enc) Embeddings of a text can be generated by encoding a text with a pre-trained *encoder*. If the two texts are encoded separately, and then we compute the cosine similarity between their embeddings, we refer to such models as *bi-encoders*. This group of models is usually trained in a supervised manner. The encoders can be trained on the translation task (Laser (Artetxe and Schwenk, 2019), LaBSE (Feng et al., 2020)), paraphrase identification task (SIMILE (Wieting et al., 2019)), or text generation task (BARTScore (Yuan et al., 2021)). They potentially can compare the meanings of texts that are very different in terms of structure and vocabulary.

[1]https://huggingface.co/SkolkovoInstitute/Mutual_Implication_Score

[2]https://github.com/skoltech-nlp/mutual_implication_score

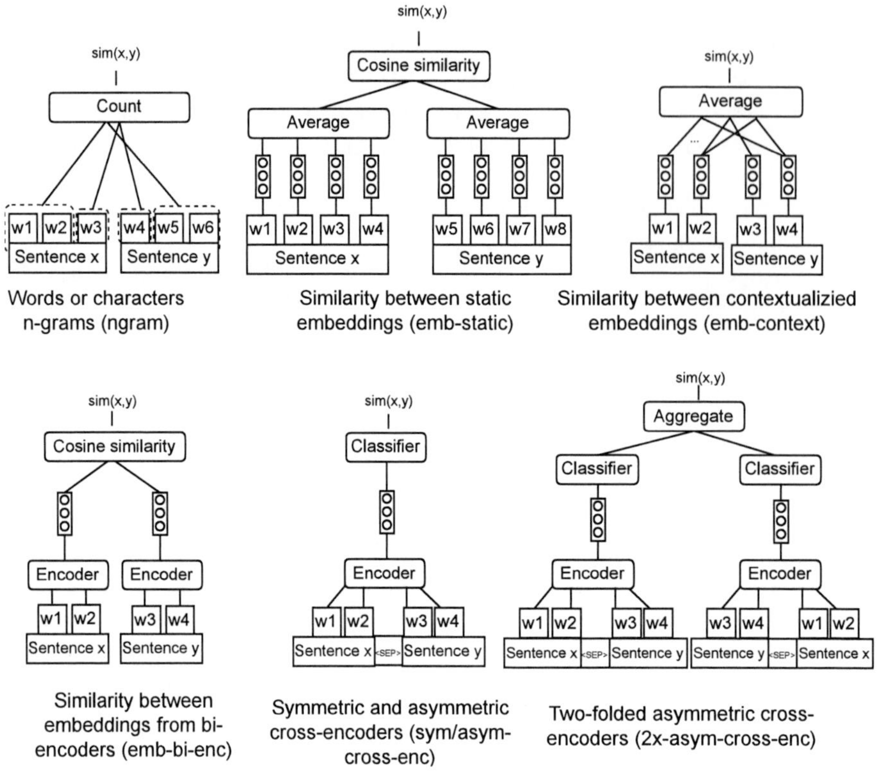

Figure 1: Different approaches to calculating content preservation between two sentences.

Symmetric and asymmetric cross-encoders (sym/asym-cross-enc) The models called *cross-encoders* process both texts simultaneously using cross-attention and directly predict the relationship between the texts. They can perform symmetrically (score is independent of the order of the texts being compared) or asymmetrically (score strongly depends on the order of the texts). Due to their supervised nature, such models can reflect content preservation more accurately than word-based approaches, but they depend on labeled data and may not generalize well to new domains. The presence of symmetry is defined by the task the model was trained on. Thus, models trained on the Natural Language Inference (NLI) task data (such as BLEURT (Sellam et al., 2020) or NUBIA (Kane et al., 2020)) are asymmetric, while cross-stsb-base model trained solely on STS-B dataset (Cer et al., 2017) for semantic textual similarity, or APD model (Nighojkar and Licato, 2021) trained on paraphrase datasets perform symmetrically.

Two-folded asymmetric cross-encoders (2x-asym-cross-enc) A textual entailment model can be used for scoring semantic relations between two phrases. Nighojkar and Licato (2021) propose to use a natural language inference (NLI) model for paraphrase identification, and Deng et al. (2021) suggest a similar model for evaluation of summarization and text style transfer. The main idea of these works is to use NLI models in a two-fold manner (direct and reverse). NLI models are generally asymmetric cross-encoders, so we classify this group of approaches as a two-fold asymmetric encoder.

As shown in Figure 2, despite the wide variety of measures, n-gram-based measures are still used most often, while embedding-based measures and cross-encoders are much less popular. In some papers, no automatic content preservation measures are used.

2.2 Evaluation of content preservation measures

Our work in many respects follows the setup of Yamshchikov et al. (2021) and extends it in several directions. In this work, the authors collected crowdsource estimates of content preservation for 14,000 sentence pairs from 14 sources and compared these estimates with 13 automatic

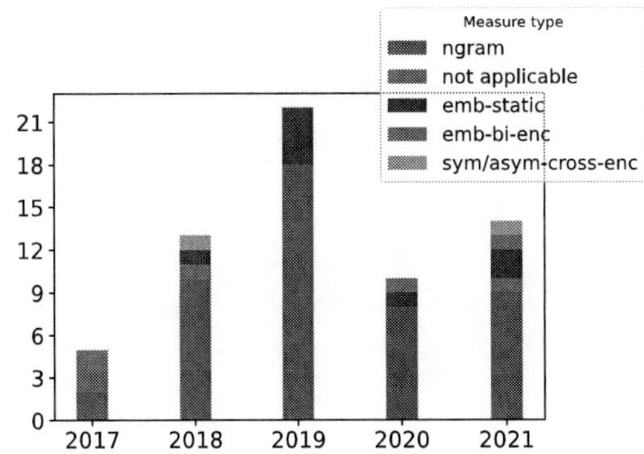

Figure 2: The number of research papers on TST and PG which use automatic content preservation measures from different groups, based on 58 publications listed in Appendix (Table 7).

measures. They evaluated the quality of automatic measures by the correlation between rankings provided by these measures and rankings created by human scores. This scoring showed that the WMD over GloVe embeddings and L2 distance between the ELMo embeddings outperform other measures. However, no supervised sentence encoders or cross-encoders were considered in this work.

In the work by Briakou et al. (2021), the authors evaluated measures of formality transfer in four languages. The main subject of this work is a thorough analysis of multilingual formality style transfer, including a high-level analysis of all aspects of style transfer quality: style accuracy, content preservation, and fluency. The authors used chrF and a cross-encoder (XLM-R) trained on a semantic text similarity dataset to calculate content preservation. They also cautioned against using BLEU in this context, because it has a lower correlation with human judgments than many other measures. However, automatic measures of content preservation were not the main focus of this work, so we extend its results by applying more diverse measures on the English part of their dataset, among others.

3 Datasets used in comparative study

We run our analysis of measures on parallel datasets manually labeled for semantic similarity or content preservation. To make the comparison more generalizable, we fetch a large number of datasets generated by different models.

3.1 Text style transfer datasets

The text style transfer task is aimed at transforming a text to change its *style* (a particular attribute of its text) while keeping the content intact. Since in some cases the style cannot be separated from the content (e.g. if the style is positive/negative sentiment), strict preservation of all content is sometimes impossible in the TST task. Therefore, we consider the parallel TST datasets separately from other data used for the analysis.

In many TST works, outputs were evaluated with human judgments, but the raw similarity labels are rarely published. We managed to find datasets that include human similarity scores for various TST tasks

- Detoxification:
  - Tox600 (Dale et al., 2021),
  - CAE (Laugier et al., 2021)
- Formality transfer:
  - xformal-FoST (Briakou et al., 2021),
  - STRAP_form, (Krishna et al., 2020)
  - Yam. GYAFC (Yamshchikov et al., 2021)[3]
- Sentiment transfer:
  - PG-YELP (Pang and Gimpel, 2019)
  - Yam. Yelp (Yamshchikov et al., 2021)
- Transfer to Old English:
  - Yam. Bible (Yamshchikov et al., 2021),
  - STRAP_coha (old American English), (Krishna et al., 2020)
  - STRAP_SP (Shakespearean English) (Krishna et al., 2020)

3.2 Paraphrases datasets

Unlike TST, the paraphrase generation task requires full preservation of content. There exist a large number of parallel datasets of paraphrases manually labelled for content preservation. The majority of them have binary labels ("same"/"different"). We use the following datasets in our analysis:

- MSRP (Dolan and Brockett, 2005),
- Twitter-URL (Lan et al., 2017),
- PIT (Xu et al., 2014),
- PAWS (Yang et al., 2019b),
- ETPC (Kovatchev et al., 2018),

[3]We use the datasets collected and/or used in the analysis by Yamshchikov et al. (2021). For clarity, we prepend their names with "Yam." prefix.

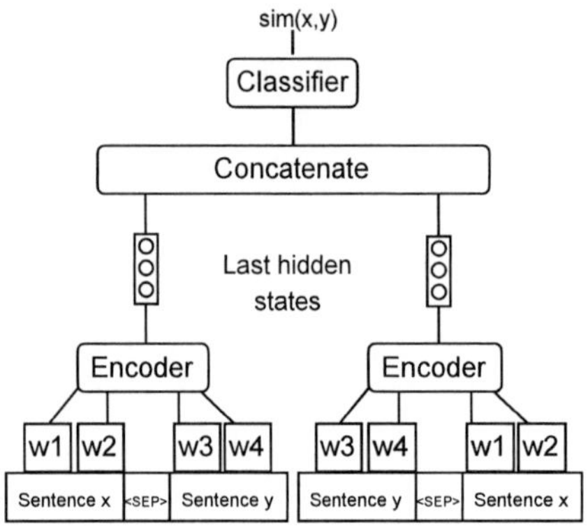

Figure 3: Mutual Implication Score (MIS).

- APT (Nighojkar and Licato, 2021),
- Yam. Para (Yamshchikov et al., 2021).

We provide detailed information about the datasets in the Appendix tables 5 and 6.

4 Mutual Implication Score (MIS)

The goal of our research is not only to analyze the existing measures of content preservation but also to suggest a new measure that can outperform the existing ones. We devise a new measure that is based on measuring content similarity with NLI, as described by Nighojkar and Licato (2021). In this work, the authors exploit the assumption that implies the two sentences with the same meaning should be equivalent in their inferential properties, i.e. each sentence should textually entail the other. This means that the NLI model is supposed to return similar entailment scores when applied to semantically equal sentences regardless of the sequence these sentences are sent to the input of the model. The authors used this assumption to propose an adversarial method of dataset creation for paraphrase identification.

NLI models predict whether one text logically entails another, and are, therefore, asymmetric. High entailment probability in the forward direction means that the second text accurately follows the first one and does not contain hallucinated information. A high entailment score in the backward direction means that all the information from the first text is retained in the second text.

The most natural way to aggregate scores from both directions is to multiply them or compute their arithmetic or harmonic mean. We use this approach as a baseline. We yield NLI scores from the following models:

PG		TST	
Measure	ρ	Measure	ρ
MIS	**0.61**	MIS	**0.54**
DeBERTa	0.60	RobNLI	0.47
RobNLI	0.59	DeBERTa	0.46
FBrobNLI	0.55	FBrobNLI	0.43

Table 1: Mean Spearman correlations of MIS and baseline NLI-based measures on PG and TST datasets. For baseline NLI measures, the forward and backward scores are averaged.

- **RobNLI** (Nie et al., 2020) — RoBERTA-Large (Zhuang et al., 2021) pre-trained on SNLI (Bowman et al., 2015), MNLI (Williams et al., 2018), FEVER-NLI (Nie et al., 2019), and ANLI (Nie et al., 2020),
- **FBrobNLI** (Liu et al., 2019) — RoBERTA-Large pre-trained only on MNLI,
- **DeBERTa** (He et al., 2021) pre-trained on the MNLI dataset.

Although these NLI models are a good starting point, they might not be fully suitable for measuring content preservation, because they were trained for a different task. We suggest that further fine-tuning them on the data annotated with content preservation scores might yield better models.

Thus, we modify the RoBERTA architecture used for NLI. Namely, we use the original encoder in both forward and backward directions, concatenate the last hidden states, and then send them to the classification module which is tuned on data annotated with content preservation scores. We refer to this model as **Mutual Implication Score (MIS)**. The scheme of our model is given in Figure 3.

We initialize the model with pre-trained weights from the RobNLI model. We tune it on Quora Question Pairs dataset (Sharma et al., 2019) for 2 epochs with a learning rate $4e^{-6}$ and all but the last encoder layer and classifier layer frozen.

We evaluate the model with the Spearman rank correlation coefficient of the automatic content preservation scores with human judgments. We evaluate all TST and PG datasets introduced in Section 3. We evaluate MIS and baseline NLI-based measures (we aggregate the NLI scores for both directions with the arithmetic mean because it showed the best results in our preliminary experiments).

The results are shown in Table 1. Fine-tuning the (slightly modified) NLI model on content preservation data slightly improves its performance on datasets generated by paraphrasing models and yields significantly higher correlation on TST datasets.

5 Measures analysis

We compute the content preservation scores for paraphrasing and style transfer datasets using measures of different types. We analyze the performance of individual measures and compare the performance of different groups of measures. We also look into the difference in measures performance on PG and TST tasks and analyze the individual datasets.

5.1 Experimental setting

We analyze 57 content preservation measures of different types. As described in Section 2.1, the measures can be divided into the following groups: a word or character n-gram based (ngram), the measures based on the distance between static (emb-static) or contextualized (emb-context) embeddings, or embeddings from bi-encoders (emb-bi-enc), different groups of encoders-based measures: symmetric (sym-cross-enc), asymmetric (asym-cross-enc) or two-fold asymmetric (2x-asym-cross-enc) cross-encoders. This grouping is used explicitly during analysis. The full list of measures is given in Table 8.

We compute the content preservation scores for 19 datasets listed in Section 3. The full information about the datasets is given in Appendix Tables 5 and 6.

We evaluate measures using the Spearman rank correlation coefficient of the automatic scores with human judgments. Since we use a large number of measures and datasets, we report only aggregated results. The full results are available in the Appendix Figures 7 and 8.

5.2 Measure-level analysis

Figure 4 shows the correlations of the best-performing measures from different groups for individual datasets. The last columns of the plots show the performance of each measure averaged across datasets. The plot shows that MIS and similar measures based on two-folded asymmetric cross-encoders have the best average performance on the paraphrase datasets. For TST datasets, there is no clear winner: symmetric cross-encoders (cross-stsb-large/base), bi-encoders (SIMCSE-SL/SB), asymmetric cross-encoders (BLEURT, NUBIA), and two-folded asymmetric cross-encoder (MIS) demonstrate almost equal performance.

Measure	Toxic	Old_Eng	Form	Sent
BLEURT-B128	0.47	0.52	0.61	**0.39**
BLEURT-L128	**0.54**	0.57	0.64	0.35
MIS	0.50	0.60	0.69	0.28
NUBIA	0.43	0.60	0.66	0.33
SIMCSE-SL	0.46	0.60	0.69	0.36

Table 2: Mean Spearman correlation of measures which perform best on different text style transfer tasks. Tasks: *Toxic* — detoxification, *Old_Eng* — old-style to modern English, *Form* — formal to informal, *Sent* — sentiment transfer. The best scores are shown **in bold**.

Paraphrase Generation (PG)			
	ρ_{max}	ρ_{avg}	$\#wins$
2x-asym-cross-enc	**0.61**	**0.56**	3
sym-cross-enc	0.55	0.51	**5**
asym-cross-enc	0.54	0.49	2
emb-bi-enc	0.54	0.45	2
emb-context	0.47	0.42	0
ngram	0.42	0.34	0
emb-static	0.32	0.27	0
Text Style Transfer (TST)			
	ρ_{max}	ρ_{avg}	$\#wins$
sym-cross-enc	**0.55**	**0.51**	**3**
emb-bi-enc	0.55	0.49	3
asym-cross-enc	0.54	0.46	3
2x-asym-cross-enc	0.54	0.45	0
emb-context	0.5	0.45	2
emb-static	0.4	0.36	1
ngram	0.41	0.35	1

Table 3: Spearman correlations of measures belonging to different groups: ρ_{max} — correlation of the best-performing in the group, ρ_{avg} — correlation averaged over the group, $\#wins$ — the number of times the model from the group performs best on any of the datasets.

The performance of content preservation measures on TST datasets varies from style to style. The TST datasets we use contain style transformations of four types: detoxification, formal to informal, positive to negative sentiment, and modern to old-style English. Thus, it seems natural to average the measures performance not only by all TST datasets but also by TST datasets of different styles. The averaged scores are shown in Table 2. There is no clear winner for old-style English and formality transfer: MIS and SIMCSE-SL show almost equal performance. However, we can see that BLEURT measures are clear leaders in detoxification and sentiment transfer.

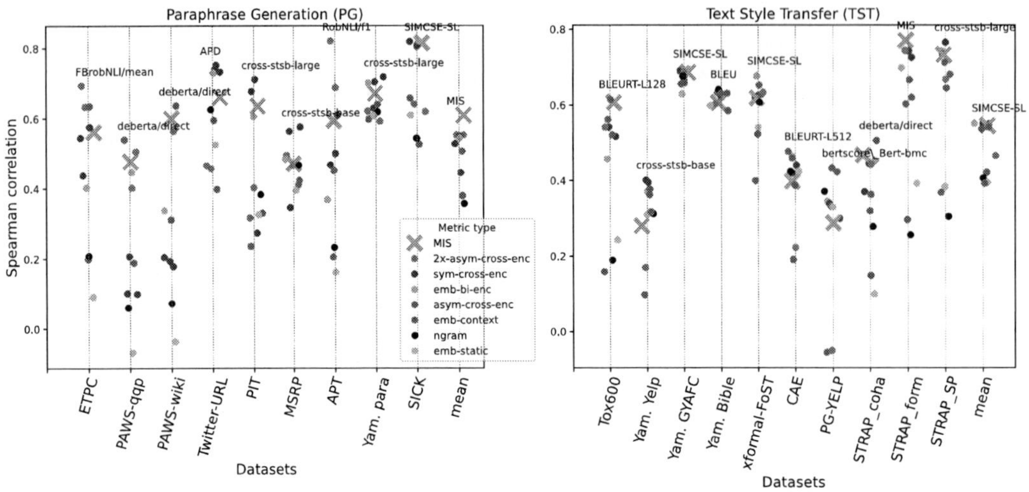

Figure 4: Correlation of measures of different classes with human judgments on paraphrase and text style transfer datasets. The text above each dataset indicates the best-performing measure. The rightmost columns show the mean performance of measures across the datasets.

5.3 Group-level analysis

To get more generalizable results of the analysis, we perform a group-level comparison of measures in Table 3. We report the Spearman correlation scores averaged over datasets of PG and TST tasks (as before, we do not merge all datasets and consider the two tasks separately). We report the mean and maximum correlations of all measures of a group. We also compute the number of times when a measure of a group performs best on the particular dataset. This indicator can be somewhat biased due to the nature of each dataset, however, it can still serve as an additional source of information. If the difference between correlations is not significant (by Williams test (Graham and Baldwin, 2014)) we assign one winning time to each group.

From this point of view, we can even better see that two-folded asymmetric models are the best choice for paraphrases detection because the mean correlation outperforms the next best-performing group by 0.05. Symmetric cross-encoders can also be an alternative option for this task because they show the largest number of wins. Symmetric cross-encoders show the highest mean correlation on the TST task. At the same time, the number of wins and correlations of the best models from this class are similar for all encoder-based classes.

Finally, from the measure-level and group-level perspective, we can see that encoder-based measures outperform ngrams-based measures in the absolute majority of datasets on TST and PG tasks.

5.4 Data-level analysis

So far we relied on the correlations averaged across different datasets. However, it is also natural to have a closer look at how the behavior of different measures changes across datasets.

For this purpose, we represent each dataset as a vector of correlations of each measure with the human judgments and plot a dendrogram (see Figure 5) to show the clustered structure of the obtained vectors. The dendrogram should be interpreted as follows. The height at which each dataset is connected to another dataset or group of datasets indicates the distance between the dataset vectors. We additionally plot a heatmap of cosine similarities of these datasets vectors in Appendix Figure 9.

Datasets related to sentiment transfer (PG-YELP, Yam. Yelp) look different from others, thus, they form a separate cluster in the dendrogram. The reason for this dissimilarity is probably the fact that in this type of TST task (sentiment transfer) the content of the utterance changes more significantly than in other tasks. Moreover, PG-YELP is originally distributed as a pairwise comparison dataset. To yield sentence-level scores, we apply Luce Spectral Ranking (Maystre and Grossglauser, 2016). This preprocessing might affect the quality of labels.

In general, the datasets are clustered into two rather dense groups and this clustering does not match the separation of the datasets among TST and PG tasks. The different behavior of the tested

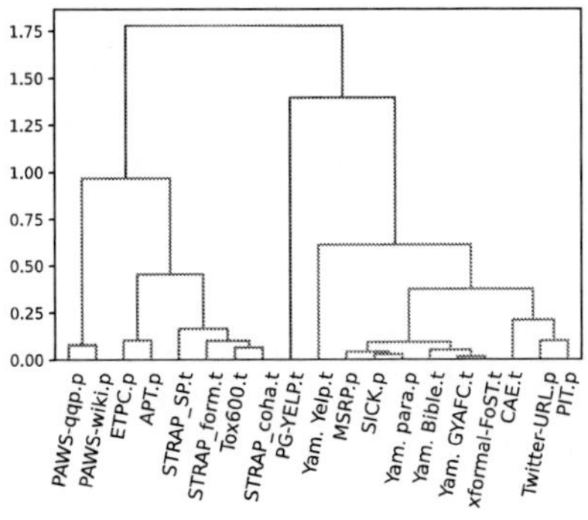

Figure 5: Dendrogram of vectors of measures correlations on a dataset. The height of the bar indicates the distance between vectors or groups of vectors. Postfixes 'p' and 't' denote the datasets for PG and TST tasks, respectively.

measures might be explained by the way the data is annotated. For example, the PAWS datasets were collected in an adversarial manner (by shuffling the words in sentences), STRAP datasets were generated with TST models, and Yam. datasets were annotated by a similar group of workers — these three sets form clusters in the dendrogram.

6 Using automatic measures to rank text style transfer systems

While above we compared automatic and human ranking of individual text pairs, our final goal is to find a measure to rank TST or PG *systems*. Six TST datasets used in our analysis were created by running several TST models on the same dataset and manually assessing the degree of content preservation in the resulting text pairs. They cover diverse tasks: formality transfer (xformal-FoST and STRAP_form datasets), text detoxification (Tox600 and CAE datasets), Shakespeare style transfer (STRAP_SP), and sentiment transfer (PG-YELP). We use the human judgments on content preservation from these datasets to rate the ability of various measures to rank text style transfer systems.

For brevity and clarity, we do not report the results of this analysis for all measures. Instead, we select the best-performing measure from each group:

- **cross-encoders**: MIS, RobNLI/mean, BLEURT-L128 and cross-stsb-base,
- **bi-encoders**: LaBSE and SIMCSE-SL (supervised, using ROBERTa-large),
- **embedding-based models**: SIMILE, BERTScore (with microsoft/deberta-xlarge-mnli model), and WMD,
- **ngram-based measures**: BLEU and ChrF.

Measure	Measure type	ρ	*acc*
MIS	2x-asym-cross-enc	0.93	0.50
BLEURT-L128	asym-cross-enc	0.92	0.83
RobNLI/mean	2x-asym-cross-enc	0.83	0.50
cross-stsb-base	sym-cross-enc	0.63	0.50
SIMCSE-SL	emb-bi-enc	0.60	0.50
LaBSE	emb-bi-enc	0.58	0.67
bertscore-Mic-Deberta	emb-context	0.55	0.50
SIMILE	emb-bi-enc	0.38	0.33
BLEU	ngram	0.10	0.17
w2v_wmd	emb-static	0.03	0.17
chrf	ngram	0.03	0.17

Table 4: Mean rank correlation (ρ) of text style transfer system-level automatic scores with human judgments, and percentage of cases when they correctly identify the best system (*acc*).

We show the results aggregated across the datasets in Table 4. The scores for individual datasets and measures and a list of measures managed to identify the best-performing model for a given dataset are given in Appendix C.

No measure can fully match the system rankings produced by humans. However, our MIS measure and BLEURT have the highest correlations with human judgments. BLEURT performs best on this task because it correctly identifies the winner on 5 datasets out of 6. The popular measures BLEU, ChrF, and WMD identify the best system only on the xformal-FoST dataset.

7 Computational efficiency of the measures

While the correlation of measures with human judgments is important, the usability of the measure in real tasks can not be treated in isolation from its computational efficiency. The main capabilities of such measures are robustness and inference speed.

One of the key functions of content preservation measures is to compare different TST or PG approaches with each other and ensure that different runs of the learning-based measure yield similar results. This problem does not apply to words or character n-grams-based models. However, this could yield some issues with trainable model-based measures. That is why it is crucial for all such measures to open-source trained weights. Moreover, when using such measures for comparison it is nec-

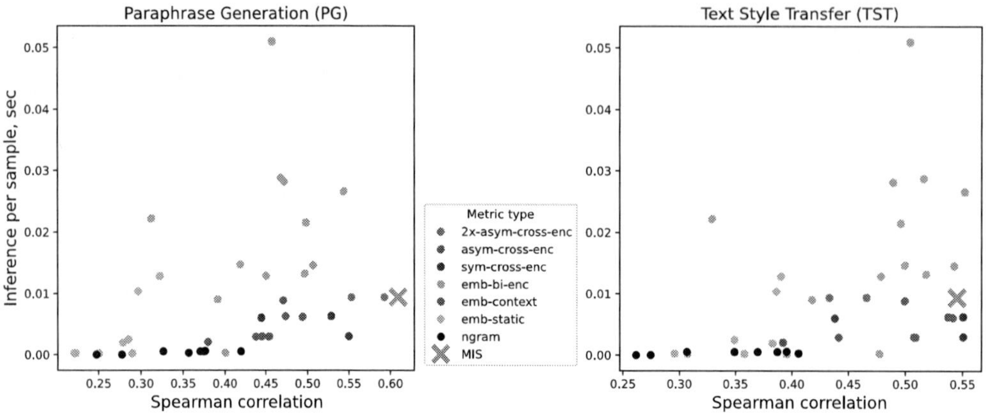

Figure 6: Dependence of time necessary for calculating similarity score for one sample and average correlation of a measure on text style transfer and paraphrases generation tasks.

essary to put the model into inference mode and freeze all layers. In such a case the model-based measures yield similar scores to similar text pairs regardless of the number of attempts or any hardware properties.

Another blocker to the usage of a certain measure could be a long inference time. We conduct additional experiments by calculating the average inference time per sample for a subset of measures representing each class w.r.t. the average correlation of the measure on the task. We concatenate texts from both tasks into two united datasets. For trainable measures, we use a data loader with a batch size equal to eight. We load all trainable models to NVIDIA GeForce RTX 2080 Ti. All other measures are calculated sample-wise on Intel(R) Xeon(R) Gold 5217 CPU @ 3.00GHz . We plot the results on Figure 6.

The most optimal measures are located at the bottom right corner of these plots, which means that the measure requires the least possible computational time and at the same time demonstrates a high correlation with human judgments. For the PG task, the MIS measure demonstrates the best performance and its average inference time is at the approximately same level as most of the other model-based measures. For TST task symmetric and asymmetric cross-encoders are the most optimal.

8 Conclusions

As our experiments show, encoder-based measures of content preservation correlate with human judgments much better than the traditional word or character-based measures such as BLEU on a wide range of datasets. In all paraphrase datasets and 9 out of 10 text style transfer datasets, the best-performing measures are based on the cross-encoder or bi-encoder architecture.

We suggest a measure called MIS which is based on the idea that texts with similar meanings mutually entail each other. We show that the proposed architecture outperforms other measures in the evaluation of paraphrases and performs on par with the top-performing measures in the evaluation of text style transfer. More specifically, it is particularly successful in transferring between contemporary and old English and between formal and informal styles. Thus, we recommend using this measure for content preservation scoring for paraphrases and TST tasks in the aforementioned tasks and to use BLEURT for other TST tasks.

While the best measures in our analysis improve over the popular ones (e.g. BLEU) by a large margin, their correlation with human judgments is still far from perfect. We expect that even better measures of content preservation will be proposed in the nearest future. We also hope that the MIS measure and the performed large scale computational study could be applied to other NLP tasks, such as machine translation, text summarization, etc.

Acknowledgements

This work was supported by MTS-Skoltech laboratory on AI.

References

Mikel Artetxe and Holger Schwenk. 2019. Massively multilingual sentence embeddings for zero-shot cross-lingual transfer and beyond. *Transactions of the Association for Computational Linguistics*, 7:597–610.

Satanjeev Banerjee and Alon Lavie. 2005. METEOR: An automatic metric for MT evaluation with improved correlation with human judgments. In *Proceedings of the ACL Workshop on Intrinsic and Extrinsic Evaluation Measures for Machine Translation and/or Summarization*, pages 65–72, Ann Arbor, Michigan. Association for Computational Linguistics.

Piotr Bojanowski, Edouard Grave, Armand Joulin, and Tomas Mikolov. 2017. Enriching word vectors with subword information. *Transactions of the Association for Computational Linguistics*, 5:135–146.

Samuel R. Bowman, Gabor Angeli, Christopher Potts, and Christopher D. Manning. 2015. A large annotated corpus for learning natural language inference. In *Proceedings of the 2015 Conference on Empirical Methods in Natural Language Processing*, pages 632–642, Lisbon, Portugal. Association for Computational Linguistics.

Eleftheria Briakou, Sweta Agrawal, Joel Tetreault, and Marine Carpuat. 2021. Evaluating the evaluation metrics for style transfer: A case study in multilingual formality transfer. In *Proceedings of the 2021 Conference on Empirical Methods in Natural Language Processing*, pages 1321–1336, Online and Punta Cana, Dominican Republic. Association for Computational Linguistics.

Yixin Cao, Ruihao Shui, Liangming Pan, Min-Yen Kan, Zhiyuan Liu, and Tat-Seng Chua. 2020. Expertise style transfer: A new task towards better communication between experts and laymen. In *Proceedings of the 58th Annual Meeting of the Association for Computational Linguistics*, pages 1061–1071, Online. Association for Computational Linguistics.

Keith Carlson, Allen Riddell, and Daniel Rockmore. 2018. Evaluating prose style transfer with the bible. *Royal Society open science*, 5(10):171920.

Daniel Cer, Mona Diab, Eneko Agirre, Iñigo Lopez-Gazpio, and Lucia Specia. 2017. SemEval-2017 task 1: Semantic textual similarity multilingual and crosslingual focused evaluation. In *Proceedings of the 11th International Workshop on Semantic Evaluation (SemEval-2017)*, pages 1–14, Vancouver, Canada. Association for Computational Linguistics.

Daniel Cer, Yinfei Yang, Sheng-yi Kong, Nan Hua, Nicole Limtiaco, Rhomni St. John, Noah Constant, Mario Guajardo-Cespedes, Steve Yuan, Chris Tar, Brian Strope, and Ray Kurzweil. 2018. Universal sentence encoder for English. In *Proceedings of the 2018 Conference on Empirical Methods in Natural Language Processing: System Demonstrations*, pages 169–174, Brussels, Belgium. Association for Computational Linguistics.

David Chen and William Dolan. 2011. Collecting highly parallel data for paraphrase evaluation. In *Proceedings of the 49th Annual Meeting of the Association for Computational Linguistics: Human Language Technologies*, pages 190–200, Portland, Oregon, USA. Association for Computational Linguistics.

Mingda Chen, Qingming Tang, Sam Wiseman, and Kevin Gimpel. 2019. Controllable paraphrase generation with a syntactic exemplar. In *Proceedings of the 57th Annual Meeting of the Association for Computational Linguistics*, pages 5972–5984, Florence, Italy. Association for Computational Linguistics.

Ning Dai, Jianze Liang, Xipeng Qiu, and Xuanjing Huang. 2019. Style transformer: Unpaired text style transfer without disentangled latent representation. In *Proceedings of the 57th Annual Meeting of the Association for Computational Linguistics*, pages 5997–6007, Florence, Italy. Association for Computational Linguistics.

David Dale, Anton Voronov, Daryna Dementieva, Varvara Logacheva, Olga Kozlova, Nikita Semenov, and Alexander Panchenko. 2021. Text detoxification using large pre-trained neural models. In *Proceedings of the 2021 Conference on Empirical Methods in Natural Language Processing*, pages 7979–7996, Online and Punta Cana, Dominican Republic. Association for Computational Linguistics.

Mingkai Deng, Bowen Tan, Zhengzhong Liu, Eric Xing, and Zhiting Hu. 2021. Compression, transduction, and creation: A unified framework for evaluating natural language generation. In *Proceedings of the 2021 Conference on Empirical Methods in Natural Language Processing*, pages 7580–7605, Online and Punta Cana, Dominican Republic. Association for Computational Linguistics.

William B. Dolan and Chris Brockett. 2005. Automatically constructing a corpus of sentential paraphrases. In *Proceedings of the Third International Workshop on Paraphrasing (IWP2005)*.

Elozino Egonmwan and Yllias Chali. 2019. Transformer and seq2seq model for paraphrase generation. In *Proceedings of the 3rd Workshop on Neural Generation and Translation*, pages 249–255, Hong Kong. Association for Computational Linguistics.

Fangxiaoyu Feng, Yinfei Yang, Daniel Cer, Naveen Arivazhagan, and Wei Wang. 2020. Language-agnostic bert sentence embedding. *arXiv preprint arXiv:2007.01852*.

Yao Fu, Yansong Feng, and John P. Cunningham. 2020. Paraphrase generation with latent bag of words.

Zhenxin Fu, Xiaoye Tan, Nanyun Peng, Dongyan Zhao, and Rui Yan. 2018. Style transfer in text: Exploration and evaluation. In *Proceedings of the Thirty-Second*

AAAI Conference on Artificial Intelligence, (AAAI-18), the 30th innovative Applications of Artificial Intelligence (IAAI-18), and the 8th AAAI Symposium on Educational Advances in Artificial Intelligence (EAAI-18), New Orleans, Louisiana, USA, February 2-7, 2018, pages 663–670. AAAI Press.

Tianyu Gao, Xingcheng Yao, and Danqi Chen. 2021. SimCSE: Simple contrastive learning of sentence embeddings. In *Proceedings of the 2021 Conference on Empirical Methods in Natural Language Processing*, pages 6894–6910, Online and Punta Cana, Dominican Republic. Association for Computational Linguistics.

Hongyu Gong, Linfeng Song, and Suma Bhat. 2020. Rich syntactic and semantic information helps unsupervised text style transfer. In *Proceedings of the 13th International Conference on Natural Language Generation*, pages 113–119, Dublin, Ireland. Association for Computational Linguistics.

Tanya Goyal and Greg Durrett. 2020. Neural syntactic preordering for controlled paraphrase generation. In *Proceedings of the 58th Annual Meeting of the Association for Computational Linguistics*, pages 238–252, Online. Association for Computational Linguistics.

Yvette Graham and Timothy Baldwin. 2014. Testing for significance of increased correlation with human judgment. In *Proceedings of the 2014 Conference on Empirical Methods in Natural Language Processing (EMNLP)*, pages 172–176, Doha, Qatar. Association for Computational Linguistics.

Ankush Gupta, Arvind Agarwal, Prawaan Singh, and Piyush Rai. 2018. A deep generative framework for paraphrase generation. *Proceedings of the AAAI Conference on Artificial Intelligence*, 32(1).

Hua He, Kevin Gimpel, and Jimmy Lin. 2015. Multi-perspective sentence similarity modeling with convolutional neural networks. In *Proceedings of the 2015 Conference on Empirical Methods in Natural Language Processing*, pages 1576–1586, Lisbon, Portugal. Association for Computational Linguistics.

Junxian He, Xinyi Wang, Graham Neubig, and Taylor Berg-Kirkpatrick. 2020. A probabilistic formulation of unsupervised text style transfer. In *8th International Conference on Learning Representations, ICLR 2020, Addis Ababa, Ethiopia, April 26-30, 2020*. OpenReview.net.

Pengcheng He, Xiaodong Liu, Jianfeng Gao, and Weizhu Chen. 2021. Deberta: Decoding-enhanced bert with disentangled attention. In *International Conference on Learning Representations.*

Mingxuan Hu and Min He. 2021. Non-parallel text style transfer with domain adaptation and an attention model. *Appl. Intell.*, 51(7):4609–4622.

Zhiting Hu, Zichao Yang, Xiaodan Liang, Ruslan Salakhutdinov, and Eric P. Xing. 2017. Toward controlled generation of text. In *Proceedings of the 34th International Conference on Machine Learning, ICML 2017, Sydney, NSW, Australia, 6-11 August 2017*, volume 70 of *Proceedings of Machine Learning Research*, pages 1587–1596. PMLR.

Parag Jain, Abhijit Mishra, Amar Prakash Azad, and Karthik Sankaranarayanan. 2019. Unsupervised controllable text formalization. In *The Thirty-Third AAAI Conference on Artificial Intelligence, AAAI 2019, The Thirty-First Innovative Applications of Artificial Intelligence Conference, IAAI 2019, The Ninth AAAI Symposium on Educational Advances in Artificial Intelligence, EAAI 2019, Honolulu, Hawaii, USA, January 27 - February 1, 2019*, pages 6554–6561. AAAI Press.

Matthew A Jaro. 1989. Advances in record-linkage methodology as applied to matching the 1985 census of tampa, florida. *Journal of the American Statistical Association*, 84(406):414–420.

Harsh Jhamtani, Varun Gangal, Eduard Hovy, and Eric Nyberg. 2017. Shakespearizing modern language using copy-enriched sequence to sequence models. In *Proceedings of the Workshop on Stylistic Variation*, pages 10–19, Copenhagen, Denmark. Association for Computational Linguistics.

Vineet John, Lili Mou, Hareesh Bahuleyan, and Olga Vechtomova. 2019. Disentangled representation learning for non-parallel text style transfer. In *Proceedings of the 57th Annual Meeting of the Association for Computational Linguistics*, pages 424–434, Florence, Italy. Association for Computational Linguistics.

Tomoyuki Kajiwara. 2019. Negative lexically constrained decoding for paraphrase generation. In *Proceedings of the 57th Annual Meeting of the Association for Computational Linguistics*, pages 6047–6052, Florence, Italy. Association for Computational Linguistics.

Hassan Kane, Muhammed Yusuf Kocyigit, Ali Abdalla, Pelkins Ajanoh, and Mohamed Coulibali. 2020. NUBIA: NeUral based interchangeability assessor for text generation. In *Proceedings of the 1st Workshop on Evaluating NLG Evaluation*, pages 28–37, Online (Dublin, Ireland). Association for Computational Linguistics.

Venelin Kovatchev, M. Antònia Martí, and Maria Salamó. 2018. ETPC - a paraphrase identification corpus annotated with extended paraphrase typology and negation. In *Proceedings of the Eleventh International Conference on Language Resources and Evaluation (LREC 2018)*, Miyazaki, Japan. European Language Resources Association (ELRA).

Ben Krause, Akhilesh Deepak Gotmare, Bryan McCann, Nitish Shirish Keskar, Shafiq Joty, Richard Socher, and Nazneen Fatema Rajani. 2021. GeDi: Generative discriminator guided sequence generation. In *Findings of the Association for Computational Linguistics: EMNLP 2021*, pages 4929–4952, Punta

Cana, Dominican Republic. Association for Computational Linguistics.

Kalpesh Krishna, John Wieting, and Mohit Iyyer. 2020. Reformulating unsupervised style transfer as paraphrase generation. In *Proceedings of the 2020 Conference on Empirical Methods in Natural Language Processing (EMNLP)*, pages 737–762, Online. Association for Computational Linguistics.

Matt Kusner, Yu Sun, Nicholas Kolkin, and Kilian Weinberger. 2015. From word embeddings to document distances. In *International conference on machine learning*, pages 957–966. PMLR.

Chih-Te Lai, Yi-Te Hong, Hong-You Chen, Chi-Jen Lu, and Shou-De Lin. 2019. Multiple text style transfer by using word-level conditional generative adversarial network with two-phase training. In *Proceedings of the 2019 Conference on Empirical Methods in Natural Language Processing and the 9th International Joint Conference on Natural Language Processing (EMNLP-IJCNLP)*, pages 3579–3584, Hong Kong, China. Association for Computational Linguistics.

Huiyuan Lai, Antonio Toral, and Malvina Nissim. 2021. Thank you BART! rewarding pre-trained models improves formality style transfer. In *Proceedings of the 59th Annual Meeting of the Association for Computational Linguistics and the 11th International Joint Conference on Natural Language Processing (Volume 2: Short Papers)*, pages 484–494, Online. Association for Computational Linguistics.

Wuwei Lan, Siyu Qiu, Hua He, and Wei Xu. 2017. A continuously growing dataset of sentential paraphrases. In *Proceedings of the 2017 Conference on Empirical Methods in Natural Language Processing*, pages 1224–1234, Copenhagen, Denmark. Association for Computational Linguistics.

Léo Laugier, John Pavlopoulos, Jeffrey Sorensen, and Lucas Dixon. 2021. Civil rephrases of toxic texts with self-supervised transformers. In *Proceedings of the 16th Conference of the European Chapter of the Association for Computational Linguistics: Main Volume*, pages 1442–1461, Online. Association for Computational Linguistics.

Dongkyu Lee, Zhiliang Tian, Lanqing Xue, and Nevin L. Zhang. 2021. Enhancing content preservation in text style transfer using reverse attention and conditional layer normalization. In *Proceedings of the 59th Annual Meeting of the Association for Computational Linguistics and the 11th International Joint Conference on Natural Language Processing (Volume 1: Long Papers)*, pages 93–102, Online. Association for Computational Linguistics.

Vladimir I Levenshtein et al. 1966. Binary codes capable of correcting deletions, insertions, and reversals. In *Soviet physics doklady*, volume 10, pages 707–710. Soviet Union.

Mike Lewis, Yinhan Liu, Naman Goyal, Marjan Ghazvininejad, Abdelrahman Mohamed, Omer Levy, Veselin Stoyanov, and Luke Zettlemoyer. 2020. BART: Denoising sequence-to-sequence pre-training for natural language generation, translation, and comprehension. In *Proceedings of the 58th Annual Meeting of the Association for Computational Linguistics*, pages 7871–7880, Online. Association for Computational Linguistics.

Dianqi Li, Yizhe Zhang, Zhe Gan, Yu Cheng, Chris Brockett, Bill Dolan, and Ming-Ting Sun. 2019a. Domain adaptive text style transfer. In *Proceedings of the 2019 Conference on Empirical Methods in Natural Language Processing and the 9th International Joint Conference on Natural Language Processing (EMNLP-IJCNLP)*, pages 3304–3313, Hong Kong, China. Association for Computational Linguistics.

Juncen Li, Robin Jia, He He, and Percy Liang. 2018. Delete, retrieve, generate: a simple approach to sentiment and style transfer. In *Proceedings of the 2018 Conference of the North American Chapter of the Association for Computational Linguistics: Human Language Technologies, Volume 1 (Long Papers)*, pages 1865–1874, New Orleans, Louisiana. Association for Computational Linguistics.

Xiao Li, Guanyi Chen, Chenghua Lin, and Ruizhe Li. 2020. DGST: a dual-generator network for text style transfer. In *Proceedings of the 2020 Conference on Empirical Methods in Natural Language Processing (EMNLP)*, pages 7131–7136, Online. Association for Computational Linguistics.

Zichao Li, Xin Jiang, Lifeng Shang, and Qun Liu. 2019b. Decomposable neural paraphrase generation. In *Proceedings of the 57th Annual Meeting of the Association for Computational Linguistics*, pages 3403–3414, Florence, Italy. Association for Computational Linguistics.

Chin-Yew Lin. 2004. Rouge: A package for automatic evaluation of summaries. In *Text summarization branches out*, pages 74–81.

Yinhan Liu, Myle Ott, Naman Goyal, Jingfei Du, Mandar Joshi, Danqi Chen, Omer Levy, Mike Lewis, Luke Zettlemoyer, and Veselin Stoyanov. 2019. Roberta: A robustly optimized bert pretraining approach. *arXiv preprint arXiv:1907.11692*.

Lajanugen Logeswaran, Honglak Lee, and Samy Bengio. 2018. Content preserving text generation with attribute controls. In *Advances in Neural Information Processing Systems 31: Annual Conference on Neural Information Processing Systems 2018, NeurIPS 2018, December 3-8, 2018, Montréal, Canada*, pages 5108–5118.

Fuli Luo, Peng Li, Jie Zhou, Pengcheng Yang, Baobao Chang, Xu Sun, and Zhifang Sui. 2019. A dual reinforcement learning framework for unsupervised text style transfer. In *Proceedings of the Twenty-Eighth International Joint Conference on Artificial*

Intelligence, IJCAI 2019, Macao, China, August 10-16, 2019, pages 5116–5122. ijcai.org.

Lucas Maystre and Matthias Grossglauser. 2016. Fast and accurate inference of plackett – luce models supplementary material.

Tomas Mikolov, Kai Chen, Greg Corrado, and Jeffrey Dean. 2013. Efficient estimation of word representations in vector space. *arXiv preprint arXiv:1301.3781*.

Remi Mir, Bjarke Felbo, Nick Obradovich, and Iyad Rahwan. 2019. Evaluating style transfer for text. In *Proceedings of the 2019 Conference of the North American Chapter of the Association for Computational Linguistics: Human Language Technologies, Volume 1 (Long and Short Papers)*, pages 495–504, Minneapolis, Minnesota. Association for Computational Linguistics.

Jonas Mueller, David K. Gifford, and Tommi S. Jaakkola. 2017. Sequence to better sequence: Continuous revision of combinatorial structures. In *Proceedings of the 34th International Conference on Machine Learning, ICML 2017, Sydney, NSW, Australia, 6-11 August 2017*, volume 70 of *Proceedings of Machine Learning Research*, pages 2536–2544. PMLR.

Yixin Nie, Haonan Chen, and Mohit Bansal. 2019. Combining fact extraction and verification with neural semantic matching networks. In *Association for the Advancement of Artificial Intelligence (AAAI)*.

Yixin Nie, Adina Williams, Emily Dinan, Mohit Bansal, Jason Weston, and Douwe Kiela. 2020. Adversarial NLI: A new benchmark for natural language understanding. In *Proceedings of the 58th Annual Meeting of the Association for Computational Linguistics*, pages 4885–4901, Online. Association for Computational Linguistics.

Animesh Nighojkar and John Licato. 2021. Improving paraphrase detection with the adversarial paraphrasing task. In *Proceedings of the 59th Annual Meeting of the Association for Computational Linguistics and the 11th International Joint Conference on Natural Language Processing (Volume 1: Long Papers)*, pages 7106–7116, Online. Association for Computational Linguistics.

Alexander Panchenko and Olga Morozova. 2012. A study of hybrid similarity measures for semantic relation extraction. In *Proceedings of the Workshop on Innovative Hybrid Approaches to the Processing of Textual Data*, pages 10–18.

Richard Yuanzhe Pang and Kevin Gimpel. 2019. Unsupervised evaluation metrics and learning criteria for non-parallel textual transfer. In *Proceedings of the 3rd Workshop on Neural Generation and Translation*, pages 138–147, Hong Kong. Association for Computational Linguistics.

Kishore Papineni, Salim Roukos, Todd Ward, and Wei-Jing Zhu. 2002. Bleu: a method for automatic evaluation of machine translation. In *Proceedings of the 40th annual meeting of the Association for Computational Linguistics*, pages 311–318.

Jeffrey Pennington, Richard Socher, and Christopher Manning. 2014. GloVe: Global vectors for word representation. In *Proceedings of the 2014 Conference on Empirical Methods in Natural Language Processing (EMNLP)*, pages 1532–1543, Doha, Qatar. Association for Computational Linguistics.

Maja Popović. 2015. chrF: character n-gram F-score for automatic MT evaluation. In *Proceedings of the Tenth Workshop on Statistical Machine Translation*, pages 392–395, Lisbon, Portugal. Association for Computational Linguistics.

Shrimai Prabhumoye, Yulia Tsvetkov, Ruslan Salakhutdinov, and Alan W Black. 2018. Style transfer through back-translation. In *Proceedings of the 56th Annual Meeting of the Association for Computational Linguistics (Volume 1: Long Papers)*, pages 866–876, Melbourne, Australia. Association for Computational Linguistics.

Alec Radford, Rafal Józefowicz, and Ilya Sutskever. 2017. Learning to generate reviews and discovering sentiment. *CoRR*, abs/1704.01444.

Chinmay Rane, Gaël Dias, Alexis Lechervy, and Asif Ekbal. 2021. Improving neural text style transfer by introducing loss function sequentiality. In *SIGIR '21: The 44th International ACM SIGIR Conference on Research and Development in Information Retrieval, Virtual Event, Canada, July 11-15, 2021*, pages 2197–2201. ACM.

Sudha Rao and Joel Tetreault. 2018. Dear sir or madam, may I introduce the GYAFC dataset: Corpus, benchmarks and metrics for formality style transfer. In *Proceedings of the 2018 Conference of the North American Chapter of the Association for Computational Linguistics: Human Language Technologies, Volume 1 (Long Papers)*, pages 129–140, New Orleans, Louisiana. Association for Computational Linguistics.

Nils Reimers and Iryna Gurevych. 2019. Sentence-BERT: Sentence embeddings using Siamese BERT-networks. In *Proceedings of the 2019 Conference on Empirical Methods in Natural Language Processing and the 9th International Joint Conference on Natural Language Processing (EMNLP-IJCNLP)*, pages 3982–3992, Hong Kong, China. Association for Computational Linguistics.

Parker Riley, Noah Constant, Mandy Guo, Girish Kumar, David Uthus, and Zarana Parekh. 2021. TextSETTR: Few-shot text style extraction and tunable targeted restyling. In *Proceedings of the 59th Annual Meeting of the Association for Computational Linguistics and the 11th International Joint Conference on Natural Language Processing (Volume 1:*

Long Papers), pages 3786–3800, Online. Association for Computational Linguistics.

Thibault Sellam, Dipanjan Das, and Ankur Parikh. 2020. BLEURT: Learning robust metrics for text generation. In *Proceedings of the 58th Annual Meeting of the Association for Computational Linguistics*, pages 7881–7892, Online. Association for Computational Linguistics.

Lakshay Sharma, Laura Graesser, Nikita Nangia, and Utku Evci. 2019. Natural language understanding with the quora question pairs dataset.

Shikhar Sharma, Layla El Asri, Hannes Schulz, and Jeremie Zumer. 2017. Relevance of unsupervised metrics in task-oriented dialogue for evaluating natural language generation.

Tianxiao Shen, Tao Lei, Regina Barzilay, and Tommi S. Jaakkola. 2017. Style transfer from non-parallel text by cross-alignment. In *Advances in Neural Information Processing Systems 30: Annual Conference on Neural Information Processing Systems 2017, December 4-9, 2017, Long Beach, CA, USA*, pages 6830–6841.

Tianxiao Shen, Jonas Mueller, Regina Barzilay, and Tommi S. Jaakkola. 2020a. Educating text autoencoders: Latent representation guidance via denoising. In *Proceedings of the 37th International Conference on Machine Learning, ICML 2020, 13-18 July 2020, Virtual Event*, volume 119 of *Proceedings of Machine Learning Research*, pages 8719–8729. PMLR.

Tianxiao Shen, Victor Quach, Regina Barzilay, and Tommi Jaakkola. 2020b. Blank language models. In *Proceedings of the 2020 Conference on Empirical Methods in Natural Language Processing (EMNLP)*, pages 5186–5198, Online. Association for Computational Linguistics.

Yukai Shi, Sen Zhang, Chenxing Zhou, Xiaodan Liang, Xiaojun Yang, and Liang Lin. 2021. GTAE: graph transformer-based auto-encoders for linguistic-constrained text style transfer. *ACM Trans. Intell. Syst. Technol.*, 12(3):32:1–32:16.

Eric Michael Smith, Diana Gonzalez-Rico, Emily Dinan, and Y-Lan Boureau. 2019. Zero-shot fine-grained style transfer: Leveraging distributed continuous style representations to transfer to unseen styles. *CoRR*, abs/1911.03914.

Matthew Snover, Bonnie Dorr, Rich Schwartz, Linnea Micciulla, and John Makhoul. 2006. A study of translation edit rate with targeted human annotation. In *Proceedings of the 7th Conference of the Association for Machine Translation in the Americas: Technical Papers*, pages 223–231, Cambridge, Massachusetts, USA. Association for Machine Translation in the Americas.

Sandeep Subramanian, Guillaume Lample, Eric Michael Smith, Ludovic Denoyer, Marc'Aurelio Ranzato, and Y-Lan Boureau. 2018. Multiple-attribute text style transfer. *CoRR*, abs/1811.00552.

Akhilesh Sudhakar, Bhargav Upadhyay, and Arjun Maheswaran. 2019. "transforming" delete, retrieve, generate approach for controlled text style transfer. In *Proceedings of the 2019 Conference on Empirical Methods in Natural Language Processing and the 9th International Joint Conference on Natural Language Processing (EMNLP-IJCNLP)*, pages 3269–3279, Hong Kong, China. Association for Computational Linguistics.

Jiao Sun, Xuezhe Ma, and Nanyun Peng. 2021. AESOP: Paraphrase generation with adaptive syntactic control. In *Proceedings of the 2021 Conference on Empirical Methods in Natural Language Processing*, pages 5176–5189, Online and Punta Cana, Dominican Republic. Association for Computational Linguistics.

Youzhi Tian, Zhiting Hu, and Zhou Yu. 2018a. Structured content preservation for unsupervised text style transfer. *arXiv preprint arXiv:1810.06526*.

Youzhi Tian, Zhiting Hu, and Zhou Yu. 2018b. Structured content preservation for unsupervised text style transfer. *CoRR*, abs/1810.06526.

Ke Wang, Hang Hua, and Xiaojun Wan. 2019. Controllable unsupervised text attribute transfer via editing entangled latent representation. In *Advances in Neural Information Processing Systems 32: Annual Conference on Neural Information Processing Systems 2019, NeurIPS 2019, December 8-14, 2019, Vancouver, BC, Canada*, pages 11034–11044.

Su Wang, Rahul Gupta, Nancy Chang, and Jason Baldridge. 2018. A task in a suit and a tie: paraphrase generation with semantic augmentation. *CoRR*, abs/1811.00119.

John Wieting, Taylor Berg-Kirkpatrick, Kevin Gimpel, and Graham Neubig. 2019. Beyond BLEU:training neural machine translation with semantic similarity. In *Proceedings of the 57th Annual Meeting of the Association for Computational Linguistics*, pages 4344–4355, Florence, Italy. Association for Computational Linguistics.

Adina Williams, Nikita Nangia, and Samuel Bowman. 2018. A broad-coverage challenge corpus for sentence understanding through inference. In *Proceedings of the 2018 Conference of the North American Chapter of the Association for Computational Linguistics: Human Language Technologies, Volume 1 (Long Papers)*, pages 1112–1122, New Orleans, Louisiana. Association for Computational Linguistics.

Chen Wu, Xuancheng Ren, Fuli Luo, and Xu Sun. 2019a. A hierarchical reinforced sequence operation method for unsupervised text style transfer. In *Proceedings of the 57th Annual Meeting of the Association for Computational Linguistics*, pages 4873–4883, Florence, Italy. Association for Computational Linguistics.

Xing Wu, Tao Zhang, Liangjun Zang, Jizhong Han, and Songlin Hu. 2019b. "mask and infill" : Applying masked language model to sentiment transfer. *CoRR*, abs/1908.08039.

Jingjing Xu, Xu Sun, Qi Zeng, Xiaodong Zhang, Xuancheng Ren, Houfeng Wang, and Wenjie Li. 2018. Unpaired sentiment-to-sentiment translation: A cycled reinforcement learning approach. In *Proceedings of the 56th Annual Meeting of the Association for Computational Linguistics (Volume 1: Long Papers)*, pages 979–988, Melbourne, Australia. Association for Computational Linguistics.

Peng Xu, Jackie Chi Kit Cheung, and Yanshuai Cao. 2020. On variational learning of controllable representations for text without supervision. In *Proceedings of the 37th International Conference on Machine Learning, ICML 2020, 13-18 July 2020, Virtual Event*, volume 119 of *Proceedings of Machine Learning Research*, pages 10534–10543. PMLR.

Ruochen Xu, Tao Ge, and Furu Wei. 2019. Formality style transfer with hybrid textual annotations. *CoRR*, abs/1903.06353.

Wei Xu, Alan Ritter, Chris Callison-Burch, William B. Dolan, and Yangfeng Ji. 2014. Extracting lexically divergent paraphrases from Twitter. *Transactions of the Association for Computational Linguistics*, 2:435–448.

Ivan P. Yamshchikov, Viacheslav Shibaev, Nikolay Khlebnikov, and Alexey Tikhonov. 2021. Style-transfer and paraphrase: Looking for a sensible semantic similarity metric. *Proceedings of the AAAI Conference on Artificial Intelligence*, 35(16):14213–14220.

Qian Yang, Zhouyuan Huo, Dinghan Shen, Yong Cheng, Wenlin Wang, Guoyin Wang, and Lawrence Carin. 2019a. An end-to-end generative architecture for paraphrase generation. In *Proceedings of the 2019 Conference on Empirical Methods in Natural Language Processing and the 9th International Joint Conference on Natural Language Processing (EMNLP-IJCNLP)*, pages 3132–3142, Hong Kong, China. Association for Computational Linguistics.

Yinfei Yang, Yuan Zhang, Chris Tar, and Jason Baldridge. 2019b. PAWS-X: A cross-lingual adversarial dataset for paraphrase identification. In *Proceedings of the 2019 Conference on Empirical Methods in Natural Language Processing and the 9th International Joint Conference on Natural Language Processing (EMNLP-IJCNLP)*, pages 3687–3692, Hong Kong, China. Association for Computational Linguistics.

Zichao Yang, Zhiting Hu, Chris Dyer, Eric P Xing, and Taylor Berg-Kirkpatrick. 2018. Unsupervised text style transfer using language models as discriminators. In *Advances in Neural Information Processing Systems*, volume 31. Curran Associates, Inc.

Weizhe Yuan, Graham Neubig, and Pengfei Liu. 2021. Bartscore: Evaluating generated text as text generation.

Tianyi Zhang, Varsha Kishore, Felix Wu, Kilian Q Weinberger, and Yoav Artzi. 2019. Bertscore: Evaluating text generation with bert. *arXiv preprint arXiv:1904.09675*.

Yi Zhang, Tao Ge, and Xu Sun. 2020. Parallel data augmentation for formality style transfer. In *Proceedings of the 58th Annual Meeting of the Association for Computational Linguistics*, pages 3221–3228, Online. Association for Computational Linguistics.

Yi Zhang, Jingjing Xu, Pengcheng Yang, and Xu Sun. 2018a. Learning sentiment memories for sentiment modification without parallel data. In *Proceedings of the 2018 Conference on Empirical Methods in Natural Language Processing*, pages 1103–1108, Brussels, Belgium. Association for Computational Linguistics.

Zhirui Zhang, Shuo Ren, Shujie Liu, Jianyong Wang, Peng Chen, Mu Li, Ming Zhou, and Enhong Chen. 2018b. Style transfer as unsupervised machine translation. *CoRR*, abs/1808.07894.

Junbo Jake Zhao, Yoon Kim, Kelly Zhang, Alexander M. Rush, and Yann LeCun. 2018. Adversarially regularized autoencoders. In *Proceedings of the 35th International Conference on Machine Learning, ICML 2018, Stockholmsmässan, Stockholm, Sweden, July 10-15, 2018*, volume 80 of *Proceedings of Machine Learning Research*, pages 5897–5906. PMLR.

Wei Zhao, Maxime Peyrard, Fei Liu, Yang Gao, Christian M. Meyer, and Steffen Eger. 2019. MoverScore: Text generation evaluating with contextualized embeddings and earth mover distance. In *Proceedings of the 2019 Conference on Empirical Methods in Natural Language Processing and the 9th International Joint Conference on Natural Language Processing (EMNLP-IJCNLP)*, pages 563–578, Hong Kong, China. Association for Computational Linguistics.

Liu Zhuang, Lin Wayne, Shi Ya, and Zhao Jun. 2021. A robustly optimized BERT pre-training approach with post-training. In *Proceedings of the 20th Chinese National Conference on Computational Linguistics*, pages 1218–1227, Huhhot, China. Chinese Information Processing Society of China.

A Datasets

Name	Comment	Size
ETPC	all data from textual_np_pos and textual_np_neg files	6004
PAWS-qqp	dev_and_test.tsv from qqp part used	677
PAWS-wiki	Test split from PAWS-Wiki Labeled (Final)	8000
Twitter-URL	Test split used	10120
PIT	Test split used	972
MSR	Test split used	1630
APT	Test split used (ap-h-test)	1252
Yam. para	Data from Paralex,Parphrase folder used	3223
SICK	Test split form SICK_test_annotated used	4927

Table 5: Paraphrase generation (PG) datasets used in the experiments.

Name	Comment	Size	Style
Tox600	All data used	600	Toxic
Yam. Yelp	Yelp subset of annotated data	2000	sentiment
Yam. GYAFC	GYAFC subset of annotated data	6000	Formality
Yam. Bible	Bible subset of annotated data	2000	Old-style English
xformal-FoST	English subset of annotated data use (meta_gyafc_en.tsv)	2458	Formality
CAE	All data used. For each sentence pair, the mean human score was used. The dataset was obtained by direct request to Laugier et al. (2021)	500	Toxic
PG	All data used. Individual ranks were induced from side-by-side comparisons using the Luce spectral ranking model. The dataset was obtained by direct request to Pang and Gimpel (2019).	886	Sentiment
STRAP_coha	For each sentence pair, the mean human score was used. All data used	100	Historical American English
STRAP_form		684	Formality
STRAP_SP		550	Old-style English

Table 6: Text style transfer (TST) datasets used in the experiments.

B Measures analysis

Citation	Measure	Task
Hu et al. (2017)	Automatic content preservation measures are not used	CG
Shen et al. (2017)	Automatic content preservation measures are not used	TST
Mueller et al. (2017)	Edit distance	CG
Jhamtani et al. (2017)	PINC (Chen and Dolan, 2011), BLEU	TST
Radford et al. (2017)	Only style accuracy analyzed	TST
Logeswaran et al. (2018)	round-trip BLEU	CG
Subramanian et al. (2018)	self-BLEU	TST
Zhang et al. (2018b)	BLEU	TST
Prabhumoye et al. (2018)	Manual pairwise comparison only	TST
Tian et al. (2018b)	self-BLEU, POS-distance - noun difference between the original and transferred sentences	TST
Yang et al. (2018)	self-BLEU	TST
Rao and Tetreault (2018)	STS CNN model (He et al., 2015)	TST
Carlson et al. (2018)	PINC, BLEU	TST
Zhao et al. (2018)	BLEU	TST
Fu et al. (2018)	Cossim between averaged or max/min-pooled GloVe (Pennington et al., 2014) embeddings	TST
Xu et al. (2018)	BLEU	TST
Zhang et al. (2018a)	BLEU	TST
Gupta et al. (2018)	BLEU, ROUGE, METEOR	PG
Pang and Gimpel (2019)	Cossim between GloVe (Pennington et al., 2014) embeddings weighted by inverse document frequency	TST
Li et al. (2018)	BLEU	TST
Smith et al. (2019)	self-BLEU	TST
Sudhakar et al. (2019)	self-BLEU	TST
Wu et al. (2019b)	BLEU	TST
John et al. (2019)	Cossim between averaged or max/min-pooled GloVe (Pennington et al., 2014) embeddings	TST
Luo et al. (2019)	BLEU	TST
Dai et al. (2019)	self-BLEU	TST
Jain et al. (2019)	BLEU, spacy.docsim	TST
Lai et al. (2019)	self BLEU	TST
Wang et al. (2019)	BLEU	TST
Xu et al. (2019)	BLEU	TST
Kajiwara (2019)	BLEU, F1-score over added, deleted, adn kept words	PG
Wu et al. (2019a)	Case insensitive BLEU	TST
Li et al. (2019a)	BLEU	TST
Li et al. (2019b)	BLEU, ROUGE	PG
Chen et al. (2019)	BLEU, ROUGE, METEOR	PG
Yang et al. (2019a)	BLEU, METEOR, TER (Snover et al., 2006)	PG
Egonmwan and Chali (2019)	BLEU, ROUGE, METEOR,GMS and EACS (Sharma et al., 2017)	PG
Wang et al. (2018)	BLEU, METEOR, TER (Snover et al., 2006)	PG
Krishna et al. (2020)	SIMILEWieting et al. (2019)	TST
Shen et al. (2020b)	self-BLEU	CG
Li et al. (2020)	self-BLEU	TST
Xu et al. (2020)	self-BLEU	TST
Gong et al. (2020)	Cossim between averaged or max/min-pooled GloVe embeddings	TST
Zhang et al. (2020)	BLEU	TST
Shen et al. (2020a)	BLEU	CG
He et al. (2020)	self-BLEU	TST
Goyal and Durrett (2020)	BLEU	PG
Fu et al. (2020)	BLEU, ROUGE	PG
Laugier et al. (2021)	BLEU, cosine sinilarity of USE (Cer et al., 2018)	TST
Lai et al. (2021)	BLEU, BLEURT (Sellam et al., 2020)	TST
Shi et al. (2021)	WMD (Kusner et al., 2015), BLEU, BERTScore (Zhang et al., 2019)	TST
Riley et al. (2021)	self-BLEU	TST
Krause et al. (2021)	Only detoxicifcation and fluency analyzed	CG
Lee et al. (2021)	BLEU, BERTScore (Zhang et al., 2019)	TST
Cao et al. (2020)	BLEU	TST
Rane et al. (2021)	BLEU	TST
Hu and He (2021)	Word Overlap, BLEU, cosine similarity between avearged or max/min-pooled GloVe (Pennington et al., 2014) embeddings	TST
Sun et al. (2021)	BLEU, ROUGE, METEOR	PG

Table 7: Automatic content preservation measures used in recent works on text style transfer (TST), paraphrase generation (PG), and controllable generation (CG).

Measure name in report	Comment	Article
RobNLI/*	Combination or separate use of NLI scores in direct or reverse direction	Nie et al. (2020)
SIMILE	Cosine similarity between embeddings generated with LSTM-based model	Wieting et al. (2019)
w2v_wmd_norm	Word mover distance with word2vec normalized	Kusner et al. (2015)
w2v_wmd	Word mover distance with word2vec	
w2v_l2	Euclidean distance vetween word2vec	
w2v_cossim	Cosine similarity over word2vec	
USE	Cosine similarity between embeddings generated with Universal Sentence Encoder	Cer et al. (2018)
SIMCSE-UL SIMCSE-UB SIMCSE-ULu SIMCSE-UBu SIMCSE-SL SIMCSE-SB SIMCSE-SBertUnc	Unsupervised and supervised version of SIMCSE:Simple Contrastive Learning of Sentence Embeddings. Unsupervised version trained to predict the input sentence itself with only dropout used as noise. Supervised version trained to produce embeddings on NLI data in contrastive manner using entailing sample as positive sample and contradiction as negative.	Gao et al. (2021)
LaBSE BERT-base-NLI-STSB	Cosine similarity between language-agnostic cross-lingual sentence embeddings	Feng et al. (2020) Reimers and Gurevych (2019)
ROUGEL	ROUGE Longest Common Subsequence	Lin (2004)
ROUGE3	ROUGE with trigram	
ROUGE2	ROUGE with bigram	
ROUGE1	ROUGE with unigram	
NUBIA	Multi-module pipeline consisting of Feature Extraction, Aggregation and Calibration for semantic similarity scoring	Kane et al. (2020)
FBrobNLI/*	Combination or separate use of Facebook roberta NLI model's scores in direct or reverse direction	Liu et al. (2019)
MoverScore	Special case of Earth Mover's Distance applied to BERT embeddings	Zhao et al. (2019)
METEOR	The measure is based on the harmonic mean of unigram precision and recall	Banerjee and Lavie (2005)
Levenshtein	The minimum number of single-character edits	Levenshtein et al. (1966)
Jaro_winkler	String measure measuring an edit distance between two sequences with special modification giving more rating to strings that match from the beginning for a set prefix	Jaro (1989)
fasttext_wmd_norm	Normalized word mover distance over fasstext vectors	Kusner et al. (2015)
fasttext_wmd	Word mover distance over fasstext vectors	
fasttext_l2	Euclidean distance between fasttext vectors	
fasttext_cossim	Cosine similarity between fasttext vectors	
facebook/bart-large-cnn	Weighted log probability of one text y given another text x. The weights are used to put different emphasis on different tokens	Lewis et al. (2020)
BLEURT-L512 BLEURT-L128 BLEURT-B512 BLEURT-B128	BERT fine-tuned for semantic similarity evaluation task in cross-encoder manner on sythetic data	Sellam et al. (2020)
deberta/*	Combination or separate use of NLI scores from deberat model in direct or reverse direction	He et al. (2021)
cross-stsb-large cross-stsb-base	Base and Large version of CrossEncoder trained on STSb	Reimers and Gurevych (2019)
APD	Paraphrase detector trained on the Adversarial Paraphrasing dataset from the correponding paper	Nighojkar and Licato (2021)
chrf	Character n-gram F-score	Popović (2015)
BLEU	Modified unigram precision score	Papineni et al. (2002)
bertscore/roberta-large bertscore_Bert-bmc bertscore-Mic-Deberta	F1-score over BERT-embeddings between tokens from initial and target setneces. The packages are: roberta-large, Bert base multilingal cased, microsoft/deberta-xlarge-mnli correspondingly	Zhang et al. (2019)

Table 8: The full list of the automatic measures of content preservation used in the analysis.

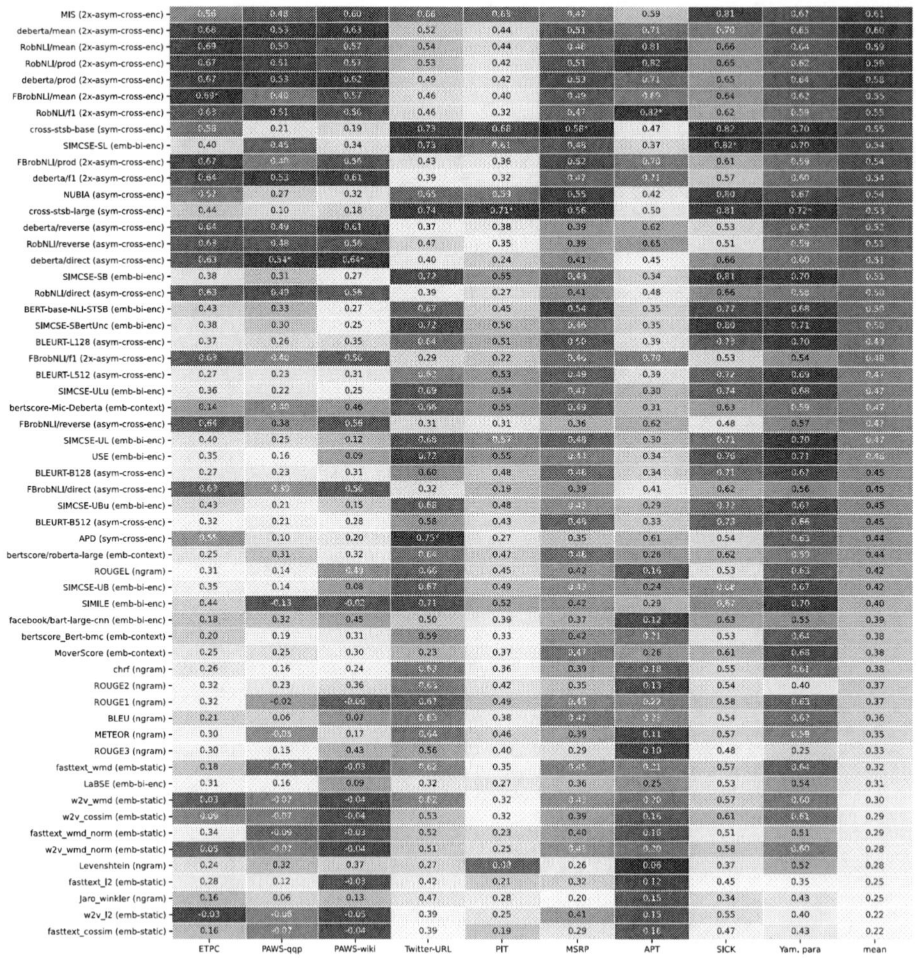

Figure 7: Spearman correlations of all the evaluated measures with human judgments for paraphrase generation (PG) datasets. The measures are sorted by the mean correlation across all datasets. The top correlations for individual datasets are marked with *. The color palette of the heatmap is based on the regret, which is the difference between the correlation of the measure on a particular dataset and the best correlation on this dataset. The lower the value of regret, the higher quality.

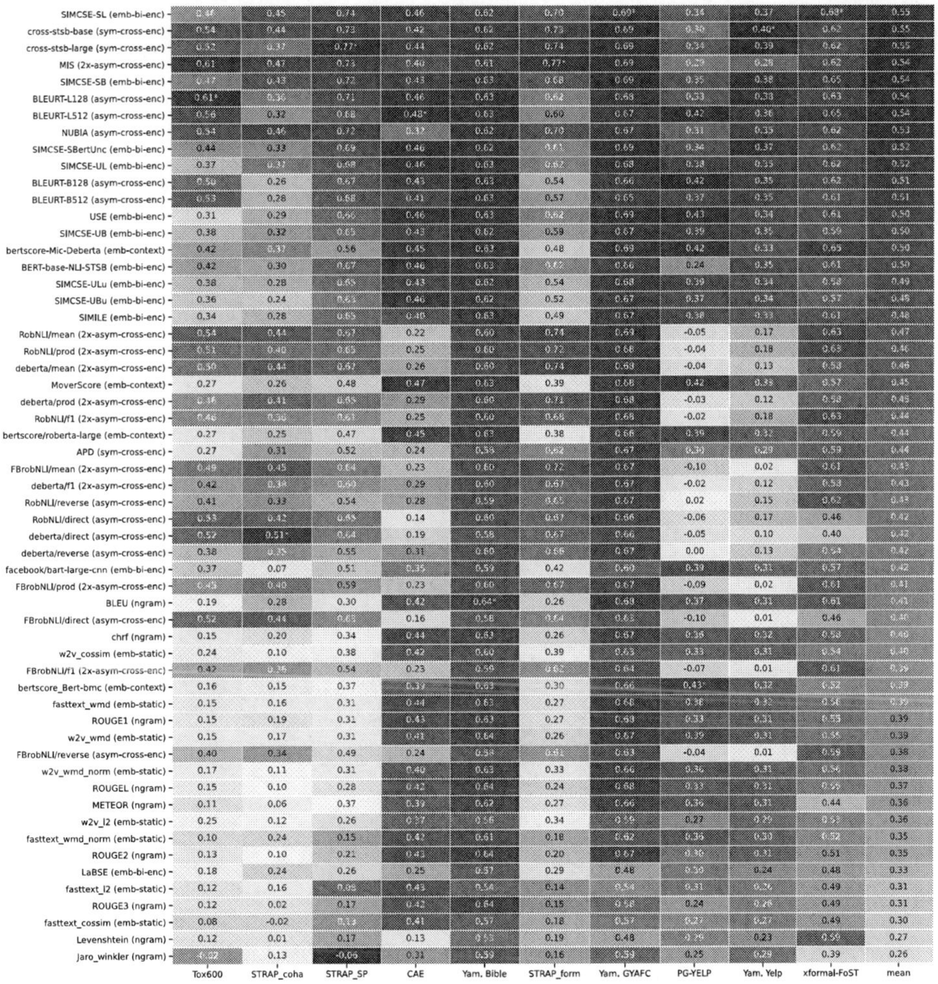

Figure 8: Spearman correlations of all the evaluated measures with human judgments for text style transfer (TST) datasets. The measures are sorted by the mean correlation across all datasets. The top correlations for individual datasets are marked with *. The color palette of the heatmap is based on the regret, which is the difference between the correlation of the measure on a particular dataset and the best correlation on this dataset. The lower the value of regret, the higher quality.

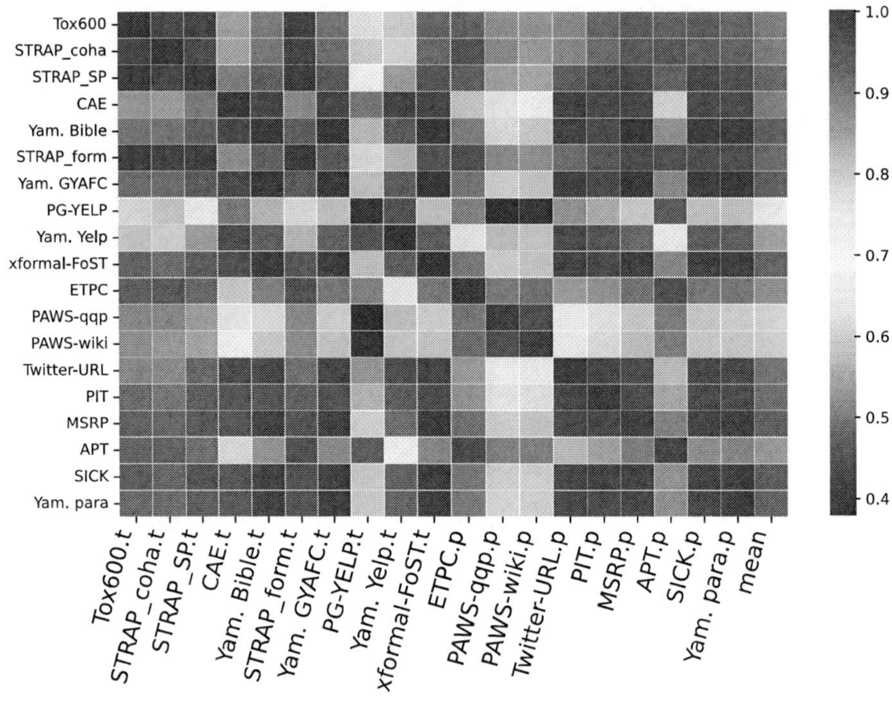

Figure 9: Cosine similarities of vectors of measures' correlations on individual datasets. The last column shows the mean cosine similarity of a dataset vector and vectors of all other dataset (excluding self-similarity). Postfixes 'p' and 't' indicate datasets for to PG and TST tasks, respectively.

C System-level ranking

system	human	MIS	RobNLI/mean	BLEURT-L128	cross-stsb-base	LaBSE	SIMCSE-SL	bertscore-Mic-Deberta	SIMILE	w2v_wmd	BLEU	chrf
paragedi	0.65	0.52	0.39	-0.25	0.82	0.95	0.68	0.76	0.67	-0.67	0.48	0.41
condbert	0.64	0.41	0.27	-0.26	1.07	0.96	0.75	0.83	0.76	-0.34	0.72	0.73
mask_infill	0.59	0.39	0.29	-0.29	0.96	0.99	0.82	0.87	0.82	-0.21	0.79	0.80

Table 9: System ranking on Tox600 (Dale et al., 2021), text detoxification.

system	human	MIS	RobNLI/mean	BLEURT-L128	cross-stsb-base	LaBSE	SIMCSE-SL	bertscore-Mic-Deberta	SIMILE	w2v_wmd	BLEU	chrf
nmt_combined	4.67	0.91	0.90	0.78	4.35	0.98	0.96	0.95	0.93	-0.15	0.88	0.85
pbmt	4.64	0.89	0.88	0.71	4.08	0.98	0.95	0.94	0.91	-0.17	0.85	0.81
ref	4.56	0.87	0.84	0.32	2.98	0.95	0.89	0.86	0.76	-0.44	0.64	0.59
nmt_copy	3.99	0.74	0.72	0.40	3.04	0.97	0.88	0.88	0.82	-0.26	0.77	0.73
nmt_baseline	3.90	0.73	0.70	0.40	3.00	0.96	0.87	0.89	0.82	-0.25	0.77	0.74

Table 10: System ranking on xformal-FoST (Briakou et al., 2021), formality transfer.

system	human	MIS	RobNLI/mean	BLEURT-L128	cross-stsb-base	LaBSE	SIMCSE-SL	bertscore-Mic-Deberta	SIMILE	w2v_wmd	BLEU	chrf
CAET rephrasing	2.63	0.34	0.28	-0.63	0.56	0.92	0.62	0.70	0.56	-0.66	0.47	0.44
IE rephrasing	2.20	0.37	0.36	-0.73	0.55	0.96	0.60	0.73	0.56	-0.56	0.58	0.56
ST (multi) rephrasing	2.10	0.26	0.22	-1.16	-0.22	0.91	0.52	0.63	0.60	-0.67	0.46	0.46
ST (cond) rephrasing	2.08	0.25	0.23	-1.11	-0.07	0.92	0.53	0.66	0.62	-0.65	0.49	0.47
CA rephrasing	1.88	0.05	0.08	-1.54	-2.22	0.90	0.18	0.51	0.16	-0.95	0.23	0.18

Table 11: System ranking on CAE (Laugier et al., 2021), text detoxification.

system	human	MIS	RobNLI/mean	BLEURT-L128	cross-stsb-base	LaBSE	SIMCSE-SL	bertscore-Mic-Deberta	SIMILE	w2v_wmd	BLEU	chrf
m7	3.41	0.16	0.09	-1.03	-0.84	0.95	0.45	0.76	0.52	-0.56	0.52	0.45
m6	3.03	0.18	0.11	-1.16	-0.58	0.95	0.45	0.74	0.56	-0.52	0.58	0.53
m2	3.03	0.14	0.07	-1.23	-1.10	0.94	0.37	0.73	0.47	-0.56	0.53	0.46
m0	2.31	0.10	0.06	-1.50	-1.80	0.91	0.28	0.64	0.30	-0.80	0.34	0.29

Table 12: System ranking on PG-YELP (Pang and Gimpel, 2019), sentiment transfer.

system	human	MIS	RobNLI/mean	BLEURT-L128	cross-stsb-base	LaBSE	SIMCSE-SL	bertscore-Mic-Deberta	SIMILE	w2v_wmd	BLEU	chrf
paraphrase_base	0.79	0.64	0.53	-0.39	1.19	0.94	0.77	0.74	0.65	-0.69	0.45	0.39
paraphrase_0.0	0.76	0.73	0.64	-0.08	1.91	0.94	0.82	0.77	0.71	-0.63	0.50	0.43
paraphrase_0.9	0.59	0.56	0.44	-0.45	1.04	0.93	0.73	0.71	0.61	-0.74	0.42	0.35
unmt	0.31	0.23	0.19	-0.95	-0.31	0.93	0.50	0.69	0.51	-0.61	0.51	0.43
he_2020	0.26	0.21	0.19	-0.99	-0.82	0.90	0.45	0.67	0.46	-0.65	0.45	0.40

Table 13: System ranking on STRAP_form, (Krishna et al., 2020), formality transfer.

system	human	MIS	RobNLI/mean	BLEURT-L128	cross-stsb-base	LaBSE	SIMCSE-SL	bertscore-Mic-Deberta	SIMILE	w2v_wmd	BLEU	chrf
paraphrase_0.0	0.81	0.62	0.58	-0.11	1.48	0.95	0.79	0.76	0.72	-0.69	0.44	0.37
paraphrase_base	0.58	0.44	0.43	-0.52	0.77	0.94	0.69	0.70	0.62	-0.79	0.37	0.31
he_2020	0.35	0.19	0.21	-1.07	-0.28	0.93	0.49	0.68	0.49	-0.65	0.46	0.40
unmt	0.26	0.12	0.13	-1.23	-0.92	0.93	0.41	0.66	0.41	-0.72	0.42	0.34

Table 14: System ranking on STRAP_SP (Krishna et al., 2020), Shakespeare style transfer.

dataset	measures
Tox600	MIS, BLEURT-L128
xformal-FoST	BLEURT-L128 , cross-stsb-base, SimCSE, BERTScore, and all other models
CAE	BLEURT-L128 , cross-stsb-base, SimCSE
PG-YELP	BLEURT-L128 , LaBSE, BERTScore
STRAP_form	LaBSE
STRAP_SP	MIS, BLEURT-L128 , cross-stsb-base, LaBSE, SimCSE, BERTScore, SIMILE

Table 15: The measures that correctly identify the best text style transfer system for each dataset.

Explicit Object Relation Alignment for Vision and Language Navigation

Yue Zhang
Michigan State University
zhan1624@msu.edu

Parisa Kordjamshidi
Michigan State University
kordjams@msu.edu

Abstract

In this paper, we investigate the problem of vision and language navigation. To solve this problem, grounding the landmarks and spatial relations in the textual instructions into visual modality is important. We propose a neural agent named Explicit Object Relation Alignment Agent (EXOR), to explicitly align the spatial information in both instruction and the visual environment, including landmarks and spatial relationships between the agent and landmarks. Empirically, our proposed method surpasses the baseline by a large margin on the R2R dataset. We provide a comprehensive analysis to show our model's spatial reasoning ability and explainability.

1 Introduction

Vision and Language Navigation (VLN) problem (Anderson et al., 2018) requires the agent to carry out a sequence of actions in an indoor photo-realistic simulated environment in response to corresponding natural language instructions. The first VLN benchmark to appear was Room-to-Room navigation (R2R) (Anderson et al., 2018) , as shown in Figure 1, the agent needs to generate a navigation trajectory in a visual environment rendered from real images following an instruction.

This task is challenging because, apart from understanding the language and vision modalities, the agent needs to learn the connection between them without explicit intermediate supervision.

To address this challenge, several recent work started to consider the semantic structure from both language and vision sides. Hong et al. (2020a) train an implicit entity-relationship graph allowing an agent to learn the latent concepts and relationships between different components (scene, object and direction). They use the object features extracted from Faster-RCNN (Ren et al., 2015) instead of only using ResNet visual features which can easily overfit on the training environment (Hu et al., 2019).

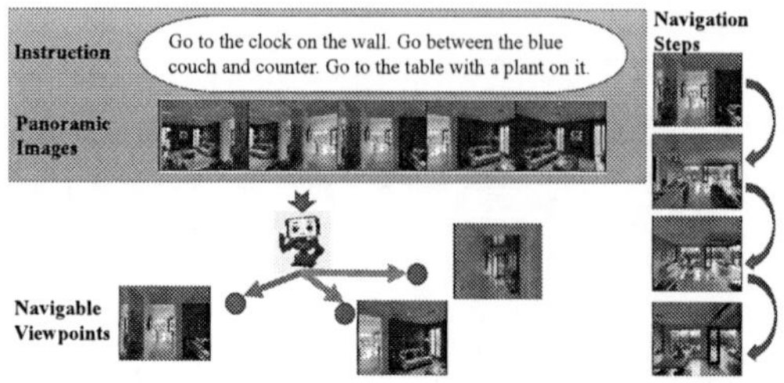

Figure 1: **VLN Task Demonstration.** The agent generates a navigation trajectory composed of navigable viewpoints selected based on the given instruction and the panoramic images at each step. The red arrow shows the ground-truth navigable viewpoint.

Although the grounding ability of their agent improves, their experimental results show that the object features do not help the navigation independently unless their relationships to the scene and direction are modeled. This issue indicates their loosely modeled latent space and motivates us to explore the ways the object features can be further exploited.

The recent research finds that indoor navigation agents rely on both landmark and direction tokens in the instruction when taking actions (Zhu et al., 2021). However, it is difficult to identify which landmarks the agent should pay attention to at each navigation step. Previous works (Tan et al., 2019; Ma et al., 2018; Wang et al., 2019; Zhu et al., 2020) mainly use the surrounding visual information as a clue to indicate the landmark tokens that the agent should focus on. However, the semantics of instruction should also play an important role. For example, with the understanding of the instruction "go to the table with chair, and then walk towards the door", the agent needs to give the same attention to "table" and "chair", and less attention to "door" at the first navigation step. In terms of direction tokens, the prior works concentrate most on the direction tokens related to motions, such as "turn left", and ignore the spatial description of

Proceedings of the 60th Annual Meeting of the Association for Computational Linguistics Student Research Workshop, pages 322 - 331
May 22-27, 2022 ©2022 Association for Computational Linguistics

landmarks, such as "table on the left". We believe distinguishing those different direction tokens can benefit the navigation performance. The last but not least, modeling the landmarks and their spatial relations can improve the explainability of the agent's actions.

In this paper, we propose a neural agent, called *Explicit Object Relation Alignment Agent* (EXOR), to explicitly align the spatial semantics between linguistic instructions and the visual environment. Specifically, we first split the long instruction into spatial configurations (Dan et al., 2020; Zhang et al., 2021), and then we select the important landmarks based on such configurations. After that, in the visual environment, we retrieve the most relevant objects according to their similarity with the selected landmarks in the instructions. Moreover, we obtain **textual spatial relation encoding** to model the spatial relations between the agent and landmarks in the textual instructions, and use **visual spatial relation encoding** to represent the relation between agent and the image in the visual environment. We then establish a mapping between the two encodings to achieve a better alignment. Finally, we use the representations of the aligned objects and spatial relations to enrich the image representations. To the best of our knowledge, none of the previous work modeled the explicit spatial relations considering the agent's perspective for this task.

Our contribution is summarized as follows:

1. Our model achieves the explicit alignments between textual and visual spatial information, and such alignments guide the agent to pay more attention to the objects in the visual environment given landmark mentions in the instructions.

2. We explicitly model the spatial relations between the agent and landmarks from both instruction and visual environments, which enhance their alignments and improve the overall navigation performance.

3. Our method surpasses the baseline performance by a large margin. Also, we provide a comprehensive analysis to show the spatial reasoning ability and explainability of our model.

2 Related Work

Vision and Language Navigation The vision-language navigation problem nowadays has gained an increasing popularity, and various navigation datasets and platforms(Savva et al., 2019; Kolve et al., 2017) are proposed to assist the development of this topic in the community, for example, R2R (Anderson et al., 2018) and Touchdown (Chen et al., 2019) datasets, which have extended navigation to the photo-realistic simulation environments. More broadly, there are work also related to instruction-guided household task benchmarks such as ALFRED (Shridhar et al., 2020). RXR (Ku et al., 2020) is a multilingual navigation dataset with spatial-temporal grounding, CVDN and HANNA are a dialog-based interactive navigation dataset (Thomason et al., 2020; Nguyen and Daumé III, 2019), and REVERI (Qi et al., 2020b) navigates to localize a remote object.

Accompanied with these benchmark works, numerous deep learning methods (Tan et al., 2019; Hong et al., 2021, 2020a) have been proposed. For R2R task, Anderson et al. (2018) propose a Sequence-to-Sequence baseline model to encode the instructions and decode the embeddings to the low-level action sequence with the observed images. Speaker-Follower agent proposed by Fried et al. (2018) trains a speaker model to generate the augmented samples to improve the generalizability. They also start modeling a panoramic action space for navigation, which further promotes fast iteration of different VLN approaches.

Grounding in VLN It has been observed that the connection between linguistic instruction and visual environment can yield a great improvement in VLN task, hence many research efforts for modeling such visual-linguistic relation have recently been developed. In general, we categorize these research works into three directions.

The first main thread (Anderson et al., 2018; Ma et al., 2018; Tan et al., 2019; Wang et al., 2019; Ma et al., 2019) tends to adopt attention mechanisms for establishing language and vision connections in neural navigation agents. For instance, Ma et al. (2019) apply a visual-textual co-grounding module and a progress monitor to guide the execution progress. The second branch of prior works (Hu et al., 2019; Hao et al., 2020; Majumdar et al., 2020; Hong et al., 2021; Shen et al., 2021) explores the pre-trained Vision and Language (VL) representation from the transformer-based models. Hong et al. (2021) design a recurrent unit on the VL transformer models, and fine-tune them on the down stream VLN task. Notably, the increased model size and additional training process help improve navigation performance and surpass the previous performance by a large margin.

The third branch works model the semantic structure, based on both language and vision perspectives, to improve the grounding ability, such as (Qi et al., 2020a; Zhang et al., 2021; Hong et al., 2020a,b; Li et al., 2021), and our work also follows such paradigm. From the language side, Hong et al. (2020b) segment the long instruction into sub-instructions and annotate their corresponding trajectories to supervise the agent to learn the alignments. From the image side, instead of using only the ResNet visual features that easily over-fits on the training environment, some recent work (Hu et al., 2019; Qi et al., 2020a; Zhang et al., 2020) use object representations to improve the generalizability. Most importantly, one should bridge both linguistic and visual semantics, and Ent-Rel (Hong et al., 2020a) obtains the best results in the third branch of work by building an implicit language-visual entity relation graph to learn the connections between the two modalities. Our work serves as a new method in the third method category. We explicitly model the alignments between landmarks and visual objects and model the spatial relations to improve the spatial reasoning ability of the agent.

3 Method

3.1 Problem Description

In our study, the agent is given an instruction with length l, denoted as $w =< w_1, w_2, \cdots, w_l >$. At each time step t, the agent observes its surrounding and receives 360-degree panoramic views of images, which are denoted as $v^p =< v^p_1, v^p_2, \cdots, v^p_{36} >$.[1] In those panoramic views, there are q candidate navigable viewpoints which the agent can navigate. We denote the viewpoints as $v^c =< v^c_1, v^c_2, \cdots, v^c_q >$. The goal of the task is to select the next viewpoint among the navigable viewpoints for generating a trajectory that takes the agent close to a goal destination. The agent terminates when the current viewpoint is selected, or a predefined maximum number of navigation steps have been reached.

3.2 Base Model

We follow the modeling approach of (Tan et al., 2019) which uses an Long short-term Memory (LSTM) based sequence-to-sequence architecture. The encoder is a bidirectional LSTM-RNN with an embedding layer to obtain language representation, denoted as, $[s_1, s_2, \cdots, s_l] = BiLSTM(F(< w_1, w_2, \cdots, w_l >)$, where F represents the embedding function. The decoder is also an attentive LSTM-RNN. At each decoding step t of navigation, the agent first attends to the panoramic image representation f^p with the previous hidden context feature $\tilde{h}_{t-1}$. The visual representation of ith panoramic image is denoted as $f^p_i = [ResNet(v^p_i); d_i]$, which is the concatenation of the ResNet visual features $ResNet(v^p_i)$ and the corresponding 128 dimensional direction encoding d_i. The direction encoding for panoramic images d_i is the replication of $[cos\theta_i, sin\theta_i, cos\phi_i, sin\phi_i]$ by 32 times, where θ_i and ϕ_i are the angles of heading and elevation of ith panoramic image. The attentive panoramic visual feature $\tilde{f}^p_t$ is computed by $\tilde{f}^p_t = SoftAttn(Q = \tilde{h}_{t-1}, K = f^p_t, V = f^p_t)$, and then is used as input to the LSTM of the decoder to represent the agent's current state as,

$$h_t = LSTM([a_{t-1}; \tilde{f}^p_t], \tilde{h}_{t-1}), \quad (1)$$

where a_{t-1} is the selected action direction of the previous navigation step, and $\tilde{h}_{t-1}$ is the hidden context after considering the grounded objects. The details will be discussed in the following sections.

3.3 Landmark-object alignment and spatial relations modeling

The proposed model has been shown in Figure 2, and we describe its four components as follows.

Spatial Configuration Representation

We split the long instructions into smaller sub-instructions, called spatial configurations. A spatial configuration contains fine-grained spatial roles, such as motion indicator, landmark, spatial indicator, and trajector (Dan et al., 2020). For example, the instruction "go to the bathroom and stop" can be split into two spatial configurations, which are "go to the bathroom" and "stop". In the first configuration, "go" is the motion indicator; "bathroom" is the landmark. In the second configuration, "stop" is the motion indicator.

We follow Zhang et al. (2021) to split a navigation instruction w into m spatial configurations based on the verbs or verb phrases. Each spatial configuration contains the flexible number of tokens and a [SEP] token as the last token. Formally, we re-organize the contextual embeddings of tokens into the array of spatial configurations representation $C = [C_1, C_2 \ldots C_m]$, where m is the number of configurations. Each configuration

[1] 12 headings and 3 elevations with 30 degree intervals.

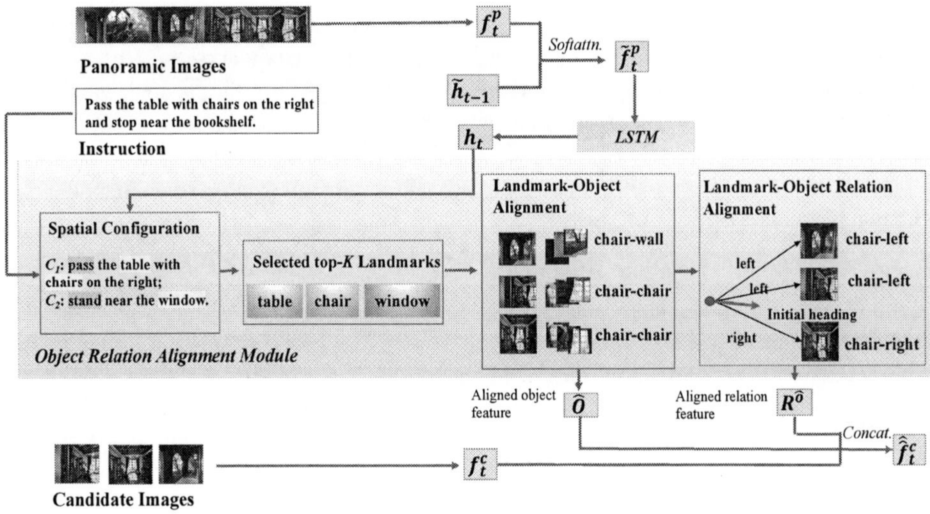

Figure 2: **Model Architecture.** The model has four sub-modules, (1) Spatial Configuration (2) Select top-k landmark selection (3) Landmark-Object alignment (4) Landmark-Object Spatial Relation relation alignment. The text highlighted in green and yellow in (1) shows motion indicators and landmarks, respectively. The red arrow in (4) is the initial agent heading (i.e. orientation).

is composed of tokens generated by the encoder, denoted as $[s_1, s_2, \cdots s_p]$, where s_p is the embedding of [SEP] token that contains the most comprehensive contextual information about the preceding words. This is because LSTM encoder is used for propagating the information throughout the sequence. Also, to enrich the spatial configuration representations, we consider the spatial semantic elements. We extract the verbs or verb phrases as motion indicators, s_m, and nouns or noun phrases as landmarks, s_l. Then we apply soft attention to each configuration representation with the representations of the [SEP] token s_p, the motion indicator s_m, and landmark s_l separately. The enriched spatial configuration is represented as $\bar{C} = [\bar{C}_1, \bar{C}_2 \ldots \bar{C}_m]$. In the base model, we attend the current hidden context h_t of the LSTM to the spatial configuration features C to form the weighted spatial configurations output $\tilde{C}$. This process is defined as follows,

$$\beta_{t,j} = softmax(\bar{C}_j^T W_c h_t), \tag{2}$$

$$\tilde{C}_t = \sum_j \beta_{t,j} C_j, \tag{3}$$

where β is the attended configuration weights, j is the index of spatial configuration and W_c is the learned weights.

Landmark Selection

Landmark phrases in instructions are split into groups according to the spatial configuration. We assign the attention weights of each spatial configuration to all its included landmarks. The attention weights of landmarks are the same once they appear in the same configuration. Then we sort all weighted landmarks and select the top-k important ones for the agent to focus on at each navigation step. Formally, each configuration contains n landmarks, denoted as $L =< L_1, L_2, \cdots, L_n >$. The total number of landmarks is $m * n$ in m spatial configurations. After sorting all landmarks based on the spatial configuration weights β, we can obtain top-k selected landmark representations, as $\tilde{L} =< \tilde{L}_1, \tilde{L}_2, \cdots, \tilde{L}_k >$. We obtain the best result when k is 3 (see 5.1 for the experiment).

Landmark-Object Alignment

After selecting top-k landmarks, the next step is to align them with the corresponding objects in the image. We use Faster-RCNN to detect 36 objects in each image, and the object representation of the i-th image is $O_i = [o_{i,1}, o_{i,2}, \cdots, o_{i,36}]$. We compute the cosine similarity scores between the j-th landmark in top-k landmarks and all objects in the i-th image, and select the object with the highest similarity score as the most relevant object to the j-th landmark, as $\hat{O}_{i,L_j} = max(cos\_sim(\tilde{L}_j, O_i))$. The aligned objects in the i-th image are denoted as

$\hat{O}_i = [\hat{O}_{i,L_1}, \hat{O}_{i,L_2}, \cdots, \hat{O}_{i,L_k}]$. We get k aligned objects since we have top-k landmarks. Finally, we concatenate the aligned object representations with the candidate image features f^c. The ith candidate image is represented as $f_i^p = [ResNet(v_i^c); d_i]$. After aligned with the corresponding objects, its representation is updated as $\hat{f}_i^c = [f_i^c; \hat{O}_i^c]$.

Landmark-Object Spatial Relation Alignment We model both textual spatial relations and visual spatial relations. On the text side, there are mainly three different cases of spatial relations described in the navigation instructions.

- Case 1. Motions verbs, such as "turn left to the table";
- Case 2. Relative spatial relationships between agent and landmarks, such as "table on your left";
- Case 3. Spatial relationships between landmarks, such as "vase on the table".

This work mainly investigates the spatial relations from the agent's perspective, and we only model the first two cases. We extract "landmark-relation" pairs for each landmark in the instructions (based on syntactic rules). For Case 1, we pair the spatial relation with all landmarks in the configuration. For example, "turn left to the table with chair", the extracted pairs are {table-left} and {chair-left}. For Case 2, we pair the relation with the related landmark. For example, "go to the sofa on the right.", the extracted pair is {sofa-right}.

We encode the spatial relations for the landmarks in six bits $[left, right, front, back, up, down]$ as the **textual spatial relation encoding**. Each bit is set to 1 for the landmark if its paired relation has the corresponding relation. On the image side, we encode the same six spatial relations as the **visual spatial relation encoding**. We obtain the spatial relations of objects in the visual environment based on the relative angle, the differences between the agent's initial direction and the navigable direction. The spatial relations are the same for all objects if they are in the same image.

Formally, for the obtained top-k landmarks, we denote their spatial encoding as $R^{\hat{L}} = [R_1^{\hat{L}}, R_2^{\hat{L}}, \cdots, R_k^{\hat{L}}]$. For the top-$k$ objects aligned with those landmarks, the spatial relations in i-th navigable image are represented as $R_i^{\hat{O}} = [R_{i,1}^{\hat{O}}, R_{i,2}^{\hat{O}}, \cdots, R_{i,k}^{\hat{O}}]$. We compute the inner product of the spatial encoding between top-k landmarks and the top-k aligned objects to obtain the spatial similarity score between the instruction and the i-th image, that is, $sim_i^R = R^{\hat{L}} \cdot R_i^{\hat{O}}$. Then we concatenate each aligned object spatial encoding with the corresponding similarity score, denoted as $\hat{O}_{i,R} = [[R_{i,1}^{\hat{O}}; sim_{i,1}^R], [R_{i,2}^{\hat{O}}; sim_{i,2}^R], \cdots, [R_{i,k}^{\hat{O}}; sim_{i,k}^R]]$. Finally, we further concatenate $\hat{O}_{i,R}$ with the candidate image features $\hat{f}_i^c$ which is concatenated with the aligned object features , and i-th candidate images features is updated as $\hat{\hat{f}}_i^c = [\hat{f}_i^c; \hat{O}_{i,g}]$. The updated image representations are then used to make action decisions for the agent.

3.4 Action Prediction

After modeling alignment between landmark tokens in the instruction and visual objects, the panoramic image feature is enriched with the aligned visual objects, and candidate image feature is enriched with both visual objects and their spatial relations. Then based on the backbone sequence to sequence agent, the probability of moving to the k-th navigable viewpoint $p_t(a_{t,k})$ is calculated as softmax of the alignment between the navigable viewpoint features and a context-aware hidden output $\tilde{h_t}$, which can be calculate as

$$\tilde{h_t} = tanh(W_{\tilde{c}h}[\tilde{C}; h_t]) \quad (4)$$

$$p_t(a_{t,k}) = softmax(\hat{\hat{f}}_i^c W_{\tilde{c}} \tilde{h_t}) \quad (5)$$

where $W_{\tilde{c}h}$ and $W_{\tilde{c}}$ are learnt weights.

3.5 Training and Inference

We follow the work of (Tan et al., 2019) for training the model with a mixture of Imitation Learning (IL) and Reinforcement Learning (RL). Imitation Learning minimizes the cross-entropy loss of the prediction and always samples the ground-truth navigable viewpoint at each time step, and Reinforcement Learning samples an action from the action probability p_t and learns from the rewards. During inference, we use a greedy search with the highest probability of the next viewpoints to generate the trajectory.

4 Experimental Setups

Dataset

We use Room-Room(R2R) dataset (Anderson et al., 2018) that is built upon the Matterport3D dataset.

	Method	Val Seen			Val Unseen			Test(Unseen)	
		SR ↑	**SPL ↑**	**SDTW ↑**	**SR ↑**	**SPL↑**	**SDTW↑**	**SR ↑**	**SPL ↑**
1	Speaker-Follower (Fried et al., 2018)	0.54	-	-	0.27	-	-	-	-
2	Env-Drop (Tan et al., 2019)	0.55	0.53	-	0.47	0.43	-	-	-
3	Env-Drop* (Tan et al., 2019)	0.63	0.60	0.53	0.50	0.48	0.37	0.50	0.47
4	SpC-NAV* (Zhang et al., 2021)	0.65	0.61	-	0.45	0.42	-	0.46	0.44
5	OAAM* (Qi et al., 2020a)	0.65	0.62	0.53	0.54	0.50	0.39	0.53	0.50
6	Entity-Relation (Hong et al., 2020a)	0.62	0.60	0.54	0.52	0.50	0.46	0.51	0.48
7	EXOR (ours)	0.60	0.58	0.53	0.52	0.49	0.46	0.49	0.46

Table 1: **Experimental Results Comparing with Baseline Models** (* means data augmentation).

		Ent-Rel		EXOR(ours)	
		SR↑	**SPL↑**	**SR↑**	**SPL↑**
1	Mask Scene	0.47	0.44	0.48	0.46
2	No Mask	0.52	0.50	0.50	0.48

Table 2: **Results on Scene & Object Alignment.**

	Method	Val Seen			Val Unseen		
		SR↑	**SPL↑**	**SDTW↑**	**SR↑**	**SPL↑**	**SDTW↑**
1	Baseline	0.55	0.53	0.49	0.47	0.43	0.37
2	Lan-Obj	0.59	0.55	0.52	0.50	0.48	0.43
3	Lan-Obj+Rel	**0.60**	**0.58**	**0.53**	**0.52**	**0.49**	**0.46**
4	Lan-Obj+Rel_v	0.59	0.56	0.52	**0.52**	0.47	0.44

Table 3: **Ablation Study.**

R2R dataset contains 7198 paths and 21567 instructions with an average length of 29 words. The whole dataset is partitioned into training, seen validation, unseen validation, and unseen test set. The seen set shares the same visual environments with the training set, while unseen sets contain different environments.

Evaluation Metrics

We mainly report three evaluation metrics. (1) Success Rate (SR): the percentage of the cases where the predicted final position lays within 3 meters from the goal location. (2) Success rate weighted by normalized inverse Path Length (SPL) (Anderson et al., 2018): normalizes Success Rate by trajectory length. It considers both the effectiveness and efficiency of navigation performance. (3) the Success weighted by normalized Dynamic Time Warping (SDTW) (Ilharco et al., 2019): penalizes deviations from the referenced path and also considers the success rate.

Baseline Models

Env_Drop (Tan et al., 2019) proposes a neural agent trained with the method of the mixture of Imitation Learning and Reinforcement Learning. Our model is built based on Env_Drop.

SpC-NAV (Zhang et al., 2021) models instructions using spatial configurations and designs a state attention to guarantee the sequential execution. Besides, it uses a similarity score between landmarks in the instruction and objects in the image to control this attention.

OAAM (Qi et al., 2020a) proposes an object-and-action aware model to learn the object and action attention separately, and also learns the object-vision and action-orientation matching.

Ent-Rel (Hong et al., 2020a) proposes a language and visual entity relation graph to exploit the connection among the scene, objects, and direction clues during navigation.

Implementation Details

We use PyTorch to implement our model[2]. We use 768 dimensional BERT-base (Devlin et al., 2018) (frozen) as the embedding of the raw instruction, and get its 512 dimensional contextual embedding by LSTM. We encode the representations of the motion indicator and the landmark in each configuration with 300 dimensional GloVe embedding respectively, and concatenate them with the 512 dimensional configuration representation to obtain the enriched configuration representation (1112 dimensional). We use 300 dimensional GloVe (Pennington et al., 2014) embedding to represent motion indicator, landmark, and object label. The optimizer is ADAM, and the learning rate is $1e-4$ with a batch size of 32.

5 Results and Analysis

Table 1 shows the performance of our model compared with baselines and the competitive models of the third branch of work as aforementioned in the related work (section 2) on unseen validation and test set. Our result is better than the baseline (Env-Drop) even with their augmented data (Tan et al., 2019) (Row#1 and Row#2), showing our improved generalizability. We obtain significantly improved

[2]Our code is available at `https://github.com/HLR/Object-Grounding-for-VLN`

results compared to SpC-NAV which models the semantic structure in language and image modalities. Compared with OAAM, which learns the object-vision matching with the augmented data, we get better SDTW, indicating that our agent can genuinely follow the instruction to the destination. However, Ent-Rel achieves better results that ours, for which we provide further analysis in the next section.

5.1 The Number of Selected Landmarks

We experimentally validated the best number of important landmarks the agent should select. Figure 3 shows the SPL results with different k values on validation seen and unseen dataset. We find that the best result is obtained when k is 3. It also shows that letting the agent focus on only one landmark or all landmarks in the instruction will hinder their navigation performance. Table4 shows the statistics of the extracted spatial configurations in train and validation seen/unseen dataset. On average, each instruction can be split into about four spatial configurations, and about 76% of spatial configurations contain landmarks. In fact, selecting top 3 landmarks means that the agent mainly focuses on the landmark-object alignment in 3 spatial configurations at most at each navigation step.

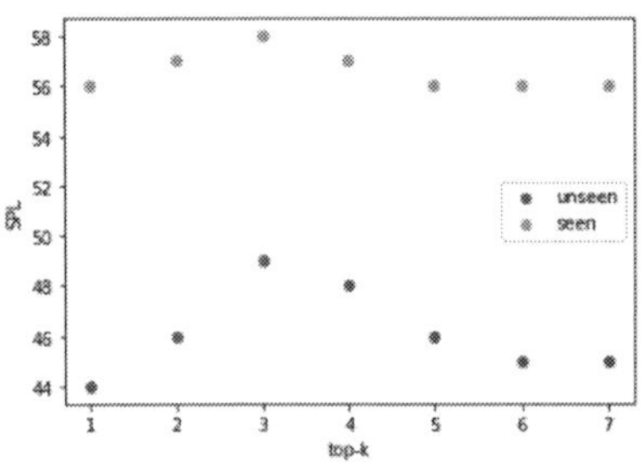

Figure 3: **SPL Results with Different K Values.**

5.2 Scene & Object Alignment

Ent-Rel(Hong et al., 2020a) distinguishes the landmarks which are *scenes* from *objects*. Scene tokens describe the location at a coarse level, such as "bathroom", while object tokens describe the exact landmarks, such as "table". To evaluate the agent's performance given the instructions with only object tokens, we mask all scene tokens in the instructions and evaluate on Ent-Rel and our model. Table 2 shows the experimental results in the unseen validation set. Compared with Ent-Rel, our model performs slightly better given the instruction with only object tokens but worse with scene and object tokens. One of the reasons for such a phenomenon is that Faster-RCNN often fails to detect the scenes correctly. For example, the aligned object labels in the image for the landmark "bedroom" are "floor", "roof", "wall", which are parts of the bedroom. The explicitly modeling makes our model more sensitive to the wrong alignments, which further impacts the navigation performance.

5.3 Ablation Study

Table 3 shows the ablation study results. Row#1 is the baseline model. Row#2 (*Lan-Obj*) shows that explicitly modeling important landmarks and aligned objects improves the performance compared to the baseline. *Rel* (row#3) is the result after modeling the spatial relation tokens describing the relative relation between agent and landmark. *Rel_v* (row#4) is the result after modeling the spatial relations in motions. The improved SDTW shows the modeling of spatial relations can help the agent to follow the instructions. However, the spatial terms directly describing the landmark are more helpful than the spatial terms in motions.

5.4 Qualitative Analysis

Figure 4 shows qualitative analysis examples. The selected k-important landmarks are "door", "table", "painting" in Figure 4a. The agent makes a correct decision by selecting the viewpoint that contains the objects aligned with all three landmarks. Figure 4b shows an example after modeling spatial relations. Although three navigable viewpoints have the object "door", the agent selects the aligned object with the "left" direction. Also, in Figure 5, we provide an example to visualize the navigation process using the selected landmark based on the spatial configurations.

However, we find that relation alignments will be helpful when the object alignments are done correctly. Figure 4c shows another example of landmark and object alignments. It contains two spatial configurations: "walk past the kitchen towards the dining room" and "stop before you reach the table". In the first configuration, the landmarks are "kitchen' and "dining room"; in the second configuration, the landmark is "table". By merely using the visual environment as a clue for viewpoint selection, the agent will select the second navigable viewpoint because of its detected "kitchen" view.

Nevertheless, based on the instruction semantics, the "kitchen" is an object the agent passes by, and

(a) Enter the "door" to the small "table" with a "painting" above.
v1: [door-door; table-table; painting-wall]
v2: [door-door; table-wall; painting-wall]
v3: [door-door; table-table; painting-picture]

(b) Head towards the "doors" on the left towards "kitchen".
v1:left; v2:right; v3:right

(c) Walk past the "kitchen" towards the "dining room". Stop before you reach the "table".
v1: [kitchen-room; dining room-room; table-table]
v2: [kitchen-kitchen; dining room-room; table-kitchen]

(d) Turn right toward "bathroom". Stop at the top of the steps.
v1:left; v2:right;

Figure 4: **Qualitative Examples.** Blue bounding boxes are the aligned objects. Green arrow is the selected correct viewpoint. v is the viewpoint, the alignment between landmarks and objects is [landmark-object].

		Train	Val Seen	Val Unseen
1	Instructions	14025	1021	2349
2	Configs	58277	4301	9625
3	Configs with Landmark	44053	3225	7303
4	Configs with Relation	13543	1142	2566

Table 4: **Statistics of Spatial Configuration**

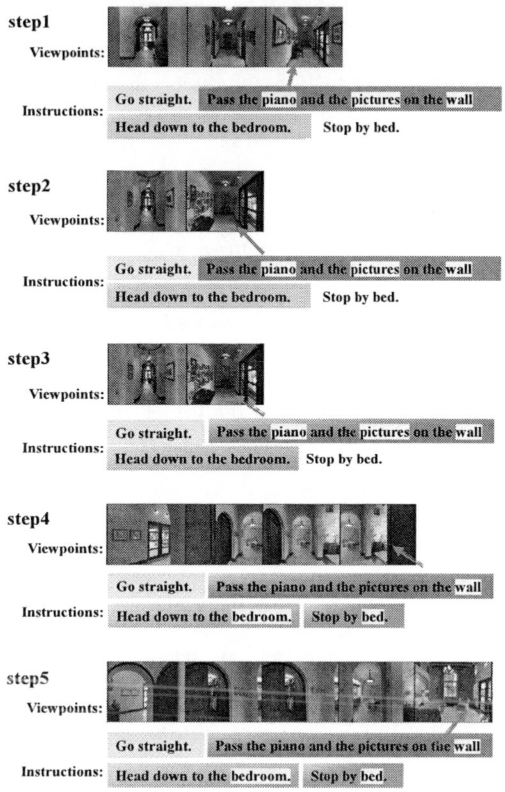

Figure 5: The green boxes are spatial configurations; darker green means higher weights; yellow boxes are the selected landmarks; the orange arrows are the path.

the "table" is the final goal. In some cases, our method can handle such situations by using the selected landmarks. In this example, the model allows the agent to focus on the aligned object such as "table", which appear later in the spatial configuration. It increases the probability of selecting the first viewpoint. Also, we find that relation alignments modeling will be helpful only when the object alignments are done correctly. If the object alignments fail, for example, when the agent makes mistakes during navigation or the aligned objects can not be detected, modeling relations can worsen the situation. For instance, in Figure 4d, for both navigable viewpoints, the object "bathroom" can not be detected, and in this case, further modeling relations leads to making wrong decisions.

6 Conclusion

In this work, we propose a neural architecture to solve the vision and language navigation problem. Our method achieves the alignments between textual landmarks and visual objects. In particular, we first select important landmarks based on spatial configurations, and then encourage the agent to concentrate on the relevant objects in the visual environment given the selected landmarks. Besides, We are the first to explicitly model the spatial relations between the agent and the landmarks from the agent's perspective on both instruction and image sides. Our experiments show that explicit object-landmark alignments and the perspective information are important factors and lead to competitive results compared with strong baselines. We have conducted comprehensive analysis to support our conclusion that explicitly modeling the objects and spatial relation alignments improving the spatial reasoning ability, generalizability and explainability of the model. Though we do not achieve the SOTA compared to transformer-based models that rely on pre-training, we plan to apply the same ideas on top of such recent models in the future.

7 Acknowledgement

This project is supported by National Science Foundation (NSF) CAREER award 2028626 and partially supported by the Office of Naval Research (ONR) grant N00014-20-1-2005. Any opinions, findings, and conclusions or recommendations expressed in this material are those of the authors and do not necessarily reflect the views of the National Science Foundation nor the Office of Naval Research. We thank all reviewers for their thoughtful comments and suggestions.

References

Peter Anderson, Qi Wu, Damien Teney, Jake Bruce, Mark Johnson, Niko Sünderhauf, Ian Reid, Stephen Gould, and Anton Van Den Hengel. 2018. Vision-and-language navigation: Interpreting visually-grounded navigation instructions in real environments. In *Proceedings of the IEEE Conference on Computer Vision and Pattern Recognition*, pages 3674–3683.

Howard Chen, Alane Suhr, Dipendra Misra, Noah Snavely, and Yoav Artzi. 2019. Touchdown: Natural language navigation and spatial reasoning in visual street environments. In *Proceedings of the IEEE/CVF Conference on Computer Vision and Pattern Recognition*, pages 12538–12547.

Soham Dan, Parisa Kordjamshidi, Julia Bonn, Archna Bhatia, Zheng Cai, Martha Palmer, and Dan Roth. 2020. From spatial relations to spatial configurations. In *Proceedings of the 12th Language Resources and Evaluation Conference*, pages 5855–5864.

Jacob Devlin, Ming-Wei Chang, Kenton Lee, and Kristina Toutanova. 2018. Bert: Pre-training of deep bidirectional transformers for language understanding. *arXiv preprint arXiv:1810.04805*.

Daniel Fried, Ronghang Hu, Volkan Cirik, Anna Rohrbach, Jacob Andreas, Louis-Philippe Morency, Taylor Berg-Kirkpatrick, Kate Saenko, Dan Klein, and Trevor Darrell. 2018. Speaker-follower models for vision-and-language navigation. *arXiv preprint arXiv:1806.02724*.

Weituo Hao, Chunyuan Li, Xiujun Li, Lawrence Carin, and Jianfeng Gao. 2020. Towards learning a generic agent for vision-and-language navigation via pre-training. In *Proceedings of the IEEE/CVF Conference on Computer Vision and Pattern Recognition*, pages 13137–13146.

Yicong Hong, Cristian Rodriguez, Yuankai Qi, Qi Wu, and Stephen Gould. 2020a. Language and visual entity relationship graph for agent navigation. *Advances in Neural Information Processing Systems*, 33:7685–7696.

Yicong Hong, Cristian Rodriguez, Qi Wu, and Stephen Gould. 2020b. Sub-instruction aware vision-and-language navigation. In *Proceedings of the 2020 Conference on Empirical Methods in Natural Language Processing (EMNLP)*, pages 3360–3376.

Yicong Hong, Qi Wu, Yuankai Qi, Cristian Rodriguez-Opazo, and Stephen Gould. 2021. Vln bert: A recurrent vision-and-language bert for navigation. In *Proceedings of the IEEE/CVF Conference on Computer Vision and Pattern Recognition*, pages 1643–1653.

Ronghang Hu, Daniel Fried, Anna Rohrbach, Dan Klein, Trevor Darrell, and Kate Saenko. 2019. Are you looking? grounding to multiple modalities in vision-and-language navigation. In *Proceedings of the 57th Annual Meeting of the Association for Computational Linguistics*, pages 6551–6557.

Gabriel Ilharco, Vihan Jain, Alexander Ku, Eugene Ie, and Jason Baldridge. 2019. General evaluation for instruction conditioned navigation using dynamic time warping. *arXiv preprint arXiv:1907.05446*.

Eric Kolve, Roozbeh Mottaghi, Winson Han, Eli VanderBilt, Luca Weihs, Alvaro Herrasti, Daniel Gordon, Yuke Zhu, Abhinav Gupta, and Ali Farhadi. 2017. Ai2-thor: An interactive 3d environment for visual ai. *arXiv preprint arXiv:1712.05474*.

Alexander Ku, Peter Anderson, Roma Patel, Eugene Ie, and Jason Baldridge. 2020. Room-Across-Room: Multilingual vision-and-language navigation with dense spatiotemporal grounding. In *Conference on Empirical Methods for Natural Language Processing (EMNLP)*.

Jialu Li, Hao Tan, and Mohit Bansal. 2021. Improving cross-modal alignment in vision language navigation via syntactic information. In *Proceedings of the 2021 Conference of the North American Chapter of the Association for Computational Linguistics: Human Language Technologies*, pages 1041–1050.

Chih-Yao Ma, Jiasen Lu, Zuxuan Wu, Ghassan AlRegib, Zsolt Kira, Richard Socher, and Caiming Xiong. 2018. Self-monitoring navigation agent via auxiliary progress estimation.

Chih-Yao Ma, Jiasen Lu, Zuxuan Wu, Ghassan AlRegib, Zsolt Kira, Richard Socher, and Caiming Xiong. 2019. Self-monitoring navigation agent via auxiliary progress estimation. *arXiv preprint arXiv:1901.03035*.

Arjun Majumdar, Ayush Shrivastava, Stefan Lee, Peter Anderson, Devi Parikh, and Dhruv Batra. 2020. Improving vision-and-language navigation with image-text pairs from the web. In *European Conference on Computer Vision*, pages 259–274. Springer.

Khanh Nguyen and Hal Daumé III. 2019. Help, anna! visual navigation with natural multimodal assistance via retrospective curiosity-encouraging imitation learning. *arXiv preprint arXiv:1909.01871*.

Jeffrey Pennington, Richard Socher, and Christopher D Manning. 2014. Glove: Global vectors for word representation. In *Proceedings of the 2014 conference on empirical methods in natural language processing (EMNLP)*, pages 1532–1543.

Yuankai Qi, Zizheng Pan, Shengping Zhang, Anton van den Hengel, and Qi Wu. 2020a. Object-and-action aware model for visual language navigation. In *Computer Vision–ECCV 2020: 16th European Conference, Glasgow, UK, August 23–28, 2020, Proceedings, Part X 16*, pages 303–317. Springer.

Yuankai Qi, Qi Wu, Peter Anderson, Xin Wang, William Yang Wang, Chunhua Shen, and Anton van den Hengel. 2020b. Reverie: Remote embodied visual referring expression in real indoor environments. In *Proceedings of the IEEE/CVF Conference on Computer Vision and Pattern Recognition*, pages 9982–9991.

Shaoqing Ren, Kaiming He, Ross Girshick, and Jian Sun. 2015. Faster r-cnn: Towards real-time object detection with region proposal networks. *Advances in neural information processing systems*, 28:91–99.

Manolis Savva, Abhishek Kadian, Oleksandr Maksymets, Yili Zhao, Erik Wijmans, Bhavana Jain, Julian Straub, Jia Liu, Vladlen Koltun, Jitendra Malik, et al. 2019. Habitat: A platform for embodied ai research. In *Proceedings of the IEEE/CVF International Conference on Computer Vision*, pages 9339–9347.

Sheng Shen, Liunian Harold Li, Hao Tan, Mohit Bansal, Anna Rohrbach, Kai-Wei Chang, Zhewei Yao, and Kurt Keutzer. 2021. How much can clip benefit vision-and-language tasks? *arXiv preprint arXiv:2107.06383*.

Mohit Shridhar, Jesse Thomason, Daniel Gordon, Yonatan Bisk, Winson Han, Roozbeh Mottaghi, Luke Zettlemoyer, and Dieter Fox. 2020. Alfred: A benchmark for interpreting grounded instructions for everyday tasks. In *Proceedings of the IEEE/CVF conference on computer vision and pattern recognition*, pages 10740–10749.

Hao Tan, Licheng Yu, and Mohit Bansal. 2019. Learning to navigate unseen environments: Back translation with environmental dropout. In *Proceedings of the 2019 Conference of the North American Chapter of the Association for Computational Linguistics: Human Language Technologies, Volume 1 (Long and Short Papers)*, pages 2610–2621.

Jesse Thomason, Michael Murray, Maya Cakmak, and Luke Zettlemoyer. 2020. Vision-and-dialog navigation. In *Conference on Robot Learning*, pages 394–406. PMLR.

Xin Wang, Qiuyuan Huang, Asli Celikyilmaz, Jianfeng Gao, Dinghan Shen, Yuan-Fang Wang, William Yang Wang, and Lei Zhang. 2019. Reinforced cross-modal matching and self-supervised imitation learning for vision-language navigation. In *Proceedings of the IEEE/CVF Conference on Computer Vision and Pattern Recognition*, pages 6629–6638.

Yubo Zhang, Hao Tan, and Mohit Bansal. 2020. Diagnosing the environment bias in vision-and-language navigation. *arXiv preprint arXiv:2005.03086*.

Yue Zhang, Quan Guo, and Parisa Kordjamshidi. 2021. Towards navigation by reasoning over spatial configurations. *arXiv preprint arXiv:2105.06839*.

Wang Zhu, Hexiang Hu, Jiacheng Chen, Zhiwei Deng, Vihan Jain, Eugene Ie, and Fei Sha. 2020. Babywalk: Going farther in vision-and-language navigation by taking baby steps. In *Proceedings of the 58th Annual Meeting of the Association for Computational Linguistics*, pages 2539–2556.

Wanrong Zhu, Yuankai Qi, Pradyumna Narayana, Kazoo Sone, Sugato Basu, Xin Eric Wang, Qi Wu, Miguel Eckstein, and William Yang Wang. 2021. Diagnosing vision-and-language navigation: What really matters. *arXiv preprint arXiv:2103.16561*.

Mining Logical Event Schemas From Pre-Trained Language Models

Lane Lawley and **Lenhart Schubert**
University of Rochester
Department of Computer Science
{llawley,schubert}@cs.rochester.edu

Abstract

We present NESL (the Neuro-Episodic Schema Learner), an event schema learning system that combines large language models, FrameNet parsing, a powerful logical representation of language, and a set of simple behavioral schemas meant to bootstrap the learning process. In lieu of a pre-made corpus of stories, our dataset is a continuous feed of "situation samples" from a pre-trained language model, which are then parsed into FrameNet frames, mapped into simple behavioral schemas, and combined and generalized into complex, hierarchical schemas for a variety of everyday scenarios. We show that careful sampling from the language model can help emphasize stereotypical properties of situations and de-emphasize irrelevant details, and that the resulting schemas specify situations more comprehensively than those learned by other systems.

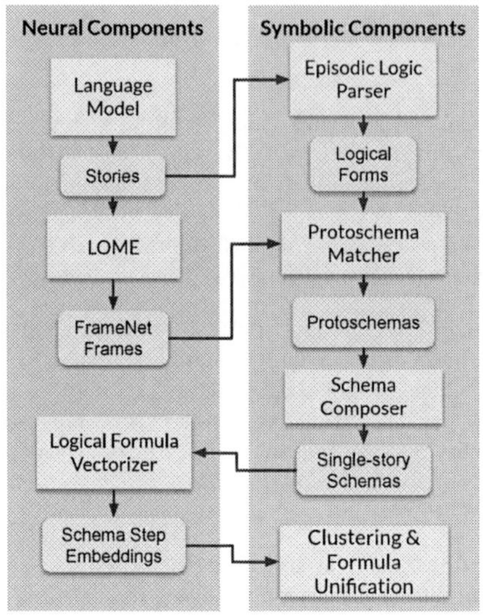

Figure 1: A diagram of the NESL schema learning pipeline. Peach-colored rounded rectangles represent data, while gray rectangles represent NESL's neural and symbolic components.

1 Introduction

Work on the task of event schema acquisition is largely separable into two main camps: the *symbolic* camp, with its structurally rich but infamously brittle representations (Lebowitz, 1980; Norvig, 1987; Mooney, 1990); and the *statistical* camp, which utilizes complex models and vast amounts of data to produce large numbers of conceptually varied event schemas at the cost of representational richness and control over what schemas are learned (Chambers and Jurafsky, 2008; Pichotta and Mooney, 2016; Wanzare et al., 2017).

In an attempt to bridge these camps together, we introduce the Neuro-Episodic Schema Learner (NESL), a composite pipeline model bringing together (1) a large, pre-trained language model; (2) word vector embedding techniques; (3) a neural FrameNet parsing and information extraction system; (4) a formal logical semantic representation of English; and (5) a hierarchical event schema framework with extraordinary expressive power.

Besides the enriched schema framework, a key contribution of NESL is the idea of *latent schema sampling* (LSS), in which a pre-trained language model is induced, via prompt-engineering, into acting as a distribution over stories, parameterized by an implicit *latent schema* coarsely established by the prompt. By finding commonalities between multiple samples from this distribution and discarding infrequent details, NESL attempts to generate more accurate, less noisy schemas. In addition to eliminating NESL's need for its own training corpus, LSS allows NESL to generate schemas for user-provided situation descriptions on demand, greatly increasing the control over what sorts of event schemas are generated.

The remainder of this paper is organized into a description of our chosen semantic representation and event schema framework (Section 2); a description of each of NESL's components (Sec-

Proceedings of the 60th Annual Meeting of the Association for Computational Linguistics Student Research Workshop, pages 332 - 345
May 22-27, 2022 ©2022 Association for Computational Linguistics

tion 3); and a description of future evaluation work we intend to complete in the near future (Section 4).

2 Schema Model

2.1 Episodic Logic

We use Episodic Logic (EL) (Hwang and Schubert, 1993) as our semantic representation of stories and of schema formulas. EL is an intensional semantic representation that is both well-suited to inference tasks and structurally similar in its surface form to English. A unique feature of EL is its treatment of *episodes* (events, situations) as first-class individuals, which may be characterized by arbitrary formulas. For a formula ϕ and an episode denoted by E, $(\phi ** E)$ expresses that E is characterized by ϕ; i.e., E is an "episode of" ϕ occurring. In the EL schema in Figure 2, for example, each formula in the `STEPS` section implicitly characterizes an episode (not displayed). The "header" formula at the top of that figure also characterizes an episode variable, `?E`. EL can temporally relate episodes using predicates implementing the Allen Interval Algebra (Allen, 1983), allowing for complex and hierarchical situation descriptions.

2.2 EL Schemas

Past approaches to statistical schema learning have largely represented schemas as sequences of lexical event tuples (Chambers and Jurafsky, 2008; Pichotta and Mooney, 2016). Seeking a richer representation, we adopt the rich, EL-based schema framework presented by Lawley et al. (2021), henceforth referred to in this paper as *EL schemas*. EL schemas are section-based: the main two sections, `STEPS` and `ROLES`, enumerate the temporal events ("steps") that make up the schema, and the type and relational constraints on the schema's participants, respectively (see Figure 2).

Designed as a suitable representation of human-centric events, EL schemas can also specify preconditions, postconditions, arbitrary temporal relationships between steps, and the *goals* of individual participants in the schema. All schema participants are represented as typed variables, all sharing a scope within the same schema, and formulas may include any number of variables as arguments. EL schemas also allow for recursive *nesting*: a schema may be embedded as a step in another schema, and implicitly expanded to check constraints or generate inferences.

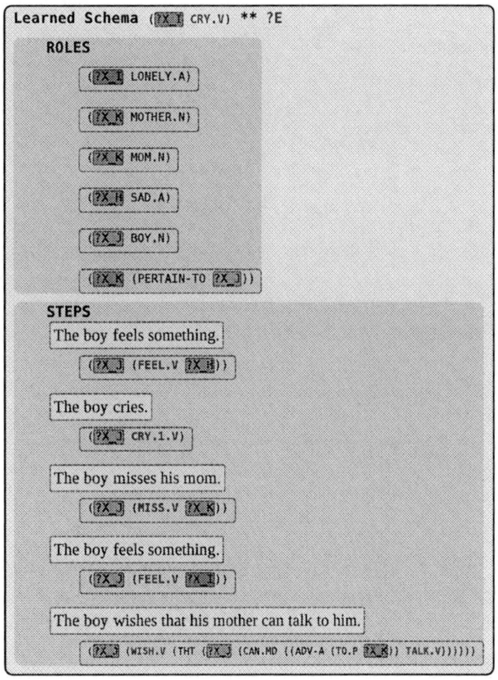

Figure 2: A schema generated by NESL from a single GPT-J 6B story sample. Note that the second step's verb predicate, `CRY.1.V`, contains a number: this identifies it as the header of a unique *protoschema* instance that was matched to the story.

For more information on the EL schema framework, see (Lawley et al., 2019) and (Lawley et al., 2021).

2.2.1 Protoschemas

The schema system we use here, due to Lawley et al. (2021), is designed to acquire schemas in the manner a very young child might. In his theory of the origin of intelligence in children, Jean Piaget hypothesized that event generalization, in babies, "always proceeds from the undifferentiated schema to the individual and to the general, combined and complementary" (Piaget and Cook, 1952). While we don't assert any particular theory of child development in this work, we follow the spirit of Piaget's claim and propose a system wherein complex schemas are learned from simple, universal ones.

As a way of modeling general actions a very young child would be likely to understand, we start with a handwritten corpus of several dozen "*protoschemas*", such as "X helps Y with action A", "X eats food F to alleviate hunger", etc.; the aim of this schema learning framework is to first match

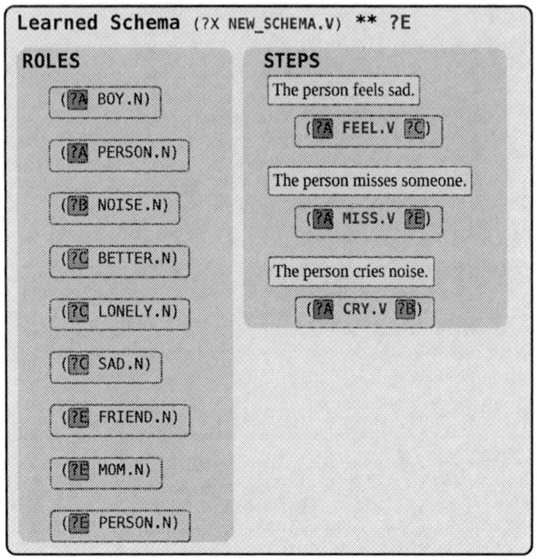

Figure 3: A schema generated by NESL combining multiple single-story schemas, such as the one shown in Figure 2. Note that some details from the single-story schema have been removed, and that variables have multiple possible types, sometimes conflicting; displaying these as certainty-weighted disjunctions is intended for a future version of NESL.

these protoschemas to stories, and then build progressively more complicated schemas from them.

The schemas built using protoschema matches may add complexity to them in two dimensions: the *compositional* dimension, in which new schemas temporally compose sequences of matched protoschemas to describe a new situation; and the *taxonomic* dimension, in which a protoschema is conceptually narrowed by additional type and relational constraints on its participants, such as "eating something" being narrowed to "eating an apple from a tree".

Protoschemas provide a rich semantic basis for understanding complex situations in terms of basic human behaviors, and this benefit is also reflected in an immediate practical convenience: protoschemas can be employed as a way of *canonicalizing* multiple distinct linguistic phrasings of the same basic action type. For more information on how we use protoschemas for this in NESL, see Section 3.2.

3 Learning Pipeline

NESL learns schemas using a multi-step pipeline, briefly described in order here, and further expounded upon in following subsections:

1. Using a procedure we call *latent schema sampling*, N short stories are sampled from the same topic-parameterized distribution defined by a language model and a task-specific prompt. (Section 3.1)

2. The N stories are then parsed into Episodic Logical Form (ELF), the formal semantic representation underlying the event schemas.

3. Simple protoschemas are then matched to each of the N EL-parsed stories with the help of LOME, a state-of-the-art neural FrameNet parser, whose identified FrameNet frames are mapped to corresponding EL protoschemas. (Section 3.2)

4. For each of the N stories, all identified protoschemas, and all unmatched ELF episodes and type formulas from the story, are composed into a *single-story schema*, in which constants are abstracted to variables and type-constrained, and events are related with a time graph. (Section 3.3)

5. The N single-story schemas are generalized into a single schema, incorporating common details and excising specious, incidental information from the entire set. (Section 3.4)

3.1 Latent Schema Sampling

Any story may have a generic schema formed from it. However, stories often contain incidental details: the sequence of going to school, taking an exam, and waving hello to a friend should likely have its third event discarded in a suitably general "school" schema. We adopt the hypothesis that the language model can generate stories according to a distribution implicitly parameterized by one or more *latent schemas*, from which it may deviate, but according to which it abstractly "selects" subsequent events. By inducing the language model into this distribution via prompt-engineering, and then sampling from it, we hypothesize that high-probability events will occur frequently across samples, and that incidental details will occur less frequently. By generating schemas for each sampled individual story, and generalizing them based on shared events and properties, we may approximate the language model's latent schemas and encode them into interpretable Episodic Logic schemas.

We implement latent schema sampling (LSS) with a sequence of two passes through the GPT-J

6B language model (Wang and Komatsuzaki, 2021) [1], each pass performing a different task induced by a "prompt-engineering" approach, in which the language model is not fine-tuned, but instructed in natural language to perform a task on some input via its context window. The two language model-based tasks of LSS are described below, and illustrated in the top half of Figure 4.

3.1.1 Topic Extraction

To ensure that the stories generated by LSS share common and salient topics, and that the story topics conform to a degree of conceptual simplicity that will work well with the child-like protoschemas and the early-stage EL parsing pipeline, we estimate the set of topics from a known collection of simple stories. We assemble a collection of short, five-sentence stories by filtering the ROCStories dataset (Mostafazadeh et al., 2016), taking the 500 stories with the highest proportion of words shared with a classic collection of child-level stories (McGuffey, 1901).

We created a few-shot task prompt for GPT-J 6B to extract one to three simple topics, such as *"going to a store"* or *"playing baseball"*, for a given story. We inserted each filtered ROCStory into this prompt and saved the generated topics for use in the next step.

3.1.2 Story Sampling

Adopting the hypothesis that story topics encode latent schemas instantiated by the story, we created a second few-shot prompt for the task of story generation given an extracted topic. For each topic generated in the previous step, we sample N stories from the language model with a temperature setting of 0.4 and a repetition penalty of 0.11. Sampled stories are filtered through a blacklist of 375 inappropriate words (Inflianskas, 2019), and stories caught in the content filter are "re-rolled" until N content-appropriate stories have been generated.

3.2 Protoschema Matching as FrameNet Parsing

To begin forming schemas, we bootstrap by matching general behavioral *protoschemas* to the stories. Protoschema matching is complicated by several issues, including the large number of actions that may evoke a general protoschema (e.g. walking, running, driving, riding, and flying are all kinds of self-motion), and the large number of phrasings that express the same action. To help address these concerns, we first observe that the FrameNet project (Baker et al., 1998) contains many conceptual frames with protoschema analogs, such as self-motion, ingestion, and possession frames. While FrameNet frames lack hierarchical, compositional, and formal internal semantics, and are thus not suitable for the mechanistic inferences these schemas are meant to enable, these frames may be *mapped* to analogous protoschemas as a way to leverage existing work on FrameNet frame parsing.

[1]We chose GPT-J 6B due to its number of parameters; at the time of this work, we believe it to be the largest publicly-downloadable auto-regressive language model.

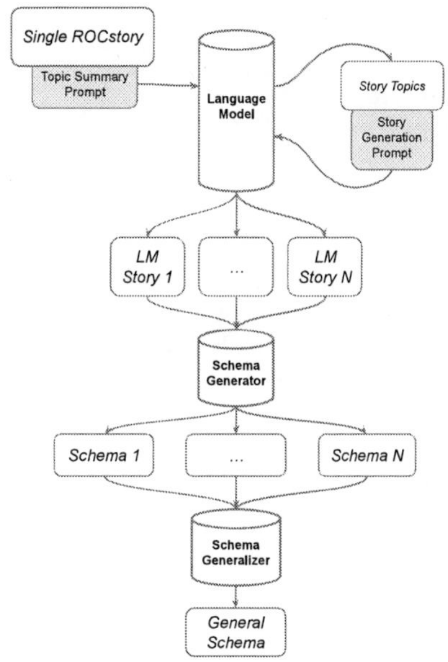

Figure 4: A diagram of the Latent Schema Sampling (LSS) procedure used to generate stories from a fixed-topic distribution.

Using LOME (Xia et al., 2021), a state-of-the-art neural FrameNet parsing system, we identify FrameNet frames in sampled stories. The invoking actions and roles of the frames are given as spans of text, which we reduce to single tokens using a dependency parser, selecting the first token in each span with a `NSUBJ`, `DOBJ`, or `POBJ` tag. The token indices are then aligned with those in the Episodic Logic parser to identify individuals in the logical domain whose type predicates were derived from those tokens. Finally, the frame, now with EL domain individuals as its roles, is mapped to a corresponding protoschema with hand-written mapping rules.

This FrameNet-based protoschema matching

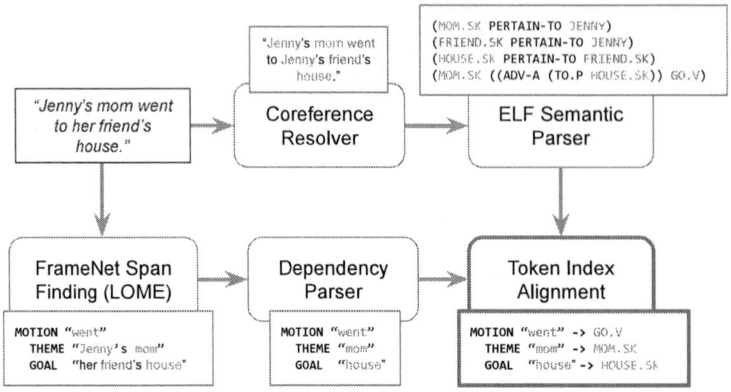

Figure 5: A presentation of the process by which FrameNet parsing with LOME is used for protoschema matching. The coreference resolver is provided by AllenNLP (Gardner et al., 2017), and the dependency parser is provided by spaCy (Honnibal and Montani, 2017).

process is illustrated, with an example, in Figure 5.

3.3 Single-Story Schema Formation

After parsing a story into Episodic Logic and using LOME to find protoschema matches in the story, we create a *single-story schema* to encapsulate the story's events and participants. This schema will be general in that the story's specific individuals will be abstracted to variables, and also in that the story's exact verbiage will be "normalized" into the semantic representations of EL and protoschemas. However, the schema will be non-general in that all of the story's details, without regard to what "usually" happens in the latent schema that generated it, will be kept, and only removed during multi-schema generalization (see Section 3.4).

The process of single-story schema generation is fairly simple:

1. The event formulae of the story are ordered as steps in a schema. If any of those steps matched to protoschemas, we instead substitute the header of that protoschema as the step; the full specification of the nested protoschema will be output separately, and may be freely expanded.

2. All individual constants that are arguments to any of the verbs of those steps are replaced with variables.

3. All type and relational constraints on those variables are extracted from the EL parse of the story, as well as from any recursively nested protoschema steps, and enumerated in the `ROLES` section of the schema.

4. A verbalization of the schema, generated with the GPT-2 model described in Section 3.5, is fed to a GPT-J 6B model with a prompt designed for single-sentence story summaries. The summary sentence is then parsed back into EL, and its arguments are aligned, based on type, with participants in the schema. This formula is then used as the "header" episode of the schema, as seen in the generated header of the schema in Figure 2.

3.4 Multi-Story Schema Generalization

Once N stories have been sampled and N corresponding schemas obtained from them, those schemas must be generalized into a single schema. The remainder of this section describes the four main steps of the multi-schema generalization process:

1. Schema step clustering: similar steps of each of the N un-merged schemas are generalized together using vector embeddings. (Sections 3.4.1 and 3.4.2)

2. Step argument co-reference resolution: the verb arguments of the events of each general step are linked to one another based on co-reference information in the N un-merged schemas. (Section 3.4.3)

3. Temporal step ordering: the general schema's steps are put into a partial "happens-before" order. (Section 3.4.4)

4. Occurrence frequency filtering: infrequent details across the N un-merged schemas are assumed to be unimportant to the latent schema

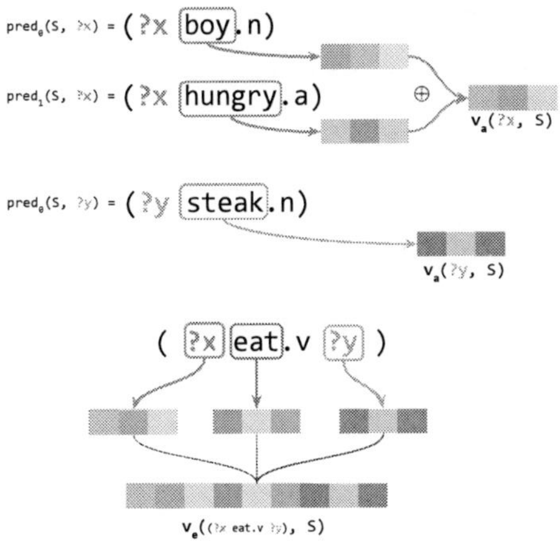

Figure 6: The procedure for embedding EL formulas as vectors. word2vec embeddings for each argument's lexical predicates are averaged together to form vector representations of each argument. These are concatenated, in subject-verb-object order, with verb predicates, to form vector representations of event formulas. Here, $\oplus$ denotes an element-wise vector mean operation.

and discarded from the general schema approximating it. (Section 3.4.5)

Figure 3 shows a schema generalized from multiple single-story schemas, such as the one shown in Figure 2.

3.4.1 Logical Formula Vector Embeddings

When generalizing several schemas sampled from the same "latent schema", we would like to combine and generalize non-identical, but functionally similar, steps, e.g. "the boy eats cake" and "the girl eats pie".

To do this, we define a function $v_a(a, S)$, which takes an argument symbol a and a schema S and returns the element-wise mean of the word vectors of all lexical predicates in S applied to argument a:

$$v_a(a, S) = \bigoplus_i [v_w(\text{pred}_i(S, a))]$$

We also define a function $v_s(\phi, S)$, which takes a step formula ϕ and a schema S and returns vector concatenation of ϕ's verb predicate and the vector representations of each of ϕ's arguments:

$$v_s(\phi, S) = v_w(\phi_{\text{verb}}) \;\; +\!\!+ \;\; \underset{i}{+\!\!+} [v_a(\phi_{\text{arg}_i}, S)]$$

Figure 6 illustrates this vectorization process using three "argument type" formulas as the values of the $pred$ function. The lexical word vector function, v_w, is implemented by word2vec. $\oplus$ and $+\!\!+$ refer to element-wise mean and vector concatenation operations, respectively.

3.4.2 Formula Vector Clustering

After vector embeddings have been created for the EL formulas for each step of each of the N sampled schemas, we form clusters of similar formula embeddings. Because the vector elements for the formula's verb and for each argument are independent, clusters can correlate not only similar actions, like "boy draws tree" and "boy sketches tree", but also similar argument types, like "boy eats cake" and "girl eats pie". When suitably similar steps have been clustered from across each of the sampled schemas, the clusters form the basis for steps in a new, generalized schema.

Given N schemas, each generated from one of N sampled stories, we denote the sets of step vectors for schema $0 < i < N$ as $ST_i = \{\vec{s}_{i,0}, ..., \vec{s}_{i,M}\}$. For each step vector $\vec{s}_{i,a}$, we construct a list L of each step vector in each other schema, $\vec{s}_{j\neq i,b}$, and sort the elements of L in descending order according to their cosine similarity with $\vec{s}_{i,a}$. Steps suitably similar to $\vec{s}_{i,a}$ are defined as the set of all elements $L_{i\leq k}$ where $k = \underset{k}{\text{argmax}}[sim(L_k) - sim(L_{k+1})]$, that is, all steps prior to the largest drop in cosine similarity values in the ordered list.

Once each step s has an associated cluster L_s of suitably similar steps, symmetricity is enforced by merging all similarity clusters with shared elements: each L_{s_1} and L_{s_2} are set to $L_{s_1} \cup L_{s_2}$ if and only if $L_{s_1} \cap L_{s_2} \neq \emptyset$. When this is done, each final cluster L_s represents one step in the generalized schema.

3.4.3 Schema Slot Co-Reference Resolution

After forming clusters of similar steps across N schemas, we would like to use these clusters as abstract steps in the merged, general schema. However, some clustered steps may not have specific instances in some schemas, even if they should ultimately share arguments with other steps in those schemas. Furthermore, specious co-reference may occur in LM-generated stories or in imperfect ELF parses, e.g., a person incorrectly being equivocated with their dog in the parsed logical domain; we would like to exclude such co-references from our merged, general schema on the basis of their (hoped-for) infrequency among the N samples.

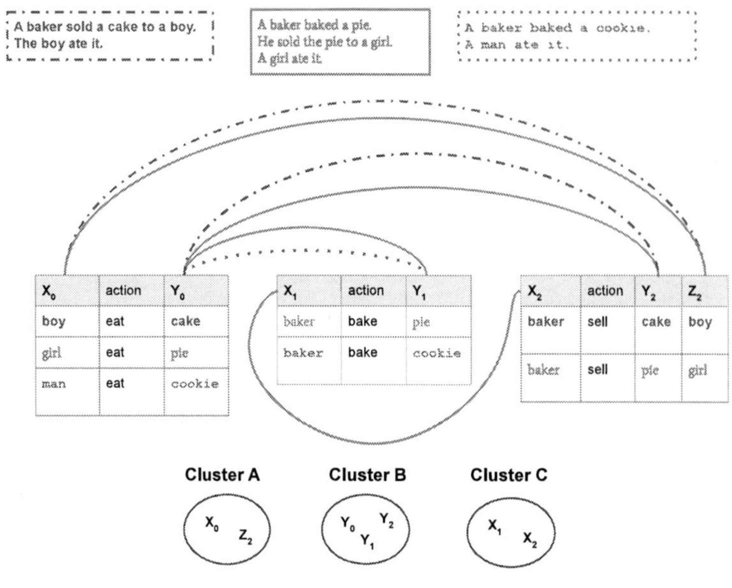

Figure 7: An illustration of the multigraph argument co-reference technique used to merge multiple sampled schemas into one general schema. Each action-argument table represents a cluster of steps obtained by the vector clustering approach in Section 3.4.2. Lines between pairs of argument columns correspond to an argument co-reference in one specific story instance. Each story instance is assigned a unique line pattern, color, and font, for easy identification. The transitive closures of the multigraph's edge relation form the clusters seen at the bottom of the figure; these clusters will form the variables of the eventual merged, generalized schema, whose abstracted steps will be, in no particular order, `(A eat B)`, `(C bake B)`, and `(C sell B A)`. Note that this final `sell` action is only present in two of the three story instances.

To address these concerns, we perform argument co-reference resolution across step clusters by constructing a multigraph $G = (V, E)$ where V is the set of all unique argument positions across all clusters, and a single edge between cluster arguments $\texttt{arg}_i \in V$ and $\texttt{arg}_j \in V$ signifies that, in at least one of the N sampled schemas, formulas from each cluster existed and shared an argument value in those two positions. One such edge between any two vertices may exist for each schema being merged.

After construction, the multigraph is reduced to a standard graph, $G' = (V', E')$ with weighted edges: the set of all edges $E_{i,j}$ between each pair of vertices $\texttt{arg}_i$ and $\texttt{arg}_j$ is converted to a single edge $E'_{i,j} \in E'$ whose weight is given by:

$$W_{E'_{i,j}} = \frac{|E_{i,j}|}{|S(\texttt{arg}_i) \cap S(\texttt{arg}_j)|}$$

where $S(v_x)$ is the set of all schemas with a step found in the step cluster for which $\texttt{arg}_x$ is an argument. Informally, this weight is the ratio of the number of schemas in which the argument co-reference *was* detected to the number of schemas in which it *could have been* detected. To remove specious, infrequent co-references, E' is filtered to remove edges with $W_{E'_{i,j}} < 0.25$.

Argument clusters are formed by the transitive closure of the edge relation given by E', and each argument cluster then forms a final variable for the merged, general schema. The types for each of the final variables are taken from the union of all possible types across all schema instances, and each type predication is assigned a certainty score proportional to its frequency across all N schemas.

An example of the multigraph and final argument clusters generated by this process is illustrated in Figure 7.

3.4.4 Temporal Sorting of Schema Steps

Once steps from specific schema instances have been clustered into general steps, and shared arguments have been created across these general steps, we must finally derive their temporal order in the general schema. Episodes in Episodic Logic may be continuous intervals, and EL schemas support complex temporal relations between the episodes characterized by their steps. The schema step intervals, however, are slightly simplified from the full semantics of EL, and represented as a "time graph" specifying before- and after-relationships between the start and end times of each episode.

Much like the argument co-reference resolution done in Section 3.4.3, we solve this with a *temporal* multi-graph. To build the graph, we further simplify the temporal model by assuming that step episodes never overlap and are defined solely by their start times. This assumption is desirable for its simplicity and computational efficiency, and suitable because the current version of the EL parser makes the same assumption. However, this algorithm could, in theory, be extended to operate on both start and end times.

We define the temporal multi-graph $G^T = (V^T, E^T)$ such that the vertices V^T are the start times of each step in the merged, general schema, and, for all steps i and j in the general schema, one edge exists between each V_i^T and V_j^T for each occurrence of an instance of V_i^T happening before an instance of V_j^T in the same un-merged schema.

Similarly to how edges were assigned weights in the argument co-reference graph based on the ratio of the number of edges to the number of possible edges, we say that, in the general schema, step i happens before step j if and only if:

$$|E_{i,j}^T| > \frac{|S(i) \cap S(j)|}{2}$$

Informally, step i happens before step j if and only if the majority of un-merged schemas that contain both also have a happens-before edge between them.

3.4.5 Occurrence Frequency Filtering

Recall that the idea behind latent schema *sampling* is to filter out events that are unimportant to a core schema by exploiting their low frequency of generation by a large language model. Therefore, to finish our general schema, we must finally remove general steps that do not occur in enough of the N sampled schemas to distinguish themselves from "noise". We currently define this threshold for "enough" as $\frac{N}{3}$: at least one third of sampled schemas must contain an instance of a general step for the step to remain in the general schema.

3.5 Verbalization and Rendering

Once finalized, we post-process learned general schemas for human readability. To verbalize the formal ELF representations of the schema steps, we first apply rule-based transductions to serialize the formula's lexical EL predicates into a pseudo-English representation. Then, using a pre-trained, fine-tuned, 774M-parameter GPT-2 model (Radford et al., 2019), we convert these pseudo-English symbol sequences into proper English. Using the Huggingface Transformers library (Wolf et al., 2020), we fine-tuned this GPT-2 model on 1,200 pairs, manually annotated by a research assistant, for this task [2].

After verbalizing the steps, we render the general schemas into an HTML representation for human review, automatically color-coding the variables with maximum mutual contrast for enhanced readability. An example of a verbalized and rendered schema is shown in Figure 2.

4 Future Evaluation

This project is a work in progress; although NESL can generate one general schema every 10 minutes, and has generated several hundred to date, qualitative evaluation of the generated schemas has not yet been performed. Imminently, we intend to carry out two human-judged studies: one evaluating the quality of *inferences* generated by the learned schemas when given unseen stories, and another evaluating the quality of the schemas themselves.

Logical schemas enable consistent, structured, and interpretable inferences about novel text, by matching pieces of the text to pieces of the schema, replacing schema variables with entities from the story, and treating other formulas in the schema that use those newly-filled variables as inferences. It is crucial that we demonstrate the inferential capacity of these learned schemas, and as future work, we will be sourcing suitable inference datasets, designing a means of presenting inferences to human judges, and collecting quality evaluations.

In addition to inferences, we would like to evaluate whether the schemas we obtain are both *topically cohesive*, i.e., focused descriptions of one kind of situation; and *interesting*, i.e., capable of generating useful and novel inferences about situations, rather than obvious or redundant ones.

Using our GPT-2 verbalization model and schema rendering software, described in Section 3.5, to make our schemas and inferences readable to untrained human judges, we intend to immediately move forward with the design and execution

[2] Our work on GPT-2 for formula verbalization is preliminary; as we continue this work, a more robust annotation protocol may be required, employing multiple annotators.

of these quality evaluation studies to complete the work.

5 Conclusion

We have described NESL, a hybrid neural and formal-logical schema learning system with which we aim to combine a richly structured schema representation, a human learning-inspired approach to schema acquisition, the linguistically flexible sentence understanding characteristic of neural NLP systems, and the large amount of knowledge contained in large language models.

By bringing a large and varied number of components from across the literature to bear, we have shown that general, semantically rich, and seemingly sensical schemas may be extracted from large language models and represented interpretably. In the immediate future, we also plan to demonstrate that these schemas are useful for inference tasks.

References

James F. Allen. 1983. Maintaining knowledge about temporal intervals. *Commun. ACM*, 26(11):832–843.

Collin F. Baker, Charles J. Fillmore, and John B. Lowe. 1998. The berkeley framenet project. In *Proceedings of the 36th Annual Meeting of the Association for Computational Linguistics and 17th International Conference on Computational Linguistics - Volume 1*, ACL '98/COLING '98, pages 86–90. Association for Computational Linguistics.

Nathanael Chambers and Dan Jurafsky. 2008. Unsupervised learning of narrative event chains. *Proceedings of ACL-08: HLT*, pages 789–797.

Matt Gardner, Joel Grus, Mark Neumann, Oyvind Tafjord, Pradeep Dasigi, Nelson F. Liu, Matthew Peters, Michael Schmitz, and Luke S. Zettlemoyer. 2017. Allennlp: A deep semantic natural language processing platform.

Matthew Honnibal and Ines Montani. 2017. spaCy 2: Natural language understanding with Bloom embeddings, convolutional neural networks and incremental parsing. To appear.

Chung Hee Hwang and Lenhart K Schubert. 1993. Episodic logic: A situational logic for natural language processing. *Situation Theory and its Applications*, 3:303–338.

Roman Inflianskas. 2019. profanity-filter: A python library for detecting and filtering profanity. `https://github.com/rominf/profanity-filter/blob/master/profanity_filter/data/en_profane_words.txt`.

Lane Lawley, Gene L. Kim, and Lenhart Schubert. 2019. Towards natural language story understanding with rich logical schemas. In *Proceedings of the IWCS workshop on Natural Language and Computer Science*.

Lane Lawley, Benjamin Kuehnert, and Lenhart K. Schubert. 2021. Learning general event schemas with episodic logic. In *NALOMA*.

Michael Lebowitz. 1980. *Generalization and Memory in an Integrated Understanding System*. Ph.D. thesis, Yale University, New Haven, CT, USA. AAI8109800.

William Holmes McGuffey. 1901. *The New McGuffey First Reader*. American Book Company.

Raymond J Mooney. 1990. *A general explanation-based learning mechanism and its application to narrative understanding*. Morgan Kaufmann.

Nasrin Mostafazadeh, Nathanael Chambers, Xiaodong He, Devi Parikh, Dhruv Batra, Lucy Vanderwende, Pushmeet Kohli, and James Allen. 2016. A corpus and cloze evaluation for deeper understanding of commonsense stories. In *Proceedings of the 2016 Conference of the North American Chapter of the Association for Computational Linguistics: Human Language Technologies*, pages 839–849, San Diego, California. Association for Computational Linguistics.

Peter Norvig. 1987. Inference in text understanding. In *AAAI*, pages 561–565.

Jean Piaget and Margaret Cook. 1952. *The origins of intelligence in children*, volume 8. International Universities Press New York.

Karl Pichotta and Raymond J Mooney. 2016. Learning statistical scripts with lstm recurrent neural networks. In *Thirtieth AAAI Conference on Artificial Intelligence*.

Alec Radford, Jeff Wu, Rewon Child, David Luan, Dario Amodei, and Ilya Sutskever. 2019. Language models are unsupervised multitask learners.

Ben Wang and Aran Komatsuzaki. 2021. GPT-J-6B: A 6 Billion Parameter Autoregressive Language Model. `https://github.com/kingoflolz/mesh-transformer-jax`.

Lilian Wanzare, Alessandra Zarcone, Stefan Thater, and Manfred Pinkal. 2017. Inducing script structure from crowdsourced event descriptions via semi-supervised clustering. In *Proceedings of the 2nd Workshop on Linking Models of Lexical, Sentential and Discourse-level Semantics*, pages 1–11.

Thomas Wolf, Lysandre Debut, Victor Sanh, Julien Chaumond, Clement Delangue, Anthony Moi, Pierric Cistac, Tim Rault, Rémi Louf, Morgan Funtowicz, Joe Davison, Sam Shleifer, Patrick von Platen, Clara Ma, Yacine Jernite, Julien Plu, Canwen Xu, Teven Le

Scao, Sylvain Gugger, Mariama Drame, Quentin Lhoest, and Alexander M. Rush. 2020. Transformers: State-of-the-art natural language processing. In *Proceedings of the 2020 Conference on Empirical Methods in Natural Language Processing: System Demonstrations*, pages 38–45, Online. Association for Computational Linguistics.

Patrick Xia, Guanghui Qin, Siddharth Vashishtha, Yunmo Chen, Tongfei Chen, Chandler May, Craig Harman, Kyle Rawlins, Aaron Steven White, and Benjamin Van Durme. 2021. LOME: Large ontology multilingual extraction. In *Proceedings of the 16th Conference of the European Chapter of the Association for Computational Linguistics: System Demonstrations*, pages 149–159, Online. Association for Computational Linguistics.

A Learned Schema Examples

The following are additional examples of schemas learned by NESL.

A.1 From the prompt "going fishing"

```
Learned Schema (?X NEW_SCHEMA.V) ** ?E
  ROLES
      (?B SEAFOOD.N)
      (?G PERSON.N)
      (?K FOOD.N)
      (?L SUPPER.N)
      (?M LOT.N)
  STEPS
    The person cooks the sea food for the food.
      (?G ((ADV-A (FOR.P ?K)) COOK.V) ?B)
    The person cleans the sea food.
      (?G CLEAN_PROTO.V ?B)
    The person cooks the sea food.
      (?G COOK.V ?B)
    The person eats sea food.
      (?G EAT_PROTO.V ?B)
    The person goes somewhere.
      (?G GO.V)
    The person catches the sea food.
      (?G CATCH_PROTO.V ?B)
    The person catches the lot.
      (?G CATCH.V ?M)
  GOALS
    The person wants the sea food to be not dirty.
      (?G (WANT.V (THAT (NOT (?B DIRTY.A)))))
    The person wants to not be hungry.
      (?G (WANT.V (THAT (NOT (?G HUNGRY.A)))))
```

A.2 From the prompt "going to the library"

```
Learned Schema (?X NEW_SCHEMA.V) ** ?E
  ROLES
      (?A BOOK.N)
      (?E PERSON.N)
      (?I LIBRARY.N)
      (?J ENTITY.N)
      (?L BOY.N)
      (?LO LOCATION.N)
      (?LX LOCATION.N)
      (?T EVENT.N)
  STEPS
    The person looks for a book.
      (?E ((ADV-A (FOR.P ?A)) LOOK_PROTO.V))
    The person reads a book about an event.
      (?E ((ADV-A (ABOUT.P ?T)) READ_PROTO.V) ?A)
    The person likes the book.
      (?E LIKE_PROTO.V ?A)
    The person finds a book.
      (?E FIND_PROTO.V ?A)
    The person goes to the library.
      (?E ((ADV-A (FROM.P ?J)) GO_PROTO.V) ?I)
    The person reads a book.
      (?E READ.V ?A)
  GOALS
    The person wants to find the book.
      (?E (WANT.V (KA (FIND.V ?A))))
    The person wants to possess a book.
      (?E (WANT.V (KA (POSSESS.V ?A))))
    The person wants to be at the library.
      (?E (WANT.V (KA ((ADV-A (AT.P ?I)) BE.V))))
```

A.3 From the prompt "mailing a letter"

```
Learned Schema (?X NEW_SCHEMA.V) ** ?E
  ROLES
      (?A PERSON.N)
      (?B DOCUMENT.N)
      (?C LETTER.N)
      (?D ENVELOPE.N)
      (?F LOCATION.N)
      (?G STAMP.N)
      (?J PAPER.N)
  STEPS
    The person writes on the paper.
      (?A ((ADV-A (ON.P ?J)) WRITE.V) ?A)
    The person puts the letter in the envelope.
      (?A PUT_PROTO.V ?C ?D)
    The person writes a letter to the person.
      (?A ((ADV-A (TO.P ?F)) MAIL.V) ?C)
    The person puts the stamp on the envelope.
      (?A PUT_PROTO.V ?G ?D)
    The person writes on the envelope.
      (?A ((ADV-A (ON.P ?D)) WRITE.V))
    The person writes to the person.
      (?A MAIL.V ?A)
    The person's document is from them.
      (?B ((ADV-A (FROM.P ?A)) BE.V))
  GOALS
    The person wants the letter to be at the envelope.
      (?A (WANT.V (THAT (?C (AT.P ?D)))))
    The person wants the stamp to be at the envelope.
      (?A (WANT.V (THAT (?G (AT.P ?D)))))
```

B Language Model Prompts

B.1 Story Topic Summarization Prompt

This is the story generation prompt provided to GPT-J to obtain latent story schemas, or topics, from given stories. The format string at the end, `%s`, is replaced with the input story, and a completion from the language model is truncated at a newline to obtain a topic. The prompt stories and latent schemas were written by research assistants and chosen based on subjective downstream schema acquisition quality on a development set of schema topics estimated from ROCstories.

```
Story:

Tom loved playing baseball.
He had a big game.
He was up to hit.
He hit a long drive.
He made a run and won the game.

Core story schemas:

playing a game
playing baseball
winning a game
--------
Story:

The man took a shower.
The hot water went cold.
He still had soap in his hair.
He washed his hair quickly.
He was shivering when he got out of the
    shower.

Core story schemas:

bathing
taking a shower
--------
Story:

Oran bought binoculars.
He took them outside.
He saw birds.
He watched them.
They became his friends.

Core story schemas:

watching animals
using binoculars
buying something
--------
Story:

Emma went to school.
She studied math.
She ate lunch.
Her teacher gave her a lot of homework.
Later, she went home.

Core story schemas:

going to school
studying something
--------
Story:

A farmer got up in the morning.
He put his boots on.
He went outside.
```

```
He milked the cow.
He went back to bed.

Core story schemas:

farming
milking a cow
--------
Story:

My son is a little child.
He ran outside to play.
His friend was out there with him.
They played together with sticks.
My son came in from outside.

Core story schemas:

children playing
playing with a friend
playing outside
--------
Story:

I went to my door yesterday.
I saw there was a new book.
It came right to me.
I was pretty happy about that.
I couldn't wait to read it.

Core story schemas:
getting mail
reading a book
--------
Story:

The hedge started to grow.
Spring came around.
The hedge started to bud flowers.
The flowers grew.
The roses were very beautiful.

Core story schemas:

springtime
plants growing
--------
Story:

%s

Core story schemas:
```

B.2 Story Generation Prompt

This is the story generation prompt provided to GPT-J to obtain a story given a topic as input. The format string at the end, `%s`, is replaced with the input topic, and a completion from the language model is truncated at a double-newline to obtain a story. The prompt stories were written by research assistants and chosen based on subjective downstream schema acquisition quality on a development set of schema topics estimated from ROCstories.

```
Stories about baseball:

Tom loved playing baseball.
He had a big game.
He was up to hit.
He hit a long drive.
He made a run and won the game.

Bob went to see a baseball game.
The players had nice bats.
The players swung at the ball.
One player hit the ball.
He hit a home run.

Jenny was playing baseball.
She took a bat and got ready.
She swung her bat at the ball.
She hit the ball.
She won the game.

--------
Stories about showers:

The man took a shower.
The hot water went cold.
He still had soap in his hair.
He washed his hair quickly.
He was shivering when he got out of the
    shower.

Jenny took a shower.
She used soap to wash her body.
She washed her hair.
The water was warm.
She dried off with a towel.

Jack was dirty.
He needed to get clean.
He took a long shower.
The shower water was very hot.
He used plenty of soap.

--------
Stories about plants:

Jessie loved plants.
She had plants in her apartment.
She watered the plants every day.
Her favorite plant was her fern.
Jessie wanted to buy more plants.

Alan bought a plant at the store.
The plant died.
He bought another plant.
He watered it.
It didn't die.

Plants are usually green.
Some plants are different colors.
Sometimes people keep plants in their
    houses.
They water those plants.
People like plants.

--------
Stories about school:

Emma went to school.
She studied math.
She ate lunch.
```

```
Her teacher gave her a lot of homework.
Later, she went home.

Jason was at school.
He ate lunch in the cafeteria.
After lunch, he went to class.
His teacher taught him about math.
He went home and ate dinner.

Abhishek loved to go to school.
His teacher gave him fun homework.
He finished his homework and gave it
    back to the teacher.
The teacher said Abhishek did a good job
    .
The teacher gave him a good grade.

Stories about %s:
```

Exploring Cross-lingual Textual Style Transfer with Large Multilingual Language Models

Daniil Moskovskiy[1] **Daryna Dementieva**[1,2] **Alexander Panchenko**[1]
[1]Skolkovo Institute of Science and Technology, Russia
[2]Technical University of Munich, Germany
{daniil.moskovskiy,daryna.dementieva,a.panchenko}@skoltech.ru

Abstract

Detoxification is a task of generating text in polite style while preserving meaning and fluency of the original toxic text. Existing detoxification methods are designed to work in one exact language. This work investigates multilingual and cross-lingual detoxification and the behavior of large multilingual models like in this setting. Unlike previous works we aim to make large language models able to perform detoxification without direct fine-tuning in given language. Experiments show that multilingual models are capable of performing multilingual style transfer. However, models are not able to perform cross-lingual detoxification and direct fine-tuning on exact language is inevitable.

1 Introduction

The task of Textual Style Transfer (Textual Style Transfer) can be viewed as a task where certain properties of text are being modified while rest retain the same[1]. In this work we focus on detoxification textual style transfer (dos Santos et al., 2018a; Dementieva et al., 2021a). It can be formulated as follows: given two text corpora $D^X = \{x_1, x_2, \dots x_n\}$ and $D^Y = \{y_1, y_2, \dots, y_n\}$, where X, Y - are two sets of all possible text in styles s^X, s^Y respectively, we want to build a model $f_\theta : X \to Y$, such that the probability $p(y_{gen}|x, s^X, s^Y)$ of transferring the style s^X of given text x (by generation y_{gen}) to the style s^Y is maximized (where s^X and s^Y are toxic and non-toxic styles respectively).

Some examples of detoxification presented in Table 1.

Textual style transfer gained a lot of attention with a rise of deep learning-based NLP methods. Given that, Textual Style Transfer has now a lot of specific subtasks ranging from formality style transfer (Rao and Tetreault, 2018; Yao and Yu, 2021) and simplification of domain-specific texts (Devaraj et al., 2021; Maddela et al., 2021) to emotion modification (Sharma et al., 2021) and detoxification (debiasing) (Li et al., 2021; Dementieva et al., 2021a).

There exist a variety of Textual Style Transfer methods: from totally **supervised** methods (Wang et al., 2019b; Zhang et al., 2020; Dementieva et al., 2021a) which require a parallel text corpus for training to **unsupervised** (Shen et al., 2017; Wang et al., 2019a; Xu et al., 2021) that are designed to work without any parallel data. The latter sub-field of research is more popular nowadays due to the scarcity of parallel text data for Textual Style Transfer. On the other hand, if we address Textual Style Transfer task as a Machine Translation task we get a significant performance boost (Prabhumoye et al., 2018).

The task of detoxification, in which we focus in this work, is relatively new. First work on detoxification was a sequence-to-sequence collaborative classifier, attention and the cycle consistency loss (dos Santos et al., 2018b). A recent work by (Laugier et al., 2021) introduces self-supervised model based on T5 model (Raffel et al., 2020) with a denoising and cyclic auto-encoder loss.

Both these methods are unsupervised which is an advantage but it comes from the major current problem of the textual style transfer. There is a lack of parallel data for Textual Style Transfer since there exist only few parallel datasets for English (Rao and Tetreault, 2018) and some other languages (Briakou et al., 2021). When it comes to detoxification there are only two parallel detoxification corpora available now and they both appeared only last year (Dementieva et al., 2021b). Most state-of-the-art methods rely on large amounts of text data which is often available for some well-researched languages like English but lacking for other languages almost entirely. Therefore, it is important to study whether cross-lingual (or at least multilingual) detoxifica-

[1]Hereinafter the data-driven definition of style is used. Therefore, we call style a characteristic of given dataset that differs from a general dataset (Jin et al., 2020).

Proceedings of the 60th Annual Meeting of the Association for Computational Linguistics Student Research Workshop, pages 346 - 354

Source text	Target text
What the f*ck is your problem?	What is your problem?
This whole article is bullshit.	This article is not good.
Yeah, this clowns gonna make alberta great again!	Yeah, this gonna make Alberta great again

Table 1: Examples of desired detoxification results.

tion is possible.

Multilingual language models such as mBART (Liu et al., 2020), mT5 (Xue et al., 2021) have recently become available. This work explores the possibility of multilingual and cross-lingual textual style transfer (Textual Style Transfer) using such large multilingual language models. We test the hypothesis that modern large text-to-text models are able to generalize ability of style transfer across languages.

Our contributions can be summarized as follows[2]:

1. We introduce a novel study of multilingual textual style transfer and conduct experiments with several multilingual language models and evaluate their performance.

2. We conduct cross-lingual Textual Style Transfer experiments to investigate whether multilingual language models are able to perform Textual Style Transfer without fine-tuning on a specific language.

2 Methodology

We formulate the task of **supervised** Textual Style Transfer as a sequence-to-sequence NMT task and fine-tune multilingual language models to translate from "toxic" to "polite" language.

2.1 Datasets

In this work we use two datasets for Russian and English languages. Aggregated information about datasets could be found in Table 2, examples from datasets can be found in A.1 and A.2.

Language	Train	Dev	Test
English	18777	988	671
Russian	5058	1000	1000

Table 2: Aggregated datasets statistics.

Russian data We use detoxification dataset[3] which consists of 5058 training sentences, 1000 validation sentences and 1000 test sentences.

English data We use ParaDetox (Dementieva et al., 2021b) dataset. It consists of 19766 *toxic* sentences and their *polite* paraphrases. This data is split into training and validation as 95% for training and 5% for validation. For testing we use a set of 671 toxic sentences.

2.2 Experimental Setup

We perform a series of experiments on detoxification using parallel data for English and Russian. We train models in two different setups: **multilingual** and **cross-lingual**.

Multilingual setup In this setup we train models on data containing both English and Russian texts and then compare their performance with baselines trained on these languages solely.

Cross-lingual setup In cross-lingual setup we test the hypothesis that models are able to perform detoxification without explicit fine-tuning on exact language. We fine-tune models on English and Russian separately and then test their performance.

2.3 Models

Scaling language models to many languages has become an emerging topic of interest recently (Devlin et al., 2019; Tan et al., 2019; Conneau and Lample, 2019; Conneau et al., 2020). We adopt several multilingual models to textual style transfer in our work.

Baselines We use two detoxification methods as baselines in this work - **Delete** method which simply deletes toxic words in the sentence according to the vocabulary of toxic words and **CondBERT**. The latter approach works in usual masked-LM setup by masking toxic words and replacing them with non-toxic ones. This approach was first proposed by (Wu et al., 2019) as a data augmentation

[2]All code is available online: `https://github.com/skoltech-nlp/multilingual_detox`

[3]`https://github.com/skoltech-nlp/russe_detox_2022`

method and then adopted to detoxification by (Dale et al., 2021).

mT5 mT5 (Xue et al., 2021) is a multilingual version of T5 (Raffel et al., 2020) - a text-to-text transformer model, which was trained on many downstream tasks. mT5 replicates T5 training but now it is trained on more than 100 languages.

mBART mBART (Liu et al., 2020) is a multilingual variation of BART (Lewis et al., 2020) - denoising autoencoder built with a sequence-to-sequence model. mBART is trained on monolingual corpora across many languages. We adopt mBART in sequence-to-sequence detoxification task via fine-tuning on parallel detoxification dataset.

2.4 Evaluation metrics

Unlike other NLP tasks, one metric is not enough to benchmark the quality of style transfer. The ideal Textual Style Transfer model output should *preserve the original content* of the text, *change the style* of the original text to target and the generated text also should *be grammatically correct*. We follow Dale et al. (2021) approach in Textual Style Transfer evaluation.

2.4.1 Content Preservation

Russian Content preservation score (**SIM**) is evaluated as a cosine similarity of LaBSE (Feng et al., 2020) sentence embeddings. The model is slightly different from the original one, only English and Russian embeddings are left.

English Similarity (**SIM**) between the embedding of the original sentence and the generated one is calculated using the model presented by Wieting et al. (2019). Being is trained on paraphrase pairs extracted from ParaNMT corpus (Wieting and Gimpel, 2018), this model's training objective is to select embeddings such that the similarity of embeddings of paraphrases is higher than the similarity between sentences that are not paraphrases.

2.4.2 Grammatic and language quality (fluency)

Russian We measure fluency (**FL**) with a BERT-based classifier (Devlin et al., 2019) trained to distinguish real texts from corrupted ones. The model was trained on Russian texts and their corrupted (random word replacement, word deletion and insertion, word shuffling etc.) versions. Fluency is calculated as a difference between the probabilities of being corrupted for source and target sentences. The logic behind using difference is that we ensure that the generated sentence is not worse than the original one in terms of fluency.

English We measure fluency (**FL**) as a percentage of fluent sentences evaluated by the RoBERTa-based[4] (Liu et al., 2019) classifier of linguistic acceptability trained on CoLA (Warstadt et al., 2019) dataset.

2.4.3 Style transfer accuracy

Russian Style transfer accuracy (**STA**) is evaluated with a BERT-based (Devlin et al., 2019) toxicity classifier[5] fine-tuned from RuBERT Conversational. This classifier was additionally trained on Russian Language Toxic Comments dataset collected from `2ch.hk` and Toxic Russian Comments dataset collected from `ok.ru`.

English Style transfer accuracy (**STA**) is calculated with a style classifier - RoBERTa-based (Liu et al., 2019) model trained on the union of three Jigsaw datasets (Jigsaw, 2018). The sentence is considered toxic when the classifier confidence is above 0.8. The classifier reaches the AUC-ROC of 0.98 and F_1-score of 0.76.

2.4.4 Joint metric

Aforementioned metrics must be properly combined to get one *Joint* metric to evaluate Textual Style Transfer. We follow Krishna et al. (2020) and calculate **J** as an average of products of sentence-level *fluency*, *style transfer accuracy*, and *content preservation*:

$$\mathbf{J} = \frac{1}{n}\sum_{i=1}^{n} \mathbf{STA}(x_i) \cdot \mathbf{SIM}(x_i) \cdot \mathbf{FL}(x_i) \quad (1)$$

2.5 Training

There is a variety of versions of large multilingual models available. In this work we use small and base versions of mT5[6,7] (Xue et al., 2021) and large version of mBART[8] (Liu et al., 2020).

[4] `https://huggingface.co/roberta-large`

[5] `https://huggingface.co/SkolkovoInstitute/russian_toxicity_classifier`

[6] `https://huggingface.co/google/mt5-base`

[7] `https://huggingface.co/google/mt5-large`

[8] `https://huggingface.co/facebook/mbart-large-50-many-to-many-mmt`

	STA↑	SIM↑	FL↑	J↑	STA↑	SIM↑	FL↑	J↑
	Russian				English			
	Baselines							
Delete	0.532	0.875	0.834	0.364	0.81	0.93	0.64	0.46
condBERT	0.819	0.778	0.744	0.422	**0.98**	0.77	0.82	0.62
	Multilingual Setup							
mT5 base	0.772	0.676	0.795	0.430	0.833	0.826	0.830	0.556
mT5 small	0.745	0.705	0.794	0.428	0.826	0.841	0.763	0.513
mT5 base*	**0.773**	0.676	0.795	0.430	0.893	0.787	**0.942**	**0.657**
mBART 5000	0.685	**0.778**	**0.841**	**0.449**	0.887	**0.889**	0.866	0.640
	Cross-lingual							
mT5 base ENG	0.838	0.276	0.506	0.115	0.860	0.834	0.833	0.587
mT5 base RUS	0.676	0.794	0.846	0.454	0.906	0.365	0.696	0.171
mT5 small ENG	0.805	0.225	0.430	0.077	0.844	0.858	0.826	0.591
mT5 small RUS	0.559	0.822	0.817	0.363	0.776	0.521	0.535	0.169
mBART 3000 RUS	0.699	0.778	0.858	0.475	*0.547*	*0.778*	*0.888*	*0.299*
mBART 5000 RUS	0.724	0.746	0.827	0.457	*0.806*	*0.484*	*0.864*	*0.242*
mBART 10000 RUS	0.718	0.735	0.827	0.448	*0.517*	*0.840*	*0.903*	*0.342*
mBART 3000 ENG	*0.923*	*0.395*	*0.552*	*0.202*	0.842	0.856	0.876	0.617
mBART 5000 ENG	*0.900*	*0.299*	*0.591*	*0.160*	0.857	0.840	0.873	0.616

Table 3: Results of evaluation of Textual Style Transfer models. Numbers in **bold** indicate the best results. ↑ describes the higher the better metric. Results of unsuccessful Textual Style Transfer depicted as *italic*. ENG and RUS depicts the data model have been trained on (English and Russian data respectively). mT5 base* was trained on all English and Russian data available (datasets were not equalized).

Multilingual training In multilingual training setup we fine-tune models using both English and Russian data. We use Adam (Kingma and Ba, 2015) optimizer for fine-tuning with different learning rates ranging from $1 \cdot 10^{-3}$ to $5 \cdot 10^{-5}$ with linear learning rate scheduling. We also test different number of warmup steps from 0 to 1000. We equalize Russian and English data for training and use 10000 toxic sentences and their polite paraphrases for multilingual training in total. We train mT5 models for 40 thousand iterations[9] with a batch size of 8. We fine-tune mBART (Liu et al., 2020) for 1000, 3000, 5000 and 10000 iterations with batch size of 8.

Cross-lingual training In cross-lingual training setup we fine-tune models using only one dataset, e.g.: we fine-tune model on English data and check performance on both English and Russian data. Fine-tuning procedure was left the same: 40000 iterations for mT5 models and 1000, 3000, 5000 and 10000 iterations for the mBART.

[9]According to (Xue et al., 2021) mT5 was not fine-tuned on downstream tasks as the original T5 model. Therefore, model requires more fine-tuning iterations for Textual Style Transfer.

3 Results & Discussion

Table 3 shows the best scores of both multilingual and cross-lingual experiments. In multilingual setup mBART performs better than baselines and mT5 for both English and Russian. Note that the table shows only the best results of the models. It is also notable that for mT5 increased training size for English data provides better metrics for English while keeping metrics for Russian almost the same. We also depict some of the generated detoxified sentences in the Table 3 in the part B of Appendix.

As for cross-lingual style transfer, results are negative. None of the models have coped with the task of cross-lingual Textual Style Transfer. That means that models produce the same or almost the same sentences for the language on which they were not fine-tuned so that toxicity is not eliminated. We provide only some scores here in the Table 6 for reference.

Despite the fact that our hypothesis about the possibility of cross-language detoxification was not confirmed, the presence of multilingual models pretrained in many languages gives every reason to believe that even with a small amount of parallel data, training models for detoxification is possible.

A recent work by (Lai et al., 2022) shows that cross-lingual formality Textual Style Transfer is possible. Lai et al. (2022) achieve this on XFORMAL dataset (Briakou et al., 2021) by adding language-specific adapters in the vanilla mBART architecture (Liu et al., 2020) - two feed-forward layers with residual connection and layer normalization (Bapna and Firat, 2019; Houlsby et al., 2019).

We follow the original training procedure described by Lai et al. (2022) by training adapters for English and Russian separately on 5 million sentences from News Crawl dataset[10]. We use batch size of 16 and 200 thousand training iterations. We also then train cross-attentions on our parallel detoxifcation data in the same way. However, models tend to duplicate input text without any detoxification. Thus, while the exact same original setup did not work for detoxification, more parameter search and optimization could lead to more acceptable results and we consider the approach by Lai et al. (2022) as a promising direction of a future work on multilingual and cross-lingual detoxification.

4 Conclusion

In this work we have tested the hypothesis that multilingual language models are capable of performing cross-lingual and multilingual detoxification. In the multilingual setup we experimentally show that reformulating detoxification (Textual Style Transfer) as a NMT task boosts performance of the models given enough parallel data for training. We beat simple (Delete method) and more strong (condBERT) baselines in a number of metrics. Based on our experiments, we can assume that it is possible to fine-tune multilingual models in any of the 100 languages in which they were originally trained. This opens up great opportunities for detoxification in unpopular languages.

However, our hypothesis that multilingual language models are capable of cross-lingual detoxification was proven to be false. We suggest that the reason for this is not a lack of data, but the model's inability to capture the pattern between toxic and non-toxic text and transfer it to another language by itself. This means that the problem of cross-lingual textual style transfer is still open and needs more investigation.

[10]`https://data.statmt.org/news-crawl/`

Acknowledgements

This work was supported by MTS-Skoltech laboratory on AI.

References

Ankur Bapna and Orhan Firat. 2019. Simple, scalable adaptation for neural machine translation. In *Proceedings of the 2019 Conference on Empirical Methods in Natural Language Processing and the 9th International Joint Conference on Natural Language Processing (EMNLP-IJCNLP)*, pages 1538–1548, Hong Kong, China. Association for Computational Linguistics.

Eleftheria Briakou, Di Lu, Ke Zhang, and Joel R. Tetreault. 2021. Olá, bonjour, salve! XFORMAL: A benchmark for multilingual formality style transfer. In *Proceedings of the 2021 Conference of the North American Chapter of the Association for Computational Linguistics: Human Language Technologies, NAACL-HLT 2021, Online, June 6-11, 2021*, pages 3199–3216. Association for Computational Linguistics.

Alexis Conneau, Kartikay Khandelwal, Naman Goyal, Vishrav Chaudhary, Guillaume Wenzek, Francisco Guzmán, Edouard Grave, Myle Ott, Luke Zettlemoyer, and Veselin Stoyanov. 2020. Unsupervised cross-lingual representation learning at scale. In *Proceedings of the 58th Annual Meeting of the Association for Computational Linguistics, ACL 2020, Online, July 5-10, 2020*, pages 8440–8451. Association for Computational Linguistics.

Alexis Conneau and Guillaume Lample. 2019. Cross-lingual language model pretraining. In *Advances in Neural Information Processing Systems 32: Annual Conference on Neural Information Processing Systems 2019, NeurIPS 2019, December 8-14, 2019, Vancouver, BC, Canada*, pages 7057–7067.

David Dale, Anton Voronov, Daryna Dementieva, Varvara Logacheva, Olga Kozlova, Nikita Semenov, and Alexander Panchenko. 2021. Text detoxification using large pre-trained neural models. In *Proceedings of the 2021 Conference on Empirical Methods in Natural Language Processing, EMNLP 2021, Virtual Event / Punta Cana, Dominican Republic, 7-11 November, 2021*, pages 7979–7996. Association for Computational Linguistics.

Daryna Dementieva, Daniil Moskovskiy, Varvara Logacheva, David Dale, Olga Kozlova, Nikita Semenov, and Alexander Panchenko. 2021a. Methods for detoxification of texts for the russian language. *Multimodal Technol. Interact.*, 5(9):54.

Daryna Dementieva, Sergey Ustyantsev, David Dale, Olga Kozlova, Nikita Semenov, Alexander Panchenko, and Varvara Logacheva. 2021b. Crowdsourcing of parallel corpora: the case of style transfer for detoxification. In *Proceedings of the 2nd Crowd*

Science Workshop: Trust, Ethics, and Excellence in Crowdsourced Data Management at Scale co-located with 47th International Conference on Very Large Data Bases (VLDB 2021 (https://vldb.org/2021/)), pages 35–49, Copenhagen, Denmark. CEUR Workshop Proceedings.

Ashwin Devaraj, Iain Marshall, Byron Wallace, and Junyi Jessy Li. 2021. Paragraph-level simplification of medical texts. In *Proceedings of the 2021 Conference of the North American Chapter of the Association for Computational Linguistics: Human Language Technologies*, pages 4972–4984, Online. Association for Computational Linguistics.

Jacob Devlin, Ming-Wei Chang, Kenton Lee, and Kristina Toutanova. 2019. BERT: pre-training of deep bidirectional transformers for language understanding. In *Proceedings of the 2019 Conference of the North American Chapter of the Association for Computational Linguistics: Human Language Technologies, NAACL-HLT 2019, Minneapolis, MN, USA, June 2-7, 2019, Volume 1 (Long and Short Papers)*, pages 4171–4186. Association for Computational Linguistics.

Cicero Nogueira dos Santos, Igor Melnyk, and Inkit Padhi. 2018a. Fighting offensive language on social media with unsupervised text style transfer.

Cícero Nogueira dos Santos, Igor Melnyk, and Inkit Padhi. 2018b. Fighting offensive language on social media with unsupervised text style transfer. In *Proceedings of the 56th Annual Meeting of the Association for Computational Linguistics, ACL 2018, Melbourne, Australia, July 15-20, 2018, Volume 2: Short Papers*, pages 189–194. Association for Computational Linguistics.

Fangxiaoyu Feng, Yinfei Yang, Daniel Cer, Naveen Arivazhagan, and Wei Wang. 2020. Language-agnostic BERT sentence embedding. *CoRR*, abs/2007.01852.

Neil Houlsby, Andrei Giurgiu, Stanislaw Jastrzebski, Bruna Morrone, Quentin de Laroussilhe, Andrea Gesmundo, Mona Attariyan, and Sylvain Gelly. 2019. Parameter-efficient transfer learning for NLP. In *Proceedings of the 36th International Conference on Machine Learning, ICML 2019, 9-15 June 2019, Long Beach, California, USA*, volume 97 of *Proceedings of Machine Learning Research*, pages 2790–2799. PMLR.

Jigsaw. 2018. Toxic comment classification challenge. https://www.kaggle.com/c/jigsaw-toxic-comment-classification-challenge. Accessed: 2021-03-01.

Di Jin, Zhijing Jin, Zhiting Hu, Olga Vechtomova, and Rada Mihalcea. 2020. Deep learning for text style transfer: A survey. *CoRR*, abs/2011.00416.

Diederik P. Kingma and Jimmy Ba. 2015. Adam: A method for stochastic optimization. In *3rd International Conference on Learning Representations, ICLR 2015, San Diego, CA, USA, May 7-9, 2015, Conference Track Proceedings*.

Kalpesh Krishna, John Wieting, and Mohit Iyyer. 2020. Reformulating unsupervised style transfer as paraphrase generation. In *Proceedings of the 2020 Conference on Empirical Methods in Natural Language Processing (EMNLP)*, pages 737–762, Online. Association for Computational Linguistics.

Huiyuan Lai, Antonio Toral, and Malvina Nissim. 2022. Multilingual pre-training with language and task adaptation for multilingual text style transfer. *CoRR*, abs/2203.08552.

Leo Laugier, John Pavlopoulos, Jeffrey Sorensen, and Lucas Dixon. 2021. Civil rephrases of toxic texts with self-supervised transformers. In *Proceedings of the 16th Conference of the European Chapter of the Association for Computational Linguistics: Main Volume, EACL 2021, Online, April 19 - 23, 2021*, pages 1442–1461. Association for Computational Linguistics.

Mike Lewis, Yinhan Liu, Naman Goyal, Marjan Ghazvininejad, Abdelrahman Mohamed, Omer Levy, Veselin Stoyanov, and Luke Zettlemoyer. 2020. BART: denoising sequence-to-sequence pre-training for natural language generation, translation, and comprehension. In *Proceedings of the 58th Annual Meeting of the Association for Computational Linguistics, ACL 2020, Online, July 5-10, 2020*, pages 7871–7880. Association for Computational Linguistics.

Mingzhe Li, Xiuying Chen, Min Yang, Shen Gao, Dongyan Zhao, and Rui Yan. 2021. The style-content duality of attractiveness: Learning to write eye-catching headlines via disentanglement. In *Thirty-Fifth AAAI Conference on Artificial Intelligence, AAAI 2021, Thirty-Third Conference on Innovative Applications of Artificial Intelligence, IAAI 2021, The Eleventh Symposium on Educational Advances in Artificial Intelligence, EAAI 2021, Virtual Event, February 2-9, 2021*, pages 13252–13260. AAAI Press.

Yinhan Liu, Jiatao Gu, Naman Goyal, Xian Li, Sergey Edunov, Marjan Ghazvininejad, Mike Lewis, and Luke Zettlemoyer. 2020. Multilingual denoising pre-training for neural machine translation. *Trans. Assoc. Comput. Linguistics*, 8:726–742.

Yinhan Liu, Myle Ott, Naman Goyal, Jingfei Du, Mandar Joshi, Danqi Chen, Omer Levy, Mike Lewis, Luke Zettlemoyer, and Veselin Stoyanov. 2019. Roberta: A robustly optimized BERT pretraining approach. *CoRR*, abs/1907.11692.

Mounica Maddela, Fernando Alva-Manchego, and Wei Xu. 2021. Controllable text simplification with explicit paraphrasing. In *Proceedings of the 2021 Conference of the North American Chapter of the Association for Computational Linguistics: Human Language Technologies, NAACL-HLT 2021, Online, June 6-11, 2021*, pages 3536–3553. Association for Computational Linguistics.

Shrimai Prabhumoye, Yulia Tsvetkov, Alan W. Black, and Ruslan Salakhutdinov. 2018. Style transfer through multilingual and feedback-based back-translation. *CoRR*, abs/1809.06284.

Colin Raffel, Noam Shazeer, Adam Roberts, Katherine Lee, Sharan Narang, Michael Matena, Yanqi Zhou, Wei Li, and Peter J. Liu. 2020. Exploring the limits of transfer learning with a unified text-to-text transformer. *J. Mach. Learn. Res.*, 21:140:1–140:67.

Sudha Rao and Joel Tetreault. 2018. Dear sir or madam, may I introduce the GYAFC dataset: Corpus, benchmarks and metrics for formality style transfer. In *Proceedings of the 2018 Conference of the North American Chapter of the Association for Computational Linguistics: Human Language Technologies, Volume 1 (Long Papers)*, pages 129–140, New Orleans, Louisiana. Association for Computational Linguistics.

Ashish Sharma, Inna W. Lin, Adam S. Miner, David C. Atkins, and Tim Althoff. 2021. Towards facilitating empathic conversations in online mental health support: A reinforcement learning approach. In *WWW '21: The Web Conference 2021, Virtual Event / Ljubljana, Slovenia, April 19-23, 2021*, pages 194–205. ACM / IW3C2.

Tianxiao Shen, Tao Lei, Regina Barzilay, and Tommi S. Jaakkola. 2017. Style transfer from non-parallel text by cross-alignment. In *Advances in Neural Information Processing Systems 30: Annual Conference on Neural Information Processing Systems 2017, December 4-9, 2017, Long Beach, CA, USA*, pages 6830–6841.

Xu Tan, Yi Ren, Di He, Tao Qin, Zhou Zhao, and Tie-Yan Liu. 2019. Multilingual neural machine translation with knowledge distillation. In *7th International Conference on Learning Representations, ICLR 2019, New Orleans, LA, USA, May 6-9, 2019*. OpenReview.net.

Ke Wang, Hang Hua, and Xiaojun Wan. 2019a. Controllable unsupervised text attribute transfer via editing entangled latent representation. In *Advances in Neural Information Processing Systems 32: Annual Conference on Neural Information Processing Systems 2019, NeurIPS 2019, December 8-14, 2019, Vancouver, BC, Canada*, pages 11034–11044.

Yunli Wang, Yu Wu, Lili Mou, Zhoujun Li, and Wenhan Chao. 2019b. Harnessing pre-trained neural networks with rules for formality style transfer. In *Proceedings of the 2019 Conference on Empirical Methods in Natural Language Processing and the 9th International Joint Conference on Natural Language Processing, EMNLP-IJCNLP 2019, Hong Kong, China, November 3-7, 2019*, pages 3571–3576. Association for Computational Linguistics.

Alex Warstadt, Amanpreet Singh, and Samuel R. Bowman. 2019. Neural network acceptability judgments. *Trans. Assoc. Comput. Linguistics*, 7:625–641.

John Wieting, Taylor Berg-Kirkpatrick, Kevin Gimpel, and Graham Neubig. 2019. Beyond bleu: Training neural machine translation with semantic similarity. In *Proceedings of the Association for Computational Linguistics*.

John Wieting and Kevin Gimpel. 2018. ParaNMT-50M: Pushing the limits of paraphrastic sentence embeddings with millions of machine translations. In *Proceedings of the 56th Annual Meeting of the Association for Computational Linguistics (Volume 1: Long Papers)*, pages 451–462, Melbourne, Australia. Association for Computational Linguistics.

Xing Wu, Shangwen Lv, Liangjun Zang, Jizhong Han, and Songlin Hu. 2019. Conditional bert contextual augmentation. In *Computational Science – ICCS 2019*, pages 84–95, Cham. Springer International Publishing.

Haoran Xu, Sixing Lu, Zhongkai Sun, Chengyuan Ma, and Chenlei Guo. 2021. VAE based text style transfer with pivot words enhancement learning. *CoRR*, abs/2112.03154.

Linting Xue, Noah Constant, Adam Roberts, Mihir Kale, Rami Al-Rfou, Aditya Siddhant, Aditya Barua, and Colin Raffel. 2021. mt5: A massively multilingual pre-trained text-to-text transformer. In *Proceedings of the 2021 Conference of the North American Chapter of the Association for Computational Linguistics: Human Language Technologies, NAACL-HLT 2021, Online, June 6-11, 2021*, pages 483–498. Association for Computational Linguistics.

Zonghai Yao and Hong Yu. 2021. Improving formality style transfer with context-aware rule injection. In *Proceedings of the 59th Annual Meeting of the Association for Computational Linguistics and the 11th International Joint Conference on Natural Language Processing, ACL/IJCNLP 2021, (Volume 1: Long Papers), Virtual Event, August 1-6, 2021*, pages 1561–1570. Association for Computational Linguistics.

Yi Zhang, Tao Ge, and Xu Sun. 2020. Parallel data augmentation for formality style transfer. In *Proceedings of the 58th Annual Meeting of the Association for Computational Linguistics, ACL 2020, Online, July 5-10, 2020*, pages 3221–3228. Association for Computational Linguistics.

A Data

A.1 English Dataset

Table 4 shows examples of sentence pairs from ParaDatex parallel detoxification corpora. There are several polite paraphrases for each toxic sentence in this dataset (Dementieva et al., 2021b), this is a consequence of the way these parallel data are collected. Leaving only one paraphrase for one source sentence we could get 6000 unique pairs of toxic sentences and their polite paraphrases. However, in this work we use data as is.

Original	my computer is broken and my phone too!! wtf is this devil sh*t???
Detoxed	My computer is broken and my phone too! So disappointed!
	My computer is broken and my phone too, what is this?
	Both my computer and phone are broken.
Original	sh*t is crazy around here
Detoxed	It is crazy around here.
	Stuff is crazy around here.
	Something is crazy around here.
Original	delete the page and shut up
Detoxed	Delete the page and stay silent.
	Please delete the page.
	Delete the page.
Original	massive and sustained public pressure is the only way to get these b*stards to act.
Detoxed	Massive and sustained public pressure is the only way to get them to act.
	Massive and sustained pressure is the only way to get these people to act.
Original	f*ck you taking credit for some sh*t i wanted to do
Detoxed	You are taking credit for something I wanted to do
	You're taking credit fro something i wanted to do.
Original	you gotta admit that was f*ckin hilarious though!
Detoxed	you got to admit that was very hilarious though!
	you gotta admit that was hilarious though!

Table 4: Example sentences from ParaDetox parallel detoxification corpora. Sentence in red is original (toxic) sentence, below are its polite paraphrases. Note that for the purpose of an overall correctness explicit words are masked with "*".

A.2 Russian Dataset

Table 5 shows examples from Russian parallel detoxification corpus.

Original	Х*рню всякую пишут,из-за этого лайка.v Долбо**изм.
Translation	*They write all sorts of bullshit, because of this like. Stupidity.*
Detoxed	Чушь всякую пишут, из- за этого лайка.
Translation	*They write all sorts of nonsense, because of this like.*
Original	А нахрена тогда ты здесь это писал?
Translation	*Why the f*ck did you post it here?*
Detoxed	Зачем ты это писал?
Translation	*Why did you post it?*
Original	Е*анутые. Отобрать оружие и лодку и штраф тысяч 500
Translation	*F*ckers. Take away weapons, boat and give a fine of 500 thousand.*
Detoxed	Отобрать оружие и лодку и штраф тысяч 500.
Translation	*Take away weapons, boat and give a fine of 500 thousand.*
Original	Не поверишь, сколько е**нутых на планете.
Translation	*You won't believe how many f*cked up people are on the planet.*
Detoxed	Не поверишь сколько таких на планете.
Translation	*You won't believe how many people like that are there on the planet.*

Table 5: Example sentences from Russian parallel detoxification corpora. Sentence in red is original (toxic) sentence, below are its polite paraphrases.

B Generation Examples

Table 6 contains detoxification examples for different models. It is notable that in some cases models generate almost the same results. This can be explained by the similarity of the training procedure and the fact that the reference answer was the same.

Original	After all its hard to get a job if you're stupid.
mBART 5000 ENG	After all its hard to get a job if you don't understand.
mBART 3000 ENG	After all its hard to get a job if you are not smart.
mT5 base (multilingual)	It's hard to get a job if you don't know.
Original	Fuck minimum security, put him in real prison.
mBART 5000 ENG	Put him in a real prison with minimum security.
mBART 3000 ENG	I don't care about minimum security, put him in real prison.
mT5 base	I don't care about minimum security, put him in real prison.
Original	Sure he should get punished ,but three f*cking years?
mBART 5000 ENG	Sure he should get punished, but three years?
mBART 3000 ENG	He should get punished, but three years?
mT5 base	He'd get punished, but three years?
Paraphrase	Что у этих людей в башке!? походу насрато!
Translation	*What's going on in these people's heads!? It looks like shit!*
mBART 5000 ENG	Что у этих людей в голове!? Походу бесчеловечно.
mBART 3000 ENG	Что у этих людей в голове? Походу ненормально!
mT5 base	походу этих людей!? походу!

Table 6: Some detoxified sentences produced by our fine-tuned models. Gray text refers to the original sentence, below are its paraphrases.

MEKER: Memory Efficient Knowledge Embedding Representation for Link Prediction and Question Answering

Viktoriia Chekalina[1], **Anton Razzhigaev**[1,2], **Alexander Panchenko**[1], **Albert Sayapin**[1], **and Evgeny Frolov**[1]

[1]Skolkovo Institute of Science and Technology, [2]Artificial Intelligence Research Insitute (AIRI)

Abstract

Knowledge Graphs (KGs) are symbolically structured storages of facts. The KG embedding contains concise data used in NLP tasks requiring implicit information about the real world. Furthermore, the size of KGs that may be useful in actual NLP assignments is enormous, and creating embedding over it has memory cost issues. We represent KG as a 3rd-order binary tensor and move beyond the standard CP decomposition (Hitchcock, 1927) by using a data-specific generalized version of it (Hong et al., 2020). The generalization of the standard CP-ALS algorithm allows obtaining optimization gradients without a backpropagation mechanism. It reduces the memory needed in training while providing computational benefits. We propose a MEKER, a memory-efficient KG embedding model, which yields SOTA-comparable performance on link prediction tasks and KG-based Question Answering.

1 Introduction

Natural Language Processing (NLP) models have taken a big step forward over the past few years. For instance, language models can generate fluent human-like text without any problems. However, some applications like question answering and recommendation systems need correct, precise, and trustworthy answers.

For this goal, it is appropriate to leverage knowledge graphs (KG) (Bollacker et al., 2008; Rebele et al., 2016) a structured repository of essential facts about the real world. For convenience, the knowledge graph can be represented as a set of triples. A triple is two entities bound with relation and describes the fact. It takes the forms of $\langle e_s, r, e_o \rangle$, where e_s and e_o represent objects and subject entities, respectively.

For efficient use of information from KG, there is a need for the low-dimensional embedding of graph entities and relations. KG embedding models usually use a standard Neural Networks (NN) backward mechanism for parameter tuning, duplicating its memory consumption. Hence, existing approaches to embedding learning have substantial memory requirements and can be deployed only on small datasets under a single GPU card. Processing large KGs appropriate for the custom downstream task is a challenge.

There are several libraries designed to solve this problem. Framework LibKGE (Ruffinelli et al., 2020) allows the processing of large datasets by using sparse embedding layers. Despite the memory saving, sparse embedding has several limitations - for example, in the PyTorch library, they are not compatible with several optimizers. PyTorch-BigGraph (Lerer et al., 2019) operates with large knowledge graphs by dividing them into partitions - distributed subgraphs. Subgraphs need a place for storing, embedding models need modifications to work with partitions and perform poorly.

The main contribution of our paper is a memory-efficient approach to learning Knowledge Graph embeddings MEKER (Memory Efficient Knowledge Embedding Representation). It allows more efficient KG embedding learning, maintaining comparable performance to state-of-the-art models. MEKER leverages generalized canonical Polyadic (CP) decomposition (Hong et al., 2020), which allows a better approximation of given data and analytical computation of the parameters' gradient. MEKER is evaluated on a link prediction task using several standard datasets and large datasets based on Wikidata. Experiments show that MEKER achieves highly competitive results on these two tasks. To demonstrate downstream usability, we create a Knowledge Base Question Answering system Text2Graph and use embeddings in it. The system with MEKER embeddings performs better as compared to other KG embeddings, such as PTBG (Lerer et al., 2019).

Proceedings of the 60th Annual Meeting of the Association for Computational Linguistics Student Research Workshop, pages 355 - 365
May 22-27, 2022 ©2022 Association for Computational Linguistics

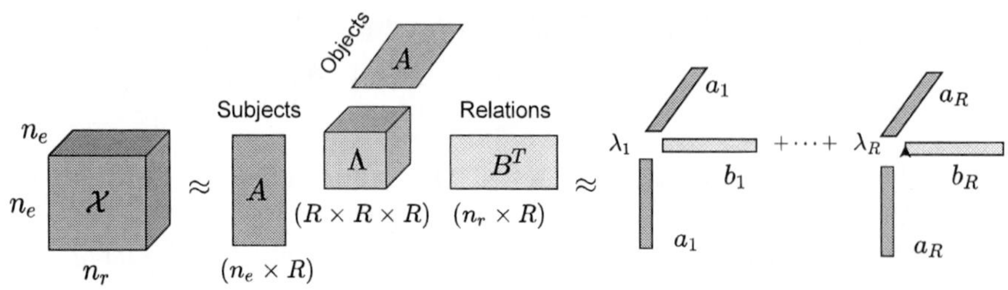

Figure 1: The CP decomposition scheme in the case of entity and relation KG embedding in MEKER. This is a binary 3-dimensional tensor $\mathcal{X}$ of knowledge graph facts that introduces objects, relations, and subjects indexes along the three axes. B contains relation embedding, while A represents entity vectors for the subject and object simultaneously. Λ is the diagonal core tensor, identity in our case.

2 Related Work

There are three types of approaches for learning KG embedding: distance-based, tensor-based, and deep learning-based models. The first group is based on the assumption of translation invariance in the embedding vector space. In model **TransE** (Bordes et al., 2013) relations are represented as connection vectors between entity representations. **TransH** (Wang et al., 2014) implies relation as a hyperplane onto which entities are being projected. **QuatE** (Zhang et al., 2019) extends the idea with hypercomplex space and represents entities as embeddings with four imaginary components and relations as rotations in the space.

Tensor-based models usually represent triples as a binary tensor and look for embedding matrices as factorization products. **RESCAL** (Nickel et al., 2011) employs tensor factorization in the manner of DEDICOM (Harshman et al., 1982), which decomposes each tensor slice along the relationship axis. **DistMult** (Yang et al., 2015) adapts this approach by restricting the relation embedding matrix to diagonal. On the one hand, it reduces the number of relation parameters, on the other hand, it losses the possibility of describing asymmetric relations. The **ComplEX** (Trouillon et al., 2016) represents the object and subject variants of a single entity as complex conjugates vectors. It combines tensor-based and translation-based approaches and solves the asymmetric problem. **TuckER** (Balazevic et al., 2019) uses Tucker decomposition (Tucker, 1966c) for finding representation of a knowledge graph elements. This work can also be considered a generalization of several previous link prediction methods.

Standard Canonical Polyadic (CP) (Hitchcock, 1927) decomposition in the link prediction task does not show outstanding performance (Trouillon et al., 2017). Several papers address this problem by improving the CP decomposition approach. **SimplIE** (Kazemi and Poole, 2018) states that low performance is due to different representations of subject and object entity and deploys CP decomposition with dependently learning of subjects and objects matrices. **CP-N3** (Lacroix et al., 2018) highlights the statement that the Frobenius norm regularizing is not fit for tensors of order more than 3 (Cheng et al., 2016) and proposes a Nuclear p-norm instead of it. Our approach also uses CP decomposition with enhancement. We consider remark from **SimplIE** and set the object and subject representations of one entity to be equals. At the same time, inside the local step of the CP decomposition algorithm, the matrices of subjects and objects consist of different elements and are different (see Appendix). In contradistinction to **CP-N3**, we do not employ a regularizer to improve training but change the objective. Instead of squared error, we use logistic loss, which is appropriate for one-hot data. We abandon the gradient calculation through the computational graph and count gradient analytically, which makes the training process less resource-demanding.

Approaches based on Deep Learning convolutions and attention mechanisms **ConvE, GAT, GAAT** (Dettmers et al., 2017; Nathani et al., 2019; Wang et al., 2020) achieve high performance in link prediction. Besides, they have their disadvantages - it necessitate more time and memory resources than other types of models and usually needs pre-training.

3 MEKER: Memory Efficient Knowledge Embedding Representation

Our approach to entity embeddings relies on generalized CP tensor decomposition (Hitchcock, 1927). Namely, R-rank CP decomposition approximates an N-dimensional tensor as a sum of R outer products of N vectors. Every product can also be viewed as a rank-1 tensor. This approximation is described by the following formula: $\mathcal{X} \approx \mathcal{M} = [|A, B, C|]$, where $\mathcal{X} \in \mathbb{R}^{I \times J \times K}$ is original data and $\mathcal{M} \in \mathbb{R}^{I \times J \times K}$ is its approximation. Factors have the following shape $A \in \mathbb{R}^{I \times R}$, $B \in \mathbb{R}^{J \times R}$, $C \in \mathbb{R}^{K \times R}$. The scheme of CP decomposition applied to the KG elements representation task is in Figure 1. We set matrix A equal to matrix C and simultaneously corresponding to subject and object entities.

3.1 Generalization of Canonical Poliyadic (CP) Decomposition

Following the determination of the approximation type, the next task is to find the parameters of the factor matrices that best match the ground truth data. Battaglino et al. (2018); Dunlavy et al. (2011) describe the most widely used CP decomposition algorithm, CP-ALS. The update rules for the factor matrices are derived by alternating between minimizing squared error (MSE) loss. Hong et al. (2020) demonstrates that MSE corresponds to Gaussian data and is a particular case of a more general solution for an exponential family of distributions. In general, the construction of optimal factors originates the minimization problem:

$$\min F(\mathcal{M}; \mathcal{X}) \equiv \sum_{i \in \Omega} f(x_i, m_i), \qquad f(x, m) \equiv \log p(x | l^{-1}(m)), \tag{1}$$

where f - elementwise loss function, Ω - set of indices of known elements of $\mathcal{X}$, l - link function, x_i and m_i - the i-th elements of $\mathcal{X}$ and $\mathcal{M}$, respectively. We also introduce $\mathcal{Y}$ - the tensor of derivatives of the elementwise loss with the same size as $\mathcal{X}$ and being filled by zeros for $i \notin \Omega$. The data in the sparse one-hot triple tensor has a Bernoulli distribution. The link function for Bernoulli is $l(\rho) = log(\rho/(1-\rho))$ and associated probability is $\rho = \exp(m)(1 - \exp(m))$ so the loss function and elements of the $\mathcal{Y}$ are defines as follows:

$$f(x_i, m_i) = \log(1 + \exp m_i) - x_i m_i, \qquad y(x_i, m_i) = \frac{\partial f(x_i, m_i)}{\partial m_i} = \frac{\exp m_i}{1 + \exp m_i} - x_i. \tag{2}$$

Hong et al. (2020) derives partial derivatives of F w.r.t. factor matrices and presents gradients G of it in a form similar to standard CP matrix update formulas:

$$G_A = \mathcal{Y}_{[0]} (B \odot C)^{T\dagger}, \qquad G_B = \mathcal{Y}_{[1]} (A \odot C)^{T\dagger}, \qquad G_C = \mathcal{Y}_{[2]} (A \odot B)^{T\dagger}, \tag{3}$$

where $\dagger$ - pseudo-inverse matrix, $\odot$ - Khartri-Rao operator, $\mathcal{X}_{[n]}$ - mode-n matricization, a reshaping of tensor $\mathcal{X}$ along the n axis. The importance of representation (3) is that we can calculate the gradients via an essential tensor operation called the matricized tensor times Khatri-Rao product (MTTKRP), implemented and optimized in most programming languages. Algorithm 1 describes the procedure for computing factor matrices gradients (3) in a Bernoulli distribution case (2).

3.2 Implementation Details

We use PyTorch (Paszke et al., 2019) to implement the MEKER model. We set the object and subject factors equal and correspond to matrix A for the decomposition of the one-hot KG triplet tensor. Sparse natural and reconstructed tensors are stored in Coordinate Format as a set of triplets (COO). We combine actual triples and sampled negative examples in batches, and process them. The corresponding pieces from the ground-truth tensor and current factor matrices are cut out for each batch. Then the pieces are sent to Algorithm 1 for the calculation of gradients of the matrix elements with appropriate indexes. Algorithm 2 describes the pseudocode of factorization KG tensor using GCP gradients.

We train the MEKER model using Bayesian search optimization to obtain the optimal training parameters. We use the Wandb.ai tool (Biewald, 2020) for experiment tracking and visualizations. The complete sets of tunable hyperparameters are in the Appendix. Table 2 shows the best combinations of it for the proposed datasets.

3.3 Baselines

As a comparison, we deploy related link prediction approaches that meet the following criteria:

1) it should learn KG embedding from scratch 2) it should report high performance 3) the corresponding paper should provide a runnable code. We use the Tucker, Hyper, ConvKB, and QuatE implementations from their respective repositories. For TransE, DistMult, ComplEx, and ConvE, we use LibKGE (Ruffinelli et al., 2020) library with the best parameter setting for reproducing every model. We run each model five times for each observed value and provide means and sample standard deviation.

Algorithm 1 GCP GRAD Bernuilli

Input: $\mathcal{X}$ ▷ Ground Truth Tensor
A, B, C ▷ Factor matrices

Output: F, G_A, G_B, G_C

$\mathcal{M} = \{A, B, C\}$ ▷ Model Restored tensor

$F = \sum_i f(x_i, m_i) = \sum log(1 + e_i^m) - x_i m_i$ ▷ Loss

$\mathcal{Y} = \sum_i \frac{\delta f(x_i, m_i)}{\delta m_i} =$ ▷ Derivative tensor
$= \sum \frac{1}{1+e^{(-m_i)}} - x_i$

$G_A = \mathcal{Y}_{[0]}(B \odot C)^{T\dagger}.$ ▷ Element-wise gradient for A
$G_B = \mathcal{Y}_{[1]}(A \odot C)^{T\dagger}$ ▷ Element-wise gradient for B
$G_C = \mathcal{Y}_{[2]}(A \odot B)^{T\dagger}$ ▷ Element-wise gradient for C

Algorithm 2 Factorization of the KG tensor using GCP gradients

Input: $\mathcal{X}$ ▷ Ground Truth Tensor
Triplets ▷ List of triplets
LR ▷ learning rate
R ▷ Desired size of embeddings
N ▷ Number of epoch

Output: A, B ▷ Updated factor matrices

Initialize factor matrices $A \in \mathbb{R}^{R \times n_e}$, $B \in \mathbb{R}^{R \times n_r}$

for $i = 1 \dots N$ **do**
  for [inds$_a$, inds$_b$, inds$_c$] **in** Triplets **do**
    $\mathcal{X}_{batch} = \mathcal{X}$[inds$_a$, inds$_b$, inds$_c$]
    $g_a, g_b, g_c, loss =$
GCP_GRAD($\mathcal{X}_{batch}$, A[inds$_a$], B[inds$_b$], A[inds$_c$])
    A[inds$_a$].grad $= g_a$
    B[inds$_b$].grad $= g_b$
    A[inds$_c$].grad $= g_c$
    UPDATE(A, B, LR)

4 Experiments on Standard Link Prediction Datasets

4.1 Experimental settings

The Link prediction task estimates the quality of KG embedding. Link prediction is a classification predicting if triple over graph elements is true or not. The scoring function $\Phi(e_s, rel, e_o)$ returns the probability of constructing a true triple. We test our model on this task using standard Link prediction datasets.

FB15k237 (Toutanova and Chen, 2015) is a dataset based on the FB15k237 adapted Freebase subset, which contains triples with the most mentioned entities. FB15k237 devised the method of selecting the most frequent relations and then filtering inversions from test and valid parts. The **WN18RR** (Bordes et al., 2013) version of WN18 is devoid of inverse relations. WN18 is a WordNet database that contains the senses of words as well as the lexical relationships between them. Table 3 shows the number of entities, relations, and train-valid-test partitions for each dataset used in the proposed work. As an evaluation, we obtain complementary candidates from the entity set for each pair entity-relation from each test triple and estimate the probability score of the received triple being true. The presence of a rising real supplement entity at the top indicates a hit. Candidate ranking is provided using a filtered setting, which was first used in (Bordes et al., 2013). In a filtered setting, all candidates who completed a true triple on the current step are removed from the set, except for the expected entity. We use Hit@1, Hit@3, Hit@10 as evaluation metrics. We also use mean reciprocal rank (MRR) to ensure that true complementary elements are ranked correctly.

4.2 Link Prediction

Table 1 shows the mean value of the experiment on small datasets for the embedding of size 200. The Hit@10 standard deviation for MEKER is 0.0034 for the FB15k237 dataset and 0.0026 for the WNRR18 dataset. Due to space constraints, the table with deviations from all experiments, comparable to Table 1, is in Appendix.

The best score belongs to QuatE (Zhang et al., 2019) model due to its highly expressive 4-dimensional representations. Among the remaining approaches, MEKER outperforms its contestants' overall metrics except for the Hit@10 - Tucker model surpasses MEKER for Fb15k237, ComplEX by LibKGE for WNRR18. In general, MEKER shows decent results comparable to strong baselines (Zhang et al., 2019; Balazevic et al., 2019). It is also worth noting that MEKER significantly improves MRR and Hit@1 metrics on freebase datasets, whereas on word sense, according to data, it has been enhanced in Hit@10.

Dataset	FB15k237				WNRR18			
Model	MRR	Hit@10	Hit@3	Hit@1	MRR	Hit@10	Hit@3	Hit@1
ConvKB (Nguyen et al., 2018)	0.2985	0.4785	0.3270	0.2296	0.2221	0.5074	0.3777	0.0347
HypER (Balazevic et al., 2018)	0.3423	0.5228	0.3774	0.2536	0.4653	0.5228	0.4774	0.4361
TuckER (Balazevic et al., 2019)	0.3455	<u>0.5408</u>	0.3899	0.2606	0.4654	0.5215	0.4784	0.4368
QuatE (Zhang et al., 2019)	**0.3614**	**0.5538**	**0.4014**	**0.2711**	**0.4823**	**0.5719**	**0.4955**	**0.4360**
CP-N3 (Lacroix et al., 2018)	0.3514	0.5294	0.3876	0.2646	0.4402	0.4858	0.4485	0.4207
LibKGE ConvE (Dettmers et al., 2017)	0.3367	0.5213	0.3682	0.2381	0.4282	0.5049	0.4492	0.3934
LibKGE TransE (Bordes et al., 2013)	0.3121	0.4962	0.3175	0.2195	0.2274	0.5189	0.3677	0.0516
LibKGE DistMult (Yang et al., 2015)	0.3331	0.5185	0.3673	0.2410	0.4505	0.5215	0.4634	0.4162
LibKGE ComplEx (Trouillon et al., 2016)	0.3390	0.5265	0.3724	0.2468	0.4752	<u>0.5467</u>	0.4809	0.4366
MEKER	<u>0.3588</u>	0.5393	<u>0.3915</u>	<u>0.2682</u>	<u>0.4768</u>	0.5447	<u>0.4875</u>	<u>0.4371</u>

Table 1: Link Prediction scores for various models on the FB15k237 and WN18RR datasets. The embedding size is 200. The winner scores are highlighted in bold font, and the second results are underlined.

Dataset	FB15k237	WN18RR
Optimizer	AdamW	AdamW
LR	0.01	0.009
Batch Size	156	128
L2 reg	0.001	0.0
Number of negative	6	8
Step of decay LR	3	15
Gamma of decay LR	0.8	0.6

Table 2: The best hyperparameters of the MEKER.

Dataset	#ents	#rels	Number of Triplets Train	Valid	Test
Fb15k237	14,541	237	$27.2 \cdot 10^4$	17,535	20,466
WN18RR	40,943	11	$8.6 \cdot 10^4$	30,034	3,134
Wiki4M	$4{,}316 \cdot 10^4$	1,245	$1{,}367 \cdot 10^4$	30,000	35,815
Wikidata5m	$4{,}594 \cdot 10^4$	822	$2{,}061 \cdot 10^4$	5,163	5,133

Table 3: Statistics of link prediction datasets.

4.3 Model efficiency in case of parameter size increasing

With a strong memory assumption, we can reduce the size of pre-trained MEKER embeddings by tenfold while losing only a few percent of performance.

Figures 2, 3 show MRR and Hit@1 scores for MEKER, TuckER, and ComplEX models at various embedding sizes. Each model approaches a constant value on both metrics around rank 100. For ranks 200 and 300, the performance difference between the three models is approximately consistent for both metrics, with MEKER scoring the highest on rank 20. It means that the number of MEKER parameters can be reduced while maintaining or improving quality. The quality loss is significant for other presented models.

4.4 Memory Complexity Analysis

The theoretical space complexity of models mentioned in the current work is shown in the right column of Table 4. In the context of the Link Prediction task, all approaches have asymptotic memory complexity $\mathcal{O}((n_e + n_r)d)$, which is proportional to the size of the full dictionary of KG elements, i.e. the embedding layer or look-up table. Other aspects of the proposed models are less significant: the convolutional layers are not very extensive. The implementation determines the amount of real memory used by the model during the training process. The Neural Network backpropagation mechanism is used to tune parameters in the most related work. Backpropagation in Figure 4 creates computational graph in which all model parameters are duplicated. It results in a multiplicative constant 2, insignificant in a small dictionary but becomes critical in a large one. To summarize, the following factors account for the decrease in MEKER's required memory:

1. In the MEKER algorithm gradients are computed analytically.

2. MEKER does not have additional neural network layers (linear, convolutional, or attention).

To measure GPU RAM usage, we run each considered embedding model on FB15k-237 into a single GPU and print peak GPU memory usage within the created process. The left column of a Table 4 demonstrates that MEKER has objective memory complexity that is at least twice lower than that of other linear approaches. This property reveals the possibility of obtaining representations of specific large databases using a single GPU card.

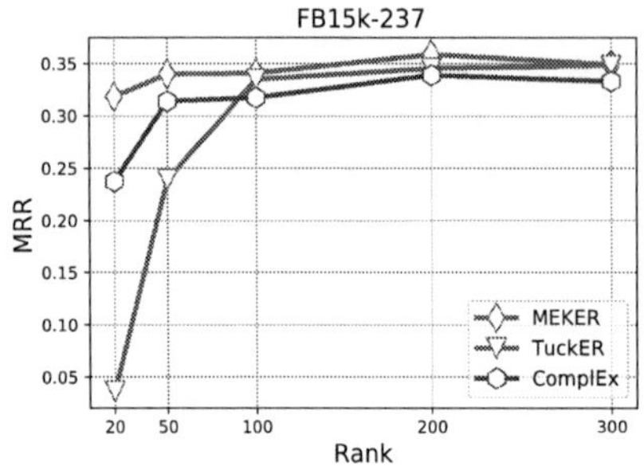

Figure 2: MRR score in dependence of embedding ranks

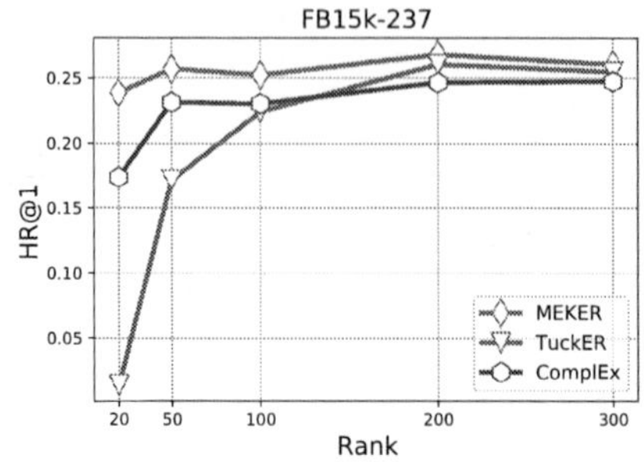

Figure 3: Hit@1 score in dependence of embedding ranks

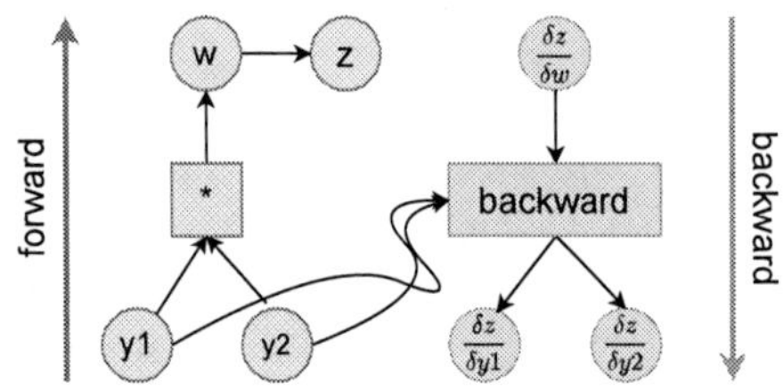

Figure 4: The scheme of the augmented computational graph of the Neural Network.

Model	GPU Memory Usage, MB	Theoretical Approximation of Space Complexity
TuckER	357	$2 \cdot ((n_e + n_r + c \cdot lin) \cdot d)$
HypER	208	$2 \cdot ((n_e + n_r + c \cdot lin) \cdot d)$
ConvKB	3 563	$2 \cdot ((n_e + n_r) \cdot d + c \cdot conv)$
ConvE	229	$2 \cdot ((n_e + n_r) \cdot d + c \cdot conv)$
ComplEX	252	$2 \cdot (n_e + n_r) \cdot d$
DistMult	174	$2 \cdot (n_e + n_r) \cdot d$
QuatE	2 367	$2 \cdot 4 \cdot (n_e + n_d + c \cdot lin)$
CP (N3)	138	$2 \cdot (n_e + n_r) \cdot d$
MEKER	79	$((n_e + n_r) \cdot d)$

Table 4: Memory, reserved in the PyTorch Framework during the training process and theoretical approximation of given implementations' complexity. On the FB15k237 dataset, we train 200-size representations with a batch size of 128. *Lin* denotes the number of output features in a linear layer, *conv* denotes the size of convolutional layer parameters. The constant c represents the number of different layers.

5 Experiments on Large-Scale KG Datasets

5.1 Experimental settings

To test the model on large KG, we employ two WikiData-based datasets. The first English dataset, **Wikidata5m** (Wang et al., 2021)[1], is selected due to the presence of related works and reproducible baseline (Ruffinelli et al., 2020). This dataset is created over the 2019 dump of WikiData and contains of elements with links to informative Wikipedia pages. Our experiments use the transductive setting of Wikidata5m - triplet sets to disjoint across training, validation, and test.

The second English-Russian dataset is formed since its suitability for the NLP downstream task. We leverage KG-based fact retrieval over Russian Knowledge Base Questions (RuBQ) (Rybin et al., 2021) benchmark. This benchmark is a subset of Wikidata entities with Russian labels. Some elements in RuBQ are not covered with Wikidata5m, so we created a link-prediction **Wiki4M** dataset over RuBQ. We select triples without literal objects and obtain approximately 13M triples across 4M entities (see Table 3). Wiki4M also fits the concept of multilingualism is intended to be used in a cross-lingual transfer or few-shot learning.

[1] https://deepgraphlearning.github.io/project/wikidata5m

5.2 Link Prediction

We embed the datasets for ten epochs on a 24.268 Gb GPU card with the following model settings: LR $2.5 \cdot 10^{-4}$, increasing in 0.5 steps every 10 epoch, batch size 256, number of negative samples 4 for Wiki4M and 2 for Wikidata5m.

As a comparison, we use the PyTorch-BigGraph large-scale embedding system (Lerer et al., 2019). PyTorch-BigGraph modifies several traditional embedding systems to focus on the effective representation of KG in memory. We select ComplEX and TransE and train graphs for these embedding models, dividing large datasets into four partitions. With a batch size of 256, the training process takes 50 epochs.

We also deploy LibKGE (Ruffinelli et al., 2020) to evaluate TransE and ComplEX approaches. For

Model	MRR	Hit@1	Hit@3	Hit@10	Memory, GB	Storage, GB
English: Wikidata5m dataset						
PTBG (ComplEX)	0.184	0.131	0.210	0.287	45.15	9.25
PTBG (TransE)	0.150	0.091	0.176	0.263	43.64	9.25
LibKGE sparse (TransE)	0.142	0.153	0.211	0.252	33.29	0.00
LibKGE sparse (ComplEX)	0.202	**0.160**	0.233	0.316	**21.42**	0.00
MEKER (ours)	**0.211**	0.149	**0.238**	**0.325**	22.27	0.00
Russian: Wiki4M dataset						
PTBG (ComplEX)	0.194	0.141	0.212	0.293	42.83	9.25
LibKGE sparse (TransE)	0.183	0.126	0.191	0.275	26.75	0.00
LibKGE sparse (ComplEX)	0.247	0.196	0.275	0.345	**20.22**	0.00
MEKER (ours)	**0.269**	**0.199**	**0.303**	**0.410**	21.04	0.00

Table 5: Unfiltered link prediction scores for MEKER and PyTorch-BigGraph approaches for Wiki4M and Wikidata5m datasets and memory needed in leveraging every model. Storage means additional memory demanded for auxiliary structures. Batch size 256. Here "RAM" is GPU RAM or main memory RAM if GPU limit of 24 GB is reached. *Sparse* means sparse embeddings. Models without *sparse* mark employ dense embeddings matrix.

ComplEX model training, we use the best parameter configuration from the repository, for TransE, we obtain a set of training parameters by greed search. The learning rate for TransE is 0.5, decaying in factor 0.45 every 5 step and train model in 100 epochs. In both cases, we use sparse embedding in the corresponding model setting and batch size of 256. Models from both wrappers that did not fit in 24 GB, we train on the CPU.

Embedding sets yielded by we these experiments we then test on the link prediction task. We provide scoring without filters because the partition-based setup of PyTorch-Biggraph does not support filtering evaluation. Tables 5 shows that MEKER significantly improves the results of PyTorch-Biggraph models across all proposed metrics. The ComplEX model with sparse embedding, fine-tuned by LibKGE, gives results almost approaching the MEKER and exceeding the Hit@1 in Wiki4M. The right part of Tables 5 shows that the baseline approaches consume twice as much memory as MEKER, but sparse ComplEX slightly improves memory consumption. TransE does not give such significant results as ComplEX.

5.3 Knowledge Base Question Answering (KBQA)

In this section, to further evaluate the proposed MEKER embeddings we test them in an extrinsic way within on a KBQA task on two datasets for English and Russian.

5.3.1 Experimental Setting

We perform experiment with two datasets: for English we use the common dataset SimpleQuestions (Bordes et al., 2015) aligned with Wiki4M KG[2] (cf. Table 3), and for Russian we use RuBQ 2.0 dataset (Rybin et al., 2021) which comes with the mentioned above Wiki4M KG (cf. Table 3). RuBQ 2.0 is a Russian language QA benchmark with multiple types of questions aligned with Wikidata. For both SimpleQuestions and RuBQ, for each question, an answer is represented by a KG triple.

For training we use a training set of SimpleQuestions for verification we use a test set of SimpleQuestions and RuBQ 2.0 dataset for English and Russian, respectively. These Q&A pairs provide ground truth answers linked to exact this version of KG elements.

More specifically, in these experiments, we test answers to 1-hop questions which are questions corresponding to one subject and one relation in the knowledge graph, and takes their object as an answer.

We want to leverage the KBQA model, which can process questions both in English and Russian. To measure the performance of a KBQA system, we measure the accuracy of the retrieved answer/entity. This metric was used in previously reported results on SimpleQuestions and RuBQ. If the subject of the answer triple matches the reference by ID or name, it is considered correct.

5.3.2 KBQA methods

The key idea of the KBQA approaches is mapping questions in natural language to the low-dimensional space and comparing them to graph elements' given representation. In **KEQA** (Huang

[2]https://github.com/askplatypus/wikidata-simplequestions

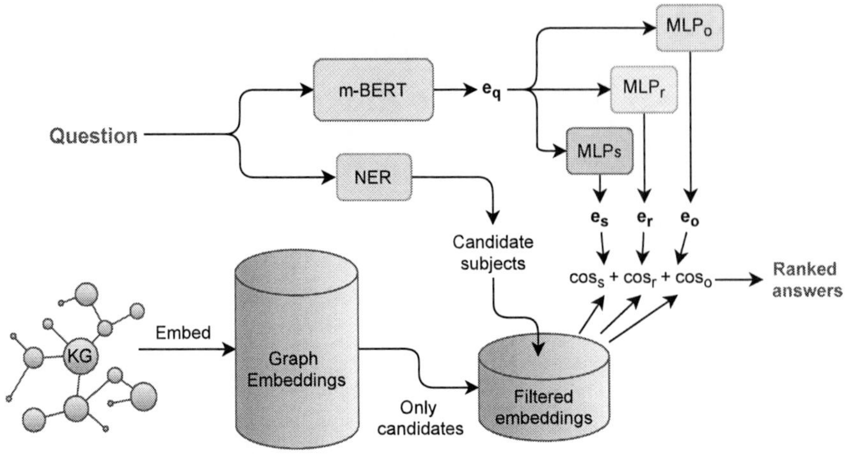

Figure 5: Text2Graph method used in our experiments: 1-Hop QA pipeline. First, we take original entity and relation embeddings. The question is embedded using m-BERT. This embedding is then processed by MLP, yielding candidate representations of an object, relation, and subject. The sum of the subject, relation, and object cosines is the final score of triple candidates.

et al., 2019) LSTM models detect the entity and predicates from the question text and project it further into the entity and predicate embedding spaces. The closest subject in terms of similarity to the entity and predicate embeddings is selected as the answer.

We created a simple approach **Text2Graph** which stems from the **KEQA** and differs from the original work in improved question encoder, entity extractor, additional subject embedding space and simplified retrieval pipeline. The Algorithm 3 describes the procedure of projecting the input question to graph elements. The multilingual-BERT (Devlin et al., 2019) model encodes the input question, and all word vectors are averaged into a single deep contextualized representation e_q. This representation then goes through three MLPs jointly learning candidate embeddings of an object, relation, and subject. We minimize MSE between predicted embeddings and the corresponding KGE model's embeddings. The appropriateness score of every fact in KG is a sum of cosine similarity between MLP outputs and ground truth model representation for every element in the triple. The triple with the highest score is considered to be an answer. The scheme is trained using an AdamW optimizer with default parameters for 10 epochs.

5.4 Baselines

5.4.1 RuBQ 2.0

We compare our method to several QA approaches compatible with questions from this benchmark.

Algorithm 3 Text2Graph question projection algorithm

Input: $\mathcal{Q}$, $\mathcal{G}$, **E**,
text encoder M_{enc},
projection modules: M_s, M_r, M_o,
Subject Candidates Extractor: NER
Output: answer $\langle o_a, r_a, s_a \rangle$

```
e_q = M_enc(Q)
Initialize answers-candidates list with empty list A=[]
Initialize scores list with empty list S=[]
Initialize entities-candidates list with empty list C=[]
for entity in G do
    if entity.name in NER(Q) then
        C.append(entity)
for entity in C do
    for relation in entity.relations do
        s = entity.id
        r = relation.id
        o = entity[r]
        triple = ⟨s, r, o⟩
        A.append(triple)
        e_s = E[s]
        e_r = E[r]
        e_o = E[o]
        y_s = M_s(e_q)
        y_r = M_r(e_q)
        y_o = M_o(e_q)
        score = cos(e_o, y_o) + cos(e_r, y_r) + cos(e_s, y_s)
        S.append(score)
ind = argmax(S)
⟨s_a, r_a, o_a⟩ = A[ind]
return ⟨s_a, r_a, o_a⟩
```

KBQA Model	Embedding Model	Accuracy 1-Hop
DeepPavlov	-	30.5 ± 0.04
SimBa	-	32.3 ± 0.05
QA-En	-	32.3 ± 0.08
QA-Ru	-	30.8 ± 0.03
Text2Graph	PTBG (ComplEX) Wiki4M	48.16 ± 0.05
Text2Graph	PTBG (TransE) Wiki4M	48.84 ± 0.06
Text2Graph	MEKER Wiki4M	49.06 ± 0.06

Table 6: Comparison of the Text2Graph system with the various KG embeddings with existing solutions (QA-Ru, QA-En, SimBa) on RuBQ 2.0 benchmark.

KBQA Model	Embedding Model	Accuracy 1-Hop
KEQA	TransE FB5M	40.48 ± 0.10
Text2Graph	PTBG (TransE) Wikidata5m	59.97 ± 0.15
Text2Graph	MEKER Wikidata5m	61.81 ± 0.13

Table 7: Comparison of the Text2Graph system with the various KG embeddings with existing embedding-based solution on the SimpleQuestions benchmark.

QAnswer[3] is a rule-based system addressing questions in several languages, including Russian. **SimBa** is a baseline presented by RuBQ 2.0 authors. It is a SPARQL query generator based on an entity linker and a rule-based relation extractor. KBQA module of **DeepPavlov Dialogue System Library** (Burtsev et al., 2018) also based on query processing.

5.4.2 SimpleQuestions

Simple Question is an English language benchmark aligned with FB5M KG - the subset of Freebase KG. Its train and validation parts consist of 100k and 20k questions, respectively. As a baseline solution we employ **KEQA** (Huang et al., 2019). We realign answers from this benchmark to our system, which is compatible with Wikidata5m. Not all of the questions from FB5M have answers among Wiki4M, that is why we test both systems on a subset of questions whose answers are present in both knowledge graphs.

5.4.3 Experimental Results

We compare the results of the Text2Graph with PTBG embeddings versus MEKER embedding and baseline KBQA models. Results on the RuBQ 2.0 dataset are shown in Table 6. Text2Graph outperforms baselines. Using MEKER embeddings instead of the PTBG version of ComplEX and TransE demonstrates slightly better accuracy.

Table 7 presents results on the SimpleQuestions dataset. As Huang et al. (2019) model uses FB5M KG and Text2Graph uses Wikidata5m KG we test both models on the subset of questions, which answers are present in both knowledge graphs for a fair comparison. Our model demonstrates superior performance and regarding the comparison within different embeddings in a fixed system, MEKER provides better accuracy of answers than TransE embeddings on the SimpleQuestions benchmark.

6 Conclusion

We propose MEKER, a linear knowledge embedding model based on generalized CP decomposition. This method allows for the calculation of gradient analytically, simplifying the training process under memory restriction. In comparison to previous KG embedding linear models (Balazevic et al., 2019), our approach achieves high efficiency while using less memory during training. On the standard link prediction datasets WN18RR and FB15k-237, MEKER shows quite competitive results.

In addition, we created a Text2Graph — KBQA system based on the learned KB embeddings to demonstrate the model's effectiveness in NLP tasks. We obtained the required representations using MEKER on the Wikipedia-based dataset Wiki4M for questions in Russian and on Wikidata5m for questions in English. Text2Graph outperforms baselines for English and Russian, while using MEKER's embeddings provides additional performance gain compared to PTBG embeddings. Furthermore, our model's link prediction scores on Wiki4M and Wikidata5m outperform the baseline results. MEKER can be helpful in question-answering systems over specific KG, in other words, in systems that need to embed large sets of facts with acceptable quality.

All codes to reproduce our experiments are available online.[4]

Acknowledgements

The work was supported by the Analytical center under the RF Government (subsidy agreement 000000D730321P5Q0002, Grant No. 70-2021-00145 02.11.2021).

[3] https://www.qanswer.eu

[4] https://github.com/skoltech-nlp/meker

References

Ivana Balazevic, Carl Allen, and Timothy Hospedales. 2019. TuckER: Tensor factorization for knowledge graph completion. In *Proceedings of the 2019 Conference on Empirical Methods in Natural Language Processing and the 9th International Joint Conference on Natural Language Processing (EMNLP-IJCNLP)*, pages 5185–5194, Hong Kong, China. Association for Computational Linguistics.

Ivana Balazevic, Carl Allen, and Timothy M. Hospedales. 2018. Hypernetwork knowledge graph embeddings. *CoRR*, abs/1808.07018.

Casey Battaglino, Grey Ballard, and Tamara G. Kolda. 2018. A practical randomized CP tensor decomposition. *SIAM J. Matrix Anal. Appl.*, 39(2):876–901.

Lukas Biewald. 2020. Experiment tracking with weights and biases. Software available from wandb.com.

Kurt Bollacker, Colin Evans, Praveen Paritosh, Tim Sturge, and Jamie Taylor. 2008. Freebase: A collaboratively created graph database for structuring human knowledge. pages 1247–1250.

Antoine Bordes, Nicolas Usunier, Sumit Chopra, and Jason Weston. 2015. Large-scale simple question answering with memory networks.

Antoine Bordes, Nicolas Usunier, Alberto Garcia-Durán, Jason Weston, and Oksana Yakhnenko. 2013. Translating embeddings for modeling multi-relational data. In *Proceedings of the 26th International Conference on Neural Information Processing Systems - Volume 2*, NIPS'13, page 2787–2795, Red Hook, NY, USA. Curran Associates Inc.

Mikhail Burtsev, Alexander Seliverstov, Rafael Airapetyan, Mikhail Arkhipov, Dilyara Baymurzina, Nickolay Bushkov, Olga Gureenkova, Taras Khakhulin, Yuri Kuratov, Denis Kuznetsov, Alexey Litinsky, Varvara Logacheva, Alexey Lymar, Valentin Malykh, Maxim Petrov, Vadim Polulyakh, Leonid Pugachev, Alexey Sorokin, Maria Vikhreva, and Marat Zaynutdinov. 2018. DeepPavlov: Open-source library for dialogue systems. In *Proceedings of ACL 2018, System Demonstrations*, pages 122–127, Melbourne, Australia. Association for Computational Linguistics.

Hao Cheng, Yaoliang Yu, Xinhua Zhang, Eric Xing, and Dale Schuurmans. 2016. Scalable and sound low-rank tensor learning. In *Proceedings of the 19th International Conference on Artificial Intelligence and Statistics*, volume 51 of *Proceedings of Machine Learning Research*, pages 1114–1123, Cadiz, Spain. PMLR.

Tim Dettmers, Pasquale Minervini, Pontus Stenetorp, and Sebastian Riedel. 2017. Convolutional 2d knowledge graph embeddings. *CoRR*, abs/1707.01476.

Jacob Devlin, Ming-Wei Chang, Kenton Lee, and Kristina Toutanova. 2019. BERT: Pre-training of deep bidirectional transformers for language understanding. In *Proceedings of the 2019 Conference of the North American Chapter of the Association for Computational Linguistics: Human Language Technologies, Volume 1 (Long and Short Papers)*, pages 4171–4186, Minneapolis, Minnesota. Association for Computational Linguistics.

Daniel M. Dunlavy, Tamara G. Kolda, and Evrim Acar. 2011. Temporal link prediction using matrix and tensor factorizations. *ACM Trans. Knowl. Discov. Data*, 5(2):10:1–10:27.

Richard A. Harshman, Paul E. Green, Yoram Wind, and Margaret E. Lundy. 1982. A model for the analysis of asymmetric data in marketing research. *Marketing Science*, 1(2):205–242.

F. L. Hitchcock. 1927. The expression of a tensor or a polyadic as a sum of products. *J. Math. Phys*, 6(1):164–189.

David Hong, Tamara G. Kolda, and Jed A. Duersch. 2020. Generalized canonical polyadic tensor decomposition. *SIAM Review*, 62(1):133–163.

Xiao Huang, Jingyuan Zhang, Dingcheng Li, and Ping Li. 2019. Knowledge graph embedding based question answering. In *Proceedings of the Twelfth ACM International Conference on Web Search and Data Mining*, WSDM '19, page 105–113, New York, NY, USA. Association for Computing Machinery.

Seyed Mehran Kazemi and David Poole. 2018. Simple embedding for link prediction in knowledge graphs. In *Proceedings of the 32nd International Conference on Neural Information Processing Systems*, NIPS'18, page 4289–4300, Red Hook, NY, USA. Curran Associates Inc.

Timothee Lacroix, Nicolas Usunier, and Guillaume Obozinski. 2018. Canonical tensor decomposition for knowledge base completion. In *Proceedings of the 35th International Conference on Machine Learning*, volume 80 of *Proceedings of Machine Learning Research*, pages 2863–2872. PMLR.

Adam Lerer, Ledell Wu, Jiajun Shen, Timothee Lacroix, Luca Wehrstedt, Abhijit Bose, and Alex Peysakhovich. 2019. PyTorch-BigGraph: A Large-scale Graph Embedding System. In *Proceedings of the 2nd SysML Conference*, Palo Alto, CA, USA.

Deepak Nathani, Jatin Chauhan, Charu Sharma, and Manohar Kaul. 2019. Learning attention-based embeddings for relation prediction in knowledge graphs. *CoRR*, abs/1906.01195.

Dai Quoc Nguyen, Tu Dinh Nguyen, Dat Quoc Nguyen, and Dinh Phung. 2018. A novel embedding model for knowledge base completion based on convolutional neural network. In *Proceedings of the 16th Annual Conference of the North American*

Chapter of the Association for Computational Linguistics: Human Language Technologies (NAACL-HLT), pages 327–333.

Maximilian Nickel, Volker Tresp, and Hans-Peter Kriegel. 2011. A three-way model for collective learning on multi-relational data. In *Proceedings of the 28th International Conference on International Conference on Machine Learning*, ICML'11, page 809–816, Madison, WI, USA. Omnipress.

Adam Paszke, Sam Gross, Francisco Massa, Adam Lerer, James Bradbury, Gregory Chanan, Trevor Killeen, Zeming Lin, Natalia Gimelshein, Luca Antiga, Alban Desmaison, Andreas Kopf, Edward Yang, Zachary DeVito, Martin Raison, Alykhan Tejani, Sasank Chilamkurthy, Benoit Steiner, Lu Fang, Junjie Bai, and Soumith Chintala. 2019. Pytorch: An imperative style, high-performance deep learning library. In H. Wallach, H. Larochelle, A. Beygelzimer, F. d'Alché-Buc, E. Fox, and R. Garnett, editors, *Advances in Neural Information Processing Systems 32*, pages 8024–8035. Curran Associates, Inc.

Thomas Rebele, Fabian M. Suchanek, Johannes Hoffart, Joanna Biega, Erdal Kuzey, and Gerhard Weikum. 2016. YAGO: A multilingual knowledge base from wikipedia, wordnet, and geonames. In *The Semantic Web - ISWC 2016 - 15th International Semantic Web Conference, Kobe, Japan, October 17-21, 2016, Proceedings, Part II*, pages 177–185.

Daniel Ruffinelli, Samuel Broscheit, and Rainer Gemulla. 2020. You CAN teach an old dog new tricks! on training knowledge graph embeddings. In *International Conference on Learning Representations*.

Ivan Rybin, Vladislav Korablinov, Pavel Efimov, and Pavel Braslavski. 2021. Rubq 2.0: An innovated russian question answering dataset. In *The Semantic Web - 18th International Conference, ESWC 2021, Virtual Event, June 6-10, 2021, Proceedings*, volume 12731 of *Lecture Notes in Computer Science*, pages 532–547. Springer.

Kristina Toutanova and Danqi Chen. 2015. Observed versus latent features for knowledge base and text inference. In *Proceedings of the 3rd Workshop on Continuous Vector Space Models and their Compositionality*, pages 57–66, Beijing, China. Association for Computational Linguistics.

Théo Trouillon, Christopher R. Dance, Éric Gaussier, Johannes Welbl, Sebastian Riedel, and Guillaume Bouchard. 2017. Knowledge graph completion via complex tensor factorization. *J. Mach. Learn. Res.*, 18(1):4735–4772.

Théo Trouillon, Johannes Welbl, Sebastian Riedel, Eric Gaussier, and Guillaume Bouchard. 2016. Complex embeddings for simple link prediction. In *Proceedings of The 33rd International Conference on Machine Learning*, volume 48 of *Proceedings of Machine Learning Research*, pages 2071–2080, New York, New York, USA. PMLR.

L. R. Tucker. 1966c. Some mathematical notes on three-mode factor analysis. *Psychometrika*, 31:279–311.

Rui Wang, Bicheng Li, Shengwei Hu, Wenqian Du, and Min Zhang. 2020. Knowledge graph embedding via graph attenuated attention networks. *IEEE Access*, 8:5212–5224.

Xiaozhi Wang, Tianyu Gao, Zhaocheng Zhu, Zhengyan Zhang, Zhiyuan Liu, Juanzi Li, and Jian Tang. 2021. Kepler: A unified model for knowledge embedding and pre-trained language representation. *Transactions of the Association for Computational Linguistics*, 9:176–194.

Zhen Wang, Jianwen Zhang, Jianlin Feng, and Zheng Chen. 2014. Knowledge graph embedding by translating on hyperplanes. In *Proceedings of the Twenty-Eighth AAAI Conference on Artificial Intelligence*, AAAI'14, page 1112–1119. AAAI Press.

B. Yang, Wen tau Yih, X. He, Jianfeng Gao, and L. Deng. 2015. Embedding entities and relations for learning and inference in knowledge bases. *CoRR*, abs/1412.6575.

Shuai Zhang, Yi Tay, Lina Yao, and Qi Liu. 2019. Quaternion knowledge graph embeddings. In *Advances in Neural Information Processing Systems*, volume 32. Curran Associates, Inc.

Discourse on ASR Measurement: Introducing the ARPOCA Assessment Tool

Megan Merz
Rose-Hulman Institute of Technology
merzm@rose-hulman.edu

Olga Scrivner
Rose-Hulman Institute of Technology
scrivner@rose-hulman.edu

Abstract

Automatic speech recognition (ASR) has evolved from a pipeline architecture with pronunciation dictionaries, phonetic features and language models to the end-to-end systems performing a direct translation from a raw waveform into a word sequence. With the increase in accuracy and the availability of pre-trained models, the ASR systems are now omnipresent in our daily applications. On the other hand, the models' interpretability and their computational cost have become more challenging, particularly when dealing with less-common languages or identifying regional variations of speakers. This research proposal will follow a four-stage process: 1) Proving an overview of acoustic features and feature extraction algorithms; 2) Exploring current ASR models, tools, and performance assessment techniques; 3) Aligning features with interpretable phonetic transcripts; and 4) Designing a prototype ARPOCA to increase awareness of regional language variation and improve models feedback by developing a semi-automatic acoustic features extraction using PRAAT in conjunction with phonetic transcription.

1 Introduction

Automated speech recognition (ASR) is the process of automatically detecting and recognizing the words that have been said in a sample of speech. ASR has a wide variety of uses, such as voice assistants, automatic transcription, speech-to-text, and closed-caption generation. Many recent ASR models have been created using deep learning, with other methods including neural networks, hidden Markov models, and Gaussian mixture models (Papastratis, 2021).

ASR models are generally trained on a corpus, which is a collection of audio recordings. Corpora are widely available for more common languages, such as English. However, they are either small or nonexistent for less common languages and dialects. This is due to the resources needed to construct a corpus and lack of available speakers. Constructing a corpus involves gathering audio recordings from a variety of speakers and is a time-consuming and costly process. As a result, less common languages remain under-resourced in the ASR field. The performance accuracy will also vary with regional language variation and among different groups of users. ASR performs especially poorly when given the task of recognizing the speech of nonnative speakers of a language, leading to model biases in common AI-assisted speech technologies (DefinedCrowd, 2021).

Furthermore, there is a lot of variation in ASR systems. In the last decade, the ASR technology has evolved from probabilistic frameworks with hand-crafted features and pronunciation dictionaries to deep learning models in which features are extracted and learned in hidden layers (Georgescu et al., 2021). Speech signals also consist of various components, such as acoustic, phonetic, and language-dependent, which jointly provide a representation of word sequences. While some features are interpretable by humans (e.g., place of articulation, vowel formants, pitch), others are the results of transformations and cannot be directly associated with any specific phonetic sound.

Finally, various evaluation systems are put forth to measure speech model accuracy (Negri et al., 2014). Grapheme-based metrics (a written word) are commonly used to compare results, such as word error rate (WER). These measurement systems, however, are not able to diagnose whether phonetic errors resulted from a variation in pronunciation, speech boundary misalignment, noise, or the lack of sufficient data.

This research is focused on existing ASR evaluation systems and speech signal features used for training. We explore solutions for improving measuring performance metrics. Our goal is to 1) develop a semi-automatic phonetic classification be-

Proceedings of the 60th Annual Meeting of the Association for Computational Linguistics
Student Research Workshop, pages 366 - 372
May 22-27, 2022 ©2022 Association for Computational Linguistics

tween vowels and consonants as these classes are traditionally associated with different salient features (e.g., vowel formants, consonant intensity, aspiration), 2) help ASR developers to identify improvement areas by focusing on specific feature engineering tasks, and 3) design an alternative evaluation system to encourage the ASR research for less-commonly used languages by incorporating development cost, corpus size, and phonetic transcript as compared to a traditional word error rate evaluation metric.

The paper is organized as follows. Section 2 presents the overview of ASR performance evaluation metrics, current ASR models and corpora. Section 3 describes the most common types of speech features and tools for their generation. In Section 4, we present our proposed evaluation system ARPOCA (Assessment of ASR using phonemes, originality, cost, and accent performance). Finally, we provide our preliminary results in Section 5, followed by conclusion and future direction.

2 Literature Review

2.1 Measuring ASR Performance

One common way of measuring the performance of automatic speech recognition (ASR) models is word error rate (WER). WER is a way to measure the accuracy of ASR. The best possible value is 0% error, and higher percentages are considered worse. WER is counted by letting a model transcribe a section of audio, then comparing it to the correct transcription. Both transcriptions are normalized before comparing, which standardizes the transcripts by removing stop words, forming contractions, etc. The words that the model has inserted, deleted, or substituted are counted and used to calculate WER using the formula illustrated in Eq.1, where S is a word substitution, D is a deletion, and I is a word insertion:

$$WER = \frac{(S + D + I)}{TotalWords} \quad (1)$$

WER is a commonly used method to assess the performance of ASR models, and creating a model with a low WER is assumed to result in a model with better language understanding accuracy. However, a better WER may not actually result in a model with a better understanding of spoken language, meaning that even if a transcript is mostly accurate, it may not correctly represent the meaning of the spoken language (Wang et al., 2003).

This problem of accuracy is especially pertinent for models that are trained with small corpora, since these models often have a poor WER. The early study comparing different spoken language models (Wang et al., 2003) found that, while the Model developed using Hidden Markov and Context Free Grammar (HMM/CFG) had a worse WER than other language models (e.g. a trigram model) it achieved a better task classification error rate, which is a way to measure how well the model understands the spoken language. This result was even more pronounced for models trained with small amounts of data: the HMM/CFG model was able to use less training data and still generate a model with a better level of understanding than the trigram model. It is worth noting that the HMM/CFG model used domain knowledge and a grammar library, which helped it achieve good results without a large training dataset (Wang et al., 2003). So, while WER can be used as a way to measure performance, other metrics (e.g., task classification error rate) may be more useful, especially for models trained with smaller corpora.

In addition, WER does not provide much feedback for developers. While it measures the number of mistakes a model made, it does not help in revealing why the mistakes were made or whether similar mistakes were made repeatedly. Providing more feedback could aid developers in diagnosing problems with their models more quickly and in the end, creating better models. This project discusses the possibility of providing more feedback for ASR models by identifying commonly mistaken sounds and recognizing different pronunciations for words.

Another metric for the accuracy of ASR is phoneme error rate (PER), which is calculated similarly to WER. However, while WER is at the word level, PER counts the number of deleted, inserted, and substituted phonemes. Phonemes are smaller than words, which could potentially help pinpoint errors better.

2.2 Methods for ASR

Deep learning is commonly used for ASR. There are typically four steps in ASR: 1) pre-processing, 2) feature extraction, 3) classification, and 4) language modeling. Pre-processing is a process applied to recordings which reduces noise and filters the audio. Feature extraction converts the audio to features, which are then analyzed and converted to language in the classification step. Mel-frequency

Cepstral coefficients (MFCC) is commonly used for the feature extraction step. MFCC converts audio signals into a linear model of human auditory processing, which is non-linear.

Deep neural networks can be used for ASR, such as recurrent neural networks (RNN), convolutional neural networks, and transformer networks. One limitation of RNNs is that they process speech using only the previous input. However, speech depends on both what comes before and what comes after. This problem can be solved using bi-directional RNNs, which process speech forward and backward. Furthermore, Connectionist temporal classification (CTC), can be used to find the most probable alignment, which is the arrangement of speech and silence. Silence can be either not speaking or transitioning between words or sounds. CTC must be used in combination with a decoding step, such as the best-path decoding algorithm. The best-path decoding algorithm aims to find the most likely word for each sequence of sound. A method called RNN-transducer uses an RNN with CTC to analyze input and also a separate RNN to predict likely words in the sequence based on previous words (Papastratis, 2021).

Dialect detection uses similar methods as ASR, so dialect detection could be used to help improve ASR. There are several motivations for dialect identification, including determining the regional origin and ethnicity of a speaker in order to adapt content (Ismail, 2020). For example, deep neural networks have been used to distinguish between dialects of Arabic. A recent study by Lulu and Elnagar (2018) used an existing dialectal dataset called the AOC (Arabic Online Commentary), which has about 110 thousand labeled sentences. The motivation for the study was to improve dialect detection for Arabic as informal dialects of Arabic are widely used on the internet, especially for applications such as blogs, forums, social media, and more. The study showed that dialect detection is also useful for machine translation and sentiment analysis. Four different types of deep neural network were used: long-short term memory (LSTM), convolutional neural networks (CNN), bi-directional LSTM (BLSTM), and convolutional LSTM (CLSTM). Three different dialects were examined - Egyptian, Gulf (which included the similar Iraqi dialect) and Levantine. Of the neural networks, the LSTM was the most accurate overall, with approximately 80% accuracy on average, which is below the human accuracy of about 90% (Lulu and Elnagar, 2018).

2.3 Data for ASR

There is a large amount of variability in the corpora used for ASR. Often, corpora are built at the word or phrase level. However, for some languages, such as Tibetan, a corpus at the syllable level can work better due to the lack of accuracy for word and phrase recognition (Dao et al., 2021). Many corpora use speech samples that have been recorded with minimal environmental noise and are of good quality, which results in models that work best in these ideal conditions. However, real life conditions can result in noisier speech, so models that have not been trained with noisy speech can struggle under such conditions (Borský, 2016).

Corpus creation can be a difficult and expensive process, which often results in smaller or nonexistent corpora for less spoken and under-resourced languages. Even if corpora exist for a language, they may not be suitable for certain applications, as was the case for an experiment conducted by Zissman et al. (1996). They found that while Spanish corpora existed, there was no corpus that had enough speakers of a variety of dialects. This led to the creation of the Miami corpus, which collected speech from Spanish speakers from Peru, Cuba, and other countries (Zissman et al., 1996). There are a number of steps involved in corpus creation. First, recordings must be obtained. This means researchers either have to find people to record their speech or find existing recordings. There are a variety of sources for existing recordings, such as audio books or YouTube videos (Ismail, 2020). If a transcript does not exist for the recording, then one must be created. Then, the transcript and audio must be aligned to ensure that the words shown in the transcript are placed where the same words are spoken in the recording (Panayotov et al., 2015). Recordings may also be cleaned of background noise and normalized. While there have been efforts to automate the corpus creation process, it is not guaranteed to be accurate. Therefore, much of this process is done manually.

3 Speech Signal Features

Feature extractions is a pre-processing task which transforms sound files into feature vectors that can be processed and analyzed by a computer. This tasks can be classified into two main groups: segment and suprasegmental prosodic features versus speaker-dependent and speaker independent features (Georgescu et al., 2021; Shahnawazuddin et al., 2020). While most of acoustic phonetics utilize interpretable features (e.g. vowel formant, duration, voice onset time) to describe phonemes (mental representation of sound) and phones (actual sounds), the ASR field relies on transformed feature vectors optimized for Machine learning tasks (e.g. Linear Prediction and Mel-Frequency coefficients).

3.1 Acoustic Features

Formant is a common interpretable measurement that correspond to resonance frequencies in a vocal tract. The first formant (F1) is correlated with high-low dimension and inversely related to vowel height, where high values represent open vowels (e.g. /a/) as compared to low values for low vowels (e.g. /i/). The second formant (F2) is correlated with front-back dimension, namely the degree of backness for a vowel. For example, front vowels (e.g., /i/) will have higher F2 values than back vowels (e.g., /o/). The third formant (F3) indicates the round shape of a vowel (Ladefoged, 2006; Kent and Vorperian, 2018). These values can be seen in a spectogram as dark bands. It should be noted that these values are not uniform across speakers, speech style, morphological context, and language variation, as can be seen from Spanish acoustic data illustrated in Fig.1, where solid line represents a vowel space obtained in a controlled laboratory sampling of Peninsular Spanish and dotted lines demonstrate a much smaller vowel space from a spontaneous speech of Venezuelan Spanish (Scrivner, 2014).

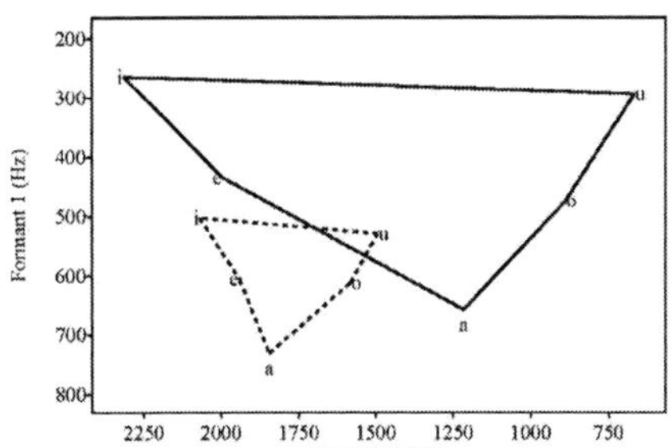

Figure 1: Comparison of Spanish vowel formants between controlled (solid line) and spontaneous speech (dotted line) and between two Spanish dialects (Venezuelan and Peninsular).

Similarly, consonants have three dimensions but related to 1) place of articulation (e.g. dental, glottal), 2) manner of articulation (e.g., nasal, fricative), and 3) voicing (Ladefoged, 2006).

In sum, three classes of distinct sound landmarks have been proposed: 1) abrupt discontinuity of consonants, 2) steady periods of vowels, 3) non-abrupt transition of glides (e.g. /w/) (Park, 2008).

3.2 Feature Vectors Extraction Algorithms

One of the preliminary operations to generate vector features is framing. Framing breaks the sound into small frames, typically 25ms long with 10ms overlap with neighboring frames. The overlap is important due to the dependence which speech has on preceding and following sounds. During framing, windowing is carried out, in which a Hamming or Han (sometimes referred to as Hanning) filter is performed. The window function decreases the amplitude at the beginning and end of the frame, which again, makes overlapping frames necessary to prevent anomalies (Georgescu et al., 2021).

Several feature extraction methods can be applied after framing, namely, Fast Fourier Transform (FFT), Linear Prediction Coefficients (LPC), Mel-Frequency Ceptrum Coefficients (MFCC), Mel-Filterbanks, Discrete Cosine Transform (DCT). FFT is a common technique used to transform speech signal from a time domain to a frequency domain. The FFT separates the air exhaled from the lungs and the time response of the vocal tract by converting from the time domain to the frequency domain, which allows these two features to be separated. When framing, windowing, and FFT are applied to an audio sample, a spectrogram can be created from the results. In contrast, LPC relies on linear prediction. It uses past samples to predict the current sample. However, this method has some drawbacks, such as inability to distinguish similar vowel sounds and its inaccurate analysis of speech signals due to the assumption that speech signals are stationary. Finally, MFCCs can be obtained by applying DCT to the log power spectrum of mel frequencies (Gupta et al., 2018).

4 ARPOCA Approach

In response to the problems previously identified in the field of speech recognition, this proposal aims to develop a more in-depth evaluation system called ARPOCA. ARPOCA is an acronym for Assessment of ASR using Phonemes, Originality, Cost, and Accent performance. The main goal is to develop a phoneme recognition system using phoneme classification and transcription, independent from a grapheme representation used in WER.

First, we selected open source existing tool Praat, a software designed for sound processing (Boersma, 2001; Styler, 2011), to extract interpretable feature representations for each phoneme. Second, we identified the following salient features for phoneme classification: frequency formants, dispersion (also called standard deviation), center of gravity, and intensity. Standard formant ranges for F1, F2, F3 are used to identify vowels. Dispersion, center of gravity, and intensity are used to identify consonants. Center of gravity measures at what frequency a sound is most concentrated, while dispersion measures how widely the frequencies of a sound are spread. Intensity measures the loudness of a sound in decibels. For testing, we obtained a non-transcribed free sample Spanish audio corpus (Defined.ai, n.d.).

In our next stage, we will create a manual phonetic transcription of utterances from the corpus, in addition to segmenting and labeling the utterances for usage in PRAAT. We will collect information about expected values of acoustic features used for identifying phonemes and compare our manual phonetic transcription with the output from an available speech recognizer library in python. In addition, we will analyze several existing models to establish a baseline for originality and cost in these models, and use this to create a rating system. Furthermore, the phoneme recognition system will incorporate an accent performance analysis. That is, the phoneme recognition system will identify whether a model has a wide pronunciation gap and identify particular areas where a model struggles, which will help close the accent gap.

5 Preliminary Results

In the first stage of this proposal, we are exploring features extracted from spectogram and speech-wave. Fig. 2 displays an example of Spanish word 'necesito' (I need). The sound waves help distinguish between sound and silence, amplitude and intensity of sounds, while the spectrogram provides a view of formant frequencies, consonants obstruction and frication.

While PRAAT includes scripting, using Python in addition makes running the PRAAT script easier to automate, especially for large amounts of audio samples. Python code calls a PRAAT script, then

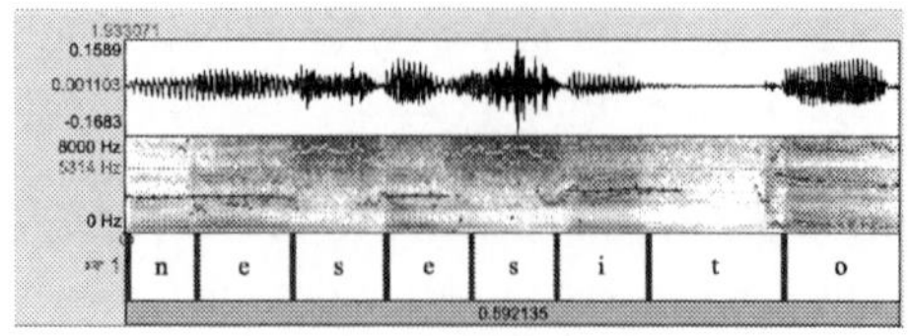

Figure 2: An example of using Praat to segment speech and label phonemes. Sound waves are shown at the top, followed by a spectrogram, then the segmentation. Red dots in the spectrogram show formants, while the blue line shows pitch.

performs additional operations on the results of the PRAAT script, such as matching the formants to the correct phoneme class. Table 1 demonstrates preliminary results from using PRAAT in conjunction with Python. The PRAAT script obtained formant values at the median time of each segment. Then, the results are matched to the phoneme based on formant range. For example, the /e/ phoneme typically has F1 values between 485 and 565 and F2 values between 2170 and 2430. While some of the vowels fell within the expected ranges of formants during testing, others did not. This could be for several reasons. One such reason is not normalizing speech prior to attempting to recognize phonemes. Normalization could help reduce variance between individual speakers. Dialectal variation may also be a factor, since vowel frequencies can vary between different dialects.

Phoneme	Duration	F1	F2	F3
n	0.0522	-	-	-
e	0.0726	572	2438	2960
s	0.0713	-	-	-
e	0.0657	484	2086	2964
s	0.0654	-	-	-
i	0.0708	489	2575	3439
t	0.1040	-	-	-
o	0.0932	6034	1274	2862

Table 1: Preliminary results from formant analysis using Praat and Python to identify formants in the audio segment 'necesito' (I neeed). F1, F2, and F3 are values for formants 1, 2, and 3 respectively.

Since consonants cannot be identified using formants only, we use different measurements, including center of gravity, intensity, and standard deviation. Currently, using these measurements is only precise enough to differentiate between fricative and non-fricative consonants. More work must be done to refine the expected ranges for consonants to be able to identify individual consonants.

Originality is another aspect of ARPOCA. We have determined that a scoring rubric would likely be best to assess originality, since there is little research on this topic. Thus, research that is an addition or improvement on an existing model will receive a lower score than more novel research. Cost is also an important element of ARPOCA. Preliminary research suggests that a budget of $500,000 would be attainable for many researchers (NIH, n.d.). An overall cost, including corpus cost and compute cost, which does not exceed $500,000 would score the highest, with score decreasing as total cost increases. The reason for this is twofold. Firstly, there are many applications that require smaller, less costly models. For instance, such models could be used to assist people with hearing loss by providing real-time transcriptions. Secondly, many costly models with large corpora already exist and are prioritized under the prevalent measurement system of WER. Therefore, in order to encourage innovation in the field of ASR, smaller, less costly models will be encouraged.

There are several important outcomes from the preliminary results. In its current state, the phoneme recognizer is unlikely to work with English, due to the presence of a large number of vowels which are not easily distinguishable. The phoneme identifier has been tested using Spanish, which is better suited to this purpose due to the smaller number of vowels, which are relatively easy to distinguish. An additional flaw in the phoneme identifier is its difficulty distinguishing between vowels and voiced consonants. Table 2 shows that the /n/ phoneme is identified as a vowel, but should be identified as a voiced consonant. The speech segments used were relatively noiseless; the phoneme recognizer is likely to be less accurate in a more noisy environment.

Time	Phoneme ID	SR
1.935	vowel	n
1.987	e	e
2.059	voiceless fricative	s
2.129	e	e
2.184	voiceless fricative	s
2.275	e	i
2.331	voiceless non-fricative	t
2.441	o	o

Table 2: A comparison of preliminary results from the phoneme identifier and a transcript created by the speech recognizer. Phoneme ID represents the results from the phoneme identifier, while SR represents the results from the python speech recognition.

6 Conclusion and Future Work

The objective of this work is to supplement ASR models and developers with an additional tool providing not only a feedback but also more interpretable representation of sound models via phonetic transcription. Such feedback could include highlighting phonemes that have been consistently misidentified and/or measuring performance of the model when given audio samples produced by non-native speakers, which is an area in which ASR models typically struggle. This feedback could improve the accuracy of ASR models and lessen the accent gap. Accuracy of models could also be improved by providing developers more feedback on their models than just using standard performance metrics. For instance, commonly mistaken sounds (phonemes) could be used as a form of feedback to help improve models and augment existing corpora. Furthermore, a phonetic approach could help create dictionaries with dialectal variation (regional alternative pronunciation) that can be added to training corpora. Finally, language transfer (using the resources from one language to develop resources in another similar language or dialect) could help provide resources for underrepresented spoken languages.

ARPOCA needs more development in order to become more accurate. This could include additional data for improving the cost baseline and grading in addition to more research into expected values of formants, center of gravity, intensity, and dispersion. In its current state of research, ARPOCA serves as a proof of concept for the development of a more robust assessment tool for ASR models. We envision ARPOCA being used in settings such as peer reviews and conferences to promote discussion and improvement of ASR models. ARPOCA can aid in supporting different research goals than WER. For instance, a model with a smaller corpus typically costs less to produce and would therefore score better in the cost section of WER. This could encourage the production of models for under-resourced and less widely spoken languages, even if such models do not immediately have a good enough WER score to compete with models for languages such as English. Another possible benefit of using ARPOCA is closing the accent gap. Although the accent performance analysis system has not been developed yet, the existing phoneme identification could help developers determine if there are specific groups of formants that a model has misidentified. On the other hand, ARPOCA must be carefully revised to ensure that the scoring system is fair and accurate. If there are inaccuracies in ARPOCA or top scores are unattainable, this could result in a variety of unwanted outcomes, such as giving models the wrong scores or discouraging developers. In addition, while ARPOCA has been developed with collaboration and discussion in mind, it has the possibility to fuel competition as well, due to its role as a tool for assessment. Therefore, ARPOCA must be used with care and consideration as to whether its use is appropriate for a given situation.

Acknowledgements

We would like to thank Dr. Michael Wollowski and anonymous reviewers for their valuable feedback.

References

Paul Boersma. 2001. Praat, a system for doing phonetics by computer. *Glot International*, 5(9/10).

Michal Borský. 2016. *Robust recognition of strongly distorted speech.* Ph.D. thesis.

Jizhaxi Dao, Zhijie Cai, Rangzhuoma Cai, Maocuo San, and Mabao Ban. 2021. A method of constructing syllable level Tibetan text classification corpus. *MATEC Web of Conferences*, 336:06013.

Defined.ai. n.d. Inclusive Speech Recognition Technology.

DefinedCrowd. 2021. Preventing Bias in Speech Technologies. Technical Report September.

Alexandru Lucian Georgescu, Alessandro Pappalardo, Horia Cucu, and Michaela Blott. 2021. Performance vs. hardware requirements in state-of-the-art automatic speech recognition. *Eurasip Journal on Audio, Speech, and Music Processing*, 2021(1):1–30.

Divya Gupta, Poonam Bansal, and Kavita Choudhary. 2018. The State of the Art of Feature Extraction Techniques in Speech Recognition. *Advances in Intelligent Systems and Computing*, 664:195–207.

Tanvira Ismail. 2020. A Survey of Language and Dialect Identification Systems. *Adalya*, 6(1).

Raymond D Kent and Houri K Vorperian. 2018. Static measurements of vowel formant frequencies and bandwidths: A review. *Journal off Communication Disorders*, 74:74–97.

Peter Ladefoged. 2006. *A course in phonetics.* Thomson, Wadsworth.

Leena Lulu and Ashraf Elnagar. 2018. Automatic Arabic Dialect Classification Using Deep Learning Models. In *The 4th International Conference on Arabic Computational Linguistics*, volume 142.

Matteo Negri, Marco Turchi, José G C De Souza, Daniele Falavigna,) Fbk -Fondazione, and Bruno Kessler. 2014. Quality Estimation for Automatic Speech Recognition. *Proceedings of COLING*, pages 1813–1823.

NIH. n.d. Data Book.

Vassil Panayotov, Guoguo Chen, Daniel Povey, and Sanjeev Khudanpu. 2015. Librispeech: An ASR corpus based on public domain audio books. In *IEEE International Conference on Acoustics, Speech and Signal Processing (ICASSP)*. IEEE.

Ilias Papastratis. 2021. Speech Recognition: a review of the different deep learning approaches.

Chiyoun Park. 2008. *Consonant Landmark Detection for Speech Recognition by.* Ph.D. thesis, Massachusetts Institute of Technology.

Olga Scrivner. 2014. Vowel Variation in the Context of /s/: A Study of a Caracas Corpus. In Rafael Orozco, editor, *New Directions in Hispanic Linguistics*, chapter Vowel Vari. Cambridge Scholars Publishing.

S. Shahnawazuddin, Nagaraj Adiga, Hemant Kumar Kathania, and B. Tarun Sai. 2020. Creating speaker independent ASR system through prosody modification based data augmentation. *Pattern Recognition Letters*, 131:213–218.

Will Styler. 2011. Using Praat for Linguistic Research.

Ye Yi Wang, Alex Acero, and Ciprian Chelba. 2003. Is word error rate a good indicator for spoken language understanding accuracy. *2003 IEEE Workshop on Automatic Speech Recognition and Understanding, ASRU 2003*, pages 577–582.

Marc A. Zissman, Terry P. Gleason, Deborah M. Rekart, and Beth L. Losiewicz. 1996. Automatic dialect identification of extemporaneous, conversational, Latin American Spanish speech. In *ICASSP, IEEE International Conference on Acoustics, Speech and Signal Processing - Proceedings*, volume 2.

Pretrained Knowledge Base Embeddings for improved Sentential Relation Extraction

Andrea Papaluca[1], Daniel Krefl[2], Hanna Suominen[1,3], Artem Lenskiy[1]

[1] School of Computing, The Australian National University, Canberra, ACT, Australia
[2] Department of Computational Biology, University of Lausanne, Switzerland
[3] Department of Computing, University of Turku, Turku, Finland
{andrea.papaluca, hanna.suominen, artem.lenskiy}@anu.edu.au, daniel.krefl@unil.ch

Abstract

In this work we put forward to combine pre-trained knowledge base graph embeddings with transformer based language models to improve performance on the sentential Relation Extraction task in natural language processing. Our proposed model is based on a simple variation of existing models to incorporate *off-task* pre-trained graph embeddings with an *on-task* finetuned BERT encoder. We perform a detailed statistical evaluation of the model on standard datasets. We provide evidence that the added graph embeddings improve the performance, making such a simple approach competitive with the state-of-the-art models that perform explicit on-task training of the graph embeddings. Furthermore, we observe for the underlying BERT model an interesting power-law scaling behavior between the variance of the F1 score obtained for a relation class and its support in terms of training examples.

1 Introduction

Besides large quantities of unstructured textual data, also structured data has become widely available to machine learning researchers in recent years. Knowledge Bases (KBs), such as Wikidata (Vrandečić, 2012) (formerly Freebase Bollacker et al., 2007; Pellissier Tanon et al., 2016), Yago (Suchanek et al., 2007) and UMLS (Bodenreider, 2004), organise various kinds of information in structured form and constantly grow in size and richness of included information.

They are represented in terms of relations between entities, forming a graph structure that makes retrieval and processing of the included information easier and finds particular application in various language related tasks, such as question answering (QA), search engine development and knowledge discovery. Distant supervision (Mintz et al., 2009) is another notable example that employs a KB to improve Relation Extraction (RE). For each pair of entities found in a sentence, distantly supervised models check whether a link between the entities in the KB graph exists, and, if there is a match, the sentence is then used as a training example for supervised learning.

Note that the utility of KBs for RE extends beyond being just a useful source of supervision labels. A natural question arises whether one can develop models which combine unstructured textual data with structured information to further improve performance, for general natural language processing tasks.

One particular class of approaches that has been gaining momentum is based on the idea of dynamically learning representations of KB entities simultaneously with word representations (Bastos et al., 2021; Nadgeri et al., 2021; Vashishth et al., 2018). The motivation behind this class of methods is whether such combined representations could improve performance for a downstream NLP task, due to a more representative embedding.

However, although in theory this could result in optimally finetuned word and graph representations for the downstream task, it might be challenging in practice. On-task training of the graph embeddings requires significantly more complex models, and therefore increases the training cost and is more prone to overfitting.

Therefore, instead of training both, graph and word embeddings, we investigate in this work whether combining static pre-trained graph embeddings, such as those provided in Lerer et al. (2019), with *on-task* learned word embeddings already achieves a significant performance boost for downstream tasks. The underlying question being whether a neural model is able to transfer the topological information contained in the pre-trained graph embeddings in a useful manner to the task at

Proceedings of the 60th Annual Meeting of the Association for Computational Linguistics
Student Research Workshop, pages 373 - 382
May 22-27, 2022 ©2022 Association for Computational Linguistics

hand.

2 Related Work

In the following, we would like to briefly review three particular works in the literature that make use of the information contained in a KB to improve classification performance on the RE task, and explain how our work relates to these previous works.

In Vashishth et al. (2018) the authors propose to use KBs as a supplementary source of information to improve on the multi-instance learning paradigm for RE. Note that in multi-instance RE one aims at identifying the relation between two targeted entities, for a given bag of sentences. In particular, the authors of Vashishth et al. (2018) match the relation predicted by the Stanford OpenIE (Angeli et al., 2015) pipeline with the set of relation aliases found in the KB. Out of this they obtain a *matched relation embedding*, h^{rel}, that is then concatenated to the sentence representation. Similarly, they build an *entity type embedding*, h^{type}, using the entity type found in the KB, which is concatenated as well to the sentence encoding.

In Bastos et al. (2021) the authors make use of the KB information to improve on the sentential RE task. They propose to construct an *Entity Attribute Context* embedding, h^o, by processing several entity properties found in the KB with the help of a BiLSTM (Schuster and Paliwal, 1997) encoder. Additionally, a *triplet context* embedding, h^r, is learned for each relation triplet by imposing the translational property in the embedding space (Bordes et al., 2013) to the triplet and its KB neighbours. Finally, the two different representations obtained are aggregated with the sentence encodings by a GP-GNN (Zhu et al., 2019) and fed to a classifier for relation prediction.

The authors of Nadgeri et al. (2021), however, suggest that statically adding all the available KB information might be counterproductive in some case. They rather propose to dynamically select the useful information. To do so, for each entity they extract and encode several KB properties with a BiLSTM (Schuster and Paliwal, 1997), that are then combined together with the sentence encoding to form a *Heterogenous Information Graph*. The relevant context information is then obtained by pruning this graph with the help of a combination of graph convolutional neural network (Kipf and Welling, 2017), pooling and self-attention layers, and finally aggregated and fed to the relation classifier, similarly to what is done in Bastos et al. (2021).

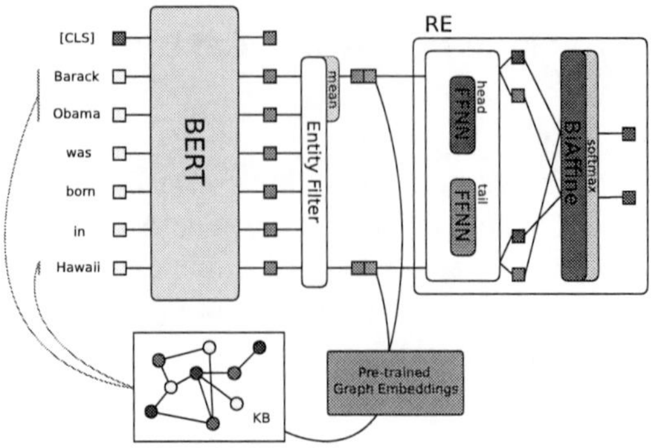

Figure 1: The RE model we make us of, inspired by Giorgi et al. (2019). The initial encodings of the sentences are provided by a pre-trained language model. The encodings corresponding to named entities are extracted, and averaged in case of multi-token entities. For the graph embedding augmented model the graph embeddings are in addition concatenated to the relative entity encodings. Each entity is then decomposed in a *head-tail* representation to form the (h, t) candidate pairs passed to the Biaffine Attention Layer (Dozat and Manning, 2017) for relation classification.

Note that the KB embedding is dynamically learned in all above cited works. Furthermore, in these examples, it derives from a wide variety of entity properties and information retrieved from the KB, but not directly from the graph structure itself. The only exception being the *triplet-context* embedding h^r of Bastos et al. (2021), which comes closest to the graph embedding (Lerer et al., 2019) we are going to make use of. However, their embedding is trained only on the downstream task, but not on the full KB.

Therefore, what is so far missing in the literature, is the basic baseline of simply adding a pre-computed *topology-based* KB embedding in order to improve the RE task performance. In this work we aim to fill this gap. We provide a detailed evaluation of such a model, which takes pre-computed KB embeddings into account. As we will show below, such a simple model extension is in fact competitive with the more advanced models mentioned above on standard benchmark datasets.

3 Model

To perform RE, we make use of the model introduced in Nguyen and Verspoor (2019); Giorgi et al. (2019). The only difference being that we do not perform Named Entity Recognition (NER), but instead train the model using gold entities, i.e. the correct span of the entity mentions is fed to the model as input. Thereby, we are able to evaluate RE performance without contamination with wrongly predicted entities. We chose this model for its relative simplicity, while still providing close to state-of-the-art performance in RE and its high modularity that allows for easy modifications and extensions.

The RE classifier we use resembles the one introduced in Nguyen and Verspoor (2019), except that it is combined with a pre-trained transformer-based (Devlin et al., 2019; Vaswani et al., 2017) encoder, as proposed in Giorgi et al. (2019). For illustration, the complete model is sketched in Figure 1.

The information flows from left to right and the errors are free to backpropagate through all the preceding layers. The input of the model is a sentence of N tokens, $w_1, w_2, ..., w_N$, containing two or more known entities, $e_i = w_j, w_{j+1}, ..., w_{j+k}$. The output is one or more triplets (h, t, r) representing the relations found in the input sentence. h and t represent the head and the tail of the relation respectively, while r is the type of relationship between h and t.

A more detailed description of our model pipeline is given in the remainder of this section. For reproducibility, we made our model source codes available on Github [1].

3.1 Pre-trained Language Model

The pre-trained language model provides the initial encodings for the tokens contained in the sentence. We opted to use variants of the BERT (Devlin et al., 2019; Liu et al., 2019) model (specifically, the implementation of *bert-base-cased* and *roberta-base* by Huggingface (Wolf et al., 2020)), but in general the encoder can be replaced by any other encoder capable of providing context-dependent embeddings of a sentence. We leave the encoder unfrozen during training such that the gradients can propagate through it. Thereby its parameters are fine-tuned to optimize the token representation for the specific task at hand.

In more detail, we start with the encoder completely frozen and gradually unfreeze the last four layers over the first epochs of training, as suggested for instance in Araci (2019). It has been shown that such training procedure does not necessary yield a decrease in accuracy, but it does significantly reduce the computational burden, c.f., Araci (2019).

3.2 Entity Filter

The purpose of the entity filter is to filter out each token that does not compose an entity. Two common choices for multi-token entities are to keep either the last token or the average of tokens as identifier of the complete entity. We tested both cases and did not find any evidence of one being superior to the other in our application. Therefore, we opted to take the average encoding among the tokens composing the entity as identifier.

Note that for the model augmented by a graph-embedding, we concatenate to the average encoding obtained for each entity, $\mathbf{x}_i^{BERT}$, the relative graph embedding $\mathbf{x}_i^{graph}$ of Lerer et al. (2019), such that we obtain for the final input $\mathbf{x}_i$ of the RE module

$$\mathbf{x}_i = [\mathbf{x}_i^{BERT}, \mathbf{x}_i^{graph}] \,. \tag{1}$$

3.3 RE Module

For details of the RE module we refer to the original works (Dozat and Manning, 2017; Nguyen and Verspoor, 2019; Giorgi et al., 2019). In a nutshell, the RE module consists of two steps. Firstly, the *head-tail* decompositions of the inputs are constructed:

$$\mathbf{x}_i^{h|t} = \mathcal{F}_{h|t}\left([\mathbf{x}_i^{BERT}, \mathbf{x}_i^{graph}]\right), \tag{2}$$

where $\mathbf{x}_i^h$ and $\mathbf{x}_i^t$, are the representation of the inputs viewed as the head or the tail of a relation triplet (h, t, r). The projection is performed by two simple feed forward neural networks, $\mathcal{F}_{head}$ and $\mathcal{F}_{tail}$, composed of two linear layers separated by ReLU activation and dropout ($p = 0.1$) for regularization.

Secondly, all pairs $\{(\mathbf{x}_j^{head}, \mathbf{x}_k^{tail})\}_{j \neq k}$ are constructed by combining all the heads with each possible tail (Miwa and Bansal, 2016; Nguyen and Verspoor, 2019; Giorgi et al., 2019), and fed to a biaffine attention layer (Dozat and Manning, 2017; Nguyen and Verspoor, 2019; Giorgi et al., 2019) for relation classification. The biaffine layer $\mathcal{B}(\cdot, \cdot)$ performs a combination of a bilinear transformation and a linear projection:

$$\mathcal{B}(\mathbf{x}_1, \mathbf{x}_2) := \mathbf{x}_1^\top \mathbf{U}\mathbf{x}_2 + \mathbf{W}(\mathbf{x}_1 \| \mathbf{x}_2) + \mathbf{b} \,, \tag{3}$$

$$\mathbf{x}_i^{RE} = \mathcal{B}(\mathbf{x}_j^{head}, \mathbf{x}_k^{tail}) \,, \tag{4}$$

[1] https://github.com/BrunoLiegiBastonLiegi/Pretrained-KB-Embeddings-for-RE

where we indicate with || the column-wise concatenation. A final softmax activation layer provides the scores for each of the relation classes. The RE loss is taken to be the crossentropy,

$$\mathcal{L}_{RE} = \sum_{i=1}^{M} \frac{\exp \mathbf{x}_{i,T}^{RE}}{\sum_{j \neq T} \exp \mathbf{x}_{i,j}^{RE}}, \quad (5)$$

where $\mathbf{x}_{i,T}^{RE}$ represents the score assigned to the correct class.

Note that if a sentence contains n_e entities, the RE module is going to provide $2\binom{n_e}{2} = \frac{n_e!}{(n_e-2)!}$ relation predictions. One for each of the possible entity combinations

$$(e_i^{head}, e_j^{tail})_{i \neq j} \quad i, j = 1, ..., n_e$$

and, therefore, allowing for multiple relations extracted from a single sentence.

4 Results

In order to quantify the benefit of adding pre-trained graph embeddings to a RE model, we have considered two popular RE datasets: the *Wikidata* (Sorokin and Gurevych, 2017) and *NYT* (Riedel et al., 2010) corpora.

Since we make use of pre-trained graph embeddings, we decided to discard all sentences in the training set containing entities not present in the graph embedding (Lerer et al., 2019). Note that in order to be able to fairly compare the models with and without graph embeddings, we also exclude these sentences in training the basic model without graph embeddings. For the test set, we keep all the sentences regardless of the available embeddings. In case no embedding for the entity is available, we simply substitute the graph embedding with a zero tensor.

For each dataset we train the model with a different random initialization ten times with and without the addition of the pre-trained graph embeddings. Hence, in total we train twenty models per experiment. Note that we always use the *AdamW* (Loshchilov and Hutter, 2019) optimizer with learning rate $2 \cdot 10^{-5}$. For the implementation of the optimizer and of the whole model depicted in Figure 1 we rely on the Pytorch Library (Paszke et al., 2019).

For evaluation, we compare the performance of the two models (with and without graph embeddings) using Precision, Recall and F1 score. Both, for each single relation class, and on average with micro- and macro-averaging. In detail we rely on the two following evaluation methods:
At first, for each relation class, we collect the F1 score obtained by the ten different trained models and we plot the complete distribution of the results as a violin plot. The mean of the ten F1 values obtained is also reported as a colored dot inside the violin. The same is done for the global micro- and macro-average. We do this for both, the model with added graph embeddings and the baseline model without graph embeddings.

Then, we generate the micro *Precision-Recall* curve for each of the ten models trained. The ten curves obtained are interpolated and averaged to form a single mean PR curve both, for the model provided with the graph embeddings and the baseline model. At each value of recall we compute the standard deviation of the precision over the ten different curves. The deviation is shown in shaded color around the mean curve.

4.1 Pre-Trained Graph Embeddings

For all examples, we rely on the Wikidata KB (Vrandečić, 2012) with pre-trained graph embeddings of the entities provided by Lerer et al. (2019). In detail, the authors of Lerer et al. (2019) propose a memory efficient and distributed implementation of several popular graph embedding methods, such as RESCAL (Nickel et al., 2011), TransE (Bordes et al., 2013) and DistMult (Yang et al., 2015). This new implementation was specifically developed for dealing with very large graphs while being competitive with the original implementation of the state-of-the-art models aforementioned.

The pre-trained embeddings we use were trained on the so-called "truthy" Wikidata dump dated 2019-03-06, making use of the TransE (Bordes et al., 2013) approach with embedding dimension of size 200.

4.1.1 Wikidata

The *Wikidata* (Sorokin and Gurevych, 2017) dataset is a RE corpus built by distant supervision with entities aligned to the Wikidata Knowledge Base (Vrandečić, 2012). We rely on the dataset version provided by Bastos et al. (2021). Some statistics of the dataset are shown together with our training configuration in Table 1. Note that in the evaluation we ignore the results for the NA relation class (i.e. the "no relation" class), as is usually done in the literature (Bastos et al., 2021; Nadgeri

Dataset	train	train$_{ours}$	test	relations	KB entities	batchsize	epochs
Wikidata	$372,059$	$369,577$	$360,334$	353	$464,535$	8	1-2
NYT	$455,771$	$\sim$ 453-$455,000$	$172,448$	58	$63,601$	8	3

Table 1: Statistics and training settings for all the datasets considered. **train$_{ours}$** indicates the actual number of training sentences used after discarding part of the data, as described in the main text. Note that for the NYT dataset the **train$_{ours}$** is given as a range, as for each repetition we sampled a different subset of the training and validation set, as described in Section 4. For the Wikidata dateset, we experimented with training for 1 and 2 epochs.

			Micro			Macro		
			P	R	F1	P	R	F1
Wikidata		RECON (Bastos et al., 2021)	87.24	87.23	87.23	**63.59**	33.91	44.23
		KG-Pool (Nadgeri et al., 2021)	**88.60**	**88.59**	**88.60**	-	-	-
	Ours	*bert-base*	85.43	78.37	81.74	51.42	37.24	40.02
		roberta-base	85.50	80.30	82.81	49.33	36.77	39.22
		roberta-base$_{1e}$	83.71	83.01	83.35	46.09	34.52	36.38
	Ours$_{ge}$	*bert-base*	88.34	79.19	83.51	55.72	39.62	43.24
		roberta-base	87.66	82.07	84.77	54.42	**41.64**	**44.33**
		roberta-base$_{1e}$	86.83	83.93	85.36	50.88	38.52	40.57
NYT	Ours	*bert-base*	47.13	75.57	57.98	28.35	45.27	33.05
	Ours$_{ge}$	*bert-base*	**51.13**	**76.46**	**61.24**	**31.66**	**47.31**	**36.20**

Table 2: Summary of the P, R and F1 scores (averaged over ten runs) obtained in our experiments for the three datasets considered. We indicate with the subscript *ge* the results obtained by the model with the graph embeddings added. For the *Wikidata* experiment we even specify with the subscript $1e$ the models that have been trained for 1 single epoch instead of 2. If avaliable, we include the results obtained by others on the same dataset, we leave blank (-) otherwise. In particular, for the *NYT* dataset, we are not aware of other works in the literature measuring the performance under the F1 metric.

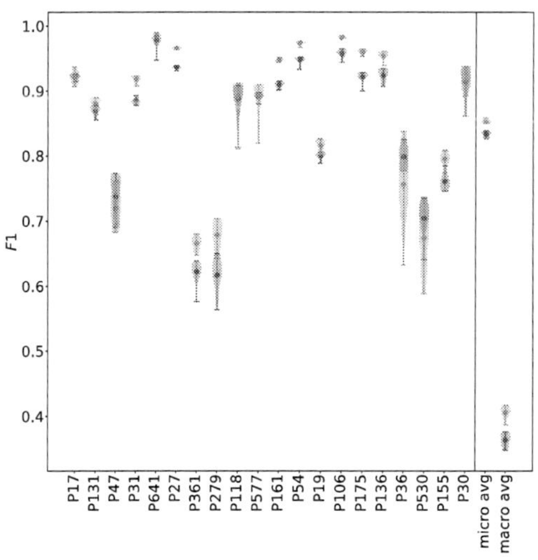

Figure 2: F1 scores on the Wikidata corpus for each relation. The micro- and macro-averages are also shown. Only the top 20 relations are plotted, ordered by decreasing support. The F1 score distribution of the ten different trained models is illustrated via violin plots. The baseline model is shown in blue and the model with added graph embeddings in orange. The means of the distributions are indicated by bullet points inside the violin plots.

	P@10	P@30
RESIDE (Vashishth et al., 2018)	73.6	59.5
RECON (Bastos et al., 2021)	87.5	74.1
KG-Pool (Nadgeri et al., 2021)	92.3	86.7
Ours	96.6	83.1
Ours$_{ge}$	**97.5**	**86.8**

Table 3: Comparison of the P@10 and P@30 for the NYT dataset. We indicate with the subscript *ge* the results obtained by the model with the graph embeddings added.

et al., 2021).

For this dataset, in addition to the *bert-base-cased* (Devlin et al., 2019) model, we also tested the *roberta-base* (Liu et al., 2019) language model. For the latter, we also experimented with training for just one epoch instead of two, obtaining slightly better micro F1, at the cost of lower macro F1.

The F1 score violin plots for the top 20 relation classes in the dataset are shown in Figure 2. The illustrated results were obtained with the *roberta-base* model as sentence encoder, the whole model was trained for 1 epoch. Although some relations do not benefit from the inclusion of graph embeddings, the majority of them show a consistent improvement. On average, we measure a performance boost, both, in micro- and macro-averaged F1 score, of around ~ 2 - 4% depending on the specific language model, c.f. Table 2.

Even so the addition of graph embeddings yields a significant performance boost to the base model, as discussed above, the boosted model does not outperform the current state-of-the-art (Nadgeri et al., 2021) in the micro-averaged metrics. In particular, only the micro precision metric (*bert-base*$_{ge}$: 88.34 ± 0.33), is statistically in range of the state of the art model[2]. However, for macro-averaged scores, our model (*roberta-base*$_{ge}$) surpasses the current state-of-the-art (Bastos et al., 2021), both, in recall (R) and F1.

4.2 NY Times

Another popular RE dataset built by distant supervision is the *NYT* corpus (Riedel et al., 2010), obtained by aligning a set of over 1.8 million articles from the *NY Times* journal to the *Freebase* Knowledge Base. We made use of the *Wikidata SPARQL* query service [3] to obtain the mapping from the old Freebase id scheme to the new Wikidata one. We make use of the dataset version provided by Bastos et al. (2021). In Table 1 are reported some statistics of the dataset together with the settings we used in our experiments.

We train on the validation ($114,317$ sentences) and training sets ($455,771$ sentences) by randomly discarding 20% of the sentences for each one of the ten runs, such that we obtain a number of train sentences comparable to Bastos et al. (2021); Nadgeri et al. (2021); Vashishth et al. (2018). Note that we had to further discard between $1,000$ to $3,000$ train sentences, depending on the run, due to the missing graph embeddings. We train the model with the settings listed in Table 1, and evaluate the performance at P@10 and P@30 (precision at fixed recall 10% and 30%), as proposed in the literature. As before, we ignore the score of the NA relation class in averaging.

Figure 3 illustrates the comparison of the performance of the two models trained. We observe that the model with the added graph embeddings shows a slower decay of the precision with increasing recall and, in particular, an improved precision on average and through the whole curve. The F1 score calculation confirms this trend, as both micro- and macro-F1 exhibit an improvement of about $\sim 3\%$, as reported in Table 2.

[2]For reference, we observed standard deviations in the range ~ 0.1 - 1 for the results reported in Table 2.

[3]https://query.wikidata.org/

The comparison with the results obtained by others in the literature, reported in Table 3, demonstrates the solid performance of our model. In particular, the model is able to surpass the current state-of-the-art (Nadgeri et al., 2021), both, under P@10 and P@30.

4.3 Discussion

To better understand under which circumstances the additional information contained in the graph embeddings is beneficial, some of the results given above are analyzed below. We are going to consider each relation separately, and we will look at four different variables characterizing them:

- $\sigma^2(F1)$: Variance of the F1 score obtained across the ten runs.
- $\overline{F1}$: Mean F1 score obtained across the ten runs.
- S: Support, i.e. the amount of training examples available.
- $\Delta\overline{F1} := \overline{F1}_{ge} - \overline{F1}_b$: Gap between the average scores obtained by the model with the additional graph embeddings and the baseline model.

Note that the *Wikidata* corpus provides the largest number of relation classes and thereby features a wider statistical variety. Therefore, we focus on the results for the *Wikidata* corpus in the remainder of this section, in particular the ones obtained by our *roberta-base* based model trained for 1 epoch. For some relations we have always obtained $\overline{F1} = 0$ with zero variance $\sigma^2(F1) = 0$, and, surprisingly, not all of them had close to zero support S. Those with higher support, however, were usually semantically similar to relations provided with much larger support that were constantly preferred by our model. We exclude all these $\overline{F1} = 0, \sigma^2(F1) = 0$ relations since their identically null variance is an artifact and thus they do not provide a good representation of the $\sigma^2(F1)$ behaviour.

As shown in Figure 2 we observe a large variance of results for several relations across the ten different runs. The relationship between the variance, $\sigma^2(F1)$, and the support S of each relation is plotted in Figure 4 (*left*). Note that we take the log scale for both axis. Both, the baseline, and the graph embedding augmented models, show an approximately linear relationship of $\sigma^2(F1)$ with

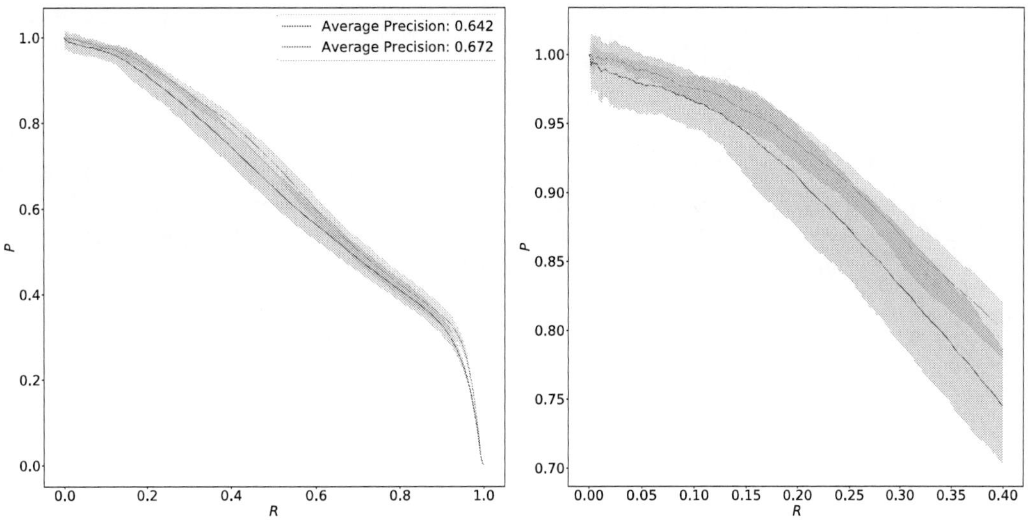

Figure 3: Micro Precision-Recall curves for the baseline model (blue) and the model augmented with graph-embeddings (orange) trained on the *NYT* dataset. The right plot gives a more detailed view into the region with Recall $\leq$ 0.4. The solid lines represent the average P-R curve for the ten trained models. The shaded regions represent the corresponding standard deviations of the Precision at given Recall.

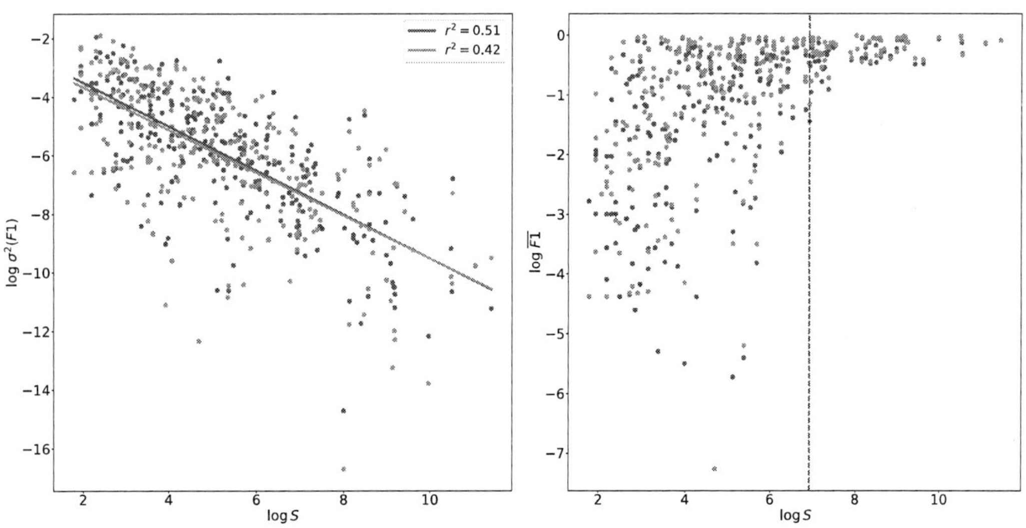

Figure 4: Distribution of the *Wikidata* dataset relations according to their score variance $\sigma^2(F1)$ (*left*) and their average score $\overline{F1}$ (*right*) against relation support S. Note that each point represents a different relation. The color of the points indicates from which model the datapoint originates. Blue for the baseline and orange for the graph embedding augmented model. Both axis are plotted in logarithmic scale. The distributions in the (*left*) plot are fitted with the linear regression (6) with the r^2 value of the fits reported in the legend. The support $S = 1000$ threshold is indicated as a dashed line in the (*right*) plot.

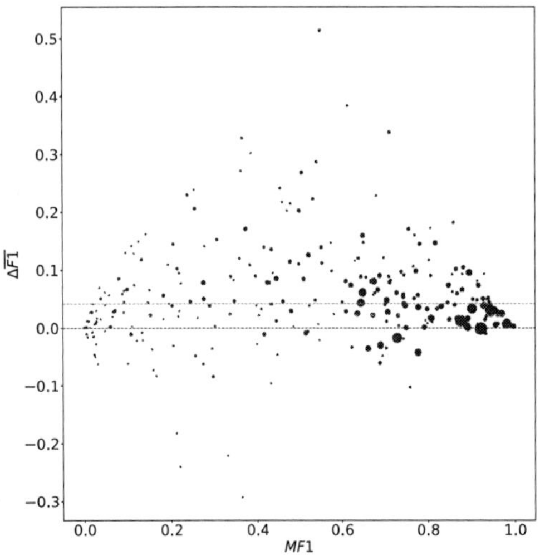

Figure 5: Gap $\Delta\overline{F1}$ for each relation in the *Wikidata* dataset plotted against the average score $MF1$ (8) obtained across the ten runs. The red and green dashed lines indicate the average and the median gap, respectively, whereas the gray dashed line a gap of zero. The size of each dot is given by the squareroot of the support of its corresponding relation.

increasing support, under the log – log transformation. We infer the following linear relationships (with and without graph embeddings):[4]

$$\begin{aligned} y &= -0.75x - 2.01\,, \\ y &= -0.73x - 2.21\,, \end{aligned} \tag{6}$$

with standard errors of 0.05 for the slopes and 0.26, respectively, 0.30, for the intercepts (note that we have taken $y = \log \sigma^2(F1)$ and $x = \log S$).

This implies a *power-law* scaling behavior of $\sigma^2(F1)$:

$$\sigma^2(F1) \propto \mathrm{S}^{-0.74}\,, \tag{7}$$

where we took as exponent the mean of the two regression coefficients given above.

In Figure 4 (*right*) the $\overline{F1}$ against the support is plotted using logarithmic scale, as for $\sigma^2(F1)$. However, we do not observe a linear relationship in log – log space as before, but rather some non-linear dependence. In particular, it appears that the larger the support of a given relation is, the better the model is able to learn it, as one would naively expect. The plot indicates that a support of at least S $\approx$ 1000 is a sufficient condition for good classification performance with an expected low variance of performance.

The gap $\Delta\overline{F1}$ is plotted against the averaged $\overline{F1}$ score,

$$MF1 = \frac{1}{2}\left(\overline{F1}_{ge} - \overline{F1}_b\right), \tag{8}$$

for each relation in Figure 5. Note first that we observe a mean and median gap of $\sim +0.05$, respectively $\sim +0.025$. The performance boost is inline with the micro- and macro- average based observation in the previous section. In the plot also the size of support is indicated for each relation. We clearly observe that relations with large support are clustered at high $MF1$, in accord with the discussion above.

It is interesting to notice that, both, for very high $MF1$ as well as very low $MF1$ the augmentation with graph embeddings only gives mild performance gains with low variance. In contrast, for $MF1 \sim 0.1$ - 0.9 we observe a larger variance of $\Delta\overline{F1}$, that leads to gaps in the wider range ~ -0.3 - 0.5.

5 Conclusion

In both the experiments discussed in Section 4, we measured on average a noticeable improvement over the baseline for the model with included pre-trained graph embeddings. Tables 2 and 3 summarize the numeric outcomes of our experiments, and also include for comparison results of the state-of-the-art methods obtained by others on the same datasets. In particular, our model is able to reach performance close to the current state-of-the-art in the *Wikidata* dataset under the micro-averaged metrics and sets a new state-of-the-art under the macro F1 metric. Similarly, for the *NYT* dataset our model achieves a new state-of-the-art under the P@10 and P@30 metric.

In common with related works in the literature, our model rests on the assumption of having the correct entity identification at hand (gold entities). Identifying entities in a sentence, however, is itself a challenging task, usually referred to as *Named Entity Recognition*. This task is further complicated by the need to map the entities to corresponding nodes in the KB (*Entity Linking*). This currently limits the practical applicability of ours, and models akin to it in the literature, and warrants further research.

We also analyzed in detail the performance of our model for each relation of the *Wikidata* dataset,

[4]The coefficients are rounded off to the first two decimals.

finding an interesting *power-law* scaling of the variance of the F1 score with increasing support of the relation. In particular, this study provided us with an estimate of around $\sim$ 1000 training occurences per relation needed for good prediction performance with small uncertainty. However, further investigation is needed to explore the validity of this finding in more generality.

Therefore, we like to highlight that we were not only able to verify that the inclusion of general pre-trained graph embeddings is helpful for the RE task, but also that such a simple model extension is competitive with other state-of-the-art models that directly perform on-task training of those embeddings. This implies that the inclusion of such pre-trained graph embeddings might be helpful across a wider spectrum of language related tasks to improve performance at a relatively low additional cost of complexity and computational burden.

We see this work as giving further support to the wider adoption of pre-computed graph embeddings in natural language processing tasks. We envisage that their adoption may become comparable to the popular Glove (Pennington et al., 2014) and Word2vec (Mikolov et al., 2013) pre-trained word embeddings.

Acknowledgements

We would like to thank the NCI Australia (National Computational Infrastructure) for providing computing resources, and the anonymous reviewers for their valuable comments and suggestions. AP was supported by an Australian Government Research Training Program International Scholarship. This research was delivered in partnership with, and funded in part by, Our Health in Our Hands (OHIOH), a strategic initiative of the Australian National University, which aims to transform healthcare by developing new personalized health technologies and solutions in collaboration with patients, clinicians, and healthcare providers.

References

Gabor Angeli, Melvin Jose Johnson Premkumar, and Christopher D. Manning. 2015. Leveraging linguistic structure for open domain information extraction. In *Proceedings of the 53rd Annual Meeting of the Association for Computational Linguistics and the 7th International Joint Conference on Natural Language Processing (Volume 1: Long Papers)*, pages 344–354, Beijing, China. Association for Computational Linguistics.

Dogu Araci. 2019. Finbert: Financial sentiment analysis with pre-trained language models.

Anson Bastos, Abhishek Nadgeri, Kuldeep Singh, Isaiah Onando Mulang', Saeedeh Shekarpour, Johannes Hoffart, and Manohar Kaul. 2021. Recon: Relation extraction using knowledge graph context in a graph neural network.

Olivier Bodenreider. 2004. The Unified Medical Language System (UMLS): integrating biomedical terminology. *Nucleic Acids Research*, 32(suppl_1):D267–D270.

Kurt Bollacker, Robert Cook, and Patrick Tufts. 2007. Freebase: A shared database of structured general human knowledge. In *Proceedings of the 22nd National Conference on Artificial Intelligence - Volume 2*, AAAI'07, page 1962–1963.

Antoine Bordes, Nicolas Usunier, Alberto Garcia-Durán, Jason Weston, and Oksana Yakhnenko. 2013. Translating embeddings for modeling multi-relational data. In *Proceedings of the 26th International Conference on Neural Information Processing Systems - Volume 2*, NIPS'13, page 2787–2795, Red Hook, NY, USA. Curran Associates Inc.

Jacob Devlin, Ming-Wei Chang, Kenton Lee, and Kristina Toutanova. 2019. Bert: Pre-training of deep bidirectional transformers for language understanding.

Timothy Dozat and Christopher D. Manning. 2017. Deep biaffine attention for neural dependency parsing.

John Giorgi, Xindi Wang, Nicola Sahar, Won Young Shin, Gary D. Bader, and Bo Wang. 2019. End-to-end named entity recognition and relation extraction using pre-trained language models.

Thomas N. Kipf and Max Welling. 2017. Semi-supervised classification with graph convolutional networks.

Adam Lerer, Ledell Wu, Jiajun Shen, Timothee Lacroix, Luca Wehrstedt, Abhijit Bose, and Alex Peysakhovich. 2019. Pytorch-biggraph: A large-scale graph embedding system.

Yinhan Liu, Myle Ott, Naman Goyal, Jingfei Du, Mandar Joshi, Danqi Chen, Omer Levy, Mike Lewis, Luke Zettlemoyer, and Veselin Stoyanov. 2019. Roberta: A robustly optimized bert pretraining approach.

Ilya Loshchilov and Frank Hutter. 2019. Decoupled weight decay regularization.

Tomas Mikolov, Kai Chen, Greg Corrado, and Jeffrey Dean. 2013. Efficient estimation of word representations in vector space.

Mike Mintz, Steven Bills, Rion Snow, and Daniel Jurafsky. 2009. Distant supervision for relation extraction without labeled data. In *Proceedings of the Joint Conference of the 47th Annual Meeting of the ACL and the 4th International Joint Conference on Natural Language Processing of the AFNLP*, pages 1003–1011, Suntec, Singapore. Association for Computational Linguistics.

Makoto Miwa and Mohit Bansal. 2016. End-to-end relation extraction using LSTMs on sequences and tree structures. In *Proceedings of the 54th Annual Meeting of the Association for Computational Linguistics (Volume 1: Long Papers)*, pages 1105–1116, Berlin, Germany. Association for Computational Linguistics.

Abhishek Nadgeri, Anson Bastos, Kuldeep Singh, Isaiah Onando Mulang', Johannes Hoffart, Saeedeh Shekarpour, and Vijay Saraswat. 2021. Kgpool: Dynamic knowledge graph context selection for relation extraction.

Dat Quoc Nguyen and Karin Verspoor. 2019. End-to-end neural relation extraction using deep biaffine attention. *Advances in Information Retrieval*, page 729–738.

Maximilian Nickel, Volker Tresp, and Hans-Peter Kriegel. 2011. A three-way model for collective learning on multi-relational data. In *Proceedings of the 28th International Conference on International Conference on Machine Learning*, ICML'11, page 809–816, Madison, WI, USA. Omnipress.

Adam Paszke, Sam Gross, Francisco Massa, Adam Lerer, James Bradbury, Gregory Chanan, Trevor Killeen, Zeming Lin, Natalia Gimelshein, Luca Antiga, Alban Desmaison, Andreas Kopf, Edward Yang, Zachary DeVito, Martin Raison, Alykhan Tejani, Sasank Chilamkurthy, Benoit Steiner, Lu Fang, Junjie Bai, and Soumith Chintala. 2019. Pytorch: An imperative style, high-performance deep learning library. In H. Wallach, H. Larochelle, A. Beygelzimer, F. dAlché-Buc, E. Fox, and R. Garnett, editors, *Advances in Neural Information Processing Systems 32*, pages 8024–8035. Curran Associates, Inc.

Thomas Pellissier Tanon, Denny Vrandečić, Sebastian Schaffert, Thomas Steiner, and Lydia Pintscher. 2016. From freebase to wikidata: The great migration. In *Proceedings of the 25th International Conference on World Wide Web*, WWW '16, page 1419–1428, Republic and Canton of Geneva, CHE. International World Wide Web Conferences Steering Committee.

Jeffrey Pennington, Richard Socher, and Christopher D. Manning. 2014. Glove: Global vectors for word representation. In *Empirical Methods in Natural Language Processing (EMNLP)*, pages 1532–1543.

Sebastian Riedel, Limin Yao, and Andrew McCallum. 2010. Modeling relations and their mentions without labeled text. In *Machine Learning and Knowledge Discovery in Databases*, pages 148–163, Berlin, Heidelberg. Springer Berlin Heidelberg.

M. Schuster and K.K. Paliwal. 1997. Bidirectional recurrent neural networks. *IEEE Transactions on Signal Processing*, 45(11):2673–2681.

Daniil Sorokin and Iryna Gurevych. 2017. Context-aware representations for knowledge base relation extraction. In *Proceedings of the 2017 Conference on Empirical Methods in Natural Language Processing*, pages 1784–1789, Copenhagen, Denmark. Association for Computational Linguistics.

Fabian Suchanek, Gjergji M Kasneci, and Gerhard M Weikum. 2007. Yago: A Core of Semantic KnowledgeUnifying WordNet and Wikipedia. In *16th international conference on World Wide Web*, Proceedings of the 16th international conference on World Wide Web, pages 697 – 697, Banff, Canada.

Shikhar Vashishth, Rishabh Joshi, Sai Suman Prayaga, Chiranjib Bhattacharyya, and Partha Talukdar. 2018. RESIDE: Improving distantly-supervised neural relation extraction using side information. In *Proceedings of the 2018 Conference on Empirical Methods in Natural Language Processing*, pages 1257–1266, Brussels, Belgium. Association for Computational Linguistics.

Ashish Vaswani, Noam Shazeer, Niki Parmar, Jakob Uszkoreit, Llion Jones, Aidan N. Gomez, Lukasz Kaiser, and Illia Polosukhin. 2017. Attention is all you need.

Denny Vrandečić. 2012. Wikidata: A new platform for collaborative data collection. In *Proceedings of the 21st International Conference on World Wide Web*, WWW '12 Companion, page 1063–1064, New York, NY, USA. Association for Computing Machinery.

Thomas Wolf, Lysandre Debut, Victor Sanh, Julien Chaumond, Clement Delangue, Anthony Moi, Pierric Cistac, Tim Rault, Rémi Louf, Morgan Funtowicz, Joe Davison, Sam Shleifer, Patrick von Platen, Clara Ma, Yacine Jernite, Julien Plu, Canwen Xu, Teven Le Scao, Sylvain Gugger, Mariama Drame, Quentin Lhoest, and Alexander M. Rush. 2020. Huggingface's transformers: State-of-the-art natural language processing.

Bishan Yang, Wen tau Yih, Xiaodong He, Jianfeng Gao, and Li Deng. 2015. Embedding entities and relations for learning and inference in knowledge bases.

Hao Zhu, Yankai Lin, Zhiyuan Liu, Jie Fu, Tat-Seng Chua, and Maosong Sun. 2019. Graph neural networks with generated parameters for relation extraction. In *Proceedings of the 57th Annual Meeting of the Association for Computational Linguistics*, pages 1331–1339, Florence, Italy. Association for Computational Linguistics.

Improving Cross-domain, Cross-lingual and Multi-modal Deception Detection

Subhadarshi Panda
Hunter College
City University of New York
spanda@gc.cuny.edu

Sarah Ita Levitan
Hunter College
City University of New York
sarah.levitan@hunter.cuny.edu

Abstract

With the increase of deception and misinformation especially in social media, it has become crucial to be able to develop machine learning methods to automatically identify deceptive language. In this proposal, we identify key challenges underlying deception detection in cross-domain, cross-lingual and multi-modal settings. To improve cross-domain deception classification, we propose to use inter-domain distance to identify a suitable source domain for a given target domain. We propose to study the efficacy of multilingual classification models vs translation for cross-lingual deception classification. Finally, we propose to better understand multi-modal deception detection and explore methods to weight and combine information from multiple modalities to improve multi-modal deception classification.

1 Introduction

Deception detection is a deliberate choice to mislead to gain some advantage or avoid some penalty (DePaulo et al., 2003). Deception detection is an important goal of law enforcement, military and intelligence agencies, as well as commercial organizations. In recent years, automatic deception detection in text has gained popularity in the Natural Language Processing (NLP) community, and researchers have studied cues to deception in a diverse set of domains. These include detecting deception in news (Wang, 2017), online reviews (Ott et al., 2011), interview dialogues (Levitan et al., 2018), trial testimonies (Fornaciari and Poesio, 2013), and in games (Soldner et al., 2019). These studies have been useful for identifying linguistic characteristics of deception, and for developing machine learning techniques to automatically detect deceptive language. However, we are still a long way from applying these state-of-the-art deception detection models in real-world deception scenarios. We currently lack information about how deception detection models perform across domains, languages, and in multiple modalities. In this proposal we outline current limitations in these three areas of deception detection: across domains, across languages and in multiple modalities. We propose work to address these limitations, with the goal of developing robust deception detection models that can generalize from lab-based datasets to real-world deception.

For each of the three topics of deception detection, we discuss current limitations, formulate research questions, and state proposed work to address the research questions. For some of our research questions, we present completed or ongoing work to answer the questions. For cross-domain deception classification, we first establish baseline performance at within and cross-domain deception classification using the well-established NLP model BERT. We identify major performance gaps between within and cross-domain deception classification. To understand the cross-domain performances, we formulate distance metrics and propose a cross-domain classification model that does not require target domain labeled training data and outperforms several baseline models. We also discuss ongoing and future research to further our understanding of and further imrpove cross-domain deception detection.

For cross-lingual deception classification, we formulate the task for deception detection in two non-English languages: Bulgarian and Arabic. We discuss the effectiveness of using a wide range of classifiers including multilingual BERT (Devlin et al., 2019), and propose additional experiments to further understand and improve cross-lingual deception detection.

Finally, we present proposed work in deception detection in a multi-modal setting from text and image features. Learning to identify deception is a challenging task, especially when there is one modality, and we propose to dynamically fuse in-

Proceedings of the 60th Annual Meeting of the Association for Computational Linguistics
Student Research Workshop, pages 383 - 390
May 22-27, 2022

formation from multiple modalities. The thorough experiments in the proposed work will contribute substantially to our understanding of cross-domain, cross-lingual, and multi-modal deception detection, and to the development of robust deception detection technologies.

2 Current limitations

2.1 Cross-domain deception classification

Although deception detection is a popular task in the NLP research community, and there is a strong interest in commercial applications of this work, there exists a large gap between deception models trained under laboratory conditions, and the performance level that is needed in real-world deception. Although researchers have in some cases obtained very strong performance at deception detection, these studies have focused on single domains, often using small datasets. We currently lack information about how small-scale, single-domain models of deception may or may not generalize to real-world data and new domains. We directly address this gap by first benchmarking the within- and cross-domain deception classification performance using five popular deceptive text datasets. We then attempt to understand performance gaps by analyzing the features of the datasets and the learned embeddings representations by the models. Finally, we propose a novel approach to leverage distance between domains to improve cross-domain deception classification.

Studying cross-domain deception detection is critical for understanding and contextualizing the successes of deception detection models thus far and gaining insights about the unique challenges of deception detection. The insights gained will motivate and inform the development of more robust models of deception.

2.2 Cross-lingual deception classification

There has been recent work in the NLP community aimed at identifying general misinformation on social media (Shu et al., 2017; Mitra et al., 2017) and particularly COVID-19 misinformation (Hossain et al., 2020).

However, most of this prior work has focused on data in English. There is a severe data shortage of high quality datasets that are labeled for misinformation in multiple languages. Because of this, we need to develop models of deception and misinformation that can utilize smaller datasets in non-English languages or leverage large amounts of training data in a source language, such as English, and generalize to new target languages.

2.3 Multi-modal deception classification

To build classifiers that can detect deception at a high accuracy, it is necessary to have high quality training data. Although a lot of prior work has focused on predicting deception from text (Potthast et al., 2017; Ott et al., 2011; Fornaciari and Poesio, 2014; Levitan et al., 2018), it is generally harder to identify deception from just one modality.

Nakamura et al. (2020) propose models to combine the image and text modalities by simple concatenation, addition, subtraction or taking dimension-wise maximum of image and text feature vectors. However, it still seems unclear how much importance should be attributed to each modality. Whether there are better ways to combine modalities is still unknown.

3 Proposed work and preliminary exploration

To address the limitations discussed above, we formulate concrete research questions that would help study deception classification across domains, languages and modalities. We now discuss proposed work and findings from initial experiments for each research question.

3.1 Cross-domain deception classification

RQ1. How do current models of deception perform within domain and across domain?

To address this research question, we select five deception datasets from different domains for our analysis. They were selected because they are all publicly available, and have been widely used for training and evaluating within-domain deception detection performance. This collection of datasets includes (1) *Fake news* containing fake and legitimate news compiled via a combination of crowdsourcing and webscraping (Pérez-Rosas et al., 2018), (2) *Open-domain deception* consisting of short, open-domain truths and lies obtained via crowdsourcing (Pérez-Rosas and Mihalcea, 2015), (3) *Cross-cultural deception* consisting of a set of deceptive and truthful essays about three topics: opinions on abortion, opinions on death penalty, and feelings about a best friend (Pérez-Rosas and Mihalcea, 2014), (4) *Deceptive opinion spam* containing truthful and deceptive hotel reviews of 20

Domain	Deception type	Number of tokens				Number of samples			
		Mean	Std.	1%ile	99%ile	Truthful	Deceptive	Train	Test
FakeNews	Self reported	324.50	692.35	78.58	1936.71	490	490	784	196
OpenDomain	Self reported	10.59	5.19	5.00	31.00	3584	3584	5734	1434
CrossCultural	Self reported	81.47	32.06	24.99	177.04	200	200	320	80
DeceptiveOpinion	Self reported	167.79	98.93	40.99	504.00	800	800	1280	320
Liar	Obs. reported	20.21	11.46	6.00	46.00	4507	8284	10232	2559

Table 1: Summary statistics for datasets from different domains along with distribution of truthful and deceptive classes and train/test sizes.

Chicago hotels (Ott et al., 2011), and (5) *Liar liar pants on fire* containing a set of short statements, mostly by politicians, in various contexts spanning across a decade (Wang, 2017). Since each dataset was collected under different experimental settings and have different topics and styles, we consider each dataset to represent a different domain without loss of generality. The summary statistics of the datasets in each domain are shown in Table 1. 4 of the 5 datasets have perfectly balanced classes, while *Liar* has approximately 35% truthful samples and 65% deceptive samples. It is important to note that the method of obtaining deception labels can vary for different datasets. Broadly, each dataset can be categorized into self reported deception or observed reported deception, based on whether they were reported by the speakers/writers or by human labelers respectively. We show the deception type for various datasets in Table 1. We perform a stratified splitting of the dataset of each domain into training and test splits with 80% of the data used for training and 20% used for testing, sizes of which are shown in Table 1. These train/test splits are used consistently across all experiments in this work to ensure a fair comparison of results across experiments.

We applied a state-of-the-art NLP model BERT (Devlin et al., 2019) to establish a strong baseline for cross-domain deception detection. We used a 10% random split of the source domain training data as the development data. For deception classification, we fine-tuned a BERT-based sequence classification model.[1] For training the BERT-based model the Adam optimizer (Kingma and Ba, 2014) was used with a learning rate of 1e-5. The training was stopped when the development accuracy did not improve for 5 consecutive epochs.

We observe in Table 2 that for any given target domain, the in-domain accuracies are generally higher than the cross-domain accuracies. This finding is consistent with observations made by Glenski et al. (2020). In some cases, the gap between within and across domain performance is egregious. For example, BERT classifier fine-tuned on *DeceptiveOpinion* has a within domain accuracy of 0.909, while the cross-domain performance of a model trained on *DeceptiveOpinion* ranges from 0.453-0.550 for the four other target domains. Further, the cross-domain performance of models trained on other domains and tested on *DeceptiveOpinion* ranges from 0.456-0.572. Although the *DeceptiveOpinion* model has very strong within domain performance and is a useful model of deceptive hotel reviews, it is clearly not a robust model of deception and cannot generalize to other deception domains.

RQ2. When there is a performance gap between within and across domain deception detection, can we explain why that occurs?

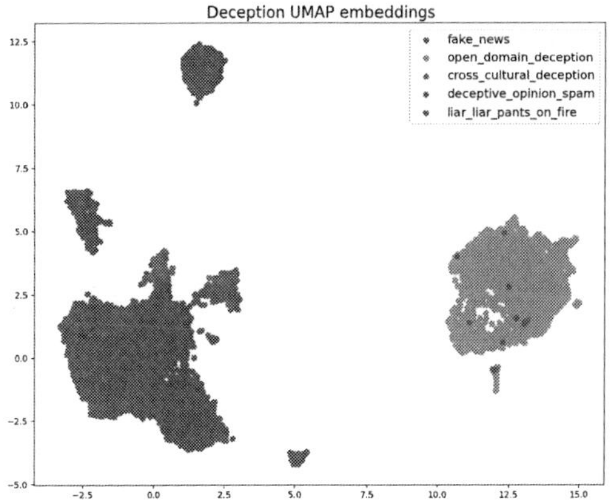

Figure 1: Deception sentence embeddings from different domains using pre-trained BERT.

To gain a deeper understanding of the classification results, we take BERT `[CLS]` token's representation to extract sentence level embedding of each sentence. To visualize the deception sentence embeddings, we project the sentence embeddings into a 2D space using UMAP (McInnes et al.,

[1] `bert-base-uncased` model in Transformers library (Wolf et al., 2020).

Target domain →	*FakeNews*	*OpenDomain*	*CrossCultural*	*DeceptiveOpinion*	*Liar*
FakeNews	0.786	**0.518**	0.5	**0.572**	**0.62**
OpenDomain	0.474	0.642	0.4	0.478	0.581
CrossCultural	**0.566**	0.504	0.613	0.456	0.501
DeceptiveOpinion	0.52	0.5	**0.55**	0.909	0.453
Liar	0.5	0.504	0.5	0.506	0.674

Table 2: In-domain and cross-domain accuracies of deception detection. For each target domain, the in-domain accuracy is underlined and the best cross-domain accuracy is bold-faced.

2018). We observe from Figure 1 that there are well-defined clusters of embeddings for most domains, for example *DeceptiveOpinion*, in red). In contrast, the *Liar* dataset, shown in purple, appears to have more broad and diverse embeddings, with several purple data points appearing in each of the other clusters.

We analyze the sentence embeddings further by defining a distance metric which can be used to measure the distance between a pair of domains. We first formulate the general notion of distance. Let D_S and D_T be the source and target domains respectively. We denote the distance from D_S to D_T as $distance(D_S, D_T)$. The distance between D_S and D_T can be computed using sentence embeddings as

$$distance(D_S, D_T) = \frac{1 - \cos(SD_S, SD_T)}{2}, \quad (1)$$

where SD_S is the mean of all the sentence embeddings in D_S and SD_T is the mean of all the sentence embeddings in D_T. Upon computing the Pearson correlation between cross-domain distances and accuracies, the correlation coefficient is found out to be -0.519, asserting that $distance(D_S, D_T)$ is negatively correlated with the cross-domain accuracy as expected.

We propose to understand the cross-domain deception performance by analyzing linguistic features of text in different domains. The list of linguistic features include politeness (Danescu-Niculescu-Mizil et al., 2013), concreteness (Kleinberg et al., 2019), complexity (Lu and Ai, 2015), readability (Dubay, 2004), sentiment and lexical features such as sentence length. Our analysis will include finding out the linguistic features correlated to deception for each domain and comparison of these features across domains.

RQ3. Can we leverage our understanding of these performance gaps to improve cross-domain deception detection?

We aim to develop a classification approach that leverages the notion of domain distance to improve cross-domain deception detection. The main idea is as follows: given a target domain, find the optimal source domain to use for training a deception detection model. We compute the domain distance between the target domain and all possible source domains. Then, we recommend the source domain which has the smallest distance from the target domain.

We compare the performance of this recommender system with 2 baselines: (1) A random recommendation system which chooses a source domain uniformly at random for a given target domain. To get a reliable cross-domain accuracy, we consider 100,000 trials of random recommendation and calculate the average cross-domain accuracy across all trials. (2) Multi-source leave-one-out training, which combines all source domains, excluding the target domain, for classification. The recommendation results are shown in Table 3. The table shows the accuracy upon using the recommended source domain for a given target domain. We observe that the recommendation using sentence embeddings based distance metrics is better than both random recommendation and leave one out multisource recommendation. This is an important use case of distance metrics, showing that they can reliably be used for improving cross-domain performance.

We find in Table 3 that while recommending a source domain is a relatively easier task for some target domains, recommendation is difficult in some other domains. For example, for the target domains *FakeNews* and *OpenDomain*, the recommendation using average sentence embeddings is right in a majority of cases. However, this is more challenging for *Liar* as the target domain, since no model achieves an accuracy that is substantially above 50%. To improve recommendation for such cases, we propose to compute the distance between a sample and all the potential source domains using sentence embeddings. By doing the recommendation at a sample level, we hope to improve the overall prediction on the target domain.

Recommendation	Target domain				
	FakeNews	*OpenDomain*	*CrossCultural*	*DeceptiveOpinion*	*Liar*
Random recommendation	0.553	0.484	0.507	0.506	0.503
Multisource leave one out	0.541	0.500	**0.550**	0.447	**0.521**
Avg. sentence embed.	**0.620**	**0.581**	0.501	**0.550**	0.500
Best possible recommendation	0.620	0.581	0.566	0.550	0.506

Table 3: Cross-domain accuracies upon recommending for various target domains.

Language →	English	Bulgarian	Arabic
Train	869	3000	2536
Dev	53	350	520
Test	418	357	1000
Total	1340	3707	4056

Table 4: Data sizes of English, Bulgarian and Arabic datasets for COVID-19 misinformation detection.

Setup	Eng. → Bulgarian	Eng. → Arabic
Zero shot	0.810	0.672
Few-50	0.819	0.775
Few-100	0.823	0.824
Few-150	0.821	0.791
Full shot	0.834	0.787
Target	0.843	0.738

Table 5: Cross-lingual (source language → target language) F1 scores when tested on the target language. *Few-n* setup denotes that only *n* samples in the target language are used for training.

3.2 Cross-lingual deception classification

RQ4. How effective are state of the art multilingual NLP models at cross lingual deception classification?

To answer this question, we use the findings from Panda and Levitan (2021) who used the tweet data provided for the Fighting the COVID-19 Infodemic shared task (Shaar et al., 2021) for analysis. The data was created by answering 7 questions about COVID-19 for each tweet about the following aspects: verifiable factual claim, false information, interest to general public, harmfulness, need of verification, harmful to society, and require attention. Each question has a Yes/No (binary) annotation. The data includes tweets in three languages: English, Bulgarian and Arabic. The data falls in the observed reported deception category (see the data discussion in Section 3.1). The training, development and test data sizes for each of the three languages are shown in Table 4. An example of an English tweet from the dataset is *Anyone else notice that COVID-19 seemed to pop up almost immediately after impeachment failed?* The 7 corresponding labels are *Q1 Yes, Q2 Yes, Q3 Yes, Q4 Yes, Q5 No, Q6 Yes, Q7 No.*

When the features from multilingual BERT (Devlin et al., 2019) are used for training on the source language and then testing is done on the target language, the scores as reported in Panda and Levitan (2021) are shown in Table 5. This is the *Zero shot* setup. The source language is set to English and the target languages are Bulgarian and Arabic. The scores for training using the target language (*Target* setup) are also shown for comparison. We observe that the cross-lingual F1 scores in the *Zero shot* setup are lower than the scores in the *Target* setup. Without the target language training data, the model as expected finds it harder to predict accurately when tested on the target language.

RQ5. What is the impact of amount of target language training data on prediction quality?

To answer this question, all the source language training data combined with n training samples from the target language is used for training. n is to 50, 100 and 150. This is called the *Few shot* setup. A special case of this setup is the *Full shot* setup, where n is set to the total size of the target language training data. We observe in Table 5 that as we increase the target language training samples in the few shot setup, the performance increases in general, as one would expect. Notably, even with just 50 samples from the target language training data, there is a noticeable increase in the cross-lingual performance in comparison to the *Zero shot* setup.

RQ6. How effective is using machine translation for cross lingual deception classification?

We propose to study the effectiveness of translation with multilingual COVID-19 misinformation classification models. In most cases, training data is available in English. The main idea is to translate either the training or the test non-English data to English using a pre-trained machine translation system. We plan to use the state-of-the-art machine translation systems by Tiedemann and Thottingal (2020) to

1. Translate the non-English test set to English and use an English model for prediction.

2-way classification			
Category	**Train**	**Dev**	**Test**
True	215490	22585	22798
Fake	337449	35567	35309
— Total —	552939	58152	58107
3-way classification			
Category	**Train**	**Dev**	**Test**
Completely True	215490	22585	22798
Fake with False text	323721	34217	33835
Fake with True text	13728	1350	1474
— Total —	552939	58152	58107
6-way classification			
Category	**Train**	**Dev**	**Test**
True	215490	22585	22798
Misleading content	104136	10970	10959
False connection	167471	17766	17429
Manipulated content	21437	2161	2286
Satire/parody	32718	3438	3419
Imposter content	11687	1232	1216
— Total —	552939	58152	58107

Table 6: Data sizes for different categories for multi-modal deception classification.

2. Translate English training data to a target language and train the m-BERT classification model using this translated data.

Results from the above experiments will help quantify the effectiveness of using translation for deception detection.

3.3 Multi-modal deception classification

RQ7. Are there better ways to fuse text and image features in comparison to static fusion?

Recent work such as Nakamura et al. (2020) have created multimodal deception datasets and also provided baselines of fusing multiple modalities. The dataset by Nakamura et al. (2020), called Fakeddit, is the largest publicly available multi-modal deception dataset. It contains two modalities: text and image. There are three labels for each data sample, varying on granularity. The fine-grained labels are true content, misleading content, false connection, manipulated content, satire/parody and imposter content. These labels come from subreddits in from which the content is taken from (see details in Nakamura et al. (2020)). This dataset can be used to train a classifier to predict deception on a desired fine-grained level, the choices of which are 2-way, 3-way and 6-way. The Fakeddit dataset falls under the self reported deception category (see the data discussion in Section 3.1). The sizes of the Fakeddit dataset are shown in Table 6.

We propose to use an attention module (Luong et al., 2015) that dynamically fuses the text and image feature vectors as shown in Figure 2. The text feature vector comes from the `[CLS]` token's representation of BERT. The image feature vector comes from ResNet. The attention module decides how much weight to assign for each modality. Specifically it uses the input features for each modality and computes as many attention scores as the number of modalities. These attention scores are positive and sum to 1 when added together. The feature vector from each modality is scaled using the corresponding attention score. Then the scaled feature vectors are added together to obtain a single vector, which can be passed through a final linear layer to produce logits. We plan to answer the following questions by analyzing the results of attention-based fusion.

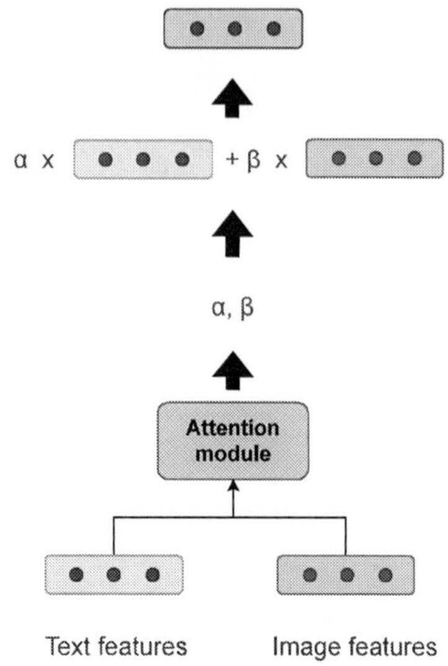

Figure 2: Fusion of text and image features using an attention module.

1. For each category of samples, what is the average attention on each modality?
2. Are there samples for which the attention to one modality is negligible? Are there patterns among these samples?
3. Does dynamic fusion of the text and image feature vectors lead to better overall prediction than static fusion?

4 Ethical considerations

Although automatic deception detection has the potential to benefit society, there are several ethical concerns within this line of research. Automatic deception detection has varying degrees of severity depending on the application area. The impact of a false positive is substantially lower when detecting deceit in informal activities such as gaming. However, when detecting dishonesty in a criminal investigation, a false positive can have serious implications. In general, automatic deception detection should be employed with caution, especially when there is no manual human verification involved.

For the case of cross-domain deception detection applications, it is important to test the model on the target domain before deploying it, as mentioned in Section 1. To understand the differences between deception domains, a linguistic feature analysis should be performed, as we mention in Section 3.1. Finally, to increase transparency in multi-modal deception detection, it is critical to compute importance scores for each modality as mentioned in Section 3.3. As automatic deception detection across domains, languages and modalities becomes a more widely studied subject, it is important to be aware of the ethical considerations and also take the necessary precautions to avoid harm to society.

5 Conclusion

We identify key challenges in deception detection in cross-domain, cross-lingual and multi-modal scenarios. For cross-domain deception classification, we quantified the gap between in-domain and cross-domain accuracies. Our proposed recommender based on distance measures improves cross-domain performance over two baselines. We plan to extend the completed work by improving the recommendation process by recommending at the sample level instead of the domain level. We also plan to analyze the cross-domain results using linguistic features. For cross-lingual deception classification, we discuss the challenges in predicting deception in a target language with no or little training data. We propose to study the effectiveness of using translation text for training and testing. For multi-modal deception classification, we discuss the merits and limitations of the current state-of-the-art models. We propose to dynamically fuse the text and image feature vectors using an attention module to better understand the importance of each modality.

References

Cristian Danescu-Niculescu-Mizil, Moritz Sudhof, Dan Jurafsky, Jure Leskovec, and Christopher Potts. 2013. A computational approach to politeness with application to social factors. In *Proceedings of the 51st Annual Meeting of the Association for Computational Linguistics (Volume 1: Long Papers)*, pages 250–259, Sofia, Bulgaria. Association for Computational Linguistics.

Bella DePaulo, James J Lindsay, Brian Malone, Laura Muhlenbruck, Kelly Charlton, and Harris Cooper. 2003. Cues to deception. *Psychological bulletin*, 129:74–118.

Jacob Devlin, Ming-Wei Chang, Kenton Lee, and Kristina Toutanova. 2019. BERT: Pre-training of deep bidirectional transformers for language understanding. In *Proceedings of the 2019 Conference of the North American Chapter of the Association for Computational Linguistics: Human Language Technologies, Volume 1 (Long and Short Papers)*, pages 4171–4186, Minneapolis, Minnesota. Association for Computational Linguistics.

William Dubay. 2004. The principles of readability. *CA*, 92627949:631–3309.

Tommaso Fornaciari and Massimo Poesio. 2013. Automatic deception detection in italian court cases. *Artificial intelligence and law*, 21(3):303–340.

Tommaso Fornaciari and Massimo Poesio. 2014. Identifying fake amazon reviews as learning from crowds.

Maria Glenski, Ellyn Ayton, Robin Cosbey, Dustin Arendt, and Svitlana Volkova. 2020. Towards trustworthy deception detection: Benchmarking model robustness across domains, modalities, and languages. In *Proceedings of the 3rd International Workshop on Rumours and Deception in Social Media (RDSM)*, pages 1–13, Barcelona, Spain (Online). Association for Computational Linguistics.

Tamanna Hossain, Robert L Logan IV, Arjuna Ugarte, Yoshitomo Matsubara, Sean Young, and Sameer Singh. 2020. Covidlies: Detecting covid-19 misinformation on social media. In *Proceedings of the 1st Workshop on NLP for COVID-19 (Part 2) at EMNLP 2020*.

Diederik P. Kingma and Jimmy Ba. 2014. Adam: A method for stochastic optimization. Cite arxiv:1412.6980Comment: Published as a conference paper at the 3rd International Conference for Learning Representations, San Diego, 2015.

Bennett Kleinberg, Isabelle van der Vegt, Arnoud Arntz, and Bruno Verschuere. 2019. Detecting deceptive communication through linguistic concreteness.

Sarah Ita Levitan, Angel Maredia, and Julia Hirschberg. 2018. Linguistic cues to deception and perceived deception in interview dialogues. In *Proceedings of the 2018 Conference of the North American Chapter of the Association for Computational Linguistics: Human Language Technologies, Volume 1 (Long Papers)*, pages 1941–1950.

Xiaofei Lu and Haiyang Ai. 2015. Syntactic complexity in college-level english writing: Differences among writers with diverse l1 backgrounds. *Journal of Second Language Writing*, 29:16–27. New developments in the study of L2 writing complexity.

Thang Luong, Hieu Pham, and Christopher D. Manning. 2015. Effective approaches to attention-based neural machine translation. In *Proceedings of the 2015 Conference on Empirical Methods in Natural Language Processing*, pages 1412–1421, Lisbon, Portugal. Association for Computational Linguistics.

Leland McInnes, John Healy, Nathaniel Saul, and Lukas Grossberger. 2018. Umap: Uniform manifold approximation and projection. *The Journal of Open Source Software*, 3(29):861.

Tanushree Mitra, Graham P Wright, and Eric Gilbert. 2017. A parsimonious language model of social media credibility across disparate events. In *Proceedings of the 2017 ACM conference on computer supported cooperative work and social computing*, pages 126–145.

Kai Nakamura, Sharon Levy, and William Yang Wang. 2020. Fakeddit: A new multimodal benchmark dataset for fine-grained fake news detection. In *Proceedings of the 12th Language Resources and Evaluation Conference*, pages 6149–6157, Marseille, France. European Language Resources Association.

Myle Ott, Yejin Choi, Claire Cardie, and Jeffrey T. Hancock. 2011. Finding deceptive opinion spam by any stretch of the imagination. In *Proceedings of the 49th Annual Meeting of the Association for Computational Linguistics: Human Language Technologies*, pages 309–319, Portland, Oregon, USA. Association for Computational Linguistics.

Subhadarshi Panda and Sarah Ita Levitan. 2021. Detecting multilingual COVID-19 misinformation on social media via contextualized embeddings. In *Proceedings of the Fourth Workshop on NLP for Internet Freedom: Censorship, Disinformation, and Propaganda*, pages 125–129, Online. Association for Computational Linguistics.

Verónica Pérez-Rosas, Bennett Kleinberg, Alexandra Lefevre, and Rada Mihalcea. 2018. Automatic detection of fake news. In *Proceedings of the 27th International Conference on Computational Linguistics*, pages 3391–3401, Santa Fe, New Mexico, USA. Association for Computational Linguistics.

Verónica Pérez-Rosas and Rada Mihalcea. 2014. Cross-cultural deception detection. In *Proceedings of the 52nd Annual Meeting of the Association for Computational Linguistics (Volume 2: Short Papers)*, pages 440–445, Baltimore, Maryland. Association for Computational Linguistics.

Verónica Pérez-Rosas and Rada Mihalcea. 2015. Experiments in open domain deception detection. In *Proceedings of the 2015 Conference on Empirical Methods in Natural Language Processing*, pages 1120–1125, Lisbon, Portugal. Association for Computational Linguistics.

Martin Potthast, Johannes Kiesel, Kevin Reinartz, Janek Bevendorff, and Benno Stein. 2017. A stylometric inquiry into hyperpartisan and fake news. *arXiv preprint arXiv:1702.05638*.

Shaden Shaar, Firoj Alam, Giovanni Da San Martino, Alex Nikolov, Wajdi Zaghouani, Preslav Nakov, and Anna Feldman. 2021. Findings of the NLP4IF-2021 shared task on fighting the COVID-19 infodemic and censorship detection. In *Proceedings of the Fourth Workshop on Natural Language Processing for Internet Freedom: Censorship, Disinformation, and Propaganda*, NLP4IF@NAACL' 21, Online. Association for Computational Linguistics.

Kai Shu, Amy Sliva, Suhang Wang, Jiliang Tang, and Huan Liu. 2017. Fake news detection on social media: A data mining perspective. *ACM SIGKDD explorations newsletter*, 19(1):22–36.

Felix Soldner, Verónica Pérez-Rosas, and Rada Mihalcea. 2019. Box of lies: Multimodal deception detection in dialogues. In *Proceedings of the 2019 Conference of the North American Chapter of the Association for Computational Linguistics: Human Language Technologies, Volume 1 (Long and Short Papers)*, pages 1768–1777.

Jörg Tiedemann and Santhosh Thottingal. 2020. OPUS-MT – building open translation services for the world. In *Proceedings of the 22nd Annual Conference of the European Association for Machine Translation*, pages 479–480, Lisboa, Portugal. European Association for Machine Translation.

William Yang Wang. 2017. "liar, liar pants on fire": A new benchmark dataset for fake news detection. In *Proceedings of the 55th Annual Meeting of the Association for Computational Linguistics (Volume 2: Short Papers)*, pages 422–426, Vancouver, Canada. Association for Computational Linguistics.

Thomas Wolf, Lysandre Debut, Victor Sanh, Julien Chaumond, Clement Delangue, Anthony Moi, Pierric Cistac, Tim Rault, Remi Louf, Morgan Funtowicz, Joe Davison, Sam Shleifer, Patrick von Platen, Clara Ma, Yacine Jernite, Julien Plu, Canwen Xu, Teven Le Scao, Sylvain Gugger, Mariama Drame, Quentin Lhoest, and Alexander Rush. 2020. Transformers: State-of-the-art natural language processing. In *Proceedings of the 2020 Conference on Empirical Methods in Natural Language Processing: System Demonstrations*, pages 38–45, Online. Association for Computational Linguistics.

Automatic Generation of Distractors for Fill-in-the-Blank Exercises with Round-Trip Neural Machine Translation

Subhadarshi Panda
CUNY Graduate Center
spanda@gradcenter.cuny.edu

Frank Palma Gomez
Queens College, CUNY
frankpalma12@gmail.com

Michael Flor
Educational Testing Service
mflor@ets.org

Alla Rozovskaya
Queens College, CUNY
arozovskaya@qc.cuny.edu

Abstract

In a fill-in-the-blank exercise, a student is presented with a carrier sentence with one word hidden, and a multiple-choice list that includes the correct answer and several inappropriate options, called distractors. We propose to automatically generate distractors using round-trip neural machine translation: the carrier sentence is translated from English into another (pivot) language and back, and distractors are produced by aligning the original sentence and its round-trip translation. We show that using hundreds of translations for a given sentence allows us to generate a rich set of challenging distractors. Further, using multiple pivot languages produces a diverse set of candidates. The distractors are evaluated against a real corpus of cloze exercises and checked manually for validity. We demonstrate that the proposed method significantly outperforms two strong baselines.[1]

1 Introduction

A cloze (fill-in-the-blank) exercise is a common method of teaching vocabulary, as well as assessing non-native speaker performance in a foreign language: a passage (sentence) is presented to the learner with one word (*target*) being removed. The target word is presented along with a list of *distractors* (usually 3), and the task is to correctly identify the target word from that list. Table 1 shows a sample cloze item with the target word "vital". The *carrier sentence* along with a multiple-choice list is referred to as *cloze item*. A cloze item is valid if and only if one word on the list (the target) fits the context. We also show valid and invalid distractors.

Carrier sentence
Are these old plates of ______ importance or can I put them into storage?
Target word: *vital* **Valid distractors:** *main, urgent, lively* **Invalid distractors:** *great, utmost*

Table 1: A sentence for a fill-in-the-blank exercise with the target word "vital" removed. Multiple-choice list will include the target and 3 distractors. Examples of valid and invalid distractors are shown.

A valid distractor is a word that does not fit the context. For example, "great" and "utmost" are invalid distractors, since they both fit the context.

Given a carrier sentence and the target word, the problem is to generate challenging distractors. In typical high-stakes tests, such as Test of English as a Foreign Language (TOEFL), distractors are generated manually by educational testing experts, a time-consuming procedure. An automated method to generate distractors would be extremely valuable. The problem becomes more challenging once the exercises are aimed at high-proficiency learners, since distractors that are not semantically close to the target word or grammatically unfit will be too easy for advanced speakers (Zesch and Melamud, 2014). To address this, previous work used context-sensitive inference rules (Zesch and Melamud, 2014), common collocation errors from large-scale learner corpora (Sakaguchi et al., 2013), co-occurrence likelihoods (Hill and Simha, 2016), and word embeddings (Jiang and Lee, 2017).

In this work, we propose to generate distractors using round-trip neural machine translation (MT). Word choice errors are commonly affected by the speaker's first language, and even advanced learn-

[1]The code is available at `https://github.com/subhadarship/round-trip-distractors`

Proceedings of the 60th Annual Meeting of the Association for Computational Linguistics Student Research Workshop, pages 391 - 401
May 22-27, 2022

ers struggle with word usage nuances and may inappropriately use semantically related words (Leacock et al., 2010). Our assumption is that lexical challenges common with non-native speakers will also manifest themselves in the round-trip machine translation as back-translated words that are semantically close to the target. Such words should therefore serve as challenging distractors for advanced learners. Unlike previous work, this method also opens up a possibility of *customizing* the cloze task for speakers of different languages.

We focus on exercises aimed at *advanced* English as a Second Language (ESL) learners. A carrier sentence is translated from English into another *pivot* language, where top n translation hypotheses are generated. For each hypothesis, top m back-translations into English are generated. The back-translated words aligned to the target are treated as potential distractors. We use five round-trip MT systems and show that *using multiple pivot languages encourages diversity in the distractor generation*, as the distractors produced with different pivot language systems are often unique.

Using a corpus of cloze exercises for advanced ESL learners, we demonstrate that the proposed method retrieves over 31% of the gold distractors used in the exercises and over 70% percent of cloze items have at least one gold distractor retrieved with our approach. Evaluation shows that the proposed method outperforms two strong baselines – the word embeddings approach (Word2vec) and BERT. Manual evaluation of the distractor validity indicates that over 72.3% of all distractors are valid with our approach compared to 56.1% and 38.0% using Word2Vec and BERT, respectively.

Our contributions are as follows: (1) we propose to use round-trip machine translation to generate challenging distractors for cloze exercises and tests. We use hundreds of round-trip translations and multiple pivot languages, and generate challenging diverse distractors; (2) we validate our approach using a dataset of real cloze exercises for advanced ESL learners and show that it significantly outperforms the Word2vec and BERT baselines both in automatic and manual evaluation; (3) unlike previous work, we find that different pivot languages provide rather unique distractors for the same item, thereby allowing for customizing the exercises on the basis of the native language of the student.

The next section presents related work. Section 3 describes the dataset of cloze exercises. Section 4 describes the baseline methods, and Section 5 presents our approach. Section 6 presents the results of the automatic and manual evaluation of the generated distractors. Section 7 further discusses the results, while Section 8 concludes.

2 Related work

The general approach to automatic distractor generation can be broken down into candidate *generation* (identification), and candidate *ranking*.

Candidate generation Most of the work on automatic distractors focuses on generating distractor candidates. These include word frequency, phonetic and morphological similarity, and grammatical fit (Hoshino and Nakagawa, 2005; Pino and Eskénazi, 2009; Goto et al., 2010).

For advanced speakers, distractors should be picked more carefully, so that they are reasonably hard to distinguish from the target. Consider, for example, the target word "error" in the carrier sentence: "It is often only through long experiments of trial and *error* that scientific progress is made." The word "mistake" is semantically close to it but is not appropriate in the sentence context, and thus could serve as a valid distractor. However, note that "mistake" can be substituted for "error" in the context of "He made a lot of mistakes in his test." and would therefore not be a valid distractor. Thus, on the one hand, challenging distractors should be *semantically close* to the target word, yet, on the other hand, a valid distractor *should not produce an acceptable sentence*.

Most of the approaches to generating challenging distractors rely on methods of semantic relatedness, such as n-grams and collocations (Liu et al., 2005; Hill and Simha, 2016), thesauri (Sumita et al., 2005), or WordNet (Brown et al., 2005). (Zesch and Melamud, 2014) use semantic context-sensitive inference rules. Sakaguchi et al. (2013) propose generating distractors using errors mined from a learner corpus. The approach, however, assumes an annotated learner corpus, and is quite limited, as both the choice of the target word and of the distractors are constrained by the errors in the corpus. Several recent studies showed that word embeddings are effective in distractor generation: Jiang and Lee (2017) and Susanti et al. (2018) generated distractors using semantically similar words obtained from Word2vec (Mikolov et al., 2013).

We propose to use round-trip neural machine translation to generate distractors. The only previous mention of using MT is that of Dahlmeier and Ng (2011) who aim at correcting ESL collocation errors using a statistical machine translation technique. To the best of our knowledge, ours is the first dedicated study that uses state-of-the-art NMT systems with 5 pivot languages and large sets of back-translations for generating distractors.

Several studies, while they do not generate distractors, address the complexity of the cloze task for language learners. Felice and Buttery (2019) focus on the contextual complexity of the generated gap itself. Marrese-Taylor et al. (2018) use LSTM models for gap generation. Gao et al. (2020) show that BERT is helpful in measuring the fit of the distractor in the context, and thus can be used for estimating distractor difficulty. Finally, we also note that there is a significant body of work on a task of generating reading comprehension (RC) items, that test a different set of examinee abilities, such as inference. That work (Chung et al., 2020) deals with generating phrases and complete sentences for distractors. RC item generation is a distinct problem from vocabulary item generation that is addressed in this work.

Candidate ranking can be used as an additional step to (re-)rank the candidates produced during candidate generation. One reason for this is that context is typically not taken into account when generating candidates. Yeung et al. (2019) used BERT (Devlin et al., 2018) to re-rank the candidate distractors generated with Word2vec for Chinese. We show that BERT is not effective at generating or re-ranking candidate distractors.

3 Data

It is important to note that there is no benchmark dataset for the task. Previous studies evaluate either on artificially created items with random words as targets or proprietary data. In contrast, we obtain cloze exercises from a reputable test preparation website, ESL Lounge.[2] The website contains study materials and preparatory exercises for ESL tests, such as FCE First Certificate, TOEFL, and International English Language Testing System (IELTS). There was significant effort put into the development of the exercises, which were manually curated for ESL students, and the exercises are of high quality. This is the first dataset that can be used by researchers working on the task.[3]

Since we wish to generate distractors for advanced learners, we use the C1 advanced level multiple choice cloze exercises.[4] C1 level is part of CEFR scale.[5] It is used to prove high-level achievement in English and is designed for learners preparing for university or professional life.

We extract a total of 142 cloze items.[6] Each *item* consists of a carrier sentence with the target word removed and is accompanied by four word choices that include the target word and three distractors. We show two sample items in Table 2. 44.4% of the target words are verbs, 38.7% are nouns, 14.1% are adjectives, and 2.8% are some other part of speech.

4 The Baselines

We compare the round-trip MT method against Word2vec and BERT. Both Word2vec embeddings and BERT can be used *to generate* candidates, and *to rank* candidates generated with MT. Here, we describe how we generate candidates with Word2vec and BERT. In Section 5.3, we describe how we use the two methods for candidate ranking. Using Word2vec, we generate words that have the highest similarity to the target word and use these as potential distractors. We use the 300-dimensional Word2vec embeddings trained on Google News. For a given target word, we find k nearest neighboring words using cosine similarity in the word embedding space. With BERT, we produce a set of candidates by passing the carrier sentence with the target word replaced by a masked token. BERT returns a list of words that best fit the context of the carrier sentence at the position of the masked token. Each word is associated with probability; we select the top k candidates with the highest scores. The candidates are filtered out using the same filtering algorithm applied in round-trip MT (see Section 5.2). In addition, we filter out misspellings by using a wordlist of about 130,000 English wordforms.

[2] https://www.esl-lounge.com

[3] A csv copy of the dataset for research purposes can be obtained from the authors on paper acceptance.

[4] https://www.esl-lounge.com/student/advanced-multiple-choice-cloze.php

[5] https://www.coe.int/en/web/common-european-framework-reference-/languages/level-descriptions

[6] Our data collection is in conformity with the website's terms as described at https://www.esl-lounge.com/student/copyright.php.

Sentence: *Much of the neighbourhood was demolished in the 1940s when living ______ had deteriorated.* **Choices**: *situations, conditions*, circumstances, states*
Sentence: *Scientists are yet to understand the full nutritional ______ of the humble olive.* **Choices**: *favours, helps, goods, benefits**

Table 2: Examples of multiple choice cloze exercises from the ESL Lounge website. Each item has exactly one correct choice, marked with a star (*).

5 Generating Distractors with Neural MT

Formally, given a sentence $X = \{x_1, x_2, \ldots, x_n\}$ and a position $k \in [1, n]$ of the target word, the task is to generate a set of candidate distractors D such that $d \in D$ can be used as a challenging semantically-confusing distractor for the target word occupying position k in X. Since challenging distractors should be more similar to the target word (Zesch and Melamud, 2014), and because many word sense nuances are challenging for non-native speakers due to the differences between word usage in their native language and in English, we expect that candidates generated with round-trip MT that uses the target word together with the surrounding context will make good distractors for advanced ESL learners.

5.1 Candidate generation

Round-trip machine translation Given a carrier sentence X with the target word, a forward machine translation system from English to a pivot language trg and backward MT system from trg to English, we can generate a round-trip translation for X. Importantly, we generate multiple hypotheses in each direction.

We first translate the sentence X in English using a forward MT system S_{en-trg} to obtain a set of top N_f translation hypotheses $Y = \{Y_1, Y_2, \ldots, Y_{N_f}\}$ in the target language trg. We then translate the sentences in Y using a backward MT system S_{trg-en} and obtain a set of top N_b translation hypotheses for $Y_i \in Y$. Finally, we obtain the set of round-trip translations $X_{RT} = \{X_{RT_1}, X_{RT_2}, \ldots, X_{RT_{N_f \times N_b}}\}$.

We use state-of-the-art NMT systems with German, Russian, Italian, French, and Czech as pivots. For German and Russian, we use the systems of Ng et al. (2019), and for the other languages we use the systems of Tiedemann and Thottingal (2020). We use $N_f = 1$, $N_b = 1,500$ for German, $N_f = 1, N_b = 1,000$ for Russian, and $N_f = N_b = 16$ for the other languages, and generate $1,500$ round-trip translations for German, $1,000$ for Russian, and 256 for Italian, French, and Czech. The number of hypotheses varies due to system specifications as well as the memory constraints in the machines we used. We do not attempt at comparing the machine translation models with various pivot languages and leave it for future work.

Alignment computation Given a round-trip translation X_{RT_i} for carrier sentence X, we need to compute the alignment between the two sentences. Then the word in X_{RT_i} that is aligned to the target word in X is considered to be the back-translation of the target.We use Simalign[7] (Sabet et al., 2020) that employs contextual word embeddings (Devlin et al., 2018) to produce an alignment model for a pair of sentences in the same or different language, without parallel training data.

Given the original sentence and the round-trip translation, first the similarity between each source token is computed with each target token using contextual embeddings from multilingual BERT. This results in a matrix that stores similarity scores between all the source and target tokens. The alignment computation is framed as an alignment problem where we search for a maximum-weight maximal matching in the bipartite weighted graph induced by the similarity matrix (see details in Sabet et al. (2020)).

5.2 Candidate filtering

Not all the words obtained by alignment can serve as distractors because (a) the candidate might fit the context, which would make the item invalid, or (b) a word may make the sentence grammatically incorrect and thus too easy for advanced students. We use two filtering mechanisms.

Filtering distractors that are synonymous with the target We use the synonyms provided in WordNet (Fellbaum, 1998) to determine the candidate words that are synonymous with the target word. We note that this approach will not weed out distractors that are synonymous in specific contexts. For example, in the sentence *Though we always turn right here, I often ______ what's down*

[7]https://github.com/cisnlp/simalign

the other road. with the target "wonder", the algorithm generates "think" as a candidate distractor. Although "think" and "wonder" are not synonyms, they are equivalent in the context of the sentence.

Filtering distractors based on POS tag An obvious approach to filter out grammatically inappropriate distractors is to ensure that the candidate word is of the same part-of-speech as the target word in the carrier sentence. We use NLTK (Bird et al., 2009) to compute the POS tag for the candidate words and only keep those which have the same part-of-speech as the target word. Both for the target word and the distractor candidates, the POS tag is obtained by applying the tagger to the entire carrier sentence with the target position filled by the appropriate word.

5.3 Candidate ranking with BERT and word2Vec

Typically, fewer than 5 distractors are used in a cloze exercise, however, as we show below, the MT method typically generates more than 5 candidates. One approach to selecting distractors from the available pool is uniformly at random. However, previous studies typically rank candidates based on their difficulty, assumed to be related to the degree of semantic similarity to the target. We thus wish to determine whether we can use Word2vec and BERT to rank the distractors instead of simply selecting candidates uniformly at random.

Using Word2vec, we define the difficulty of a candidate distractor d for sentence X with target t as the cosine similarity of their word embeddings as in Equation 1:

$$\text{difficulty}(d, t) = \frac{Emb(d) \cdot Emb(t)}{|Emb(d)||Emb(t)|} \quad (1)$$

The $Emb(w)$ is a pre-trained embedding for word w. We use the 300 dimensional Word2vec embeddings trained on Google news (Mikolov et al., 2013). We pick candidates with the highest similarity values. Similarly, we rank the candidates using the scores obtained with BERT.

6 Evaluation

We evaluate the generated distractors using both automatic and manual evaluation.

6.1 Automatic evaluation

Number of distractors generated We first show the average number of unique candidate distractors retrieved with each pivot language system and with the union of all the pivot systems, with and without filtering (Figure 1). The number of unique distractors is smaller than the total number of back-translated sentences since many of the hypotheses result in the same round-trip translation of the target word. The smallest average number of distractors is 18.1 for Italian, and the largest average number is 51.8 for German, when no filtering is used. Notably, the union produces an average of 104.6 distractors per target word, suggesting that round-trip translations from different pivot languages contribute unique distractor candidates. Filtering removes a significant number of generated candidates by reducing the average number of candidates from 104.6 to 51.1 for the union.

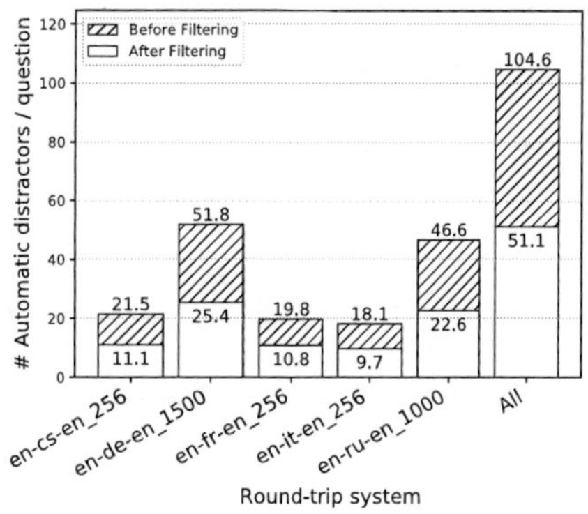

Figure 1: Average number of automatic distractors generated per cloze item using different pivots before and after filtering. The average is computed over 142 cloze items.

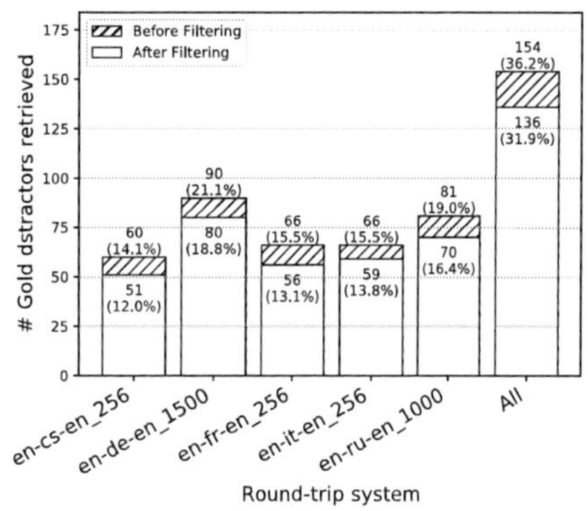

Figure 2: The number and percentage of gold distractors retrieved as a function of round-trip translations used, before and after filtering.

Gold distractor retrieval While there may be many valid challenging distractors for a given ex-

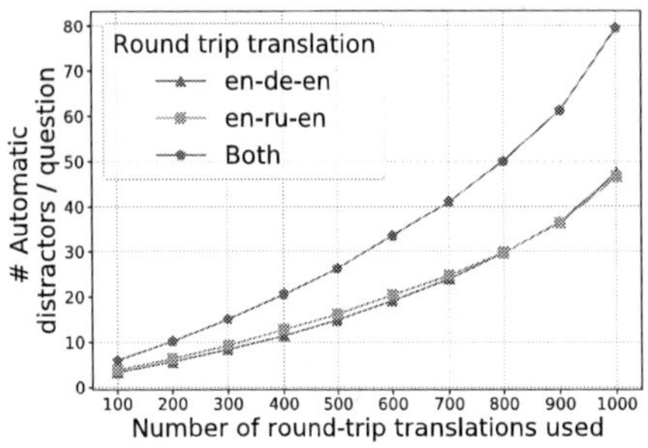

Figure 3: Average number of automatic distractors per item as a function of the number of round-trip translations used. The average is computed over 142 cloze items.

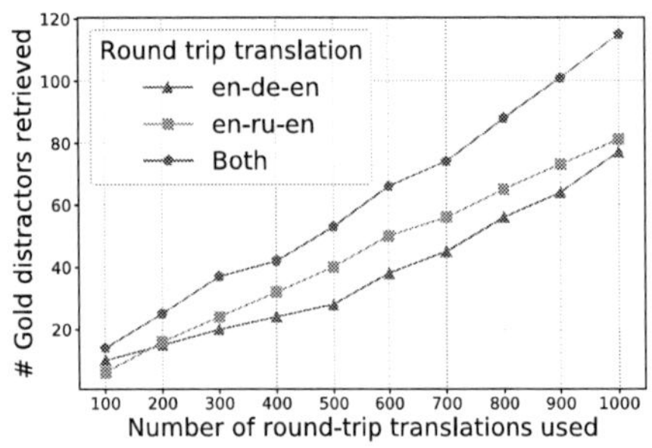

Figure 4: Number of gold distractors retrieved as a function of round-trip translations used.

ercise item, we nevertheless wish to evaluate the distractors generated automatically against the set of gold distractors (distractors used in the cloze items in the dataset). Given a cloze item with its set of 3 gold distractors D_{gold}, and an automatic distractor d generated for this cloze item, we compute the distractor retrieval score following Equation 2.

$$r(d, D_{gold}) = \begin{cases} 1 \text{ if } d \in D_{gold} \\ 0 \text{ otherwise} \end{cases} \quad (2)$$

We compute cumulative retrieval score[8] $\sum r(d, D_{gold})$ across all the generated distractors and across all cloze items (the total number of gold distractors is 426, since we have 142 cloze items, each containing 3 gold distractors). Figure 2 shows the cumulative retrieval score (and percentage of gold distractors retrieved) by pivot language and for the union of all pivot languages before and after filtering is applied: 36.2% of gold distractors are retrieved with the automatic approach (without filtering). Filtering reduces this number to 31.9%, however, as we showed above, filtering removes about 50% of the generated candidates. We also note that by-pivot performance is surprisingly consistent: for German and Russian, we retrieve 21.1% and 19.0% of gold distractors, and for the other pivots – between 14.1% and 15.5%. We attribute the differences between the first and second group to the number of round-trip translations we generate ($1,000$ and $1,500$ for Russian and German, respectively, and 256 for the other pivots). Importantly, the union of the pivot languages is able to retrieve almost twice as many gold distractors as the individual languages, indicating that *multiple pivots produce diverse candidate distractors*.

We stress that, while the distractors are not uniquely defined, it is encouraging that over 30% of gold distractors are retrieved with our approach.

Gold distractor retrieval as a function of the number of round-trip translations Next, we evaluate how increasing the size of the round-trip translations affects the number of distractors generated, and whether it improves gold distractor retrieval. We use 2 pivot languages, German and Russian, since we generate a large number of translations with these pivots. We limit the number of round-trip translations to $1,000$ since this is the maximum number of translations we can generate with the Russian pivot. These NMT models also have similar implementations, which would allow for a fair cross-pivot comparison. We use $N_f = 1$ in all cases, and vary N_b between 100 and 1,000.

Figure 3 shows that *the average number of distractors generated per item* increases with the number of round-trip translations. With 100 hypotheses, fewer than 5 candidates are generated with each pivot, but this number increases to around 50 when $1,000$ are used. Interestingly, the number of candidates for each pivot is almost the same, but the union of the pivots generates almost twice as many candidates indicating that the pivots generate non-overlapping candidates.

While the number of candidates increases with the number of round-trip translations used, it is not obvious if the lower-ranked hypotheses are useful or they simply generate noise. Figure 4 shows the gold retrieval scores as a function of the number of translations. Both systems behave similarly in terms of the number of gold distractors retrieved, and the retrieval score continues to increase as the

[8]We do not evaluate precision here, as the set of potential valid distractors is not unique, and candidates that are not in the gold set can also serve as valid distractors, so precision cannot be computed in automatic evaluation.

	Gold distractors retrieved		
	Word2vec	BERT	MT
Before filt.	66 (15.5%)	144 (33.8%)	**154** (36.2%)
After filt.	39 (9.2%)	97 (22.8%)	**136** (31.9%)

Table 3: **Word2vec** vs. **BERT** vs. **round-trip MT**: Number of gold distractors retrieved.

Method	% of valid distractors				Gold distr.
	R1	R2	R3	Avg.	retrieved
MT-no-ranking	**67.9**	**73.5**	**75.4**	**72.3**	16 (3.8%)
Word2vec	57.2	48.7	62.4	56.1	23 (5.4%)
BERT	22.7	46.3	45.1	38.0	24 (5.6%)
MT (word2Vec rank.)	50.4	47.1	52.1	49.9	47 (11.0%)
MT (BERT rank.)	27.7	41.8	55.4	41.6	36 (8.5%)

Table 4: Percentage of valid distractors in the top-5 list by rater and distractor generation method. The last column shows the number and percentage of the gold distractors in the top-5 list.

number of translations goes up. For example, with 200 round-trip translations, each language generates around 15 gold distractors among its candidates, and this number increases linearly, to almost 80 when 1,000 translations are used. This suggests that lower-ranked hypotheses are still very useful. Furthermore, the information produced by each pivot system is complementary: *the union of the pivots retrieves almost twice as many gold distractors as the individual languages*. This motivates the use of multiple round-trip translation systems.

Finally, Figure 5 shows the percentage of cloze items for which at least $x \in \{1, 2, 3\}$ gold distractors were retrieved for the German and Russian round-trip translations. For both pivots, when using 1,000 translations, less than 5% of cloze items have all 3 distractors retrieved. However, at least 1 gold distractor is retrieved in around 40 % of the cloze items. With the union of the two pivots, we retrieve at least 1 gold distractor for about 55% of the items, which, again, demonstrates that using multiple pivots introduces diversity and provides complementary information. We also find that some of the distractors might be more difficult to retrieve using the MT approach, as discussed further in Section 7.

Comparing generated distractors with BERT and Word2vec Using Word2vec and BERT, we generate a list of n nearest neighbors for each target word. Since the round-trip MT method produces a different number of candidate distractors per target, whereas Word2vec and BERT generate a long list of candidates, we use the average number of candidates produced with round-trip MT with the union of 5 pivot languages, and generate 104 neighbors without filtering and 51 neighbors with filtering applied. Table 3 shows the results. Round-trip MT retrieves significantly more gold distractors compared to Word2vec and BERT.

Method	Annotators			Avg.
	1,2	1,3	2,3	
MT-no-ranking	0.573	0.619	0.590	0.594
Word2vec	0.379	0.389	0.624	0.463
BERT	0.294	0.705	0.364	0.454
MT (Word2vec rank.)	0.496	0.476	0.696	0.556
MT (BERT rank.)	0.439	0.495	0.413	0.449

Table 5: Pairwise agreement for the 3 annotators.

6.2 Manual evaluation of item validity

Evaluation of the item validity needs to ensure that the distractors cannot be used in the carrier sentence (see Table 1). Many invalid examples involve contextual synonyms that have not been filtered out with WordNet, as well as other, non-synonymous candidates that simply fit the context.

For each carrier sentence, we compare 5 sets of automatically-generated distractors:[9] (1) round-trip MT (without ranking);[10] (2) round-trip MT with Word2vec ranking; (3) round-trip MT with BERT ranking; (4) using Word2vec for generation; (5) using BERT for generation.

The manual evaluation is performed by three annotators who are college students and native English speakers. The annotators were presented with a carrier sentence, the target, and manually evaluated 5 sets of distractors by marking each distractor as valid or invalid.

We obtain the "precision" of each method, i.e. the percentage of the distractors judged as valid (Table 4). MT without ranking produces the highest percentage of valid candidates with all three annotators. On average , 72.3% of candidates are valid for MT without ranking, vs. 56.1% with Word2vec and 38.0% with BERT. Using BERT and word2Vec for ranking reduces the percentage of valid candidates in the top-5 list. The last column shows the retrieval scores for the top-5 list. Interestingly, BERT and word2Vec retrieve more gold candidates than the MT method, however, the proportion of invalid candidates is much higher for these methods, pos-

[9]The number of candidates is set to 5 because in a typical setting one would need to use 3 distractors for creating the exercises, and some of the automatic distractors would turn out to be invalid.

[10]5 distractors are selected uniformly at random.

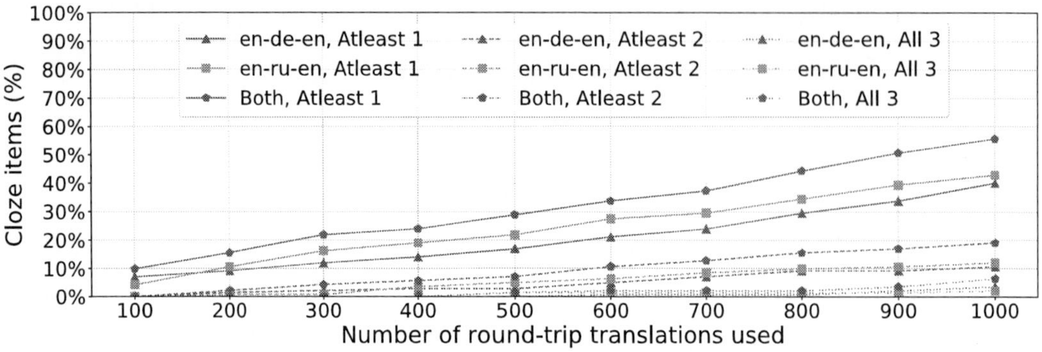

Figure 5: Percentage of cloze items with at least 1, 2, and 3 (all) gold distractors retrieved as a function of the number of round-trip translations used.

Sentence: *When choosing for this role, don't ______ the talents of Brian, one of the best actors in the academy.* **Choices**: *overlook*, overvalue, oversee, overrate*
Sentence: *You simply must invite Carol to the party. She's always the life and ______ of any evening.* **Choices**: *light, soul*, blood, flesh*

Table 6: Examples of multiple choice cloze exercises where none of the gold distractors were identified with the round-trip NMT approach. Each item has exactly one correct choice, marked with a star (*).

sibly, due to the higher proportion of synonyms of unrelated words that fit the sentence context.

Overall, manual evaluation demonstrates the superiority of the MT approach over Word2vec and BERT. We also find that neither Word2vec nor BERT are effective at ranking the candidates. With Word2vec, we conjecture this is due to the nature of the word embedding models that tend to prefer words that are not simply semantically similar but also synonymous with the target. Similarly, BERT is good at producing words that are most likely in the context of the carrier sentence.

Inter-annotator agreement We compute pairwise agreement using Cohen kappa's (Cohen, 1960) and present the results in Table 5. Our average pairwise agreement values are shown in the last column. These values are better than those obtained by Yeung et al. (2019), although their annotation task included 3 classes. Cohen's kappa results indicate moderate agreement in all cases.

7 Analysis and Discussion

We further analyze the distractors generated with round-trip MT. First, we examine the gold distractors that have not been identified with the MT approach. We find that some gold distractors are not semantically close to the target. Table 6 shows two such examples. In the first sentence, the gold distractors are based on morphology/phonology (common prefix), while in the second sentence, the distractors ("light", "blood", and "flesh"), arguably, are not semantically close to the target "soul".

Next, we focus on the differences between the distractors generated with Word2vec, BERT, and MT, and show an example that demonstrates the ability of round-trip MT to model sentential context. First example in Table 7 illustrates that Word2vec distractors are independent of the context of the sentence: the distractors are all latched on the "music" sense of the target word "band". However, round-trip MT models the context of the complete sentence and generates more appropriate distractors. The second example compares BERT-generated and MT-generated distractors: while not all of the MT distractors are valid, BERT is more likely to generate candidates that are synonymous with the target, and thus are invalid as distractors. In fact, Zhou et al. (2019) successfully use BERT for the task of lexical substitution, while Qiang et al. (2020) use BERT for lexical simplification. The idea of using BERT in such tasks is to provide good substitutes that are close synonyms in the given context. This is precisely the opposite of our goal: difficult distractors for a gap-filling task should not be substitutes of the target word.

Finally, the example below demonstrates that MT systems are capable of generating unique pivot-dependent distractors. Consider the carrier sentence "Despite being such a *frequent* visitor to Paris, Sam never bored of exploring it." with the

Sentence: *The ______ of thieves had been captured.* **Target word**: *band*; **gold distractors**: *bunch, crew, range* **Top-5 word2vec distractors**: *keyboardist, vocalist, drummer, quintet, guitarist* **Round-trip MT distractors**: *crew, group, orchestra, gang, squad*
Sentence: *The ______ of the report have yet to be analysed by the government so they can formulate new policies.* **Target word**: *findings*; **gold distractors**: *invenstions, discoveries, rulings* **Top-5 BERT distractors**: *recommendations, assertions, observations, results, conclusions* **Round-trip MT distractors**: *outcomes, familiarities, shows, results, achievements*

Table 7: Word2vec and BERT distractors vs. round-trip MT distractors.

target word "frequent" the French system generates "usual" as a distractor, while the Russian system does not. We believe this might be related to the fact that one of the translations of "frequent" into French is "habituel", which also has a meaning of "usual", and thus "usual" can be produced as a round-trip translation with the French pivot. This is not the case for Russian.

8 Conclusion

We present a novel approach to generating challenging distractors for cloze exercises using round-trip neural machine translation. We show that using multiple pivot systems and a large set of round-trip translations produces diverse candidates, and each pivot language contributes unique distractors. This opens up a possibility of customizing the cloze generation task for speakers of different languages (groups), an interesting promise that BERT-based and other models cannot do. We conducted a thorough evaluation of the distractors, using a set of real cloze exercises for advanced ESL learners. Comparison with Word2vec and BERT showed that the round-trip MT retrieves substantially more gold distractors given the same size of the candidate set.

For future work, we will focus on customizing distractors based on the learner's native language, by prioritizing that language as pivot for MT. We will also conduct a study with language learners to determine whether the automatic distractors produced with our approach result in cloze items of the same difficulty as those that use gold distractors.

For the current work for English, we used high-quality machine translation systems. However, for many language pairs that do not include English as one of the languages, high-quality MT systems are not available. Further, high-quality MT systems are also rarely available for low-resource languages paired with English. The future work will also focus in determining whether and how translation quality might affect the quality of generated distractors. We hypothesize that the proposed method might require special approaches when used to develop exercises for languages other than English and when generating English distractors using low-resource pivots. This is another exciting direction for future work.

Acknowledgments

We thank the anonymous reviewers for their insightful comments.

References

Steven Bird, Ewan Klein, and Edward Loper. 2009. *Natural Language Processing with Python*. O'Reilly Media.

Jonathan Brown, Gwen Frishkoff, and Maxine Eskenazi. 2005. Automatic question generation for vocabulary assessment. In *Proceedings of Human Language Technology Conference and Conference on Empirical Methods in Natural Language Processing*, pages 819–826, Vancouver, British Columbia, Canada. Association for Computational Linguistics.

Ho-Lam Chung, Ying-Hong Chan, and Yao-Chung Fan. 2020. A BERT-based distractor generation scheme with multi-tasking and negative answer training strategies. In *EMNLP*. Association for Computational Linguistics.

Jacob Cohen. 1960. A coefficient of agreement for nominal scales. *Educational and Psychological Measurement*, 20(1):37–46.

Daniel Dahlmeier and Hwee Tou Ng. 2011. Correcting semantic collocation errors with L1-induced paraphrases. In *Proceedings of the 2011 Conference on Empirical Methods in Natural Language Processing*, pages 107–117, Edinburgh, Scotland, UK. Association for Computational Linguistics.

Jacob Devlin, Ming-Wei Chang, Kenton Lee, and Kristina Toutanova. 2018. BERT: pre-training of deep bidirectional transformers for language understanding. *CoRR*, abs/1810.04805.

Mariano Felice and Paula Buttery. 2019. Entropy as a proxy for gap complexity in open cloze tests. In *Proceedings of the International Conference on Recent Advances in Natural Language Processing (RANLP 2019)*. INCOMA Ltd.

Christiane Fellbaum. 1998. *WordNet: An Electronic Lexical Database*. Bradford Books.

Lingyu Gao, Kevin Gimpel, and Arnar Jensson. 2020. Distractor analysis and selection for multiple-choice cloze questions for second-language learners. In *Proceedings of the Fifteenth Workshop on Innovative Use of NLP for Building Educational Applications*. Association for Computational Linguistics.

Takuya Goto, Tomoko Kojiri, Toyohide Watanabe, Tomoharu Iwata, and Takeshi Yamada. 2010. Automatic generation system of multiple-choice cloze questions and its evaluation. *Knowledge Management & E-Learning: An International Journal*, 2(3):210–224.

Jennifer Hill and Rahul Simha. 2016. Automatic generation of context-based fill-in-the-blank exercises using co-occurrence likelihoods and Google n-grams. In *Proceedings of the 11th Workshop on Innovative Use of NLP for Building Educational Applications*, pages 23–30, San Diego, CA. Association for Computational Linguistics.

Ayako Hoshino and Hiroshi Nakagawa. 2005. A real-time multiple-choice question generation for language testing: A preliminary study. In *Proceedings of the Second Workshop on Building Educational Applications Using NLP*, pages 17–20, Ann Arbor, Michigan. Association for Computational Linguistics.

Shu Jiang and John Lee. 2017. Distractor generation for Chinese fill-in-the-blank items. In *Proceedings of the 12th Workshop on Innovative Use of NLP for Building Educational Applications*, pages 143–148, Copenhagen, Denmark. Association for Computational Linguistics.

Claudia Leacock, Martin Chodorow, Michael Gamon, and Joel Tetreault. 2010. *Automated Grammatical Error Detection for Language Learners*. Morgan and Claypool Publishers.

Chao-Lin Liu, Chun-Hung Wang, Zhao-Ming Gao, and Shang-Ming Huang. 2005. Applications of lexical information for algorithmically composing multiple-choice cloze items. In *Proceedings of the Second Workshop on Building Educational Applications Using NLP*, pages 1–8, Ann Arbor, Michigan. Association for Computational Linguistics.

Edison Marrese-Taylor, Ai Nakajima, Yutaka Matsuo, and Ono Yuichi. 2018. Learning to automatically generate fill-in-the-blank quizzes. In *Proceedings of the 5th Workshop on Natural Language Processing Techniques for Educational Applications*.

Tomas Mikolov, Ilya Sutskever, Kai Chen, Greg S Corrado, and Jeff Dean. 2013. Distributed representations of words and phrases and their compositionality. In *Advances in neural information processing systems*, pages 3111–3119.

Nathan Ng, Kyra Yee, Alexei Baevski, Myle Ott, Michael Auli, and Sergey Edunov. 2019. Facebook FAIR's WMT19 news translation task submission. In *Proceedings of the Fourth Conference on Machine Translation (Volume 2: Shared Task Papers, Day 1)*, pages 314–319, Florence, Italy. Association for Computational Linguistics.

Juan Pino and Maxine Eskénazi. 2009. Semi-automatic generation of cloze question distractors effect of students' l1. In *SLaTE*.

Jipeng Qiang, Yun Li, Yi Zhu, Yunhao Yuan, and Xindong Wu. 2020. Lexical simplification with pretrained encoders. In *Proceedings of The Thirty-Fourth AAAI Conference on Artificial Intelligence (AAAI-20)*. Association for the Advancement of Artificial Intelligence.

Masoud Jalili Sabet, Philipp Dufter, and Hinrich Schütze. 2020. Simalign: High quality word alignments without parallel training data using static and contextualized embeddings. *arXiv preprint arXiv:2004.08728*.

Keisuke Sakaguchi, Yuki Arase, and Mamoru Komachi. 2013. Discriminative approach to fill-in-the-blank quiz generation for language learners. In *Proceedings of the 51st Annual Meeting of the Association for Computational Linguistics (Volume 2: Short Papers)*, pages 238–242, Sofia, Bulgaria. Association for Computational Linguistics.

Eiichiro Sumita, Fumiaki Sugaya, and Seiichi Yamamoto. 2005. Measuring non-native speakers' proficiency of English by using a test with automatically-generated fill-in-the-blank questions. In *Proceedings of the Second Workshop on Building Educational Applications Using NLP*, pages 61–68, Ann Arbor, Michigan. Association for Computational Linguistics.

Yuni Susanti, Takenobu Tokunaga, Hitoshi Nishikawa, and Hiroyuki Obari. 2018. Automatic distractor generation for multiple-choice english vocabulary questions. *Research and Practice in Technology Enhanced Learning*, 13(1):15.

Jörg Tiedemann and Santhosh Thottingal. 2020. OPUS-MT — Building open translation services for the World. In *Proceedings of the 22nd Annual Conferenec of the European Association for Machine Translation (EAMT)*, Lisbon, Portugal.

Chak Yan Yeung, John Lee, and Benjamin Tsou. 2019. Difficulty-aware distractor generation for gap-fill items. In *Proceedings of the The 17th Annual Workshop of the Australasian Language Technology Association*, pages 159–164, Sydney, Australia. Australasian Language Technology Association.

Torsten Zesch and Oren Melamud. 2014. Automatic generation of challenging distractors using context-sensitive inference rules. In *Proceedings of the Ninth Workshop on Innovative Use of NLP for Building Educational Applications*, pages 143–148, Baltimore,

Maryland. Association for Computational Linguistics.

Wangchunshu Zhou, Tao Ge, Ke Xu, Furu Wei, and Ming Zhou. 2019. BERT-based lexical substitution. In *Proceedings of the 57th Annual Meeting of the Association for Computational Linguistics*. Association for Computational Linguistics.

On the Locality of Attention in Direct Speech Translation

Belen Alastruey*, **Javier Ferrando***, **Gerard I. Gállego** and **Marta R. Costa-jussà**
TALP Research Center, Universitat Politècnica de Catalunya, Barcelona
{belen.alastruey,javier.ferrando.monsonis
gerard.ion.gallego,marta.ruiz}@upc.edu

Abstract

Transformers have achieved state-of-the-art results across multiple NLP tasks. However, the self-attention mechanism complexity scales quadratically with the sequence length, creating an obstacle for tasks involving long sequences, like in the speech domain. In this paper, we discuss the usefulness of self-attention for Direct Speech Translation. First, we analyze the layer-wise token contributions in the self-attention of the encoder, unveiling local diagonal patterns. To prove that some attention weights are avoidable, we propose to substitute the standard self-attention with a local efficient one, setting the amount of context used based on the results of the analysis. With this approach, our model matches the baseline performance, and improves the efficiency by skipping the computation of those weights that standard attention discards.

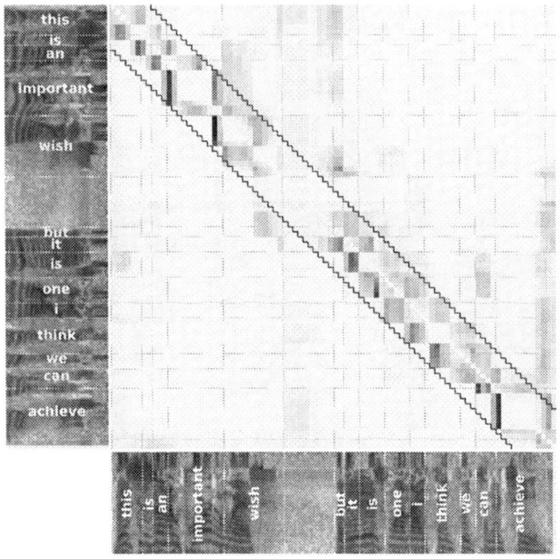

Figure 1: Spectrogram and contributions matrix[1] in Layer 11, after training for En-De ST. Tokens attend locally, creating a diagonal pattern. Highlighted is shown our proposed adaptive local attention window.

1 Introduction

Recently, Transformer-based models have gained popularity and have revolutionized Natural Language Processing (NLP) (Vaswani et al., 2017; Devlin et al., 2019; Brown et al., 2020). In the speech-to-text setting, the Transformer works with audio features like the mel-spectrogram (Dong et al., 2018; Di Gangi et al., 2019). These features provide longer input sequences compared to their raw text counterparts. This can be a problem when regarding complexity, since the Transformer's attention matrix computational cost is $O(n^2)$, where n is the sequence length. In speech, a common approach used to overcome this issue and reduce the input sequence length is to employ convolutional layers with stride before the Transformer encoder. However, even with the addition of convolutional layers, time and memory complexity is still an issue.

An active area of research has investigated ways to make the Transformer more efficient in tasks involving long documents, that exhibit the same problem as speech tasks (Tay et al., 2020). These models explore different techniques on how to avoid the computation of some attention weights, hence reducing the complexity of the self-attention layer. Some of these models, such as the Reformer (Kitaev et al., 2020) or the Routing Transformer (Roy et al., 2021), only compute attention weights on those queries and keys that are more related according to different clustering techniques. The authors of the Linformer (Wang et al., 2020b) state that the attention matrix is low-rank, so they project keys and values to reduce the size of the attention matrix. The Synthesizer (Tay et al., 2021) directly avoids computing token-to-token interac-

* Equal contribution.

[1] The main diagonal, which accounts for 65% of the total contributions, is hidden for visualization purposes.

Proceedings of the 60th Annual Meeting of the Association for Computational Linguistics
Student Research Workshop, pages 402 - 412
May 22-27, 2022 ©2022 Association for Computational Linguistics

tions by learning synthetic attention weights. The Longformer (Beltagy et al., 2020) and the Big Bird (Zaheer et al., 2020) modify the attention matrix with patterns such as local or random attentions. In this paper, we focus on local attention by using a sliding window centered on the diagonal of the attention matrix.

We build upon recent advances in the explainability of the Transformer to analyze the amount of context used by self-attention when dealing with speech features. Recent interpretability works have moved beyond raw attention weights as a measure of layer-wise input attributions and have integrated other modules in the self-attention, such as the norm of the vectors multiplying the attention weights (Kobayashi et al., 2020), the layer normalization, and the residual connection (Kobayashi et al., 2021). In the Automatic Speech Recognition (ASR) domain, the usefulness of the self-attention has been argued (Zhang et al., 2021; Shim et al., 2022), showing that its exposure to the full context might not be necessary, especially in the top layers. We carry out this analysis for Direct Speech Translation (ST) systems, which are capable of translating between languages from speech to text with a single model. The encoder of these systems needs to jointly perform acoustic and semantic modeling, while in ASR the latter is not that relevant (Liu et al., 2020). To the best of our knowledge, this is the first work that uses interpretability methods to understand how the Transformer's self-attention behaves in the Direct ST task.

In this work, we use the layer-wise contributions proposed by Kobayashi et al. (2021) to analyze the patterns of self-attention in Direct ST in En-De, En-Es and En-It tasks, unveiling their strong local nature. Consequently, using self-attention might not be entirely useful, but it is computationally costly. To verify this hypothesis, based on our analysis, we propose a new architecture designed to maximize the efficiency of the model while minimizing the information loss, and demonstrate no hinder in the model's performance in any of the three directions. We achieve this by substituting regular self-attention with local attention in those layers where the contributions are placed around the diagonal. Finally, we analyze the performance of the proposed model.

2 Speech-to-text Transformer

Recent works have attempted to adapt the Transformer to speech tasks (Di Gangi et al., 2019; Gulati et al., 2020). In the Direct ST domain, a usual approach is adding two convolutional layers with a stride of 2 before the Transformer (Wang et al., 2020a). By doing this, the sequence length is reduced to a fourth of the initial one. After the two convolutional layers, the speech-to-text Transformer (S2T Transformer) consists of a regular Transformer model, composed of 12 encoder layers and 6 decoder layers.

The main component of the Transformer is the multi-head attention mechanism, in particular, the self-attention is in charge of mixing contextual information. Given a sequence of token representations $\{\mathbf{x}_1, \cdots, \mathbf{x}_N\}$, each of the H heads projects these vectors to queries $\mathbf{Q}^h \in \mathbb{R}^{N \times d_h}$, keys $\mathbf{K}^h \in \mathbb{R}^{N \times d_h}$ and values $\mathbf{V}^h \in \mathbb{R}^{N \times d_h}$, with head dimension $d_h = d/H$, where d is the model embedding dimensionality. The self-attention attention (SA) computes:

$$\mathrm{SA}(\mathbf{Q}^h, \mathbf{K}^h, \mathbf{V}^h) = \sum_h^H \mathbf{A}^h \mathbf{V}^h \mathbf{W}_O^h + \mathbf{b}_O \quad (1)$$

Where $\mathbf{W}_O^h \in \mathbb{R}^{d_h \times d}$ and $\mathbf{b}_O \in \mathbb{R}^d$ are learnable parameters, and

$$\mathbf{A}^h = \mathrm{softmax}\left(\frac{\mathbf{Q}^h (\mathbf{K}^h)^T}{\sqrt{d_h}}\right) \quad (2)$$

Training details. We reproduce the S2T Transformer training with FAIRSEQ (Ott et al., 2019; Wang et al., 2020a). The training procedure consists of two phases. First, we pre-train the model in the ASR setting (Bérard et al., 2018). Then, we substitute the decoder with a randomly initialized one, and both are finally trained in the ST task (see Appendix C for more details on the hyperparameters). For the trainings, we use the MUST-C English-German, English-Spanish and English-Italian subsets (Cattoni et al., 2021).

3 Model Analysis

In this section, we present the analysis of the encoder self-attention in the S2T Transformer.

Interpretability method. Kobayashi et al. (2021) propose an interpretability method that measures the impact of each layer input, i.e token representations ($\mathbf{x}_j$), to the output of the layer,

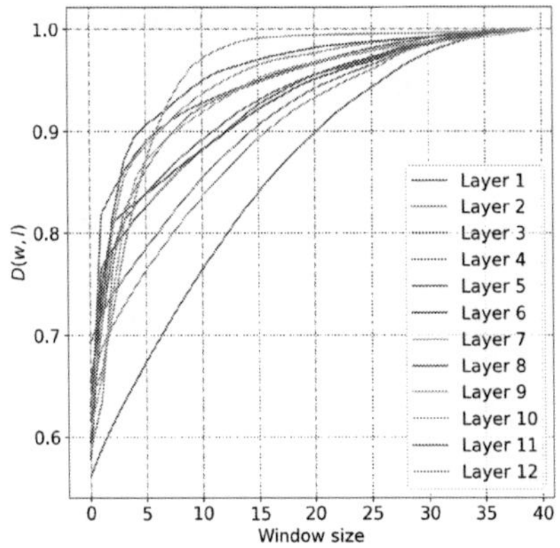

Figure 2: Contribution diagonality $D(w, l)$ after ST training, for a single En-De example. The greater the area under the curve (CCD), the higher the diagonality.

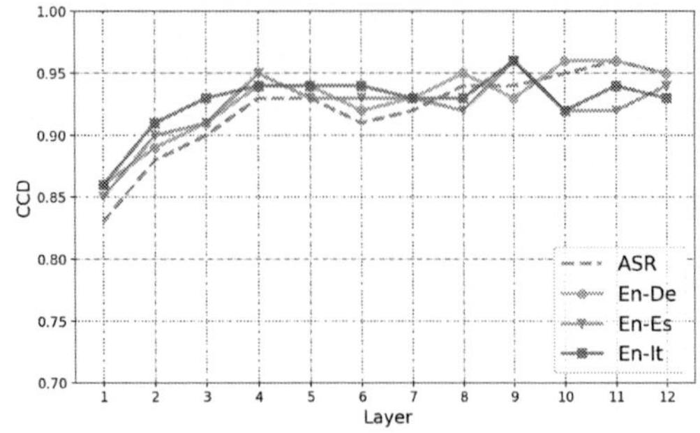

Figure 3: Average cumulative contribution diagonality (CCD) score across layers, over 100 samples. Results shown for models trained in ASR (dashed line) and ST (solid line).

considering also the layer normalization and the residual connection. They provide the formulation for the attention block of the original Transformer architecture, which has layer normalization on top of the self-attention module. In this work, we give an adaptation to the group of models that normalize before the multi-head attention (Pre-LN), such as the S2T Transformer. The complete chain of computations in the Pre-LN attention block can be reformulated as a simple expression of the layer inputs:

$$\hat{\mathbf{x}}_i = \sum_j^N \sum_h^H \mathbf{A}_{i,j}^h \mathrm{LN}(\mathbf{x}_j) \mathbf{W}_V^h \mathbf{W}_O^h + \mathbf{b}^O + \mathbf{x}_i \quad (3)$$

We can now express the attention block output as a sum of transformed input vectors ($F_i(\mathbf{x}_j)$):

$$\hat{\mathbf{x}}_i = \sum_j^N F_i(\mathbf{x}_j) + \mathbf{b}^O \quad (4)$$

Where $F_i(\mathbf{x}_j)$ is defined as:

$$F_i(\mathbf{x}_j) = \begin{cases} \sum_h^H \mathbf{A}_{i,j}^h \mathrm{LN}(\mathbf{x}_j) \mathbf{W}_V^h \mathbf{W}_O^h & \text{if } j \neq i \\ \sum_h^H \mathbf{A}_{i,j}^h \mathrm{LN}(\mathbf{x}_j) \mathbf{W}_V^h \mathbf{W}_O^h + \mathbf{x}_i & \text{if } j = i \end{cases}$$

Kobayashi et al. (2021) measure the contribution $C_{i,j}$ of each input vector $\mathbf{x}_j$ to the layer output $\hat{\mathbf{x}}_i$ with the Euclidean norm of the transformed vector:

$$C_{i,j} = \|F_i(\mathbf{x}_j)\| \quad (5)$$

Layer-wise analysis. We analyze the contribution scores obtained with Eq. 5 from the encoder layers in both ASR (pre-training) and ST tasks. From the results shown in Figure 4 (see also Appendix E) we observe that most layers' contributions are dense around the diagonal. To measure the degree of diagonality in the contribution matrices at each layer l, we build upon the attention diagonality proposed by Shim et al. (2022), originally defined with attention weights and proportions of the sequence length. We reformulate it with the obtained contributions, and token ranges w (see Appendix A for more details on the differences):

$$D(w, l) = \frac{1}{N} \sum_i \sum_j C_{i,j}^l \quad (6)$$

where $j \in [\max(1, i - \lfloor \frac{1}{2}w \rfloor), \min(N, i + \lfloor \frac{1}{2}w \rfloor]$, $i \in [1, N]$. $D(w, l)$ computes the average of the contributions restricted by the diagonal window range w. In order to measure how fast the contribution density increases over the window length, we calculate the cumulative contribution diagonality (CCD), that corresponds to the area under the curve of the accumulated $D(w, l)$ within the range[2] $w \in [1, 2N]$. That is, we approximate the integral of $D(l, d)$ along the distance d, but for the discrete variable w (Figure 2).

In Figure 3 we show the CCD results for ASR and ST across layers, where we can observe a strong diagonal pattern. We can see that, surprisingly, CCD is very similar in both tasks. This contradicts the belief that, because of the need for deeper semantic processing when translating, ST

[2]Note that a window of size w contains $\lfloor \frac{1}{2}w \rfloor$ tokens on each side of the main diagonal, so $w = 1$ represents the main diagonal and $w = 2N$ every possible diagonal.

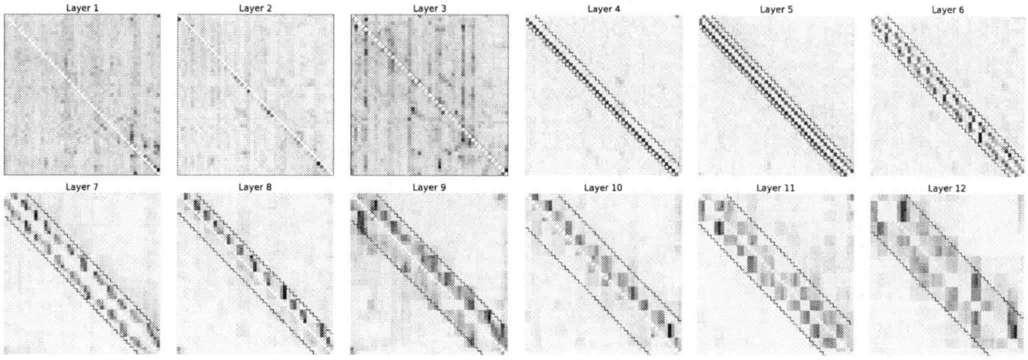

Figure 4: Contribution matrices[3] of encoder layers on a sample after training for En-De ST. Windows used in the efficient architecture highlighted.

needs more context than ASR. Furthermore, we see different behaviors along the encoder, and a trend towards uniformly distributed contributions in the first layers.

Moreover, in Figure 4, we can see differences between those layers that show local patterns. Layers 4, 5 and 6 attend to close context. Instead, those layers at the end of the encoder, as 11 or 12, need larger context, and we can see how the contributions create patterns corresponding to words in the spectrogram, enabling us to see interactions between them (Figure 1). Additionally, we see that contribution matrices reveal silences in the speech sequence. However, we believe that further research is needed to fully understand the meaning of these patterns.

Algorithm 1: Window size selection

Input:
C^l: contribution matrix, N: number of tokens,
t: min diagonal contribution threshold
Output:
w^l: optimal window size

$counter \leftarrow 0$
$w^l \leftarrow 0$
while $counter < (N/10)$ **do**
  for $i \leftarrow 0, N$ **do**
    if $mean(C^l_{diag}[i]) > t$ ***or*** $mean(C^l_{diag}[-i]) > t$
    then
      $w^l \leftarrow 2i + 1$
      $counter \leftarrow 0$
    else
      $counter \leftarrow counter + 1$

4 Efficient Speech-to-text Transformer

From the previous analysis, we hypothesize that suitable local attention patterns may potentially avoid the computation of unused attention scores. Note that if a token does not contribute to the output of a layer, its attention score can be canceled. Our objective is to maximize the efficiency of the model while minimizing the performance drop.

Window size selection. CCD could serve as a starting point to obtain optimal window lengths. However, it requires predefining the amount of total contribution required inside the window, which makes it fragile to properly detect local patterns. On one hand, it can be too sensitive to a strong main diagonal. On the other, it may overestimate random distant contributions. We propose an alternative based on the average contribution of every sub/superdiagonal (Alg. 1). Starting from the main diagonal $C_{diag}[0]$, it keeps adding tokens to the window length until it finds $N \cdot 10\%$ consecutive sub/superdiagonals below the t threshold[4]. We repeat this procedure with a random set of 400 sentences, and we compute each layer's window length mean (μ^l) and standard deviation (σ^l). To ensure that most significant contributions are considered, we define as the optimal window size (w^l) the result of the operation[5] $w^l = \lceil \mu^l + \sigma^l \rceil$. The results obtained are similar in every language pair (Table 1 and Appendix D). In Figure 4, we can see how w contains most of the relevant contributions for En-De ST (see more examples in Appendix E).

[3]The main diagonal, which accounts for around 65% of the total contributions in each layer, is hidden for visualization purposes.

[4]Hyperparameter that defines the minimum average value of the sub/superdiagonals to be considered. We choose 0.01 after empirical study.

[5]If w^l is even, we set $w^l = w^l + 1$ so that it is odd and hence the window can be centered around the diagonal.

Layer	$\mu \pm \sigma$	w	CL
1 *	3.41 ± 13.15	*17*	*0.35 ± 0.07*
2 *	1.18 ± 3.45	*5*	*0.32 ± 0.04*
3 *	0.51 ± 1.56	*3*	*0.30 ± 0.04*
4	2.25 ± 1.30	5	0.23 ± 0.04
5	4.03 ± 0.28	5	0.17 ± 0.03
6	7.03 ± 1.03	9	0.23 ± 0.04
7	11.37 ± 1.13	13	0.18 ± 0.04
8	7.94 ± 1.16	11	0.18 ± 0.04
9	12.56 ± 1.85	15	0.19 ± 0.05
10	16.47 ± 2.40	19	0.13 ± 0.05
11	13.28 ± 1.90	17	0.13 ± 0.04
12	16.28 ± 3.86	21	0.16 ± 0.05

Table 1: Optimal window size study in En-De ST. (*) For the first three layers, we use standard self-attention.

	En-De	En-Es	En-It
Baseline	22.53 ± 0.15	27.49 ± 0.22	22.98 ± 0.15
Ours	22.49 ± 0.11	27.46 ± 0.12	22.97 ± 0.27

Table 2: BLEU obtained on the Speech Translation task (mean ± std after training with 5 different seeds).

Contribution loss. We can now calculate the percentage of the total contributions that are left outside the window. This allows us to discover the amount of contribution that is lost because of the use of local attention. To do so, we employ Eq. 6, but since we are interested in the contributions outside each window w^l, we define $CL(l, w^l) = 1 - D(l, w^l)$.

Proposed architecture. From the previous results, we see that the first three layers are the ones with the weakest local pattern (See Figure 4). In these layers, $CL(l, w^l)$ is large, and CCD (Figure 2) shows smaller areas. For these reasons, we believe that using the entire self-attention in the first three layers is necessary. In the following layers, we use local attention with window size w^l. Our proposed architecture is an efficient adaptation of the S2T Transformer, and therefore it is exactly equal with exception of the self-attention layers (detailed architectures in Section 2 and Appendix B).

Experiments. Finally, we train our model under the same specifications and dataset as the baseline (see Section 2 for details on the dataset, and Appendix C for the training hyperparameters).

As we see in Table 2, our model matches the performance of the S2T Transformer in every analyzed language pair. However, we achieve it while reducing the complexity in most layers from $O(n^2)$ to $O(n \cdot w^l)$. This difference can be highly significant, considering the usual length of speech sequences and the size of the windows used. In particular, w^l goes from 5 to 25 tokens between the different languages. However, the average length of an input sequence in studied splits of the MUST-C dataset after the two convolutional layers used in the S2T Transformer, is 166 tokens, even reaching a maximum of 1052.

5 Conclusions

Transformer-based models are the current state-of-the-art in many different fields. However, the quadratic complexity of the self-attention module usually hinders the usefulness of the model in real-life applications. This problem worsens when working with long sequences, as is the case with speech. In this paper, we have questioned the need of computing all attention weights in ST. We have analyzed the contribution matrices, and we have seen that, in many layers, the relevant scores are placed in a diagonal pattern. Therefore, we have hypothesized that these weights do not need to be calculated. To verify our hypothesis, we have trained a model that substitutes regular self-attention with local attention, with a suitable window size for each layer. We have seen that as we expected, the results are almost equal to the ones obtained with the baseline model, but the complexity has been lowered significantly.

Regarding interpretability, we have found how the Transformer establishes connections between words in speech sequences. Furthermore, we have seen that, in contrast to what was expected, diagonality scores are similar in both ST and ASR tasks, meaning that they use the same amount of context.

6 Acknowledgments

This work was partially funded by the project ADAVOICE, PID2019-107579RB-I00 / AEI / 10.13039/501100011033, and the UPC INIREC scholarship n°3522. We would like to thank Ioannis Tsiamas and Carlos Escolano for their support and advice, and the anonymous reviewers for their useful comments.

7 Ethical Considerations

This work analyzes the inner workings of a particular architecture in Direct Speech Translation. Based on the analysis, we propose a more efficient model, that maintains the baseline performance.

Our proposed solution can help reduce the ecological footprint of Speech Translation systems based on the Transformer architecture. We believe this work has no direct negative social influences. However, we should underline that the dataset used in this paper consists of high-resource languages such as English, German, Spanish, and Italian. Although the interpretability method does not depend on specific languages, there may be differences in the degree of efficiency that can be achieved when experimenting with other languages.

References

Iz Beltagy, Matthew E. Peters, and Arman Cohan. 2020. Longformer: The long-document transformer. *ArXiv*, abs/2004.05150.

Tom Brown, Benjamin Mann, Nick Ryder, Melanie Subbiah, Jared D Kaplan, Prafulla Dhariwal, Arvind Neelakantan, Pranav Shyam, Girish Sastry, Amanda Askell, Sandhini Agarwal, Ariel Herbert-Voss, Gretchen Krueger, Tom Henighan, Rewon Child, Aditya Ramesh, Daniel Ziegler, Jeffrey Wu, Clemens Winter, Chris Hesse, Mark Chen, Eric Sigler, Mateusz Litwin, Scott Gray, Benjamin Chess, Jack Clark, Christopher Berner, Sam McCandlish, Alec Radford, Ilya Sutskever, and Dario Amodei. 2020. Language models are few-shot learners. In *Advances in Neural Information Processing Systems*, volume 33, pages 1877–1901. Curran Associates, Inc.

Alexandre Bérard, Laurent Besacier, Ali Can Kocabiyikoglu, and Olivier Pietquin. 2018. End-to-end automatic speech translation of audiobooks. In *2018 IEEE International Conference on Acoustics, Speech and Signal Processing (ICASSP)*, pages 6224–6228.

Roldano Cattoni, Mattia Antonino Di Gangi, Luisa Bentivogli, Matteo Negri, and Marco Turchi. 2021. Must-c: A multilingual corpus for end-to-end speech translation. *Computer Speech & Language*, 66:101155.

Jacob Devlin, Ming-Wei Chang, Kenton Lee, and Kristina Toutanova. 2019. BERT: Pre-training of deep bidirectional transformers for language understanding. In *Proceedings of the 2019 Conference of the North American Chapter of the Association for Computational Linguistics: Human Language Technologies, Volume 1 (Long and Short Papers)*, pages 4171–4186, Minneapolis, Minnesota. Association for Computational Linguistics.

Mattia Antonino Di Gangi, Matteo Negri, and Marco Turchi. 2019. Adapting Transformer to End-to-End Spoken Language Translation. In *Proc. Interspeech 2019*, pages 1133–1137.

Linhao Dong, Shuang Xu, and Bo Xu. 2018. Speech-transformer: A no-recurrence sequence-to-sequence model for speech recognition. *2018 IEEE International Conference on Acoustics, Speech and Signal Processing (ICASSP)*, pages 5884–5888.

Anmol Gulati, James Qin, Chung-Cheng Chiu, Niki Parmar, Yu Zhang, Jiahui Yu, Wei Han, Shibo Wang, Zhengdong Zhang, Yonghui Wu, and Ruoming Pang. 2020. Conformer: Convolution-augmented Transformer for Speech Recognition. In *Proc. Interspeech 2020*, pages 5036–5040.

Nikita Kitaev, Łukasz Kaiser, and Anselm Levskaya. 2020. Reformer: The efficient transformer. In *International Conference on Learning Representations*.

Goro Kobayashi, Tatsuki Kuribayashi, Sho Yokoi, and Kentaro Inui. 2020. Attention is not only a weight: Analyzing transformers with vector norms. In *Proceedings of the 2020 Conference on Empirical Methods in Natural Language Processing (EMNLP)*, pages 7057–7075, Online. Association for Computational Linguistics.

Goro Kobayashi, Tatsuki Kuribayashi, Sho Yokoi, and Kentaro Inui. 2021. Incorporating Residual and Normalization Layers into Analysis of Masked Language Models. In *Proceedings of the 2021 Conference on Empirical Methods in Natural Language Processing*, pages 4547–4568, Online and Punta Cana, Dominican Republic. Association for Computational Linguistics.

Yuchen Liu, Junnan Zhu, Jiajun Zhang, and Chengqing Zong. 2020. Bridging the modality gap for speech-to-text translation. *ArXiv*, abs/2010.14920.

Myle Ott, Sergey Edunov, Alexei Baevski, Angela Fan, Sam Gross, Nathan Ng, David Grangier, and Michael Auli. 2019. fairseq: A fast, extensible toolkit for sequence modeling. In *Proceedings of the 2019 Conference of the North American Chapter of the Association for Computational Linguistics (Demonstrations)*, pages 48–53, Minneapolis, Minnesota. Association for Computational Linguistics.

Aurko Roy, Mohammad Saffar, Ashish Vaswani, and David Grangier. 2021. Efficient content-based sparse attention with routing transformers. *Transactions of the Association for Computational Linguistics*, 9:53–68.

Kyuhong Shim, Jungwook Choi, and Wonyong Sung. 2022. Understanding the role of self attention for efficient speech recognition. In *International Conference on Learning Representations*.

Yi Tay, Dara Bahri, Donald Metzler, Da-Cheng Juan, Zhe Zhao, and Che Zheng. 2021. Synthesizer: Rethinking self-attention in transformer models. In *International Conference on Machine Learning*. PMLR.

Yi Tay, Mostafa Dehghani, Dara Bahri, and Donald Metzler. 2020. Efficient transformers: A survey. *ArXiv*, abs/2009.06732.

Ashish Vaswani, Noam Shazeer, Niki Parmar, Jakob Uszkoreit, Llion Jones, Aidan N Gomez, Ł ukasz Kaiser, and Illia Polosukhin. 2017. Attention is all you need. In *Advances in Neural Information Processing Systems*, volume 30. Curran Associates, Inc.

Changhan Wang, Yun Tang, Xutai Ma, Anne Wu, Dmytro Okhonko, and Juan Pino. 2020a. Fairseq S2T: Fast speech-to-text modeling with fairseq. In *Proceedings of the 1st Conference of the Asia-Pacific Chapter of the Association for Computational Linguistics and the 10th International Joint Conference on Natural Language Processing: System Demonstrations*, pages 33–39, Suzhou, China. Association for Computational Linguistics.

Sinong Wang, Belinda Z. Li, Madian Khabsa, Han Fang, and Hao Ma. 2020b. Linformer: Self-attention with linear complexity. *ArXiv*, abs/2006.04768.

Manzil Zaheer, Guru Guruganesh, Kumar Avinava Dubey, Joshua Ainslie, Chris Alberti, Santiago Ontanon, Philip Pham, Anirudh Ravula, Qifan Wang, Li Yang, and Amr Ahmed. 2020. Big bird: Transformers for longer sequences. In *Advances in Neural Information Processing Systems*, volume 33, pages 17283–17297. Curran Associates, Inc.

Shucong Zhang, Erfan Loweimi, Peter Bell, and Steve Renals. 2021. On the usefulness of self-attention for automatic speech recognition with transformers. In *2021 IEEE Spoken Language Technology Workshop (SLT)*, pages 89–96.

A Cumulative Attention Diagonality (CAD)

Shim et al. (2022) propose the cumulative attention diagonality (CAD) as the integral of the attention diagonality $D(r, l)$ along the variable r, which defines the window length as a proportion of the sequence length:

$$CAD^l = \int_{r=0}^{r=1} D(r, l)\ dr$$

where $D(r, l)$ is defined over the attention weight matrix A^l:

$$D(r, l) = \frac{1}{N} \sum_{i=1}^{N} \sum_{\substack{j=\max(1,\\ i-r(N-1)}}^{\substack{\min(N,\\ i+r(N-1))}} A^l_{i,j}$$

To approximate the result of the integral, Shim et al. (2022) use the Trapezoidal Rule with the discretized variable $\hat{r} \approx r$.

$$\int_{r=0}^{r=1} D(r, l)\ dr \approx \sum_{\hat{r}=0}^{\hat{r}=1} \frac{D(\hat{r}, l) + D(\hat{r}+1, l)}{2}$$

For each step in the summation, the window range around the diagonal increases $2r(N-1)$, which may lead to different increments based on the sentence length. For instance, for a sentence with $N = 11$, in a 0.1 increase of $\hat{r}$, the window size range increases by 2. However, with $N = 101$ we get an increment of 20. For this reason, we redefine the diagonality measures with token-wise increments.

B Architecture Details

Both our efficient model and the S2T Transformer (Wang et al., 2020a) share the same architecture, with the exception of the self-attention modules. The models consist 12 encoder layers and 6 decoder layers with sinusoidal positional encodings. In the encoder and decoder we use 4 attention heads, an embedding dimension of 256, and of 2048 in the FFN layers. We use a dropout probability of 0.1 in both the attention weights and FFN activations. We use ReLU as the activation function.

Regarding the convolutional layer applied to reduce sequence length, it consists of a 1D convolutional layer, with a kernel of size 5, a stride of 2, and with the same number of output channels than input channels.

C Training Hyperparameters

To ensure a reliable comparison, we performed all ASR and ST experiments under the same conditions and hyperparameters. In ASR training we fixed a maximum of 40000 tokens per batch. We used Adam optimizer and a learning rate of $1 \cdot 10^{-3}$ with an inverse square root scheduler. We applied a warm-up for the first 10000 updates. We clipped the gradient to 10 to avoid exploding gradients. We used label smoothed cross-entropy as a loss function, with a smoothing factor of 0.1. We used an update frequency of 8 on a single GPU. We set a maximum of 50000 updates for every training. In ST training, we use the same hyperparameters as for ASR, but we use a learning rate of $2 \cdot 10^{-3}$. We conducted the training of all our experiments using NVIDIA GeForce RTX 2080 Ti GPU.

D Optimal window analysis in En-Es and En-It ST

Layer	$\mu \pm \sigma$	w	CL
1 *	4.68 ± 14.77	*21*	*0.39 ± 0.08*
2 *	3.21 ± 6.17	*11*	*0.29 ± 0.04*
3 *	0.99 ± 3.6	*5*	*0.28 ± 0.04*
4	2.58 ± 1.96	5	0.2 ± 0.02
5	4.52 ± 2.38	7	0.24 ± 0.04
6	15.88 ± 2.92	19	0.21 ± 0.06
7	11.32 ± 1.91	15	0.16 ± 0.03
8	9.52 ± 2.5	13	0.22 ± 0.05
9	14.96 ± 1.78	17	0.07 ± 0.05
10	15.94 ± 3.0	19	0.19 ± 0.05
11	13.83 ± 3.66	19	0.21 ± 0.05
12	20.38 ± 3.42	25	0.1 ± 0.05

Table 3: Optimal window size study in En-Es ST. (*) For the first three layers, we use standard self-attention.

Layer	$\mu \pm \sigma$	w	CL
1 *	6.16 ± 17.57	*25*	*0.34 ± 0.09*
2 *	2.56 ± 7.47	*11*	*0.29 ± 0.05*
3 *	2.44 ± 2.84	*7*	*0.27 ± 0.05*
4	4.08 ± 0.65	5	0.19 ± 0.03
5	14.05 ± 2.08	17	0.15 ± 0.03
6	10.82 ± 1.31	13	0.18 ± 0.04
7	7.37 ± 4.54	13	0.23 ± 0.05
8	8.62 ± 2.18	11	0.22 ± 0.04
9	12.49 ± 1.65	15	0.09 ± 0.03
10	16.06 ± 3.80	21	0.17 ± 0.04
11	18.15 ± 3.20	23	0.11 ± 0.05
12	17.34 ± 4.83	23	0.15 ± 0.05

Table 4: Optimal window size study in En-It ST. (*) For the first three layers, we use standard self-attention.

E Contribution Matrices

Below, we show more examples of contribution matrices for the different languages that have been studied. Note that, although in some cases a diagonal a pattern appears in the first three layers, the diagonality score is still low. Local diagonal patterns are not strictly related to high diagonality, since contributions outside the pattern might be uniformly distributed, and thus difficult to observe in the heatmap. For this reason, contribution matrices can be misleading, and we focus on the use of CL scores to determine which layers should use full attention.

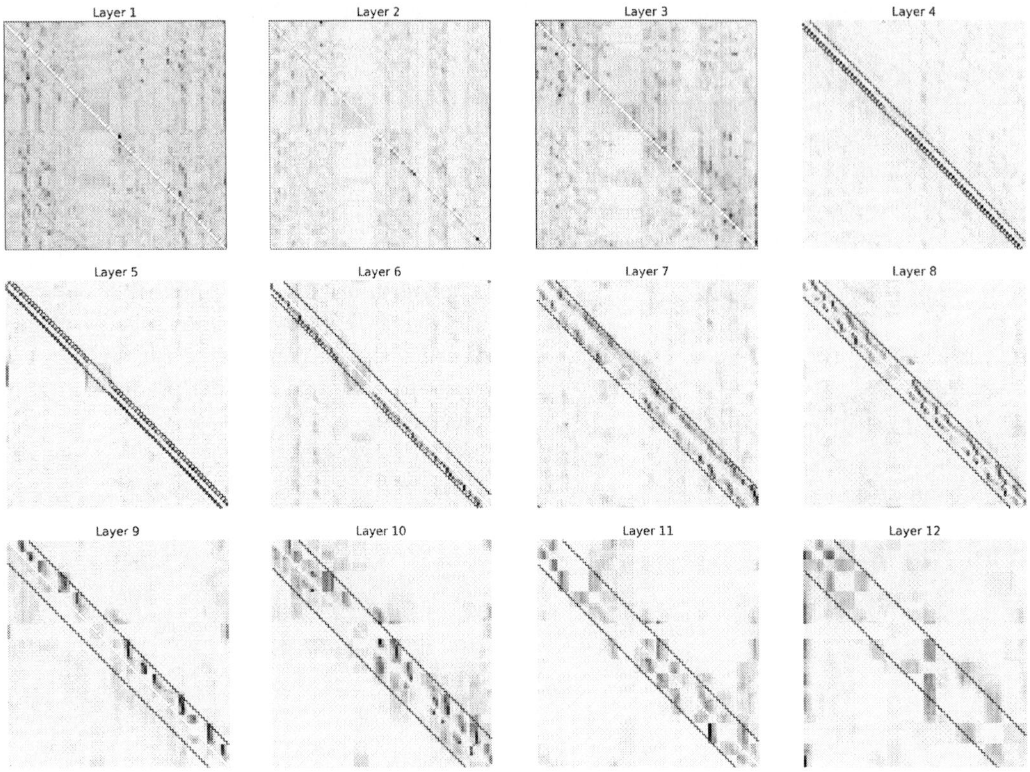

Figure 5: Contribution matrices for a sample after En-De ST training.

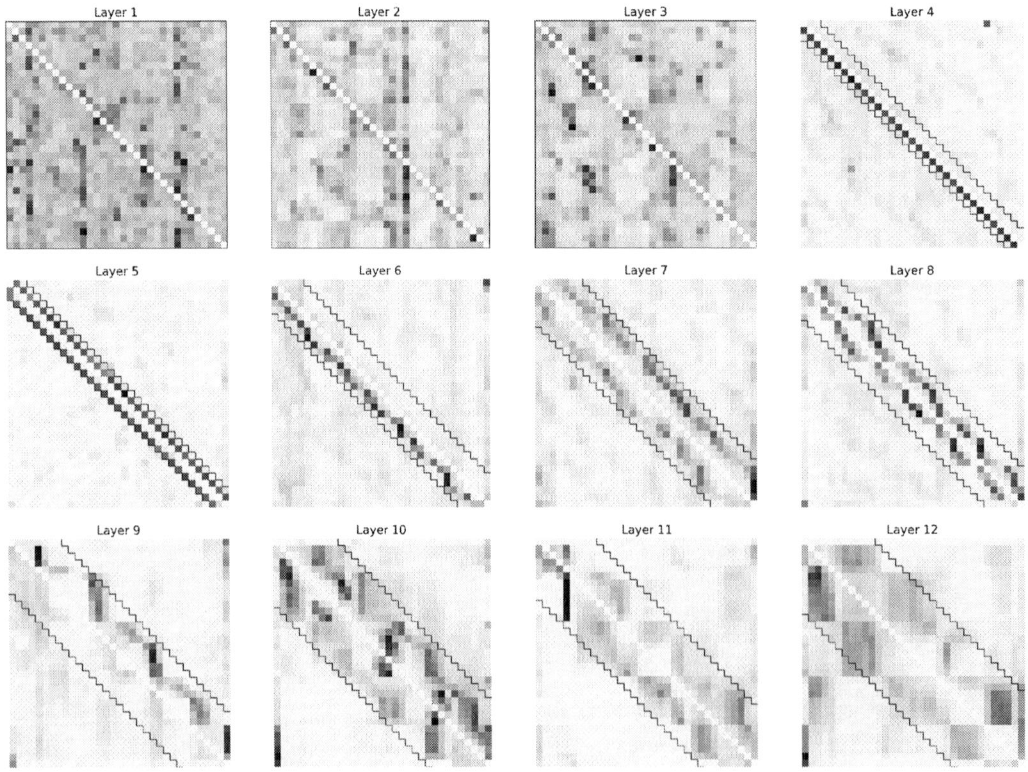

Figure 6: Contribution matrices for a sample after En-De ST training.

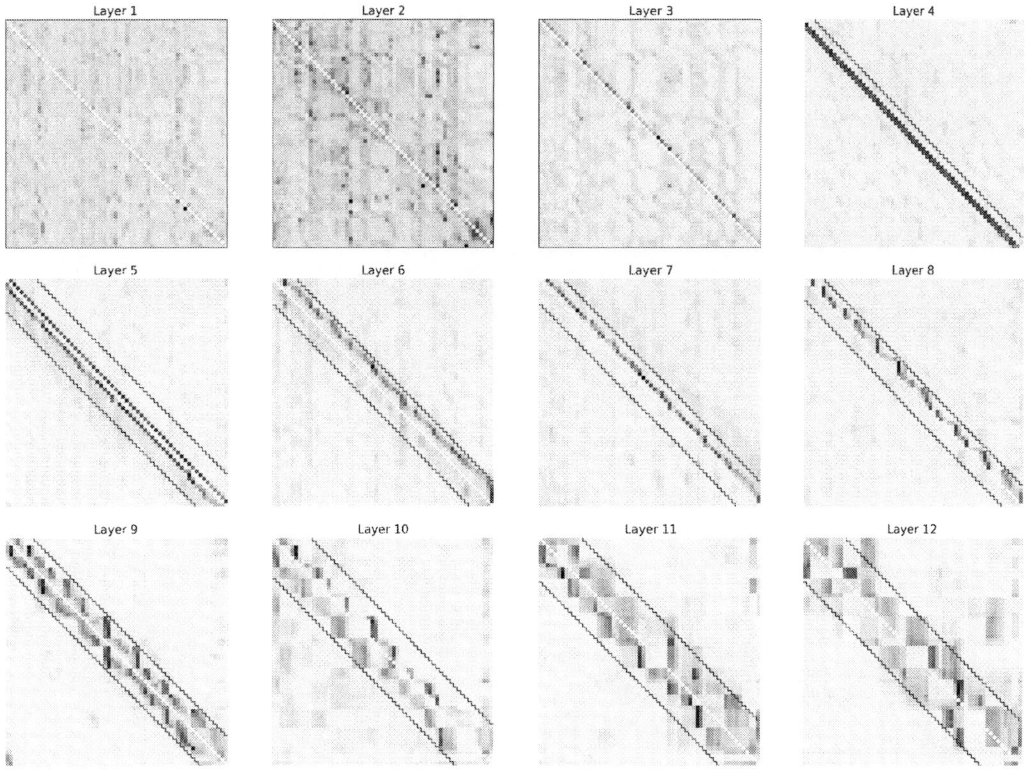

Figure 7: Contribution matrices for a sample after En-It ST training.

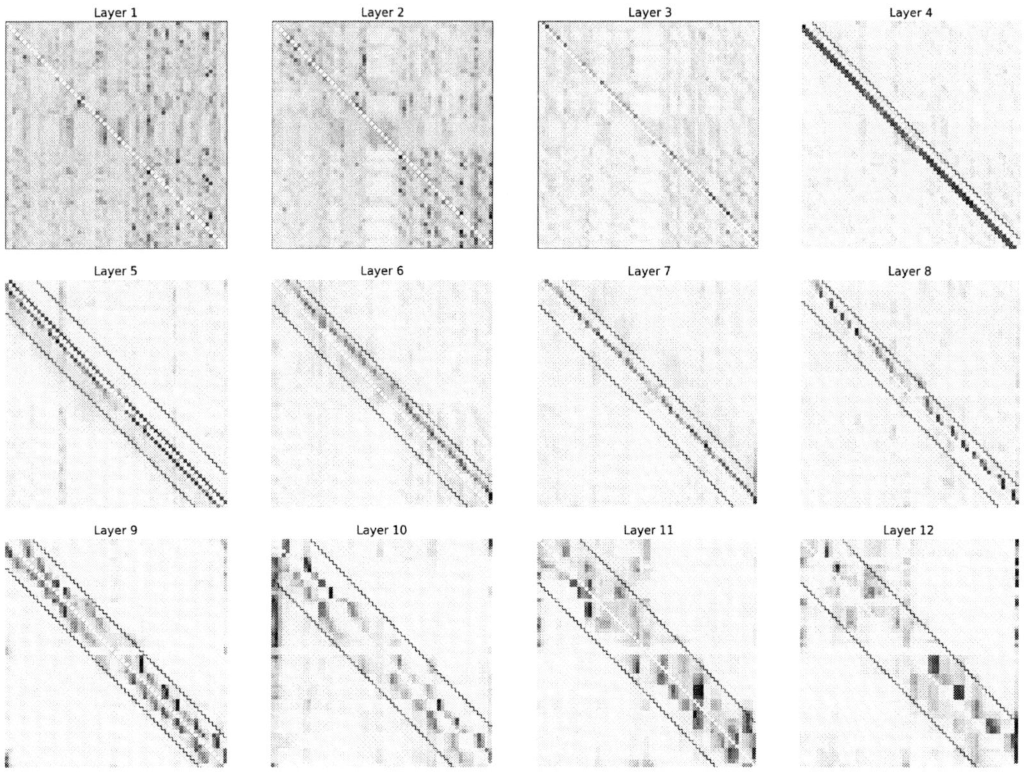

Figure 8: Contribution matrices for a sample after En-It ST training.

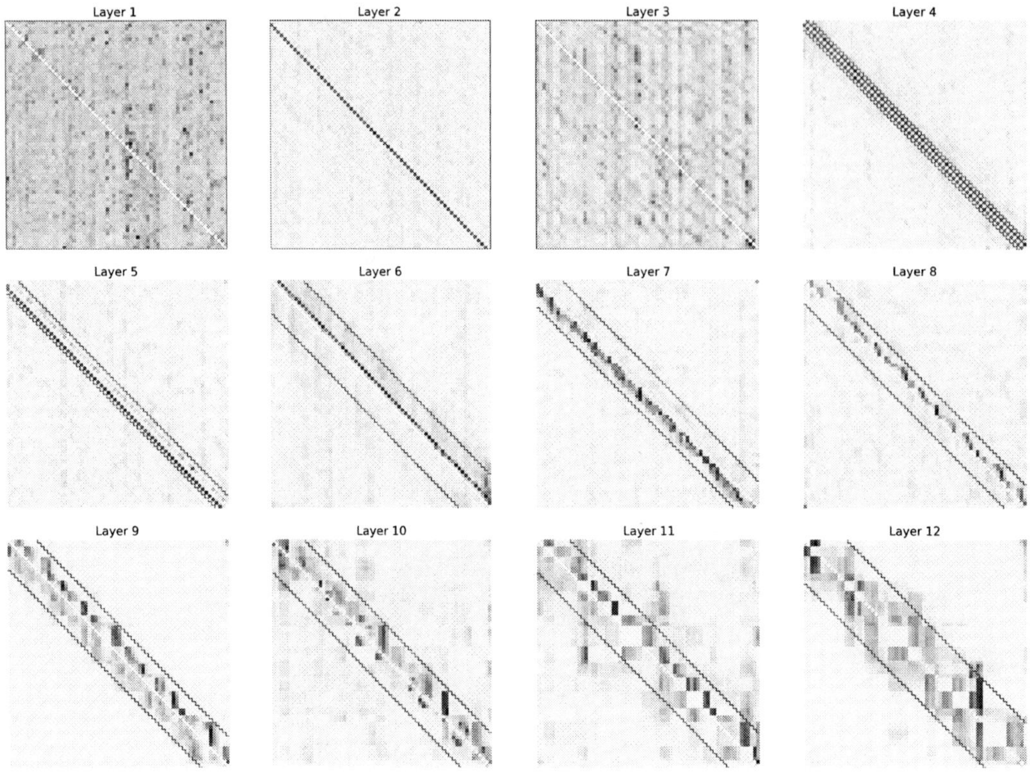

Figure 9: Contribution matrices for a sample after En-Es ST training.

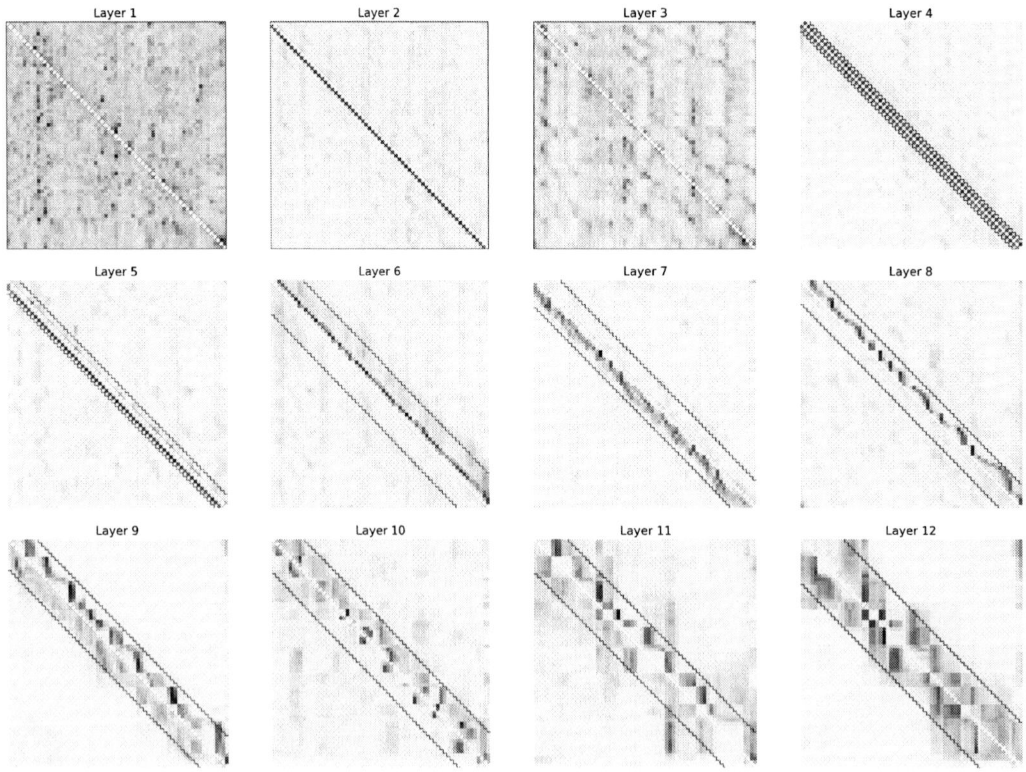

Figure 10: Contribution matrices for a sample after En-Es ST training.

Extraction of Diagnostic Reasoning Relations for Clinical Knowledge Graphs

Vimig Socrates
Yale University / New Haven, CT
vimig.socrates@yale.edu

Abstract

Clinical knowledge graphs lack meaningful diagnostic relations (e.g. comorbidities, sign/symptoms), limiting their ability to represent real-world diagnostic processes. Previous methods in biomedical relation extraction have focused on concept relations, such as *gene-disease* and *disease-drug*, and largely ignored clinical processes. In this thesis, we leverage a clinical reasoning ontology and propose methods to extract such relations from a physician-facing point-of-care reference wiki and consumer health resource texts. Given the lack of data labeled with diagnostic relations, we also propose new methods of evaluating the correctness of extracted triples in the zero-shot setting. We describe a process for the intrinsic evaluation of new facts by triple confidence filtering and clinician manual review, as well as extrinsic evaluation in the form of a differential diagnosis prediction task.

1 Introduction

Knowledge graphs (KGs) are increasingly utilized in key knowledge-intensive applications, such as recommendation and question answering. However, their utility in these systems can be limited due to missing facts (triples) among entities (Balazevic et al., 2019). The missing knowledge in KGs largely comes from three main sources: missing unknown entities, missing unknown relations, and missing existing relations between known entities. Significant advances have been made in the general and biomedical domains in recent years to tackle each of these problems, using techniques from the NLP and graph communities such as entity linking (EL) (Thibault Févry, 2020), relation extraction (RE) (Trisedya et al., 2019), and link prediction (Kazemi and Poole, 2018).

In the clinical domain, SNOMED-CT[1] is the most comprehensive and broadly used knowledge base, containing over 350,000 medical concepts and 1 million relations organized into a poly-hierarchy. When mapping documentation to SNOMED-CT, Travers and Haas (2006) found high coverage of clinical concepts. However, its taxonomic structure leads to a lack of clinically meaningful relations between concept hierarchies. Therefore, in this work we focus on the problem of missing unknown relations.

Relation Name	# of Rel. (%)
isa	567356 (19.0)
mapped_to	140394 (4.7)
finding_site_of	95138 (3.2)
same_as	90158 (3.0)
possibly_equivalent_to	80502 (2.7)
associated_morphology_of	70230 (2.4)
method_of	64902 (2.2)
interprets	37094 (1.2)
direct_procedure_site_of	35592 (1.2)
pathological_process_of	21719 (0.7)

Table 1: Names and occurrences of top 10 relations in SNOMED-CT.

As shown in Table 1, SNOMED-CT largely contains hierarchical *is-a/has-a* relations and lacks important diagnostic relations between clinical concept hierarchies. For instance, since SNOMED-CT lacks a *is_contraindicated_by* relation, associations between medications and clinical findings are largely missing. Those existing inter-hierarchy relations are often trivial and would not meaningfully contribute to downstream knowledge representation (e.g. litigation of aneurysm of popliteal artery $\rightarrow$ direct_morphology_of $\rightarrow$ aneurysm). Explicit relations (e.g. comorbidities, sign/symptoms, risk factors) that draw meaningful connections between entities in different hierarchies have the potential to better model clinical reasoning and understand text describing diagnostic processes, such as progress notes and discharge summaries.

[1] https://www.nlm.nih.gov/healthit/snomedct

Proceedings of the 60th Annual Meeting of the Association for Computational Linguistics
Student Research Workshop, pages 413 - 421
May 22-27, 2022 ©2022 Association for Computational Linguistics

In this work, we define a set of missing clinically meaningful diagnostic relations based on an existing clinical reasoning ontology (CRO). We then propose two methods of adding such relations to the SNOMED-CT knowledge graph (KG) using distinct and complementary data sources. We describe a relation extraction task using a semi-structured emergency department (ED)-focused wiki and a zero-shot relation classification (RC) task using a newly gathered corpus of consumer health information derived from MedlinePlus[2] and Merck Manuals (Bullers, 2016), described in detail in section 3.2. Throughout this work, we will address the following research questions:

RQ1. Can we leverage the semi-structured form of a wiki to extract reasoning relations?

RQ2. Do consumer health resources provide distinct missing relations from those found in RQ1?

RQ3. How do we evaluate the accuracy of new relations in a clinical KG?

In RQ1 and RQ2, we limit ourselves to a predetermined set of relations to minimize hand curation by domain experts, such as would be required with free text relations extracted using an open information extraction system (Juric et al., 2020). However, we still need to determine the accuracy of our new facts to evaluate the model. This leads us to RQ3, in which we determine how to evaluate the accuracy of new relations in a clinical KG, given that such relations don't currently exist. We propose intrinsic and extrinsic methods of evaluation in this zero-shot setting.

The rest of this proposal will be structured as follows. In section 2, we will describe the existing biomedical and clinical relation extraction datasets and methods, as well as the CRO we define our relation label set on. In section 3, we describe our methodology for RQ1 and RQ2. Finally, in section 4, we discuss two strategies to address RQ3: manual evaluation by clinician review after pruning low confidence triples and prediction on a proxy clinical diagnostic reasoning task.

2 Related Work

2.1 Biomedical Relation Extraction

Considerable progress has been made in biomedical relation extraction, with large language models achieving state of the art results on a variety of tasks (Lee et al., 2020). Biomedical relation extraction datasets largely concentrate on relations between a few entity types such as chemicals and diseases (Li et al., 2016) or chemicals and proteins (Krallinger et al., 2017). A number of these tasks have been consolidated as part of a large biomedical language understanding benchmark known as BLURB (Tinn et al., 2021). The authors also pretrained a BERT model, PubMedBERT, on PubMed abstracts, achieving over 80% micro F1, averaged over three RE tasks. In the autoregressive setting, SciFive (Phan et al., 2021) further improved on these results, achieving an average of 84% micro F1, averaged over two RE datasets.

However, biomedical RE tasks do not capture clinical relationships. Due to the cost of anonymization, clinical RE datasets tend to be smaller and more limited. Many are focused on particular tasks such as adverse event and medication treatment relations. For instance, the 2010 i2b2/VA challenge (Uzuner et al., 2011) requires assigning relation types between conditions, tests, and treatments. Similarly, Henry et al. (2020) propose a RE task in which adverse events and signatures are related to medications. Outside of the pharmaceutical relation space, we only found one task with available data, involving temporal relation extraction (Sun et al., 2013).

Despite considerable progress, most clinical datasets don't effectively model real world settings in which the class of relations can be large, include both existing and missing relation types, and few training examples for a particular relation may exist. Our task of identifying and extracting new diagnostic relations falls within this category. The models developed in this project may help us better understand the real world challenges of extracting new meaningful relation types for KG construction.

2.2 Clinical Reasoning Ontologies

Clinical decision tools often need to model diagnostic axioms employed by clinicians to derive decision rules and provide users with relevant alerts and recommendations. Many of these tools use existing ontologies (Mohammed and Benlamri, 2014) or domain experts (Abidi et al., 2007) to develop a controlled set of reasoning terms. In order to standardize the vocabulary used to model the clinical reasoning process, Dissanayake et al. (2020) identified a set of preexisting ontologies through literature review. They then propose a consolidated ontology, normalizing reasoning concepts and relations. In this work, we model our reasoning relation extrac-

[2]https://medlineplus.gov

tion task as a classification task among a relevant subset of relationships Dissanayake et al. (2020) propose, including important inter-hierarchical relations such as *complication_of* and *comorbidity_of*. We describe a subset of relevant relations, along with the SNOMED-CT hierarchies they involve, in Table 2.

The full list of relations that define our label set can be found in Appendix B.

3 Research Plan

3.1 Wiki-Based Relation Extraction

In order to extract relations relevant to diagnostic reasoning, we select WikEM (Donaldson et al., 2016), a domain-specific point-of-care reference wiki under active development by ED residents at Harbor-UCLA Medical Center for clinical use during diagnostic processes. It has over 7000 pages and is based on Mediawiki[3], the same wiki engine underlying Wikipedia. Unlike Wikipedia's Wikidata project (Vrandečić and Krötzsch, 2014), smaller domain-specific wikis rarely have an accompanying structured knowledge base. Therefore, in the first part of this work we plan to automatically extract an open KG based on the existing structure within WikEM. Then, we will link these entities and relations to SNOMED-CT and the CRO, leveraging recent advances in medical EL methods. An overview of the system is shown in Figure 1.

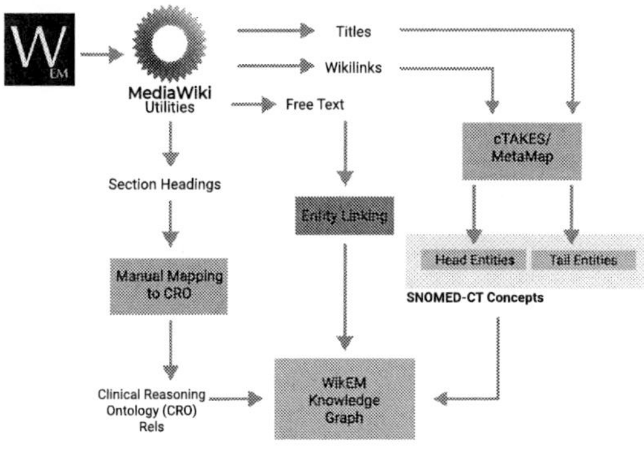

Figure 1: System overview for extraction of knowledge triples from WikEM

We first employ a wikicode parser to extract open text entities that serve as nodes. The link label will act as the head entity and the title of the link destination will become the tail entity. We also extract section titles (e.g. *Differential Diagnosis, Evaluation, Management*) that serve as open text edges. In order to use this open KG in downstream tasks and integrate new triples back into SNOMED-CT, we need to link all three components of the knowledge triple. To determine the range of relations in WikEM, we visualized meaningful extracted section titles, shown in Figure 2. The relations found in WikEM encompass a subset of our full relation set which we can manually map to the predetermined CRO labels. Exploratory testing has also shown that existing named entity recognition and linking methods like cTAKES (Savova et al., 2010) are effective in mapping named entity lists, like those that appear in WikEM sections (example in Appendix A). However, we will also test BERT-based models such as SapBERT (Liu et al., 2021). These two approaches allow us to map the head, relation, and tail entities of new reasoning fact triples.

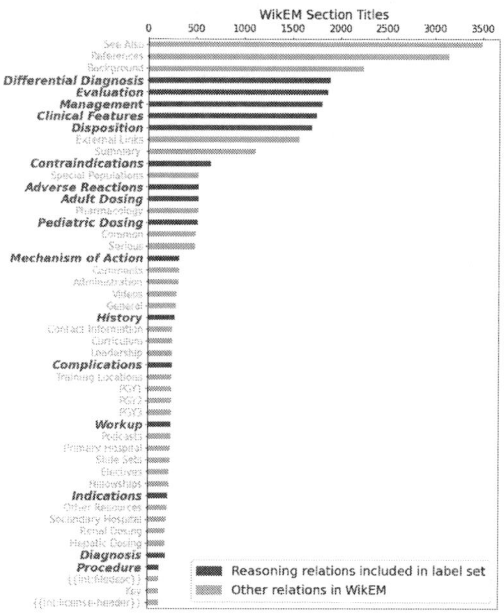

Figure 2: Most common relations extracted from WikEM section titles (relations highlighted in purple correspond to relations in our CRO label set)

3.2 Zero-Shot Relation Classification from Consumer Education Resources

While we can take advantage of the wiki structure to identify high quality triples in WikEM, relation types that aren't captured by section titles may be missed. Therefore, we also perform RC using consumer education resources. By employing these

[3]https://www.mediawiki.org/wiki/MediaWiki

SNOMED-CT Head	CRO Relation	SNOMED-CT Tail
clinical finding	cause_by	clinical finding, procedure
clinical finding	is_symptom_of	clinical finding
clinical finding	hasSyndrome	clinical finding
clinical finding	has_treatment	procedure, substance
substance	Can_be_combined_with	substance
substance	has _effect_on_disease	clinical finding
substance	may_prevent	clinical finding

Table 2: Sample of relation label set for RQ1 and RQ2, including domain of SNOMED-CT top level hierarchy concepts for head and tail entities

two data sources, we may also gain some insight into different relation frequencies common to either physician- or patient-facing resources.

Similar to (Juric et al., 2020), we plan to use MedlinePlus, a curated consumer health resource developed by the National Library of Medicine. We combine this with the consumer edition of the Merck Manuals, medical references published by Merck geared towards patient education. These two sources constitute a new consumer health corpus from which we extract new clinical reasoning triples. We develop this corpus, as opposed to using a preexisting resource such as PubMed because these texts describe primary care and contain relevant reasoning relations, like side effects and comorbidities, unlike the research articles in PubMed. Unlike in RQ1, we must extract and link both entities and relations from free text in this setting.

Similar to Riedel et al. (2010)'s distantly supervised NYT corpus, we first detect and link named entities in our corpus using an end-to-end entity linker. Namely, we will fine-tune SciFive, a new T5 model (Raffel et al.) pretrained on PubMed articles, on the newly proposed autoregressive entity retrieval task (De Cao et al., 2021). Having identified a set of entities, we can take advantage of recent zero-shot relation classification methods. Many of these models use auxiliary information, like relation descriptions (Chen and Li, 2021), to reason about unseen relations. However, they don't take advantage of semantic types. For instance, the relation *contradict_with* can only have a pharmaceutical product as its head entity and a disease as its tail entity. We propose training a BERT model to embed relations and descriptions, while restricting the search space to relevant semantic types, hopefully improving zero-shot RC results.

4 Evaluation

From RQ1 and RQ2, we have a set of new clinical reasoning triples, grounded in SNOMED-CT entities and the CRO relation set. However, without existing labeled reasoning relations, we have no way to use conventional confusion matrix-based evaluation measures. Therefore, to tackle **RQ3**, we propose two evaluation approaches.

Filtering and Evaluation By Clinicians As a first step, we plan to evaluate our zero-shot RE system on BioRel (Xing et al., 2020), a large distantly-supervised RE dataset for the biomedical domain, carefully selecting train/test splits to model the zero-shot setting. While this provides a comparison to baselines, the noisy nature of distant supervision and lack of external validation of the training data by the authors may obscure the accuracy of the model. Furthermore, this evaluation scheme doesn't measure our final goal of contributing new facts to SNOMED-CT.

To that end, we will first calibrate our extraction model and filter out any low confidence triples. This reduces potentially noisy triples and allocates clinical resources to the most promising triples. Then, we randomly sample triples from the model and have several clinicians determine the proportion of accurate predicted relations, measuring inter-rater reliability.

Evaluation Using Proxy Discharge Diagnoses Prediction Task To investigate whether extracted diagnostic reasoning relations improve downstream clinical prediction tasks, we choose a relevant auxiliary task: differential diagnosis prediction of ED patients presenting with abdominal pain. Given a patient's ED triage information and their past medical history, the goal is to rank the list of relevant differential diagnoses that a physician may assign the patient upon discharge in order of likelihood.

To accomplish this task, we augment patient representations with a clinical KG that includes relations derived in RQ1 and RQ2. Bisk et al. (2020) discuss the importance of augmenting language with other modalities in representation learning, and so we include other clinical variables (e.g. demographics, lab measurements, vitals) in our patient representations. To combine a drug-drug interaction network with an external knowledge base, Yu et al. (2021) extracted KG subgraphs and attended on relevant relations. Similarly, we compute a patient similarity graph and extract subsets of our 3 versions of SNOMED-CT with the goal of comparing predictive performance on a set of differential diagnoses for each ED patient. Using the attention maps, we also plan to investigate the importance of clinical reasoning relations in prediction, as compared to pre-existing relations in SNOMED-CT.

5 Societal Impact

Extraction of triples using the relation set described in this proposal and their alignment with an existing clinical KG has the potential to significantly improve automated diagnostic reasoning. For instance, a KG-augmented system may be able to remind the physician to order labs based on probable diagnoses or extract disease-specific, relevant past medical history from patient records in real-time. We can also expect improvement in conventional NLP tasks such as reading comprehension of progress notes and reports (e.g. radiology summaries) and clinical knowledge question answering (QA) involving multi-hop reasoning. Benchmarks to evaluate such tasks exist, like MMLU-Professional Medicine (Hendrycks et al., 2021) and MedQA (Jin et al., 2021), both of which draw QA pairs from medical licensure exams.

However, such benchmarks are abstractions that do not fully align with complex real-world use cases. To better model the challenges of clinical reasoning, we suggested the particular task of differential diagnosis prediction, which involves incorporating additional clinical data modalities. However, additional considerations may be necessary for evaluating KG use in real-world applications, such as modeling temporality. A task involving prediction of changing disease states over time may focus on the longitudinal nature of diagnostic reasoning. A portion of this work will involve continuing to define tasks that consider the challenges of real-world clinical reasoning use cases.

6 Summary

In this thesis proposal, we suggest methods to address the problem of missing reasoning relations in clinical knowledge graphs. We select a subset of relations from a clinical reasoning ontology and extract relations from two data sources: a point-of-care reference for ED physicians and a newly created consumer health resource corpus. We plan to train a T5-based EL model to link entities and develop a zero-shot RE method to extract relations. Finally, we discuss methods of evaluation in the real world context of zero-shot relation extraction using filtered expert review and a proxy diagnostic reasoning prediction task. Our work should provide a case study for the complex task of introducing new types of knowledge into an existing structured knowledge base.

Acknowledgements

We are grateful to Richard Andrew Taylor and Sarah Mullin for their helpful advice and discussion and the anonymous reviewers for their detailed feedback.

References

Samina R. Abidi, Syed S. R. Abidi, Sajjad Hussain, and Mike Shepherd. 2007. Ontology-based modeling of clinical practice guidelines: A clinical decision support system for breast cancer follow-up interventions at primary care settings. *Studies in Health Technology and Informatics*, 129:845–849.

Ivana Balazevic, Carl Allen, and Timothy Hospedales. 2019. TuckER: Tensor Factorization for Knowledge Graph Completion. In *Proceedings of the 2019 Conference on Empirical Methods in Natural Language Processing and the 9th International Joint Conference on Natural Language Processing (EMNLP-IJCNLP)*, pages 5185–5194. Association for Computational Linguistics.

Yonatan Bisk, Ari Holtzman, Jesse Thomason, Jacob Andreas, Yoshua Bengio, Joyce Chai, Mirella Lapata, Angeliki Lazaridou, Jonathan May, Aleksandr Nisnevich, Nicolas Pinto, and Joseph Turian. 2020. Experience Grounds Language.

Krystal Bullers. 2016. Merck Manuals. *Journal of the Medical Library Association : JMLA*, 104(4):369.

Chih-Yao Chen and Cheng-Te Li. 2021. ZS-BERT: Towards Zero-Shot Relation Extraction with Attribute Representation Learning. In *Proceedings of the 2021 Conference of the North American Chapter of the*

Association for Computational Linguistics: Human Language Technologies, pages 3470–3479. Association for Computational Linguistics.

Nicola De Cao, Gautier Izacard, Sebastian Riedel, and Fabio Petroni. 2021. Autoregressive Entity Retrieval.

Pavithra I Dissanayake, Tiago K Colicchio, and James J Cimino. 2020. Using clinical reasoning ontologies to make smarter clinical decision support systems: A systematic review and data synthesis. *Journal of the American Medical Informatics Association*, 27(1):159–174.

Ross I Donaldson, Daniel G Ostermayer, Rosa Banuelos, and Manpreet Singh. 2016. Development and usage of wiki-based software for point-of-care emergency medical information. *Journal of the American Medical Informatics Association*, 23(6):1174–1179.

Dan Hendrycks, Collin Burns, Steven Basart, Andy Zou, Mantas Mazeika, Dawn Song, and Jacob Steinhardt. 2021. Measuring massive multitask language understanding. *Proceedings of the International Conference on Learning Representations (ICLR)*.

Sam Henry, Kevin Buchan, Michele Filannino, Amber Stubbs, and Ozlem Uzuner. 2020. 2018 n2c2 shared task on adverse drug events and medication extraction in electronic health records. *Journal of the American Medical Informatics Association : JAMIA*, 27(1):3.

Di Jin, Eileen Pan, Nassim Oufattole, Wei-Hung Weng, Hanyi Fang, and Peter Szolovits. 2021. What disease does this patient have? a large-scale open domain question answering dataset from medical exams. *Applied Sciences*, 11(14):6421.

Damir Juric, Giorgos Stoilos, Andre Melo, Jonathan Moore, and Mohammad Khodadadi. 2020. A System for Medical Information Extraction and Verification from Unstructured Text. *Proceedings of the AAAI Conference on Artificial Intelligence*, 34(08):13314–13319.

Seyed Mehran Kazemi and David Poole. 2018. SimplE embedding for link prediction in knowledge graphs. In *Proceedings of the 32nd International Conference on Neural Information Processing Systems*, NIPS'18, pages 4289–4300. Curran Associates Inc.

Martin Krallinger, Obdulia Rabal, Saber A Akhondi, Martın Pérez Pérez, Jesús Santamaría, Gael Pérez Rodríguez, Georgios Tsatsaronis, Ander Intxaurrondo, José Antonio López, Umesh Nandal, et al. 2017. Overview of the BioCreative VI chemical-protein interaction Track. In *Proceedings of the Sixth BioCreative Challenge Evaluation Workshop*, volume 1, pages 141–146.

Jinhyuk Lee, Wonjin Yoon, Sungdong Kim, Donghyeon Kim, Sunkyu Kim, Chan Ho So, and Jaewoo Kang. 2020. BioBERT: A pre-trained biomedical language representation model for biomedical text mining. *Bioinformatics*, 36(4):1234–1240.

Jiao Li, Yueping Sun, Robin J. Johnson, Daniela Sciaky, Chih-Hsuan Wei, Robert Leaman, Allan Peter Davis, Carolyn J. Mattingly, Thomas C. Wiegers, and Zhiyong Lu. 2016. BioCreative V CDR task corpus: A resource for chemical disease relation extraction. *Database*, 2016:baw068.

Fangyu Liu, Ehsan Shareghi, Zaiqiao Meng, Marco Basaldella, and Nigel Collier. 2021. Self-alignment pretraining for biomedical entity representations. In *Proceedings of the 2021 Conference of the North American Chapter of the Association for Computational Linguistics: Human Language Technologies*, pages 4228–4238, Online. Association for Computational Linguistics.

Osama Mohammed and Rachid Benlamri. 2014. Developing a Semantic Web Model for Medical Differential Diagnosis Recommendation. *Journal of Medical Systems*, 38(10):79.

Long N. Phan, James T. Anibal, Hieu Tran, Shaurya Chanana, Erol Bahadroglu, Alec Peltekian, and Grégoire Altan-Bonnet. 2021. SciFive: A text-to-text transformer model for biomedical literature.

Colin Raffel, Noam Shazeer, Adam Roberts, Katherine Lee, Sharan Narang, Michael Matena, Yanqi Zhou, Wei Li, and Peter J. Liu. Exploring the limits of transfer learning with a unified text-to-text transformer. 21(140):1–67.

Sebastian Riedel, Limin Yao, and Andrew McCallum. 2010. Modeling Relations and Their Mentions without Labeled Text. In *Machine Learning and Knowledge Discovery in Databases*, Lecture Notes in Computer Science, pages 148–163. Springer.

Guergana K. Savova, James J. Masanz, Philip V. Ogren, Jiaping Zheng, Sunghwan Sohn, Karin C. Kipper-Schuler, and Christopher G. Chute. 2010. Mayo clinical Text Analysis and Knowledge Extraction System (cTAKES): Architecture, component evaluation and applications. *Journal of the American Medical Informatics Association : JAMIA*, 17(5):507.

Weiyi Sun, Anna Rumshisky, and Ozlem Uzuner. 2013. Evaluating temporal relations in clinical text: 2012 i2b2 Challenge. *Journal of the American Medical Informatics Association : JAMIA*, 20(5):806.

Nicholas FitzGerald Thibault Févry. 2020. Empirical Evaluation of Pretraining Strategies for Supervised Entity Linking. Automated Knowledge Base Construction (AKBC).

Robert Tinn, Hao Cheng, Yu Gu, Naoto Usuyama, Xiaodong Liu, Tristan Naumann, Jianfeng Gao, and Hoifung Poon. 2021. Fine-Tuning Large Neural Language Models for Biomedical Natural Language Processing.

Debbie A. Travers and Stephanie W. Haas. 2006. Unified Medical Language System Coverage of Emergency-medicine Chief Complaints. *Academic Emergency Medicine*, 13(12):1319–1323.

Bayu Distiawan Trisedya, Gerhard Weikum, Jianzhong Qi, and Rui Zhang. 2019. Neural Relation Extraction for Knowledge Base Enrichment. In *Proceedings of the 57th Annual Meeting of the Association for Computational Linguistics*, pages 229–240. Association for Computational Linguistics.

Özlem Uzuner, Brett R. South, Shuying Shen, and Scott L. DuVall. 2011. 2010 i2b2/VA challenge on concepts, assertions, and relations in clinical text. *Journal of the American Medical Informatics Association : JAMIA*, 18(5):552.

Denny Vrandečić and Markus Krötzsch. 2014. Wikidata: A free collaborative knowledgebase. *Communications of the ACM*, 57(10):78–85.

Rui Xing, Jie Luo, and Tengwei Song. 2020. BioRel: Towards large-scale biomedical relation extraction. *BMC Bioinformatics*, 21(16):543.

Yue Yu, Kexin Huang, Chao Zhang, Lucas M Glass, Jimeng Sun, and Cao Xiao. 2021. SumGNN: Multi-typed drug interaction prediction via efficient knowledge graph summarization. *Bioinformatics*, 37(18):2988–2995.

A WikEM Sample Page with Entities

In Figure 3, we show the head, relation, and tail entities as they appear in an example WikEM page. In this case, if another wikilink linked to *Peritonitis*, it would act as the tail entity, and the section headings (i.e. Background, Clinical Features, Differential Diagnosis) act as relations. Finally, the link texts act as open text head entities.

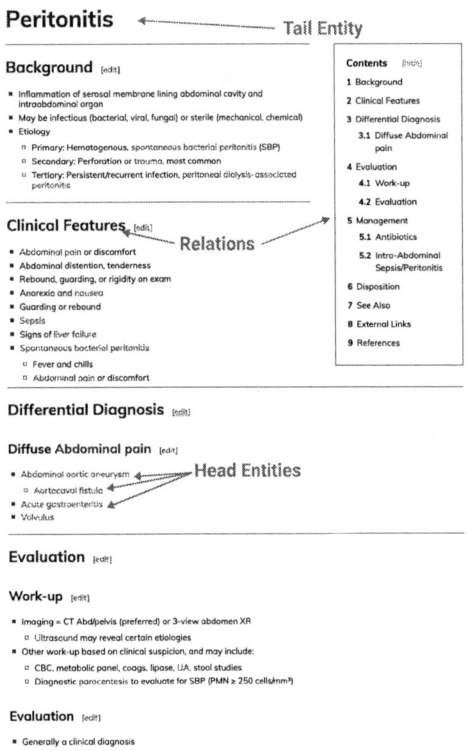

Figure 3: Example of a WikEM page with Links. Each entry in the table of contents can act as a relation.

B Full Clinical Reasoning Relation Set

In Table 3, we show the full set of labels we selected from the clinical reasoning ontology developed by (Dissanayake et al., 2020), along with the domain and semantic types that the relation accepts.

Domain	Relation Name	Range
Diagnostic process	observationMethod	observation method
	Assessment_Reason	reason
	has_device	medical device
	has_Assessment	assessment
	has_Recommendation	recommendation
Signs & Symptoms	Is_assessed_by	assessment name
	is_not_caused_by	factors
	cause_by	causing factor
	is_symptom_of	disease
Diagnosis & Disease	hasSyndrome	syndrome name
	has_severity	severity level
	has_treatment	treatment
	has_Contraindication	contraindication
	has_causing_factors	causing factor
	hasRisk	risk factor
	affected_Body_Site	body part
	hasLabTest	lab test name
	has_Sign_and_Symptom	sign and symptoms
	is_transmitted_by	vector
	has_complication	complication list
	occurs_with	disease, symptom, risk factor
	hasExperimentalData	experimental data related to disease
Treatment	has_ part	order list
	part_of	treatment plan
	has_intervention_goal	intervention goal
	has_pharmacological_plan	medication list
	hasSurgicalProcedure	surgery type
	is_recommended_for_illness	recommendation
Medication	Can_be_combined_with	medication
	Contradict_with	drug ingredient
	has_treatment_target	treatment target
	has_active_ingredient	active ingredient
	has_administrationProcess	medication administration process
	has_cost	medication cost
	has_dose	dose
	dosage_Measurement_Unit	measurement unit
	has_cumulative_dose	accumulative dose
	has_drug_Form	dosage form
	has_maximum_dose	medication dosage
	has_treatment_duration	time
	has_frequency	drug Frequency
	has _effect_on_disease	medication effect on disease
	has_application_route	medication application route
	has_explanation	explanation
	has_toxicity	toxicity
	component_interact_with	drug, ingredient
	may_prevent	disease

Table 3: Full set of clinical reasoning labels selected from the CRO

Scene-Text Aware Image and Text Retrieval with Dual-Encoder

Shumpei Miyawaki[1], **Taku Hasegawa**[2], **Kyosuke Nishida**[2], **Takuma Kato**[1], **Jun Suzuki**[1]
[1]Tohoku University, [2]NTT Human Informatics Laboratories

Abstract

We tackle the tasks of image and text retrieval using a dual-encoder model in which images and text are encoded independently. This model has attracted attention as an approach that enables efficient offline inferences by connecting both vision and language in the same semantic space. However, whether an image encoder as part of a dual-encoder model can interpret scene-text, i.e., the textual information in images, is unclear. We propose pre-training methods that encourage a joint understanding of the scene-text and surrounding visual information. The experimental results demonstrate that our methods improve the retrieval performances of the dual-encoder models.

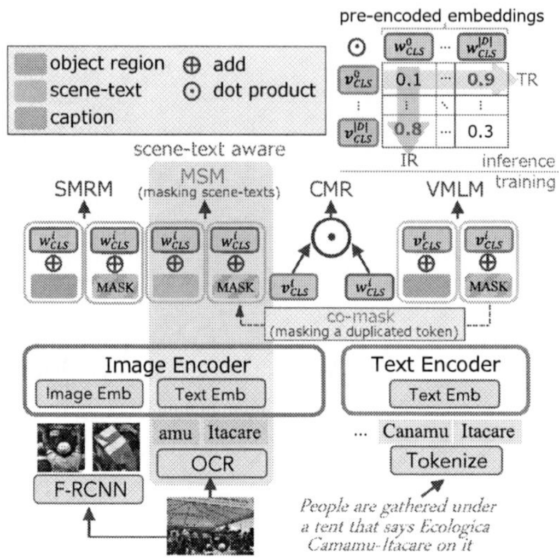

Figure 1: **Overview of the proposed architecture.** We propose pre-training methods to enable the image encoder to jointly interpret the scene-text and surrounding visual information.

1 Introduction

When pre-trained on a large-scale corpus of image and text pairs, vision and language models can obtain effective multi-modal representations that bridge the semantic gap between visual and textual information. In general, two approaches are used: 1) the cross-encoder approach, in which textual and visual information are jointly fed into a single Transformer-based model (Vaswani et al., 2017), and 2) the dual-encoder approach, in which the textual and visual information are independently fed into two modality-specific encoders. Cross-encoder models use cross-modal attention, which facilitates the interpretation of the different modalities. However, such models are not suitable for image retrieval and other tasks requiring fast and large-scale inferences (Miech et al., 2021; Luan et al., 2021). In contrast, dual-encoder models can make quick inferences, but their interpretation of concomitant modalities is insufficient; in particular, such models have difficulty jointly interpreting scene-text and the surrounding visual information.

Given the above background, this paper investigates the effectiveness of incorporating scene-text into a dual-encoder. The contributions of this study are as follows. 1) We introduce pre-training methods for a dual-encoder to facilitate a joint interpretation of the textual information in the images and surrounding visual information (Figure 1). The performance of the model is then evaluated for image and text retrieval tasks. 2) We experimentally show that, similar to cross-encoder approaches, the joint scene-text and semantic representations improve the retrieval performance of the dual-encoder.

2 Related Work

To make sense of visual and textual semantics, recent studies concerning vision and language pre-training, such as image captioning and text-aware VQA (Singh et al., 2019; Biten et al., 2019; Mishra et al., 2019; Mathew et al., 2021), incorporate concomitant textual information, such as scene-text and object tags, in terms of regions-of-interest to

Proceedings of the 60th Annual Meeting of the Association for Computational Linguistics Student Research Workshop, pages 422 - 433

enable cross-modal interactions using self-attention in a Transformer-based model (cross-encoder) (Hu et al., 2020; Li et al., 2020; Yang et al., 2021; Tanaka et al., 2021; Biten et al., 2021). However, cross-encoders are not suitable for image retrieval or other tasks requiring fast and large-scale inferences. Although cross-encoder models typically allow expressive token-wise interactions for an input pair of a query and retrieval target, the similarity score cannot be decomposed and is not indexable (Miech et al., 2021; Luan et al., 2021). Therefore, such models are impractical for application in tasks with many queries requiring quick responses, such as retrieval tasks.

In contrast, dual-encoder approaches (Sun et al., 2021; Alec et al., 2021; Jia et al., 2021; Yao et al., 2021) can successfully perform downstream tasks, enabling efficient offline inferences of all pre-encoded image and text embeddings. However, the effectiveness of incorporating concomitant modalities, such as scene-text, in dual-encoder models has not been thoroughly investigated or demonstrated in the community.

3 Scene-Text Aware Dual-Encoder

This paper proposes the incorporation of textual information in images into the dual-encoder architecture. We build our method based on the LightningDOT (Sun et al., 2021) framework, a cutting-edge dual-encoder that encodes both object-wise and token-wise representations. We first briefly introduce LightningDOT in its current use. We then describe the proposed method, including the learning objectives, to incorporate the textual information in the images into the image encoder.

3.1 LightningDOT

LightningDOT outputs a visual feature $\boldsymbol{V}$ and a textual feature $\boldsymbol{W}$[1]. To obtain a visual feature, LightningDOT first extracts multiple objects from an input image using a pre-trained object detector based on Faster R-CNN (Anderson et al., 2018). The obtained visual feature $\boldsymbol{V}$ is a list of vectors, namely, $\boldsymbol{V} = (\boldsymbol{v}_{\texttt{CLS}}, \boldsymbol{v}_1, \ldots, \boldsymbol{v}_I)$, where I is the number of extracted objects and $\boldsymbol{v}_{\texttt{CLS}}$ is the vector for a special object "CLS." Similarly, the textual feature is a list of vectors $\boldsymbol{W} = (\boldsymbol{w}_{\texttt{CLS}}, \boldsymbol{w}_1, \ldots, \boldsymbol{w}_J)$, where J is the number of tokens in a given caption and $\boldsymbol{w}_{\texttt{CLS}}$ is the vector for a special token "CLS."

[1]Appendix A provides additional details of LightningDOT.

LightningDOT attempts three pre-training objectives: (1) visual-embedding fused masked language modeling (VMLM), (2) semantic-embedding fused masked region modeling (SMRM), and (3) cross-modal retrieval (CMR). Both VMLM and SMRM predict masked tokens from their surrounding context. Let $\mathcal{M}$ represent a set of mask indices. $\boldsymbol{W}_{\setminus\mathcal{M}}$ denotes $\boldsymbol{W}$ after substituting all m-th vectors of $m \in \mathcal{M}$ in $\boldsymbol{W}$ with the special vector assigned to the `[MASK]` token. Similarly, $\boldsymbol{V}_{\setminus\mathcal{M}}$ is $\boldsymbol{V}$ after substituting the m-th indices of all $m \in \mathcal{M}$ with the `[MASK]` vector[2]. The training objectives of VMLM and SMRM are formulated as follows:

$$\mathcal{L}_\theta^{(*)}(\mathcal{M}) = \frac{1}{|\mathcal{M}|} \sum_{m \in \mathcal{M}} \mathcal{L}_\theta^{(*)}(m, \mathcal{M}). \quad (1)$$

Here, the mask index for the caption feature $\mathcal{M}_w$ lies in the range of $2, \ldots, I+1$ because an index of 1 corresponds to $\boldsymbol{w}_{\texttt{CLS}}$, which is not masked. The VMLM objective $\mathcal{L}_\theta^{(\texttt{VMLM})}(\mathcal{M}_w)$ can then be written by substituting $\mathcal{L}_\theta^{(*)}(m, \mathcal{M})$ into Eq. 1 with

$$\mathcal{L}_\theta^{(\texttt{VMLM})}(m, \mathcal{M}_w) = \ell_\theta(\boldsymbol{w}_m | \boldsymbol{W}_{\setminus\mathcal{M}_w}, \boldsymbol{v}_{\texttt{CLS}}), \quad (2)$$

where $\ell_\theta(\cdot) = -\log(P_\theta(\cdot))$. Similarly, the SMRM objective $\mathcal{L}_\theta^{(\texttt{VMLM})}(\mathcal{M}_v)$ can be obtained with

$$\mathcal{L}_\theta^{(\texttt{SMRM})}(m, \mathcal{M}_v) = \mathcal{D}_\theta(\boldsymbol{v}_m | \boldsymbol{V}_{\setminus\mathcal{M}_v}, \boldsymbol{w}_{\texttt{CLS}}) \quad (3)$$

where $\mathcal{M}_v = \{2, \ldots, J+1\}$ and D_θ is any differentiable distance function[3].

The CMR task leverages the paired semantics between the visual and textual representations. Specifically, the similarity (obtained by calculating the inner product $\text{sim}(\boldsymbol{w}_{\texttt{CLS}}, \boldsymbol{v}_{\texttt{CLS}}) = \boldsymbol{w}_{\texttt{CLS}} \cdot \boldsymbol{v}_{\texttt{CLS}}$ is optimized to promote pair matching with in-batch negative sampling. The details of CMR are omitted here because this objective is not related to the presented extensions of the proposed method.[4]

3.2 LightningDOT with scene-text

To obtain scene-text features from images, we apply an optical character recognition (OCR) system to each input image. Each token in the scene-text obtained by OCR is then converted to a d_v-dimensional token embedding ("Text Emb" in Figure 1). Let $\boldsymbol{s}_k$ be the embeddings corresponding to

[2]The `[MASK]` for the visual feature is the zero vector.

[3]The goal of the model prediction is to reconstruct the masked features themselves (masked region feature regression) or their object class (masked region classification with the Kullback–Leibler divergence)

[4]See Appendix A.2 for additional details concerning CMR.

the k-th token in the scene-text, and let K denote the number of tokens in the scene-text. We then modify and redefine the visual feature $\boldsymbol{V}$ as the concatenation of the visual features explained in Section 3.1 and the textual features $\boldsymbol{s}_k$ in the images, that is, $\boldsymbol{V} = (\boldsymbol{v}_{\texttt{CLS}}, \boldsymbol{v}_1, \ldots, \boldsymbol{v}_I, \boldsymbol{v}_{\texttt{SEP}}, \boldsymbol{s}_1, \ldots, \boldsymbol{s}_K)$, where $\boldsymbol{v}_{\texttt{SEP}}$ is a vector of separators.

3.3 Masked scene-text modeling (MSM)

This section proposes masked scene-text modeling (MSM) for training the scene-text features. We extended VMLM such that the mask prediction is applied directly to the scene-text. By masking only the textual information in the scene-text, the model can read the scene-text from the surrounding visual information. Let $\mathcal{M}_s = \{I+2, \ldots, I+K+2\}$. $\mathcal{M}_s$ is the mask for the scene-text.[5] Similar to the SMRM objective, the MSM objective $\mathcal{L}_\theta^{(\texttt{MSM})}(\mathcal{M}_s)$ can be obtained via Eq. 1 by substituting $\mathcal{L}_\theta^{(*)}(m, \mathcal{M})$ with

$$\mathcal{L}_\theta^{(\texttt{MSM})}(m, \mathcal{M}_s) = \ell_\theta(\boldsymbol{s}_m | \boldsymbol{V}_{\setminus \mathcal{M}_s}, \boldsymbol{w}_{\texttt{CLS}}). \quad (4)$$

3.4 Cross-modal VMLM (co-mask)

Inspired by Alexis and Guillaume (2019); Zhou et al. (2021), we also propose a cross-modal co-masking strategy (co-mask) that leverages the cross-modal correspondence. Following the same strategy as VMLM, we randomly replace a token from a caption and then simultaneously replace the duplicated token from the scene-text in `[MASK]` to promote cross-modal relationships. When at least one paired token exists between a caption and a scene-text and is outside the targets for masking, we randomly select one masked token and switch the masking target to the paired token. While both VMLM and MSM promote multi-modal relationships between the textual information in the images and a caption describing the scene image, the "co-mask" promotes textual semantic alignment to leverage cross-modal relationships.

4 Experiments

We designed experiments to investigate the effectiveness of incorporating the scene-text as an additional feature for visual features in image and text retrieval tasks.

4.1 Experimental setup

Dataset As the training and evaluation dataset, we selected TextCaps (Sidorov et al., 2020) because it provides "caption," "image," and "scene-text"[6] triples. TextCaps includes 22,953 images and 109,764 captions on training set, and 3,166 images and 15,830 captions on development set. Each image is described by five human-annotated captions. Textual information in an image context can be correctly extracted from the TextCaps data because 96.9% of the images and 81.3% of the captions contain scene-text.

Base model Following Sun et al. (2021), we used BERT (Devlin et al., 2019) as the text encoder and UNITER (Yen-Chun et al., 2020) as the image encoder. Note that we used UNITER as the image encoder only, not as the cross-encoder, although it can also simultaneously model text. This is because the inference speed of UNITER, as reported by Sun et al. (2021), is too slow for practical use in retrieval tasks[7]. In our setting, we employed the dual-encoder to model captions and images. However, the scene-text was concatenated with the visual features and input to the image encoder because this text is part of the visual information. The scene-text vocabulary of the image encoder was initialized with that of the text encoder.

Pre-training setting To pre-train LightningDOT with four tasks, MSM, CMR, VMLM (with co-mask), and SMRM, we randomly sampled one task for each mini-batch with $1:2:1:1$ weightings[8] for 300,000 optimization steps.[9]

Conventional models To reveal the effectiveness of the proposed method, we compared its retrieval performance with those of the SCAN (Lee et al., 2018), VSRN (Li et al., 2019), and STARNet (Mafla et al., 2021) models, which were tested by Mafla et al. (2021). All models were trained on TextCaps and evaluated on its development set. We compared STARNet as a baseline for modeling the interaction among scene text, visual objects, and captions. The difference from the proposed method

[5]The index for the scene-text starts at $I+2$ because we redefine $\boldsymbol{V} = (\boldsymbol{v}_{\texttt{CLS}}, \boldsymbol{v}_1, \ldots, \boldsymbol{v}_I, \boldsymbol{v}_{\texttt{SEP}}, \boldsymbol{s}_1, \ldots, \boldsymbol{s}_K)$.

[6]To obtaining the scene-text using OCR, Sidorov et al. (2020) employed Rosetta-en (Borisyuk et al., 2018).

[7]In an identical setting, the inference speed of LightningDOT is 639× faster than that of UNITER on the Flickr30K (Plummer et al., 2015) test set, in which the retrieval target includes 1K images

[8]SMRM was divided into MRFR and MRC-kl tasks. These weights were allocated with a ratio of $1:1$.

[9]Appendix A.3 describes the implementation details.

	IR@k			TR@k		
	k=1	k=5	k=10	k=1	k=5	k=10
VSRN	9.5	26.2	37.2	14.3	34.9	46.2
SCAN	14.1	37.6	52.1	23.2	50.5	63.5
STARNet	19.8	40.1	51.6	28.7	53.7	65.1
LightningDOT	16.6	36.0	46.2	21.3	43.6	54.5
w/ ST	38.7	60.4	68.4	50.6	73.7	81.3
w/ ST+co-mask	39.4	61.6	70.2	52.3	74.8	82.2
w/ ST+MSM	**40.5**	**63.0**	**71.1**	**52.9**	**76.4**	**83.2**

Table 1: **Results of the image (IR) and text retrieval (TR) performances with recall@k on the TextCaps development set.** We extended LightningDOT to input scene-text (w/ ST). In addition, we evaluated our proposed method with the co-mask and MSM.

modality	model	IR@k			TR@k		
		k=1	k=5	k=10	k=1	k=5	k=10
IMG+ST	w/ ST	38.7	60.4	68.4	50.6	73.7	81.3
	+co-mask	39.4	61.6	70.2	52.3	74.8	82.2
	+MSM	**40.5**	**63.0**	**71.1**	**52.9**	**76.4**	**83.2**
IMG	w/ ST	11.6	28.2	37.9	14.1	31.3	41.6
	+co-mask	**13.3**	**31.5**	**42.1**	**16.0**	**34.1**	**45.3**
	+MSM	11.7	29.1	39.3	13.8	32.0	41.6
ST	w/ ST	0.0	0.1	0.3	5.0	15.4	24.7
	+co-mask	0.0	0.2	0.4	12.9	28.8	37.9
	+MSM	**16.7**	**31.4**	**37.8**	**16.1**	**33.3**	**42.0**

Table 2: **Ablation study on selecting visual modalities.** The "modality" indicates the input for the image encoder, which is used as the retrieval target in image retrieval (IR) and as the query in text retrieval (TR).

is that STARNet is trained by using the triplet ranking loss. Moreover, the final visual representations are obtained via a dot product following a graph convolutional network (Kipf and Welling, 2017)[10] on scene-text and visual objects.

Inference The visual and textual embeddings ($\boldsymbol{v}_{\texttt{CLS}}, \boldsymbol{w}_{\texttt{CLS}}$) from the development set were independently indexed using FAISS (Johnson et al., 2021). We then conducted an exact maximum inner product search (IndexFlatIP) for each query embedding, that is, for each $\boldsymbol{w}_{\texttt{CLS}}$ in the image retrieval (IR) and each $\boldsymbol{v}_{\texttt{CLS}}$ in the text retrieval (TR). The image retrieval (IR@k) and text retrieval (TR@k) tasks were evaluated in terms of the recall at k.

4.2 Retrieval results

Table 1 shows the retrieval performances of the tested methods on the TextCaps development set. In our experimental setting, the baseline Lighting-DOT model consistently delivered an inferior performance compared with that of STARNet. After considering scene-text (w/ ST), the performances in both the IR and TR settings were significantly improved and surpassed that of STARNet. Our proposal, which incorporates the co-mask (w/ ST+co-mask) and the MSM objective (w/ ST+MSM), further improved the retrieval performance. These observations indicate that modeling the scene-text directly is effective for modeling visual information that enhances semantic affinities with captions.

4.3 Ablation study on visual modalities

To investigate whether the image encoder can interpret the joint visual information in scene-text and object regions, we evaluated the retrieval performance by excluding one of the modalities. When the object regions or the scene-text alone was input into the image encoder, the retrieval performance was significantly reduced in the TR and IR settings (see Table 2). The cross-modal masking strategy (w/ ST+co-mask) improved the modeling compared with that of the scene-text strategy (w/ ST) on both modalities but was especially effective in the object regions. MSM (w/ ST+MSM) for multi-modal optimization improved the modeling of the scene-text but had a small effect on the images. These results suggest the necessity of modeling not only joint representations of visual and textual semantics in images but also fine-grained cross-modal relationships in future work.

4.4 Benefit of duplicated tokens

Here, we define the term **duplicated token** as a token that appears both in the caption and in the scene-text. To investigate whether the retrieval model leverages cross-modal relationships, we focus on the duplicated tokens because we will obtain a higher performance if such tokens share an adequate amount of information. For example, given a query that includes "Coca-Cola," the model was able to leverage the modality of the scene-text when retrieving an image of a can or a bottle that was labeled not as "Pepsi" but as "Coca-Cola." We evaluated the retrieval performance via accuracy@k on the development set in TextCaps (Sidorov et al., 2020) versus the number of duplicated tokens. We used spaCy[11] to narrow down the content tokens [12]

[10]The output of the scene-text and visual objects are fed into the average pooling layer and gated recurrent unit (Cho et al., 2014), respectively.

[11]https://spacy.io/

[12]Their part of speech tags are in "ADJ," "ADV," "NOUN," "PROPN," and "VERB".

task (retrieval targets)		IR (image and scene-text)				TR (caption)			
# of duplicated tokens		0	1	2	3	0	1	2	3
total # of tokens for retrieval targets		2,302	512	212	94	11,785	2,484	1,004	342
w/ ST	acc@1	**51.13**	47.85	50.94	52.13	36.25	41.14	51.10	**55.56**
	acc@5	**74.28**	71.48	73.58	68.09	57.92	62.80	71.31	**82.46**
	acc@10	81.75	80.08	**82.08**	76.60	66.26	70.57	78.39	**86.55**
w/ ST+co-mask	acc@1	52.48	**52.54**	51.89	50.00	37.07	41.14	50.10	**61.70**
	acc@5	**75.33**	74.61	70.75	70.21	59.30	62.76	72.11	**84.80**
	acc@10	82.41	81.64	79.72	**85.11**	68.25	71.30	78.69	**89.47**
w/ ST+MSM	acc@1	**53.52**	52.54	50.47	50.00	38.22	41.67	52.09	**62.28**
	acc@5	**77.15**	75.20	72.64	74.47	60.76	63.93	75.50	**80.12**
	acc@10	**84.06**	81.64	79.72	78.72	69.29	71.70	81.18	**86.55**

Table 3: **Retrieval accuracy versus the number of duplicated tokens between the caption and the scene-text.**

	IR@k			TR@k		
	$k=1$	$k=5$	$k=10$	$k=1$	$k=5$	$k=10$
LightningDOT	**17.2**	**37.7**	**48.9**	22.6	45.4	55.5
(mul - en)	$+0.6$	$+1.7$	$+2.6$	$+1.3$	$+1.8$	$+1.0$
w/ ST+MSM	0.0	44.5	57.8	**35.0**	**61.3**	**71.2**
(mul - en)	-40.5	-18.5	-13.3	-17.9	-15.1	-12.0

Table 4: **Retrieval performance on the development set in a multilingual setting.** We employed multilingual BERT and show differences obtained by subtracting the recall@k of the monolingual BERT (en) from that of the multilingual BERT (mul).

because the scene-text detected by an OCR system contains a large number of false positive tokens.

From Table 3, we can see that the retrieval performance in TR is proportional to the number of duplicated tokens. This indicates that duplicated tokens are one of the factors that enhance the semantic affinity between a caption and the scene-text[13]. In the IR setting, conversely, the retrieval performance does not depend on the number of duplicated tokens when the objectives are "w/ ST" and "w/ ST+co-mask." However, when using the MSM objective, the retrieval performance in IR is degraded depending on the number of duplicated tokens. According to these results, the performance gap is the result of differences in the modality of the retrieval target (textual or visual semantics) and in the inclusion of informative tokens between the scene-text and caption.

4.5 Effectiveness of multilingual text encoder

Modeling scene-text is not so easy; we have to essentially deal with various languages since they depend on where the picture was taken and where the product was made in scene-text (Chen et al., 2021). Recently, Biten et al. (2021) pre-trained a model on a large text corpus and reported the robustness of their model with respect to the OCR errors. We also investigated the model performance with multilingual (mul) BERT (Devlin et al., 2019) as the text encoder in the baseline LightningDOT and LightningDOT with MSM settings. Note that the vocabulary size $(119,547)$ of the multilingual BERT is approximately four times as large as that of its monolingual counterpart $(28,996)$.

Compared with the monolingual encoder, the multilingual encoder increased the retrieval performance in the baseline method (LightningDOT) but degraded the performance when using the scene-text (w/ ST+MSM). In the multilingual setting, the LightningDOT baseline could model the joint representations well because the pre-training corpus size and token fertility between the multilingual and monolingual BERT were nearly the same (Rust et al., 2021). In contrast, the degradation resulting from using scene-text in the multilingual setting indicates that scene-text may still be underrepresented or that false positive tokens due to OCR errors may harm the model. A better usage of multilingual BERT in scene-text needs to be explored in future work.

5 Conclusion

We proposed a framework that incorporates the textual information in images into the dual-encoder architecture. An evaluation on the TextCaps dataset confirmed that modeling the scene-text-aware cross-modal relationships benefited the dual-encoder architecture. In future research, we will attempt a more robust exploration of scene-text modeling (Singh et al., 2021; Wang et al., 2021b,a).

[13]Note that it may be possible to make the prediction easier because captions and images in TextCaps contain scene-text.

Acknowledgments

We thank the three reviewers for their valuable comments and suggestions to improve our paper.

References

Radford Alec, Wook Kim Jong, Hallacy Chris, Ramesh Aditya, Goh Gabriel, Agarwal Sandhini, Sastry Girish, Askell Amanda, Mishkin Pamela, Clark Jack, Krueger Gretchen, and Sutskever Ilya. 2021. Learning Transferable Visual Models From Natural Language Supervision. In *Proceedings of the 38th International Conference on Machine Learning, ICML 2021, 18-24 July 2021, Virtual Event*, pages 8748–8763.

Conneau Alexis and Lample Guillaume. 2019. Cross-lingual Language Model Pretraining. In *Advances in Neural Information Processing Systems 32: Annual Conference on Neural Information Processing Systems 2019, NeurIPS 2019, December 8-14, 2019, Vancouver, BC, Canada*, pages 7057–7067.

Peter Anderson, Xiaodong He, Chris Buehler, Damien Teney, Mark Johnson, Stephen Gould, and Lei Zhang. 2018. Bottom-Up and Top-Down Attention for Image Captioning and Visual Question Answering. In *2018 IEEE Conference on Computer Vision and Pattern Recognition, CVPR 2018, Salt Lake City, UT, USA, June 18-22, 2018*, pages 6077–6086.

Ali Furkan Biten, Ron Litman, Yusheng Xie, Srikar Appalaraju, and R. Manmatha. 2021. LaTr: Layout-Aware Transformer for Scene-Text VQA. *CoRR*.

Ali Furkan Biten, Ruben Tito, Andres Mafla, Lluis Gomez, Marcal Rusinol, Ernest Valveny, C.V. Jawahar, and Dimosthenis Karatzas. 2019. Scene Text Visual Question Answering. In *2019 IEEE/CVF International Conference on Computer Vision, ICCV 2019, Seoul, Korea (South), October 27 - November 2, 2019*.

Fedor Borisyuk, Albert Gordo, and Viswanath Sivakumar. 2018. Rosetta: Large Scale System for Text Detection and Recognition in Images. In *Proceedings of the 24th ACM SIGKDD International Conference on Knowledge Discovery & Data Mining, KDD 2018, London, UK, August 19-23, 2018*, pages 71–79.

Xiaoxue Chen, Lianwen Jin, Yuanzhi Zhu, Canjie Luo, and Tianwei Wang. 2021. Text Recognition in the Wild: A Survey. *ACM Comput. Surv.*, pages 42:1–42:35.

Kyunghyun Cho, Bart van Merrienboer, Çaglar Gülçehre, Dzmitry Bahdanau, Fethi Bougares, Holger Schwenk, and Yoshua Bengio. 2014. Learning phrase representations using RNN encoder-decoder for statistical machine translation. In *Proceedings of the 2014 Conference on Empirical Methods in Natural Language Processing (EMNLP)*, pages 1724–1734.

Jacob Devlin, Ming-Wei Chang, Kenton Lee, and Kristina Toutanova. 2019. BERT: Pre-training of Deep Bidirectional Transformers for Language Understanding. In *Proceedings of the 2019 Conference of the North American Chapter of the Association for Computational Linguistics: Human Language Technologies, Volume 1 (Long and Short Papers)*.

Ronghang Hu, Amanpreet Singh, Trevor Darrell, and Marcus Rohrbach. 2020. Iterative Answer Prediction With Pointer-Augmented Multimodal Transformers for TextVQA. In *2020 IEEE/CVF Conference on Computer Vision and Pattern Recognition, CVPR 2020, Seattle, WA, USA, June 13-19, 2020*, pages 9989–9999.

Chao Jia, Yinfei Yang, Ye Xia, Yi-Ting Chen, Zarana Parekh, Hieu Pham, Quoc V. Le, Yun-Hsuan Sung, Zhen Li, and Tom Duerig. 2021. Scaling Up Visual and Vision-Language Representation Learning With Noisy Text Supervision. In *Proceedings of the 38th International Conference on Machine Learning, ICML 2021, 18-24 July 2021, Virtual Event*, pages 4904–4916.

Jeff Johnson, Matthijs Douze, and Hervé Jégou. 2021. Billion-Scale Similarity Search with GPUs. *IEEE Trans. Big Data*, pages 535–547.

Thomas N. Kipf and Max Welling. 2017. Semi-supervised classification with graph convolutional networks. In *5th International Conference on Learning Representations ICLR*.

Kuang-Huei Lee, Xi Chen, Gang Hua, Houdong Hu, and Xiaodong He. 2018. Stacked Cross Attention for Image-Text Matching. In *Computer Vision - ECCV 2018 - 15th European Conference, Munich, Germany, September 8-14, 2018, Proceedings, Part IV*, pages 212–228.

Kunpeng Li, Yulun Zhang, Kai Li, Yuanyuan Li, and Yun Fu. 2019. Visual Semantic Reasoning for Image-Text Matching. In *2019 IEEE/CVF International Conference on Computer Vision, ICCV 2019, Seoul, Korea (South), October 27 - November 2, 2019*, pages 4653–4661.

Xiujun Li, Xi Yin, Chunyuan Li, Pengchuan Zhang, Xiaowei Hu, Lei Zhang, Lijuan Wang, Houdong Hu, Li Dong, Furu Wei, Yejin Choi, and Jianfeng Gao. 2020. Oscar: Object-Semantics Aligned Pre-training for Vision-Language Tasks. In *Computer Vision - ECCV 2020 - 16th European Conference, Glasgow, UK, August 23-28, 2020, Proceedings, Part XXX*, pages 121–137.

Ilya Loshchilov and Frank Hutter. 2019. Decoupled weight decay regularization. In *7th International Conference on Learning Representations ICLR*.

Yi Luan, Jacob Eisenstein, Kristina Toutanova, and Michael Collins. 2021. Sparse, dense, and attentional representations for text retrieval. *Trans. Assoc. Comput. Linguistics*, pages 329–345.

Andres Mafla, Rafael S. Rezende, Lluis Gomez, Diane Larlus, and Dimosthenis Karatzas. 2021. StacMR: Scene-Text Aware Cross-Modal Retrieval. In *IEEE Winter Conference on Applications of Computer Vision, WACV 2021, Waikoloa, HI, USA, January 3-8, 2021*, pages 2220–2230.

Minesh Mathew, Dimosthenis Karatzas, and C. V. Jawahar. 2021. DocVQA: A Dataset for VQA on Document Images. In *IEEE Winter Conference on Applications of Computer Vision, WACV 2021, Waikoloa, HI, USA, January 3-8, 2021*, pages 2199–2208.

Antoine Miech, Jean-Baptiste Alayrac, Ivan Laptev, Josef Sivic, and Andrew Zisserman. 2021. Thinking fast and slow: Efficient text-to-visual retrieval with transformers. In *IEEE Conference on Computer Vision and Pattern Recognition CVPR*, pages 9826–9836.

Anand Mishra, Shashank Shekhar, Ajeet Kumar Singh, and Anirban Chakraborty. 2019. OCR-VQA: Visual Question Answering by Reading Text in Images. In *2019 International Conference on Document Analysis and Recognition, ICDAR 2019, Sydney, Australia, September 20-25, 2019*, pages 947–952.

Bryan A. Plummer, Liwei Wang, Chris M. Cervantes, Juan C. Caicedo, Julia Hockenmaier, and Svetlana Lazebnik. 2015. Flickr30k entities: Collecting region-to-phrase correspondences for richer image-to-sentence models. In *International Conference on Computer Vision (ICCV)*, pages 2641–2649.

Phillip Rust, Jonas Pfeiffer, Ivan Vulić, Sebastian Ruder, and Iryna Gurevych. 2021. How Good is Your Tokenizer? On the Monolingual Performance of Multilingual Language Models. In *Proceedings of the 59th Annual Meeting of the Association for Computational Linguistics and the 11th International Joint Conference on Natural Language Processing (Volume 1: Long Papers)*, pages 3118–3135.

Oleksii Sidorov, Ronghang Hu, Marcus Rohrbach, and Amanpreet Singh. 2020. TextCaps: A Dataset for Image Captioning with Reading Comprehension. In *Computer Vision - ECCV 2020 - 16th European Conference, Glasgow, UK, August 23-28, 2020, Proceedings, Part II*, pages 742–758.

Amanpreet Singh, Vivek Natarajan, Meet Shah, Yu Jiang, Xinlei Chen, Dhruv Batra, Devi Parikh, and Marcus Rohrbach. 2019. Towards VQA Models That Can Read. In *IEEE Conference on Computer Vision and Pattern Recognition, CVPR 2019, Long Beach, CA, USA, June 16-20, 2019*, pages 8317–8326.

Amanpreet Singh, Guan Pang, Mandy Toh, Jing Huang, Wojciech Galuba, and Tal Hassner. 2021. TextOCR: Towards Large-Scale End-to-End Reasoning for Arbitrary-Shaped Scene Text. In *IEEE Conference on Computer Vision and Pattern Recognition, CVPR 2021, virtual, June 19-25, 2021*, pages 8802–8812.

Siqi Sun, Yen-Chun Chen, Linjie Li, Shuohang Wang, Yuwei Fang, and Jingjing Liu. 2021. LightningDOT: Pre-training Visual-Semantic Embeddings for Real-Time Image-Text Retrieval. In *Proceedings of the 2021 Conference of the North American Chapter of the Association for Computational Linguistics: Human Language Technologies*, pages 982–997.

Ryota Tanaka, Kyosuke Nishida, and Sen Yoshida. 2021. VisualMRC: Machine Reading Comprehension on Document Images. In *Thirty-Fifth AAAI Conference on Artificial Intelligence, AAAI 2021, Thirty-Third Conference on Innovative Applications of Artificial Intelligence, IAAI 2021, The Eleventh Symposium on Educational Advances in Artificial Intelligence, EAAI 2021, Virtual Event, February 2-9, 2021*, pages 13878–13888.

Ashish Vaswani, Noam Shazeer, Niki Parmar, Jakob Uszkoreit, Llion Jones, Aidan N Gomez, Ł ukasz Kaiser, and Illia Polosukhin. 2017. Attention is All you Need. In *Advances in Neural Information Processing Systems 30: Annual Conference on Neural Information Processing Systems 2017, December 4-9, 2017, Long Beach, CA, USA*, pages 5998–6008.

Hao Wang, Xiang Bai, Mingkun Yang, Shenggao Zhu, Jing Wang, and Wenyu Liu. 2021a. Scene Text Retrieval via Joint Text Detection and Similarity Learning. In *IEEE Conference on Computer Vision and Pattern Recognition, CVPR 2021, virtual, June 19-25, 2021*, pages 4558–4567.

Jing Wang, Jinhui Tang, Mingkun Yang, Xiang Bai, and Jiebo Luo. 2021b. Improving OCR-Based Image Captioning by Incorporating Geometrical Relationship. In *IEEE Conference on Computer Vision and Pattern Recognition, CVPR 2021, virtual, June 19-25, 2021*, pages 1306–1315.

Zhengyuan Yang, Yijuan Lu, Jianfeng Wang, Xi Yin, Dinei Florencio, Lijuan Wang, Cha Zhang, Lei Zhang, and Jiebo Luo. 2021. TAP: Text-Aware Pre-Training for Text-VQA and Text-Caption. In *IEEE Conference on Computer Vision and Pattern Recognition, CVPR 2021, virtual, June 19-25, 2021*, pages 8751–8761.

Lewei Yao, Runhui Huang, Lu Hou, Guansong Lu, Minzhe Niu, Hang Xu, Xiaodan Liang, Zhenguo Li, Xin Jiang, and Chunjing Xu. 2021. FILIP: Fine-grained Interactive Language-Image Pre-Training. *CoRR*.

Chen Yen-Chun, Li Linjie, Yu Licheng, El Kholy Ahmed, Ahmed Faisal, Gan Zhe, Cheng Yu, and Liu Jingjing. 2020. UNITER: UNiversal Image-TExt Representation Learning. In *Computer Vision - ECCV 2020 - 16th European Conference, Glasgow, UK, August 23-28, 2020, Proceedings, Part XXX*, pages 104–120.

Mingyang Zhou, Luowei Zhou, Shuohang Wang, Yu Cheng, Linjie Li, Zhou Yu, and Jingjing Liu. 2021. UC2: Universal Cross-Lingual Cross-Modal Vision-and-Language Pre-Training. In *IEEE Conference on Computer Vision and Pattern Recognition, CVPR 2021, virtual, June 19-25, 2021*, pages 4155–4165.

A Detailed Explanation of LightningDOT

A.1 Input tokens for the image encoder

As mentioned in Section 3.1, LightningDOT (Sun et al., 2021) first extracts multiple object regions from an input image using a pre-trained object detector based on Faster R-CNN (Anderson et al., 2018). Let I represent the number of extracted objects. In fact, the object detector provides two features: object regions and their locational features[14]. From these features, "Image Emb" (Figure 1) regenerates the input features to the image encoder. Specifically, an object feature and its locational feature are projected into the same d_v-dimensional space using an independent fully connected layer and then their embeddings are summed and finally fed into the normalization layer. By this means, input features $\boldsymbol{O}$ for object regions can be obtained, that is, $\boldsymbol{O} = (\boldsymbol{o}_1, \ldots, \boldsymbol{o}_I)$.

The proposed method described in Section 3.2 also extracts multiple tokens of scene-text from an input image using an OCR system (Rosetta-en (Borisyuk et al., 2018)). Let K represent the number of tokenized tokens for the scene-text. In addition, we apply positional indices to each token instead of the locational features. Similar to "Image Emb," the input feature of the scene-text is obtained by "Text Emb" (Figure 1). Specifically, a scene-text token and its positional index are looked up in their d_v-dimensional embeddings and then their embeddings are summed and finally fed into the normalization layer. By this means, the input features $\boldsymbol{T}$ for the scene-text tokens can be obtained, that is, $\boldsymbol{T} = (\boldsymbol{t}_1, \ldots, \boldsymbol{t}_K)$.

We denote an image encoder as f_{θ_v}. In the baseline setting, the image encoder encodes $\boldsymbol{V} = f_{\theta_v}(\tilde{\boldsymbol{v}}_{\text{CLS}}, \boldsymbol{o}_1, \ldots, \boldsymbol{o}_I)$, where $\tilde{\boldsymbol{v}}_{\text{CLS}}$ is a special object "CLS." In our setting of a scene-text aware framework, the image encoder encodes $\boldsymbol{V} = f_{\theta_v}(\tilde{\boldsymbol{v}}_{\text{CLS}}, \boldsymbol{o}_1, \ldots, \boldsymbol{o}_I, \tilde{\boldsymbol{v}}_{\text{SEP}}, \boldsymbol{t}_1, \ldots, \boldsymbol{t}_K)$, where $\tilde{\boldsymbol{v}}_{\text{SEP}}$ is a special object "SEP."

A.2 Cross modal retrieval

Cross modal retrieval (CMR) is a task leveraging the paired semantics between the visual and textual representations. Specifically, the similarity according to the inner product $\text{sim}(\boldsymbol{w}_{\text{CLS}}, \boldsymbol{v}_{\text{CLS}}) = \boldsymbol{w}_{\text{CLS}} \cdot \boldsymbol{v}_{\text{CLS}}$ is optimized to promote a matched pair and vice versa with in-batch negative sampling[15]:

$$\mathcal{L}^{(\text{CMR})}(B) = \frac{1}{2B}\sum_{b=1}^{B} \mathcal{L}^{(\text{TR})}(b) + \mathcal{L}^{(\text{IR})}(b) \quad (5)$$

$$\mathcal{L}^{(\text{TR})}(b) = -\log\left(\frac{e^{\text{sim}(\boldsymbol{v}^b_{\text{CLS}}, \boldsymbol{w}^b_{\text{CLS}})}}{\sum_{j=1}^{B} e^{\text{sim}(\boldsymbol{v}^b_{\text{CLS}}, \boldsymbol{w}^j_{\text{CLS}})}}\right) \quad (6)$$

$$\mathcal{L}^{(\text{IR})}(b) = -\log\left(\frac{e^{\text{sim}(\boldsymbol{w}^b_{\text{CLS}}, \boldsymbol{v}^b_{\text{CLS}})}}{\sum_{i=1}^{B} e^{\text{sim}(\boldsymbol{w}^b_{\text{CLS}}, \boldsymbol{v}^i_{\text{CLS}})}}\right), \quad (7)$$

where B is the number of instances in a single (mini-)batch during the training process.

A.3 Implementation details

The model dimensions of both encoders are set to 12 Transformer layers, 768 hidden dimensions, and 12 attention heads. In our masking strategy, following Devlin et al. (2019), we decomposed 15% of the total input tokens into 80% `[MASK]`, 10% random tokens, and 10% unchanged. We used AdamW (Loshchilov and Hutter, 2019) as the optimizer for pre-training with $\beta_1 = 0.9 and \beta_2 = 0.98$ and set the learning rate to $5e-5$. We adopted a learning rate warmup strategy, where the learning rate was linearly increased during the first $10,000$ training steps, followed by a linear decay to 0. We set the L2 weight decay to 0.01. We set the batch size to 4096 per GPU with six accumulation steps.

A.4 Qualitative examples

In this section, we show several qualitative results of the top-5 image retrievals using the TextCaps development set (Sidorov et al., 2020). We compare two models, "LightningDOT" and "LightningDOT w/ST+MSM," which showed the best scores in Table 1. Figure 2 and 3 show true positive examples when employing the MSM objective with the scene-text. The results indicate that both models can retrieve similar images given the entity level information and that the model using the MSM objective retrieved appropriate images, including the scene-text of *"Voll-Damm"* (Figure 2b) and *"Sibelius Symphonies from Minnesota Orchestra"* (Figure 3b). Figure 4 shows true negative examples. In the case when it is necessary to achieve reading comprehension, our proposed method does not work well. For a more robust and fine-grained comprehension, we need to consider the geometrical relationships between multiple scene-texts (Wang

[14] Each locational feature consists of seven-dimensional vectors: normalized top, left, bottom, and right coordinates, width, height, and area.

[15] Other images and captions in the mini-batch are selected as negative instances

et al., 2021b), as well as a pre-training framework with a large-scale text corpus (Biten et al., 2021), in future work.

(a) LightningDOT (out of top-100 range)

(b) LightningDOT w/ ST+MSM (1)

Figure 2: Top-5 retrieval images from the query *"A glass bottle and glass of Voll-Damm beer."* The ground truth is indicated by the green rectangle. The number in parentheses indicates the ranking index of the retrieval result for the positive image.

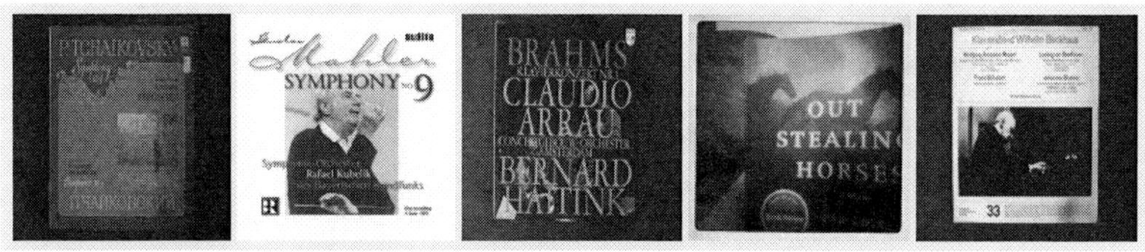

(a) LightningDOT (33)

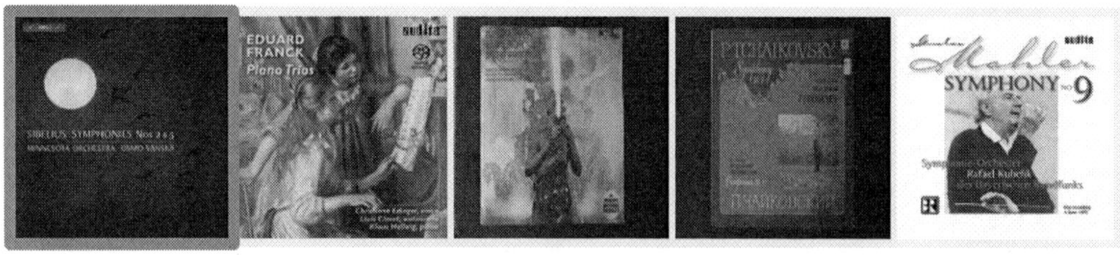

(b) LightningDOT w/ ST+MSM (1)

Figure 3: Top-5 retrieval images from the query *"The music book cover with Sibelius Symphonies from Minnesota Orchestra."* The ground truth is indicated by the green rectangle. The number in parentheses indicates the ranking index of the retrieval result for the positive image.

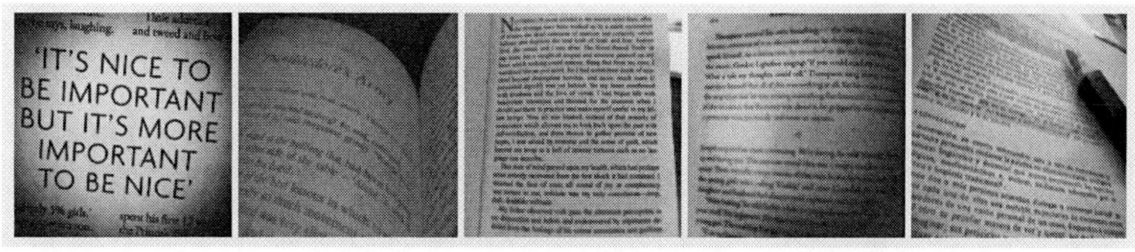

(a) LightningDOT (86)

(b) LightningDOT w/ ST+MSM (20)

Figure 4: Top-5 retrieval images from the query *"Open book on a page that says the young man dried up his tears."* The number in parentheses indicates the ranking index of the retrieval result for the positive image.

Towards Fine-grained Classification of Climate Change related Social Media Text

Roopal Vaid, Kartikey Pant and **Manish Shrivastava**
International Institute of Information Technology, Hyderabad, India
{roopal.vaid, kartikey.pant}@research.iiit.ac.in,
m.shrivastava@iiit.ac.in.

Abstract

With climate change becoming a cause of concern worldwide, it becomes essential to gauge people's reactions. This can help educate and spread awareness about it and help leaders improve decision-making. This work explores the fine-grained classification and Stance detection of climate change-related social media text. Firstly, we create two datasets, *ClimateStance* and *ClimateEng*, consisting of 3777 tweets each, posted during the 2019 United Nations Framework Convention on Climate Change and comprehensively outline the dataset collection, annotation methodology, and dataset composition. Secondly, we propose the task of Climate Change prevention stance detection based on our proposed *ClimateStance* dataset. Thirdly, we propose a fine-grained classification based on the *ClimateEng* dataset, classifying social media text into five categories: *Disaster*, *Ocean/Water*, *Agriculture/Forestry*, *Politics*, and *General*. We benchmark both the datasets for climate change prevention stance detection and fine-grained classification using state-of-the-art methods in text classification. We also create a Reddit-based dataset for both the tasks, *ClimateReddit*, consisting of 6262 pseudo-labeled comments along with 329 manually annotated comments for the label. We then perform semi-supervised experiments for both the tasks and benchmark their results using the best-performing model for the supervised experiments. Lastly, we provide insights into the *ClimateStance* and *ClimateReddit* using part-of-speech tagging and named-entity recognition.

1 Introduction

The effects of climate change are becoming increasingly apparent, with various natural disasters, including floods, droughts, storms, and fires, increasing in intensity and frequency. The biosphere is changing, endangering the natural resources and agriculture that are essential for our survival. According to the Fifth Assessment Report of the Intergovernmental Panel on Climate Change (IPCC) [1], continued climate change will have severe and irreversible impacts on people and ecosystems worldwide. According to the report, climate change is predicted, with high confidence, to lead to increased intensity and frequency of daily temperature extremes, sea-level rise, ocean acidification, and reduced crop yields. Climate change and its effects have become major causes of concern globally, leading to increased participation in public discourse. They have been the subject of various newspaper articles, scientific papers, blogs, and social media threads.

Although many steps can help control the intensity and effects of climate change, integrating these steps with public policy depends on the vox populi of climate change. There are multiple ways to study and quantify public opinion on climate change. However, traditional methods, including polling, do not take advantage of the growing prevalence and the abundance of public discourse in social media. Twitter is one of the most popular social media and serves as a vital data source for determining public opinion and perception of climate change. Globally, it has more than 200 million daily active users, with an average annual growth of around 20% in the number of active users. Linden (2017) discusses the impact social networks have on developing climate change risk perception, which suggests the importance of understanding discourses in social media for this domain.

One of the primary concerns around climate change is polarization, with social media being one of the key influencers of the same. As has been observed in previous works, climate change skepticism has achieved a higher level of visibility in media than scientific literature (Boykoff and Boykoff, 2004). Nevertheless, it may help mit-

[1] https://www.ipcc.ch/assessment-report/ar5/

Proceedings of the 60th Annual Meeting of the Association for Computational Linguistics
Student Research Workshop, pages 434 - 443
May 22-27, 2022 ©2022 Association for Computational Linguistics

igate differences and spread awareness of information related to climate change. Social media also creates an open space for organizations, climate activists, and scientists to reach more people worldwide. *UKCOP26* and *Greenpeace* are a few examples that use social media platforms to share knowledge about current climate conditions and collaborate with artists, activists, politicians, and academic institutions. Hence, the importance of social media outreach in climate change awareness campaigns is immense for effectively reaching a large global audience.

This work proposes climate change prevention stance detection and fine-grained classification of climate-change-related social media text. We release two Twitter-based English datasets [2], *ClimateStance* and *ClimateEng*, consisting of 3777 tweets, manually annotated for both the tasks. Thirdly, we benchmark state-of-the-art text classification models including *BERT*, *RoBERTa* and *DistilBERT* on both the tasks. Fourthly, we create a Reddit-based pseudo-labeled dataset ClimateReddit from the best performing model for ClimateStance and ClimateEng and benchmark its performance based on a smaller manually annotated test dataset. Finally, we perform a linguistic feature-based analysis for both the datasets based on part-of-speech tagging and named entity recognition.

2 Related Works

Early work in analyzing climate-change-related text in the social media setting is primarily focused on statistical analysis (Kirilenko and Stepchenkova, 2014; Pearce et al., 2013; Kirilenko et al., 2014; Cody et al., 2015). Kirilenko et al. (2014) collected tweets on climate change and global warming in five languages and studied the effect of geography, time, major news events that inspired central topics of discussion over climate change. Pearce et al. (2013) presented the tweet authors and topics associated with the publication of the *IPCC's AR5* on the physical science basis for climate change based on the Tweet's hashtags. Moreover, Kirilenko et al. (2014) performed the analysis on tweets during 2012-2013 to conclude that users are establishing a relationship between temperature anomalies and climate change. On the other hand, Cody et al. (2015) used Hedonometer to determine how collective sentiment differs in response to climate change-related events, news, natural disasters, oil drillings. They conclude that natural disasters and other phenomena related to climate change contributed to a decrease in overall happiness. Although the works mentioned above are immensely helpful in understanding climate change-related discourses in social media, recent advances in natural language processing enable the fine-grained detection of climate-change-related social media text. The advent of contextualized word representation for improving natural language representation for various downstream tasks, including text classification, has been particularly significant.

Recent work in the area employs the techniques of topic modeling (Dahal et al., 2019), and lexicon-based sentiment analysis (Loureiro and Alló, 2020). Dahal et al. (2019) provided an overview of high-impact areas where machine learning and AI can assist the fight against climate change and highlighted climate mitigation and adaptation, as well as meta-level tools that enable other strategies. Loureiro and Alló (2020) analyzed Twitter conversations related to climate change in UK and Spain and employed NLP tools to access the sentiment associated and various emotions evoked by these tweets. They used the lexicon developed by the National Research Center Canada (NRC), denoted as EmoLex (Mohammad and Turney, 2013). Luo et al. (2020) released the Global Warming Stance Detection Dataset, specifically focused on identifying stance on global-warming-related sentences from news articles. Sobhani et al. (2016) released a Twitter dataset for stance detection and further concluded that sentiment features assist in stance classification but are not sufficient on their own. Moreover, Maynard and Bontcheva (2015) release an open-source toolkit for enabling researchers to use Twitter to analyze and understand the engagement of the society regarding climate change.

3 Dataset

This section outlines the dataset creation process for both fine-grained classification of climate-change-related tweets and climate change prevention stance detection. First, we detail the data collection process, which entails scraping, filtering, and preparing the text for annotation. Secondly, we outline the data annotation schema for the fine-grained climate-change-related tweet classification task, along with examples of each of the five categories. We then detail the data annotation schema

[2] `https://github.com/serendipity5497/finegrained-climate-change-social-media`

Stance	Example
Favor	*"It's time for the American electorate to make #climate change a political do-or-die, up and down the ticket." #ClimateCrisis* *It's not TOO late, but it's late to start reversing climate change.*
Against	*UN not satisfied with hysteria over "Global Warming", "Climate Change". They are seeking language to scare us line "Climate Calamity" to push their fake narrative. #ClimateHoax* *You want to solve climate change, become an electrician.*
Ambiguous	*It's going to be an interesting week in the UK, with elections looming - from a climate change perspective, this is what the major parties are saying* *BBC News - General election 2019: Your questions on climate change and the environment*

Table 1: Examples of Climate Change Prevention Stance Detection Task

for the climate change prevention stance detection task. Finally, we calculate the inter-annotator agreement to evaluate the efficacy of the annotation process.

3.1 Data Collection

3.1.1 Twitter Data Collection

Using the Twitter Application Programming Interface (API) [3], we collected a sample of tweets between 1st December 2019 and 14th December 2019 as the UN Climate Change Conference COP 25 was held from 2 – 13 December 2019. To accommodate different time zones, we start collecting data one day before the conference and collect it until one day after the conference. In total, we collected 378772 tweets along with their metadata. In order to extract climate-change-related tweets from this dataset, we constructed a list of keywords relevant to the concerns regarding climate change - *Climate Change*, *Global Warming*, *Warming Planet*. Apart from these keywords, we also collect tweets containing the following hashtags *#climatechange*, *#climateaction*, *#globalwarming*,*#fossilfree*, *#climatehoax*, *#climatetaxfraud*. After removing non-English tweets, we were left with 263041 tweets. We used Twitter ID deduplication to remove overlapping redundant tweets from multiple hashtags or keywords. Further, we deduplicate tweets based on tweet text to remove duplicates leaving us with 243781 tweets. Lastly, for performing the human annotation process, we sampled 3777 tweets.

[3] `https://developer.twitter.com/en/docs/twitter-api`

3.1.2 Reddit Data Collection

We use Pushshift (Baumgartner et al., 2020) for extracting Reddit comments related to climate change. For this purpose, we use four subreddits that engage in climate change discourse, namely: r/climate, r/Climateskeptics, r/ClimateActionPlan, r/climatechange. Through this method, we extracted 6591 comments in total. We then preprocess these comments to remove hyperlinks and markdown symbols representing stylized text (i.e., bold and italic). Finally, we split the dataset into two parts: 6262 comments for creating the pseudo-labeled dataset and 329 comments for manual annotation for benchmarking the pseudo-labeled dataset.

3.2 ClimateStance: Climate Change Prevention Stance Detection

We use the term stance as a broad concept covering sentiment, evaluation, appraisal, or attitude and its associated information that is stance target and further use this to evaluate the stance. Similar to Sobhani et al. (2016) we use favor, against and ambiguous labels. We categorize each tweet into one of the three categories in terms of its stance towards climate change prevention:

- **Favor**: Expressions of opinion, action, concern against the climate change phenomenon.
- **Against**: Expressions of distance, ignorance towards signs of climate change, extreme climates, and the opposition of climate change policies or actions taken by the governing bodies.

Class	Examples
Disaster	Take a swim in the charcoal, kids - Sydney beach today (Malabar) #NSWfires #ClimateChange #AustraliaFires Too late to act on fires after they start - need to stop them by acting on climate change #qana
Ocean/Water	IUCN report: Oceans losing oxygen at rapid rate due to #CLIMATE change, #POLLUTION Good news, when climate change melts all of Greenland's ice and deflects the gulf stream away from Europe, you'll get all the snow you could ever ask for!
Agriculture/Forestry	Our most important mountains are under threat—thanks to climate change Extensive livestock farming in rainfed pastures and grazing land could mitigate climate change while being more humane and just.
Politics	It's astonishing that battling climate change is politicized, mainly because it hurts republicans right in their pockets. Vote and vote for someone sees the importance of mitigating climate change by any necessary means
General	Everything is due to climate change? This sounds like a propaganda Am committed and will expect all of the below and more - including tackling homelessness and climate change issues with determination

Table 2: Examples of Fine-grained Classification Task

- **Ambiguous**: Do not express any clear stance towards climate change. Tweets with sarcastic tones were also marked as ambiguous.

3.3 ClimateEng: Fine-grained Classification

The collected data was then manually annotated on the following categories: Disaster, Ocean/Water, Agriculture/forestry, Politics, General.

3.3.1 Disaster

This category contains tweets related to various climate-change-influenced natural disasters, including wildfires, floods, hurricanes, and droughts. These references entail:

- References containing opinions about specific instances of natural disasters.
- Information regarding specific instances of natural disasters.

3.3.2 Ocean/Water

This category contains tweets that are:

- References to the effects of climate change on biodiversity on ocean, seas, and other water bodies.
- References to water-based activities that accelerate climate change.
- References to how biodiversity on land adapts to the effects of climate change.

3.3.3 Agriculture/forestry

This category contains tweets that are:

- References to the effects of climate change on biodiversity on land, crop yields.
- References to activities including deforestation and fossil fuel burning accelerating climate change.
- References to how biodiversity on land is adapting itself to the effects of climate change.

3.3.4 Politics

This category contains tweets that are related to:

- Quotes of different world leaders on the topic of climate change.
- References about actions taken by institutions like UN to spread awareness about the increasing concerns about climate change.
- References to policies being put in place like Newgreendeal, COP25.

3.3.5 General

This category contains tweets that are:

- References of people discussing and spreading awareness about climate change without a specific focus like ocean, water.
- References of climate change affecting suburban lives.

3.4 Semi-supervised Experiments

We also create *ClimateReddit* dataset to perform experiments with semi-supervised learning for the task of stance detection and Fine-grained Classification for a Reddit-based dataset. Semi-supervised learning is often used for utilizing a large amount of unlabeled data to improve the predictive performance of models across various machine learning tasks (Blum and Mitchell, 2000; Chapelle et al., 2006). For our semi-supervised experiments, we use the method of pseudo-labeling. In this method, we first train a "teacher" model based on our Twitter-based annotated datasets, namely, *ClimateEng* and *ClimateStance*. We then use this model to predict the labels for the un-annotated Reddit dataset and create a pseudo-labeled dataset from the predictions. We denote this pseudo-labeled dataset of Reddit comments along with its predicted stance and fine-grained climate-based classification labels as *ClimateReddit*.

3.5 Inter-annotator Agreement

Two human annotators with a linguistic background and proficiency in English conducted the annotation of the dataset to classify the tweets according to the schemas mentioned above. We selected a sample annotation set consisting of 100 tweets per class from all across the dataset. Throughout the annotation process, these sample annotation sets served as the reference baseline of each category.

We also analyze the disagreements between the two annotators on both the fine-grained classification task and the stance detection task. The use of sarcasm in the tweets led to disagreements in many such cases, particularly in the case of stance detection. To accurately capture the stance for those cases, we marked them to be ambiguous. Moreover, the implicit bias of the annotators towards specific entities also led to disagreements between the annotators. We tried our best to select the more objective answer from those labels for creating our corpus.

We calculated the Inter-Annotator Agreement (IAA) to validate the annotation quality. For both annotation tasks, we compute the IAA between the two annotation sets of 3777 tweets using Cohen's Kappa coefficient (Fleiss and Cohen, 1973). We obtained the Cohen Kappa scores of 0.817 and 0.739 for the *ClimateStance* and the *ClimateEng* respectively. Moreover, we also calculate the Cohen Kappa score to be 0.850 for the fine-grained classification task and 0.864 for the stance detection task between the two annotation sets for the manually annotated test split of the *ClimateReddit* dataset. These denote that the quality of the annotations and the presented datasets are significantly productive.

4 Methodology

This section briefly describes the various state-of-the-art models that we used for our benchmarking experiments.

4.1 FastText

FastText (Joulin et al., 2017) is an open-source library for efficient learning of word representations and sentence classification. It allows training both supervised and unsupervised word and sentence representations, also supporting training using both continuous bag-of-words and skip-gram techniques. Since *FastText* uses character n-grams while generating embeddings, it can create representations for words that do not appear in the training corpus. Moreover, *FastText* is capable of achieving good predictive performance efficiently without a pre-trained corpus.

4.2 BERT

BERT released by Devlin et al. (2019) is a bidirectionally trained language model. It exploits a novel technique called Masked LM (MLM) Masking processing text in both directions and using the full context of the sentence, i.e., words to both left and right of the masked word, to predict the masked word. It relies on the Transformer model, which works by performing a small, constant number of steps applied to understand relationships between all words in a sentence, regardless of their respective position, using an attention mechanism. In terms of the type of training data used, it can be classified into cased and uncased variants, based on the letter casing of the training data. We use the Base cased and Large cased variants for our benchmarking experiments.

4.3 RoBERTa

RoBERTa (Liu et al., 2019) is *BERT*-based contextualized word embedding that uses modified key hyperparameters, simpler pre-training objectives, and a different size of training data. Unlike *BERT*, *RoBERTa* does not use the next sentence prediction training objective while using dynamic masking for changing the masked token during training epochs. It uses a larger batch-training size and ten times the training data when compared to *BERT*. These improvements enable *RoBERTa* to obtain significant gains in the predictive performance in various downstream tasks, including *GLUE* (Wang et al., 2018) for text classification. Similar to *BERT*, it also comes in two variants in terms of transformer architecture: Base and Large. Unlike *BERT*, it only comes in the cased variant in terms of the type of training data used. We benchmark both Base and large variants of *RoBERTa*.

4.4 DistilBERT

DistilBERT (Sanh et al., 2019) is a distilled version of *BERT* that uses 40% fewer parameters and is 60% faster while retaining the majority of its predictive performance. It does not use token-type embeddings while removing the pooler in its architecture, reducing the number of layers compared to *BERT* by half. *DistilBERT* uses a composite loss combining distillation, cosine-distance, and language modeling losses to leverage the inductive biases learned by undistilled models during pre-training. In terms of the type of training data used, it can be classified into two variants:- *cased* and *uncased*. We use the cased version of *DistilBERT* for our benchmarking experiments.

5 Experiments

5.1 Experimental Settings

5.1.1 Supervised Experimental Setting

We evaluate our models on a held-out test dataset for all experiments that consist of 10% of the total dataset. For validation purposes, we split the training dataset was further divided in 8 : 1 training:validation split. We use *F1*, *Precision*, *Recall*, and *Accuracy* for evaluating the models. We use the macro variant of the *F1*, *Precision*, and *Recall* which treats all classes equally by taking an unweighted arithmetic mean of all per-class scores.

We use *FastText*'s recently open-sourced automatic hyperparameter optimization functionality and run 100 trials of optimization. For *BERT*, *RoBERTa* and *DistilBERT*, we fine-tune with a learning rate of $1 * 10 - 5$, batch size of 12, and a maximum sequence length of 128 tokens. We validate the models for up to five epochs using the validation dataset and report the best-performing model in our results.

5.1.2 Semi-Supervised Experimental Setting

For generating pseudo-labels and performing the benchmarking experiments, we use the best-performing model in terms of *F1* score for both tasks of stance detection and fine-grained classification. We use the same methodology for training the models as explained in Subsection 5.1.1.

We use all splits of the Twitter-based datasets, namely *ClimateStance* and *ClimateEng*, for their respective tasks, for training the generating the pseudo-labels from the Reddit dataset. For validation, we re-split the dataset into a 9 : 1 split. Now, upon pseudo-labeling, we use the aggregated dataset consisting of both Twitter and Reddit text and re-split the dataset again into a 9 : 1 split for validation. For all our evaluation experiments, we use the same manually annotated dataset split of *ClimateReddit* as the test dataset.

5.2 Experimental Results

5.2.1 Supervised Experiments

From Table 3 which illustrates the results of the climate change prevention stance detection experiment, we observe *RoBERTa-Base* outperform all models in *F1* with a score of 0.510. In contrast, *RoBERTa-Large* outperforms all models in *Accuracy* and *Recall* with *Accuracy* 82.54% and 0.507 *recall* score. *BERT-LARGE* achieved the best *precision* score of 0.530.

Model / Metric	F1	Accuracy	Precision	Recall
FastText	0.343	79.63%	0.503	0.354
BERT-Base	0.464	77.51%	0.507	0.446
BERT-Large	0.489	77.78%	**0.530**	0.470
RoBERTa-Base	**0.510**	81.22%	0.528	0.502
RoBERTa-Large	0.489	**82.54%**	0.473	**0.507**
DistilBERT	0.448	79.37%	0.497	0.430

Table 3: Results for the Stance Detection using *ClimateStance* dataset

Table 4 illustrates the results of the fine-grained-classification experiment. For this task, we observe *RoBERTa-Large* to outperform all models in *F1*, *Accuracy*, and *Precision*, obtaining an *F1* score of 0.735, *accuracy* of 83.07%, and *Precision* of 0.738

in the experiments. At the same time, *RoBERTa-Base* was able to achieve a better *Recall* score of 0.756.

Model / Metric	F1	Accuracy	Precision	Recall
FastText	0.638	73.55%	0.730	0.594
BERT-Base	0.696	78.84%	0.697	0.701
BERT-Large	0.695	78.31%	0.730	0.689
RoBERTa-Base	0.734	80.16%	0.725	**0.756**
RoBERTa-Large	**0.735**	**83.07%**	**0.738**	0.742
DistilBERT	0.694	77.51%	0.695	0.713

Table 4: Results for the Fine-grained Classification using *ClimateEng* dataset

Apart from these, *DistilBERT* and *FastText* also perform competitively while being trained significantly faster than the others. *DistilBERT* obtains an *F1* score of 0.448 in the Climate Change Prevention Stance Detection task and an *F1* of 0.694 in the fine-grained classification task. In contrast, *FastText* obtains an *F1* score of 0.343 in the Climate Change Prevention Stance Detection and an *F1* of 0.638 in the fine-grained classification task.

5.2.2 Semi-Supervised Experiments

For this experiment, we use the best performing models in terms of *F1* score for the Climate Change Prevention Stance Detection task using *ClimateStance* (*RoBERTa-Base*) and Fine-grained Classification task using *ClimateEng* dataset (*RoBERTa-Large*).

Training Data	F1	Accuracy	Precision	Recall
ClimateEng	0.775	88.15%	0.800	0.769
ClimateEng + Pseudo-labelled Reddit Data	0.834	90.27%	0.850	0.823

Table 5: Results for the Semi-Supervised Fine-grained Classification Task

From Table 5, for the task of fine-grained classification, we find that *RoBERTa-Large* trained with all splits of *ClimateEng* performs significantly well in the fine-grained classification task for ClimateReddit dataset, obtaining an F1 of 0.775 and an accuracy of 88.15%. Moreover, using the pseudo-labeled Reddit dataset for training along with *ClimateEng*, we find an even higher F1 of 0.834 and an accuracy of 90.27%.

Training Data	F1	Accuracy	Precision	Recall
ClimateStance	0.343	60.79%	0.403	0.387
ClimateStance + Pseudo-labelled Reddit Data	0.311	60.49%	0.396	0.369

Table 6: Results for the Semi-Supervised Stance Detection Task

In contrast, as illustrated in Table 6, the predictive performance of *RoBERTa-Base* reduces sharply for the task of Stance detection in the semi-supervised setting. It obtains an F1 score of 0.343 and an accuracy of 60.7% when only trained with the *ClimateStance* dataset. Upon adding the additional Reddit-based pseudo-labeled corpus for the Stance detection, we find the model's performance to dip even further, reaching an F1 score of 0.311 and an accuracy of 60.49%. This drop can be attributed to the significant imbalance in class distribution as highlighted in Subsection 6.1.

6 Discussion

6.1 Dataset Composition

In the annotated *ClimateStance* dataset, we observe the primary stance to be in *favor* with a count of 2990 (79.16%), i.e., in conclusion, most discussions showed concern and proposed actions to mitigate climate change. Further, we observed the *ambiguous stance* state with no clear stance on climate change 414 (10.96%) times. In contrast, the tweets against and with confusion towards climate change, i.e., those having a *against stance* state, occurred 373 (9.87%) times.

In the annotated *ClimateEng* dataset, we found the popularity of *General* tweets with a count of 2159 (57.16%) followed by *Politics* class with a count of 1045 (27.67%), which sheds light on how different governing bodies are acting against climate change and citizens' expectations from the governing parties for climate change mitigation. We observed *Ocean/Water* class has a count of 204 (5.40%) as we see the signs of climate change, including rising shorelines and melting glaciers. The *Agriculture/Forestry* class consisted of 197 (5.21%) tweets due to the rising effects of climate change on agricultural practices and biodiversity. We also observed that disastrous events around the globe did follow an increase in discussions regarding climate change and global warming; in the dataset, we were able to capture 172 (4.55%) tweets that could be classified as *Disaster*.

Class	Part-of-Speech						Named Entities				
	PROPN	VERB	NOUN	ADJ	PRON	ADV	PERSON	GPE	MONEY	ORG	DATE
Favor	4.22	3.69	7.76	2.00	1.39	1.15	0.29	0.29	0.39	0.99	0.26
Against	3.22	3.71	7.18	2.26	1.76	1.41	0.30	0.17	0.20	0.71	0.24
Ambiguous	3.55	3.01	6.47	1.81	1.47	1.16	0.31	0.20	0.35	0.82	0.24

Table 7: Mean Value of Part-of-Speech tags and Named Entities in the *ClimateStance* dataset per Class.

Class	Part-of-Speech						Named Entities				
	PROPN	VERB	NOUN	ADJ	PRON	ADV	PERSON	GPE	MONEY	ORG	DATE
General	3.58	3.33	7.08	1.92	1.47	1.13	0.28	0.16	0.35	0.85	0.23
Politics	4.75	4.26	8.14	2.21	1.68	1.34	0.38	0.41	0.39	1.12	0.28
Ocean/ Water	4.94	3.17	7.96	1.78	0.82	0.86	0.22	0.40	0.37	0.97	0.32
Agriculture/ Forestry	4.10	3.51	8.73	1.92	0.72	0.95	0.16	0.22	0.47	0.95	0.19
Disaster	4.46	3.81	8.24	2.23	1.09	1.34	0.27	0.61	0.42	0.95	0.35

Table 8: Mean Value of Part-of-Speech tags and Named Entities in the *ClimateEng* dataset per Class.

In the *ClimateReddit* dataset consisting of 6591 Reddit comments, we observe the primary stance to be in favor with a count of 6269 (95.11%). Further, we observed the *against* stance 251 (3.80%) times and those having a *ambiguous* stance, occurred 71 (1.08%) times. Moreover, upon observing in terms of the fine-grained labels, we found 4699 (71.29%) comments to lie in the *General* category. The next most frequent category was *Politics*, having 1197 (18.16%) comments. The next three categories of comments had a fairly equivalent number of occurrences having 243 (3.69%), 227 (3.44%), and 225 (3.41%) comments for *Ocean/Water*, *Agriculture/Forestry*, and *Disaster* respectively.

6.2 Linguistic Feature Analysis

We compare our annotated features with various linguistics features including part-of-speech (POS) and named entities (NE) on *ClimateStance* and *ClimateEng* datasets. To perform this analysis, we exploit SpaCy [4], an open-source library for advanced natural language processing. We use the *en_core_web_sm* for extracting the part-of-the-speech tagging and performing named-entity recognition from all 3777 tweets.

Table 7 illustrates the results for the part-of-speech tagging and named entity recognition for the *ClimateStance* dataset. We observe that tweets in *favor* stance use proper nouns and nouns the most when compared to other classes. In contrast, tweets with stance *against* displayed a higher use of adjectives, pronouns, and adverbs. While observing NEs, we found the highest occurrence of GPE, MONEY, and ORG tagged NEs in tweets with in *favor* stance. The arguments to support this observation could be stated as in favor stance towards climate change would lead to concern and demand action against climate change. Organizations (ORG) and geopolitical entities (GPE) would be required to make significant changes to bring a systematic change that could slow down climate change. Moreover, the economy needs to adapt to the changing climate, which might be the reason for using entities with the MONEY tag in tweets having stance in *favor* of climate change.

Table 8 illustrates the results for the part-of-speech tagging and named entity recognition for the *ClimateEng* dataset. Tweets classified as *Disaster* had the majority of GPE NEs as well as DATE NEs. We believe this could be due to the localization of disastrous events and tweets holding the political body of the geography for action for mitigation and relief work. Tweets classified as *General* observed the least mention of MONEY NEs. In contrast, we see a higher count of the MONEY NEs in *Agriculture* and *Disaster* classes, which might be due to the cost associated with agricultural industries and disaster mitigation and relief organizations to adapt to the climate change effects witnessed during a disaster. We also observe the most leading mention of ORG NEs in *Politics* class. This observation could be due to references of actions needed to be adopted or are adopted by different organizations to mitigate climate change.

This analysis of linguistic features can be fur-

[4]https://spacy.io/

ther extended to entail a study on the correlation of these features alongside fine-grained labels and stance labels created in *ClimateStance* and *ClimateEng* dataset. The study may lead to interesting sociolinguistic findings while helping out in general understanding of how we use language in a social setting while writing climate-related short-form text. Moreover, this study may also help with information retrieval (Li et al., 2022) based on the named entities alongside our created labels.

7 Conclusion

In this work, we proposed the task of predicting Stance in social media texts related to climate change. We further proposed the task of categorizing these texts into five categories. We benchmarked the datasets using state-of-the-art contextualized word embeddings and provided baselines for both the proposed tasks. We observed that *RoBERTa-Large* outperforms all other models in three of the four evaluation metrics for the fine-grained classification task, obtaining an *F1* of 0.735. Moreover, we also observed that *RoBERTa-Base* obtained the best *F1* score in the Stance detection task with a 0.510 *F1* score. We further extend this work to the semi-supervised setting and use pseudo-labeling to predict for the Stance detection and fine-grained classification tasks in a Reddit-based dataset. This work can be further expanded to analyze people's reactions to climate change in multi-modal and multilingual settings to get a broader understanding.

Ethical Considerations

This paper uses data obtained from the Twitter Developer API [5] and freely available social media data from the Reddit platform using the Pushshift API (Baumgartner et al., 2020). Moreover, we only provide the Tweet ID in the annotated datasets along with a data preparation script in accordance with the Twitter Terms of Service. We also compensated the human annotators with a stipend more than the minimum wage in India.

Acknowledgements

We would like to thank the annotators Kumar Abhishek and Shreya Chandorkar for their immensely useful contribution to this work. We would like to thank the anonymous reviewers for providing critical suggestions.

[5] https://developer.twitter.com/en/docs/twitter-api

References

Jason Baumgartner, Savvas Zannettou, Brian Keegan, Megan Squire, and Jeremy Blackburn. 2020. The pushshift reddit dataset. In *ICWSM*.

Avrim Blum and Tom Mitchell. 2000. Combining labeled and unlabeled data with co-training. *Proceedings of the Annual ACM Conference on Computational Learning Theory*.

M. Boykoff and Jules Boykoff. 2004. Balance as bias: global warming and the us prestige press. *Global Environmental Change-human and Policy Dimensions*, 14:125–136.

Olivier Chapelle, Bernhard Schölkopf, and Alexander Zien, editors. 2006. *Semi-Supervised Learning*. The MIT Press.

Emily M. Cody, A. J. Reagan, Lewis Mitchell, P. Dodds, and C. Danforth. 2015. Climate change sentiment on twitter: An unsolicited public opinion poll. *PLoS ONE*, 10.

Biraj Dahal, S. Kumar, and Zhenlong Li. 2019. Topic modeling and sentiment analysis of global climate change tweets. *Social Network Analysis and Mining*, 9:1–20.

J. Devlin, Ming-Wei Chang, Kenton Lee, and Kristina Toutanova. 2019. Bert: Pre-training of deep bidirectional transformers for language understanding. In *NAACL*.

J. Fleiss and Jacob Cohen. 1973. The equivalence of weighted kappa and the intraclass correlation coefficient as measures of reliability. *Educational and Psychological Measurement*, 33:613 – 619.

Armand Joulin, Edouard Grave, Piotr Bojanowski, and Tomas Mikolov. 2017. Bag of tricks for efficient text classification. In *EACL*.

A. Kirilenko, T. Molodtsova, and S. Stepchenkova. 2014. People as sensors: Mass media and local temperature influence climate change discussion on twitter. *Global Environmental Change-human and Policy Dimensions*, 30:92–100.

Andrei P. Kirilenko and Svetlana O. Stepchenkova. 2014. Public microblogging on climate change: One year of twitter worldwide. *Global Environmental Change*.

Jing Li, Aixin Sun, Jianglei Han, and Chenliang Li. 2022. A survey on deep learning for named entity recognition. *IEEE Transactions on Knowledge and Data Engineering*, 34(1):50–70.

S. Linden. 2017. Determinants and measurement of climate change risk perception, worry, and concern. *Social Science Research Network*.

Yinhan Liu, Myle Ott, Naman Goyal, Jingfei Du, Mandar Joshi, Danqi Chen, Omer Levy, M. Lewis, Luke Zettlemoyer, and Veselin Stoyanov. 2019. Roberta: A robustly optimized bert pretraining approach. *ArXiv*, abs/1907.11692.

M. Loureiro and M. Alló. 2020. Sensing climate change and energy issues: Sentiment and emotion analysis with social media in the u.k. and spain. *Energy Policy*, 143:111490.

Yiwei Luo, D. Card, and Dan Jurafsky. 2020. Desmog: Detecting stance in media on global warming. *ArXiv*, abs/2010.15149.

D. Maynard and Kalina Bontcheva. 2015. Understanding climate change tweets: an open source toolkit for social media analysis. In *EnviroInfo/ICT4S*.

Saif M. Mohammad and Peter D. Turney. 2013. Crowdsourcing a word–emotion association lexicon. *Computational Intelligence*, 29.

W. Pearce, K. Holmberg, I. Hellsten, and B. Nerlich. 2013. Climate change on twitter: topics, communities and conversations about the 2013 ipcc report.

Victor Sanh, Lysandre Debut, Julien Chaumond, and Thomas Wolf. 2019. Distilbert, a distilled version of bert: smaller, faster, cheaper and lighter. *ArXiv*, abs/1910.01108.

Parinaz Sobhani, Saif M. Mohammad, and Svetlana Kiritchenko. 2016. Detecting stance in tweets and analyzing its interaction with sentiment. In *SEMEVAL.*

Alex Wang, Amanpreet Singh, Julian Michael, Felix Hill, Omer Levy, and Samuel R. Bowman. 2018. Glue: A multi-task benchmark and analysis platform for natural language understanding. *ArXiv*, abs/1804.07461.

Deep Neural Representations for Multiword Expressions Detection

Kamil Kanclerz and **Maciej Piasecki**
Department of Artificial Intelligence,
Wrocław University of Science and Technology, Wrocław, Poland
{kamil.kanclerz,maciej.piasecki}@pwr.edu.pl

Abstract

Effective methods for multiword expressions detection are important for many technologies related to Natural Language Processing. Most contemporary methods are based on the sequence labeling scheme applied to an annotated corpus, while traditional methods use statistical measures. In our approach, we want to integrate the concepts of those two approaches. We present a novel weakly supervised multiword expressions extraction method which focuses on their behaviour in various contexts. Our method uses a lexicon of English multiword lexical units acquired from The Oxford Dictionary of English as a reference knowledge base and leverages neural language modelling with deep learning architectures. In our approach, we do not need a corpus annotated specifically for the task. The only required components are: a lexicon of multiword units, a large corpus, and a general contextual embeddings model. We propose a method for building a silver dataset by spotting multiword expression occurrences and acquiring statistical collocations as negative samples. Sample representation has been inspired by representations used in Natural Language Inference and relation recognition. Very good results (F1=0.8) were obtained with CNN network applied to individual occurrences followed by weighted voting used to combine results from the whole corpus. The proposed method can be quite easily applied to other languages.

1 Introduction

Multiword expressions (henceforth MWEs) have been studied for decades, defined in different ways in literature with different denotations of this term, e.g. see the overview in (Ramisch, 2015). Probably, the most genuine, but the least operational, definition is multiword lexemes stored as single lexical units in the mental lexicon ready to be retrieved. In the spirit of this fundamental property, we consider MWEs from the lexicographic point of view as lexical units that "has to be listed in a lexicon" (Evert, 2004) and we seek for methods of automated extraction of MWEs from text corpora to expand a large semantic lexicon with *multi-word lexical units*. Summarising a longer definition given in (Ramisch, 2015), MWEs are "lexical items decomposable into multiple lexemes", "present idiomatic behaviour at some level of linguistic analysis" and "must be treated as a unit" and, thus, should be described in a semantic lexicon, e.g. from (Stevenson, 2010) *air corridor* (an agreement between two countries), *slow food* ("traditional food and ways of producing, cooking and eating it"), *fast food*, *fire door*, *first lady* etc. A similar definition was adopted in the PARSEME Shared Task resource (Ramisch et al., 2018, 2020a). As we target the construction of a general lexicon expressing good coverage for lexical units occurring frequently enough in a very large corpus, we need also to take into account *multiword terms*, i.e. (Ramisch, 2015) "specialised lexical units composed of two or more lexemes, and whose properties cannot be directly inferred by a non-expert from its parts because they depend on the specialised domain".

Several MWE characteristics or identifying properties have been postulated, e.g.: arbitrariness, institutionalisation, limited semantic variability (especially non-compositionality and non-substitutability), domain specificity, and limited syntactic variability (Ramisch, 2015). Among them, semantic non-compositionality seems to be one of the strongest identifying factors. However, the challenge is to trace them using some corpus-based evidence and guide the extraction process. In addition, MWEs should be some how correlated with higher or more prominent frequency in language use in order to be worth inclusion in a lexicon.

Extraction of MWEs and their description in a semantic lexicon (e.g. as a reference resource) is important for many NLP applications like semantic

Proceedings of the 60th Annual Meeting of the Association for Computational Linguistics Student Research Workshop, pages 444 - 453

indexing, knowledge graph extraction, vector models, topic modelling etc. Due to the specific properties of MWEs as whole units, their automated description by the distributional semantics method, e.g. embeddings, is not guaranteed, especially in the case of MWEs of lower frequency.

Traditionally, MWEs extraction is preceded by finding collocations (frequent word combinations) by statistical or heuristic *association measures* and filtering them by syntactic patterns. However, in this way mainly the frequency-related aspect is covered. The peculiar behaviour of MWEs as a language unit may be observed in linguistic contexts, and methods based on the well-known *sequence labelling* scheme try to do that. They explore MWE specific behaviour of as a language expressions across text contexts, where the contexts are represented by contextual embeddings (neural language models). However, such approaches require a lot of hard manual work on text annotation. In addition, due to the corpus size limitation, most potential MWEs are observed only in a few, if not singular uses, while a lexicon element by a definition is a ready-to-use unit to be included in different contexts and, as such, should be studied.

Thus, we want to fully explore the expected MWE characteristic aspects, including frequency, and to reduce the amount of manual work required. MWE annotated corpora are very rare and small, e.g. PARSEME (Ramisch et al., 2020b), but MWEs are listed in dictionaries and lexical resources. We propose a weakly supervised approach in which a lexicon of MWEs is used to build a kind of silver data on the basis of general text corpus. Concerning negative examples, i.e. language expressions rejected to be MWEs, that are hardly listed in any lexical resources, we use association measures (frequency aspect) to find collocations very likely not being MWEs. Next we feed a system combining contextual embeddings, deep neural learning and weighted voting scheme across individual MWE occurrences with the silver data. As a result, the system can be next used to filter potential MWEs extracted from a corpus with association measures (the frequency aspect in a positive role). In contrast to many methods from literature, we neither need a corpus laboriously annotated with MWE occurrences, nor language models specially trained for this task. In addition we aim at jointly encompass most of the MWE characteristic aspects with the majority of them recognised in a kind of overlap of MWE contextual embeddings across their different occurrences. The proposed approach is illustrated with good results achieved on English MWEs coming from several dictionaries and the British National Corpus. However, our method can be quite easily adapted to any language, the only required elements are: a corpus and an initial lexicon of MWEs, and a general contextual embeddings model.

2 Related Work

Initially statistical association measures calculated on the basis of word co-occurrence statistics in corpora were used for discovering and ranking collocations as potential MWEs (Evert, 2004). Single measures can be also combined into complex ones, e.g. by a neural network (Pečina, 2010). Syntactic information from parsing (Seretan, 2011) or from lexico-syntactic constraints based on morpho-syntactic tagging (Broda et al., 2008) were used in counting statistics and post-filtering collocations. Several systems for MWE extraction were proposed, combining different techniques, e.g. *mwe-toolkit* by Ramisch (Ramisch, 2015) combines statistical extraction and morpho-syntactic filtering, but also describes collocations with feature vectors to train Machine Learning (ML) classifiers. Lexico-syntactic patterns, measures, length and frequency are used as features in ML-based MWE extraction (Spasić et al., 2019). Linguistic patterns were used to extract MWEs and post-filter the outcome of association measures (Agrawal et al., 2018). MWEs were also detected by tree substitution grammars (Green et al., 2013) or finite state transducers (Handler et al., 2016).

Recently, attention was shifted to MWE extraction perceived as a sequence labelling problem, e.g. (Chakraborty et al., 2020), where corpora are annotated on the level of words, typically, BIO annotation format (Ramshaw and Marcus, 1995): B – a word begins an MWE, I is inside, O – outside. Sequence labelling approaches can also be combined with heuristic rules (Scholivet and Ramisch, 2017) or supersenses of nouns or verbs (Hosseini et al., 2016). Such heuristics are applied to extract linguistic features from texts for training a Bayesian network model (Buljan and Šnajder, 2017). Convolutional graph networks and self-attention mechanisms can be used to extract additional features (Rohanian et al., 2019). There are many challenges related to the nature of the MWEs, e.g.: discontinuity – another token occurs between the MWE components or overlapping – another MWE occurs between the components of the given MWEs. To counteract this, a model based on LSTM, the long short-term memory networks and CRF is proposed (Berk et al., 2018). The model from (Taslimipoor et al., 2020) combines two learning tasks: MWE recognition and dependency parsing in parallel. The approach in (Kurfalı, 2020) leverages feature-independent models with standard BERT embeddings. mBERT was also tested, but with lower results. An LSTM-CRF architecture combined with a rich set of features: word embedding, its POS tag, dependency relation, and its head word is proposed in (Yirmibeşoğlu and Güngör, 2020).

MWEs can be also represented as subgraphs enriched with morphological features (Boros and Burtica, 2018). Graphs can be next combined with the *word2vec* (Mikolov et al., 2013) embeddings to represent word relations in the vector space and then used to predict MWEs on the basis of linguistic functions (Anke et al., 2019). Morphological and syntactic information can be also delivered to a recurrent neural network (Klyueva et al., 2017). Two approaches to MWE recognition within a transition system were compared in (Saied et al., 2019): one based on a multilayer perceptron and the second on a linear SVM. Both utilise only lemmas and morphosyntactic annotations from the corpus and were trained and tested on PARSEME Shared Task 1.1 data (Ramisch et al., 2018).

However, such sequence labeling approaches focus on word positions and orders in sentences, and seem to pay less attention to the semantic incompatibility of MWEs or semantic relations between their components. Furthermore, sequence labeling methods do not emphasize the semantic diversity of MWE occurrence contexts. Thus, they overlook one of the most characteristic MWE factors: components of a potential MWE co-occur together regardless of the context. It allows us to distinguish a lexicalised MWE from a mere collocation or even a term strictly related to one domain. To the best of our knowledge, the concept of using deep neural contextual embeddings to describe the semantics of the MWEs components and the semantic relations between them in a detection task has not been sufficiently studied, yet. Moreover, due to the sparsity of the MWEs occurrences in the corpus, the corpus annotation process is very time consuming and can lead to many errors and low inter-annotator agreement. For this reason, we propose a lexicon-based corpus annotation method. We assume that the vast majority of MWEs are monosemous, automatically extract the sentences containing the MWE occurrences, and treat all sentences including a given MWE (as a word sequence) as representing the same multiword lexical unit.

3 Datasets

The conducted analysis of the existing resources has shown that it is difficult to find a large annotated dataset for the multiword expressions detection task. PARSEME shared task and multilingual corpus (Ramisch et al., 2020b) is a very valuable initiative, but focused mainly on verbal MWEs and quite small, especially its English part. Moreover, dictionaries containing MWEs follow different definitions and lexicographic practices, which makes it difficult to unambiguously determine whether a given multiword entity is a valid MWE. Therefore, in order to obtain a large dataset, we followed our idea of silver dataset and selected The Oxford Dictionary of English (ODE) (Stevenson, 2010) as a reference point to obtain the list of correct MWEs. The proposed method is in some way parameterised by a selected reference dictionary.

Concerning language expressions that are not MWEs, i.e. negative samples from the ML perspective, they are not listed or mentioned in the dictionaries. Having a corpus annotated with MWE occurrences we could extract expressions that are not as negative samples. However genuine MWEs are more frequent or statistically specific. Thus, 'normal' language expressions would be too obviously different. Instead, we noticed that statistical association measures produce very long ranking lists of collocations. Further down the ranking, MWE occurrences are quickly dwindling away. In addition, we are interested only in specific structural types of collocations that match structural types of MWEs acquired from a dictionary.

To generate the list of incorrect MWEs, we selected three popular association measures[1]: (1) the Pointwise Mutual Information (PMI) (Church and Hanks, 1990), (2) the Sørensen–Dice coefficient (Dice) (Dice, 1945), and (3) Pearson's chi-square (Chi2) (Manning and Schutze, 1999) and used them

[1]A combined association measure could produced a better ranking, but only moderately better and would require optimisation on the given dictionary and corpus. Moreover, our dictionary seems to be too small, with too small coverage for the optimisation.

to extract collocation ranking list from the British National Corpus (BNC) (Burnard, 1995). In order to find relevant examples of multiword units, we decided to select those collocations that were in the third quartile of the list sorted in descending order based on the value of the selected measure. We quickly skimmed the list in order to ensure that it is hard to spot anything looking as a MWE (but we do not exclude the possibility that some MWEs may occur, perfect precision does not seem to be necessary). We combined the list of the correct MWEs (from the dictionary) separately with the lists of collocations obtained via each of the three selected measures. In all experiments we concentrated on two word MWEs and collocations, as the statistical association measures we applied are naturally defined for two word combinations. However, as it will be presented later, some of the MWE representation we propose can be easily expanded to k-word cases. Moreover, two word MWEs form the vast majority of all in the dictionaries. Collocations extracted from the corpus were restricted only to those that represent structural types of MWEs from the dictionary.

We then used the three resulting lists to search for sentences including collocation or MWE occurrences in the BNC corpus. The searched expressions were simply recognised by comparing lemma sequences. Some recognition error may appear, but the potential error ration seems to be very small (single percents). If multiple MWE/collocation lemma sequences were detected among the sentence lemmas, then their occurrences were considered as separate *training samples* (positive or negative), see Alg. 1. In order to evaluate our method of detecting sentences containing MWEs, we extracted 4 randomly selected samples containing 100 found sentences each. A linguist conducted the analysis and found that 99% of the sentences contained correct MWE occurrences. The analysis was performed only on sentences corresponding to positive samples – MWEs from the dictionary, but similar results can be expected for collocations from the lists. Our work resulted in the creation of three datasets of MWE and collocation occurrences, named on the basis of the sources of knowledge:

- **ODE–PMI dataset** – dataset containing occurrences of correct MWEs from the ODE dictionary and the incorrect ones obtained via the PMI measure,
- **ODE–Dice dataset** – dataset containing occurrences of correct MWEs from the ODE dictionary and the incorrect ones obtained via the Dice measure,
- **ODE–Chi2 dataset** – dataset containing occurrences of correct MWEs from the ODE dictionary and the incorrect ones obtained via the Chi2 measure.

Algorithm 1 Procedure of obtaining sentences (s) containing MWEs from the corpus (C) by comparing sentence word lemmas ($l_i \in [l_0, l_1, \ldots, l_n]$) to the list ($M$) of lemmatised MWEs ($m_j \in [m_0, m_1, \ldots, m_k]$)

$sentence\_list \leftarrow [\,]$
for $s \in C$ **do**
  for $l_i \in s$ **do**
    for $m_j \in M$ **do**
      if $l_i \in m_j$ **then**
        $sentence\_list$.insert(s)
      end if
    end for
  end for
end for
return $sentence\_list$

4 Deep Neural Representations for MWE Detection

4.1 Baseline

As our *baseline*, we decided to use a concatenation of vectors consisting of:

1. a component embedding ($\overrightarrow{c_{sent}}$),
2. an MWE embedding ($\overrightarrow{m_{sent}}$) in the context of the sentence ($sent$),
3. the absolute difference between the MWE embedding and the component embedding ($|\overrightarrow{m_{sent}} - \overrightarrow{c_{sent}}|$),
4. and the Hadamard product between the MWE embedding and the component embedding ($\overrightarrow{m_{sent}} \odot \overrightarrow{c_{sent}}$).

The proposed representation has been inspired by the ones often used in the Natural Language Inference domain and also in the task of semantic relations extraction (Fu et al., 2014; Levy et al., 2015). Our idea is to represent syntactic and semantic relations between the whole MWE and its components. We want to analyse the relation between the picture of the whole MWE used in a context and one of its components used in the same context, but separately, i.e. we exchange the whole MWE with one of its components and vice versa to see their contextual picture and interactions alone. The obvious target is the potential compositionality of an expressions: MWE or non-lexicalised collocation. In the case of compositional expressions we expect to see some kind of inclusion relation. However, we assumed that contextual embeddings allow us to go beyond focusing only on semantic compositionality, e.g. some syntactic idiosyncrasy should be also visible in relation between contextual embeddings of the whole expression and its component. Moreover, in order to minimise the effect of accidental properties of some specific context we try to collect representations of the same expressions (MWEs and collocations) across as many contexts as possible.

The obtaining of contextual MWE embeddings is described in Eq. 1. An MWE embedding ($\overrightarrow{m_{sent}}$) in the sentence context ($sent$) is an average of the WordPiece subtoken ($s \in S_{m_{sent}}$) vectors ($\overrightarrow{v_s}$) related to the MWE components.

$$\overrightarrow{m_{sent}} = \frac{\sum_{s \in S_{m_{sent}}} \overrightarrow{\nu_s}}{|S_{m_{sent}}|} \quad (1)$$

In the next step, the MWE occurrence was replaced subsequently with each of its components in order to obtain their contextual embeddings ($\overrightarrow{c_{sent}}$) by averaging the corresponding subtoken vectors representations ($\overrightarrow{\nu_s}$) related to the substituted components ($S_{c_{sent}}$), see Eq. 2.

$$\overrightarrow{c_{sent}} = \frac{\sum_{s \in S_{c_{sent}}} \overrightarrow{\nu_s}}{|S_{c_{sent}}|} \quad (2)$$

The final baseline embedding ($\overrightarrow{B}$) of a training sample related to a sentence ($sent$) containing MWE (m) and one of its components (c) is described in Eq. 3.

$$\begin{aligned}\overrightarrow{B_{c,m,sent}} = &\overrightarrow{c_{sent}} \oplus \overrightarrow{m_{sent}} \oplus (\overrightarrow{m_{sent}} - \overrightarrow{c_{sent}}) \\ &\oplus (\overrightarrow{m_{sent}} \odot \overrightarrow{c_{sent}})\end{aligned} \quad (3)$$

4.2 Difference vector based representation Diff-Emb

Our element-wise difference vector based representation *Diff-Emb* ($\overrightarrow{D}$), described in Eq. 5 leverages the absolute difference between non-contextual component embeddings ($\overrightarrow{w_1} - \overrightarrow{w_2}$) obtained via the skipgram model from the *fastText* library (Bojanowski et al., 2017) and the averaged element-wise difference between the component embeddings and MWE embedding ($\overrightarrow{avg\_diff_{m,sent}}$) in the context of the sentence ($sent$). Eq. 4 describes the averaged difference vector for the MWE (m) containing components ($c \in m$). The non-contextual, static word embeddings were introduced into the representation in order to take into account semantic characteristics of expression components collected from a large corpus. In this way we want to take a yet another perspective on relation between the components.

$$\overrightarrow{avg\_diff_{m,sent}} = \frac{\sum_{c \in m} (\overrightarrow{m_{sent}} - \overrightarrow{c_{sent}})}{|m|} \quad (4)$$

$$\overrightarrow{D_{m,sent}} = |\overrightarrow{w_1} - \overrightarrow{w_2}| \oplus \overrightarrow{avg\_diff_{m,sent}} \quad (5)$$

4.3 Product based representation

We also decided to consider the relevance of Hadamard product vectors, which we included in our *Prod-Emb* representation ($\overrightarrow{P}$), explained in Eq. 7. It consists of the Hadamard product of non-contextual *fastText* component embeddings ($\overrightarrow{w_1} \odot \overrightarrow{w_2}$) and the averaged vector of Hadamard products between the component ($c \in m$) embeddings and MWE (m) embedding ($\overrightarrow{avg\_prod_{m,sent}}$) in the context of the sentence ($sent$) described in Eq. 6

$$\overrightarrow{avg\_prod_{m,sent}} = \frac{\sum_{c \in m} (\overrightarrow{m_{sent}} \odot \overrightarrow{c_{sent}})}{|m|} \quad (6)$$

$$\overrightarrow{P_{m,sent}} = (\overrightarrow{w_1} \odot \overrightarrow{w_2}) \oplus \overrightarrow{avg\_prod_{m,sent}} \quad (7)$$

4.4 Combined representation: differences and products

In order to combine the difference-based and product-based approaches we developed the *Mean-Emb* representation ($\overrightarrow{M}$), explained in Eq. 8. It consists of the averaged difference vector ($\overrightarrow{avg\_diff_{m,sent}}$) and the averaged Hadamard product vector ($\overrightarrow{avg\_prod_{m,sent}}$) described in Eq. 4 and 6 respectively.

$$\overrightarrow{M_{m,sent}} = \overrightarrow{avg\_diff_{m,sent}} \oplus \overrightarrow{avg\_prod_{m,sent}} \quad (8)$$

5 Experimental Setup

For all conducted experiments we selected a single-task binary classification, where the classifier aims to predict the correct label out of 2 possible ones (lexicalised vs non-lexicalised) for the expression represented by one of the vector representations: baseline, Diff-Emb, Prod-Emb or Mean-Emb. In the process of generating the contextual embeddings we used the XLM-RoBERTa (Conneau et al., 2020) language model as it is considered as one of the best transformer models for English. We decided to use the convolutional neural network (CNN) architecture as the classifier to better extract the knowledge from our vector representations. We used the TensorFlow library (Abadi et al., 2015) to implement the CNN model. Our convolutional neural network contains three convolutional layers, each followed by the pooling layer and the dropout layer and is shown in Fig. 1. We used the F1-macro metric to measure the performance of the classifier on each of the representations. To prevent data leakage, we applied the *lexical split* to avoid the risk of testing on the same multiword unit, which was used in the training procedure (even if the sentence samples are obviously not overlapping). We leveraged the 10-fold cross-validation and used statistical tests to measure the significance of the difference between different experiment configurations. We checked the assumptions and then applied the independent samples t-test with the Bonferroni correction if they were met. Otherwise we used the Mann-Whitney U-test.

6 Results

Tab. 1 shows the evaluation results for each representation on the ODE–PMI dataset. Each value is averaged over ten folds. The Mean-Emb representation combining both the knowledge based on the difference vector and the Hadamard product vector achieved the best results.

The performance of the CNN model trained on all representations and evaluated on the ODE–Dice dataset is shown in Tab. 2. The best performance can be observed for the Mean-Emb model. Each of the developed representations achieved better results than the baseline vector representation.

The evaluation results for the classifier trained on each representation and evaluated on the ODE–Chi2 dataset are shown in Tab. 3. The Mean-Emb model achieved the best results among other representations. The worst performance can be observed for the baseline vector representation.

Representation	Cor F1	Inc F1	F1
baseline	0.77	0.77	0.77
Diff-Emb	0.77	0.78	0.78
Prod-Emb	0.78	0.78	0.78
Mean-Emb	**0.79**	**0.79**	**0.79**

Table 1: The results of the CNN model trained on various representations on the ODE–PMI dataset. Measures: Cor F1 – F1 score for lexicalised MWEs; Inc F1 – F1 score for non-lexicalised MWEs; F1 – macro average of the F1 scores for lexicalised and non-lexicalised MWEs. Values in **bold** are significantly better than others.

Representation	Cor F1	Inc F1	F1
baseline	0.75	0.75	0.75
Diff-Emb	0.76	0.76	0.76
Prod-Emb	0.76	0.76	0.76
Mean-Emb	**0.77**	**0.77**	**0.77**

Table 2: Evaluation results on the ODE–Dice dataset. Measures: Cor F1 – F1 score for lexicalised MWEs; Inc F1 – F1 score for non-lexicalised MWEs; F1 – macro average of the F1 scores for lexicalised and non-lexicalised MWEs. Values in **bold** are significantly better than others.

Representation	Cor F1	Inc F1	F1
baseline	0.77	0.77	0.77
Diff-Emb	0.77	0.78	0.78
Prod-Emb	0.77	0.78	0.78
Mean-Emb	**0.79**	**0.80**	**0.80**

Table 3: Evaluation results on the ODE–Chi2 dataset. Measures: Cor F1 – F1 score for lexicalised MWEs; Inc F1 – F1 score for non-lexicalised MWEs; F1 – macro average of the F1 scores for lexicalised and non-lexicalised MWEs. Values in **bold** are significantly better than others.

7 Discussion

The idea of silver dataset enables transformation of any corpus into a dataset for MWE extraction, only if a limited lexicon of MWE examples is provided as a starting point – a kind of seed lexicon to be expanded. We can leverage a MWE annotated corpus, too, in the same way as a lexicon to extract the initial list of MWEs, but a large non-annotated corpus stays the basis. Several linguistic resources can be also merged, any MWE annotated text, as well as lexicons. Time-consuming and expensive corpus annotation is avoided. Moreover, it seems to be

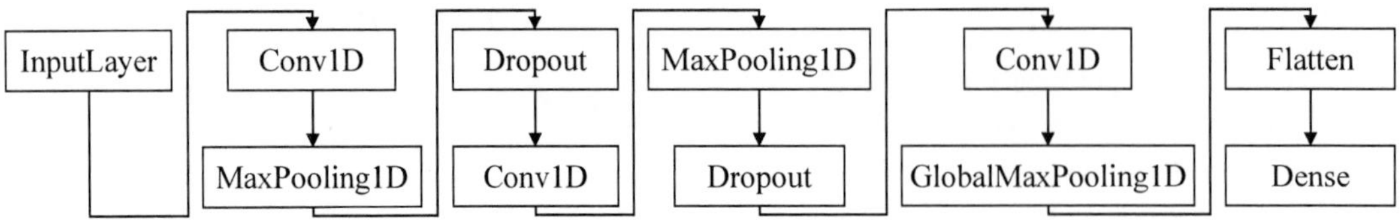

Figure 1: Convolutional neural network classifier structure.

easier to maintain high quality lexicon than corpus annotation, e.g. due to potential errors and discrepancies between single annotations. A lexicon can be edited by several linguists, and metrics such as inter-annotator agreement can be easily calculated.

What is more, such a transformation of lexicon-based knowledge into a dataset enables the use of deep neural network models that require large number of training samples. This is one of the reasons why our CNN method, pre-trained on contextual embeddings with weighted voting, applied to MWE recognition achieved several times better results than methods based on contextual embeddings and recurrent neural in the PARSEME shared task in general (Ramisch et al., 2020a), not mentioning the English part alone that is very small.

Our approach may be applied to texts in different languages, both to obtain multilingual collections and to apply transfer learning to facilitate the knowledge about MWEs in one language to MWE recognition in another language. This may be particularly relevant for low-resource languages, and it definitely a direction for further research.

Another advantage of the proposed method is faster training and prediction in comparison to sequence labeling methods. In our case, the model gets the full sample representation only once before prediction. This shortens the inference time.

Our vector representations support MWEs longer than two words. In the case of multiword units containing three and more words, the difference and product vectors calculated between two MWE components can be replaced with the vector obtained via the same operation, but averaged over all MWE component pairs.

The obtained results show that non-lexicalised representations, i.e. those that do not include vectors for components and the whole expression[2] perform better independently of the kind of a measure used to extract collocations. All representations except the baseline are built from differences and products of vectors, not the vectors itself. Thus they are more focused on representing relations between a potential MWE and its components. It is worth to be emphasised that lexical split was also implemented in order to prevent the models to remember concrete words instead of learning patterns for behaviour of proper MWEs. There are no large differences between results for different measure, but, with some caution, we can observe that results obtained with PMI are slightly better, while in the case of PMI the measure is naturally is filtered by 0 threshold and produces potentially more interesting collocations, thus harder to be distinguished from the proper MWEs.

8 Conclusions and Future Work

Our three representations allowed classifier to achieve significantly better results in comparison to the baseline approach focused on the component and MWE embedding.

The context provided additional information on the MWE semantics, which improved the model performance. This is related to the non-compositional nature of the MWEs, which meaning cannot be inferred from their component meanings.

Our approach based on difference and product vectors forced the models significantly reduced the training time. It may be more important in practice, when the training time and inference time are more important than the quality of prediction. On the other hand, the method based on contextual embeddings allows transforming any set of texts with the use of dictionary knowledge into an annotated corpus containing occurrences of the MWEs and their components. The model, by examining the semantic differences between the component and the entire expression, takes into account the variability of the context, which should allow for the extraction of the MWE meaning following the assumption of its monosemous character.

In future work, we want to use our methods to generate corpora in other languages, which will be later used to train models in the multilingual MWEs

[2]A contextual vector of the whole expression somehow includes a picture of the particular expression and its lexemes.

detection task and to explore the transfer learning mechanism in a language-independent MWE detection.

Acknowledgements

This work was financed by (1) the National Science Centre, Poland, project no. 2019/33/B/HS2/02814; (2) the Polish Ministry of Education and Science, CLARIN-PL; (3) the European Regional Development Fund as a part of the 2014-2020 Smart Growth Operational Programme, CLARIN – Common Language Resources and Technology Infrastructure, project no. POIR.04.02.00-00C002/19; (4) the statutory funds of the Department of Artificial Intelligence, Wroclaw University of Science and Technology.

References

Martín Abadi, Ashish Agarwal, Paul Barham, and et al. 2015. TensorFlow: Large-scale machine learning on heterogeneous systems.

Shaishav Agrawal, Ratna Sanyal, and Sudip Sanyal. 2018. Hybrid method for automatic extraction of multiword expressions. *Int. Journal of Engineering & Technology*, 7:33.

Luis Espinosa Anke, Steven Schockaert, and Leo Wanner. 2019. Collocation classification with unsupervised relation vectors. In *Proc. of the 57th Annual Meeting of the ACL*, pages 5765–5772, Florence, Italy. Association for Computational Linguistics.

Gözde Berk, Berna Erden, and Tunga Güngör. 2018. Deep-BGT at PARSEME shared task 2018: Bidirectional LSTM-CRF model for verbal multiword expression identification. In *Proc. of the Joint Workshop on Linguistic Annotation, Multiword Expressions and Constructions (LAW-MWE-CxG-2018)*, pages 248–253, Santa Fe, New Mexico, USA. Association for Computational Linguistics.

Piotr Bojanowski, Edouard Grave, Armand Joulin, and et al. 2017. Enriching word vectors with subword information. *Transactions of the ACL*, 5:135–146.

Tiberiu Boros and Ruxandra Burtica. 2018. GBD-NER at PARSEME shared task 2018: Multi-word expression detection using bidirectional long-short-term memory networks and graph-based decoding. In *Proc. of the Joint Work. on Linguistic Annotation, Multiword Expressions and Constructions (LAW-MWE-CxG-2018)*, pages 254–260, Santa Fe, New Mexico, USA. Association for Computational Linguistics.

B. Broda, M. Derwojedowa, and M. Piasecki. 2008. Recognition of structured collocations in an inflective language. *Systems Science*, 34(4):27–36.

Maja Buljan and Jan Šnajder. 2017. Combining linguistic features for the detection of Croatian multiword expressions. In *Proc. of the 13th Workshop on Multiword Expressions (MWE 2017)*, pages 194–199, Valencia, Spain. Association for Computational Linguistics.

Lou Burnard. 1995. *British National Corpus: Users Reference Guide British National Corpus Version 1.0.* Oxford Univ. Computing Service.

Sritanu Chakraborty, Dorian Cougias, and Steven Piliero. 2020. Identification of multiword expressions using transformers.

Kenneth Ward Church and Patrick Hanks. 1990. Word association norms, mutual information, and lexicography. *Computational Linguistics*, 16(1):22–29.

Alexis Conneau, Kartikay Khandelwal, Naman Goyal, Vishrav Chaudhary, Guillaume Wenzek, Francisco Guzmán, Edouard Grave, Myle Ott, Luke Zettlemoyer, and Veselin Stoyanov. 2020. Unsupervised cross-lingual representation learning at scale. In *Proceedings of the 58th Annual Meeting of the Association for Computational Linguistics*, pages 8440–8451, Online. Association for Computational Linguistics.

Lee R Dice. 1945. Measures of the amount of ecologic association between species. *Ecology*, 26(3):297–302.

Stefan Evert. 2004. *The Statistics of Word Cooccurrences: Word Pairs and Collocations.* Ph.D. thesis, Institut für maschinelle Sprachverarbeitung, Univ. of Stuttgart.

Ruiji Fu, Jiang Guo, Bing Qin, Wanxiang Che, Haifeng Wang, and Ting Liu. 2014. Learning semantic hierarchies via word embeddings. In *Proceedings of the 52nd Annual Meeting of the Association for Computational Linguistics (Volume 1: Long Papers)*, pages 1199–1209, Baltimore, Maryland. Association for Computational Linguistics.

Spence Green, Marie-Catherine de Marneffe, and Christopher D. Manning. 2013. Parsing models for identifying multiword expressions. *Computational Linguistics*, 39(1):195–227.

Abram Handler, M. Denny, H. Wallach, and et al. 2016. Bag of what? simple noun phrase extraction for text analysis. In *NLP+CSS@EMNLP*, pages 114–124, Austin, Texas. Association for Computational Linguistics.

Mohammad Javad Hosseini, Noah A. Smith, and Su-In Lee. 2016. UW-CSE at SemEval-2016 task 10: Detecting multiword expressions and supersenses using double-chained conditional random fields. In *Proc. of the 10th International Workshop on Semantic Evaluation (SemEval-2016)*, pages 931–936, San Diego, California. Association for Computational Linguistics.

Natalia Klyueva, Antoine Doucet, and Milan Straka. 2017. Neural networks for multi-word expression detection. In *Proc. of the 13th Workshop on Multiword Expressions (MWE 2017)*, pages 60–65, Valencia, Spain. Association for Computational Linguistics.

Murathan Kurfalı. 2020. TRAVIS at PARSEME shared task 2020: How good is (m)BERT at seeing the unseen? In *Proceedings of the Joint Workshop on Multiword Expressions and Electronic Lexicons*, pages 136–141, online. Association for Computational Linguistics.

Omer Levy, Steffen Remus, Chris Biemann, and Ido Dagan. 2015. Do supervised distributional methods really learn lexical inference relations? In *Proceedings of the 2015 Conference of the North American Chapter of the Association for Computational Linguistics: Human Language Technologies*, pages 970–976, Denver, Colorado. Association for Computational Linguistics.

Christopher Manning and Hinrich Schutze. 1999. *Foundations of statistical natural language processing*. MIT press.

Tomás Mikolov, Kai Chen, Greg Corrado, and et al. 2013. Efficient estimation of word representations in vector space. In *1st International Conference on Learning Representations, ICLR 2013, Scottsdale, Arizona, USA, May 2-4, 2013, Workshop Track Proc.*

P. Pečina. 2010. Lexical association measures and collocation extraction. *Language Resources and Evaluation*, 44:137–158.

Carlos Ramisch. 2015. *Multiword Expressions Acquisition. A Generic and Open Framework.* Springer.

Carlos Ramisch, Silvio Ricardo Cordeiro, Agata Savary, Veronika Vincze, Verginica Barbu Mititelu, Archna Bhatia, Maja Buljan, Marie Candito, Polona Gantar, Voula Giouli, Tunga Güngör, Abdelati Hawwari, Uxoa Iñurrieta, Jolanta Kovalevskaitė, Simon Krek, Timm Lichte, Chaya Liebeskind, Johanna Monti, Carla Parra Escartín, Behrang QasemiZadeh, Renata Ramisch, Nathan Schneider, Ivelina Stoyanova, Ashwini Vaidya, and Abigail Walsh. 2018. Edition 1.1 of the PARSEME shared task on automatic identification of verbal multiword expressions. In *Proceedings of the Joint Workshop on Linguistic Annotation, Multiword Expressions and Constructions (LAW-MWE-CxG-2018)*, pages 222–240, Santa Fe, New Mexico, USA. Association for Computational Linguistics.

Carlos Ramisch, Agata Savary, Bruno Guillaume, Jakub Waszczuk, Marie Candito, Ashwini Vaidya, Verginica Barbu Mititelu, Archna Bhatia, Uxoa Iñurrieta, Voula Giouli, Tunga Güngör, Menghan Jiang, Timm Lichte, Chaya Liebeskind, Johanna Monti, Renata Ramisch, Sara Stymne, Abigail Walsh, and Hongzhi Xu. 2020a. Edition 1.2 of the PARSEME shared task on semi-supervised identification of verbal multiword expressions. In *Proceedings of the Joint Workshop on Multiword Expressions and Electronic Lexicons*, pages 107–118, online. Association for Computational Linguistics.

Carlos Ramisch, Agata Savary, Bruno Guillaume, Jakub Waszczuk, Marie Candito, Ashwini Vaidya, Verginica Barbu Mititelu, Archna Bhatia, Uxoa Iñurrieta, Voula Giouli, Tunga Güngör, Menghan Jiang, Timm Lichte, Chaya Liebeskind, Johanna Monti, Renata Ramisch, Sara Stymne, Abigail Walsh, and Hongzhi Xu. 2020b. Edition 1.2 of the PARSEME shared task on semi-supervised identification of verbal multiword expressions. In *Proceedings of the Joint Workshop on Multiword Expressions and Electronic Lexicons*, pages 107–118, online. Association for Computational Linguistics.

Lance Ramshaw and Mitch Marcus. 1995. Text chunking using transformation-based learning. In *Third Workshop on Very Large Corpora*.

Omid Rohanian, Shiva Taslimipoor, Samaneh Kouchaki, and et al. 2019. Bridging the gap: Attending to discontinuity in identification of multiword expressions. In *Proc. of the 2019 Conference of the North American Chapter of the ACL: Human Language Technologies, Volume 1 (Long and Short Papers)*, pages 2692–2698, Minneapolis, Minnesota. Association for Computational Linguistics.

Hazem Al Saied, Marie Candito, and Mathieu Constant. 2019. Comparing linear and neural models for competitive MWE identification. In *Proc. of the 22nd Nordic Conference on Computational Linguistics*, pages 86–96, Turku, Finland. Linköping University Electronic Press.

Manon Scholivet and Carlos Ramisch. 2017. Identification of Ambiguous Multiword Expressions Using Sequence Models and Lexical Resources. In *Proc. of the 13th Workshop on Multiword Expressions (MWE 2017)*, pages 167–175, Valencia, Spain. Association for Computational Linguistics.

V. Seretan. 2011. *Syntax-Based Collocation Extraction*, volume 44 of *Text, Speech and Language Technology*. Springer Netherlands.

Irena Spasić, David Owen, Dawn Knight, and et al. 2019. Unsupervised multi-word term recognition in Welsh. In *Proc. of the Celtic Language Technology Workshop*, pages 1–6, Dublin, Ireland. European Association for Machine Translation.

Angus Stevenson. 2010. *Oxford Dictionary of English*. Oxford University Press.

Shiva Taslimipoor, Sara Bahaadini, and Ekaterina Kochmar. 2020. MTLB-STRUCT @parseme 2020: Capturing unseen multiword expressions using multitask learning and pre-trained masked language models. In *Proceedings of the Joint Workshop on Multiword Expressions and Electronic Lexicons*, pages 142–148, online. Association for Computational Linguistics.

Zeynep Yirmibeşoğlu and Tunga Güngör. 2020. ERMI at PARSEME shared task 2020: Embedding-rich multiword expression identification. In *Proceedings of the Joint Workshop on Multiword Expressions and Electronic Lexicons*, pages 130–135, online. Association for Computational Linguistics.

A Checkpoint on Multilingual Misogyny Identification

Arianna Muti and **Alberto Barrón-Cedeño**
Department of Interpreting and Translation
Alma Mater Studiorum–Universitá di Bologna
Forlì, Italy
{arianna.muti2,a.barron}@unibo.it

Abstract

We address the problem of identifying misogyny in tweets in mono and multilingual settings in three languages: English, Italian and Spanish. We explore model variations considering single and multiple languages both in the pre-training of the transformer and in the training of the downstream task to explore the feasibility of detecting misogyny through a transfer learning approach across multiple languages. That is, we train monolingual transformers with monolingual data and multilingual transformers with both monolingual and multilingual data. Our models reach state-of-the-art performance on all three languages. The single-language BERT models perform the best, closely followed by different configurations of multilingual BERT models. The performance drops in zero-shot classification across languages. Our error analysis shows that multilingual and monolingual models tend to make the same mistakes.

Disclaimer: Due to the nature of the topic, this paper contains offensive words.

1 Introduction

Misogynous contents express hate towards women in the form of insulting, sexual harassment, male privilege, patriarchy, gender discrimination, belittling, violence, body shaming and sexual objectification (Srivastava et al., 2017). According to a study by *Vox–Osservatorio Italiano sui diritti* on hate speech against minorities (women, homosexuals, migrants, people with disabilities, Jews and Muslims) in Italian tweets,[1] women are the most targeted group. They observed a significant increase in the number of misogynous tweets from 2019 to 2021: shifting from 26% to 44% of all hateful posts. Blake et al. (2021) observed a correlation between misogyny on Twitter and domestic violence in specific areas has, stressing the importance of flagging such contents to try to dim their impact online.

We target the problem of identifying misogyny in multiple languages. This work represents a first step towards investigating the specificity of misogyny with respect to language and culture. To address this novel research question, we test two hypotheses:

H1 More data boosts the model performance, even if it is in a different language; therefore, considering training material in diverse languages benefits in the prediction of misogyny in such languages.

H2 misogyny is language-specific and therefore a monolingual model performs better, even if it is trained on smaller data.

We rely on: (a) data in each of the languages in isolation; or (b) data in various languages in conjunction, through the training of a single multilingual model.[2] We exploit monolingual transformers (BERT (Devlin et al., 2019)) for three languages — English, Italian, and Spanish — and one multilingual transformer (Multilingual BERT (Devlin et al., 2019)). We perform a thorough exploration combining different settings, which include training monolingual transformers with monolingual data, multilingual transformers with monolingual data, and multilingual transformers with multilingual data.

Section 2 summarizes the related work on misogyny identification, both in mono- and multilingual settings. Section 3 describes the datasets. Section 4 describes the methodology, whereas Section 5 discusses the obtained results. Section 6 shows our

[1] http://www.voxdiritti.it/la-nuova-mappa-dellintolleranza-6/

[2] Our settings avoid resorting to machine translation because the jargon used to convey hateful messages tends to produce faulty target texts, causing the classifiers to struggle (Casula and Tonelli, 2020; Pamungkas and Patti, 2019).

Proceedings of the 60th Annual Meeting of the Association for Computational Linguistics Student Research Workshop, pages 454 - 460

error analysis. Section 7 and 8 provide a conclusion and an overview on the societal impact and limitations of our work.

2 Related Work

Monolingual Approaches The increasing number of hateful posts against women has attracted the interest of the scientific community, but it remains an underexplored field compared to other types of hate speech (Tontodimamma et al., 2021). Work on automatic misogyny identification has been carried out in a limited number of languages. For instance, the Automatic Misogyny Identification (AMI) series of shared tasks launched in EVALITA (Fersini et al., 2018, 2020) and IberEval (Anzovino et al., 2018) has produced evaluation frameworks to identify misogynous tweets in English, Italian and Spanish. HatEval at SemEval 2019 (Basile et al., 2019) focused on the detection of hate speech towards women and immigrants in English and Spanish.

Participants in those shared tasks mostly used TF–IDF representations (e.g., Frenda et al. (2018)), word embeddings (e.g., Fabrizi (2020)), and sentence embeddings (e.g., Ahluwalia et al. (2018)). When extracting lexical features from social media, it is common to represent hashtags, emoticons and mentions as well. For instance, Pamungkas and Patti (2019) considered both a bag of hashtags and a bag of emojis. They also encoded information about the occurrence of swear words.

Among the most commonly-used classifiers there are recurrent neural networks (Goenaga et al., 2018; Buscaldi, 2018), convolutional neural networks (da Silva and Roman, 2020), shallow models (Pamungkas et al., 2018) and transformer-based models (Lees et al., 2020; Muti and Barrón-Cedeño, 2020), which perform the best.

Multilingual Approaches Few works are focused on the multilingual identification of misogyny. Basile and Rubagotti (2018) adopted a bleaching approach, i.e. transforming lexical strings into more abstract features (van der Goot et al., 2018), and tested their model on Italian and English. They use an SVM with n-gram features. This is a close work to ours: they train on L1 and test on L1, train on L2 and test on L2, and they also train and test on both languages in combination.

Pamungkas and Patti (2019) created bilingual misogynist data in English, Italian and Spanish with machine translation to train in a source language and predict in a target language with an LSTM. We neglect the use of machine translation at all stages.

	training		testing	
Dataset	**not mis**	**mis**	**not mis**	**mis**
en EVALITA 2018	2,215	1,785	540	460
es IberEval 2018	1,658	1,649	416	415
it EVALITA 2018	2,171	1,828	509	491

Table 1: Class distribution for the three corpora in English (en), Spanish (es) and Italian (it).

Pamungkas et al. (2020) adopted an approach similar to ours, using multilingual transformers to identify English, Spanish and Italian misogynist tweets. The difference is that they only train a model on one language and test it on a different one, without considering all language combinations.

Differently from the previous works, we do not focus on model performance or engineering, but we head toward investigating a novel research question: is misogyny language-specific?

3 The multi-AMI Evaluation Framework

We consider misogyny datasets in three languages, released under two editions of the AMI shared task: AMI at IberEval 2018 (Anzovino et al., 2018) and AMI at EVALITA 2018 (Fersini et al., 2018). AMI at IberEval 2018 focused on identifying misogyny on English and Spanish tweets, and in classifying misogynistic instances in different categories. AMI at EVALITA 2018 focused on two tasks in Italian. Task A addressed misogyny identification, whereas Task B aimed at recognizing whether a misogynous tweet is person-specific or generally addressed towards a group of women. We address the binary problem alone: whether a tweet is misogynist or not. Table 1 shows statistics for the three corpora.

We stick to the evaluation metric of AMI: the F_1 measure. For direct comparison with our models we consider the best-performing approaches in both shared tasks. For Italian, Bakarov (2018) used TF-IDF weighting combined with singular value decomposition and an ensemble of classifiers. For English, Saha et al. (2018) concatenated sentence and average word embeddings with TF–IDF weights coupled with a logistic regression model. For Spanish, Pamungkas et al. (2018) applied an SVM with a series of lexical features, including lexicons of abusive words. The bottom row of Table 2 shows the performance of the three models.

4 Model Description

Our models to identify misogynous tweets are built on different variations of BERT (Devlin et al., 2019). In the monolingual settings, we use bert-base-uncased for English (Devlin et al., 2019), bert-base-spanish-wwm-uncased for Spanish (Cañete et al., 2020) and AlBERTo for Italian (Polignano et al., 2019). For the multilingual settings, we use multilingual BERT (mBERT) (Devlin et al., 2019). mBERT has the same architecture as BERT, but it is trained on Wikipedia articles in multiple languages (Liu et al., 2020). We also apply mBERT in monolingual settings, to observe its behaviour in zero-shot classification across languages.

Our output layer is a soft-max with two units. We use the categorical cross-entropy loss function and the AdamW optimizer with a learning rate of 1-8 (Loshchilov and Hutter, 2017), batch size of 16 and 4 training epochs.

5 Experiments and Results

Our objective is to assess whether and to what extent considering training material in diverse languages benefits in the prediction of misogyny in multiple languages. We carried out a number of experiments to test hypotheses H1 and H2 (cf. Section 1).

We head toward investigating the way in which misogyny is expressed in different languages. Even if the impact of shared vocabulary in multilingual settings remains unclear (Liu et al., 2020), we explore the feasibility of using multilingual embeddings to produce zero-shot classifications across languages —training on L_1 to predict on L_2— and as a data augmentation technique —training on L_1+L_2 to predict on L_1.

We trained ten models considering all combinations of data in English (en), Spanish (es) and Italian (it): (*i*) one BERT model per language, (*ii*) one mBERT model per language, (*iii*) one mBERT model per each language pair, and (*iv*) one mBERT model with all three languages. Table 2 shows the results when predicting on data in each language and all together. The scores under columns en, es and it are comparable, whereas those under all are not, because the testing sets are different.

The monolingual BERT models consistently perform the best, improving over the best AMI approaches (cf. Section 3). There is a performance drop when monolingual models are trained on top of mBERT, with the model trained on English achieving the poorest performance: as low as F_1=0.14 and 0.17 when tested on Spanish and Italian and six points lower on English than the monolingual BERT alternative. The results suggest that this transfer learning approach is not suitable for languages which are relatively far from each other, e.g., a Romance and a Germanic one. Considering a second language during training improves the predictions of the mBERT models (*i*) on English in all three cases, (*ii*) on Spanish with pair en–es, but (*iii*) not on Italian. Indeed, combining English and Spanish produces better results for both languages than when combining either with Italian. Considering all three languages results in mixed effects. It has the best mBERT performance on English, but runs short by one point with respect to the pairwise combinations on the other two languages. The best performance on all three languages together is obtained when neglecting the training data in English: F_1=0.84.

train	**en**	**es**	**it**	**all**
BERT en	**0.71**	–	–	–
BERT es	–	**0.85**	–	–
BERT it	–	–	**0.87**	–
mBERT en	0.65	0.14	0.17	–
mBERT es	0.62	0.81	0.50	–
mBERT it	0.47	0.63	0.87	–
mBERT en-es	0.67	0.83	–	0.75
mBERT en–it	0.66	–	0.86	0.77
mBERT es–it	–	0.80	0.86	0.84
mBERT en–es–it	0.68	0.82	0.86	0.78
best-AMI	0.70	0.81	0.84	–

Table 2: F_1 performance for the different language combinations. Best AMI shared task models shown at the bottom for comparison (cf. Section 3).

These results confirm H1 only partially. On the one hand, monolingual models built on top of a monolingual BERT performs the best. On the other hand, considering multilingual training data with a multilingual BERT improves over considering monolingual data alone.

We performed an additional experiment to verify that the performance shifts are not caused by the increase in the volume of training data, rather than the inclusion of another language. We trained a bilingual English–Italian model considering only 2,000 instances per language (conforming to the volume of the monolingual datasets). The performance on the English test set drops from F_1=0.65

it	FN	FP	en	FN	FP	es	FN	FP
bel	1	17	hysterical	27	20	puta	16	25
tette	0	8	woman	16	33	polla	3	13
culo	0	12	women	12	35	cállate	0	6
culona	3	12	fuck	9	27	acoso	7	5
porca	6	0	pussy	5	23	callate	2	4
figa	0	8	rape	3	27	madre	3	3
cazzo	3	4	bitch	4	22	mujer	6	5

Table 3: The most common words (sorted by inverse frequency) with the number of false positives and negatives in which they occur in the monolingual settings.

it	FN	FP	en	FN	FP	es	FN	FP
culo	2	16	hysterical	28	20	puta	24	25
bel	2	20	woman	19	34	polla	2	25
figa	2	11	women	28	31	cállate	6	5
cazzo	0	7	fuck	3	37	callate	1	8
troia	7	3	rape	4	39	madre	4	3
tette	3	3	fucking	4	29	acoso	5	9
culona	1	12	bitch	3	26	escoria	1	7

Table 4: The most common words (sorted by inverse frequency) with the number of false positives and negatives in which they occur in the multilingual settings.

es	en	it	en
acoso	harassment	bel	beautiful
callate	shut up	cazzo	dick
cállate	shut up	culo	ass
escoria	scum	culona	big ass
madre	mother	figa	pussy
mujer	woman	porca*	slut
polla	dick	tette	boobs
puta	whore	troia	whore

*in most of the cases it refers to the expression *porca puttana* ≈ holy shit.

Table 5: Translation of the most common words in both Spanish and Italian into English.

to 0.54; on Italian it does from 0.87 to 0.85.

These results play in favour of H2: with the same amount of training data, the models do not benefit from data in other languages. Although this hints that H2 is true, these experiments are not enough to prove that misogyny is language-specific. The results obtained with the mBERT models when trained on single languages — no difference when compared against BERT models on Italian, but a drop of six and four points on English and Spanish— give more confidence that H2 might be true.

6 Error Analysis

We conducted an error analysis to assess how and which kind of errors are transferred from the mono- to the multilingual setting. We want to answer two questions. Question Q1 allows observing the behavior of the multilingual model with respect to the monolingual ones. Question Q2 helps to identify the words that are most likely responsible for the misclassification in the three languages.

Q1 Which instances are classified differently by the monolingual and the multilingual model?

The number of false positives and false negatives behave similarly in all languages. We discuss instances in English for the sake of clarity. We analyse the instances that the monolingual model (BERT en) classified correctly and the multilingual one (mBERT en-es-it) got wrong. We find 122 instances, with 51 false negative (FN) and 71 false positive (FP). Among the FN, the five most common lexical words are *hysterical*, *woman*, *skank*, *women* and *ass*. Among the FP, the words *rape* and *women* are very present, followed by *fucking*, *fuck* and *shut*. We notice that FN instances are more lexically diverse.

We also observe the intersection of misogynist tweets between the two models. The mono and multilingual model judged 543 and 541 tweets as misogynist. The intersection is of 438 instances, with 307 being correctly identified. Therefore, the majority of misogynist instances are detected by both models. This hints that there is no big difference between the models.

Q2 Which words are most present in instances misclassified by both mono and multilingual models?

We first observe instances misclassified by both models. We find 70 FNs and 131 FPs. Table 3 shows the most frequent words in misclassified tweets in the mono- and Table 4 in the multilingual settings. Table 5 shows the translations of the Spanish and Italian words. No significant differences are observed across datasets of the same language, but there are big differences in how misogyny is expressed. In Italian, most words are related to the physical appearance of a woman, linked to sexual objectification. Italian language shows more linguistic creativity. Whereas English contains more insults, Spanish is more aggressive.

For English, the most frequent words are the

1	La ragazza che lavora nel negozio dove vado a fare sempre shopping mi ha detto che ho un bel culo :3333 *The girl working at the place where I always do shopping told me I have a nice ass.*
2	He said she said di Ashley Tisdale fa uscire il puttanone che è in me *He said she said by Ashley Tisdale brings out the bitch in me.*
3	ciao kikka buon pm quanto 6 figa e sexy [...] *hi kikka good evening you are so hot and sexy*
4	figa stai zitta che sono a casa da sola *oh don't tell me I'm home alone*

Table 6: Instances of tweets misclassified by both the monolingual and multilingual models (original Italian tweets followed by English translations).

same in both settings: *hysterical*, *woman*, *women*, *fuck* and *rape*. The fact that *woman* and *women* lie in the second and third positions might indicate an unintended identity-term bias (Fersini et al., 2020), for which the model learnt that *woman* occurs in misogynistic contexts. In both cases, the words *hysterical*, *rape* and *kitchen* (linked to women's stereotyped role) have a strong co-occurrence with the terms *women, woman*, therefore we can assume that these words trigger an error. The word *rape* is common in highly offensive contexts, making it a decisive feature for misogyny; it is frequently present in false positives.

For Spanish, words *puta*, *polla* and *cállate* are common for both settings. We focus the rest of the analysis on Italian, since it shows the biggest discrepancies. Table 6 shows examples. In both cases, *bel* always co-occur with *culo*. In FPs, it is commonly used by women to comment on themselves in a positive way, as in example 1. The same happens with the word *tette*, where in FP instances women usually complain about their breast size. These words tend to occur in offensive contexts and therefore are inclined to be classified as misogynist. Another interesting phenomenon that triggers FPs is the presence of slur reappropriation, i.e. women reclaiming certain negative terms (Felmlee et al., 2020), as in example 2 of Table 6. Another word that triggers FPs is *figa*, as it is typically used in hypersexualised contexts (example 3) but also in neutral way as a filler word in northern Italy (example 4).

7 Final Remarks

We explored the contribution of adding multilingual training material in the automatic identification of misogynist tweets in three languages: English, Spanish and Italian. Our models trained on monolingual data achieve state-of-the-art performance. The inclusion of data in one or two other languages impacts the performance negatively when compared to BERT models, but positively when compared to mBERT models. Multilingual models can be used as data augmentation technique — train on L_1+L_2 to predict on L_1, but they are not suitable for zero-shot classification across languages — train on L_1 to predict on L_2, hinting that misogyny might be language-specific, but further experiments are required.

8 Societal Impact and Limitations

This work represents a starting point toward investigating whether misogyny is language-specific. Analysing the differences of misogyny across languages and cultures is important, since it can help policymakers to develop country-specific policies to mitigate its impact. On Twitter, as well as on other platforms, interactions can be carried out in different languages. We head toward a real-world application, which considers the multilingualism of the platform. Users would benefit from a system able to flag misogynous tweets in multiple languages. Such system would raise awareness and ultimately make a more enjoyable online environment for women.

Among the limitations of this work, we currently focus on three languages only, neglecting geographical information. As a result, not enough attention is paid to culture. Moreover, currently our models are not interpretable, and that would be an important aspect to raise awareness in the general public.

References

Resham Ahluwalia, Evgeniia Shcherbinina, Edward Callow, Anderson Nascimento, and Martine De Cock. 2018. Detecting misogynous tweets. In *Proceedings of the Third Workshop on Evaluation of Human Language Technologies for Iberian Languages (IberEval 2018), co-located with 34th Conference of the Spanish Society for Natural Language Processing (SEPLN 2018)*, page 2150:242–248, Sevilla, Spain. CEUR-WS.org.

Maria Anzovino, Elisabetta Fersini, and Paolo Rosso. 2018. Automatic identification and classification of misogynistic language on Twitter. In *International Conference on Applications of Natural Language to Information Systems*, pages 57–64. Springer.

Amir Bakarov. 2018. Vector space models for automatic misogyny identification. In *Proceedings of the sixth evaluation campaign of natural language processing and speech tools for Italian. Final workshop (EVALITA 2018) co-located with the fifth Italian conference on computational linguistics (clic-it 2018)*. CEUR-WS.org.

Angelo Basile and Chiara Rubagotti. 2018. Crotonemilano for AMI at evalita2018. A performant, cross-lingual misogyny detection system. In *Proceedings of the Sixth Evaluation Campaign of Natural Language Processing and Speech Tools for Italian. Final Workshop (EVALITA 2018) co-located with the Fifth Italian Conference on Computational Linguistics (CLiC-it 2018), Turin, Italy, December 12-13, 2018*, volume 2263 of *CEUR Workshop Proceedings*. CEUR-WS.org.

Valerio Basile, Cristina Bosco, Elisabetta Fersini, Debora Nozza, Viviana Patti, Francisco Manuel Rangel Pardo, Paolo Rosso, and Manuela Sanguinetti. 2019. SemEval-2019 task 5: Multilingual detection of hate speech against immigrants and women in Twitter. In *Proceedings of the 13th International Workshop on Semantic Evaluation*, pages 54–63, Minneapolis, Minnesota, USA. Association for Computational Linguistics.

Khandis R. Blake, Siobhan M. O'Dean, James Lian, and Thomas F. Denson. 2021. Misogynistic tweets correlate with violence against women. *Psychological Science*, 32(3):315–325.

Davide Buscaldi. 2018. Tweetaneuse@AMI EVALITA2018: character-based models for the automatic misogyny identification task (short paper). *CEUR Workshop Proceedings: 2263. Proceedings of the sixth evaluation campaign of natural language processing and speech tools for italian. final workshop (EVALITA 2018) co-located with the fifth italian conference on computational linguistics (clic-it 2018), turin, italy, december 12-13, 2018 (pp. 1–4). CEUR-WS.org.*

Camilla Casula and Sara Tonelli. 2020. Hate speech detection with machine-translated data: The role of annotation scheme, class imbalance and undersampling. *Proceedings of the Seventh Italian Conference on Computational Linguistics (CLiC-it 2020).*

José Cañete, Gabriel Chaperon, Rodrigo Fuentes, Jou-Hui Ho, Hojin Kang, and Jorge Pérez. 2020. Spanish pre-trained bert model and evaluation data. In *PML4DC at ICLR 2020.*

Adriano dos S. R. da Silva and Norton T. Roman. 2020. No place for hate speech@AMI: Convolutional neural network and word embedding for the identification of misogyny in italian (short paper). *Proceedings of the 7th evaluation campaign of Natural Language Processing and Speech tools for Italian (EVALITA 2020).*

Jacob Devlin, Ming-Wei Chang, Kenton Lee, and Kristina Toutanova. 2019. BERT: Pre-training of deep bidirectional transformers for language understanding. In *Proceedings of the 2019 Conference of the North American Chapter of the Association for Computational Linguistics: Human Language Technologies, Volume 1 (Long and Short Papers)*, pages 4171–4186, Minneapolis, MN. ACL.

Samuel Fabrizi. 2020. fabsam@AMI: A convolutional neural network approach. In *Proceedings of the 7th evaluation campaign of Natural Language Processing and Speech tools for Italian (EVALITA 2020).*

Diane Felmlee, Paulina Inara Rodis, and Amy Zhang. 2020. Sexist Slurs: Reinforcing Feminine Stereotypes Online. *Sex Roles*, 83(1):16–28.

Elisabetta Fersini, Debora Nozza, and Paolo Rosso. 2018. Overview of the Evalita 2018 task on automatic misogyny identification (AMI). In *EVALITA Evaluation of NLP and Speech Tools for Italian: Proceedings of the Final Workshop 12-13 December 2018, Naples*, pages 59–66. Torino: Accademia University Press.

Elisabetta Fersini, Debora Nozza, and Paolo Rosso. 2020. AMI @ EVALITA2020: Automatic misogyny identification. In *Proceedings of the 7th evaluation campaign of Natural Language Processing and Speech tools for Italian (EVALITA 2020)*, Online. CEUR.org.

Simona Frenda, Bilal Ghanem, and Manuel Montes y Gómez. 2018. Exploration of misogyny in spanish and english tweets. In *Proceedings of the Third Workshop on Evaluation of Human Language Technologies for Iberian Languages (IberEval 2018), co-located with 34th Conference of the Spanish Society for Natural Language Processing (SEPLN 2018).*

Iakes Goenaga, Aitziber Atutxa, Arantza Casillas, Arantza Díaz de Ilarraza, Nerea Ezeiza, Koldo Gojenola, Maite Oronoz, Alicia Pérez, and Olatz Perez de Viñaspre. 2018. Automatic misogyny identification using neural networks. *Proceedings of the Third Workshop on Evaluation of Human Language Technologies for Iberian Languages (IberEval 2018).*

Alyssa Lees, Jeffrey Scott Sorensen, and Ian D. Kivlichan. 2020. Jigsaw@AMI and haspeede2: Fine-tuning a pre-trained comment-domain bert model. In *Proceedings of the 7th evaluation campaign of Natural Language Processing and Speech tools for Italian (EVALITA 2020).*

Chi-Liang Liu, Tsung-Yuan Hsu, Yung-Sung Chuang, and Hung yi Lee. 2020. What makes multilingual bert multilingual? *arXiv*.

Ilya Loshchilov and Frank Hutter. 2017. Fixing weight decay regularization in adam. *CoRR*, abs/1711.05101.

Arianna Muti and Alberto Barrón-Cedeño. 2020. UniBO@AMI: A Multi-Class Approach to Misogyny and Aggressiveness Identification on Twitter Posts Using AlBERTo. In *Proceedings of the 7th evaluation campaign of Natural Language Processing and Speech tools for Italian (EVALITA 2020)*.

Endang Wahyu Pamungkas, Valerio Basile, and Viviana Patti. 2020. Misogyny detection in twitter: a multilingual and cross-domain study. *Information Processing & Management*, 57.

Endang Wahyu Pamungkas, Alessandra Teresa Cignarella, Valerio Basile, and Viviana Patti. 2018. 14-ExLab@UniTo for AMI at IberEeal2018: Exploiting lexical knowledge for detecting misogyny in English and Spanish tweets. In *Proceedings of the Third Workshop on Evaluation of Human Language Technologies for Iberian Languages (IberEval 2018), co-located with 34th Conference of the Spanish Society for Natural Language Processing (SEPLN 2018)*.

Endang Wahyu Pamungkas and Viviana Patti. 2019. Cross-domain and cross-lingual abusive language detection: A hybrid approach with deep learning and a multilingual lexicon. In *Proceedings of the 57th Annual Meeting of the Association for Computational Linguistics: Student Research Workshop*, pages 363–370, Florence, Italy. Association for Computational Linguistics.

Marco Polignano, Pierpaolo Basile, Marco de Gemmis, Giovanni Semeraro, and Valerio Basile. 2019. AlBERTo: Italian BERT Language Understanding Model for NLP Challenging Tasks Based on Tweets. In *Proceedings of the Sixth Italian Conference on Computational Linguistics (CLiC-it 2019)*, volume 2481, Bari, Italy. CEUR.

Punyajoy Saha, Binny Mathew, Pawan Goyal, and Animesh Mukherjee. 2018. Indian institute of engineering science and technology (shibpur), indian institute of technology (kharagpur). In *Proceedings of the Sixth Evaluation Campaign of Natural Language Processing and Speech Tools for Italian. Final Workshop (EVALITA 2018) co-located with the Fifth Italian Conference on Computational Linguistics (CLiC-it 2018) (pp.1-9)*.

Kalpana Srivastava, Suprakash Chaudhury, P.S. Bhat, and Samiksha. Sahu. 2017. Misogyny, feminism, and sexual harassment. *Industrial psychiatry journal*, 26(2):111–113.

Alice Tontodimamma, Eugenia Nissi, Annalina Sarra, and Lara Fontanella. 2021. Thirty years of research into hate speech: topics of interest and their evolution. *Scientometrics*, 126(1):157–179.

Rob van der Goot, Nikola Ljubešić, Ian Matroos, Malvina Nissim, and Barbara Plank. 2018. Bleaching text: Abstract features for cross-lingual gender prediction. In *Proceedings of the 56th Annual Meeting of the Association for Computational Linguistics (Volume 2: Short Papers)*, pages 383–389, Melbourne, Australia. Association for Computational Linguistics.

Using dependency parsing for few-shot learning in distributional semantics

Ștefania Preda
University College London
United Kingdom
stefipredacs@gmail.com

Guy Emerson
University of Cambridge
United Kingdom
gete2@cam.ac.uk

Abstract

In this work, we explore the novel idea of employing dependency parsing information in the context of few-shot learning, the task of learning the meaning of a rare word based on a limited amount of context sentences. Firstly, we use dependency-based word embedding models as background spaces for few-shot learning. Secondly, we introduce two few-shot learning methods which enhance the additive baseline model by using dependencies.

1 Introduction

Distributional semantics models create word embeddings based on the assumption that the meaning of a word is defined by the contexts it is used in (for an overview, see: Sahlgren, 2008; Lenci, 2018; Boleda, 2020; Emerson, 2020). A fundamental challenge for these approaches is the difficulty of producing high-quality embeddings for rare words, since the models often require vast amounts of training examples (Adams et al., 2017; Van Hautte et al., 2019). To address this problem, various few-shot learning methods have been previously introduced. The goal of a few-shot learning technique is to learn an embedding that captures the meaning of a word, given only a few context sentences. The rare word's vector has to be placed in an existing *background* space of embeddings.

Few-shot learning in distributional semantics is a relatively underexplored area, with important practical applications. Having good representations of rare words is highly desirable in applications aiming to understand dialects or regionalisms, as well as specific technical language.

In this work, we explore the idea of incorporating information from the dependency parse of sentences in the context of few shot-learning. An intuition why this might be useful is provided in Figure 1. In the given sentence, the most relevant word for inferring the meaning of the target rare word "conflagration" is "destroyed". Even if this word is located far from the target, it is directly connected to it through a nominal subject dependency. Moreover, the fact that the target word is used in a certain dependency structure might reveal important characteristics related to its meaning. Since in the case of few-shot learning the data is limited, using dependency parsing information is a resource with great potential to boost existing models.

As a first effort in this direction, this work provides three contributons. Firstly, we explore the effect of using dependency-based word embeddings as background spaces. Secondly, we introduce new few-shot learning methods leveraging the dependency parsing information. Lastly, we update a previous dependency-based background model to make it more suitable for few-shot learning.

2 Background: dependency-based word embeddings

The widely-used Skip-Gram model introduced by Mikolov et al. (2013) takes the contexts of a word to be those words surrounding it in a pre-defined window size. The model learns the embeddings in an unsupervised manner, using a feed-forward neural network trained on large amounts of sentences.

Levy and Goldberg (2014) proposed a different way to construct the contexts of a target word in the training process of the Skip-Gram model. Instead of taking the words from a pre-defined window, one takes the words that are connected to the target word by a syntactic dependency. The contexts were defined as the concatenation of the connected word and the label of the dependency. This allowed the model to differentiate between same words used in different syntactic roles.

The dependency-based word embeddings were found to be better at capturing similarity, while the window-based models capture relatedness. For example, a dependency-based model would produce close embeddings for "Rome" and "Florence", which are *syntactically similar* since they can be

Proceedings of the 60th Annual Meeting of the Association for Computational Linguistics
Student Research Workshop, pages 461 - 466

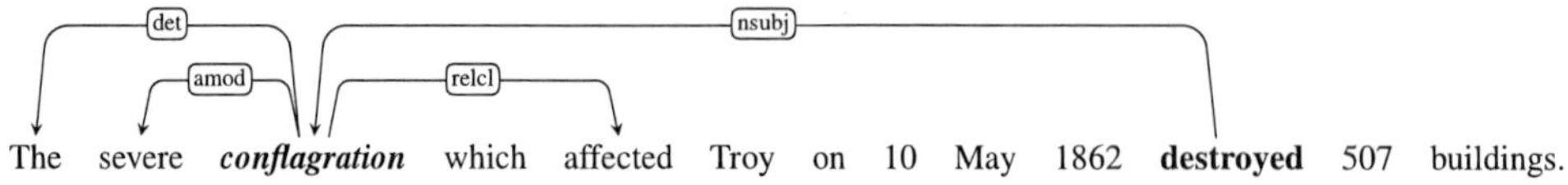

Figure 1: A dependency parse, illustrating that context words connected by a dependency can be important for inferring meaning in a few-shot setting, such as "destroyed" for the rare word "conflagration".

used in the same grammatical contexts, while a window-based model is likely to place closely the embedding of highly related terms such as "Rome" and "ancient", even if they cannot be used interchangeably since they are different parts of speech.

Levy and Goldberg's model successfully captured syntactic similarity, but failed to express how different dependency types affect relations between words. Moreover, it introduced sparsity issues. Czarnowska et al. (2019) developed the Dependency Matrix model to address these shortcomings. Instead of incorporating the dependency labels in the context vocabulary, each dependency type d is associated with a matrix T_d, which acts as a meaning representation of the link between the target and the context words. The matrices T_d, as well as the vectors holding the target vectors e and context vectors o, are learned during training. Let $\mathcal{D}$ be the set of training examples given by tuples of target word t, context word c and dependency type d. For each tuple, we generate a set $\mathcal{D}'$ of negative samples (t, c', d) by drawing context words c' from a noise distribution and maintaining the same target word t and dependency type d. The learning goal is to maximise the function in (1), where σ is the sigmoid function and e_t and o_c are the vectors of the target and context word.

$$\sum_{(t,c,d)\in\mathcal{D}} \Big(\log \sigma(u^{t,c,d}) + \sum_{(t,c',d)\in\mathcal{D}'} \log \sigma(-u^{t,c',d}) \Big) \quad (1)$$

$$u^{t,c,d} = e_t \cdot T_d \cdot o_c \quad (2)$$

3 Background: few-shot learning

As a straight-forward yet successful baseline, the vector of the rare word is estimated by the sum of the vectors of the words in contexts, as proposed by Lazaridou et al. (2017) and Herbelot and Baroni (2017). The latter noticed that not including the stop-words greatly improves the performance on the evaluation tasks. To optimise the performance of the additive model, Van Hautte et al. (2019) proposed weighting the context words according to distance and frequency, as well as subtracting a "negative sampling" vector. These modifications take hyperparameters that are important for Skip-Gram's strong performance, such as number of negative samples k and window size n (Levy et al., 2015), and apply them to the few-shot setting. For each word w in the vocabulary V, with frequency $f(w)$ and distance m from the target rare word t, and for a frequency threshold τ, we calculate the subsampling weight $s(w)$, the window weight $r(w)$ and negative sampling coefficient $n(w)$.

$$s(w) = \min\left(1, \sqrt{\frac{\tau}{f(w)}}\right) \quad (3)$$

$$r(w) = \max\left(0, \frac{n-m+1}{n}\right) \quad (4)$$

$$n(w) = \frac{f(w)^{0.75}}{\sum_{w\in V} f(w)^{0.75}} \quad (5)$$

Assume C is the collection of non-stop context words for the given target rare word t and v_c is the vector in the background space for each $c \in C$. The vector of the target rare word t will is:

$$v_t = \sum_{c\in C} v_c^{\text{add}} \quad \text{where} \quad (6)$$

$$v_c^{\text{add}} = s(c)r(c)\Big(v_c - k \sum_{w\in V} n(w)v_w\Big) \quad (7)$$

More involved models have been proposed for the task of few-shot learning. Khodak et al. (2018) introduced A La Carte, which applies a linear transformation to the sum of the context words obtained by the additive model. The weights of the linear transformation are optimised based on the co-occurrence matrix of the corpus. Van Hautte et al. (2019) takes this approach further in the Neural A La Carte model, by using a neural network with a hidden layer to produce a non-linear transformation matrix, which adds flexibility.

The meaning of a rare word can often be deduced from the word form itself. This information has been leveraged in few-shot learning models. For example, the Form-Context Model (Schick and Schütze, 2019) is a hybrid method which retrieves the weighted sum between the surface form embedding of the rare word, obtained using FastText

(Bojanowski et al., 2017) and the context-based embedding, produced using the A La Carte model.

In this paper, we focus on additive methods, which do not require additional training on few-shot learning examples. This keeps the inference fast and in line with the *true few-shot learning* setting proposed by Perez et al. (2021).

4 Dependency-based FSL methods

Dependency relations proved to be an informative tool in the context of creating distributional semantics models. Based on this success, we introduce two dependency-based few-shot learning methods which build on top of the Additive model. In this section, we assume we have already trained a background space of embeddings v_i for each word i. In our setup, we chose to consider only the target embeddings learnt by the aforementioned background models, i.e. $v_i = e_i$. Alternatively, one could use the concatenation of the target and context embeddings.

Dependency Additive Model The starting point of our methods is the assumption that the closer a word is to the target word in the dependency graph, the more relevant it is for inferring the target's meaning, as seen in Figure 1.

Our method assigns weights for each word in the sentence by considering the distances from the rare word in the dependency parse. For each context word c, let d_c be the number of dependency links from the target rare word t to c in the parse. Note that we consider links in both directions. The inferred vector v_t of the rare word is the weighted sum of the vectors of context words, where the weight w_c of each context word c is given in (8). The weight is chosen so that it is inversely proportional to the distance from the target, and we add 1 in order to avoid discarding context words which are far from the target in the dependency tree.

$$v_t = \sum_{c \in C} w_c v_c^{\text{add}} \quad \text{where } w_c = 1 + \frac{1}{d_c} \tag{8}$$

Initially, we experimented with simply applying the coefficients w_c on the vectors of the context words v_c. However, a better performance was achieved when we incorporated the the weighting steps in (7), so we used v_c^{add} instead of v_c.

Dependency Matrix Additive Model The Dependency Additive model above does not take into account the type of dependency on each edge in the graph, which, as we have seen, plays an important role in capturing the meaning of the words in relation to each other. We thus devised a strategy to make use of this information.

Czarnowska et al. proposed the idea of using the learnt dependency matrices of the Dependency Matrix model for the task of semantic composition, by multiplying word embdeddings with matrices over chains of dependencies. We apply the same idea in the context of few-shot learning. More precisely, instead of giving a weight for each vector of a context word, we multiply it with corresponding dependency matrices on the chain of dependencies from the target to the context. To be able to do this based on the original Dependency Matrix model, we would have to take into account that when we advance in the dependency parse, we have to switch between using the context vector (retrieved from o) and target vector (retrieved from e).

To simplify this process, we modified the Dependency Matrix model to use only one embedding per word, instead of separate context and target embeddings.[1] This also reduces the training time of the model. More precisely, we have the same training loss as in (1), but (2) is replaced by:

$$u^{t,c,d} = v_t \cdot T_d \cdot v_c \tag{9}$$

Having trained this model, we then make use of the matrices T_d, optimised for each dependency type d. For the target rare word t and each non-stop context word c, Let $D(t, c)$ be the path of dependency types from t to c. The vector of the target rare word is calculated as:

$$v_t = \sum_{c \in C} v'_c \quad \text{where } v'_c = \left(\prod_{d \in D(t,c)} T_d \right) v_c^{\text{add}} \tag{10}$$

5 Experiments

In our setup, we considered three background models: window-based Skip-Gram, dependency-based Skip-Gram and the modified Dependency Matrix model which only uses one embedding for each

[1]This cannot be applied to Skip-Gram without causing every word to predict itself as a context. To allow Skip-Gram to use only one vector per word, Zobnin and Elistratova (2019) propose using an indefinite inner product, which corresponds to T in (9) being a diagonal matrix of 1s and -1s. In a similar vein, Bertolini et al. (2021) propose a more radical simplification of the Dependency Matrix model, which uses matrices that are non-zero only on the diagonal and off-diagonal.

Backgr. Model	FSL Model	DN		Chimera			CRW				
		MRR	MR	L2	L3	L6	1	2	4	8	16
Skip-Gram	Additive	0.010	5312	0.12	0.19	0.20	0.11	0.12	0.13	0.15	0.15
	Dep. Additive	0.021	4007	0.13	0.20	0.21	0.12	0.13	0.14	0.15	0.16
Dependency Skip-Gram	Additive	0.023	4671	0.14	0.21	0.21	0.11	0.14	0.15	0.16	0.17
	Dep. Additive	0.027	3785	**0.16**	0.21	0.23	0.12	0.15	0.16	0.17	0.18
Dependency Matrix	Additive	0.017	3367	0.13	0.23	0.25	0.15	0.17	0.20	0.22	0.22
	Dep. Additive	**0.034**	**3140**	0.14	**0.26**	0.29	**0.18**	**0.20**	**0.22**	**0.24**	**0.25**
	DM Additive	0.019	3163	0.15	0.24	**0.31**	0.16	0.20	0.20	0.21	0.22

Table 1: Results for different combinations of background and few-shot learning model, on three evaluation datasets. The best result for each column is marked in bold. Higher is better for all columns except MR.

word. To allow a direct comparison, we trained them all on the WikiWoods (Flickinger et al., 2010) snapshot of English Wikipedia. The same hyperparameters were used: a dimensionality of 100, 15 negative samples, a batch size of 5, and an Adagrad optimiser with an initial learning rate of 0.025. For the dependency models, we used the universal dependency parser provided by `spaCy` (Honnibal et al., 2020). We applied the two few-shot methods we devised, as well as the Additive model with window weighting, subsampling and negative sampling described in §3. The hyperparameters were $t = 10^{-6}$, $k = 15$ and $n = 5$.

5.1 Few-shot learning tasks

Definitional Nonce (DN) This task (Herbelot and Baroni, 2017) provides a single definition sentence for each test word. The test words are frequent words, which have gold vectors of high quality in the background space. At evaluation time, a new vector is computed for each test word, based on the few-shot learning model. The rank of the gold vector relatively to the inferred vector is then calculated, i.e.the number of words from the vocabulary which are closer to the inferred vector than the gold vector is. The distance metric is cosine similarity - the bigger the similarity, the smaller the distance. The metrics retrieved are the Mean Reciprocal Rank (MRR) and median rank.

Chimera The Chimera task (Lazaridou et al., 2017) provides non-existing words (chimeras) with 6 context sentences, as well as similarity scores between the chimera and other existing words. The way in which the dataset was built simulates few-shot learning for humans, since the participants of the experiment needed to infer the meaning of a word they never saw before and rate its similarity with other concepts, based only on the 6 context sentences. Trials with 2, 4 and 6 context sentences are conducted. After each trial, the similarity scores between the inferred vector and the vectors of the words provided is compared against the human similarity scores by retrieving the Spearman's rank correlation coefficient.

Contextual Rare Words (CRW) Like Chimera, the CRW task (Khodak et al., 2018) is based on human ratings between pairs of words. This time the pairs contain a rare word and a frequent one, with an assumed reliable embedding in the background model. For each rare word, 255 context sentences are provided. The vector is generated using the few-shot model for 1, 2, 4, 8, 16 context sentences, selected at random. For each such experiment, the similarity scores between the few-shot vector and the background embedding of the non-rare word are calculated and compared against the human scores using the Spearman's rank correlation coefficient. The scores are averaged out across 10 random selections of context sentences.

5.2 Results and Discussion

The results in Table 1 show that the dependency-based background models performed better than window-based Skip-Gram on all three evaluation tasks. For all background models, applying the Dependency Additive technique consistently improved the results of the Additive model. For the DN task and DM background model, there were three cases where the Additive model gave a rank of over 30,000, while the Dependency Additive model gave a rank of 1 or 2, showing the method's potential for sentences of specific structures. The DM additive model showed a promising result for the Chimera task, but was still outperformed by the Dependency Additive model, and its scores had the biggest variance across all combinations. This suggests that more careful weighting might be required.

6 Conclusion

We investigated the use of dependency information for few-shot learning in distributional semantics. We found that dependency-based contexts are more useful than window-based contexts, with better performance across three evaluation datasets. We proposed a simplified version of the Dependency Matrix model, using only one vector per word, which makes it easier to apply in a few-shot setting.

An important next step would be to investigate the use of the proposed methods for other languages, since our work was limited to English data and it is possible that the dependency structure is more relevant for few-shot learning in the case of specific languages. In order to do such an analysis, one would additionally need to create test data for the few shot-learning tasks, which would require the participation of speakers of the selected languages.

In future work, performance might be further improved by training an A La Carte model (discussed in §3), where the use of dependencies would make it possible to use a graph-convolutional network (Marcheggiani and Titov, 2017).

References

Oliver Adams, Adam Makarucha, Graham Neubig, Steven Bird, and Trevor Cohn. 2017. Cross-lingual word embeddings for low-resource language modeling. In *Proceedings of the 15th Conference of the European Chapter of the Association for Computational Linguistics: Volume 1, Long Papers*, pages 937–947, Valencia, Spain. Association for Computational Linguistics.

Lorenzo Bertolini, Julie Weeds, David Weir, and Qiwei Peng. 2021. Representing syntax and composition with geometric transformations. In *Findings of the Association for Computational Linguistics: ACL-IJCNLP 2021*, pages 3343–3353, Online. Association for Computational Linguistics.

Piotr Bojanowski, Edouard Grave, Armand Joulin, and Tomas Mikolov. 2017. Enriching Word Vectors with Subword Information. *Transactions of the Association for Computational Linguistics*, 5:135–146.

Gemma Boleda. 2020. Distributional semantics and linguistic theory. *Annual Review of Linguistics*, 6:213–234.

Paula Czarnowska, Guy Emerson, and Ann Copestake. 2019. Words are vectors, dependencies are matrices: Learning word embeddings from dependency graphs. In *Proceedings of the 13th International Conference on Computational Semantics - Long Papers*, pages 91–102, Gothenburg, Sweden. Association for Computational Linguistics.

Guy Emerson. 2020. What are the goals of distributional semantics? In *Proceedings of the 58th Annual Meeting of the Association for Computational Linguistics*, pages 7436–7453, Online. Association for Computational Linguistics.

Dan Flickinger, Stephan Oepen, and Gisle Ytrestøl. 2010. WikiWoods: Syntacto-semantic annotation for English Wikipedia. In *Proceedings of the 7th International Conference on Language Resources and Evaluation (LREC)*, pages 1665–1671. European Language Resources Association (ELRA).

Aurélie Herbelot and Marco Baroni. 2017. High-risk learning: acquiring new word vectors from tiny data. In *Proceedings of the 2017 Conference on Empirical Methods in Natural Language Processing*, pages 304–309, Copenhagen, Denmark. Association for Computational Linguistics.

Matthew Honnibal, Ines Montani, Sofie Van Landeghem, and Adriane Boyd. 2020. spaCy: Industrial-strength natural language processing in Python.

Mikhail Khodak, Nikunj Saunshi, Yingyu Liang, Tengyu Ma, Brandon Stewart, and Sanjeev Arora. 2018. A la carte embedding: Cheap but effective induction of semantic feature vectors. In *Proceedings of the 56th Annual Meeting of the Association for Computational Linguistics (Volume 1: Long Papers)*, pages 12–22, Melbourne, Australia. Association for Computational Linguistics.

Angeliki Lazaridou, Marco Marelli, and Marco Baroni. 2017. Multimodal word meaning induction from minimal exposure to natural text. *Cognitive Science*, 41 Suppl 4.

Alessandro Lenci. 2018. Distributional models of word meaning. *Annual review of Linguistics*, 4:151–171.

Omer Levy and Yoav Goldberg. 2014. Dependency-based word embeddings. In *Proceedings of the 52nd Annual Meeting of the Association for Computational Linguistics (Volume 2: Short Papers)*, pages 302–308, Baltimore, Maryland. Association for Computational Linguistics.

Omer Levy, Yoav Goldberg, and Ido Dagan. 2015. Improving distributional similarity with lessons learned from word embeddings. *Transactions of the Association for Computational Linguistics*, 3:211–225.

Diego Marcheggiani and Ivan Titov. 2017. Encoding sentences with graph convolutional networks for semantic role labeling. In *Proceedings of the 2017 Conference on Empirical Methods in Natural Language Processing*, pages 1506–1515, Copenhagen, Denmark. Association for Computational Linguistics.

Tomas Mikolov, Ilya Sutskever, Kai Chen, Greg S Corrado, and Jeff Dean. 2013. Distributed representations of words and phrases and their compositionality. In C. J. C. Burges, L. Bottou, M. Welling, Z. Ghahramani, and K. Q. Weinberger, editors, *Advances in Neural Information Processing Systems 26*, pages 3111–3119. Curran Associates, Inc.

Ethan Perez, Douwe Kiela, and Kyunghyun Cho. 2021. True few-shot learning with language models. In *Advances in Neural Information Processing Systems*.

Magnus Sahlgren. 2008. The distributional hypothesis. *Italian Journal of Disability Studies*, 20:33–53.

Timo Schick and Hinrich Schütze. 2019. Learning semantic representations for novel words: Leveraging both form and context. In *Proceedings of the AAAI Conference on Artificial Intelligence*, volume 33, pages 6965–6973.

Jeroen Van Hautte, Guy Emerson, and Marek Rei. 2019. Bad form: Comparing context-based and form-based few-shot learning in distributional semantic models. In *Proceedings of the 2nd Workshop on Deep Learning Approaches for Low-Resource NLP (DeepLo 2019)*, pages 31–39, Hong Kong, China. Association for Computational Linguistics.

Alexey Zobnin and Evgenia Elistratova. 2019. Learning word embeddings without context vectors. In *Proceedings of the 4th Workshop on Representation Learning for NLP (RepL4NLP-2019)*, pages 244–249, Florence, Italy. Association for Computational Linguistics.

A Dataset and BERT-based Models for Targeted Sentiment Analysis on Turkish Texts

M. Melih Mutlu
Department of Computer Engineering
Boğaziçi University
melih.mutlu@boun.edu.tr

Arzucan Özgür
Department of Computer Engineering
Boğaziçi University
arzucan.ozgur@boun.edu.tr

Abstract

Targeted Sentiment Analysis aims to extract sentiment towards a particular target from a given text. It is a field that is attracting attention due to the increasing accessibility of the Internet, which leads people to generate an enormous amount of data. Sentiment analysis, which in general requires annotated data for training, is a well-researched area for widely studied languages such as English. For low-resource languages such as Turkish, there is a lack of such annotated data. We present an annotated Turkish dataset suitable for targeted sentiment analysis. We also propose BERT-based models with different architectures to accomplish the task of targeted sentiment analysis. The results demonstrate that the proposed models outperform the traditional sentiment analysis models for the targeted sentiment analysis task.

1 Introduction

The increasing availability of the Internet and the growing number of online platforms allowed people to easily create online content. Because of the value of mining the people's opinions, the sentimental information contained in this online data makes sentiment analysis (SA) an interesting topic. It is an area that is attracting the attention not only of academic researchers, but also of businesses and governments (Birjali et al., 2021) and has become a rapidly growing field, as evidenced by the number of recent SA papers published (Mäntylä et al., 2018).

The problem with traditional sentiment analysis is that it cannot capture the different attitudes toward multiple aspects in a given text. For example, if the given text is *"Phones from this brand are great, but I don't really like their laptops"*, the sentiment towards the two targets *"phone"* and *"laptop"* are positive and negative, respectively. Traditional sentiment analysis methods would not be able to detect this opposing sentiment for *"phone"* and *"laptop"*, but would assign an overall sentiment for the text. Targeted Sentiment Analysis (TSA) aims to overcome this challenge and extracts sentiment from a given text with respect to a specific target. One of the challenges of TSA is the lack of available datasets. Both TSA and SA require labeled datasets. Collecting data from various sources and labeling them, which is mostly done manually, is an expensive process. Although the number of datasets suitable for SA has recently increased due to new studies in the SA area, not all SA datasets are usable for TSA (Pei et al., 2019). TSA requires more refined datasets. The labels should reflect the sentiment toward targets rather than the overall sentiment of the sentences.

English is the most studied language for sentiment analysis (Dashtipour et al., 2016). SA models that perform satisfactorily for English do not seem to always work with similar performance for Turkish (Kaya et al., 2012). In this work, we create a manually annotated dataset from Twitter specifically labeled for both traditional and targeted sentiment analysis in Turkish. Then, we experiment with different model architectures for the Turkish TSA task. Experimental results demonstrate that our techniques outperform traditional sentiment analysis models.

1.1 Problem Definition

Let E denotes all entities in a given document D such that:

$$D = \{w_1, \ldots, w_k\} \text{ each } w \text{ is a word; } k \in Z^+$$
$$E = \{e_1, \ldots, e_l\} \text{ each } e \text{ is an entity; } l \in Z^+$$
$$T = \{t_1, \ldots, t_m\} \; t_i \text{ is a target; } t_i \in E; m, i \in Z^+$$

The objective of targeted sentiment analysis is to find all sentiment (s_i, t_i) pairs in document D where t_i is a target from T and s_i is the sentiment toward t_i.

Proceedings of the 60th Annual Meeting of the Association for Computational Linguistics
Student Research Workshop, pages 467 - 472

Tweet	Sentence Sentiment	Targeted Sentiment
coca cola daha iyi lezzet olarak (*coca cola*'s taste is better)	positive	positive
whatsapp çöktü de biraz rahatladım bildirimlerden kurtuldum (*whatsapp* is crashed so I'm little relieved, got rid of notifications)	positive	negative

Table 1: Sample tweets from the dataset. Targets are shown in italics. Sentences are annotated with respect to overall sentence sentiment and targeted sentiment which represent the sentiment towards the target. English translations are provided in parenthesis.

2 Related Work

One of the challenges of targeted sentiment analysis is identifying contexts associated with target words in the sentiment classification. Early methods for understanding the relationship between the target and the rest of the sentence rely on handcrafted feature extractions and rule-based techniques (Ding et al., 2008; Jiang et al., 2011). Recurrent neural networks (RNN) have been implemented for sentiment analysis in the recent years. It achieved improved results compared to earlier methods (Dong et al., 2014; Nguyen and Shirai, 2015; Baktha and Tripathy, 2017). Two RNNs are used to obtain the context from both left and right and combine the context knowledge in (Tang et al., 2016). Attention mechanisms are recently added into RNN-based methods to model the connection between each word and the target (Wang et al., 2016; Ma et al., 2017; Zhang et al., 2020).

Vaswani et al. (2017) introduced the transformer architecture consisting of encoder and decoder blocks based on self-attention layers. Bidirectional Encoder Representations from Transformers (BERT) has been introduced and shown to achieve the state-of-the-art in various NLP tasks in (Devlin et al., 2019). BERT has recently become a widely used approach for sentiment analysis in many languages (Sun et al., 2019; Li et al., 2019). Köksal and Özgür (2021) provide a Twitter dataset in Turkish for sentiment analysis called BounTi. It consists of Twitter data which are about predefined universities and manually annotated by considering sentimental polarities towards these universities. They propose a BERT model fine-tuned using the BounTi dataset to identify sentiment in Turkish tweets.

3 Dataset

Twitter is a commonly used source of sentiment classification dataset in the literature (Jiang et al., 2011; Severyn and Moschitti, 2015; Kruspe et al., 2020). In this study, we also create a Twitter dataset with 3952 tweets whose timestamps span a six-month period between January 2020 and June 2020. The tweets are collected via the official Twitter API by separately searching our 6 targets selected from famous companies and brands.

This dataset is manually annotated with three labels, positive, negative, and neutral. Two factors are considered in the annotation process, namely sentence sentiment and targeted sentiment. Each tweet has the following two labels. The sentence sentiment label expresses the overall sentiment of the sentence, regardless of the target word, as in traditional sentiment analysis techniques. On the other hand, the targeted sentiment label reflects the sentiment for the target in that sentence. The collected tweets are annotated separately by two annotators (one of the authors and a volunteer annotator) who are native Turkish speakers. Cohen's κ (Cohen, 1960) is used to demonstrate inter-annotator agreement and is calculated as 0.855. In case of conflict between annotators, they re-evaluated the conflicting tweets. After re-evaluation, tweets on which the annotators agree are retained and conflicting tweets are removed from the dataset.

Table 1 shows example sentences from the dataset. The first tweet is a positive comment about the target and the sentence is also positive overall. The second tweet indicates a negative opinion about the target, since it has stated as crashed, although the sentence expresses a positive situation overall. Both sentence and targeted sentiment are the same for most of the tweets as in the first example. Only in 21% of the tweets, targeted sentiment differs from the overall sentence sentiment. This means that the rest of the dataset is similar to a standard sentiment analysis dataset. The number of negative tweets in the dataset is significantly higher than the number of positive and neutral tweets for

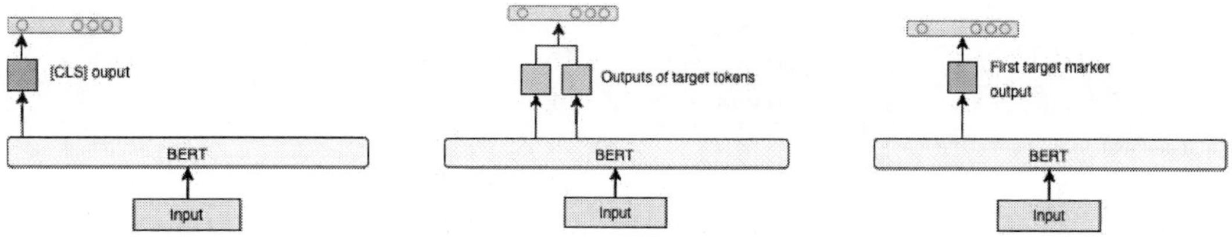

(a) [CLS] output

(b) Max-pooling outputs of target tokens

(c) The output of the first target marker

Figure 1: An overview of architectures to get and handle outputs from BERT

each target. The strikingly high number of negative tweets may be caused by the tendency of customers to write a review when they have had a bad experience. The total percentages of positive, negative and neutral classes are 19%, 58% and 23%, respectively. The dataset is randomly divided into train, test, and validation sets by 65%, 20% and 15%, respectively. The distribution of labels for each subset is kept similar to the distribution of labels for the entire dataset.

The dataset contains ungrammatical text, slang, acronyms, as well as special Twitter characters. During pre-processing URLs and mentions (@) are deleted. Hashtag signs (#) are removed, but hashtags are kept for two reasons: hashtags have been shown to express sentiment (Alfina et al., 2017; Celebi and Özgür, 2018) and some tweets contain the targets as hashtags.

4 Methodology

Baldini Soares et al. (2019) has introduced a novel method with transformer structure in the field of relation extraction. The key idea behind this work is to tag the entities with additional tokens before feeding the BERT model with the input. Different combinations of input and output types are evaluated. The best results are obtained when entity markers are added to the input and when the output of the starting entity markers are taken as the output from BERT. Motivated by the results of Baldini Soares et al.'s work, this paper evaluates several BERT architectures with different input and output techniques for the targeted sentiment analysis task.

Two input representation techniques are investigated. In the standard input representation, the inputs are simply entered into the model without modification. In the second input representation approach, the targets are highlighted by adding additional special target tokens [TAR] at the beginnings and ends of targets, as shown in Table 2. These target tokens are expected to collect information about the target, just as the [CLS] token collects knowledge about the entire sentence. The three approaches for outputs explored in this study are shown in Figure 1. The [CLS] output approach uses only the output of the first token from the last hidden state of BERT, as proposed for classification in the original paper (Devlin et al., 2019). In the second approach, the outputs of the tokens originating from the target, including the outputs of the [TAR] tokens, are max-pooled. The first target marker approach considers only the output of the first [TAR] token in the input instead of the output of the standard [CLS]. All output approaches utilize a softmax layer at the end for classification.

Tweets with [TAR] tokens
[TAR]*whatsapp*[TAR] çöktü de biraz rahatladım bildirimlerden kurtuldum
([TAR]*whatsapp*[TAR] is crashed so I'm little relieved, got rid of notifications)
[TAR]*coca cola*[TAR] daha iyi lezzet olarak
([TAR]*coca cola*[TAR]'s taste is better)

Table 2: Example tweets with target marker representation

4.1 Model Descriptions

First, two baseline models are defined in order to show the drawbacks of the traditional SA models. One baseline is the BERT-based BounTi model (Köksal and Özgür, 2021). The second baseline is also a BERT-based traditional SA model, but fine-tuned with our new dataset using sentence sentiment. Both have similar architectures and use the [CLS] output for sentiment classification.

Four other variants of BERT-based models are proposed for targeted sentiment analysis. **T-BERT** is a model with a similar architecture to our base-

Model	F1-Score
Baseline Model	0.591
BounTi Model	0.498
T-BERT	0.610
T-BERT$_{marked}$	0.659
T-BERT$_{marked}$-TS	0.653
T-BERT$_{marked}$-MP	0.669

Table 3: Performance of all models for TSA with test dataset against targeted sentiment labels

Model	F1-Score
Baseline Model	0.256
BounTi Model	0.233
T-BERT	0.401
T-BERT$_{marked}$	0.428
T-BERT$_{marked}$-TS	0.459
T-BERT$_{marked}$-MP	0.444

Table 4: Performance of all models for TSA with data whose targeted and sentence sentiment are different.

line models. It makes no changes to the input and takes its output from the [CLS] token. The main difference is that targeted sentiment labels are used in the training phase. Therefore, the model is trained to learn targeted sentiment, whereas the baseline models are not aware of the target. **T-BERT$_{marked}$** employs only the target marker representation on top of T-BERT and adds [TAR] tokens into the input. [TAR] token is introduced to BERT's tokenizer and the vocabulary is resized. Hence, the tokenizer accepts [TAR] as one of its special tokens such as [SEP]. **T-BERT$_{marked}$-MP** is another model with target marker representation, additionally it max-pools all outputs of target tokens. **T-BERT$_{marked}$-TS** also utilizes target markers. However, it takes its output only from the first target token [TAR] unlike T-BERT$_{marked}$-MP.

In the training phase of all models, BERTurk (Schweter, 2020) is chosen as the base BERT model. Class weights are set inversely proportional to the class distribution to reduce the effects of an unbalanced data set. The batch size is chosen as 24. Hyperparameters like weight decay, learning rate, and warm-up steps are selected as 0.1, $1e-5$, and 300 respectively. As optimizer, AdamW is used.

5 Results

All proposed BERT variants and baselines are evaluated for targeted sentiment analysis over our introduced dataset. Macro averaged F1-Score is used as the evaluation metric in these experiments. The results are presented in Table 3. All targeted BERT variants outperform both baseline models for TSA. T-BERT$_{marked}$-MP achieves the best results with 67% F1-score, while T-BERT is relatively the worst performing targeted model with 61% F1-score. T-BERT$_{marked}$-TS and T-BERT$_{marked}$ obtain performance quite close to each other, the difference between those models is insignificant. They both have approximately 65% F1-scores.

Only 21% of the dataset has different sentence and targeted sentiment. These portion of data can demonstrate the distinction between targeted and sentence sentiment classification better. If both labels are the same, then traditional SA models may seem to accurately predict targeted sentiment. However, such sentences do not show how accurate the predictions from neither TSA nor SA models are. For this reason, a subset of our dataset such that all sentences have different targeted and sentence sentiment is used for another round of experiments. Table 4 shows the results for the TSA task with this subset. Baseline models' F1-score decreases dramatically to 25%, and it's 23% for BounTi model. Targeted BERT model with the lowest score (40% F1-score) outperforms both models. T-BERT$_{marked}$-TS achieves better targeted sentiment predictions with 46% F1-score. T-BERT$_{marked}$-TS improves the baseline performance by 79% on F1-score.

6 Discussion

Our results suggest that target oriented models can significantly improve the performance for targeted sentiment analysis. BERT architectures that perform successfully in the relation extraction field are shown to be successful for the targeted sentiment analysis task. Target markers make BERT models understand target related context better compared to the [CLS] token. All three models with target markers outperform the baselines and T-BERT. Hence, adding target markers is an effective approach for improving TSA performance.

T-BERT$_{marked}$-TS and T-BERT$_{marked}$-MP are shown to perform slightly better than the other target oriented models. The common aspect of these models, apart from the target tokens, is that they both focus on the outputs of the target-related tokens rather than the [CLS] tokens. Therefore, it can be concluded that target outputs improves the performance for the TSA task.

We only considered one target in each sentence and annotated according to that target. Other targets in the sentence, if any, are ignored. Multiple targets with conflicting targeted sentiment in the same sentence can be a problem to consider. There are cases where a sentence has more than one target, and each target has a different targeted sentiment. For example, in a comparison, the sentiment toward one target may actually depend on the sentiment of another target in the same sentence. In this work, the scope is limited to only one target in each sentence. Target markers are also used only for this one target in the sentence and other possible targets are ignored. The lack of proper treatment of such cases in this work may affect the performance of all models.

Sentence and targeted sentiment are identical for 79% of the dataset. Thus, if a traditional SA model, which is designed to predict the overall sentence sentiment, is used for the TSA task, its success for this task would be overestimated. The results demonstrate that targeted sentiment analysis models perform significantly better than traditional sentiment analysis models on the TSA task. However, the performance of the TSA models increases when they are tested on the entire test dataset, rather than on a subset containing only tweets with different sentence and targeted sentiment labels. This highlights that they may still be biased in favor of sentence sentiment to some extent.

7 Ethical Considerations and Limitations

The dataset contains public tweets in Turkish that are provided by the official Twitter API for research. Only tweet ID's and labels of the tweets are shared publicly to follow Twitter's terms and conditions. The annotators have no affiliation with any of the companies that are used as targets in the dataset, so there is no potential bias due to conflict of interest.

The models developed in this work are not yet satisfactory to use their results without human monitoring. It is recommended to manually check the predictions of these models before using them.

8 Conclusion and Future Work

We presented a manually annotated Turkish Twitter dataset specifically created for targeted sentiment analysis and is also suitable for the traditional sentiment analysis task. This allowed us to develop and evaluate novel models for targeted sentiment analysis in a low-resource language such as Turkish.

We adapted and investigated BERT-based models with different architectures for targeted sentiment analysis. Experiments show significant improvement on baseline performance.

As future work, we plan to expand our dataset so that it contains more sentences with different sentence and targeted sentiment. Moreover, novel methods for sentences with multiple targets will be investigated.

Acknowledgements

We would like to thank Abdullatif Köksal for helpful discussions and Merve Yılmaz Mutlu for annotations. GEBIP Award of the Turkish Academy of Sciences (to A.Ö.) is gratefully acknowledged.

References

Ika Alfina, Dinda Sigmawaty, Fitriasari Nurhidayati, and Achmad Nizar Hidayanto. 2017. Utilizing hashtags for sentiment analysis of tweets in the political domain. In *Proceedings of the 9th international conference on machine learning and computing*, pages 43–47.

Kiran Baktha and BK Tripathy. 2017. Investigation of recurrent neural networks in the field of sentiment analysis. In *2017 International Conference on Communication and Signal Processing (ICCSP)*, pages 2047–2050. IEEE.

Livio Baldini Soares, Nicholas FitzGerald, Jeffrey Ling, and Tom Kwiatkowski. 2019. Matching the blanks: Distributional similarity for relation learning. In *Proceedings of the 57th Annual Meeting of the Association for Computational Linguistics*, pages 2895–2905, Florence, Italy. Association for Computational Linguistics.

Marouane Birjali, Mohammed Kasri, and Abderrahim Beni-Hssane. 2021. A comprehensive survey on sentiment analysis: Approaches, challenges and trends. *Knowledge-Based Systems*, page 107134.

Arda Celebi and Arzucan Özgür. 2018. Segmenting hashtags and analyzing their grammatical structure. *Journal of the Association for Information Science and Technology*, 69(5):675–686.

Jacob Cohen. 1960. A coefficient of agreement for nominal scales. *Educational and psychological measurement*, 20(1):37–46.

Kia Dashtipour, Soujanya Poria, Amir Hussain, Erik Cambria, Ahmad YA Hawalah, Alexander Gelbukh, and Qiang Zhou. 2016. Multilingual sentiment analysis: state of the art and independent comparison of techniques. *Cognitive computation*, 8(4):757–771.

Jacob Devlin, Ming-Wei Chang, Kenton Lee, and Kristina Toutanova. 2019. BERT: Pre-training of deep bidirectional transformers for language understanding. In *Proceedings of the 2019 Conference of the North American Chapter of the Association for Computational Linguistics: Human Language Technologies, Volume 1 (Long and Short Papers)*, pages 4171–4186, Minneapolis, Minnesota. Association for Computational Linguistics.

Xiaowen Ding, Bing Liu, and Philip S Yu. 2008. A holistic lexicon-based approach to opinion mining. In *Proceedings of the 2008 international conference on web search and data mining*, pages 231–240.

Li Dong, Furu Wei, Chuanqi Tan, Duyu Tang, Ming Zhou, and Ke Xu. 2014. Adaptive recursive neural network for target-dependent Twitter sentiment classification. In *Proceedings of the 52nd Annual Meeting of the Association for Computational Linguistics (Volume 2: Short Papers)*, pages 49–54, Baltimore, Maryland. Association for Computational Linguistics.

Long Jiang, Mo Yu, Ming Zhou, Xiaohua Liu, and Tiejun Zhao. 2011. Target-dependent Twitter sentiment classification. In *Proceedings of the 49th Annual Meeting of the Association for Computational Linguistics: Human Language Technologies*, pages 151–160, Portland, Oregon, USA. Association for Computational Linguistics.

Mesut Kaya, Guven Fidan, and Ismail Toroslu. 2012. Sentiment analysis of turkish political news. pages 174–180.

Abdullatif Köksal and Arzucan Özgür. 2021. Twitter dataset and evaluation of transformers for turkish sentiment analysis. In *2021 29th Signal Processing and Communications Applications Conference (SIU)*, pages 1–4. IEEE.

Anna Kruspe, Matthias Häberle, Iona Kuhn, and Xiao Xiang Zhu. 2020. Cross-language sentiment analysis of European Twitter messages during the COVID-19 pandemic. In *Proceedings of the 1st Workshop on NLP for COVID-19 at ACL 2020*, Online. Association for Computational Linguistics.

Xin Li, Lidong Bing, Wenxuan Zhang, and Wai Lam. 2019. Exploiting BERT for end-to-end aspect-based sentiment analysis. In *Proceedings of the 5th Workshop on Noisy User-generated Text (W-NUT 2019)*, pages 34–41, Hong Kong, China. Association for Computational Linguistics.

Dehong Ma, Sujian Li, Xiaodong Zhang, and Houfeng Wang. 2017. Interactive attention networks for aspect-level sentiment classification. In *Proceedings of the 26th International Joint Conference on Artificial Intelligence*, pages 4068–4074.

Mika V Mäntylä, Daniel Graziotin, and Miikka Kuutila. 2018. The evolution of sentiment analysis—a review of research topics, venues, and top cited papers. *Computer Science Review*, 27:16–32.

Thien Hai Nguyen and Kiyoaki Shirai. 2015. PhraseRNN: Phrase recursive neural network for aspect-based sentiment analysis. In *Proceedings of the 2015 Conference on Empirical Methods in Natural Language Processing*, pages 2509–2514, Lisbon, Portugal. Association for Computational Linguistics.

Jiaxin Pei, Aixin Sun, and C. Li. 2019. Targeted sentiment analysis: A data-driven categorization. *ArXiv*, abs/1905.03423.

Stefan Schweter. 2020. Berturk - bert models for turkish.

Aliaksei Severyn and Alessandro Moschitti. 2015. UNITN: Training deep convolutional neural network for Twitter sentiment classification. In *Proceedings of the 9th International Workshop on Semantic Evaluation (SemEval 2015)*, pages 464–469, Denver, Colorado. Association for Computational Linguistics.

Chi Sun, Luyao Huang, and Xipeng Qiu. 2019. Utilizing BERT for aspect-based sentiment analysis via constructing auxiliary sentence. In *Proceedings of the 2019 Conference of the North American Chapter of the Association for Computational Linguistics: Human Language Technologies, Volume 1 (Long and Short Papers)*, pages 380–385, Minneapolis, Minnesota. Association for Computational Linguistics.

Duyu Tang, Bing Qin, Xiaocheng Feng, and Ting Liu. 2016. Effective lstms for target-dependent sentiment classification. In *Proceedings of COLING 2016, the 26th International Conference on Computational Linguistics: Technical Papers*, pages 3298–3307.

Ashish Vaswani, Noam Shazeer, Niki Parmar, Jakob Uszkoreit, Llion Jones, Aidan N Gomez, Łukasz Kaiser, and Illia Polosukhin. 2017. Attention is all you need. *Advances in neural information processing systems*, 30.

Yequan Wang, Minlie Huang, Xiaoyan Zhu, and Li Zhao. 2016. Attention-based lstm for aspect-level sentiment classification. In *Proceedings of the 2016 conference on empirical methods in natural language processing*, pages 606–615.

Ji Zhang, Chengyao Chen, Pengfei Liu, Chao He, and Cane Wing-Ki Leung. 2020. Target-guided structured attention network for target-dependent sentiment analysis. *Transactions of the Association for Computational Linguistics*, 8:172–182.

Author Index